AN EXACT TRANSCRIPT OF THE

CODEX AUGIENSIS,

A GRÆCO-LATIN MANUSCRIPT OF S. PAUL'S EPISTLES,
DEPOSITED IN THE LIBRARY OF TRINITY
COLLEGE, CAMBRIDGE.

TO WHICH IS ADDED

A FULL COLLATION OF FIFTY MANUSCRIPTS

CONTAINING VARIOUS PORTIONS OF THE GREEK NEW
TESTAMENT IN THE LIBRARIES OF CAMBRIDGE,
PARHAM, LEICESTER, OXFORD, LAMBETH,
THE BRITISH MUSEUM, &c.

WITH A CRITICAL INTRODUCTION

BY THE

REV. FREDERICK HENRY SCRIVENER, M.A.

LATE SCHOLAR OF TRINITY COLLEGE, CAMBRIDGE,
PERPETUAL CURATE OF PENWERRIS, FALMOUTH.

"QUOD POTUI."

WIPF & STOCK · Eugene, Oregon

Wipf and Stock Publishers
199 W 8th Ave, Suite 3
Eugene, OR 97401

An Exact Transcript of the Codex Augiensis
A Graeco-Latin Manuscript of S. Paul's Epistles, Deposited in the Library of Trinity College, Cambridge.
By Scrivener, Frederick H.
ISBN 13: 978-1-60608-843-2
Publication date 5/14/2009
Previously published by Cambridge University Press, 1859

CONTENTS.

ILLUSTRATIONS.

INTRODUCTION.

CHAPTER I.

ON THE PRINCIPLES OF COMPARATIVE CRITICISM.

THE term "Comparative Criticism" has been happily applied to that delicate and important process of investigation whereby we seek to trace the relative value and mutual connexion of the authorities upon which the Greek Text of the New Testament is based, whether they be manuscripts of the original, early versions, or citations by the Christian Fathers. Our *accurate* acquaintance with these authorities is very limited, much that we know about them being due to the exertions of scholars yet living: but we are sufficiently aware of the extent of the subject[1], and the minute and perplexing inquiries which beset the Biblical student at every step, not to seize with hearty welcome any clue that may promise to guide us through a labyrinth thus dark and doubtful. To this natural feeling, far more than to any external evidence or internal probability of the theories themselves, I would ascribe the favour extended to the schemes of recension promulgated by Griesbach and his imitators in the last generation. *Men wished such compendious methods of settling the sacred text to be true*, and as demonstrated truths they accordingly accepted them. These systems, bold, ingenious, imposing, but utterly groundless, I have elsewhere discussed at length (*Collation of the Holy Gospels*, Introd. Chap. I.); it were needless to revert to them, for I believe that no one at the present day seriously entertains any one of them.

As Griesbach's scheme and its subsequent modifications were gradually abandoned by critics, a more simple, but (I am persuaded) a no less mistaken theory grew up in its place, which, under the seemly profession of recurring to ancient authorities alone for the remodelling of the text, deliberately refuses so much as to hearken to the testimony of the vast majority of documents that freely offer themselves to the researches of patient industry. This certainly appears a short and easy road to Scriptural science, but, like some other short routes, it may

[1] I can hardly estimate the number of copies containing the Gospels alone (including Evangelistaria) to be much under a thousand, nineteen-twentieths of which are for critical purposes as good as uncollated.

prove the longest in the end: yet it is recommended to us by names I cannot mention without deference and respect. The countenance which Dr Davidson lends to this principle is neither unreserved, nor supported by arguments he can well deem conclusive. Tischendorf practically adopted it in his earlier works, but even then made concessions amounting to nearly all a discreet adversary would be disposed to claim: in Dr Tregelles, however, it finds an advocate learned, able, uncompromising[1]. In my endeavour to refute what I conceive to be erroneous in his views on this subject, I trust I shall not be betrayed into one expression that may give him pain. I honour the devotion and singleness of purpose he has brought to bear on these divine pursuits; I am sure that his edition of the New Testament *by reason of the large accession it will make to our existing store of critical materials*, and of its great accuracy so far as it has yet been tested, will possess, when completed[2], what he modestly hopes for it, "distinctive value to the Biblical student:" I am not the less earnest in hailing the fruits of his long and persevering toil, because I fear that, as a clergyman of the English Church, I differ from him on matters of even more consideration than systems of Comparative Criticism.

I. For Dr Davidson a short notice will suffice. In his chapter (an excellent one on the whole) entitled "General Observations on MSS." he tells us that "The first thing is to collate the oldest thoroughly and accurately, publishing the text in facsimile or otherwise, so that they need not be re-examined. All the rest, or the great mass of juniors, may be dispensed with. They are scarcely needed, because the uncials are numerous. At present they do nothing but hinder the advancement of critical science, by drawing off to them time and attention which might be better devoted to older documents" (Davidson, p. 328, &c.) He then states (I am not concerned to say how truly) that Scholz, from attempting too much, accomplished little, and adds, "Critics have discovered a better way than Scholz's diffuse perfunctory method." No profound discovery surely: that it is better to do a little well than much carelessly is an axiom tolerably familiar to most of us. Yet why must what is well done be of necessity but little?

Dr Davidson's judgment with regard to the *order* in which the work should be executed must be assented to by every reasonable person. Of course there is a presumption beforehand that the older MSS. written in uncial characters will prove of more weight than comparatively modern copies in cursive letters: the

---

[1] I refer to Davidson's "Treatise on Biblical Criticism," Vol. II. 1852; Tischendorf's Prolegomena to his manual Greek Testament, Lips. 1849; and Tregelles' "Account of the Printed Text of the Greek New Testament," 1854. These three works I shall cite throughout the present chapter, simply by the page affixed to their authors' names.

[2] At present (July 1858) but one part of this laborious work has issued from the press, for the use of Subscribers only. It contains the Gospels of St Matthew and St Mark.

rule of common sense is to examine first what promises the most richly to reward our pains. *Yet has not this been done?* Which of the uncial codices of the Greek Testament not previously published in full, has escaped the unwearied zeal of Tischendorf on the continent, of Tregelles at home? I really know of none, except those printed in my present and former volume, and four Evangelistaria in England (Barocc. 202, Canonici Græci, 85 and 92 in the Bodleian, and Wheeler 3 at Lincoln College), and perhaps a few abroad. Now respecting Evangelistaria and Lectionaries, Dr Davidson holds that "till the ancient codices are collated and applied, it were better not to meddle with them. They must have been oftener copied, and therefore are more liable to errors of transcription." I may question alike his fact, his inference and his conclusion on this point, yet at any rate we have here a reason, *satisfactory to himself*, why the whole process of collation should not be suspended till a few Evangelistaria shall be examined, hardly any of which date higher than the tenth century.

But the mass of juniors, he tells us, are scarcely needed, "*because the uncials are numerous.*" On a first perusal I was fairly at a loss to account for such a statement from so well-informed a source. At length I came to recollect that "numerous," like some others, is only a relative term, conveying to different minds widely different ideas. One person will think it a "long distance" from London to Lancashire; another uses the same expression when speaking of the space between this earth and 61 Cycni, some sixty-three billions of miles. We shall therefore best see Dr Davidson's meaning when we come to simple numbers. In the Apocalypse the uncial MSS. are *three:* one of first-rate consequence, complete and well-known (A); another very ancient and well-known, but a mere heap of fragments (C); the third of late date, hastily collated, and now virtually inaccessible (B). These, I conceive, are not so "numerous" as to tempt us to dispense with further information, when we fortunately have it within our reach. In the case of the Acts and Epistles matters are not much better. In the Acts, three MSS. are very old (ABC); the last of them a fragment: two incomplete (DE) exceedingly precious, but not so early; one (F^{a}) a fragment containing just seven verses; one (I) of 42 verses: two (GH) imperfect copies of the ninth century; in all *nine*. In the Catholic Epistles we find *four* entire MSS., *one* fragment. The list for the Pauline Epistles is nominally *thirteen;* from which deduct E a mere transcript of D, make allowance for the intimate connexion subsisting between F and G (see below, Chap. II. 1,) and reckon several as mere fragments, three of but a few passages (F^{a}IL): not one of the thirteen is complete.

Dr Davidson will probably tell us that he used the term "numerous" with reference to the uncial MSS. of the *Gospels;* if so the fact should be stated, lest we be induced to throw aside the cursive copies of other parts of the New Testament as if they might be "dispensed with." Yet I really know not that his case is materially strengthened even in the Gospels. True, the list of uncials is formidable enough at a rapid glance. Tischendorf's catalogue (N. T. 7th edition, 1856) extends to *thirty-two:* let us briefly analyse its contents. In the first place we notice *ten* which consist of only a few leaves, some of but a few verses ($F^a JNOR^1 TWY^1 \Theta\Lambda$): they are beyond all price as specimens of the state of the text at periods varying from the sixth to the tenth century, yet I doubt whether all put together contain as much matter as St Luke's Gospel. PQZ exhibit larger fragments, Z indeed a considerable portion of the single Gospel of St Matthew: these three may contain about as much as the sum of the other ten. The Nitrian palimpsest R consists of fragments of St Luke on 45 leaves: the two Bodleian MSS. Γ and Λ are considerable, and between them contain about as much matter as one complete copy (see Tischendorf. Anecdota Sacra et Profana, pp. 4—6). Then we must in fairness deduct six, which, being not earlier and some of them decidedly later than the tenth century (GHMSUX), are entitled to no more weight than many "junior copies" of the same age. This observation applies, though with diminished force to five (FKVΓΔ) ascribed to the ninth, and even to three (ELΛ) of about the eighth century. There will then remain but the four primary authorities ABCD, of which B alone is complete, A and C being seriously mutilated. I cannot imagine that many will judge this *apparatus criticus* so comprehensive, as to render further investigation superfluous.

Notwithstanding the sentiments on which I have commented, it were wrong to regard Dr Davidson as a willing advocate for the suppression of all manuscript evidence not written in uncial letters. I shall presently have occasion to confirm my own argument by statements of his respecting the importance of the cursive or later codices, quite as full as anything I could hope to say. The fact is that Davidson, himself no mean example of the dignity of intellectual toil, despairs of a thorough collation of all existing materials from the languid students of our age. "It is sufficient for one man to *collate well* several important documents, whether they be versions, MSS., or patristic citations. It exhausts his patience and energy" (Davidson, p. 105). So discouraging a representation of energy and patience exhausted by a few slight efforts cannot, *must not*, be true of the younger school of Biblical critics in our two great Universities; I will leave Dr Dobbin, the editor of the Codex Montfortianus, to speak for that of Dublin. These men will not surely much longer suffer the manuscript treasures of their public libraries to lie neglected or unapplied. The very repulsiveness of this task, at its first aspect, is to the earnest student only one reason the more for prosecuting it with ever-growing interest;

Et non sentitur SEDULITATE labor.

II. The reputation of Tischendorf is so firmly grounded on his editions of the famous Codices Ephraemi and Claromontanus, on his Monumenta Sacra Inedita and other learned works, that his opinion on the great questions of sacred criticism cannot fail to be regarded with considerable interest. In his manual edition of the N. T. 1849 his practice must be regarded on the whole as adverse to me. His list of authorities in the Gospels is limited to the uncial MSS., and to a few of the cursive whose variations from the common standard text are most conspicuous (e.g. 1, 13, 33, 69, 102, 131). Occasionally indeed he estimates (very roughly of course) the *number* of later copies supposed to countenance a reading of his uncials, yet I nowhere perceive that he gives much weight to such testimony in the arrangement of his text. The edition of 1849, however, must be considered as quite superseded by another (which, reckoning several little known in England, Tischendorf calls his *seventh*), now issuing in parts from the Leipsic Press. This, the latest fruits of his persevering toil, is far more comprehensive in plan and (*experto credite*) more accurate in execution than its predecessor. In compiling it he has freely availed himself of the labours of others in this field of Biblical research, has cited the cursive MSS. as much perhaps as is expedient in a volume intended for general use, and in exercising his judgment on the materials he has brought together, has produced a text (as Dr Wordsworth has observed before me) much more closely resembling the textus receptus than that he had formed before[1]. I cannot help believing this gradual and (as it would appear) almost *unconscious* approximation to the views I am advocating, into which more exact study and larger experience have led so eminent a scholar, to be no slight assurance that those views are founded in reasonableness and truth[2].

---

[1] Thus, for example, Tischendorf's 7th edition, in St Matthew alone, returns to the received readings he had rejected in 1849 in no less than 187 passages. The instances in which he abided by the common text in 1849, but subsequently deserts it, are 56 in St Matthew's Gospel, but about nine-tenths of them consist of Alexandrine forms (e. g. *εἶδαν, εἶπαν, ἦλθαν* &c.) which he now prefers to the common ones.

[2] It has been said indeed ("Journal of Philology, Vol. IV. March 1858, p. 207") that "the impression that Tischendorf is now beginning to entertain some respect for the *textus receptus* is quite unfounded. Many of his present readings accidentally coincide with the 'received' readings, but that is all. It is not that he prefers the bulk of late evidence to the weight of early evidence: but that he makes the worst or at least very bad evidence, if supported by a canon of probability, outweigh the best evidence standing alone." On a point of this kind there is nothing like coming to the test of facts. I select the third chapter of St Matthew partly for its brevity, partly because the loss of cod. A (the *first-rate* authority which most resembles the later text) in this chapter, will so far assist the learned reviewer's case. Exclusive of his constant use of *ν εφελκυστικον* and *οὕτως* (v. 15), Tischendorf in his edition of 1849 departs from the *textus receptus* 13 times: in his seventh edition he returns to it seven times out of the thirteen. Now one of these seven instances I think favourable to the reviewer: certainly there is considerable, perhaps even preponderating evidence (for versions can be relied on in such a variation) for adding *ποτάμῳ* to Ἰορδάνῃ in v. 6; Tischendorf *now* rejects it, as if it were borrowed from Marc. i. 5. The other six passages seem fatal to the notion that internal evidence, not diplomatic authority, is the operating cause which is bringing Tischendorf's text so much nearer what we believe to be the true one. These passages are v. 2 *καὶ* restored before λέγων; v. 7 *αὐτοῦ* restored after *βάπτισμα*; v. 14 Ἰωάννης restored; v. 15 *πρὸς αὐτὸν* of the common text replaces *αὐτῷ*; v. 16 *καὶ βαπτισθεὶς* replaces *βαπτισθεὶς δέ*; v. 16 *καὶ* is restored before *ἐρχόμενον*. In each of these texts Tischendorf in 1849 rejected the common reading on the slender testimony of a single uncial B, countenanced by one or more of the Egyptian and Latin versions or Fathers, and

Yet even in the Prolegomena to his edition of 1849 (no critical Introduction to his 7th edition has yet appeared) I find little from which I should withhold my assent. "Textus" he observes "petendus est unicè ex antiquis testibus, et potissimum quidem e græcis codicibus, sed interpretationum patrumque testimoniis minimè neglectis" (*Proleg.* p. XII). The drift of this self-evident proposition appears from the next sentence: "Itaque omnis textûs nostri confirmatio ab ipsis testibus proficisci debebat, non a receptâ quam dicunt editione." Very true: I for one see nothing in the history or sources of the received text to entitle it, *of itself*, to peculiar deference. I esteem it so far as it represents the readings best supported by documentary evidence, and no further: if in my judgment the Elzevir text approaches nearer *on the whole* to the sacred autographs than that formed by Tischendorf, it is only because I believe that it is better attested to by the very witnesses to whom Tischendorf himself appeals; the MSS., the versions, the Primitive Fathers. I enquire not whether this general purity (for it is but general) arises from chance, or editorial skill, or (as some have piously thought) from Providential arrangement: I am content to deal with it as a fact. Perhaps Dean Alford's plan is preferable (*N. T. Proleg.* p. 69, Vol. I. 1st edition), who, in difficult cases, where testimony seems evenly balanced, would give "the benefit of the doubt" to the Textus Receptus; but the practical difference between the two principles will be found, I imagine, very slight indeed.

And now recurs the question what we shall understand by "*antiqui testes*" in the case of Greek Manuscripts? In the first rank Tischendorf justly places those dating from the fourth to the ninth century; and among them, to the oldest he attributes the highest authority. "Hæc auctoritas ut magnoperè augetur si interpretationum ac patrum accedunt testimonia, ita non superatur dissensione plurimorum vel etiam omnium codicum recentiorum, i.e. eorum qui a decimo sæculo usque ad decimum sextum exarati sunt" (p. XII). If this canon is to extend only to cases wherein the most ancient witnesses in competent numbers *unanimously* support a variation from the common text, I do not conceive that any judicious critic would object to its temperate application: though he may reasonably suspect that where the earliest available evidence is thus overwhelming, a portion of the later manuscripts will always be found to accord with it. What we *do* resist is a scheme, which, however guardedly proposed, shall exclude the cursive MSS. from all real influence in determining the sacred text. This is Dr Tregelles' avowed principle: that it is not Tischendorf's (however much he may have once seemed to countenance it by his practice) plainly appears from his own distinct assertions: "codices post octavum vel nonum sæculum scriptos

---

by a very few cursive MSS., sometimes by none at all! Surely it is because he has seen the insufficiency of such evidence, that he has judiciously retraced his steps, rather than from "an increasing tendency to set private canons above the authority of manuscripts, versions, and Fathers."

negligendos aut parvi æstimandos non esse......recentiorum codicum lectiones quas easdem antiquissimi interpretes ac patres testimonio suo confirment, antiquitatis commendatione minimè destitutas esse" (*Proleg.* p. XIII). On this ground he praises the design of Reich, "præstantissimis codicibus minusculis denuo examinandis," declaring of it "ea perquam utilia fore arbitror et ad historiam et AD EMENDATIONEM TEXTUS (p. XXXIII. *not.*).

III. I am unfeignedly anxious to present to the reader a clear and even forcible statement of the principlès of textual criticism maintained in Dr Tregelles' "Account of the Printed Text of the Greek Testament:" I assure him I do not criticise his book unread[1], or reject his theory without patient examination. I presume he would wish it to be enunciated in such terms as the following:

The genuine text of the Greek New Testament must be sought exclusively from the most ancient authorities, especially from the earliest uncial copies of the Greek. The paramount weight and importance of the last arises not from the accidental circumstance of their age, but from their agreement with the other independent and most ancient authorities still extant, viz. the oldest versions and citations by the fathers of the first four centuries.

To which proposition must be appended this corollary as a direct and necessary consequence:

"The mass of recent documents [i.e. those written in cursive characters from the tenth century downwards] possess no determining voice, in a question as to what we should receive as genuine readings. We are able to take the *few* documents whose evidence is *proved* to be trustworthy, and safely discard from present consideration the eighty-nine ninetieths, or whatever else the numerical proportion may be" (Tregelles, p. 138).

In the ordinary concerns of social life, one would form no favourable estimate of the impartiality of a *judge* (and such surely is the real position of a critical editor) who deemed it safe to discard unheard eighty-nine witnesses out of ninety that are tendered to him, unless indeed it were perfectly certain that the eighty-nine had no means of information, except what they derived from the ninetieth: on that supposition, but on that supposition alone, could the judge's reputation for wisdom or fairness be upheld. That mere numbers should decide a question of sacred criticism never ought to have been asserted by any one; never has been asserted by a respectable scholar. Tischendorf himself (*Proleg.* p. XII.) cannot condemn such a dogma more emphatically than the upholders of the general integrity of the Elzevir text. But I must say that the counter-proposition, that

[1] "Let me request any one who may wish to understand the principles of textual criticism which I believe to be true, to *read* what I have stated, &c." (Tregelles, *Addenda*, p. 2). A moderate request certainly, but I should hope it was hardly needed.

numbers have "no determining voice," is to my mind full as unreasonable, and rather more startling. I agree with Dr Davidson (p. 333) in holding it to be "an obvious and natural rule" that the reading of the majority is *so far* preferable. Not that a bare majority shall always prevail, but that numerical preponderance, especially where it is marked and constant, is an important element in the investigation of the genuine readings of Holy Scripture. For on what grounds shall we justify ourselves in putting this consideration wholly aside? Is the judge convinced to a moral certainty that the evidence of the eighty-nine is drawn exclusively from that of the ninetieth? It has never I think been affirmed by any one (Dr Tregelles would not be sorry to affirm it, if he could with truth) that the mass of cursive documents are corrupt copies of the uncials *still extant:* the fact has scarcely been suspected in a single instance, and certainly never proved. I will again avail myself of Davidson's words, not only because they admirably express my meaning, but because his general bias is not quite in favour of the views I am advocating. "*Cœteris paribus,*" he observes, "the reading of an ancient copy is more likely to be authentic than that of a modern one. But the reading of a more modern copy may be more ancient than the reading of an ancient one. A modern copy itself may have been derived not from an extant one more ancient, but from one still more ancient no longer in existence. *And this was probably the case in not a few instances*" (p. 101). No one can carefully examine the readings of cursive documents, as represented in any tolerable collation, without perceiving the high probability that Davidson's account of them is true. But it is not essential to our argument that the fact of their being derived from ancient sources now lost should be *established,* though internal evidence points strongly to their being so derived: it is enough that such an origin is *possible,* to make it at once unreasonable and unjust to shut them out from a "determining voice" (of course jointly with others) on questions of doubtful reading. I confess that Tregelles is only following up his premises to their legitimate conclusion in manfully declaring his purpose in this respect; but we are bound to scutinize with the utmost jealousy and distrust a principle which involves consequences so extensive, and he must forgive me if I add, so "perilous."

It is agreed then on all hands that the antiquity of a document is only a presumption, a *primâ facie* ground for expectation, that it will prove of great critical importance. "The oldest MSS." writes Dr Davidson again, "bear traces of revision by arbitrary and injudicious critics. GOOD READINGS MAKE GOOD MANUSCRIPTS" (p. 101). "It ought to be needless for me to have to repeat again and again," insists Dr Tregelles, whose reviewers I suppose were δυσμαθέστεροι, "that the testimony of very ancient MSS. is *proved* to be good on grounds of evidence (not mere assertion); and that the distinction is not between the ancient MSS. on the one hand, and all other witnesses on the other,—but between the *united evidence* of the *most ancient documents*—MSS., versions, and early citations—

together with that of the few more recent copies that accord with them, on the one hand, and the mass of modern MSS. on the other" (Tregelles, *Addenda*, p. 2). Very well: this immeasurable superiority claimed for the early uncials over all later authorities (so that the former shall be every thing in criticism, the latter absolutely nothing) rests not on an axiom intuitively true; it has to be *proved* by an induction of scattered facts; and we are bound to watch the process of proof with the greater care, from our previous knowledge that when once established it will inevitably lead us to conclusions which seem hardly consistent with even dealing towards a whole legion of honest and reputable witnesses.

Now Dr Tregelles produces no less than SEVENTY-TWO passages from various parts of the New Testament (pp. 133—147), as a kind of sample of some two or three thousand which he reckons to exist there, wherein "the more valuable ancient versions (or some of them) agree in a particular reading, or in which such a reading has *distinct* patristic testimony, and the mass of MSS. stand in opposition to such a lection, [while] there are certain copies which *habitually* uphold the older reading" (Tregelles, p. 148). Of course I cannot follow him step by step through this long and laboured catalogue; an adequate specimen *taken without unfair selection* will amply suffice to shew my opponent's drift and purpose. I will therefore transcribe all the places he cites from the Gospel of St Mark (they amount to seven), making choice of that Gospel partly for its shortness, partly because I wish, in justice to Dr Tregelles, to discuss in preference those texts which remain unmutilated in the four uncial codices of the first class (see above, *vide supra*, p. vi.); in the following list they all are complete, except C in Mark xiii. 14 alone. As Tregelles "for the sake of brevity" has laid before us these passages "without any attempt to state the balance of evidence" (p. 148), I have ventured to supply within brackets an omission which I cannot help considering a little unfortunate.

(1). "Mar. iii. 29. Common text, *αἰωνίου κρίσεως*. Vulg. has, however, '*reus erit æterni delicti;*' so too the *Old* Latin [*a. b. c. e. ff*^{2}. g^1. *l.* Tregelles N. T., 1857], the Memph., Goth., Arm.; and this is the reading of Cyprian [*bis*, Treg. N. T.], Augustine, and Athanasius. Corresponding with this BLΔ, 33 (and one other MS. [28; add 2^{pe}]), read *αἰωνίου ἁμαρτήματος*, and C* (ut videtur), D, 69 (and two others [13. 346]), have *αἰωνίου ἁμαρτίας*, a perfectly cognate reading." (p. 141).

[But *κρίσεως* is found in AC** (whose primitive reading seems quite doubtful) EFGHKMSUVΓ[1] being all the other uncials that contain the passage. Of the

[1] Of the uncials cited for these texts B (Tregelles' favourite) is least accurately known. ACD LΔ have been edited in full; EFGHKMSUXΓ have been so repeatedly collated (recently by Tischendorf or Tregelles or both) that when they are not cited as supporting variations so marked as those under discussion, their testimony even *sub silentio* in behalf of the received text may be fully relied on. In these seven texts, however, they are expressly cited by Tischendorf's seventh edition for the readings here ascribed to them.

cursive copies all go with the received text, except the six named above, and three which have κολάσεως. The Peshito Syriac reads ܕܕܝܢܐ *judicii:* thus also the Harclean Syriac of the 7th century, the Æthiopic ("in condemnatione"), the Codex Brixianus *f.* of the Italic (or Old Latin), the Codex Toletanus of the Vulgate, and any Fathers not named by Tregelles, many of whom must have cited this remarkable passage.]

(2). "Mar. iv. 12. τὰ ἁμαρτήματα of the common text is omitted by Origen *twice;* by one MS. of the *Old* Latin [two *b. i.* in Treg. N. T.], the Memph., and Arm., with BCL, 1 (and some other MSS.)" [i. e. "22. 118. 209. 251. 340* *al.*" Scholz: τὰ παραπτώματα Theophyl. and eight MSS.].

[τὰ ἁμαρτήματα is read in ADEFGHKMSUVΔ (*hiat.* Γ), all cursives not named above, Syrr. both Pesh. and Harc., Æthiopic, Gothic, Vulg., all Italic MSS. except two].

(3). "Mar. iv. 24. τοῖς ἀκούουσιν omitted by the Old Latin, Vulg., Memph., Æth., with BCDLΔ, and some other copies." [credentibus *f.* Goth., Treg. N. T.].

[Tischendorf, even in his seventh edition, adds G (Harl. 5684), but on reference to the MS., I find he is wrong. Griesbach adds "*item* 13. 69 *semel,*" yet 69 *in this verse* reads τοῖς ἀκούουσιν, as do AEFGHKMSUV (*hiat.* Γ), all other cursive MSS., both Syrr.].

(4). "Mar. x. 21. ἄρας τὸν σταυρὸν omitted by the Old Latin in most copies [*b. c. f. ff. g*[1. 2] *k. l.* Treg. N. T.], Vulg., Memph. [by Schwartze], (so too Clem. Alex. and Hil.), with BCDΔ." [L is here defective, and so for the first time deserts its allies: add to the list Scholz's 406].

[ἄρας τὸν σταυρὸν is read in AEFHKMSUVXΓ, the whole mass of cursive copies, the Harclean Syriac, Wilkins' Memphitic and the Gothic. The words are placed before δεῦρο in G 1. 13. 69. 118. 124 and four other cursives; in Peshito Syr., Æth., Arm., the Vercelli MS. *a.* of the Old Latin, and Irenæus].

(5). "Mar. xii. 4. λιθοβολήσαντες omitted by Old Latin, Vulg., Memph., [Theb., Treg. N. T.], Arm., with BDLΔ, 1, 33 and four other copies." [i.e. 28. 91. 118. 299.]

[But λιθοβολήσαντες is found in ACEFGHKMSUVXΓ, all other cursive copies, both Syrr., Goth., Æth.].

(6). "Mar. xii. 23. ὅταν ἀναστῶσιν *om.* some copies of Old Latin [*b* (ut vid.). (*c*). (*k*). Treg. N. T.], Memph., Syr., [i. e. Peshito; Treg. N. T. adds Theb. Æth.] with BCDLΔ, 33."

[ὅταν ἀναστῶσιν is read in AEFGHKMSUVXΓ, all cursives but one (13. 69. 346 *alio ordine*), Vulg., *a. ff. g*[2]. *i.* of Old Latin, Harclean Syr., Goth., Arm.].

(7). "Mar. xiii. 14. τὸ ῥηθὲν ὑπὸ Δανιὴλ τοῦ προφήτου *om.* most copies of Old Latin [*a. ff. g*[1]. only in Treg. N. T., where he adds Theb.], Vulg., Memph, Arm., also Augustine *expressly,* with BDL." [Scholz adds "nec attingunt Victor et Theophylact."]

[The words are read in AEFGHKMSUVXΓΔ, all cursives (with some variation in my y and eight others), both Syrr., Æth., *c. k.* of Old Latin].

I do not think the reader will desire more than these specimens, transcribed as they are consecutively from Dr Tregelles' list *without the possibility of undue selection:* I fully believe him that they may be increased twenty-fold. It is time to offer a few remarks on the facts that have been alleged by each of us. Meanwhile I must beg that the design of my learned opponent in producing his examples be carefully borne in mind. He does not so much aim at shewing that the readings of Codex B and its adherents are preferable to those of the received text (though this he implies throughout), as at demonstrating that the united testimonies of early uncials, primitive versions, and ecclesiastical authors of the first four centuries form together such a mass of evidence as will overbear the voice of the vast majority of witnesses of all ages and countries. We may grant that his favourite documents are entitled to great weight in the process of critical investigation, and this I admit fully and without reserve: we might even prefer many of their readings to those of the received text, which on the whole I am not quite disposed to do: and yet we must demur as firmly as ever to the claim of paramount and exclusive authority he sets up for them. With these preliminary observations I pass on to an analysis of the state of evidence in the passages Dr Tregelles has brought to our notice.

(1). First then it is obvious that the uncial documents, even the earliest of them, are much divided in every place he has cited. I hardly know why the Alexandrine MS. (A) has come to be considered a little younger than the Codex Vaticanus (B); we have free access to and minute knowledge of the one; through the jealousy of the Papal librarians our acquaintance with the other is still very imperfect[1]; much doubt hangs over many of its readings; it seems barely certain

[1] Since writing the above I have examined Cardinal Mai's long-expected edition of the Vaticanus (5 Tom. Romæ 1857) the text of which was ten years passing through the press (1828—38), and was then kept back from publication till within the last few months. I regret that I cannot even now modify my statement of the precariousness of our knowledge of this great document: I must needs add my voice to the loud chorus of disappointment this work has called forth throughout Europe. It is impossible to study Vercellone's letter to the reader, prefixed to the first volume, without seeing the strange incompetency both of Mai and of himself, for the task they had undertaken: in fact, Vercellone's frank admission of the great Cardinal's inaccuracy would be amusing if it were not most vexatious. Finding his sheets full of errors and misrepresentations of the Codex Vaticanus (some of them inserted from printed books!), Mai tries to get rid of them as well as he can, sometimes by cancelling a few leaves, sometimes by *manual* corrections made in each copy; while he reserves the mass for a table of errata, to be placed at the end of each volume. In this unpromising state was the work found by Vercellone after Mai's death in 1854, when, anxious to decorate the Cardinal's memory "novâ usque gloriâ atque splendidiore coronâ" (Tom. I. p. III), he drew up the tables of errata projected by his predecessor, and at length submitted this deplorable performance to the judgment of Biblical scholars. His lists of errata are obviously most imperfect; as regards orthography he only professes to give us "selectiora," for Mai, it seems, did not care much about such points; at any rate it was not worth while to delay publication on their account: and so "reliqua quæ supererunt eruditis castiganda permittimus; immo ut summâ ἀκριβείᾳ castigentur optamus" (*ib.* p. XIII). Add to all this that the lacunæ throughout the MS. are supplied from later sources; that even accidental omissions and errors of the

whether its accents and breathings are *primâ* or *secundâ manu*[1]. We will adopt however the usual opinion about them: no competent critic places A later than the fifth, or B earlier than the fourth century[2]. *Now in each of these seven places A sides with the Elzevir text against B.* Is it an argument in favour of B that its readings are ancient? The same plea might be entered for those of A. And their divergencies, it will be noted, are not merely accidental exceptions to a general coincidence, but perpetual, almost systematic. While I confess freely the great importance of B, I see not why its testimony ought, *in the nature of things*, to be received in preference to that of A. I cannot frame a reason why the one should be listened to more deferentially than the other.

(2). In the next rank, yet decidedly below A or B, stand the palimpsest fragment C (Codex Ephræmi) and the Codex Bezæ or D. This latter is generally considered much the least weighty of the four great MSS. of the Gospels (see for instance Alford, *N.T. Proleg. on D.*): and that not so much on account of its later date (perhaps about the middle of the sixth century), as from the violent corrections and strange interpolations wherewith it abounds. "Its singularly corrupt text," observes Davidson, "in connexion with its great antiquity, is a curious problem, which cannot easily be solved" (p. 288)[3]. Now in the seven passages under consideration C accords with B in four cases, with A once; once its reading is doubtful, once its text has perished. Codex D agrees with B five times, much resembles it once, and once sides with A. Thus these documents of the second class favour B rather than A, C however less decidedly than D.

---

pen are corrected in the text, though noted in the margin; that the breathings, accents, and ι subscriptum are accommodated to the modern fashion; and that a slight Preface of a few pages by Mai supplies the place of the full Prolegomena once promised and so urgently required.

[1] On this point however Vercellone's testimony should be heard. After correcting Birch's statement that the breathings and accents are *primâ manu*, he adds, "etenim amanuensis ille, qui cunctas totius codicis litteras, vetustate pallescentes, atramento satis venuste, servatâ vetere formâ, renovavit, idem accentus etiam spiritusque imposuit, qui nulli fuerant a primâ manu; ut illæ codicis particulæ ostendunt, quas certis de causis (id est vel quia repetitas in codice vel ab eo improbatas) non attigit. Rei hujus veritatem codicis spectatores ipsi per se deprehendent." (Cod. Vatican. Tom. v. p. 499.) I presume it is for this reason that while the facsimile of one column, Mark i. 1—9, prefixed to Tom. v. of Mai's edition contains no breathings or accents, they are represented in the splendid plate of the three columns of the first surviving page (commencing Gen. xlvi. 28 πολιν) prefixed to Tom. I.

[2] I find no traces in Mai's Codex Vaticanus of the absurd opinion once imputed to him, that this MS. dates as far back as the *second* century; Vercellone acquiesces in the date usually assigned to it, that of the fourth or early in the fifth century, but refers to Hug for the proof.

[3] Dr Tregelles, indeed, in partial reference to Codex D, is good enough to say, "Some people rest much on some one incorrect reading of a MS., and then express a great deal of wonder that such a MS. could be highly valued by critics. The exposure of such excessive ignorance as this might be well dealt with by one who knows Greek MSS. as well as Mr Scrivener" (p. 137 *note*). Thus appealed to I will reply, that, putting aside the case of mere errors of the scribe, I do think that the admitted corruptions and deliberate interpolations which we *all* recognize in the Codex Bezæ, have a natural tendency to detract from the credibility of its testimony in more doubtful cases.

(3). When we descend to uncials of the third rank, from the eighth century downwards, the case is entirely reversed. One of them indeed (L of the eighth or ninth century) edited by Tischendorf (*Monumenta sacr. ined.* pp. 57—399) is here and elsewhere constantly with B: Δ also (Codex Sangallensis of the ninth century, which will be spoken of in Chapter II.) supports B five times, A only twice[1]; while all the rest extant (EFGHKMSU and X where it is unmutilated) unanimously support A. Some of these are as ancient as L, several quite as valuable as Δ.

(4). On coming down from uncial to cursive MSS. the preponderance is enormous. Dr Tregelles does not object to the rough estimate of ninety to one; and those few copies which often maintain the readings of BL are by no means stedfast in their allegiance. Yet even here the resemblance to A or B or to each other is but general. The materials accumulated in the present volume and elsewhere shew isolated readings of the most recent codices, even of those which approach nearest to the Elzevir edition, for which no ancient authority can be produced except the Codex Vaticanus. No one who has at all studied the cursive MSS. can fail to be struck with the *individual character* impressed on almost every one of them. It is rare that we can find grounds for saying of one manuscript that it is a transcript of some other now remaining. The fancy which was once taken up, that there existed a standard Constantinopolitan text, to which all copies written within the limits of that Patriarchate were conformed, has been "swept away at once and for ever" (Tregelles, p. 180) by a closer examination of the copies themselves. Surely then it ill becomes us absolutely to reject as unworthy of serious discussion, the evidence of witnesses (whose mutual variations vouch for their independence and integrity) because their tendency on the whole is to uphold the authority of one out of the two most ancient documents against the other.

(5). One of the arguments on which Dr Tregelles lays most stress is the accordance of the oldest versions with Codex B rather than with A. So far as the Latin versions are concerned the passages he has alleged must be admitted to prove the correctness of his assertion. The Vulgate agrees with A but twice, with B five times. The Old Latin translations (for the term *Italic* it seems is obsolete), though in six instances some of them countenance A, give a clear majority for B. I do not like to speak of the Coptic or Armenian translations, as I am totally ignorant of the languages wherein they are written: Tregelles, I perceive, labours under the same disadvantage (p. 171), and will be as reluctant

[1] Observe, however, that "The text of St Mark's Gospel is that which especially gives this MS. a claim to be distinguished from the mass of the later uncial copies." (Introductory Notice to Tregelles' N. T., 1857, p. iv.); which intimates that our selection of the passages in St Mark's Gospel is peculiarly favourable to Dr Tregelles, so far as Δ is concerned. Elsewhere its readings are much nearer the *textus receptus*.

as I am to dogmatise about matters on which we are both disqualified from pronouncing a trustworthy opinion. Certainly these versions incline powerfully to the Latin, if we may rely on the common representation of them, and one of the editors of the Armenian (*Zohrab*) denies the correctness of the suspicion revived by Tischendorf, "Ætate multo seriori [than its origin in the fourth or fifth century] armenos codices passim ad latinam versionem correctos esse, virorum doctorum opinio fert" (*Proleg.* p. LXXVIII).

It is time to turn to the Queen of the primitive versions, the graceful and perspicuous Peshito Syriac. Here, at any rate, there is no ambiguity as to the preference bestowed on Codex A: it is supported by the Syriac in six cases out of the seven. Nor is this the result of mere accident in the Gospel of St Mark: no one who has studied its readings will question that a like proportion is steadily maintained throughout the New Testament. Here then is a venerable translation, assigned by eminent scholars to the first century of our æra, undoubtedly not later than the second, which habitually upholds the readings of *one* of the two oldest uncial copies, of the later uncials, and of the vast majority in cursive characters. Our conclusion shall now be drawn, *mutatis mutandis*, in the words of Tregelles, when he sums up the results of his induction of the seventy-two passages I have so often alluded to. "Here then is a sample of very many passages, in which, by the testimony of the most ancient version, that such a reading was current in very early times, the fact is proved indubitably; so that even if no existing MS. supported such readings, they would possess a strong claim on our attention: and such facts might have made us doubt, whether the old translators were not in possession of better copies than those that have been transmitted to us. Such facts so proved might lead to the inquiry, whether there are not *some* MSS. which accord with these ancient readings; and when examination shews that such copies actually exist (nay that they are the *many* in contrast to the *few*), it may be regarded as a demonstrated point that such MSS. deserve peculiar attention" (Tregelles, p. 147) . . . . But here I pause; it is enough that I claim for Codex A and its numerous companions "peculiar attention" by reason of their striking conformity with the Peshito Syriac. I ask not, I have no right to ask, that Codex B and its scanty roll of allies, strengthened as they are by the Latin, perhaps by other versions, should be overlooked in forming an estimate of the merits of conflicting readings. I am content to lay myself open to the poet's humorous reproof,

νήπιοι, οὐδὲ ἴσασιν ὅσῳ πλέον ἥμισυ παντός.

How is this divergency of the Peshito version from the text of Codex B explained by Tregelles? He feels of course the pressure of the argument against him, and meets it, if not successfully, with even more than his wonted boldness. The translation degenerates in his hands into "*the version commonly printed as the Peshito*" (p. 170). Now let us mark the precise nature of the demand here made on our faith by Dr Tregelles. He would persuade us that the whole Eastern Church, distracted as it has been and split into hostile sections for the space of 1400 years, Orthodox and Jacobite, Nestorian and Maronite alike, those that could agree about nothing else, have laid aside their bitter jealousies in order to substitute in their monastic libraries and liturgical services another and a spurious version in the room of the Peshito, that sole surviving monument of the first ages of the Gospel in Syria! Nay more, that this wretched forgery has deceived Orientalists profound as Michaelis and Lowth, has passed without suspicion through the ordeal of searching criticism, to which every branch of sacred literature has been subjected during the last half-century! We will require solid reasons indeed before we surrender ourselves to an hypothesis as novel as it appears violently improbable.

And what is the foundation on which our opponent rests his startling conjecture? The reader is aware that besides the Peshito, several other Syriac versions, some grounded upon it, *and therefore implying its previous existence and popularity* (e.g. the Philoxenian, executed A.D. 508, and Cardinal Wiseman's Karkaphensian), others seemingly independent of it (e.g. Adler's Jerusalem Syriac, and a palimpsest fragment lately discovered by Tischendorf) have been more or less applied to the criticism of the New Testament. About the year 1847 Canon Cureton, in his most fruitful researches among the MSS. purchased for the British Museum from the Nitrian monasteries, met with extensive fragments of the Gospels, which Tregelles has collated, and found to contain "altogether *ancient* readings," and thus to be "an important witness to the ancient text" (p. 161). As this MS., assigned to the fifth century, is still unpublished, we can only say at present that it affords us "AN HITHERTO UNKNOWN VERSION;" certainly not "*the version commonly printed as the Peshito*" with mere various readings[1]. To this version has been given the appellation of the

[1] As this sheet is going to press (July 1858) Dr Cureton's "Remains of a very antient recension of the four Gospels in Syriac, hitherto unknown in Europe," has at length appeared. The Syriac text had been printed in 1848, but was doubtless withheld by the learned editor in the hope of finding leisure to write Prolegomena more full, and possibly containing more definite conclusions, than those with which he has favoured us. It would ill become me to express a hasty judgment respecting theories on which so eminent a scholar has bestowed thought and time and much labour. He will naturally expect Biblical critics to hesitate before they implicitly admit, for instance, the persuasion which he hardly likes to embody in words, that we have in these precious Syriac fragments, at least to a great extent (Preface, p. xciii), the very Hebrew original of St Matthew's Gospel, so long supposed to have been lost, that even its existence has been questioned. But topics like this are sure to be warmly debated by abler pens than mine: I will confine myself to those points that concern my argument, *the relation these fragments bear to the Peshito*. And here I would say in all humble deference (for my knowledge of Syriac, though of long standing, is not extensive) that my own hurried comparison of the Curetonian and Peshito texts would have led me to take them so far for quite separate versions. Even Dr Tregelles, who, through the editor's kindness, has been enabled to use the text for years, and whose bias is very strong, can only venture to say "the differences are great; and yet it happens not unfrequently that such coincidences of words and

Curetonian Syriac, and long may it bear that honoured name: but for regarding it as the true Peshito, in the room of that commonly so known, I perceive *at present* no cause whatever except the strong exigency of Dr Tregelles' case.

Yet has not the Peshito Syriac been suspected by previous writers of exhibiting a corrupt or modernised text? Undoubtedly the reconciliation of the Maronites with the see of Rome, and the channels through which its earlier editions were conveyed to us, induced certain critics to hazard a conjecture that this version, like the Armenian, had been tampered with, in order to bring it into closer conformity with the Latin Vulgate. *This, however, is a change in precisely the opposite direction to that which Tregelles' hypothesis demands:* his complaint against the Peshito is not its accordance with the Latin, but its consent with Codex A and the junior MSS. against it. I vouch not for the correctness of this surmise as regards the Armenian; its injustice towards the Peshito is demonstrated by the evidence of that old MS. Rich 7157 in the British Museum, of the eighth century, a period long anterior to that when a "*fœdus cum Syris*" was possible on the part of the admirers of the Vulgate. This precious document has been collated throughout by Tregelles; together with several others of high antiquity in the Museum, it has been carefully examined by Dr Cureton, by Mr Ellis, and two German scholars (Bloomfield, *Preface* to *N. T.*, *ninth edition*, p. viii, *note*). The reports of all concur to the same effect: these venerable MSS. exhibit a text, singularly resembling that of the printed editions; which last were consequently drawn from purer and more ancient sources than, reasoning from the analogy of the Greek text, the warmest advocates of the Peshito had been led to anticipate.

(6). We have little to say about citations from the Fathers. That the Latin ecclesiastical writers should accord with the Latin versions is nothing strange: perhaps some of them could not read, none of them used familiarly the Greek original. As witnesses for the readings of the Italic or Vulgate they are of course valuable: unless in the very rare instances where they expressly appeal to the Greek, their influence upon it is but indirect and precarious. As regards the Greek Fathers I am bound to state, that no branch of Biblical criticism has been

---

renderings are found (and that too, at times, through a great part of a passage) as to shew that they can hardly be *wholly* independent" (Tregelles, Horne's *Introd.* p. 268). To the same effect also Dr Cureton speaks: "It seems to be scarcely possible that the Syriac text published by Widmanstad, which, throughout these pages, I have called the Peshito, could be altogether a different version from this. It would take up too much space to institute here a comparison of passages to establish this fact, which, indeed, any one may easily do for himself" (Preface, p. lxx). I heartily wish that Dr Cureton had fully investigated the subject; he might have removed the difficulties at least of those who love truth, and are ready to embrace it wherever they shall find it. As it is, we can but say with Tregelles, "Such a point as this can only be properly investigated after the publication of this version shall have given sufficient time to scholars to pursue a thorough investigation" (Tregelles, *ubi supra*). In the mean while neither he nor I are at liberty to *assume* the truth of that hypothesis which may happen to harmonise best with our preconceived opinions.

so utterly neglected as the application of their citations to the discussion of various readings; indeed I know almost nothing that has been seriously attempted with respect to it, except Griesbach's examination of the quotations of Origen in his *Symbolæ Criticæ*. The whole question, however, is so replete with difficulties, that Bishop Fell (*N. T. Oxon.* 1675) thought the bare allusion to them sufficient to absolve him from entering upon it at all. The ancient Fathers were better theologians than critics; they often quoted loosely, often from memory; what they actually wrote has been found peculiarly liable to change on the part of copyists: their testimony therefore can be implicitly trusted, even as to the MSS. which lay before them, only in the comparatively few places where the course of their argument, or the current of their exposition, renders it manifest what reading they support. At present we have many intimations in our critical editions that this or that ecclesiastical author countenances a *variation* from the Textus Receptus, but few cases, very few indeed, are recorded in which they *agree with it:* the latter point being confessedly no less essential to our accurate acquaintance with the state of the evidence than the former. Any enlarged discussion on this head of our argument must at any rate be postponed till we possess more reliable information on the facts it involves: most thankful should I be to any student who has leisure and disposition to enter upon this wide yet almost unoccupied field. Meantime I am constrained to admit that many examples have been established by Griesbach and his successors, wherein Origen agrees with Codices BL against Codex A and the received text, one or both. I will not dissemble, I strive not to evade, the force of such early testimony where it is unambiguous and express: let such readings be received with "peculiar attention," let them never be rejected without grave and sufficient reason. Yet the support given to B or L by Origen is *very far* from being uniform or "habitual." While I can well understand the importance of his confirmation where he countenances the readings they exhibit, I fail altogether in apprehending what service he can do them, where he is either silent or positively hostile[1].

Those who have followed me through this prolonged investigation (which I knew not how to abridge without sacrificing perspicuity to conciseness) will readily anticipate my reply to Dr Tregelles' "statement of his case," comprehended in the following emphatic words: "It is claimed that the *united* testimony of versions, fathers, and the oldest MSS. should be preferred to that of the mass of modern

---

[1] e.g. Origen sides with the received text or with A against B, Matth. xxi. 29 cited by Tregelles (p. 107), and in the course of the next few chapters in xxv. 27; 29; xxvi. 48; 53; xxvii. 3; 11; 54 *bis*; xxviii. 15; 18. I could multiply references *lectoris ad fastidium*. It may tend to shew the precariousness of patristic testimony if I add that in five of the above-named passages Origen's authority may be cited on *both* sides.

copies; and farther, that the character of the few ancient MSS. which agree with versions and fathers, must be such (*from that very circumstance*) as to make their general evidence the more trustworthy" (p. 141). Unquestionably, I rejoin, your claim is reasonable, it is irresistible. If you shew us all, or nearly all, the uncials you prize so deservedly, maintaining a variation from the common text which is recommended by *all* the best versions and most ancient Fathers, depend upon it we will not urge against such overwhelming testimony the mere number of the cursive copies, be they ever so unanimous on the other side. But are we not discussing a purely abstract proposition? Do we ever find the "united" testimony of the ancients drawing us one way, that of the juniors another? I will not assert that such instances may not occur, though at this moment I can hardly remember one: it is enough to say that principles broad as those laid down by Tregelles must be designed to meet the rule, not the exception. In the seven texts we have been reviewing, in the sixty-five that remain on his list, in the yet more numerous cases he tells us he has passed over, the uncial MSS. are not unequally divided; or where there is a preponderance, it is not often in our adversary's favour. The elder authorities being thus at variance, common sense seems to dictate an appeal to those later authorities, respecting which one thing is clear, that they were *not* copied immediately from the uncials still extant. Such later codices thus become the representatives of others that have perished, as old, and (to borrow Davidson's suggestion, p. viii) not improbably more old than any now remaining. These views appear so reasonable and sober, that they have approved themselves to the judgment even of Dr Tregelles: for he does not by any means disdain the aid of the few cursive copies (*e.g.* 1. 33. 69. &c.) which "preserve an ancient text," whereby of course is implied one coinciding with his *preconceived* opinion of what an ancient text ought to be[1].

Perhaps I shall be expected to say a few words respecting the scheme devised by Bentley for settling the sacred text on a firmer basis, since both Tregelles and his precursor Lachmann (*N. T. Proleg.* Vol. I. p. xxx) have sheltered their practice of recurring *exclusively* to the most ancient extant documents beneath the shadow of that great name. We shall all agree on one point, that no authority, however imposing, can supply the place of *argument* in enquiries of this kind; nor do I scruple to confess that were I disposed to swear allegiance to any earthly teacher, it would be to that illustrious scholar,

---

[1] Dean Alford had constructed the text of his first volume of the Greek Testament (1st edition) on nearly the same plan as Tregelles would, and thoroughly was he dissatisfied with the result. "The adoption of that text," he writes with admirable frankness, "was, I do not hesitate to confess, *a great mistake*. It proceeded on altogether too high an estimate of the most ancient existing MSS., and too low an one of the importance of internal evidence." (*N. T.* Vol. II. *Proleg.* p. 58.)

whose learning and genius shed a bright ray across the darkness of his evil generation. It is painful to say of the most highly gifted man that ever devoted himself to the study of Biblical criticism, that his leading principle was taken up hastily and on precarious grounds; yet if the fact be so, why need we hesitate to avow it? Bentley's theory, as most of my readers will remember, was built on the idea, that the oldest MSS. of the Greek original and of Jerome's Latin version, resemble each other so marvellously, even in the very order of the words, that by means of this agreement he could restore the text as it stood in the fourth century, "so that there shall not be twenty words, or even particles, difference!" "By taking two thousand errors out of the Pope's [Clementine] Vulgate, and as many out of the Protestant Pope Stephens's [1550], I can set out an edition of each in columns, without using any book under nine hundred years old, that shall so exactly agree word for word, and, what at first amazed me, order for order, that no two tallies, nor two indentures, can agree better." Thus wrote Bentley to Archbishop Wake in 1716: the tone of his "Proposals," in 1720, after considerable progress had been made in the work of collation, is not *materially* less confident. Yet to those who have calmly examined the subject, the wonder is not the closeness of agreement between the Greek and Latin Codices, but that a man of so vast erudition and ability should have imagined that he perceived it, to any thing approaching the extent the lowest sense of his words demands. Accordingly when his collations came to be examined, and compared, and weighed, keen indeed must have been the disappointment of our English Aristarchus. With characteristic fearlessness he had been at no trouble to *select* his materials (at least I trace no indication of such choice in his surviving papers), and thus the truth would burst upon him all the sooner, that the theory on which he had staked a noble reputation, in the face of watchful enemies, must either be abandoned or extensively modified. We can well understand the struggle which silently agitated that proud spirit. Had the subject of his labours been Terence or Milton, it were easy to conjecture the course he would have adopted: if MSS. refused to support his system, they must have been forced to yield to it. But Bentley, with all his faults of temper, was an honest and a pious man; he dared not make the text of Holy Scripture the victim of his sportive ingenuity; and so, soon after the year 1721, we come to hear less and less of his projected Greek Testament. Though he lived till 1742, it does not appear that he ever made serious progress in arranging the stores collected by himself and his coadjutors. As I have turned over his papers in the Library of Trinity College, with a heart saddened by the spectacle of so much labour lost, I could not persuade myself that the wretched dissensions which embittered his declining days had, of themselves, power enough over Bentley's mind to break off in the midst a work that he had once regarded as his best passport to undying fame.

From the facts we have been discussing I feel entitled to draw two or three practical inferences.

(*a*). That the true readings of the Greek New Testament cannot safely be derived from any one set of authorities, whether MSS., versions, or Fathers, but ought to be the result of a patient comparison and careful estimate of the evidence given by them all.

(*b*). That where there is a real agreement between all the documents prior to the tenth century, the testimony of later MSS., though not to be rejected unheard, is to be regarded with much suspicion, and, unless supported by strong internal evidence[1], can hardly be adopted.

(*c*). That in the far more numerous cases where the most ancient documents are at variance with each other, the later or cursive copies are of great importance, as the surviving representatives of other codices, very probably as early, possibly even earlier, than any now extant[2].

I do not lay down these propositions as any new discovery of my own, but as being (*even the second of them*) the principles on which all reasonable defenders of the *Textus Receptus* have upheld its GENERAL INTEGRITY.

IV. I have a good hope that the foregoing investigation of the laws of Comparative Criticism will have convinced an impartial reader, that the cursive or junior copies of the Greek New Testament have, in their proper place and due subordination, a real and appreciable influence in questions relating to doubtful readings. If I have succeeded thus far, it results that the time and pains I have bestowed on studying them have not been wasted: the collations I have accumulated cannot fail to be of some service to the Biblical critic, even though he may think I have a little exaggerated their value and importance. I am not so sanguine as to the degree of popular acceptance my views may obtain, nor (without affecting absolute indifference on the subject) am I by any means so anxious on this head. I have always thought that the researches and labours of the scholar—of the theological scholar above all others—are

[1] If I have hitherto said nothing on the important head of internal evidence, it is from no wish to disparage its temperate and legitimate use. Yet how difficult it is to hinder its degenerating, even in skilful hands, into vague and arbitrary conjecture!

[2] Even Mr Green, from whom I fear I differ widely on some of the topics discussed in this chapter, does not shrink from saying, "In a review of authorities special regard will reasonably be paid to antiquity; but this must not be overstrained into a summary neglect of more recent witnesses, as necessarily offering nothing worthy of notice:" finely adding, "The critic should not suffer himself to be encumbered by prepossessions or assumptions, nor bind himself to the routine of a mechanical method of procedure. If he allows himself to be thus warped and trammelled, instead of ever maintaining the free employment of a watchful, calm, and unfettered mind, he abandons his duty and mars his work" (*Course of Developed Criticism, Introduction*, p. x.).

their own highest and purest reward[1]. Let me plead guilty to having read with sensations akin to scorn, the manuscript note appended by Cæsar de Missy (a person who might have known better) to the copy of Hearne's scarce edition of the Codex Laudianus (published in 1715), now preserved in the British Museum. To Hearne's miserable list of just *forty-one* subscribers to his book, De Missy subjoins the sarcastic comment "*Après cela, Docteur, va pâlir sur la Bible!*" Yet why should he not have grown pale in the study of God's Word? Why not have handed down to happier times a treasure of sacred learning which the princes and prelates of George the First's reign (that nadir-point of public virtue and intellectual cultivation in England) were too slothful to appreciate, too negligent even to despise? The pursuits of Scriptural criticism are so quiet, so laborious, that they can have few charms for the votary of fame, or the courtier of preferment: they always have been, perhaps they always must be, the choice employment mainly of those, who, feeling conscious (it may be) of having but one talent committed to their keeping, seek nothing so earnestly as TO USE THAT ONE TALENT WELL.

---

[1] I should have wished to add some noble sentiments of Dr Dobbin (*Codex Montfortianus, Preface*, p. xx.) on this point, but that I trust they are known to my readers, as they well deserve to be.

CHAPTER II.

DESCRIPTION OF CERTAIN MANUSCRIPTS COLLATED BY F. H. SCRIVENER.

THE following contributions to the criticism of the Greek Testament are now submitted to the Biblical student.

I. A transcript of the uncial CODEX AUGIENSIS GRÆCO-LATINUS OF ST PAUL'S EPISTLES. The importance of this venerable document, no less than its countless variations from the printed text in both languages, seems to make a full publication of its contents very advisable. No pains or diligence has been spared to render the copy here exhibited a faithful representation of the original manuscript.

II. A full and exact collation of eight manuscripts of the Gospels (three being Evangelistaria in uncial letters), of fifteen containing the Acts and Catholic Epistles, of fifteen copies of St Paul's Epistles, and thirteen of the Apocalypse, few of which have been previously used for critical purposes.

I have set down the variations of these fifty-one documents from the standard text (Elzevir, 1624) with a minuteness not before deemed necessary by others, or indeed by myself in my "Collation of Manuscripts of the Holy Gospels." Not only have I noted the various readings strictly so called, but every peculiarity of grammatical inflexion or breathing, every erasure or error of the pen, every *remarkable* change, whether of accent or punctuation, will be found recorded in these pages. In adopting this plan, I have acted not so much on my own judgment, as the earnest desire of several scholars, who have wished my labours to present them with as true an image as possible of the original codices. Undoubtedly the real value of our materials, the degree of care exercised by the respective scribes, together with many interesting and significant peculiarities of each document, may thus be preserved for the curious inquirer: nor in consulting a book of reference like the present can any one be seriously incommoded by what he may think an error of excess on my part. A portion of my task whose usefulness is less open to dispute is my anxiety to state, in the case of every important variation, not only which of my authorities differ from the received text, but which of them agree with it.

I proceed to lay before the reader, as clearly and briefly as I may, some account of the manuscripts I have collated, beginning with that whose transcript covers so many of the following pages.

I. The CODEX AUGIENSIS is a Greek and Latin Manuscript of St Paul's Epistles, written in uncial letters, probably of the ninth century, deposited in the Library of Trinity College, Cambridge (B. 17. 1), to the Master and Fellows of which society I am deeply indebted, as well for the munificent aid they have afforded me in the publication of this volume, as for their liberal permission to use this and other precious documents at my own residence. The Codex Augiensis is written on 136 quarto leaves of fine vellum, 9 inches long by 7¼ broad, and has a rude binding in wood, such as was common in Germany and the Low Countries some centuries ago: on the leathern back are stamped the initials of one of its late owners (G. M. W.). Each page contains 28 lines and is divided into two columns, wherein the Latin version is set alongside of the Greek text, the Latin column being always placed outside. This copy commences, Rom. iii. 19, μω λεγει, and the Greek ends, Philem. v. 20, εν χρω. There also occur the following hiatus in the Greek; 1 Corinth. iii. 8 to v. 16, οικει εν υμιν: *ibid.* vi. 7 to the end of v. 14: and Coloss. ii. 1, after λαοδικια to v. 8, κοσμου[1]. In all these places *after* Rom. iii. 19, the Latin version is complete, being carried on to the end of the Epistle to the Hebrews; but the very same hiatus are found in the Greek text and *Latin version* of the CODEX BOERNERIANUS (*Matthæi*, 1791), although this latter document contains portions of the Epistle to the Romans before the place where the Codex Augiensis begins.

The recent history of our manuscript may be traced by means of the inscriptions and notes at its beginning and end, which I have copied below, p. 272, and need not here repeat. It was first the property of the monastery whence it derives its name, that of Augia Major, or Augia Dives, Reichenau (*rich meadow*) on a fertile island in the lower part of Lake Constance in Baden; not Augia Rheni, Rheinau (*meadow of the Rhine*) on an island near the cataract of Schaffhausen, as Michaelis and others state (Reeves' edition of Adamnan's "Life of St Columba," Pref. p. xxii): Bentley's note "Monasterium Augiae, *in Belgis*, ubi institutus est Goddeschalchus" seems to point to Orbais in the diocese of Soissons and modern Department of the Marne, some thirty miles east of Paris. If Wetstein be right in supplying "Concilii" after "Basiliensis" [A.D. 1431] in the earliest inscription, p. 272, the book must have belonged to that monastery in the fifteenth century; whence it came into the possession of G. M. Wepfer, of Schaffhausen, and then of L. Ch. Mieg, who permitted Wetstein to examine it. Wetstein induced Bentley to purchase this Codex at Heidelberg in 1718, the German bookseller parting with it at cost price (250 Dutch florins) in consideration for the fame and learning of the prince of English scholars[2]. Bentley, as

---

[1] Eight leaves of the Codex Augiensis, which ought to follow fol. 55, have been placed by the binder after fol. 102.

[2] Or rather perhaps as Bentley states the case when writing to Wetstein at the time (*Bentley Correspondence*, p. 541), "ob beneficia a me partim

will be seen from his manuscript notes, formed a high estimate of the Codex Augiensis, and used it for his projected edition of the Greek Testament. I have compared his collation (consisting of the Greek text only) with my own transcript, and extracted (*infra*, p. 284) the few notes interspersed with it from the margin of his copy of the Oxford Greek Testament 1675, now preserved with his other papers and books in Trinity College Library (B. 17. 8). The first published collation of our manuscript was that of Wetstein, in whose notation it is marked F of the Pauline Epistles; but as this was easily seen to be very imperfect, it was again examined by Tischendorf in 1842, and by Dr Tregelles in 1845, for their editions of the Greek Testament. The result of Tischendorf's labours appears in his manual N. T. of 1849, but it is obviously impossible in so small a volume to do anything like justice to such a document as this: indeed I may fairly apply to his case the language of Matthæi respecting the kindred Códex Boernerianus: "Etenim nec Kusterus nec Wetstenius satis accuratè omnia hujus Codicis singularia notaverant, *nec vero etiam, nisi totum transcribere voluissent, potuerant.* Plura enim prorsus singularia nullus inter Codices N. T. habet, nisi fortasse Evangeliorum et Actuum Bezæ seu Cantabrigiensis" (*Præf. Cod. Boern.* p. III.)[1]. I should add that Tischendorf was the first to pay attention to the Latin translation in F (denoted by f), remarkable and in some measure perplexing as it is. "Primus contuli et passim citavi" is his statement (*Nov. Test. Proleg.* p. LXXXII.); yet his citations are comparatively few (no less than eight variations being omitted in Rom. viii.), and convey no adequate representation of its peculiar character. I have reason to know that this defect will be supplied in his seventh edition.

In estimating the age and country of this manuscript we are scarcely left to conjecture. The style of writing both in its Latin and Greek columns, its manifest connexion with the Codex Boernerianus, and *consequently* with the Codex Sangallensis of the Gospels (Δ) published in lithograph *facsimile* by Rettig (Turici, 1836); no less than the extraneous matter it contains, written in the same hand as the sacred text, all seem to point distinctly to the West of Europe, and the middle of the ninth century.

This foreign matter consists of a Latin Prologue to the Epistle to the Hebrews (*infra*, p. 252), the only Argument in the Codex Augiensis, and a kind of Epilogue to the same Epistle (pp. 268—272), having however but little reference to it. Both the Prologue and Epilogue are found in the works of Rabanus Maurus, Archbishop of Mayence, who died A.D. 856, and is justly termed by Dean Waddington (*History of the Church*, p. 259, first edition)

---

accepta, partim adhuc sperata:" yet who would not gladly impute their courtesy to the higher motive?

[1] "Nam de Augiensi," Matthæi strangely adds, "quia ubi nunc lateat, ignoratur, non attinet commemorare." This was in 1791, yet the Cod. Augiensis was then at Trinity College, having been placed there in 1787, after the death of Richard Bentley the nephew.

"the most profound theologian of the age." The Prologue is prefixed to that prelate's Commentary on the Hebrews (Migne, *Patrologia*, Tom. 112, Paris, 1851; *Rabani Opera*, Tom. VI. p. 711); the Epilogue is annexed to Rabanus' Treatise "*De Modo Pœnitentiæ,*" comprising the twenty-third and concluding chapter of that work, with the title "DICTA ABBATIS PINOPHI" (Migne, *Patrologia*, Tom. 112, p. 1329); yet, as in the case of the Codex Augiensis, it has no special connection with the preceding matter, only that it was manifestly familiar to Rabanus, who has employed its sentiments, and sometimes its very words, throughout his own Treatise[1]. Now when we consider that *both* the Prologue and Epilogue are found in the volumes of Rabanus, it need not materially modify our estimate of the date of the Codex Augiensis were we to learn that one or both of them has been traced *separately* to an earlier source. The Prologue is read almost verbatim, in the Codex Amiatinus edited by Tischendorf (1850, 1854), the most venerable existing MS. of the Latin Vulgate, whose date is the sixth century: while a marginal note has been affixed by a modern hand to the Epilogue in our MS. (fol. 139, p. 2)[2], directing our attention to Cumianus, an Irish writer of the middle of the seventh century. On comparing the passage cited (*Bibliotheca Patrum Maxima*, Lugduni 1677, Tom. XII. p. 42) with our Postscript, the resemblance between them appears so slight and general that it is hard to believe that the writer of the note could have ever read both pieces throughout: in the few opening sentences alone is there any real similarity. There seems, therefore, at present no reason for disturbing the general opinion which has assigned the date of our Manuscript to the next generation after Charlemagne.

We are led to much the same conclusion when we regard the Codex Augiensis in connexion with the Codices Sangallensis and Boernerianus: I name them together, for no one that has read Rettig's elaborate Prolegomena to the former (Cap. IV. pp. 18—23) will hesitate to consider them as portions of one and the same document. The close affinity subsisting between the Codices Augiensis

---

[1] The Codex Augiensis should be used for correcting the text of Rabanus: thus, both it and the Cod. Amiatinus supply an important sentence in the Argument to the Hebrews, and it confirms Migne's conjecture "elemosinarum," fol. 140, p. 1, col. 1, l. 6. After "jam non recordabor," fol. 141, p. 1, col. 2, l. 1, there is no resemblance between our MS. and the "Dicta Pinophi," either in the words or sense. For this Abbot Pinophus I have searched in vain every index of mediæval literature I could meet with. I must leave him to some one who may be more fortunate.

[2] I subjoin the whole note, the cramped handwriting of which has perplexed more readers than one: "respondent sæc [sequentia?] quadantenus variis illis remittendi peccata modis, quorum meminit Origenes Homil. II. in Levit." A later scribe adds, "imo potius conveniunt iis quæ Cumianus habet in l. de Poenitentiarum mensura· qui auctor vixit an̄ 640. et iis quæ extant B. Patr. T. XII. p. 42." For *habet in* Tischendorf reads *Rabani*, for *habet* Mr Hort (in Tregelles' Horne, p. 198 note) reads *Fata* or *Fota*, and obligingly points out to me that "Fota" or "the Long" was the *sobriquet* of Cumianus or Commin (nat. A.D. 592; Cave, *Histor. Literar.* Tom. I. p. 584, Oxon. 1740). I believe, however, that when he shall next consult the MS., he will find my reading of the word correct. I have placed an asterisk on p. 268, at the place where this marginal note begins.

and Boernerianus has indeed no parallel in this branch of literature, for the Codex Sangermanensis of St Paul's Epistles (E) is nothing but a bad copy of the great Codex Claromontanus (D), and having as such no critical value whatever, ought long since to have been expunged from the list of authorities. No suspicion of this kind can be reasonably entertained in the present case. The Latin versions in the two copies are *essentially* different, and though the circumstance that the same hiatus are met with in the Greek text of each, and their intimate correspondence even in errors of the scribe, abundantly prove that they are derived from the same Greek prototype ("ejusdem veteris exemplaris apographo," as Bentley expresses it, *infra*, p. 284), yet the supposition that the one was immediately derived from the other, will be found quite irreconcileable with ascertained phenomena. I have made an accurate collation of the Codex Augiensis with Matthæi's edition of the Codex Boernerianus, which was lately ascertained by Böttiger to be very exact, and have placed its results at the foot of each page in my transcript in the following pages. Hence it appears that the two documents vary from each other in 1984 places; whereof 579 are mere blunders of the pen; 968 *itacisms*, or changes of one vowel into another[1]; 166 relate to a similar interchange of consonants; 71 to grammatical or orthographical forms; while the real various readings amount to 200, of which 32 arise from the omission or insertion of the article. Elsewhere the Greek texts of these manuscripts are identical, coinciding in the minutest points.

The 166 instances of interchange of consonants are chiefly corrections in the Codex Boernerianus of anomalies found in the Codex Augiensis; yet many remain common to both, from which might be drawn up a catalogue to the full as curious as that of Rettig in his Prolegomena to the Codex Sangallensis, and much of the same character. *A few examples will suffice for a thousand*, and it is quite evident that the scribe who adopted them had a most imperfect acquaintance with Greek. Thus Δ and Θ are perpetually confused in F; e.g. ανδρωπος, Gal. iii. 15; v. 3; Eph. vi. 6; Phil. ii. 7; Col. iii. 22: but αθελφος Phil. ii. 25; iii. 1; 13; 17; iv. 1; 21; Coloss. i. 1; 2; 1 Thess. iv. 10, *bis;* 13; v. 1 *p.m.*; 4 *p.m.*; 12 *p.m.*; 1 Tim. iv. 6 *p.m.*; v. 1; 2; αληδιαν, 1 Tim. iv. 3 *p.m.*: αγωνιζομεδα, *ibid.* v. 10 *p.m.*; παραδεκην, 2 Tim. i. 12: λυδαδην (pro αυθαδη), Tit. i. 7. So Ν and Π, τουπαντιον, Gal. ii. 7: συνυνεκριθησαν, *ibid.* v. 13: λυνειται, Ephes. iv. 30: πρενει, v. 3: περινατιτε, *ibid.* v. 8: especially κονος (pro κοπος), 2 Cor. x. 15; xi. 23; 27, *passim.* Thus also Τ and Θ are interchanged, ενειχεσται, 2 Cor. xi. 4: απολογουμετα, xii. 19 *p.m.*: καθαρτιζεσθαι, xiii. 11: ανθεστην, Gal. ii. 11. Similarly with ζ and ξ, Rom. vii. 11 has εζηπατησεν both in F and G; but Phil. iii. 8 εξημειωθην: see also F in Col. i. 29; iii. 13; 1 Thess. v. 3; 2 Thess. i. 3;

---

[1] In both MSS. the vowels are interchanged as much as in any copy I know, none perhaps so frequently as ο and ω: yet I would not quite assert with Tregelles (Horne, p. 198), that the writer of F "used them without discrimination. The interchange of ε and η is nearly as frequent.

1 Tim. i. 6; Tit. i. 2; ii. 9. Η and Ν are constantly interchanged in G, and sometimes in F, e.g. Eph. i. 17; iii. 8; 2 Tim. iii. 13. The confusion of μ and ν, noted by Matthæi in G, is also found in F, e.g. Rom. xv. 26; 1 Cor. i. 9; as is the more natural error of Α for Δ (1 Cor. iii. 19), Λ for Α (Tit. i. 7), Λ for Δ (2 Cor. xii. 6). The decided Latinism Π for Ρ (e.g. 1 Tim. ii. 1) and *vice versâ* is very frequent: σρερμα, Rom. ix. 7: παραρτωματι, xi. 11: αγαρητοι, 1 Cor. x. 14 *p.m.*: but πληποφορεισον, 2 Tim. iv. 5. Mutations of π and β (1 Tim. iv. 14), of κ and χ (especially in εκθρος and εκθρα, e.g. Rom. v. 10; viii. 7; xii. 20), of ξ and χ (Rom. xi. 14, G; 1 Cor. vi. 2, F; 2 Cor. iii. 18, F; 1 Tim. i. 15) of νχ for γχ (σπλανχνα, Philem. vv. 7; 12) constantly occur, and need not here be further cited.

There are no signs of the ordinary breathings and accents in this manuscript. Codex F occasionally, and G more often places a straight line *nearly* horizontal over the initial vowel of a word, which may be designed for the aspirate, but is found in some few places where the vowel takes the lenis (ιδιον, 1 Cor. vi. 18; vii. 4; 37; ισσα, Phil. ii. 6; see also 1 Tim. iv. 15). This mark is of some importance from the circumstance that both in F and G it is placed over OC in 1 Tim. iii. 16, for which various reading in the place of ΘC these codices are well known to be the chief, I had almost said the only *unequivocal* witnesses. Yet I do not believe that the line was intended to denote that OC was the familiar abbreviation for θεος, for not only is there not the faintest trace of such a line *within* the O as shall make it become Θ[1], but the line is placed *over* too many initial and aspirated omicrons to render it probable that anything more was intended here (1 Thess. i. 9 F G; 1 Tim. iii. 1 G; iv. 14 G; 15 FG; vi. 15 *bis* FG). Another peculiarity of these codices is the strange and sometimes indeed the absurd manner in which the words are separated from each other. The continuous mode of writing, with no space or division between the words, which prevailed in the elder Greek uncial copies, was by this time laid aside, and the scribe of the Codex Augiensis seems to have intended to place a *middle* point or stop (·) after the last letter of each word he wrote. These points I have faithfully retained in my transcript, and though the penman neglects them in some passages (about fol. 12 and elsewhere they almost disappear for a while), yet on the whole they are found pretty uniformly in all parts of the MS. Parts of the *same* word, originally separated, are often linked (*p.m.* as it would seem) by a curve (‿), the point once between them being partially or wholly erased. In the Codex Boernerianus few such stops are found, but an interval is left between the several words much in the fashion of modern writing. Now the point I would draw attention to is this: that while the mode in which the words

[1] Of course I speak of the Codex Augiensis from close and repeated examination, and the reader will judge for himself by the photograph contained in this volume. The facsimile of this passage from the Codex Boernerianus is given in Matthæi's *Greek Testament*, Vol. I. p. 4.

are divided in each copy displays much ignorance on the part of the penman, there is no striking resemblance in the actual blunders: the two documents therefore were derived *separately* from some early codex, in which there was probably no interval between the words; and consequently in those places where F and G *agree*, they must not be estimated as two distinct authorities, but as one; the surviving representatives of a manuscript now lost, perhaps a century or two older than themselves.

This is true as regards the Greek text: their respective Latin versions are quite independent and even more interesting than the Greek to a Biblical critic. "Codex Augiensis latinam interpretationem eamque veterem vulgatam adscriptam habet, Boernerianus vero græcis superscriptam eamque veterem italam," is Tischendorf's decision (*Proleg. N. T.* p. LXXIII). Tregelles again terms the Latin version of F a very good copy of that of Jerome, "far superior to that generally current" (Tregelles' Horne, p. 198). I am not sure whether Dr Davidson has closely examined this subject, as his description of this copy is not quite free from error, yet I conceive his view of the version to be more correct, when he regards it as "patched and mended so as to be a mixture of the Old Latin and Jerome's" (*Treatise on Biblical Criticism*, Vol. II.). But in fact the internal history of the Latin Vulgate translation, and its relation to the Italic or old Latin, under the various forms wherein the latter has been preserved to us, remain yet to be investigated, nor is this the place to venture on so large a field of inquiry. The Latin portion of the Codex Augiensis (called f by Tischendorf) will I believe prove very useful to the scholar who shall undertake the thorough examination of this question: for the present it shall suffice to offer a few general remarks.

Our version then will be found to approximate much nearer to the Clementine Vulgate, or to the best MSS. of Jerome's version, such as the Codices Amiatinus and Fuldensis, in those parts of the manuscript where the Greek is lost: indeed to differ from one or more of them only in affording some good various readings. There is wider divergency in other places, yet even there it very much consists of readings assimilated to those of the Greek text in the parallel columns, or of changes in the order of words, which are thus made to approach to that of the original, a tendency too natural under the circumstances to excite surprise. Sometimes, when the variation in order is more extensive than usual, marks are placed over the Greek words, referring them to the corresponding Latin (e.g. Rom. xi. 22). In some parts of this MS. (e.g. 1 Cor. x.) the divergences of the Latin version in our copy from the Vulgate are considerable: its renderings approaching nearer to those of the Italic MSS. In many passages, however, the Latin reading agrees with the *printed* Vulgate against the Greek (e.g. Rom. xii. 11; 1 Cor. xi. 2; 24; xiv. 18; xv. 51; 2 Cor. i. 20; iii. 13; v. 3; 19; xi. 23; Gal. i. 6 *p.m.*; v. 25; Ephes. vi. 19; Phil. ii. 11; iii. 8; 17; 20; 2 Tim. i. 9; iv. 22): while in some instances it departs from the Greek and *present* Vulgate text jointly (*e. g.*

Rom. ix. 4; 1 Cor. x. 1; 29; xv. 23; Eph. iii. 11; Phil. iii. 7; 1 Tim. v. 1; 2 Tim. i. 15 *bis*); and often sides with the Greek against the Vulgate (e.g. 1 Cor. vi. 20; ix. 24; x. 2; 19; Gal. v. 22; *et passim*).

Throughout the whole MS. many Latin words will be seen placed over the Greek, probably by a later[1], certainly by an ancient hand, a large portion of which, viz. 86 cases out of the whole 106, are derived from the interlinear version of the Codex Boernerianus[2]: of the remainder, one rendering "*waltet*" 1 Cor. vii. 4 is in German, which was doubtless the native language of this scribe. Either therefore a later hand must have corrected the Cod. Augiensis by its kindred copy (which from other improvements *in the Greek* may be deemed not impossible), or the interlinear Latin in both documents was taken from their common prototype, which in that case must have exhibited the old Italic and not Jerome's revised translation. The Latin version in F is somewhat carelessly written, at least in parts (e.g. foll. 49, 50). I have thought it my duty to retain in my copy all the original errors of the pen.

I would not positively assert that the Codex Augiensis is the work of a single scribe: certainly when the misplaced leaves 56—63 are seen in the later part of the MS. after fol. 102, the contrast in style of writing is rather striking. Yet those who are most conversant with palæography will often feel the most diffident in pronouncing judgment on this point, so greatly does the hand change in the course of a long task; and so much is it influenced by the prospect of an abundance or scarcity of vellum or paper. Yet in a case like that before us, where the same document was faithfully copied at the same time and place, the question respecting the identity of the copyist is hardly worth discussing[3].

Wetstein, I believe, was the first to speak of the Anglo-Saxon form of the Latin characters (*N. T. Proleg.* Tom. II. 8), but I perceive no real difference between the style of this MS. and of many of the same date which abound in public libraries (*e.g. Bodleian, Douce,* 322). Hence I would rather acquiesce in the statement of the late accomplished John Wordsworth (*infra*, p. 272): "This MS. is not written in Anglo-Saxon characters, as has been described, but in the renovated minuscule of the Caroline period." While the Greek portion is executed in a neat but rather rude uncial character, the Latin is in a cursive hand, the intervals between the words well marked, and the whole appearance one of singular elegance and clearness. The reader will observe from my copy

---

[1] *pota illum*, Rom. xii. 20, and perhaps some other words, are clearly *p. m.*

[2] From which, I presume, h was inserted before *υποκρισει*, Fol. 118, p. 2, l. 18.

[3] I am quite willing to acquiesce in Dr Tregelles' statement, in his edition of Horne's *Introduction*, Vol. II. p. 189: "If different parts of the Codex Augiensis are compared, it may seem as if it had been written by several hands from the variety in the character of the Greek; but if the leaves are looked at consecutively (and not in the order in which some of them are *now* transposed) [*vid. supra, p.* xxiii, *note* 1.], it will be seen that the changes are so gradual as to indicate the same hand having become more practised (or more wearied) in tracing Greek letters."

that prepositions, &c. are often joined closely with the following word. Here again a few of the consonants are repeatedly interchanged, b with p[1], d with t, c with s, x with ch (1 Cor. xii. 31), and p with r in $\overline{\text{xps}}$ or $\overline{\text{xpc}}$, both which forms perpetually occur, the latter perhaps the more frequently. The letter r has often the shape of ϲ, and twice (Rom. ix. 19; 2 Tim. iii. 17) r is used where ϲ is plainly meant. On the other hand, a few Latin letters and forms have crept into the Greek text, as in Gal. v. 24; 1 Tim. iv. 2; 2 Tim. iii. 4 *p.m.*; iv. 1. Indeed υ, u and y are much confounded: the genitive ι for ου occurs 2 Cor. ii. 15; v. 10; 1 Tim. iv. 6; Philem. 9 *p.m.*: ι for the pl. nom. οι, 1 Cor. ix. 5; xv. 48; 2 Thess. iii. 8: ις for οις, 1 Cor. xvi. 16: k is read in karissimus, but not (I think) elsewhere.

The abbreviations or contractions in the Greek text are confined to the words, θεος, κυριος, ιησους, χριστος, πατηρ, πνευμα, and their oblique cases; these are common to most uncial copies. The Codex Augiensis however (thus resembling the Cod. Boernerianus) is peculiar in reading $\overline{\iota\eta\upsilon}$, $\overline{\iota\eta\nu}$, $\overline{\chi\rho\upsilon}$, $\overline{\chi\rho\nu}$, although the more usual forms $\overline{\iota\upsilon}$, $\overline{\iota\nu}$, $\overline{\chi\upsilon}$, $\overline{\chi\nu}$ are often met with. It also sometimes reads ȣ for ου. All these peculiarities I have, of course, studiously retained.

The Latin version has many more contractions, though these are so unequally distributed that on many pages (especially near the beginning) there are scarce any. The page we represent in photograph exhibits an average number. Most of them will be found in other MSS. of about the same date, but since I have not exhibited them in my transcript except for special reasons, I have been the more careful to draw up the following complete list of them.

Both in the middle and end of a word – over a letter denotes *m*: over *m* it stands for *en* (e. g. $\overline{\text{am}}$), over *t* or *v* for *er* (e.g. tali$\overline{\text{t}}$), over the last written

---

[1] Since Reichenau, like St Gall and other neighbouring foundations, was much frequented in the ninth century by Irish monks and pilgrims, the Codex Augiensis has been thought to have been written by a scribe of that nation. I note however a considerable difference both in style of writing and in neatness between the *Latin* of this MS., and the rude coarse hand of the Codices Sangallensis and Boernerianus, which strikingly resemble the interlined copy of the Lord's Prayer appended to the Reichenau MS. of the Life of St Columba, founder of Hy [Icolmkill] by Adamnan, and published with it in 1857 for the Irish Archæological Society by Dr Reeves, the Celtic scholar, to whom we were indebted ten years ago for the interpretation of the *Irish* stanzas at the foot of fol. 23 of the Codex Boernerianus. The learned editor has also laboriously collected from this MS. of Adamnan (which he assigns to the eighth century), from the Book of Armagh (A.D. 807) and other kindred sources, those orthographical peculiarities which he considers to characterise Irish MSS. of about the ninth century (Preface, p. xvi). I believe that his list would have been more useful had he excluded mere errors of the pen, and made it rather more select: some of his forms, e. g. *-is* for *-es*, *c* and *t* interchanged, *adinpletus* for *adimpletus*, are common to all ages and MSS. Yet not a few of his examples occur in the Codex Augiensis, e. g. *b* for *p*; *p* for *b* (*prespiter*); *f* for *ph*; *t* for *d*; *habunde*; *eclesia*; *oboedientia*; and especially the coherence of the preposition to the word it governs, so constant in our MS. Dr Reeves (Preface, pp. xx. xxi.) incidentally states that the capricious sub-division of words, of which we see so much in the Greek of the Codex Augiensis, is a marked peculiarity of old Irish writing. But in our Latin version (f) we find nothing of this kind, nor am I on the whole inclined to impute it to an Irish scribe.

of a verb for the terminations *it, at,* or *unt.* The mark ɪ above the itten letter of a verb is for *ur;* the termination *us* is often represented apostrophe (e.g. man'), rarely by û (Hebr. xiii. 4), uˢ or u', or even r the apostrophe. The mark ⨯ seen on ll. 18 and 27 of the photographed s for the ending *um* of the genitive plural; b̄ is for the termination *bis;* r b; for *bus* final. A comma *under* e (l. 17 photograph) is for ae diph- and though it is often found under *e* in *ę̧lum*, yet that word when written is always spelt *cœlum* not *cœlum:* so also *pęnitentia*, pp. 268, 269. What nt by the comma *over* e (which I retain whenever it is found) I know A kind of flourished tail appended to *h, m,* or *n* stands for *i* (e.g. *h,*); are often written N, N̄; *a* is sometimes written small below the line onnected with the other letters by a species of flourish, as *a*, *h*ₐ, *ha*[1].

the subjoined list of ABRIDGED WORDS the appended reference shews that rm occurs only in the passages cited:

ebr. vii. 21) .... *æternum.*
.... *aliquid* or *aliquod.*
sls .... *apostolus.*
(au& Ephes. vi. 21) .... *autem.*
.... con prepos.
1 Cor. iv. 5), *dn̄i* &c......... *Dominus &c.*
lo, dm̄ .... *Deus &c.*
clsae, eclam.......................... *ecclesia &c.*
or. xii. 20; xiii. 17)................. *enim.*
.... *epistolis.*
'it. i. 7) .... *episcopum.*
.... *ergo.*
.... *est.*
eent .... *esse, esset, essent.*
a joined with other letters), or 7 ...... *et.*
Eph. vi. 19) .... *evangelii.*
frem, fres, fribus .... *frater &c.*
ie .... *gloria &c.*
se, gram, gras .... *gratia &c.*
(Hebr. vii. 22) .... *hierusalem.*
ihs (ih 2 Thess. ii. 8), ihu, ihm .*Jesus &c.*
ū (1 Cor. iii. 7) .... *incrementum.*
rre .... *in.*

irl, isrl .... *Israhel.*
kmi (Eph. v. 1; Phil. ii. 12) .... *carissimi.*
micda, miserda, miae, miam ... *misericordia &c.*
ms (Hebr. x. 38) .... *meus.*
n̄ .... *non* (*ne* p. 270, l. 27 ?)
nr, nra, nrm, nrorum, nris .... *noster &c.*
numqd or numqd .... *numquid.*
nc (Hebr. ix. 24) .... *nunc.*
obsecrat (Eph. vi. 18) .... *obsecratione.*
omis, oms, ome, omi, oma .... *omnis &c.*
p .... *per.*
p' (only in Hebr. and Postscript) .... *post.*
p̄ (even joined with other letters)... *præ* or *pre.*
pbros (once in Postscript) .... *presbyteros.*
pⁱ mu (Eph. iv. 9) .... *primum.*
p (l. 20 photograph) .... *pro.*
qd, qd or qⁱd, quⁱd .... *quid.*
quid .... *quidem.*
q .... *quæ.*
q .... *quæ* or *quam.*
quiᵃ or qⁱa .... *quia.*
qⁱ, qⁱs or quⁱs, q°, qᵃ .... *qui, quis, quo, qua.*

---

[1] *pugnas*, 1 Tim. vi. 4; *habitans*, ib. 16; *habeam*, 2 Tim. i. 3; *habitavit*, ib. 5; *criminatores*, iii. 3.

qd or qu°d	*quod.*
quo, qm, quom	*quoniam.*
q· q; q'	*que.*
sclm, sacla (scl *gen.* 1 Cor. ii. 6) &c.	*sæculum &c.*
scs, sca, scm, sce, scorum, scis &c.	*sanctus &c.*
scdm or secdm	*secundum.*
ſ, or ɔd	*sed.*
sic	*sicut.*
simil (1 Cor. vii. 4)	*similiter.*
sps, spm, spu	*spiritus &c.*
s	*sunt.*
l[1]	*vel.*
v° (h 1 Cor. xi. 15)	*vero.*
vr, vestr, vrae, vrum, vrs &c.	*vester &c.*
xpc or xps, xpi, xpo, xpm	*Christus &c.*

The liturgical matter, numbers of κεφαλαια, marginal annotations, &c. of the Codex Boernerianus are totally wanting in the Codex Augiensis, which contains, however, a few marks at the foot of the second pages of folios 95, 111, 119, 127, and of the first page of 113[2]. The stops in F are the full point (·) between the Greek words, and a note of interrogation ? often employed in the Latin, where the colon also prevails. The other chief marks are the horizontal line discussed above (p. xxvii.), double or single points or commas over ι and υ, a *large* comma, and a kind of circumflex ^ sometimes placed over a Greek vowel or diphthong (usually ι or ει), on no regular principle that I can make out. The sign ⁊ or ⁊⁊, which perplexed Matthæi in the Codex Boernerianus, is rarely found in F, nor can I throw any light upon it. The titles and initial lines of each epistle, as also the first letter of each κεφαλαιον, are in rubric and *secundâ manu*, though many of the last are still wanting, letters being placed in the margin (often *p.m.*) to guide the rubrician, and a few are placed erroneously, e.g. 1 Thess. iv. 1; 13; 2 Thess. ii. 1; iii. 1. No trace exists in F of that strange announcement with which G *concludes*, Προς λαουδακησας αρχεται επιστολη, which raises our curiosity as if only to baulk it. Some writers have observed that F resembles the Codex Bezæ in adopting the abbreviations χρς, ιης, &c. instead of the more usual forms χς, ις, &c. But, as I intimated above, the latter occur in this manuscript scarcely less often than in the former: see 1 Cor. viii. 6 and many other places. Both in the Greek and Latin texts I have often hesitated whether a letter somewhat larger than the rest should be printed as a capital; and on this minute point my judgment has probably been sometimes at fault.

I had purposed to lay before the student a selection from the remarkable readings and extraordinary grammatical inflexions which abound in this Codex, but in plain truth they are innumerable, and, at the same time, of such

---

1 Matthæi Cod. Boerner. p. 101, describes a similar abbreviation in that MS. as t for *aut*: yet both in the Cod. Augiensis (e.g. fol. 102, p. 2) and in his own facsimile of the Cod. Boerner. 1 Tim. i. 3, the letter is clearly l for *vel*.

2 I do not understand ρα on fol. 113, or on fol. 127 repetit. The numerals ιγ on fol. 95, ιδ on fol. 111, ιε on fol. 119, and ιϛ on fol. 127, occur at intervals of eight leaves, and shew that the MS. consisted originally of 143 leaves, of which 8 are misplaced after fol. 102, and the first seven (probably including a title-leaf) lost.

a character that they will be sure to arrest the interest and reward the best attention of every one into whose hands this volume is likely to fall.

As the Codex Augiensis exhibits throughout many traces of erasures and corrections, the reader will please, while using it, to make constant reference to the ANNOTATIONES EDITORIS (*infra*, pp. 273—284), in which these alterations are carefully recorded. I only hope my notes may prove serviceable to others, in some proportion to the pains and anxiety I have expended on them. But no one versed in these studies is ignorant how much doubt and uncertainty often exists, as to whether a change has been introduced by the first penman, or by some later hand[1]. I have arranged these corrections into three classes, those *primâ manu*, those *secundâ manu*, and those again *recenti manu*, according as I conceive them to have been made by the original scribe, by a second yet ancient corrector (AND TO HIM I IMPUTE THE GREAT MASS OF THESE CHANGES), or by a recent critic, whose judgment should have no weight whatever. Alterations of the last kind are easily detected, but for the others I am sensible that another eye will often decide differently from mine. I have taken no notice of a *mala seges* of Latin annotations scribbled over the earlier leaves of this Codex by some one who must have been profoundly unconscious of its value; from the similarity of handwriting I fear the culprit is Mieg, one of the former possessors of this priceless treasure. Several places are also disfigured by grotesque sketches in ink, such as often offend the reverential student of Biblical MSS. I am inclined to think, however, that they are least frequently found in copies of the Holy Gospels[2].

My transcript of Cod. F has been compared with the original six times, before it was submitted to the reader. For the photograph copy of the page containing the important variation in 1 Tim. iii. 16, I am indebted to the skill and Christian kindness of my friend and neighbour, the Rev. R. F. B. Rickards, Vicar of Constantine.

II. 1. I proceed to describe the eight copies of the Gospels which have been collated for this volume.

(i) TRIN. COLL. CANTAB. B. x. 17. This manuscript and the next but one belong to the Library of Trinity College, and although they are not in the list of Bentley MSS., since they never passed into the younger Richard Bentley's possession, are said in the general catalogue to have been "brought from Mount Athos,

[1] "Passim difficile dictu est utrum emendatio ad ipsum auctorem an manum ejus æqualem, an ad correctorem posteriorem sit referenda," is Tischendorf's admission as regards the Codex Amiatinus (Proleg. p. XXXII. 1850).

[2] One of the least repulsive examples of this evil habit I have met with occurs in the Bodleian MS. Canonici Græci 110 of the Acts and Epistles, wherein a poor priest is portrayed in a humorous and triumphant attitude, pointing to 1 Tim. v. 19, a text which had doubtless proved of some use to him when in difficulties.

purchased by Dr Bentley, and bequeathed by him to the College." Unquestionably they are both paged and the modern chapters noted by his hand. My attention was first drawn to them by Mr Field, the editor of Chrysostom's Homilies, and I have found them both well worthy of the labour bestowed upon them. This copy is on vellum, quarto, on 317 leaves (exclusive of 6 leaves of paper at the beginning) with 20 lines in a page, written in a neat set style, and in good condition, though the ink has faded in parts. I should assign it to the 13th century. The binder has happily lettered it "*Hymni in dies festos.*" The paper leaves contain Liturgical matter and an ὑποθεσις to St Matthew (the other Gospels have none) in a good hand, though somewhat more recent than that of the MS. itself. Here also, and on the last page of vellum we have an illegible scrawl in modern Greek, seemingly about the owner, one Sylvester. The vellum MS. contains κεφαλαια majora before each Gospel, and (foll. 311—317) the ordinary γνωσις του ευαγγελ. του ὁλου ενιαυτου, including the Saints' Days. On the ample margin of this fine copy are found the numbers of the Ammonian sections and capitals to each (but no Eusebian Canons, or Epistola ad Carpianum or Eusebian tables); αρχη, τελος constantly in the text; the titles of the κεφαλαια majora and beginnings of lessons at the top and foot of each page: all these in bright red.

As Codex i presents us with a pretty fair specimen of the character of such itacisms as prevail in MSS. of this date, I have formed a list of them, stating how often each occurs. We meet with ω for ο, 109 times; ο for ω, 105; ει for η, 81; η for ει, 78; ι for ει, 35; ει for ι, 36; ε for αι, 41; αι for ε, 35; ε for η, 11; η for ε, but twice; η for ι, 84 times (with πιστης *always*); ι for η, 76; ει for οι, 4; οι for ει, once; ι for υ, 5 times; υ for ι, 4; υ for οι, 4; οι for υ, once; υ for η, 14 times; η for υ, 3; ει for υ, once; υ for ει, 4 times; οι for ι, 7; ι for οι, twice; οι for η, 5 times; η for οι, twice; ο for οι, once; ω for ου, 4 times; ου for ω, 4: total in the four Gospels 759 itacisms. The ν εφελκυστικον is read 171 times (chiefly with ειπεν), but is so unequally distributed that there are only nine after Luke viii. 29. No ι ascript is met with, but ι subscript is as often inserted as omitted (28 times in Matth. i—iv.), not rarely where it has no place, e.g. μεγαλῃ, Matth. vii. 27, κεφαλῃ, *ibid.* xiv. 11, and in 15 other passages.

The breathings in i are a little irregular, though much less so than in some other copies: we often find ὀχλος, ὀλιγος, οἰδα, ὀδοντων, ὀστεων, αἰτεω, &c. and verbs whose initial letter is η improperly aspirated: on the other hand, ἁρπαζω, ἑτερος, ἑταιρος, ὁλος, εἱστηκει &c. The accents are somewhat inaccurate, and occasionally neglected, especially in δια or προς before articles and nouns; yet verbs compounded with prepositions frequently have both parts of the compound accented. I have noted ten cases where the circumflex is thrown upon the ante-penultima, e.g. οἶδατε, Matth. xxv. 13. Of grammatical and orthographical peculiarities this MS. has no great number; the following list is I believe pretty complete: αποσταλμενους

Matth. xxiii. 37; Luc. xiii. 34; λελαμψ, Marc. iv. 37; παρελθηναι, vi. 48; μειζω (for -ων) ix. 34; xii. 31; παρεδωκησαν, xv. 10; εμπροσθε, Luc. v. 19 *p.m.*; εσιωπουν, vi. 9; διαμερισμενοι, xii. 52; κοπριαν (with some editions), xiii. 8; θυγατεραν, *ibid.* 16; θυρα (*accus.*) *ibid.* 25 *bis*; σαρει, xv. 8; αροτριουντα, xvii. 7; εκαθερισθησαν, *ibid.* 14; χηρα (*accus.*), xviii. 5; μασθοι, xxiii. 29; γαλλιλαια, xxiii. *quinquies*; κριμαν, xxiv. 20; πολλος, Johan. vii. 12; δοξασθη, xv. 8. In the two earlier Gospels we usually find ῥαμβι, βαραβας. We mostly read ὠδε, always I think ἀβρααμ, οὕτως, ἠλιας, οὐχ'. Other forms which frequently occur are ἑορακα, διατοῦτο, κατιδίαν, διαπαντὸς, ἆρα (for ἄρα), ἐξευωνύμων, ὡσαῦτως, ὅτ' ἂν, ἐπ' ἂν. A few proper names in τ are followed by the apostrophe, e.g. ναζαρετ', ἐλισαβετ': ν is occasionally rejected so as to generate the hiatus, e.g. Johan. xiii. 26, and 6 other places.

Of various readings Codex i supplies a large variety, and is somewhat partial to glosses: it will occasionally be found to accord with the received text, in passages where few MSS. support it. Though not negligently written, it exhibits at least 16 omissions from the ὁμοιοτελευτον: ἡμεις and ὑμεις are confounded in about 25 places. A reviser's hand has been somewhat busy with this document, and a few corrections are very late. The rubric portions are not quite contemporary with the MS., for some letters are erased that they may be rewritten in red ink. On the last page of the vellum, after the Synaxarion, or table of lessons, we read the following *rubro:*

> τον δακτυλοις γραψαντα, τον κεκτημενον
> τον αναγινωσκοντα μετ' ευλαβειας
> φυλαττε τους τρεις ή τριας τρισολβιως.

I subjoin a list of a few principal readings of Cod. i. which will be seen to be in frequent agreement with the Codex Leicestrensis, to be described hereafter, and with Codd. cgpy and sometimes l of my "Collations of the Gospels." Matth. vii. 14 *p.m.* (*Elzev.*); x. 36; xiii. 10; 14 (c); 15; 17 (y); xix. 28; xx. 23; xxvii. 6; Marc. iv. 21; 29; 38; v. 9; 15; vi. 29; vii. 4; 8; 13; 15; 20; xii. 29; xiv. 33; 44 (cy); Luc. i. 23; 59; iii. 23 (*stops*); v. 6; 36; vi. 7 (*Elzev.*); vii. 4 (g); 42; viii. 50; x. 2; 22; 36 (*Elzev.*); xvii. 26; 27 (g); xix. 8 (g); 21; xxii. 10; 65; Johan. i. 27; v. 12; 16; vi. 1; xvii. 11; 13 (p); xviii. 5 (y); 40 (g); xix. 21; 41 (y); xx. 26 (c); 31.

(v)[1]. Cantab. Mm. 6. 9 is a copy of the whole Greek Testament except the Apocalypse, and belongs to the University of Cambridge; it was lent me for collation from the Public Library through the kind offices of the Vice-Chancellor for the years 1856—8, the Rev. Dr Philpott, Master of St Catharine's College.

---

[1] As I have elsewhere designated by v the readings of one of the Lambeth MSS. (1180) in Marc. i. 1—iv. 16; Johan. vii. 53—viii. 11; I have in these places distinguished the Cambridge MS. by the notation *v*.

It was doubtless once the property of Dr More, Bishop of Ely, for it was presented to the University by George I. in 1715, with the other books of that prelate; a royal gift which provoked one of the wittiest epigrams in our language. It is written on 294 leaves of vellum (foll. 233, 234, and 235, 236 being misplaced by the binder) in small quarto (7 inches by 5½), each page containing 28 lines in a minute, clear, neat and regular hand, of the 12th or 13th century. This copy is numbered by Scholz, 440 in the Gospels, 111 in the Acts, 221 in St Paul, but he collated only six chapters, and those so hastily, that out of 101 various readings they contain, he has neglected 34 and misstated 4.

While engaged on the Epistles I soon detected the identity of this MS. with 61 of Griesbach, the unknown English copy indicated by *Hal.*, whose readings that critic transcribed from the margin of Mill's own copy of his Greek Testament preserved in the Bodleian, and published for the first 17 chapters of St Matthew and all the Epistles in his *Symbolæ Criticæ*, Tom. I. pp. 247—304. Whether these readings had been collected by Mill or Hearne, they must not be regarded as a complete collation, since full three variations out of every four are passed by unnoticed. On comparing the result of my own labours with the readings exhibited by Griesbach, and consulting the original MS. wherever we differed, I find that *Hal.* or 61 agrees with Cantab. Min. 6. 9 in about a thousand passages, and (excluding a few obvious misprints in the *Symbolæ Criticæ*) differs from it only in 24[1], most of which may be fairly imputed to the circuitous route by which the extracts from *Hal.* have come round to us. No one will question that the two authorities are identical who shall weigh the many strange readings wherein they stand quite alone, or compare them at Matth. xii. 32; 1 Cor. vii. 35 (where α is mistaken by the collator for ευ); 1 Tim. i. 10. These instances (to which many might be added) are quite decisive.

The Eusebian canons in rubric cover the first nine pages, but the Epistola ad Carpianum is wanting. Three pages which follow and eight others throughout the MS., originally left blank, are scribbled over with tables of Church lessons in a recent hand. There are no tables of κεφαλαια majora before the several books, but each κεφαλαιον and its contents are written in bright red at the head of their proper pages. In the Gospels the Ammonian sections (but no references to the Eusebian Canons) are placed in the margin in red, and throughout the MS. the beginnings, endings and initial words of the Church lessons are fully given *rubro*, sometimes indeed the initial words have crept into the body of the text in black ink: to each lesson is prefixed a rubric capital. There is no preliminary matter except υποθεσεις to the Catholic and first eight Pauline Epistles; after the Acts,

---

[1] I subjoin a list of these texts, that 61 may no longer be falsely cited for readings it does not contain; in each case the true reading is given in the following pages: Matth. i. 4; ii. 3; v. 28; vii. 22; xvii. 25; Rom. vii. 23; 1 Cor. vii. 35; 2 Cor. i. 6; iii. 6; 7; Gal. i. 21; Eph. v. 19; Phil. iv. 12; 1 Thess. i. 9; 1 Tim. i. 8; vi. 4; 2 Tim. ii. 1; Heb. ii. 8; 9 [?]; vi. 9; vii. 2; xi. 8; 1 Johan. v. 20; Jud. v. 1.

1 and 2 Peter, 3 John and before the Romans large *blank* squares are ruled in red, apparently to receive subscriptions. The hands of two separate correctors can be traced both in the text and margin; the one being the original scribe or else the person who wrote the rubric portions, the other much later: a few changes were made by the recent hand which wrote the ecclesiastical tables: the modern chapters are noted and the leaves numbered by a yet later writer, whom I believe to be Bentley. Not fewer than 28 instances of omission by ὁμοιοτελευτον occur, some of them extensive; on the whole the accents and breathings are accurately represented: only that there is a tendency to throw them somewhat out of place. We find ι *subscriptum* twice in Matth. v. 39: ι *ascriptum* Luc. ii. 25; Johan. xii. 12: nowhere else. Ν εφελκυστικον occurs before a consonant 98 times: but is wanting before a vowel 30 times. The itacisms are not particularly numerous; I count 445 in all, chiefly of the ordinary character; e.g. ο interchanged with ω, η with ει and ι, ε with αι. A large portion of these is met with in the last 22 leaves (comprising 2 Thess. to Hebrews) the text of which is quite different from that of other parts of the volume, either because the scribe had grown careless, or was copying from a different exemplar. On these leaves are found several remarkable readings, for which there exists no other authority than Griesbach's 61 Act. and Paul: e.g. 1 Tim. iii. 9; 16; Hebr. iv. 8; ix. 9?; 28?; x. 3: see also 1 Cor. xv. 11; Eph. iii. 8. The mixed character of its text attracted Scholz's attention, as he observes that in the Gospels it is "ex familiâ utrâque conflatum." In fact, without exhibiting such perpetual and conspicuous variations as are found in the Cod. Leicestrensis and a few others, it abounds in readings either peculiar to itself or attested only by a few of the most ancient documents: this is especially true for St Luke's Gospel, the Acts and the last six Pauline Epistles. In Johan. vii. 53—viii. 11, and some other places it closely resembles the MS. I shall presently denote w: it often supports the Cod. Leicestrensis, and eg of my previous collations. Throughout the Acts and Epistles it is very much with our b (Lambeth 1183) in passages where they stand quite alone.

Few unusual forms, either of orthography or inflexion, are met with in this document: we read however χειραν, Matth. xii. 10; διαν, Act. xiv. 12; εσυραν, *ibid.* v. 19; ψυχω, 2 Cor. xi. 27. The reduplication is sometimes lost, Johan. xi. 52; Act. xi. 11; Hebr. ix. 6; xi. 5: sometimes the augment, Luc. iii. 18; vii. 32; 1 Tim. vi. 7; 12; 17; 2 Tim. i. 16. The punctuation often differs from that of the printed books, but the scribe has been too negligent in this respect to deserve much attention where he is unsupported (e.g. ; and · are frequently put for each other): I have noted such peculiarities as seemed of any importance. This MS., though a beautiful specimen of caligraphy, contains an unusual proportion of contractions, some of them rather uncommon; yet all may be read with certainty after a little practice: η and ν almost interchange their shapes. The colophon merely consists of the words σωσον με κς ὁ θς μου · σωσον με κς *rubro* on the last page. Far in the margin on fol. 151, p. 2, we read, ἁγιος ὁ θ̅ς̅ in a later hand. Occasionally, though not often, citations from Scripture &c. are indicated by rubric marks in the margin. The last few leaves are dirty and somewhat damaged. Here, as elsewhere, we meet with ἀβρααμ, οὑτως uniformly, ἑστη, ἡλιας, ὁραμα, ὁριων, ὁρκος, ὥρα, ὦτα mostly, but ὁταν, ὡδε more frequently than ὡδε, ὅτ' ἄν. We see μὴ, but only joined with ου or used interrogatively; sometimes ὁ μὲν, ὁ δὲ, τέ, ἐξ', ἐν', οὐχ'. No one who shall attentively examine the readings of this MS. will hesitate to regard it as one of the most important of its date, and to deem it well worthy of the minute examination to which I have subjected it.

(w). Trin. Coll. Cantab. B. x. 16, the remaining manuscript of Bentley's collection, contains, like the last, the whole New Testament, with the ordinary exception of the Apocalypse, the Catholic Epistles as usual following the Acts. It is written on thick oriental paper, in small quarto, on 363 leaves, containing 28 lines on a page. Its date is fixed by a note at the end of St John's Gospel: αὑτη ἡ· βιβλος ηγουν το ἁγιον ευαγγελιον, ὁμοιως και ὁ αποστολος εγραφησαν εν τω ορει τω ἁγιω σινα, ενθα μωυσης οιδεν [sic] την ἁγιαν βατον και εδεξατο τον νομον· εγραφησαν δε εν ετη ϛωκδ, δια χειρος εμου ἁμαρτωλου ιακωβου ἱερομοναχου (*cætera eraduntur*). Though written so late as A. D. 1316 [6824 of the Greek æra], it was doubtless copied from one of those more antient volumes, wherewith the region of Mount Sinai abounded, as it is rich in various readings of high value. Mr Field, in an obliging communication, notices its frequent resemblance to the Codex Cyprius (K of the Gospels), on which Scholz, and more recently Tischendorf and Tregelles, have bestowed so much pains: but in the other parts of the N. T. also, it will be found in company with the best authorities, and with the Lambeth MSS. acd. The Liturgical matter in this document is pretty copious. The table of Eusebian canons, the ὑποθεσις and κεφαλαια majora to St Matthew seem to be lost, for the margin of every page in the Gospels contains the numbers of the Eusebian canons, in their proper place under the Ammonian sections: while the three later Gospels have the larger κεφαλαια prefixed to them in rubric, and references are made to them in the margin throughout. The beginnings, endings and proper days for the Church lessons are given at the top and foot of each page in rubric. This copy is in fair condition, being only a little torn about Hebr. xi. 18; 32, 33, and portions of the first six leaves of the Acts being restored in a late hand, which I have indicated by *k;* see especially Acts vii. 48—60. Otherwise the whole MS. seems written by one scribe (in no very elegant style), only that in the Acts and Epistles the words are much abridged, I suppose because paper was running short (*vid. supra*, p. xxix). A second hand has been busy throughout the volume; the erasures are numerous, and many curious glosses are found in the margin, together with some variations otherwise well vouched for; so that it is clear the corrector derived them from a good source. The itacisms of this MS. are *much* fewer than those of Cod. i, the instances of ν εφελκυστικον far more frequent (in *ειπεν* almost uniform) in the Gospels, but much more rare afterwards. In the Gospels ι ascript occurs 67 times (mostly with the article), ι subscript but thrice in the whole MS. A remarkable feature of w is the capricious, or at least unusual arrangement of its breathings, in this respect much resembling the Parham Evangelistarium (P) hereafter to be described: the irregularities of i being nothing in comparison. The penman seems to aspirate all initial etas with verbs, most omicrons and omegas: e. g. *ἧν* (*imperf.*) often, *ἥλθον, ἥκουσα, ἡκολουθει*: so *ὁφθαλμος, ἑνιαυτος, ὧν, αἱγιαλος, αἱτεω, αἱτια, ἥδη, αἱγυπτος, ὁφειλω, αὕριον, ἑπαινος, ὁκτω, ὁπισω, ὁχλος, ὁνομα, ὁψε, ὁψομαι*[1], &c. but mostly *ὡδε, εἱστηκει, ἑνεκεν, οἱτινες*. When a word begins with *ρ*, he puts the aspirate over the first vowel, as *ρῆματα*: he reads *ἁβρααμ, ἱσαακ, ἡλιας*, the last two not uniformly. As in Cod. i, the accents are not very correct; sometimes they are placed over each part of a compound word, sometimes the preposition and noun are treated as one word. We often have *ιδου, ἐπ'ἂν, οὕτως* (for *οὕτω*): in Matth. ix. 35 *υ* and *β* are confounded (*θεραπεβων*): so Acts iv. 36 *sec. man.* &c. The hiatus is not rare, e.g. Matth. xvii. 23, and 14 other places. Grammatical peculiarities are not many: such are *ειπαν*, Matth. xvi. 14; Johan. vii. 20; 52: *ανταλαγμα*, Matth. xvi. 26; Marc. viii. 37: *συνκαθημενος*, Marc. xiv. 54: *προεφητευσεν*, Luc. i. 67: *αριθμηνται*, xii. 7: *την θυρα*, Johan. xviii. 16: *εὕροιαν*, Act. xvii. 27; *αναδοσαντες*, xxiii. 33: *ἡμερα* (*accus.*), xxvi. 7: *ειπα*, *ibid.* 15; Hebr. iii. 10: *ποτοθε*, Hebr. ix. 4: *αντεκατεστητε*, xii. 4. The augment is omitted in Act. xiii. 14; xv. 14; xxiii. 14; 1 Pet. i. 10. This copy contains its share of *ὁμοιοτελευτα*, of which I have noted 14 examples: for peculiarities in punctuation see (among others) Matth. x. 42; Act. v. 39; xvi. 12; Jac. v. 3; Jud. *v.* 20; Rom. vi. 10; xiii. 4; 1 Cor. v. 1; Gal. iii. 6; iv. 10; 16; Eph. vi. 6; 19; Phil. i. 4; ii. 28; 1 Thess. v. 25; Hebr. iii. 10. The celebrated passage Johan. v. 4 is marked with an obelus in the margin *rubro*, as in dk among my "Collations," the uncials S Λ &c. Besides much foreign matter of an ordinary character before the three later Gospels (lists of *κεφαλαια* majora, prefaces of Cosmas Indicopleustes, rude iambic verses &c.), foll. 161—175 contain *εκλογαδιν των δ̄ ευαγγελιστων...ὁμοιως και των αποστολου*, including *συναξαριον του ὁλου ἐνιαυτου* (fol. 166). The Acts have no preface, but on fol. 219 is *προλογος των καθολικων επιστολων*, each of which and all the Pauline Epistles have *ὑποθεσεις* prefixed. Fol. 333, p. 2 to fol. 363 consist of *supplementary* matter. (1) Lives of the Apostles, pp. 5. (2) Another *εκλογαδιν των δ̄ ευαγγελιστων...τελειουν εν τω μηνολογιω* pp. 14. (3) *συναξαριον συν θ̄ω αρχομενον απο μηνος σεπτεμβριου* pp. 7. (4) The omitted or lost preliminary matter to St Matthew, *κεφαλαια* majora, iambic lines, preface of Cosmas &c. (5) On the *same* leaf 350, a Life of St James, Bishop of Jerusalem, liturgical tables, canonical questions, *ὑποθεσις της βιβλου των πραξεων* (fol. 355), prayers and miscellaneous

---

[1] In Matth. xxiii. 21, 23, we find *ὁμνυει*, but *ὁμοσας*, though *ὁμοσας* had been given in v. 20, so that it is vain to look for consistency: thus in Luc. vi. 41, *ὀφθαλμω* and *ὀφθὰλμῳ* both occur.

pieces, to fol. 363, where the MS. concludes abruptly, being mutilated at the end.

In the following passages Cod. w will often be found to agree not only with the Codex Cyprius (K), but with several of the best of the MSS. I have before collated, in their most singular readings, e.g. cegy and especially op. Matth. ix. 4 (D); xv. 32 (K); xviii. 35 (BDKL); xxiii. 25 *semel cum* de, *semel cum* BDL. *Elzev.*; xxvii. 34 (BDK); Marc. v. 10; xii. 22 (c); xv. 47 (ABCDo); xvi. 2 (D); 19 *p. m.* (CK); Luc. i. 2 *p. m.* (Ko); 39 (AKo); 65 (AKo); ii. 42 (ABKc); vii. 25 (DKp); viii. 24 (Kp); x. 16 (AKp); xxiv. 43 (K); Johan. ii. 12 (Kp); v. 4 (K); 25 (K); vi. 5; ix. 8; xi. 12 (Kop); xii. 15; xvii. 4 (ABC); 8 (p); xix. 17 (z); xx. 16 (BDL); xxi. 11 (ABCp). In the Acts and Epistles it often resembles acd: unusual readings are Act. iii. 26; iv. 16; 22; 31; v. 5 (ABD); 30; 36 (DE); 37 (E); vi. 2; 15; xii. 25 (B); xiii. 16; xiv. 19; xvii. 16 (ABEa); 34; xviii. 6; xx. 7 (ABEa); 8; xxi. 2 (a); xxii. 23; xxiii. 23; xxv. 11; 13 (c); Jac. iii. 8; iv. 5; 1 Pet. i. 22; 24; ii. 24; iii. 8; 2 Pet. ii. 22; iii. 5 (h); Jud. *vv.* 12; 23; 24; 25 (ABC); Rom. vii. 16; viii. 23; 27; ix. 31; xii. 3; xiii. 3; xv. 29; 30; 1 Cor. vii. 28; x. 19; xi. 25; xiv. 35; xv. 8; 2 Cor. iii. 9 (D); 16; iv. 14; v. 5; 21; xi. 26; xii. 20; xiii. 13 *secund. man.*; Gal. iii. 14 (DFG); Eph. ii. 11; iii. 4; iv. 32; Phil. ii. 23; Coloss. i. 26; 1 Thess. iv. 5 (*Syriac*); 2 Thess. ii. 15; iii. 1 (FG); 1 Tim. i. 2; ii. 2; iii. 1: 2 Tim. iii. 3; iv. 17 (FG); Tit. i. 6; 12; ii. 10; Philem. *v.* 6; Hebr. vi. 14; ix. 14; 15 (l); 19; 25; x. 1; 10 (*cum Elzev.*); xi. 29; xiii. 11; 12: not a few of which are found in no other document, so far as I know.

(L). Codex Leicestrensis. This famous and most valuable document is the property of the Corporation of Leicester, which kindly allowed me to remove it from the Public Library for full examination at my own house, where for several months I bestowed upon it the labour its weight and interest imperatively required. It is one of the very few Codices which contain the whole New Testament (the others in England being the great Codex Alexandrinus, two "Additional MSS.," 11837 and 17469 in the British Museum, and Canonici Græci 34 in the Bodleian), in large folio, 14¾ inches long by 10 broad, on 212 complete leaves, followed by one fragment, besides which the margins of foll. 77; 86, and the upper corner of fol. 201, are cut and mutilated. This copy is written on 91 leaves of vellum, and 122 of coarse paper, not "temerè permixtis" as Wetstein states, but arranged pretty regularly in series of two vellum followed by three paper leaves, evidently from previous calculation how far the more costly material would hold out. The paper is so bad that four of the leaves would bear the writing only on one side. There are 38 lines on every page; the instrument employed seems to have been a reed rather than a pen, and the style of writing is very singular, yet certainly neither elegant nor remarkably perspicuous. The smooth and rough breathings are often very hard to distinguish, and ε is usually placed in a recumbent posture, so much resembling α that it is not easy to say at

Codex Leicestrensis. I Tim. III. 10.16.

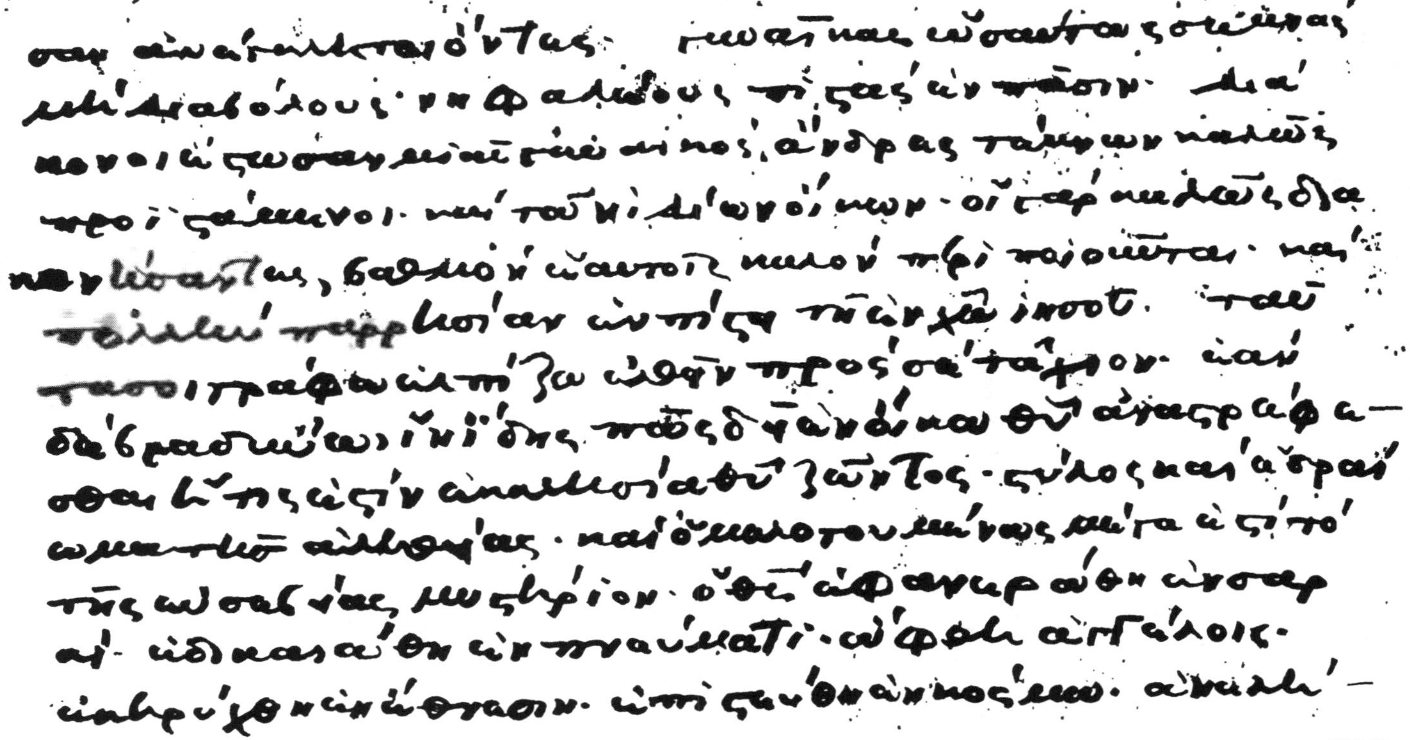

J.P. Jobtms

all times which was meant[1]. An eminent mediæval scholar to whom I shewed the MS., remarked that the letters were formed much like the earliest Greek type used in Italy towards the end of the 15th century. No one who has inspected the Codex Leicestrensis has estimated its age as earlier than the 14th century, but in this, as in so many other instances, the antiquity of the actual volume has nothing to do with its critical importance. It commences Matth. xviii. 15, *σου και αυτου μονου*: after Acts x. 45, *πιστοι*, we read in the same line, with absolutely no break, *ουρανοθεν*, xiv. 17, the intervening matter, upwards of three chapters, being wholly omitted: the mutilation on fol. 201 has destroyed portions of 2 Johan. vv. 1—5; 3 Johan. vv. 5—10; after Jud. v. 7, *και αἱ*, one leaf is lost, containing the rest of St Jude, and perhaps a preface to the Apocalypse. Mill and Wetstein state that the MS. ended Apoc. xx. 15, *και πυρος*, and give its various readings up to that point, which I have copied and digested. There must then have been 214 leaves, the last of which is quite gone, but about one third of fol. 213 is yet legible, and its variations have been recorded in my collation: the last complete leaf (212) ends with *εστρηνιασεν*, Apoc. xviii. 7; the fragment, fol. 213, terminates with *και των αδελφων σου των εχον ibid.* xix. 10.

At the top of the first page this Codex exhibits in a beautiful hand the words Ειμι Ιλερμου Χαρκου, then in a later hand "Thomas Hayne." The book is now well bound, and on the cover in very recent gold letters we read, "Town Library, Leicester, the gift of Mr Thomas Hayne, 1640," under the Town arms. William Chark was one of the former owners of the celebrated Codex Montfortianus, and is supposed to have lived in the reign of Elizabeth (see *Dobbin's Codex Montfortianus, Introduction*, p. 7); some of the later changes in the Cod. Leicestrensis were made by him, chiefly however in the margin: I suppose he obtained the book from one of the dissolved monasteries. Wetstein, I believe on John Jackson's authority, states that Thomas Hayne, M.A. of Trussington in Leicestershire, gave the volume to the Leicester Library in 1660. A collation of the MS. was first published by Mill; Cæsar de Missy in 1748 lent to Wetstein a much more accurate one made by John Jackson and William Tiffin, which he used for his great edition of the Greek Testament; since that period nothing further has been published on the subject which has not been servilely borrowed from Mill and Wetstein. Yet nothing can be more unsatisfactory than their representation of this important document. Not to mention instances in which the various readings exhibited in Cod. Leicestrensis are *passed over* by both these editors (for they are innumerable), I have made out a list of more than 300 places in which the actual reading is falsely cited by Mill alone, by Wetstein alone, and very

---

[1] Thus, for instance, this MS. is cited as reading ἐχθῆραι, Marc. vi. 27, by Dobbin and Tregelles, and by Tregelles ἀπέκτεινεν, *ibid.* xii. 5; ἐπέσπασε Matth. xxvi. 51; where I must think *α* was meant by the scribe: see also Marc. xiii. 9; xiv. 15; Luc. xvii. 24; Johan. i. 28; vi. 70; xi. 56.

often by both. When Matthæi met with some such instances in another MS., he breaks forth against these illustrious critics in the exclamation, "Quæ diligentia? quæ fides?" (*Cod. Boerner.* p. 107): I must be allowed to rejoin to him, *Eheu! quam temerè in nosmet legem sancimus iniquam!* The task of a collator calls for vigilance so perpetual, powers of observation so minute and unflagging, that although I have the fullest confidence both in the "diligentia" and "fides" of Matthæi, I doubt not he will be found as peccable as the rest of us, whenever his work shall come to be tested. I have avoided therefore, as much as possible, such invidious annotations as "*malè Millius,*" "*falsò Wetsteinius,*" requesting the reader once for all to bear in mind, that I have anxiously verified all passages wherein I differ from my predecessors: occasionally however, chiefly when this copy agrees with the received text against the testimony of the editors, I have expressly notified the fact.

Unpublished collations of this MS. are (1) one by Carte, which I am informed[1] used to be kept at Leicester with the Codex, but has now disappeared; at least it could not be found when I was there. If two leaves of the MS. have been destroyed within a century, we need not be surprised at any other loss: but their treasure is *now* valued by the Corporation, which is justly proud of possessing it: (2) a collation of Jo. Jackson (not identical, it would seem, with that lent to Wetstein) contained in his copy of Mill's N.T., now in Jesus College Library, Cambridge. The kindness of the Rev. Dr Corrie, the Master of that College, gave me access to this collation, which I compared with those of Mill and Wetstein in that part of the Apocalypse which, though extant in Jackson's time, is now lost (see the result at the end of this volume): (3) another by Dr Tregelles for his N.T., the fruits of which are not yet fully published; I did not know that he had collated the book, till I had publickly pledged myself to undertake the task: nor can he possibly in an edition of the N.T. lay before the reader all the characteristic variations of such a document as this[2]: (4) a selection of some thousands of readings made by Dr Dobbin when arranging his edition of the "Codex Montfortianus," which that gentleman most considerately put at my disposal. His extracts enabled me severely to test my own accuracy, and as our judgment sometimes differs respecting the actual reading, I have in such cases set down his testimony as well as my own. He will be pleased to learn that Dr Barrett's statement, to which he alludes (*Introd.* p. 23) without vouching for it, "In Apocalypsi tam fideliter [Codex Montfortianus] in textu exprimit Leicestrensem, ut vix unquam discrepent" is too strongly asserted:

[1] In 1845, by Mr Combe, the bookseller there.

[2] I have now (1858) compared Dr Tregelles' collation of this MS. with my own, so far as he has published it (Matth. xviii. 15—Mark xvi. 20). Although mine is of necessity much the fuller, I most cheerfully bear testimony to his great accuracy. I have noted a few places in which we differ as to what the scribe intended to write, and have corrected two or three of his looser citations by simply inserting (*sic*).

e. g. there are seven variations between the two MSS. in Cap. I., fourteen in Cap. VIII.[1]

The Codex Leicestrensis contains the list of *κεφαλαια* majora (without corresponding numerals in the margin of the text) before the three later Gospels, but with so extensive variations that I have adopted the unusual course of presenting them to the curious reader (*infra*, p. xlvi); besides these there is no Liturgical matter whatever, no divisions into sections, or Eusebian canons, or notes about Lessons, except a marginal mark or two, as at Mark vii. 6, and a few words, which are often illegible, scribbled at the foot of the first page of each leaf. The Pauline Epistles immediately follow the fourth Gospel, and have no *ὑποθεσεις* except the Προλογος to the Hebrews, *ἡ δε προς ἑβραιους κ. τ. λ.* (*Kuster's Mill*, p. 519, col. 2, *vid infra*, p. xlvii). Between the Hebrews and Acts of the Apostles are five pages of foreign matter. (1) An exposition of the Creed and statement of the errors condemned by the seven general Councils, ending with the second of Nice: (2) the ordinary Lives of the Apostles, followed by an exact description of the limits of the Five Patriarchates. The opening chapters of the Acts have rubric capitals and breaks of line at the beginning of each *κεφαλαιον*, but these disappear after Cap. VI. and there is nothing like them elsewhere. The remarkable titles of the Gospels attracted Mill's notice (*Proleg.* 67); those of the other books are short and simple. As I never saw the Cod. Montfortianus, I cannot confirm Dr Dobbin's opinion, "The titles to the sacred books, in pale red ink, are by the same person who added those of the Codex Montfortii, none of these portions of either MS. being by the transcribers of the text" (*Introd.* p. 24). Such a notion would not have occurred to me on viewing the Cod. Leicestrensis only; but I distrust myself on a point like this.

We cannot praise the care of the scribe in copying this MS. Many words occur which are only begun, broken off perhaps after the first syllable, and I have counted the large number of 74 omissions from *ὁμοιοτελευτον* and the like causes. Yet the accents are represented with much accuracy, and the breathings (if indistinct at times) are regular; we have *ἀβρααμ*, *ὧδε*, *οὕτω* often; yet sometimes *αἱρω*, *αὐριον* and *ὁραμα* once: the acute accent is much used where the grave is commonly written by others. The vowels *ι* and *υ* have mostly a single dot over them; other peculiarities of this Codex are *τέ* sometimes, *ἰοῦδας*, *διατοῦτο*, *ἀπάρτι*, *ἀπαρχῆς*, *κατιδιαν* (*ferè*), *ἐξευωνυμων*, *αραβων*, *μελλει* (*pro* *μελει*: so *εμελλεν* Acts xviii. 17), *φιλιξ* *semper*, *ουθεν*, *μηθεν*, *ηυδοκησα*, *ανθρωποπαρεσκοι*, *κεντηριων* (Mark xv. *ter*), *γιγνομαι* in the Acts, *εγκακειν* (*pro* *εκκακειν*), *ποιειν* (*pro* *πιειν*). The *ν εφελκυστικον* is much used with *ειπεν* and *εστιν*, and in cases where emphasis is

[1] So that we can hardly resort to the Cod. Montfort., as Tregelles suggests (Horne's Introduction, Vol. II. p. 216), for the readings of the Cod. Leicestrensis in those parts of the Apocalypse which are defective in the latter MS.

meant or where there is a pause in the sense. Yet in Johan. ix. 30 and 16 other places an hiatus arises from the absence of ν. Respecting ι ascript I cannot speak decidedly: in seven places I have noted what may be ι, but is more probably a rude stop (e. g. Acts v. 25); ι subscript is clearly read in six places (e. g. Matth. xxvii. 28), two of them being with verbs (Rom. ii. 3); elsewhere it is not found. This copy is remarkable for always writing ιησους at full length up to Johan. xxi. 15, where we meet with ις̅, and in 41 other places 19 of which are in the Acts: thus too ιερουσαλημ is usually unabridged. Of itacisms I count 1129 throughout the Codex, viz. ο *pro* ω, 190; ω *pro* ο, 126; η *pro* ει, 93; ει *pro* η, 104; ι *pro* ει, 77; ει *pro* ι, 62; η *pro* ι, 87; ι *pro* η, 46; ε *pro* αι, 73; αι *pro* ε, 72; ε *pro* η, 24; η *pro* ε, 20; υ *pro* η (*rare elsewhere*), 27; η *pro* υ, 28; ου *pro* ω, 13; ω *pro* ου, 16; οι *pro* ι, 3; ι *pro* οι, 3; ου *pro* η, Act. vii. 59; η *pro* ευ, Luc. xii. 16; υ *pro* ι, 15; ι *pro* υ, 14; υ *pro* η 6; *pro* ε, 1; *pro* οι, 4; *pro* ει, 3; οι *pro* υ, 4; *pro* η, 9; ο *pro* ου, 3; η *pro* οι, 3; α *pro* η, Apoc. xiii. 17: which list may be compared with the analysis of Cod. i, *supra*, p. xxxiv. We have also θ for τ, Marc. x. 40; Luc. xi. 7. The following are the unusual grammatical forms: ηλθατε Matth. xxv. 36; ειπαν *ibid.* xxvi. 35; Luc. xx. 2; εξηλθατε Matth. xxvi. 55; Marc. xiv. 48; Luc. vii. 24; 25; 26; xxii. 52; εισηλθατε *ibid.* xi. 52; ανεπεσαν Johan. vi. 10; επεπεσαν Rom. xv. 3; επεσαν 1 Cor. x. 8; επεσα Act. xxii. 7; εξειλατο Act. vii. 10; επαθατε Gal. iii. 4; παραγεναμενος Luc. xiv. 21; Hebr. ix. 11; εὑραμενος Hebr. ix. 12; γεναμενης Act. ii. 6. So accusatives in -αν for -α, νυκταν Luc. ii. 37; θυγατεραν xiii. 16; χειραν Johan. vii. 30; σακραν Eph. vi. 12; θυατειραν Apoc. i. 11; (*cf.* ii. 18, 24). The gender is sometimes altered: thus λιμος *fem.* Luc. iv. 25; οφρυς *masc. ibid.* 29; νοσος *masc. ibid.* 40. Verbs in αω or οω are formed as those in -εω, επηρωτουν Luc. iii. 10; xx. 27; επετιμουν xviii. 15; ετολμουν xx. 40; ηρωτουν Johan. iv. 31; εμβριμουμενος xi. 38; κινει Marc. vii. 20; 23; σαρει Luc. xv. 8; μαστιγει Hebr. xii. 6; and the contrary, αγανακτωντες Marc. xiv. 4. Irregularities in verbs in -μι are αφιουσι Marc. iv. 36; τιθων x. 16; περιτιθουσιν xv. 17; συνετιθοντο Johan. ix. 22; επιτιθε 1 Tim. v. 22; επιτιθειναι Act. xv. 10; αποδωσης Luc. xii. 59; διδοασιν Apoc. xvii. 13. I note also μεγα *masc.* Matth. xxvii. 60; μεγαν *neut.* Luc. xiv. 16; μεγαλη *accus.* Act. ii. 20; εχαρην 3rd *pers.* Johan. viii. 56; ἡκασιν Marc. viii. 3; εκκεχωρητωσαν Luc. xxi. 21; εκαθεριστε Act. x. 15; κατασκευασμενον Luc. i. 17; Hebr. ix. 6; συγγενευσι Marc. vi. 4; Luc. ii. 44 (ν); δραγχμας xv. 8; εμπροσθε Johan. i. 30. In the Apocalypse we always read ιδον except in xvii. 3; εφιδεν Luc. i. 25. I add ανηγγελαν Act. xiv. 27; παραγγελειν Act. xv. 5 (*sic v.* 27; xvi. 17; 21); ἀπαγγελλῶ *fut.* Hebr. ii. 12; ανηγγελλη 1 Pet. i. 12; εξεχεθην Tit. iii. 6; ανεπιλημπτον 1 Tim. iii. 2. The augment is omitted Luc. x. 34 and 22 other passages; but we have a double augment in ηπηντησαν Johan. iv. 51; αντεκατεστητε Hebr. xii. 4.

The wide variations of this document from the received editions are well known, and it is a favourite authority with those who wish to base the sacred text upon what Scholtz would have us call the Alexandrine family of MSS. Mill (who did not particularly value it) first observed its striking affinity with the Codex Bezæ; perhaps the result of my collation is to diminish that resemblance, though not materially. Wetstein compares it with Paris 6 (13), Hensler with Havn. 3 (44 Evst.) of the Gospels: add too the uncial U, and note how much it coincides with the great cursive 1 (e. g. in the space of a few verses, Marc. xiii. 14; 19; 20; 32; 34; xiv. 1, &c.). In the Acts and Epistles it approaches much nearer to the received text: in parts quite as much as our Cod. k for example, which (as well as ad) it is much like. Though totally destitute of Liturgical matter, many of its various readings may easily be seen to have arisen from Evangelistaria and Lectionaries: the particles of time are often omitted in L when they are necessarily wanting in such books, *initio pericopæ*, and clauses are perpetually inserted from the same source. I cite a very few instances out of many: Marc. iv. 10; v. 1; Johan. xii. 1; xiii. 3; xvii. 1; xviii. 28; xx. 11; 19; xxi. 1; Act. xxviii. 1; 1 Tim. ii. 1; 2 Tim. iii. 10; iv. 5. This copy has always been noted for two capital innovations; the pericope adulteræ (Joh. vii. 53—viii. 11) is wholly wanting in its proper place, but is found after Luc. xxi.; that position being suggested I suppose by comparing το ορος το καλουμενον ελαιων Luc. xxi. 37 with Johan. viii. 1; and ωρθριζε Luc. xxi. 38 with ορθρου Johan. viii. 2. The other transfer is that of Luc. xxii. 43, 44 (which verses too are wanting in their place) to Matth. xxvi. where they follow v. 39, as if they belonged to St Matthew's narrative. This arrangement also is derived from Evangelistaria, in several of which it is still read (e. g. our Pz *sem.*); just as in P (to be described below) Johan. xix. 31—37 is put after Matth. xxvii. 54, after which v. 55 follows, as if nothing foreign had been inserted.

Many of the changes met with in this MS. arise from inversion of order, the substitution of simple for compound words, and *vice versâ*. The accusative is often found for the dative; Marc. vi. 36; ix. 7; Luc. vi. 28; viii. 32; xiv. 29; xvii. 7; xviii. 5; 43; xxiii. 36; 40; 1 Tim. i. 18: and the contrary, Matth. xxv. 42; 43; Marc. i. 43; x. 49; xii. 43; xiv. 7; Luc. v. 14; vi. 29; x. 35; xix. 44 *sec. man.*; xxii. 47; xxiii. 11; 39; Act. x. 8. Thus dative for genitive, Marc. iii. 10; xv. 3; Johan. i. 37, and accusative for genitive, Luc. xxii. 47; Act. xviii. 26. In the celebrated passage 1 Tim. iii. 16 this MS. has ὁ θ̄ς, seemingly a *mixture* of the common reading and that of the Cod. Claromontanus (D). In about 50 instances the Codex Leicestrensis supports the Elzevir text against the general mass of copies: see particularly Matth. xxiii. 13, 14; 21; 25; Marc. iii. 32; vi. 33; 52; xii. 33; Luc. v. 8; vi. 7; 9; xxiv. 18; Johan. iii. 25; iv. 5.

A corrector's hand has been busy throughout this copy, whom Dr Dobbin considers to have been the original scribe; I have deemed the changes to be *secundâ manu*, but nearly as old as the first. There are catch words at the foot of many pages. The familiar form υ for β occurs Luc. ix. 3; xviii. 30 (where

Mill is strangely perplexed); Johan. i. 39. The stop ; is rarely found. The Latin chapters and many various readings (e. g. Johan. xv. 10; xvii. 5; 9; xviii. 16; 20; xix. 39) are noted by a recent hand (seemingly Chark's), and there are two or three *very modern* marginal notes, which might easily be dispensed with.

Subjicitur collatio κεφαλαιων *majorum in Codice Leicestrensi cum Kusteri editione Novi Testamenti Milliani* (1723): (*hiat S. Matthæi Evangelium usque ad Cap.* XVIII, *v.* 15).

S. Marci: εκ του κατα μαρκον ἁγιου ευαγγελιου τα κεφαλαια. ϛ'. –του *prim.* θ'. περι της παραβολης του σπορου. ια'. περι του εχοντος τον λεγεωνα. ιβ'. αρχησυναγωγου. ιγ'. αἱμοροουσης. ιϛ'. –και των δυο ιχθυων. ιθ'. φοινίκισης. κ'. μογγιλαλου. κδ'. μακαρια (*pro* καισαρειᾳ). κε'. –του ιησου. κϛ'. σελίνιαζομενου. κζ'. μειζον. κη', κθ'. *Desunt omnia ab* των κη' *usque ad* περι του, κθ' (επερωτησαντος αυτον πλουσιου). λα'. –του. λε'. γραμματεων (*pro* πρεσβυτερων). λϛ'. *fin.* +παραβολης. λζ'. εκκαθετων (*pro* επερωτησαντων τον κ̅ν̅). κυνσον. λη'. σαδουκαιων. λθ'. των γραμματεων. μα'. –βαλουσης. μβ'. +της (*ante* συντελειας). μδ'. μυρου. μϛ'. προφητειας. μζ'. +της (*ante* αρνησεως).

S. Lucæ: εκ του κατα λουκαν ἁγιου ευαγγελιου τα κεφαλαια. γ'.–του. ε'. +τον (*ante* ιωαννην). ζ'. σ̅ρ̅σ̅ (*pro* χ̅υ̅). θ'. –του. ι'. ποικιλου νοσου. ιϛ'. διαταγης. κδ'. περι του εχοντος τον λεγεωνα. κε'. αρχησυναγωγου. κθ'. των μαθηματων (*pro* του κ̅υ̅). λδ'. αναδιδαχθεντων (–ἑβδομηκοντα). μ'. εν τω οχλω. φωνης. μα'. σημειων. μβ'. ιησουν (*pro* κ̅ν̅). μϛ'. οὐ (του *Mill*:). εφωρισεν. ν'. ει (*pro* οἱ). να'. του ειποντος του ιησου. ἡρωδου. νγ'. πρωτοκλησιας. νδ'. εν τω δειπνω. νε'. περι παραβολης οικοδομης πυργου. νϛ'. περι παραβολης ἑκατον προβατων. νθ'. –του *bis.* ξβ'. –του *secund.* ξγ'. τον ιησουν πλουσιου. ξϛ'. –ἑαυτῳ. ξζ'. του λαβοντα. ξη'. πολου. ξθ'. ηρωτησαντων. οἱ αρχϊερεις και οἱ πρεσβυτεροι. οα'. *Deest.* οβ'. σαδουκαιων: *deinde post spatium* περι της του κ̅υ̅ επερωτησεως. ογ'. –του. –εστιν. *fin.* ὁ χί (*sic*). οδ'. –βαλουσης. οε'. –της. –ερωτησις. οη'. εξετασεως. –και αρνησεως πετρου. οθ'. Ἐξουθενωσις ἡρωδου (–περι). πβ'. περι αιτησεως του κυριακου σωματος. πγ'. –του.

S. Johannis: εκ του κατα ιωαννην ευαγγελιου τα κεφαλαια. γ'. –και ιησου. δ'. ζητησις περι καθαρμου (καθαρισμου L**). ε'. ἁμαρτιδος (*pro* σαμαρειτιδος). ϛ'. καθαρισμου και (*pro* υἱου). ζ'. ετων. *fin.* +αυτου. η'.

–και των δυο ιχθυων. ι'. –εκ γενετης. ια'. –της εγερσεως. ιβ'. μυρου. ιγ'. ιουδας. ιδ'. του (*pro* της). ιε'. –και ερωτωντων τον φιλιππον.

Desunt omnino in L *literæ numerales Evangeliorum* κεφαλαιοις *præponi solitæ: nec leguntur* κεφαλαια *in reliquis S. Fœderis libris.*

Collatio ὑποθεσεως *in Hebræos apud Cod. Leicestrensem cum Millii N. T. editione Kusterianâ, p.* 519, *col.* 2.

Προλογος ητουν ὑφηγησις της προς ἑβραιους επιστολης. *Init.* Ἡ δε προς. ταις αλλαις (*pro* αλλαις ταις). τω λεγειν. –του (*ante* λαλεισθαι). ὑπο του κυ δια (*Hebr.* II. 3). τερασιν. –ουν. ηλαχθαι. λελεκται. δ' οἱ. αυτου (*pro* τουτου). –και (*ante* σωζει). οὐχ' ἰουδαιων. εδωκεν. λοιποις (*pro* τοις *ante* αποστ.). γραφειν (*pro* προγραφειν). μαρτυρει. εν τοις δεσμοις (*Hebr.* X. 34). περισσοτερως ευχεσθαι. *Deest* και εκ του λεγειν γινωσκετε *usque ad* επαγγελλεται. ειναι (*pro* τυγχανειν). διδαξει.

The next four copies on my list are Evangelistaria, two of them (P and P_2) belonging to the princely collection of Manuscripts at Parham Park, Sussex, brought from the East by the Hon. Robert Curzon, jun. They are best known to the general reader by the notices of them scattered throughout that gentleman's lively and most interesting "Visits to Monasteries in the Levant." A more formal yet succinct account of them will be found in his "Catalogue of materials for writing, early writings on tablets and stones, rolled and other MSS. and Oriental MSS. books in the Library of Robert Curzon at Parham," fol. 1849: a scarce work, of which a copy is in the British Museum. For the privilege of collating these Evangelistaria (both of them in uncial letters) and two copies of the Apocalypse to be described in their place, I am indebted to Mr Curzon's kindness and liberality, for which I am bound to tender him my earnest thanks. Twelve other manuscripts of the Greek Testament remain unexamined at Parham, several of which (especially a very early copy of the Gospel in cursive characters, and a splendid Evangelistarium which belonged to the Emperor Alexius Comnenus) are of considerable critical value. Before we describe the Parham books we will first speak of

(H) HARLEIAN, 5598, in the British Museum, being Scholz's Evangelistarium, 150. Its splendour has been admired by many; facsimiles of its penmanship have been published by Woide in his edition of the Cod. Alexandrinus (Præf. p. xv.), by Horne in his Introduction, and by Scott Porter in his "Principles of Textual Criticism" (Belfast, 1848); in the Catalogue of the Harleian MSS., published as far back as 1808, it had been most justly described as "collatione dignissimum," yet up to this time its readings have not been available to the critic. This copy consists of 748 pages on vellum in large folio, and usually contains 21 lines in each of the two columns on a page, the characters being bold yet elegant uncial letters, while fortunately the date is fixed by a colophon on p. 748, in the hand of the original scribe: εγραφη δια χειρος κῶνσταντίν^{υ} πρεσβυτερ, μ^{υη} μαιω $\overline{κζ}$, ινδ. $\overline{η}$, ετους $\overline{ςφγ}$: i. e. in the year of the Greek æra, 6503, or A. D. 995. I believe that but two older *dated* MSS. of the Greek Testament are extant, nor can I account on any reasonable principle, for the neglect this volume has met with. It is at least as early as several of the uncial copies of the Gospels in their proper order; and when allowance is made for the necessary liturgical changes at the beginnings of the Church lessons (an allowance which the veriest tiro in these studies could make with ease) I can not even conjecture why an Evangelistarium should be thought of less value than another MS. of the same age[1].

This is one of the *five* copies of the Greek Testament (the others are Harleian 5537, 5557, 5620, 5778: I have used two of them in the Apocalypse) brought from the East in 1677 by Dr John Covell, for seven years Chaplain to the British Embassy at Constantinople; then Chaplain to the Princess Mary at the Hague, from which office he was summarily dismissed by her churlish husband; and from 1688 till his death in 1722 (æt. 85) Master of Christ's College, Cambridge. He seems to have been an unpopular, perhaps an unamiable person, but his services rendered to Biblical criticism entitle his memory to respect. This MS. was paged and the lessons diligently noted in the margin by his hand: between pp. 726 and 727 are bound up ten paper leaves, comprising useful indices of the Church lessons contained in the book, and certain notes, chiefly on the various readings he had observed in a cursory perusal, a few of them referring to the Epistles, and therefore extracted from some of his other MSS.[2]

This magnificent codex contains all the Church lessons daily throughout the year, the services of the Holy Week, the proper lessons for the Great Feasts and Saint days, followed by the Gospels set apart for special occasions, εις εγκαινια ναου, εις γυναικας, εις κοιμηθεντας, εις ανομβριαν, and such like. There is an

---

[1] It is pleasant to be able to confirm one's own judgment, however decided, by such authority as Tischendorf's. I believe he has individually done nothing in this field of labour, yet he does not shrink from confessing "Evangelistariorum codices literis uncialibus scripti, nondum sic ut decet, in usum criticum conversi sunt." (*Proleg. N. T. Præfat.* p. lxviii. ed. 1849.)

[2] This year (1858) I find the MS. newly bound and Dr Covell's papers placed at the end of the volume. On the initial fly-leaf is written in pencil, "Sclavonice, vid. 5684, 5787, Rev. Mr. Woide and H. G." Below this are two old scraps pasted on the leaf, in different hands. The one runs, "Observandum est in hisce Pericopis, multa ex uno Evangelio in lectionem sumptam et alio transferri, ad illustrandam et augendam Historiam. Inde in ipsis Evangeliis oritur mira aliquando varietas lectionis, eorum quæ in ipsum textum irrepserunt." The other, which seems somewhat more recent, runs, "Manuscriptum τὸ παρὸν videtur seculi novi: literæ autem cum Russicis [Slavonicis] prorsus conveniunt." The writer had not observed that the MS. is dated.

apparent hiatus after p. 639, which ends abruptly with τα σωματα εν Johan. xix. 31, but the missing verses are taken up a few pages later, so that nothing is lost. There is a slight illumination on the first page (on which all the letters are gilded) and elsewhere throughout the volume at the commencements of its several parts; each lesson also begins with a large flourished capital, gaudily colored: in other respects the book is destitute of ornament, which indeed it can well spare, when we consider its intrinsic value.

The text of Harl. 5598 is much more widely removed from the textus receptus than either the Arundel (X) or Parham (P) Evangelistaria, though it is of a somewhat later date. It approximates rather closely to that of the cursive Lectionary I shall hereafter describe as z, though in parts they are not at all alike. The *Pericope Adulteræ* is not found in this MS., for it is not only absent here, as in all other Service Books I know, from the Greek lesson for the Pentecost (Johan. vii. 37—viii. 12), but it is not read among the Saints' Day lessons, as in P and z. Many documents contain more instances of itacism than Codex H: I have counted 528 in the whole MS., quite of the ordinary character. The breathings, however, have given me great trouble, as they are very irregular, and in a copy of such importance I thought it right to represent them all. We read ού, ούκ, ούδεις, pretty constantly; αἱ, οἱ (the articles), ἀγιος, ἀρπαζω, ἀλιεις, ἐως, εἱς gen. ἑνος, ἑκαστος, ἑορτη, ἑτερος, ἑτοιμος, οὐκ', ὡδε, and on the contrary, ὁλιγος, ὁπισω, ὀζος, &c. Once we have the form αὑτων (Matth. xxiii. 30) so rare in MSS. of the Greek Testament. The accents are so ill placed that to note their peculiarities would be to transcribe the whole volume. We meet with no ι *subscript.* or *ascript.*, and ν εφελκυστικον, at least *primâ manu*, not frequently (yet ειπεν always), but a later hand has taken the trouble to insert it often where it was originally absent: yet above nine instances remain where it is wanting before a vowel. Two correctors have been employed on this book; one quite recent and so of little weight, the other (who writes a few marginal notes[1] in a small uncial hand) nearly as early as the scribe Constantine himself, though I do not agree with Dr Covell that the colophon containing the date is by this second hand[2]. Not more than six errors by ὁμοιοτελευτον occur in this MS. and χειραν Matth. xii. 10, ανταλαγμα Marc. viii. 37, and ναζαρεθ *semper*, are the only Alexandrian forms I notice. Yet there are frequent interchanges of the cases after verbs: e.g. dative for accusative, Marc. vi. 48; xiv. 7; Luc. ix. 2; 18; xi. 46; Johan. xviii. 7: accusative for dative, Matth. xxvii. 44; Marc. iv. 2; v. 13; vi. 37; xv. 23; Luc.

---

[1] Wherever this early uncial hand is used, I have stated that the correction is *antiquâ manu.* I have noted twenty-three such cases.

[2] Such I suppose is Covell's meaning when he writes (Harl. 5598, p. 748), "vid. p. 403, ubi in margine scribuntur hujusmodi characteres [sc. και μετα τρεις ἡμερας αναστηναι, Marc. viii. 31], unde manifestè collig|*o perfec*|tum esse hoc anno" (*o perfec* is barely legible). Perhaps, however, he means that the writer of the small uncials is the original scribe when correcting his copy, which may possibly be the fact.

vi. 34; ix. 55; xvi. 9; xxii. 19; 29; xxiii. 9; Johan. xix. 3: accusative for genitive, Marc. iii. 2; xv. 3; Luc. xxiii. 2. In the present copy, as in most other Lectionaries, many marks are found, which seem to be musical notes, designed for guiding the reader's voice: } seems often interrogative. This is beyond question a most important document.

(P) Parham Evangelistarium unciale, No. 18, is a noble folio, written on 222 leaves of delicately white vellum, each page containing two columns of 27 or 22 lines each[1], written in clear and elegant uncial characters. Like Arundel, 547, this volume contains the lessons for every day between Easter and Pentecost, with the Saturday and Sunday lessons only for the rest of the year: the full service for the Holy Week, with lessons for Saints' Days somewhat different to those in our other Evangelistaria, for many of the minor festivals were more or less specially observed at different periods and in different regions. The age and country of this copy appears from an inscription on the last page (of which Mr Curzon's catalogue contains a fac-simile) evidently *primâ manu*: ϵγραφη το τιμιον και ἁγιον ευαγγελιον επι στεφανου του θεοφιλου επισκοπου κισκισσης· μηνι ιουνιω· ινδ. η· ετους ϛυπη· γραφεν δια χειρος νικ̄ χ̄ ⳨ (*sic*). The year ϛυπη is A. M. 6488 of the Greek æra, or A. D. 980. This copy, therefore, with the single exception of Vatican 354 (S of the Gospels), collated by Birch, and written A. D. 949, is the oldest *dated* MS. of any portion of the Greek Testament. Ciscissa, where no doubt the document was written, was a small town and Bishop's See in Cappadocia Prima, some thirty-five miles E. S. E. of Cæsarea, its capital and metropolitan see (*Bingham, Antiquit.* Vol. III. p. 93; *see also*, p. 191). Its country is further established by a kind of colophon scrawled on the fly-leaf (fol. 222) under a rude arcade, with other irrelevant and almost illegible matter: ανεκαινισθη το τιμιον και ἁγιον ευαγγελιον επι νικητα του ἁγιωτατου επισκοπου κισκισσης του . . . δια χειρος μιχαηλ νοταριου και ἀνου (?) αυτου· ετους ϛφνζ, μηνι μαρτ ά· ινδ. β΄· επι κωνσταντινου μονομαχου ζωης και θεοδωρας των θεοσεπτων βασιλεων· μιχαηλ του ἁγιωτατου και οικουμ . . . . πατριαρχου κηρουλλου· στυλιανου του ἁγιωτατου μητροπολιτου καισαρειας καππαδοκιας και [*cætera vix legibilia*]. This colophon bears date A. D. 1049 [A. M. 6557] and was written, I presume, by the person who made the numerous changes *secundâ manu*, both in small uncial and cursive characters, which abound throughout the MS.: to him also we may be indebted for the two lessons in cursive letters on the margin of the book (foll. 146, 147) which I have indicated by *P* (Luc. xi. 47—52; Johan. x. 9—16). As a notary, or official scribe (*vid.* Suicer, *Thesaur. Ecclesiast.* Tom. II. p. 431), he takes care to apprise us of the names of the three joint-sovereigns of the Eastern Empire (one of whom, I fear, little deserved the epithet θεοσεπτην), of the Patriarch of Constantinople, of the Metropolitan of Cæsarea, and of the Bishop of Ciscissa. This volume is now superbly bound in purple velvet, with the original clasp and

[1] Observe that foll. 140, 141, and 142, 143, are misplaced by the binder.

five golden bosses; it was disinterred by Mr Curzon in 1837 (together with both copies of the Apocalypse described below) from the Library of Caracalla, a monastery on Mount Athos.

Both this MS. and Arundel 547, which I consider to be older, approximate much more closely to the received text than others of a later date and less promising appearance: from which fact I leave the reader to draw his own inference. Yet the collation of this copy cost me much labour, through my desire to exhibit all its peculiarities whether of breathing or orthography. The accents indeed, like those of Arundel 547, seem to be put almost at random, and I have not noticed them except in special cases: the system of breathings, such as it is, is tolerably uniform. Thus Codex P always gives ἧν or ἧν for the imperfect of ειμι, ἦλθον or ἦλθον (as our w), οὗν, οὐκ', ἐξ", ὀχλος, ὀνομα: in fact all verbs beginning with η and many words whose initial vowel is ο, seem to take the aspirate as a matter of course: ῑ often has no breathing. In accentuation ῑδοῦ, ἀληθῆs, οὐδεῖs, μὴ *interrogativè*, νὺν, ὅτ' ἂν, ἐὰν, ἐπὰν, are pretty constant: but the circumflex and grave accent are repeatedly interchanged. After proper names such as ἀβρααμ, δᾱδ, ῑλημ, we often see the apostrophe ' even before consonants. Ν εφελκυστικον may be said to be almost universal, but I noticed no example of ι ascript or subscript. This codex is not much illuminated; there are slight ornaments on the first page and at foll. 112, 144, p. 2, besides the initial letters of each lesson: the rubrical and musical notes are in red ink, and the form of the mark of breathing square (⊣ ⊢). Though written in uncial letters the mutation of β for υ occurs, Johan. x. 1 *sem.*, and of υ for β Luc. vi. 34: but this is found even in the Arundel 547. Itacisms are not so numerous as in some documents of this period, yet still plentiful (υ *pro* οι *sæpe*): I have represented them all.

I now pass on to grammatical inflexions. We have the 3rd declension accusative in -αν, νυκταν, Luc. ii. 37 *p.m.*; θυγατεραν, xiii. 16 *sem.*; χειραν, Marc. iii. 1; Luc. xv. 22; on the other hand, μαχαιρα, Matth. xxvi. 52; καιαφα, *ib.* 57 *sem.*; accusatives: ασθενην Matth. xxv. 39; 44 *sem.*; μειζον *fem.* Johan. xix. 11 *sem.*: in verbs εισελθατε Matth. vii. 13; ηλθατε xxv. 36 *sem.* (ἡλθατε *sem.*); ηλθαμεν *ibid.* 39 *sem.*; παρελθατο xxvi. 39; εξηλθατε *ibid.* 55; προσεπεσαν vii. 25; ανεπεσαν Johan. vi. 10; ειπαν ix. 28; γεναμενης Matth. xxvi. 20: of verbs in μι, δυνομενη Luc. xiii. 11 *sem.*; παραδιδουντα Johan. xiii. 11; αφιειμην xiv. 27 *sem.*: note also εωρουν Johan. vi. 2; ελεγουν xix. 21 *sem.*; ἑωρακαν Luc. ix. 36; εκαθερισθη Marc. i. 42; so Luc. xvii. 14; but ἐκαθερεῖσθη Luc. iv. 27; εφοβηθην Johan. xix. 8; ηδυνηθην Marc. vii. 24 (3rd person); προσκυμψας Luc. xxiv. 12 *p.m.*; ανταλαγμα Marc. viii. 37. We often see γαλλιλαια, μνημιον, περισευμα, διορυσω, διαγγελω, κατετος, κατιδιαν, κατοναρ, κατονομα. The accusative is put for the dative Matth. xx. 4; xxi. 2 *p.m.*; xxvi. 15 *sem.*; xxvii. 31 *sem.*; 44 *bis*; xxviii. 9; 17; Marc. i. 43; ii. 4; vi. 19[1]; x. 34 *bis in versu;* xv. 19; Luc. xvii. 7;

[1] επηχεν αυτον: on p. 327 of our collation read αυτον (*pro* αυτῳ) Pz: αυτου is a misprint.

xxiii. 26; xxiv. 42; Johan. vi. 8; vii. 26: the dative for accusative, Matth. xxvi. 71; Luc. iv. 31; x. 35; xvii. 14; xxiv. 51: the accusative for the genitive, Marc. i. 41. The pericope adulteræ is once omitted in the middle of a lesson, but Johan. viii. 3—11, and Luc. vii. 36, &c. comprise the proper service for the feast της ἁγιας θεοδωρας on Sept. 18. Theodora's strange story is told in the great *Acta Sanctorum* (Antwerp, 1765), September, Tom. III. p. 789: she lived in the fifth century.

This document contains as many as 32 examples of ὁμοιοτελευτον, e. g. Johan. xiv. 3; 12; but on the whole is accurately written. Glosses (Matth. xvii. 20; xix. 12; Johan. vi. 11; viii. 44; xix. 11 *sem.*), itacisms (Matth. xxvi. 60; xxvii. 2 *rubro:* 41), or rare variations (Luc. xxiii. 35; Johan. x. 36; xx. 12), are often introduced by later hands, of which probably more than one was engaged in making alterations and erasures. This MS. rarely departs from the received text as widely as in Marc. vii. 25, 26; Luc. ix. 28—36; yet the following passages deserve notice: Matth. v. 32; vii. 2 (*cum Elzev.*); 14; viii. 30; ix. 18; xxiii. 10; xxv. 20; 26; 45 *p.m.*; Luc. vi. 4; vii. 39 *p.m.*; 44; viii. 17; 31; xxi. 8; xxiii. 1; 15 (D *Leicest.*); 28; 33; xxiv. 7; Johan. vii. 8 (ου καταβαινω); x. 28 *sem.*; xxi. 3 (*Elzev.*) *p.m.*

(P_2) PARHAM EVANGELISTARIUM UNCIALE, No. 1. This volume contains many specimens of early writing on papyrus, vellum and other materials, in Coptic and other languages, which are minutely described in the Parham Catalogue. The only Biblical fragment in Greek among them consists of three 'eaves of an Evangelistarium in large uncial characters, removed from the binding of a MS. of the twelfth century, found at the Monastery of Docheirou on Mount Athos. Mr Curzon obtained them for asking. The Evangelistarium must have been of about the ninth century, and much resembles in style the fragment I have called X (2), at the end of Arundel 547 (*Collation of the Holy Gospels*, Introd. p. lx.); indeed as both fragments have two columns of nineteen lines each on each page, they are very possibly parts of the same book. This Codex contains Matth. i. 1—11; 11—22; vii. 7, 8; Marc. ix. 41; xi. 22—26; Luc. xi. 1—4: the vellum has been so hacked as to cut away much of the margin and many letters of the text; the leaves seem to belong to that portion of an Evangelistarium which relates to the Feasts; before Marc. xi. 22 we read σεπτ. κβ̄. ληψης της ἁγιας αννης. There are but few variations from the received text in these three leaves, but the breathings and accents are as irregular as in Arund. 547, my remarks on which exactly apply to P_2. Some corrections are made in small uncials, seemingly by a later hand (Matth. i. 14; 22). Marc. ix. 41 is perhaps unique.

(z) CHRISTI COLL. CANTAB. F. 1, 8, is a fine Evangelistarium on vellum, consisting of 218 thick folio leaves, with two columns on a page: a modern hand has numbered *the columns* (871): there are *about* 30 lines in a column, in a clear bold style, and good preservation, only that the ink is somewhat faded and a few

Coll. Christ. Cantab. F.1.8.

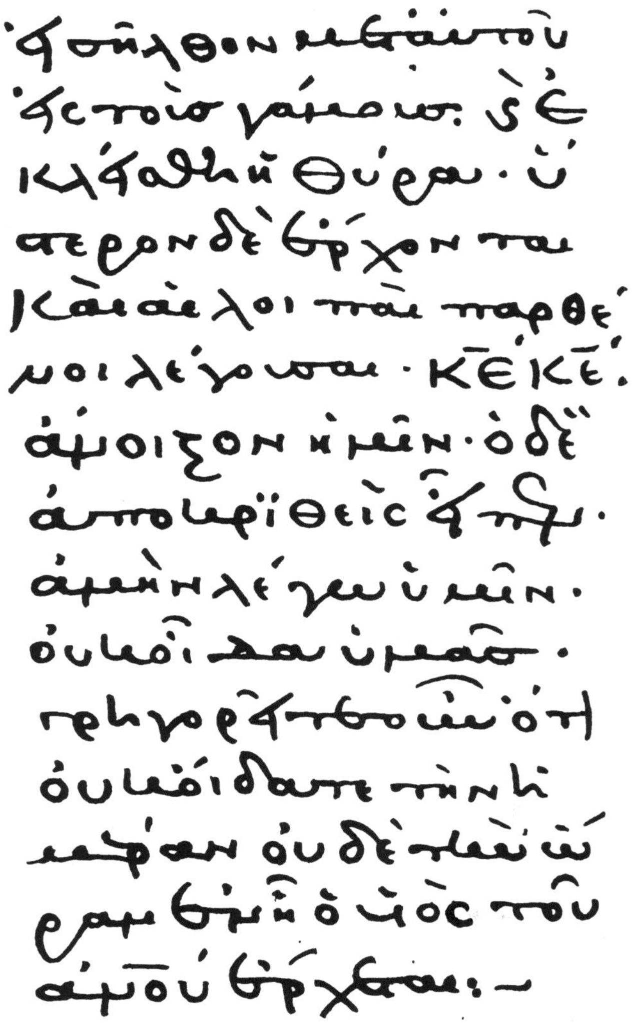

3.

Coll. Emmanuel Cantab 1.4.35.

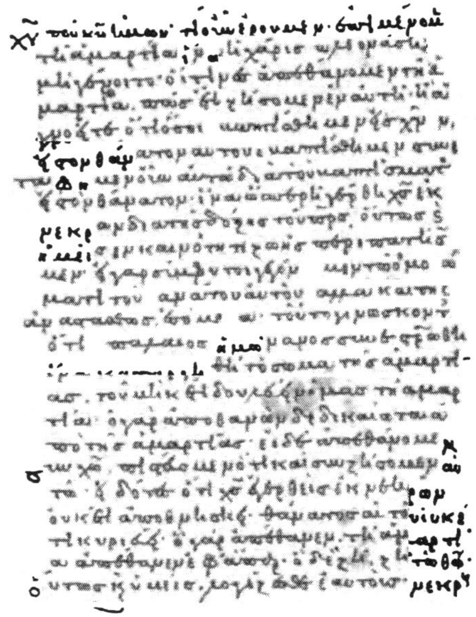

J.R. Jobbins

leaves are lost[1]. On a paper fly-leaf we read, "E dono Francisci Tayleri, in Theologiâ Licenciati olim Collegii Christi apud Cantabrigienses alumni, nunc vero verbi divini in Æde Christi apud Cantuarienses concionatoris: data Julij 24, 1654." As Mill overlooked this document when he collated the copy of the Acts and Epistles in the same library (to be described below), it has never been inserted in Catalogues of Greek Testament MSS.; I am indebted for my knowledge of its existence to the truly learned Dr Kaye, late Bishop of Lincoln, who had been Master of the College. The present Master and Fellows of the Society granted me permission to collate both their MSS. at my own house, with a courtesy and readiness for which I cannot be too grateful. At the foot of col. 871 we find *primâ manu*, δοξα τω λογω τω δοντι τελος· αμην, and on the second page of this last leaf (218), much illegible scrawl in later hands, among which occurs the following: ἀπουλείθη τὸ παρὼν εὐαγγέλειων καὶ ηγῶράσθη παρὰ ἀθα[να]σιου τοῦ τάγκρι ἀπὸ τὸν.... [*illegibilia*].... γραθ. σεβτεμβρι δ̄ τὸ ἔτος ςψο̄ · ινδον δ. This date is 6770 or A.D. 1261, and since it is considerably more recent than the Evangelistarium, we may fairly place the latter as early as the eleventh or twelfth century. There are a few poor illuminations on the first page and elsewhere, the initial letter of each lesson is colored and flourished, and the rubrical notes are partly in red. The hand which paged the columns and noted the modern chapters in the margin seems less recent than that which wrote on the paper fly-leaves at the end of the volume a convenient table of references to the lessons taken from the three first Gospels: a similar table is met with in Harleian. 5598; Dr Covell perhaps compiled both.

This Evangelistarium contains no example of ι ascript, except perhaps ηιδειτε, Luc. ii. 49, and only 17 of ι subscript, almost always with the article. In the earlier pages ν εφελκυστικον is quite rare, but as we proceed it gets more common, until with ειπεν it is quite the rule. The hiatus, however, takes place for want of ν in Matth. vii. 9 *sec. man.*; xxi. 30; Luc. xv. 27; Johan. xx. 5. The itacisms are about the same in amount as in Cod. i, but somewhat differently distributed: thus η for ει occurs 159 times; ει for η, 92; ω for ο, 104; ο for ω, 105; η for ι, 52; ι for η, 32; ε for αι, 32; αι for ε, 40; ου for ω, 10; ω for ου, 8; υ for οι, 4; οι for υ, 3; υ for ι, 1; ι for υ, 2; υ for η, 2; η for υ, 1; ι for ει, 28; ει for ι, 16; ε for η, 12; η for ε, 7; ει for οι, 1; οι for ει, 2: in all 713: ἡμεις and ὑμεις are confounded, Matth. vii. 11; 15, *sem.*; Luc. ix. 49; xxii. 31, *sem.*; xxiii. 30, *sem.*; xxiv. 20; Johan. xi. 11; xvi. 17, *sem.*; xix. 35, *p.m. sem.*

Of grammatical inflexions &c. we mark the following: of nouns, θυρα, Matth. vi. 6; χηρα, Luc. xviii. 5, *accus.*; but χειραν, Marc. vii. 32; Luc. vi. 8; νυκταν, ii. 37;

[1] About eight leaves are wanting which gave the lessons from the Saturday for the fourth week after Easter to the Tuesday of the sixth, col. 56, Johan. xii. 24, μονος μενει: also about five leaves between the 12th Saturday of Luke, c. xiii. 24, λεγω υμιν, col. 438, to the 15th Sunday, xix. 4, ανεβη.

θυγατεραν, xiii. 16: *ιεροις*, Matth. xii. 4; *μεγισταναις*, Marc. vi. 21; so *μειζων*, *neut. pl.* Johan. i. 51, *sem.: accus. sing.* v. 36; *πολλυν*, *ibid.* 6; of verbs, *προσεπεσαν*, Matth. vii. 25; *εκβαλατε*, xxii. 13; *εξελθατε*, xxiv. 26, *sem.*; *ηλθατε*, xxv. 36, *sem.*; *εξηλθατε*, Luc. vii. 25; *ειπαν*, xx. 16; *ειδατε*, Johan. xiii. 17, *sem.*; *ηδυνηθην*, 3 *pers.* Marc. vii. 24: and *ν* rejected in *απεσταλη*, Matth. xv. 24; *εδιδου*, Johan. xix. 3: note also, *παραδιδουντα*, Johan. xiii. 11 *sem.*; *κατεγελουν*, Matth. ix. 24; *συνηκων*, Marc. vi. 52; *απηγασι*, Johan. xviii. 13; and in orthography observe *διδραγματα*, Matt. xvii. 24; *σκυλεις*, Marc. v. 35; *όπισθεν*, Matt. xv. 23; *εμπροσθε*, Johan. i. 15; 27. We read also *δειση* and *εδεισεν* for *δηση* and *εδησεν* (quite a peculiarity of this copy), *κυλος*, *γεενα* constantly. In the following places the reduplication of verbs is omitted, Matth. ix. 36; Marc. v. 4; Johan. iii. 21; vi. 42. The preposition receives the augment in *επροφητευσαμεν*, Matt. vii. 22; *ηφισταто*, Luc. ii. 37. The augment is lost in Matth. xi. 17; xiii. 24; xiv. 6; xviii. 23; xxii. 2; 7; xxv. 1; xxvii. 44 *sem.*; Marc. xv. 44 *sem.*; Luc. ii. 38; vi. 14; vii. 32; xiii. 13; xxii. 6 *sem.*; Johan. xii. 42, *sem.*

The breathings and accents are very regular, though (as in most of the copies I have examined) the accent of an enclitic is not often thrown back when the preceding word is properispomenon. We have, however, *μὴδὲ*, *μηδὲμία*, &c. *μὴκέτι*, *οἶδατε*, *πῶποτε* and other such anomalies, *παρὰχρῆμα*, *ὑπὸκάτω*, *οὐδ᾽ εἰς*, *ἐὰν*, *ἐπὰν* (but *ὅταν*), *οὐχ᾽*, *ὧδε*, *αἴρω*, *κατιδίαν*, *κατόναρ*, *διαπαντὸς*, *διατοῦτο*, *οὐκέτι*, *ρρ* not *ῤῥ*.

Besides the Gospels in full, several portions of which are always written more than once in an Evangelistarium (see *Collation of the Holy Gospels*, Introd. p. lxiii.), this copy is remarkable for containing among the services for the Holy Week, four passages from the Septuagint version, Isaiah iii. 9—13; lii. 13—liv. 1; Jerem. xi. 18—xii. 15; Zechar. xi. 10—14; and four from the Pauline Epistles, Rom. v. 6—10; Gal. vi. 14—18; 1 Tim. vi. 11—16; Hebr. x. 19—31. The various readings of these last are recorded in their proper places and noted z.

This MS. is carefully written, though it contains 23 omissions by *ὁμοιοτελευτον*: a second hand has sometimes made alterations, but these are not many: it introduces an itacism Marc. iv. 29, and scrawled a rubrical note over coll. 161, 2. In noticing peculiarities of punctuation we must bear in mind that ; is often equivalent to a *comma*; this may perhaps apply to Johan. i. 43; v. 45; viii. 13; and is also true in Cod. i. For stops see Matth. xii. 28; xx. 12; Marc. viii. 18; xiv. 31.

Few copies of the Gospels contain more numerous and interesting yet *minute* variations from the printed text than Cod. z, which much resembles in that respect iL of my present, and cegop and especially y of my previous collations; but in very many places it stands almost, often quite alone. Thus the patient student will find it a document of singular importance, well meriting his best consideration. Matth. xxiii. 35 omits the perplexing *υἱου βαραχιου*; in xxvii. 9, *ιερεμιου* is wanting in one place, but read in another; the genealogy in Luc. iii. abounds with variations; Luc. xxii. 43, 44 is wanting in its place, but once placed after Matth. xxvi. 39; Johan. vii. 53—viii. 11 is wanting in its place (Whitsunday), but Johan. viii. 1—11 is given on August 31 (the last day of the ecclesiastical year) εις την ἑορτην πελαγιου και εις λοιπας ἁγιας. This MS. has some solecisms and many changes of case: e.g. genitive for dative, Luc. ix. 23; 57; and *vice versâ*, Matth. xxvi. 62: dative for accusative, Matth. vii. 24; 26; 29; xviii. 32; xxvii. 1; Marc. v. 24 and 14 other texts: accusative for dative, Matth. xi. 1; xiv. 7; xvi. 22; xxii. 16 *sem.*; Marc. iv. 2; x. 21, and 25 others.

The following readings, selected from a very large number, may serve to shew the choice character of this Evangelistarium. Matth. i. 8; ii. 9 (o); 13; iii. 5 (b); 7; 8 (*Elz.*); 9 (r); iv. 2 (our P*); 24(g); v. 11; 12 (D); 31; 38; vii. 18; viii. 4 (s); ix. 15 (Dg); x. 4 *sem.* (BCD); 10; xii. 8; 12; 39; 40; 50; xvi. 10 (c); 11; 12; xxiii. 26; Marc. i. 22 (Ccv); 27; 33; iii. 11; 28 (ABCD); iv. 4 (*Elz.*); 5 (D); 7 (CDc); 9 (*Elz.*); 11 (y); 14; 16; 19 (our L); 22; vi. 3; 4; 9; 45 (Dc); 49 (Bc); 55; Luc. i. 26; 30 (C); iv. 4 (*gloss*); vi. 17 *sem.*; 49 (By); vii. 32; xi. 13, *sem.*; 20; xvi. 26; xvii. 36 (*Elz.*); xx. 10 (Cy); 27; xxii. 19, *sem.*; 32; xxiii. 50; 56 (s); xxiv. 10; Johan. i. 26 *sem.* (c); 41; 51 *sem.* (B); ii. 5; 10 (B); 15; 17 (*Elz.*); iii. 2; 11; 23; 24; 25 (*Elz.*); v. 19; 22; 25 (BD); 32; vi. 1; 2 (ABD); 17; 19; vii. 13; 17; xii. 26, &c.

II. 2. As our list of MSS. for the Acts and Catholic Epistles is with four exceptions the same as that for the Epistles of St Paul, it will be convenient to describe both series under the same head.

The Lambeth MSS. of the Carlyle collection comprise the first six on our catalogue (abcd, e of Acts, e of St Paul): of these I have elsewhere given a sufficient general account[1]. When I collated them, now twelve years ago, by the permission of the late Archbishop Howley (who was pleased to countenance my exertions in this department of sacred learning), they had merely been inspected so far as to ascertain that none of them contained the disputed passage, 1 John v. 7, 8. Dr Bloomfield has since used four of them and some lectionaries in the same collection to enrich his critical notes in the ninth edition of his Greek Testament: he kindly permitted me to verify my references in many places while they continued in his possession. I proceed to describe them in detail.

(a). Lambeth, 1182. This copy is in quarto, of 793 pages, on paper, and must date from the 12th century at the earliest. Professor Carlyle marked it I 8, thus indicating that he procured it from one of the Greek Islands. The MS. itself is written in a bold round hand, but as many leaves are lost, they have been supplied in a more careless style by a scribe full two centuries later: the passages so supplied are Acts i. 1—xii. 3 (68 pages; the more ancient writing commencing at προσεθετο); Acts xiii. 5, συναγωγαις to v. 15 και των (pp. 75, 76); 2 and 3 John

[1] Collation of the Holy Gospels. Introduction, pp. xxiv—vi.

and Jude (pp. 755—793)[1]. The books are arranged in a very unusual order, the Pauline Epistles following the Acts, and preceding the Catholic Epistles, as in our modern Bibles. The older part of this MS. is much damaged, in fact most of the leaves are remounted. Before the Acts in the later hand are Liturgical αντιφωνα for Easter (*vid.* Suicer, *Thes. Ecc.* Tom. I. p. 387), αποδημιαι παυλου, an ὑποθεσις to the Acts, and an arrangement of the contents in order, *the Catholic Epistles being here made to follow the Acts.* After the Acts, *primâ manu*, follow πραξεις των ἁγιων αποστολων 5 pp., as their sequel. Each Epistle has an ὑποθεσις, and at the end, in the later hand, are a Synaxarion of the Πραξαποστολος throughout the year, and lessons from Phil. ii. 5—11; Hebr. ix. 1—7; 1 Thess. iv. 13—17 (marked a^2 in this collation). This volume contains a few coarse illuminations, *rubro;* κεφαλαια numbered in the margin, with capitals commencing each; αρχαι, τελη of the lessons noted, their proper days at the top of the page, and such initial supplements as αδελφοι, &c. all in red.

The breathings and accents of Cod. a are very regular; we have only a few such forms as ἀλοων, ἐνεστωσαν, ἑδραιωμα, but ἀβρααμ, ὧδε, καθ' ὃ, κατ' ἐνωπιον, καθημεραν, τοιγὰροῦν, and in orthography, καταγγελω, ενατος, οὑτως (οὑτω only four times) φιληξ nine times; οφθαλμο_δουλεια, ταπειφροσυνη (Col. ii. 23; iii. 12), νηφαλεος. The ν εφελκυστικον occurs only Hebr. vii. 2; xi. 8. We never read ι ascript, but ι subscript 67 times, often with relatives. Itacisms are rare, though somewhat thicker in the more recent portion of the MS.: they are even inserted *secundâ manu*, e.g. Act. iii. 22; iv. 13; of grammatical forms we find ηλλατο, Act. xiv. 10; εσυραν, xvii. 6; ηφωριζεν, Gal. ii. 12; ειπα, Hebr. iii. 10; εὑραμενος (*cum multis*) ix. 12. There are 27 instances of ὁμοιοτελευτον, and the writing is in some places injured by damp and the ink faded. On the top of p. 384 is some faded writing, now illegible. The corrections are in two hands, one ancient (perhaps *primâ manu*), the other more recent, and some are in vermilion. Δε and τε, ἱεροσολυμα and ἱερουσαλημ (Act. xvi. 4; xx. 16; xxi. 14; 15) are often confounded: there are many transpositions in the order of words (sometimes noted α, β *secundâ manu*), and the copy is so liturgical as often to omit particles of time *initio pericopes.* The more modern hand (Acts i.—xii. 3, &c.) agrees closely with Cod. h, to be described below, and has some good readings: e.g. Acts ii. 13 (ABC); 24: but the older hand represents a very interesting and valuable text, and is full of rare variations, especially in the Acts and Catholic Epistles, being there found in harmony with cdh (described below), with the most ancient MSS., and very conspicuously with that most precious document, designated below as p (consult, for instance, Acts xiii.—xvii. *throughout*). It has $\overline{κυ}$ for $\overline{θυ}$, Acts xx. 28, with ACDE, and very few cursive copies. Compare also Act. xiv. 19; xv. 4; 18; 20 (69); 1 Pet. ii. 8;

---

[1] The binder has misplaced pp. 371-2 and 369-70; 375-6 and 373-4; 457-8, 455-6 and 453-4; 463-4, 461-2 and 459-60; 473-4 and 471-2; 477-8 and 475-6.

11 (*ambobus locis cum* 57**, 69); 12; 19 (C. 69); iii. 12 (57. 69); iv. 14 (57**. 69. c.); 2 Pet. i. 10 (A.c. 69); 1 Cor. xii. 13 (74); xv. 8 (τφ); 2 Cor. iii. 9 (ACD*, 74); iv. 4 (74); v. 17; Eph. ii. 16, *p.m.*; iii. 19 (A 74); Col. ii. 23; iii. 16 (74); 1 Thess. ii. 2; 7 (CD* 74); iv. 5 (74); v. 8 (74); 24 (74); 2 Tim. i. 15; ii. 11; Hebr. vii. 26 (74); xii. 9; xiii. 22 (D); 24 (74). The close resemblance to Knittel's Guelpherbyt. xvi. 7 (69 Acts, 74 Paul) is very remarkable.

(b). LAMBETH 1183, Carlyle I 9, like the preceding, contains the Acts and all the Epistles in their modern order, on paper, pp. 472 quarto, with 27 lines on each page. On the last page is read εγραφη εν ετει ςωξς · ιν · ια · θυ το δωρον και πονος : θς ἁγιος: after which

γονυ μεν ζευξας και ὑποκλινας καραν
χειρας εκτεινας προς τας θειας τετραδας
εκπεπληρωκα την θεοσδοτον δελτον.

μην μαῖος κγ του Cὅ (?) μῖχαηλ συναδων του δμολογητου [*sic*]. ἡμερα δ[1]. και οἱ τηδε τη γραφη εντυχανοντες [*sic*] το κε συγχωρησον και ελεησον τον γραφεα του παροντος βιβλιου λεγετε, ἱν ὁπως και ὑμας αλλοι παλιν μνησθωσι: all this *p.m.*: the date is A.D. 1358. This copy is written in a noble and beautiful hand, and is in pretty good preservation, except that the binder has cut off the tops of many pages[2]. The MS. contains the following hiatus: 1 Cor. xi. 7, κατακαλυπτεσθαι την to v. 27 ενοχος (one leaf); 1 Tim. iv. 1, προσεχοντες to v. 8, νοει την πιστιν (one leaf). The first pages contain fragments of a synaxarion, chants, &c. Before the Acts and all the Epistles are ὑποθεσεις and tables of κεφαλαια: their titles are repeated at the top and bottom of each page of the MS., the number of each κεφαλαιον, the αρχαι, τελη and proper day for each lesson, and the initial capitals, are all in the margin in red. The accents and breathings are very accurate (yet we have ὀσμην, 2 Cor. ii. 14; ἀφης, Eph. iv. 16 *p.m.*; so Col. ii. 19); ι ascript or subscript nowhere occurs, and ν εφελκυστικον only at 1 Cor. i. 18; 25; xv. 58; Hebr. iii. 18; vii. 14. Itacisms are very rare, only one being met with in the first twelve chapters of the Acts (θυγατεραις, ii. 17), and nearly all with proper names (e.g. Acts xiii. 1; xvi. 12; xx. 15; xxiii. 24; 26; xxvii. 6; xxviii. 11 *bis*). They are introduced *sec. man.* Act. xxvii. 2; 40; and in δηραντες, xvi. 37, &c.: there are not above 14 more in the whole MS. Of peculiar forms I note only ἥλλατο, Act. xiv. 10, κατῖδιαν, ἀβρααμ, καθημεραν, ενατος, ἀπαρχῆς, (not in 1 Johan.); οὑτως always except in Act. xiii. 47; xx. 13 *sec. man.*; 1 Thess. iv. 14; 17. Notice also σαρωναν, Act. ix. 35, *p.m.*; εσυραν, xiv. 19; xvii. 6; ει τυχη, 1 Cor. xiv. 10; μεγα, *acc. mas.* Hebr. iv. 14, *p.m.*

In critical value Cod. b may be somewhat inferior to cd and several others in this collection. Yet it has not a few rare and observable readings, of which I

---

[1] A festival of the Apparition of St Michael is set down in the Calendar for May 8, not May 4 or 23.

[2] He has also misplaced pages 165-6, 163-4 and 161-2; 207-8 and 205-6; 243-4 and 241-2; 247-8 and 245-6; 253-4 and 251-2; 431—44 and 415—30; 467-8 and 465-6; 149-50 is bound up after 304.

subjoin a specimen, though on the whole it does not depart from the common text in many *important* places; in the following list it is almost always found in company with Cantab. Mm. 6, 9, which is o of the Acts and Epistles (*supra*, pp. xxxv—vi), i.e. with 61 of Griesbach: Act. iv. 14 (o); xiii. 23; xiv. 19; xv. 20 (Do); xxiii. 15; xxiv. 8; xxv. 8; xxvi. 5 (o); Jac. iii. 7 (o); v. 15 (o); 1 Pet. v. 2 (o); 2 Pet. i. 14 (o); ii. 14; 1 Johan. i. 7 (o); Rom. viii. 10 (o); 23; xi. 4 *p.m.* (o); xiv. 13 *p.m.* (o); 1 Cor. i. 29 (o); xi. 4 (o); xiv. 33 (FG.o); 40 (o); xvi. 3; 2 Cor. xii. 12 (o); Eph. ii. 12 (o); v. 11 (o); Phil. ii. 11, *p.m.* (o); Col. ii. 2, *p.m.* (o); 2 Thess. i. 5. Δε and τε are often interchanged, and the subscriptions to St Paul's Epistles are a little unusual: these are in red, and apparently *primâ manu*. This MS. has only nine examples of ὁμοιοτελευτον, a proof that the scribe exercised some care; in many places where the old writing has become faded, it has been restored, I think by the same person who made the numerous alterations *secundâ manu*.

(c). Lambeth 1184, Carlyle I[slands] 10, of the Acts and Epistles, having been returned with five other MSS. of this collection to the Patriarch of Jerusalem in 1817[1], I am indebted for a knowledge of its contents to some papers in a case (Lambeth 1255, 10—14), which contains (with other matter) a scholar-like and seemingly accurate collation of it with the Greek text of Mill, made by the Rev. W. Sanderson of Morpeth, in or about the year 1804. In Archdeacon Todd's Lambeth Catalogue of MSS. Codex 1184 is described as "Codex chartaceus, in quarto, Sæc. xv.: Acta Apostolorum, Epp. Catholicas et Pauli omnes complectitur... In initio mutilus. Incipit Act. vi. 10, τη σοφια. A diversâ manu duo folia, codicem claudentia, exarata sunt. I. 10." Now Sanderson's collation shews no such defect as the Catalogue mentions, yet he so often cites his copy as I 10, that it is hard to suppose they are speaking of different books. If we were able to form any estimate of the age of a document from the readings it exhibits, we should certainly assign to it a much earlier date than the fifteenth century. In the Acts it is one of our best authorities, being full of weighty and probable variations from the common herd, and we cannot but be too thankful for the diligence which has recorded them for our use; in the Catholic Epistles it is scarcely less valuable, but in the Epistles of St Paul it presents us with little worthy of particular notice. There is an hiatus from Act. vii. 52 ὑμων to viii. 25 εις. At the end of his collation Sanderson adds "In antecedenti collatione differentia in ν paragogico (i. e. ν addito verbis desinentibus ab ε vel ι, proximâ dictione a vocali exorsâ) cum a variâ lectione profluit, non notatur; *ex more enim fit*." Of other peculiarities in regard to the writing he says nothing; but shews

---

[1] See Archdeacon Todd's "Account of Greek Manuscripts, chiefly Biblical, which had been in the possession of the late Professor Carlyle, the greater part of which are now deposited in the Archiepiscopal Library at Lambeth Palace." London, 8vo. [1818].

his ignorance of the fact that *υ* is only another form for *β* (e. g. 2 Johan. 8; Gal. iv. 5); an error into which Fenton, who collated Cod. e of the Acts, and other novices in these studies, have constantly fallen. Sanderson takes laudable care to notice those places where his manuscript was doubtful or illegible, and his performance indicates that he was a diligent student, of whose labours we may avail ourselves with some degree of confidence. He does not state what reprint of Mill's New Testament he used: from the wretched blunders whereof he subjoins a list, it must have been a very bad one[1]. This circumstance sometimes renders his notes unintelligible; in which case I have simply transcribed them with the warning "sic." There are pretty many itacisms in this MS., especially *ω* for *ο*; *ἰλ͞ημ* and *ἱεροσολυμα* are much interchanged; e. g. Acts viii. 25; xx. 16; xxi. 17; xxv. 20; xxviii. 17. We read *οὕτε* Act. xix. 37; *θυρα accus.* xii. 13; *ενκοπτεσθαι* 1 Pet. iii. 7; *ανηγγελλη* Rom. xv. 21; *ειπα* Hebr. iii. 10; *επιλανθανασθε ibid.* xiii. 16: besides which the following unusual readings may give the reader some notion of the genius of Cod. c. Act. i. 12; ii. 33 (B); 36; 43; iii. 9 (B); 11 (ABCE); iv. 15; 16 (ABD); v. 42; vi. 1; 15; vii. 35 (ADE); viii. 28; ix. 6; 30; 39; x. 6; 9; 11 (*sic* MS. 13); 31; xi. 8; 20 (AD*); xii. 22; xviii. 9; xx. 19 (C); xxi. 34; xxiv. 16; xxvii. 40; Jac. i. 18; 1 Pet. iii. 19; v. 13; many of which resemble Scholz's 180 in its rarest variations: moreover MS. c will be found pretty much with our am. This most interesting document will be seen to contain not a few errors of the pen.

(d). LAMBETH 1185, Carlyle I. 11, is a small quarto of 417 pages, having about 26 lines in a page, on bad paper, vilely written, and in a dirty state: in fact nothing could well be more unpromising than this MS. on a first glance. Todd assigns it to the fifteenth century: I should be disposed to date it somewhat earlier. It comprehends the Acts and the Epistles in the usual *Greek* order. On pp. 1—5, is a mutilated *ὑποθεσις* to the Acts, the table of *κεφαλαια* being lost; pp. 395—404 exhibit an ill-written synaxarion of the Praxapostolos; pp. 405—417 *ὑποθεσεις* and *κεφαλαια* of the Epistles, from the Galatians to the Hebrews, much torn. In fact the MS. might almost be considered a series of fragments in several different hands: it has the following hiatus; from Act. ii. 36 *ὅτι και* to iii. 8 *και εξαλλομενος* (one leaf): from vii. 3 *προς αυτον* to *v.* 59 *επικαλουμενον* (three leaves): from xii. 7 *λεγων ανα* to *v.* 25 *παραλαβοντες και ιω* (one leaf): from xiv. 8 *ουδεποτε περι* to *v.* 27 *μετ' αυτων* (one leaf)[2]: from xviii. 20 *αυτοις ου* to xix. 12 *σουδαρια* (one leaf): from xxii. 7 *λεγουσης μοι* to xxiii. 11 *ὁ κυριος* (two leaves): 1 Cor. viii. 12 *συνειδησιν* to ix. 18 *ἵνα* (one

[1] When Mill's text differs from that of *my* standard, Elzevir 1624, I have assumed from the silence of c and e of the Acts that they correspond with Mill, i. e. with R. Stephens' 3rd edition, nearly. I then cite them for a reading thus, "c e *tacitè*."

[2] The binder has also misplaced Acts xv. 40—xvi. 10; xviii. 20—xix. 12 is put as pp. 91, 92 in cap. xxvi. The leaves containing the following are torn, Rom. iii. 27—30 and iv. 9—11; iv. 17—19 and v. 2—4; v. 12—15 and 18—21; vi. 6—12 and 18—21.

leaf): 2 Cor. part of the ὑποθεσις to i. 10 ῥυεται (one leaf): from Eph. iii. 2 οικονομιαν της to Phil. i. 24 μενειν εν: 2 Tim. iv. 12 απεστειλα to Tit. i. 6 κος ανηρ (one leaf): Hebr. vii. 19 ελπιδος to ix. 12 ιδιου (two leaves). I trace distinctly *at least* four hands in this copy: pp. 1—218 seem to be written by one scribe: pp. 219—21 (1 Cor. ii. 11—v. 2) are in an antient hand, so small as to be barely legible; there are 31 lines on each page and the ink is pale: p. 222 is a large scrawl, in dark ink, comparatively modern, containing 1 Cor. v. 2 ὁ το εργον to *v.* 12 εξω κρινειν. On p. 223 begins 1 Cor. v. 11 νυν δε (so that *v.* 11 and part of *v.* 12 are in two different hands) on thick ribbed paper, perhaps by the writer of pp. 219—21, pretty wide and legible but in a wretched style: we have now the form α as an abridgement for ει, and the particles of time &c. which were dropped at the beginning of each lesson are here written in red, a unique yet convenient arrangement: in this portion of the MS. aspirates are scarcely used at all but with initial η: this scribe breaks off with p. 280, 2 Cor. x. 15 καυχομενος, the last two pages being written very large, *in order to cover the space;* the part of the text on ribbed paper was therefore posterior in time to what immediately follows. On p. 281 a new hand begins with 2 Cor. x. 8 καθαιρεσιν, so that *vv.* 8—15 are twice written, and their various readings are separately indicated in my collation (d¹ for those on p. 280, d² for those on p. 281). This portion is so much damaged by damp as to be hardly readable in parts (e. g. p. 284): it may possibly be the work of the scribe that executed pp. 1—218, but I could not bring myself to think so: it is full of itacisms, errors of the pen, corrections *sec. man.*, and various readings, some of rarity and importance. This hand terminates on p. 312, Eph. iii. 2, after which there occurs an hiatus, and another scribe (p. 313) commences Phil. i. 24, who goes on to the end of the Synaxarion which follows the Hebrews (p. 404) in a rather neat style, closely written, there being 30 lines on each page. The concluding pages 405—417 are by the penman of the ribbed-paper portion (pp. 223—280), who may be regarded as the person that brought this Codex into its present shape. The reader will pardon this long detail when he observes that the genius and worth of the manuscript vary much, according to the periods at which its parts were severally written.

All the Catholic Epistles are preceded by ὑποθεσεις and tables of κεφαλαια: so also are Rom., 1, 2 Corinth. The κεφαλαια alone are found before the rest, but Gal. and Eph. have not even these, except at the end, pp. 405—417. In the early part of the MS. the breathings and accents are very irregular, the aspirate being almost constant in words beginning with η or ο, e.g. ἤκουσα, ἥγερθη, ἥτησατο, ὅνομα, ὅπισω, οἶκος, ὄχλος, ὄντα, αἵτησας, even εἵς (Act. xx. 13), οἱκτειρμων (Jac. v. 11), ὁμνυητε (*v.* 12), ἅβυσον (Rom. x. 7). Some words are but half-written *p.m.*, and there are not a few instances of ὁμοιοτελευτον. Ν εφελκυστικον is rare, and the itacisms are pretty numerous, some being inserted *secundâ manu* (e. g. Heb. i. 3); πνεμα for πνευμα is always used, unless the word be abridged. Of peculiar forms we have ανειλατε Act. ii. 23; καταγγελειν iv. 2; κατηγγελλη xvii. 13; επεσα xxii. 7; ἡλιας (Jac. v. 17); ενκεντρισθω Rom. xi. 19; οὑτω, οὐχ'. ἀβρααμ, nearly always: yet the hand which wrote the Hebrews reads ἀβρααμ and has besides αδελφος for *acc.* 2 Thess. iii. 15; αποληψασθε Col. iii. 24; ιδατε Phil. iv. 15 *sec. man.*; εμπροσθε 1 Thess i. 3; ii. 19; iii. 9; 13; ἑορακασι Col. ii. 1 (so v. 18) and such like, and αντεκατεστητε (with many other authorities) Heb. xii. 4. The only instance of ι subscript is 1 Cor. v. 11. The letter β is put for υ (a rare change elsewhere) 1 Cor. xv. 30; xvi. 4; 2 Cor. xi. 25; xiii. 11; Gal. i. 8; iv. 9; 25; v. 13; Eph. i. 16; ii. 11; Heb. xi. 15; besides the ordinary υ for β 2 Cor. xii. 16; Gal. iii. 1; 27.

Codex d has the αρχαι, τελη and proper days for lessons in a coarse rubric at the top and bottom of each page, and capitals at the beginning of each lesson. There are many various readings of a curious character, inversions of order, glosses, &c. throughout the Catholic Epistles, and more than usual in the Pauline. I subjoin a list of some passages which seem to deserve special notice, and from them it will be seen how much this MS. is countenanced by the best uncials: Act. i. 11; ii. 1 (c); iii. 23 (ACe); iv. 12; v. 16; vi. 14; ix. 21; xv. 22; xvi. 15 (E); 23; xviii. 2; xix. 19; 29; 39 (B); xxi. 5, 6 (ABCE); 30; xxv. 8; 20; xxvi. 1; xxviii. 16 (*cf.* A); Jac. ii. 25 (C); 3 Johan. 9; Rom. xv. 12; 1 Cor. x. 11 (ABC); 2 Cor. xi. 1; 8; Gal. i. 22; iii. 23; v. 8; vi. 11; Eph. ii. 8; 10; 2 Thess. iii. 8; Philem. 16; 20; Hebr. i. 3; iv. 5; vi. 9; xi. 23; xii. 9.

(e). LAMBETH—of the Acts of the Apostles. I have obtained this unfinished collation of Act. i. 1—xxvii. 12 from the same source as Sanderson's collation of Codex c, viz. the case of papers at Lambeth numbered 1255 (27—33). It was made by the Rev. John Fenton for Professor Carlyle, and was probably broken off at the death of the latter[1].

As Codex e is certainly not identical with any of the MSS. I have just described (abcd), it must have been one of the two remaining copies of the Acts that were returned in 1817, which were marked Lambeth, 1181 and C (Constantinople). Though Mr Fenton's is a well-executed collation (so far at least as we can judge in the absence of the original) I do not find any account of the document itself among his papers. Lamb. 1181, is termed in the Printed Catalogue "Codex Chartaceus in quarto, Sec. xiv. I. 7. Acta Apost. Epist. Cath. et Pauli omnes complectens." C is merely mentioned in Archdeacon Todd's *Account of Greek Manuscripts*, &c. p. 68. Fenton, like the rest of Carlyle's friends, collated his copy with Mill's text, but uses no breathings or accents, though he carefully marks the places where the reading of his MS. was dubious or illegible. It contained many strong itacisms and so rich an array of variations from the common

---

[1] Professor Carlyle died Vicar of Newcastle, April 12, 1804, æt. 45.

text, that we cannot help regretting that we possess not a fuller knowledge of its contents. The following places are more or less remarkable: Acts ii. 6 (E); iii. 4; 7; 9; 21; iv. 11; 18; 30 (DE); 33; v. 9; 21; 30 (E); 33 (ABE); vi. 7; vii. 34; 38; viii. 16; 24; 37 (*habet cum E et Elzev.*); ix. 8; 10; 11; 27; 28; x. 15 (g); 16; 25 (g); 31; xi. 21; 28; xii. 25; xiii. 33 (ABC); 34; xiv. 10 (CDa *ferè*); 17; 20; xv. 29 (Da); xvii. 13; 16; 26 (AB); xx. 26 (E); 29 (g); xxii. 21; 24; xxv. 7.

(e). LAMBETH 1186, contains St Paul's Epistles and the Apocalypse. It is a fine copy 4to on vellum, of 144 leaves and 23 lines in a page. Todd (who reasonably assigns it to the eleventh century, and has given a fac-simile of Apoc. I. 1, in the Lambeth Catalogue) calls it "the best in the collection;" yet its critical value in St Paul's Epistles is the least of any I examined in that Library: in the Apocalypse it is indeed of singular weight and importance. It begins Rom. xvi. 15, *παν και τους*, and ends Apoc. xix. 4, *αμην*: but there are also hiatus from 1 Cor. iv. 19, *ταχεως προς ὑμας* to vi. 1, *εχων* (one leaf); from x. 1, *οἱ πρ̄ες ἡμων* to *v.* 21, *ναcθε ποτηριον* (one leaf); from Hebr. iii. 14, *μετοχοι γαρ γε* to ix. 19, *λαληθεισης γαρ*; from Apoc. xiv. 16, *επι την secund.* to xv. 7, *ωνας των* (one leaf). This MS. is marked I. 12 and 13 in Carlyle's notation. It is written in a good clear hand with a broad margin, although the copy is in bad condition, and the ink much faded; the last leaf especially is torn and damaged by mildew. Each Epistle is preceded by an *ὑποθεσις*, but not the Apocalypse. The cases of *ν εφελκυστικον* in Cod. e are very numerous; in fact, it is quite the ordinary usage: there is no *ι* subscript, though *ι* ascript occurs about 67 times, chiefly with articles and relatives. The Apocalypse has nothing in the margin, but throughout the Epistles the titles of the *κεφαλαια*, the beginnings and endings of lessons, &c. are placed at the tops of the pages, and the following passages have curious marginal notes, *primâ manu:* 1 Cor. xv. 33; 2 Cor. viii. 21; Gal. vi. 15; Col. iv. 16; Tit. i. 12, besides references to quotations from the Old Testament. The accents are very carefully given, but the breathings of compound words are often doubled, or otherwise separately written (e.g. *προεῖπον*, Gal. v. 21): we find also *ἑργοις* (1 Tim. v. 10), *ἀλοων* (1 Cor. ix. 10), *ἀψινθος*, *ὑάκινθινος*, *μὴκέτι*, *ὡσαῦτως*, *ὅτ' ἂν*, *δίὸ*, *δι' ὅπερ*, *δι' ὅτι*, *καθ' ὅ*, *οὐκέτι*: note also such abridgements as *ερωμη*, (2 Tim. i. 17), *εκω̃*, where *ε* stands for *εν*, and *ἑορακα* (1 Cor. ix. 1), *ἑορακασι*, &c. *constantly*. Itacisms are unusually scarce; I have counted but 29 throughout the whole MS. Alexandrine forms are so rare that they are rejected even when found in the Elzevir text, e.g. Gal. v. 4; 1 Thess. iv. 6; Apoc. i. 17; v. 14; vi. 13; xi. 16; xvii. 10. There are a few erasures (1 Cor. vi. 15) and changes *sec. man.* (2 Cor. xiii. 1), and before each book are pale blue initials. Few copies approach so near the common text as this does in the Epistles, yet some good readings may be selected from it: e.g. 1 Cor. ii. 12; 2 Cor. xi. 23; xiii. 12 (AFG); Gal. i. 15; vi. 18; Hebr. x. 7; xi. 26 (BD).

The next three Manuscripts, fgh of the Acts and Epistles, have been described in my "Collation of Greek MSS. of the Holy Gospels," where their readings in the Gospels are recorded: I shall therefore repeat as little as possible of what I said respecting them in that volume.

(f). Codex Theodori (*Collation, Introd.* p. li.) contains the whole N.T. except the Apocalypse, on vellum, bearing date A.D. 1295. I know not what has become of it, and have not seen it since 1845. Its variations in the Gospels I have indicated by the letter q: those in the Acts and Epistles are not extensive.

(g). Codex Wordsworth (*Collation, Introd.* p. xliii.) also contains the Gospels (which I have noted by the letter l), the Acts and all the Epistles. I presume it is still in Canon Wordsworth's possession: it is of the 13th century, on vellum. Many of its readings will be found to accord with e of the Acts.

(h). Codex Butler 2. British Museum, Additional MS. 11837 (*Collation, Introd.* p. xliv.) contains the whole New Testament on vellum, the various readings in the Apocalypse, like those of Lambeth 1186, being of great value. This MS. is our m of the Gospels, and, in common with the two preceding copies, does not differ widely from the received text, though it exhibits many lesser changes of considerable interest. Notice especially several peculiarities in the punctuation. It bears date A.D. 1357.

(j). Burney 48, in the British Museum, contains the Catholic Epistles only. They are found at fol. 221 of the second volume of a large folio paper MS. of Chrysostom's Homilies from the Galatians to the Hebrews, but not in the same hand with them. The Epistles are in a neat and even elegant style, of about the 14th century. This copy accords very often with c and d in their less usual variations, and affords perhaps a more antient text than many others which were written earlier; a circumstance easily accounted for, yet always worth notice when we meet with it. Before each epistle is an ὑποθεσις and εκθεσις κεφαλαιων, but of St Jude nothing remains except a part of the ὑποθεσις. Here we have ι ascript and subscript used indifferently, e.g. both in Jac. iii. 7: ν εφελκυστικον, is not found. There are not above five itacisms in the Catholic Epistles, but in breathings we have ἑοικε, Jac. i. 6; 23; ὀλολυζοντες, v. 1; ἑστηκεν, v. 9; ὡδε, ἀβρααμ. This codex is carefully written, having but one example of ὁμοιοτελευτον (2 Johan. 3, 4), but few corrections and one erasure (1 Johan. i. 9), *sec. man.*: we have, however, καταλειτε, Jac. iv. 11, *p.m.*; καταλουσιν, 1 Pet. iii. 16, and προ for προς. The following readings should be noticed: Jac. i. 5; 25, *p.m.*; iii. 3; 14; v. 3; 15; 16; 19; 1 Pet. i. 8 (BC); 10; ii. 19; iii. 3; iv. 3 (ABC); v. 1; 11; 12; 2 Pet. i. 2; 4; 20; ii. 1 *p.m.*; 21; iii. 10; 14; 15; 1 Johan. i. 9; ii. 4 (AB); 7; 9, 10; 20; 23 (ABC); v. 13; 2 Johan. 8 (A); 12.

(j). Burney 18 is a mere fragment of the Pauline Epistles, containing Hebr. xii. 17, μετα δακρυων, to the end of that epistle. It is found in the MS. I have described as n of the Gospels (*Collation, Introd.* p. xlvi.) dated A.D. 1366, between δηλωσις ακριβης των καθ' ἑκαστην ἡμεραν αναγινωσκομενων αποστολοευαγγελιων (foll. 210—214) and a συναξαριον των ἑορτων του ὁλου χρονου, δηλουν τα οφειλομενα αποστολοευαγγ. αναγινωσκεσθαι (foll. 218—222). It is on five pages (foll. 215—217) in the same hand as the Gospels, and with the same decorations, viz. Capitals, αρχαι, τελη, the proper days and commencements of the lessons, all in gold. The last verses Hebr. xiii. 17—25 are spread over two pages in a cruciform shape[1], shewing that this was the end of the whole manuscript, which doubtless once contained the Acts and all the Epistles. Hebr. xii. 24, reads το, with B; v. 26 has αγγ$^{ου}_{αι}$ in the margin; otherwise this fragment is not at all remarkable.

(k). TRIN. COLL. CANTAB. B. x. 16. This important MS. is the same as w of the Gospels, and has been fully described above, p. xxxviii.

(l). CHRISTI COLL. CANTAB. F. i. 13 is another interesting document, liberally lent me by the Master and Fellows of Christ's College. It is noted by Mill, Cant. 2, and was written on vellum (606 pages, quarto) about the end of the twelfth century: it is 8½ inches long by 6 broad. The first leaf being lost, it begins with εμβλεποντες Act. i. 11: there are also hiatus from Act. xviii. 20 χρο to xx. 14 ηλθομεν; and from Jac. v. 14 προσευξασθωσαν to 1 Pet. i. 4 και αμαραντον (one leaf): pp. 115—16 (Act. xx. 24—28; 30—32) and p. 170 Jac. i. 6, 7 are torn; pp. 529, 530 are misplaced after p. 542: the last two leaves are also decayed. Mill states that Thomas Gale had seen this MS. and Wetstein that he had given extracts from its readings to the editor of the Oxford New Testament of 1675, but the first person who examined it throughout was Mill himself, who speaks of it as "sedulo a me collatum" (*Proleg. Nov. Testament.* § 1419). I have now followed Mill's footsteps over no inconsiderable space, but no where have I found less reason to be satisfied with the accuracy of his labours. The first chapter I tested happened to be Act. xii. wherein he notes but one out of the ten variations that occur in Cant. 2: in fact the proportion of one in three is a favourable estimate of the readings he cites compared with those he omits. Bentley next collated this MS. and inserted its readings among those of 32 others collected for him by J. J. Wetstein in 1716: his collation remains at Trinity College (B. xvii. 10, 11). It was next used by Jo. Wigley, Fellow of Christ's College, for John Jackson of Leicester, who projected an edition of the Greek Testament, and inserted the results of Wigley's diligence, with many other stores he had accumulated, in the margin of that copy of Mill now preserved at Jesus College, Cambridge (*vid. supra*, p. xlii.). While very much remains to be done in these studies, it is sad to see so many efforts of honest and well-directed industry thus absolutely

[1] A few very costly copies exist exhibiting throughout a cruciform shape: perhaps the most splendid of them yet known is the Parham Evangelistarium, said to be written in part by the imperial hand of Alexius Comnenus.

thrown away[1]. The fly-leaf of this MS. contains an extract from Jackson's memorandum respecting it in the Jesus College copy of Mill: this extract had previously been published in Sutton's Life of that eccentric and unhappy scholar (*Memoirs of the life and writings of Jackson*, 1764, pp. 200, 265). He there states that Wigley had brought to light more than five hundred readings of Cant. 2 which Mill had neglected, and adds, "Hic MS. congruit maxime cum Complut. et Leicestr." I have not myself seen Wigley's or examined Bentley's collation, but after a close comparison of my own papers with the MS. and Mill's edition, I think I may claim the reader's confidence when I say that where I differ from Mill, the error is not mine. There are no ὑποθεσεις before any of the books, or lists of κεφαλαια; only that rubric capitals are placed at the beginning of each section, there would be no divisions in the text of each book. Before St James' Epistle alone stands a slight illumination; the whole MS. is written in the same clear bold hand, but a second scribe has made *many* changes throughout, even in the punctuation: these it is the more necessary to note, as Mill perpetually cites the changes of this later pen for the original readings of his Cant. 2; e.g. Rom. xv. 7; 2 Cor. i. 21; 1 Thess. v. 21. This Codex contains no ι subscript, but 60 cases of ι ascript, *yet in three instances out of four at the end of the line*, as if to fill it up. This is one of the most accurately written MSS. extant; a few errors of the pen however are caused by the rubric capitals, and a few various readings, e. g. Act. xxi. 20; Gal. i. 13. The only unusual breathings are ἀλοωντα 1 Tim. v. 18; ἑλιξεις Hebr. i. 12; 'Αβρααμ ('Α *rubro*) Hebr. vi. 13; xi. 8 for the ordinary form ἀβρααμ. No ν εφελκυστικον is found. Of grammatical peculiarities we read αναδοσαντες Act. xxiii. 33 *p. m.*; ειπα xxvi. 15; επεσαν 1 Cor. x. 8; αποκτεννει 2 Cor. iii. 6; εξεπεσατε (*with Elzev.*) Gal. v. 4; παραγγελε 1 Tim. iv. 11; εὑραμενος Hebr. ix. 12; αντεκατεστητε xii. 4. Of itacisms I count but 47, whereof 23 are interchanges of ο and ω. Ἡμεις and ὑμεις are confused, sometimes even to the detriment of the sense: e. g. 1 Cor. iv. 6; 10; xi. 24 *p. m.*; xv. 14; 2 Cor. viii. 19; xi. 8; Col. i. 8; 1 Thess. ii. 19; 2 Thess. ii. 2; 13. The interrogation (;) is so often omitted when absolutely required, that no great weight can be given to its absence in more doubtful cases. Other forms worth notice are οὑτως (always except 2 Cor. vii. 14), διατοῦτο, ἐπὶ τὸ αὐτὸ, ἐπ' ἀληθειας, τὰ νῦν, διαπαντὸς, μὴ interrog. (even οὐ μὴ), τὲ often, κρίμα and νίκος always, κῆρυξ, κατ' ἐνωπιον (not Col. i. 22), ὑπὲρ ἄνω, ὑπερεκπερισσοῦ, ἐξ αὐτῆς, καθημεραν, ἀπ'ἀρχῆς, δηλονότι, ἐξεναντίας, καταρχὰς, οὐκέτι always, οὐχ', ὡδε, ἑστησαν. The breathings are sometimes placed falsely over the

[1] I will give one more instance of this *waste* of energy. No student of late years has ever spent an hour in the Bodleian Library, but left it a debtor to the courtesy and zeal of the Rev. H. O. Coxe. Many years since that gentleman forwarded to one versed in Biblical criticism his *only* copy of a most laborious collation he had made of two Bodleian MSS. (Codex Ebnerianus of the Gospels, Acts and Epistles, and Can. Græc. 110 of the Acts and Epistles). It has not been published so far as I know, nor am I aware of there being any prospect of publication.

rubric letters (Act. ix. 23; xiii. 4; xxi. 27; 1 Pet. iii. 15; Rom. xi. 5; 1 Thess. i. 4; Hebr. ii. 11), and the red letter, which is in most MSS. later than the original writing, is here, as in many other instances, often omitted altogether. The title of each epistle is *repeated* rubro at the head of its first page, and we meet with some scrawling notes in later hands here and there, which deserve no further mention.

The various readings of Codex 1 are not so numerous as in some others, but always valuable: it well merits Mill's commendation "liber est probæ notæ," and will I am sure be the more highly esteemed, now that it may be better known. I do not agree with Jackson in perceiving much resemblance to the Leicester MS., but it will often be found in concert with the Æthiopic version (as Mill cites it) and my codices e Act. and j, k. It frequently places simple verbs for their compounds, e. g. Act. ix. 36; xv. 4; 32; xxi. 4; Jac. i. 20; Phil. i. 21; ii. 30; Hebr. ix. 6; 27. I subjoin a specimen of the variations in which it is so rich: Act. ii. 14; 37; 38; 41; iii. 26; iv. 26 *p.m.*; v. 2; 26; vi. 6; vii. 5; 8; 38; 50; 55 *p.m.*; viii. 21; ix. 1; 4; 26; x. 3; 7; 17; xiii. 7; 41; 45; xiv. 11; 12; 13; xv. 2; 23; 36; xvi. 10; 13; 15; xvii. 12 *p.m.*; xviii. 12; xx. 25 (E); xxi. 14 *p.m.*; 19; 25 (BD); 39; xxii. 7; 13; 18; xxiii. 2; 10; 15; 17; 18; 24; xxiv. 12; xxv. 26; 27; xxvi. 10; 14; 29; xxvii. 6 (A); 10; 20; 28; xxviii. 6; 14; 21; Jac. i. 25; 27 (*Syr. Vulg.*); ii. 19; iii. 8; iv. 4; 7; 1 Pet. i. 9; iii. 17; iv. 12 *p.m.*; 14; 17 *p.m.*; 18; v. 2; 13 *p.m.*; 2 Pet. i. 17; iii. 10; 16; 1 Johan. i. 8; ii. 8; 15; iii. 2; 14; iv. 1; 2 Johan. 3; 4; Rom. i. 23; ii. 16; iv. 7; 11; 12; 24; vi. 20; 22 (*Æthiop.*); vii. 21; viii. 34; ix. 7; 32; x. 11; 16 *p.m.*; xiii. 9; xiv. 1; 14; xv. 20 *p.m.*; 24; 30; 1 Cor. i. 9; viii. 10; x. 29; xi. 17; xii. 2 *p.m.*; xiii. 13; xiv. 25 *p.m.*; 37 *p.m.*; xvi. 1 *p.m.*; 23 (*Æth.*); 2 Cor. i. 5; ii. 4; v. 15; vi. 10; 12; viii. 2; 19; ix. 5; 13; xii. 21 (*Æth.* cf. xiii. 2); Gal. i. 6; 8; ii. 9 *p.m.*; 16; iv. 19; Eph. i. 10; iii. 10; 18; v. 3 *p.m.*; Phil. i. 7; 27 (*Æth.*); iii. 7; iv. 14; Col. i. 15; ii. 2; 16; iii. 13; iv. 9 *p.m.*; 12; 1 Thess. ii. 9; iv. 3; v. 3 *p.m.*; 2 Thess. iii. 4 *p.m.*; 8; 11; 18; 1 Tim. i. 16; ii. 3 *p.m.*; v. 9; 13; 2 Tim. i. 17; iv. 18; Tit. i. 9; Philem. 7; 8; 21; Hebr. iii. 6; vii. 19?; viii. 6; ix. 1 (ABD); 15; 22 *p.m.*; 23 *p.m.*; x. 25; 34; xii. 15 *p.m.*; 19; 24 *p.m.*; xiii. 21. This MS. is Wetstein's 24 Act., 29 Paul.

(m). Codex Leicestrensis (which I have called L of the Gospels) has been fully described above, p. xl.

(n). Emmanuel. Coll.: Cantab.: i. 4. 35, is a copy of St. Paul's and part of the Catholic Epistles, in the Library of Emmanuel College, Cambridge, the Master and Fellows of which Society were pleased to lend it me for collation: it is Mill's Cant. 3, Wetstein's Act. 53, Paul. 30. This is the smallest manuscript I have examined, measuring only 4½ inches square. The writing being very minute (though singularly beautiful) and the ink much faded in parts, I was compelled to read it by small portions at a time, and usually with a good glass. It is written on 144 leaves of vellum, with 24 lines on a page, and is of the 12th or 13th century, or perhaps a little earlier. At the beginning of the volume we read "Collegio Emmanuelis in Testimonium grati animi D.D. Samuel Wright, ejusdem Collegii alumnus: Anno 1598, Pridie Nonas Julias." It was used by Walton for his Polyglot, but the readings he extracts from it are very few, and he merely says of it "liber (teste D. James in Cat. libr. MSS. utriusque Academiæ) præstans ob antiquitatem, minutis characteribus descriptum" (*Polygl.* Tom. vi.) Mill first collated it throughout, (and I am glad to be able to add) with much more than his habitual accuracy, though by no means so satisfactorily as to supersede the necessity of another's labours: my collation is quite independent of his, but its results have been diligently compared with his volume, and with the original document. Unfortunately this valuable book is but a fragment. The first half of p. 1 is quite illegible from damp; it contained the opening verses of 2 Pet. ii. but the first letters I can read are on line 13, *μαρτηα*, v. 4, and much on this leaf can only be deciphered by a glass in a strong light: all the earlier portions of the Catholic Epistles (James, 1 Peter, 2 Peter i.) have perished, and at 1 Johan. iii. 20 *της καρδι* is an hiatus which continues to the *ὑποθεσις* to the Romans (from Œcumenius, given in Mill) *ελθειν δια*[1]. Another hiatus occurs from 1 Cor. xi. 7, *οφειλει* to xv. 56, *θανατου ἡ ἁμαρτια*. The MS. ends Hebr. xi. 27, *τον γαρ*. At 1 Tim. vi. 5, *την ευσεβειαν* commences another hand, less careful than that of the former scribe; *ι* ascript (which had been used but five times before) now becomes very frequent, nor are the breathings and accents placed so accurately: the circumflex especially is often used falsely. We find *ι* subscript 14 times in this MS., and *ν εφελκυστικον* is not rare. I number 184 itacisms, chiefly interchanges of *ω* and *ο*, of *η* and *ει*: of irregular forms only *ηπειααν*, Rom. xv. 3; *μαρτυραν*, 2 Cor. i. 23; *εξεπεσατε* (*with Elzev.*) Gal. v. 4; *προειπαμεν* (*with Elzev.*) 1 Thess. iv. 6, and *ὑγειαινω* often: the augment is neglected, 1 Cor. iii. 14; the reduplication, 2 Pet. ii. 21: *συν* in composition remains unaltered, Rom. viii. 16; 17; ix. 1, &c. The breathings and accents throughout this MS. are somewhat peculiar, and on a pretty uniform system; compounds have them on both parts of the word[2], and many monosyllables receive a double accent, e.g. *δὲ̃*, *καὶ̃*, *γὰ̀ρ*, *μὲ̃ν*, *μὴ̃* interr.: but not always; so *ἐπεὶ̀* sometimes. Otherwise the breathings are tolerably regular; we usually find *οὐκ'*, *ἐξ'*, *ἀβρααμ*, and often such forms as *οὐκέστι*, *ἐναυτῷ*. Codex n has also *δι' ὅτι*, *καθῶς*, *ὅτ' ἂν*, *ὀθεν*, and often such arrangements as *σπέρμά ἐστε*: *ῑ* has frequently no breathing. This copy exhibits several compendious forms of writing which are not very common, e.g. h = *αυ*, b = *ερ*, ᵔ = *αρ*, ¯ = *α*, ʿ = *αν*, ˇ = *ας*, _ = *ω*, ˋ = *ον*, ˜ = *ως*, ˢ = *ης*, ᵛ = *ου* (besides

---

[1] Mill cites Cant. 3 in error for 2 Johan. 8: *απολεσητε*. The binder has also misplaced 2 Cor. viii. 6—ix. 14 by five leaves, and two leaves containing part of the *ὑποθεσις*, the *κεφαλαια* and Eph. i. 1—ii. 3 stand after Hebr. ii. A few words are lost by mutilation of the leaf, Rom. ix. 27—29; and x. 3—5. Hebr. xi. 19—26 is but just legible.

[2] This practice in our MS. renders the various reading *ὡς περὶ καθάρματα* 1 Cor. iv. 13, which I cite after Mill, rather doubtful.

° = ος, ¯ = ν which are usual): τγ is used for ττ, as in codices owz of the Gospels and others: the shape of ζ is here very peculiar. Of omissions by ὁμοιοτελευτον I have noted but four in this accurate MS.

Of extraneous matter this document contains the ὑποθεσεις ascribed to Œcumenius and tables of κεφαλαια before each epistle: the titles and numbers of the κεφαλαια are also placed at the top and foot of each page. A later scribe has made some alterations in deeper ink, but many of the marginal notes certainly seem to be *primâ manu:* e.g. Rom. xiii. 7; xiv. 15; 1 Cor. xvi. 22; 2 Cor. xiii. 1 (δευτερονομιου); Gal. v. 14; 2 Thess. i. 5. Citations from Scripture are usually indicated by marks of quotation, e.g. 2 Cor. vi. 16—18; but this book contains nothing in red or coloured ink. I annex a few of the less usual variations: 1 Johan. iii. 18 (*with Elzev.*); Rom. xi. 3; xiv. 14; 18; xv. 3; 14 (B); xvi. 19; 1 Cor. ix. 18 (AC); 2 Cor. v. 10; x. 12; Gal. iii. 16; Eph. ii. 4; iii. 8; Phil. iii. 13 *p.m.*; 15; iv. 22; Col. iii. 1; 1 Thess. ii. 17; iv. 5; 17; 2 Thess. ii. 10; 1 Tim. i. 1 (AD*FG); iii. 15; 2 Tim. i. 15; iii. 7; Tit. iii. 15 *sec. man.* (FG); Philem. 15; 18; 22; Hebr. i. 9; iii. 15; iv. 4; v. 4; vi. 2; vii. 9; ix. 26; x. 10: some of these appear quite unique.

(o). Cantab. Mm. 6. 9, described above as v of the Gospels, p. xxxv.

(p). Brit. Mus. Additional MS. 20,003. This copy contains only the Acts of the Apostles in a mutilated condition, but it is unquestionably the most valuable cursive MS. of that book yet known. It was sold to the British Museum in 1854 by Tischendorf, who seems to have brought it from the East, though on this point we lack information. A slight inspection having satisfied me of its great importance, I collated it with much care and minuteness: I have since learnt that it had previously been collated both by Tischendorf[1] and Tregelles. The latter will no doubt use it for his edition of the Greek Testament. Tischendorf has published his report in the "Anecdota Sacra et Profana," pp. 7, 8; 130—146. I have diligently compared the result of his labours with my own, and find that I have extracted many variations which he has discarded as beside his purpose (e.g. itacisms, peculiarities of spelling, breathing, or accent, and not a few readings of some consideration); wheresoever our accounts *differed*, the original MS. was consulted, so that I may state with confidence that the collation given in the following pages has been rendered by our joint labours unusually accurate: that made by Tischendorf is certainly open to the charge of carelessness brought against it by Tregelles. The MS. consists of 57 leaves of vellum in small quarto, with 23 lines on each page. The following serious hiatus occur:

[1] In the current number of Tischendorf's N.T., 7th edition (October, 1858), I observe that this MS. is cited throughout the Acts as "lo^{tt}", which notation will doubtless be explained in his forthcoming Prolegomena.

from iv. 8, *αρχοντες* to vii. 17, *ὁ χρονος*, and from xvii. 28, *ὡς και τινες* to xxiii. 9, *ουδεν*. Its date appears from the subscription, on fol. 57, p. 1, of which Tischendorf has given a lithographed facsimile: *ἐγράφη ἡ πνευματοκείνιτος ϗ ἱερᾶ βίβλος αὖτι κατεπιτρωπεῖν τοῦ κυ ἰακῶβ α ϗ πρ ϗ ἰωᾶννου α, διαχειρὸς ιω α · ἔτουσ ς φνιβ · ιν ιβ μ ἀπρὶ κ.* By ς φνιβ Tischendorf and Tregelles understand the year of the Greek æra 6562 or A.D. 1054: I would rather say A.M. 6552 or A.D. 1044[1]. The handwriting of this "John the Monk" is small and not inelegant, but it abounds in contractions and sometimes degenerates into a scrawl: in this and some other copies H and N seem almost to interchange their forms. Some of the numerous corrections seem *primâ manu*, (e. g. vii. 47; 52; viii. 15; 28; 29; xvi. 22; 27; xvii. 14; xxiii. 27 *prim. loco;* xxvi. 1; xxvii. 1?; xxviii. 7; 20; 21; 25) others (e. g. iii. 3; viii. 5; xi. 14; xvii. 10; xxiii. 19; 27 *secundo loco;* xxiv. 27) are manifestly later. There are no rubrical marks, divisions into chapters, or numerals denoting the usual *κεφαλαια*, but notes on the beginnings and endings of the Church Lessons and their dates in a coarse later hand (in viii. 25 *τελ* seems *p.m.*), in the text, margin, and at the top and bottom of the pages. We simply read *πραξεις των αποστολων* in common ink at the head of Chap. i. and the end of Chap. xxviii. On fol. 56, p. 2, the *κεφαλαια* of St James are commenced, so that this MS. once contained the Catholic Epistles. There occur a few small capitals in black ink, and one or two larger (e. g. Chap. xiv): marks of citation are pretty constant in the margin, *primâ manu*.

As this copy must be supposed to be drawn from some purer and earlier source than usual, it seems specially deserving of notice that its itacisms, 185 in number, but little exceed the average, and are of the ordinary type, only that *υ* is often put for *οι*, as in *κυνος*, *λυπος*. I observe no *ι* ascript or subscript, but *ν εφελκυστικον* with verbs before a consonant is universal, except in ix. 22; xiii. 31; xxiii. 24; xxvi. 5; xxviii. 7. Such forms as *ειπαν*, *ανειλατε*, *καταγγελω*, *μωϋσης* are constant; *λιμος* is fem. xi. 28 (so Bion, VI. 4); notice also *παραγεναμενος*, x. 33; *ανειλαν*, *ibid.* 39; *διαστειλαμαθα*, xv. 24: the following accusatives in *αν* for *α* are rarer, *τινᾶν*, vii. 34; *τερσεαν*, *p.m.*, ix. 11; *σαρωνᾶν*, *ibid.* 35; *βασιλεαν*, xiii. 21; *διαν*, xiv. 12; *τρωαδαν*, xvi. 8; *μυραν*, xxvii. 5. The only stop is (·); for unusual punctuation see viii. 32, 33; xvi. 9; 37; xvii. 6; 25; xxvi. 2; 7; 22; 29; xxvii. 40. The breathings are nearly as irregular, and much of the same kind as in the later uncials (e. g. Harl. 5598 and the Parham Evangelistaria): such are, *ἑσται*, *ἑστιν*, *ἑχω*, *οἱκος*, *ὀλιγος*, *ὁνομα*, *ὁρει*, *οἱν* (yet *ἀβρααμ'*), but *ἑκαστος*, *ἑτερος*, *ἱλημ*, *ἱερον*, &c. The accents are pretty correct,

[1] Surely $\overline{\nu\iota\beta}$ instead of $\overline{\xi\beta}$ for 62 is very strange, if not unprecedented, and both in the original and Tischendorf's facsimile the mark between *ν* and *β* is not a plain *ι* as elsewhere, but a jagged line, as if a mere slip of the pen: hence I would read *νβ* (52), not *νιβ*. Besides, the indiction for A.D. 1054 is 7, for A.D. 1044 is 12, the number given in the subscription. This last fact seems decisive of the question.

yet the circumflex is wrongly placed in *οἶδατε*, *οἶκω*, *παῦλω*, &c.; enclitics often receive an accent, especially *τὲ*: compound verbs have a double accent, as *περὶέτεμεν*, or on the contrary, a preposition and its case are accented as one word, e.g. *διαλόγου*.

A clear idea of the critical value of this document may be obtained by noting the great number of places in which its readings support those of the principal uncials ABCDE against the received text. For this purpose I have merely used Griesbach's and Tischendorf's (1849) editions of the Greek Testament, yet in the 710 verses of which this MS. consists (297 being lost), I count no less than 699 such passages, in 594 of which it agrees with A, in 561 with B, in 372 with C, in 225 with D, in 298 with E: bear in mind also that portions of CDE are lost[1], and that B is not even yet very accurately known. Now since our MS. accords only 29 times with A *alone* of the five uncials, but 28 times with B, 10 with C, 4 with D, and 7 with E, it follows that this valuable cursive copy countenances the uncials *chiefly where two or more of them agree*, a plain indication of its sterling worth: and we may remark in passing that this closer agreement of the principal authorities ABC, &c., in the Acts, renders the task of settling the text of this book so far easier than it is in the Gospels. The nearest of my other MSS. to p are doubtless a (in its more ancient portions), c, and m; but the nearest to it of all the rest of the cursives may perhaps be considered *longo proximus intervallo*. In a few remarkable readings it stands quite alone: e.g. i. 20; vii. 28; x. 2; xiii. 37; xv. 12; xxiii. 30; xxiv. 12; xxv. 1; 10; xxvii. 7; 23; 32; xxviii. 26. In short, "the excellence of this MS." (I employ the words of Dr Tregelles, *Horne's Introd.* p. 211, &c.) "can hardly be estimated too highly," while "it differs sufficiently from the other copies with which it must be classed, to shew that it cannot be regarded as a mere duplicate of any of them[2]."

II. 3. It only remains for me to speak briefly of the MSS. of the Apocalypse collated for this volume.

(a). LAMBETH, 1186, is e of the Pauline Epistles, and is described above, p. lxii.

(b). BUTLER 2, ADDITIONAL MS. 11837 is m of the Gospels, h of the Acts and Epistles, and is named above, p. lxiii.

(c). HARLEIAN: 5678, also in the British Museum, as are Codices d e j. The first eight chapters of this copy were very loosely collated for Griesbach by Paulus (31 in Griesbach's list), otherwise it has not been examined before. The volume which contains it is of about the fifteenth century, on glazed paper in quarto, of 244 leaves. On the top of its first page it is inscribed "Coll. Agen. Soc. Jesu.

[1] Of these 710 verses, 187 are lost in C, 256 in D, 72 in E.

[2] To the same purport Tischendorf writes "Quo pauciora summæ antiquitatis monumenta textum actuum conservarunt, eo pluris codex noster æstimandus est; haud dubie enim antiquissimi codicis uncialis, qui ipse periit, exemplum est." *Anecd. Sacr. et Prof.* p. 8.

Cat. Inscr." It embraces (1) ἑρμηνεια λεξεων κατα στοιχειον εμφερομενων τηδε τη βιβλω. (2) γεωργιου ἱερομνημονος της ἁγιωτατης του θεου μεγαλης εκκλησιας του παχυμερου παραφρασις εις τον ἁγιον ἱερομαρτυρα διονυσιον τον αρεοπαγιτην[1]. (3) The Apocalypse on the reverse of the same leaf (223) which finishes Pachymer's Commentary. The title and initial letter are in rubric; the broad margin contains no κεφαλαια or liturgical matter, but there are 17 capital letters throughout the book. This whole volume is written in the same clear neat small hand: at the end we read *rubro* τω εχοντι και γραφαντι χε̄ μου σωσον. The stops in this copy are , and :. There is no instance of ι ascript or subscript, but ν εφελκυστικον once occurs viii. 6, and an hiatus in the place of it two or three times. About four itacisms are met with (x. 7; xiii. 1; xv. 5; xviii. 13), and the breathings and accents are regular; we have however ἐστηκα, iii. 20; ἑστηκεν, xiv. 1; ἤξουσιν, xviii. 8; μῦλον, xviii. 21; μεγιστάνες, xviii. 23; ἴσα, xxi. 16; ὑπὸκάτω, but ὦδε. I note one case of ὁμοιοτελευτον, xiii. 15, and the anomaly τον δρεπανον, xiv. 15: the Apocalypse however is so full of violations of the ordinary rules of Greek syntax, that the practice of a single copy should not be noticed, unless it stand nearly alone. This MS. approaches nearer the common text than ab and most others, yet it exhibits many grave variations from it. Rare readings are xii. 9; xiii. 6; xiv. 13; xvii. 15; xviii. 13 (AC); 14; 17; xix. 9; xxii. 2; 18, some of which are mere glosses. A second hand has been employed, chiefly in supplying omissions: e. g. iii. 15; v. 10, and about eight other places.

(d). Harleian: 5778, is called by Mill the Sinai MS., because Dr Covel procured it thence (*supra*, p. xlviii.). It contains the Acts, Epistles and Apocalypse. In the two former Dr Bloomfield has examined it after Mill, and on his report of Mill's inaccuracy I took it up for the Apocalypse, which I found to have been most imperfectly collated. The copy is in a very bad state, quite illegible indeed in parts, and it must have been ill treated *since* Mill's time, for he has preserved many readings of which I could not trace a vestige. In such cases I have cited "d (Mill)," and would wish it to be understood that the variation rests on his authority. In all places where we differ I have ascertained that I am correct, but have not deemed it necessary to be always complaining of my illustrious predecessor. This MS. is Wetstein's Act. 28, Paul. 34, Apoc. 8, and is on vellum of about the twelfth century (see Mill, *N. T. Proleg.* § 1488): it has an hiatus from vi. 14 ειλισσομενον και to viii. 1 τω ουρανω (one leaf), and breaks off xxii. 19 ἁγιας και των. Here ν εφελκυστικον is perpetual, but neither ι ascript or subscript. We may note θυατειραν i. 11; θυατειρη ii. 18; ἦ (*pro* ἡ) iii. 12; επεσαν v. 14 (*with Elzev.*); xi. 16 (*with Elzev.*); xvi. 19; xvii. 10 (*with Elzev.*): εὗρες ii. 2; ὧδε iv. 1; ἱστωτας, ἑστηκεν (*not always*), ὁτ' ἂν, ταλαντιαῖα, οὐδ' εἷς, σφραγίδα, σφραγίσιν. This is an

[1] George Pachymer flourished about A.D. 1280. On the title ἱερομνημων consult Suicer *Thesaurus Ecclesiast.* Tom. I. p. 1443, that real treasure to the theological student.

important MS., more resembling ab than c: observe xvii. 1; 14; xviii. 1; xix. 14 &c. I often cite d? in doubtful passages.

(e). HARLEIAN: 5613, has also been collated before by no less a scholar than Griesbach, who gives the results of his labours very negligently in his edition of the Greek Testament (Act. 60; Paul. 63; Apoc. 29), but more fully in his Symbolæ Criticæ, Tom. I. p. 226, &c. I must confess that I was first led to this MS by a desire to test Griesbach's exactness as a collator, and was rather startled to find our differences in this single book amounted to more than *sixty*, all of which except eleven a comparison with the original document shewed to be errors on Griesbach's part: in fact he began his work well enough, but grew careless and weary towards the end. This copy contains also the Acts and Epistles, collated only in 55 select chapters by Griesbach, and well deserving a thorough examination. It is on paper, and at the end of the Epistle to the Hebrews we read τελειωθεν κατα μηνα μαΐον, ινδικτιωνος πεντε και δεκατης, ετους ἑξακισχιλιοστου εννακοσιοστου πεντεκαιδεκατου (A.D. 1407). Griesbach minutely describes a most interesting vellum fragment in red letters and a semi-uncial character (he calls it early cursive) of about the ninth or tenth century, containing 1 Cor. xv. 52—2 Cor. i. 15; x. 13—xii. 5, and barbarously employed for the binding of the paper volume (*Symb. Crit.* Tom. II. p. 162; *N. T.* Paul. 64)[1]. In this fragment ι subscript is used 3 times, ascript twice, but in the paper MS. we find ι subscript almost universally: I have remarked but one (xiv. 15) instance of ν εφελκυστικον. This copy of the Apocalypse ends xxii. 2 καρπον, one leaf being lost, but is finished from v. 18 λιω to the end of v. 19 on the vellum fly-leaf. It contains about eleven ordinary examples of itacism, and one of ὁμοιοτελευτον (xiii. 4). Of forms we may observe διψασουσιν vii. 16; μασθοις i. 13; μετρος xxi. 17; ὧδε, ὦδε and ᾧδε (xiv. 12 &c.), ὑασπις *ter*, ζωνης (i. 13 &c), σφραγίδας, σφραγίσιν, but σφραγῖδα vi. 7; 9 *p. m.* In many places this document closely resembles Cod. a, but on the whole it comes closer than some others to the Elzevir text. The following are rare: i. 2; ii. 24; ix. 15; xi. 1; 2; 3 (so xii. 6); xii. 9; 13; 17.

(f). CODEX LEICESTRENSIS is L of the Gospels, m of the Acts and Epistles. It is described above p. xl.

(g). PARHAM No. 17 I believe to yield in value and importance to no copy of the Apocalypse except the three uncials. Mr Curzon tells us in his best manner the history of his acquisition of it in 1837 at Caracalla in Mount Athos (*Visits to Monasteries in the Levant*, p. 350): this precious document certainly

---

[1] Tischendorf has recently published these precious fragments, together with some leaves *of the same MS.*, containing portions of the Epistle to the Hebrews, preserved in the Public Library of Hamburgh, in his *Anecdota Sacra et Profana*, pp 147—205.

ιad a most narrow escape from the ignorant wastefulness of his friend the Abbot. t is written on vellum, on 16 leaves, quarto, the 12th and 13th leaves being nisplaced: it breaks off xx. 11, *και τοπος*. In this MS. (which is dirty and damaged, specially near the end) *ι* ascript is uniformly employed, never being omitted, hough often inserted falsely (e. g. *ζωιον*): *ν εφελκυστικον* is found seven times. One reat peculiarity regards the breathings, than which nothing can be imagined nore capricious: thus in the few opening verses we have *ἐσημανεν v.* 1; *ἰωαννης*, *ρφῃ*, *ἐνωπιον v.* 4; *ἁμαρτιων v.* 5; both *αἰωνας* and *αἰωνων v.* 6. After this it is seless to multiply examples, but we have pretty consistently *ὀνομα*, *ὡδε*, *ἐργα*, *ἐχεις*, *ξω*, *ὀρος*, *ἐπτα* (not xv. 7), *ἱππων*: the accents are just as ill put; sometimes they re placed over each part of a compound, and often neglected altogether. Words re repeatedly written twice over, and there are about five examples of *ὁμοιοτελ-των*: the itacisms are 46, quite of an ordinary complexion. The text of the Apocalypse is *surrounded* by a commentary in a cramped and less distinct style, evidently however by the same hand, which exhibits several forms of abridgement ot very usual, some of them being nearly the same as we met with in Codex n of he Epistles (*see above*, p. lxvii.): such are : = *α*, ' = *ον*, ͬ = *αν*, √ = *ας*. The comment-ry, which is not very rare in MSS. of the Apocalypse, is a kind of epitome of hat of Arethas, Archbishop of the Cappadocian Cæsarea in the tenth century appended to the Paris Œcumenius, 1631); so that this copy cannot well be placed earlier than the eleventh century, nor do I think it later than the twelfth. The title and initial A alone are in rubric; there is no division into sections, but each longer lesson has a capital letter at its commencement: these however are later than the text, for they are often written where the smaller letter was already found: e.g. ii. 5; 8. There are perpetual notes of reference to the commentary, above and in the body of the sacred text. This MS. frequently supports the readings of Cod. a, which I presume is of about the same age, and will merit attentive study: yet it is not seldom found to agree with the Elzevir text against the majority of our copies: e. g. xii. 8; 9; 14; xiii. 2; 3; 5; 8; 18; xiv. 3; 4; 7; 8; 19; xvii. 16; xviii. 2; 13; 15; 19; xix. 2; 6; 12; 17; xx. 11: in many of which g is attended by our copies h or n. The alterations in this MS. seem to have been made *primâ manu* (except v. 9), but are certainly early.

(h). Parham, No. 2, contains the Apocalypse complete, on glazed paper, quarto, 22 leaves, with 28 lines on a page, in a very neat hand, which much reminded me of Lambeth 1350 (t of the Gospels: see my *Collation, Introd.* p. lv): I should assign it to the 14th century. This MS. also came from Caracalla in 1837, and is in beautiful preservation. There is a scrawling inscription at the end, of which I can decipher *βοηθη του δουλου σου ιωαννη του παπα δημητριου του τρυχωαργαρ* [??]... We find some *short* glosses or comments in the margin of this book; e.g. on ii. 22 *κλινην ασθενειας*: these are in a later hand. The title, initial

10

letters of the sections, and numerals indicating the κεφαλαια are in pale red: the only traces of a second hand in the text are vii. 17; xvii. 10; xix. 10; and a few erasures. The breathings and accents are correct, though a few are omitted: we read ἂν, μὴ, ὧδε, ἀφοῦ, ἕωσοῦ, ἄχρισοῦ, μεταταῦτα, οὕτως always; nor is the accent of the enclitic ever thrown back, when the preceding word is properispomenon, e. g. εἶπε μοι. The only ν ἐφελκυστικον is erased xvii. 10: ι subscript is used but six times, always with ᾠδῆς and ᾄδουσιν; ι ascript never: the itacisms are but eight, of the commonest kind. This MS. resembles efg most of ours, and is remarkable for coming nearer to the Elzevir text than perhaps any other in existence. The examples (which I have carefully noted in my collation) are so numerous, that it may suffice to state the fact once for all (e.g. i. 5; 14; 17; ii. 1; 5; 7; 10; 17; 25, &c.). Other unusual readings are i. 2; 13 (A); vi. 5 (AC: *sic v.* 7); 9; viii. 9 (A); 13; x. 4; 7; xi. 3 (AB); xvii. 10; xviii. 3; 17, &c.

(j). British Museum, Additional MS. 17469. This copy of the whole New Testament is one of the most precious of the Biblical MSS. added to our National Library within the last ten years[1]. It was purchased from T. Rodd, the bookseller, in 1848. It is a small folio on vellum of 186 leaves and 35 lines in a page; not much earlier, I should imagine, than the 14th century. I have hitherto collated it for the Apocalypse alone, but on inspecting cursorily the other books (we all know by this time how little a *cursory* inspection is worth) I observed nothing very striking: there is an hiatus about 1 Tim. iii. 16. Before certain liturgical tables at the end of the volume we read *rubro* τῳ συντελεστη των καλων θῳ χαρις | * * * (*a line erased*) | τῆρι των καλων πλαστου γε μου; | Σοι τω δοξα τιμη και κρατος πρεπει μονω |. This document is neatly written, though the abridged forms are rather numerous; the breathings and accents are full and correct: we find ὧδε, οὐχ', ῥάβδος (*vid. supra*, p. xxxix); ἑστησαν xviii. 17; ἐξουσιαν xvi. 9; οἰκουμενης *ibid.* 14; ὀνοματα xxi. 12, διατοῦτο, and (as in Cod. h &c.) εἶπε μοι, οἶδα σου, κ.τ.λ. μὴ is used almost always, as is οὕτως: we read απηλθα x. 9; επεσαν xix. 4; επεσα *ibid.* 10. I observe no instance of ν ἐφελκυστικον, and only twelve itacisms: ι subscript is perpetual (not however with αδης or ωδη), and in four places where it ought not to be (e.g. ii. 11 ακουσατῳ). The title and initial letter of each section are in rubric, and six examples of error by ὁμοιοτελευτον occur. This copy is of great value and full of interesting variations from the general mass, especially in the earlier chapters. Of our codices it most resembles ce. There will be found to exist a tendency to omit the article, and the following passages well merit examination: i. 14; 15; 18; 20; ii. 17; xii. 1; xiii. 10; 18; xiv. 4; 14; 20; xviii. 7; xx. 9; xxi. 19; xxii. 6; 12.

---

[1] The following fresh copies, *of the Gospels alone*, await a patient labourer in this field of Biblical science; Addit. MSS.: 16183 (12th cent.?); 16943 (11th cent.?); 17470; 17741; 17982; 19387; a noble harvest for some fortunate scholar.

(k). Liber Canonicus 34 in the Bodleian at Oxford. The Libri Canonici comprise a splendid collection of 576 Greek Manuscripts, purchased by Dr Bandinel, the Principal Librarian of the Bodleian, at Venice in 1817, from the heirs of Abbot M. L. Canonici, for the University of Oxford. They are described by Mr Coxe, in the Bodleian Catalogue, Part iii. (1854). This document contains the whole New Testament, neatly written in quarto, on 319 paper leaves, having 25 lines on a page, the Pauline Epistles preceding the Acts, as in the Codex Leicestrensis. At the end of the Apocalypse (the only portion of the MS. yet collated) we read Μιχαηλος δαμασκηνος ὁ κρης τω εκλαμπροτατω και πανσοφωτατω ιωαννη φραγγισκω πικω μοιρανδου...ἡγεμονι και ταυτην την θειον βιβλον...ψεν ετει απο της χριστου γεννησεως $\overline{\text{αφις}}$[1], μηνι ιουλλιω $\overline{\text{ιη}}$ (fol. 319), i.e. A.D. 1516. This John Francis Picus was the nephew and biographer of the illustrious John Picus of Mirandola, who died in 1494. A little lower on fol. 319 is written in the same hand εγραφη το παρον βιβλιον εν μοιρανδουλιᾳ, [Mirandola, now in the Grand Duchy of Modena] and still lower in a later but ancient hand "[Si quis[2] h]uic exemplari parvam fidem adhibendam putet. descriptum noverit e vetustissimo codice manu scripto. Nam ipse Jo. Fran. Picus olim Mirand. dux in Annotationibus Erasmi, quas ipsi in bibliothecâ illius invenimus, id manu propriâ testatum reliquit. Ego hieronymus Teggetæus, qui in præsenti libri hujus sum possessor, quæ vidi hic annotandum putavi; manum autem illius nos probè novimus." The truth of this statement is established by the character of the text exhibited in the MS.; the slightest examination will shew that the scribe has not used Erasmus' *editio princeps* of the Greek Testament, whose Preface by Frobenius bears date March 1, 1516. In the Apocalypse this copy abounds in peculiar readings; in some places much resembling e described above, while in others it stands quite alone: e.g. i. 3, 4; 14; 19; ii. 1; iv. 1; 8; vi. 11; vii. 13; viii. 1; ix. 14; 15; x. 1; xi. 7; 18; xii. 3; 14; xiii. 3; 4; 12; xiv. 9; xvi. 5; xvii. 5; 12; 13; 16; xviii. 4; 14; xix. 9; xx. 3; 14; xxii. 12: it often resembles Griesbach's 30 (Guelpherbyt. xvi. 7) in its rarest readings. The writer seems scarcely familiar with Greek (e.g. xvii. 3), and sometimes employs the article rather strangely (e.g. 1 Johan. v. 8, ὅτι οἱ τρεις εισιν οἱ μαρτυρουντες το πνευμα, κ.τ.λ. *omisso versu septimo*). From Apoc. ii. 11 to *v.* 23 και γνωσονται there is a chasm, yet the text runs on *uno tenore*, with no signs of omission (*vid. supra*, p. xli.). There occur no less than 13 instances of ὁμοιοτελευτον in the Apocalypse. The breathings and accents are pretty regular, but we have ὁρη, ἑστηκα, ἑστηκως (*ferè*), χρυσοὺς, and such forms as οἶδα σου. Of itacisms there are few or none. The augment is omitted x. 7; we read χειραν x. 5, *p. m.* Θεος, χριστος &c.

---

[1] Mr Coxe reads $\overline{\text{αφιζ}}$, but we find ς with a similar shape in Apoc. xviii. 6, not to mention that the Gospels have a like colophon bearing date May 23, 1515 (fol. 131), and the Pauline Epistles are dated October 11, 1515 (fol. 229).

[2] A few letters are illegible. Mr Coxe supplies "Nemo:" I prefer "Si quis," supposing the point after *putet* to represent no more than a comma. The second g in Teggetæus is erased.

are rarely abridged: we find ὧδε, οὕτω, ὅταν. It is usual to write ι *subscriptum* (never *ascriptum*), six times where it should be absent. Ν ἐφελκυστικὸν before a consonant is met with three times, the hiatus for lack of it twice. Corrections are few, and seem *p. m.* Throughout the MS. is no liturgical or marginal matter: the Apocalypse begins on the same page as the Catholic Epistles end, with a simple initial capital letter, *rubro*. I am indebted to Dr Bandinel's kind attention for bringing this interesting copy under my notice.

(l). HARLEIAN: 5537, is Mill's Covell 2, and Wetstein's Act. 25, Paul. 31, Apoc. 7; containing the whole New Testament except the Gospels. This very important copy was loosely collated by Mill, whose readings I have compared with my own throughout the Apocalypse. It is a *small* quarto of 286 vellum leaves, having 23 lines on each page, in a very neat and clear hand. On fol. 100 b, between the Catholic and Pauline Epistles, after other matter (which seems to fix the country of the MS. to the shores of the Ægean sea) we read ετελειωθη δε ὁ ἁγιος αποστολος μετα και της αποκαλυψεως μή μαιω ηγουν τη Ν̄ [i.e. the Pentecost] ·ινδ̄.ῑ· ετ. ϛφϟε [A.D. 1087]· βασιλευοντος αλεξιου του κομ....και νικολαου πατριαρχου. Mill justly remarks "est certè hic ex libris nostris probatioribus" (Proleg. § 1482). The following specimens of its unusual readings will prove acceptable: i. 5 (*Arab.*); ii. 3; 16 (*Arab.*); iii. 7 *p. m.*; 11; 18; iv. 5; 8 (*Arab.*); v. 8; 11 (*Arab.*); vii. 5; viii. 13 (*Arab.*); ix. 6; 12; x. 10; xiii. 10; xiv. 10 (A); 11; 15 (*Arab.*); xv. 2; 7; xvi. 3; 15; xx. 10; xxii. 3; 12; 14 (A *ferè*); 20. It is often thus found with the polyglot Arabic version almost alone; also with our h and the Elzevir text, where they are countenanced by few others. We find no ι *ascriptum* or *subscriptum*, but ν εφελκυστικον is frequent, though mostly erased by a more recent hand, whereof I observe no other trace, except in xxi. 22, which change is very late. An hiatus occurs xi. 6 *secund. manu*; the augment is omitted xiv. 18; we find τεσσαρεις and επεσαν (v. 8). Here the itacisms are many and strong, especially ει interchanged with η: εδωθη, ιδον are almost perpetual. A few breathings are irregular (ἀμμος, ὀλιγος, ἑνιαυτος, ἑστηκα, ἱματια), though even here the usage fluctuates. The circumflex is often misplaced: e.g. ζῶον, πρῶτον, οἶκον, ζῶων· on the contrary see μήνας, πάσαν, γήν, χρυσούς, &c. and such forms as οὐκέχουσιν, οὐκευρέθη, ὅτ' ἄν, ὢν (for ὂν), οὐαὶ and οὐαῖ indifferently, but ὧδε always. There are five instances of ὁμοιοτελευτον in the Apocalypse, which has no ὑποθεσις, and no κεφαλαια noted in the margin, but rubric capitals often. One rubric title is inserted in the body of the text (iv. 1).

(m). Codex Mediomontanus 1461, olim Meermann. 118, is a MS. on vellum, on 229 leaves 8vo, of the eleventh or twelfth century at the latest, purchased by Sir Thomas Phillipps, Bart. at the Meermann sale in 1824, and now forming a part of his unrivalled collection of Manuscripts at Middle Hill, Worcestershire. It contains the Acts, Epistles and Apocalypse, unhappily in a mutilated condition, beginning Act. iv. 24 αυτοις· ὁ δια, ending Apoc. xxi. 12 υιων ιηλ. Many leaves are lost, though only one other in the Apocalypse, containing from after απαρχη τω θω xiv. 4 to v. 14 και επι την νεφελην· several leaves have also been misplaced[1]. This copy is numbered by Scholz Act. 178, Paul. 242, Apoc. 87: he probably *saw* it abroad, but does not once cite it throughout the whole Apocalypse, which book the present owner most obligingly allowed me to collate at Middle Hill: I do not imagine that the rest of the MS. was ever examined. It is written in a bold clear hand, the number of lines on each page varying from 23 to 31: it is worn in parts, and occasionally retouched: e. g. in five passages of the Apocalypse (i. 1; xiii. 2; xvii. 13, 14; xviii. 1; 22, 23): five cases of ὁμοιοτελευτον occur. Each of the Epistles has an ὑποθεσις before it, and both they and the Acts exhibit in the margin the usual κεφαλαια, αρχαι of Church lessons, liturgical directions and rubric capitals: the Apocalypse however has no ὑποθεσις or κεφαλαια, but a small illumination over the title, and flourished capitals to the 72 κεφαλαια in faded red. This MS. abounds with rare and singular readings; e. g. i. 5; 7 (*article*); 13; 16; ii. 1; 8; 9; 13; 17; iii. 1; 7; iv. 8; v. 2; 9; vi. 9; 11; 17; vii. 1; 12; viii. 1; 12; x. 10; xi. 2; 14; 19; xii. 3; 4; 7; 11; 16; 18 (AC); xiii. 10; 17; xv. 2; 3; xvi. 20 (*article*); xvii. 4; 6 (*article*); 14; 15; 16; xviii. 6; 7; 10 (*article*); 13 (ACc); 22; xix. 3; 6 (c); 13 (g); 17; 21; xx. 10; xxi. 9 (A). It is often found with our gn. This copy frequently agrees with the Elzevir text with few others: i. 8; 9; ii. 7; iii. 2; v. 6; vi. 4; 12; viii. 7; 8; ix. 7; 10; 12; x. 1; xiii. 7; 14; 18; xv. 2; xviii. 19; xix. 20; xx. 8; xxi. 12. We meet with no ι *ascriptum* or *subscriptum*; ν εφελκυστικον is frequent, but less so towards the end of the book. Only eleven ordinary itacisms occur in the Apocalypse: μετοπων is read once, φυαλη three times (these forms are *constant* in Codex n, to be described next): many breathings are irregular, e. g. ἠγαπησεν, ἠνοιξε, ἠνοιγη, ἠνεωγμενον, ἠρημωθη, ἠκουσα, ἑμεσαι, ἀπισω, ὀλιγα, οὐπω, ὀπωρα, ὀφελον, and on the contrary ἡξουσιν, εἱστηκει, ἑστηκοτες (but ἑστωτα), ὡδε. The circumflex is often put over nominatives in η, as συναγωγῆ, στολῆ, λευκῆ &c., and over the *short* penultima, as βαστᾶσαι, θερῖσαι, καυματῖσαι, ἀγορᾶσαι, πατᾶξαι, yet we have προφῆται, αἰῶνας: we see also γλῶσσας, θυατεῖροις, ὑπὸ κάτω, μὴδὲν, οὐ μῆ, both ὅτἂν and ὅτ' ἄν.

(n). Barocc. 48, in the Bodleian, is a volume in small quarto, consisting of various pieces in several hands, some on vellum and others on paper, of about the 15th century. Mr Coxe describes its general contents in his Catalogue[2]. The Apocalypse commences at fol. 51 b, and ends abruptly at fol. 74 b, after the

[1] After Apoc. xi. 2, read the four following leaves in this order, 4, 2, 3, 1. After Apoc. xix. 1 two leaves are transposed and turned upside down. The present is hardly the place for giving a list of the chasms in the Acts and Epistles.

[2] On fol. 18 (paper, of the 14th century) are five verses of the Apocalypse (v. 1—5) differing in several places from the text of the copy I have called n. The readings of this small fragment are cited as n[2].

words *βδελυγματων αυτης* xvii. 5. It is neatly and clearly written on paper, with 22 lines on the page, and bears date from the 14th or 15th century. This copy was collated (together with three others at Oxford) for Wetstein's Greek Testament by Caspar Wetstein, his kinsman, Chaplain to the Prince of Wales, and its readings are numbered 28 in Wetstein's edition; but the collator has done his work most negligently, though I have been glad to use his labours for the correction of my own throughout the book. Codex n is one of the most important of our cursive MSS., containing wide and frequent variations from the mass of authorities: it somewhat resembles our h in its close approximation to the Elzevir text, and next to h, it approaches nearest to bgl. For its resemblance to the Elzevir editions, see i. 6; 9; 12; 18; 20; ii. 3; 9; iii. 9; 11; v. 14; vi. 8; 9; ix. 2; xvi. 1. The following readings are also remarkable: ii. 20; 27; iii. 7; 12; 13; 14; 18; iv. 7; 8; vi. 5; vii. 4; 11; viii. 12; ix. 13; xi. 1; 5; 8; 15; xii. 1; 4; xiii. 3; 11; 13; xiv. 6; 8; 16; xvii. 3. In this very recent codex we find no *ι ascriptum* or *subscriptum*; *ν εφελκυστικον* is read but six times before a consonant, the hiatus in its absence once (i. 4). There are five cases of *ὁμοιοτελευτον*, and many itacisms, chiefly between *ο* and *ω*: we always have *μετοπων*, *φυαλη*, and *εδωθη*, *ερριθη*, each twice. Of grammatical forms I note only *ειδα*, ii. 2. There is a slight illumination at the opening of the Apocalypse, and its first three verses are in rubric. The headings of the several *κεφαλαια* are interspersed with the text, the *κεφαλαια* numbered in the margin, and their commencements marked by rubric capitals. Numerals are invariably expressed by letters, not words. The breathings are not very accurate or consistent, e. g. *ἱππος*, *αἱμα*, *ἀδουσιν*, *ἥκουσα*, *ἤνοιξε*, *ἤξουσι*, *ὁδοντες*, *ὁλιγα*, *οὖς* (*auris*), *ὡδε*. The accents are more carefully given: we find however *ὑπομονῆ* *nom.*, *φωνὴ* *dat.*, *χρυσάς*, *οἶδα σου*, *μὴδεὶς*, &c. A few corrections seem *primâ manu*, but several are very recent, as are some Latin notes which disfigure the margin. I believe that this manuscript merits peculiar attention.

As it is admitted on all hands that the text of the Apocalypse is less satisfactorily represented in our printed editions than that of any other part of the New Testament, I deeply regret that scholars should have published a revision of it, even within the last few years, without having previously sought to add to our existing store of materials, or at least to test their accuracy. Up to this time we have an *exact* knowledge of but two copies of this book of Holy Scripture, the Codex Alexandrinus (A) and the Codex Ephraemi (C), the latter a mere fragment. Tischendorf's transcript of the only remaining uncial, the Codex Vaticanus 2066 (B), is, in fact, the result of a hurried collation (*Monument. sacr. ined.* pp. 407—432), made under circumstances I should not wish to happen to me[1]. I cannot doubt then that the present contribution will be

[1] I praise as little as any one the childish jealousy displayed by the authorities at the Vatican, but it is now their fixed rule to permit no stranger to *collate* their more precious manuscript treasures. Tregelles however in 1845, and Tischendorf in 1843, obtained leave to make facsimiles of one or

lcome to those who desire to see the text of the Apocalypse settled on a ner basis: a task not only less toilsome, but (I will venture to say) less preca- us in its results than the criticism of the Gospels: so much easier is it in s instance to distinguish the broad tide-wave of ancient evidence from those al currents which bewilder the inexperienced voyager.

I annex a list of examples of enallage of cases which occur in one or more of : manuscripts of the Acts, Epistles, and Apocalypse. Those in the Gospels l be found under their separate heads.

Genitive for accusative: Phil. iii. 14; 1 Thess. ii. 9; Hebr. iii. 6; vi. 2; Apoc. i. 3; x. 2 (*cf. v.* 5); xvii. 8; xx. 4. Genitive for dative: Apoc. ix. 19.

Dative for genitive: Apoc. v. 13; vi. 16; vii. 10; 15; xix. 4; xxi. 5.

Dative for accusative: Act. x. 23; xi. 26; xiii. 32; xvi. 10; 20; xxi. 24; xxii. '; xxiii. 12; 14; Jac. i. 22; 1 Pet. iii. 15; 2 Cor. iii. 1; Gal. i. 9; iii. 1; Apoc. i. 4; 15; xiv. 16; xvii. 3; xviii. 20.

Accusative for genitive: Act. xxi. 30; 33; Rom. ii. 4; xi. 7; 1 Cor. vi. 19; ebr. vi. 13; Apoc. ii. 10; xiii. 16; xiv. 14; xx. 11.

Accusative for dative: Act. x. 3; xii. 17; xxi. 24; 39; 40; xxiii. 28; Rom. vii. ; xii. 9; 2 Cor. iv. 4; x. 11; Gal. i. 8; v. 26; 2 Thess. ii. 8; Tit. ii. 14; Apoc. i. ; ii. 21; iv. 1; vi. 2; 4; 5; viii. 13; x. 7; xiii. 8; xiv. 7; 14; xviii. 9; xx. 4.

To the variations in punctuation found in MSS., of which I gave a list in my *llation of the Holy Gospels, Introd.* p. lxv., we must now add Matth. x. 42; Luc. . 23; Johan. v. 45; viii. 44; xiv. 9. I have noticed the following in the other oks of the N. T.: Act. i. 24, 25; vii. 9; viii. 33; xii. 19; xiv. 11; xv. 7; 24;); xvi. 12; xix. 4; 8; xx. 19; xxi. 7; xxii. 27; xxv. 24; xxvi. 29; xxvii. 13; c. ii. 23; iii. 8; 10; iv. 5; 16; v. 3; 5, 6; 1 Pet. i. 13; ii. 16, 17; 2 Pet. ii.), 11; Jud. 7; 20; Rom. i. 10; ii. 4; viii. 21; ix. 5; xiii. 4; 1 Cor. i. 26; iv. 9; 1; 2; xi. 22; xii. 15, 16; xvi. 3; 2 Cor. v. 19; viii. 13; ix. 5; 10; x. 7; Gal. ii. '; iv. 10; v. 13; Eph. iii. 1; 8; iv. 10; 16; v. 5; 13; vi. 19; Phil. i. 27; ii. 18; . 10; Col. iii. 16; 1 Thess. i. 4; iv. 11; 1 Tim. ii. 6; iii. 12; 15; 2 Tim. iii. 16; ilem. *v.* 4; Hebr. iv. 7; vii. 6; xi. 1; 34; xii. 23; xiii. 18; Apoc. iii. 15; ix. 12; ii. 8; xviii. 11; 21; xix. 10; xxii. 1; and perhaps a few other places.

It is so difficult to ensure accuracy in collation, and I have detected so many rors in the volumes of my most eminent predecessors, that I am unwilling to eak with confidence of the character of my own labours in this respect. I

› passages of Codex B (2066). And now the er shall tell his own story. "Mihi vero aestate i 1843, cum concessum esset aliquos codicis sus facsimili exprimere, contigit ut in confi-ciendo facsimili variantes lectiones omnes editioni meae Lipsiensi adscriberem." (N.T. ed. 1849, Proleg. p. lxxiv.) *Contigit ut!*

may say with truth that I have cheerfully devoted time and care and untiring diligence to this pursuit, in the full belief that whatever aims at the illustration of God's Word demands and *deserves* our best: the rest I must leave to the candour and intelligence of my readers. I will only add that I have taken as my standard the Elzevir New Testament of 1624, even in its few obvious misprints and inconsistencies. Thus we find *ν εφελκυστικον* Apoc. ii. 14, and an hiatus for lack of it, Act. ii. 7; xxii. 14; 1 Cor. xv. 28; Apoc. xiv. 20. Of typographical errors the chief are Act. ix. 3, *περιεστραψεν*; 1 Cor. v. 7, *εθυθη*; 1 Cor. xiii. 3, *ψωμιζω*; 2 Cor. v. 19, *θημενος*; Col. ii. 13, *συνεζωποιησε*; 1 Thess. ii. 17, *αποφανισθεντες*; Hebr. xii. 9, *εντρεπομεθα*; 2 Pet. i. 7, *φλιαδελφιαν*; Apoc. xviii. 16, *κεχρυσωμενοι*. *Οὕτως* is used before a consonant 1 Cor. iii. 15; 2 Tim. iii. 8; 1 Johan. ii. 6. We read *ἠλιᾳ* Rom. xi. 2, but *ἠλιας* Jac. v. 17: *ἠσαυ* Rom. ix. 13; Hebr. xii. 16, but *ἠσαυ* Hebr. xi. 20. Omissions of *ι* subscript (Eph. iv. 16; Hebr. ix. 26), mistakes in breathing (*ἀλλ'* 1 Tim. ii. 10; *ἑπτα prim.* Apoc. i. 20), in accents, and such like minutiæ, it is needless for us to notice in detail.

POSTSCRIPT.

Among Bentley's papers, deposited in Trinity College Library, I have found a collation by that great scholar of the Uncial Evangelistarium, Arundel 547, whose various readings I have published in my "Collation of Greek Manuscripts of the Holy Gospels." It is contained in the margin of his copy of the Oxford New Testament of 1675 (B. 17. 8), the same volume which preserves his collation of the Codex Augiensis, mentioned above in the Introduction, p. xxiii. He describes the manuscript as "vetustum lectionarium 800 ann. in Bibliotheca Regiæ Societatis Londini, literis capitalibus scriptum (num. 31 in Catalogo). Hic codex *η ι* et *ει* passim confundit: sic *οι* et *ο*: *ν* in *εστιν*, *ελεγεν*, &c.: sic passim habet ante consonantem." On comparing my published collation with that of Bentley, I perceived that we differed in many places, chiefly (indeed almost exclusively) through our respective *omissions* of various readings. These variations I have compared with the venerable original in the British Museum, and while it is no part of my duty to note the errors committed by Bentley, I am bound to take this opportunity of correcting my own. I truly regret that the list of my errata is so large (26), and can only hope (what from other circumstances I am inclined to believe) that my collation of this document is no favourable specimen of my general care and accuracy.

To my collation of Evangelistarium Arund. 547 (x) the following variations should be added: MATTHÆI xviii. 15. –*και prim.* 30. *παν το οφειλομενον*. xx. 2. *και συμφωνησας* (–*δε*). 30. *υἱε*. xxi. 9. *ὡσαννα*. 23. *τι* (*pro τις*). 31. *προσαγουσιν*. MARCI i. 10. *εκ* (*pro απο*). ix. 38. –*δε*. –*εν*. 41. *επι* (*pro εν*). xi. 25. *αφιση*. xii. 30. *εστιν πρωτη*. xv. 10. *παρεδωκεισαν*. xvi. 1. *legas* –*ἡ του* x *semel*, –*του secund. semel.* LUCÆ ii. 51. *ἡ δε μητηρ* (–*και*). vii. 24. *τοις οχλοις* (–*προς*). xii. 8. *ὁμολογησω καγω*, *non καγω ὁμολογησω*. xxi. 34. *βαρηθωσιν*. 36. –*ταυτα*. xxii. 45. –*αὐτου*. 62. –*ὁ πετρος*. JOHANN. iii. 4. *γεννηθηναι bis.* vii. 24. *fin. κρινετε Bentl. at κριντε MS.* x. 24. –*ει συ ει ὁ χ̅ς̅*. xi. 7. + *αυτου* (*post μαθηταις*).

Perhaps I ought to add Marc. ii. 7. *οὑτος· οὑτος*, and Johann. ii. 11. –*εν κανᾳ της γαλιλαιας*, but these are scarcely various readings. Bentley is very capricious in noting itacisms, *ν εφελκυστικα*, &c., though he usually neglects the great mass of them. He specially observes *εὐδομην* for *ἑβδομην* Johann. iv. 52, (which is I think a proof that the cursive hand was familiar when this copy was written) and the form *εγνωκαν* Johann. xvii. 7.

CODEX AUGIENSIS GRÆCO-LATINUS

EPISTOLARUM PAULINARUM.

II. 19 μω·λεγει·ινα·παν·στομα·	dicit·ut omne os
φραγη·και·υποδικοσ·γενη	obstruatur·et subditus fi
ται·πασ·οκοσμοσ·τω·θω·	at omnis mundus do·
20 διοτι·ου·δικαιω_θησεται·	quia non justificabitur·
εξεργων·νομου·πασα·	ex operibus legis omnis
σαρξ·ενοπιον[1]·αυτου·	caro coram illo·
Δια·γαρ·νομου·επιγνωσεωσ·	per legem enim agnitio
αμαρτιασ·	peccati· ~~~~~
21 Νυν·ιδε·χωρισ·νομου·	Nunc autem sine lege
δι_και_οσυνη·του[2]·θυ·	÷ sine lege :
πεφανερωται·μάρτυρου_	justitia di
μενη·υπο·του·νομου·και·	manifestata est·testi
22 των·προφητων·δικαι_οσυ	ficata a lege et
νη·δε·θυ·δια·πίστεωσ·ιηυ	prophetis·Justitia
χρυ·εισπαντασ·και·επιπαντασ·	autem di·per fidem ihm
τυυσ·πιστευοντασ·ου·γαρ·	xpi·inoms et super omnes
23 εστιν·διαστολη·παντεσ·γαρ·	qui credunt·non enim
η·μαρτον·και·υστερουνται·	est distinctio·oms enim
24 τησ·δοξησ·του·θυ·δι_και_	peccaverunt et egent
ου_μαινοι·δωρα_ιαν·τη·αυτου	gloria di justifica
χαριτι·δια·τησ·απολυτρω	ti gratis per ipsius
25 σεωσ·τησ·εν χρω ιυ·ον·	gratiam·per redempti
προεθετο·ο·θσ·ιλαστηρεϊον·	onem·quæ est in xpo ihu quem
δια·πιστεωσ·εν·τω·αυτου·	proposuit ds·propitiationem
αιματι·εισ·ενδιξιν·τησ, δι	per fidem in illius·
26 και_οσυν_ησ·αυτου·εν·τω·	sanguine·ad ostensionem·
νυν·καιρω·εισ·το·ειναι·αυτον	justitiæ suæ in hoc
	tempore·ut sit ipse

CODICIS BOERNERIANI VARIANTES LECTIONES.

[1] ενωπιον. [2] – του at rasura in loco. + δια πιστεωσ ιηυ χρυ εισ παντασ και επι παντασ (post θυ).

Latin	Greek
CAP. III. justus justificans eum qui	δικαιον·δικαιουντα·τον·
v. 27 ex fide est. Ubi est ergo	εκ·πιστεωσ·Που·ουν·η·
gloriatio tua? exclusa	καυχησισ·σου? εξεκλεισ
est·per quam legem?	θη·δια·πο‿ιου·νομου? των
factorum·non·sed per	εργων? ου·αλλα·δια·
28 legem fidei·arbitra	νομου·πιστεωσ·λογειζομε
mur enim justificari ho	θα·γαρ·δικαιουσ‿θαι·ανθρο
minem per fidem sine ope	πον[1]·δια·πιστεωσ·χωρισ·ερ
29 ribus legis·an judæorum	γον[2]·νομου· Η·ϊου‿δαιων·
d̅s̅ tantum·nonne et gentium·	ο·θ̅σ̅·μονον·ουχε·και·εθνων·
30 utique et gentium· Q̅m̅ quidem	ναι και εθνων·επε·ιπερ·
unus d̅s̅ qui justificavit circum	εισ·οθ̅σ̅·οσ·δικαι‿ωσει·πε
cisionem ex fide·et	ριτομην·εκπιστεωσ·και·
præputium per fidem	ακροβυστιαν·δια·τησ·πισ
31 legem ergo destru	τεωσ·νομον·ουν·καταρ
imus per fidem·	γουμεν·δια·τησ·πιστεωσ·
absit sed legem	μηγενοιτο·αλλα·νομον·
statuimus;	στανομεν·
CAP. IV. 1 Qui‿d ergo dicemus invenisse	Τι·ουν·ερουμεν·ευρηκεναι·
Abraham patrem nostrum	αβρααμ·τον·πατερα·ημων·
2 secundum carnem·si enim abraham	κατα·σαρκα·ει·γαρ·αβρααμ·
ex operibus justificatus est habet	εξ εργ(ω)ον[3]; εδικαιωθη·εχει
gloriam·sed non apud d̅m̅	καυχημα·αλλα‿ου[4]·προσ·θ̅ν̅·
3 Quid enim scriptura dicit·credi	Τι·γαρ·(·Η·)γραφη[5]·λεγει·επιστευ
dit abraham d̅o̅·et reputatum	σεν·αβρααμ·τω·θ̅ω̅·κα·ελο
est ei ad justitiam	γεισθη; αυτω·εισ διακαιοσυ
4 ei autem qui operatur	νην[6]·τω·δε·εργα‿ζομενω·
merces non imputatur secun	ο·μισ‿θοσ·ου λογιζεται·κα

[1] ανθρωπον. [2] εργων. [3] εξ εργων. [4] αλλου. [5] η γραφη. [6] δικαιοσυνην.

V. τα·χαριν·αλλα·κατα·οφει	dum gratiam· Sed secundum
5 λημα· Τω·δε·μη·εργα	debitum· Ei autem qui non opera
ζομενω·πιστευοντι·δε·	tur· Credenti autem
επι·τον·δικαιωντα[1]·τον·	in eum qui justificat
ασεβην·λογι‿ζεται·η·πιστισ·	impium·reputatur fides
αυτου·εισ δικαιοσυνην·	ejus ad justitiam·
6 καθωσ·και·ο·δαυιδ·λεγει·	sicut et dauid dicit
τον·μακαρισμον·του·ανου	beatitudinem hominis
ω·ο·θσ λογειζεται·δικαιοσυ	cui ds reputat adjustiti
7 νην·χωρισ·εργων·μακαρι	am sine operibus beati
οι·ων·αφεθησαν·αι·ανο	quorum remissæ sunt iniqui
μαι·και·ων·επεκαλυ φθησαν·	tates·et quorum tecta sunt
8 αι·αμαρτιαι·μακαριωσ·ανηρ?	peccata·beatus vir
ω[2]·ου μη·λογεισηται κσ·α	cui non imputabit dns pec
μαρτιαν·	catum·
9 Ο μακαρισμοσ·ουν·αυτουσ[3]·επι·	eatitudo ergo hæc in
την·πεπιτομην[4]· η·και επι·	circumcisione an etiam·in
την·ακροβυστιαν? λεγομεν·	præputio? dicimus
γαρ·οτι·ελογεισ·θη·τω αβρα	enim quō deputata est abra
αμ·η·πιστισ·εισ δικαιουσυνην[5]·	hæ fides adjustitiam·
10 πωσ·ουν·ελογεισθη? εν·περι	quomodo ergo reputata est? incircum
τομη·η·εν·ακροβυσια?[6]	cisione an inpræputio?
ουκ·εν·περιτομη·αλλεν·α	non incircumcisione·sed inpræ
11 κροβυστια·και·σημει‿ον·	putio· Et signum
ελαβεν·περιτομησ·σφραγει·	acceperat circumcisionis·signa
δα·δια·τησ·δικαιοσυνησ·τησ·	culum justitiæ
πιστωσ[7]·τησ εν·ακροβυστια·	fidei·quæ est in præputio
εισ·το·ειναι·αυτον	ut fieret

[1] δικαιουντα. [2] ου (pro ω). [3] ουτοσ. [4] περιτομην. [5] δικαιοσυνην. [6] ακροβυστια. [7] πιστεωσ.

CAP. IV.	pater omnium credenti	πατερα · παντων · τωσ[1] · πιστευ_
	um · per præputium ut	οντων · δια · ακροβυστιασ · εισ ·
	reputetur et illis	το λογεισθηναι · και αυτοισ ·
v. 12	ad justitiam · Et pa	την · δικαιοσυνην · και πα
	trem circumcisionis · eis non	τερα · περιτομησ · τοισ · ουκ ·
	ex circumcisione tantum · sed	εκ περητομησ[2] · μονον · αλλα
	et his qui sectantur	και · τοισ · στοιλουσειν · τοισ
	vestigia quæ est inpræpu	ιχνεσειν · τησ · εν · ακροβυσ
	tio fidei patris nostri	τια · πιστεωσ · του · προσ · ημων ·
13	abrahæ · Non enim per legem	αβρααμ · Ου · γαρ · δια · νομου ·
	promissio abrahæ aut	η · επαγγελια · τω · αβρααμ · η ·
	semini ejus	τω · σπερματι · αυτου · το
	ut heres ipse esset	κληρονομον · αυτον · ειναι ·
	mundi; Sed per justiti	κοσμου · αλλα · δικαιοσυ
14	am fidei · Si enim qui	νην[3] · πιστεωσ · Ει · γαρ · οι ·
	ex lege · heredes sunt ·	εκνομου · κληρονομοι ·
	et exinanita est fides et	και · καινωται · η · πιστισ, και
	obolita est promissio	κατηργηται · η · παγγελια[4] ·
15	Lex enim iram ope	Ο · γαρ νομοσ · οργην · κατεργα
	ratur · ubi enim non est	ζεται · που · γαρ ουκ · εστιν ·
	lex · nec præ varicatio ·	νομοσ · ουδε · παραβα_σεισ ·
16	ideo exfide ut	Δια · τουτο · εκπιστεωσ · Ϊνα ·
	secundum gratiam inesse	κατα · χαριν · εισ το · ειναι ·
	firmam promissionem	βαιβαιαν · την · επαγγελειαν ·
	omni semini · non ei qui	παντει · τω · σπερματι · ου · τω ·
	ex lege est · sed ei qui	εκ · του · νομου · αλλα · τω
	ex fide est abrahæ · qui	εκ · πιστεωσ · αβρααμ · οσ ·
17	est pater omnium nostrum sic	εστιν πρ παντων · ημων · κα

[1] των. [2] περιτομησ. [3] διὰκαιοσυνησ. [4] επαγγελια.

V. θοσ[1] γεγ_ραπται· Οτι·πατερα·	ut scriptum est· Quia patrem
πολλων·εθνων·τεθεικα·σε·	multarum gentium posui te
κατεναντι·ου·επιστευ σασ·	ante eum cui credidisti
θω·του·ζωοποιουντοσ·τουσ	do qui vivificat
νεκρουσ·και·καλουντοσ·	mortuos et vocat
τα·μη·οντα·ωσ·οντα· ⌈τευσεν·	ea quæ non sunt tamquam essentinalia[2]
18 οσ παρελπιδα·εφελπιδει, επισ	Qui contra spem in spe credidit
εισ·το·γενασθαι[3]·αυτον·πρα·	ut fieret pater
πολλων·εθνων·κατα·το·	multarum gentium secundum qd
ειρημενον·ουτωσ·εσται·	dictum est ei·sic erit
το·σπερμα·σου·ωσ·αι·	semen tuum sicut
αστερεσ·του ουνου[4]·και·το·	stellæ cæli et
αμμον·τησ·θαλασσισ·	arena maris·
19 και·μη·ασθενησασ·εν·τη·	Et non infirmatus in
πιστι·ουκ·ατεν·ησεν[5]·το·	fide non consideravit
εαυτου·σομα[6]·νενεκρωμε	suum corpus emortu
νον·εκατοντα·αι·τησ που	um·cum·c·fere annorum
υπαρχον[7]·και·την·νεκρω	esset·et emortu
σειν·τησ·μητρασ[8]·σαρρασ·	am vulvam saræ
20 εισ·την,επαγγελιαν·του·θυ·	in repromissione di
ου·διεκρι θη·τη·απιστια·	non hæsitavit diffidentia
αλλε·δυνα_μωθη·τη·πιστι·	sed confortatus est fide·
21 δουσ·δοξαν·τω·θω·πλη	Dans gloriam do plenis
ρο·φορηθεισ·οτι·ο·επιγ	sime sciens quia quod pro
γελται·δυνατοσ·εστιν·και·	misit potens est et
22 πο_ιησαι· Διο·ελογισ_θη·	facere· Propter qd reputatum est
αυτω·εισ·δικαιο_συνην·	ei ad justitiam
23 Ουκ·εγραφη·δε·μονον	Non est scriptum autem tantum

[1] καθωσ. [2] *In Lat.* essentialia. [3] γενεσθαι.
[4] – αι αστερεσ του ουνου *p.m.* ut videtur. [5] κατενοησεν. [6] σωμα. [7] υ'παρχων. [8] μητρασ.

CAP. IV.	propter eum quia reputatum est illi	δι·αυτον·οτι·ελογεισθε[1]·αυτω
v. 24	sed et propter nos quibus	αλλα·και·δι·ημασ·οισ μελλεισ[2]
	reputabitur credenti	λυγειζεσθαι·τοισ·πιστευ_ου
	bus in eum qui suscitavit	σειν·επι·τον·εγει_ραντα·
	ihm dnm nostrum ex	ιν·τον·κν·ημων·εκ
25	mortuis·qui traditus est propter	νεκρων·οσ·παρεδο θη·δια·τα
	delicta nostra et	παραπτωματα·ημων·και
	resurrexit propter justificationem	ηγερθη·δια·την·δικαιωσειν·
	nostram·	ημων·
CAP. V. 1	Justificati igitur exfide	δ Δικαιωθεντεσ·ουν·εκπιστεωσ·
	pacem habeamus·	ϊρηνην·εχομεν·
	addm per dominum	προσ·τον·θν·δια·του·κυ·
2	nrm ihm xpm per quem et	ημων·ιυ χυ·δι·ου·και·
	accessum habemus	την·προσαγωγιν·εσχεκαμεν[3]·
	ingratiam istam in	εισ·τιν[4]·χαριν·ταυτην·εν·
	qua stamus et gloria	η·εστηκαμεν·και·καυ_χω
	mur inspe gloriæ	μετα[5]·εφελπιδι·τησ·δοξεσ[6]·
3	di·non solum autem sed	του·θυ·ου·μονον·δε·αλλα·
	et gloriamur in	και·καυχομετα[7]·εν·ταισ
	tribulationibus·scientes qd	θλιψεσιν·ειδοτεσ·οτι·η·
	tribulatio patientiam ope	θλιψεισ·ϋπομον_ην·κατερ
4	ratur·patientia autem	γαζεται·η·δε·υπομον_η·
	probationem·probatio vero	δοκειμην·η·δε·δοκειμη·
5	spem· spes autem non con	ελπιδα·η·δε·ελπισ·ου·κατα
	fundit· Quia caritas	ισχυ_νει·οτι·η·αγαπη·του
	di diffusa est in cordi	θυ·εκκεχυται·εν·ταισ·καρ
	bus nostris per spm san	διαισ·ημων·δια·πνσ·αγιου·
	ctum qui datus est nobis	του·δο·θεντοσ·ημιν

[1] ελογεισθη. [2] μελλει. [3] εσχηκαμεν. [4] την. [5] καυχωμεθα. [6] δοξησ. [7] καυχωμεθα.

v. 6 Ει στι·γαρ χρσ ον των	Ut quid enim xps consistentibus
ημων ασθενων αιτεικα	nobis infirmis adhuc secun
τα καιρον ϋπερ ασεβων	dum tempus pro impiis
7 απεθανεν· Μολεισ γαρ ϋπερ	mortuus est· Vix enim pro
δικαιου·τισ·αποθανειται	justo quis moriatur
ϋπερ γαρ του·αγαθου·ταχα	nam pro bono forsitan
τισ και τολμα αποθανειν	quis et audeat mori·
8 Συνϊστησιν·δε·την εαυτου	Commendat autem suam
αγαπην ο θσ εισ ημασ·οτι	caritatem ds in nobis·quō
ειαιτει αμαρτωλων οντων	adhuc peccatoribus subsistentibus
ημων χρσ ϋπερ ημων απε	nobis xps pro impiis mortu
9 θανεν· Πολλω μαλλον δι	us est· Multo magis justi
καιωθεντεσ νυν εν τω αιμα	ficati nunc insan
τι αυτου·σωθησομεθα·	guine ipsius salvabimur
δι αυτου απο τησ οργησ·	per ipsum ab ira·
10 Ει γαρ εκ θροι οντεσ κατηλ	Si enim cum inimici essemus recon
λα_γημεν τω θω δια[1]·θανατȣ	ciliati sumus do per mortem
του·υιου·αυτου·πολλω μαλλον	filii ejus·multo magis
καταλλαγεντεσ σωθησομεθα	reconciliati salvi erimus
11 εν τη ζωη αυτου·ου μονον	in vita ipsius·non solum
δε τȣτο αλλα και καυχω	autem hoc·sed et gloria
μεν εν τω θω δια του κυ·	mur in do per dnm ⌈nunc
ημων ιυ χρυ διου νυν·	nrm ihm xpm per ihm xpm per quem
την καταλλαγεν[2] ελαβομεν	reconciliationem accepimus
12 Δια τουτο ωσ περ δι ενυσ	Propter ea sicut per unum
ανου εισ τον κοσμον·η·	hominem in hunc mundum
αμαρτια·εισ ηλθεν[3] και δια	peccatum intravit et per
τησ αμαρτιασ θανατοσ και	peccatum mors·et

[1] +του (post δια). [2] καταλλαγην. [3] εισηλθεν.

CAP. V.	ita inomnes homines pertrans	ουτωσ εισ παντασ ανουσ δι
	iit inquo omnes peccave	ηλθεν εφ ω παντεσ ημαρ
v. 13	runt· Usque enim adlegem pec	τον· αχρι γαρ νομου αμαρ
	catum erat in mundo· peccatum	τια ην· εν κο^{σ}·μω[1]· αμαρτια
	autem non imputabatur· non con	δε ουκ ενλογιται μη ον
14	sistente lege· Sed regna	τοσ νομου· αλλε βασιλευ ·
	vit mors ab adam	σεν[2] ο· θανατοσ απο αδαμ·
	usque ad moÿsen etiam in	μεχρι μωυσεωσ· Και επι
	non peccantes	τουσ μη αμαρτησαντασ
	in similitudine prævarica	επι τω ομοιωματι τησ πα
	tionis adæ· qui est	ραβασεωσ αδαμ οσ εστιν·
	forma futuri	τυποσ του μελλοντοσ·
15	sed dns sicut delictum	αλλ ουχ ωσ το παραπτωμα
	ita et donum	ουτοσ[3] και το χαρισμα
	i enim unius de	ι[4] γαρ τω του ενοσ παραπτομα
	licto multi mortui sunt	τι[5] οι πολλοι απεθανον
	multo magis gratia	πολλω μαλλον· η· χαρισ· του·
	di et donum in gratia	θυ και η δωραια χαριτι τη
	unius hominis ihu xpi in	του ενοσ ανου ιυ χυ εισ
	plures abundavit	τουσ πολλουσ επερισσευσεν·
16	Et non sicut per unum pecca	και ουκ ωσ διενοσ αμαρ
	tum· ita et donum· nam	τηματοσ το δωρημα[6]· τομεν
	judicium ex uno in condem	κρημα εξενοσ εισ κατα κρημα[7]·
	nationem· Gatia autem ex	το δε χαρισμα εκ
	multis delictis in	πολλων παραπτωματων εισ
17	justificationem· Si enim in uno	δικαιωμα· ει γαρ εν εινει[8]
	delicto mors regna	παραπτωμα[9] ο θανατοσ εβασιλευ
	vit per unum· multo magis	σεν δια του ενοσ· πολλω μαλλον

[1] κοσμω. [2] αλλεβασειλευσεν. [3] ουτωσ. [4] Ει. [5] παραπτωματι. [6] δορη^{ω}μα (literâ ante μα erasa). [7] κατακριμα. [8] ενει. [9] παραπτωματι.

V.	οιτην περισσιαν τησ χαριτοσ	qui abundantiam gratiæ
	και τησ δωραιασ τησ δικαιο	et donationis justiti
	συνησ λαμβοντεσ εν ζωη βα	æ · accipientes in vita regna
	σιλευσουσιν δια του ενοσ · ιυ χυ	bunt per unum ihm xpm
:8	ρα[1] ουν ωσ διενοσ το παραπ	gitur sicut per unius deli
	τομα[2] εισ παντασ ανθροπουσ[3]	ctum · in omnes homines
	εισ κατακριμα ουτοσ[4] και	in condemnationem · ita et
	διενοσ και[5] δικαιωμα εισ παντασ	per unius justitiam in omnes
	ανουσ εισ δικαιωσιν ζωησ ·	homines injustificationem vitæ ·
9	ωσπερ γαρ δια τησ παρα κο	Sicut enim per in oboedienti
	ησ του ενοσ ανου αμαρτω	am unius hominis peccato
	λοι κατεσταθησαν οι πολλοι	res constituti sunt multi ·
	ουτοσ[6] και δια τησ του ενοσ	ita et per unius
	ανου υπακοησ δικαιοι κατεσ	hominis oboedientiam · justi
	ταθησονται[7] οι πολλοι ·	constituuntur multi ·
10	ομοσ[8] δε παρεισηλθεν[9] ϊνα	ex autem subintravit ut
	πλεονασῃ το παραπτομα[10] οπου	abundaret delictum · ubi
	δε επλεονασεν η αμαρτια	autem abundavit peccatum
	ὑπερ επερισσευσεν η χαρισ ·	super abundavit gratia
11	ϊνα ωσπερ εβασιλευσεν η	ut sicut regnavit
	αμαρτια εν θανατω ουτωσ	peccatum inmortem ita
	και η χαρισ βασιλευσῃ δια	et gratia regnet per
	δικαιοσυνησ[11] εισ ζωην αιω	justitiam invitam æter
	νιον δια ιυ χυ του κυ	nam · per ihm xpm dnm
	ημων	nostrum ·
P. VI V. 1	[12] ιουν ερευμεν[13] · επι μενω	[Q]uid ergo dicemus · permane
	μεν τη αμαρτια ϊνα η χαρισ	bimus inpeccato ut gratia
2	πλεονασῃ ? μηγενοιτο οτινεσ[14]	abundet ? absit · qui

[1] Αρα. [2] παραπτωμα. [3] ανουσ. [4] ουτωσ. [5] το (pro και). [6] ουτωσ. [7] καταστaθησονται.
[8] Νομοσ. [9] ἐπαρεισηλθεν. [10] παραπτωμα. [11] δικαιονησ. [12] Τι. [13] ερουμεν. [14] οιτινεσ.

	Latin	Greek
CAP. VI.	enim mortui sumus peccato	γαρ ανεθανομεν[1] τη αμαρτια
	quomodo adhuc vivemus in eo?	πωσ ειτει[2] ζησωμεν εναυτη?
3	an ignoratis quia quicumque bap	Η αγνοειται οτι οσοι εβαπ
	tizati sumus in xpo ihu in	τισθημεν εισ χν ιν[3] εισ τον
	morte ipsius baptizati su	θανατον αυτου εβαπτισθη
4	mus·consepulti ergo cum	μεν·συνεταφημέν ουν
	illo per baptismum	αυτω δια του βαπτισματοσ
	in mortem·ut quomodo	εισ θανατον ϊνα ωσπερ
	surrexit xps a mortuis per	ηγερθη χσ εκνεκων[4] δια
	gloriam patris ita	τησ δοξησ του πρσ ουτωσ
	et nos innovitate	και ημεισ εν καινοτητι
	vitæ ambulemus	ζωησ περιπατησωμεν
5	Si enim complantati facti sumus	Ει γαρ συνφυγοιγε γοναμεν
	similitudini mortis	τω ομοιωματι του θανατου·
	ejus·simul et	αυτου αμα και τησ
	resurrectionis ejus erimus	ανασθασεωσ[5] αυτου εσομαι
6	hoc scientes·quia	θα τουτο γινωσκοντεσ·οτι
	vetus homo noster simul	ο παλλαιοσ[6] ημων ανοσ· συν
	crucifixus est·ut destruatur	εσταυρωθη ϊνα καταργηθη
	corpus peccati	το σωμα τησ αμαρτιασ·του
	ut nonultra serviamus	μηκετι δουλευειν ημασ
7	peccato · Qui enim mortu	τη αμαρτια ογαρ αποθα
	us est·justificatus est	νων δεδικαιωται απο τησ
8	a peccato · Si autem mortui	αμαρτιασ Ειγαρ αποθανο
	sumus cum xpo credimus	μεν[7] συν χρω πιστευομεν
	quia etiam convivemus xpo·.	οτι και συνζησομεθα τω χρω
9	Scientes qd xps resurgens a	Ειδοτεσ οτιχσ εγερθεισ εκ
	mortuis·jam non moritur·	νεκρων ουκ ετι αποθνησκι

---

[1] απεθανομεν. [2] ετει. [3] ιη. [4] νεκρων. [5] αναστασεωσ. [6] παλαιοσ. [7] απεθανομεν.

VI.	θανατοσ αυτου ουκ ετει κυ	mors illi non domi
10	ριευει Ο γαρ απεθανεν· τη	nabitur · Quod enim mortuum est
	αμαρτια · απεθανεν · εφαπαξ ·	peccato · mortuus est semel ·
11	Ο δε ζη · ζη τω θω · ουτοσ[1]	Quod autem vivit · vivit do · Ita
	και ϋμισ λογιζεσθαι εαυ	et vos existimate vos
	τουσ νεκρουσ μεντη αμαρ	met mortuos quidem esse pecca
	τια · ζωντασ δε τω θω · εν	to · viventes autem do in
	χρω ιηυ[2]	xpo ihu
12	Μη ουν βασειλευετω η · α	ou ergo regnet pec
	μαρτια εν · τω · θνητω ·	catum inmortali
	υμων σωματι εισ το επα	vestro corpore inoboedi
13	κουειν αυτη[3] · Μηδε παρισ_	endo ei[3] · Neque exhibeatis
	τανετε τα μελη υμων οπλα	membra vestra arma
	αδικιασ τη αμαρτια · αλλα	iniquitatis peccato sed
	παραστησαται εαυτουσ τω θω	exhibete vos do ·
	ωσ εκνεκρων ζωντεσ	tamquam ex mortuis viventes
	και τα μελη ϋμων οπλα	et membra vestra arma
14	δικαιοσυνησ τω θω αμαρ	justitiæ do · Pecca
	τια γαρ ϋμων ουκυριευσει	tum enim vobis non dominabitur
	ου γαρ εσται ϋπο νομον	non enim estis sub lege
	αλλα ϋπο χαριν	sed sub gratia
15	Τι ουν ημαρτησαμεν οτει	uid ergo? peccabimus quō
	ουκ εσμεν υπονομον αλλα	non estis sub lege sed
16	ϋπο χαριν[4] μηγενοιτο · η · ουκ	sub gratia · abeit · aut ne
	οιδαται οτει ω παρειστα	scitis quoniam cui exhibuistis
	νεται εαυτουσ δουλουσ εισ	vos servos ad
	ϋπακοην[5]? δουλοι εσται	oboediendum · servi estis
	ω ϋπακουεται ητοι αμαρ	cui oboedistis sive pec

[1] ουτωσ. [2] *Nullum spatium vacuum.* [3] *Marg.* ·|· τη αματια. [4] χαρειν. [5] υπακοην.

CAP. VI.	cati ad mortem · Sive oboe	τειασ εισ θανατον · η ὑπακο
v. 17	ditionis adjustitiam · Gra	ησ εισ δικαιοσυνην χαρεισ
	tia autem d̅o̅ quod fuistis	δε τω θ̅ω̅ οτει ητε
	servi peccati · oboe	δȣλοι τησ αμαρτιασ[1] υπη
	distis autem excorde in	κουσαται δε εκκαρδιασ[2] εισ
	quam traditi estis formam do	ον παραδοθηται[3] τυπον δι
18	ctrinæ liberati	δαχησ ελευθερω θεντεσ
	autem apeccato	δε αποτησ αμαρτειασ
	servi facti estis justi	ει δουλωθηται τησ[4] δικαι
	tiæ	οσυνη
19	umanum dico propter in	α νθρωπεινον λεγω δια[5]την
	firmitatem carnis ves	ασθενειαν τησ σαρκοσ ὑ
	træ · Sicut enim exhibu	μων ωσπερ γαρ παρεστησα
	istis membra vestra ser	ται τα μελη υμων δου
	vire inmunditiæ et	λευειν τη ακαθαρσεια και
	iniquitati adiniquita	τη ανομεια εισ την ανο μει
	tem · Ita nunc exhibete	αν ουτω νυν παραστησαται
	membra vestra servire	τα μελη ὑμων δουλευειν
	justitiæ insanctificationem ·	τη δικαιοσυνη · εισ αγειασμον
20	Cum enim servi eratis pec	Οτε γαρ δουλθιητε[6] τησ αμαρτε
	cati · liberi fuistis justi	ασ ελευθηροιητε[7] τη δικαι
21	tiæ · Quem ergo fructum	οσυνη τηνα[8] ουν καρπον
	habuistis tunc inhis in quibus nunc	ειχεται τοτε εφοισ νυν επαισ
	erubescitis · Nam finis	χυνεσθαι Το μεν γαρ τελοσ
	illorum mors est ·	εκεινων θανατοσ εστειν
22	Nunc vero liberati	νυν ειδε ελευθερω · θεντεσ
	a peccato · Servi autem	αποτησ αμαρτιασ δουλω
	facti d̅o̅ habetis fruc	θεντεσ δε τω θ̅ω̅ εχεται · τον καρ

[1] αμαρτειασ. [2] εκαρδιασ (κ written above). [3] παρεδοθηται. [4] τη. [5] δεια. [6] δουλοιητε. [7] αμαρτειασ ελευθεροιητε. [8] τινα.

L. πον υμων εισ αγειασμον	tum v̅r̅m̅ insanctificationem
το δε τελοσ ζωην αιωνιον·	finem vero vitam æternam·
3 τα γαρ οψωνια·τησ·αμαρτιασ	Stipendia enim peccati
θανατοσ Το δε χαρισμα του	mors·gratia autem
θ̅ο̅υ̅ ζωη αιωνιοσ εν χ̅ρ̅ω̅ ι̅υ̅	d̅i̅ vita æter na·in x̅p̅o̅ i̅h̅u̅
τω κ̅ω̅ ημων	d̅n̅o̅ nostro·
1 Η αγνοειται αδελφοι·γει	[An] ignoratis fratres·scien
νωσκοσιν γαρ νομον λαλω	tibus enim legem loquor·
οτει ονομοσ κυριευει του	quia lex dominatur in
α̅ν̅ο̅υ̅ εφοσον χρονον·ζη	homine quantum tempus vivit·
2 η γαρ υπαναροσ[1] γυνη	Nam quæ sub viro mulier
τω ζωντει ανδριδεδεται	vivente viro alligata est
νομω Εαν δε αποθα	legi · Si autem mortuus fu
νη ο ανηρ κατηργηται απο	erit vir · Soluta est a
3 του νομου αναροσ[2] αραουν	lege viri · Igitur
ζωντοσ[3] του αναροσ· χρη	vivente viro·judi
ματισει μοιχαλεισ εαν γε	cabitur adultera · Si fu
νηται αναρι[4] ετερω εαν	erit cum viro alio · Si
δε αποθανη ο ανηρ·αυτησ	autem mortuus fuerit vir ejus
ελευθερα εστιν[5] αποτου νομȣ	liberata est alege
του μη ειναι αυτην μοιχα	non esse eam adul
λειδα γενομενην αναρι[6]	teram sifuerit cumviro
ετερω	alio·
4 ω στε αδελφοι μοι καιυμεισ	[I]taque fratres mei etvos
εθανατωθηται τω νομω	mortificati estis legi
διατουσοματοσ[7] του χ̅υ̅ εισ	per corpus x̅p̅i̅·ut
τογενεσθαι υμασ ετερω	sitis vos alterius
τω[8] εκνεκρων εγερθεντει	amortuis resurgentis

[1] υπανδρος. [2] του ανδροσ. [3] + χ̅ρ̅ (ante του ανδρος). [4] ανδρι. [5] εστειν. [6] ανδρι. [7] σωματοσ. [8] τω^ν.

Latin	Greek
CAP. VII. ut fructificemus	ϊνα καρποφορεσωμεν τω
v. do · Cum enim essemus	θω Οτε γαρ ημεν τη
incarne · Passiones	σαρκει ταπαθηματα των
peccatorum quæ per	αμαρτειων τα δια του
legem erant operabantur in	νομου ην εργειτο εν τοισ
membris nostris · ut fructi	μελεσιν ημων εισ το καρπο‿
ficarent morti ·	φυρεσαι οτω[1] θανατω
6 Nunc autem soluti sumus	νυν δε κατηργηθημεν
a lege mortis	απο του νομου του θανατου
inqua detinebamur · ita ut	εν ω κατειχομεθα ωστε
serviamus innovitate	δουλευειν εν καινοτητει
sps et non in vetustate	πνσ · και ου παλλιοτη τι[2]
litteræ ·	γραμματοσ ·
7 Quid ergo dicemus? lex	Τι ουν ερευομεν[3]? ο νομοσ
peccatum est · abeit · sed	αμαρτια · μηγενυιτο αλλα
peccatum non cognovi	την αμαρτιαν ουκ εγνων
nisi per legem · Nam	ειμη δια νομου Την γαρ
concupiscentiam non cognovi · nisi	επυθυμιαν[4] ουκ ηδειν ειμη
lex diceret · Non concu	ονομοσ ελεγεν ουκ επει
8 pisces · Occasione ergo	θυμησισ · αφορμην δε
accepta peccatum per	λαβουσα ηαμαρτια διατησ
mandatum · operatum est in me	εντολησ · κατιργασατο · εν · ειμοι[5]
omnem concupiscentiam · sine	πασαν επιθυμιαν’ χωρισ
lege enim peccatum non	γαρ νομου αμαρτεια νεκρα
9 erat · Ego autem vivebam sine	ην Εγω δε εζων χωρισ
lege aliquando · veniente	νομου ποτε ελθουσησ
autem mandato peccatum	δε τησ εντυλησ η αμαρτεια
10 revixit · ego autem mortuus	ανεζησεν · Εγω δε απεθα

[1] τω. [2] παλαιοτη τι. [3] ερουμεν. [4] επιθυμιαν. [5] εμοι.

L νον·και ευρεθε[1]·μοι·η·εντο	sum· Et inventum est mihi manda
λη·η·εισ·ζωην·αυτη·	tum qd erat advitam hoc esse
1 εισ·θανατον·Η·γαρ·αμαρτ·ια[2]·	ad mortem · Nam peccatum
αφρμην[3]·λαβουσα·δια·τησ·	occasione accepta per
εντολησ·εζηπα‿τησεν·μαι·	mandatum seduxit me
και·διαυτησ·απεκτινεν·	et ex illa occidit me
2 Ωστε·ομεν·νομοσ·αγειοσ·	Itaque lex quidem sancta
και·η·εντολη·αγια·και·δικαια·	et mandatum scm et justum
3 και·αγαθη·το·ουν·αγαθον·	et bonum · Quod ergo bonum
εμοι·θανατοσ? με[4]γενοιτο·	mihi mors est? abeit·
αλλη·αμαρτεια·ινα·φανη·	sed peccatum ut appareat
αμαρτια[5]·δια·του·αγαθου	peccatum·per bonum
μοι·κατεργα‿ζομενη·θανα	mihi operatum est mor
τον·ινα·γενηται·καθυπερ	tem·ut fiat supra
βολην·η·αμαρτ·ια[6]·αμαρτωλοσ·	modum ipsum peccatum peccans
14 δια·τησ·εντολησ·οιδαμην[7]·	per mandatum · Scimus
γαρ·οτει·ονομοσ·πνευμα	enim quia lex spirita
τικοσ·εστειν·Εγω·δε·σαρ	lis est · Ego autem car
κινοσ·ειμει·πεπραμενοσ·υπο·	nalis sum venundatus sub
15 την·αμαρτ·ιαν[8]·Ο·γαρ·κατερ	peccato · Quod enim ope
γαζομαι·ου·γενοσκο[9]·ουγαρ	ror non intellego non enim
ο·θελω·παρασσω·αλλο·μεισω·	qd volo ago sed quod odio
16 του·το[10]·ποιω·Ει·δε·ο·ου·θελω·	illud facio · Si autem qd nolo
του·το·ποιω·συνφημει·τω·νομω·	hoc facio consentio legi
17 οτι·καλον·εστιν·Νυν·ειδε·	quia bona est · Nunc ecce
ουκετει·εγω·κατεργαζομαι[11]·	non jam ego operor
αυτο·αλλα·η·οικουσα·εν·	illud sed quod habitat in
18 εμοι·αμαρτεια·Οιδα·γαρ·	me peccatum · Scio enim

[1] ευρεθη. [2] αμαρτια. [3] αφορμην. [4] μη. [5] αμαρτια. [6] αμαρτια. [7] οιδαμεν. [8] αμαρτιαν. [9] γεινωσκω. [10] τουτ̣ο. [11] καταργαζομαι.

	Latin	Greek
P. VII.	quod non habitat in me hoc	οτι[1]·ουκ·οικει·εν·εμοι·του·τεσ
	est incarne mea bo	τειν·εν·τη·σαρκει·μου·το·αγα
	num· nam velle adjacet	θον·το·γαρ·θελειν·παρακεπαι[2]·
	mihi per ficere autem	μοι·το·γαρ·κατεργαζεσθαι·το·
v. 19	bonum non invenio·non enim	αγοθον·ουκ[3]·ευρισκω·Ου·γαρ
	qd volo facio bonum·sed quod	ο·θελω·ποιω αγαθον·αλλο
	odio malum illud ago	μεισω[4]·κακον·του·το πρασσω·
20	Si autem quod nolo illud facio	Ει·δε·ο·ουθελω·του·το ποιω·
	non jam ego operor	ουκ·ετει·εγω·κατεργαζομαι·
	illud sed quod habitat in me	αυτο·αλλη·ιοκουσα[5]·εν·εμοι·
	peccatum·	αμαρτεια·
21	Invenio igitur legem	ε Ευρισκω·αρα·τον·νομον·
	volenti mihi facere	τω·θελοντει·εμοι·ποι εινν·
22	bonum·condelector enim	το·καλον·συν·η δομαι[6]·γαρ·
	legi di secundum	τω·νομω·του·θυ·κατα·τον
23	interiorem hominem video autem	εσω·ανον·βλεπο[7]·δε·
	aliam legem in mem	ετερον·νομον·εντοισ·μελε
	bris meis repugnantem	σειν·μοι αντιστρατευ ομενον·
	legi mentis meæ et	τω·νομω·του·νοοσ·μου·και·
	captivantem me in lege	αιχμαλω τειζοντα·μαι; εν·τω·νομ
	peccati quæ est in	τησ·αμαρτιασ[8]·τω·οντει·εν·τοισ·
24	membris meis · Infelix ego	μελεσιν·μου·Ταλαιπωροσ·εγω·
	homo quis me liberabit de	ανοσ·τισ·μαι·ρυσεται·εκ·του·
	corpore mortis hujus?	σωματοσ·του θανατου·τουτου·
25	gratia dni per ihm xpm	η·χαρισ·κυ·δια·ιηυ·χρυ·του·
	dnm nostrum·	κυ·ημων·
	Igitur ipse ego mente	Αρα·ουν·αυτοσ·εγω·τω·νοει·
	servio legi di autem	δουλευω·νομω·θυ·τη·δε·

[1] οτει. [2] παρακειται. [3] αγαθον ουχ. [4] — μεισω. [5] οικουσα. [6] συνηδομαι. [7] βλεπω. [8] αμαρτιασ.

II. σαρκει νομω αμαρτειασ·	carne lege peccati
II. I ουδεν αρα·νυν·κατακριμα	Nihil ergo nunc damnatio
τοισ·εν·χρω ιηυ	nis est his·qui
	sunt in xpo ihu
[1]	qui non secundum
	car nem
	ambulant
2 ο·γαρ·νομοσ·του·πνσ·τησ·ζωησ·	lex enim sps vitæ
εν χρω·ιηυ·ελευθεροσεν[2]·σαι·	in xpo ihu liberavit te
απο·του·νομου·τησ·αμαρτιασ[3]·	alege peccati
3 και·του·θανατου· το γαρ	et mortis · Nam quod
αδυνατον·του νομου·εν·ω·	jam possibile erat legi·inquo
ησθενει·δια·τησ σαρκοσ· ο θσ·	infirmabatur per carnem·ds
τον·εναυτου[4]·υιον·πεμφψασ[5]·	suum filium misit
εν·ομοιωματε[6]·σαρκοσ αμαρ	in similitudinem carnis pec
τειασ·και·περι·αμαρτειασ·	cati·et de peccato
κατεκρινεν·την·αμαρτειαν·	damnavit peccatum
4 εν·τη·σαρκι·ϊνα·τω[7]·δικαιω	incarne ut justificatio
μα·του·νομου·πλερωθη[8]·εν·	legis inpleretur in
ημιν·τοισ·μη·κατα·σαρκα·	nobis qui non secundum carnem
περει_πατουσειν·αλλακατα·	ambulamus·sed secundum
5 πνα · Οι·γαρ·κατα σαρκα·οντεσ·	spm·qui enim secundum carnem sunt
τα·τησ·σαρκοσ·φρονουσειν·	quæ carnis sunt sapiunt·
οι·δε·κατα·πνα·τα·του	qui ergo secundum spm que sunt
6 πνσ · Το·γαρ·φρονημα·τησ	sps · Nam prudentia
σαρκοσ·θανατοσ · Το·δε·φρονη	carnis mors est·pruden
μα·του·πνσ·ζωη·και·ϊρηνη·	tia autem sps vita et pax
7 οτι·το·φρονημα·τησ·σαρκοσ·	quoniam sapientia carnis

---

[1] *Simile spatium vacuum.* [2] ελευθερωσεν. [3] αμαρτιασ. [4] εαυτου. [5] πεμψασ. [6] ομοιωματει. [7] το. [8] πληρωθη.

CAP. VIII.	inimica est do·legi enim	εκθρα εισ θν Τω γαρ νομω
	di non est subjecta	του θυ·ουχ·υποτασσε_ται[1]·
v. 8	nec enim potest · Qui autem	ου·δε·γαρ·δυναται · Οι·δε·
	incarne sunt do placere	εν·σαρκει·οντεσ·θω·αρεσαι·
9	non pos sunt·vos autem non	ου·δυνανται ·7 Υμισ δε ουκ
	estis incarne·sed inspu	εσται ενσαρκει αλλεν·πνι
	sitamen sps di habitat in	ει περ πνα θυ οικει εν
	vobis · Siquis autem spm xpi	υμιν·ει δε τησ[2] πνα χρυ
	non habet·hic non est	ουκ εχει·ουτοσ ουκεστιν·
10	ejus · Corpus quidem est	αυτου·τομεν·σωμα·εστιν·
	mortuum propter peccatum	ε. ν·κρον[3]·δια·αμαρτιαν·το·
	sps autem vivit propter justificationem	δε·πνα·ζη·δια·δικαιοσυνην·
11	Si autem sps ejus quisuscita	ει·δε·το·πνα του εγι
	vit ihm ex mortuis habi	ραντοσ·ιν·εκ νεκρον[4] (ω)·οι
	tat invobis qui suscitavit xpm	κει·εν υμιν ο·εγειρασ χν
	amortuis vivificavit et	εκ νεκρων·ζωοποιησει·και
	mortalia corpora vestra	τα·θνητα·σωματα υμων
	per inhabitantem ejus	δια το εν οικουν·αυτου
	spiritum in vobis	πνα εν υμιν
12	rgo fratres·debitores	ρα[5]·ουν·αδελφοι·οφιλεται·
	sumus non carni·ut secundum	εσμεν·ου·τη·σαρκει·του·κατα·
13	carnem vivamus·si enim secundum	σαρκα·ζην·ει γαρ κατα
	carnem vixeritis·mori	σαρκα·ζηται[6]·μελλεται (incipietis)·απο
	emini · Si autem spiritu facta	θνησκι[7]·Ει·δε·πνι·τασ·πραζισ[8]
	carnis mortificaveritis·vi	τησ σαρκοσ·θανατουτε·ζη
14	vetis · Quicumque enim spu di	σεσθαι · Οσ·οι·γαρ πνι θυ
	aguntur·hi filii sunt di·	αγονται·ουτοι·υιοι·εισειν·θυ·
·enim 15	Non·accepistis spiritum servitutis	Ου·γαρ·ελαβεται·πνα·δουλεγίασ[9]

[1] υποτασεται. [2] τισ. [3] νεκρον. [4] νεκρων. [5] Αρα.
[6] ζηται ζηται. [7] αποθνησκιν. [8] πραξισ. [9] δουλεῖασ.

II.	παλειν · εισ · φοβον · αλλε	iterum intimorė · Sed
	λαβεται · πνα · υιο · θεσε‿ιασ ·	accepistis spm adoptionis fili
	εν · ω · κραξομεν[1] · αββα ο ·	orum · Inquo clamus abba
	con	
16	παγηρ[2] · αυτο · το · πνα συν	pater · Ipse sps testimoni
	testabitur	
	μαρτυρι · τω · πνι · ημων · οτει	um reddit spui nostro quod
17	εσμεν · τεκνα · θυ · ει · δε · τεκνα ·	sumus filii di · Siautem filii
	και · κληρο νομοι · [3]	et heredes · heredes quidem
	δε χρυ ·	di · coheredes autem xpi ·
	ει · περ · συν‿πασχομεν[4] · ϊνα · και	sitamen conpatimur ut et
	συνδοξασ‿θωμεν ;	con glorificemur ·
	quia	
18	Αογειζομαι[5] · γαρ · οτι ουκ	Existimo enim quod non sint con
	nunc	
	αζια[6] · τα · παθηματα · του · νυν ·	digne passiones hujus
	temporis	
	και‿ρου · προσ · την · μελλουσαν ·	temporis adfuturam
	δοξαν · αποκαλυ‿ψθηναι ·	gloriam quæ revelabitur
19	εισ · ημασ · Η · γαρ ; αποκαραδο	innobis · Nam expecta
	κια · τεσ[7] · κτει‿σεωσ · την · απο	tio creaturæ revelati
	καλυψν[8] · των · υιων θυ · απεκ	onem filiorum di expec
20	δεχεται · Τη · γαρ · μαται‿ιοτη ·	tat · Vanitati autem
	τη[9] · η · κα‿τισεισ[10] · υπεταγη · ου	creatura subjecta est non
	subi	
	θελουσα · αλλα · δια · τον υπο	volens sed propter eum qui subje
	cientem eam	
21	ταξαντα · εφελπειδει · Διοτει ·	cit inspe · Quia
	και · αυ‿τη κτισισ[11] · ελευθερωθη	et ipsa creatura libera
	σεται · απο · τησ · δουλειασ ·	bitur aservitute
	τησ · φθορασ · εισ · την ελευ	corruptionis inliber
	θεραν · τεσ[12] · δοξησ · των · τεκνων ·	tatem gloriæ filiorum
22	του θυ · Οι δαμεν · γαρ · οτει	di · Scimus enim quia
	con	
	πασα · η · κτεισεισ · συνσ‿τεν	omnis craeatura inge
	dolet	
	αζει · και · οδυνει · αχρι του νυν ·	miscit et parturit usque adhuc

---

[1] κραζομεν. [2] πατηρ. [3] *Nullum spatium vacuum.* [4] συνπασχομεν. [5] Λογειζομαι. [6] αξια. [7] τησ. [8] αποκαλυψιν. [9] ματαιοτη τη. [10] ηκτισεισ. [11] κτισισ. [12] ελευθεριαν τησ.

CAP. VIII. v. 23	Non solum autem illa sed et	ου · μονο[1] · δε · αλλα · και ·
	nos ipsi primicias	receptaculum ημεισ · αυτοι · την · απαρχην ·
	sps habentes	του[2] · πνσ εχοντεσ αυτοι
	intra nos gemimus expec	ingemiscimus εν · αυτοισ · στεναζομεν · απεκ
	tantes redemptionem	δεχυμενοι · την · απολύτρωσιν ·
24	corporis nostri · Spe enim	τού σωματοσ · ημων · τη · γαστρ[3] ·
	salvi facti sumus	ελ πιδει · εσωθη μεν
	spes autem quæ videtur non	ελ πισθε[4] ηβλεπομενη ουκ
	est spes · Quodenim videt	εστειν · ελπισ · Ο γαρ βλεπει,
25	quis quid sperat · siautem quod	τεισ τει · ελπειζει · ειδε ο
	nonvidemus speramus per	ου βλεπομεν · ελπιζομεν · δι
	patientiam expectamus	υπομνησ[5] απεκδεχυμε θα
26	imiliter autem et sps	[Ω] σαυτοσ[6] δε και το πνευμα
	adjuvat infirmitatem	συναντειλαμβανεται · τησ
	orationis nostræ · Nam quid	δεησεωσ ημων · Το γαρ τι
	oremus · sicut oportet	προσ · ευχομεθα · καθο · δει
	nescimus · Sed ipse	ουκιοδαμεν[7] · αλλα · αυτο
	sps postulat pro nobis	το πνα · υπερεντυγχα νει[8]
	gemitibus inenarrabilibus	στεναγ μοισ αλαλ ητοισ ·
27	Qui autem scrutatur corda	Ο δε ερευνωντα[9] καρδ ιασ
	scit quid desideret	οιδεν τιτο φρονημα του
	sps quo secundum dm postulat	πισ[10] · Οτι καταθν εντυγχανει
	pro scis ·	Ϋπερ αγειων · ;
28	cimus autem quo diligenti	ιδαμεν[11] δε οτι τοισ αγανω
	bus dm omnia coope	σισ[12] · τον θν παντα σίν
	rantur inbonum · his qui secundum	ἐργει[13] εισ αγαθον · τοισ κατα
	propositum vocati sunt sci ·	προθεσιν κλητοι σούσιν ·
29	Quo quos præscivit et præ	Οτι ουσ προεγνω και · προ

[1] μονον. [2] του. [3] γαρ. [4] δε. [5] ὑπομονησ. [6] Ωσαυτοσ. [7] οιδαμεν.
[8] ὑπερεντυγχανει. [9] τασ. [10] πνσ. [11] Οιδαμεν. [12] αγαπωσιν. [13] συνεργει.

II. ωρεισεν συν μορ φουσ τησ	distinavit conformes fieri
ικονοσ · τού · υιοι αυτου · εισ το	imaginis filii sui ut
ειναι αυτον πρωτοτοκον	sit ipse primogenitus
30 εν πολλοισ αδελφοισ · Ουσ	inmultis fratribus · Quos
δε προωρεισεν τουτοισ[1] και	autem predistinavit hos et
εκαλε σεν · και ουσ εκαλεσεν	vocavit · Et quos vocavit
τουτουσ καιεδικαωσεν[2] ·	hos et justificavit
ουσ · δε · εδ ικαιωσεν · τουτουσ ·	Quos autem justificavit illos
glorificavit και · εδοξασεν · ;	et imagnificavit
31 Τιουν · ερουμεν · προσ ταυτα ·	uid ergo dicemus ad hæc?
ει · ο · $\overline{θσ}$ · Ϋπερ · ημων · τησ[3] ·	si $\overline{ds}$ pro nobis quis (æ)
32 καθ · $\overline{η}$μων οσ · ουδε · υίου ·	contra nos qui neque filio
ἴδιου · εφεισατο · αλλα · υπερ · ημων ·	proprio pepercit sed pro nobis
παντων · παρεδωκεν · αυτων[4] ·	omnibus tradidit illum
πωσ · ουχι · και · συν · αυτω ·	Quomodo non etiam cum illo
παντα · ημιν χαρι_σεται ·	omnia nobis cum illo donavit ·
33 τισ · εν · καλεσει · κατα · εκ	quis accusabit adversus e
λε_κτων · $\overline{θυ}$ · $\overline{Θσ}$ · ο · δικαιων ·	lectos $\overline{di}$ · $\overline{ds}$ qui justificat
34 τισ · ο · κατα · κρινων · $\overline{χσ}$ · $\overline{ισ}$ ·	quis est qui condemnet · $\overline{xpc}$ $\overline{ihc}$
ο · αποθανων · μαλλον · δε ·	qui mortuus est · immo autem
και · εγερθισ · οσ · και εστιν ·	et resurrexit · qui et est
εν · δεξεια · του · $\overline{θυ}$ · οσ · και	ad dexteram $\overline{di}$ qui etiam
εν · τυγχανει · υπερει · ημων · ;	interpellat pro nobis ·
35 Τισ ουν · ημασ χωρησει · απο	uis ergo nos separabit a
τησ · αγαπη[5] (σ.) · του · $\overline{χυ}$ · Θλιψεισ ·	caritate $\overline{xpi}$ · tribulatio
η · στενχαωρια[6] (t) · δι · ωγμοσ ·	an angustia an persecutio
η · λειμοσ · Η · γυμνοτησ ·	an fames · an nuditas ·
η · κιν_δυνοσ · η · μαχαιρα ·	an periculum · an gladius

---

[1] τουτουσ. [2] εδικαιωσεν. [3] τισ. [4] αυτον. [5] αγαπησ. [6] στενσαωρία (tχ).

CAP. VIII v. 36	sicut scriptum est· Quia	καθωσ · γεγραπται · Οτι ·
	propter te mortificamur	ενεκεν · σου · θανατουμεθα ·
	tota die æstima	ολην · την · ημεραν · ελογει
	ti sumus · ut oves oc	σθ͜ημεν · ωσ · προβατα σφα
	cisionis ·	γησ · ;
37	ed inomnibus supe	λλεν[1] · του · τοισ · πασιν · υπερ
	ramus propter eum qui di	νει͜κωμεν · δια · του · αγαπη
		confido
38	lexit nos · certus sum	σαντα · ημασ · πεπισμαι ·
	enim quia neque mors neque	γαρ · οτι · ουτε · θανατοσ · ουτε
	vita · neque angelus neque	ζωη · ουτε · ανγελοσ · ουτε ·
	principatus neque instantia	αρχια[2] · ουτε · ενεσ͜τωτα ·
	neque futura · neque vir	ουτε · μελλοντα · Ουτε · δινα
39	tus · Neque altitudo · neque	μεισ[3] · ουτε · Ϋψωμα · ουτε ·
	profundum · neque creatura	βαθασ[4] · Ουτε · κτει͜σεισ ·
	alia poterit nos	ετερα · δυνησεται · ημασ ·
	separare acaritate	λωρεισαι · απο · τησ · αγαπησ ·
	di · quæ est in xpo ihu	του · θυ · τησ · εν χρω · ιηυ ·
	dno nostro ·	του · κυ · ημων · ;
CAP. IX. 1	[V]eritatem dico inxpo ihu non	ληθιαν[5] · λεγω · εν χρω · ιηυ · ου
	mencior · testimonium red	ψευδομαι · συνμαρτυρου ·
	dente mihi conscientia	σησ · μοι · τησ · συ · ϊδεσεωσ[6] ·
2	mea in spu sco · quoniam	μου · συν · πνι · αγειω · Οτι ·
	tristicia mihi est magna et	λυπη μοι · εστιν · μεγαλη · και
	continuus dolor cor	αδιαλειπτοσ · οδυνη · τηκαρ
3	di meo · Obtabam enim	διάμου · Ηυχομην · γαρ
	anathæma esse ipse ego	ανθεμα[7] · ειναι · αυτοσ · ẹγω ·
	axpo pro	απο[8] · του : χρυ · ὑπερ · των ·
	fratribus meis · qui sunt cogna	αδελφων · μου · τωνσυνγε

---

[1] Αλλεν. [2] αρχαι. [3] δυναμεισ. [4] βαθοσ. [5] Αληθιαν. [6] συνίδησεωσ. [7] αναθεμα. [8] ὑπο (*pro* απο).

IX. 4 νων των · κατα σαρκα · Οιτινεσ[1] ·	ti mei secundum carnem · qui
εισειν · ισραηλειται · ων	sunt israhelitæ quorum
Ϋιο · θεσεια · και η δοξα	adoptio est filiorum · et gloria
και · η · διαθ_ηκη · και η · νομο	et testamenta · et legis
θεσια[2] · και · η · λατρια · και	latio · et obsequium · et
5 επαγγελια[3] · Ων · πατερεσ ·	promissa · Quorum patres
εξων · ο · χρσ κατα σαρκα ·	ex quibus xpc secundum carnem ·
ο, ων · επιπαντων θσ ευ	qui est super omnia ds bene
λογητοσ εισ · τουσ · αιωνασ · αμην · ;	dictus insecula amen ·
6 υχ[4] · οιον δε οτι εκπεπτωκεν ·	onautem quod exciderit
ο λογοσ · του · θυ · Ου · γαρ ·	verbum di · Non enim
παντεσ · οι εξ_ισραηλ · ουτοι ·	oms qui ex israhel sunt · hi sunt
7 ισ ραηλειται · ου_δοτι · εισιν ·	israhelitæ · Neque
σρερμα[5] · αβρααμ · παντ εσ ·	semen abrahæ omnes ·
τεκνα · αλλεν · ισαακ[6] ·	filii · sed in isahac
κληθησεται · σοι · σπερμα ·	vocabitur tibi semen ·
8 του · εστιν · ουτα · τεκνα της	Idest non qui filii
σαρκοσ · ταυτα · τεκνα · θυ	carnis hi filii di
αλλατα · τεκνατησ επαγγε	sed filii promissio
λειασ[7] · λογειζεται · εισ · σπερ	nis æstimantur in se
9 μα · Επαγγελειασ · γαρ · ο	mine · Promissionis enim
λογοσ ουτοσ κατα τον	verbum hoc est · ad
καιρον τουτον ελευσομαι ·	tempus hoc veniam
και εσται · τη σαρρα Ϋιοσ	et erit saræ filius ·
10 Ου μονον · δε · αλλα · και ρε	Non solum autem sed et re
βεκκα · εξενοσ · κοιτην ·	becca exuno concubitu
εχουσα · ισαακ · του · πρσ	/. /. hisaac habens patris
11 ημων · (non cum) Μηπο[8] · γαρ · γεννη	nostri · Nam cum nondum na

---

[1] οιτινεσ. [2] νομοθεσία. [3] ηπαγγελεια. [4] ουχ. [5] σπερμα. [6] ϊσακ. [7] *Spatium ante* λογειζ. [8] πω.

CAP. IX.	ti fuissent·aut egissent	θεντων·Η·πραξαντων·
	aliquid boni aut mali ut	τι·αγαθον·η·κακον·ινα·
	secundum electionem pro	ηκατε·κλογην·προ
	positum di maneret	θεσεισ·του·θυ·μεινη·
	non ex operibus sed ex	ουκεξεργων·αλλεκ·του·
v. 12	vocante dictum est ei	καλουντοσ·ερρεθη·αυτη
	quia major serviet	Οτι·ο μειζων·δου·λευ‿σει·
13	minori sicut scrip	τω·ελασσονει·καθ ωσ·γε
	tum est · Jacob dilexi	γραπται · Τον ιακοβ[1]·ηγαπησα·
	esau autem hodio habui	τον·δε εσαυ[2] εμει‿σησα·
14	uid ergo dicemus·numquid iniqui	Τι ουν·ερουμεν·μη αδικει·
15	tas apud dm · absit·	απαρα·θω·μη·γενοιτο·Τω·
	moÿsi enim dicit·miserebor	μωυσει·γαρ·λεγει·ελεησω·
	cui misereor·et misericordiam prestabo	οναν·ελεω·και·οικτειρησω[3]·
16	cui miserebor · Igitur non	οναν·οικτειρω·αρα·ουνου·
	volentis·neque curren	του·θελοντοσ·ουδε·του·τρεχον‿
	tis·sed miserentis est di·	τοσ·αλλα·τονελαιωντοσ·θυ·
17	Dicit enim scriptura pharaoni·	λεγει·γαρ·η γραφη·τω φ·ραω[4]·
	Quia in hoc ipsum excita	οτι·εισ·αυτο·τουτο·εξηγει
	vite uostendam in	ρα‿σε·οπωσ·ενδειζομαι[5], εν·
	te virtutem meam et	σοι·την·διναμιν[6]·μου·και
	ut adnuntietur nomen	οπωσαν·διαγγελητο·ονομα·
18	meum inuniversa terra ergo	μου·ενπαση·τη·γη·αρα·ουν·
	cui vult miseretur et quem vult	ον·θελει·ελαια·ον·δε·θελει·
	indurat	σκληρυνει·;
19	icis itaque mihi quod dr adhuc	Ερεισ·ουν·μοι·τι·ουν·ετει
	queritur · Voluntati enim	μεν φεται · Το[7]·γαρ·βουλημα
	ejus quis resistit?	τει·αυτου·τισ·ανθεστηκεν

---

[1] ιακωβ. [2] ησαυ. [3] οικτειρώησω. [4] φαραω. [5] ενδειξωμαι. [6] δυναμιν. [7] μεμφεται Τω.

20 Ω ανθρωπε · συ · τισει · Ο	O homo tuquis es
ανταπο‿κρινομενοσ · το[1] θ̅ω̅ ·	qui respondeas d̅o̅
μη · ερει · το · πλασμα · τω · πλα	numquid dicit figmentum ei qui se
σαντει · Τι · μαι εποιη‿σασ ·	finxit · Quid me fecisti
21 ουτωσ · Η · ουκ · εχει · εξου	sic aut non habet potesta
σειαν · οκεραμευσ · του · πηλου	tem figulus luti
εκ του · αυτου · φυραματοσ ·	ex eadem massa
ποιησαι · ο μεν · εισ · τιμην ·	facere aliud quidem in honorem
σκευοσ · Ο · δε · εισ · ατειμει‿	vas · aliud v° in contu meli
22 αν · Ει · δε · θελων ο θ̅σ̅	am · Quod si volens d̅s̅
ενδιξασθαι την · οργην ·	ostendere iram
και · γνωρεισαι · το · δυνατον ·	et notam facere potentiam
αυτου · εν · πολλη · μακροθυ	suam inmulta pacienti
μια · εισ σκευη · οργησ ·	a · invasa iræ
κατηρ‿τεισ‿μενα · εισ · απω	preparata ininteri
23 λειαν · και · ι̅να · γνωρει	tum · et ostende
σητο · πλουτοσ · τησ · δοξησ ·	re divicias gloriæ
αυτου · επι · σκευη · ελαι	suæ invasa misericor
ουσ[2] · απροη‿τοιμασεν ·	diæ · quæ preparavit
24 εισ · δοξαν · ουσ · και · εκα	ingloriam · Quos et vo
λεσεν · ημασ · Ου · μονον ·	cavit nos · Non solum
εξιου‿δαιων · αλλα · και εξ	exjudæis · sed etiam ex
25 εθνων · ωσ · και εν · τω · ωση ·	gentibus · Sicut et inosee
λεγει · καλεσω · τον · ου ·	dicit · vocabo non
λαον · μουλαον · μου και	plebem meam plebem meam et
την ουκ · ηγαπημενην · ηγα	non dilectam di
26 πημενην · και εσται · εν · τω ·	lectam · Et erit in
τοπω · οΥαν · κληθησονται ·	loco ubi dictum est

[1] τω.

[2] ελαιουσ‿ουσ.

CAP. IX.	non pleps mea vos · Ibi	ουλαοσ μου Ϋμισ · εκει ·
	vocabuntur filii di vivi ·	κληθησονται Ϋιοι θυ · ζωντοσ ·
v. 27	Esaias autem clamat pro	Ησαιασ · δε · κραζει · Ϋπερ του
	israhel · Sifuerit numerus	ισραηλ · Εαν · η · ο · αρειθμοσ
	filiorum israhel tamquam	των · Ϋιων ισραηλ · ωσ
	harena maris ·	η · αμμοσ · τησ · θαλασσησ · το ·
	reliquiæ salve fient	κατα λιμμα · σωθησεται ·
28	verbum enim con sum mans et	λογον · γαρ · συντελων · και ·
	brevians inæquitate	συντεμνων · εν · δικαιοσυνη ·
	Quia verbum breviatum	οτει · λογον · συντεγμημενον[1] ·
	faciet dns super terram ·	ποιησει · κσ · επι · τησ · γησ ·
29	Et sicut predixit esaias ·	και καθωσ · προιρηήκεν[2]; ησαιασ ·
	Nisi ds sabaoth reli	ειμη · κσ σαβαωθ · ω · εν κα
	quisset nobis semen	τελειπεν · ημιν · σπερμα ·
	quasi sodoma facti esse	ωσ · σοδομα · ανεγεν‿ηθη
	mus · Et quasi gomorra	μεν · και ωσ · γομρρα[3] ·
	fuissemus · similes	ανομοι · ω · θημεν ; ·
30	[Q]uid ergo dicemus quod gentes	Τι ουν ερουμεν · οτι · εθνη ·
	quæ non sectabantur justi	τα · μηδηωκοντα · δικαι
	ciam · appreheenderunt juti	οσυνην · κατελαβεν[4] · δικαι
	ciam · Justiciam autem quæ	οσυνην · Δικαιοσυνην · δε ·
31	ex fide est · Israhel vero	τησ · εκπιστεωσ · Ισραελ[5] · δε ·
	sectando legem justiciæ	διωκων · νομον · δικαιοσυνησ ·
	Inlegem justiciæ non	εισ · νομον ÷ δικαιοσυνησ[6] · ουκ ·
32	pervenit Quare · quia non	εφθοχεν · Διατει ? · οτει · ουκ
	ex fide sed quasi ex ope	εκπιστωσ[7] · αλλωσ · εξ ερ
	ribus · Offenderunt enim in lapidem	γον[8] · Προσ · εκο φαν, τω · λιθω
33	offensionis sicut	του · προσ · κομματοσ · καθωσ ·

---

[1] συντετμημενον. [2] προϊρηκεν. [3] γομορρα. [4] + την (post κατελαβεν). [5] Ϊσραηλ. [6] — δικαιοσυνησ. [7] πιστεωσ. [8] εργων.

X. γεγραπται · Ιδου τιθιμει · εν	scriptum est · Ecce pono in
σειων · λιθων · προσκοματοσ[1]	sion lapidem offensionis
και πετραν σκανδολου[2] · και	et petram scandali · et
επιστευων[3] · επ · αυτω · ου · μη ·	qui crediderit ineum non
κατα‿ισχυνθη ·	confundetur ·
X. I Αδελφοι · ημεν · ευδοκεια ·	[F]ratres voluntas quidem
της · εμησ · καρδιασ · και · η · δαι	cordis mei · et obsecra
ηεισ προσ · τον · θν · υπερ · αυτων	tio ad dm pro illis
2 εισ · σωτηρίαν · Μαρτυρω · γαρ ·	insalutem · Testimonium enim
αυτοισ · οτει ζη	perhibeo illis · quia ze
λον · θυ εχουσιν αλλον‿	lum di habent · sed non
3 κατε‿πει‿γνωσιν · αγνο ουν	secundum scientiam · Ignoran
τησ[4] · γαρ · την · του θυ · δικαι	tes enim di justi
οσυνην · και · την · ιδιαν ·	tiam · Et suam
δικα‿ιοσυνησ[5] · ζητουντεσ · στι	justiciam quærentes statu
σαι · τη · δικαι οσιυνην[6] · του · θυ ·	ere · Justitiæ di
4 ουχ · υπεται · ησαν[7] · Τελοσ · γαρ ·	non sunt subjecti · Finis enim
νομου · χρσ εισ · δικαιοσυνην ·	legis xpc adjusticiam
παντει · τω · πιστευοντει ·	omni credenti
5 Μωυσεσ[8] · γαρ · γραφει · την · δικαι	Moÿses enim scribit · Justi
οσυνην · την · εχτου[9] · νομου ·	tiam quæ ex lege est
οτει · οποιησασ · αυταζησεται ·	quo qui fecerit ea · vivet
6 εν · αυτοισ · Η · δε · εκπιστεωσ ·	in eis · quæ autem ex fide est
δικαιουσυνη[10] · ουτωσ λεγει ·	Justicia sic dicit
μη · ειπισ[11] · εν · τη · καρδια ·	nedixeris incorde
σου · τισ · αναβησεται · εισ ·	tuo · Quis ascendit in
τον · ουρανον του · τεστιν ·	cælum hoc est
7 χν · κατα γαγειν · Η · τισ	xpm deducere · aut quis

[1] λιθον προσκομματοσ. [2] σκανδαλου. [3] ὁ πιστευων. [4] αγνο ουντεσ. [5] δικαιοσυνην. [6] δικαιοσυνη. [7] υπερταιησαν. [8] Μωυσεησ. [9] εκ του. [10] δικαιοσυνη. [11] ειπησ.

CAP. X.	descendit in abys	κατα βησεται · εισ · την · αβυσ
	sum hoc est xpm exmor	σον · του · τεστιν · χν · εκνε
v. 8	tuis redure [ce] · Sed quid	κρων · αναγαγειν[1] · αλλα · τι ·
	scriptura dicit prophete est	Η · γραφηλετει[2] · εγγυσ · σον · εστιν ·
	verbum in ore tuo	το · ρημα · εν · τω · στοματι · σου ·
	et incorde tuo · Hoc est	και · εν · τι[3]καρδια · σου · του · τεστιν ·
	verbum fidei quod	το · ρημα · τησ · πιστεωσ ο
9	predicamus · Quia si confi	κηρυσσομεν · Οτι · εαν ομο
	tearis inore	λογησησ · εντω στοματι
	tuo dnm ihm et credideris	σου κν ιν και · πιστευσεσ[4] ·
	incorde tuo quod ds	εν · τη · καρδια · σου · οτι · ο · θσ ·
	illum suscitavit amortuis	αυτον · η · γειρεν · εκ νεκρων ·
10	salvus eris · Corde enim credi	σωτηση[5] · καρδια · γαρ · πιστευ
	tur adjusticiam · O	εται · εισ δικαιοσυνην · στο
	re autem confessio fit in	ματει δε · ομολογειται · εισ ·
11	salutem · Dicit enim scriptu	σωτηριαν · λεγει · γαρ · η · γρα
	ra · Omnis qui credit in	φη · Πασ · ο · πιστευων · επ
	illum · non con fun	αυτω ουμη · καταισχυν θη
12	detur · nonenim est distincti	σεται · ου · γαρ · εστιν · Διαστο
	o judæi et greci	λη · ϊουδιαι[6] · ουτε και ελλενοσ[7] ·
	Nam idem dns omnium	Ο · γαρ · αυτοσ · κσ · παν των ·
	dives inomnes qui	πλουτων · εισ · παντασ · τουσ
	invocant illum	επεικαλȣμενουσ · αυτον ·
13	Omnis enim quicumque invocave	Πασ · γαρ · οσανεπει καλεση
	rit nomendni salvus	ται · το · ονομα · κυ · σωθησ ·
	erit ·	εται ·
14	[Q]uomodo ergo invocabunt	Πωσ · ουν · επικαλε σωνται ·
	in quem non crediderunt	εισ · ον · ουκ · επιστευ σαν

[1] αναγγαγειν. [2] λεγει. [3] τη. [4] πιστευσησ. [5] σωθηση. [6] ϊουδαι. [7] ελληνοσ.

X. η · πωσ · δε · επιστευσω‿σιν ·	aut quomodo credent ei
ου · ουκ · ηκουσαν · Πωσ δε	quem non audierunt · Quomodo autem
ακουσονται · χωρισ · κηρυσσον	audient sine predican
15 τοσ · Πωσ · δε · εκηρυσ‿σουσιν ·	te · quomodo autem p̄dicabunt
εαν · μη · αποσταλωσιν · καθωσ ·	nisi mittantur · sicut
γεγραπται · 7 ωσ · ωραιοι · οι ·	scriptum est · Quam spetiosi
ποδεσ · των ευαγγελιζομε	pedes evangelizanti
νων · ῑρηνην · ευαγγελιζομε	um pacem · evangelizanti
16 νων · αγα‿θα · αλλ ου · παντεσ ·	um bona · Sed non omnes
υπηκουσαν · του · ευαγγελιου ·	obediunt evangelio ·
ησαιασ · γαρ · λεγει · κ̅ε̅ · τισ ·	esaias enim dicit · D̅n̅e quis
επιστευσεν · τηακοη · ημων ·	credidit auditui nostro?
17 αρα · ουνηπιστισ · εξ ακο‿ησ ·	Ergo fides · exauditu ·
η · δε · ακοη · δια · ρηματοσ ·	auditus autem per verbum
18 αλλα · λεγω · μη · ουκ · ηκου	sed dico · numquid non audie
σαν? εισπασαν · την · γην ·	runt · Inomnem terram
εξηλθεν · οφεογγοσ[1] · αυτων ·	exivit sonus eorum
και · εισ · ταπερατα · τησ · οικου	et infines orbis ter
μενησ · τα · ρηματα · αυτων · ;	ræ verba eorum ·
19 αλλαλεγο[2] · μη · ι̅σ̅ραηλ · ουκ ·	[S]ed dico num quid israhel non
εγνω · Πρωτοσ · μωυσησ · λεγει ·	cognovit · Primus moÿses dicit ·
Εγω · παραζηλωσω, Ϋμασ · επ	ego ademulandum provoco vos in
ουκ · εθνη · επι · εθνι · ασυνε	non gentem · Ingentem insi
20 τω · παροργειω · Ϋμασ · Ησα	pientem irritabo vos · Esa
ιασ · δε · λεγει · ευρεθην · εν ·	ias autem dicit · Inventus sum in
.τοισ · εμαι · μη · ζητουσιν ·	me non quærentibus ·
εν · φανησ · εγενομην · τοισ ·	inmanifesto factus sum ·
21 εμαι · μη · ε περωτωσιν · προσ	me noninterrogantibus · 7

---

[1] φθογγοσ.

[2] λεγω.

CAP. X.	adisrahel autem dicit · Totam	δε · τον · ισραηλ · λεγει · Ολην[1] ·
	diem expandi	την · ημεραν · εξεπετασα · τασ
	manus meas ad plebem non cre	χειρασ · μου · προσλαον · απει
CAP. XI. V. 1	dentem · Dico ergo numquid	θουντα · Λεγω · ουν · μη
	reppulit ds heredi	απωσατο · ο θσ · την · κληρο ·
	tatem suam · absit ·	νομειαν · αυτου · Μηγενοιτο ·
	et enim ego israhelita sum	και · γαρ · εγω · ισραηλ · ιτησεμει[2] ·
	ex semine abraham · De tribu	εκ · σπερματοσ · αβρααμ · φυλησ
2	beniamin non repulit	βενιαμιν · ουκ · απ ᵖ ωσατο[3] · ο ·
	ds plebem suam quam	θσ · τον · λαον · αυτου · ον ·
	præscivit · An nescitis	προεγνω · Η ουκ οιδαται ·
	inelia quid dicit scriptura	ενηλεια · τι · λεγι · η · γρα φη
	quomodo postulabat	ωσεν · τυγ χανει · τω ·
3	dm adversus israhel · Dne	θω · κατα · του · ισηλ[4] · κε τουσ ·
	prophetas tuos occiderunt	προ φετασ[5] · σου · απεκτιναν ·
	altaria tua destru	τα · θυσειασ · τηρεια · σου · κατεσ
	xerunt et ego relictus sum	καψαν · καγω · ὑπελειφθην ·
	solus · Et quærunt	μονοσ · και · ζητουσειν · την ·
4	animam meam · sed quid dicit	ψυχην μου · αλλα · τι · λεγει ·
	illi responsum divinum ·	αυτω · οχρημα · τισμοσ ·
	reliqui mihi septem	κατελειπον · εμαυτω · επτακισ ·
	milia viros quinon	χιλιουσ · ανδρασ · Οιτινεσ · ουκ ·
	curvaverunt genu baal	εκαμψαν · γονυ · το[6] · βααλ ·
5	sic ergo et nunc inhoc	Ουτοσ[7] · ουν · και · εν · τω · νυν ·
	tempore · reliquiæ secundum electi	καιρω · λιμμα · κατε κλο
	onem græ salvæ factæ sunt,	γην · χαριστοσ[8] · γεγονεν ·
6	Si autem gra non etiam	ει · δε · χαριστι[9] · ουκ · ετει ·
	ex operibus alioquin gra	εξεργων · επει · Η · χαρισ ·

---

[1] ονν (λ above). [2] ειμει. [3] αππωσατο. [4] ισηλ, *vid.* Matthæi in loco.
[5] προφητασ. [6] τω. [7] ουτωσ. [8] χαριτοσ. [9] χαριτι.

L ουκ ετι · γεινεται · χαρισ ·
7· Τιουν · ο · επεζηται[1] · ισρα
ηλ · τουτο · ουκ · επετυχεν ·
Η · δε · εκλογη · επτυχεν[2] ·
οι · δε · λοιποι · επωρωθησαν ·
8 καθωσ · γεγραπται · εδωκεν ·:
αυτοισ · ο · θσ · πνα · κατανυ
ξεωσ · οφθαλ_μουσ · του · μη ·
βλεπειν · και · ωτα · του · μη ·
ακουειν · εωσ · τησ · σημερον ·
/. /.
9 λεγει · γενηθητω · Η · τραπεζα ·
αυτων · εισ · παγιδα · και · εισ ·
θηραν · και · εισ · σκανδαλον ·
και · εισ · ανταποδωμα · αυτοισ ·
10 Cκοτεισ_θητωσαν · οι · οφθαλ
μοι · αυτων · του · μη · βλεπ
πειν[3] · και · τον · νωτον · αυτων ·
διαπαντοσ · συνκαμ_ψον ·
11 Λεγω · ουν · μη · επτε_σαν
ινα · πεσωσειν · Μηγενοιτο ·
αλλα · τω · αυτων · παραρτωμα
τι[4] · η · σωτηρεια · τοισ · εθνε
σειν · εισ · το · παραζηλωσαι · αυτουσ ·
12 ει · δε · το · παραπτωμα · αυτων ·
πλουτοσ · κοσμου · και το ·
ηττημα · αυτον[5] · πλουτοσ ·
εθνων · ποσω · μαλλον · το ·
/.
ημερασ · και δαυιδ ·[6]

nonjam erit gratia
uid ergo quod querebat isra
hel · noninvenit ·
Electio autem consecuta est
ceteri vero excecati sunt
sicut scriptum est · Dedit
eis ds spm conpuncti
onis · occulos ut non
videant · et aures ut non
audiant usque inhodier
num diem · Et david
dicit · fiat mensa
eorum · inlaqueum et in
captionem · et inscandalum
et inretribucionem illis ·
Obscurentur oculi
eorum ut non vi
deant et dorsum eorum
semper incurva ·
Dico ergo numquid sic offenderunt
ut caderent · absit ·
sed illorum delic
to salus genti
bus ut emulentur illos · 7
Quod si delictum eorum
divitiæ mundi et
diminutio eorum divitiæ
gentium · quanto magis ·

---

[1] επεζητει. [2] επετυχεν. [3] βλεπειν. [4] παραπτωματι. [5] αυτων. [6] *Non ita Cod. Boern.*

CAP. XI. v. 13	plenitudo eorum·vobis	πληρωμα·αυτων · Υμιν·
	enim dico gentibus	γαρ·λεγω·τοισ·εθνεσειν·
	quam diu ego sum gentium	εφοσον·εγω·ειμει·εθνων·
	apostolus·ministerium	αποστολοσ·την·διακονειαν·
14	meum glorificabo · Si quoniam	μου·δοξασω·Ει·πωσ·
	emuler carnem meam	παραζηλωσω·την·σαρκαμου·
	et salvabo aliquos exillis	και·σωσω·τινασ·εξαυτων[1]·
15	Si enim amissio eorum recon	Ει·γαρ·η·αποβολη·αυτων·κα
	ciliacionem mundi · Quæ as	ταλλαγη·κοσμω·τησ·η·προ
	sumtio·nisi vita ex mortuis	λημψισ·ειμη·ζωη·εκνκρων[2]·
16	uod si delibatio sc̄a et	Ει·δε·η̄·απαρχη·αγεια·και
	massa·et radix sc̄a	το·φυραμα·και·η·ρειζα·αγεια·
17	et rami · Quod si aliqui	και·οι·κλαδοι · Ει·δε·τεινεσ·
	ex ramis·fracti sunt·	των·κλαδων·εξεκλασθησαν[3]·
	tu autem cum esses oleaster in	συ·δε·αγρει·ελαιοσων·εν·
	sertus es in ipsos·et	εκεν·τρισθησ·εν·αυτοισ·και
	socius factus es	συν·κοινωνοσ·εγενου·τησ·
18	pinguedinis olivæ·noli	πειοτητοσ·τησ·ελαιασ · Μη·
	gloriari adversum ramos	κατα·καυχω·των·κλαδων·
	quod situ gloriaris·non	ει·δε·συ·καυχασαι·ου·συ·την·
	tu radicem portas·sed ra	ρειζαν·βασταζεισ·αλλη·ρει
19	dix te · Dicis ergo si frac	ζα·σε·γερεισ·ουν·ει·κλασ
	ti sunt rami·ut ego in	θησαν·κλαδοι·ῑνα·εγω·εν·
20	serar · Bene·incredu	κεντρισθω·καλωσ·την·απισ
	litate fracti sunt · Tu autem	τεια·εκλασθησαν·συ·δε·τη·
	fide sta · Noli altum	πειστει·εστηκασ·μη·υψη
21	sapere·sedtime · Si enim	λοφρονει·αλλα·φοβου·ειγαρ
	d̄s natura libus ra	ο θ̄σ·των·κατα φυσειν·κλα

[1] εχαυτων, v. Matthæi in loco. [2] νεκρων. [3] εχξεκλασθησαν.

11 δων · ουκ · εφεισατο · μη	mis nonpepercit · Ne
πωσ · ου · δε · σου · φεισεται · ;	forte nectibi parcat
12 Ει · δε · ουν · χρηστοτητα · και ·	ide ergo bonitatem et
αποτομιαν · θυ · επει · μεν	severitatem di · severitatem
τουσ · πεσοντασ · αποτομιαν ·	quidem · in eos quica dunt ·
Επει · δε · σε χρηστοτητα · εαν ·	Inte autem bonitatem si
επει · μεινησ · τη · χρηστοτητι ·	permanseris inbonitate
13 Επει · και · συ · εκκπησῃ[1] · κα · και	Alioquin et tu excideris · et il
νοι[2] · δε · εαν · μη · επειμει_νω	li sinon perman se
σειν · τη · απεστεια[3] · ενκεντρεισ	rint inincredulitate inse
θησονται · Δυνατοσ · γαρ · εστιν ·	rentur · Potens est enim
ο θσ · παλιν · εν · κεντρισαι · αυτοισ[4] ·	ds iterum inserere illos ·
14 Ει · γαρ · συ · εκ · τησκαταφυσειν · εξ	Si enim tu exnaturali ex
εκοπησ · αγριελαιου · και · παρα	cisus es oleastro · et contra
φυσειν · ενεκεντρεισθησ · εισ ·	naturam insertus es in
καλλει · ελαιον · Ποσω μαλ	bonam olivam · Quanto ma
λον, ουτοι · οι · κατα φυσειν · εν	gis hisecundum naturam in
κεντρισθησονται · τη · ϊδεια	serentur suæ
ελαια ·	olivæ ·
25 Ου · γαρ · θελω · ῆμασ[5] · αγνο	on enim volo vos igno
ειν · αδελφοι · το μυστηρει	rare fratres mysteri
ον · τουτο · Ϊνα · μη · ητε ·	um hoc · ut non sitis
εαυτοισ · φρονειμοι · Οτι · πωρω	vobis met ipsis sapientes quia cæ
σεισ · απομερουσ · τω · ισραηλ	citas · exparte israhel
γεγονεν · αχρισου · το πλη	contigit · donec pleni
ρωμα · των εθνων · εισ · ελθη ·	tudo gentium intraret ·
26 και · ουτωσ · πασ · ϊσραηλ · σωθησ	et sic omnis israhel salvus
εται · καθωσ · γεγραπται · Ηξ	erit · sicut scriptum est · veni

[1] εκκοπησῃ. [2] κακεινοι. [3] απε ι στεια. [4] αυτουσ. [5] ῦμασ.

CAP. XI.	et ex sion quieripiat·	ει·εκ·σειων·ο·ρυομενοσ·
	et avertat impietatem abia	αποστρε‿ψαι·ασεβειασ·απο ι̅α̅
v. 27	cob et hoc illis erit	κωβ·και·αυτη·αυτοισ·η·
	ame testamentum cum abstu	παρε·μου·δια·θηκη·οταν·αφε
	lero peccata eorum	λω μαι·τασ·αμαρτειασ·αυτων·
28	Secundum evangelium quidem in	κατα·μεν·το·ευαγγελιον·εκ
	imici propter vos·secundum ele	θροι·δι·ὑμασ·κατα·δε·την·
	ctionem autem dilecti propter	ε̣κλογην[1]·αγαπητοι·δια·τουσ·
29	patres·sine poenitentia enim	πατερεσ[2]·αμε·ταμελητα·γαρ·
	sunt dona et vocatio	τα·χαρεισματα·και·η·κλησεισ·
30	d̅i̅ · Sicut enim vos	του θ̅υ̅·ωσπερ·γαρ·υμεισ·
	aliquando non credidistis d̅o̅	ποτε·ηπειθησαται·τω·θ̅ω̅·
	Nunc autem micd̅a̅ consecuti estis propter	νυν·δε·ηλεηθηται·τη·τουτων·
31	diffidentiam · Ita et isti nunc	απειθια·Ουτωσ·και·αυτοι·νυν·
	non crediderunt vestræ miseri	ηπειθησαν·τω·υμετερω·ελαι
	cordiæ·ut et ipsi misericordiam	ει·ι̅να·και·αυτοι·ελαιη·θω
32	consequent · Conclusit enim d̅s̅	συν[3]·Cυνεκλισεν·γαρ·ο θ̅σ̅·
	omnia inincredulitatem·ut	παντα·εισ·απειθειαν·ι̅να·
	omnibus misereatur	τουσ·παντασ·ελεηση·;
33	[O] altitudo diviciarum et sapien	Ω βαθοσ·πλουτου·και σοφει
	tiæ et scientiæ d̅i̅ · Quam	ασ·και·γνωσεωσ·του·θ̅υ̅·ωσ·
	inscrutabilia sunt judicia ejus	ανεξερευνητα·τα·κριματα·αυτου·
	et investigabiles viæ	και·ανεξειχνιασ·τοι·αιοδοι·
34	ejus quis enim cognovit sensum d̅n̅i̅	αυτου · Τισ γαρ·εγνω·νουν·κ̅υ̅·
	aut quis consilia rius ejus fuit	η·τισ·συμβουλοσ·αυτου·εγενετο·
35	aut quis prior dedit illi·et	η·τισ·προεδωκεν·αυτω·και
36	retribuetur ei quo̅ ex	ανταποδοθησεται·αυτω; οτι·εξ
	ipso·et per ipsum·et in ip	αυτου·και·δι·αυτου·καιεισ·αν‿

[1] εκλογ(η)ιν. [2] πατερασ. [3] ελαιηθωσιν.

I. τον·ταπαντα·αυτω·η·δο
ξα·εισ·τουσ·αιωνασ·των·
αιωνων[1]·αμην·
II.
1 αρακαλω[2]·ουν·ὑμασ·αδελ
φοι·δια·των·οικτειρων·του·
$\overline{θυ}$·παραστησαι·τα·σωματα·
υμων·θυσιαν·ζωσαν·
αγειαν·ευαρεστον[3]·τω·$\overline{θω}$·την·
λογεικην·λατριαν·ὑμων·
2 και·μη·συνσχηματιζεσ‿θαι·
τω·αιωνει·τουτω·αλλα·με
τα·μορφουσται[4]·τη·ανα·και
νοσει[5]·του·νοοσ[6]·εισ·το·δοκει‿
μαζιν·ὑμασ·τι·το θελημα·
$\overline{θυ}$·το·αγαθον·και·ευα‿ρεσ
3 τον·και·τελειον·λεγω·γαρ·
δια·τησ·χαρειτοσ·τησ·δοθει
σησ·μοι·παντει·τω·οντει·
εν·ϋμιν·μη·ϋπερ·φρονειν·
αλλα·φρονε‿ιν·εισ[7]·το·σöφρο ω̈
νειν[8]·εκαστω·ωσ·ο $\overline{θσ}$·εμε
ρεισεν·μητρον[9]·πιστεωσ·
4 ωσ·περ·γαρ·εν·ενει·σωματει·
πολλα·μελη·εχομεν·τα·δε·
παντα·μελη[10]·ου την·αυτην·
/. /.
5 πραξειν·εχει[11]·Ουτωσ·οι·πολ
λοι εν·σωμα·εν$\overline{χρω}$·Το·δε·
alterius
καθεισ·αλληλων·μελη·

so sunt omnia · Ipsi glori
a insæcula
sæculorum amen·
[O]bsecro itaque vos fra
tres permisericordiam
$\overline{\text{di}}$ utexhibeatis corpora
$\overline{\text{vra}}$ hostiam viventem
$\overline{\text{scam}}$ placentem $\overline{\text{do}}$
rationabile obsequium vestrum
et nolite ɔformari
sæculo huic·sed refor
mamini innovita
te sensus vestri·ut probe
tis quæ sit voluntas
$\overline{\text{di}}$ bona·et bene pla
cens et perfecta·dico enim
per gratiam quæ data
est mihi omnibus qui sunt
inter vos · Non plus sapere
sed sapere ad sobrieta
tem · Unicuique sicut $\overline{\text{ds}}$ di
visit mensuram fidei·
Sicut enim inuno corpore
multa membra habemus autem
omnia membra non eundem
habent actum · Ita mul
ti unum corpus in $\overline{\text{xpo}}$ autem
singuli alter alterius membra

---

[1] - των αιωνων, habet supra, *sec. manu.* [2] Παρακαλω. [3] $\overset{a}{\varepsilon}$υρεστον. [4] μεταμορφουσθαι. [5] ανακαινωσει. [6] νουσ. [7] - εισ, habet supra, *sec. manu.* [8] σωφρονειν. [9] μετρον. [10] μελη παντα. [11] εχει πραξειν.

CAP. XII. v. 6	Habentes autem donationes secundum gra	Εχοντεσ · δε · χαρισματα · κατα · την
	tiam quæ data est nobis	ρειν · την · δοθεισαν · ημιν ·
	differentes · Sive prophetiam	διαφορα · Ει · τε · προφητειαν ·
	secundum rationem fi	κατα · την · αναλογιαν · τησ · πισ
7	dei · Sive ministerium in	τεωσ · Ει · τε · διακονειαν · εν · τη ·
	ministrando · Sive qui docet	διακονεια · Ει · τε · ο · διδασκων
8	in doctrina · Qui exorta	εν · τη · διδασκαλεια · ο · παρακα
	tur · inexortando · Quitri	λων[1] · εν · τη · παρακλεσει[2] · ο · με
	buit insimplicitate · Qui	τα · διδουσ · εν · απλοτητει · ο ·
	preest insollicitudine ·	προ · ϊστα · μενοσ · ενσπουδη ·
	Qui miseretur inhilaritate ·	Ο · ελαιων · εν ϊλαροτειτει ·
9	dilectio sine simulatione ·	η · αγαπη · αν · υποκριτο ·
	odientes malum adhe	μει · σουντεσ · το πονηρον · καλ
10	rentes bono · Caritate fra	λομενοι[3] · τω · αγαθω · τη · φει
	ternitatis invicem beni	λαδελφια · εισ · αλλ(η)ελουσ[4] · φιλοσ
	gni · Honore invicem	τοργοι · τη · τειμη · αλληλουσ[5] ·
11	p̄ venientes · sollicitudine non	προηγου‿μενοι · τη · σπουδη · μη ·
	pigri · spū ferventes	οκνηροι · τω · πν̄ι · ζεοντεσ · τω ·
12	dn̄o servientes · spe	tempore καιρω · δουλευοντεσ · τη · ελ‿
	gaudentes intribulatione	πιδει · χαιροντεσ · τη · θλειψει ·
	patientes · orationi	υπομενοντεσ · τη , προσευ‿χη ·
13	instantes · necessitatibus	προσ καρτερουντεσ[6] · Ταισμνιασ[7] ·
	scōrum communicantes	των αγιων · κοινω νουντεσ[8] ·
	hospitalitatem secta·(n)tes ·	την · φιλοξενιαν · διωκοντεσ ·
14	Benedicite et nolite male	ευλογειταε[9] · και · μη · κατα
15	dicere · gaudere cum gauden	ρασθαι · χαιρειν · μετα · χε
	tibus flere cum	ροντων[10] · κλαιειν · μετα
16	flentibus · id ipsum in	κλαιοντων · το · αυτο · εισ ·

---

[1] παρακαλων. [2] εν τη εν τη παρακλησει. [3] κολλομενοι. [4] αλληλουσ. [5] δλληλουσ s. m. at λλληλουσ p. m.
[6] Marg. δον̄. [7] ταισ μνιαισ. [8] κοι:νουντεσ (νω above). [9] ευλογειται. [10] χαιροντων.

L. αλληλουσ · φρονουντεσ ·	vicem sentientes
μη · τα · υψηλα · φρονουντεσ ·	non alta sapientes
αλλα · τοισ · τα · πεινοισ · συν͜	sed humilibus con
απα͜γομενοι ·	sentientes ;
η[1] · γεινεσθαι · φρονειμοι · παρε ·	olite esse prudentes apud
17 αυτοισ · μεδενει[2] · κακον ·	vosmet ipsos · Nulli malum
αντικακ · ουαποδειδοντεσ ·	promalo reddentes
Προνο͜ου͜μενοι · καλα · ουμο	Providentes bona non so
νον · ενωπειον · του · $\overline{θυ}$ · αλλα ·	lum coram $\overline{do}$ · sed
κειενωπιον · των · $\overline{ανων}$ ·	etiam coram omnibus hominibus
18 ει · δυνατον · τοεξυμων · με	si fieri potest quod ex vobis est
τα · παντων · $\overline{ανων}$ · ιρηνευον	cum omnibus hominibus pacem ha
19 τεσ · Μη · εαυτουσ · εκδικουν	bentes · Non vosmet ipsos defen
τεσ · αγαπιτοι[3] · αλλα · δοτε	dentes karissimi sed date
τονον [π][4] · τηοργη · γεγραπται · γαρ ·	locum iræ · Scriptum est enim
εμοι · εκδεικησεισ · εγω · αντα	mihi vindictam · ego retri
20 ποδω · λεγει ; $\overline{κσ}$ · εαν · πεινλο ·	buam dicit $\overline{dns}$ · si esurierit
εκθροσ · σου · ψωμειζαι · αυτον ·	inimicus tuus · ciba illum ·
εαν · δειψα · ποτειζαι [pota] · αυτον [illum] ·	si sitit potum da illi ·
Τουτο · γαρ · ποιων · ανθρακασ ·	Hoc enim faciens carbones
πυροσ · σωρευσεισ · επι · την , κε	ignis congeres super ca
21 φαλην · αυτου · Μη · νει͜κω ·	pud ejus · Noli vinci
απο · του · κακου · αλλα · νεικα ·	a malo sed vince
εν · τω · αγαθω · το · κα͜κον ·	in bono malum ;
C. XIII 1 ασαισ[5] · εξουσειαισ · υπερ ·	[O]mnibus potestatibus subli
εχου͜σαισ · υποτασ͜εσται[6] ·	mioribus subtiti estote ·
Ου · γαρ · εστειν · εξουσια · ειμη ·	Non enim est potestas nisi
απο · $\overline{θυ}$ · αι · δε · ουσαι · απο$\overline{θυ}$	a$\overline{do}$ · Quæ autem sunt a$\overline{do}$

---

[1] Μη. [2] μηδενει. [3] αγαπητοι. [4] τοπον. [5] Πασαισ. [6] ὑποτασσεσθαι.

	Latin	Greek
CAP. XIII. v. 2	ordinate sunt Itaque	τεταγμεναι · εισειν · Ωστε ·
	qui resistit potesta	ο · αντειτασσομενοσ · τη · εξου
	ti · d̅i̅ ordinationi re	σια · τη · τουθ̅υ̅ · διαταγη · ανθεσ
	sistit · Qui autem resistunt ·	τηκεν · οι · δε · ανθεστηκο‿
	ipsi sibi damnationem adqui	τεσ · εαυτοι · σκριμα · λημψον
3	runt · Nam principes non	ται · Οι · γαρ · αρχοντεσ · ουκ
	sunt timori bono operi	εισειν · φοβοσ · τω · αγαθο[1] · εργω ·
	sed malo · Vis autem	αλλα · τω · κακω · Θελεισ · δαι
	nontimere potestatem ·	μη · φοβισθαι · την · εξουσιαν ·
	bonum fac et habebis	το · αγαθον · ποιει · ϗ εξεισ ·
4	laudem ex illa · d̅i̅ enim	επαινον · εξαυτησ · Θ̅υ̅ · γαρ ·
	minister est tibi inbo	διακονοσ · εστιν · εισ · το · αγα
	num · Si autem malum feceris	θον · εαν · δε · το · κακον · ποιησ ·
	time · Non enim sine causa	φοβου · ουγαρ · εικη · την · μα
	gladium portat · D̅i̅ enim mi	χαιραν · φορει · θ̅υ̅ · γαρ · δια‿
	nister est · Vindex	κονοσ · εστιν · εκδικοσ · τω
	malum facienti	το κακον · πρασσοντει ·
5	deoque subditi estote · Non solum	διο · ϋποτασσεσθαι · ουμονον ·
	propter Iram · Sed et propter	δια · την · οργην · αλλα · δια ·
6	conscientiam · Ideo	την · συδησειν[2] · Δια · τουτο ·
	enim · et tributa penditis mi	γαρ · και · φορουσ · τελειται · λει
	nistri enim d̅i̅ sunt · In	τουργοι · γαρ · θ̅υ̅ · εισειν · εισ ·
	hoc ipsum · pertinaciter ser	αυτο · τουτο · προσκαρτερουν
7	vientes · Reddite ergo omnibus	τεσ · αποδοτε · ουν · πασιν · τασ
	debita · Cui tributum tributum	οφειλασ · τω · τον · φορον · τονφο
	Cui vectigal vectigal · cui	ρον · τω · το · τελοσ · το · τελοσ · Τω ·
	timorem timorem · Cui	τον · φοβον · τον · φοβον · Τω · την ·
	honorem honorem	τε · ιμην · την · τειμην ;

[1] αγαθω.

[2] συνϊδησειν.

μ 8	ηδενει[1] · μηδ_εν · οφιλεται · ειμη ·	emini quicquam debeatis nisi
	το · αλληλουσ · α_γαπαν · Ο · γαρ · γα	ut in vicem diligatis qui enim dili
	πων · τον · ετερον · νομον · πεπλη	git · proximum legem in
9	ρωκεν · γεγραπται · γαρ · ου · μηχευ	plebit · Scriptum est enim non adul
	σεισ · ου · φονευσεισ · ου · κλεψεισ ·	terabis · non occides non furaberis ·
	ουκ · επιθυμησισ · και · ειτεισ ·	non concupisces et si quod est
	ετερα · εν · τολη · εν · τω · λογω · τουτω ·	aliud mandatum in hoc verbo
	ανακαιφαλαιουται · αγαπησεισ ·	recapitulatur · Diliges
	τον · πλησειον · σου · ωσ · εαυτον ·	proximum tuum tamquam te ipsum ·
10	Η · αγαπη · τω · πλησειω · κακον · ουκ ·	Dilectio proximi malum non
	εργαζεται · πληρωμα · δε · νομου ·	operatur · Plenitudo g° legis
11	η · αγαπη · ⁊Και · τουτο · ιδοντεσ[2] ·	est dilectio · Et hoc scientes
	τον · καιρον · οτει · ωρα · ημασ · ηδη ·	tempus quia hora est nos jam
	εξυπνουσ · ε_γερθηνε · Νυν · γαρ ·	de somno surgere · Nunc autem
	εγγυτερον · ημων · η · σωτηρια ·	propior est nostra salus
12	η · οτε · επιστευσαμεν · η · νυξ · προ_	quam cum credidimus · Nox pro
	εκο_ψεν · η · δε · ημερα · ηγγικεν ·	cessit dies autem adpropinquabit
	απυ · βαλωμεθα · ουν · τα · εργα · του ·	abitiamus ergo opera tene
	σκοτουσ · και ενδυσωμεθα ·	brarum · et induamus
13	τα · οπλα · του · φωτοσ · ωσ · εν ·	arma lucis sicut in
	ημερα · ευσ_χημωνωσ · περειπα_	die honeste ambu
	τησωμεν · μη · κωμωισ[3] · και · με	lemus · non in commessationibus
	θαισ · μη · κοιταισ · και · ασελγει	et ebrietatibus non in cubilibus et in
	αισ · μη · ερειδει · και · ζηλω ·	Pudititiis non in contentione et æmulatī ·
4	αλλεν · δυσασθαι · τον · κ̅υ̅ · ι̅υ̅ ·	sed induimini d̅n̅m̅ i̅h̅m̅
	χ̅υ̅ · τησ · σαρκοσ · προνοιαν · μη ·	x̅p̅m̅ · carnis curam ne
	ποιεισθαι · εν · επιθυμειαισ ·	feceritis in desideriis ·
1.	[Τ]ον[4] · δε · ασθενουντα · τη · πιστει ·	[I]nfirmum autem fide ·

[1] Μηδενει. [2] ιδοτεσ (ν above). [3] κωμοισ. [4] Τον.

	Latin	Greek
CAP. XIV.	assumite non in disceptatio	προσ λαμβανεσθαι·μη·εισ δια_
v. 2	ne cogitationum alius quid em	κρισεισ·δια_λογεισμον[1]·οσ·μεν·
	credit manducare omnia qui autem	π^{σ}ι·τευ_ει[2]·φαγε_ιν·παντα·οσ·δε·
	infirmus est holera manducet·	ασθενων·λαχανα·αισθειετω·
3	Qui manducat non manducantem	Ο·αισθειων·τον·μη·αισ_θει_οντα·
	non spernat·neque qui non	μη·εζον_θενειτω[3]·Ουδε·ο·μη
	manducat·manducantem ju	αισθει_ων·τον·αισθειοντα·κρι
	dicet · Ds enim illum as	νετω ; · Ο·θσ·γαραυτον·προσ
4	sumpsit · Tu quis es qui judicas	ελαβετο · Cυ·τισ·ει·ο·κρινων·
	alienum servum suo·	αλλοτριον·οι·κετην·τω·ιδειω·
	dno stat aut cadit stabit	κω·στηκι·η·πειπτει·σταθησεται·
	autem · Potens est enim ds statue	δαι·δυνατει·γαρ·οθσ·στη
5	re illum · Nam alius judicat	σαι·αυτον·οσ·μεν·κρινει·
	diem inter diem · Alius autem	ημεραν·παρ·ημεραν·οσ·δε·
	judicat omnem diem·	κρινει·πασαν·η_μεραν·
	Unus quisque in suo sensu ab	εκαστοσ·εν·τω·ιδιωνοει·πληρο
6	undet · Qui sapit diem	φορισθω · Ο φρονων·την·ημεραν·
	dno sapit et qui manducat	κω·φρονει·και·ο·αισ_θειων·
	dno manducat · Gratias enim a	κω·αισθειει·ευχαριστει·γαρ·
	git do et qui non manducat	τω·θω·και·ο·μη·αισθειων·
	dno non manducat·et gratias	κω·ουκ·αισθειει·και·εὐχα
7	agit do nemo enim	ρειστει·τω·θω·ουδεισ·γαρ·
	nostrum sibi vivit·et	ημων·εαυτω·ζη·και·
	nemo sibi moritur·	υυδεισ·εαυτω·αποθνησκει·
8	Sive enim vivimus do vivi	Єαντε·γαρ·ζωμεν·τω·κω·ζω
	mus sive morimur	μεν·εαντε·αποθνησκομεν·
	dno morimur·sive	κω·αποθνησκομεν·εαντε·
	ergo vivimus sive mo	ουν·ζωμεν·εαντε·ουν·απο

[1] διαλογεισμων. [2] πιστευει. [3] εξουθενειτω.

	Graece	Latine
v.	θνησκομεν·του·κυ·εσμεν·	rimur dni sumus
9	Εισ·τουτο·γαρ·χρσ·απεθανεν·	In hoc enim xps mortuus est
	Και·ανεστι·ινα·και·νεκρων·	Et resurrexit·ut et mortuorum
	και·ζωντων·κυριευση·	et vivorum dominetur
10	Cυ·δε·τι[1]·κρινεισ·τον·αδελ	u autem quid judicas fra
	φον·σου·ειν[2]·τωμη·αισθει‿	trem tuum innon manducan
	et	
	ειν·η·και·συ·τι·εξουθε‿	do·aut tu quare sper
	νεισ·τον·αδελ‿φον·σου[3]·	nis fratrem tuum inmanducando·
	Παντεσ·γαρ·παραστησομεθα·τω·	Oms enim asstabimus
11	βηματει·του θυ Γεγραπται·	ante tribunal di·scriptum est
	γαρ·ζω·εγω λεγει·κσ·ειμη·	enim·vivo ego dicit dns·quia
	εμοι·καμ‿ψει·παν·γονυ·και	mihi flectet omne genu·et
	εξομολο‿γησεται·πασα·γλωσ	confitebitur omnis lin
12	σα·τω·θω · Αρα·εκαστοσ·	gua do · Itaque unus quisque
	ημων·περι·εαυτου·λογον·	nrm prose rationem
13	αποδωσει[4] · Μη·κετει·ουν·	reddet · Non amplius ergo
	αλληλουσ·κρινωμεν·αλλα·	invicem judicemus·sed
	τουτο·κρινεται·μαλλον·το·μη·	hoc judicate magis·ne
	τηθεναι · Προσκομμα·	ponatis offensionem
	τω·αδελφω·η·σκαν‿δαλον·	fratri·vel scandalum
14	Οιδα·και·πεπέισ‿μαι·εν·κω·	Scio et confido in dno
	ιηυ·οτι·ουδεν·κοινον·διαυτου·	ihu quia nihil commune per ipsum·
	ειμη·τω·λογει‿ζομενω[5] · Τι·κοι	nisi ei qui æstimat quid commu
	νον·ειναι·εκεινω·κοινον·	ne esse · Illi commune est·
15	Ει·γαρ·διαβρωμα·αδελφοσ·	Si enim propter escam frater
	σου·λυπιται · Ουκ·ετει·κατα	tuus tristatur · Non jam secundum
	αγαπην·περι‿πατεισ · Μη·	caritatem ambulas · Noli
	τω·βρωματει·σου·εκει‿νον·	esca tua illum

[1] + γαρ (post τι). [2] ειση. [3] του. [4] αποδωσει. [5] λοιγειζομενω.

		pro quo
CAP. XIV.	perdere propter quem xps	απολλ_υειν · υπερ · ου · χρσ ·
v. 16	mortuus est · Neblaspheme	απεθανεν · μη · βλασφημεισ_
	tur bonum vestrum	θω · ημων · το αγαθον ·
17	non est enim regnum di	ου · γαρ · εστιν · ηβασιλια · του · θυ ·
	esca et potus · sed	βρω_σεισ · και · ποσεισ · αλλα ·
	justitia et pax · Et	δικαιοσυνη · και · ιρηνη · και ·
18	gaudium in spu sco · Quienim	χαρα · εν · πνι · αγιω · Ο · γαρ ·
	inhoc servit xpo	εν · τουτω · δουλευων · χρω ·
	placet do · et proba	ευρεστοσ[1] · τω · θω · και · δοκι
	tus est hominibus ·	μοσ[2] τοισ · ανοισ ·
19	Itaque quæ pacis sunt secte	Αρα · ουν · τα · τησ · ιρηνησ · διω
	mur · et quæ ædificati	κομεν · και · τα · τησ · οικοδο_
	onis ininvicem custodi	μησ · τησ · εισ · αλληλουσ · φυ_
20	amus · Noli propter es	λαξωμεν · Μη · ενεκεν · βρω
	cam · destruere opus	ματοσ · καταλυ_ειν · το · εργον · του ·
	di · Omnia quidem munda · sed	θυ · Παντα · μεν · καθαρα · αλλα
	malum homini per offensi	κακον · τω · ανω · τω · δια · προσκομ
21	onem manducanti · Bonum est	ματοσ · αισ_θει_νοντι · καλον ·
	nonmanducare carnem · Neque	το · μη · φαγιν · κρεα · Μη · δε ·
	bibere vinum · neque inquo	πινειν · οινον · Μη · δε · εν · ω ·
	frater tuus offendit · aut	ο · αδελφοσ · σου · προσκοντει[3] · η ·
	scandalizatur · aut infirmatur ·	σκανδαλει_ζεται · η · ασ_θενει ·
22	tu fidem tenes penes temet ipsum	Cυ · πιστιν · εχει[4] · κατασ · εαυτω ·
	habe coram do · Bea	εχαι · ενωπιον · του · θυ · Μακα
	tus qui non judicat semet ipsum	ριοσ · ο · μη · κρινων · εαυτον
23	in quo probat · Qui autem dis	εν · ω · δοκιμα_ζει · Ο · δε · δια
	cernit simanducavit	κρινον_μενοσ[5] · εαν · φαγη ·
	damnatus est · Quia non ex	κατακε_κρειται · οτι · ουκ εκ

[1] ευραστοσ. [2] δοκιμοισ. [3] προσκοπτει. [4] εχεισ. [5] διακρινομενοσ.

IV.	πιστεωσ · Παν · δε · ο · ουκ ·	fide · Omne autem qd nonest
	εκ · πιστεωσ · αμαρτια · εστιν[1] ·	exfide peccatum est ·
XV. 1	Ο φειλομεν · δε · ημησ · οι · δυνατοι ·	[D]ebemus autem nos firmiores
	τα · ασθενηματα · των · αδυνατων ·	imbecillitates infirmorum
	βασταζιν · και · μη · εαυτουσ[2] ·	sustinere · et non nobis metipsis ·
2	αρεσκον · εκαστοσ · μων[3] · τω ·	placere · unusquisque vrm
	πλησειον · αρεσκετω · εισ · το · αγαθον ·	proximo suo placeat inbonum
3	προσ · οι · κοδομην · και · γαρ · χρσ ·	ad ædificationem · Et enim xpc
	ουκ · εαυτω · ηρεσεν · αλλα · καθωσ ·	non sibi placuit · Sed sicut
	γεγραπται · Οι · ονει · δεισμοι · των ·	scriptum est · Improperia
	ονει · δει‿ζοντων · σε · επεπεσαν ·	improperantium tibi · ceciderunt
4	επεμαι · Οσα · γαρ · προσε · γραφη ·	super me · Quecumque enim scripta sunt
	εισ · την · ημητεραν · διδασκαλιαν ·	ad nostram doctrinam
	εγραφη · ινα · δια · τησ · υπομο	scripta sunt · ut per patienti
	νησ[4] · και · τησ · παρακλησεωσ · των ·	am et consolationem
	γραφων · την · ελπειδα · εχωμεν ·	scripturarum · spem habeamus ·
5	ο δε · θσ τησ υπομονησ · και · τησ ·	Ds autem patientiæ et
	παρακλεσεωσ[5] · δωη · υ‿μειν · το	solatii det vobis
	αυτο · φρονειν · εν · αλληλοισ ·	id ipsum sapere in alterutrum
6	κατα · ιν · χν[6] · ϊνα · ομοθυμαδο	secundum ihm xpm · ut unani
	νεν · εν · ει · σ‿τοματι · δοξαζηται ·	mes uno ore honorificetis
	τον · θν · και · πρα · του · κυ · ημων ·	dm et patrem dni nri
7	ιυ · χυ · Διο · προσ‿λαμβανεσ	ihu xpi · Propter qd suscipi
	θαι · αλληλουσ · καθωσκαι[7] · χσ ·	te invicem · sicut et xpc
	προσε‿λαβετο · υμασ · εισ · δοζαν[8] · (glam)	susce pit vos in honorem
8	του θυ · λεγο[9] γαρ · ιν · χν ·	di · Dico enim ihm xpm
	διακονον · γενεσ‿θαι · περιτο	ministrum fuisse circumcisio
	μησ · υπερ · αληθειασ θυ ·	nis propter veritatem di

[1] *Circiter quinque lineas relinquit vacuas Cod. Boern. post caput* XIV. [2] εαυτοισ. [3] υμων. [4] ὑπομονησ. [5] παρακλησεωσ. [6] χν ιν. [7] + ο (*ante* χρσ). [8] δοξαν. [9] λεγω.

CAP. XV.	ad confirmandas promissi	εισ·το·βαιβαιωσαι·τασ·επαγ
v. 9	ones patrum · Gentes autem	γελιασ[1]·των·πατερων · Τα·δε·εθνη·
	super miserda honorare	ὑπερ·ελαιουσ·δοξασαι·τον·
	dm·sicut scriptum est·propter hoc	θν·καθωσ[2]·γεγραπται·Δια·τουτο·
	confitebor tibi ingentibus	εξομολογησομαι·Σοι·εν·εθνε
	et nomini tuo cantabo·	σειν ; Και·τω·ονοματι·σου·ψαλω[3]·
10	et iterum dicit·laetamini	και·παλειν·λεγει·εὐ φρανθηται·
	gentes cum plebe ejus·	εθνη·μετα·του·λαου·αυτου·
11	et iterum dicit·laudate	και·παλειν·λεγει·αινεται·τον
	dnm oms gentes·et conlau	κν·παντα·τα·εθνη·και·επαινε
	date eum oms populi·	σατε·αυτον·παντεσ·οι·λαοι·
12	et rursus esaias ait·erit	και·παλε‿ιν·ησαιασ·λεγει·εσται·
	radix jesse·et qui ex sur	η·ριζζα·του·ιεσσε·και·ο·ανιστα
	get regere gentes·ineum	μενοσ·αρχην·εθων[4]·επαυτω·
13	gentes sperabunt·ds autem	εθνη·ελ‿πιουσιν·Ο·δε·θσ·τησ·
	spei·repleat vos	ελπιδοσ·πληροφορησαι·υμασ·
	omni gaudio·et pace incredendo	παση·χαρα·και·ρηνη[5]·
	ut habundetis inspe	εισ·το·περισσευειν·υμασ·τη·ελπιδει· (spe)
	et virtute spiritus sancti·	(in) εν δυναμει·πνσ·αγιου·
14	[Confido] autem et ipse ego de	π επισμαι[6]·δε·και αυτο[7]·εγω·περι·
	vobis fratres · Quom pleni estis	υμων·αδελ‿φοι[8]·οτι·μεστοι·εσται·
	caritate·et repleti·om	αγαπησ·και·πεπληρωμενοι·πα
	ni scientia·ut invicem possi	πασησ[9]·γνωσεωσ·αλληλουσ·δυνα
15	tis monere · Audatius	μενοι·νου‿θετειν · Τομη‿ροτερον·
	autem scripsi vobis fr‿s·ex parte	δε·εγραψα·υμιν·αδελφοι·απο
	tanquam · Immemoriam vos re	μερουσ·ωσ·επαναμιμ‿νησ
	vocans · Propter grati	κων·υμασ·δια·την·χα
	am quæ data est mihi a	ριν·την·δοθεισαν·μοι απο[10] τȣ

[1] επαγγελειασ. [2] Καθωσ (Κλθωσ *p.m.*). [3] ψαλω τω ονοματι σου. [4] εθνων.
[5] ϊρηνη. *Nullo spatio relicto.* [6] Πεπισμαι. [7] αυτοσ. [8] Δδελφοι. [9] πασησ. [10] υπο (*pro* απο).

16	θυ · εισ · το · γενεσθαι · με · λειτουρ	do ut sim servi
	γον · χυ · ιυ · εισ · τα · εθνην[1] ·	ens xpo ihu ingentibus ·
	Ιερουργουντα[2] · το ευαγγελιον · του θυ ·	sci ficans evangelium di ·
	ινα · γενηται · η · προσ · φορα · των · εθ	ut fiat oblatio genti
	νων · ηγιασμενη · εν · πνι · αγειω ·	um sanctificata in spu sco ·
17	εχω · ουν · την[3] · καυχησην · εν · χρω ·	Habeo igitur gloriam in xpo
18	ιυ · τα · προσ · τον · θν · Ου · γαρ · τολ	ihu ad dm · Non enim au
	μησω · τι · ειπειν · ων · ου κατηρ	deo aliquid loqui eorum quæ non
	γασατο · ο · χσ · δι · εμου · εισ ὑπα	efficit xps per me in oboedi
	κοην[4] · εθνων · λογω · και · εργω ·	entia gentium verbo et factis
19	εν · δυναμει · αυτου · Cημειὼν ·	invirtute ejus · Signorum
	και · τερατων · εν · δυναμει · πνσ[5] ·	et prodigiorum in virtute sps
	αγιου · ωσ · τε · πεπληρωσθαι ·	sci · ita ut repleverim
	απο ιερουσαλημ · μεχρι · του ·	abierusalem usque ad
	ιλλυρικου · και κυκλω · το · ευαγ	illiricum et in circuitu evan
20	γελιον · του · χρυ · Ουτωσ · δε ·	gelium xpi · Sic autem
	φειλο · τιμοιμαι · εναγγελειζεσ	cupide desideravi evangeliza
	θαι · οπου · ουκ · ωνομασθη · ο ·	re · ubi non nominatus est
	χρσ · ινα · μη · επαλλοτριω · θε	xpc · Ut non supra alienum fun
21	μελειω · οικοδομω · αλλα · κα	damentum ædificarem · sed sic
	θωσ · γεγραπται · οισ · ουκ αναγ	ut scriptum est · Quibus non est nunti
	γελη · περι · αυτου · οψονται · και ; οι ·	atum deeo videbunt et qui
	ουκ · ακηκοασειν · συνη‿σουσιν ·	nonaudierunt intellegent
22	δι · ο · και · ενεκοπην · πολλακησ ·	propter quod et impediebar plurimum
	του · ελθειν · προσ · υμασ · απο	venire advos ex
	πολλων · αιτων · ωσανυν[6] ·	multis jam præcedentibus annis
23	νυν · ειδε · μη · κετειτοπον ·	nunc ergo ulterius locum non
	εχων · εν · τοισ · κλημασιν · τουτοισ ·	habens in regionibus his

---

[1] εθνη. [2] Ἱερουργουντα. [3] την. [4] ὑπακοην. [5] + αυτου (ante πνσ).
[6] ὡσανοῦν πόρευομαι. του ελθειν ὑμασ.

Latin	Greek
CAP. XV. desiderium autem habeo veniendi	επειποθειαν · δε · εχω · του · ελθειν ·
v. 24 ad vos · Sed cum proficiscar in	προσ · υμασ | · πορευομαι[1] · εισ · την ·
ispaniam spero in transitu ·	σπανιαν · ελπειζω · δια · πορευο
videre vos et avobis	μενοσ · θεασασθαι · υμασ · ϗαφυμων ·
deduci illuc si vobis	προπεμφθηναι[2] · εκει · εαν · υμων ·
primum ex parte fruitus fuero	πρωτον[3] · απομερουσ · ε̣ν̣ (μ) · πλησθω[4] ·
25 [N]unc igitur proficiscar iniero	ν νν[5] · δε · πορευομαι · εισ · ιερου
solimam ministrare scis	σαληε̣μ[6] · διακονησαι · τοισ · αγιοισ ·
26 probaverunt enim macedones	ευδοκησαν · γαρ · μακαιδονεσ ·
et achaici collationem aliquam	ϗ αχαι‿ακοι · μωνειαν[7] (ρ) · τινα ·
facere in pauperes scorum	ποιησασθαι · εισ · τουσ · πτοχουσ[8] ·
qui sunt in hierusalem	των · εν · ιερουσαλημ · αγειων ·
27 debitores enim eorum sunt	οφειλεται · γαρ · αυτων · εισειν ·
quo si spiritalium eorum	ει · γαρ · τοισ · πνευματικοισ · αυτων ·
participes factæ sunt gentes debent	εκοινω · ησαν[9] (ν) · τα · εθνη · οφιλουσειν ·
et in carnalibus ministrare	ϗ · εν · τουσ[10] · σαρκει‿κοισ · λειτουρ
28 eis · Hoc igitur	γησαι · αυτοισ · τουτο · ουν ·
cum consummavero et ad signa	αρα · επειτελεσασ · και · σφραγεισ ·
vero eis fructum hunc	αμενοσ · αυτοισ · τον · καρπον · τουτον ·
proficiscar pervos in ispani	απελευ‿σομαι · δι · υμασ · εισ · σπα
29 am · Scio enim quia ad	νειαν · γεινωσκω · γαρ · οτι · προσ ·
vos in abundantia benedicti	υμασ · ινπλε̣ροφορία[11] (η) · ευλογίασ ·
onis xpi veniam ·	χυ · ευλευ‿σομαι ·
30 bsecro autem vos frs per	π αρακαλω[12] · δε · υ‿μασ · αδελφοι ; δια ·
dnm ihm xpm et per	του · κυ · ημων · ιυ · χυ · και · δια · τησ
caritatem sps · ut sollicitudinem	αγαπε̣σ[13] (η) · του · πνσ · συναγονεισασ‿
animi · mihi in orationibus	θαι · μοι · εν · ταισ · προσευχαισ ·
31 vris ad dm ut liberer	υμων · προσ · τον · θν · ϊνα · ρισθω[14]

1 + απο πολλων αιτων ωσανουν (ante πορευομαι). 2 προπεμθιφθηναι. 3 πρωντον. 4 εμπλησθω. 5 νυν. 6 ιερουσαλημ. 7 νωνειαν. 8 πτωχουσ. 9 εκοινωνησαν. 10 τοισ. 11 εν πληροφορία. 12 Παρακαλω. 13 αγαπησ. 14 ρυσθω.

XV.	απο · των · απειθουντων : εν · τηϊου	ab infidelibus qui sunt In
	δαια · και · η · δωροφορια · μου ·	judea · et ut ministratio mea
	η · εν · ιερυσαλημ[1] · προσ_δεκτοσ ·	hierusalem acceptalis
32	γενηται · τοισ · αγειοισ · Ινα · εν ·	fiat scis ut in
	χαρα · ελθω · πρ°· σ[2] · ὑμασ · δια · θε	gaudio veniam ad vos per volun
	ληματοσ · χυ · ιυ · και · αναψυ	tatem xpi ihu · et refrige
33	χω · μεθυμων · Ο δε · θσ ·	tur vobiscum · Ds autem
	τησ · ιρηνησ · ητω · μετα · παντων ·	pacis sit cum omnibus
	υμων ·	vobis ·
XVI. 1	ν νισ_τημει[3] · ὑμειν · φοιβην ·	[C]ommendo vobis phoeben
	την · αδελφην · υμων · ουσαν ·	sororem nram quæ est
	διακονον[4] · τησ · εκκλησειασ ·	inministerio aecclesiae
2	τησ · εν · κενχρεαισ[5] · Ινα · προσδε	quæ est cenchris ut suscipi
	ξησθαι · αυτην · εν · κω · αξιωσ ·	atis eam indno digne
	των · αγειων · κ · παραστητε ·	scis · et assistatis
	αυτη · ενωαν · υμων · χρη_	ei in quocumque vestri indigu
	ζη πραγματει · Και · γαρ · αυτη ·	erit · et enim ipsa
	και · εμου · και αλλων · παρασ	astitit multis ·
	τατεισ · εγενετο ;	et mihi ipsi ·
3	σπασθαι[6] · πρισκαν · κ ακυλαν ·	alutate priscam et aquilam
	τουσ συνεργουσ · μου · εν · χρω ·	adjutores meos in xpo
	ιηυ · και · την · κατοικον · αυτων ·	ihu · Et domesticam eorum
4	εκκλησείαν · Οι · τινεσ · υπερ ·	aecclesiam qui pro
	τησ · ψυχησ · μου · τον · εαυτων ·	anima mea suam
	τραχηλον · υπεθηκαν · οισ · ουκ ·	suppo/suerunt cer/vicem quibus non
	εγω · μονοσ · ευχαρειστω ·	ego solus gratias ago
	αλλα και πασαι αι εκκλη	sed et cunctæ aeccle
	σειαι[7] των εθνων ·	siae gentium

---

[1] Ιερουσαλημ. [2] προσ. [3] Συνιστημει. [4] δι·ά·κονον. [5] κεν χρεαισ. [6] Ασπασθαι. [7] εκκλησειαι.

CAP. XVI. v. 5	Salutate epenetum	Ασπασθαι επαινετον τον
	dilectum meum qui est	αγαπητον μου · οσ εστιν
	primitivus asiæ in xpo ·	απαρχη τησ ασειασ εν χρω ·
6	Salutate mariam quæ mul	Ασπασθαι μαριαμ · ητεισπολ
	tum laboravit indno ·	λα εκοπειασεν ενυμιν ·
7	Salutate andronicum et	Ασπασθαι ανδρονικον και
	juniam cognatos meos	ιουνιαν τουσ συνγενεισ μου
	et concaptivos	και συναιχμαλωτουσ[1]
	meos · qui sunt nobiles	μου · οιτινεσ εισιν[2] επισημοι
	in apostolis · Qui et ante	εντοισ αποστολοισ · Τοισ προ
	me fuerunt in xpo ihu ·	εμου εν χρω ιυ ·
8	Salutate ampliatum	Ασπασθαι[3] αμπλιατον
	dilectum meum indno ·	τον αγαπητον εν[4] κω ·
9	Salutate urbanum coope	Ασπασθαι ουρβανον τον συνερ
	ratorem nrm indno · et stachin	γον ημων εν κω · ϗ · σταχυν
	dilectissimum meum	τον[5] αγαπιτον[6] μου[7]
10	Salutate apellen prol	Ασπασθαι απελλην τον δοκει
	bum in xpo	μον εν χρω
	Salutate eos qui sunt exari	Ασπασθαι τουσ εκτωναρι
11	stoboli · Salutate ero	στοβολου[8] · ασπασθαι ηρω
	d^{e}ianum cognatum meum	δειωνα τον συνγενη μου
	Salutate eos qui sunt ex nar	Ασπασθαι τουσ εκτων ναρ
	cissi qui sunt in dno ·	κεισσου τουσ οντασ εν κω
12	Salutate tryphenam et try	Ασπασθαι τρυφεναν και τρυ
	phosam laborantes in dno ·	φωσαν τασ κοπειωσασ εν κω
13	Salutate rufum electum	Ασπασθαι ρουφον τον εκλεκ
	in dno et matrem	τον εν κω και την μητερα
	ejus et meam	αυτου και εμου

---

[1] συν αιχμαλωτουσ. [2] εισειν. [3] Ασπασασθαι. [4] + μου (ante εν).
[5] – τον p.m. (habet super rasuram sec. man.) [6] αγαπητον. [7] fin. + εν κω. [8] αριστοβολοιν.

L. 4 ασπασθαι ασυνκριτον φλε	Salutate asincretum fle
γοντα · ερμην · πατροβαν · ερ	gonta · ermen · patrobam ·
μαν · καιτουσ συν αυτοισ	erman · et quicumque eis sunt
αδελφουσ ·	frs ·
5 ασπασθαι φιλολογον και ϊουνι	Salutate filologum · et ju
αν · νηρεαν · ϗ την αδελφεν[1]	liam · Nereum et sororem
αυτου · και ολιμπειδα[2] · και	ejus · et olimpiadem · et
τουσ συν αυτοισ παντασ αγει	qui cum eis sunt oms sanc
16 ουσ · ασπασθαι[3] αλλη λουσ	tos · salutate invicem ·
ενφειληματι αγιω	inosculo sco ·
17 αρακαλω[4] δευμασ αδελφοι ·	ogo autem vos frs
ασφαλωσ σκοπειται τουσ	diligenter observate eos
τασδειχοστασιασ · ϗ τα σκαν	qui dissensiones faciunt et
δαλα · παρατην διδαχην ·	scandala pter doctrinam
ην · ὑμεισ εμαθεται · λεγον	quam vos didicistis · dictis
τασ · η · ποιουντασ · και εκκλι	vel factis et decli
18 νατε απαντων · Ουγαρτοιουται[5]	nate abillis · hujusmodi enim
κω χρω ημων ου δουλευ	dno xpo nonservi
σουσειν · αλλα τη εαυτων	unt sed suo
κοιλια · καιλια[6] τησ χρηστο · λο	ventri et perdulces ser
γιασ εξαπατωσειτασ καρδιασ	mones seducunt corda
19 των ακακων · ηγαρ υπακοη	innocentium · oboedientia enim
ὑμον[7] εισ παντασ αφικετο	vestra in omnes divulgata est
χαιρω · ουν · εφυμιν · και · θελω ·	gaudeo igitur invobis · Etvolo
ὑμασ · σοφουσ · ειναι · εισ · το · αγα	vos sapientes esse inbo
θον · ακερεῦυσδε · εισ · το · κα	no et simplices inma
20 κον · Ο · δε θσ · τησ · ιρηνησ ·	lo · Ds autem pacis
συντρι ψει · τον · σαταναν · υπο	conterat satanan sub

[1] αδελφην. [2] ολυμπειδα. [3] Ασπασασθαι. [4] Παρακαλω δε ημασ. [5] Οι γαρ τοιουτοι. [6] και δια. [7] ὑμων.

CAP. XVI. pedibus vestris velociter·
v. 21 Salutat vos timotheus
adjutor meus · Etlucius
et iason·et sosipater
cogniti mei·et universæ
ecclesiæ xpi·
22 Saluto vos ego terti
ius · Qui scripsi epistolam hanc
23 indno · Salutat vos ga
ius hospes meus·et univer
sæ ecclesiæ · Salutat
vos erastus·arcarius
civitatis·et quartus
24 frater · Gratia dni
nri cum omnibus vobis·
25 i autem qui potens est vos ↄfirmare
juxta evangelium meum et prædi
cationem ihu xpi secundum revelati
onem mysterii temporibus æternis
26 taciti·quod nunc patefactum
est per scripturas prophetarum secundum
præceptum æterni di adoboedi
tionem fidei incunctis gentibus
27 cognito · Soli sapienti do per
ihm xpm honor et gloria
insæcula sæculorum·amen

τουσ·ποδασ·ὑμων·ενταχει·
Ασπαζεται·ὑμασ·τιμοθεοσ·
οσυνεργοσ·μου·και·λουκειοσ·
ϗ·ιασων·ϗ σωσει͜πατροσ·
οι·συνγενεισ·μου·ϗ·αι·εκκλη
σειαι·πασαι·του χυ·
Ασπαζομαι·υμασ·εγω·τερτει͜
οσ·ο·γραψασ·την·επιστολην·
εν·κω · Ασπαζεται·ὑμασ·γα
ἰοσ·οξενοσ·μου·και·ό·λαι
αι·εκκλησιαι · Ασπαζεται[1]·
ὑμασ·εραστοσ·ο·οι·κονομοσ·
τησ·πολεωσ·και·κου͜αρτοσ·
ο·αδελφοσ · Η·χαρ·ισ[2]·του·κυ
ημων·μετα·παντων·ὑμων·
αμην[3]

---

[1] – ασπαζεται (*habet supra, sec. man.*). [2] χαρεισ.
[3] >>>>> *Nullum spatium inter* αμην >>>>> *et* Προσ ρωμαιουσ Ετελεσθη.

Προσ Κορινθι
ουσ·αρχεται·α[1]·

P. I
V. 1 Παυλοσ κλη
τοσ·αποστολοσ·χυ·
ιηυ·δια·θεληματοσ·θυ·
και·σωσθενησ·ο·αδελφοσ·
2 τη·εκκλησεια·του·θυ·η·γειασ
μενοισ·εν·χρω·ιυ·τη·ουση·
εν·κορεινθω·κλητοισ·αγιοισ·
συν·πασιν·τοισ·επικαλουμενοισ·
το·ονομα·του·κυ·ημων·ιυ·χυ·
εν·παντι·τοπω·αυτων·και·
3 ημων·χαρισ·ὑμιν·και·ειρη
νη·απο θυ·πρσ·ημον[2]·και
4 κυ·ιυ·χρυ · Ευχαριστω·
τω·θω·μου·παντοτε·περι
μων·επι·τη·χαριτει·του·θυ
τη·δοθειση·υμιν·εν·χρο[3]·ιυ·
5 οτι·εν παντει·Επλουτισ‿θηται
εν·αυτω·ενπαντι·λογω·και
6 παση·γνωσει·καθωσ·τομαρ
τυριον·του·θυ·εβαιβαιωθη·
7 εν·υμιν·ωσ·τε·υμασ·μη·
υστερισ θαι[4]·εν·μηδενη·χα
ρισματι·απεκδεχομενουσ·
την·αποκαλ‿υψιν·του·κυ·ημον[5]·

Ad Corinthi
os Prior inc'

Paulus voca
tus apostolus xpi
ihu·pervoluntatem di
et sostenes frater
aecclesiæ di·sanctifica
tis in xpo ihu quæ est
corinthi·vocatis sanctis
cum omnibus invocantibus
nomen dni nri ihu xpi
in omni loco ipsorum et
nro · Gratia vobis et pax
a do patre nro·et dno
ihu xpo · Gratias ago
do meo semper pro
vobis ingratia di
quæ data est vobis in xpo ihu
qm inomnibus locupletati estis
in illo·in omni verbo et
in omni scientia·sicut testi
monium di confirmatum est
invobis · Ita ut vos non
indiegeatis·in ulla gra
tia expectantibus
revelationem dni nri

---

1 — ·α·   2 ημων.   3 χρω.   4 ὑστερεισθαι.   5 ημων.

CAP. I. v. 8	ihu xpo · qui et confirmavit vos	ιυ χυ · Οσ · και · βαιβαιωσει · υμασ
	usque infinem sine crimine in	αχρι · τελουσ · αν · εγκλητου[1] · εν ·
	adventu dni nostri	τη · παρουσεια · του · κυ · ημων ·
	ihu xpi	ιυ · χρυ ·
9	Fidelis ds per quem vocati	Πιστοσ · οθσ · υφου εκληθη
	estis insocietatem filii	ται · εισ · κοιμωνιαν[2] · του · υιου ·
	ejus · ihu xpi dni nri	αυτου · ιυ · χυ · του · κυ · ημων ·
10	Obsecro autem vos fratres	Παρά‿καλω · δε · υμασ · αδελφοι ·
	per nomen ihu xpi dni	δια · του · ονοματοσ · ιυ · χρυ[3] κυ
	nri · utidipsum dicatis	ημων · ινα · το · αυτο · λεγηται ·
	omnes · et non sint invobis	παντεσ · και · μη · η · εν · υμιν ·
	scismata · sitis autem per	σχισματα · Ητε · δε · κατηρτεισ‿
	fecti ineodem sensu	μενοι · εν · τω · αυτω · νοει ·
	et in eadem scientia	και · εν[4] · τη · αυτη · γνωμη ·
11	Revelatum est enim mihi de vobis	Εδηλωθη · γαρ · μοι · περι · υμων ·
	fratres mei ab his qui sunt chlo	αδελφοι · μου · υπο · των · χλο
	es · quod contentiones inter vos	ησ · οτι · ερειδεσ · εν · υμιν
12	sint · Hoc autem dico quia	εισειν · Λεγω · δε · τουτο · οτι ·
	unusquisque vrm dicit · Ego	εκαστοσ · υμον[5] · λεγει · εγο[6] ·
	quidem sum pauli · ego autem	μεν · ειμει · παυλου · εγο[7] · δε ·
	apollo · ego autem caeph · ego	απολλο[8] · Εγω · δε · κηφα · εγω ·
13	autem xpi · Divisus est xpc	δε · χρυ · Μεμερεισται · ο · χρσ ·
	Numquid paulus crucifixus est pro	Μη · παυλοσ · εσταυρωθη · υπερ ·
	vobis · aut in nomine pau	υμων · Η · εισ · το · ονομα παυ
	li baptizati estis ·	λου · εβαπτεισθη‿ται ·
14	Gratias ago do quod neminem	Ευχαρειστω · το[9] · θω · οτι · ουδενα ·
	vrm baptizaverim nisi crispum	υμων · εβαπτεισα · ειμη · κρισπον ·
15	et gaium · Utnequis dicat	κ̗ · γαιον · Ινα · μη · τισ · ειπη[10] ·

[1] αν εγκλητουσ. [2] κοινωνιαν. [3] + του (*ante* κυ). [4] — εν (*habet supra sec. man.*) [5] υμων. [6] εγω. [7] εγω. [8] απολλω. [9] τω. [10] — ειπη *et* — δε v. 16, *membranæ vitio, ut videtur.*

	baptizaverim	
P. I.	οτι · εισ · το·εμον · ονομα · εβαπτεισα ·	qd in nomine meo baptizati estis
16	Βεβαπτικα · δε · και · τον · στεφανα ·	Baptizavi autem et stephanæ
	οικον · Τολοιπον · ουκοιδα · ει	domum · Ceterum nescio si
17	τινα · εβαπτεισα · Ου · γαρ · απεστει	quem baptizaverim · Non enim mi
	λ ν[1] · μαι · ο · χσ βαπτιζιν · αλλευ_	sit me xpc baptizare · sed evan
	αγγελειζεσθαι · ουκ · εν · σοφεια	gelizare · Non in sapientia
	λογον · ῑνα · μη · κενωθη · ο · σταυ_	verbi utevacuætur crux
18	ροσ · τον · χρυ · Ο · λογοσ · γαρ · του[2] ·	xpi · Verbum enim
	σταυρου · τοισ · μεν · απολλυ	crucis pereuntibus quidem stulti
	μενοισ · Μωρεια · εστιν · τοισ · δε ·	tia est · His vero
	σωζομενοισ · δυναμεισ · θυ · εστιν · 7	quisalvi fiunt virtus di est ·
19	Γεγραπται · γαρ ; απολω · την · σοφιαν	Scriptum est enim · perdam sapientiam
	των σοφων · ϗ · την ; συνεσῖν · των · ασινετων[3]	sapientium · et prudentiam prudentium ·
20	αθετησο[4] · Που · σοφοσ · που · γραμματεὺσ ·	reprobabo ubi sapiens · ubi scriba ·
	Που · συν_ζητητησ · του · αιωνοσ ·	Ubi conquisitor saeculi
	τουτου · Ουχι · εμωρανεν · οθσ ·	hujus · Nonne stultam ds fecit
	την · σοφιαν · του · κοσμου · τουτου ·	sapientiam mundi hujus ·
	quia na	
21	Επει · δη[5] · εν · τη · σοφια · του · θυ · ουκ ·	Nam quia in sapientia di non
	εγνωο · κοσμοσ · δια · τησ · σοφιασ	cognovit mundus per sapientiam
	τον · θν · Ευδοκησεν · τω · θω · δια ·	dm · placuit do per
	τησ · μωρειασ · του · κηρυγματοσ ·	stultitiam predicationis
	σωσαι · τουσ · πιστευοντασ ·	salvare credentes
22	Επει · ιουδαιοι · σημια · αυτουσειν ·	Quoniam judæi signapetunt
	και · ελληνεσ · σοφιαν · ζητουσειν ·	et greci sapientiam quærunt ·
23	Ημισ · δε · κηρυσσόμεν · χν · εσταυ_	Nos autem prædicamus xpm cru
	ρωμενον · Ιουδαιοισ · μεν · σκαν	cifixum judæis quidem scan
	δαλον · εθνεσιν δε · μωριαν ·	dalum gentibus autem stultitiam
24	Αυτοισ · δε · κλητοισ · ιουδαιοισ ·	Ipsis autem vocatis judæis

[1] απεστειλεν. [2] γαρ ο του. [3] ασυνετων. [4] αθετησω. [5] Επει δὲ ἡ.

CAP. I.	atque grecis · xpm di virtutem	και · ελλησειν · χρν · θυ · δυν · μιν[1] ·
v. 25	et di sapientiam quia qd stultum est	και · θυ · σοφιαν · οτι · το · μωρον[2] ·
	di · sapientius est	του · θυ · σοφωτερον · εστιν · των ·
	hominibus · et quod infirmum est di	ανων · και · ο · ασθενεσ · του · θυ ·
	fortius est hominibus	ισχυροτερον · εστιν · των · ανων
26	Videte ergo vocationem	Βλεπεται · ουν · την · κλησιν ·
	vram fratres quia non multi	υμων · αδελφοι · Οτι · ουπολ
	sapientes secundum · carnem non multi	λοι · σοφοι · κατα · σαρκα · ου · πολλοι ·
27 ÷	potentes : non multi nobiles · sed quæ stulta sunt	ευγενεισ[3] · αλλα · τα · μωρα · του · deest
	mundi elegit ds · ut confundat sapientes	κοσμου · εξελεξατο · ο · θσ · Ινα ·
28	et infirma mundi elegit ds ut confundat fortia	κατα · ισχυνη · τα · ισχυρα · και ·
	et ignobilia et contempti	τα · αγενη · του · κοσμου · και · τα ·
	bilia elegit	εξουθενημηνα · εξελεξατο ·
	ds etquæ non sunt · ut ea quæ sunt	ο · θσ · τα · μη · οντα · Ινα · τα · οντα
29	destrueret · ut non glori	καταργηση · Ο · πωσ · μη · καυχη
	etur omnis caro coram	σεται · πασα · σαρξ · εν · ωπειον · (inconspectu)
30	illo · Ex ipso autem vos	του · θυ · Εξαυτου · δε · υμεισ ·
	estis in xpo ihu · qui factus	εσται · Εν · χρω · ιυ · Οσ · εγενηθη ·
	sapientia nobis a do · et justi	η · σοφία · ημην[4] · απο θυ · ϗ · διϗο
	tia · et scificatio · et redempti	συνη · ϗ · αγίασμοσ · ϗ · απολυτρω
31	o · utquemadmodum scriptum est · Qui	σεισ · Ινα · καθωσ · γεγραπται · ο · και
	gloriatur · in dno glorietur ·	χωμενοσ · εν · κω · καυχαρισθω[5] ·
CAP. II. 1	Et ego veniens ad vos frs · veni	Καγω, ελθων · προσ · υμασ · αδελφοι
	non in sublimitate sermonis aut sapi	ουκ · αθυπεροχην · λογου · η · σοφιασ
	entiæ · annuntians vobis testimonium	καταγγελλων · υμιν · του · αρτιριον[6] ·
2	di · Non enim judicavi scire me aliqd	του · θυ · Ουγαρ · εκρινα · ειδεναι · τι ·
	in vobis · nisi xpm ihm et hunc	εν · υμιν · ειμη · χρμ · ιημ[7] · ϗ · τουτον ·
3	crucifixum · Et ego ininfirmita	εσταυρωμενον · ϗ · εγω · εν · ασθε

[1] δυναμιν. [2] μερ μωρον. [3] αγανον *in margine.* [4] ημιν. [5] καυχασθω. [6] το μαρτυριον. [7] χν ιν.

C. II	νεια · ϗ · φοβω · ϗ τρομω · πολλο[1] ·	te et timore et tremore multo
v. 4	εγενομην · προσ · ὑμασ · ϗ ολογοσ ·	fui apudvos · et sermo meus
	μου · ϗ · το · κηρὑγμα · μου · ουκ · εν ·	et prædicatio mea non in
	πειθοισ · σοφιασ · αλλεν · αποδειξει ·	persuasione sapientiæ sed in ostensi
5	πνσ · ϗ · δυναιωσ · Ινα · η · πιστισ ·	one sps et virtutis · utesset fides
	ὑμων · μη · εν · σοφια[2] · ανων · αλλεν ·	vra non insapientia hominum sed in
6	δυναμει · θυ · σοφιαν · δε · λαλουμεν ·	virtute di ; Sapientiam autem loquimur
	εν · τοισ · τελιοισ · Σοφιαν · δε · ου[3] · αιωνοσ ·	inter perfectos · Sapientiam autem non scl
7	τουτου · των · καταργουμενων · αλ	hujus quæ destruitur · Sed
	λα · λαλουμεν · θυ · σοφιαν · εν · μυσ	loquimur di sapientiam in my
	τηρειω[4] · την · αποκεκρυμμενην ·	sterio absconditam
	Ην · προωρεισεν · ο · θσ προτων · αιω	quam predistinavit ds ante sae
8	νων · εισ δοξαν · ημων · Ην · ουδεισ ·	cula ingloriam nostram quam nemo
	των · αρχον_των · τουαιωνοσ · τουτου ·	principum hujus seculi ſsent
	εγνωσεν[5] · ει · γαρ · εγνωσαν · ουκαν ·	cognovit · Si enim cognovissent
	τον · κν · τησ · δοξεσ[6] · εσ_ταυρωσαν ·	numquam dnm gloriæ crucifixis
9	Αλλα · καθοσ[7] · γεγραπται[8] · αοφθαλ	Sed sicut scriptum est quod ocu
	μοσ · ουκ · ειδεν · ϗ ουσου · ουκ · (auris)	lus non vidit · nec auris
	ηκουσεν ϗ · επικαρδιαν · ανθρω	audivit · et in cor homi
	που · ουκ · ανεβη · α · ητοιμασεν ·	nis non ascendit · quæ pparavit
10	ο θσ · τοισ · αγαπωσιν · αυτον · Ημιν ·	ds diligentibus se · Nobis
	δε · απεκαλυψεν · ο · θσ · δια · του · πνσ ·	autem revelavit ds per spiritum
	αυτου · Το · γαρ · πνα · παντα · ερευνα ·	suum ; Sps enim omnia scrutatur
11	ϗ · ταβαθη · του · θυ · Τισ · γαρ · οιδεν ·	etiam alta di · Quis enim scit
	ανων · τα · του · ανου · ειμη · το · πνα	hominum quæ sunt hominis nisi sps
	το · εναντω · Ουτωσ · ϗ · τα · εν ·	qui in ipso est · Sic et quæ di
	το[9] · θω · ουδεισ · εγνω · ειμη · τοπνα ·	sunt · nemo cognovit nisi sps
12	του · θυ · Ημεισ · δε · ουτο · πνα · του · κοσ	di · Nos autem non spm mun

[1] πολλω. [2] σοφεια. [3] + του (hujus) (post ου). [4] μυστερειω (η). [5] γοδδισκ' in margine (sic etiam Rom. III. 5). [6] δοξησ. [7] καθωσ. [8] in αποκαλιψι ενοχ και ηλιασ (in margine). [9] τω.

CAP. II.	di hujus accepimus·sed	μου·τουτου·ελαβομεν·αλλα·
	spm qui ex do est·ut sciamus	το·πνα·το·εκτου·θυ·Ϊνα·ϊδωμεν·
	quæ a do donata sunt nobis	τα·υπο·του·θυ·χαρισθεντα·ημειν·
v. 13	quæ et loquimur non in doctrina	ϗ·λαλουμεν·ουκ·εν·διδακτοισ·
	humanæ sapientiæ·verbis	ανθρωπεινησ·σοφεῖασ·λογουσ·
	sed in doctrina sps · Spiritali	αλλεν·διδακτοισ·πνσ · Πνευμαται
	bus spiritalia comparantes	κοισ[1]·πνευματεικα·συνκρινομεν[2]
14	Animalis autem homo non percipit ea quæ	Ψυχει·κοσ·δε·ανοσ·ου·δεχεται·τα
	sunt sps di · Stultitia enim illi	του·πνσ·του·θυ·Μωρία·γαρ·αυτω
	est·et non potest scire·quo	εστιν·ϗ·ου·δυναται·γνωναι·οτι·
	spiritaliter judicatur	πν·υματικοσ[3]·ανακρινεται·
15	Spiritalis autem dijudicat omni	Οδε·πνευματικοσ[4]·ανακριναι[5]·παν
	a · Ipse autem anemine judi	τα·αυτοσ·δε·υπο·υδενοσ·ανα
16	catur · Quis enim cognovit sensum	κρινεται[5]·Τισ·γαρ·εγνω·νουν·
	dni qui instruat eum · Nos	κυ·οσ·συνβ·ιβασαι·αυτων[6], ημεισ
CAP. III. 1	autem sensum dni habemus·et ego fra	δε·νουν·κυ·εχομεν·καγο[7]·αδελ
	tres non potui loqui	φοι·ουκ·ηδυνηθην·λαλησαι·
	vobis quasi spiritalibus·sed quasi	υμιν·ωσ·πνευματεικοισ·αλλωσ·
	carnalibus quasi parvulis in xpo	σαρκαικοισ[8]·ωσ·νηπειοισ·εν·χρω·
2	lac vobis potum dedi et non escam·	γαλα·υμασ·εποτεισα·ϗ·ου·βρω
	Nondum enim poteratis·sed neque	μα·ου·πω·γαρ·εδυνασ·αλουδε[9]·
3	adhuc quidem potestis · Adhuc enim	ετεινυν·δυνασθαι·ετει·γαρ·εσ
	estis carnales·cum enim sit inter vos	ται·σαρκινοι·Ό·που·γαρ·εν·ημιν·
	zelus et contentio·et dissensiones	ζελοσ[10]·ϗ·ερεισ·ϗ διχοστασειαι·
	nonne carnales estis·et secundum ho	ουχει·σαρκεινοι·εσται·και κατα·αν
4	minem ambulatis · Cum enim quis	θρωπον·περιπατειτε · Οταν·γαρτισ
	dicit·ego quidem sum pauli·	λεγε[11]·Εγω·μεν·ειμει·παυλου·
	alius autem ego apollo·nonne ho	ετεροσ·δε·εγω·απολλω·Ουχι·αν

[1] πνευματεικοισ. [2] συνκρρινομεν. [3] πνευματικωσ. [4] πνευματεικοσ. [5] ανακρεινει. [6] συνβιβασει αυτον. [7] κα γω. [8] σαρκεικοισ. [9] εδυνασθαι αλλουδε. [10] ζηλοσ. [11] λεγη.

III 5 θρωποι εσται · Τισ · ουνεστιν · απολ
λω · Τισ δε παυλοσ · Διακονοι · δι
ων · επιστευσατε · ϗ εκαστω · ωσ
6 ο κ̄σ · εδωκεν · Εγωεφιτευσα[1] · απολ
λω · εποτισεν · αλλα · ο θ̄σ · η · υξανεν ·
7 Ωστε · ουτε · ο · φυτευων · εστιν · τι ·
ουτε · ο · ποτειζον · αλλω[2] · αυξανων ·
θ̄σ[3]

Vide pag. 39. Defuit folium in Autographo: nam utrobique et hic et 39, et 94: par est spatium. Nec vero exscriptus est ex Cod. Claromontano [sic]: *quia et iste et Germanensis utroque loco integer est.* R. B.

mines estis · Quis ergo est apol
lo · quis vero paulus? Ministri ejus
cui credidistis · et unicuique sicut
dn̄s dedit · Ego plantavi apollo
rigavit · sed d̄s incrementum dedit
Itaque neque qui plantat est aliquid
neque qui rigat · sed qui īmentū dat
8 d̄s · Qui plantat autem et
qui rigat unum sunt
Unusquisque autem pro
priam mercedem accipiet
secundum suum laborem
9 D̄i enim sumus adjutores
d̄i agrigultura estis
d̄i aedificatio estis
10 Secundum gratiam quæ
data est mihi ut sapiens
architectus fundamentum
posui · Alius autem superaedificat
Unusquisque autem videat
quomodo super aedificet
11 Fundamentum enim aliud nemo
potest ponere preter id quod
positum est quod est xp̄c ih̄s
12 Si quis autem sup̄ aedificaverit supra
fundamentum hoc aurum argentum
lapides preciosus · ligna fenum
13 stipulam uniuscujusque opus

[1] εφυτευσα. [2] ποτειζων αλλο. [3] deest in græco (*in margine*).
[4] *Hoc spatium prorsus vacuum relinquit scriptor Codicis Boerneriani.*

CAP. III. manifestum erit·dies enim dni
declarabit·quia inigne revela
bitur·et uniuscujusque opus q[a]le sit
v. 14 ignis probabit · Si cujus opus manserit
qd sup aedificavit mercedem accipiet
15 Si cujus opus arserit detrimentum
patietur · Ipse autem salvus
erit·sic tamen quasi per ignem
16 Nescitis quia templum di estis et
sps di habitat in vo
17 bis·siquis templum di viola
verit·disperdet illum ds·templum enim
di scm est·quod estis
18 vos · Nemo vos sedu
cat·si quis videtur sapiens esse inter
vos in seculo hoc·stultus
fiat ut sit sapiens
19 Sapientia enim mundi hujus
stultitia est apud dm · Scriptum est
enim · Comprehendam sapientes
20 in astutia eorum · Et iterum·
Dns novit cogitationes
sapientium·quo vanæ sunt
21 Itaque nemo glorietur in ho
mine · Omnia enim vestra sunt
22 sive paulus·sive apollo·sive
cephas·sive mundus·sive vita sive
mors·sive presentia·sive futu

οικει·εν·ῦ
μιν·Ειτισ·τον·ναον·τȣ·θυ·φθει
ρει·φθειρει·αυτον·ο·θσ·Ο γαρ·ναοσ·
του·θυ·αγειοσ·εστιν·οιτιν·εσε(σ)·ται[1]
υμισ · Μηδεισ·εαυτον·εξαπατα
τω·Ειτισ·δυκει·σοφοσειναι·εν·
υμιν·εν·τω·αιωνι·τȣτω·Μοροσ[2]·
γενεσθω·Ινα·γενεται[3]·σοφοσ·
Η·γαρ·σ(ο)·φια[4]·τȣ·κοσμου·τουτου·
μωρεια·παρα·θω·εστιν·γεγ·(α)ρπται[5]·
γαρ·αρασσομενοσ·σοφυσ[6] εν
τη·πανȣργει·αυτων·ȣ·παλειν·
κσ·γινωσκει·τουσ·διαλογισμȣσ·
των·σοφων·οτι·εισειν (sunt)·ματαιοι (vanæ)
Ωστε·μηδεισ·καυχασθο[7]·εν·ανθρω
πω[8]·παντα·γαρ·υμων·εστειν·
ειτε·παυλοσ·ειτε·απολλω·ειτε·
κηφασ·ειτε·κοσμοσ·ειτε·ζωη·ειτε
θανατοσ·ειτε·ενεσ‿τωτα·ειτε·με

---

[1] οιτιν εσεσται. [2] μωροσ. [3] γενηται. [4] σοφια. [5] γεγραπται. [6] Δρασσομενοσ σοφουσ. [7] καυχασθω. [8] ανθωπω.

C. III. v. 23 λοντα · παντα · δι · υμων · Ὑμεισ ·	ra · Omnia enim vra sunt · Vos
δε · χυ · χσ · δε · θυ ·	autem xpi · xpc autem di
C. IV. 1 Ουτωσ · ημασ · λογιζεσθω · ανοσ · ωσ ·	Sic nos existimet homo ut
ὑπερετασ · χυ · ϗ · οικονομουσ ·	ministros xpi et dispensatores
2 μυστηριων[1] · τοὺ · θυ · ω δε λοιπον ·	mysteriorum di ; · Hic jam
ζητητε · εν · τοισ · οικονομουσ[2] · Ινα ·	quæritur inter dispensatores ut
3 τισ · πιστοσ · ευρεθη · Εμοι · δε · εισ ·	quis fidelis inveniatur · Mihi autem pro
ελαχιστον · εστιν · Ινα · ὑφὑμων ·	minimo est ut a vobis
ανακριθω · Η · υπο · ανθρωπεινησ ·	judicer · aut ab humano
ημερασ · αλλȣ̓δεμαυτον · ανα	die · sed neque me ipsum ju
4 κρεινω · ουδεν · γαρ · εμαιτο · σιν	dico · Nihil enim mihi consci
ȣδα[3] · αλλουκ · εν · τουτω · δε · δι_και	us sum · sed non in hoc justificatus
ωμαι · ὁ · δε · ανακρινων · μαι ·	sum · qui autem judicat me
5 κσ · εστιν · Ωσται · μη · προκαιȣ[4]	dns est · Itaque nolite ante tempus
τι · κρινετε · εωσαν · ελθη · ο · κσ ·	aliqd judicare · donec veniat d
ϗ · φωτεισει · τα · κρυπτα · τȣ · σκο	et inluminet abscondita tenebra
τουσ · ϗ · φανερωσει · τασ · βουλασ ·	rum · et manifestabit consilia
τω[5] καρδιων · ϗ τοτε · ο · επαι	cordium · Et tunc laus
νοσ · γενησεται · εκαστω · αποτȣθυ ·	erit unicuique a do
6 Ταυτα · δε · αδελφοι · μετα · σχη	Hæc autem fratres transfigu
ματισα[6] · εμαυτον · ϗ απολλω ·	ravi in me ipsum et apollo
δι · ὑμασ · Ινα · εν · ημειν · μαθη	propter vos · ut in nobis disca
τε · Μη · ὑπερ · ο · γεγραπται · ινα ·	tis ne supra quod scriptum est ut
μη · εισ · κατα · του · ενοσ · φυσειωνσ_	non unus adversus alterum infle
7 θαι · κατα · του · ετερου · Τισ · γαρ ·	tur pro alio ; Quis enim
σε · δια · κρινει · τι · δε · εχεισ · ο · ουκ	te discernit · quid autem habes qd non
ελαβεσ · ει · δε · και · ελαβεσ · τι ·	accepisti · si autem accepisti · quid
καυ_χασαι · ωσ · μη · λαβων ·	gloriaris quasi non acceperis

---

[1] μυτηριων. [2] οικονομοισ. [3] εμαυτω συνουδα. [4] καιρου. [5] των. [6] μετασχηματισα.

	Latin	Greek
CAP. IV. v. 8	Jam saturati estis jam	Ηδη · κεκορεσμενοι · εσται · ηδη ·
	divites facti estis · Sine nobis	επλουτησετε[1] · Χωρισ · ημων ·
	regnatis · et utinam	εβασειλευσαται · ϗ · οφελον ·
	regnaretis · ut et nos	εβασαιλευσαται[2] · Ινα · ϗ · ημεισ ·
	vobicum regnaremus	υμιν · σινβασειλευσωμεν[3] ·
9	Puto enim ds nos aposto	Δοκω · γαρ · οθσ · ημασ · τȣσ · αποσ
	los novissimos ostendit [ctaculum	τολουσ · αισχατουσ · απεδιξεν[4] ·
	tamquam morti destinatos quo spe	ωσ · επι · θανατι · ȣ[5] · Οτι · θεατρον ·
	facti sumus huic mundo et	εγενηθημεν · τωκοσμω · και ·
	angelis et hominibus ·	αγγελοισ · καιανθρωποισ ·
10	Nos stulti propter xpm vos autem	Ημεισ · μωροι · δια χν · Ϋμεισ · δε ·
	prudentes in xpo · nos in	φρονιμοι · εν · χρω · Ημεισ · αεθε
	firmi · vos autem fortes · vos	νεισ[6] · Ϋμεισ · δε · ισχὺροι · ὑμεισ ·
	nobiles · nos autem ignobiles	εν · δοξοι · ημεισ · δε · ατειμοι ·
11	usque in hanc horam et esurimus	Εωσ · αργει[7] · ωρασ · ϗ · πεινωμεν ·
	et sitimus et nudi	ϗ · δειψωμεν ϗ γιμνι_τεὺ_
	sumus et colaphizamur	ομεν[8] · ϗ κολαφειζομεθα ·
12	et instabiles sumus et lobora	ϗ αστατυὺμεν · ϗ κοπειω_
	mus · operantes propriis	μεν · εργα_ζομενοι · ταισ · ιδι
	manibus · Maledicimur	αισ · χερσειν · Λοιδορουμενοι[9] ·
	et benedicimus · persecutionem	ϗ ευλογουμεν · Διω_κομε
13	patimur · et sustinemus · Blas	νοι · καὶ ανεχομεθα · Βλασ
	phemamur · et obsecramus	φημουμενοι · παρακαλȣμεν ·
	Tamquam purgamenta hujus mundi	Ωσ · περικαθαρματα · του · κομου[10] ·
	facti sumus omnium pipsi	εγενηθημεν · παντων · περιψη
14	ma usque adhuc · Non ut confundam	μα · εωσ · αρτει · Ουκ · εντρεπων ·
	vos hæc scribo · sed ut	υμασ · ταυτα · γραφο[11] · αλλωσ ·
	filios meos carissimos mo	τεκνα · μου · αγαπηταν · ουθε

[1] επλουστησατε. [2] εβασειλευσαται. [3] συνβασειλευσωμεν. [4] απεδιζεν *marg. sec. manu.* [5] επι θανατι ουσ. [6] Υ.μεισ ασθενεισ. [7] αρτει. [8] γυμνιτευομεν. [9] Λοδορουμενοι. [10] κοσμον. [11] γραφω.

· Εαν · γαρ · μὺριοὺσ · παιδα	neo · Si enim · x · milia peda
γουσ · εχηται · ενχρω · αλ	gogos habeatis in xpo sed
ν · πολλουσ · πατερασ · Εν · γαρ ·	non multos patres · Nam in
ω · ιυ · Δια · τοὺ · εὺαγγελιοὺ[1] ·	xpo ihu perevangelium
ω · ὺμασ · εγεννησα · Παρακαλο[2]	ego vos genui · Obsecro ita
· ὺμασ · Μειμηται · μοὺ · γεινεσ	que vos · Imitatores mei esto
ι · Δια · τοὺτο · επε · ψα · ὺμην[3] ·	te · Ideo misi advos
ειμοθεον · Οσ · εστιν · τεκνον ·	timotheum · qui est filius
ον · αγαπητον · ϗ · πιστοσ · εν κω ·	meus karissimus et fidelis in dno
)σ · ὺμασ · αναμνησει · τασ · οδουσ ·	Qui vos admonebit vias
ιοὺ · τασ · εν · κω · ιηὺ · καθοσ[4] · παν	meas · quæ sunt in dno ihu sic u
ταχου · ενπαση ; εκκλησεια · διδασκο[5]	bique in omni aecclesia doceo
Ωσ · μη · ερχομενου · μου ·	Tamquam non venventurus sim
προσ · υμασ · εφυσειωθησαν ·	ad vos inflati sunt
τινεσ · Ελεὺσομαι · δε · ταχαιωσ	quidam · Veniam autem
προσ · ὺμασ · εαν · οκσ · θηλησῃ[6]	advos si dns voluerit ·
ϗ · γνωσομαι · ουτον · λογον ·	et cognoscam nonverbum
ιυτων · των · πεφυσειωμενον[7] ·	eorum qui inflati sunt
λλα · την · δυναμιν · οὺ · γαρ · εν · λο	sed virtutem · Non enim in ser
ω · η · βασιλεια · του θυ · αλλα · εν	mone est regnum di sed in
ναμει · Τι · θελεται · εν · ραβδω	virtute · Quid vultis in virga
θω · προσ · υμασ · Η[8] · ναγαπη ·	veniam advos · an incaritate
νεὺματι · τεπραοτητοσ ·	et spu mansuetudinis ·
λοσ[9] · ακουεται · εν · ὺμιν · πορ	[O]mnino auditur inter vos fornica
ια · ϗ · τοι · αυτη · πορνία · ητισ ·	tio · et talis fornicatio qualis
δε · εν · τοὺσ[10] · εθνεσιν · ωστε ·	nec inter gentes · ita ut
ναικα · τοὺ · προ · εχειν · τινα ·	uxorem patris habeat aliquis ·
· ὺμεισ · πεφυσειωμενοι · εσται ·	Etvos inflati estis ·

---

caput paginæ : φιλοσοφια φισικη εθικη λογικη nos generat mater generamus nos quoque matrem
[1] εναγγειον. [2] παρακαλω. [3] επεμψα ὺμιν. [4] καθωσ. [5] διδασκω. [6] θελησῃ. [7] πεφυσειωμενων, cf. Matthæi *in loc.* [8] η εν. [9] Ολῶσ. [10] τοισ.

	Latin	Greek
CAP. V.	et non potius luctum · habuistis ut	ϗ ουμαλλον · επενθησαται · Ινα ·
	tollatur demedio vestrum qui hoc o	αρθη · εκμεσου · ὑμων · ο · το · ερ
v. 3	pus fecit · Ego equidem	γον · τουτο · ποιησασ · Εγωμεν · γαρ ·
	ut absens corpore · psens autem	ωσ · απων · τω · σωματι · παρων · δε
	spu · Jjam judicavi ut presens	το · πνι[1] · Ηδη · κεκρικα · ωσ · παρων ·
	eum qui sic operatus est	τον · ουτο[2] · κατεργασαμενον ·
4	innomine dni nostri	Εντω · ονοματι · του · κυ · Ημων
	ihu xpi congregatis vobis	ιυ · χυ · Cυναχθεντων · υμων ·
	et meo spu · Cum virtu	ϗ του · εμου · πνσ · συν · τη · δυνα
5	te dni nri ihu xpi trade	μι · του · κυ · ημων · ιυ · χυ · παρα
	re ejusmodi satanæ in	δουναι · αυτον · τω · σατανα · εισ ·
	interitum carnis · ut	ολεθρον · τησ · σαρκοσ · Ινα · το
	sps salvus sit in die dni	πνα · σωθη · εν · τη · ημερα · του · κυ ·
6	nri ihu xpi · Non bona	ημων · ιυ · χυ · Ου · καλοντο ·
	gloriatio vestra · Nescitis	καυχημα · ὑμων · ου · κοιδατε
	qd modicum fermentum totam mas	οτι · μεικρα · ζημη · ολοντο · φυ
		fermentat
7	sam corrumpit · Expurgate	ραμα · ζυμοι · Εκκαθαραται ·
	vetus fermentum · ut sitis	την · παλαιαν · ζυμην · Ινα · ητε
	nova conspersio sicut estis	νεον · φυραμα · καθωσ · εσται ·
	azimi · Etenim pasca nrum	αζυμοι · ϗ γαρ · το · πασχα · ημων ·
8	immolatus est xps · Itaque epule	ετυθη · ο · χσ · Ωστε · ορτα_ζω
	mur · Non in fermto veteri · neque	μεν · μη · εν · ζυμη[3] · παλαια · μηδε ·
	in fermto malitiæ et nequitiæ ·	εν · ζυμη · κακιασ · ϗ · πορνειασ ·
	Sed in azimis sinceritatis	αλλεν · αζυμοισ · ιλει · κρινιασ ·
	et veritatis ·	ϗ · αλέθειασ[4] ·
9	Scripsi vobis in epistola	Εγραψα · υμειν · εν · τη · επιστολη ·
	necommisceamini fornicariis	μη · συναναμειγνυσθαι · πορνοισ ·
10	non utique fornicariis hujus mun	ου · παντωσ · τοισ · πορνοισ · του · κοσ

[1] τω πνι. [2] ουτω. [3] ζημη. [4] αληθειασ.

	Graece	Latine
V.	μον · τουτου · Ητοισ · πλεονεκτα ·	di aut avaris
	ϗ · αρπαζεἰν[1] · η ιδω‿λολατραισ ·	et rapacibus aut idolatris ·
	επει · ω · φειλεται · αρα · εκτου · κοσ	alioquin debueratis de hoc num
11	μον · εξελθειν , Νυν · δε · εγρα	do exisse · Nunc autem scri
	ψα · ὑμιν · μη · συν · αναμειγνὺσ	psi vobis necommisceami
	θαι · Εαν · τισ · αδελφοσ · ονομαζο	ni · Siquis frater nomina
	μενοσ · η · πορνοσ · η · πλεονεκ‿	tur aut fornicator · aut ava
	τησ · η · ιδωλολατρησ · η · λοιδο	rus · aut idolatra · aut male
	cum	
	ροσ · η · μεθυσοσ · η · αρπαξ · τω ·	dicus · aut ebriosus · aut rapax ·
	τοιουτω[2] ; μητε · συνεσθειειν ·	cum hujusmodi nec cibum sumere
12	Ει · γαρ · μοι τουσ · εξωκρινειν ·	Q̄d enim mihi de his qui foris sunt judicare ·
	ȣχὶ[3] · τουσ · εσω · υμισ · κρινεται ·	nonne de his qui intus sunt vos judicatis ·
	auferte	
13	τυυσ · δε · εξω · ο · θ̄σ̄ · κρινει · εξαραται ·	qui autem foris sunt d̄s judicabit · Au
	τον · πονηρον · εξυμων · αὐτων ·	ferte malum ex vobis ipsis
VI. 1	Ολματισ · ὑμων · προσ · τον · ετερον ·	Videt aliquis vr̄m adversus alterum
	πραγμα · εχων · κρινεσθαι · επει ·	nogotium habens · judicari apud
	των · αδικων · ϗ ουχι · επει · των	iniquos · et non apud
2	αγιων · Η · ου · κουδατε · οτι · οι ·	sc̄os · an nescitis quia
	αγιοι · τον · κοσμον · κρινȣσιν · ϗ	sc̄i mundum judicabunt · et si
	εαν · εν · ὑμειν · κρινεται · ο · κοσμοσ	in vobis judicabitur mundus
	αναχει · οι[4] · εσται · κρητηριων · ελα‿	indigni estis qui deminimis ju
3	χειστων · Ουκοιδατε · οτι · αγ	dicetis · Nescitis quō an
	γελουσ · κρινουμεν · ποσω · μαλλον	gelos judicabimus · quanto magis
4	βιοτικα[5] · Βιωτικα · γοὺν · κρητη	saecularia · Saecularia igitur ju
	ρια · εαν · εχεται[6] · τουσ · εξου	dicia sihabueritis · c̄temtibi
	θεν‿ημενουσ · εν · τη εκκλεσεια ·	les qui sunt in aecclesia
5	τουτουσ · καθειζεται · Προσ · εν ·	illos c̄stituite · ad verecun
	τροπιν[7] · ὑμιν · λεγω · Ουτωσ · ȣκ	diam vobis dico · Sic non

[1] αρπαξεἰν s.m. at ζ p.m. [2] τοὐιουτω. [3] ουχι. [4] αναξειοι. [5] βιατικα primum. [6] εχηται. [7] εντροπην.

CAP. VI. est inter vos quisquam sapiens
qui possit judicare inter
proximum et fratrem ejus·
v. 6 sed frater cum fratre
judicio contendit·et hoc apud in
fideles·et non apud scos·
7 Jam quidem omnino delictum
est in vobis quod judicia
habetis inter vos · Quare
non magis injuriam accipi
tis·quare non magis frau
8 dem patimini · Sed vos in
juriam facitis et fraudatis
9 et hoc fratribus · An nescitis
quia iniqui regnum di non
possidebunt · Nolite erra
re·neque fornicarii neque
idolis servientes·neque adul
teri·neque molles·neque mas
10 culorum concubitores·neque
fures·neque avari neque e
briosi·neque maledici·neque
rapaces regnum di posside
11 bunt·et hæc quidem fuistis·sed
abluti estis·sed sanctifi
ati estis·sed justifacati
estis in nomine dni nri
ihu xpi et spu di nostri

εστιν·εν·ὑμιν·ουδεεισ·σοφοσ·
οσ·δυνησεται·διακριναι·ανα
μεσον·τού·αδελφου·αὐτού
αλλα·αδελφοσ·μετα·αδελφου
κρινατε[1]·Και·τουτο·επι·α
πιστον[2]·και·ου·επι·αγιων[3]·

Vide p. 35. [R. B.]

[1] *κριναιτε.* [2] *απιστων.* [3] *fin.* + *ουκ οιδατε, post quod spatium prorsus vacuum est usque ad v.* 15, H. *ουκ* ‹

CAP. VI. V. 12 Omnia mihi licent·sed
non omnia expediunt
omnia mihi licent sed sub
nullius redigar pote
13 state · Esca ventri
et venter escis · Ds autem
et hunc et hæc destruet
Corpus autem non
fornicationi sed dno
et dominus corpori·
14 Ds vero et dnm sus
citavit·et nos susci
tabit pervirtutem suam

Graece	Latine
P. VI. 15 Η·ουκ·οιδατε[1]·οτι·τα·σωματα·	An nescitis quia corpora
υμον[2]·μελη·χρυ[3] · Η (an)·αρα ουντα·	vra membra sunt xpi · Tollens ergo
μελετου (η[4])·χρυ·ποιησω·μελη·πορ	membra xpi·faciam membra mere
16 νησ[5]·Με[6]γενοιτο·Ηουκ·οιδατε·	tricis·absit·aut nescitis
οτι·οκολλωμενοσ·τη·πορνη·	quia qui adheret meretrici
εν·σομα[7] (ω)·εστιν: Εσονται·γαρ·φη	unum corpus est · Erunt enim in
17 σιν·οι·δυο·εισ·σαρκα·μια[8] · Ο·δε·	quit duo in carne una·qui autem
κολλωμενοσ·τω κω·εν·πνα·εστιν·	adheret dno·unus sps est
18 φυγετε·την·πορνιαν·παν·αμαρ	Fugite fornicationem · Omne pec
τημα·ο·εαν·ποιηση·ανοσ·εκ	catum qdcuq' fecerit homo ex
τοσ·του·σωματοσ·εστιν · Ο·δε·	tra corpus est · Qui autem
πορνευων·εισ·το·ιδιον·σωμα·	fornicatur in corpus suum
19 αμαρταννει · Η·ουκοι͜δατε·	peccat · An nescitis
οτι·το·σωμα·υμων·ναοσ·του·	quia corpus vrm templum est qui
εν·υμιν·αγιου·πνσ·εστιν·Ου	in vobis est sps sci quem

[1] ουδατ^ε. [2] ὑμων. [3] + ποιησω μελη πορνησ μη γενοιτο (ante Η. Αρα ουν). [4] μελη (prim.). [5] πορ^ν ησ. [6] μη. [7] σωμα. [8] μια.

CAP. VI. betis a do · et non estis
v. 20 vri · Empti enim estis preti
o glorificate et portate dm in
corpore vestro
CAP. VII. 1 De quibus autem scipsistis mihi bo
num est homini mulierem non tan
2 gere · Propter fornicationem autem
unusquisque suam uxorem
3 habeat · Uxori vir
debitum reddat · Similiter
autem et uxor viro
4 Mulier sui corporis non
habet potestatem sed vir · Simil
autem et vir proprii corporis
non habet potestatem sed mulier
5 Nolite fraudare invicem nisi
forte ex consensu adtempus
ut vacetis orationi · et iterum
in id ipsum revertimini · ut ne
temptet vos satanas · propter
6 incontinentiam vestram · Hoc autem dico
secundum consilium non secundum impe
7 rium · Volo autem omnes homines
esse sic me ipsum · sed unusquisque
proprium habet donum ex do · alius
quidem sic · alius vero sic
8 Dico autem non nuptis et vidu
is · bonum est illis si sic perman

εχεται · απο · θυ · ϗ · ουκ · εσται ·
εαυτων · Η · γορασθηται · γαρ · τι
μησ · δοξασαται · δη · τον · θν · εν ·
τω · σωματι · υμων ·
Περι · δε · ων · εγραψαται · μοι · κα
λον · ανω · γυναι‿κοσ · μη απ
τεσται[1] · Δια[2] · δε · την · πορνιαν ·
εκαστοσ · την εα · τού[3] · γυναικα ·
εχετω · Τη · γιναικι · ανηρ[4] · την ·
οφιλην · αποδιδοτω · Ομοιωσ ·
δε · ϗ η · γύνη · τω · ανδρι ·
Η · γύνη · τού · ιδιού · σωματοσ · oὐκ
[uualtit?]
εξούσειαζει · ανηρ[5] · Ομοιωσ ·
δε · και · ο · ανηρ · τού · ιδιού · σωματοσ
oὐκ · εξούσειαζει αλλη · γύνη ·
Μη · αποστερειται · αλληλούσ · ειμη
τειαν · εκ · σύμφο‿νού[6] · προσ · ϗρον -
ινα · σχολασηται · τη · προευχη[7], ϗ
παλιν · επι · το · αυτοητε · Ινα · μη ·
πειραξη[8] · ὑμασ · ο · σατανασ · δια · τ
ακρασειαν · ὑμων · Τούτοδε · λεγω
κατα · σύνγνωμον[9] · ὑκατε · πειτα
γην · Θελω · δε · παντα · ανθρωπουσ[10]
ειναι · ωσ · ϗ εμαυτον · αλλε · καστοσ
ιδιον · εχει · χαρισμα · εκ · τού · θύ · ο ·
μεν · ούτωσ · Ο · δε · ὑυτωσ ·
Λελω[11] · δε · τοισ · αγομοισ[12] · ϗ · ταισ
ραισ[13] · καλον · αὐτοισ · Εαν · μει

[1] απτεσθαι. [2] αγα in marg. (cf. I. 26.) [3] εαυτου. [4] γυναικι ο ανηρ. [5] + αλλο (ante ανηρ). [6] συμφωνου. [7] προσευχη. [8] πειραζη. [9] συν. γνωμιν (η above). [10] παντασ ανθρωπουσ. [11] Λεγω. [12] αγαμοισ. [13] χηραι

VII 9 νωσειν · ωσ · και · εγω · ει · δε · ου	serint · sicut et ego · Quod si se non
κρατευονται · γαμειτωσαν · κρισ	continent nubant · Meli
σον · γαρ · γαμησαι · Η πυρουσθαι ·	us est nubere quam uri
10 οισ[1] · δε · γεγαμηκοσιν · παραγγελλω ·	is autem qui matrimonio juncti sunt · p̄cipio
ουκ · εγο · αλλω[2] κσ γυναικα · απο	non ego sed dns · uxorem
11 ανδροσ · μη · χωρειζεσται[3] · εαν · δε ·	a viro non discedere · quod si
ϗ χωρισθημενειν · αγαμον · η ·	discesserit manere innuptam aut
τω · ανδρι · καταλλαγηναι · ϗ ανδρα ·	viro reconciliari · et virum
12 γυναικα · μη · αφειεναι · Τοισ · δε ·	uxorem nontimittere · Ceteris
λοιποισ · εγω · λεγω:ουκ[4] · ο · κσ · Ειτισ	autem ego dico non dns · Sitis
αδελφοσ · γυναικα · εχει · απιστον ·	frater uxorem habet infidelem
ϗ αυτη · συνευδοκι · οικειν ·	et hac consentit habitare
μεταυτο[5] · μη · αφιετω · αυτην ·	cum illo · non dimittat illam
13 Και · γυνη · ειτε · ισ · εχει · ανδρα · απισ	Et si qua mulier habet virum infide
των[6] · ϗ ουτοσ · συν · ευδοκι · οικειν ·	lem et hic consentit habitare
μεταυτησ · μη · αφειετω · ταν[7] · αν	cum ea · non dimittat virum ·
14 δρα · Η · γιασται · γαρ · ο · ανηρ · ο · απισ	Scificatur enim vir infide
τοσ · εν · τη · γυναικι · τη · πιστι · και	lis · in muliere fideli et
ηγιασται · ηγυνη η · απιστοσ · εν ·	scificata est mulier infidelis in
τω αδελφο[8] · Επι · αρα · τα · τεκνα ·	fratre · Alioquin filii
υμων · ακαθαρτα · εστιν · νυν ·	vri inmundi sunt · Nunc
15 ει · δε · αγεια · εστιν[9] · Ει · δε · ο · απι	vero sci sunt · Quod si infide
στοσ · χωρι ζεται · χωριζεσθω[10] ·	lis discedit discedat ·
Ουδε · δουλωται · ο · αδελφοσ ·	Non est servituti subjectus frater
η · αδελφη · εν · τοισ τοιουτοισ ·	aut soror in ejus modi
Εν · δε · ιρηνι · κεκληκεν · ημασ ·	In pace enim vocavit nos
16 ο · θσ · Τι · γαρ · οιδασ · γυνη · ει · τον ·	ds · Quid enim scis mulier si
ανδρα · σωσεισ · Η · τι · οδασ[11] · ανηρ ·	virum salvum facies · aut quid scis vir

[1] τοισ. [2] εγω αλλο. [3] χωρειζεσθαι. [4] ουχ. [5] μεταυτου. [6] απιστον. [7] τον. [8] αδελφω. [9] εστειν. [10] χωριςζεσθω. [11] οιδασ.

CAP. VII. v. 17	si uxorem salvam facies · Nisi	ει · την · γὺναικα · σωσεισ · ειμη ·
	unicuique sicut divisit dns · et	εκαστω · ωσ · εμερισεν · ὸ κσ · και ·
	unumquemque sicut vocavit ds	εκαστον · ωσ · κεκληκεν · οθσ[1] ·
	ita ambulet · sicut	οὑτωσ · περιπατιτω · ϗ οὑτωσ ·
	in ecclesiis omnibus do	ενταισ · εκκλησειαισ · πασαισ · δ̑ι
18	ceo · Circum cisus aliquis	δασκω · Περι · τεμνη μενοσ ·
	vocatus · n adducat preputium · in	εκληθητισ · μη · επισπασθω · εν ·
	prepucio aliquis vocatus · non	ακροβὺστεια · τισ[2] · κεκληται · μη ·
19	circum cidatur · Circumcisio ni	περιτεμνη‿σθω[3] · Περιτομη · οὺ-
	hil est · sed observatio mandato	δεν · εστιν · αλλα · τη · ρησεισ · εν · το‿
20	rum di · Unus quisque invocatio	λων · θῦ · Ꞓκαστοσ · εν · τη · κλη
	ne · qua vocatus est · inea perma	σι · η · εκληθη · εν · ταὺτη · μενε‿
21	neat · Servus vocatus es · n tibi	τω · Δου[4] · εκληθησ · Μη · σοι
	sit curæ · Sed si potes li	μελετω · αλλειδ̑ὺνασαι · ελεὺ
	ber · fieri magis utere ·	θεροσ · γενεσθαι · μαλλον · χρησαι ·
22	Qui enim indno vocatus est servus ·	Ο · γαρ · εν · κω · κληθησ[5] · δ̑οὺ
	libertus dni est ·	λοσ · απελεὺθεροσ · κῦ · εστιν ·
	Similiter autem et quiliber voca	Ομοιωσ · δ̑ε · και · ο · ελευθεροσ · κλη
23	tus est · servus xpi est · precio	θεισ · δ̑οὺλοσ · χῦ · εστιν · Τιμησ ·
	empti estis · Nolite fieri ser	εγορασθηται[6] · μη · γινεσθαι · δ̑ȣ
24	vi hominum · Unusquisque fratres	λοι · ανων · Ꞓκαστοσ · αδελφοι ·
	inquo vocatus est ineo permaneat	εν · ω · εκληθη · εν · τοὺτω · μενετω ·
	aput deum ·	παρα · θω ·
25	Devirginibus autem preceptum	Περι · δ̑ε · των · παρθενων · επιταγην ·
	dni non habeo · consilium autem	κῦ · οὺκ · εχω · Γνωμην · δε · δ̑εδι
	do · tamquam misericordiam consecutus	δωμι · ωσ · ηλεημονοσ · ὺπο · κῦ ·
26	adno · ut sim fidelis · existimo ego	πιστοσ · ειναι · νομειζω · ουν
	hoc bonum esse propter	τουτο · καλὸν · ὺπαρχειν · δια ·

(λοσ. written above Δου)

[1] ο κσ ο θσ. [2] τησ. [3] περι τεμνεσθω. [4] δουλοσ. [5] κληθισ. [6] ηγορασθηται.

VII. την·ενεστωσαν·αναγκην·	instantem necessitatem
οτι·καλον·εστιν·ανω·ουτοσ[1]·	quia bonum est homini sic
27 ειναι·Δεδεσαι·γυναικι·μηζητει·	esse·Alligatus es uxori noli quærere
λυσειν·λελυσαι·απογυναικοσ·μη·	solutionem·solutus ab uxore ne
28 ζητει·γυναικα[2]·Εαν·δε·και·λα	quæras uxorem·Si autem et accepe
βησ·γυναικα·ουχ·ημαρτεσ·	ris uxorem non peccasti
ϗ·εαν·γαμη·παρθηνοσ·ουκ[3]·	et si nupserit virgo Non
ημαρτεν·Θλιψιν·δε·εν·τη	peccabit·Tribulationem tam
Cσαρκι[4]·εξουσειν·οιτοι·ουτοι·	carnis habebunt hujus modi·
29 Εγω·δε·υμων·φιδομαι·Τουτο·δε·	Ego autem vobis parco·hoc autem
εφημει·αδελφοι·οτι·ο·καιροσ·	dico fratres·tempus
συνεσταλμενοσ·εστιν·Λοιπον·	breve est·Reliquum
εστιν·Ινα·ϗ·οι·εχοντεσ·γυ	est·ut et quihabent uxo
30 ναικασ·ωσ·μη·εχοντεσ·ϗ·οι·	res·tamquam non habentes et qui
κλεθοντεσ·ωσ·μη·κλεθοντεσ·	flent·tamquam non flentes
ϗ·οι·χαροντεσ·ωσ·μη·χαιρον	et qui gaudent·tamquam non gauden
τεσ·ϗ·οι·αγοραζοντεσ·ωσ·μη·	tes·et qui emunt tamquam non
31 κατεχοντεσ[5]·ϗ·οι·χρωμενοι·	possidentes·et qui utuntur
τον·κοσμον·τουτον·ωσ·μη·	huic mundo·tamquam non
κατα χρωμενοι·Παραγει·γαρ·	utantur·Preterit enim figura
το·σχημα·του·κοσμου·τουτου·	hujus mundi·
32 Θελω·υμασ·αμεριμνουσ·ειναι·	Volo vos sine sollicitudine esse
Ο·αγαμοσ·μεριμνα·τα·του·κυ·	Qui sine uxore est sollititus est quæ sunt di
33 πωσ·αρεση·τω·θω·Ο·δε·γαμησασ·	quomodo placeat do·Qui autem matrimonio
sollicitat	
μερ·ιμνα·τατου·κοσμου·πωσ·	.junctus est sollicitus est quæ sunt mundi·quomodo
34 αρεση·τη·γυναικι·Μεμε ρισται·	placeat uxori·et divisa
η αγαμοσ innupta	
ϗ·ηγυνη·ϗ·η·παρθενοσ·	mulier·et virgo
Η·αγαμοσ·μεριμνα·τα·του·κυ·	inmaculata·cogitat quæ sunt dni

[1] ουτωσ. [2] αγα *in margine.* [3] παρθενοσ ουχ. [4] σαρκι. [5] χα κατεχοντεσ.

CAP. VII.	ut sit sca et corpore et	ινα · η · αγεια · και · σωματι · και
	spu · Quæ autem nupta est cogi	πνι · Η · δε · γαμησασα · Μεριμ
	tat quæ sunt mundi quomodo placeat	να · τα · τού · κοσμού · ποσ[1] · αρεση ·
v. 35	viro · hoc autem ad	τω · ανδρι · Τούτο · δε · προσ · το ·
	vram utilitatem dico ·	ὑμων · αὐτων · σύμφερον · λεγω ·
	non ut laqueum vobis iniciam	οὐκ[2] · ινα · βροχον ὑμιν · επιβαλω ·
	sed ad id quod honestum est · et	αλλα · προσ · το · εὐσχημον · και ·
	bene stabile dno · inadducibili	ευπαρεδρον · το · κο[3] · απερεισπασ
36	ter · si autem quis turpem se existimat	τωσ · Ει · δε · τισ · ασχημονει ·
	super virgine sua · quod sit	επι · την · παρθενον · αὐτού · εαν · η ·
	super adulta · et ita oportet	ὑπερακμοσ · ϗ · οὐτοσ[4] · οφιλει ·
	fieri · qd vult faciat · non	γενεσθαι · Ο · θελι · ποιειτω · οὐκ ·
37	peccat sinubat · Qui autem	αμαρταννει · γαμειτο[5] · Οσ · δε ·
	statuit incorde suo	εστηκεν · εν · τη · καρδια · αὐτού ·
	non habens necessitatem · potestatem	μη · εχων · αναγκην · εξουσιαν ·
	autem habens propriæ volunta	δε · εχει · περι · τού · ιδιού · θελημα
	tis · et hoc statuit in	τοσ · ϗ · τουτο · κεκρικεν · εν · τη ·
	corde suo servare	καρδια · αὐτού · τού · τηρειν · την ·
	suam virginem benefaciat	εαὐτού · παρθενον · καλωσ · ποιει ·
38	et qui non dat nuptum melius facit	ϗ · ο · μη · γαμειζων · κρισσον · ποιει ·
39	Mulier alligata est legi · quanto	Γύνη · δεδεται · νομω · εφοσον ·
	tempore vivit vir ejus · Si	χρονον · ζη · ανηρ[6] · αὐτησ · Εαν ·
	autem dormierit vir ejus	δε · κεκοιμηθη · ο · ανηρ · αὐτεσ[7]
	liberata est · Cui vult nubat	ελεύθερα · εστιν · ω · θελει · γαμηθη ·
40	tantum indno · Beatior autem	μονον · εν · κω · Μακαριοτερα[8] · δε ·
	est · si sic permanserit secundum meum	εστιν · εαν · οὐτωσ · μινη · κατα
	consilium · Puto autem	την · εμην · γνωμην · Δοκω · δε ·
	qd et ego spm di habeam ·	καγω · πνα · θύ · εχω ·

[1] πωσ. [2] ουχ. [3] τω κω. [4] ουτωσ. [5] γαμειτω. [6] + ο (ante ανηρ). [7] αυτησ. [8] μακαριωτερα.

Greek	Latin
VIII. v. 1 Περι·δε·των·ϊδωλοθυτων·οιδαμεν·	De his autem quæ idolis immolantur sci
οτι·παντεσ·γνωσιν·εχομεν · Η·γνω	mus qa oms scientiam habemus · Sci
σισ·φυσιοι · Η·δε·αγαπη·οικοδο	entia inflat·caritas aedifi
2 μει · Ει·δε·τισ·δοκει·εγνωκεναι_	cat · Si quis autem putat se scire
τι·ουδε·πωεγνω·καθοσ[1]·δει_	aliquid·nondum cognovit quemadmodum
3 γνωναι · Ει·δε·τισ·αγαπα·τον·θν·	oporteat scire · Si autem quis diligit dm
ουτοσ·εγνωσται·Υπαυτου·	hic cognitus est abillo·
4 Περι·τησ·βρωσεωσ·ουν·του[2]·ιδω_	De esca ergo sacrifici
λοθυτων·ουδαμεν·οτι·ουδεν·	orum·scimus quia nihil
εστιν·ιδωλον·εν·κοσμω·κ̣ οτι·	est idolum inmundo et quia
5 ουδεισ·θσ·ειμη·εισ·κ̣ γαρ·ει·	nullus ds nisi unus·etenim si
περισειν·οι·λεγομενοι·θεοι·ειτε·	sunt quidicantur dii·sive
εν·ουρανω·ειτε·επι·γησ·Ωσ·περ	incaelo sive interra·sicut
εισιν·θεοι·πολλοι·κ̣·κυριοι·πολλοι·	sunt dii multi·et domini multi
6 αλλημιν·εισ·ο θσ·ο·πηρ·εξου·	sed nobis unus ds pat ex quo
τα·παντα·κ̣·ημεισ·εισ·αυτον·	omnia·et nos in ipso·
κ̣ εισ·κσ·ισ·χσ·διου·τα·παντα·κ̣	et unus dns ihc per quem omnia et
7 ημεισ·δι·αυτου·αλλουκ·εν·πασιν·	nos per ipsum·sed non in omnibus est
η·γνωσισ · Τινεσ·δε·τη·συνιδησι·	scientia · Quidam autem inconscientia
εωσαρτι·του·ιδωλου·ωσ·ιδωλο_	usque adhuc idoli·quasi idolothi
θυτον·αισ·θει·ουσιν·κ̣ ιδησεισ[3]·	tum manducant·etcscientia
αυτων·ασθενησ·ουσαμολυνεται·	eorum cum sit infirma inquinabitur
8 Βρωμα·δε·ημασ·ου·σινιστησιν[4]·	esca autem nos non commendat
τω·θω · Ουτε·γαρ·εαν·φαγωμεν·	do · Neque enim si manducaverimus
περισσευομεν · Ουτε·εαν·μη·φα	abundavimus · Neque si non manduca
γωμεν·υστερουμεθα·	verimus deficiemus·
9 Βλεπετε·δε·μη·ποσ[5]·η·εξουσια·	Videte autem ne forte hæc licentia
υμων[6]·προσ·κομμα·γενηται·τοισ· (αυτη.)	vra · Offendiculum fiat

[1] καθωσ. [2] των. [3] ηιδησεισ. [4] συνιστησιν. [5] πωσ. [6] υμων αυτη.

Latin	Greek
CAP. VIII. v. 10 infirmis · Si enim quis viderit	ασθενεσιν · Εαν · γαρ · τισ · ἰδει · τον ·
habentem scientiam in idolio re	εχον · τα · γνωσιν · εν · ϊδωλειω · κατα
cumbentem · Nonne conscientia	κειμενον · Οὐχι · η · σὐνιδησισ ·
ejus cum sit infirma · aedifica	αὐτοὐ · ασθενοὐσοντοσ · οικοδο
bitur admanducandum	μηθησεται · εισ το · αισ · θειειν · τα ·
11 idolothita · et peribit in	ιδολωθὐτα · ϗ · απολειται · ο · ασ
firmus intua scientia frater	θενων · εν · τη · ση · γνωσει · ο · αδελφοσ ·
12 propter quem xpc mortuus est · Sic autem	διον · χσ · απεθανεν · Οὐτωσ · δε ·
peccantes infratres	αμαρτανοντεσ · εισ · αδελφοὐσ ·
percutientes eorum conscientiam ·	τὐπτοντησ · αὐτων · την συνιδη
am infirmam · in xpm pec	σιν[1] · ασθενουσαν · εισ · χν · αμαρ
13 catis · Quapropter si esca	τανεται · Διοπερ · ειτο · βρομα[2] ·
scandalizat fratrem non	σκανδαλειζει · Τον · αδελφον · οὐ
manducabo carnem in æternum ·	μη · φαγω · κρεα · εισ · τον · αιωνα ·
ut non fratrem scandali	ινα · μη · τον · αδελφον · σκανδαλει
CAP. IX. 1 zem · Non sum apls, non sum	σω · ουκ · ειμει · αποστολοσ · οὐκ · ειμει ·
liber · nonne xpm ihm dnm	ελεὐθεροσ · οὐ · χν · ιν[3] · τον · κρν[4] ·
nrm vidi · Nonne opus meum	ημων · εορακα[5] · Ουτο · εργων[6] · μοὐ ·
2 vos estis indno · Si aliis non	ὐμισ · εσται · εν · κω · Ει · αλλοισ · οὐκ ·
sum apostolus · sed tamen vobis	ειμει · αποστολοσ · αλλα · γε · ὐμειν
sum · nam signaculum mei apo	ειμει · Η · γαρ · σφαγεισ · τησ · εμησ · α
3 stolatus vos estis indno · mea	στολησ · ὐμεισ · εσται · εν · κω · Η · μη[7] ·
defensio aput eos qui me · judicant	απολυγεια · τοισ · εμαι · ανακρινουσιν ·
haec est ·	αὐτη · εστιν ·
4 Numquid non habemus potestatem mandu	Μη · οὐκ · εχομεν · εξοὐσιαν · φαγειν ·
5 candi et bibendi · numquid non habemus potes	ϗ πιν · μη · ουκ · εχομεν · εξου
tatem mulieris circum ducendi	σιαν · γυναικασ · περιαγειν · ωσ · ϗ
sic et alii apli et fratres	οι · λοιποι · αποστολι[8] · ϗ · οι · αδελφοι ·

1 τυπτοντεσ αυτων την συν ἰδεσιν. 2 βρωμα. 3 ιη. 4 κν. 5 εορακα. 6 εργον. 7 Ηεμη. 8 αποστολοι.

Greek	Latin
P. IX v. 6 του κυ ꝫ · κηφασ[1] · Η · μονοσ · εγω ·	dni · et caephas · aut solus ego
ꝫ · βαρνα · σ · ε · ουκ[2] · εχομεν · εξου (βα.)	et barnabas non habemus potesta
7 σιαν · μη · εργαζεσθαι · τισ · (σ) τρατευεται[3] ·	tem hoc operandi · quis militat
ιδειοι σ · οψωνειοισ · ποτε · τισ · φυ	suis stipendiis umq · quis plan
τενει · αμπελωνα · ꝫ · τον · καρπον ·	tat vineam et fructum
αυτου · ου · κ · αι · (σ.) θειει · και · εκαιπινι[4] ·	ejus non manducat et bibit ·
Τισ · ποιμενει · ποιμνην · ꝫ · εκτου ·	Quis pascit gregem · et de
γαλακτοσ · αὐτησ · οὐκ · αισθειει ·	lacte ejus non edit ·
8 Μη · κατα · ανον · ταυτα · λεγω · Η · ει ·	Nun quod secundum hominem dico · An si
9 ꝫ · ονομοσ · ταυτα · λεγει · Γεγραπ	et lex haec dicit · Scriptum est
ται · γαρ · οὐκ · ημωσεισ · Βουη[5] ·	enim · Non alligabis os bovi
αλοωντα · Μη · περι · των · βοων ·	trituranti · Numqd debubus
10 μελει · τω · θω · Η · δι · ημασ · παντωσ ·	cura est do · An propter nos utique
λεγει · Δι · ἡμασ · γαρ · εγραφη · οτι ·	dicit · Propter nos enim scriptum est qm
οφε(ι)λει[6] · ο · εφελπιδει · αροτριων ·	in spe quiarat ·
οφε(ι)λει[7] · αροτριαν · ꝫ · ο · αλων	debet arare · et qui triturat
τ(η)εσ[8] · ελπειδοσ · αὐτου · μετεχειν ·	in spe fructus percipiendi ·
11 Ει · ημεισ · ὑμιν · τα · πνευματι κα ·	Si nos vobis spiritalia
εσπιραμεν · Μεγα · ει · ημεισ · Ὑμων ·	seminavimus · Magnum est si vestra
12 τα · σαρκει κα ; θερισωμεν · ει · αλλοι ·	carnalia metamus · Si alii vestrae
τησ · ὑμων · εξουσιασ · μετεχου	potestatis participes sunt quare
σιν · οὐ · μαλλον · ημεισ · αλλο · ουκ[9] ·	non potius nos · Sed non
εχρησαμεθα · τη · εξουσια · αὐτη ·	usi sumus potestate hac ·
Αλλα · παντασ · τεγομεν · Ινα · μη ·	Sed omnia sufferimus · v non
ενκοπην · τινα · δωμεν[10] · τω · εὐαγ	offendiculum demus evan
13 γελιω · του · χυ · Ουκ · οιδατε · οτι ·	gelio di · Nescitis qm
οι · τα · ἱερα · εργα ζομενοι · Τα εκτου	qui in sacrario operantur · quæ
ἱερου · αισθειουσιν · Οι · τω · θυσει	desunt edunt · Qui altario

[1] κυ και κηφασ. [2] βαρναβασ ουκ. [3] στρατευεται. [4] αισθειει και πινι. [5] βουν.
[6] οφιλει. [7] οφειλει. [8] τησ. [9] αλλουκ. [10] εν κοπην τιν(λ) αδωμεν.

Latin	Greek
CAP. IX. deserviunt · Cum alta	αστηρια · παραδρεύοντεσ · τω · θῡ
rio participantur ·	σειαστηρειω · συνμεριζονται ·
v. 14 Ita et dns ordinavit his	Ουτωσ · ϗ · οΚσ · διεταξεν · τοισ ·
qui evangelium adnunti	το · ευαγγελιον · καταγγελλού_
ant de evangelio vivere	σειν[1] · εκτού · εύαγγελιού · ζην ·
15 Ego autem non usus sum ullo	Εγω · δε · ούκ · εχρημαι · ούδενει ·
horum · non scripsi autem hæc	τούτων · Ούκ · εγραψα · δε · ταύτα
ut ita fiant inme ·	ινα · ουτοσ[2] · γενηται · εν · εμοι ·
Bonum enim mihi est magis mo	Καλον · γαρ · μοι · μαλλον · αποθα
ri · quam ut gloriam meam quis	νειν · Η · το · καύχημα · μού · τισ ·
16 evacuet · Si enim evangelizavi	ϗ · νωσει · Εαν · γαρ · εαγγελλισω
vero · non est mihi gratia · Ne	μαι[3] · ούκ · εστιν · μοι · χαρισ · αναγ
cessitas enim mihi incumbit · Ve enim	κη · γαρ · μοι · επικειται · Ούαι · γα
mihi erit · si non evangeliza	μοι · εσται · Εαν · μη · εύαγγελεισω
17 vero · Si enim volens hoc ago	μαι · Ει · γαρ · αικων · τούτο · πρασ
mercedem habeo · Si autem invitus	μεισθον · εχω · Ει · δε · ακων[4] · οι ·
18 dispensatio mihi credita est · Quæ	κονομει_αν · πεπειστεύμαι · Τισ ·
ergo erit mihi merces · Ut	ούνεσται · μοι · ομεισθοσ · Ινα ·
evangelizans sine sumptu	εύαγγελειζομενοσ · αδαπανον ·
ponam evangelium xpi	θησω · το · εύαγγελιον · τού · χ̄ῡ ·
ut non abutar ·	Εισ · το · μη · κατα · χρησαθαι · την
potestate mea inevange	εξούσειαν · μοι · Εν · το[5] · εύαγγε
19 lio · Nam cum liber essem ab	λιω · Ελευθερυσ · γαρ · ων · εκ ·
omnibus · omnium me servum	παντων · πασιν · εμαύτον · εδου
feci · Ut plures lucriface	λωσα · Ινα · τουσ · πλιονασ · κερ
20 rem · et factus sum judae	δησω · ϗ · εγενομην[6] · τοισ · ῑού_
is tamquam judæus · ut judæos	δαιοσ[7] · ϊούδαιοισ · Ιν[8] ῑούδαιούσ ·
lucrifacerem · Quisublege quasi	κερδησω · Τούσ · Ύπο · νομον · ωσ

[1] καταγγελουσειν. [2] ουτωσ. [3] ευαγγελεισωμαι. [4] αίκων. [5] μου εν τω.
[6] ωσ (quasi) in margine. [7] ῑουδαιοίσ. [8] ϊοδαιοισ Ῑνα.

IX	ὑπο · νομον · μη · ων · αὐτοσ · ὑπο ·	sub lege e̅e̅m̅ · Cum non e̅e̅m̅ ipse sub
	νομον · ινα · τοὺσ · ὑπο · νυμον · κερ	lege · ut eos qui sub lege erant · lu
21	δησω · Τοισ · α · νομοισ · ωσ · α · νομοσ ·	crarer · his qui sine lege sunt ta̅q̲ sine lege
	μη · ων · α · νομοσ · θ̅υ̅ · αλλεν · νομοσ ·	cum non e̅e̅m̅ sine lege d̅i̅ · sed in lege e̅e̅m̅
	χ̅ὺ̅ · Ινα · κερδανω · α · νομοὺσ ·	x̅p̅i̅ ut lucrarer eos quisine lege sunt
22	Εγενομη[1] · δε · ϗ · τοισ · ασθενοὺ	Factus sum autem et infir
	σιν · ωσ · ασθενησ · Ινα · τοὺσ · ασ	mis tamquam infirmus · ut in
	θενεισ · κερδησω · Τοισ · πασιν	firmos lucrifacerem · Omnibus
	εγενομην · παντα · Ινα · παντασ ·	factus sum omnia · ut omnes sal
23	σωσω · Παντα · δε · ποιω · δια · το ·	vos facerem · Omnia autem facio propter
	ἐυαγγελειον · Ινα · σὺνκοι · ω	evangelium · ut particeps
	νοσ[2] · αὐτου · γενωμαι ·	ejus efficiar ·
24	Ουκ · οιδατε · οτι · οι · εν · σταδιω · τρε	Nescitis q̅d̅ hi qui in stadio cur
	χοντεσ · Παντεσ · μεν · τρεχου	runt omnes quidem cur
	σιν · εισ · δε · λαμβανι · το · βραβι	runt · sed unus accipit pravi
	ον · Εγω · δε · λεγω · ὑμιν · Ουτωσ ·	um · Ego autem dico vobis · Sic
	τρεχεται · ι̅να · κατα · λα · βηται[3] ·	currite ut conprehendatis
25	Πασ · δε · ο · αγωνει · ζομ · νοσ[4] · παντα ·	Omnis autem qui in agone contendit ab omnibus
	εν · κρατεὺεται · εκεινοι · μεν ·	se abstinet · et illi quidem
	ουν · Ινα · φαρτον[5] · στεφανον ·	ut corruptibilem coronam
	λαβωσειν · ημεισ · δε · αφθαρτον ·	accipiant · Nos autem incorruptam
26	Εγω · τοινυν · ουτοσ[6] · τρεχω · ωσ ·	Ego igitur sic curro · non quasi
	ουκ · αδηλωσ · οὐτοσ[7] · πυκτευω ·	in incertum · Sic pugno
27	ωσ · ουκ · αερα · δερων · αλλὺπο	non quasi aerem verberans · Sed
	πειαζω · μοὺ · το · στομα · ϗ · δοὺ	castigo corpus meum et inservi
	λα · γωγω · μη · πωσ · αλλοισ · κηρὺ	tutem redigo · ne forte cum aliis p̅dica
	ξασ · αὐτοσ · αδοκειμοσ · γενωμαι ·	verim ipse reprobus efficiar ·
X. 1	Ου · θελω · γαρ · ὑμασ · αγνοειν · αδελ	Nolo autem vos ignorare fra

[1] εγενομην. [2] συνκοινωνοσ. [3] καταλαβηται. [4] αγωνειζομενοσ. [5] ; φθαρτον. [6] ουτωσ. [7] ουτωσ.

CAP. X. res · quo patres nri onis	φοι · οτι · οι · πατερεσ · ημων · παντε
sub nube fuerunt · et oms	ὑπο · την · νεφελην ησαν · ϗ · παν
mare transierunt ·	τεσ · δια · τησ θαλασσησ · διηλθον ·
v. 2 et omnes inmoyse bap	ϗ παντεσ · εισ · τον · μωυσην · εβαπ
tizati sunt inmari et in	τισθησαν · εν · τη · θαλασση · ϗ · εν ·
3 nube · et omnes eandem	τη · νεφελη · ϗ · παντεσ · το · αὐτο ·
aes cam spiritalem manducaverunt	βρωμα · πνεὑματικον · εφαγον ·
4 et omnes eundem potum spirita	ϗ παντεσ · τοαὐτο · πομα · πνεὑ
lem biberunt · Bibebant enim de	ματικον · επἰον · Επεινον · γαρ · εκ
spiritali sequenti ·	πνεὑματικησ · ακολοθουσ · ησ[2] ·
petra · petra autem erat xpc	πετρασ · πετρα · δε · ην · ο · χρσ ·
5 Sed non in pluribus eorum	Αλλοὐκ · εν · τοισ · πλιοσιν · αὐτων ·
bene placuit ds · prostra	ευδοκησεν · Οθσ · κατεσ_τρω
6 ti sunt enim indeserto · Haec	θησαν · γαρ · εν · τη · ερημω · Ταὑτι
autem in figura nri facta sunt	δε · τὑποι · ημων · εγενηθησαν ·
ut non simus nos concupis	εισ · το · μη · ειναι · ημασ · επιθυμη
centes malorum · sicut et illi	τασ · κακον · καθοσ[3] · ϗ · κεινοι ·
7 concupierunt · nec idola	επεθὑμησαν · Μη · δε · ιδωλολα
tres efficiamini sicut scriptum est	τρασ · γεινεσθαι · καθοσ[4] · γεγραπτα
Sedit populus manducare et bibere ·	Εκαθησεν[5] · ο · λαοσ · φαγειν · ϗ πειν
8 et surrexerunt ludere · Neque	ϗ ανεστη · παιζειν · Μη · δε · εκ
fornicemur sicut quidam ex	πορνεὑωμεν · καθωσ · τινεσ · αὐ
ipsis fornicati sunt · et ceciderunt	των · εξεπορνευσαν · ϗ · επεσαν ·
una die · xx · tria milia ·	μια · ημερα · εικοσει · τρισ · χιλιαδασ
9 Neque temptemus	Μη · δε · εκπιρασω_μεν · τον
xpm sicut quidam eorum tempta	χν καθυσ · τε · νεσ[6] · αὐτων · εξεπι_
verunt · et a serpentibus	ρασαν · ϗ · ὑπυ · των · οφεων
10 perierunt · Neque murmurave	απωλοντο · Μη · δε · γογγυζω

---

[1] *e μαp in margine.* [2] *απολουθουσ ησ.* [3] *κακων.καθωσ.* [4] *καθωσ.*
[5] Θκαθησε (cf. Matthæi *ad locum*). [6] *καθωσ τεινεσ.*

10 μεν·καθοσ[1]·τεινεσ·αυτων·	ritis sicut quidam eorum
εγογγυσαν·ϗ·απολοντο[2]·υπο·	murmuraverunt·et perierunt ab
11 του·ολεθρου · Παντα·δε·ταυτα·	exterminatore · Omnia autem haec
τυποι·συνεβενον·εκεινοισ·	infigura contingebant illis·
Εγραφη·δε·προσ·νουθεσιαν·	Scripta sunt autem adcorreptionem
ημων·εισ·ουστα·τηλη[3]·των·αι	nostram·inquos fines sclorum
12 ωνων·κατην·τηκεν · Ωστε·ο·	lorum devenit · Itaque qui
δοκων·εσταναι βλεπετω·μη·	se existimat stare videat ne
13 πεση · Πιρασμοσ·υμασ·ουκατα.	cadat · Temptacio vos non apre
λαβη·ειμη·ανθρωπινοσ · Πιστοσ·	hendat·nisi humana · Fidelis
δε·ο·θσ·οσ·ουκ·αφησει·υμασ·	autem ds quinonpacietur vos
πιρασθηναι·υπερ·ο·ου·δυνασ	temptari super id qd non pote
θαι·υπενεγκειν·αλλα·ποιησει	stis sustinere·sed fàciet
συν·τω·πιρασμω·ϗ·την·εκβα	cumtemptacione etiam proven
σειν·του·δυνασθαι·υπενεγκην·	tum·ut possitis sustinere·
14 Διοπερ·αγαρητοι[4]·μου·φευγεται·	Propter qd carissimi mei fugite
15 απο·τησ·ιδωλολατριασ·ωσ·	abidolorum cultura·sicut
φρονιμοισ·λεγω · κρινεται[5]·	prudentibus dico · Judicate
16 υμισ·ο·φημι · Το·ποτηριον·τησ·	vos quod dico · Calix be
ευχαριστιασ·ο·ευλογου μεν·	nedictionis quem benedicimus
ουχι·κοινωνεια·του·αιματοσ·	nonne communicatio sanguinis
του·χρυ·εστιν · Τον·αρτον·ον·	xpi est · Panem quem
κλωμεν·ουχι·κοινωνια·του·	frangimus·nonne communicatio
17 σωματοσ·του·κυ·εστιν·Οτι·	corporis dni est·quo
εισ·αρτοσ·ενσωμα·οι·πολλοι	unus panis unum corpus·multi
εσμεν·Οι·γαρ·παντεσ·εκτου·	sumus · Oms enim de
ενοσ·αρτου·ϗ του·ενοσ·ποτη	uno pane·et uno cali
ριου[6]·μετε_χομεν	ce participam·

[1] καθωσ. [2] απωλοντο. [3] τελη. [4] αγαπητοι. [5] κρινατε. [6] αρτου ποτηριου.

CAP. X. v. 18 Videte irl secundum carnem
nonne quiedunt sacrificia
ficia · participes alta
19 ris sunt · Quid ergo dico quod
idolis immolatum est · aliq'd non qd
20 idolum fuit aliquid · sed
q gentes immolant doemonis
immolant etnondo · No
lo autem vos doemoniorum so
21 cios fieri · Non potestis
calicem dni bibere et cali
cem demoniorum · Non potestis
mensæ dni participare · et
22 mensæ demoniorum · An emula
mur dnm · Nuquid forti
23 ores illo sumus · Omnia
licent · sed non omnia ex
24 pediunt · nemo qd suum est quæ
rat · sed quod alterius
25 Omne quod inmacello ve
niat · edite · nihil interro
gantes propter conscientiam
26 dni enim est terra · et pleni
27 tudo ejus · siquis vocat vos ·
exinfidelibus ad cænam · et
volueritis ire · Omne qd
appositum fuerit vobis edi
te · Nihil interrogantes

Βλεπετε · τον · ιηλ · κατα · σαρκα ·
ουχ οι · αισθειοντεσ · τασ, θυσει
ασ · κοινωνοι · του · θυσιασ · τη
ρει · εισειν · Τι · ουν · φημει · οτι · ιδ
λοθυτον · εστιν · τι · ουχ · οτι ·
ιδωλοθυτον · εστιντι · αλλα ·
α · θυουσειν · δαιμονει οισ ·
θυουσειν · και · ουχ[1] · θω · Ουθε
λω · δε · υμασ · δαιμονειων · κοι
νωνουσ · ειναι · Ουχ[2] · δυνασθαι ·
ποτηριον · κυ · πινιν · και · ποτηρι
ον · δαιμονιων · Ουχ[3] · δυνασθαι ·
τραπεζησ · κυ · μετεχειν · και ·
τραπεζησ · δαιμονειων · Η · παρα
ζηλουμεν · τον · κν · μη · ισχυρο
τεροι · αυτου · εσμεν · Παντα ·
εξεστειν[4] · αλλου · παντα · συμ
φερει · μη · δεισ · το · εαυτου · ζη
τειτω · αλλα · τοτου · ετερου ·
Παντο · εν · μακελλω · πωλουμε
νον · αισθει εται · μηδεν · ανα
κρινοντεσ · δια · την · συνιδησιν ·
του · κυ · γαρ · η · γη · και · το · πληρ
μα · αυτησ · Ειτισ · καλι · υμασ ·
των · απιστων · εισ · διπνον · και
θελεται · πορευεσθαι · παντο ·
παρατηθεμενον · υμιν · αισθι
εται · μηδεν · ανακρινοντεσ ·

---

[1] ου. [2] ου. [3] δαιμονιων .Ου. [4] + μηδεισ το εαυτου (post εξεστειν).

X. 18 δια · την · σὺν ῑδησειν · Εαν · δε ·	propter conscientiam · Siquis
τισ · ειπη · τοὺτο · ἰδολωθυτον[1] ·	autem hoc immolaticium est
εστιν · Μη · αισθει · εται · δια · την ·	est nolite manducare propter
29 σὺν ῑδησιν · Cὺν · ιδησειν · δε · λε	conscientiam · Conscientiam autem
γω · οὺχι · την · εαὺτοὺ · αλλα · την · τȣ ·	dico nontuam sed alterii
ετεροὺ · Ινατι · γαρ · η · ελεὺθερια ·	us · Ut quid enim libertas
μοὺ · κρινεται · ὺπο · απιστοὺ · συν	mea judicabitur · ab alia con
30 ἰδησεωσ · Ει · εγω · χαριτει · μετε	scientia · Si enim ego cum gratia parti
χω · τι · βλασφημοὺ · μαι · ὺπερ ·	cipo · quid plasphe mor · pro eo q̅d̅
31 οὺ · εγω · εὺχαριστω · ειτε · ουν ·	gratias ago · Sive ergo
αισθιετε · ειτε · πινεται · ειτε ·	manducatis sive bibitis · Ī aliud
ποιειτε · τι · παντα · εισ · δοξαν · θ̅ῡ̅ ·	quid facitis omnia ingl̄am d̄i
32 απροσκοποι · γεινεσθαι · ῑουδαι	Sine offensione estote judæ
οισ · τεκαι · ελλησειν · ϗ · τη · εκ	is et gentibus et eccle
33 κλησεια · θ̅ῡ̅[2] · Καθωσ · καγω · πα	siæ d̄i · Sicut et ego omni
σειν · κατα · παντα · αρεσκω · μη ·	bus per omnia placeo · Non
ζητων · το · εμαυτου · συμφε	quærens · q̅d̅ mihi utile est
ρον · αλλα · των · πολλων · ινα ·	sed q̅d̅ multis ut salvi
P. XI. 1 σωθωσειν · Μειμηται · μου ·	fiant · Imitatores mei
γινεσθαι · καθ(ω)οσ[3] · καγω · χ̅ῡ̅ ·	estote sicut et ego x̅p̅i̅
2 Επαινω · δε · ὺμασ · αδελφοι · οτι ·	Laudo autem vos fratres q̅d̅
παντα · μου · μεμν(η)εσθαι[4] ·	per omnia mei memores estis
και · καθ(ω)οσ[5] · παντα · (ubique) χοὺ · παρα	et sicut tradidi vobis
δωκα · τασ · τασ[6] · παραδοσισ · μου ·	precepta mea
3 καταιχεται · Θελω · ὺμασ ·	tenetis · Volo autem vos
ειδεναι · οτι · παντυσ · ανδροσ ·	scire · q̅d̅ omnis viri
η · κεφαλη · χ̅σ̅ · εστιν · Κεφαλη ·	caput x̅p̅e̅ est · Caput
δεγυναι κυσ[7] · ο · ανηρ · κεφα	autem mulieris vir · Caput

---

[1] Ἰδωλοθυτον. [2] εκκλησειααὺτου θ̅υ̅. [3] καθωσ. [4] μεμνησθαι. [5] καθωσ. [6] τασ *semel*. [7] χ̅υ̅ γυναικοσ.

CAP. XI v. 4 vero xpi ds·omnis vir o
rans aut prophetans ve
lato capite·deturpat
caput suum·
5 Omnis autem mulier orans
aut prophetans · Nonve
lato capite·deturpat
caput suum · Unum est enim
ac si de calvetur·
6 Nam sinon velatur
mulier et tondeatur·
Sivero turpe est mulieri tonde
ri aut decalvari velet ca
7 put suum · Vir quidem non
debet velare
caput suum·quo imago et glo
ria di est · Mulier autem
8 gloria viri est · Non
enim vir exmuliere est·
9 sedmulier exviro·et enim
non est creatus vir propter
mulierem·sed mulier prop
10 propter virum · Ideo
debet mulier potestatem
habere super caput propter
11 angelos · Verumtamen neque
mulier sine viro·neque
vir sine muliere in dno·

λη·δε·χυ·ο·θσ·πασ·ανηρ·προ
σευχομενοσ·η·προφητευων·
κατα·κεφαλησ·εχων καταισ
χυνει·την·κεφαλην·αυτου·
Πασα·δε·γυνη·προσευχομενη·
η·προφητευουσα ακατα·κα
λυπτω·κεφαλη·κατα ισχυνει·
την·κεφαλην·αυτησ · Εν·γαρ·
εστιν·και·το·αυτο·τη·εξυρη
μενη · Ει γαρ·ουκατα·καλυπ
τεται·γυνη·και·κερασθω[1]·
Ει·δε·αισχρον·γυναικι·το·κει
ρασθαι · Η·ξυρασθαι·κατα·κ·λ
πτεσθω[2]·ανηρ·μεν·γαρ·ουκ·
οφιλει·κατα·καλυπτεσθαι·
την·κεφαλην·εικων·και·δο
ξα·θυ·υπαρχων·Η·γυνη·δε·
δοξα·του·ανδροσ·εστιν · ουχ[3]·
γαρ·εστιν·ανηρ·εκ·γυναικοσ·
αλλα·γυνη·εξανδροσ·και·
γαρ·ουκ·εκτεισθη·ανηρ·δια·
την·γυνεκα·αλλα·γυνη·
δια·τον·ανδρα · Δια·τουτο·
οφειλει·η·γυνη·εξουσιαν·
εχιν·επι·τησ·κεφαλησ·δια·
τουσ·αγγελουσ · Πλην·ουτε·
γυνη·χωρισ·ανδροσ·ουτε·
ανηρ·χωρισ·γυναικοσ[4]·ενκω·

---

[1] κειρασθω. [2] κατακαλυπτεσθω. [3] ου. [4] ἀγυναικοσ.

Graece	Latine
XI 12 Ωσπερ γαρ · ηγὑνη · εκτου ανδροσ	Nam sicut mulier deviro
οὑτωσ · και ανηρ[1] δια τησ γὑ	ita et vir permulierem
ναικοσ · Ταδε παντα εκ τοὺ θ̅υ̅	erem · Omnia autem ex d̅o̅ ·
13 Εν · ὑμιν · αυτοισ · κρινατε · πρε	Vos ipsi judicate · decet
πον εστιν · γὑναικα · ακατα͜κα	cet mulierem non ve
λυπτον[2] · προσεὑχεσθαι · τω · θ̅ω̅ ·	latam orare d̅m̅
14 Ουδε · η · φὑσισ · διδασκαι[3] · ὑμασ[4] ·	Nec ipsa natura docet vos
οτι · ανηρ · μεν · εαν · κομα ·	quod vir quidæm sicomam
15 [α]τιμια[5] · αυτω · εστιν · Γὑνη δε ·	nutriat ignominia est illi mulier h
εαν · κομα[6] · δοξα · αυτη · εστιν ·	sicomat nutriat g̅l̅a̅ est il
οτι · η · κομη · αντει · περιβο	li · q̅u̅o̅ capilli pro velamine ei
16 λεου · δεδοτε · Ει · δε · τισ · δοκει ·	dati sunt · Siquis autem videtur
φειλονεικοσ · ειναι · Η · μεισ ·	contentiosus esse · Nos
τοι · αυτην · συν · ηθιαν · ουκ · εχο	talem consuetudinem non habe
μεν · ουδε · αι εκκλησειαι · τοὺ	mus neque ecclesia
17 θ̅υ̅ · Τουτο · δε · παραγγελλων ·	d̅i̅ · Hoc autem precipio
ουκ · αιπαινω · οτι · ουκ · εισ · το ·	non laudans q̅d̅ non in
κρισσον · αλλεισ · το · ελαττον ·	melius · sed in deterius
18 σὑνερχεσθαι · Προτον[7] · μεν ·	convenitis · Primum quidem
γαρ · σὑνερχομενων · Ὑμων ·	venientibus vobis
ενεκκλησεια · ακοὑω · σχισ	in e̅c̅c̅l̅a̅ audio scis
ματα · ὑπαρχειν · εν · ὑμιν ·	mata esse intervos
19 και · μερασ[8]τι · πιστεὑω · Δει ·	et exparte credo · Nam oport
γαρ · ꝗ · αιρεσεισ · ειναι · Ινα ·	tet et hereses esse · ut
οιδοκειμοι · φανεροι · γενων	probati manifesti fiant ·
20 ται · εν · ὑμιν · Σὑνερ͜χομε	invobis · Convenientibus
νων · Ὑμων · επιτο · αὑτο ουκ ·	ergo vobis inunum · jam non est
ετει · κὑριακον · διπνον · φαγειν ·	dominicam caenam manducare ·

---

[1] + ο (*ante* ανηρ). [2] ακατακαλυπτον. [3] διδασκει. [4] contra graecos *in marg.* [5] Τιμια. [6] $\overline{\mu\alpha\rho}$ *in marg.* [7] πρωτον. [8] μεροσ.

CAP. XI. V. 21	Unus quisque enim suam caenam	Εκαστοσ · γαρ · το · ιδιον · διπνον ·
	presumit admanducandum	προλαμβανει · επι · τω · φαγειν ·
	et alius quidem esurit alius autem ebrius est ·	και · οσ · μεν · πινα · οσ · δε · μεθὐει
22	Numquid domos non habetis adman	Μη γαρ · οικιασ · οὐκ · εχεται · φα
	ducandum et bibendum · aut ecclesiam ·	γειν · καιπειν · η · τησ · εκκλησιασ ·
	di contemnitis · et	του · θυ · κατα · φρονειται · και ·
	con funditis · eos · qui non ha	καταισχυνεται · τὐυσ · μη · εχον
	bent · Quid dicam vobis · laudo	τασ · Τι · ειπω · ὑμιν · επαι‿νω ·
	vos inhoc · Non laudo ·	ὑμασ · εν · τοὐτω · ουκ · επαινω ·
23	Ego enim accepi adno qd	Εγω · γαρ · παρελαβον · απο · θὐ · ο ·
	et tradidi vobis · quo dns	και · παρεδωκα · ὑμιν · οτι · ο · κσ ·
	ihc inqua nocte tradebatur	ισ · εν · η · νὐκτι · παρεδειδετο ·
24	accepit panem · et gratias a	ελαβεν · τον · αρτον · και · εὐχα
	gens · fregit et dixit ·	ριστησασ · εκλασεν · και · ειπεν ·
		ω
	hoc est corpus meum quod	τοὐτο · μοὐ · εστιν · το · σομα[1] · το ·
		frangetur
	pro vobis tradetur · hoc	ὑπερ · ὑμων · κλω‿μενον · τοὐ
		ε
	facite inmeam commemora	το · ποιειται · εισ · μην[2] · αναμ
25	tionem · Similiter et cali	νησιν · ωσ · αὐτοσ[3] · και · το πο
	cem postquam caenavit · di	τηριον · μετατο · διπνησαι · λε
	cens · hic calix	γων · Τοὐτο · το · ποτηριον · η ·
	novum testamentum est in	καινη · διαθηκη · εστιν · εν · τω ·
	meo sanguine · hoc facite	εμω · αιματι · τοὐτο · ποιειται
	quotiens cumque bibitis in meam	οσ · ακἰσ · αν πειν ηται · εισ · την ·
26	commemorationem · quoties cuq · enim	εμην · αναμ‿νησειν · οσ · ακἰσ · γαρ ·
	manducabitis panem hunc	αναισθειηται · τον · αρτον · του‿
	et calicem bibetis ·	τον · και · το · ποτηρον[4] · πεινηται ·
	mortem dni adnuntiabi	τον θανατον · του · κυ · καταγγελ
27	tis · donec veniat · Itaque	λεται · αχρισ · ου · ελθη · ωστε ·

[1] σωμα. [2] εμην. [3] Ωσαυτωσ. [4] ποτηριον.

XI	ο σαν·αισθειηται·τον·αρτον·η·	quicumque manducaverit panem aut
	πινηται το·ρ̣οι_τηριον[1]·του·κυ·ανα_	biberit calicem dni in di
	ξιωσ·ενοχοσ·εσται·του·σωμα	gne reus erit corpo
	τοσ·και·του·αιμα_τοσ·του·κυ·	ris et sanguinis dni
28	Δοκειμαζετω·δε·εαυ τον·ανθρω	Probet autem se ipsum ho
	ποσ·και·ουτωσ·εκ·του·αρτυ[2]·αισ	mo et sic de pane illo e
	θειετω·και·εκ_του·ποτερι_ου[3]·	dat·et de calice
29	πεινε_τω·Ογαρ·αισθειων·και	bibat·qui enim manducat et
	πεινων·αναξιωσ·κριμα·εαυτω·	bibit indigne·judicium sibi
	αισθειει·ϗ πινει·μη·δια_κρινων·	manducat et bibit non dijudicans
30	το·σωμα·του·κυ·διατουτο·εν	corpus dni · Ideo inter
	υμιν·πολλοι·ασθενεισ·και αρ	vos multi infirmi et imbe
	ρωστοι·και·κοιμωνται·ι_κα	ciles·et dormiunt mul
31	νοι[4] · Ει·δε·εαυτον[5]·διε_κρινο	ti · Qd si nosmet ipsos dijudica
32	μεν·ουκ·ανεκρινομεθα·κρι	remus non utique judicaremus · Dum
	νομενοι·δε·αποκυ·παιδε Υο	judicamur autem adno corripi
	μεθα·Ιναμησυν·το[6]κοσμω	mur·ut non cum hoc mundo
33	τουτο[7] κατακριθωμεν·Ωστε·	damnemur · Itaque
	αδελφοι·μου·συν_ερχομενοι·	fratres mei cum con venitis
	εισ·το·φαγειν·αλληλουσ·εκδε	ad manducandum invicem ex
34	χεσθαι · Ειτισ·πεινα·εν·οι_κω·	pectate · Si quis esurit·domi
	αισθει_ετω·Ινα·μη·εισ·κριμα·	manducet ut non in judicium
	συν ερχεσθαι[8] · Τα·δε·λοιπα·ωσαν·	conveniatis · Cetera autem cum
XII. 1	ελθω·δια·ταξωμαι[9] · Περι·δε·	venero disponam · Despiri
	των·πνευματικων·ουθελω · Υμασ·	talibus autem nolo vos
2	αγνοειν·αδελφοι · Οιδαται·οτι·	ignorare frs · Scitis qm cum
	εθνη·ηται·προσ·τα·ιδωλα·τα·	gentes essetis·adsimulacra
	αμορφα·ωσ·ανηγεσθαι·απαγο	muta prout ducebamini eun

[1] ποτηριον. [2] αρτου. [3] ποτηριου. [4] ἱ ϊκανοι. [5] εαυτουσ.
[6] τω. [7] τουτω. [8] συν ερχησθαι. [9] διαταγησ in marg.

CAP. XII. v. 3 tes · Ideo vobis facio notum quod
nemo in spu di loquens dicit anathe
ma ihu et nemo potest di
cere dns ihc nisi in spu sco
4 Divisiones gratiarum sunt
5 idem autem sps et divi siones
ministracionum sunt · idem autem
6 dns · et divisiones operatio
num sunt · Idem autem ds qui
operatur omnia In omnibus
7 Unicuique autem datur manifesta
tio sps adutilitatem ·
8 Et alii quidem per spm datur
sermo sapientiæ · Alii autem sermo
scientiæ · secundum eundem spiritum
9 Alteri fides in eodem spiritu ·
Alii gratiæ sanitatum
10 In uno spu · Alii operatio
virtututum · Alii prophetatio
alii discretio spirituum
um · Alii genera linguarum ·
Alii interpretatio sermonum ·
11 Hæc autem omnia operatur
unus atque idem sps · Dividens
12 singulis prout vult · Sicut
enim corpus unum est et membra
habet multa · Omnia menbra
corporis cum sint multa · unum

μενοι · Διο · γνοριζω[1] · υμιν · οτι ·
ουδεισ · εν · πνι · θυ · λεγει · αναθε
μα · ιηυ[2] · ϗ · ουδεισ · δυναται · ει_
πειν · κυ · ιν · ειμη · εν · πνι · αγιω ·
Διαιρεσεισ · δε · χαρισματων · εισειν ·
το · δε · αυτο · πνα · και · διαιρεσεισ ·
διακονειων · εισιν · ϗ · ο · αυτοσ ·
κσ · ϗ · διαρεσεισ[3] · ενεργημα_
των · εισειν · ο · αυτοσ · δε · θσ · ο ·
ενεργων · τα · παντα · εν · πασιν
Εκαστω · δε · διδοτε · η · φανερω_
σισ · του · πνσ · προσ · το · συμφερον ·
Ωμεν · γαρ · δια · του · πνσ · διδοται ·
λογοσ · σοφιασ · Αλλω · δε · λογοσ ·
γνοσεωσ[4] · κατα · το · αυτο · πνα ·
Ετερω · πιστισ · εν · τω · αυτω · πνι ·
curarationum
Αλλω · χαρισματα · τα ιαματων
eodem
εν · τω αυτω · πνι · αλλω · ενεργεια ·
virtutis
δυναμαιωσ · Αλλω · προφητια ·
Αλλω · δια_κρισισ · πνευ_
ματων · Ετερω · γενη · γλωσ_
linguarum
σων · Αλλω · δε · ερμηνια · γλωσ
σων · Ταυτα · δε · παντα · ενεργει_
εν · και · το · αυτο · πνα · διαιρουν ·
unicuique
εκαστω · καθοσ[5] · βουλεται · καθα ·
περ · γαρ · το · σωμα · εν εστιν · μελη ·
δε · εχει · πολλα · παντα · δε · τα · μελη ·
του · σωματοσ · πολλ · οντα[6] · ενεσ

---

[1] γνωριζω. [2] ιν. [3] διαιρεσεισ. [4] γνωσεωσ. [5] καθωσ. [6] πολλα οντα.

XII.	τιν·σωμα·οὑτωσ·και·ο·χρσ·	corpus sunt ita et xps
13	και·γαρ·εν·πνι·ημισ·παντεσ·εισ	etenim in uno spu·omnes nos in
	εν·σωμα·εβαπτισθημεν·ειτε·	unum corpus baptizati sumus·sive
	greci	
	ιουδαιοι·ειτε·ελληνεσ[1]·ειτε·	judei sive gentiles sive
	δουλοι·ειτε·ελευθεροι·ϗ·παν	servi sive liberi·et omnes in
14	τεσ·εν·πνα·εποτισθημεν·ϗ·γαρ·	uno spu potati sumus·nam et
	το·σωμα·ουκ·εστιν·εν·μελοσ·αλ .	corpus non est unum membrum·sed
15	λα·πολλα · Εαν·ειπη·ο πουσ·οτι·	multa · Si dixerit pes quo
	ουκ·ειμει·χειρ·ουκ·ειμει·εκτου·	non sum manus·non sum de
	σωματοσ·ουκ[2]·παρατουτο·ουκ·	corpore · non ideo non
16	εστιν·εκ·του·σωματοσ·ϗ·εαν·	est de corpore et si
	ειπη·το·ουσ·οτι·ουκ·ειμει[3]·οφ	dixerit auris quia non sum o
	θαλμοσ·ουκ·ειμι·εκ·του·σωμα	culus·non sum decorpo
	propterea	
	τοσ·ου·παρα τουτο·ουκ·εστιν·	re·non ideo non est
17	εκ·του·σωματοσ · Ει·ολον·το·	de corpore · Si totum
	σωμα·οφθαλμοσ·που·η·ακοη?	corpus oculus·ubi auditus?
	ει·ολον·ακοη·που·η·οσ·φρησισ?	Si totum auditus ubi odoratus?
	nunc posuit	
18	Νυν·δε·ο·θσ·εθετο·τα·μελη·	Nunc autem posuit ds membra
	ενεκασ_τον·αυτων·εν·το[4]·σωμα_	unumquodque eorum in corpo
19	τι·καθωσ·η·θελησεν · Ει·δε ην	re sic voluit · Qd si essent
	παντα·εν·μελοσ·που·το·σωμα·	omnia unum membrum·ubi corpus?
20	Νυν·ειδε·πολλα·μεν·μελη·εν·	Nunc autem multa quidem mbra·1·
21	δε·σωμα·ου·δυναται·ο·οφθαλ	autem corpus·non potest oculus
	ι necessitatem tui	
	μοσ·ε·πιν[5]·τη·χειρει·χριαν·σου·	dicere manui·opera tua non
	non habeo	
	ουκ·εχω·η·παλιν·η·κεφαλη·τοισ·	indigeo · Aut iterum caput
	necessarium vos	
	ποσιν·Χριαν·υμων·ουκ·εχω·	pedibus non estis mihi necessarii
22	αλλα·πολλω·μαλλων[6] · Τα·δοκουν·	Sed multo magis quæ videntur
	τα·μελη·του·σωματοσ·ασθενεσ	membra corporis infirmio

[1] Αλησεσ. [2] ου. [3] ειμι. [4] τω. [5] ειπιν. [6] πολλω μαλλον.

Latin	Greek
CAP. XII. ra esse·necessariora sunt	τερα·υπαρχιν·ανακαια·εστιν·
v. 23 et quæ putamus ignobiliora	και·οδοκουμεν·ατιμοτερα·
membra esse corporis his	ειναι·μελη·του·σωματοσ·του
honorem abundantiorem·cir	τοισ·τιμην·περισσοτεραν·περιτι
cum damus·et quæ inhonesta sunt nra	θεμεν·και·τα·ασχημονα·ημων·
nra abandantiorem honestatem	ευσχΥμοσυνην·περισσοτεραν·
24 habent · Honesta autem nra	εχειν · Τα·δε·ευσχημονα·ημων·
nullius egent · Sed ds	ουχριαν·εχειτημησ[1]·αλλο θσ·
temperavit corpus·ei cui de	συνεκερασεν·το·σωμα·τω·υστε
erat·abundantiorem tribuendo	ρουντι·περισσοτεραν·δουστιμην·
25 honorem·ut non sit scisma in corpore	ινα·μη·η·σχισματα·εν·τω·σωματι·
re sed id ipsum pro in vicem	αλλα·τα·αυτα·υπερ·αλληλων·
26 sollicita sunt membra·et si quid	μεριμνα·τα·μελη·και·ειτι·
patitur unum membrum·compatiuntur	πασχει·εν·μελοσ·συν·πασχει·παν
omnia membra · Sive gloriatur unum	τα·τα·μελη · Ειτε·δοξαζεται·εν·
membrum·congaudent omnia mem	μελοσ·συνχαιρει·παντα·τα·με
27 bra · Vos autem estis corpus xpi et	λη · Υμασ·δε·σωμαι[2]·εσται·χυ·και
28 membra demembro·et quosdam qui	μελη·εκ·μερουσ·και·ουσ μεν·
quidem posuit ds in ecclesia·	εθε το·ο·θσ·εν·τη·εκκλεσια[3]·
primum apostolos · Secundo	πρωτον·αποστολουσ·δευτερον·
prophetas tertio doctores·	προφητασ·τριτον·διδασκαλουσ·
deinde virtutes·exinde gratias	ειπει·τα·δυναμεισ·Χαρισματα·
curationum·opitulationes·gu	ιαματων·αντειλημψεισ·κυ
bernationes·genera linguarum·	βερνησεισ·γενη·γλωσσον[4]·
29 Numquid omnes apostoli nuqd oms	Μη[5]·παντεσ·αποστολοι·μη·παντεσ
oms prophete? nuqd oms doctores?	προφηται·μη·παντεσ·διδασκαλοι·
30 nuqd oms virtutes? nuqd oms	μη·παντεσ·δυναμισ·μη·παντεσ·χα
gratia habent curationum?	ρισματα·εχουσειν·ιαμα·των·

[1] εχειτιμησ. [2] σωμα. [3] εκκλησια. [4] γλωσσων. [5] γυσαι vel γυσω in marg.

II. μη[1] · παντεσ · γλωσσαισ · λαλουσειν ·	nuquid oms linguis lo cuntur?
μη · παντεσ · διερμηνευ͜ουσειν ·	nuqd oms interpretantur?
31 Ζελουται · δε · χαρισματα · (τα.) κρισ	aemulamini autem xarismatama
σονα[2] · ειτει[3] · καθΎπερβολην · οδον ·	jora · et adhuc excellentiorem viam
II I δικνυμι · ὑμιν · Εαν · ταισ · γλωσ	vobis demonstro · Si linguis
σαισ · των · ανθρωρ̣πων[4] · λαλω · κ̣ ·	hominum loquar et
των · αγγελων · αγαπην · δε · μη ·	angelorum · caritatem autem non
(unum) εχω · εν · ειμει · η · χαλικοσ · ηχων ·	habeam · factus sum velut aes so
2 η · κυμβαλον · αλαλαζον · και · εαν ·	nans aut cẏmbalum tinniens · et si
εχω · προφητεῖαν · και · ουδα ·	et si habuero prophetiam · et noverim
τα · μυστηρια · τα · παντα · κ̣ · πασαν ·	mẏsteria omnia · et omnem
την · γνωσιν · κ̣ · εαν · εχω · πασαν ·	scientiam · et habuero omnem
(ν.) τη[5] · πιστιν · Ωστε · ορη · μεθεισ͜	fidem ita ut montes transfe
ταναι · αγαπην · δε · μη · εχω · ουδεν ·	ram · caritatem autem non habuero nihil
3 ειμει · κ̣ · εαν · ψωμεισω[6] · παν	nihil sum · et si distribuero in ci
(substantias) τα · τα · υπαρχοντα · μου ·	bos pauperum omnes
[7]	facultates meas ·
κ̣ · εαν · παραδωσω · το · σωμα · μου ·	Et si tradiro corpus meum
ἵνα · καυθησομαι · αγαπην · δε ·	ita ut ardeam · caritatem autem
ϊ ι η[8] · εχω · ουδεν · ωφελουμαι[9] ·	non habuero · nihil mihi prodest
4 Η · αγαπη · μακροθυμάι[10] · χρησ	Caritas patiens est benigna est
τευεται · η · αγαπη · ου · ζηλοι ·	caritas non aemulatur ·
η · αγαπη · ου · περπερευεται · ου ·	non agit perperam · Non
5 φυσει · ου · ται · ουκ · κ̣ασχημονοι[11] ·	inflatur · non est ambitiosa
ου · ζητει · τα · ε αυτησ · ου · παροξυ	non quærit quæ sua sunt · Non irta
νεται · ου · λογιζεται · το · κακον ·	irritatur · non cogitat malum
6 ου · χαιρει[12] · επι · αδικια · συν χαιρι ·	non gaudet super iniquitate · congaudet
7 δε · τη · αληθια · παντα αστατι	gaudet autem veritati · Omnia suffert

[1] γισω in marg. [2] τα κρισσονα. [3] ετει. [4] ανθρωπων. [5] την. [6] ψωμ̣̇μεισω. [7] Spatium vacuum. [8] μη. [9] Spatium breve in fin. vers. [10] μακροθυμει. [11] ασχημονει. [12] χαιρι.

CAP. XIII. omnia credit · omnia sperat ·
v. 8 omnia sustinet · caritas num
quam excidet · sive prophetiæ
evacuabuntur · sive linguæ
cessabunt sive scientia destru
9 etur · Ex parte enim cognosci
mus · et ex parte prophetamus ·
10 Cum autem venerit quod
perfectum est · evacuabitur · q̄d ex
11 parte est · Cum essem parvulus lo
loquebar ut parvulus · sapiebam ut
bam ut parv̄ulus · cogitabam ut parvul̄
Quando autem factus sum vir evacuav̄i q
12 erant parvuli · Videmus nunc
per speculum in enigmate
tunc autem facie ad faciem ·
nunc cognosco exparte · tunc
autem cognoscam sicut et
13 cognitus sum Nunc autem manet fides
spes · caritas · tria hæc · major
CAP. XIV. 1 autem his est caritas · Sectami
ni caritatem emulamini autem
spiritalia · magis autem ut pro
·te 2 phētis · Qui enim loquitur
lingua · non hominibus loquitur
sed d̄o · Nemo enim audit · s̄pu
3 autem loquitur mÿsteria · nam qui pro
phetat hominibus loquitur adæ

παντα · πιστευει · παντα · ελπιζει ·
παντα · ὑπομενι · Η · αγαπη · ουδε ·
ποτε · εκπιπτι · Εἰτε · προφητειαι ·
καταργηθησονται · ειτε · γλωσσαι ·
παυσονται · ειτε · γνωσεισ · καταρ_
γηθησονται · Εκ · μερουσ · γαρ · γει
νωσκομεν · ϗ εκ · μερουσ · πρὸ
φητευομεν · Οταν · δε · ελθη · το ·
τελειον · καταργηθησεται · τα · εκ
μερούσ · Οτε · ημην · νηπιοσ · ωσ ·
νηπιοσ · λαλουν · ωσ · νηπιοσ · εφρο_
νουν · ωσ · νηπιοσ · λογειζομην ·
Οτε · δε · γεγονα · ανηρ · τα · τȣ · νηπιου
κατηργηκα · Βλεπομεν · αρτει ·
διεσοπτρου · εν · αινειγματι ·
τοτε · δε · προσωπον · προσ · προσωπον
αρτει · γινωσκω[1] · εκ · μερȣσ · τοτε ·
δε · επιγνωσομαι[2] · καθωσ · ϗ · εγω
επι · γνωθην[3] · Μινειδε · πιστισ ·
ελπισ · αγαπη · Τα · τρια · ταυτα · μει
ζων · δε · τουτων · η · αγαπη · Αιω
κεται · την · αγαπην · Ζελουται[4] · δε ·
τα · πνευματικα · μαλλον · δε · ινα ·
προφητευεται · Ο · γαρ · λαλων ·
γλωσσαισ · οὐκ · αν̄ουσ · λαλει · αλ
λα · θ̄ω · ȣ̇ · δεισ · γαρ · ακουει · π̄να ·
δε · λαλει · μυστηρια · ει · γαρ · ο · προ
φητευων · ανθρωπȣσ · λαλει · οι_

---

[1] γυνωσκω. [2] εκ μερουσ επι γνωσομαι. [3] επι γνωσθην. [4] Ζηλουται.

IV.	κοδομην·και·παρακλησιν·και·	dificationem·et exortationem et
Γ. 4	παραμυθειαν · Ο·λαλει[1]·γλωσση·	consolationem · Qui loquitur lingua
	εαυτον·οικοδμι[2]·Οδε·προ φη	semetipsum aedificat · Qui autem prophe
	τευων·εκκλησειαν·θυ·οικοδο	tat·aecclesiam aedificat·
5	μι · Θελω·δε·παντασ·υμασ·λα	Volo autem omnes vos lo
	λειν[3]·γλωσσαισ·μαλλον·δε·ινα·	qui linguis·magis autem
	προφητευετε · Μιζων·γαρ·εστιν·	prophetare · Nam major est
	ο·προφητευων·η·ο·λαλων·γλωσ	qui prophetat·quam qui loquitur lin
	σαισ·εκτυσ·ειμη·η·ο·διερμηνευ_	guis·nisi forte interprete
	ων·ινα·η·εκκλησεια·οικοδομην·	tur·ut ecclesia aedificationem
6	λαβη · Νυν·δε·αδελφοι·εαν·ελθω·	accipiat · Nunc autem frs si venero
	προσ·υμασ·γλωσσαισ·λαλων·τι·	ad vos linguis loquens·quid
	υμασ·ωφελησω·εαν·μη·υμιν·	vobis prodero·nisi si vobis
	λαλησω·η·εν·αποκαλυψι·η·εν·	loquar·aut in revelatione aut in
	γνωσι·η·εν·προφητια·η·διδαχη·	scientia·aut prophetia·aut i doctrina
7	Ομοσ[4]·τα·αψυχα·φωνην·διδον_	Tam quæ sine anima sunt vocem dan
	τα·ειτε·αυλοσ·ειτε·κιθαρα·	tia·sive tibia·sive cithara
	εαν·μη·διαστολη·φθογγοισ·δω·	nisi distinctionem sonituum dederint
	πωσ·γνωσθη·το·αυλουμενον·	quomodo scietur·qd canitur
8	η·το·κιθαριζομενον·και·γαρ·	aut qd citharizatur·et enim
	tuba εαν·αδηλον·φωνην·σαλπινξ·	si incertam vocem det tuba
	det paratur δω·τισ·παρασ_κευασεται·εισ·πο	quis parabit se ad bel
9	λεμον·ουτωσ·και·υμεισ·δια·	lum · Ita et vos per
	τησ·γλωσσην[5]·εαν·μη·ευσημον·	linguam nisi manifestum
	λογον·δωτε·πωσ·γνωσθησεται·	sermonem dederitis quomodo scietur
	το·λαλουμενον·Εσεσ_θαι·γαρ·	id qd dicitur · Eritis enim
10	εισ·αερα·λαλουντεσ·ειτυχου·	in aera loquentes tam multa ut puta
	vocum γενη·φωνων·εισιν·εν·τω·κοσμω·	genera linguarum sunt in hoc mundo

[1] λαλειῦ λαλων (*in textu*). [2] οικοδομι. [3] αλλειν. [4] Ομωσ. [5] γλωσσ.

CAP. XIV. V. 11	et nihil sine voce est · Si	ϗ · ουδεν · αφωνον · εστιν · Εαν ·
	ergo nesciero virtutem	ουν · μη · γινωσκω · την · δυναμην ·
	vocis · ero ei cui loquor	τησ · φωνησ · εσομαι · τω · λαλουντι ·
	barbarus · et qui loquitur mihi	βαρβαροσ · και · ο · λαλων · εμοι ·
12	barbarus · Sic et vos	βαρβαροσ · Ουτοσ[1] · και · υμεισ ·
	quo emulatores estis spirituum	επι · ζηλωται · εσται · πνευματων ·
	ad ædicationem eccles	προσ · την · οικοδομην · τησ · εκκλη
	ae · quærite ut abundetis	σιασ[2] · ζητιτε · ινα · περισσευηται ·
13	et ideo qui loquitur lingua oret	διο · ο · λαλων γλωσση · προσεύ_χεσ_
14	ut interptetur · Nam si	θω · ινα · διερμηνευη · εαν ·
	orem lingua · spiritus	προσ · εύχομαι · γλωσση · το · πνα ·
	meus orat · mens autem	μού · προσ · ευχεται · Ο · δε · νούσ ·
15	mea sine fructu est · Quid ergo est	μου · ακαρποσ · εστιν · Τι · ουν · εστιν ·
	orabo spu · orabo	προσ · ευξωμαι[3] · τω · πνι · προσ · ευξω_
	et mente · Psallam spu psal	μαι · και · τωνοι · ψαλω · πνι · ψα_
16	lam et mente · Ceterum si	λο[4] · και · τω νοει · Επει · εαν ·
	benedixeris spu qui sup	ευλογησησ · πνευματι · ο · ανα
	plet locum idiotae	πληρων · τον τοπον · του · ιδιωτού ·
	quomodo dicet am super tuam bene	πωσ · ερει · αμην · επι · τησ · η · ευχα
	dictionem · quo quid dicas ne	ριστία · επι · δη · ουκοιδεν · τι · λε
17	scit · Nam tu quidem bene grati	γισ · Cυμεν · γαρ · καλωσ · ευχα
	as agis · sed alter non aedifi	ριστεύσ[5] · αλλω[6] · εταιροσ · ουκ · οι_
18	catur · Gratias ago	κοδομιται · Ευχαριστω · τω ·
	quod omnium vestrum lingua	θω · οτι · παντων · υμων γλωσση ·
19	loquor · Sed in aecclesi	μαλλον · λαλο[7] · αλλεν[8] · εκκλη
	a volo quinque verba loqui	σεία · θελω · πενται · λογουσ · λαλη
	sensu meo · ut et alios	quidem ο μεν · τω · νοι · μου · ίνα · καλλουσ ·
	instruam quam · x · milia verborum	κατηχησω · η · υμυριουσ · λογουσ

[1] Ουτωσ. [2] εκκλεσιασ. [3] προσευξωμαι *p.m.* (utrum non liquet). [4] ψαλω. [5] ευχαριστεισ. [6] Αλλο. [7] λαλω. [8] αγαρο *in margine*

XIV. εν·γλωσση·	inlingua·
20 Αδελφοι·μη·παιδια·γεινεσθαι·	Fratres mei nolite pueri effici
ταισ·φρεσιν · αλλα·τη·κακια·	sensibus·sed malitia
νηρει·αζεται[1]·Ινα·ταισ·φραισειν·	parvuli estote·ut sensibus
21 τελιοι·γενησθαι · Εν·τω·νομω·	perfecti sitis · Inlege
γεγραπται · Οτι·εν·ετεραισ·γλωσ	scriptum est $\overline{\text{quo}}$ inaliis lin
σαισ·ϗ εν·χιλεσειν·ετεροισ·	guis·et labiis aliis
λαλησω·τω·λαω·τουτω · και·	loquar populo huic·et
ουδε·πωεισ·ακουσεται·μου·λε	nec sic exaudient me di
22 γι·$\overline{\kappa\sigma}$ · ωστε·αιγλωσσαι·εισ·σημι	cit $\overline{\text{dns}}$ · Itaque linguae insi
ον·εισιν·εισ·ουτουσ[2]·πιστευουσιν·	gnum sunt non fidelibus
αλλα·τοισ·απιστοισ · Η·δε·προφη	sed infidelibus · Prophetiae
τεια·ουτοισ·απιστοισ·αλλα·τοισ	autem non infidelibus sed
23 πιστοισ · Εαν·συν ελθη[3]ολη·η·εκ	fidelibus · Siergo conveniat univer
κλησεια·επι·το·αυτο·ϗ·παντεσ·	sa ecclesia inunum·et omnes
λαλησωσιν[4]·γλωσσαισ·εισ·ελθω‿	linguis loquantur · Intrent
σιν·δε·ιδιωται·η·απιστοι·	autem idiotæ·aut infideles
ουκ·αυρουσειν·οτι·μενεσθαι·	nonne dicent $\overline{\text{qd}}$ insanitis·
24 Εαν·δε·παντεσ·προφηευωσιν[5]·	Si autem omnes prophetent·
εισ ελθη·δε·τισ·απιστοσ·η·ιδιωτησ·	intret autem quis infidelis aut idiota
ελεγχεται·υπο·παντων·ανακρι	convincitur abomnibus dijudica
25 νεται·υποπαντων·τα·κρυπτα·τησ·	tur abomnibus · Occulta cordis
καρδιασ·αυτου·φανερα·γεινεται·	cordis ejus manifesta fiunt·
Και·ουτωσ·πεσων·επι·προσωπον·	et ita cadens in faciem
προσ·κυνησει·τω·$\overline{\theta\omega}$·αναγγελλων[6]·	adorabit $\overline{\text{dm}}$ pronuntians
οτι·οντωσ·$\overline{\theta\sigma}$·εν·υμιν·εστιν·	$\overline{\text{qd}}$ vere $\overline{\text{ds}}$ in vobis sit·
26 Τι·ουν·εστιν·αδελφοι·οταν·συν·ερ	Quid ergo est $\overline{\text{frs}}$·cum conve
χησθαι·εκαστοσ·υμων·ψαλμον	nitis·unus quisque vestrum psalmum

[1] νηπειαζεται. [2] Ου τοισ. [3] συν ελθη. [4] λαλησωσιν. [5] προφητευωσιν. [6] απαγωνγελλων.

CAP. XIV.	habet · doctrinam habet · apocalipsin ·	εχει · διδαχην · εχει · αποκαλυψιν ·
	habet · linguam habet · interptationem	εχει · γλωσσαν · εχει[1] · διερμηνειαν ·
	habet · Omnia adaedificationem	εχει · Παντα · προσ · οικοδομην · γει
v. 27	fiant · Sive lingua quis loquitur scdm ·	νεσθω · Ειτε · γλωσση · τισ · λαλει · κατα ·
	duos · aut multum tres · et per partes	δυο · η · το · πλιστον · τρισ · και · αναμε_
28	et unus interpretetur · Si autem	ροσ · και · εισ · διερμη_νευτω · Εαν · δε ·
	non fuerit interpres · taceat in ec	μη · η · υ · ερμηνεύτησ · σιγατω · εν · εκκλη
	clesia · sibi autem loquatur · et do	σια · αυτω · δε · λαλιτω · ϗ τω · θω ·
29	Prophetæ duo aut tres dicant ·	Προφηται · δε · δυο · η · τρεισ · λαλειτωσαν ·
30	et ceteri dijudicent · Quod si	και · αλλοι · ανακρινετωσαν · Εαν ·
	alii revelatum fuerit sedenti	αλλω · αποκαλυφθη · καθημενω ·
31	prior taceat · Potestis enim oms	ο · πρωτοσ · σειγατω · Δυνασθαι · γαρ · πα
	per singulos prophetare · Ut	τεσ · καθενα · προφητευεσιν[2] · Ινα ·
	oms discant · et oms	παντεσ · μανθανωσιν[3] · ϗ παντεσ ·
32	exortentur · et sps propheta	παρακαλωνται · ϗ πνα · προ
	rum prophetis subjecti	φητων · προφηταισ · υποσ τασσε
33	sunt · Non enim est dissensionis	ται[4] · Ου · γαρ · εστιν · ακαταστασταστασε –
	ds sed pacis · sicut inomnibus	θσ · αλλιρηνησ · ωσ · εν · πασαισ · ταισ ·
	ecclesiis sanctorum doceo ·	εκκλησιαισ · των · αγιων · διδασκω ·
36	an avobis verbum di proces	Η · αφυμων · ο · λογοσ · του · θυ · εξηλ_
	sit invos solos pervenitur?	θεν · η · εισ · υμασ · κατην_τησεν[6] · μο
37	Siquis videtur propheta es	νουσ · Ειτισ · δοκει · προφητησ · ει_
	se · aut spiritalis · cognoscat	ναι[7] · η · πνευματικοσ[8] · επι · γινωσ_
	quæ scribo vobis quia dni mandata	κετω · αγραφω · ὑμιν · οτι · κυ · εσ
38	sunt · Siquis autem ignorat ignorabitur ·	τιν[9] · Ειδε · τισ · αγνοει[10] · η · γνοειται ·
39	Itaque frs emulamini prophe	Ωστε · αδελφοι · ζηλουται · προφὺ
	tare · et loqui linguis	τευειν · ϗ · το · λαλειν · εν γλωσ
40	nolite prohibere · Omnia autem hones	σαισ · μη · κωλευετε[11] · Παντα · δε · ευσ

1 εχι *secundum*. 2 προφητευειν. 3 μανθανωσιν. 4 ἱποτασσεται. 5 ακαστασταστασειασ. 6 κατηντησεν. 7 ειναι. 8 πνευματεικοσ. 9 εστειν. 10 αγνοει. 11 κωλυετε.

V.	χημωνοσ[1] · και · καταταξιν · γινεσθο[2] ·	ste et secundum ordinem fiant ·
	vestrae	
34	Αιγυνεσκαισ[3] · υμων · εν · ταισ · εκκλη	ulieres in ecclesiis
	σειαισ · σιγατωσαν · ȣ · γαρ · επι · τρε	taceant · non enim permittit
	πεται · αυταισ · λαλειν · αλλυπο	titur eis loqui sed subditas
	·σ	
	τασσεσθαι · καθω[4] · κ̄ϛ · ονομοσ · λε	esse · Sicut et lex di
35	γι · Ειτι · δε · μαθειν · θελουσεν ·	cit · Siquid autem discere volunt
	ενοικω · τοισ[5] · ῑδιουσ · ανδρασ · επε‿	domi viros suos interro
	ρωτα‿τωσαν · Αισχρον · γαρ · εστιν ·	gent · Turbe enim est
	mulieribus	
	γυναιξιν · εν · εκκλησιαισ · λαλῖν	mulieri loqui in ecclesia
	notesco	
XV. 1	Γνωριζω · δε · υμιν · αδελφοι · το	Notum aut vobis facio fratres
	ευαγγελιον · ο · ευηγγλεισαμην[6] ·	evangelium quod predicavi
	ὑμιν · ο · και παρελαβετε · εν · ο[7] ·	vobis · quod et accepistis · in quo
2	και · στηκεται · διου̇ · κ̄ϛ · σωζεσθαι ·	et statis per q̄d̄ et salvamini ·
	τινι · λογω · εὐηγγελεισαμην · ὑμιν ·	qua ratione p̄dicaverim vobis
	οφιλεται · κατεχειν · εκτοσ · ειμη ·	sitenetis · nisi frustra
3	ει · κη · επιστεὐσαται · Παρεδωκα ·	credidistis · Tradidi enim vobis
	ω	
	γαρ · ὑμιν · εν · προ τοισ[8] · ο · και · πα	enim vobis inprimis q̄d̄ et ac
	ρελαβον · Οτι · χ̄σ̄ · απεθανεν ·	cepi quia x̄p̄c̄ mortuus est
	ὑπερ · των · αμαρτιων · η · ὑμων[9] ·	pro peccatis nostris · secundum
4	κατα · τασ · γραφασ · κ̄ϛ οτι · εταφη ·	dum scrpturas · et quia sepultus est
	κ̄ϛ · οτι · εγηγερται · τη · τριτη · ημε	et quia surrexit tertia die
5	ρα · κατα · τασ · γραφασ · κ̄ϛ · οτι · ωφ	secundum scripturas · et quia visus
	illis	
	θη · κηφα · και · μεταταὐτα · τοισ ·	sus est cephae et post haec
6	ενδεκα · Επιτα · ωφθη · επανω ·	undecim · Deinde visus est plus q̲
	πεντα‿κοσιοισ · αδελφοισ · εφαπαξ ·	quingentis fratribus simul
	εξων · οι · πλιονεσ · μενȣσιν · εωσ	ex quibus multi manent usque ad
	αρτι · τινεσ · δε · εκοιμηθησαν ·	huc · quidam autem dormierunt
7	Επιστα · ωφθη · ῑακωβο[10] · επιτα	Deinde visus est iacobo · deinde

---

[1] ευσχημονωσ. [2] γινεσθω. [3] γυνεκαισ. [4] καθωσ. [5] τουσ. [6] ευηγγελεισαμην. [7] ω. [8] πρωτοισ. [9] αμαρτιων ημων. [10] επιτα ωφθη ῐακωβω.

CAP. XV. v. 8 apostolis omnibus · Novissi
me autem omnium tamquam abor
9 tivo visus est et mihi · Ego
enim sum minimus aposto
lorum · qui non sum dignus
vocari apostolus · quo perse
cutus sum ecclesiam di ·
10 Gratia autem di sum id qd sum · et
gratia ejus · in me vacua
non fuit · sed abundantius
illis omnibus laboravi · non
autem ego · sed gratia di mecum ·
11 Sive autem ego sive illi ·
sic praedicamus · et sic
12 credidistis · Si autem xpc pdi
catur · qd resurrexit a mortuis
quo modo quidam dicunt in vobis ·
qm resurrectio mortuorum non est ·
13 Si autem resurrectio mortuorum non
es · neque xpc resurrexit ·
14 Si autem xpc non resurrexit inanis
est ergo praedicatio nostra
15 inanis est et fides vestra · Inve
nimur autem et falsi te
stes di qm testimonium dixi
mus adversus dm · qd suscitave
rit xpm quem non suscitavit
16 si mortui non resurgunt

τοισ · αποστολοισ · πασιν · Λισχα
τον · δε · παντων · ωσ · περι εκτρο
ματι[1] · ωφθη · και · εμοι · Εγω ·
γαρ · ειμι · ο · ελαχιστοσ · των · απο
στολων · οσ · οὐκ · ειμι · ἱκανοσ ·
καλισθαι · αποστολοσ · δι · οτι · εδει
ωξα · την · εκκλησειαν · τοὐ θυ ·
Χαριτι · δε · θὐ · ειμι · ο · ειμι · και · η ·
χαρισ · αὐτοὐ · εισ · εμαι · πτωχη ·
οὐ · γεγονεν · αλλα · περισσοτερον ·
αὐτων · παντων · εκοπειασα · ȣκ ·
εγω · δε · αλλη · χαρισ · τȣ · θυ · σὐνε
μοι · Ειτε · δε εγω · ειτε · εκεινοι ·
ȣτωσ · κηρυσσομεν · και · οὐτωσ ·
επιστεὐσαται · Ειδε · χσ · κηρὐσ
σεται · εκνεκρων · οτι · εγιγερται[2] ·
πωσ · λεγοὐσιν · τινεσ · εν · ὐμιν ·
οτι · αναστασεισ · νεκρων · οὐκ · εστιν ·
Εαν · δε · αναστασισ · νεκρων · οὐκ ·
εστιν · οὐδε · χσ · εγηγερται ·
Ειδε · χσ · οὐκ · εγηγερται · καινον ·
αρα · και · το · κηρὐγμα · ημων ·
καινη · και · η · πιστισ · ὐμων · Εὐ
ρισκομεθα · δεκαι[3] · ψευδομαρ
τυρεσ · τοὐ · θυ · οτι · εμαρτὐρη
σαμεν · κατα · τοὐ · θυ · οτι · εγιγεν
τον · χν · ον · οὐκ · ηγειρεν · ειπερ ·
αρα · οι · νεκροι · ουκ · εγιρονται · ει

---

1 εκτρωματι.

2 εγηγερται.

3 ᾳδεκαι.

ιρ·νεκροι·οὐκ·εγειρονται·ουδε·
σ εγηγερται· Ειδε·χσ·οὐκ·εγη
ρται·ματαια·η·πιστισ·ὑμων·
ι·εσται·εν·ταισ·αμαρτιασ[1]·ὑμων·
ρα·και·οι·κυιμηθεντεσ·εν·χω·
πολοντο[2]·Ει·εν·τη·ζωη·ταὐτη·
·χρω·ηλπ_ικοτεσ·εσμεν·μο
ον·ελεινοτεροι·παντων·ανων·
σμεν· Νὐν·δε·χσ·εγηγερ
ται·εκτων·νεκρων·απαρχη·
των κεκοιμη_μενων[3]·επει·δη·γαρ·
δια·ανοὐ·ο·θανατοσ·κ·δια[4]·ανου·
αναστασισ·νεκρον[5]·ωσ·περ·γαρ
εν·τω·αδαμ·παντεσ·αποθνησκοὐ_
σιν·οὐτωσ·κ·εν·τω·χω·παν
τεσ·ζω_οποιηθη_σονται· Εκαστοσ·
δε·εν·τω·ϊδιωταγματι·απαρχη·
χσ·επειτα·οι·τοὐ·χὐ·οι·εν·τη·
παροὐσια·αὐτοὐ·ελπισαντεσ· (sperantes)
ειτα·το·τελοσ· Οταν·παραδειδοι·
την·βασιλιαν·τω·θω·κ·πνι[6]·οταν·
καταργηση·πασαν·αρχην·κ·πα
σαν·εξοὐσειαν·κ·δὐναμειν·
Δει·γαρ·αὐτον·βασιλεὐιν·αχρι
οὐ·θη·παντασ·τοὐσ·εκθροὐσ·
ντου·υπο·τοὐσ·ποδασ· αισ
χτοσ·εκθροσ·καταργιται·ο·
νατοσ· Παντα·γαρ·ὐπεταξεν

nam si mortui non resurgunt·neque
xpc resurrexit· Si autem xpo non resur
rexit·vana est fides vestra·
adhuc enim estis inpeccatis vestris·
ergo et qui dormierunt in xpo
perierunt· Si in hac vita tantum
in xpo·sperantes sumus
miserabiliores sumus omnibus
hominibus· Nunc autem xps re
surrexit amortuis·primitiæ
dormientium·quo enim
p hominem mors·et p hominem
resurrectio mortuorum·et sicut
in adam oms moriuntur
ita et in xpo oms·vivifi
cabuntur· Unus quisque
autem insuo ordine·primitiae
xpc·deinde hi qui sunt xpi in
adventu ejus·
deinde finis cum tradiderit
regnum do et patri·cum
evacuerit omnem principatus
et potestatem et virtutem·
Oportet enim illum regnare donec
ponat omnes inimicos
suos sub pedibus ejus Novis
sima autem inimica destruetur
mors· Omnia enim subjecit·

---

[1] αμαρτιαισ. [2] απωλοντο. [3] κεκοιμημενων. [4] δι secundum. [5] νεκρων. [6] πρι.

CAP. XV. sub pedibus ejus · Cum
autem dicit · quia omnia subjecta sunt
ei · sine dubio praeter eum qui sub
v. 28 jecit ei omnia · Cum autem
subjecta fuerint ei omnia · tunc
et ipse filius subjectus erit
ei qui sibi subjecit omnia
ut sit d̅s̅ omnia inomnibus
29 Alioquin quid facient qui bapti
zantur pro mortuis · si omni
no mortui non resurgunt ·
ut quid baptizantur pro illis
30 ut quid et nos periclitamur om
31 ni hora · Cotidie morior
pro vestra gloria · quam abeo in x̅p̅o̅ i̅h̅u̅
quam abeo in x̅p̅o̅ i̅h̅u̅ d̅n̅o̅
32 nostro · Si secundum hominem ad
bestias pugnavi effesi · quid mihi
prodest si mortui nonresurgunt ·
manducemus · et bibamus · cras
33 enim moriemur · Nolite seduci ·
corrumpunt mores bonos
34 colloquia mala · Evigilate justi
et nolite peccare ·
Ignorantiam enim d̅i̅ quidam habent
35 adreverentiam vobis dico ·
seddicit aliquis · quomodo resurgent
mortui · quali autem corpore venient ·

ὑπο · τοὑσ · ποδασ · αὑτου · Οταν ·
δε επη[1] · οτι · παντα · ὑποτε · τακται ·
αὑτω · δελον[2] · οτι · εκτυσ · τοὑ ὑπο
ταξαντοσ · αὑτω · παντα[3] · Οταν ·
δε · ὑποταγη · αὑτω · τα · παντα · τοτε ·
αυτοσ · ο · ὑιοσ · ὑποταγησεται ·
τω · ὑποταξαντι · αὑτω · τα · παντα ·
ἱνα · η · ο · θ̅σ̅ · τα · παντα · εν · πασειν ·
Επει · τι · ποι · ουσειν · οι · βαπτιζο
μενοι · ὑπερ · των νεκρον[4] · ει ·
ολωσ · νεκροι · οὑκ · εγειρονται ·
τι · και · βαπτιζονται · ὑπερ · αὑτων ·
τι · και · ημεισ · κινδὑνευὁμεν · πα
σαν · οραν[5] · καθημεραν · αποθνησ
κω · νη · την · ὑμετεραν · καὑχη
σιν · ἑν · εχω[6] · εν · χ̅ω̅ · ι̅υ̅ · τω · κ̅ω̅ ·
ημον[7] · Ει · κατα · ανθρωπον · εθη
ριο · μαχησα · εν εφεσσω · Τι · μοι ·
οφελοσ · ει · νεκροι · οὑκ · εγιρονται ·
φαγωμεν · και · πιωμεν · αὑριον ·
γαρ · αποθνησκομεν · μη · πλανασ
θαι · φθιροὑσειν · ηθηρ[8] · χρησ · τα
sobrii estote
ομιλιαι · κακαι · Εκνη ψαται · δι
καιωσ · και · μη · αμαρτανεται ·
Αγνωσἱαν · γαρ · θ̅υ̅ · τινεσ · εχοὑσειν ·
προσ · εν · τροπην · ὑμιν · λεγω · Αλ
λερει · τισ · πωσ · εγιρονται · οι · νε
κροι · ποιω · δε · σωματι · ερχονται ·

---

[1] ειπη. [2] δηλον. [3] + τα (*ante* παντα). [4] νεκρων. [5] ωραν.
[6] ην εχω. [7] ημων. [8] η . θηρ.

αφρων · σὺ · οσ · πειρεισ · οὐ · ζω_οποι_	insipiens tu q̅d̅ seminas · non vivi
ειται · εαν · μη · πρωτων[1] · αποθανη ·	ficatur · Nisi prius moriatur ·
Και · οσπιρεισ · οὐτο · σωμα · το · γεν_	et q̅d̅ seminas non corpus q̅d̅
nasciturum νησομενον · σπειρεισ · αλλα · γὺμ	futurum est seminas · sed nu
νον · κοκον · ειτὺχοισ · ει τοὺ ·	dum granum · utputa tritici
η · τινοσ · των · λοιπων · Ο · δε · θ̅σ̅ · αὺ	aut alicujus cæterorum · D̅s̅ autem
τω · διδωσιν · σωμα · καθωσ · ηθε	dat illi corpus sicut volu
λησεν · ϗ · εκαστω · των · σπερμα	it · et unicuique semi
των · ϊδιων[2] · σωμα · Οὺ · πασα · σαρξ ·	num proprium corpus · Non omnis caro
η · αὺτη · αλλ_αλλη · μεν · α̅ν̅ω̅ν̅ ·	eadem caro · Sed alia hominum
αλλη · δε · κτηνοὺσ[3] · αλλη · δε · ιχθὺ_	alia pecorum · alia vero pisci
40 ων · αλλη · δε · σαρξ · πετινον[4] · και ·	um · alia volucrum · et cor
σωματα · επουρανια · ϗ · επηγια	pora caelestia · et corpora tr̄estria
Αλλετερα · μεν · η · των · επούρα	Sed alia quidem caelestium
νιων · δοξα[5] · ετερα · δε · η · των ·	gla · alia autem terrestrium
41 επιγιων · αλλη · δε · δοξα · ηλιοὺ ·	Alia claritas solis
αλλη · δε · δοξα · σεληνησ · και ·	alia claritas lunae et
αλλη · δοξα · αστερον[6] · αστηρ ·	alia claritas stellarum · Stella
γαρ · αστεροσ · διαφερει · εν · δοξη ·	autem abstella differt inclaritate ·
42 οὺτωσ · και · η · αναστασισ · των · νε	sic et resurrectio mortuo
κρων · Cπιρεται · εν · φθορα · εγι	rum · Seminatur incorruptione
43 ρεται · εν · αφθαρσια · Cπιρεται · εν ·	surgit inincorruptione · Seminatur
ατιμια · εγιρεται · εν · δοξη · Cπι	inignobilitate · surgit in g̅l̅a̅ · Semi
ρεται[7] · εν · ασθενια · εγειρεται · εν ·	natur ininfirmitate · surgit in
δὺναμει · Cπιρεται · σωμα · ψὺ	virtute · Seminatur corpus ani
χικον · εγιρεται · σωμα · πνεὺμα	male · surgit corpus spiri
τικον · Ει[8] · εστιν · σωμα · ψὺχικον ·	tale · Si est corpus animale
εστιν · και · πνεὺματικον · καθωσ ·	est et spiritale · Sicut scri

[1] πρωτον. [2] ἴδιον. [3] κτηνουσ. [4] πετινων. [5] *In margine* δοξα *gloria claritas majestas.* [6] αστερων. [7] Cπειρεται. [8] Καθωσ ει.

CAP. XV. ptum est·factus est primus
homo adam inanimam viventem·
Novissimus adam in spm vivi
v. 46 ficantem · Sed non prius qd
spiritale est sed qd animale
deinde qd spiritale·
47 Primus homo deterra terrenus·
secundus homo decælo
48 celestis · Qualis terrenus·ta
les et terreni·et qualis
caelestis·tales et caelestes·
49 Igitur sicut portavimus imaginem
terreni·portemus et ima
50 ginem caelestis · Hoc
autem dico frs quia caro et
sanguis regnum di non possidebunt
neque corruptio incor
51 ruptelam possidebit · Ecce
mysterium vobis dico · Omnes
quidem resurg[illegible]·sed non
52 omnes immutabi[illegible] · In
momen[illegible] inictu [illegible]li·in
novissima tuba · Canet enim
tuba·et mortui surgent
incorrupti·et nos inmutabi
53 mur · Oportet enim corruptibile hoc
induere incorruptionem·et mor
talo hoc induere immortalita

γεγραπται·εγενετο·ο·προτοσ[1]·
ανοσ·αδαμ·εισ·ψύχην·ζωσαν,
Ο·αισχατοσ·αδαμ·εισ·πνα·ζω-
οποιοὺν·αλλοὺ·πρωτον·το·
πνεὺματικον·αλλα·το ψὺχι
κον·επιτα·το·πνεὺματικον·
Ο·πρωτοσ·ανοσ·εκγησ·χοικοσ·
ο·δεὺτερυσ·ανοσ·εξοὺρανοὺ·
υ·οὺρανιοσ·ο·ιοσ·ο·χοικοσ·τοι·
οὺτοι·οι·χοικοι·ꙗ·ο·ιοσ·ο·
οὺρανιοσ·τοι·οὺτι[2]·ꙗ·οι·οὺρανοι
Αρα[3]·καθωσ·εφορεσαμεν·την·ἶκονα
τȣ·χοικοὺ·φορεσωμεν·ꙗ·την·
ἶκονα·τοὺ·επου(ρα)·νιου[4] · Τοὺτο·
γαρ·φιμει[5]·αδελφοι·οτι·σαρξ·ꙗ·
αιμα·βασιλιαν·θυ·οὺ·κληρονομη-
σοὺσιν·οὺδε·η·φθορα·την·αφ
θαρσιαν·κληρυνομησει·Ἶδοὺ·
μυστηριον·ὺμιν·λεγω·Παντεσ·
dormiemus
μενοὺν·κοιμηθη·σωμεθα[6]·οὺ
παντεσ·δε·αλλα·γησομεθα·εν·
ατομο[7]·Єν·ροπη·οφθαλμοὺ·εν
τη·αισχατῆ·σαλπιγγι · Cαλπισει·
γαρ·ꙗ·οι·νεκροι·αναστησονται·
αφθαρτοι·ꙗ ημεισ·αλλα·γησο
μεθα · Δει·γαρ·οφθαρτον·τοὺτο
εν·δὺσασθαι·αφθαρσειαν[8]·ꙗ·το
θνητον·ενδὺσασθαι·αθανασει-[9]

igitur
1 πρωτοσ. 2 τοιουτοι. 3 *In margine tantum* αρα. 4 επουρανου. 5 φημει.
6 κοιμηθησομεθα. 7 ατομω. 8 Μαρ *in margine.*
9 *Desunt a* 1 *Cor.* XV. 53, *ad* 2 *Cor.* v. 20. *Sed habentur hic p.* 103. [R.B.]

αν[1] · Τοτε · γενησετα · ι ο · λογοσ · ο · γε
γραμμενοσ · κατεπυθη · ο · θανα
τοσ · εισ · νικοσ · πού · σού · θανατε ·
το · κεντρον · πού · σού · θανατε · το ·
νικοσ · Τοδε · κεντρον · τȣ · θανα
τού · η · αμαρτιασ[2] · Η · δε δύναμισ ·
τησ · αμαρτιασ · ο · νομοσ · Το[3]δε · θω ·
χαρισ · το · διδοητι[4] · ημιν · το · νικοσ[5] ·
δια · τού · κυ · ημων · ιύ · χρύ ·
Ωστε · αδελφοι · μού · αγαπητοι ·
αιδρεοι · γινεσθαι · αμετακινητοι ·
περισσεύοντεσ · εν · τω · εργω · τού ·
κυ · παντοτε · ιδοτεσ · οτι · ȣκ · εστιν ·
ο · κοπ̣ο̣σ[6] · ύμων · χ̣ν̣οσ · εν · κω ·
I. 1 Περι · δε · τησ · λογιασ · τησ · εισ · τουσ ·
αγιούσ · ωσ · περ διεταξα · ταισ · εκκλη
σιαισ · τησ · γαλατιασ · Ούτωσ · και
2 ύμισ · ποιησαται · κατα · μιαν · σαββα
τού · Εκαστόσ · ύμων · παρε · αύτο[7] ·
τιθετω · θεσαύριζον[8] · οτι · ανεύο
δωτε · Ινα · μη · οταν · ελθω · τοτε ·
λογιαι · γινονται[9] · Οταν · δε · παρα
γενωμαι · ȣσαν · δοκειμασηται ·
διεπιστολον[10] · τούτούσ · πεμψω ·
απενεγκειν · την · χαριν · ύμων ·
εισ · ιημ · Εαν · δε · η · αξιον · του · κα
μαι πορευεσθαι · σύνεμοι · πορεύ
σονται · Ελ̣ευσομαι · δε · προσ

tem · Tunc fiet sermo · qui scri
ptus est · absorta est mors
invictoria · ubi est mors
aculeus tuus · ubi est mors
victoria tua · Aculeus autem mor
tis peccatum est · Virtus vero
peccati lex · do autem
gratias · qui dedit vobis victoriam
p dnm nrm ihm xpm
Itaque frs mei dilecti
stabiles estote et inmobiles
abundantes in opere
dni semper · scientes quod labor
vr · non est inanis in dno
Decollectis autem quæ fiunt in
scis · sicut ordinavi ecclesi
is galatiae · Ita et
vos facite per unam sabba
ti · unusquisque vrm apud se
ponat recondens quod ei bene
placuerit · ut non cum venero · tunc
collectae fiant · Cum autem psens
fuero · quos probaveritis
per epistolas · hos mittam
perferre gratiam vrm inhie
rusalem · Quod si dignum fuerit
ut et ego eam · mecum i
bunt · Veniam autem ad

[1] *Vide fol.* 56 [R.B.] [2] αμαρτια. [3] Τω. [4] τω διδοντι. [5] νεικοσ. [6] κοποσ. [7] παρε αυτω. [8] θησαυριζων. [9] γινωνται. [10] διεπιστολων.

CAP. XVI.	vos · cum macedoniam ptransi	ὑμασ · οταν · μακεδονιαν · διελ
	ero · Nam macedoniam ptransibo	θω · Μακαιδονιαν · δε[1] · διερχομαι ·
v. 6	apud vos autem forsitan mane	προσ · ὑμασ · δε · τὑχον · παρατο
	bo vel etiam hiemabo · Utvos	μεινο[2] · και · παραχιμασω · ειμη ·
	me deducatis quocumque	ὑμεισ · μαιπροπεμψηται · οὑ · αν
7	iero · Nolo enim vos	πορεὑωμαι · Οὑ · θελω · γαρ · ὑμασ ·
	modo intransitu videre · Spero	αρτι · εν · παραδω[3] · ῑδιν · Ελπειζω ·
	enim me aliquantum temporis manere	γαρ · χρονον · τεινα · επι · μιναι ·
	apud vos si dns permiserit ·	προσ · ὑμασ · εαν · ο · κσ · επιτρεπη ·
8	pmanebo autem ephesi usque ad	επιμενω · δε · εφεσσου[4] · εωσ · τησ
9	pentecosten · Ostium enim mihi	πεντηκοστησ · Θυρα · γαρ · μοι ·
	apertum est magnum · et evidens	ανεωγεν · μεγαλη · ϗ · ενεργισ[5] ·
10	et adversarii multi · Si autem	ϗ · αντικημενοι πολλοι · Εαν ·
	venerit timotheus · Videte	θε[6]ελθη · τημοθεοσ · Βλεπεται[7] ·
	ut sine timore sit apud vos	ῑνα · αφοβωσ · γενηται · προσ · ὑμασ ·
	Opus enim dni operatur · sicut et	Το · γαρ · εργον · κυ · εργαζεται · ωσ · ϗ
11	ego · Nequis ergo illum spernat ·	εγω · Μητισ · αὑτον · εξουθενηση ·
	deducite autem illum in pa	προπεμψαται · δε · αὑτον · εν · ῑρη
	ce ut veniat adme · Expecto	νη · ῑνα · ελθη προσ · εμαι · Εχδεχο
	enim illum cum fratribus	μαι · γαρ · αὑτον · μετα · τον[8] αδελφων
12	De apollo autem fratre	Περι · δε · απολλω · τοὑ · αδελ
	significo vobis qia multum ro	φοὑ · δελω[9] · ὑμιν · οτι · πολλα · πα
	gavi eum · ut veniret ad	ρεκαλεσα · αὑτον · ῑνα · ελθη · προσ ·
	vos cum fratribus et	ὑμασ · μετα · των · αδελφων · και
	utique non fuit voluntas · ut	παντω[10] · οὑκ · ην · θελημα · ῑνα ·
	nunc veniret · Veniet autem cum	νὑν ελθη · Ελεὑσεται · δε · οταν ·
13	ei vacuum fuerit · Vigilate sta	εὑκαιρεση[11] · Γρηγορειται · στηκε
	te in fide · viriliter agite et con	ται · εν · πιστι · ανδριζεσθαι · κρα

[1] γαρ (pro δε). [2] παραπομεινω. [3] παροδω. [4] εν εφεσσω. [5] ενεργησ, at in marg. ενεργια.
[6] δε. [7] τιμοθεοσ . Βλεπετε. [8] των. [9] δηλω. [10] παντωσ. [11] ευκαρεση.

14	ται · οὐσθαι · παντα · ὑμων · εν · α	fortamini · Omnia vestra Incari
15	γαπη · γινεσθω · Παρακαλω · δε ·	tate fiant · Obsecro autem
	ὑμασ · αδελφοι · Ο.ιδαται · την ·	vos fratres · nostis
	οικιαν · στεφανα · ϗ · φορτοὐνα‿	domum stephane · et fortuna
	τοὐ · και · αχαὐκοὐ[1] · οτι · εισιν ·	ti et achaici · quoniam sunt ·
	απαρχη της · αχαιασ · ϗ · εισ · δια	primitiae achaiae · et inmi
	κονιαν · τοισ · αγιοισ · εταξαν · εαὐ	nisterium s̅c̅o̅rum ordinaverunt se
16	τοὐσ · Ι̅να · και · ὑμισ · ὑποτασσησ‿	ipsos ut et vos subtiti si
	θαι · τοισ · τοι · ȣ · τισ[2] · ϗ · παντι ·	tis ejusmodi · et omni
	τω σὐνεργοὐντι · ϗ · κοπιωντι ·	cooperanti et laboranti
17	εν · ὑμιν · Χαιρω · δε · επι · τη ·	In vobis · Gaudeo autem Inprae
	παροὐσια[3] · στεφανα · ϗ · φορτοὐ	sentia stephanae et fortuna
	να‿τοὐ · ϗ αχαικοὐ · οτι · τοὐ	ti · et achaici · Quoniam id quod
	μετερον · ὐστερημα · αὐτοι · ανε	vobis deerat · Ipsi supple
18	πλσ̣ηρωσαν[4] · Ανεπαὐσαν · γαρ · ϗ ·	verunt · Refecerunt enim et
	το · εμον · π̅ν̅α̅ · και · το · ὑμων ·	meum s̅p̅m̅ et v̅r̅m̅ ·
	Επιγινωσκεται · οὐν · τοὐστοι · οὐ	Cognoscite ergo qui ejus mo
19	τουσ · ασπαζονται · ὑμασ · αι	di sunt · Salutant vos
	εκκλησιαι · τησ · ασιασ · ασπα	aecclesiae asiae · Salutant
	ζονται · ὑμασ · εν · κ̅ω̅ · πυλλα ·	vos In d̅n̅o̅ multum
	ακὐλα[5] · ϗ · πρισκιλλα · σὐντη	aquila et priscilla · cum
	κατοικον · αὐτων · εκκλησια ·	domestica sua ecclesia
20	παρουσ[6] · ϗ · ξενζομαι · ασπα	apud quos et hospitor · salu
	ζονται · ὑμασ · οι · αδελφοι · παν	tant vos f̅r̅s̅ om
	τεσ · ασπασασθαι · αλληλουσ ·	nes · salutate Invicem
21	εν · φιληματι · αγιω · Ο · ασπασ	Inosculo s̅c̅o̅ · Salutati
22	μοσ · τη · εμη · χιρι · παὐλοὐ · Ητισ ·	o mea manu pauli · siquis
	ου · φιλι · τον · κ̅ν̅ · ι̅ν̅ · χ̅ν̅ · Η · τω · ανα	non amat d̅n̅m̅ i̅h̅m̅ x̅p̅m̅ · sit ana

[1] αχαικου. [2] τοιουτοισ. [3] παρουσιασ̣. [4] ανεπληρωσαν. [5] ακυλασ.
[6] παρ οισ p.m. at παρ ουσ s.m.

CAP. XVI. thema maranatha · Gratia	θεμα · μαρανναθα[1] · Η · χαρισ · του
v. 23 24 dni ihu vobiscum · Caritas	κυ ιυ χυ · μεθύμων · Η · αγαπη ·
mea cum omnibus vobis in xpo	μου · μετα · παντων · υμων · εν · χω ·
ihu · EXPLICIT AD COR PRIOR ·	ιηυ, Ετελεσθη · προσκορινθιυσ · α[2] ·
Incip ad Corin	**Αρχεται προσ Κοριν**
thios secunda ·	**θιουσ · Δευτερη ·**
CAP. I. 1 **Paulus Apsls ·**	**Παυλοσ · αποστολοσ ·**
per boluntatem Di ·	**δια[3] · θεληματοσ · θυ ·**
et timotheus frater ecclesiae	ϗ τιμοθεοσ · ο · αδελφοσ · τη · εκκλη
di quæ est corinthi	σια · τού · θυ · τη · ούση · εν · κορινθω ·
cum sanctis omnibus	συν · τοισ · αγιοισ · πασιν ·
qui sunt In universa achaia ·	τοισ · ούσειν · εν · ολητη · αχαΐα ·
2 Gratia vobis et pax ado patre	Χαρισ · ὑμιν · ϗ · ἰρηνη · αποθυ · προ ·
3 nro et dno ihu xpo · Bene	ημων · ϗ · κυ · ιυ χυ · Ευλογη
dictus ds et pater dni nri	τοσ · ο · θσ · και πηρ · του · κυ · ημων ·
ihu xpi · pater misericordiarum	ιυ χυ · Πηρ · των · οικ‿τιρμων ·
et ds totius consolationis ·	ϗ · θσ · πασησ · παρακλησεωσ ·
4 qui consolatur nos In omni	οπαρακαλών · ημασ · επι · παση · τη ·
tribulatione nra · ut possimus	θλιψι · ημον[4] · Ἰνα · το · δυνασθαι ·
et ipsi consolari eos qui In omni	ημασ · παρακαλιν · τουσ · εν · πα
præssura sunt per exortationem	ση · θλιψι : δια · τησ · παρακλησε
qua exortamur et	ωσ · Ησ · παρακαλού · μεθα · και ·
5 ipsi a do · Quoniam sicut	αύτοι · απο[5] τού · θυ · Οτι · καθωσ ·
abundant passiones	περισσεύει · τα · παθηματα · του ·
xpi In nobis Ita et per	χρυ · εισ · ημασ · Ουτωσ · ϗ · δια ·
xpm abundat consolatio	τού · χρυ · περισσεύει · ϗ · η · παρακλη

---

[1] μαραν^ν αθα. [2] *Ad finem habet* γενεθητω γενεθητω Ετελεσθη Προσ Κορινθιουσ Πρωτη. Αρχεται προσ Κορινθιουσ. Δευτερη. B. [3] + ιυ χυ (*ante* δια). [4] ημων. [5] υπο (*pro* απο).

ιεσ · ημων · Ειτε · δε · θλιβομεθα ·	nra · Sive autem tribulamur
ὑπερ · τησ · ὑμων · παρακλησεωσ ·	pro vestra exortatione
ϗ · σωτιριασ[1] · τησ · ενεργοὐμε‿	et salute · quæ operatur
νησ · εν · ὑπομονη · των · αὐτων ·	intolerantia earundem
παθηματων · ωσ · ϗ · ημισ · πασ	passionum quas et nos pati
χομεν · ϗ · η · ελπισ · ημων · βλι	mur · et spes nra firma
βαια · ὑπερ · ὑμων · Ειτε · παρακα	pro vobis · Sive exortamur
λοὐ‿μεθα · ὑπερ · τησ · ὑμων · παρα	pro vestra exortatio
κλησεωσ · ϗ · σωτηριασ · Ειδοτεσ ·	ne et salute · Scientes
οτι · οικοι‿νωνοι · των · παθηματων ·	quo sicut socii passionum
εσται · ϗ · τησ · παρακλησεωσ ·	estis · sic eritis et consolationis
8 Οὐ · γαρ · θελομεν · ὑμασ · αγνοειν · αδελ	Non enim volumus ignorare frs
φοι · περι · τησ · θλιψεωσ · ημων · τησ ·	detribulatione nra · quae
γενομεν‿ησ · εν · τη · ασια · οτι · καθ‿	facta est indno · quo supra
ὑπερ βολην[2] · εβαρηθημεν · παρα	modum gravati sumus · supra
δὐναμιν · Ωστε · εξαπορεθηναι ·	virtutem · Ita ut tederet
9 ημασ · ϗ · τοὐ · ζην · αλλαὐτοι · εν ·	nos etiam vivere · Sed ipsi in
εαυτοισ · το · αποκριμα · τοὐ · θανα	nobis ipsis · responsum mor
τοὐ · εσχηκαμεν · ινα · μη · πεποιθοτεσ ·	tis habuimus · ut non simus fiden
ωμεν · εφεαὐτοισ · αλληπι[3] · θν · τον ·	tes in nobis · sed in do qui
10 εγιροντα · τοὐσ · νεκρουσ · οσ · εκτη ·	suscitat mortuos · qui de
periculo λικοὐ · τϐ · θανατοὐ · ερρὐσα‿το	tantis periculis eripuit
ημασ · ϗ · ρὐεται · εισ · ον · ηλπικα	nos et eruit · In quem spera
μεν · ϗ · οτι · ρὐεται · σὐνὐ‿ποὐρ‿	mus · quo et adhuc eripiet ad
γοὐντων · ϗ · ὐμων · περι · ημων[4] ·	juvantibus et vobis in oratione
τη · δεησι · Ινα · εν · πολλο · πρωσοπω‿[5]	pro nobis · ut ex multarum facierum perso
το · εισ · ημασ · χαρισμα · διαπολλων ·	nis · ejus quæ in nobis est donationis per
εὐχαριστηθη · υπερ · ὐμων[6] · Η · γαρ	multos gratiae aguntur pro nobis · Nam

[1] σωτηριασ. [2] καθ, υμ περβολην. [3] αλλεπι. [4] περι υμων. [5] πολλω προσωπω. [6] ημων.

CAP. I.	gloria nostra haec est	καὺχησισ · ημων · αὺτη · εστιν · το
	testimonium conscientiae no	μαρτὺριον · τησ · σὺνιδησεωσ · η
	stræ · qd in simplicitate et since	μων · οτι εν απλοτητι · και · ιλι
	ritate di et non in sapientia car	κρινια · θυ · ουκ · εν σοφια[1] · σαρκι
	nali sed in gratia di conversati	νη · αλλεν · χαριτι · θυ · ανεστρα‿
	sumus in hoc mundo abundan	φημεν · εν · το[2] · κοσμω · Περισσο
v. 13	tius autem advos · Non enim alia	τερωσ · δε · προ[3] · ὺμασ · Οὺ · γαρ · α
	scribimus vobis quam quae le	γραφομεν · ὺμιν · η · α · αναγινωσ‿
	gistis et cognovistis · Spero	κεται · και · επιγινωσκεται · ελπι
	autem quod usque in finem cognos	ζω · δε · οτι · εωσ · τελοὺσ · επι γνωσ
14	cetis sicut et cognovistis nos	εσται[4] · καθωσ · ϗ · επεγνωται · η
	ex parte quia gloria	μασ · απομεροὺσ · οτι · καὺχημα ·
	vestra sumus sicut et	ὺμων · εσμεν · καθα · περι · και ·
	vos nostra in die dni	ὺμισ · ημων · εν · τη · ημερα · τοὺ ·
15	nri ihu xpi et hac	κυ ημων · ιυ · χυ · ϗ ταὺτη ·
	confidentia volui	τη · πεποιθησει · Εβοὺλομεν[5] ·
	prius venire ad vos	προτερον · ελθιν · προσ · ὺμασ[6]
16	ut secundam gratiam haberetis et	ινα · δεὺτεραν · χαριν εχηται · ϗ
	per vos transire in mace	δια · ὺμων[7] · απελθιν · ε σ[8] μακαι
	doniam · et iterum a macedo	δονιαν · ϗ · παλιν · απο μακαι
	nia venire advos et	δονιασ · ελθειν · προσ · ὺμασ · ϗ ·
	a vobis deduci in	αφὺμων · προπεμφθηναι · ε·στιν[9] ·
17	judeam · Cum hoc ergo vo	ιοὺδαιαν · Τοὺτο · οὺν · βουλομε
	luissem numquid levitate u	νοσ · μητι · αρα · ελαφρια · εχρησα
	sus sum aut quae cogito secundum	μην · η · α · βοὺλεὺομαι · κατασαρ
	carnem cogito · ut sit apud me	κα · βοὺλεὺομαι · ινα · η[10] · παρεμοι ·
18	est et non · Fidelis	το ναι ναι · και · το · οὺ οὺ · Πιστο
	autem ds quia sermo noster qui sit ad	δε · ο · θσ · οτι · ο · λογοσ · ημων · ο,πρ

---

1 σοφιασ. 2 τω. 3 προσ. 4 επιγνωσεσθαι. 5 Εβουλομην. 6 *Post* ὺμασ *addit.* και αφυμων προπεμφθηναι εισ την ἴουδαιαν. 7 δι υμων. 8 εισ. 9 εισ την. 10 ητω *super* η.

CAP. I ὑμασ·οὐκ·εστιν·ναι·και·οὐ·	vos·non est in illo est·et non·sed est
v. 19 Ο·γαρ·θυ·ὑιοσ·ιησ·χρσ·	in illo est·Di enim filius ihs xps
ο·εν·ὑμιν·οδι·ημων·κηρ ὑχ	in vobis per nos praedica
θισ[1]·διεμοὐ·κ̣·σιλβανοὐ·και·	tus est per me et s(i)alvanum et
τιμοθεοὐ·οὐκ·ετενετο[2]·ναι·	timotheum·Non fuit est
και·ου·αλλα·ναι·εν·αὐτω·γενο	et non·Sed /. inillo fu /. est
20 με(ν)[3]·οσαι·γαρ·επαγγελιαι·θυ·εν·	it·quotquot enim promissiones di
αὐτω·τοναι·Διο·και·δι·αὐτοὐ·	sunt in illo est·Ideo et per ipsum
το·αμην·τω·θω·προσ·δοξαν·κ̣·	amen deo adgloriam nostram
honorem per nos	
21 τιμην·δι·ημων·Ο·δε·βαιβα(ω)ων[4]·	qui autem confirmat
ημασ·σὐν·ὑμιν·εισ·χν·κ̣·χρι	nos nobiscum in xpo et qui un
22 σασ·ημασ·θσ·και·οσ·φραγισαμε	xit nos ds et qui signavit nos
νωσ[5]·ημασ·και·δοὐσ·των·αραβο	et dedit pignus
να[6]·του·πνσ·εν·ταισ·καρδιαισ·	sps in cordibus
23 ημων·Εγω·δε·μαρτυρα·τον·θν·	nostris·Ego autem testem dm
επικαλοὐμαι·επι·την‿εμην·	invoco in animam meam
ψὐχην·οτι·φιδομενοσ·ὑμων·	quod parcens vobis
24 οὐκ·ηλθον·εισ·κορινθον·Οὐκ[7]·	non veni ultra corinthum·Non
οτι·κυριεὐομεν·τησ·πιστεωσ·	quia dominantur fidei
ὑμων·αλλα·σὐνεργοι·εσμεν·	vestrae sed adjutores sumus
τησ·χαρασ·υμων·τη·γαρ·πιστει·	gaudii vestri·Nam fide
CAP. II 1 εστηκατα·Εκρινα·δε·εμαὐ	statis·Statui autem hoc ipsum·
τω·τοὐτο·Το·μη·παλιν·εν·λυπη	apud ut non in tristicia ve
2 ελθιν·προσ·ὑμασ·Ει·γαρ·εγω·	nirem ad vos·Si enim ego con
λὐπω·ὑμασ·Και·τισ·εστιν·ο·εὐ	tristo vos·et quis est qui me
φραινων·Μαι·ειμη·ολὐπουμε	laetificet·nisi qui contrista
νοσ·εξεμοὐ·και·τουτ(ο.)[8]·αὐτο·	tur ex me·et hoc ipsum
εγραψα·ὑμιν·ινα·μη·ελθων·	scripsi vobis·ut non cum venero

---

[1] κυρυχθισ (η above υ). [2] εγενετο. [3] γενονεν. [4] βαιβαιων. [5] οσ φραγισαμενοσ. [6] τον αραβωνα. [7] Ουχ secundum. [8] τουτο.

CAP. II. tristitiam super tristiam habeam de quibus
oportuerat me gaudere confidens in
omnibus vobis qa (i) mecum gaudium om
v. 4 nium vestrum est · Nam ex multa
tribulatione et angustia cordis
scripsi vobis per multas lacri
mas non ut contristemini · sed
ut sciatis quam caritatem habeo
5 abundâtius in vobis · Si quis
autem contristav̄ · non me contrista
vit · sed ex parte ut non one
6 rem omnes vos · Sufficit illi qui ejusmodi est
objurgatio haec · quæ fit a pluribus
7 Ita ut econtrario magis
donetis et consolemini · ne
forte · abundantiori tristitia
absorbeatur qui ejusmodi est
8 Propter q̄d obsecro vos ut confirmetis
9 in illum caritatem · Ideo enim et
scripsi vobis · ut cognoscam experi
mentum vestrum · an in omnibus
10 obedientes sitis · Cui autem aliq̄d do
nastis et ego · Nam et ego q̄d
donavi · si quid donavi
propter vos in persona x̄p̄i · Ut
non circumveniamur · a
11 satana · Non enim ignoramus
cogitationes ejus

λύπην · επιλύπην · εχω · εφων ·
εδι · μαι · χαριν · πεποιθωσ · επι
παντασ · ὑμασ · Οτι · η · εμη · χαρα · παν
των · ὑμων · εστιν · Εκ · γαρ · πολλησ ·
θλιψεωσ · ϗ συνοχησ · καρδιασ ·
εγραψα · ὑμιν · δια · πολλον · δ α
κριων[1] · Οὐχ · ῑνα · λύπηθηται · αλ
λῑνα · γνωται · την · αγαπην · ε̣ν̓[2] (η) · εχω ·
περισσοτερωσ · προσ · ὑμασ · Ει · δε ·
τισ · λελύπηκεν · οὐκ · εμαι · λελύπη
κεν · αλλαπο · μερουσ · Ῑνα · μη · επι
βαρων · παντασ · ὑμασ · Ικανον ·
τωτοι · ουτω · Η · επιτιμια · αὐτη ·
ωστε · του · ναντιον · υμασ · μαλλον ·
χαρισασθαι · ϗ · παρακαλεσαι · μη ·
πωσ · τη · περισσοτερα · λύπη · κατα
ποθ‿η · Ο · τοι · οὐτοσ ·
Δι · ο · παρακαλω · ὑμασ · κύρωσαι · ει▭
αυτον · αγαπην · Εισ · τοὐτο · γαρ · ϗ
εγραψα · ὑμων · ῑνα · γνω · την · δοκι
μην · παντων · ὑμων · ει · εισ · παντα
ὑπηκο οι · εσται · Ω · δε · τι · χαρι
ζεσθαι[3] · ϗ · εγω · και · γαρ · εγω · ο ·
και · χαρισμαι[4] · ει · τι · κεχαρισμαι ·
δι · ὑμασ · εν · προσωπω · χ̄ῡ · ῑνα ·
μη · πλεον‿εκτηθωμεν · ὑπο · τοὐ ·
σατανα · Οὐ · γαρ · αυτου · τα · νο (ver)
(sutias) ηματα · αγνο‿οὐμεν

[1] πολλων δακρυων. [2] ην. [3] χαριζεσθαι. [4] και χαρεισμαι *primum*.

II. 12 Ελθων · δε · εισ · την · τρωαδα · δια ·	Cum venissem autem troade propter
το · ευαγγελιον · του · χυ · και · θυ	evangelium xpi · et osti
ρα · μοι · ην · εωγμενη · εν · κω ·	um mihi aptum esset in dno
ουκ · εσχηκα · ανεσειν · τω · πνι ·	non habui requiem spu
μου · Τω · μη · ευριαν μαι[1] · τιτον ·	meo · eo qd non invenerim titum
13 τον · αδελφον · μου · αλλα · απο	fratrem meum · Sed vale faci
ταξαμενοσ · αυτοισ · εξηλθον ·	ens eis · profectus sum
14 εισ · μακαιδονιαν · Τω · δε · θω ·	in macedoniam · Do autem
χαρισ · το[2] παντοτε · θριαμ · βευ	gratias qui semp trium
οντι · ημασ · εν · τω · χρω · και · την ·	phat nos inxpo · et odo
οσμην · τησ · γνωσεωσ · αυτου ·	rem notitiae suæ
φανερουντει · δι · ημων · εν · παντι ·	manifestat p nos in omni
15 τοπω · Οτι · χρι · ευωδρια[3] · εσμεν ·	loco · Quia xpi bonus odor sumus
τω · θω · εν · τοισ · σωζομενοσ[4] · χ ·	do in his qui salvi fiunt et
16 εν · τοισ · απολλυμενοισ · Οισ · μεν ·	in his qui pereunt · aliis quidem
οσμη · θανα · του · εισ · θανατον · οισ ·	odor mortis in mortem · Aliis
δε · οσμη · ζωησ · εισ · ζωην · και ·	autem odor vitæ in vitam · et
17 προσ · ταυτα · τισ · ικανοσ · Ου · γαρ ·	haec quis ta idoneus · Non enim
εσμεν ; ωσ · οιλοιποι · καπηλευ	sumus sicut plurimi adulte
οντεσ · τον · λογον · του · θυ · αλλεξ ·	rantes verbum di · Sed ex
ιλικρινιασ · ωσ · εκ · θυ · κατενω	sinceritate sic ex do co
πον[5] · του · θυ · εν · χρω · λαλουμεν ·	ram do in xpo loquimur
AP. III. 1 Αρχομεθα · παλιν · εαυτουσ · συνισ	Incipimus iterum nosmetipsos co
ταναι · ημη · χρηζομεν · ωσ · τινεσ ·	mdare vobis · aut nuqd egemus
συν · στατικον · επιστολον[6] · προσ ·	sic quidam commdaticiis epistolis ad
comendaticiis	
υμασ · η · εξ · υμων · συν στατικων[7] ·	vos aut ex vobis
epistolis	
2 επιστολον[8] · Η · επιστολη · ημων ·	Epistola nostra
υμισ · εσται · εν · γεγραμμενι[9] · εν ·	vos estis scripta in

---

[1] ευρωμαι. [2] τω. [3] χρυ ευωδεια. [4] σωζομενοισ. [5] κατενωπιον. [6] συνστατικων επιστολων. [7] συνστατεικων. [8] επιστολων. [9] ενγεγραμμενη.

CAP. III.	cordibus nostris quæ scitur	ταισ · καρδιαισ[1] · ημων · γινωσκο ·
	et legitur ab omnibus	μενη · και · αναγινωσ · κομενη
v. 3	hominibus manifestati ·	ὑπο · των · ανων · φανερουμενοι ·
	qm epistola estis xpi minisstra	οτι · εσται · επιστολη · χυ · διακο
	ta anobis et scripta	νηθισα · ὑφημων · εν · γεγραμμε
	non atramento sed spu di	νη · οὐμελανι[2] · αλλα · πνι · θυ ·
	vivi · Non in tabulis lapide	ζωντωσ[3] · Οὐκ · εν · πλαξιν[4] · λιθει
	is · sed in tabulis cordis	ναισ · αλλεν · πλαξειν · καρδιασ[5] ·
4	carnalibus · Fiduciam autem ta	σαρκιναισ · Πεποιθεσιν[6] · δε · τοι ·
	lem habemus per xpm	αυτην · εχομεν · δια · του · χυ ·
5	ad dm non quod sufficientes	προστον · θν · ουχ · οτι · ἰκανοι ·
	simus cogitare aliquid ano	εσμεν · λογιζεσθαι · τι · αφεαυ
	bis quasi ex nobis sed sufficien	των · ωσ · εξ · αυτων · αλλη · ἰκανο
6	tia nostra ex do est qui et ido	τησ · ημων · εκ · τοῦ · θυ · οσ · και · ἰκα
	néos nos fecit ministros novi	νωσεν · ημασ · διακονουσ · κ̄ς · νησ
	testamenti non littera sed	διαθηκησ · οὐ · γραμματοσ · αλ
	spu · Littera enim occi dit	λα · πνσ · Το · γαρ · γραμμα · αποκτε
7	sps autem vivificat · Quod si	νει[7] · Το · δε · πνα · ζωοποιει · Ειδε ·
	ministratio litteris mortis litte	η · διακονία · του · θανατοῦ · εν · γραμ
	ris deformata in lapidibus fu	ματι · τε · τυπωμενη · λιθοισ · εγενη
	it in gloria · Ita ut non possent	θη · εν[8] · δοξη · ωστε · μη · δυνασθαι ·
	intendere filii isra hel in	ατενισαι · τοὺσ · ὑιοὺσ · ιηλ · εισ · το ·
	faciem moysi propter glori	προσωπον · μουσεωσ[9] · δια · την · δο
	am vultus ejus quae	ξαν · τοῦ · προσωποῦ · αὐτοῦ · την ·
8	evacuatur quomodo non ma	καταργουμενην · πωσ · ουχι · μαλ
	gis ministratio sps erit	λον · η · διακονεια · τοῦ · πνσ · εσται ·
9	in gloria · Nam si ministratio	εν · δυξη · Ει · γαρ · τη · διακονία · τησ
	damnationis gloria est multo	κατακρισεωσ[10] · δοξα · εστιν · πολλω ·

[1] καρδάιαισ. [2] μεχλανι. [3] ζωντοσ. [4] πλαξιν *p. m.* [5] καρδιαισ. [6] Πεποιθησιν.
[7] αποκτεννει. [8] ε. εν. [9] Μωυσεωσ. [10] *In margine* κατακρισισ.

αλλον · περισσευει · η · διακονια ·	magis abundet ministerium
ησ · δικαι͜οσυνησ · εν · δοξη ·	justiciae in gloria
και · γαρ · ουδε · δοξασ͜ται · το · δε · δο	Nam nec glorificatum est quod cla
ασ · μενον · εν · τουτω · τω · μερι	ruit in hac parte
ενεκεν · τεσ[1] · υπερβαλλουσησ ·	propter excellentem
δοξησ · Ει · γαρ · το , καταρ͜γουμε	gloriam · Si enim quod evacu
νον[2] · δια · δοξησ · Πολλω · μαλλον ·	tur per gloriam est multo magis
το · μενον · εν · δοξη · Εχοντεσ ·	quod manet in gloria est · Habentes
ουν · το · αυτην[3] · ελπιδα · Πολλη ·	ergo talem spem · multa
παρρησια · χρωμεθα · και · ουκ ·	fiducia utimur · et non
καθα · περ · μουσησ[4] · ετιθη · καλυμ	sicut moyses ponebat vela
μα[5] · επι · το · προσωπον · αυτου[6] · προσ ·	men super faciem suam · ut
τομη · ατενισαι · τουσ · υιουσ · ιηλ ·	non intenderent filii isrl
finem ω εισ · τελοσ[7] · του · καταργουμενου ·	in faciem ejus quae evacuatur
4 Αλλε · πωρωθητα · νοηματα · αυ	Sed si obtunsi sunt sensus eo
των[8] · αχρι · γαρ · τησ · ημερων · ημε	rum · Usque in h odiernum enim di
ρασ[9] τοαυτο · καλυμμα · εν · τη ·	em idipsum velamen in
αναγνωσι · τησ · παλαιασ · διαθηκησ ·	lectione veteris testamenti
μενει · Μη · ανακαλυπτομενον ·	non revelatum
5 οτι · εν · χρω · καταργιται · αλλεωσ ·	quia in xpo evacuatur · Sed usque
σημερον · ηνικα · αναγινωσκε	in hodiernum diem quotiens
ται · μουσησ[10] · καλυμμα · καιται[11] ·	legitur · moyses velam est posi
6 επι · την · καρδιαν · αυτων · Οτα ·	tus super cor eorum · Cum
vero δαν · επιστρεψη · προσ · κν · περι	autem convsus fuerit ad dm au
εριται · το · καλυμμα · Ο δε · κσ ·	feretur velamen · Dns autem
το · πνα · εστιν · Που · δε · το · πνα · κυ ·	sps est · Ubi autem sps dni
εκει · ελευθερια · Ημεισ · δε · παντεσ ·	ibi libertas · Nos autem omnes
ανακεκαλυμμενω[12] · προσωπω · την ·	revelata faciae

[1] εινεκεν τησ [2] καταργο^{υ}μενον. [3] τοι αυτην s. m. του αυτην p.m. [4] μωυσησ. [5] καλκαλυμμα. [6] *In margine* Μαρ. [7] τελοσ. [8] *In marg.* contra judaeos. [9] τησ ημερον ημερασ. [10] μωϋσησ. [11] κειται. [12] ανακεκαλλυμενω.

CAP. III.	gloriam dni contemplantes	δυξαν · κυ · αποπτριζομενοι · την ·
	in eandem imaginem transformamur	αὐτην · ἰκονα · μεταμορφοὺμεθα ·
	a claritate in claritatem tamquam	αποδοχησ[1] · εισ · δοξαν · καθα · περ
CAP. IV. V. 1	a dni spu · Ideo habentes	απο · κυ · πνσ · Δια · τουτο · εχοντ
	hanc ministrationem juxta quod	την · διὰκονιαν · αυτην · καθωσ ·
	misericordiam ɔsecuti sumus non deficiamus	ελεηθημεν[2] · Οὐκ · εν · κακουμεν ·
2	sed abdicemus occulta	αλλα · πιπαμεθα · τακρὺπτα · τησ ·
	dedecoris · non ambulantes	αισχὺνησ · Μη · περιπατοὺντεσ ·
	in astutia · neque adulteran	εν · πανουργια · μηδε · δολουν
	tes verbum di · sed in	τεσ · τον · λογον · τοὺ · θυ · αλλα · τη
	manifestatione veritatis commen	φανερωσει · τησ · αληθιασ[3] · σὺνιστ
	dantes nosmet ipsos ad omnem csci	τεσ · εαὺτουσ · προσ · πασαν · σὺνϊ
	enciam hominum coram do ·	δησιν · ανων · εν · ωπιον · τοὺ · θυ ·
3	Quod si etiam opertum est	Εἰδε · και · εστιν · κεκαλὺμμενον ·
	evvangelium nrm in his qui pere	το · ευαγγελιον · ημων · εν · τοισ · απ
	unt est opertum	λὺμμενοισ · εστιν · κεκαλὺμμε
4	In quibus ds hujus saeculi	νον · Εν · οισ · ο · θσ · τοὺ · αιωνοσ ·
	et caecavit mentes	τοὺτοὺ · ετὺφλωσεν · τα · νοηματα
	infidelium · Ut non fulgeat	των · απιστων · εισ · τω[4] · μη · αὺγασ
	illuminatio evangelii	τον · φωτισμον · τὸ · εὐαγγελιοὺ ·
	gloriae xpi · qui est ima	τησ · δοξησ · του χυ · ο · εστιν ϊ
5	go di · Non enim nosmetipsos	κων · του θυ · Ου · γαρ · εαυτοὺσ ·
	predicamus · sed ihm xpm dnm	κηρισσομεν[5] · αλλα · κν · ιν · χν ·
	nos autem servos vestros per	εαυτουσ · δε · δουλουσ · ὺμων · δια,
6	ihm · quo ds qui dix de tenebris	ιυν · οτι · οθσ · ο · ειπων εκ σκοτὸσ
	lucem splendescere illux in	φωσ · λαμψαι · ελαμψεν · εν · ταισ
	cordibus nostris · ad illuminationem	καρδιασ[6] · ημων · προσ · φωτισμον ·
	scientiae claritatis di in fa	γνωσεωσ · τησ · δοξησ · αυτὸ · εν · τ

---

[1] απο δοξησ. [2] ηλεηθημεν. [3] αλιθηῑασ (η written above). [4] το. [5] κηρυσσομεν. [6] καρδιαισ.

πω · χυ · ιυ ·	ciae xpi ihu ·
ζομεν · δε · τον · θησαυρὸν · τȣτο[1] · εν ·	Habemus autem thesaurum istum in
τρακινοισ · σκευεσιν · ἳνα · Η · ὑπερ	vasis fictilibus · Ut sublimi
λη · τησ · δυναμαιωσ · η[2] · του · θυ · ϗ ·	tas sit virtutis di et
	· εξ ημων · Εν · παντι · θλιβο	non ex nobis · In omnibus tribulati
νοι · [3]αλλου · στενοχωρουμενοι ·	onem patimur · sed non angustiamur ·
πορουμενοι · αλλουκ · εξαπορου̇	aporiamur · sed non distitui
ενοι · Διωκομενοι · αλλουκ ·	mur · Persecutionem patimur sed non
ν · καταλιμπαν ͜ νομενοι · κατα · βαλ	derelinquimur · Deicimur
λομενοι · αλλου̇κ · απολλυ̇μενοι ·	sed non perimus ·
Παντοτε · την · νεκρωσιν · του · χρυ ·	Semper mortificationem xpi
εν · το[4] · σωματι · ημων · περιφερον	in corpore nro circum feren
τεσ · ἳνα · και · η · ζωη · ιυ · χρυ · εν ·	tes · Ut et vita ihu in
τω · σωματι · ημων · φανερωθη ·	corpore nro mani festetur ·
Ει · γαρ · ημεισ · οι · ζωντεσ · εισ · θανα	Si enim nos qui vivimus In mor
τον · διδομεθα · δια · ἳν · ινα · και ·	tem tradimur propter ihm · ut et
η · ζωη[5] · ιυ · χυ · φανερωθη · εν · τη ·	vita ihu manifestetur Incar
θνητη · σαρκι · ημων · Ωστε · ο ·	ne nra mortali · ergo
θανατοσ · εν · ημιν · ενεργιται · η · δε ·	mors innobis operatur · Vita
ζωη εν · υμιν[6] · Εχοντεσ · δε · το αυ	autem in nobis · Habentes autem eun
το · πνα · τησ · πιστεωσ · κατα · το · γεγραμ	dem spm fidei · sicut scriptum
μενον · Επιστευσα · διοϗ · ελαλη	est · Credidi · propter qd locutus
σα · ϗ · ημισ[7] · πιστευ ομεν · διο · και	sum · et nos credimus · propter qd et
λαλουμεν · Ιδοτεσ · οτι · ο · εγιρασ ·	loquimur · Scientes qm susci
τον · κν · ιν · και · ημασ · συν · ιυ · εγι	tavit dnm ihm · et nos cum ihu sus
ρει · ϗ παρασ͜τησ͜ει · σὺν · ὑμιν ·	citabit · et constituet vobiscum ·
τα · γαρ · παντα · δι · ὑμασ · Ἳνα · η · χαρισ ·	Omnia enim propter · Ut gratia
λεονα ͜ σασα · δια · των · πλιονον[8] · την ·	abundans per multos

---

[1] τουτον. [2] η (÷ ητω). [3] + Διωκομενοι (*ante* αλλου). [4] τω. [5] ζωη.
[6] *In marg.* contra rufum. [7] ημεισ. [8] πλιονων.

CAP. IV. gratiarum actio habundet in
v. 16 gloriam di·propter quod non de
ficimus · Sed licet is qui foris est nr
homo corrumpitur tamen is qui in
tus est renovatur dedie
17 indiem · Id enim quod in presenti
est momentaneum et leve tri
bulationis nostrae supra modum
in sublimitatem·Æternum glori
18 ae pondus operatur in nobis
non contemplantibus nobis quæ videntur
sed quae non videntur · Quae enim vi
dentur temporalia sunt · Quæ autem
non videntur æterna sunt
CAP. V. 1 Scimus enim qm si terrestris do
mus nra hujus habitationis dis
solvatur·qd aedificationem ex
do habemus·domum non manufactam
2 aeternam in caelis · Nam et
inhoc ingemiscimus·
habitationem nram quaedecælo est
super indui cupientes·
3 sitamen vestiti·non nu
4 di inveniamur · Nam et qui su
mus intabernaculo hoc · In ge
miscimus gravati·eo qd nolu
mus exspoliari·sed super
vestiri · Ut absorbeatur qd mor

ευχαριστίαν·περισσευση εισ·την
δοξαν·του·θυ·Διο·ουκ·εγκακου
μεν·αλλει·και·ο·εξω·ημων·αν
δροποσ[1]·διαφειρεται·αλλο·εσω·
ημων·ανακαι_νουται·ημερα·
και ημερα · Το·γαρ·παραυτικα·
και_ρον·και·ελαφρον·τησ·θλι
ψαιωσ·ημων·καθὑ·περβολην·
εισ·ὑπερβολην·αιωνιον·βαροσ·
δοξησ·κατεργαζεται·ημιν·μη·
σκοπουν_τεσ·τα·πλεπομενα·αλ
λα·τα·μη·βλεπομενα · Τα·γαρ·
πομενα·προσ·καιρα·εστιν · Τα·δ
μη·βλεπομενα · Αιωνία·
Οιδαμεν·γαρ·οτι·εαν·η·επιγιωσ[2]
μων·οικεια·τοὺ·σκηνοὺσ·καταλὺ
θη·οτι·οικοδομην·εκ·θυ·εχο
μεν·οικιαν·ουκ·αχιρο,πι ητον[3]·
αιωνιον·εν·τοισ·ουρανοισ·και·
γαρ·εν·τουτω·στεναζομεν·το·
οικη·τηριον·ημον[4]·το·εξ·ουρανου
επενδυσασθαι·επιποθουντεσ[5]·
expoliati
ειπερ·και·εκλυσαμενοι·ου·γυμ
νοι·ευρεθησομεθα·κ̔αι·γαρ·οι·ον
τεσ·εν·το[6]·σκηνι·τουτω·στενα_ζο
μεν·βαρυνομενοι·εφω·ουθε
λομεν·εκδυσασθαι·αλλεπεν
δυσασται[7]·Ινα·καταποθη[8]·το·θνη

[1] ανθρωποσ. [2] επιγιοσ. [3] αχιροποιητον. [4] ημων. [5] *In marg.* Μαρ. [6] τω. [7] Αλλεπενδυσασθαι. [8] *In marg.* absorbitio καταποτια.

ον·τουτο·ὑπο·τησ·ζωησ · Ο·δε·	tale est a vita · Qui autem
ιτεργα_ζομενοσ·η μασ·εισ·αυτο·	efficit nos in hoc ipsum
ωτο·θσ·ο·δουσ·ημιν·τον·αρρα	ds·qui dedit nobis·pignus
ονα[1]·τοὐ·πνσ·Θαρρουντησ[2]·	sps · Audentes
ν·παντοτε·και·ειδοτεσ·οτι·	igitur semper·et scientes quo
τλημουντεσ·εν·το[3]·σωματι·	dum sumus in corpore
πολημουμεν·υπο·του·θυ · Δια·	peregrinamur adno · Per
ιστεωσ·γαρ·περιπατουμεν·ου·	fidem enim ambulamus·et
ν·δει·ιδειδουσ·Θαρρου_μεν·	non per speciem · Audemus
consentimus	
ων[4]·και·ευδοκουμεν·μαλλων[5]·	autem·et bonam voluntatem habemus ma
εκδημησαι·εκ·του·σωματοσ·	gis peregrinari a corpore
ad η	
και·ενδιμησαι[6]·προσ·τον·κν·	et presentes esse ad dnm·
διο·και·φιλο_τειμουμεθα·ειτε·	et ideo contendimus sive
ντ	
εν·δημου·τεσ[7]·ειτε·εκδημμουν	absentes·sive presentes
τεσ·εναρεστοι·αυτω·ειναι · Τουσ·	placere illi · Omnes enim
γαρ·παντασ·ημασ·φανερωθηναι·	nos manifestari opor
δει·εν·προσ_θεν[8]·του·βηματοσ·του·	tet·ante tribunal
χρι[9]·Ινα·κομισηται·εκαστοσ·	xpi·ut referat unusquisque
quae. per. corpus	
α·δια·του·σωματοσ·επραξεν·	propria corporis prout gessit
ειτε·αγαθον·ειτε·κακον·	sive bonum sive malum
Ειδοτεσ·ουν·τον·φοβον·του·κυ·	Scientes ergo timorem dni
ανθρωπουσ·πειθομεν · Θω·δε·	hominibus suademus · Do autem
πεφανερωμεθα·ελπι_ζω·δε·ου·	manifesti sumus · Spero autem et
νταισ·συνιδησεσιν·υμων·πεφα	in conscientiis vestris·manifestos
ερωσθαι · Ου·παλιν·εαυτουσ·συν_	nos esse · Non iterum commenda
τα_νομεν·υμιν·αλλα·φορμην·	mus nosmetipsos vobis·sed occasionem
αυ.	
δοντεσ·υμιν·κ·χηματοσ[10]·υπερ·	damus vobis gloriandi pro
ιων·ινα·εχηται·προσ·τουσ·εν	nobis · Ut habeatis ad eos qui in

---

[1] αρραβωνα. [2] Θαρρουντεσ. [3] επιλημουντεσ εν τω. [4] + δε (post ουν) forsan p.m. [5] μαλλον. [6] εν δημησαι. [7] ενδημουντεσ. [8] In marg. Μαρ. [9] χρυ. [10] καυχηματοσ.

CAP. V.	facie gloriantur et non	προσωπω · καὐχωμενουσ · ϗ · ουκ ·
v. 13	in corde · Sive enim mente excedimus	εν · καρδια · Ειτε · γαρ · εξεστημεν ·
	do · sive sobrii sumus vobis	θω · Ειτε · σωφρονουμεν · υμιν ·
14	Caritas enim xpi urguet nos	Η · γαρ · αγαπη · του · χυ · συνεχει · ημι
15	aestimantes hoc · Quia si unus pro	κριναντεσ · τουτο · Οτι · εισ · υπερ
	omnibus mortuus est · ergo om	παντων · απεθανεν · αρα · οι · παν
	nes mortui sunt · et pro omnibus	τεσ · απεθανον · και · υπερ · παντων ·
	mortuus est xpe · ut et qui vivunt	απεθανεν · χσ · Ινα · οι · ζοντεσ[1] ·
	jam non sibi vivunt · sed ei	μηκετει · εαυτοισ · ζωσειν · αλλα ·
	qui pro ipsis mortuus est · et	τω · υπερ · αυτον[2] · αποθανοντι · ϗ ·
16	resurrexit · Itaque nos ex hoc	εγερθεντι · ωστε · ημεισ · αποτȣ
	neminem novimus secundum	νυν · ȣδενα · οιδαμεν · κατα ·
	carnem · Et si cognovimus secundum	σαρκα · ϗ · ει · εγνωκαμεν · κατα ·
	carnem xpm · sed nunc jam non	σαρκα · χν · αλλα · νυν · ουκ · ετει ·
17	novimus · Si qua ergo	γινωσκομεν · κατα · σαρκα · Ωστε ·
	in xpo nova creatura · Ve	ειτεισ · εν · χρω · και · νηκτισισ · τα ·
	tera transierunt · Ecce facta sunt	αρχαια · παρηλθεν · ῑδου · γεγοναν ·
18	nova · Omnia autem ex do · qui	καινα · Τα · δε · παντα · εκθυ · του ·
	reconciliavit nos sibi	καταλλα_ξαντοσ · ημασ · εαυτω ·
	per xpm · et dedit nobis ministe	δια · χυ · ϗ · δοντοσ · ημιν · την · δια_
19	rium reconciliationis · Quo quidem	κονιαν · τησ · καταλλαγησ · ωσ · οτι ·
	ds erat in xpo · mundum reconci	οθσ · ην · εν · χρω · κοσμον · καταλ
	lians sibi · Non reputans	λασσων · εαυτω · Μη · αστιζομενοσ ·
	illis delicta ipsorum	αυτοισ · τα · παραπτ[ω]οματα[3] · αυτων ·
	et posuit in nobis	[evangelii] και · θεμενοσ · εν · ημιν · ευαγγελιȣ ·
20	verbum reconciliationis ·	τον · λογον · τησ · καταλλαγησ · ον ·
	pro xpo ergo legatione fungimur tamquam do	υπερ · χρυ · πρεσβευομεν · ωσ · τȣ · θυ ·
	exortante pernos · Obsecra	παρακαλοῦντοσ · δι · ημων[4] · Λαιο[5]

[1] ζωντεσ. [2] αυτων. [3] παραπτωματα. [4] ημον. [5] Vide p. 56. [R. B.]

ιαινοι · ὑπερ · χῡ · καταλλαγεναι[1] · θω ·
του · μηγ_νοντα · αμαρτειαν · υπερ ·
fecit
ημων · αμαρτιαν · εποιησεν · ινα ·
ημεισ · ενωμέα · δικαιοσυνη · θῡ ·
εν · αυτω · Cυνεργουντεσ · δε · και ·
παρακαλουντεσ · Μη · εισ · καινον
την · χαριν · του · θῡ · δεξασθαι · ὑμασ ·
καιρω · γαρ · λεγει · δεκτω · επηκυ
σα · σου · και · εν · ημερα · σωτηριασ ·
εβοηθησα · σου[2] · Ιδου · νυν · καιροσ ·
δεκτοσ · Ιδου · νυν · ημερα · σωτη
3 ριασ · Μη · δεμιαν · εν · μηδενι · δι ·
δοντεσ · προσκοπην · ϊνα · μη : μωμη
4 θη · η · διακονία · ημων · αλλεν · παν
τει · συνϊσταντεσ · εαυτυοσ[3] · ωσ ·
θῡ · διακονοι · Εν · υπομονη · πολλη ·
εν · θλιψεσιν · ειν · αναγκαισ[4] · εν · στε
5 νοχωριαισ · εν · πληγαισ · εν · φυλ · καισ[5] ·
εν · καταστασιαισ · εν · κοποισ ·
6 εν · αγριπνιαισ[6] · εν · νηστιαισ · εν ·
αγνοτητι · εν · γνωσι · εν · μακρο
θυμία · εν · χρηστοτητι · εν · π̄ν̄ι̅ · αγι
ω · εν · αγαπηαν · υποκρεῖτω · εν · λο
γω · αληθιασ · εν · δυναμει · θῡ · δια ·
των · οπλων · τησ · δικαισυνησ[7] · των ·
δεξειων · καιαρειστερων · δια · δοξησ ·
ϗ ατιμιασ · δια · δυσ_φημίασ · και ·
υφημίασ · ωσ · πλανοι · και · αληθισ ·

mus pro xpo reconciliamini do ·
eum quinon noverat peccatum pro
nobis peccatum factus est · Ut
nos efficeremur justitia di
in ipso · | Adjuvantes autem et
exortamur ne in vacuum
gratiam di recipiatis ·
Ait enim · tempore accepto ex
audivi te · et indie salutis
adjuvi te · Ecce nunc tempus
acceptabile ecce nunc dies sa
lutis · Nemini dantes ullam
offensionem ut non vitupere
tur ministerium nostrum · Sed inom
nibus exhibeamus nosmet ipsos sic
di ministros · In multa patientia ·
In tribulationibus in necessitatibus in
angustiis · in plagis · in carceribus ·
in seditionibus · in tribulationibus
in vigiliis · in jejuniis in
castitate · in scientia · in longani
mitate · in suavitate · in spu sco ·
In caritate non ficta · in ver
bo veritatis · in virtute di · per
arma justitiae a
dextris et a sinistris · per gloriam
et ignobilitatem per infamiam et
bonam famam · Ut seductores et veraces

---

[1] καταλλαγηναι. [2] σοι (pro σου). [3] εαυτουσ. [4] εν αναγίκαισ. [5] φυλακαισ. [6] αγρυπνιαισ. [7] δικαιοσυνησ.

CAP. VI. v. 9	sicut qui ignoti et cogniti	ωσ · αγνο‿ουμενοι · και · επιγινω·κο‿
	quasi morientes et ecce	μενοι[1] · ωσ · αποθνησ‿κομυντ‿εσνοι ·
	vivimus · Ut castigati	και · ετει · ζωμεν · ωσ · πιρα‿ζομενοι ·
10	et non mortificati · Quasi tris	και · μηθανατȣμενοι · ωσ · λυπȣ‿
	tes semper autem gaudentes · Sic̄ egen	μενοι · αει · δε · χαιροντεσ · ωσ · πτω
	tes multos autem locupletantes ·	χοι · πολλουσ · δε · πλȣτειζοντεσ ·
	Tanquam nihil habentes et omnia	ωσ · μιδεν · εχοντεσ · και · παντα · κα
	possidentes ·	τεχοντεσ ;
11	Os nostrum patet ad	Το : στομα · ημων · ανεωγεν · προσ ·
	vos o' corinthii cor	υμασ · ω · κορινθειοι · η · καρδια ·
12	nostrum dilatatum est · Non an	ημον · πεπλατυνται[2] · ου · στενοχω
	gustiamini in nobis · angustiamini	ρισθαι · εν · ημιν · στενοχωρει·θαι[3]
	autem invisceribus vestris.	δε · εν · τοισ · σπλαγχνοισ · υμων ·
13	Eandem autem habentes remune	την · δε · αυτην · αν·ιμισθίαν[4] · ωσ ·
	rationem · tanquam filiis dico · Dilatamini et	τεκνοισ · λεγω · πλαγυνθητε · και ·
14	vos · et nolite jugum ducere	υμασ · και · μη · γινεσθαι · ετερο · ζυ
	cum infidelibus · Quae enim	γουντεσ · Μη · τα · απιστον[5] · Τησ · γα
	participatio justitiæ cum ini qui	μετοχη[6] · δκαιοσυνησ · μη · τα[7] ανο‿
	tate · aut quae societas luci ad	μιασ · η · τισ · κοινωνία[8] · φωτι · προσ
15	tenebras · Quae autem conventio xp̄i	σκοτοσ · τησ · δε · συμφωνη · εισ · χρ̄ω ·
	ad belial · aut quæ pars fideli cum	προσ βελιαβ · η · τισ[9] · μερισ · πιστω ·
16	infidele · Qui autem consensus	απιστȣ · τησ · δε · συν καταθεσισ ·
	templo dī cum idolis · Vos enim	ναω · θ̄υ · μητα[11] · ιδωλων · υμισ · γαρ ·
	estis templum dī vivi · sicut dicit	ναοσ · θ̄υ · εσται · ζωντωσ[12] · λεγει · γαρ ·
	d̄s · Quō inhabitabo in illis	ο θ̄σ · οτι · εν · οικησωνεν · αυτοισ ·
	et inambulabo et ero	και · εν · περιπατησω · και · εσομαι ·
	illorum d̄s · et ipsi erunt	αυτοισ · θ̄σ · και αυτοι · εσονται ·
17	mihi populus · Propter qd̄ exite demedio	μοι · λαοσ · Διο · εξελθατε · εκμεσσȣ ·

[1] επιγινωσκομενοι. [2] ημων πεπλατυνται. [3] στενοχωρεισθαι. [4] αντιμισθίαν. [5] μετα απιστων. [6] *In marg.* μετοχη. [7] δικαιοσυνησ μετα. [8] η τησ κονωνία. [9] η τησ. [10] μετα. [11] μετα. [12] ζωντοσ.

VI. αυτων · και · αφωρισθητε · λεγει · κσ̄ ·
και · ακαθαρτου · μη · απθεσθε[1] κα
18 γω · εισ · δεξομαι · υμασ · και · εσομαι ·
υμιν · εισ · πατεραν · και · υμισ · εσεσ
θαι · μοι · εισ · υιω · σ[2] · και · θυγατερασ ·
II. 1 λεγει · κσ̄ παντο · κρατωρ[3] · Ταυτασ ·
ουν · εχονταισ · τασ · επαγγελειασ ·
αγαπη · τοι · καθαρισωμεν · εαυτουσ ·
αποπαντοσ · μολυσμου · σαρκοσ ·
και · πνσ̄ · επιτελουντεσ · αγιοσινην[4] ·
2 εν · φοβω · θῡ · χωρησαται · υμασ[5] ·
ουδενα · ηδικησαμεν · ου δενα ·
εφθιραμεν · ουδενα · επλεον · εκτ
3 τησαμεν · ου · προσ · κατακρι σιν ·
λεγω · προιρηκα · γαρ · οτι · εν · ταισ
καρδιαισ · ημων · εσται · εισ · το · συν
αποθανιν · και συν ζην ·
4 Πολλη · μοι · παρρησία · προσ · υμασ ·
πολλη · μοι καυχησισ · υπερ · υμον[6] ·
πεπληρωμαι · τη · παρακλησει · υπερ
περισσευομαι · τη · χαρα · επι · παση ·
θλιψει · υμων[7] ·
5 Και · γαρ · ελθον · των · υμων[8] · εισ ·
μακαιδονίαν · ου · δε · μιαν · ανε
σιν · εσχεν · η · σαρξ · ημον[9] · αλλεν ·
παντι · θλιβομενοι · εξωθεν · μα
6 χαι · εσοθεν[10] · φοβοι · αλλο · παρα ·
καλων · τουσ · ταπινουσ · παρεκα

eorum · et separamini dicit dn̄s
et inmundum netetigeritis et
ego recipiam vos et ero
vobis in patrem · et vos eri
tis mihi in filiös et filias
dicit dn̄s omnipotens · Has
igitur habentes promissiones
karissimi · mundemus nos
ab omni inquinamento carnis
et sp̄s · perficientes sanctificationem
In timore dī · Capite nos
neminem lesimus neminem
corrupimus neminem circum ve
nimus · Non ad condemnationem
dico · Praedixi enim quod in
cordibus nostris estis ad com
moriendum et ad convivendum ·
Multa mihi fiducia apud vos
multa mihi gloriatio pro vobis ·
repletus sum consolatione · super
abundo gaudio In omni
tribulatione nr̄a
Nam cum et venissemus
macedoniam nullam requi
em habuit caro nostra · sed om
nem tribulationem passi · foris
pugnae · intus timores · Sed qui
consolatur humiles consolatus

---

[1] απτεσθαι. [2] υιουσ. [3] *In marg.* phor̄. [4] αγιοσυνην. [5] ημασ. [6] υμων. [7] ημων. [8] ημων. [9] ημων. [10] εσωθεν.

CAP. VII. est nos d̅s̅ in adventu
v. 7 titi · Non solum autem in adven
tu ejus sed etiam in consola
tione qua consolatus est invobis·
referens nobis vestrum
desiderium · vestrum fletum·
vestram emulationem pro me·
8 Ita ut magis gauderem·quoniam
et si contristavi vos in episto
la mea·non me poenitet·et si
me poeniteret · Video enim
quod epistola illa et si ad
9 horam vos contristavit · Nunc gau
deo·non quia contristati estis sed
quia contristati estis ad poenitentiam·
contristati enim estis secundum d̅m̅·ut in
nullo detrimentum patiamini ex nobis
10 Quae enim scdm (d̅m̅.) · tristitia est poenitentiam
in salutem stabilem ope
ratur · Saeculi autem tristiti
11 a mortem operatur · Ecce
enim hoc ipsum q̅d̅ s̅c̅d̅m̅ d̅m̅ contri
stavi vos·quantam in vobis opera
tur sollicitudinem·sed defensionem·
sed indignationem·sed timorem·
sed desiderium·sed emulationem
sed vindictam · In omnibus exhibu
istis vos incontaminatos esse

λεσεν·υμασ[1]·ο θ̅ς̅·εν·τη·παρουσια·
τειτου[2]·Ου·μονον·εν·τη·παρου
σια·αυτου·αλλα·και·εν·τη·πα
ρακλησει·η·παρακληθη[3]·εφυμιν·
αναγγελλων·ημιν·την·υμων·
επιποθηον·τον·υμων·οδυρμον
τον·υμων·ζηλον·υπερ·εμου·
Ωστε·μαλλον·χαριναι[4]_μαι·οτι·
εικαι·ελυπησα·υμασ·εν·τη·επισ
τοληιμου·ου·με·τα·μελομαι[5]·ει·και·
με·τε·μελομιν[6] · Βλεπω·γαρ·
οτι·επιστολη[7]·εκεινη·ει·και·προσ·
ωραν·υμασ·εληπησεν[8]·νυν·χαι
ρω·ουχ·οτι·ελυπηθηται·αλλοτι·
ελυπηθηται·εισ·μετανοιαν·ελυ
πηθηται·γαρ·κατα·θ̅ν̅·ἵνα·εν·
μηδε_νει·ζημειω_θηται·εξ·ημων·
Η·γαρ·κατα·θ̅ν̅·λυπη[9]·μετα_νοιαν·
εισ·σωτηριαν·αμεταμελητον·κα
τεργα_ζεται · Η·δε·του·κοσμου·λυ
πη θανατον·κατεργ·(α)ζεται[10]·Ιδου·
γαρ·αυτο·τουτο·το·κατα·θ̅ν̅·λυπη
θηναι·ποσην·κατιργασατο·εν
υμιν·σπουδην·αλλα·πολογειαν·
αλλα·γανακτησιν·αλλαφοβον·
αλλαεπιποθησιν[11]·αλλα·ζ(η)ελον[12]·
αλλα·εκδικησιν·εν·παντει·συνεστη_
σαται[13]·εαυτουσ·αγνουσ_ειναι·τω·

---

1 ημασ. 2 αυτου τειτου. 3 παρεκληθη. 4 χαρηναι. 5 μεταμελο μαι. 6 μετεμελομην. 7 + η. (ante επιστολη). 8 ελυπησεν. 9 λυπη. 10 κατεργαζεται 11 αλλεπι ποθησιν. 12 ζηλον. 13 συν εστηκαται.

VII. 12	πραγματι · Αρα · ει · και · εργαψα[1] · υμιν ·	negotio · Igitur et si scripsi vobis
	injuriatorem	
	ου · χενεκεν · του · αδικησαντοσ · ου ·	non propter eum qui fecit injuriam · neque
	δε · ενεκεντου · αδηκηδεντοσ[2] · αλ	propter eum qui injuriam passus est sed
	propter	
	λε · νεκεντου · φανερω͜θηναι · την ·	ad manifestandam sollici tu
	σπουδην · υμων · την · υνερ · υμων[3] ·	dinem nostram quam pro vobis habemus
	π	
13	προσ · υμασ ενογειον[4] · του · θ̄υ · Δια ·	ad vos coram d̄o · Ideo
	τουτο · παρακεκλημεθα · επι · δε · τη ·	consolati sumus · in consolati
	παρακλησῖ · υμων[5] · περισσοτερωσ ·	one autem nostra abundantius
	μαλλον · εχαρημεν · επι · τη · χαρα ·	magis gavisi sumus super gaudium
	τευτου[6] · οτι · αναπεπαυται · το · π̄να ·	titi · quia refectus est s̄ps
14	αυτου · αποπαντων · υμων · Οτι	ejus ab omnibus vobis · Et si quid
	ειτι · αυτω · κεκαυχημαι · υπερ ·	apud illum de vobis gloriatus
	υμων · ουκατησ · χυνθην · αλλωσ ·	sum · non sum confusus · sed sicut
	παντοτε · εν · αληθεία · ελαλησαμεν ·	omnia vobis inveritate locuti
	υμιν · Ουτωσ · ꝁ · η · καυχησισ · υμων[7] ·	sumus · Ita et gloriatio nostra quae
	Η · προσ · τεῖτον · αληθῖα · εγενη͜θη ·	fuit ad titum veritas facta est
15	και · τα · σπλαγχνα · αυτου · περισσο	et viscera ejus abundantius
	τερωσ · εισ · υμασ εστιν · αναμι͜	in vobis sunt · reminis
	μνησ͜κομενου · την · παντων · υμων ·	centis omnium vestrum
	υπακοην · ωσ · μετα · φοβου ·	obedientium · quomodo cum timore
	και · τρομου εδεξασθαι · αυτον,	et tremore excepistis eum ·
16	χαιρω · οτι · εν · παντι · θαρρω · εν · υμιν ·	Gaudeo quod in omnibus confido in vobis ·
VIII. 1	Γνω͜ριζομεν · δε · υμιν · αδελ	Notam autem facimus vobis fra
	φοι · την · χαριν · του · θ̄υ · την · δεδομε	tres gratiam d̄i quae data est
	νην · εν · ταισ · εκκλησιαισ · τησ · μακαι	in aecclesiis macedo
2	δονιασ · οτι · εν · πολλη · δοκειμη ·	niae quod in multo experimento
	θλειψεωσ · η · περισσîα · τησ · χαρασ ·	tribulationis abundantia gaudii
	αυτων · και · η · καταβαθουσ · πτο	ipsorum et altissima pauper

[1] εγραψα. [2] αδικηθεντοσ. [3] ημων την ὑπερ ἡμων. [4] ενωπειον. [5] η̄μων. [6] τεῖτου. [7] ημων.

CAP. VIII.	tas eorum abundavit in di	χία[1] · αυτων · επερισσευσεν · εισ
	vitias simplicitatis eo	τον · πλουτον · τησ · απλοτητοσ αυ
v. 3	rum · Quia secundum virtutem testimo	των · Οτι · κατα · δυναμιν · μαρτυ
	nium illis reddo et supra virtutem vo	ρω · και · παρα · δυναμειν · αυθερετοι[2] ·
4	luntarii fuerunt cum multa exortatione	μετα · πολλησ · παρακησεω[3] · δυμο
	obsecrantes nos · gratiam et	μενοι · ημων · την · χαριν · και · την ·
	comunicationem ministerii quod	κοινονιαν · τησ · δι · κονιασ[4] · τησ · εισ ·
5	fit in sanctos et non sicut spera	τουσ · αγιουσ · και · ου · καθωσ · ελπι
	vimus · sed semet ipsos dederunt	σαμεν · αλλεαυτουσ · εδωκαν ·
	primum do deinde nobis per	προτων[5] · τωκω · και · ημιν · δια
6	voluntatem di · Ita ut roga	θεληματοσ · θυ · εισ · το · παρακαλε
	remus titum · Ut quem admodum	σε · ημασ · τιτον · Ινα · καθωσ · προ
	coepit · Ita ut perficiat	ενη · ξατο[6] · Ουτωσ · και · επιθελε
	in vobis etiam gratiam istam ·	σε[7] · ευσ[8] · υμασ · κ̄ · την · χαριν · ταυτη
7	Sed sicut in omnibus abundatis	Αλλωσπερ · εν · παντι · περισσευεται ·
	fide et sermone et scientia · et omni	πιστι · και · λογω · και · γνωσει · κ̄ · πασα
	sollicitudine · Insuper et caritate	σπουδε[9] · κ̄ · τη · εξυμων · εν · ημιν ·
	vestra in nos · ut et in hac gratia	αγαπη · ινα · καιενταυτη · τη · χαριτα
8	abundetis · Non quasi imperans	περισσευσηται · ου · κατεπειγαγην[10]
	dico · sed per aliorum sollicitudi	λγω[11] · αλλα · δια · τησ · ετερων · σπου
	nem etiam vestrae caritatis · Inge	δησ · και · το · τησ · υμετερασ · αγαπησ (pro)
9	nium bonum comprobans · Scitis	γνησιον · δοκειμαζω · Γινοσκεται[12] ·
	enim gratiam dni nri ihu xpi	γαρ · τεν[13] · χαριν · του · κυ · ημων · ιυ · χυ
	quoniam propter vos egenus factus est	οτι · δι · υμασ · επτωχευσεν · πλουσει
	cum esset dives · ut illius inopia	οσων · ινα · τη · αυτου · πτωχεια ·
10	vos divites essetis · et consilium	υμεισ · πλουτησηται · και · γνωμην[14] ·
	In hoc do · hoc enim vobis	εν · τουτω · δειδωμει · τουτω[15] · γαρ ·
	vobis utile est quia non solum	υμιν · συνφερει · οτι · ου · μονον · το ·

[1] *In marg.* ξενοπτοχιον. [2] αυ, θερετοι (λυ above). [3] παρακλησεωσ. [4] διακονιασ. [5] πρωτον. [6] προενηρξατο. [7] επιτελεση. [8] εισ. [9] σπουδη. [10] κατεπειταγην. [11] λεγω. [12] Γινωσκεται. [13] την. [14] γνωμην. [15] τουτο

ποιησαι · αλλα · και · το · θελειν · εν_	·facere sed et velle coepistis
ρξαθαι[1] · απο · περσυ · νυνιδαι · και ·	ab anno priore · Nunc vero et
ο · ποιησαι · επι · τελεσαται · Ο̄ · πωσ · καθα ·	fact perficite · Ut quem admodum
τερ · η · προθυμια · του · θελειν ·	promptus est animus volendi
[2] Ουτωσ και	ita sit et
το · επιτελεσαι · εκ του εχειν ·	perficiendi ex eo quod habetis
Ει γαρ η · προθυμια · προκειται · καθο ·	Si enim voluntas propterea est scdm id
ινεχη · ευπροσδεκτοσ · ου · καθο ·	quod habet accepta est · non scdm
ουκ εχει τισ · ου · γαρ · ινα αλλοισ ·	quod non habet · Non enim ut aliis sit
ανεσεισ υμιν · δε · θλιψισ · αλλεξ_	remissio · vobis autem tribulatio sed
ισοτητοσ · εν · τω[3] καιρω · το · υμων ·	ex æqualitate · In presenti tempore
περισσευμα · εισ το · εκεινων · υστε_	vra abundantia illorum inopiam sup
ρημα · ινακαι το εκι_νων · περισ_	pleat · ut et illorum abundan
σευμα · γενηται[4] εισ · τω[5] · υμων · υσ	tia vestrae inopiae sit supplem̄
τερημα · ο · πωσ · γενηται · ισσο_τησ ·	tum · Ut fiat aequalitas
καθωσ · γεγραπται · Ο · το · πολλυ · ουκ ·	sicut scriptum est qui multum non
επλεονασεν · και · το ολιγ_ον[6] ·	abundavit · et qui modicum
ουκ · ηλαττονησεν · χαρισ · δε · τω · θ̄ω ·	non minoravit · Gratias autem d̄o
τω · δοντι[7] · την · αυτην · σπου_δην ·	qui dedit eandem sollicitudinem
υπερ υμων · εν · τηκαρδια · τιτου ·	pro vobis in corde titi ·
Οτι · την · μεν · παρακλησιν · εδεξατο ·	quoniam exortationem quidem suscepit ·
σπουδαι · οτεροσ · δε · υπαρχων · αυ	sed cum sollicitior esset sua volun
θερετοσ[8] · εξηλθεν · προσ υμασ ·	tate profectus est ad vos ·
Συν · επεμψαμεν · δε · μεταυτου · τον ·	Misimus etiam cum illo fra
αδελφον · ου[9] · επαινοσ · εν · τω ευ	trem cujus laus est in evan
αγγελιω[10] · δια · πασων · των · εκκλη	gelio per omnes eccle
σιων · Ου · μονον · δε · αλλα · και	sias · Non solum autem sed et
χειροτονηθισ · υπω[11] · των · εκκλησιων ·	ordinatus ab ecclesiis comes

---

nunc

[1] επηρξασθαι. [2] *Spatium breve.* [3] + νυν (*ante* καιρω). [4] γενηται. [5] το. [6] ολλιγον. [7] δοντι. [8] αυθερετοσ (cf. v. 3). [9] ου ο. [10] ευαγγελειω. [11] υπο.

CAP. VIII.	peregrinationis nrae in hac gra	συνεκδημοσ · υμων[1] · συν · τη · χα
	tia quae ministratur	ριτῖ ταυτη · τη · διακονου‿μενη ·
	a nobis ad dni gloriam	υφημων · προσ · την · τȣ · κυ · δοξαν ·
	et destinatam voluntatem nostram	και · προθυμιαν υμων[2] ·
v. 20	devitantes hoc · ne quis	υποσ · τελλομενοι · τουτο · μη · τισ ·
	nos vituperet in hac ple	υμασ · μομησηται[3] · εν · τη αδροτη
	nitudine quae ministratur	τι · ταυτη · τη[4] · διακονου‿με‿νη ·
21	a nobis · Providemus enim bo	υφημων[5] · Προνο ουμεν[6] · γαρ · κα
	na non solum coram do sed	λα · ου · μονον · ενωπῖον · κυ · αλλα ·
22	etiam coram hominibus · Mi	και · ενοπῖον · ανδρωπων[7] · Cυνε
	simus autem cum illis et fra	πεμψαμεν · δε · αυτοισ · τον · αδελ
	trem nrm quem probavimus	φον υμων[8] · ον · εδοκειμασαμεν ·
	in multis sepe sollicitum	εν · πυλλοισ · πολλα‿κῖσ · σπουδαι‿
	esse · Nunc autem multo sollici	ονοντα · Νυν · ιδε · πυλλυ · σπου
	tiorem confidentia multa in	δαιοτερον · πεποιθησι τη · εισ ·
23	vos · sive protito qui est so	υμασ · ειτε · υπερ · τιτου · κο‿ινω
	cius meus et in vos adju	νοσ · εμοσ · και εισ υμασ συν‿
	tor · sive fratres nostri aposto	εργοσ · ειτε · αδελφοι · υμων[9] · απο
	li ecclesiarum gloria xpi ·	στυλοι · εκκλησειων · δοξα · κυ[10] ·
24	Ostensionem ergo caritatis	Την · ουν · ενδιξῖν · τησ · αγαπησ[11] ·
	vestrae et nostrae gloriae	υμων και · ημων · καυχησεωσ ·
	pro vobis · in illos ostendi	υπερ · υμων[12] · εισ αυτουσ εν · δικ‿
	te In faciem ecclesi	νυμενοι · εισ προσωπον · των · εκκλη‿
CAP. IX. 1	arum · Nam deministe	σιων · Περι · μεν · γαρ τησ δια‿
	rio quod fit in sanctos exabun	κονῖασ · τησ · εισ · τουσ · αγιουσ · περισ
	danti mihi est scribere vobis ·	σον · μοι · εστιν · του · γραφειν · ημιν[1]
2	Scio enim promptum animum vestrum	Οιδα · γαρ · την · προθυμῖαν · υμων ·
	pro quo de vobis glorior apud	ην · υπερ · υμων καυ χωμαι · μακε

[1] ημων. [2] ημων. [3] μωμησηται. [4] δ̣ τη. [5] In marg. Μαρ. [6] In marg. προνοια. [7] ενωπιον ανθρωπων. [8] ημων. [9] ημων. [10] χυ (pro κυ). [11] In marg. agatha. [12] ημων. [13] ὑμιν.

IX. δοσιν · οτι · αχαΐα · παρεσκευ_ασται ·	macedonas quo achaia parata est
αποπερσυ · ϗ[1] · ο · εξυμων · ζηλοσ ·	ab anno priore et vestra emulatio
v. 3 ηρεθεισεν · του[2] · πλιονασ · Επεμ	provocavit multos · Mi
ψα · δ[3] · τουσ · αδελφοισ[4] · Ινα · μη ·	si autem fratres ut ne
το · καυχημα · ημων · και · νωθη ·	quod gloriamur de vobis eva
εντο[5] μερι · τουτω · Ινα · καθ_ωσ ·	cuetur in hac parte ut quem ad
ελεγον · παρεσκευασμενοι · ηται	modum dixi parati sitis
4 Μη · πωσ · εαν · ελθωσΐν · συνε_μοι ·	Ne cum venerint mecum
μακαιδονεσ · ϗ · ευρουσιν · υμασ ·	macedones et invenerint nos
απαρασκευαστουσ · καταισχυν	imparatos erubesca
θωμεν · ημεισ · Ῑνα · μι[6] · λεγω · υμεισ ·	mus nos ut non dicamus vos
5 εν · τη · υποστασι · ταυτη · αναγκαι	in hac ssubstantia · Necessari
ον · ουν · ηγησαμην · παρακαλαισε ·	um ergo existimavi rogare
τουσ αδελφουσ · Ῑνα · προσ · ελθω	fratres ut praeveniant
σιν · προ[7] · υμασ · ϗ προκαταρτη_	ad vos et praeparent
σωσιν[8] · την · προεπηγγελμενην[9] ·	promissam hanc benedicti
ευλογΐαν · υμων · ετοιμην · ειναι ·	onem vestram paratam esse sic
ουτωσ · ωσ · ευλογιαν · μηω[10] · πλεο	quasi benedictionem non quasi ava
6 νεξΐαν · Τουτο · δε · ο, σπιρων · φιδο	ritiam- hoc autem dico quia q[i] par
μενωσ · φιδομενωσ · ϗ · θερισι ·	ce seminat parce et metet ·
και · ο, σ_πιρων · ενευλογια · επ	et qui seminat in benedictionibus de
7 ευλογια · και · θερισι · Εκαστοσ ·	benedictionibus et metet · Unusquisque
καθωσ · προειρεται[11] · τη · καρδια ·	pro ut destinavit corde suo ·
μη · εκλυπησ · η · εξαναγ_κησ ·	non ex tristitia aut ex necessitate ·
Ιλαρον · γαρ · δοτην · αγαπα · οθσ̄ ·	Hilarem enim datorem diligit ds̄ ·
8 Δυνατι · δε · ο · θσ̄ · πασαν · χαριν ·	Potest autem ds̄ omnem gratiam
περισσευσαι · εισ · υμασ · ῑνα · εν ·	abundare facere in vobis ut in
παντι · πασαν · αυταρκιαν · εχον	omnibus semper omnem sufficientiam haben

---

1 *In marg.* astronomia. 2 τουσ. 3 δε. 4 αδελφουσ. 5 τω. 6 μη. 7 προσ. 8 προκαταρτισωσιν. 9 προ επιγγελμενην. 10 μη ωσ. 11 προειρηται.

CAP. IX.	tes·abundetis in omne opus	τεσ·περισσευηται·εισ·παν·εργον·
v. 9	bonum sicut scriptum est·	αγαθον·καθωσ·γε_γραπται·
	Dispersit dedit pauperi	εσκορπισεν·εδωκεν·τοισ·πε
	bus justitia ejus	νησιν·η·δικαιοσυνη·αυτ_ου·
	manet in seculum secu	μενει·εισ·τον·αιωνα·του·αιω
10	li · Qui autem administrat semen	νοσ · Ο·δε·επιχορηγων·σπο
	seminanti·et panem ad mandu	ρον·τω·σπιροντι·και·αρτον·εισ·
	candum prestabit et multi	βρωσιν·χορηγησαι·και·πλη
	plicabit semen vestrum et auge	θυναι·τον·σπορον·υμων·ϗ·
	bit incrementa frugum justiti	αυξησει·τα·γενηματα·τησ·δικαι
11	ae vestrae·ut in omnibus lo	οσυνησ·υμον[1]·ῖνα·εν·παντι·
	cupletati abundetis in omnem sim	πλουτιζομενοι·εισ·πασαν(α)·πλο
	plicitatem·quæ operatur per nos	τητα[2]·η·τ(η)εσ[3]·κατεργαζεται·δι·ημ
12	gratiarum actionem d̄o·q̄m mini	ευχαριστῖαν·τω·θ̅ω[4] · Οτι·η·διακο
	sterium hujus officii non	νια·τησ·λιτȣργῖασ·ταυτησ·ου
	solum ea supplet	μονον·εστιν·προσ·αναπληρȣ
	quae de sunt sanctis·	σα·τα·υστερηματα·των·αγιων·
	Sed etiam abundat per multas	Αλλα·και·περισσε_υουσα·δια·πολ
13	gratiarum actiones ind̄no · Per	λων·ευχαριστειων·τω·θ̅ω·δια·
	probationem ministerii	τησ·δοκιμησ·τησ·δια_κονῖασ·
	hujus glorificantes d̄m in o	ταυτησ·δοξαζοντεσ·τον·θ̅ν·επ —
	boedientia confessionis	τη·υποταγη·τησ·ομολογῖασ·
	vestrae · In evangelium x̄pi·	υμον[5]·εισ·το·ευαγγελιον·του·χ̅ν -
	et simplicitate communicatio	και·απολτητι[6]·τησ[7]·κοινωνιασ·
14	nis vestrae in illos et in omnes et	εισ·αυτȣσ·και·εισ·παντασ·και·
	ipsorum obsecrationem pro vobis desi	αυτων·δε·ησι·υπεριμων[8]·επι
	derantium vos propter emi	ποθουντων·υμασ·δια·την·
	nentem gratiam d̄i in	υπερβαλλȣσαν·χαριν·του·θ̅υ·

---

[1] υμων. [2] απλοτητα. [3] ητησ. [4] *In marg.* M̅a̅ρ̅. [5] υμων.
[6] απλοτητι. [7] τῆσ τησ. [8] υμων.

	Graece	Latine
	εφυμιν · Χαρισ · τω · θ̅ω̅ · επι · τη ·	vobis · Gratias autem d̅o̅ super in
	ανετ διητητο[1] · αυτου · δωραια ·	enarrabili dono ejus
1	αυτοσ · δε · ετω[2] · παυλοσ · παρακαλω ·	ipse autem ego paulus obsecro
	υμασ · δια · τησ · πραυτητοσ · και ·	vos · per mansuetudinem et
	επι · κει κιασ[3] · του · χ̅υ̅ · Οσ · κατα	modestiam x̅p̅i̅ qui in fa
	προσωπον · μεν · ταπινοσ · εν · υμιν ·	cie quidem humilis Inter vos
2	απων · δε · θαρρω · εισ · υμασ · Δεο_	absens autem confido in vobis · Ro
	μαι · δε · το · μη · παρων · θαρρησαι ·	go autem ne praesens audeam
	τη · πεποιθησι · ηλογιζομαι ·	per eam confidentiam qua existimor
	τολμησαι · επι · τινασ · τουσ ·	audere in quosdam qui
	λογιζομενουσ · ημασ · ωσ ·	arbitrantur nos · tamquam
	κατα σαρκα · περιπατουντασ ·	secundum carnem ambulemus ·
3	Εν · σαρκι · γαρ · περιπατουντασ	In carne enim ambulantes
	ου · κατα σαρκα · στρατευομεθα ·	non secundum carnem militamus ·
4	Τα · γαρ · οπλα · τησ · στρατîασ ·	[N]am arma militiae
	ημων · ου · σαρκικα · αλλα · δυ	n̅r̅a̅e̅ · non carnalia sed po
	νατα · τω θ̅ω̅ · Προσ · καθερε	tentia d̅o̅ · ad distructi
5	σιν · οχυρωματων · λογισ_	onem munitionum · consi
	μουσ · καθαιρουντεσ · και ·	lia distruentes · et om
	παν · υψωμα · επαιρομενον ·	nem altitudinem extollentem se
	κατα · τησ · γνωσεωσ · του θ̅υ̅ ·	adversus scientiam d̅i̅
	αιχμαλωτι_ζοντεσ · παν ·	et in captivitatem redigentes omnem
	νοημα · εισ · την · υπακοην ·	intellectum · In obsequium
6	του · χ̅υ̅ · αγοντεσ · και ενε	x̅p̅i̅ · et in prom
	(μω.) τοι[4] · εχοντεσ · εκδικη_σαι ·	ptu habentes · ulcisci
	πασαν · παρα_κοην · οταν · πληρω	omnem oboedentiam · Cum impleta
7	θη · η̅ · ιπακοη · ημων[5] · τα · κατα	fuerit v̅r̅a̅ oboedientia · quæ secundum
	προσωπον · βλεπεται · Ει · τισ	faciem sunt videte · Si quis

---

[1] ανεκδιηγητω. [2] εγω. [3] επικειεικιασ. [4] ενετοιμω. [5] ὑπακοη υμων.

CAP. X.	confidit se xpi servum	πεποιθεν εαυτω · χρυ · δουλοσ
	esse · hoc cogitet iterum	ειναι · τουτο · λιγιζεσθω[1] · πα
	apud se quia sicut ipse	λιν · αφε αυτου · οτι · καθωσ · αυ
	xpi est ita et nos ·	τοσ · χρυ · ουτωσ · και · ημεισ[2] ·
v. 8	Nam et si amplius aliquid glo	Εαν · γατι[3] [ρ] · περισσοτερον · καυ
	riatus fuero de potestate	χησωμα · περι · τησ · εξουσιασ ·
	nra quam dedit nobis ds	ημων · ησ · εδωκεν · ο θσ · ημιν ·
	adaedificationem · et non in di	εισ · οικοδομην · και · ουκ εισ
	structionem vram non erubes	καθερεσιν · ημων[4] ουκ αισ
9	cam · Ut autem non existimer	χηνθησομαι[5] · Ινα · μη · δοξωμεν ·
	tanquam terrere vos	ωσ αν[6] εκφοβειν υμασ
10	per epistolas · quoniam quidem	δια · των επειστολων · οτι · αιμεν
	epistolae inquiunt graves sunt	επιστολαι φεσειν[7] [η] βαριαι ·
	et fortes · praesentia autem	κασχυραι[8] [ι] · η · δε παρουσεια ·
	corporis infirma et	του · σωματοσ ασθενησ · και
	sermo contemptibilis ·	ο · λογοσ εξουθενιμε νοσ[9] ·
11	hoc ergo cogitet qui ejus modi	τουτο · λογει ζεσθω · οτοι · ου
	est · quia quales sumus verbo	τοσ · οτι · οιοι · μεν · τω · λογω
	per epistolas absentes · ta	δι · εριστολων[10] [π] · αποντεσ τοι
	les et praesentes in facto ·	ουτοι · και παροντεσ τω εργω ·
12	Non audemus enim conferre	Ου γαρ τολ · ωμεν[11] [μ] · κριναι · η
	aut conparare nos quibusdam	σιν · κριναι[12] · εαυτουσ · τει σειν
	qui se ipsos com mendant ·	των εαυτουσ συν · ιστα νοντων ·
	sed ipsi in vobis nosmet ip	αλλα αυτοι εν αυτοισ[13] · εαυ
	sos metientes et comparan	τουσ · μετρουντεσ · και συν
	tes nos met ipsos nobis	κρινοντεσ εαυτουσ εαυτοισ
13	non in immensum glorian	ουκ εισ το αμετρον καυχω
	tes · sed secundum mensuram	μενοι · αλλα[14] κατα το · μετρον

---

1 λογιζεσθω. 2 ημασ [εισ]. 3 γαρ τι. 4 υμων. 5 αισχυνθησομαι. 6 ωσαν ωσ αν. 7 φησειν. 8 και σχυρ… 9 εξουθενημενοσ. 10 επιστολων. 11 τολμωμεν. 12 συνκριναι. 13 εν εαυτοισ. 14 In marg. καν…

K. X.	του · κανονοσ · ου · εμερει_σεν ·	regulae quam mensus est nobis
	ο θσ · μετρου · αφικεσθαι · αχρι ·	ds · mensuram pertingendi usque
v. 14	και υμων · Ου γαρ ωσ · μη · αφι	ad vos · Non enim quasi non per
	κομενοι · εισ υμασ υπερ · εκτι	tingentes ad vos super ex
	νομεν εαυτουσ αχρι γαρ	tendimus nos · Usque ad vos
	και υμων οφθα_σαμενεν[1] ·	enim pervenimus in
15	τω · ευαγγελιω · του χρυ · Ουκ · εισ · τα	evangelio xpi · Non in im
	αμετρα · καυχωμενοι · εν · αλ	mensum gloriantes · In ali
	λοτριουσ κονοισ[2] · ελπιδα · δε ·	enis laboribus · spem autem
	εχοντεσ · αυξανομενησ · τησ ·	habentes crescentis
	πιστεωσ υμων εν · υμιν · μεγα	fidei vestrae · In nobis magni
	λυνθηναι · κατα τον · κανονα ·	ficari secundum regulam
16	ημων εισ περισσῖαν · εισ · τα · υπε	nram in abundantiam etiam in
	ρεκεινα · υμων ευαγγελισασ_	illa quae ultra vos evange
	θαι · Ουκ εν αλλοτριω · κανονῖ	lizare · Non in aliena regula
	εισ · τα · ε · τοιμα · καυχησασθαι ·	in his quæ præparata sunt gloriari
17	Ο · δε · καυχωμενοσ εν κω καυ	Qui autem gloriatur in dno glori
18	χασθω · Ου γαρ ο · εαυτον συν	etur · Non enim qui se ipsum
	ιστανον[3] εκεινοσ · εστιν · ο · δοκῖ	commendat ille probatus
	μοσ · αλλον ο κσ συνιστησιν ·	est sed quem dns commendat ·
XI. 1	Ωφελον · ανειχεσθαι μι_κρον ·	Utinam sustineretis modicum qd
	τησ · αφροσυνησ · μου · αλλα	insipientiae meae sed
2	και ανεχεσθαι · μου · ζελω · γαρ ·	et supportate me · Emulor enim
	υμασ θυ ζελω · Ηρμοσαμεν[4] ·	vos di emulatione · Dispondi
	γαρ υμασ ενι ανδρι · παρθενον ·	enim vos uni viro virginem
	αγνην παραστησαι τωχρω	castam exhibere xpo ·
3	Φοβουμαι δε · μηποτε_ωσ · ο · οφισ[5]_	Timeo autem ne forte sic serpens
	εξηπατησεν · ευαν · εν · τι[6] · πανουρ_	evam seduxit astutia

[1] εφθασαμεν εν. [2] αλλοτριοισ κοποισ. [3] συνιστανων. [4] ζηλω Ηρμοσαμην.
[5] *In marg.* contra graecos q. e. contra graecos. [6] τη.

CAP. XI.	sua · Ita corrumpantur sensus	για · αυτου · φθαρη · τα · νοηματα ·
	vestri · et excidant a simplici	υμων · αποτηισ[1] · απλοτητοσ ·
		castitate σ.
	tate quae est in	και τησ αγνητητο[2] · τησ εισ
v. 4	xpo · Nam si is qui venit	χρν · ει,μεν · γαρ · ο · ερχομενοσ ·
	alium xpm praedicat · quem non p	αλλον · χρν · κηρυσσι · Ον · ουκ ·
	predicavimus · aut alium spm	ηκηρυ ξαμεν[3] · Η · πνα · ετερον ·
	accipitis · quem non accepistis ·	λαμβανεται · ο · ουκ · εδεξασθαι ·
	aut aliud evangelium	η · ευαγγελιον ετε‿ρον ·
	quod non recepistis	λαμβανεται · ο · ουκ · εδεξασ
5	recte pateremini · Existimo	θαι · καλοσ[4] · ενειχεσται[5] · λογι
	enim nihil me minus fecisse	ζομε · γαρ · μηδεν · υστερηκε‿
		supramodum
	magnis apostolis ·	ναι · των · υπερλιαν[6] · αποστολων
6	et si imperitus sermone	ει · δε · και · ϊδειωτησ · τω · λογω ·
	non tamen scientia · In omni	αλλου · τη · γνωσει · αλλεν · παν
	bus autem manifestatus sum vobis ·	τει · φανερω‿σαντεσ · εισ · υμασ
7	Aut nunquid peccatum feci me	Η · μη · αμαρτιαν · εποιησα · εαυ
	ipsum humilians · ut vos	τον · ταπινον[7] · ϊνα · υμεισ · υψω
	exaltemini · Quoniam gratis evan	θηται · Οτι · δωραιαν · το · του θυ
	gelium di · evangelizavi	ευαγγελιον · ευηγγελισαμε[8]
8	vobis · Alias aecclesias ex	υμιν αλλασ εκκλησει‿ασ[9]
	spoliavi accipiens stipendium	εσυλησα · λαβων · οψωνιον ·
	ad ministerium vestrum ·	προσ · την · υμων · διακονειαν[10] ·
	et cum essem apud vos et ege	και παρων προσ υμασ ϗ υστε
	rem nulli onerosus fui ·	ρηθεισ · ουκατεναρκησα · ου‿
9	Nam quod mihi de erat	δενοσ · το γαρ · υστερημα · μου ·
	suppleverunt fratres	προσαν‿επληροσαν[11] · οι · αδελ
	tres qui venerunt amacedo	φοι · ελθοντεσ · απο · μακαιδο
	nia · et in omnibus sine onere	νιασ · και · εν · παντει · α · βαρη ·

[1] τησ. [2] αγνοτητοσ. [3] ηκηρυξαμεν *p.m.* [4] καλωσ. [5] ανειχεσθαι. [6] υπερδιαν. [7] ταπινων. [8] ευηγγελισαμη. [9] εκκλεσειασ. [10] *In marg.* διακονεια. [11] προσανεπληρωσαν.

II. υμην[1] · εμαυτον · ετηρησα · κ̣	me vobis servavi et
10 τηρησω · εστην[2] · αληθια · χ̅ρ̅υ̅ ·	servabo · est veritas x̅p̅i̅
εν · εμοι · οτι · ηκαυχησισ · αυτη ·	in me quoniam haec gloria
ου · φραγησεται · εν · εμοι · εν	non infringetur in me in
11 τοισ · κλιμασιν · αχαιασ · δια · τι ·	regionibus achaiae · quare?
οτι · ουκ · αγαπω · υμασ · ο̅θ̅σ̅ · οι‿	quia non diligo vos? D̅s̅ scit
12 δεν · Ο · δε · ποιω · και · ποιησω · ῑνα ·	quod autem facio et faciam · ut
εκοψω · την αφορμην · των	amputem occasionem eorum
θελον · των[3] αφορμην · ῑνα · εν	qui volunt occasionem · ut in
ω · καυχωνται · ευρεθωσιν · κα	quo gloriantur · Inveniantur · si
13 θωσ · και υμισ[4] · Ου · γαρ · τοι · ουτοι ·	cut et nos · Nam ejusmodi
ψευδαποστολοι · εργαται ·	pseudo apostoli operarii
δολειοι μετασχηματι‿ζο‿	subdoli trans figurantes
14 μενοι · αποστολουσ · χ̅υ̅ · και	se in apostolos x̅p̅i̅ et non
ου θαυμα · αυτοσ γαρ · ο · σατανασ ·	mirum · Ipse enim satanas
μετασχηματιζε‿ται · εισ	transfigurat se In
15 αγγελον · φωτοσ · ου · μετα[5] · ουν ·	angelum lucis · Non est ergo magnum
ει και · οι · διακονοι · αυτου · με‿	si ministri ejus trans
τα σχηματιζονται · ωσ · διακο‿	figurentur velut ministri
νοι · δικαι·συνησ[6] · ων · το · τε‿	justitiae · quorum fi
λοσ εσται · κατα · τα · εργα · αυτων ·	nis erit s̅c̅d̅m̅ opera ipsorum ·
16 παλιν · λεγω · μη · τισ · μαι · δοξη ·	Iterum dico nequis me putet
αφρον[7] · ειναι · ει · δε · μη · γη[8] καν ·	insipientem esse · Alioquin
ωσ αφρονα δεξασθαι ·	velut insipientem accipite
μαι · ῑνα · καγω · μικρον · τι · καυ	me · ut et ego modicum q̄id gro
17 χησωμαι · ο · λαλω · ου · κατα	rier · q̅d̅ loquor non secundum
κ̅υ̅ · λαλω · Αλλωσ · εν αφροσυ	d̅m̅ loquor · Sed quasi in insi
νη · εν · ταυτη · τη · υποστασι · τησ ·	pientia in hac substantia

---

[1] υμιν. [2] τηρησω. Εστιν. [3] θελοντων. [4] ημισ. [5] μεγα. [6] δικαιοσυνησ. [7] αφρονα. [8] γε.

CAP. XI. v. 18 gloriae quoniam multi glorian	καυχησεωσ·επι[1]·πολλοι·καυ
tur secundum carnem et ego glori	χωνται·κατα σαρκα·καγω·καυ
19 abor · Libenter enim suf	χησομα · Η·δε‿ωσ·γαρ·ανεχεσ‿
fertis insipientes cum sitis ip	θαι·των·αφρονων·φρονειμοι
20 si sapientes · Sustinetis enim si quis	οντεσ·ανεχεσθαι γαρ·ει τησ[2]·
vos inservitutem redigit·si q'ˢ de	υμασ καταδουλοι·ειτισ·κα
vorat·si quis accipit·	τα‿ισθειοι[3]·ειτισ·λαμβανει·
si quis extollitur·si quis in faci	ειτισ·επερεται·ειτισ·εισ[4]·προ
21 em vos cedit · Secundum ignobi	σωπον·υμασ·δερει·κατα ατι
litatem dico quasi nos infirmi fu	μιαν·λεγω·ωσ·οτι·ησθενησα‿
erimus·In quo autem quis audet in in	μεν·ημεισ·εν·ωδαν·τησ[5]·τολ
sipientia dico·audeo et ego·	μα·τολμω·καγω·εν·αφροσυνη·
22 ebrei sunt et ego · Is	λεγω·εβραιοι·εισιν·καγω·ισ̄
rahelitae sunt et ego · Semen	ραηλιται·εισιν·καγω·Cπερμα
23 abrahae sunt et ego · Ministri	αβρααμ·εισιν·καγω·Διακονοι'
xpi sunt et ego·ut minus sapiens dico	εισιν·χ̄υ·Παραφρονων·λεγω·
plus ego · In laboribus pluri	Ὑπερ εγω·εν·κονοισ[6]·περισσοτε
mis · In carceribus abundantius·	ρῶσ·εν·πληγαισ·περισσοτερῶσ·
in plagis supra modum·	εν·φυλακαισ·ὑπερ·βαλλοντωσ·
24 In mortibus frequenter·a	εν·θανατοισ·πολλακεῖσ·Υπο
judeis quinquies qua dragenas	ιουδαιων·πεντακῖσ·μ̄·παρα
25 una minus accepi · Ter virgis cesus sum·	μιαν·ελαβων[7]·τρισ·εραβδι·θην[8]·
semel lapidatus sum · Ter naufragium	απαξελιθασθην · Τρισ·εναυ‿
feci · Nocte et die in profun	αγησα · Νυχ·θημερον·εν·τω·
26 do maris fui · In itineribus	βυθω·πεποι·ηκα·οδοιπορειαισ‿
sepe · Periculis flumi	πολλακῖσ·κινδυνοισ·ποτα‿
num·periculis latronum·	μων·κινδυνοισ·λησ‿των·
periculis ex genere pericu	κιν δυνοισ·εκγενουσ κιν‿

[1] *In marg.* in lucan. [2] ει τισ. [3] καταισθειει. [4] ειυσ. [5] τισ. [6] κοποισ. [7] ελαβον. [8] εραβδισ θην.

P. XI. δυνοισ·εξεθνων·κινδυνοισ·	lis ex gentibus · Periculis
εν·πολει·κινδυνοισ·εν·ερη_	incivitate · Periculis in solitu
μια·κινδυνοισ·εν·θαλασση·	dine · Periculis in mari·
κινδυνοισ·εν·ψευδαδελφοισ·	Periculis in falsis fratribus·'
v. 27 κονο[1]·και·μοχθω·εν αγρυπ	In labore et erumna·in vigili
ναισ·πολλακισ·εν·λειμω·και·	is multis · In fame et
διψει·εν[2]·νηστειαισ·πολλακισ·	siti · In jejuniis multis·
εν·ψυχι·και γυμνο_τη_τι·	In frigore et nuditate·
28 Χωρισ·των παρεκτοσ·η·επισ	Preter illa quæ extrinsecus in
·η· μ	
τασεισ·μοι·καθημερι·νη[3]·με	stantia·mea cottidiana
ριμνα·πασω ·των·εκκλησει	sollicitudo·omnium ecclesi
29 ων · Τισ·ασθενι · και·ουκ·	arum · Quis infirmatur·et ego non
ασθενω · Τισ·σκανδαλιζε	infirmor? Quis scandaliza
ται·και·ουκ·εγω·πυρουμαι·	tur·et ego nonuror·
30 Ει·καυχασθαι·δει·τα·τησ·ασ	Si gloriari oportet·quæ infirmi
θενιασ·μου·καυχησομαι[4]·	tatis meæ sunt gloriabor·
31 Ο θσ·και πατηρ του κυ ιυ	Ds et pater dni nri ihu xpi
οιδεν·ο·ων ευλογητοσ·εισ·	scit qui est benedictus in
τουσ·αιωνασ·οτι·ου·ψευδο	secula·quod non mentior·
gentis	
32 μαι·εν·δαμασκω·ο·εθ_ναρ	Damasci prepositus gen
princeps	e
χησ·αρετα·του·βασιλε_ωσ·	tis aratæ regis·
εφρουρει·την·πολιν[5]·δαμασ	custodiebat civitatem damas
33 κηνων·θελων·πισαι·μαι·και·	cenorum·ut me comprehenderet
δια·θυριδοσ·εχα·λασθην·	et per fenestram insporta dimissus sum
δια·του·τιχουσ·και·εξε φυ	per murum·et effugi
XII. 1 γον·τασ·χειρασ·αυτου · Καυ	manus ejus · Si gloria
χασθαι·δει·ου·συμφε_ρον·	ri oportet·non expedit
μεν · Ελευσομαι·δαι·εισ·τα·	quidem · Veniam autem ad

[1] κοπω. [2] εν εν. [3] η καθημερινη. [4] *In marg.* καυχημα. [5] πολιν *p.m.*

CAP. XII.	visiones et revelatio	οπτασειασ και αποκαλυ_
v. 2	nes dni · Scio hominem	ψεισ χυ[1] · Οι·δα·ανθρωπον·
	in xpo ante annos quatuor_	εν χρω προ αιτων·δεκατεσ
	decim sive in corpore ne	σαρων·ειτε·εν·σωματι·ουκ_
	scio sive extra corpus	οιδα·ειτε·εκτοσ·του σωμα
	nescio ds scit	τοσ·ουκ οιδα·οθσ οιδεν
	raptum hujusmodi	αρπαγεντα·τον·τοι·ουτον·
	usque ad tertium caelum	εωσ·του·τριτου·ουρανου·
3	et scio hujusmodi hominem	και·οιδα·τον·τοι·ουτον·ανον·
	sive in corpore sive extra	ειτε·εν·σωμαται[2]·ειτε·εκτοσ·
	corpus nescio	του σωματοσ·ουκ·οιδα·
4	ds scit quom raptus est in	ο θσ οιδεν·οτι·ηρπαγη·εισ·
	paradisum·et audivit	τον·παραλισον[3]·κ̅ ηκουσεν·
	archana verba quæ non licet	αρπη·τα[4]·ρηματα·α·ουκ·εξον·
5	homini loqui · Pro ejusmo_	ανθρωπω·αλλησαι[5]·υπερ·του·
	di gloriabor pro	τοι·ουτοι·καυχησομαι·υπερ·
	me autem nihil gloriabor	δε εμαυτοσ[6] (υ above)·ου·καυχησομαι·
	nisi in infirmitatibus meis	ει μη·εν·ταισ ασθενιαισ·μου·
6	Nam et si voluero gloriari	Εαν·γαρ·θελησω·καυχασθαι·
	non ero insipiens · Verita	ουκ·εσομαι·αφρων·αλη
	tem enim dico Parco autem	θιαν·γαρ·ερω[7] (γ above)·φειλομαι·δαι·
	nequis me existimet	μη·τισ·εισ·μαι[8] (ε above)·λογεισ_ηται·
	supra id qd videt me aut audit	υπερ·ο·βλεπειμαι·η·ακουει·
7	aliquid ex me·et ne magni	εξεμου·και·τη·υπερβολη·
	tudo revelationum	των·αποκλυψ[9] διο
	extollat me·datus est	ινα·μη·υπερ_ερωμαι·εδοθη·
	mihi stimulus carnis meae	μοι·σκολοψ-τη·σαρκι·μου·
	angelus satanae·ut mo co	αγγελοσ[10]·σατανα·Ινα·με·κολα

1 · *In marg.* evang. in graeco. 2 σωματει. 3 παραδισον. 4 αρρη;τα. 5 λαλησαι. 6 εμαυτου. 7 ερω. 8 τησ *p.m.* εισ εμαι. 9 αποκαλυψ. 10 Αν (γ above) γελοσ.

II. 8 φιζη · υπερ · τουτου · τρισ · τον · κ̅υ̅ ·
παρεκαλεσα · ινα · αποστη · απεμ8 ·
9 και · ειπεν · μοι · αρκι · σοι · η · χα‿
ρισ · μου · η · γαρ · δυναμισ · εν · ασθε
να · τελιται · Η · διστα · ουν ·
μαλλον · καυχησομαι · εν · ταισ ·
ασθενιαισ · μου · Ῑνα · επισκη
νοση[1] · επεμαι · η · δυναμεισ ·
10 του χ̅υ̅ Δι · ο · ευδοκω · εν ˀ
εν · αν · γκαισ[2] · εν · διωγμοισ ·
εν · στενο‿χωριαισ · υπερ χ̅υ̅ ·
Οτε · γαρ · ασθενο[3] · τοτε · δυνατω ·
11 Εγεγωνα[4] · αφρων · ημεισ · μαι
ηναγκασαται · Εγω · γαρ · ωφι
λον · υφυμων · συνϊστασ‿θαι ·
Ου · γαρ · υστερησα · των · υπερ ·
λιαν · αποστολων · Ει · και · ου
12 δεν · ειμι̂ αλλε · τα · μεν · σημι̂α ·
του · αποστολου · κατηργασ‿θη ·
εν · υμιν · εν · παση · υπομονη ·
και · σημειοισ · και · τερασιν · κ̷
13 δυναμεσιν · τι · γαρ · εστιν · ο ·
ελατω‿θηται · υπερ · τασ · λοιπασ ·
εκκλησι̂ασ · ειμη · οτι εγω ·
αυτοσ · ου · κατεναρκησα · υμων ·
χαρισασθαι · μοι · την · αμαρτιαν ·
14 ταυτην · Ιδου · τριτον · του το ·

ˀ ασθενιαισ · μου · εν · υβρεσιν ·

lafizet · Propter quod ter d̅n̅m̅
rogavi ut discederet a me
et dixit mihi · Sufficit tibi gra
tia mea · Nam virtus in infir
mitate perficitur · Libenter igitur
gloriabor in infirmita
tibus meis · ut inhabi
tet in me virtus
x̅p̅i̅ · Propter q̅d̅ placeo mihi*
in necessitatibus in persecutionibus
in angustiis pro x̅p̅o̅
Cum enim infirmor · tunc potens sum ·
Factus sum insipiens vos me
coegistis ego enim debui
a vobis commendari ·
Nihil enim minus fui ab his q[i] sunt supra
modum apostoli · tam et si ni
hil sum · signa tamen
apostoli sunt facta super vos
in omni patientia
signis et prodigiis et
virtutibus · Quid est enim quod
minus habuistis præ ceteris
æcclesiis · Nisi quod ego
ipse non gravavi vos ·
danate mihi hanc injuri
am · Ecce tertio hoc

* in infirmitatibus · in contumeliis

[1] επι σκηνωση. [2] αναγκαισ. [3] ασθενω. [4] εγεγονα.

	Latin	Greek
CAP. XII.	paratus sum venire ad	ετοιμωσ · εχω · ελθειν · προσ ·
	vos · et non ero gravis vobis ·	υμασ · και · ουκαταν_αρκησω · υμασ
	Non enim quaero quæ vestra sunt sed	Ου · γαρ · ζητω · τα · υμων · αλλα ·
	vos · Nec enim debent filii	υμασ · Ου γαρ · οφιλει · τα · τεκνα ·
	parentibus thesaurizare ·	τοισ · γονευ_σειν · θησαυριζιν ·
	sed parentes filiis ·	αλλοι · γονεισ · τοισ · τεκνοισ
v. 15	Ego autem libentissime impendam	Εγω · δε · η · δεισ · τα · δαπανησω ·
	et super impendar pro	και · εκδαπα_νηθησομαι · υπερ ·
	animabus vestris · Licet plus	των · ψυχων · υμων · ει · περισ
		ω
	vos diligens · minus	σοτεροσ[1] · υμασ · αγαπων · ελασσον ·
		ω
16	diligar · Sed esto ego vos	αγαπομαι[2] · Εστω · δε · εγω · δε ·
	non gravavi · Sed cum	ου · κατεν_αρκησα · υμων · αλλα ·
	essem astutus · dolo	υπαρχων · πανουργοσ · Δολω ·
17	vos coepi · Nunqd per aliquem eo	υμασ · ελαβον · Μη · τινα · ων ·
		avaricia
	rum quos misi ad vos · circumve	απεσταλκα · προσ · υμασ · επλεον ·
18	ni vos · Rogavi	εκτησα · υμασ · Παρεκαλεσα ·
	titum · et misi cum illo	τιτον[3] · και · συν · απεστειλα · τον ·
	fratrem nunquid titus vos	αδελφον · μητι · επλεον · εκτησεν ·
	circumvenit · Nonne eodem	υμασ · τιτοσ · Ουτω · αυτω ·
	spu ambulavimus · nonne	πνι · περι · επατησαμεν[4] · ου · τοισ ·
19	eisdem vestigiis · Olim puta	αυτοισ · ιχνε_σιν · Παλαι · δο
	tis quod excusemus nos apud	κειται · οτι · υμειν · απολογου
		θ
	vos · Coram do in xpo	μετα[5] · κατεναντι · θυ · εν · χρω
	loquimur · Omnia autem caris	λαλουμεν · Τα · δε · παντα · αγα
	simi propter vestram ædifica	πη_τοι · υπερ · τησ · υμων · οικο
20	tionem · Timeo enim ne	δομησ · Φοβουμαι · γαρ · μη ·
	forte cum venero non quales vo	πωσ · ελθων · ουχ · οι_ουσ · θε
	lo inveniam vos et ego inve	λω · ευρω · υμασ · και · εγω · ευ

---

[1] περισσοτερωσ. [2] αγαπωμαι. [3] τει τιτον. [4] + οτι εαν ελθω παλιν ου φισομαι (ante ου). [5] απολογουμεθα.

L. ρεθω · υμιν · οιον · ου · θελεται ·	niar a vobis qualem non vultis ·
Μη · πωσ · ερεισ · ζηλοσ · θυμον[1] · (animositates)	Ne forte contentiones æmulationes
αιρειθειαι · κατα · λαλειαι ·	animositates · dissensiones detractiones
ψιθυρισμοι · φυσειω_σεισ ·	susurrationes seditiones sint inter vos
21 Μη · παλιν · ελθον · τοσ · μου	Ne iterum cum venero
τα · πεινωσει · μαι · ο̅θ̅σ̅ μου	humilet me d̅s̅
προσ υμασ · και · πενθησω · πολ	apud vos et lugeam · mul
λουσ · των · προ · ημαρτηκοτων ·	tos ex his qui ante peccaverunt
και · μη · μετα · νοησαν · των · επι ·	et non egerunt poenitentiam sup̱
τη · ακαθαρσία · και πορνία ·	immunditia et fornicatione
και · ασελγία · η · επραξαν	et impudicitia quam gesserunt
XIII. 1 τριτον · τουτο · ερχομαι προσ	tertio hoc venio ad
υμασ επειστοματοσ · δυο · μαρ	vos · In ore duorum vel tri
τιρων[2] · και · τριων · σταθησεται ·	um testium stabit om
2 παν · ρημα · Προ · ειρηκα · και ·	ne verbum · Praedixi et
προ · λεγω · ωσ · παρων · το · δευ	praedico ut praesens bis ·
τερον · και · απον[3] · νυν · τοισ · προ ·	et nunc absens · his qui ante
η · μαρτηκοσιν · και · τοισ · λοιποισ ·	peccaverunt · et cæteris
πασιν · οτι · εαν · ελθω · παλιν ·	omnibus quo̅ si venero iterum
3 ου φισομαι · Οτι · δοκειμην · ζη	non parcam · An experimentum quæ
τει · τε · του · λαλουντοσ · εν · εμοι ·	ritis ejus qui in me loquitur ·
χ̅ρ̅υ̅ · Οσ · εισ · υμασ · ουκ · ασθε	x̅p̅c̅ · Qui in vos non infirma
νει · αλλα · δυνατει · εν · υμιν ·	tur · sed potens est in vobis ·
4 Και · γαρ · εσταυρωθη · εξασ_θε	Nam et si crucifixus est ex infirmi
νίασ[4] · αλλα · ζη · εκδυνα_μαι ·	tate sed vivit ex virtute
ωσ · θ̅υ̅ · και · ημεισ · ασθε_νου_	d̅i̅ · Nam et nos infirmi sumus
μεν · συν · αυτω · αλλα · ζησω	cum illo · sed vivemus cum ipso ex
5 μεν · συν · αυτω · εισ · υμασ · εαυ	virtute d̅i̅ in vobis · Vosmetipsos

[1] θυμοι. [2] μαρτυρων. [3] απων. [4] *In marg.* δ̅ο̅ν̅.

CAP. XIII. temptare si estis in
fide ipsi vos proba
te · An cognoscitis
vos ipsos quia xps ihs in vobis
est nisi forte reprobi
v. 6 estis · Spero quod cognosce
tis · quia nos non sumus
7 reprobi · Oramus autem
dm ut nihil*
mali faciatis non
ut nos probati parea
mus · sed ut vos quod bo
num est faciatis Nos autem ut
8 reprobi simus · Non enim
possumus aliqd adversus veri
tatem sed pro veritate
9 Gaudeamus enim quando nos in
firmi sumus · Vos autem poten
tes estis Hoc et ora
mus vestram consummati
10 onem · Ideo haec
absens scribo · ut non psens
durius agam · Secundum
potestatem quam dns de
dedit mihi in aedificationem et
11 non in distructionem · Decetero
fratres gaudete perfecti
estote Exortamini i

τουσ · πειραζεται · ει · εσται · εν
τη · πιστι · εαυτουσ · δοκειμα
ζεται · Η · ουκ · επιγινοσκεται[1] ·
εαυτουσ · οτι · χρσ · ισ · εν · υμιν
εστιν · ει · μη · τι · αδοκει μοι ·
ε · ται[2] · ελπιζω · γαρ οτι γνω
σεσθαι · οτι · ημεισ · ουκ · εσμεν ·
αδοκειμοι · Ευχομεθα · δε ·
προσ · τον · θν · μη · ποι η σαι ·
υμασ · κακον · μηθεν[3] · ουχ ·
ιν[4] · ημεισ · δοκειμοι · φανω
μεν · αλλινα · υμεισ · τοκα
λον · ποιηται · Ημεισ · δε · ωσ ·
αδοκειμοι · ωμεν · Ου · γαρ ·
δυναμεθα · τι · κατα · αληθι
ασ · αλλα υπερ αληθιασ ·
Χαιρομεν · γαρ · οτε · ημεισ · ασ
θενωμεν υμεισ[5] · δε · δυ
νατοι · ητε · Τουτο · και ευχο
μεθα · την · υμων καταρ
τισῖν · Δια · τουτο ταυτα
απων · γραφω · ῖνα · μη · παρων ·
αποτομωσ · χρησομαι · κατα
την · εξουσῖαν · ην · οκσ · εδω
κεν · μοι εισ · οικοδομην[6] · και ·
ουκ εισ καθερεσιν · Λοιπον ·
αδελφοι · χαιρεται · καθαρ
τι ζεσθαι[7] · παρακαλεισ · θαι · το ·

[1] επιγινωσκεται. [2] εσται. [3] μηδεν. [4] ἵνα. [5] Υμισ. [6] οικοδωμην. [7] καταρτιζεσθαι.

11. αυτο φρον ειτε · ιρηνευετε ·
και · ο θσ της ιρηνης εσται
12 μεθυμων · ασπασασθαι · αλ
ληλους · εν · φιληματι · αγιω ·
13 Ασπαζονται · υμας · οι · αγιοι ·
14 παντες · Η · χαρεις · του κυ ιυ
χυ · και · η · αγαπη · του θυ · και ·
ηκοι‿νωνία · του αγειου · πνς
μετα παντων · υμων ·

Ετελεσ‿θη προς κο
ρινθιους · B[1] ·

dem sapite pacem habete
et ds dilectionis et pacis erit
vobiscum · Salutate invi
cem in osculo sancto ·
Salutant vos sancti
omnes · Gratia dni nri ihu
xpi · et caritas di et
communicatio sci spiritus
sit cum omnibus vobis ·

EXPLICIT AD CO
RINTHIOS · II ·

Αρχεται προς Γα
λατας ·

Incipit ad Ga
Latas ·

CAP. I
1 Παυλος αποστο
λος ·

ουκ απ · ανθρωπων · ουδε δια
ανθρωπου · αλλα · δια · ιηυ · χρυ
και θυ πατρος του · εγιραντος ·
2 αυτον · εκ · νεκρων · ϗ · οι ; συνεμοι ·
παντες · αδελφοι · ταις · εκκλησει
3 αις[2] · της · γαλατείας · χαρεις · υμιν ·
και · ιρηνη · αποθυ · πατρος · ϗ κυ
4 ημων ιυ χυ του · δον‿τος · εαυ

Paulus aposto
lus ·

non ab hominibus neque per
hominem · sed per ihm xpm
et dm patrem qui suscitavit
eum a mortuis · et qui mecum
omnes fratres ecclesi
is galatiae · gratia vobis
et pax a do patre et dno
nro ihu xpo · qui dedit semet

[1] – B.

[2] εκκλησειας.

CAP. I.	ipsum pro peccatis nostris	τον·περιτων·αμαρτελων·υμων[1]·
	ut eriperet nos de	οπωσ·εξεληται·ημασ[2]·εκτου·
	præsenti seculo nequam	ενεστωτοσ·αιωνοσ·πονηρου[3]·
	secundum voluntatem d̅i̅ et pa	κατα·το·θελημα·του·θ̅υ̅·και πα
v. 5	tris n̅r̅i̅·cui est gloria in sae	τροσ·ημων·ω·η·δοξα·εισ·τουσ
	cula sæculorum Amen·	αιωνασ·των·αιωνων·αμην·
6	Miror quod sic tam cito trans	Μαζω·δε·οτι·ταχαιωσ·μετα_
	ferimini·ab eo qui vos vocavit·	τιθεσθαι·αποτουκαλεσαντοσ·
	in gratiam x̅p̅i̅ · In aliud	χριστου υμασ·εν·χαριτι[4]·εισ·ετερον·
7	evangelium·q̅d̅ non est aliud	ευαγγελιον·ο·ουκ·εστιν·αλλο·
	nisi sunt aliqui qui vos con	ειμη·τινεσ·εισ ιν·οι·παρασσον_
	turbant·et volunt conver	τεσ·υμασ και θελοντεσ·μετα_
	tere evangelium x̅p̅i̅·	στρεψαι·το·ευαγγελιον·του·χ̅υ̅
8	Sed licet nos aut angelus	Αλλα·και·εαν·ημεισ·η·αγγελοσ·
	de cælo evangelizet vobis	εξουρανου·ευαγγελιζηται[5]·
	preter quod evangelizavimus vobis	παρ·ο·ευαγγελι_σαμετα ημιν[6]
9	anathema sit·sicut praediximus	αναθεμα·εστω·ωσ·προιρηκαμεν·
	et tunc iterum dico·si quis vobis	και·αρτι·παλιν·λεγω·ειτισ·υμασ·
	evangelizaverit praeter id q̅d̅ ac	ευαγγελι_ζηται·παρ·ο·παρελαβε
10	cepistis anathema sit · Modo enim	ται·αναθεμα·εστω·Αρτι·γαρ·
	hominibus suadeo aut d̅o̅·	ανθρωπουσ·επιθω·η·τον·θ̅ν̅·
	aut quaero hominibus placere·	η·ζητω·ανθρωποι σ·αρεσκειν·
	si adhuc hominibus placerem x̅p̅i̅	ει·αιτει[7]·ανουσ[8]·ηρεσκον·χ̅ρ̅υ̅·
11	servus non essem · Notum enim vobis	δουλοσ·ουκ·ανεμην[9]·Γνωριζω·
	facio fratres evangelium	γαρ·υμιν·αδελφοι·τε[10] ευαγγελιον·
	quod evangeli zatum est a me	το·ευαγγελισθεν·υπε μου[11]·
	quia non est secundum hominem	οτι·ουκ·εστιν·κατα·ανθρωπον·
12	neque enim ego ab homine	ουδε·γαρ·εγω·παρα·ανθρωπου·

[1] αμαρτειων ημων. [2] ημωσ. [3] *In marg.* αγανο. [4] *Non habet* χριστου. [5] ευαγγελιζαηται. [6] ευαγγελισαμεθα υμιν. [7] αιτεια. [8] ανοισ. [9] ανημην. [10] το. [11] *In marg.* contra αγανον.

CAP. I.	παρελαβον · αυτο · Ουδε · εδιδαχ_	accepi illud neque didici ·
	θην · αλλα · διαποκαλυψαιωσ · ·	sed per revelationem
v. 13	ιυ̅ · χυ̅ · Η · κουσαται · γαρ · την · εμην ·	ihu̅ xpi̅ · Audistis enim conversa·
	αναστροφην · ποτε · εν[1] · ϊουδαισ	tionem meam aliquando in juda
	μω[2] · οτι · καθυ · περβολην · εδιω	ismo · quō supra modum perseque ·
	κον · την · εκκλησΐαν · του̅ · θυ̅	bar · ecclesiam di̅
14	και · επολεμουν · αυτην · και · προ	et expugnabam illam et profi
	εκοπτον · εν · τω · ϊουδαισ_μω ·	ciebam In judaismo
	υπερ · πολλουσ · συνελει_κειω_	supra multos coætaneos meos
	τασ · εν · τω · γενει · μου · περισσο_	ingenero meo abundanti
	τερωσ · ζηλω · τισ[3] · ὑπαρ_χων ·	us æmulator existens
	των · πατρικων · μου · παραδο_	paternarum mearum traditio
15	σαιων[4] · Οτε · δε · ευδοκησεν · ο ·	num · Cum autem placuit ei qui
	αφορισασ · μαι · εκκουλΐασ[5] · μη_	me segregavit deutero ma
	τροσ · μου · και καλεσασ · δια · τησ ·	tris meae etvocavit per
16	χαριτοσ · αυτου · αποκαλυψαι ·	gratiam suam · Ut revela
	τον υιον · αυτου · εν · εμοι · ϊνα ·	ret filium suum in me · ut
	ευαγγελειζωμαι · αυτον · εν · τοισ ·	evvangelizarem illum in
	εθνεσιν · Ευθεωσ · ου · προσ · ανε	gentibus · Continuo non ad qui
17	θεμην · σαρκι · και · αιματι · ουδε ·	evi carni et sanguuini neque
	απηλθον · εισ · ιεροσολυμα · προσ ·	veni ierosolimam ad ante ces
	τουσ · εμου · αποστολουσ · Αλλα ·	sores meos apostolos · Sed
	απηλθον · εισ · αραβεΐαν · ϗ παλιν ·	abii in arabiam · et iterum
	υπεστρεψα · εισ · δαμασκον ·	reversus sum in damascum ·
18	Επι · τα · μετα · αιτη · γ̅ · ανη · θον[6] · (λ. above)	Deinde post annos tres veni
	εισ · ιεροσολυμα · ϊστορησαι · πετρον ·	hierosolimam videre petrum
	και · επεμεινα · προσ · αυτον · ημε	et mansi apud eum die
19	ρασ · δεκαπεντε · Ετερον · δε · των ·	bus quin decim · Alium autem

[1] + τω (*post* εν). [2] *In marg.* contra judaeos. [3] ζηλωτησ : *in marg.* ζελοτεσ. [4] *In marg.* παραδισοσ. [5] κοιλΐασ. [6] ανηλθον.

CAP. I.	apostolorum vidi neminem ni	αποστολων·ειδον·ουδενα·ει
	si jacobum fratrem	μη·ιακωβων[1]·τον·αδελφον·του·
v. 20	dni · Quae autem scribo vobis·ecce	κυ·α·δε·γραφω·υμην[2]·ῒδου·
	coram do·quia non menti	ενοπιων[3]·του·θυ·οτι·ου·ψευδο
21	or · Deinde veni in par	μαι· Єπῖτα·ηλθον·εισ·τα·κλιμ
	tes syriae et cilici	ματα[4]·τησ·συριασ·και·τησ·κιλικι
22	ae · Eram autem ignotus	ασ · Ημεν[5]·δε·αγνο_ουμενοσ
	faciae ecclesiis·	προσωπω·ταισ·εκκλησιαισ·τησ·
23	judeae quae erant in xpo · Tantum	ῒουδαιασ·ταισ·εν·χρω · Μονον·
	autem auditum habebant·qm qui perse	δε·ακουοντεσ·ησαν·οτι·ο·διω
	quebatur nos aliquando nunc evange	κων·υμασ[6]·ποτε·νυν·ευαγγελι
	lizat fidem·quam aliquando	ζεται·την·πιστιν·ην ποτε·
24	expugnabat·et in me clarificabant	επολεμι·και·εν·εμοι·εδοξατον[7]
CAP. II. 1	dm · Deinde post annos quatu	τον·θν · Єπιτα·δια·δεκατεσσα
	ordecim · Iterum ascendi	ρων·αιτων·ανεβην·παλιν·
	hierosolimam·cum barnaba	εισ·ῒροσολυμα[8]·μετα·βαρναβα·
2	assumpto et tito · Ascendi	συν·παραλαβων·και·τιτον·ανε
	autem secundum revelationem et	βην·δε·κατα·αποκαλυψιν·και
	contuli cum illis evangeli	(exposui) ανεβαλομην·αυτοισ·το·εναγ
	um quod praedico in gen	γελιον·ο·κηρυσσω·εν·τοισ·
	tibus · Seorsum autem his qui vide	εθνεσιν·κατῒδιαν·δε·τοισ·
	bantur aliqd esse ne forte in vacuum	δοκουσῖν·μη·πωσ·εισ·καινον
3	currerem aut cucurrissem·sed	τρεχω·η·εδραμον·αλλουτε·
	neque titus·q[i] mecum erat cum esset gen	τιτοσ·ο·συνεμοι·ελλη_νων·
	tilis·compulsus est circum cidi·	ην·αγκασθη·περιτμηθηναι·
4	propter subintroductos fal	δια·δε·τουσ·παρεισ·ακτουσ·ψευ
	sos frs·qui subintroierunt·	δα·δελφουσ·ο·ιτῖνεσ·παρειση
	explorare liberta	λθον·κατα·σκοπησαι·την; ελευ

[1] ῒακωβον. [2] υμιν. [3] ενωπιον. [4] κλιμ̣ατα (μ.). [5] Ημην. [6] ημασ. [7] εδοξαζον. [8] ῒεροσολυμα.

Greek	Latin
II. θεριαν · ημων · ην · εχομεν · εν	tem nram · quam habemus in
χρω · ιηυ · ἱνα · μη · ημασ · κατα ·	xpo ihu Ut nos in servitu
I. 5 δουλω_σωσιν · οισ · ουδε · προσ ·	tem redigerent · quibus nec ad
ωραν · ειζαμεν · τη · υποταγη · ἱνα ·	horam cessimus subjectioni · Ut
η · αληθια · του · ευαγγελιου · δια	veritas evangelii permane
6 μεινη · προσ · υμασ · Απο · δε · των ·	at apud vos · Ab his autem qui
δοκουντων · ειν(αι)[1] · τι · οποι_οι ·	videbantur esse aliquid · quales
ποτε · ησαν · ουδεν · μοι · δια_φε_	aliquando fuerint · nihil meam consci
ρι · θσ · ανδρωπου[2] · προσωπον ·	entiam inter est · Ds personam hominis
ουλ · αμβανει · Εμοι · γαρ · οι · δοκουν_	non accipit · Mihi autem qui vide
τεσ · τι · ειναι · ουδεν · προσαν	bantur aliqd esse nihil contule
7 θεντο · αλλα του παντι ον[3] · ι_	runt · sed contra cum vidis
δοντεσ · οτι · περιστευ_ται[4] · μοι ·	sent · quod creditum est mihi
το · ευαγγελιον · τησ · ακροβυστει_	evangelium præputii ·
8 ασ · καθωσ · πετρο · περιτομησ[5] · εν ·	sicut petro circumcisionis ·
ηργησεν · καμοι[6] · εισ · τα · εθνην[7] ·	operatus est et mihi intergentes ·
9 και · γνοντεσ · την · χαριν · την ·	et cum cognovissent gratiam quae
δοθεισαν · μοι · πετροσ · και · ια	data est mihi · petrus · et ia
κωβοσ · και ἰωαννησ · οι · δοκουν	cobus · et iohannes qui videban
τεσ · (σ)τυλοι[8] ειναι · δεξειασ · εδω ·	tur columnae esse · dextras dede
καν · μοι · και · βαρναβα · κοινω	runt mihi et barnabae societa
νιασ · ἱνα · ημεισ · εισ · τα · εθνη ·	tis · Ut nos intergentes
αυτοι · δε · εισ · την · περιτομην ·	ipsi autem incircumcisonem
o μονον · ἱνα · των · πτωχων · μνη_	tantum ut pauperum memores es
μονευωμεν[9] · ο · και · εσπουδα_	semus · quod et sollicitus
I σα · αυτο · τουτο · ποιησαι · οτε ·	fui hoc ipsum facere · Cum
δε · ηλθεν · πετροσ · εισ · αντιο	autem venisset petrus antio
χειαν · κατα · προσωπον · αυτω ·	chiam in faciem ei

[1] ειναι. [2] ανθρωπου. [3] τουναντι ον. [4] πεπιστευται. [5] πετροσ τησ περι τομησ.
[6] κα μοι. [7] εθνη. [8] στυλοι. [9] μνημονευμίωμεν.

CAP. II.	restiti · quia reprachensi bi	ανθεστην · οτι · κατε_γνωσ_με_
v. 12	lis erat · Prius enim quam venirent	νοσ · ην · Προτου · γαρ · ελθειν ·
	quidam ab iacobo cum	τινασ · αποϊακωβου · μετα · των ·
	gentibus edebat · Cum autem	εθνων · συνησθειεν · Οτε · δε ·
	venissent subtrahebat et segre	ηλθεν · ὑπεστελλεν · και · αφω
	gabat se timens eos	ριζεν · εαυτον · φοβουμενοσ ·
13	qui ex circumcisione erant et simula	τουσ · εκ περιτομη_σοντασ · και
	tioni ejus consenserunt cæ	συνυνεκριθησαν[1] · αυτω · και · οι
	teri Iudaei · Ita ut et bar	λοιποι · ϊουδαιοι · ωστε · και · βαρ
	nabas duceretur ab eis in illam simula	ναβασ · συναπηχθη · τη · υπο
14	tionem · Sed cum vidissem	κρισι · αυτων · αλλοτε · ιδον ·
	quod non recte ambularet ad ve	οτι · ουκ · ορθοποδουσιν · προσ ·
	ritatem evangelii ·	την · αληθιαν · του · ευαγγελου[2] ·
	dixi petro coram	ειπον · τω · πετρω · εν · προσθεν ·
	omnibus · Si tu judæus cum	παντων · Ει · συ · ϊουδεοσ[3] · υπαρ_
	sis gentiliter · et non judaice	χων · εθνικωσ · και · ουκ ϊουδαϊ_
	vivis · quomodo gentes co	κωσ · ζησ · πωσ · τα εθνη · αναγκα
15	gis judaizare · Nos natura ju	ζεισ · ϊουδαιζιν · Ημεισ · φυσι · ϊου
	dæi et non ex gentibus peccato	δαιοι · και · ουκ · εξεθνων · αμαρ
16	res · Scientes autem q'a non justifica	τωλοι · Ειδοτεσ · δε · οτι · ου · δικαιω
	tur homo ex operibus legis nisi	ται[4] · α̅ν̅ο̅σ̅ · εξεργων · νομου · εανμη ·
	per fidem i̅h̅u̅ x̅p̅i̅ · et nos	δια · πιστεωσ · ι̅υ̅ χ̅υ̅ · και ημσισ[5] ·
	In x̅p̅o̅ i̅h̅u̅ credimus · ut	εισ · χ̅ρ̅ν̅ · ι̅ν̅ · επιστευσαμεν · Ι̅να ·
	justificemur ex fide x̅p̅i̅ et	δικαιωθωμεν · εκπιστεωσ · και
	non ex operibus legis · propter q̅d̅ ex	ουκ · εξεργων · νομου οτι · εξερ
	operibus legis non justificabitur	γων · νομου · ου · δικαιωθησεται ·
17	omnis caro · Quod si quærentes	πασα · σαρξ · Ειδε · ζητουντεσ ·
	justificari in x̅p̅o̅ Inventi su	δικαιωθηναι · εν · χ̅ρ̅ω̅ · ευρεθη_

[1] συνυπεκριθησαν. [2] ευαγγελιου. [3] ϊουδαιοσ. [4] διάκαιουται. [5] ημεισ.

17	μεν·και·αυτοι·τοι·αμαρτωλοι·	mus et ipsi peccatores
	αρα·χρσ·αμαρτιασ·διακονοσ·	nunquid xps peccati minister
18	μη γενοιτο·Ει·γαρ·ακατελυσα·	absit · Si enim quæ distruxi
	ταυτα παλιν·οικοδομω·παρα	haec iterum aedifico·prevari
	βατην·εμαυτον·συνιστα͜νω·	catorem me constituo
19	εγω·γαρ·δια·νομου νομω·απε	ego enim perlegem legi mortuus
20	θανον·ινα·θω ζησω·χρω·συν	sum·ut do vivam·Xpo confixus
	εσταυρωμαι·ζω·δε·ουκ·ετι·	sum cruci · Vivo autem jam non
	εγω·ζη·δε·εν·εμοι·ο·χρσ Ο·δε·	ego vivit vero in me xpo · Qd autem
	νυν·ζω·εν·σαρκι·εν·πιστι·ζω	nunc vivo In carne · In fide vivo
	τη·του·θυ·και·χρυ·του·αγαπη‿	filii di qui dilexit
	σαντοσ[1]·μαι·και·παραδοντοσ·εαυ	me·et tradidit semet ip
21	τον·υπερ·εμου · Ου·καθετω·	sum pro me · Non abicio
	την·χαριν·του·θυ·Ει·γαρ·δια·	gratiam di·Si enim per
	νομον·δικαιοσυνη·αρα·χρσ·	legem justitia·ergo xps
III. 1	δωρεαν·απεθανεν·ω·ανο	gratis mortuus est · O insen
	ητοι·γαλαται·τησ[2]·υμασ·εβασ	sati galatae·quis vos fascina
	καν·εν·οισ·κατοφθαλμουσ·	vit·ante quorum occulos
	ιησ·χρσ·προεγραφη·εν·υμιν·	ihs xps p scriptus est et
2	εσταυρωμενοσ · Τουτο·μονον·	crucifixus · Hoc solum
	μαθειν·θελω·αφυμων·εξερ	volo a vobis discere·ex operi
	γων·νομου·(·το·) πνα[3]·ελαβεται·	bus legis spm accepistis
3	η·εξακοησ·πιστεωσ · Ουτωσ·	an ex auditu fidei · Sic
	ανοητοι·εσται·εν·αρξαμενοι·	stulti estis ut cum spu coepe
	πνι·νυν·σαρκι·επιτελισθαι·τοσ·	ritis·nunc carnem c summamini
	αυτα·επαθεται·εικη·ει·γαικαι·	tanti passi estis sine causa · sitam
	εικη · Ο·ουν·επιχορηγων·υμιν·	sine causa · Qui ergo vobis tribuit
	το·πνα·και·εν·εργων·δυναμισ·	spm·et operatur virtutes

[1] + εαυτον (ante μαι). [2] τισ. [3] το πνα.

CAP. III. in vobis · exoperibus legis · An
v. 6 exauditu fidei · Sicut scrip
tum est · Credidit abraham
d̅o̅ et reputatum est illi ad
7 justitiam · Cognoscitis
ergo quia qui ex fide sunt hi
8 sunt filii abraham · Providens
autem scriptura · quia ex fide
justificat gentes d̅s̅ prænunti
avit Abrahæ quia
benedicentur In te omnes
9 gentes · Igitur qui ex fide
sunt · benedicentur cum fideli
10 abraham · Quicumque enim ex operi
bus legis sunt · sub maledic
to sunt · Scriptum est enim quia
maledictus omnis q[i] non permanse
rit in omnibus quae scripta
sunt in libro legis
11 ut faciat ea · Quoniam
autem in lege nemo justifica
tur apud d̅m̅ · scriptum est enim
quia · Justus ex fide
12 vivit · Lex autem non
est ex fide sed qui fece
rit ea vivet in illis ·
13 X̅p̅c̅ nos redemit demale
dicto legis · factus

εν υμιν · εξεργων νομου · Η ·
εξακοησ · πιστεωσ · καθωσ · γε
γραπται · Επιστευσεν · αβρααμ ·
τω θ̅ω̅ · και ελογισθη · αυτω · εισ
δικαιοσυνην · Γινωσ‿κεται ·
αρα · οτι · οι · εκ · πιστεωσ · Ουτοι ·
εισιν · ὑιοι · αβρααμ · Προϊδουσα ·
δε · η · γραφη · Οτι · εκπιστεωσ ·
δικαιοι · τα · εθνη[1] · οθ̅σ̅ · προευ
ηγγελισατο · τω · αβρααμ · οτι ·
ευλογηθησονται · εν · σοι παντα ·
τα · εθνη · Ωστε · οι · ἐκ πιστε
ωσ · ευλογουνται · συν · τω · πιστω -
αβρααμ · Οσ · οι · γαρ · εξερ
γων · νομου · εισιν · υποκαταρ
αν · εισιν · Γεγραπται · γαρ · οτι ·
επικαταρτοσ · πασ · οσ · ουκ · εμ
μενει · εν · πασιν · τοισ · γεγραμ
μενοισ · εν · τω · βιβλιω · του · νο
μου · του · ποιησαι · αυτα · οτι ·
δε · εν · νομω · ουδεισ · δικαιου
ται · παρα · θ̅ω̅ γεγραπται · γαρ[2] ·
οτι · ο δικαιοσ · εκ πιστεωσ ·
ζησεται · Ο · δε · νομοσ · ουκ ·
εστιν · εκπιστεωσ · αλλο · ποι
ησασ · αυτα · ζησεται · εν · αυτω ·
Χ̅ρ̅σ̅ ημασ · εξηγορασεν · εκ τησ‿
καταρασ · του[3] · νομου · γενο

---

[1] Θθνη. [2] *In marg.* in σαλομονε. [3] : του τ̣̇.

P. III. μενοσ·υπερ·υμων[1]·καταρα·	pro nobis maledictum
οτι·γεγραπται·επικαταρατοσ·	quia scriptum est maledictus
πασ·ο·κρεμαμενοσ·επι·ξυλον[2]·	omnis qui pendet in ligno·
v. 14 ινα·εισ·τα·εθνι·ευλογια·του·	ut in gentibus benedictio
αβρααμ·γενηται·εν·χρω·ιηυ·	Abrahæ fieret · In XPO IHU·
ινα·την·ευλογογιαν[3]·του·πνσ·	ut pollicitationem sps
λαβωμεν·δια·τησ·πιστεωσ·	accipiamus per fidem·
15 Αδελφοι·κατα·ανδρωπον[4]·λεγω·	FRS secundum hominem dico
ομωσ·ανου·κεκυρωμενην·	tamen hominis confirmatum
δια·θηκην·ουδεισ·αθετει·Η·	testamentum nemo spernit aut
16 επι·διατεσσεται[5]·Τω·αβρααμ·	super ordinat · Abrahae
εππεθησαν[6]αι·επαγγελεισσαι·και	dicte sunt promissiones et
τω·σπερματι·αυτου · Ου·λεγει[7]·	semini ejus · Non di cit
και·τοισ·σπερμασιν·ωσ·επιπολλων·	et seminibus·quasi in multis
αλλωσ·επι·ενοσ·και·τω	sed quasi in uno et
17 σπερματι·σου·ουεστιν·χρσ·του	semini tuo qui est xps·hoc
το·δε·λεγω·διαθηκην·κεκυρω	autem dico testamentum confir
μενην·υπο του θυ εισ χρν·	matum a de o·
Ο·μετα·υ·και·λ[8]·αιτη·γεγω	Quæ post cccc et xxx annos facta
νοσ[9]·νομοσ·ουκ·ακυροι·εισ·	est lex·non irritum facit ad
το·καταργησαι·την·επαγγελιαν·	evacuandam promissionem·
18 Ει γαρ εκ νομου·η·κληρονομια·	Nam si ex lege hereditas·
ουκ·ετει·εξεπαγγελιασ·Τω·	jam non ex promissione·
δε·αβρααμ·διεπαγγελιασ·κε	Abrahæ autem per promissionem do
19 χαρισται·θσ[10]·τι·ουν·ο·νομοσ·	navit ds · Quid igitur? Lex
των·πραξαιων·ετεθη·αχρι	propter transgressionem posita est
σου·ελθη·το·σπερμα·ω·επιγγελ	donec veniret semen cui promise
ται[11]·δια·ταγισ·διαγγελων[12]·	rat·ordinata per angelos

[1] ημων. [2] ξυλου. [3] ευλογιαν. [4] ανθρωπον. [5] επι διατασσεται. [6] ερρεθησαν. [7] λεγι. [8] a (*pro* λ) *at* xxx *Latinè*. [9] γενομωσ. [10] ο θσ. [11] επηγγελται. [12] *In marg.* ευαγ.

CAP. III. v. 20 in manu mediatoris · Mediator	εν · χιρει · μεσειτου · Ο · δε · μεσει
autem unius non est · ds autem	τησ · ενοσ · ουκ · εστιν · ο · δε · θσ · εισ ·
21 unus est · Lex ergo adversus	εετιν · ο · ουν · [ν.]ομοσ[1] · κατα ·
promissa di absit ·	των · επαγγελιων · θυ · μηγενοιτο ·
Si enim data esset lex quae pos	Ει γαρ · εδοθη · νομοσ · ο · δυ
set vivificare · Vere	ναμενοσ · ζωοποιησαι · αληθια ·
22 ex lege esset justitia · Sed	εκ νομου · δικαιοσυνη[2] · αλλα ·
conclusit scriptura omnia sub	συνεκλῖσεν · η · γραφη · παντα · υφ
peccato · ut promissio ex	αμαρτῖαν · ινα · η · επαγγελῖα · εκ
fide ihu xpi daretur creden	πιστεωσ · ιυ · χυ · δοθη · τοισ · πισ
23 tibus Prius autem quam veniret	τευ_υυσιν · Προτου · δε · ελθειν ·
fides · sub lege custodie	την · πιστιν · υπομονον[3] · εφρου
bamur conclusi in	ρου · με[θ]τα[4] · συνκλιομενοι · εστιν[5] ·
eam fidem · quae reve	μελλουσαν · πιστιν · αποκαλυφ
landa erat	θηναι ·
24 Itaque lex pedagogus noster	Ωστε · ο · νομοσ · πεδαγωγοσ[6] · ημωι
fuit in xpo ihu · ut ex	γεγονεν · εισ · χρν · ιην · ῑνα · εκ
25 fide justificemur · at ubi	πιστεωσ · δικαιωθωμεν · ελθυ
venit fides · jam non	σησ · δε · τησ · πιστ[αι]εωσ[7] · ουκ · ετει ·
26 suppedagogo sumus · Om	Ὑπο · παιδαγωγον · εσμεν · παν
nes enim filii di estis · perfi	τεσ · γαρ · υιοι · θυ · εσται · δια · τησ ·
27 dem quae est in xpo ihu · Quicumque	πιστ[αι]εωσ[8] · εν · χρω · ιυ · Οσοι · γαρ ·
enim in xpo baptizati estis xpm	εισ · χρν εβαπτισθηται · χρν · ενε
28 induistis · Non est judaeus	δυσασθαι · Ουκ · ενει · ῑουδαιοσ ·
neque grecus · Non est servus	ουδε · ελλην · ουκ · ενει · δουλοσ ·
neque liber · Non est masculus ·	ουδε · ελευτεροσ · ουκ · [·ενει·] αρσησ[9] ·
neque femina · Omnes enim vos	και · θηλυ · παντεσ · γαρ · υμεισ ·
29 unum estis in xpo ihu · Si autem	εν · εσται · εν · χρω · ιηυ ειδε ·

[1] εστιν. Ο ουν νομοσ. [2] + η (*ante* δικαιοσυνη). [3] υπο νομον. [4] εφρουρουμεθα. [5] εισ την. [6] παιδαγωγοσ. [7] πισταιωσ. [8] πισταιωσ. [9] ελευθεροσ ουκ ενει αρσησ.

II. υμεισ·παντεσ·εν εσται·ενχω·	vos xpi·ergo abrahae se
ιυ·αραουν·του·αβρααμ·σπερ	men estis·secundum promissio
μα·εσται·και·κατεπαγγελει_	nem heredes·
IV. v. 1 αν·κληρονομαι[1]·Λεγω·δε·	dico autem
αδελφοι·εφωσον[2]·χρονον·ο·κλη	frs quanto tempore he
ρονομοσ·νη·πειοσ·εστιν·ουδεν·	res parvulus est·nihil
διαφερει·δουλου·κυριοσ·παν	differt a servo·cum sit dns om
2 των ων · Αλλυπο επιτροπουσ[3]·	nium · Sed sub tutoribus
εστιν·και·οικονομουσ·αχρι	est et actoribus usque
τησ·προθέσμιασ·του·πατροσ·	ad prefinitum tempus apatre
3 Ουτοσ[4]·και·ημεισ·οτε·ημεν·νη	Ita et nos cum essemus parvu
πιοι·υποτα_στοιχεία·του·κοσ	li subelementis mundi
μου·ημεθα·δε·δουλωμενοι·	eramus servientes
4 Οτε·δε·ηλθην[5]·το·πλη_ρωμα·	A tubi venit plenitudo
του·χρονου·εξαπεστειλεν·ο·	temporis·misit
θσ·τον·υιον·αυτου·γενομενον·	ds filium suum factum
εκ·γυναικοσ·γενομενον·υπο·νο	ex muliere·factum sub le
5 μον·ινα·τουσ·υπόμονον[6]·εξα	ge uteos qui sub lege erant re
γορασηται·ινα·την·υιοθεσίαν·	dimeret·utadoptionem filiorum
6 απυλαβωμεν · Οτι·δε·εσται·υιοι	reciperemus · Quo autem estis filii
θυ[7]·εξαπεστîλεν·οθσ·το·πνα·του·	di misit ds spm
υιοι·αυτου·εισ·τασ·καρδιασ·ημων·	filii sui·in corda nra
εν·υ·κραξομεν[8]·αββα·ο·πατηρ[9]·	clamantem abba pater·
7 ωστε·ουκ·ετει·δουλοσ·αλλα·υιοισ[10]·	Itaque jam non est servus sed filius·
Ειδε·υιοισ[11]·και·κληρονομοσ·δια	Quod si filius et heres per
8 θν·αλλα·τοτε·μεν·ουκ ει_δο_	dm · Sed tunc quidem ignoran
τεσ·θν·τοισ·μη·φυσειν·ουσειν·	tes dm·his qui natura non sunt
9 θεοισ·εδουλευσαται · Νυν·ειδε·	dii serviebatis · Nunc autem

[1] κατὰ επαγγελειαν κληρονομοι. [2] εφοσον. ζ [3] επι τ τροπουσ. [4] Ουτωσ. [5] ηλθεν. [6] υπο νομον. [7] *In marg.* contra graecos. [8] κραξομεν. [9] *In marg.* Γρ eb. [10] ϋιοσ. [11] υἱοσ.

CAP. IV.	cum cognoveritis dm immo	γνοντεσ · τον · θν · μαλλον · δε ·
	cogniti estis ado · quomodo	γνωσ_θεντεσ · απο[1] θυ · Πωσ ·
	convertimini iterum · ad in	επεστρεφεται · παλιν · επι · τα ·
	firma · etegena elementa	ασθενη · και · πτωχα · στοιχια ·
	quibus denuo servire	οισ · παλιν · ανωθεν · δουλευειν ·
v. 10	vultis · Dies observatis	θελεται · Ημερασ · παρατηρισθαι ·
	etmenses · etannos · et	και · μηνασ · και · ενει · αυτουσ · ϗ
11	tempora · Timeo vos ne	καιρουσ · Φοβουμαι · υμασ · μη
	forte sine causa laboraverim in vobis ·	πωσ · εικη · εκοπειακα · εισ · υμασ ·
12	estote sicut ego · quia et ego sicut	γινεσθαι · ωσ · εγω · οτι · καγω · ωσ ·
	vos · Frs obsecro vos	υμισ · αδελφοι · δθ · ομαι[2] · υμων ·
13	nihil me lesistis · Scitis autem	ουδεν · μαι · ηδικησαται · οιδατε ·
	quia per infirmitatem carnis evan	οτι · δια · ασθενίαν · σαρκοσ · ευηγ
	gelizavi vobis jam pridem	γελεισαμην · υμιν · το · προτερον ·
14	ettemptationem vestram in	και · τον · πιρασμον · υμων · εν · τη ·
	carne mea non sprevistis ne	σαρκι · μου · ου · εξουθενησαται · ȣ
	que respuistis · sed sicut ange	δε · εξεπτυσαται · αλλα · ωσ · αγγε
	lum di excepistis me sicut xpm	λον · θυ · εδεξασθαι · μαι · ωσ · χρν ·
15	ihm · Ubi est ergo beatitudo	ιν · Που · ουν · η · ο · μακαρισ_μοσ ·
	vestra · Testimonium enim perhibeo vobis quia	υμων · μαρτυρω · γαρ · οτι · ει · δυ
	si fieri posset · oculos vestros	νατον[3] · τουσ · οφθαλμȣσ · υμων ·
	eruissetis · et dedissetis	εξορυξαντεσ · και · εδωκαται ·
16	mihi · Ergo inimicus vobis	μοι · ωστε · εγω · εκτροσ[4] · υμων ·
17	factus sum · verum dicens vobis · aemu	γεγονα · αληθευων · υμιν · ζη
	lantur vos nonbene · sed	λουσιν · υμασ · ουκαλωσ · αλλα ·
	excludere vos volunt ut	εκκλεισαι · υμασ · θελουσειν · ινα ·
	illos emulemini · aemulamini	αυτουσ · ζηλουται · ζηλουται ·
18	autem dona meliora · Bonum quoque	δε · τα · κριτω · χαρισματα · καλον ·

[1] υπο (*pro* απο). [2] δε ομαι. [3] δ δυνατον. [4] εκθροσ.

IV. το · ζηλουσθαι · παντοτε · εν · τω ·	emulamini in bono semper ·
αγαθω · και · ου · μονον · εν · τω · πα	et nontantum cum presens
v. 19 ρειν · αι μαι · προσ · υμασ · Τεκνα ·	sum apud vos · Filioli mei
μου · ουσ · παλιν · ωιδνω[1] · αχρισου ·	quos iterum parturio donec
20 μορφωθη · χρσ · εν · υμιν · Η_θε_	formetur xpc in vobis · Vellem
λον[2] · δε · παρειναι · προσ · υμασ · αρτει ·	autem apud vos esse modo
και · αλλαξαι · την · φωνην · μου ·	etmutare vocem meam
21 οτι · απορουμαι · εν · υμιν · Λεγε	quo confundor in vobis · Dici
ται · μοι · οι · υπο · νομον · θελοντε–	te mihi qui sub lege vultis
ειναι · τον · νομον · ουκ · αναγει	esse · legem non le
22 νωσκεται · γεγραπται · γαρ · οτι ·	gistis? scriptum est enim · quo
αβρααμ · δυο · ὑιουσ · εεχεν[3] · ενα ·	abraham duos filios habuit · unum
εκ · τησ · παιδισκησ · και · ενα · εκτησ ·	deancilla etunum de
23 ελευθερασ · αλλο · μεν · εκ · τησ · παι	libera · Sed qui de ancil
δισκησ · κατα · σαρκα · γεγεννηται ·	la secundum carnem natus est ·
Ο · δε · εκ · τησ · ελευθερασ · δια · τησ ·	Qui autem de libera per repro
24 επαγγελιασ · ατινα · εστιν · αλλη_	missionem · quae sunt per allegori
γορουμενα · αυτα · γαρ · εισιν · δυο ·	am dicta · Haec enim sunt duo
διαθηκη · Μια · μεν · απο · ορουσι	testamenta · Unum quidem a monte
να · εισ · δουλιαν · γενοσα[4] · ητεισ ·	syna · in servitutem generans · quae
25 εστιν · αγαρ · Το · γαρ · σινα · οροσ · εστιν ·	est agar · Syna enim mons est
εν · τη · αραβια · η · συν_στοι_	inarabia quiconjunctus est
χουσα · τη · νυν · ἱερουσαλημ · δου	ei · quae nunc est hierusalem · et
λευ_ει · γαρ · μετα · των · τεκνων · αυ_	servit cum filiis suis ·
26 τησ · η · δε · ανω · ιερουσαλημ · ε	illa autem quae sursum est hierusalem li
λευθερα · εστιν · η · τισ · εστιν · μητηρ ·	bera est · quae est mater
27 ημων · γεγραπται · γαρ · ευφραν	nostra · Scriptum est enim · Laeta
θητει · στειρα · η · μη · τικ του σα ·	re sterilis quæ non paris ·

[1] ωδινω. [2] *In marg.* αγ ε. [3] εσχεν. [4] γενωσα.

	Latin	Greek
CAP. IV.	Erumpe et clama quae non parturis	Ρηζον · και · βοησον · η · ουκ · ωδινουσα
	quia multi filii deserte	οτι · πολλα · τα · τεκνα · της · ερημου
	magis quam ejus quae habet vi	μαλλον · η · της · εχουσης[1] · τον · αν
v. 28	rum · Nos autem frs secundum isa	δρα · υμεις · δε · αδελφοι · κατα · ϊσα
29	ac promissionis filii sumus · Sed quo	ακ · επαγγελιας · τεκνα · εσται · αλ
	modo tunc qui secundum carnem na	λως · περ · τοτε · ο · κατα · σαρκα · γε
	tus est persequebatur eum qui secundum spm	νηθις · εδιωκεν · τον · κατα · πνα ·
30	ita et nunc · Sed quid dicit scrip	ουτως · και · νυν · αλλα · τι · λεγι · η ·
	tura · Eice ancillam	γραφη · εκβαλε · την · παι δισκην ·
	et filium ejus · Non enim heres	και · τον υιον · αυτης · ου · γαρ · κλη
	erit filius ancillae	ρονομηση · ο · υιος · της · παιδισκης ·
31	cum filio liberae · Itaque frs	μετα · του · υιου · μου · ϊσαακ · αρα ·
	non sumus ancille	ουν · αδελφοι · ουκ · εσμεν · παι
	filii · sed liberae ·	δισκης · τηκνα[2] · αλλα · ελευθερας ·
CAP. V. 1	qua libertate xpc nos libe	η · ελευθερια · ημας · χρς · ηλευθε
	ravit · State ergo et nolite	ρωσεν · Στηκεται · ουν · και · μη
	iterum jugo servitutis contineri ·	παλιν · δουλιας · ζυγω · ενεχεσθαι ·
2	Ecce ego paulus dico vobis · quia	Ει δε · εγω · παυλος · λεγω · υμιν · οτι ·
	sicircumcidamini · xpc vobis	εαν · περιτεμνησθαι · χρς · υμας ·
3	nihil proderit · Testificor autem rur	ουδεν · ωφελησει · Μαρτυρωμαι[3] ·
	sum omni homini circumciden	δε · παντι · ανδρωπω[4] · περιτεμνο
	ti se · quō debitor est	μενω · οτι · οφιλε της · εστιν ·
4	universae legis faciendae · eva	ολον · τον · νομον · ποι ησαι · κατηρ
	cuati estis a xpo · qui in le	γηθηται · απο · χρυ · οι · τινες · εν
	ge justificamini · a gratia	νομω · δικιουσθαι[5] · της · χαριτος ·
5	excidistis · Nos enim spu ex	εξεπεσαται · ημεις · γαρ · πνι · εκ
	fide · spem justitiae	πιστεως · ελπιδα · δικαιοσυνης ·
6	expectamus · Nam in xpo ihu	απεκδε · (χο) μεθα[6] · Εν · γαρ · χρω[7] · ιυ ·

[1] ης της ερημου εχουσης. [2] τεκνα. [3] Μαρτυρομαι. [4] ανθρωπω. [5] δικαιουσθαι. [6] απεκδεχομεθα. [7] εν : (γαρ) χρω.

V. ουτε ακροβυστία·	neque circumcisio aliquid va
[1]	let · Neque prepucium·
αλλα·πιστισ·δια·αγαπησ·ενερ	sed fides quae per caritatem ope
v. 7 γουμενη · Ετρεχεται·καλοσ[2]·	ratur · Currebatis bene·
τισ·υμασ·ενεκοψεν·τη·αλη	quis vos inpedivit? Veritati
θηα · Μη·πιθεσθαι·μηδενι·πει	non oboedire nemini consense
8 θεσθαι · Η·πισμονη·ουκ·εκτοΥ	ritis · Persuasio non est ex eo qui vo
9 καλουντοσ·ὑμασ · Μικρα·ζυ	cat vos · Modicum fermen
μη·ολον·το·φυραμα·ζυμοι·	tum totam massam corrumpit·
10 Εγω·δε·πεποιθα·εισ·υμασ·ενκω·	Ego autem confido invobis in dno·
οτι·ουδεν·αλλο·φρονησεται·ην·	quod nihil aliud sapietis·÷quam
εχι·η·αληθια·του·χρυ[3] · Ο·δε·	habet veritas xpi · Qui autem
ταρασσων·υμασ·Βασταςῖ·το·	conturbat vos portabit
11 κριμα·οστισ·αvη·Εγω·δε·	judicium quicumque est ille·ego autem
αδελφοι·ει·περιτομην·κηρυσ	frs·sicircumcisionem adhuc prædi
σω·τι·ετει·διωκομαι·αρα·κα	co·quid adhuc persecutionem patior?
τηργηται·το·σκανδαλον·του	ergo evacuatum est scandalum
12 σταυρου · Οφελον·και·αποκο	crucis · Utinam et abscidan
ψωνται·οι[4]·αναστα[1]·τουντεσ·	tur qui vos conturbant·
13 υμασ·υμεισ·δε·επελευ θερῖα·	Vos enim in libertatem
εκκληθηται·αδελφοι·μονον·	vocati estis frs·tantum
μη·την·ελευθερῖαν·εισ·αφορ	ne libertatem in occasio
μην·τη·σαρκι·δωτε·αλλα·τη·	nem carnis detis·sed per
αγαπη·του·πνσ·δουλευεται·	caritatem servite
14 αλληλοισ · Ο·γαρ·πασ·νομος·	invicem · Omnis enim lex·
εν·υμιν·εν·ενῖ λογω·πληρυυ	in uno sermone impletur
ται·αγαπησεισ·τον·πλησι ον·	diliges proximum
5 σου·ωσ·εαυτον · Ειδε·δυκνεται·	tuum·sicut te ipsum · Quod si morde

[1] *Nullum spatium vacuum.* [2] *καλωσ.* [3] *— ην usque ad χρυ. Habet margo.* [4] *ου p.m.*

CAP. V.	tis et devoratis invicem·	και καταισθιεται·αλληλουσ·
	videte neabinvicem consumma	βλεπεται·μη·αναλωθηται·υπαλ
v. 16	mini · Dico autem · Spu ambulate·	ληλων·λεγω·δε·Πνι·περιπατι
	et desideria carnis non	ται·και·επιθυμιαν·σαρκοσ·ου
17	perficietis·caro enim concupiscit	μη·γελεσηται[1]·η·γαρ·σαρξ·επι
	adversus spm·sps autem	θυμει·κατα·του·πνσ·το·δε·πνα·
	adversus carnem · Haec enim in	κατα·τησ·σαρκοσ · Ταυτα·γαρ·αλ
	vicem adversantur·ut non quae	ληλοισ·αντικειται·ινα·μη·ο
18	cumque vultis illa faciatis · Quod si	αν·θεληται·Ταυτα·ποιηται · Ει
	spu ducimini·non estis sub	δε·πνι·αγεσθαι·ουκ·εσται·υπο·
19	lege·Manifesta autem sunt ope	νομον · Φανερα·δε·εστιν τα·ερ
	ra carnis·quae sunt·adulte	γα·τησ·σαρκοσ·ατινα·εστιν·μοι
	ria·fornicatio·immunditia·	χειαι·πορνειαι·ακαθαρσει αι·
20	luxuria·idolorum servitus · Vene	ασελγειαι·ιδωλολατριαι·φαρ
	ficia·inimicitiae·contentiones·emula	μακειαι·εκθραι·ερεισ·ζηλουσ·
	tiones · Irae·rixae·dissensiones·	θυμοι·ερειθειαι·διχοστασειαι·
21	sectae·invidiae·hereses ÷ homicidia	αιρεσεισ·φθονοι·φονοι·μεθαι·
	ebrietates·commessationes·et his si	κωμοι·και·τα·ομοια·τουτοισ·
	milia·quae pdico vobis sicut pdi	απρο·λεγω·υμιν·καθωσ·προι
	xi·quō quitalia agunt	ρηκα·οτι·οι·τα·τοι·αυτα·πρασ
	regnum di non conse	σοντεσ·Βασευλιαν[2]·θυ·ου·κλη
22	quentur · Fructus autem	ρονομη σουσιν·Ο·δε·καρποσ·
	sps est·caritas·gaudium	του·πνσ·εστιν·αγαπη·χα ρα·
	pax·longanimitas·boni	ϊρηνη·μακροθυμια·χρηστο
	tas·benignitas·fides patientia	τησ·αγαθοσυνη·πιστεισ·πρα
	mansuetudo·modestia·ctinentia castitas·	οτησ·ενκρατεια · αγνεια·
23	adversus hujus modi non est	κατα·των·τοι ουτων·ουκ·εστιν·
24	lex·qui autem sunt XPI	νομοσ·Οι·δε·του·χρυ·εν·τεσ·την·

[1] τελεσηται. [2] Βασιλιαν.

AP. V.	σαρκα · αυτων · εσταυρωσαν ; συν · τοισ ·	carnem suam crucifixerunt cum
	παθημασιν · και · ταισ · επιθυμιαισ ·	vitiis etconcupiscentiis ·
v. 25	[1]πνι · ζωμεν · πνι στοιχωμεν ·	Sivivimus spu · spu et ambalemus ·
26	Μη · γεινωμεθα[2] καινοδοξοι ·	Non efficiamur inanis gloriae cupidi ·
	αλληλον[3] · προκαλουμενοι · αλλη	invicem provocantes · invi
P. VI. 1	λοισ[4] · φθονουντεσ · αδελφοι · εαν ·	cem invidentes · Frs · et si
	και · προλημφθη · ανοσ · εν · τινι · πα	preoccupatus fuerit homo in aliquo
	ραπτωματι · υμεισ · οι · πνευματι	delicto · vos qui spiritales estis
	κοι · καταρτιζεται · τον · τοιουτον ·	hujus modi instruite
	εν · πνι · πραοτητοσ · Cκοπων ; εκασ	in spu lenitatis · considerans te
	τόσ · σε · αυτον · μη · και · αυτοσ · πιραθη[5] ·	ipsum neettu tempteris ·
2	Αλληλων · τα · βαρη · βαστα	Alter alterius onera porta
	ζεται · ϗ ουτωσ · αναπληρωσε	te · et sic adimplebitis
3	ται · νομον · του χρυ · Eι · γαρ · δο	legem xpi · Nam siquis existi
	κει · τεισ · ειναι · τι · μηδεν · ων	mat se aliquid esse cum nihil sit ·
4	εαυτον · φραιναπατα · το · δε · ερ	ipse se seducit · Opus autem
	γον ; εαυτον · δοκειμαζητω[6] · ε	suum probet unus quis
	καστοσ · ϗ τοτε · εισ · εαυτον ·	que et sic in semet ipso
	μονον · το · καυχημα · εζει[7] · και	tantum gloriam habebit · et
5	ουκ · εισ τον · ετερον · εκασ_τοσ ·	non in altero · Unus quisque
	γαρ · τοιδιον · φορτιον · βασταστι ·	enim onus suum portabit
6	κοινωνιτω · δε · ο · κατεχουμε	communicet autem is qui catezizatur
	νοσ[8] · τον · λογων[9] · τω · κατηχουν	verbum · ei qui se catezizat
7	τι · εν · πασιν · αγαθοισ · μη · πλαν_	in omnibus Nolite errare
	ασθαι · θσ · ου μυκτηρει_ζε_ται ·	ds non irridetur ·
	ο · γαρ · ανσπειρη · ανοσ · ταυτα · και	quae enim seminaverit homo · haec et
8	θερισει · Οτι · ο · σπειρων · τη · σαρκι ·	metet · Quo qui seminat in carne
	αυτου · εκ · τησ · σαρκοσ · αυτου · θε_	sua · decarne et me

[1] *Initio lineæ* + ει. [2] γε,νωμεθα. [3] αλληλουσ. [4] αλληλουσ. [5] πιρασθη. [6] δοκειμαζετω. [7] εξει. [8] κατηχουμενοσ. [9] λογον.

CAP. VI.	tet corruptionem · Qui autem seminat	ρισει · φθοραν · ο · δε · σπειρω[1] · εισ · το
	in spu · de spu et metet vitam	πνατι · εκ · του · πνσ · θερισει · ζωην ·
v. 9	aeternam · Bonum autem facientes	αιωνιον · Το · δε · καλο[2] · ποιουντεσ ·
	non deficiamus; Tempore enim suo	μη · εκκακησωμεν · καιρω · γαρ · ῑδιω
10	metemus non deficientes · Ergo ·	θερισωμεν · μη · εκλυομενοι · αρα ·
	dum tempus habemus opere	ουν · ωσ · καιρον · εχομεν · εργαζω
	mur bonum ad omnes	μεθα · το · αγαθον · προσ · παντασ ·
	Maxime autem addomesticos	Μαχλιστα · δε · προσ · τουσ · οικιουσ
11	fidei · Videte qualibus	τησ · πιστεωσ · Ιδετε · πιλει‿κοισ[3] ·
	literis scripsi vobis	γραμμασιν · υμιν · εργαψα[4] · τη ·
12	mea manu · quicumque volunt	εμη · χειρει · Οσοι · θελουσιν ·
	placere in carne hi	ευπροσωπησαι · εν · σαρκι · ουτοι ·
	cogunt vos circum ci	αναγκαζουσῖν · ὑμασ · περιτεμ
	di tantum ut crucis	νεσθαι · μονον · Ινα · μη · τω · σταυρω ·
13	xpi persecutionem patiantur · Neque enim	του · χυ · διωκονται · Ου · δε · γαρ ·
	qui circum ciduntur le	οι · περιτεμνημοι[5] · αυτοι · νο
	gem custodiunt · Sed volunt	μον · φυλασσουσιν · αλλαθελου
	vos circum cidi · Ut	σιν · υμασ · περιτεμνεσθαι · ῑνα
	in carne vestra glorien	εν · τη · ὑμετερα · σαρκι · καυχη
14	tur · Mihi autem absit	σωνται[6] · Εμοι · δε · μη γενοιτο ·
	gloriari · nisi in cruce	καυχασθαι · ειμη · εν · τω · σταυρω ·
	dni nri ihu xpi · perquem	του · χυ[7] · ημων · ιυ · χυ · Διου ·
	mihi mundus crucifixus est et e	εμοι · ο · κοσμοσ · εσταυροται[8] · κα
15	go mundo · In xpo enim ihu neque	γω · κοσμω · Εν · γαρ · χρω · ιυ · ουτε ·
	circumcisio aliquod valet · neque prepu	περιτομη · τη[9] · εστιν · ουτε · ακρο
	cium · sed nova creatura ·	βυστῖα · αλλα · καινη κτι‿σῖσ
16	et quicumque hanc regulam secuti	και · οσοι[10] · τω · κανονι · τουτω ; στοι
	fuerint pax super illos et	χουσιν · ϊρηνη · επαυτουσ · και

[1] σπειρων. [2] καλον. [3] πηλεικοισ. [4] εγραψα. [5] περιτεμνημενοι. [6] καυχησονται (ω above ο).
[7] κυ. [8] εσταυρωται. [9] Τι. [10] οσοι τουτω στοιχουσιν τω κ.

VI. ελαιοσ · και · επι · τον · ιηλ · του · κυ ·	misericordia · et super israhel di
laboris mihi nemo	
17 Του · λοιποι[1] κοπουσ · μοι · μηδεισ ·	De cetero nemo mihi mo
exhibeat	
παρεχετω · Εγω · γαρ · ταστιγμα	lestus sit · Ego enim stigmata
τα · του · κυ · ημων · ιυ χυ εν · τω ·	ihu · in
18 σωματι · μου · βασταζω · Η · χαρισ ·	corpore meo porto · Gratia
του χυ[2] ημων ιυ χυ μετα του	dni nri ihu xpi cum
πνσ υμων αδελφοι · αμην[3]	spiritu vro fratres · Amen ·
Ετελεσθη επιστολη	EXPLICIT EPISTOLA
προσ γαλατασ	AD GALATAS ·
Αρχεται προσ	Incipit ad
εφεσιουσ ·	efesios ·
CAP. I. 1 Παυλοσ αποστολοσ	Paulus apostls
ιηυ χρυ ·	ihu xpi
δια · θεληματοσ · θυ · τοισ · αγιοισ ·	pervoluntatem di scis
τοισ · ουσω[4] · εν · εφεσω[5] · και · πισ	omnibus qui sunt ephesi · et fideli
2 τοισ · εν χρω ιυ · χαρισ · υμιν ·	bus in xpo ihu · Gratia vobis
και ιρηνη · απο θυ · πατροσ · ημων	et pax a do patre nostro
3 και κυ ιυ χυ ευλογητοσ ·	et dno ihu xpo · Benedictus
ο θσ · και πατηρ · του κυ ημων	ds et pater dni nri
ιυ χρυ · Ο · ευλογησασ · ημασ	ihu xpi · Qui benedixit nos
εν πασι[6] ευλογια πνευματικη ·	in omni benedictione spitali
εν τοισ επουρανι‿οισ · εν	in caelestibus in
4 χω · καθωσ · εξελεξατο · ημασ ·	xpo · sicut elegit nos in
εαυτω προσ · κατα‿βολησ · κοσ	ipso ante mundi constitutio
μου · ειναι · ημασ · αγιουσ · και	nem · ut essemus sci et

[1] λα‿του. [2] Κυ (*pro* χυ) (cf. v. 14). [3] – αμην. [4] *In marg.* ουσια. [5] εφεσω. [6] παση.

CAP. I.	inmaculati·in conspectu ejus	αμωμουσ·κατενωπιον·αυτου·
v. 5	in caritate · Qui praedestinavit nos	εν·αγαπη·προ·ορεισασ[1] ημασ
	in ad optionem filiorum per ihum xpm	εισ υιοθεσιαν·δια·ιυ·χυ·εισ·
	in ipsum·secundum prepositum	αυτον·κατα·την·ευδοκιαν·
6	voluntatis ejus · In laudem	του·θελιματοσ[2]·αυτου·εισ·επαι
	gloriæ gratiæ suae	νον·δοξησ·τησ·χαριτοσ·αυτου
	In qua gratificavit nos in	εν εχαριτωσεν[3]·ημασ·εν·τω·
7	dilecto filio suo·in	ηγαπημενω·υιω·αυτου·εν
	quo habemus redemptionem	ω·εχομεν·την·απολυτροσιν[4]
	per sanguinem ejus	δια·του·αιματοσ·αυτου·την·
	remissionem peccatorum·	αφεσιν·των·παραπτωματων·
	Secundum divitias gloriae	Κατα·του·πλουτοσ·τησ·χαριτωσ[5]·
8	ejus·quae super habundavit in	αυτου·ησ·επερισσευσεν·εισ·
	nobis in omni sapientia et pruden	ημασ·εν·παση·σοφια·και·φρονη
9	tia·ut notum faceret nobis miste	σει·γνωρεισαι·ημιν·το·μυστη
	rium·voluntatis suae secundum	ριον·του·θελιματοσ[6]·αυτου·κατα
	bonum placitum ejus·quod proposuit	την·ευδοκιαν·ην προε θετο·
10	in eo·in dispensationem	εν·αυτου·ει[7]·οικονομιαν του
	plenitudinis temporum·instau	πληρωματοσ·των·καιρων·ανα
	rare omnia in	κεφελεωσασθαι[8]·τα·παντα·εντω
	xpo·quae in caelis et quae	χρω τα·εν·τοισ·ουρανοισ · και
11	in terra sunt in ipso·In quo etiam	τα επι·τησ·γησ·εν·αυτω·Εν·ω·κ
	sorte vocati sumus·praedistinati	εκληθησαμεν[9]·προορισθεντεσ·
	secundum propositum di qui	κατα·την·προθεσιν·του·θυ·τα
	omnia operatur secundum	παντα·ενεργουντεσ[10]·κατα·την·
	consilium voluntatis ejus·	βουλην·του·θεληματοσ·αυτου·
12	ut simus in laudem	εισ·τοειναι·ημασ·εισ·επαινον·
	gloriae ejus qui ante speravimus in	δοξησ·τουσ·προηλπικοτασ·εν

1 προορειάσας. 2 θεληματοσ. 3 εν η εχαριτωσεν. 4 τηνά απολυτρωσίν. 5 χαρίτοσ.
6 θεληματοσ. 7 αυτω εισ. 8 ανακεφαλεωσασθαι. 9 εκληθημεν. 10 ενεργουντοσ.

P. I 13	χρω · ενω · και · υμεισ · ακουσαν_	xpo · In quo etvos cum audisse
	τεσ · τον · λογον · τησ αληθιασ	tis · verbum veritatis
	το · ευαγγελιον · σωτηριασ · υμων	evangelium salutis vestrae
	εν · ω πιστευσαντεσ · εσ φραγισ	in quo etcredentes signati
	θιται[1] · τω · πνι · τησ επαγγελιασ ·	estis spu promissionis
14	τω αγιω · Ο · εστιν · αραβων · τησ ·	sco · qui est pignus
	κληρονομίασ · ημων · εισ · απο	hereditatis nostrae · inredem
	. λυτρωσιν · τησ · περιποιησεωσ ·	ptionem adquisitionis ·
	εισ · επαινον · τησ · δοξησ · αυτου ·	in laudem gloriae ipsius ·
15	Δια τουτο · καγω · ακουσασ · την	Propterea et ego audiens
	καθυμασ · πιστην[2] · εν · κω · ιυ · χρω	fidem vestram quae est in dno ihu
	ϗ την · αγαπην · εισ · παντασ · τουσ	et dilectionem in omnes
16	αγιουσ · Ου πανομαι · ευχαρισ ·	scos · Noncesso gratias agens
	των · υπερ · ϋμων · μιαν · ποιου	pro vobis · memoriam vestri faci
	μενοσ · υμων · επι · των · προσ · ευ_	ens in orationibus
17	χών · μου · Ινα · ο θσ · του · κυ · ημων ·	meis · ut ds dni nri
	ιυ χυ · Ο · πατηρ · τησ · δοξησ · Δων[3] ·	ihu xpi · pater gloriae det
	ὑ μιν · πνα · σοφίασ · ϗ αποκαλυ	vobis spm sapientiae · et revela
	ψαιωσ · εν · επι · γνωσι · αυτου ·	tionis in agnitione ejus
18	πεφωτεισ_μενουσ · τουσ · οφθαλ	illuminatos ocu
	μουσ · τησ · καρδιασ · υμων · Ινα ·	los cordis vri · ut
	οιδαται · τι · εστιν · η · ελπισ ·	sciatis quae sit spes
	τησ · κλησεωσ · αυτου · Τισ · ο πλου	vocationis ejus · quae diviti
	τοσ · τησ · δοξησ · τησ · κληρονομι	ae gloriae hereditatis
19	ασ · αυτου · εν · τοισ · αγιοισ · και ·	ejus in scis · et quae sit
	τιτο · μεγεθοσ · τησ · δυναμιωσ ·	super eminens magnitudo virtutis
	αυτου · Εισ · υμασ · τουσ · πιστευ	ejus · in nos qui credi
	οντασ · κατα · την · εν,εργιαν · του	mus · secundum operationem poten

[1] εσφραγισθηται. [2] πιστιν. [3] δωη.

CAP. I. v. 20	tiae virtutis ejus quam	κρατουσ·τησ·ῑσχυοσ·αυτου·ην
	operatus est in xpo suscitans eum	ενηργησ·εν·τω·χρω·εγῑρασ·αυτον·
	amortuis·etconstituens ad dex	εκ·νεκρων·και εκαθισεν·εν·δε
	teram suam in caelestibus	ξια·αυτου·εν·τοισ·επουρανι_οισ·
21	supra omnem principatum etpotes	ὑπερανω·πασησ·αρχησ·και·εξου
	tatem et virtutem et dominati	σιασ·και·δυναμα_ιωσ·κ·κυριο
	onem·et omne nomen quod	τητοσ[1]·και·παντυσ·ονομα·τοσ·
	nominatur·non solum in	ονομα_ζεμενου[2]·ου·μονον·εν·
	hoc saeculo sed et in	τω·αιωνι·τουτω·αλλα·και·εν
22	futuro·et omnia subje	τω·με ạλλοντι[3]·και παντα·υπε
	cit sub pedibus ejus·	ταξεν·υπο·τοισ[4]·ποδασ·αυτου·
	et ipsum dedit caput super	και·αυτον·δοκεν[5]·κεφαλην·
23	omnem eclesiam·quae	υπερ·παντα·τη·εκκλησῑα·η·τισ·
	est corpus ipsius·plenitu	εστιν·το·σωμα·αυτου·τοπλη
	do ejus qui in omnia in omni	ρωμα·του·τα·παντα·εν·πα
CAP. II. 1	bus adimpletur·et vos	σιν·πληρουμενου·και·υμασ·
	cum essetis mortui delictis	οντασ·νεκρουσ·του[6]·παραπτω
	et peccatis vestris·	μασιν·και·ταισ·αμαρτῑαισ·υ_
2	in quibus·aliquando ambula	μων·εν·αισ·ποτε·περιεπατη_
	stis·scdm sclm mundi	σαται·κατα·τον·αιωνα·του·κοσ
	hujus·scdm principem	μου·τουτου·κατα·τον·αρχοντα[7]·
	potestatis aeris	τησ·εξουσιασ · του · αεροσ·
	hujus spiritus·qui nunc opera	τουτου·πνσ·του·νυν·ενεργουν
	tur in filiis diffidentiae·	τυ[8]·εν·τοισ·υιοισ·τησ·απιθῑασ·
3	in quibus et nos aliquando conver	εν·οισ·παντεσ·ανεστραφημεν·
	sati sumus·in desideriis	ποτε·εν·ταισ·επιθυμιαισ·τησ·
	carnis nostrae · facientes	σαρκοσ·υμων[9]·ποιουντεσ·τα·
	voluntatem carnis·et	θεληματα·τησ σαρκοσ·και

---

1 και,ριοτητοσ. (κυ written above) 2 ονομαζομενου. 3 μελλοντι. 4 τουσ. 5 δωκεν. 6 τοισ.
7 *In marg.* diab. 8 εν εργοιντοσ. 9 ημων.

II. των·δια νοιων·και·ημεν·φυσι·	cogitationum·eteramus natura
τεκνα·οργησ·ωσ·και·οιλοιποι	filii irae sicut etceteri·
·4 Ο·δε·θ̅σ̅·πλουσεισ·ων·εν·ελε‿ει·	D̅s̅ autem qui dives est misericordia
δια·την·πολλην·αγαπν[1]·ην·	propter nimiam caritatem suam qua
ηγαπησεν·ημασ [2]	dilexit nos
5 και οντασ·	et nos cum essemus
ημασ·νεκρουσ·τη·αμαρτια·συν‿	mortui peccatis·convivi
εζω ποιησεν[3] (·ημασ) ·τω·χ̅ρ̅ω̅·ου χαρι	ficavit nos x̅p̅o̅·cujus gratia
6 τι·εσταισ(·σ·)εωσ‿μενοι[4]·και·συν	estis salvati·etconresuscita
ηγιρεν·και·συν εκαθισεν·εν·τοισ·	vit·etconsedere fecit incae
7 επουρανιοισ·Ινα·εν·δειξηται[5]·:[6]	lestibus in x̅p̅o̅ i̅h̅u̅·utostenderet
εν·τοισ·αιωσῖν·τοισ·επερα·ομε	in saeculis super venienti
νοισ · Το·υπερ·βαλλον·πλουτοσ·	bus abundantes divitias
τησ·χαριτοσ·αυτου·εν·χρηστο	gratiae suae in bonita
8 τητι·εφημασ·εν·χ̅ρ̅ω̅·Τη·γαρ·	te·super nos in x̅p̅o̅ i̅h̅u̅ · Grati
χαριτι·εσται·σεσωσμενοι·δια·	a enim estis salvati per
πιστεωσ·και·τουτο·ουκ·εξ·	fidem·et hoc non ex
9 ημων·Θ̅υ̅·το·δωρον·ουκ·εξ	nobis·D̅i̅ enim donum est·non ex ope
εργων·Ι̅να·μητισ·καυχησε	ribus ut ne quis glorie
10 ται·αυτου·γαρ·εσμεν·ποι	tur · Ipsius enim sumus factu
ημα·κτεισ θεντεσ·εν·κ̅ω̅·επερ	ra·creati in x̅p̅o̅ i̅h̅u̅ in operi
γοισ·αγαθοισ·οισ·προ ητοιμα	bus bonis·quae prepara
σεν·ο·θ̅σ̅·Ι̅να·εν·αυτοισ·περιπα	vit d̅s̅ ut in illis ambule
11 τισωμεν[7] · Δια·τουτο·μνημο	mus · Propter quod memo
νευοντεσ·υμισ·οι·ποτε·τα εθ	res estote quod aliquando vos
νη·εν·σαρκι·οι·λεγομενοι·ακρο	qui eratis gentes in carne qui dicebamini
βυστια·υπο·τησ·λεγομενησ·	preputium ab ea quae dicitur
περιτομισ[8]·εν·σαρκι·χειρο·ποι	circumcisio·in carne manufac

[1] αγαπην. [2] *Simile spatium.* [3] – ημασ. [4] σεσωσμενοι. [5] ενδειξηται *p.m.*
[6] *In marg.* εποδιξην. [7] περιπατησωμεν. [8] περιτομησ.

CAP. II. v. 12	ta·quia eratis illo tempo	ητω·Οτι·ητε·τω·καιρω · εκει
	re sine xpo·aliena	νω·χωρισ·χρυ·απηλλοτριω
	ti a conversatione	μενοι[1]·τησ·πολειτειασ · του·
	isrl·et hospites testamento	ἰσραηλ·και·ξενοι·των·δια‿θη
	rum promissionis ejus	κων·τησ·επαγγελἷα[2]·αυτων·
	spem non habentes·et sine do	ελπιδα·μη·εχοντεσ·και·α θυ·
13	in hoc mundo · Nunc autem	εν·τω·κοσμω·τουτω·Νυν·ειδε·
	in xpo ihu vos qui aliquando eratis	εν·χρω[3]·ιυ·υμισ·οιποτε·οντεσ·
	longe facti estis prope in san	μακραν·εγγυσ εγενηθηται·εν
14	guine xpi · Ipse enim	τω·αιματι·του·χρυ · αυτοσ·γαρ
	est pax nostra qui fe	εστιν·η·ϊρηνη·ημων · ο·ποι η‿
	cit utraque unum et medi	σασ·τα·αμφοτερα·εν·και·το·
	um parietem maceriae sol	μεσο·τοιχον·του·φραγμου·λυ
15	vens inimititias in carne	σασ·την·εκθραν·εν·τη·σαρκι·
	sua·legem mandato	αυτου·τον·νομον·των·εν·το
	rum indecretis evacuans	λων; εν·δογμασἷν·καταργησασ·
	ut duos conderet in semetipso·	ἶνα·τȣσ·δυοκτειση·εν·αυτω[4]·
	inunum novum hominem faciens	ειναʹ[5]·κοινον·ανων[6]·ποι‿ων
16	pacem·et reconcilians	ἰρηνην·κα[7]·αποκαταλλα‿ζη·
	ambos inuno corpore	τουσ·αμφοτερουσ·εν·ενι·σομα
	do·percrucem interfi	τι[8]·τω·θω·δια·του·σταυρου·α
	ciens inimicitiam in semet	ποκτεινασ·την·εκθραν·εν·ε‿
17	ipso·Et veniens evangeliza	αυτω·και·ελθων·ευαγγελισα
	vit pacem vobis qui longe fuistis·	το[9] ϊρηνην·υμιν[10]·τοισ·μακραν·
18	et pacem his qui prope·quo per	και ϊρηνην·τοισ·εγγυσ · Οτι διαυ‿
	ipsum habemus accessum	του·εχομεν·την·προσ·αγωγην
	ambo in uno spu ad	οι·αμ φοτεροι·εν·ενι·πνι·προσ·τον·
	patrem·	πατερα· [11]

---

[1] απηλλοτριωμενοι. [2] επαγγελιασ. [3] χρυ. [4] εαυτω. [5] εισ εναι. [6] ανον. [7] Και. [8] σωματι. [9] ευηγγελισατο. [10] τοισ εγγυσ υμιν. [11] *Nullum spatium vacuum.*

II. 19	Αρα · ουκ · ετει · εσται · ξενοι[1] · ϗ · πα	Ergo · jam non estis hospites et ad
	ροικοι[2] · αλλεσται · συνπολειται ·	venae · sed estis cives
20	τω[3] · αγιων · ϗ οικει · οιτȣ · θυ · εποικο	scorum etdomestici di super aedifi
	δομιθεντεσ[4] · επι · τω · θεμελω[5] ·	cati supra fundamentum
	των · αποστολων · και · προφητων ·	apostolorum et prophetarum
	οντοσ · ακρογωνι‿εου · λι‿θου ·	ipso summo angulari lapide
21	αυτου · ιυ χρυ · εν · ω · πασα · οικο	xpo ihu · In quo omnis aedifica
	δομη · συναρμο‿λογουμενη · αυ	tio constructa cre
22	ξει · εισ · ναον · αιων[6] · εν κω · εν · ω ·	scit in templum scm in dno · In quo
	και · υμεισ · συν οικοδομεισ‿θαι ·	et vos coaedificamini
	εισ · κατοικητηριον · του θυ · ενπνι ·	in habitaculum di in spu sco ·
III. 1	ουτου[7] · χαριν · εγω · παυλοσ · ο	hujus rei gratia ego paulus
	δεσμοισ[8] · του · χρυ · ὑπερ · υμων ·	vinctus xpi ihu · provobis
2	των εθνων · ειγη[9] · ηκουσαται · την ·	gentibus si tamen audistis dispen
	οικονομîαν · του · θυ · τασ[10] · χαρι	sationem gratiae di
	τοσ · τησ · δοθεισ · ησμοι ; εισ · υμασ ·	quae data est mihi invobis ·
3	Κατα · απυκαλυψιν · γαρ · εγνω	Scdm revelationem enim · notum
	ρισθη · μοι · το · μυστεριον[11] · κα	mihi factum est sacramentum sicut
4	θωσ · προ εγραψα[12] · εν · ολιπω[13] · προ‿	supra scripsi in brevi pro
	σο δυνασθαι · αναγινωσκον ; τεσ‿	ut potestis legentes intel
	νοησαι · τη[14] · συνεσίν · μου · εν · τω ·	legere prudentiam meam in
5	μυστηριω · του χρυ · ο · ετεραισ ·	mysterio xpi · quod aliis
	γεναισ[15] · ουκ · εγνωρισθη · τοισ ·	generationibus non est agnitum
	ὑιοισ · των ανων · ωσ · νυν · απε	filiis hominum · sicut nunc revela
	καλυφθη · τοισ · αγιοισ · αυτου ·	tum est scis ejus
	αποστολοισ · ϗ · προφιταισ[16] · εν ·	apostolis et prophetis in
6	τω · πνι · ειναι · τα · εθνη · συνκλη	spu · esse gentes cohere
	ρονομα · ϗ · συνσωμα · ϗ · συν	des · et concorporales · et compar

[1] ξενοι p.m. [2] *In marg.* παρροικια. [3] των. [4] εποικοδομηθεντεσ. [5] θεμελιω. [6] αγιον. [7] Τουτου. [8] δεσμιοσ. [9] ειγε vel ειγθ. [10] τησ. [11] μυστηριον. [12] προ εγραψα (γ written above ρ). [13] ολλιγω. [14] την. [15] γεναιαισ. [16] προφηταισ.

CAP. III.	ticipes promissionis ejus	μετοχα[1] · τησ · επαγγελιασ · αυτου ·
	in xpo ihu per evangelium	εν · τω · χρω · Δια · του ευαγγελιου ·
v. 7	cujus factus sum minister scdm	ου · εγενηθην · διακονοσ · κατα ·
	donum gratiae di	την · δω · ραιαν · τησ · χαριτοσ · τȣ · θυ ·
	quae data est mihi · secundum ope	τησ · δοθεισησ · μοι · κατα · την · ενερ
	rationem virtutis ejus ·	γίαν · τησ · δυναμαιωσ · αυτου · ,
8	mihi omnium scorum mini	εμοι · τω · ελαχιστω · παντων · αγι
	mo data est haec gratia	ων · εδοθη · η · χαρισ · αυτη · του ·
	di in gentibus evangeli	θυ · εν · τοισ · εθνεσιν · ευαγγελι
	zare investigabiles diviti	σασται[2] · το · ανεξεχηιασ · τον[3] · πλου
9	as xpi · et illuminare omnes	τοσ · του · χρυ · ϗ φωτισαι παντασ ·
	quae sit dispensatio sacramen	τησ[4] · η · οικονομία · του μυστηρι
	ti absconditi a	ου · του · αποκεκρυμενου[5] · απο ·
	saeculis et genea	των · αιωνω[6] · ϗ απο · των · γε
	logiis indo qui omnia	νεων · εν · τω · θω · τω · παντα ·
10	creavit · utinnotescat prin	κτισαντι · ἶνα · γνωρισθη · ταισ ·
	cipibus et potestatibus · in	αρχαισ · ϗ ταισ · εξουσιαισ · εν ·
	caelestibus per ec	τοισ · επουρανιȣσ · δια · τησ · εκ
	clesiam multi formis sapien	κλησιασ · η · πολυ ποικειλοσ · σο
11	tiae di scdm prefinitionem	φία · του · θυ · κατα · πρ · θεσίν[7] · των ·
	saeculorum quam fecit in xpo	αιωνων · ην · εποι‿ησεν · εν · τω ·
12	dno nro · In quo habemus fidu	κω · ημων · εν · ω · εχομεν · την ·
	ciam etaccessum	προσ‿αγωγην · εισ · την · παρ
	inconfidentia per	ρησιαν · εν · πεποιθησι · δια · τησ ·
13	fidem ejus · Propter quod peto	πιστεωσ · αυτου · Διο · ετουμαι[8] ·
	nedeficiatis intribulatio	μη · εκκα‿κειν · εν · ταισ · θλειψε
	nibus meis pro vobis · quae est	σιν · μου · υπερ · υμων · ητισ · εσ
14	gloria vestra · Hujus rei gra	τιν · δοξα · υμων · Του του · χα

[1] *In marg.* μετοχη. [2] ευαγγελισασθαι. [3] ανεξεχνιαστον. [4] τισ. [5] *In marg.* αποκριφα και κρυπτα. [6] αυωνων *p.m.* at αιωνων *s.m.* [7] προθεσίν. [8] *In marg.* agan.

III.	ρων · καμπτω · τα · γονα · τα · μου ·	tia flecto genua mea
	προσ · τον · πατερα · του · κυ · ημων ·	ad patrem dni nostri
15	ιυ χρυ · εξου · πασα · πατρια · εν ·	ihu xpi · ex quo omnis paternitas in
	ουρανοισ · και · επι · γησ · ονομα	cælis et interra nomina
16	ζεται · ἵνα · δω · υμιν · κατα · τοπλȣ	tur · Ut det vobis secundum diviti
	τοσ · τησ · δοξησ · αυτου · ενδυνα	as gloriae suae virtute
	μει · κραταιωθηναι · δια · τȣ · πνσ ·	corroborari per spm
17	αυτȣ · εισ · τον · εσω · ανον · κατοι	ejus in interiori homine habi
	κησαι[1] · τον · χρν · δια · τησ · πιστεωσ ·	tare xpm per fidem
18	εν · ταισ · καρδιαισ · υμων · εν · αγα	in cordibus vestris · In carita
	πη · ερρειζωμενοι · και · τεθεμε	te radicati et fun da
	λειωμενοι · ἵνα · εξισχυχήται[2]; κα	ti ut possitis compre
	ταλαβεσθαι · συν · πασιν · τοισ · αγι	hendere cum omnibus scis
	οισ · τι · το · πλατοσ · και · μη · κοσ ·	quae sit latitudo · longitudo
19	και · υψοσ · ȣβαθοσ[3] · Γνωναι ·	sublimitas et profundum · Scire
	την · υπερ · βαλλουσαν · τησ · γνω	etiam super eminentem sci en
	σεωσ · αγαπην · τȣ · χυ · ἵνα · πλη	tiae caritatem xpi · Ut imple
	ρωθηται · εισ · παν · το · πληρωμα ·	amini in omnem plenitudinem
20	τȣ · θυ · Το[4] δε · δυναμαινω · παν	di · Ei autem qui potens est omnia
	τα · ποιησαι · ὑπερ · εκ περισσου ·	facere super abundanter
	ων · αιτȣμεθα · η · νο ουμεν ·	quam petimus aut intellegimus
	κατα · την · δυναμιν · την · ενερ	secundum virtutem quae ope
21	γȣμενην · εν · ημιν · αυτω ·	ratur in nobis · Ipsi
	η · δοξα · εν · χρω · ιυ · και · τη · εκ	gloria in xpo ihu et in eccle
	κλησία · εισ · πασασ · τασ · γενεασ	sia · In omnes genera
	των · αιωνων · AMHN ·	tiones saeculorum · Amen ·
CAP. IV. 1	Παρακαλω · ȣν · υμασ · εγω · ο	Obsecro itaque vos ego
	δεσμίοσ · εν · κω · αξιωσ · περι	vinctus in dno ut digne ambu

[1] καταοικησαι. [2] εξισχυσηται. [3] *In marg.* Μαρ. [4] Τω.

CAP. IV. letis vocatione qua vocati
v. 2 estis · Cum omni humilitate
et mansuetudine · cum pati
entia supportantes invi
3 cem in caritate · solliciti
servare unitatem spiritus
in vinculo pacis ·
4 Unum corpus et unus sps · sicut voca
ti estis In una spe
5 vocationis vestrae · Unus dns una
6 fides unum baptisma · unus ds et pa
ter omnium qui super omnes et
per omnia et in omnibus nobis ·
7 Unicuique autem nrm data est
gratia · scdm mensuram dona
8 tionis xpi · Propter qd dicit ascen
dens in altum · captivam duxit
captivitatem · dedit dona
9 hominibus · Quod autem ascendit
d
quis est nisi quia et descendit primum ·
10 in inferiores partes terrae · qui
descendit ipse est et qui ascen
dit super omnes cae
los ut ad impleret omnia
11 et ipse dedit quosdam quidem
apostolos · quosdam autem prophe
tas · Alios autem evangelistas ·
alios autem pastores et docto

πατησαι · τησ · κλησεωσ · ησ · εκλη
θηται · Μετα · πασησ · ταπινοφρο
συνησ · και · πραοτητοσ · μετα · μα
κροθυμιασ · ανεχομενοι · αλλη
λων · εν · αγαπη · σπουδαζοντεσ ·
τηρειν · την · ενοτητα · του · πνσ ·
εν · τω · συν · δεσμω · τησ · ϊρηνησ ·
Εν · σωμα · και · εν · πνα · καθωσ · και ·
εκληθηται · εν · μι̂α · ελπιδι · τησ ·
κλησεωσ · υμων · εισ · κσ · μια · πισ
τισ · εν βαπτισμα · εισ · θσ · ϗ πα
τηρ · παντων · ο · επι · παντων · ϗ
δια · παντων · και · επασιν[1] · ημιν ·
Εν · ειδε · εκαστω · ημων · εδοθη ·
χαρισ · κατα · το · μετρον · τησ · δω
.α.
ρ.ιασ[2] · του · χρυ · Δι · ο · λεγι · ανα
βασ · εισ · υψοσ · ηχμαλω · τευσεν ·
αιχμαλωσιαν · εδωκεν · δοματα
εν · ανθρωποισ · Το · δε · ανεβη ·
τι · εστισ[3] · ειμη · οτι · ϗ κατεβη ·
εισ · τα · κατωτερα · τησ · γησ · Ο ·
καταβασ · αυτοσ · εστιν · ϗ ο · ανα
βασ · ὑπερ · ανω · παντων · των · ȣ
ρανων · ῑνα · πληρωση · τα · παντα ·
και · αυτοσ · εδωκεν · τουσ · μεν ·
αποστολουσ · τουσ · δε · προφη
τασ · Τουσ · δε · ευαγγελιστασ ·
τουσ · δε · ποιμενασ · και · διδασ

---

[1] εν πασῖν.   [2] δωραιασ.   [3] εστιν (pro εστισ).

IV. 12 καλουσ προσ · τον · καταρτισμον ·	res ad consummationem
των · αγιων · εισ · εργον · τησ · διακο	sanctorum In opus ministe
νίασ · εισ · οικοδομην · του · σωμα	rii · in aedificationem corpo
13 τοσ · του · χρυ · Μεχρι · καταντη	ris xpi · Donec occurra
σω · παντεσ · εισ · την · ενοτητα ·	mus omnes in unitatem
τησ · πιστεωσ ϗ · τησ · επιγνωσεωσ ·	fidei · et agnitionis filii
του θυ · εισ · ανδρα · τελειων[1] · εισ	di · In virum per fectum in
μετρον · ηλεικιασ · του · πληρω	mensuram aetatis plenitu
14 ματοσ · του · χυ · Ινα · μηκετει ·	dinis xpi · Ut non jam
ωμεν · νιπιοι · κλυδωνειζομε	simus parvuli et fluctuantes ·
νοι · και · περι · φερομενοι · παντί	et circum feramur omni
ανεμω · τησ · διδασκαλίασ · εν · τη ·	vento doctrinae in nequi
τικυβια[2] · των · ανον[3] · εν · τι[4] · παν · ουρ	tia hominum · In astu
για · προσ · την · μεθοδιαν · τησ · πλα	tia adcircumventionem erro
15 νησ[5] · αληθίαν · δε · ποι ουντεσ ·	ris · Veritatem autem facientes
εν · αγαπη · αυξησομεν · εισ · αυ	in caritate crescamus in il
τον · τα · παντα · οσ · εστιν · κεφαλη ·	lo per omnia qui est caput
16 ο · χσ · εξ · ου · παντο · σωμε[6] · συναρ	xps ex quo totum corpus · com
μο · λογουμενον · και · συνβιβα	pactum et cone
ζομενον · δια · πασησ · αφησ · τησ ·	xum per omnem juncturam
επιχορηγίασ · εν · μετρω · ενοσ ·	subministrationis · in mensura uni
εκαστου · μερουσ[7] · την · αυξησιν[8] ·	us cujusque partis · augmentum
του · σωματοσ · ποιειτε εισ · οικο	corporis facit · In aedifica
17 δομεν[9] · αυτου · εν · αγαπη · Τουτο ·	tionem sui in caritate · Hoc
ουν · λεγω · ϗ · μαρτυρομαι · εν ·	itaque dico et testificor In
κω · μηκετει · Ϋμασ · περιπατειν	dno · ut jam non ambuletis
καθωσ και τα εθνη περιπατει ·	sicut gentes ambulant
εν · μαται · ο · τητι · του · νοοσ · αυτων ·	in vanitate sensus sui ·

[1] *τελειον.* [2] *— τι (ante κυβια).* [3] *ανων.* [4] *τη.* [5] *In marg.* ago q io.
[6] *σωμα.* [7] *μετρουσ.* [8] *In marg. αγα.* [9] *οικοδομην.*

		obscurati Ī obtenebricati
CAP. IV. v. 18	tenebris obscuratum habentes intellectum	εσκοτισ · μενοι · τη · διανοια · απηλ
	alienati a vita d̄i	λοτριω μενυι[1] · τησ · ζωησ · τȣ · θ̄υ ·
	per ignorantiam quae est	δια · την · αγνωσιαν · την · ουσαν ·
	in illis · propter caecitatem	εν · αυτοισ · δια · την · παρωσιν[2] · τησ ·
19	cordis ipsorum · Qui disperan	καρδιασ · αυτο̣ν[3] · οιτινεσ · αφηλ
	tes semet ipsos tradiderunt	πικοτεσ · εαυτουσ · παρεδωκαν ·
	impudicitiae · In operationem omnis	τη · ασελγία · εισ · εργασιαν · πασησ ·
	immunditiae · et avaritiae ·	ακαθαρσιασ · κα[4] · πλεονεξιασ ·
20	Vos autem non ita didicistis	Ὑμεισ · δε · ουκ[5] · ουτωσ · εμαθεται ·
21	x̄p̄m̄ · si tamen illum audistis	τον · χ̄ρ̄ν̄ · ει · γη[6] · αυτον · ηκουσαται ·
	et in ipso edocti estis · sicut	και · εν · αυτω · εδιδαχθηται · καθωσ ·
22	est veritas in ih̄ū · depone	εστιν · η · αληθία · εν · τω · ῑῡ · αποθεσ
	re vos secundum pristinam	θαι[7] · υμασ · κατα · την · προτεραν ·
	conversationem · veterem hominem	αστροφην · τον · παλαιον · ᾱν̄ο̄ν̄ ·
	qui corrumpitur secundum deside	τον · φθειρομενον · κατα · τασ · επι_
23	ria erroris · Renovamini autem	θυμιασ · τησ · απατησ ; ανανευσ
24	s̄p̄ū mentis vestrae · et	θαι · το[8] [9] · π̄ν̄ῑ · του · νοοσ · υμων · και
	induite novum hominem qui	ενδυσασθαι · τον · καινον · ᾱν̄ο̄ν̄ ·
	secundum deum creatus est in justi	τον · κατα · θ̄ν̄ · κτισθεντα · ενδι
	tia et sanctitate verita	καιοσυνη · και · οσειοτητι · ϗ αλη
25	tis · Propter quod deponentes men	θία · Διο · αποθεμενοι · του[10] · ψευ
	dacium loquimini veritatem unusquisque	δοσ · λαλιται · αληθîαν · εκαστοσ ·
	cum proximo suo · quoniam	μετα · του · πλησîον · αυτου · οτι ·
26	sumus invicem membra · Irasci	εσμεν · αλληλων · μελη · οργι
	mini et nolite peccare ·	ζεσθαι[11] · δε · ϗ μη · αμαρτανεται[12] ·
	Sol non occidat	Ō ηλîοσ · μη · επι δ υ ε τ ω ·
	super iracundiam vestram	επι · τω · παροργισμω · ὑμων ·
27	neque detis locum di abo	μηδε · δειδυτε · το · πον ; τω · διαβω_[13]

[1] εσκοτισ . μενοσ ; verba τη.διανοια : απηλλοτριωμενοι : desunt *p.m.* : habet supra *s. m.* [2] πωρωσιν.
[3] αυτων. [4] και. [5] ουχ. [6] γε. [7] *In marg.* αποθεσισ. (depositio) [8] *In marg.* collecta.
[9] ανανεουσθαι τω. [10] το. [11] Οργιο̣ζεσθαι. [12] *In marg.* αγανο. [13] διαβολω.

IV. 28	λω · ο · κλεπτων · μη · κετι · κλεπ	lo · Qui furabatur · jam non fure
	τετω · Μαλλον · δε · κοπειατω · ερ	tur · Magis autem laboret ope
	γαζομενος · ταις · ἴδιαις · χερσῖν ·	rando manibus suis
	το · αγαθον · ἵνα · εχη · μετα · δουναι	quod bonum est · uthabeat unde tribu
29	τω · χριαν · εχοντι · Πας · λογος ·	at necessitatem patienti · Omnis sermo
	σαπρος · εκ · του · στοματος · υμων ·	malus ex ore vestro
	μη · εκπορευεσθω · αλλειτις ·	non procedat · Sed si quis
	αγαθος · εστιν · προς · οικοδομη [Γ.ν.]	bonus est ad aedificationem
	της · πιστεως · ἵνα · δοι · χαρίν ·	fidei · Ut det gratiam
30	τοις · ακουουσιν · και · μη · λυπει_	audientibus · et nolite contrista
	ται[1] · το · αγιον · πνα · του · θυ · εν ·	re spm scm di · in quo
	ω · εσ_φραγισθηται · εις · ημεραν ·	signati estis in diem
31	απολυτρωσεως · Πασα · πικρια[2] ·	redemptionis · Omnis amaritudo
	και · οργη · και · θυμος · και · γραυ	et ira et indignatio · et cla
	γη[3] · και · βλασφημία · αρθητω · αφ	mor · et blasphemia · tollatur a
32	υμων · συν · παση · κακία · γινες	vobis · cum omni malitia · Esto
	θαι · ουν · εις · αλληλους · χρηστοι ·	te autem invicem benigni
	ευσπλανχνοι · χαριζομενοι ·	misericordes · Donantes
	εαυτοις · καθως · και · ο · θς · εν	invicem sicut et ds in
CAP. V. 1	χρω εχαρισατο · υμιν · Γινεσθαι ·	xpo donavit vobis · Estote
	ουν · μειμηται · του · θυ · ως · τεκνα ·	ergo imitatores di sicut filii
2	αγαπητα · και · περιπατῖτε · εν ·	kmi · et ambulate in di
	αγαπη · καθως · και · ο χρς · ηγα	lectione sicut et xps di
	πησεν · ημας · και παρεδωκεν ·	lexit vos et tradidit
	εαυτων[4] · υπερ · ημων · προσφοραν ·	semet ipsum pro nobis oblationem
	και · θυσιαν · τω · θω · εις · οσμην ·	et hostiam do in odorem
3	ευωδιας · Πορνῖα · δε · και · πασα ·	suavitatis · Fornicatio autem et omnis
	ακαθαρσία · η · πλεο·[νε]ξῖα[5] · μηδε ·	immundia · aut avaritia · Nec

[1] λυπεισται. [2] *In marg.* πιγρας. galieni*. [3] κραυγη. [4] εαυτον. [5] ακαρθαρσία · η · πλεονεξῖα.

CAP. V.	nominetur in vobis sicut	ονομα‿ζετω · εν · υμιν · καθωσ ·
v. 4	decet scos · aut turpitudo aut stul	πρενει[1] · αγιοισ · η · αισχροτησ · η ; μω
	ti loquium · aut scurrilitas quæ ad rem non	ρο‿λογîα · η · ευτραπελîα · τα · ουκ ·
	pertinet · sed magis gratiarum	ανκοντα · αλλα · μαλλον · ευχαρισ
5	actio · Hoc enim scitote intelle	τîιι · Τουτο · γαρ · ïστε · γινωσ
	gentes · qd omnis fornicator aut im	κοντεσ · οτι7πασ[2] · πορνοσ · η · ακαθαρ
	mundus aut avarus qd est idolo	τοσ · η · πλεον‿εκτησ · ο · εστιν · ιδω
	rum servitus · Non habet heredita	λολατρîα · ουκ · εχει · κληρονομι
	tem in regno xpo et	αν · εισ · την · βασιλιαν · τυ · θυ · και
6	di · Nemo vos seducat	χρυ · Μεδεισ[3] · υμασ · απατα‿τω[4] ·
	inanibus verbis · Propter hæc enim ve	κενοι[5] · λογοισ · Δια · ταυτα · γαρ · ερ
	nit ira di in	χεται · η ; οργη · του · θυ · επι · τουσ ·
7	filios diffidentiae Nolite itaque	υιουσ · τησ · απιθîασ · Μη · ουν ·
	effici participes eorum ·	γινεσθαι · συνμετοχοι · αυτων ·
8	Eratis enim aliquando tenebræ nunc autem	Ηται · γαρ · ποτε · σκοτοσ · νυν · ειδε ·
	lux in dno ut filii lucis ambu	φωσ · εν · κω · ωσ · τεκνα · φωτοσ · πε
9	late · Fructus enim lu	ρινατîτε[6] · Ο · γαρ · καρποσ · του · φω
	cis est in omni bonitate et justi	τοσ · εν · παση · αγαθοσυνηυ[7] · και
10	tia · et veritate · Pro ban	δικαιοσυνη · και · αληθîα · οκει
	tes quid sit beneblacitum	μαζοντεσ · τηειστιν[8] · ευαρεστον ·
11	do · et nolite communicare	τω θω · και · μη · συνκοι‿νονειται[9] ·
	operibus infructuosis te	τοισ · εργοισ · τοισ · ακαρποισ · του ·
	nebrarum · Magis autem et redar	σκοτουσ · Μαλλον · δε · και · ελεγ
12	guite · Quæ enim occulte fiunt	χεται · Τα · γαρ · κρυφη · γεινομεν ·
	ab ipsis · turpe est et	αυπαυτων · αισχρον · εστιν · ϗ
13	dicere · Omnia enim quæ argu	λεγειν · τα · δε · παντα · ελεγχο
	untur · A lumine manifestan	μενα · υποτουφωτοσ · φανερου
	tur · Omne enim quod manifesta	ται · Παν · γαρ · το · φαναιρουμε

[1] πρεπει. [2] οτι πασ. [3] Μηδεισ. [4] *In marg.* contra graecos. [5] κενοισ. [6] περιπατîτε. [7] αγαθοσυνη. [8] τι εστιν. [9] συνκοινωνειται.

14 νου·φωσ·εστιν·διολεγει[1]·εγει
ρε·ο·καθευδων·χ̧·αναστα·εκ
των·νεκρων·χ̧ επιφαυσει·σοι·
5 ο χρσ[2] · Βλεπεται·ουν·πωσ·ακρι
βωσ·περιπατῖτε·μη·ωσ·ασοφοι·
16 αλλωσ·σοφοι·εξαγοραζομενοι·
τον·καιρον·οτι·αι·ημεραι·πο
17 νηραι·εισιν · Διατουτο·μη·γει
νεσθαι·αφρονεσ·αλλα·συνϊοντεσ·
18 τι·το·θελημα·του·κυ·και·μη·
μεθυσκεσθαι·οινω·εν·ω·ͤστιν[3]·
ασωτία·αλλα·πληρουσθαι·εν·
19 τω·πνι·αλλουντεσ[4]·εαυτοισ·
ψαλμοισ[5]·και·υμνοισ·και·ω‿
δαισ·πνευματικαισ·αδοντεσ·
και·ψαλλοντεσ·εν·ταισ·καρδιαισ·
20 υμων·τω·κω · Ευχαριστȣντεσ·
παντωτε[6]·ὑπερ·ὑμων·εν·ονο
ματι·του·κυ·ημων·ιυ·χυ·τω·πα
21 τρι·και·θω·ὑποτάσ‿σομενοι·
αλληλοισ·εν·φοβω·ιυ·χυ·
22 Αι·γυνεκαισ·υποτασεθαι[7]·τοισ·
23 ἰδιοισ·ανδρασῖν·ωσ·τω·κω·οτι·
ανηρ·εστιν·κεφαλη·τησ·γυναικοσ·
ωσ·και·ο·χρσ·κεφαλη·τησ·εκκλη
σιασ·αυτοσ·σφτηρ[8]·του·σωματοσ·
24 Αλλωσ·η·εκκλησῖα·υποτασσε
ται·τω·χρω·ουτοσ[9]·και·αιγυ

tur lumen est propter qd dicit · Sur
ge qui dormis·et exurge a
mortuis et inluminabit tibi
xps · Videte itaque quomodo cau
te ambuletis non quasi insipientes
sed ut sapientes · Redimentes
tempus quoniam dies ma
li sunt · Propterea nolite fi
eri imprudentes·sed intellegentes
quae sit voluntas dni·et nolite
inebriari vino in quo est
luxuria · Sed implemini
spu loquentes vobis metipsis
psalmis et Ymnis·et canti
cis spiritalibus cantantes
et psallentes In cordibus
vris dno · Gratias agentes
semper pro omnibus in nomi
ne dni nri ihu xpi·do
et patri · Subjecti
invicem in timore xpi·
Mulieres subjectae sint
viris suis sicut dno·quoniam
vir caput est mulieris
sicut xps caput ecclesi
ae · Ipse salvator corporis·
Sed sicut ecclesia subjecta
est xpo · Ita et muli

[1] *In marg.* in secreto enoch. [2] *In marg.* contra graecos. [3] εστιν. [4] Αλλουντεσ.
[5] *In marg.* περι προσευχησ. [6] παντοτε. [7] ὑποτασσεσθαι. [8] σωτηρ. [9] Ουτωσ.

CAP. V.	eres viris suis in omni	ναικαισ · τοισ · ανδρασιν · εν · παν
v. 25	bus · Viri diligite	τι · Οι · ανδρεσ · αγαπαται · τασ ·
	uxores vestras · sicut et	γυναικασ · υμων · καθωσ · και
	xps dilexit ecclesi	ο · χρσ · ηγαπησεν · την · εκκλησί
	am · et semet ipsum tradidit	αν · ϗ · εαυτον · παραδωκεν[1] ·
26	pro ea · ut illam scifica	υπερ · αυτησ · Ινα · αυτην · αγι
	ret · mundans lavacro	ασῃ · καθαρεισασ · τω · λουτρω ·
27	aquae in verbo · Ut	του · υδατοσ · εν · ριματι[2] · Ινα
	exiberet ipse sibi glorio	παραστηση · αυτοσ · εαυτω · εν · δο
	sam ecclesiam · non habentem	ξον[3] · την · εκκλησιαν · μη · εχουσαν ·
	maculam · aut rugam · aut aliquid	σπειλον · η · ρυτειδα · η · τι · των · τοι
	ejusmodi · Sed ut sit sca et immacu	ουτων · αλλϊνα · η · αγια · και · αμω
28	lata · Ita et viri de	μοσ[4] · Ουτωσ · και · οι · ανδρει · σοφι[5]
	bent deligere uxores	λουσιν · αγαπαντασ · εαυτων · γυ
	suas ut corpora sua quia	νεκασ[6] · ωσ · τα · εαυτων · σωματα ·
	qui diligit suam uxorem · se ipsum	ο · αγαπων · την · εαυτου · γυναικα · εαυ
29	diligit · Nemo enim umquam	τον · αγαπα · ουδεισ · γαρ · ποτε · την ·
	carnem suam odio habuit · Sed nu	εαυτου · σαρκα · εμεισησεν · αλλεκ
	trit eam et fovet · sicut	τρεφει · αυτην · ϗ · θαλπει · καθωσ ·
30	et xps ecclesiam · quia	και · χσ[7] · την · εκκλησίαν · οτι ·
	membra sumus corporis ejus	μελη · εσμεν · του · σωματοσ · αυτου
	de carne ejus et de os	εκτησ · σαρκοσ · αυ·του · και ·
31	sibus ejus · Propter	εκτων · οσταιων · αυτου · αν
	hoc relinquet homo pa	τιτι · του · καταλειψει · ανοσ · πα
	trm et matrem · et adhære	τερα · και · μητερα · ϗ · κολληθησε
	bit uxori suæ · et erunt	ται · τη · γυναικι · αυτου · ϗ · εσον
32	duo In carne una	ται · οι · δυο · εισ · σαρκα · μιαν · το
	Sacramentum hoc magnum est	μυτηριον[8] · τουτο · μεγα · εστιν ·

---

[1] παρεδωκεν. [2] ρηματι. [3] εν δοξαν. [4] *In marg.* αμωμum. [5] ανδρεσ οφι. [6] γυναικασ. [7] + ο (*ante* χσ). [8] μυστηριον.

V. εγω · δε · λεγω · εισ · χρν · ϗ εισ · την ·
33 εκκλησίαν · Πλην · και · ύμεισ ·
οικαθενα · εκαστον · την · εαυτου ·
γυναικα · ωσ · εαυτον · αγαπατω ·
Η · δε · γυνη · ϊνα · φοβηται · τον · αν
VI. 1 δρα · τα · τεκνα · υ · πακουεται ·
τοισ · γονευσιν · υμων · τουτο · γαρ ·
2 εστιν · δικαιον · τιμα · τον · πατε
ρα · σου · και · την · μητερά · σου · η
τισ[1] · εστιν · εν · τολη · πρωτη · εν · τη ·
3 επαγγελîα · Ινα · ευ · σου · γενηται ·
και · εση · μακρωχρονειοσ[2] · επι · τησ ·
4 γησ · και · οι · πατεράσ[3] · μη · παροր
γειζεται · τα · τεκνα · υμων · αλ
λεκτρεφεται · αυτα · εν · παιδεια[4] ·
5 και · νουθεσîα · κυ · οι · δουλοι · υ
πακουεται · τοισ · κυριοισ · κατα ·
σαρκα · μετα · φοβου · και · τρομου ·
εν · απλοτητι · τησ · καρδιασ · υμων ·
6 ωσ · τω · χρω · μη · κατοφθαλμο ·
δουλêιαν · ωσ · ανδρω · παρεσκοι[5] ·
αλλωσ · δουλοι · χρυ · ποιουντεσ ·
το · θελημα · του · θευ[6] · εκ · ψυ
7 χησ · μετεύνοιασ · δουλευον
τεσ · ωσ · τω · κω · και · ουκ · ανοισ ·
8 ιδοτεσ · οτι · εκαστοσ · οαν · ποιη
ση · αγαθον · τουτο · κομεισεται ·
παρα · κυ · ειτε · δουλοσ · ειτε · ε

ego autem dico In xpo et in
ecclesia · Veruntamen et vos
singuli unus quisque suam
uxorem sicut seipsum diligat ·
Vuxor autem ut timeat vi
rum · Filii oboedite
parentibus vestris · hoc enim
est justum · honora patrem
tuum et matrem quod
est primum mandatum in
promissione · Ut bene sit tibi
et sis longævus super ter
ram · et patres nolite ad iracun
diam provocare filios vrs · sed
educate illos in disciplina
et correptione dni · Servi oboe
dite dominus carnali
bus cum timore et tremore
in simplicitate cordis vestri ·
sicut xpo · Non ad occulum
servientes quasi hominibus placen
tes · sed sicut servi xpi · facientes
voluntatem di ex ani
mo cum benignitate servien
tes sicut dno et non hominibus
scientes qd unusquisque quodcuq · fece
rit bonum hoc percipiet
a dno · sive servus sive li

---

[1] η τισ. [2] μακροχρονειοσ. [3] πατερεσ. [4] In marg. παιδîα. (disciplina.) [5] ανθρω,παρεσκοι. [6] Θυ.

CAP. VI. v. 9	ber·et vos domini eadem	λευθεροσ·και·οι·κυριοι·τα·αυτα·
	facite illis·remitten	ποιεπαι[1]·προσ·αυτουσ·ανειεν
	tes minas · Scientes quia	τεσ·την·απιλην·ειδοτεσ·οτι·
	et illorum et vester d̄n̄s est in	και·αυτων·υμων·ο·κ̄σ̄·εστιν·εν
	caelis·et personarum accepti	ουρανοισ·και·προσωπολημ
	o non est aput d̄m̄·	ψια·ουκ·εστιν·παρα·τω·θ̄ω̄
10	Decetero fratres conforta	Το·λοιπον·αδελφοι·εν·δυνα
	mini in d̄n̄o·et in potentia	μουσθαι[2]·εν·κ̄ω̄·και·εν·τω
11	virtutis ejus · Indu	κρατει·τησ·ἰσχυοσ·αυτου·εν
	ite vos armaturam	δυσασθαι·υμασ·την·πανοπλῐ
	d̄ī ut possitis	αν·του·θ̄ῡ·εισ·το·δυνασθαι·
	stare adversus insidi	υμασ·στηναι·προσ·τασ·μεθο
12	as diaboli · Quia non	διασ·του·διαβολου·οτι[3]·ουκ·
	est vobis colluctatio adversus carnem	εστιν·υμιν·η·παλη·προσ·αῖμα
	et sanguinem·sed adversus princi	και·σαρκα·αλλα·προσ·τασ·αρ
	pes et potestates·adversus mun	χασ·εξουσῖασ·προσ·τουσ·κοσ
	di rectores tenebrarum ha	μο·κρατορασ·του·σκοτουσ·ταυ
	rum·contra spiritalia	του[4]·προσ·τα·πνευματικα·τησ·
	nequitiae in caelestibus·	πονηριασ·εν·τοισ·επουρανοισ·
13	Propterea accipite armatu	Διατουτο·αναλαβεται·την·πα
	ram d̄ī ut possi	νοπλῖαν·του·θ̄ῡ·ινα·δυνηθη
	tis re sistere in die	ται·αντιστηναι·εν·τη·η̄μερα·
	mala·et in omnibus per	τη·πονηρα·και·απαντα·κατα
14	fecti stare · State ergo succin	ιργασαμενοι[5]·στηται·περιεζωσ
	cti lumbos vestros in verita	μενοι·τηνοσ·φυνυμων·εν·αλη
	te·et induti lorica	θῖα·και·εν·δυσαμενοι[6]·τον·θω
15	justitiae·et calcia	ρακα·τησ·δικαι·υνησ[7]·και·υπο (.οσ. above)
	ti pedes in praeparati	δησαμενοι·τουσ·ποδασ·εν·ετοι

[1] ποιειται. [2] *Marg.* phorphi. [3] *In marg.* contra γ̄ρ̄ε̄. [4] τουτου.
[5] κατ.ιργασαμενοι, σ̣. (α. above) [6] ευδυσαμενοι. [7] δυκαιοσυνησ.

VI. 16 μασῖα · τȣ · ευαγγελιȣ · τησ · ῑρηνησ · επι	one evangelii pacis · In
πασιν · αναλαβοντεσ · τον · θιραιον[1] ·	omnibus sumentes scutum
τησ · πιστεωσ · εν ; ω · δυνασθαι · παντα ·	fidei · In quo possitis omnia
τα · βελη · του · πονηρου · πεπυρωμενασ[2] ·	tela nequissimi ignea
17 βεσε · ϗ · την · περικεφαλιαν[3] · του · σω	extinguere et galeam salutis assumite
τηριου · ϗ την · μαχαιραν · του · πν̄σ ·	et gladium spiritus
18 Ο · εστιν · ρημα · θ̄υ · δια · πασισ[4] · προσ · ευχησ · ϗ	quod est verbum dī per omnem orationem et
δεησεωσ · προσ · ευχομενοι · εν · παντι · ϗρω ·	obsecrationem orantes omni tempore
εν · πν̄ι · ϗ · εισ · αυτον · αγρυπνουντεσ · παντοτε ·	in spū · et in ipso vigilantes semper
εν · παση · δεησι · υπερ · παντων · αγιων ·	In omni Instantia et obsecrāt pro omnibus scīs
19 ϗ · υπερ · εμȣ · ῑνα · μοι · δοθη ; λογοσ · εν · ανοι	et pro me ut detur mihi sermo In aperti
ξει · τȣ, στοματοσ · μȣ · εν · παρησι · α[5] γνωρεισαι ·	one oris mei · Cum fidutia notum facere
20 το, μυστηριον · ὑπερ · ου · πρεσβευω · εν	mysterium evanḡ pro quo legatione fungor in
αλυσει · ῑνα · εν · αυτω · παρρισια [η] · σομαι[6] ·	catena · Ita ut in ipso audeam
21 ως · δειμαι · λαλησαι · Ινα · δε · ϗ υμεισ ·	prout oportet loqui · Ut autem vos
ιδητε · τα · κατεμαι · Τι πρασσω · γνωρισει ·	sciatis quæ circa me sunt quid agam omnia nota faciet
υμιν · Τυχεικοσ · ο · αγαπητοσ · αδελφοσ ·	vobis tuchius [c] carissimus frt̄ et [‖] fidelis
22 ϗ πιστοσ · διακονοσ εν · κ̄ω · Ον ; επεμψα ·	minister In dn̄o · Quem misi
προσ · υμασ · εισ · αυτο · τȣτο · Ῑνα · γνωται ·	ad vos in hoc ipsum · Ut cognoscatis
τα · περι · ημων · ϗ · παρακαλεσι[7] · τασ ·	quæ circa nos sunt · et consoletur
καρδιασ · υμων ·	corda Vestra ·
23 Ειρην[8] · τοισ · αδελφοισ · ϗ · αγαπη · μετα ·	Pax frībus et caritas cum
πιστεωσ · απο · θ̄υ · πατροσ · ϗ · κ̄υ · ῑυ · χ̄υ ·	fide a dō patre et dn̄o ih̄u xp̄o ·
24 Η · χαρισ · μετα · παντων · των · αγαπων ·	Gratia cum omnibus qui diligunt
των[9] · κ̄ν · ημων · ῑν · χ̄ν · εν · αφθαρσια[10] ·	dn̄m n̄rum ih̄m xp̄m In incorruptione ·
Ετελεσθη · επιστολη ·	EXPLICIT EPISTOLA
προσ · εφεσιουσ ·	AD EPHESIOS

---

1 Θυραιον. 2 *In marg.* cogan. 3 περι καιφαλιαν. 4 πασησ. 5 παρρησια. 6 παρρησιασομαι. 7 παρακαλεση. 8 Ειρηνη. 9 αγαπων τον. 10 *In marg.* αφαρσια ·|· incorruptio

Incipit ad phi	Αρχεται προσ φι
lippenses	η λιππεσιουσ[1]
CAP. I. v. 1 **Paulus et timo**	Παυλοσ και τιμο
theus servi ihu xpi ·	θεοσ δουλοι ιυ χρυ
omnibus scis in xpo ihu	πασῖν · τοισ · αγιοισ · εν · χρω · ιυ ·
qui sunt philippis · cum	τοισ · ουσῖν[2] · εν · φιλιπποισ[3] · συν
episcopis et diaconibus ·	επισκοποισ · και · διακονοισ ·
2 Gratia vobis et pax a do	Χαρισ · υμιν · ϗ · ερηνη[4] · απο · θυ ·
patre nro et dno ihu xpo	πατροσ · ημων · ϗ · κυ · ιυ · χυ ·
3 Ego quidem gratias ago do nro	Εγω · μεν · ευχαρειστο[5] · τω · κω · ημων
4 in omni memoria vri semper	επι · παση · τη · μνιαν[6] · υμων · παν
in cunctis orationibus meis pro	τοτε · εν · παση · δεησι · μου · υπερ ·
omnibus vobis cum gaudio	παντων · υμων · μετα · χαρασ ·
deprecationem faciens	και · την · δεησιν · ποι͜ουμενοσ ·
5 super communicatione vestra in	επι · τη κοινωνια · υμων · εισ · το ·
evangelio · a prima die	ευαγγελιον · αποπρω · τησ · ἡμε
6 usque nunc · Confidens	ρασ · αχρι · του · νυν · πεποιθωσ
hoc ipsum · quia qui coepit	αυτοτουτο · οτι οεναρξαμε
in vobis opus bonum perfici	νοσ εν υμιν εργον αγαθον · επι
et usque in diem xpi ihu ·	τελεσει · αχρισ · ημερασ · ιυ · χρυ ·
7 sicut est mihi justum hoc	καθωσ · εστιν · δικαιον · εμοι · του
sentire pro omnibus vobis	το · φρονειν · υπερ · παντων · υμων ·
eo quod habeam vos in corde	δια · το · εχ·ιν[7] · μαι · εν · τη · καρδια ·
et in vinculis meis	υμασ · εν · τετοισ · δεσμοισ · μου ·
et indefensione et confirmatione	και · τη · απολογια · ϗ · βαιβαιωσει
evangelii · socios	του · ευαγγελιου · συνκοινωνουσ ·
gaudii mei omnes vos	τησ · χαριτοσ · μου · παντασ · ὑμασ

[1] Φιλιππησιουσ. [2] *In marg.* ουσια. [3] φιλιπόποισ. [4] ειρηνη. [5] ευχαρειστω. [6] δεησι μου τη μνιαν. [7] εχειν.

	Graece	Latine
AP. 1. v. 8	οντασ · μαρτυσ · γαρ · μοι · ο · κσ ·	esse · Testis enim mihi est ds
	ωσ · επι_ποθω · παντασ · υμασ · εν ·	quomodo cupiam omnes vos in
9	σπλανχνοισ · ιυ · χρυ[1] · και · τουτο ·	visceribus ihu xpi · et hoc
	προσ · ευχομαι · ῑνα · η · αγαπη · υμων ·	oro ut caritas vestra
	ετει · μαλλον · και · μαλλον · περισ	magis ac magis abun
	σευοι · εν · επιγνωσι · ꝁ · παση · αισ	det In scientia et omni sen
10	θησει · εισ · το · λοκιμαζειν · υμασ ·	su · Ut probetis
	τα · δια φεροντα · Ητει · ινα[2] · λεικρι	potiora · ut sitis sinceres
	νεισ · και · απροσκοποι · εισ · ημεραν ·	et sine offensione In diem
11	χρυ · ιυ · πεπληρωμενοι · καρπον ·	xpi ihu repleti fructu
	δικαιοσυνησ · τον · δια · ιυ · χυ · εισ ·	justitiae per ihum xpm in glo
12	δοξαν · και · επαινονμοι · Εινωσ	riam et laudem di · Sci
	κειν · δε · υμασ · βουλομαι · αδελφοι ·	re autem vos volo fratres ·
	οτι · το · κατε · μαι · μαλλον · εισ · προ	quia quae circa me sunt magis adpro
	κοπην · του · ευαγγελιου · ελησυ	profectum evangelii pervene
13	θεν[3][4] · ωστε · τουσ · δεσμουσ · μου ·	runt · Ita ut vincula mea
	φανερουσ · γενεσθαι · εν · χρω · εν	menifesta fierent in xpo in
	ολω · τω · πρετωριω · και · τοισ · λοι	omni praetorio · et in caete
14	τοισ · πασιν · και · τουσ · πλειονασ[5] ·	ris omnibus et plures
	των · αδελφων · εν · κω · πεποιθο	e fratribus in dno · confiden
	τασ · τοισ · δεσμοισ · μου · περισσοτε	tes in vinculis meis · abundan
	ροσ[6] · τολμαν · αφορωσ[7] · τον · λογον ·	tius auderent sine timore verbum
15	κυ · λαλειν · Τινεσ · μεν · και · δια ·	di loqui · Quidam quidem et propter
	φρον[8] · και · ερειν[9] · Τινεσ · δε · και	invidiam et contentionem · quidam autem
	δι ευδοκίαν · τον · χρν · κηρυσσου_	et propter bonam voluntatem xpm p
17	σιν · Οιμεν · εξαγαπησ · ειδοτεσ ·	dicant · Quidam ex caritate scientes
	οτι · εισ · απυλογίαν · του · ευαγγελι	quo indefensione evangelii
16	ου · κιμαι · οιδε · εξεριθιασ[10] ·	positus sum · Quidam autem ex contentione

---

[1] χρυ ιυ. [2] Ἵνα ητεῖ. [3] ελυλυθεν. [4] *In marg.* evang graecum. [5] πλειωνασ. [6] περισσοτερωσ. [7] αφοβωσ. [8] φρονον. [9] *In marg.* eresis. [10] εριάθιασ.

	Latin	Greek
CAP. I.	xpm annuntiant non sincere·	χρν·καταγγελουσιν·ȣκ·αγνωσ·
	estimantes pressuram suscitare	οιομενοι·θλιψι.ν·εγιρειν·τοισ
v. 18	vinculis meis · Quid enim dum om	δεσμοισ·μου · Τι·γαρ·πλην·οτιπαν
	ni modo seu per occasionem sive perveri	τι·τρωπω[1]·ειτε·προφασι·ειτε·αλη
	tatem xpc annuntiatur·et in	θια·χρσ·καταγγελλ·ται[2]·και·εν·
	hoc gaudeo·sed et gaude	τουτω·χαιρω·αλλα·ϗ χαιρησο
19	bo · Scio enim quia hoc mihi perve	μαι[3] · Οιδα·γαρ·οτι·τουτο·μοι·απο
	niet in salutem·per vestram	βησεται·εισ·σωτηρείαν·δια·τησ·
	orationem·et sub ministrationem	υμων·δεησεωσ·ϗ·επι·χορηγειασ·
20	sps xpi ihu · Secundum exspecta	του·πνσ·χυ·ιυ·κατα·την·κάρα
	tionem et spem meam quia in	δοκιαν·ϗ·ελπιδα·μου·Οτι·εν·
	nullo vestrum confundar·	ουδενὶ·υμων·αισχυνθησομαι
	Sed in omni fidutia sicut semper	Αλλεν·παση·παρρησια[4]·ωσ·παντο
	et nunc magnificabitur xps	τε·και·νυν·μεγαλυνθησεται·χρσ[5]·
	in corpore meo sive per vitam·	εν·τω·σωματι·μȣ·ειτε·δια·ζωησ
21	sive per mortem · Mihi enim vive	ειτε·δια·θανατου · Εμοι·γαρ·το
	re xps est · et mori	ζην·χρσ·εστιν·και·το·αποθα
22	lucrum·quod sivivere in	νιν·κερδοσ·ειδε·τοζην·εν·
	carne hic mihi fructus operis	σαρκι·τουτο·μοι·καρποσ·εργου·
	est·et quid eligam igno	εστιν·καιτι·αιρησομαι·ουγνω
23	ro · Coartor enim e	ριζω·συνεχομαι·δε·εκ των
	duobus desiderium habens	δυο·την·επιθυμîαν·εχων
	dissolvi·et cum xpo esse	το αναλυσαι·και·συν·χρω·ειναι·
24	multo magis melius·Perma	ποσω·μαλλον·κρισσον · Το·δε·
	nere autem incarne necessa	επιμενειν·εν·τη·σαρκι·αναγ
25	rium propter vos·et hoc	καιοταιρον·δι·υμασ·και·τουτο·
	confidens·scio quia manebo et	πεποιθωσ·οιδα·οτι·μενω·ϗ
	permanebo omnibus vobis ad	παραμενω·πασîν·υμιν·εισ·την·

---

[1] *τροπω.* [2] *καταγγελεται.* [3] *χαρησομαι.* [4] *παρρησια παση.* [5] *In marg.* contra **hereticos.**

I. υμων · προκοπην · και · χαραν ·	profectum vestrum · et gaudium
26 της · πιστεως · ἵνα · το · καυχη_	fidei · ut gratulatio
μα · ὑμων · περισσευη · εν · εμοι ·	vestra abundet · in me
εν · $\overline{χρω}$ · $\overline{ιυ}$ · δια · της · εμης · πα	in $\overline{xpo}$ $\overline{ihu}$ per meum adven
ρουσιας · παλιν · προς · υμας ·	tum iterum ad vos ·
27 Μονον · αξειως · το · ευαγγελι	Tantum digne evangeli
ο[1] · του · $\overline{χρυ}$ · πολειτευ_εσται[2] ·	o $\overline{xpi}$ conversamini
ἵνα ειτε · ελθων · και · ιδων ·	ut sive cum venero · et videro
υμας · ειτε · απων · ακουσωτα ·	vos · sive absens audiam
περι · υμων · οτι · στηκεται · εν ·	de vobis quia statis in
ενι · $\overline{πνι}$ · μια ψυχης · συναθ	uno $\overline{spu}$ · unanimes conlabo
λουντες · τη · πιστει · του · ευαγγε	rantes fidei evange
28 λιου · και · μη · πτυρομενοι ·	lii · et in nullo terre
εν · μηδενει · ὑπο · των · αντικει	amini ab adversari
μενων · η · τεις · εστιν · αυτοις ·	is · que est illis
ενδεξεις[3] · απωλειας · ημιν · δε ·	causa perdicionis · vobis autem
σωτηριας · και · τουτο · απο · $\overline{θυ}$ ·	salutis · et hoc a $\overline{do}$ ·
29 οτι · υμιν · εχαρισθη · υπερ · $\overline{χρυ}$ ·	quia vobis donatum est pro $\overline{xpo}$
ου · μονον · το · εις · αυτον · πιστευ	non solum ut in eo creda
ειν[4] · αλλα · και · το · υ_περ · αυτου ·	tis · sed etiam pro illo
30 πασχειν[5] · τον · αυτον · αγωνα ·	patiamini · Idem certamen
εχοντες · οιον · και · ιδεται · εν	habentes quale et vidistis in
εμοι · και · νυν · ακουεται · εν · εμοι	me · et nunc auditis de me ·
P. II. 1 Ειτεις · ουν · παρακλησις · εν · $\overline{χρω}$ ·	Si qua ergo consolatio in $\overline{xpo}$
ειτι · παραμυθειον · αγαπις[6] · ει	si quod solatium caritatis · si
τις · κοινωνια[7] · $\overline{πνς}$ · ειτις · σπλαν	qua societas $\overline{sps}$ · si qua viscera
2 χνα · και · οι · κτιρμοι · πληρω	miserationis · implete
σαται · μου · την · χαραν · Ἵνα · το	gaudium meum ut idem

[1] τω ευαγγελιω. [2] πολειτευεσθαι. [3] ενδειξεις. [4] — πιστευειν (*habet marg.*). [5] *In marg.* πασχα. [6] αγαπης. [7] *In marg.* αγανον.

Latin	Greek
CAP. II. sapiatis eandem	αυτο · φρονηται · την · αυτην ·
caritatem habentes · unanimes	αγαπην · εχοντεσ · συνψυχοι ·
v. 3 id ipsum sentientes · nihil per conten	το εν · φρονουντεσ · μηδεν · κα_
tionem aut inanem gloriam · sed	τερειθῖαν[1] · η · και_νοδυξῖαν[2] · αλ
in humilitate sensus superiores	λα · τη · ταπεινοφροσυνη · αλλη
sibi invicem arbitrantes	λουσ · ηγουμενοι · υπερεχο·τεσ[3] (ν. above)
4 non quæ sua sunt · singu	εαυτον[4] (ω above) · μη · τα · εαυτων · εκασ
li considerantes · Sed ea quæ	τοισ · κοπουντεσ (laborantes above) · αλλα · τα · των ·
5 aliorum · Hoc enim sentite	ετερων · τουτο · γαρ · φρονιται ·
in vobis quod et in xpo ihu ·	εν · υμιν · ο · και · εν · χρω ιυ
6 Qui cum in forma di esset	Οσ · εν · μορφη · θυ · ὑπαρχων[5] ·
non rapinam arbitratus est esse se	ουχ · αρπαγμων[6] · ηγησατο · ῖναι ·
7 aequalem do · Sed semet ipsum	ῖσσα · θω ⁚ αλλα · εαυτων[7] · εκαινω
exinanivit formam servi accipiens	σεν · μορφην · δουλου · λαβων ·
in similitudinem hominum	εν · υμοιμομ̣ατι (ω above) · ανδρωπων[8] ·
8 factus et habitu in	γενομενοσ · και · χσηματι[9] · ευ
ventus ut homo · humili	ρε_θεισ · ωσ · ανοσ · ετα_πεινω
avit se ipsum factus h'oboedi	σεν · εαυτων[10] · γενομενοσ · υπη
ens usque ad mortem mortem	κοσ · αχρι · θανατου · θανατου ·
9 autem crucis · Propter quod et ds il	δε ; σ_ταυρου · Διο · και · ο · θσ · αυ
lum exaltavit et donavit	τον · ὑπερ ὑψωσεν · και · εχα_
illi nomen quod est	ρισατο · αυτω · ονομα · εισ · το ·
10 super omne nomen · ut in no	υπερ · παν · ονομα · Ινα · εν · τω ·
mine ihu omne genu flectatur	ονοματι · ιυ · παν · γονυ · καμψη ·
cælestium · terrestrium · et	επουρανῖων · και · επιγῖων · ꙃ ·
11 infernorum · et omnis lin	καταχθονιων · και · πασα · γλωσ
gua confiteatur quia dns	σα[11] · εξομολ·γησεται[12] (ο. above) · οτι · κσ ·
ihc xpc in gloria est di patris ·	ιησ · εισ · δοξαν · θυ · πατροσ ·

[1] κατε_φ̇_ρειθῖαν. [2] *In marg.* σενοδοχια. [3] υπερεχοντεσ. [4] εαυτων *prim.* [5] *In marg.* ϙ ὑπαρχων. [6] αρπαγμον. [7] εαυτον. [8] ομοιμωματι ανθρωπον (ω above). [9] σχηματι. [10] εαυτον. [11] γλω.σα (σ. above). [12] εξομολογησεται.

Greek	Latin
II. 12 Ωστε · αγαπη · τοι · μȣ · καθωσ ·	Itaque kmi mei sicut
παντοτε · υπη_κȣσαται · μη ·	semper oboedistis non
ωσ · τη · παρȣσια[1] · μου · μονον ·	ut impresentia mei tantum · Sed
αλλα · πολλω · μαλλον · νυν · με	multo magis nunc ÷ in psentia mea
τα · φοβου · και · τρομȣ · την · έαυ	cum metu et tremore vestram
των · σωτηρίαν · κα_τεργαζεσθαι ·	salutem operamini ·
13 Θσ · γαρ · εστιν · οενεργων · εν ·	Ds est enim qui operatur in
υμιν · και · το · θελειν · και · το	vobis et velle et perfi
ενεργιν · υπερ · τησ · ευδοκίασ ·	cere · pro bona voluntate ·
14 Παντα · ποι_ειται · χωρισ · γογ	Omnia autem facite sine murmura
γισμων[2] · και · δια · λογισμων ·	tionibus · et hesitationibus
inreprehensibiles sin	
15 ινα · ητε · αμεμ_π_τοι · και · ακαι	ut sitis sine querela · et simpli
ceres inmaculati	
ραιοι · τεκνα · θυ · αμωμητα ·	ces · filii di sine rephensione
μεσον · γενεασ · σκολίασ · και ·	in medio nationis prave et
διεστραμ_μενησ[3] · εν · οισ · φαι	perverse · Inter quos lu
νεσθαι · ωσ · φωστηρεσ · εν · τω ·	cetis sicut luminaria in hoc
16 κοσμω · τουτω · λογον · ζωησ ·	mundo · Verbum vitae
επεχοντεσ · εισ καυχημα ·	continentes · ad gloriam
εμοι · εισ · ημερασ[4] · χρυ · οτι · ȣκ ·	meam in die xpi · quia non
εισ · και_νον · εδραμον · ουδε ·	In vacuum cucurri · Neque
17 εισ · καινον · εκοπειασα · αλλα ·	in vacuum laboravi · Sed
και · ει · σπεν_δομαι · επι · τη · θυ	et si immolor supra sacrifici
σια · και · λει_τουργία[5] · τησ · πιστε	um et obsequium fidei
ωσ · υμ[6] · χαιρω · και · συν	vestræ · gaudeo et con gratu
18 χαιρω · πασιν · υμιν · το · δαυτο ·	lor omnibus vobis · Id ipsum autem
και · υμισ · χαιρεται · κ · συν χαι	et vos gaudete et congrala
ραι_ται · μοι ·	mini mihi ·
19 Ελπιζω · δε, εν · χρω · ιηυ · τειμο	f Spero autem in dno ihu timo

[1] παρουσία. [2] γογγυσμων. [3] διέστραμμενησ.
[4] ημεραν. [5] λειτουγία. [6] υμων.

	Latin	Greek
CAP. II.	theum cito me mittere ad vos	θεον · ταχαιωσ · πεμ‿ψαι · ὔμιν ·
	ut et ego bono animo sim cognitis	cum cognovero ῑνα · κα̊γω · ευψυχω · γνουστα ·
v. 20	quæ circa vos sunt · Neminem enim habeo	de vobis περι ὔμων · Ουδενα · γαρ · εχω
	tam unanimem · q[1] tam sincera affec	εισοψυχον · οσ · τεισ · γνησιωσ
	tione pro vobis sollititus sit ·	τα · περι υμων · μεριμ‿νησι ·
21	Omnes enim quae sua sunt	Ου[1] · παντεσ γαρ · τα · εαυτων
22	quaerunt · Non quae i̅h̅u̅ x̅p̅i̅	ζητουσιν · ου · τα · ι̅υ̅ · χ̅ρ̅υ̅ · την ·
	Experimentum autem ejus cognoscite	δε · δο‿κει‿μην · αυτου · γινοσκεται[2] ·
	quo̅ sicut patri filius mecum	οτι · ωσ · πατρι · τεκνον · συνεμοι ·
	servivit in evangelio ·	εδουλευσεν · εισ · τω · ευαγγελιων[3] ·
23	hunc ergo spero mittere me	τουτον · μεν · ουν · ελπιζω · πεμ
	mox ut videro quae circa me sunt	ψαι · ωσ · αναφιδω · τα · περι εμαι ·
24	ex ipso · Confido autem in dn̅o	εξαυτησ · Πεποιθα · δε · ηͤν[4] · κ̅ω̅[5]
	quo̅ et ipse veniam ad vos cito,	οτι · ϗ · αυτωσ[6] · ελευσομαι · ταχαιωσ
25	Necessarium autem existimavi epa	Ανα καιον[7] · δε · ηγησαμην[8] · επα
	froditum frm̅ et cooperato	φροδῖτον · τον · αθελφον[9] · και · συν
	rem et commilitonem	εργον · και · συν‿στρατειωτην ·
	meum · Vestrum autem apostolum	μου · Ϋμων · δε · αποστολον ·
	et ministrum necessitatis mææ	και · λειτουργον · τησ · χριαν[10] · μου ·
26	mittere ad vos quo am quidem	πεψαι[11] · προσ υμασ · επι‿δη
	omnes vos desiderabat · et	επιπορθων[12] · ην · παντασ · υμασ · ϗ
	mestus erat · propterea quia audieratis	merebat αδημονων · Διοτι · ηκουσατυι ·
27	illum infirmari · Nam et infir	αυτον · ησθενη‿κεναι · και · γαρ ·
	matus est usque ad mor	prope ησθενησεν · παρα · πλησῖον · θανα
	tem · sed d̅s misertus est ejus ·	τω · αλλο θ̅σ̅ · ηλεησεν · αυτον ·
	Non solum autem ejus · Verum etiam	Ουκ · αυτον · δε · μονον · αλλα · και
	mei · ne tristiciam super tristitiam	εμαι · ῑνα · μη · λυπην · επιλυπην ·
28	haberem · Festinantius ego mi	εχω · Cπουδαιοτερον · δε · επεμ

---

[1] Οι. [2] γινωσκεται. [3] το ευαγγελιον. [4] εν. [5] *In marg.* ελευσισ περιελευσεως in evangelio graeco ◄ [6] αυτοσ. [7] Αναγκαιον. [8] ηγησαμεͪν. [9] αδελφον. [10] χριασ. [11] πεμψαι. [12] επιποθων.

L. ψα · αυτων[1] · ϊνα · ιδοντεσ · αυτον ·	si illum · Ut viso eo
παλιν · χαιρηται[2] · καγω · αλυπο	iterum gaudeatis et ego sine tristi
at vero	
29 τεροσω · Προσ · δε · εχεσθαι · ουν ·	tia sum · Excipite itaque
αυτον · ηη[3] κω · μετα · πασεσ[4] · χα	illum in dno cum omni gaudi
ρασ · και · τουσ · τοι ουτουσ · εν ·	o · et ejusmodi cum honore
30 τίμουσ · εχεται · οτι · δια · το	re habetote · Quo propter
εργον · χρυ · εωσ · θανατου · ηγ	opus xpi usque ad mortem ac
γεισεσ[5] · παρα_βολευ_σαμενοσ ·	cessit · tra dens
τη · ψυχη · αυτου · ϊνα · αναπλη	animam suam · Ut impleret
ρωση το · υμων · υστερημα · τησ ·	id quod vobis de erat
L. πρoσ · μαι · λιτουργιασ · το · λοιπον ·	erga meum obsequium · Decetero
αθελφοι[6] · μοι · χαιρεται · εν · κω ·	frs mei gaudete in dno
ταυτα · γραφειν · υμιν · εμοι · μεν ·	eadem vobis scribere mihi quidem
ουκ · οκνηρον · ϋμειν · δε · ασφα	non pigrum · vobis autem necessari
λεσ · Βλεπεται · τουσ · κυνασ ·	um · Videte canes
Βλπεται[7] · τουσ · κακουσ · εργα	videte malos operi
τασ · Βλεπεται[8] · την · κατα_τομην ·	os Videte concisionem
Ημεισ · γαρ · εσμεν · η · περι_τομη · οι	Nos enim sumus circum cisio · qui
πνι · θυ · λατρευοντεσ · ϗ · καυχω_	spu do servimus ; et gloria
μενοι · ηη[9] χρω · ιυ · και · ουκ · εν ·	mur in xpo ihu et non in car
σαρκι · πεποιθοτεσ · και · περ εγω ·	ne fidutiam habentes quanquam ego
εχων · πεποιθησειν · εν · σαρχι[10]	habeam confidentiam in carne ·
Ειτισ · δε · αλλωσ · δοκει · πεποι	Si quis autem alus videtur confide
θεναι · εν · σαρκι · εγω · μαλλων[11] ·	re in carne · Ego magis · circum
περιτομη · οκτα · ημεροσ · εκ	cisus octava die ex gene
γενουσ[12] · ιηλ · φυλησ · βενιαμην ·	re isrl detribu beniamin
εβραιοσ · εξεβραιων · κατα · τον	hebraeus ex hebraeis · secundum
νομον · φαρισαιωσ[13] · κατα · ζηλοσ ·	legem pharisæus · secundum emulationem

[1] αυτον prim. [2] χαρηται. [3] εν. [4] πασησ. [5] ηγγεισεν. [6] Αδελφοι. [7] Βλεπεται. [8] Βλεπετε. [9] εν. [10] σαρκι. [11] μαλλον. [12] γεγουσ. [13] φαρισαιοσ.

CAP. III.	persequens ecclesiam dī secundum	διωκων · εκκλησῖαν · θῡ · κατα ·
	justitiam quæ in lege est	δικαιοσυνην · την · εν · νομω ·
v. 7	conversatus sine querela · Sed	γενομενοσ · αμεμπτοσ · αλλι[1] · τι
	quae mihi fuerunt lucra hæc arbi	να · ην · μοὶ · κερδη · ταυτα · ηγη
8	tratus sum propter ihm̄ detrimenta ·	μαι · δια · τον · χρ̄ν · ζημιαν · αλ
	Verumtamen existimo omni	λαμεν · ουν · και · ηγȣμαι · παν
	a detrimentum esse propter eminen	τα · ζημιαν · ειναι · Δια · τȣ · περ
	tem scientiam ihu̅ xpi̅	εχον · τησ · γνοσεωσ[2] · χρ̄υ · ιῡ ·
	dni̅ mei · Propter quem omnia	τȣ κῡ μου · Διον · τα · παντα
	detrimentum feci · et arbitror ut	εξημει‿ωθην · και · ηγου‿μαι ·
	stercora · ut xpm̄ lucrifaciam	σκυβαλα · ῑνα · χρ̄ν · κερ‿δησω ·
9	et inveniar in illo non habens	και · ευρεθω · εν · αυτω · μη · εχων ·
	meam justiciam quae ex le	εμην · δικαιοσυνην · την · εκ
	ge est · Sed illam quae ex fide est	νομου · αλλα · την · δια · πιστεωσ ·
	xpi̅ quae ex do̅ justitia est	χρ̄υ · την · εκ θῡ · δικαιοσυνην ·
10	in fide ad cognoscendum il	επι · τη · πιστι · τȣ · γνωναι · αυ
	lum · et virtutem	τον · και την γυναμην[3] τησ
	resurrectionis ejus · et	αναστασεωσ[4] αυτου · και · την
	societatem passionum	κου‿νωνῖαν[5] · των · παθηματων ·
	illius configuratus	αυτου · συν φορτει‿ζομενοσ ·
11	morti ejus · Si quo modo	τω · θανατω · αυτου · Ειπωσ
	occurram ad resurrectionem	καταν‿τησω · εισ · την · εξαναστα‿
12	quæ est ex mortuis · Non qd̄	σιν · των · εκνεκρων · Ουκ[6] · οτι ·
	jam acceperim · aut jam justifi	ηδη · ελαβον · η · ηδη · δικαιω‿
	catus sum · aut jam perfectus sim ·	μαι[7] · η · ηδη · τετελειωμαι ·
	Sequor autem sicō prehendam a quo	Διωκω · δε · ει καταλαβω · εφω ·
	et cō prehensus sum ab ihu̅ xpo̅ ·	κατελημ‿φθην · υπο · χρ̄υ ·
13	Fr̄s ego me non arbitror	αθελφοι[8] · εγω εμαυτον · ȣλο

[1] Ά (– λλι). [2] γνωσεως. [3] δυναμην. [4] *In marg.* γυνθαρ. [5] κοινωνίαν. [6] Ουχ. [7] τετελειωμαι δικαιομαι. [8] Αδελφοι.

III 14	γει_ζομαι · κατ ι λη̣φοτα · εν · δε ·	comprehendisse · Unum autem
	τα · μεν · οπεισω · επιλαν_θανο	quae quidem retro sunt obli
	in ante μενοσ · εισ · δε · τα · εμπροσ_θεν ·	viscens · ad ea vero quæ priora sunt
	appetens secundum contemplationem απεκ_τει_νομενοσ · κατα · σκο	me extendens · ad destina
	I intentionem πον · διοκω[1] · επι · το · βραβιον · τησ ·	tum · persequor ad bravium
	ανω κλησεοσ[2] · εν · κω · ιυ · χρυ[3] ·	supernæ vocationis di in xpo ihu ·
15	Ο σοι · ουν · τελιοι · εν · χρω ιυ	Quicuque ergo per fecti ·
	τουτο · φρονωμεν · και · ειτι ·	hoc sentiamus · et si quid
	ετερωσ · φρονιται · και τουτο ·	aliter sapitis · et hoc vobis
16	ο θσ · υμιν αποκαλυψυει[4] · Πλην ·	ds revelat · Veru tamen
	εισ · οεφθασ_μεν · το · αυτο	ad quod pervenimus · ut idem
	φρονειν · τω · αυτω · συν · στοι	sapiamus · et in eadem permanea
17	χιν · Cυν · μει_μηται · μου · γι	mus regula · Imitatores mei
	νεσ_θαι · αθελφοι[5] · και · σκοπει	estote fratres et observate
	ται · Τουσ · ουτω · περιπα_τουν	eos qui ita ambulant
	τασ · καθωσ · εχεται · τυπον ·	sicut habetis formam
18	ημασ · Πολλοι · γαρ · περιπα_τουσιν ·	nostram · Multi enim ambulant
	ουσ · πολλα κισ · ελεγον · υμιν ·	quos sepe dicebam vobis ·
	Νυν · δε · και · κλαιων · λεγω · τουσ ·	Nunc autem et flens dico inimi
	εκθρουσ · του · σταυρου · του · χρυ ·	cos crucis xpi ·
19	Ων · το · τελοσ · απωλια · ων · οθσ · η ·	Quorum finis interitus · quorum ds
	κοιλια · και · η · δοξα · εν · τη · αισχυ	venter est · et gloria in c fusione
	νη · αυτων · οι · τα · επι_για · φρονουν	ipsorum qui terrena sapiunt ·
20	τεσ · ημων · γαρ · το · πολιτευμα	nostra autem conversatio
	εν · ουρανοισ · υπαρχει · εξου · και ·	in cælis est · Unde etiam
	σωτερα[6] · απεκ_δεχομεθα · κν ·	savatorem expectamus dnm nrum
21	ιν · χρν · οσ · μετα σχεματισει[7] ·	ihm xpm · qui reformavit
	το, σομα[8] · τησ · ταπινωσεωσ · ημων	corpus humilitatis nostrae

---

[1] διωκω. [2] κλησεωσ. [3] χρω. [4] Αποκαλυψει. [5] αδελφοι. [6] σωτηρα. [7] μετασχηματισει. [8] σωμα.

	Latin		Greek
CAP. III.	configuratum corpori clari		συν μορφον · τȣ · σωματοσ · τησ ·
	tatis suae · secundum opera		δοξησ · αυτου · κατα · την · ενερ
	tionem qua possit etiam		γίαν · του · δυνασθαι · αυτον · ϗ
	subicere sibi omnia ·		υποταξαι · αυτω · τα · παντα ·
CAP. IV. V. 1	Itaque frs mei carissimi		Ωστε · αθελφοί[1] · μου · αγαπη_τοι ·
	et desiderantissimi · Gaudium meum		και επι ποθητοι · χαρισ και στε
	et corona mea · sic sta		φανοσ μου · και ουτοσ[2] στη
	te in dno carissimi		κεται εν κω αγαπιτοι[3]
2	Euhodiam rogo · et sin		Ευοδίαν παρακαλω · και · συν
	tychem deprecor · id ipsum sape		τυχεν[4] · παρα καλω · το αυτο · φρο
3	re in dno · Etiam rogo et te		νειν · εν · κω · Ναι · ερωτω · και · σε ·
	germane compar		εγνη_σιε · γερμανε · συνζυγαι[5] ·
	adjuva illos · qui mecum		συν λαμβανȣ · αυταισ · αιτινεσ ·
	laboraverunt in evangelio		εν · τω · ευαγγελιω · συνηθλεσαν[6] ·
	cum clemente et		μοι[7] · μετα · κλημεντοσ · και ·
	ceteris adjutoribus meis		των · λοιπων · συν_εργων · μου ·
	quorum nomina sunt in libro vitæ ·		ων · τα · ονοματα · εν · βιβλω · ζωησ ·
g 4	Gaudete in dno semper iterum	χ	Χαιρεται · εν κω · παντοτε · παλίν ·
5	dico gaudete · modestia vestra		ερω · χαιρεται · το · επι_εικεσ · ὑμων ·
	nota sit omnibus hominibus		γνοσ_θητω[8] · πασιν · ανθρωποισ ·
6	dns prope est · Nihil solliciti		ο κσ · εγγυσ · Μηδεν · μεριμνα
	sitis sed in omni oratione		τε · αλλεν · παντι · τη · προσευ
	et obsecratione cum gratia		χη · και · τηδεησι · ματα[9] · ευχα
	rum actione petitiones vestræ		ριστίασ · τα · αι_τηματα · υμων ·
7	innotescant aput dm · et		γνοριζεσθω[10] · προσ · των[11] · θν · και
	pax di quae exuperat		η · ϊρηνη · τȣ · θυ · η · υπερ_εχουσα ·
	omnem sensum custodiat cor		παντα · νουν · φρουρησει · τασ ·
	da vestra · et intellegentias		καρδιασ · υμων · ϗ · τα · σωματα ·

[1] αδελφοι. [2] ουτωσ. [3] αγαπητοι. [4] συντυχην. [5] συνσζυγαι. [6] σύνηθλησαν s. m. at συνηθλησαν p. m. [7] μουι. [8] Γνωσθητω. [9] Μετα. [10] γνωριζεσθω. [11] τον.

Greek	Latin
εγερθηται[1] · δια · τησ · πιστεωσ ·	rexistis per fidem
τησ · ενεργίασ · του · θυ · του εγι	operationis di̅ qui susci
ραντοσ · αυτον · εκ · των · νεκρων ·	tavit illum a mortuis ·
3 Και · ϋμαὸσ · νεκρουσ · οντασ · εν ·	Et vos cum mortui essetis in
τοισ · παραπτωμασιν · και · εν ·	delictis et
τη · ακροβυστια · τησ · σαρκοσ ·	pre putio carnis
υμων · εξω‿οποι‿ησεν[2] · συν αυ	vestræ convivicavit cum
τω · χαρι‿σαμενοσ · ημιν · παν	illo · donans vobis omnia
14 τα · τα · παραπ‿τοματοσ[3] · εξα	delicta de
λει‿ψασ · το · κα‿θημων · χει	lens q̅d adversum nos erat
ρογραφον · τοισ · δ̑ογμασῖν ·	chirografum · decreti
ο · ην · ϋπεναντιον · ημιν · και	quod erat contrarium nobis et
αυτο · ηρεν · εκ · του · μεσȣ · προσ	ipsum tulit demedio af
15 ηλωσασ · αυτο · τω · σταυρω · απεκ	figens illut cruci · expo
δ̑υσαμενοσ · την · σαρκα · τασ ·	lians principatus
εξουσιασ · εδιγματισεν · εν · παρ	et potestates · traduxit confi
ρησια · θριαμ‿βευσασ · αυτουσ ·	denter · palam triumphans illos
16 εν · αυτω[4] · Μη ; ουν · τισ · ϋμασ ·	in semet ipso · Nemo ergo vos
κρι‿νετω · εν · βροσι[5] · η · εν · ποσι ·	judicet in cibo aut potu aut
η · εν · μερι εορτησ · η · νεομη	in parte diei festi · aut neome
17 νία η ; σαββατω · ο · εστιν ·	niae · au̅t sabbatorum quae sunt
σκία · των · μελλοντων · το · δε ·	umbra futurorum corpus
18 σωμα · χ̅ρ̅υ̅ · Μηδεισ · ϋμασ · κα	a̅u̅t x̅p̅i̅ · Nemo vos se
τα · βραβευτω · θελων · εν · τα	ducat · volens in hu
πεινο‿φροσυνη · ϗ · θρησ‿κῖα[6] ·	militate · et religione
των · αγγελων · α · ουκ · εωρα	angelorum · quae non vi
(sine causa) κεν · εν · βατευων · εικη · φυ	dit · ambulans frustra in
σει‿ουμενοσ · υπο · του · νοοσ ·	flatus sensu

[1] συνεγερθητε. [2] Εζωοποιησεν. [3] παραπτωματα. [4] εαυτω. [5] βρωσι.

[6] *In marg. ad* θρησκῖα *habet* visionis umbra. Vid. Matthæi ad locum.

	Latin	Greek
CAP. II. v. 19	carnis suae · et non	τησ · σαρκοσ · αυτου · και · ου
	tenens caput ex quo	κρατων · την · κεφαλην · εξου
	totum corpus per ne	παντο · σωμα · δια · των_αφι
	xum et conjunctionē	ων[1] · και · συν δεσ_μων[2] ·
	sub ministra tum et con	επιχυρη_γουμενον · και · συν
	structum crescit in au	βειβαζομενον · αυξει · την · αυ
	gmentum di	ξησιν[3] · του · θυ
20	Si mortui estis cum xpo ab	Ει · απεθανεται · συν · χρω · απο ·
	elementis mundi hujus	των · στοιχιων · του · κοσ_μου ·
	quid adhuc quasi viventes	τι · παλιν · ωσ · ζωντεσ · εν · τω ·
21	in mundo decernitis · ne tetige	κοσμω · δογματιζεσθαι · μη ·
	ritis neque gustaveritis neque con	αψη · μηδε · γευση · μηδε ·
22	trectaveritis · quæ sunt omnia	θειγησ · α · εστιν · παντα ·
	in interitu ipso usu	εισ · φθεοραν[4] · τη · αποχρησι ·
	secundum precepta et doctri	κατα · τα · εν · ταλματα · και · δι
	nas hominum	δασκαλ · ἑασ[5] · των · αν_ων ·
23	quæ sunt rationem quidem	ατινα · εστιν · λογον · μεν · εχον_
	habentia sapientiæ in superstitione	τα · σοφιασ · εν · θρεσκια[6] · και ·
	et humilitate sensus et ∫re	ταπι_νοφροσυνη · του · νοοσ · και ·
	ad non parcendum corpori · non in hono	αφιδια · σωματοσ · ουκ · εν · τιμη ·
	aliquo · ad saturitatem car	τινι · προσ · πλησμονην · τησ · σαρ
CAP. III. 1	nis · Igitur sicut resurrexistis	κοσ · Ει · ουν · συνη_γερ_θητε ·
	cum xpo quæ sursum sunt querite	τω · χρω · τα · ανω_ζητει_τε ·
	ubi xpc est · in dextera	που · ο · χρσ · εστιν · εν · δεξια ·
2	di sedens · Quæ sursum sunt	τȣ · θυ · καθημενοσ · α · ανω
	sapite · non quæ super	φρονειται · μεγα[7] · επι · τησ ·
3	terram · Mortui enim estis · et	γησ · Απεθανεται · γαρ · και · η ·
	vita vestra abscondita est cum_ IΓ	ζωη · ὑμων · κεκρυπται · συν_

[1] αφων. [2] συνδεσμον. [3] αυξεισιν (η above). [4] φθοραν. [5] διδασκαλείασ. [6] θρησκια. [7] μη τα.

II. 4 τω · χρω · εν · τω · θω · Οταν · ο · χρσ ·	xpo in do · Cum xpc
φανερωθη · ϗ · η · ξωη[1] · υμων ·	aparuerit vita vestra
τοτε · και · υμεισ · συν · αυτω ·	tunc et vos aparebitis
φανερωθησεσ‿θαι · εν · δοξη ·	cum ipso ingloria ·
5 Νεκρωσαται · ουν · τα · μελη ·	Mortificate ergo membra
υμων · τα · επι · τησ · γησ · Πορ	vestra quæ sunt super terram · Fornica
νίαν · ακαθαρσîαν · πλεονε	tionem · inmunditiam · avaritiam ·
ξίαν · παθοσ · επθυμîαν[2] ·	libidinem · concupiscentiam malam
ητεισ · εστιν · ïδω‿λατρια ·	quæ est simulacrorum servitus ·
6 Διο ερχεται · οργη · του · θυ ·	Propter quæ venit ira di ·
επι · τουσ · ϋιουσ · τησ · απιθîασ ·	super filios incredulitatis ·
7 εν · οισ · ϗ · ϋμεισ · περι‿επατησατε ·	in quibus et vos ambulastis
ποτε · οτε · εζητε · εν ·	aliquando · cum viveritis in
8 αυτουσ[3] · Νυν · ειδε · αποθεσ	illis · Nunc autem deponite
θαι · και · υμεισ · κατα · παντα ·	et vos secundum omnia
οργην · θυμον · κακîαν[4] ·	iram · indignationem · malitiam ·
βλασ‿φημîαν · αισ‿χρο‿λογιαν ·	blasphemiam · turpem sermonem ·
εκ · του · στοματοσ · ὐμων ·	de ore vestro
9 μη · εκπο‿ρευ‿εσθω · μη ·	ne emiseritis · Nolite
ψευδεσθαι · εισ αλλη‿λουσ ·	mentiri invicem
απεκδυσαμενοι · τον · παλα	expoliantes vos vete
ιον · ανον · συν · ταισ · παξεσιν[5] ·	rem hominem cum actibus
10 αυτου · ϗ · εν · δυσαμενοι · τον ·	suis · et induentes
νεον · τον · ανακαι‿νου‿με‿νον ·	novum · eum qui renovatur
εισ · επιγωσιν[6] · κατï‿κονα · αυτου ·	in agnitionem secundum imaginem ejus
11 του · κτεισαντοσ · αυτυν · Οπου ·	qui creavit eum · Ubi
ουκ · ενιαρσεν · και θηλυ[7] · ελ	non est masculus et femina genti
λην · και · ïου‿δαιοσ · περι‿τομη ·	lis et judeus circum cisio

[1] ζωη. [2] Επιθυμîαν. [3] αυτοισ. [4] κακααν? *p.m.* [5] πραξεσιν. [6] επιγνωσιν. [7] θηλὴυ.

	Latin	Greek
CAP. III.	et præputium · barbarus et	και ακροπυστια[1] · βαρβαροσ · και ·
	scytha servus et li	σκυθησ · δουλοσ · και · ελευτε_
	ber sed omnia et in	ροσ[2] · αλλα · τα · παντα · και · εν ·
	omnibus xpc ;	πασιν · χρσ ·
v. 12	Induite ergo vos sicut ele	Εν · δυσασθαι · ουν · ωσ · ει · εκ λε
	cti di · sancti et dile	κτοι[3] · θυ · αγιοι · και · ηγαπη
	cti viscera misericor di	μενοι · σπλανχναοι κτειρ
	ae · Benignitatem humili	μου · χρηστοτητα · τα_πεινο
	tatem modestiam · patien	φροσυνην · πραοτητα · Μα
13	tiam sub portantes	κρο_θυμιαν · ανεχο_μενοι ·
	invicem · et donantes vobismet	αλληλον[4] · και · χαρι_ξομενοι ·
	ipsis · si quis adversus aliquem	εαυτουσ[5] · εαν · τισ · προστινα ·
	habet quærelam · sicut et dns	εχει · οργην · καθοσ[6] · και · κσ[7] ·
	donavit vobis ita et	εχαρισα_το · υμιν · ουτοσ[8] · και ·
14	vos · Super omnia	υμεισ · (facite) ποιειτε · Επι · πασιν ·
	autem hæc caritatem	δε · του_τοισ · την · αγαπην ·
	quod est vinculum	ο, εστιν · συνδεσμοσ · τησ ·
15	per fectionis · et pax xpi ex	(unitatis) ενοτητοσ · και · ϊρηνη · του · χρυ · βρ=
	ultet in cordibus vestris ·	βευ · τω[9] · εν · ταισ · καρδειαισ · υμων ·
	In qua et vocati estis in uno	Εισ · εν[10] · και · εκληθεται[11] · εν · ενί ·
	corpore et grati esto	σωματι · και · ευχαριστοι · γινεσ_
16	te · verbum xpi habit	θαι · ο · λογοσ · του · χρυ · ενοι_και_
	tet in vobis abundanter in	το[12] · εν · υμιν · πλου_σειοσ[13] · εν ·
	omni sapientia docentes et	πασε : [14] σοφία · δικασ_κοντεσ · και -
	commonentes vosmet ipsos psal	νου_θετουντεσ · εαυτουσ · ψαλ
	mis Ymnis canticis spirita	μοισ · ϋμνοισ · ωδεσ · πνευματι
	libus in gratia cantantes	κοισ[15] · εν · τη · χαρριτι · αδοντεσ ·
	in cordibus vestris do	εν · ταισ · καρδιαισ · υμων · τω · θω ·

---

1 ακροβυστια. 2 ελευθεροσ. 3 εκλεκτοι. 4 Αλληλων. 5 χαριζομενοι εαυτοισ. 6 Καθωσ 7 + ο (ante κσ).
8 Ουτωσ. 9 βραβευετω. 10 ην. 11 εκληθηται. 12 ενοικειτω. 13 Πλουσειωσ. 14 παση. 15 πνευματικαισ.

III. v. 17	Παν·οτι·εαν·ποι_ηται[1]·εν·λογο[2]·	Omne quodcumque facitis in verbo
	η·ενεργω·παντα·εν; ονο	aut in opere · omnia in nomi
	ματι·ιηυ·χρυ·ευχαριστουν	ne dni ihu gratias agen
	τεσ·τω·θω·και·πατρι·διαυτου·	tes do · et patri per ipsum;
18	Γυνεκεσ·υποτασεσθαι·τοισ·	Mulieres subditae estote
	αν δρασιν·υμον[3]·ωσ·ανηκεν·	viris vestris sicut oportet
19	εν·το[4]·κω · Ο[5]·ανδρεσ·αγα	in dno · Viri diligite
	παται·τασ·γυναικασ·υμων·	uxores vestras
	και·μη·πικρενεσται·προσαιτασ[6]·	et nolite amari esse ad illas
20	Τα·τεκνα·υπα κουεται·τοισ·	Filii obedite
	γονευσιν·κατα·παντα·τουτο·	parentibus per omnia · Hoc
	γαρ·εστιν·ευαρεστον·εν·κω·	enim placitum est in dno
21	Οι·πατερεσ·μη·παροργιζεται·	Parentes nolite ad indignatio
	τα·τεκνα·υμων· [7]	nem provocare filios vestros
22	ινα·μη·αθυμοσιν[8]·Οι·δουλοι[9]·	ut non pusillo animo fiant · Servi
	υπα_κου_εται·κατα·παντα·	oboedite per omnia
	τοισ·κυριοισ·κατα·σαρκα·μη·	dominis carnalibus · non
	εν·οφθαλμον·δουλια[10]·ωσ·	ad locum servientes quasi
	ανδροπω·παρεσ_κοι[11]·αλλεν·α	hominibus servientes sed in sim
	πλοτετι[12]·καρδιασ·φοβουμενοι·	plicitate cordis timentes
23	τον·κν · Ο αν·ποιηται·εκ·ψυ	dnm · Quodcuque facitis ex ani
	χησ·εργαζεσθαι·ωσ·τω·κω·	mo operamini sicut dno
24	και·ουκ·ανθρωποισ·ειδοτεσ·	et non hominibus · Scientes
	οτι·απο·κυ·απολημ_ψεσθαι·	quod a dno accipietis
	retributionem	
	την·ανταποδοσιν·τησ·κλη	mercedem heredi
	ρονομιασ·του·κυ·ημων·ιυ·	tatis dni nri ihu
25	χυ·ω·δουλευτε·ο·γαρ·α	xpi cui servitis · Qui enim inju
	δικων·κομιζε_ται·ο[13]·	riam facit recipiet id qd ini

[1] ποιεται. [2] λογω. [3] υμων. [4] τω. [5] Ω (*pro* Ο). [6] πικρενεσθαι προσ αυτασ. [7] *Simile spatium.* [8] αθυμωσιν. [9] δολοι. [10] οφθαλμοδουλια. [11] ανθρωπαρεσκοι. [12] απλοτητι. [13] *In marg.* Μαρ.

	Latin	Greek
CAP. III.	que gessit et non est per so	ηδικησεν · και · ουκ · εστιν · προ
	narum acceptio aput dm	σοπο · λημψία[1] · παρα · τω · θω ·
CAP. IV. v. 1	Dni quod justum est et	Ω · κυριοι · το · δικαιον · και · την ·
	æquum · servis presta	ισσοτητα[2] τοισ τουλοισ[3] · παρε
	te scientes quod et vos	χεσθαι · ειδοτεσ · οτι · και · υμεισ ·
	dnm habetis in cælis ·	εχεται · κν · εν · ουρανοισ ·
2	Orationi instate	Η · προσευχη · προσ καρτερι ται ·
	vigilantes in ea in gratiarum	γρηγορουντεσ · εν · αυτη · εν
3	actione · Orantes	ευχαριστία · Προσευχομενοι ·
	simul et pro nobis ut ds	αμα · και · περι · ημων · ἵνα · οθσ ·
	aperiat nobis ostium sermonis	ανοιξη · ημιν · θυραν · λογου ·
	ad loquendum mysterium xpi ·	λαλησε · το · μυστηριον · του · χρυ ·
4	propter qd et junctus sum ut mani	δι · ον · και · δεδεμαι · ἵνα · φανε
	festem illud ita ut oportet me	ρωσω · αυτο · ωσδει μαι · λα
5	loqui · In sapientia ambulate	λησαι · εν · σοφια · περιπατειται ·
	ad eos qui foris sunt tempus redi	προσ · τουσ · εξο[4] · τον · καιρον · εξα
6	mentes · Sermo vester	γορα ζομενοι · Ο · λογοσ · υμων ·
	semper in gratia sale sit condi	παντοτε · εν · χαριτι · αλατι · ηρ
	tus ut sciatis qmodo oporteat vos	τυμενοσ · ιδεναι · πωσ · δει · υμασ ·
	unicuique respondere	ενειε καστω · αποκρινεσθαι ·
7	Quæ circa me sunt omnia nota faciet	Τα · κατε · μαι · παντα · γυνωρισει[5] ·
	vobis tichicus carissimus fra	μιν · τυχικοσ · ο · αγαπητοσ · αδελ
	ter et fidelis minister et	φοσ · και · πιστοσ · διακονοσ · και ·
8	conservus in dno quem misi	σινδυλοσ[6] · εν · κω · ον · επεμ ψα ·
	ad vos · ad hoc ipsum ut	προσ · υμασ · εισ · αυτο · τουτο · ἵνα
	cognoscat quæ circa vos sunt et console	γνοται[7] · τα · περι · ημων · και · παρα
9	tur corda vestra cum	καλεση · τασ · καρδιασ · ϋμων · συν ·
	onesimo carissimo et fide	ονεσιμω[8] · τω · αγαπετω[9] · και πισ

[1] προσωπολημψία. [2] ἴσσοτηρα. [3] δουλοισ. [4] εξω. [5] γνωρισει. [6] συνδουλοσ. [7] γνωται. [8] ονησιμω. [9] αγαπητω.

P. IV.	τω·αδελφω·οσ·εστιν·εξυμων·	li fratre qui est ex vobis·
	Παντα·ὑμιν·γνω‿ρεισουσειν[1]·τα·	Omnia vobis nota facient quae
v. 10	ω·δε·πραγτομενα·ασπαζεται·	hic aguntur · Salutat
	υμασ·αρισταρχοσ·οσιν·αιχμα	vos aristarchus concapti
	λωτοσ[2]·μου·και·μαρκοσ·οανε	vus meus et marchus consobri
	ψιοσ·βαρναβα·περιου·ελαβετε·	nus barnabae de quo accepistis
	εντολασ·εαν·ελθε[3]·προσ·ὑμασ·	mandata · Si venerit ad vos
11	δεξασθαι·αυτον·και·ϊησουσ·ο·	excipite illum · et iesus qui
	λεγομενοσ·ιουστοσ·οι·οντεσ·	dicitur iustus · qui sunt
	εκπεριτομεσ[4]·ουτοι·μονοι·συν	ex circumcisione · Hi soli sunt
	εργοιμου·εισιν·εισ·την·βασιλι	adjutores mei · in regno
	αν·του·θυ · Οιτινεσ·εγενηθη	di qui mihi fuerunt
12	σαν·μοι·παρηγορια·Ασπα‿ζεται·	solatio · Salutat
	υμασ·επαφρασ·ο·εξ ὑμον[5]·	vos epaphras qui ex vobis est
	δουλοσ·χρυ·παντοτε·γονι	servus xpi · semper sollici
	ζομενοσ[6]·περι·υμων εν·ταισ	tus pro vobis in
	προσευχαισ·ϊνα·στητε·τελει	orationibus ut stetis perfecti
	οι·και·πεπληρο‿φορημενοι·εν·	et pleni in
13	παντι·θεληματι·του·θυ · Μαρτι	voluntate di · Testimoni
	ρω[7]·γαρ·αυτω·οτι·εχει·πολυν[8]	um enim illi perhibeo qd habeat multum
	κοπον·ὑπερ·ὑμων·και·των·	laborem pro vobis et pro his qui sunt
	εν·λαοδικια·και·των·εν·ϊε	in laodicia et qui ie
14	ραπ·λι[9]·Ασπαζεται·υμασ·λου	rapoli · Salutat vos lu
	κασ·ο·ϊατροσ·ο·αγαπετοσ[10]·και·	cas medicus carissimus et
15	δημασ · Ασπαζεσται[11]·τουσ·εν·	demas · Salutate frs qui sunt
	λαοδικια·αδηλφουσ[12]·και·νυμ	laodiciæ · et nympham
	φαν·και·την·οι·κατοικον·αυτου·	et quæ in domo ejus est
16	εκκλησιαν·και·οταν·ανα	ecclesiam · et cum le

[1] γνωρισουσειν. [2] ο. συν αιχμαλωτοσ. [3] ελθη. [4] περιτομησ. [5] ὑμων. [6] γωνιζομενοσ s.m. seu p.m. ex correctione. [7] Μαρτυρω. [8] πολυν. [9] ϊεραπολι. [10] αγαπητοσ. [11] Ασπαζε.ται (σ above). [12] αδελφουσ.

CAP. IV. cta fuerit apud vos epistola
facite ut et in laodicen
sium ecclesia lega
tur · et eam quæ laodicensium est
v. 17 vos legatis et dici
te archippo · Vide
ministerium qd accepisti in
18 dno ut illut impleas · Salu
tatio mea manu pauli
Memores estote vinculo
rum meorum · Gratia vobiscum ·

EXPLICIT AD COLOSENSES

Incipit ad thesalo nicenses ·

CAP. I. 1 **Paulus et silbanus ·**
et timotheus · ecclesiæ
thessalonicensium in do patre
et dno ihu χρω gratia vobis et
2 pax · Gratias agimus do
semper pro omnibus vobis · memo
riam vri facientes in orati
3 onibus vestris · sine intermissione
memores operis
fidei vestri · et laboris · et
caritatis · et sustinentiae

γνωσ‿θη · παρ · ϋμυν[1] · η · επιστολη ·
ποι‿ησαται · ϊνα · και · εν · των · λαο
δικαιων · εκκλησία · ανα‿γνωσ
θη · και · την · εν · λαοδικίασ · και ·
ϊνα · υμεισ · ανα‿γνωται · και · ει
πατε · αρχιππω · Βλεπεται[2] · την ·
διακονίαν · ην · παρηλαβεσ[3] · εν ·
κω · ϊνα · αυτην · πληροισ · ο · ασ
πασ‿μοσ · τη · εμη, χειρι · παυλου ·
Μνημον · ευεται · μου · τον[4] · δεσ‿
μων · Χαρισ · μεθυ μων ·

Ετελεστη[5] · προσ · κολοσσαεισ ;

Αρχεται προσ θεσσα λονικαιουσ προτη[6].

Παυλοσ · και σιά βανοσ[7] ·
και · τιμωθεοσ[8] · τη · εκκλησία
θεσσαλνικαιον · ην[9] · θω · πατρι
κ͵ · κω · ιυ · χρω · χαρισ · Ϋμιν · και ·
ϊρηνη · Ευχαρισ · τοΥμεν[10] · τω · θω
·περι·[11]
παντοτε · παντων · υμων · μνί
αν · υμων · ποι‿ȣμενοι · επι · των ·
προσευχων · ημων · αδια‿λιπτωσ ·
μνημονευοντεσ · το · εργον · τησ ·
πιστεωσ · υμων · και · τον · κοπον ·
τησ · αγαπησ · και · την · ϋπομονην ·

---

[1] ϋ'μιν. [2] Βλεσ̣πεται. [3] παρελαβεσ. [4] των. [5] Ετελεσθη. [6] Ā Πρωτη επιστολη. [7] σιλβανοσ. [8] τιμοθεοσ. [9] Θεσσαλονικαιων εν. [10] Ευχαρειστουμεν. [11] περι in textu.

P. I.	της ελπιδοσ · του · κυ · ημων · ιυ · χρυ ·	spei dni nri ihu xpi
	εμπροσθην[1] · του · θυ · και πατροσ ·	ante dm et patrem
v. 4	ημων · Ειδοτεσ · αδελφοι · ηγα	nrm · Scientes fratres di
	πηνενοι · υπο · θυ · την · εκλοτην[2] ·	lecti a do electio nem
	υμων · οτι · το · ευαγγελιον · ημων ·	vestram · quia evvangelium nostrum
	ουκ · εγενηθη · προσ · υμασ · ην[3] · λογω ·	non fuit ad vos in sermo
	μονον · αλλα · και · ην[4] · δυναμει ·	ne tantum · sed in virtute
	και · ην[5] · πνι · αγιω · και · ην[5] · πληρο	et in spu sco et inplenitu
	φορια · πολλε · καθοσ[6] · οιδαται ·	dine multa · sicut scitis
	οιοι · εγενη_θημεν · εν · υμιν · δι	quales fuerimus · in vobis propter
6	υμασ · και · υμεισ · μι_μηται ·	vos · Et vos imitatores
	ημων · εγενηθηται · και · του · κυ ·	nri facti estis et dmi ·
	δεξαμενου[7] · τον · λογον · εν · θλι	excipientes verbum in tribula
	ψι · πολλη · μετα · χαρασ · πνσ · αγιου ·	tione multa cum gaudio sps sci
7	ωστε · γενεσθαι · υμασ · τυπουσ ·	ita ut facti sitis forma
	πασιν · τοισ · πιστευουσιν · ην[8] · τη ·	omnibus credentibus in
	μακαιδονια · και · ην · τε · αχαγια[9] ·	machedonia et in achaia ·
8	Αφυμων · γαρ · εξη_χηται · ο · λογοσ ·	A vobis enim diffamatus est sermo
	του · κυ · ου · μονον · εν[10] · τη · μακαιδο	dni · non solum in macedo
	να · και · ην[11] · τη · αχαγια · αλλην[12] ·	nia et inachia · sed in
	παντι · τοπω · η · πιστισ · υμων ·	omni loco fides vestra quæ est ·
	η · προσ · τον · θν · εξε_λελυθεν[13] ·	ad dm perfecta est ·
	ωσ - τε · μη · χριαν · εχειν · ημασ · λα	ita ut non sit nobis necesse quic
9	λειν · τι · Αυτου[14] · γαρ · πηρι[15] · ημων ·	quam loqui · Ipsi enim de nobis
	απ αγγελουσιν · ο̄ · ποιαν · εισοδον ·	adnuntiant · qualem introitum
	εσχομεν · προσ · υμασ · και · πωσ	habuerimus ad vos · et quomodo
	επισ_τρεψαται · προσ · τον · θν · απω[16] ·	conversi estis ad dm a
	των · ιδολων[17] · δουλευ_ειν · θω ·	simulacris · servire do

[1] εμπροσθεν. [2] ηγαπημενοι υπο Θυ Την εκλογην. [3] εν. [4] εν. [5] εν bis. [6] πολλη. Καθωσ. [7] Δεξαμενοι. [8] εν. [9] τη αχαϊα. [10] εν. [11] εν. [12] αχαϊα. Αλλεν. [13] εξεληλυθεν. [14] Αυτοι. [15] περι. [16] Απο. [17] των. ιδωλων.

CAP. I. v. 10	vivo et vero·et expecta	ζωντι·και·αλεθινω[1]·και·ανα
	re filium ejus de	μενεισ[2]·τον·υιον·αυτου·εκ·
	cælis quem suscitavit ex mor	των·ουρανον[3]·ον·ηγιρεσ[4]·εκ·
	tuis ihm qui eripu	των·νεκρον[5]·ιν·τον·ρυομε
	it nos ab ira	νον·ημασ·απο·τεσ[6]·οργησ·τησ·
CAP. II. 1	ventura · Nam ipsi scitis	ερχομενεσ[7]·αυτοι·γαρ·οιδαται·
	frs·introitum nostrum	αδελφοι·την·εισοδον·ημων·
	ad vos·quia non inanis	προσ·υμασ·οτι·ουκ·ενη·
2	fuit·sed ante passi et	γεγονεν·Αλλα·προπαθοντεσ·
	contumeliis afflicti·scitis	και·ϋβρεισ‿θεντεσ·καθωσ·
	scitis in philippis·	οιδαται·ην[8] φιλιπποισ·
	fidutiam habuimus in do	επαρεσειασ·αμεθα·ην·το[9]·θω·
	nostro loqui ad vos·	ημων·λαλεσαι[10] προσ·υμασ·
	evvangelium di in multa	το·ευαγγελιον·του·θυ·εν·πολλω
3	sollititudine · Exortatio enim	αγωνε[11] · Η·γαρ·παρα‿κλησεισ—
	nostra·non de errore·neque de	ημων·ουκ·εκπλανησ·ουδε·
	inmunditia·neque in dolo·	εξακαθαρσιασ·ουδε·ην[12]·δολω·
4	sed sicut probati sumus	αλλα·καθοσ[13]·δεδο·κειμασ‿μενοι
	a do·ut crederetur nobis evvan	απο·τυ·θυ[14]·πιστευ‿θηναι·
	gelium · ita loquimur·	το·ευαγγελιον·ȣτοσ[15]·λαλȣμεν—
	Non quasi hominibus placentes	ουχ·ωσ·ανοισ·αρεσ‿κοντεσ·
	sed do qui probat	αλλα·το·θω[16]·τω·δοκιμα‿ζοντι—
5	corda nostra · Neque enim	τασ·καρδιασ·ημων · Ουγε[17]·γαρ
	aliquando fuimus in sermone	ποτε·ην[18]λογω·κολακίασ·εγεν‿
	adolâtionis sicut scitis·neque	ηθημεν·καθωσ·οιδατε·ουτε·
	in occasione avaritiæ·ds	εν·προ‿φασι·πλεονε‿ξίαν[19]·ο·θ
6	testis est · Nec querentes ab	μαρτυσ · Ουτε·ζητουντεσ·εξ
	hominibus gloriam neque a	ανθροπων[20]·δοξαν·ουτε·αφ

---

1 αληθινω. 2 αναμενειν. 3 ουρανων. 4 ηγιρεν. 5 νεκρων. 6 τησ. 7 ερχομενησ. 8 εν. 9 επαρησειασαμεθα εν τω. 10 Λαλησαι. 11 αγωνει. 12 εν. 13 καθωσ. 14 ϋπο του Θυ. 15 Ουτωσ. 16 τω θω. 17 Ουτε. 18 εν. 19 πλεονεξίασ. 20 ανθρωπων.

P. II.	υμων · ουτε · απο · αλλων ·	vobis · neque ababaliis
	δυνα‿μενοι[1] εν . βαρι · ειναι · ωσ ·	cum possimus oneri esse · sicut
v. 7	χρυ̅ · αποστολοι · Αλλε · γενεθη‿ (η above)	xp̅i apostoli · Sed facti su
	μεν[2] · νεπιοι[3] (η above) · εν · μεσω · υμων ·	mus parvuli in medio vestrum
	ωσ · εαν · προ φοσ · θαλπητα · εαυ	taqua̅ si nutrix foveat fili
8	της · τεκνα · ουτωσ · ομει · ρο	os suos · ita desiderantes vos (eramus /.)
	μενοι · υμων · ευδοκουμεν ·	cupide volebamus
	μεγα[4] · δουναι · ϋμιν ·	tradere vobis
	ου · μονον · το · ευαγγελιων[5] · του	non solum evangelium
	θυ̅ · αλλα και · τασ · εαυτων · ψυχασ ·	d̅i · sed et nostras animas
	διοτι · αγαπητοι · ημιν · εγενηθη‿	qm̅ carissimi nobis facti ·
9	ται · Μνημονευεται · γαρ · αδελφοι ·	Memores enim estis fr̅s
	τον · κοπον · ημων · και · τον · μοχ	laboris nostri et fati gatio
	θον · νυκτοσ · κ̷ · ημηρασ[6] (ε above) · εργα	nis nocte et die · operan
	ζομενοι · προσ · το · μη · επιβαρ	tes ne quem vestrum grava
	ησαι · τινα · ϋμων κηριξαμεν[7] ·	remus · prædicavimus
	εισ · υμασ · το · ευαγγελιον · του · θυ̅ ·	in vobis evangelium d̅i ·
10	υμεισ · μαρτιρεσ[8] · εσται · κ̷ · οθ̅σ ·	Vos testes estis et d̅s
	προσ · αγίοσ[9] · και · δικαιωσ · και · α	quam sc̅e et juste · et sine
	μεμπτοσ[10] · υμιν · τοισ · πιστευου	querela vobis qui credidistis
11	σιν · Εγενηθη‿μεν[11] · καθαπερ · οιδα	fuimus sicut scitis
	ται · Πωσ · ενα · εκαστον · υμων ·	qualiter unumquemque vestrum
	ωσ · π̅η̅ρ · τεκνα · εαυτου · παρα‿κα‿	taqua̅ pater filios suos depre
	λουντεσ · υμασ · και · παραμυθου	cantes vos et consolantes
	μενοι · και · μαρτυρου‿μενοι ·	testificati sumus
12	εισ · το · περιπα · ειν[12] (·τ above) ϋμασ · αξιωσ ·	ut ambularetis digne
	τȣ · θυ̅ · του καλουντοσ · υμασ ·	d̅o · qui vocavit vos
	εισ · την · εαυτου · βασιλιαν · και · δο	in suum regnum et glori

[1] δυναμενοι. [2] αλλεν̓γενηθημεν. [3] νηπῖοι. [4] μετα. [5] ευαγγελιον. [6] ημερασ. [7] Κηρυξαμεν. [8] μαρτυρεσ. [9] π·Ωσ οσίωσ (pro προσ · αγίοσ). [10] α μεμπτώσ. [11] εγενηθημενέ. [12] περιπατειν.

CAP. II. v. 13 am · Ideo et nos gratias	ξαν · Δια τουτο · και · ημηισ[1] · ευχα
agimus do sine intermissione	ρισ͜τουμεν · τω · θω · α · διαλιπτοσ[2] ·
quo cu accepissetis verbum au	οτι · παρα͜λαβοντεσ[3] · λαγον[4] ακο
ditus di a nobis suscepistis non	ησ · παρ · εμων[5] · του · θυ · εδεξασθαι ·
ut verbum hominum sed sicut	ου · λογον · ανθροπων[6] · αλλα · κα
est vere verbum di	θωσ · εστιν · αληθωσ · λογον · θυ ·
qui operatur in vobis qui credi	οσ · και · ενεργειται · εν · υμιν · τοισ · π
14 distis · Vos enim imitatores	τευ͜ουσιν · Υμεισ · γαρ · μει͜μη͜τα
facti estis frs ecclesia	εγενηθηται · αδελφοι · των · εκκλεσι
rum di quæ sunt in	ων[7] · του · θυ · των · ουσων · εν · τη
judæa in xpo ihu quia eadem	ϊουδαια · εν · χρω · ιυ · οτι · τα · αυτα
passi estis et vos a vestris	επα͜θεται · και · υμεισ · απο · των ι
contribulibus · sicut et	διων · σινφυλετων[8] · καθωσ · και
15 et ipsi a judaeis	αυτοι απο · τον[9] · ϊουδαιων · των,
qui et dnm occide	[10] και · τον · κν · απεκτι
runt ihm · et prophetas	ναν · των · ιν · και · τουσ · προφητασ ·
et nos persecuti sunt et do	και · ημασ · εδιωξαντων · και · θω ·
non placent · et omnibus homi	μη αρεσαντων · και · πασιν · ανθρο
16 nibus adversantur · prohiben	ποισ[11] · εναντιων · Κω͜λυοντων[12] ·
tes nos gentibus loqui ut	ημασ · τυισ · εθνεσιν · λαλησαι[13] · ινα ·
salvae fiant · ut impleant	σωθησονται · εισ · το · ανα πληρω
peccata sua sem	σαι · αυτων · τασ · αμαρτιασ · παν
per · prevenit enim ira di	τοτε · εφθασεν · δε · επαυτουσ ·
super illos usque in finem	η · οργη · του · θυ · εισ · τελοσ[14].
17 Nos autem fratres desola	Ημεισ · δε · αδελφοι[15] · απορφα
tia vobis adtem	νεισ͜θεντεσ · αφυμων · προσ και
pus · oræ facie non corde	ρον · ωρασ · προσωπω · ου · καρδια[16].
abundantius festinavimus	περισσοτερωσ · εσπου͜δασμεν ·

---

[1] ημεισ. [2] αδιαλιπτωσ. [3] *Supra* + αφημων : (*del. s. m.*) [4] λογον. [5] ημων. [6] ανθρωπων. [7] εκκλησιων. [8] συν φυλετων. [9] των (*pro* τον). [10] *Nullum spatium vacuum.* [11] ανθρωποισ. [12] κωλυοντων. [13] *In marg.* contra judaeos. [14] *In marg.* contra judaeos. [15] αδελφοι. [16] *In marg.* γ

P. II. το·προσωπον·ϋμων·ϊδειν·	faciem vestram videre
v. 18 εν·πολλη·επιθυμία · Διοτι·	in multo desiderio · Quō quidem
ηθελησαμεν·ελθειν·προσ·υμασ·	voluimus venire ad vos
εγο[1]·μεν·παυλοσ·και·απαξ·και·	ego quidem paulus et semel et
δεισ·και·ανεκο_ψεν·ημασ·ο·	iterum·et impedivit nos
19 σατανασ · Τισ·γαρ·ημων·ελ	satanas · Quæ est enim nostra
πισ·η·χαρα·η·στεφανοσ[2]·καυ	spes aut gaudium aut corona glo
(aut non etiam) χησεωσ·η·ουχ·ει_και·ϋμεισ·	riæ · Nonne vos
ηυ·προσθεν[3]·του·κυ·ημων·ιυ·	ante dnm nrm ihm
χρυ·ηυ[4]·τη·αυτου·παρουσια·	xpm in adventu ejus
20 Ϋμεισ·γαρ·εσται·η·δοξα·ημων·	Vos enim estis gloria nostra
P. III. 1 και·εχαρα[5] · Διο·με·καιτει[6]·στε_ (jam)	et gaudium · Propter qd nos susti
γοντεσ·ευδο_κησαμεν·κατα	nens amplius·placuit nobis rema
λιφθηναι·ηυ[7]·αθηναισ·μονοι·	nere athenis soli
2 και·επεμ_ψαμεν·τιμοθεον·	et misimus timotheum
τον·αδελφον·ημων·δια κο	frm nrum diaco
νον·και·συνεργον·του·θυ·	num·et cooperatorem di
εν·τω·ευαγγελιω·του·χρυ·εισ·	in evangelio xpi ad
το·στεριξαι[8]·ϋμασ·και·παρα	confirmandos vos·et exor
κα_λεσαι[9]·ϋπερ·τησ·πιστεωσ·	tandos pro fide
3 υμων·ϊνα·μηδεν·ασιενεσθαι·	vestra ut nemo moveatur
εν·ταισ·θλιθεσιν[10]·ταυ_ταισ·	intribulationibus istis·
αυτου[11]·γαρ·οιδαται·οτι·εισ·του	ipsi enim scitis quod in hoc
4 το·και_μεθα[12]·και·γαρ·οτε·προσ·	positi sumus · Nam et cum aput
ϋμασ·ημεν·ελεγομεν·υμιν·	vos essemus ! pdicebamus vobis
οτι·ελλομεν[13]·θλι_βεσθαι·	passuros nos tribulationes
καθωσ·εγε_νετο·και·οιδαται·	sicut factum est et scitis
5 Δια τουτο·καγω·μη·κετει·στε	Propterea et ego amplius non sus

[1] Εγω. [2] *In marg.* στεφανοσ. [3] εμπροσθεν. [4] εν. [5] η χαρα. [6] μη κετει. [7] εν. [8] στηριξαι. [9] παρακαλασαι (ε). [10] θλιψ : ιν (εσ:). [11] Αυτοι. [12] κειμεθα. [13] μελλομεν.

CAP. III.	tinens·nisi ad cognoscendam	γον[1]·επεμψα·εισ·το·γνω͜ναι·
	fidem vestram · Ne forte	την·πιστῖν·ϋμων·μη·πωσ·
	temptaverit vos is qui temptat	επιρασεν·υμασ·οπιραζων·και·
	et inanis fiat labor vestr̄·	εισ·καινον·γενηται·οκοποσ·ημω
v. 6	Nunc autem veniente timotheo	Αρτι·δε·ελθον·τοσ·τιμοθεου·
	ad nos a vobis·et adnunti	προσ·υμασ[2]·αφυμων·και·ευαγ
	ante nobis fidem	γελισαμενοι[3]·ημιν·την·πιστιν·
	et caritatem vestram et quia	και·την·αγαπεν[4]·υμων·και·οτι–
	memoria nostri habetis bo	μνιαν·εχεται·ημων·αγα
	nam·semper desiderantes	θην·παντοτε·επιπο͜θευντεσ[5]·
	nos videre·sicut nos quoque	ημασ·ϊδειν·καθα·περ·κ̶·ημισ·
7	vos · Ideo consolati sumus	υμασ · Δια τουτο·παρεκληθη
	fratres in vobis·in omni	μεν·αδελφου[6]·εφυμιν · ην·πασε[7]
	necessitate·et tribulatione nostra	τη·αναγκη·και·θλιψι·ημων·
8	per fidem nostram quoniam	δια·τησ·υμων·πιστεωσ·οτι·
	nunc vivimus·si vos sta	νυν·ζωμεν·εαν·υμεισ·στη͜κε
9	tis in dn̄o · Quam enim gratia	ται·εν·κ̄ω · Τινα·γαρ·ευχα
	rum actionem·possumus d̄o	ριστῖαν·γυναμεθα[8]·τω·κ̄ω·
	retribuere pro vobis	ανταποδουναι·περι·υμων·
	in omni gaudio quo gaudemus	επιπαση·τη·χαρα·η·χερομεν·
	propter vos·ante d̄m	δι·υμασ·εμπροσθεν·του θ̄υ
10	nostrum nocte ac die	η̄μων·νυκτοσ·και·ημερασ·
	abundantius orantes	υπερ·εκπερισσου·δεο͜μενοι·
	ut videamus faciem vestram	εισ·το·ῑδειν·υμων·το·προσωπον
	et compleamus ea quæ de	και·καταρ͜τεισαι·τα·υστερημα͜
11	sunt fidei vestrae · Ipse	τα · Τησ·πιστεωσ·υμων·Αυτοσ
	autem d̄s et pater noster et	δε·οθ̄σ·και·π̄η̄ρ·ημων[9] · και·
	d̄n̄s īh̄s x̄p̄c dirigat	οκ̄σ·ημων·ῑσ·χ̄σ·κατευθυναι·

[1] στεγων. [2] ἤμασ (*pro* υμασ). [3] ευαγγελισαμενου. [4] αγαπην. [5] επιποθουντεσ. [6] αδελφοι. [7] εν παση. [8] δυναμεθα. [9] *In marg.* περι του πατροσ και χ̄ρ̄υ.

P. III.	την·οδον·ημων·προσ·υμασ·	viam nostram ad vos
v. 12	Υμασ·δε·οκσ·ισ·πλεονασ_εε[1]·	Vos autem dns multiplicet
	και·περι σευσαι·τησ αγαπεσ[2]	et abundare faciat caritatem
	εισ·αλληλουσ·και·εισ·παντασ·	in invicem·et in omnes
	καθαπερ·και·ημισ·εισ·υμασ·	quem admodum et nos in vobis
13	εισ·το·στηρειται·τασ·καρδιασ·	ad confirmanda corda
	υμων·α·μεμπτουσ·εν·αγιοσυνη·	vestra sine querela in scitate
	εμπροσθεν·του·θυ·και·πρσ·ημων·	ante dm·et patrem nostrum
	εν·τε[3]·παρουσια·του·κυ·ημων·ιυ·	in adventu dni nri ihu
	χρυ·μετα·παντων·των·αγιων·	xpi cum omnibus scis
	αυτου·	ejus·
P. IV. 1	Ποιπον[4]·ουν·αδελφου[5]·ερωτωμεν·	d Decetero ergo frs·rogamus
	υμασ·και·παρα_καλουμεν·εν·κω	vos et obsecramus in dno
	ιυ·ινα·καθωσ·παρε_λαβεται·παρ·	ihu·ut quemadmodum accepistis
	ημων · Οπωσ·δει·υμασ·περιπα	a nobis quomodo oporteat ambu
	τειν·και·αρεσ_κειν·θω·καθωσ·κ	lare et placere do sicut et
	περιπα_τειτε·ϊνα·περισσευ_ηται·	ambulatis·ut abundetis
2	μαλλον · Οιδατε·γαρ·τινασ·	magis · Scitis enim quæ
	παραγγελιασ·παρεδω_καμεν·	precepta dederim
	υμιν·δια·του·κυ·ημων·ιυ·	vobis p dnm nostrum ihm
3	χρυ · Τουτο·γαρ εστιν·το·θελη	xpm·Hæc est enim voluntas
	μα·θυ·ο·αγιασμοσ·υμων·	di sancti ficatio nostra·
	απεχεσθαι·υμασ·απο·πασι[6]·	ut abstineatis vos ab omni
4	τησ·πορνιασ·ϊδεναι·εκαστοσ·	fornicatione·ut sciat unusquisque
	υμων·κτασθαι·το·εαυτου·σκενοσ·	vestrum suum vas possidere
	εν·αγιασμω·και·τιμη[7] · Μη·	in scificatione et honore · Non
	εν·παθει·και·επιθυμιασ·καθα	in passione desiderii·sicut
	περ·και·τα·εθνη·τα·μη·ϊδοτα·	et gentes quae ignorant

[1] πλεονασσε. [2] αγαπησ. [3] τη. [4] Λοιπον. [5] αδελφοι. [6] — πασι (*habet supra sec. man.*) [7] *In marg.* αγανον.

CAP. IV. v. 6	dm · Ut nequis supergrediatur neque	τον·θν · Το·μη·υπερ·βαι_νειν·χ
	circumveniat in negotio	πλεο_νεκτειν·εν·τω·πραγματι[1]·
	frm suum·quoniam	τον·αδελφον·αυτου·δει[2]·οτι·
	.vindex est dns dehis omni	εκαι_κοσ[3]·οθσ·περι_παντων·
	bus·sicut predixi	τουτων·καθωσ·και·προειπα
	mus vobis et testificati sumus·	μεν·υμιν·και·διεμαρτυρα_μεθα·
	7 Non enim vocavit nos ds in	Ου·γαρ·εκαλεσεν·ημασ·οθσ·επι
	inmunditia·sed in scificatione	ακαθαρσια·αλλεν·αγιασμω·
	8 Itaque qui hæc spernit·non hominem	qua propter τοι·γαρουν·ο·α·θετων[4]·ουκ·ανον[5]·
	spernit sed dm qui etiam·de	αθετει·αλλα·θν·τον·και·διδον
	dit spm suum scm	τα·το·πνα·αυτου·το·αγιων[6]·εισ
	in nobis	υμασ·
	9 De caritate autem frat nitatis·non	π Περι·δε·τησ·φιλαδελφιασ[7]·ου
	necesse habemus scribere vobis	χριαν·εχομεν·γραφειν·ὑμιν,
	ipsi enim vos a do didi	αυτοι·γαρ·υμεισ·θω·διδακτοι_
	cistis·ut diligatis invicem·	εσται·εισ·το·αγαπαν·αλλελουσ (η above ε)
	10 et enim facitis illud in omnes	και·ποι_ειτε[9]·αυτο·εισ·παντασ—
	frs in universa macedo	τουσ·αθελφουσ[10]·εν·ολη·τη·μακε
	nia · Rogamus autem vos	δονια · Παρα_καλουμεν·δε·υμασ
	11 frs·ut abundetis magis·et	αθελφοι[11]·περισσευ_ειν·μαλλον·
	operam detis ut quieti sitis	studium habeatis l studere silendi l sile… φιλοτει_μεισθαι·ησυχαζειν·και-
	et ut vestrum negotium agatis et ope	πραττειν·τα·ϊδια·και·εργαζεσ…
	remini manibus vestris·sicut præce	ταισ·χερσειν·ὑμων·καθωσ·υμιν
	12 pimus vobis·et honeste am	παρεγγειλαμεν[12]·ἱνα·περιπα_τε (η above ε)
	buletis ad eos qui foris sunt	τε·ευσχημανωσ[13]·προσ·τουσ·…
	et nullius aliqd desideretis	και·μη·δενοσ·χριαν·εχηται·
n	13 Nolumus autem vos ignorare	μ Μ[14]υθελομεν·δε·ϋμασ·αγνο ειν·
	frs de dormientibus	αθελφοι[15]·περι·των·κεκοιμη_ν… (δ above θ)

Vide pag. 111. [R.B.]

[1] *In marg.* πραγμα. [2] Ċ Δει. [3] Εκδικοσ. [4] ο.α.εθετων (α above). [5] ανον ạ. [6] αγιο…
[7] *In marg.* φιλαδελφοσ amator fraternitatis. [8] αλληλουσ. [9] + γαρ (*ante* ποιειτε). [10] αδελφο…
[11] αδελφοι. [12] παρηγγειλαμεν. [13] *In marg.* honeste. [14] Ου. [15] αδελφοι.

V. ινα · μη · λυπεισ͜θαι · ωσ · και · οι	ut non contristemini sic et
λοι͜ποι · μη · εχοντεσ · ελπιδα ·	ceteri qui spem non habent ·
14 Ει · γαρ · πιστευ͜ομεν · οτι · ιησ · απε	Si enim credimus quod ihs mor
θανεν · και · ανεστη · ουτωσ[1] · και ·	tuus est et resurrexit · Ita et
οθσ · τουσ · κεκοι͜μημενȣσ · δεια · τȣ	ds eos qui dormierunt per
15 ιην · αξει · σιν[2] · αυτω · Τουτο · γαρ ·	ihm adducet cum eo · Hoc enim
υμιν · λεγομεν · ηv[3] · λογω · κυ · οτι	vobis dicimus in verbo dni quia
ημεισ · οιζωντεσ · οιπερι͜λιπομε	nos qui vivimus qui re sidui su
νοι · εισ · την · παρȣσια[4] · του · κυ ·	mus In adventu dni ·
ου · μη φθασωμεν · τουσ · κοι͜μηδεν͜	non preveniemus eos qui dor
16 τασ[5] · Οτι · αυτοσ · ο κσ · εν κελευσμα	mierunt · Quo ipse dns in jus
τι · ενφονη[6] · αρχαγγελου · και[7] · εν	su et in voce archangeli et in
σαλπιγτι · θυ · κατα͜βησεται · απου	tuba di descendet de cae
ρανου · και · οι · νεκροι · οι · εν · χρω ·	lo[7] · et mortui qui in xpo sunt
17 αναστη͜σονται · προτοι[8] · Επιτα ·	resurgent primi · Deinde
ημεισ · οι · ζοντεσ[9] αμασυν · αυ	nos qui vivimus simul rapi
τοισ · αρπαγησομεθα · εν · νε φαι	êmur cum illis in nubi
λαισ · εισ υπαν͜τησειν[10] · τωχρω εισ ·	bus obviam xpo in
αερα · και · ουτοσ[11] · παντοτε · συν ·	aera · et sic semper cum
18 κω εσομεθα · ωστε · παρα͜καλειται ·	dno erimus · Itaque consolamini
αλλε͜λουσ[12] · εν · τοισ · λογοισ · του	invicem In verbis
τοισ ·	istis
P. V. 1 Περι · δε · των · χρονων · και · των ·	d De temporibus autem et mo
καιρων · αθελφοι[13] · ου · χρια · εστιν ·	mentis frs · non indigetis ut
2 υμιν · γραφεσθαι · αυτοι · γαρ ·	scrbā vobis · Ipsi enim
ακριβωσ · οιδαται · οτι · ημερα · κυ ·	diligent scitis · quia dies dni
ωσ · κλεπ τεσ[14] · εν · νυκτι · ουτωσ ·	sicut fur in nocte ita
3 ερχεται · Οταν · λεγουσιν · ϊρηνη ·	veniet · Cum dixerint pax

---

1 Ουτωσ παντοτε συν κω εσομεθα. 2 συν. 3 εν. 4 παρουσιαν. 5 κοιμηθεντασ. 6 φωνη. 7 *In capite paginæ* Cum tuba caelesti surgere voce canet. 8 Αναστασονται πρωτοι. 9 ζωντεσ. 10 *In marg.* υποπαντη. 11 ουτωσ. 12 αλληλουσ. 13 Αδελφοι. 14 κλεπτησ.

	Latin	Greek
CAP. V.	et securitas · tunc repentinus	και ασφαλια · τοτε · εφνιδιοσ · αυ
	illis super veniet interitus · sicut	τοισ · φανεσεται[1] · ο · λεθροσ · ωσ ·
	dolor in utero habentis	περ · η̄ · ωδεινεσ · εν · γαστρι · εχȣση ·
v. 4	non et effugient · Vos autem	και · ου μη · εκφευζονται[2] · υμεισ · δε ·
	f̄rs non estis intenebris · ut	αθελφοι[3] · ουκ · εσται εν · σκοτει · ινα
	vos dies illa · tāquam fur	υμασ · η · η μερα · εκειν η · ωσ · κλεπτ
5	cōprehendat · Omnes enim vos filii	κατα λαβοι · παντεσ · γαρ · υμεισ · υι
	lucis estis · et filii diei · et	φωτοσ · εσται · ϗ υιοι · ημερασ · και –
	non estis noctis · neque tenebrarum ·	ουκ · εσται · νυκτοσ · ουδε · σκο τȣσ ·
6	Igitur non dormiamus · sicut	Αρα · ουν · μη · κα θευδωμεν · ωσ · ϗ
	ceteri · sed vigilemus · et sobrii	οιλο · ποι[4] · αλλα · γρεγορωμεν[5] · ϗ · νη
7	simus · Qui enim dormiunt noc	φομεν[6] · Οι · γαρ · καθευδοντεσ · νυκ
	te dormiunt · et qui ebrii	τοσ · καθευδοντεσ · και · οι · μεθυσκο
8	sunt · nocte ebrii sunt · Nos autem	μενοι · νυκτοσ · μεθυουσιν · Ημεισ ·
	qui diei sumus · sobrii simus · In	δε · ημερασ · οντεσ · νηφομεν[7] · εν ·
	duti lorica fidei et carita	δυσαμενοι · θορακα[8] · πιστεωσ · και ·
	tis · et galeam spem	αγαπησ · και · περικεφαλαιαν · ελπιδ
9	salutis · quō non posuit nos	σωτεριασ[9] · οτι · ουκ · εθετο · ημασ ·
	d̄s in iram · sed in adquisitionem	ο̄θ̄σ̄ · εισ · οργεν[10] · αλλεισ · περιποι
	salutis · per dn̄m nr̄m ih̄m xp̄m	σοτηριασ[11] · δια · του · κ̄ῡ · ημων · ῑῡ
10	qui mortuus est pro nobis	τȣ · αποθανοντοσ · υπερ · ημων ·
	ut sive vigilemus · sive dormi	ινα · ειτε · γρηγορωμεν · ειτε · καθευ
	amus simul cum illo vivamus	δωμεν · αμα · συν · αυτω · ζεσωμεν[12] ·
11	Propter q̄d consolamini invicem	Διο · παρα καλειται · αλλελουσ[13] ·
	et edificate alterutrum · sicut	in unum οικοδο μειται · εισ · τον · ενα · καθω
	et facitis ·	και · ποιειται · ;
12	Rogamus autem vos fratres ut	Ερωτωμεν · δε · ϋμασ · αθελφοι[14] ·
	noveritis eos qui laborant in vobis	cognoscere. ϊδεναι · τουσ · κοπειωντασ · εν · υμιν

ΙΔ

[1] Φανησεται. [2] εκφευξονται. [3] Αδελφοι. [4] λοιποι. [5] γρηγορωμεν. [6] νηφωμεν. [7] νηφωμεν. [8] Θωρακα. [9] σωτηριασ. [10] οργην. [11] σωτηριασ. [12] ζησωμεν. [13] Αλληλουσ. [14] αδελφο

P. V. και·προ ϊσταμενουσ·υμων·εν·	et presunt vobis in
κω·και·νουθετουντασ·υμασ·	dno · et monent vos
13 ωστε·ηγεισθαι·αυτουσ·υπερ·εκ	ut habeatis illos abundan
περισσωσ·εν·αγαπη·διο[1]·το·εργον·	tius in caritate·propter opus
αυτων·ϊρενευσαται[2]·εν·αυτοισ·	illorum pacem habete cum eis·
14 Παρα καλουμεν[3]·δε·υμασ·αδελφοι·	R Rogamus autem vos fratres
νουθετειν·τουσ·ατακτουσ·πα	corripite in quietos·conso
ραμυθειται[4]·τουσ·ολειγοψυχουσ·	lamini·pusillanimes
αντεχεσθαι·των·ασθενων·μα	suscipite infirmos·patientes
15 κροθυμειται·προσ·παντασ · Ορα	estote ad omnes · Vide
ται·μητισ·κακον·αντι·κακου·τι	te nequis malum pro malo alicui
νι·αποδοι·Αλλο[5]·παντοτε·το·αγα	reddat·sed semper quod bo
θον·δειωκεται·εισ·αλληλουσ·και·	num est sectamini ininvicem
16 εισ·παντασ · Παντοτε·χαιρεται·	et in omnes · Semper gaudete
17 εν τω Κω·α·διαλιπτοσ[6]·προσευ	sine inter missione ora
18 χεσθαι[7]·εν·παντι·ευχαρεισ τιται·	te · In omnibus gratias agite·
Τουτο·γαρ·εστιν·θελεμα[8]·θυ·εν·	Haec est voluntas di in
19 χρω·ιυ·εισ υμασ · Το·πνα·μεζβεν	in xpo ihu·in omnibus vobis · Spm nolite
20 νυται[9]·προφητῖασ·με[10]·εξουθενι	extinguere·prophetias nolite sperne
21 ται · Παντα·δε·δοκειμαζεται·το·	re · Omnia (autem) probate·quod bo
22 καλον·κατεχεται·Απο·παντοσ·	num est tenete·ab omni
ϊδουσ·πονηρου·απεχεσθαι·	specie mala abstinete vos
23 Αυτοσ·δε·οθσ·τησ·ϊρηνησ·αγι	Ipse autem ds pacis sanctifi
ασει·υμασ·ολοτελεισ·και·ολο κλη	cet vos per omnia·et inte
ρον·υμων·το·πνα·και·η·ψυχη·	ger sps vester·et anima
και·το·σωμα·αμεμπτοσ[11]·εν·τη·	et corpus sine querela in ad
παρουσῖα·του·κυ·ημων·ιυ·χρυ·	ventu dni nri ihu xpi
24 Ο·πιστοσ[13]·ο·κα	servetur · Fidelis ds qui voca

[1] Δια. [2] ϊρηνευσαται. [3] *In marg.* fergus. [4] Παραμυθεισ̣ται. [5] Αλλα. [6] Αδιαλιπτωσ. [7] προσευχασθαι. [8] θελημα. [9] μηζβεννυται. [10] μη. [11] αμεμπτωσ. [12] + τηρηθει. [13] Η . πιστοσ.

CAP. V. vit vos qui etiam faciet·
v. 25 Fratres orate pro nobis·
26 Salute fratres omnes
27 in osculo sco · Adjuro vos
per dnm ut legatur ae
pistola hæc omnibus fratribus
28 Gratia dni nri ihu xpi
vobiscum EXPLICIT AD THES
SALONICENSES EPA·P·AP·I·

λων·ὑμασ·οσ·και·ποι‿ησαι[1]·
Αδελφοι·προσ·ευχεσθαι·Ὑπερ·ημων
Ασπασασ‿θαι·τουσ·αδελφουσ·παντ
εν·φιληματι·αγιω·ορκιζω·υμασ·
τον·κν·ανα‿γνωσθηναι·την·ε‿
πιστολην·πασῖν·τουσ[2]·αδελφοισ·
Η·χαρισ·του·κυ·ημων·ιυ·χρυ·
μεθυμων·
Ετελεσθη προσ θεσσαλονικαιων[3]·α—

Incipit ad thes salonicenses · secunda ·

Αρχεται προσ θεσ σαλονι[4] καιων δευτερη[5] ·

CAP. I.
1 Paulus
et silvanus et ti
motheus ecclesiae
thessalonicensium in
do patre nro et dno ihu xpo·
2 Gratia vobis et pax a
do patre nro et dno ihu xpo
3 Gratias agere debemus do
·semper pro vobis fratres
sicut dignum est quo super
crescit fides vra·et abun
dat caritas unius cujusque
omnium vestrum in in vi
4 cem · Ita ut et nos ipsi in

Παυλοσ
και·σιλβανοσ·και·τι
μοθεοσ·τη·εκκλησεῖα·
θεσσαλονι‿καιων · εν·
θω·πρι·ημων·και·χρω·ιηυ·
Χαρεισ·ὑμιν·και·ϊρηνη·απο
θυ·πατροσ·ημων·κ̣ κυ·ιυ·χρυ·
Ευχαρεισ·τειν·οφιλομεν·τω·θω·
παντοτε·περι·ημων[6]·αδελφοι·
καθοσ[7]·αξιον·εστιν·οτι·υπερ·
αιξανει η·πιστεισ υμων και
πλεονα‿ξει[8]·η·αγαπε[η][9]·ενοσ‿εκασ·-
του·παντων·υμων·εισ·αλλη
λουσ·ωστε·ημασ·αυτουσ·ε εν[10].

---

[1] ποιησει. [2] τοισ. [3] Θεσσαλονι. [4] Θεσσαλονι. [5] B. [6] ὑμων.
[7] Καθωσ. [8] πλεοναζει. [9] αγαπη. [10] εν.

	Greek	Latin
1	υμιν · καυχησασθαι · εν · ταισ · εκ	vobis gloriemur in ec
	κλησιαισ · του θυ υπερ · τεσ[1] · υ	clesiis di pro patien
	πο_μονησ · υμων · και πιστεοσ[2] ·	tia vestra et fide
	εν · πασιν · τοισ · διωγμοισ · υμων ·	in omnibus persecutionibus vestris
	και · θλι_ψεσιν · αισ · ανεχεσθαι ·	et tribulationibus quas sustinetis
v. 5	εν · διγμα · τησ · δικαιασ · κρισε	in exemplum justi judi
	ωσ του θυ · εισ · το · κατα_ξειωθη	cii di · ut digni habeami
	ναι · υμασ[3] · τησ · βασιλιασ · του · θυ ·	ni in regno di
6	☧[4] περ · ησ · πασ_χεται · Περ · δι_και	pro quo et patimini · Si tam justum
	ον · παρα · θω · ανταπο_δουναι ·	est apud dm retribuere
	αυτοισ · τοισ · θλει_βουσιν · υμασ ·	his qui tribulant vos
7	θλιψιν · κα · υμιν[5] · τοισ · θλι βο	tribulationem · et vobis qui tribula
	μενοισ · ανεσιν · μεθημων · εν · τη ·	mini requiem nobiscum · in reve
	αποκαλυψει · του · κυ ιυ · απουρα	latione dni ihu de cælo
	νου · μει[6] · αγγελων · δυνα_μαιωσ[7] ·	cum angelis virtutis
8	αυτου · ☧ · εν · φλογι · πυροσ · δειδουσ ·	ejus in flamma ignis dantis
	εκδικησιν · τοισ · μη · ιδοσειν · θν ·	vindictam his qui non nover dm
	και · τοισ · μη · υπα κου_ϐσιν · τω · ευ	et qui non oboediunt evan
	αγγελιω · του · κυ · ημων · ιυ · χρυ ·	gelio dni nri ihu xpi
9	Οιτινεσ · δικην τεισ · ουσ · ειν · ολε	Qui poenas dabunt · in interi
	θρον · αιωνιον · απο · προσ_ωπου · κυ	tum · æternas ante faciem dni
	και · απο · τησ · δοξησ · τησ ισχουσ[8] ·	et agloria virtutis
10	αυτου · οταν · ελθη · εν · δοξασ_θεναι[9] ·	ejus · cum venerit glorificari
	εν · τοισ · αγιοισ · αυτου[10] · και εν · θαυ	in scis suis · et admirabilis fie
	μασ_θηναι · εν · πασιν · τουσ · πιστευ_	ri in omnibus qui credide
	σασιν[11] · Οτι · επιστευθη · το μαρτυ	runt · Quia creditum est testimo
	ριων[12] · ημων · εφυμασ · εν · τη · ημε	nium nostrum super vos in die
	ρα · εκεινη · Εισ · ο · και · προσευ_χο	illo · In quo et hora
	ρα	

[1] τησ. [2] πιστεωσ. [3] ημασ. [4] και in textu. [5] Κα υμιν. [6] μετ. [7] *In marg.* de ημερασ τησ κρισεωσ. [8] ισχυοσ. [9] ενδοξασθηναι. [10] *In marg.* contra hereticos. [11] τοισ πιστευσασιν. [12] μαρτυριον.

Latin	Greek
CAP. I. mus semper pro vobis ut	μεθα · παν‿τοτε · περ · υμων · ινα ·
dignetur vos vocatione sua	υμασ · εξειωσε[1] · τησ · κλησεοσ[2] · υμωι
ds nr · et impleat omnem	οθσ · ημων · και · πληρωσε[3] · πασαν ·
voluntatem bonitatis et o	ευδοκιαν · αγαθω‿συνησ[4] · και · ερ
v. 12 pus fidei in virtute · ut clari	ita ut γον · πιστεωσ · εν · δυναμει · ο · πωσ ·
ficetur nomen dni nri	εν · δοξασθη · το · ονομα · τȣ · κυ · ημ.
ihu xpi in vobis	ιυ χρυ εν · υμιν
R CAP. II. 1 Rogamus autem vos fratres per	π Πρωτωμεν[5] · δε · υμασ · αδελφοι · υ
adventum dni nostri	περ · τησ · παρουσιασ · τȣ κυ · ημω
ihu xpi et nrae congregationis	ιυ · χρυ · και ημων επι‿συναγω‿γ
2 in ipsum ut non cito move	εν · αυτον[6] · εισ · το · μη · ταχαιωσ · σ
amini a vestro sensu · neque	θηναι · υμασ · απο · του · νοοσ · μηδε ·
terreamini neque per spm neque per	θροεισθαι · μηδε[7] · δια · πνα · μητε[8] δ
sermonem neque per epistolam taqa	λογου · μηδε · δι επιστολεσ[9] · ωσ · δι
per nos missam quasi instet dies	ημων · ωσ · οτι · ενεστηκεν · η · ημερα
3 dni · Nequis vos seducat	κυ · Μητισ · υμασ · εξαπα‿τηση ·
ullo modo · quoniam nisi	κατα με δηνα[10] · τροπον · οτι · εαν μ
venerit discessio primum et revela	ελθη · η · αποστασία[11] · πρωτον · και
tus fuerit homo pecca	καλυφθη · ο · ανθροποσ[12] · τησ · αμαρ
4 ti filius perditionis qui adversa	τίασ · ο · υιοσ · τησ · απολίασ · ο · αντε
tur et extollitur supra	και‿μενοσ[13] · και · επαι ρομενοσ · επι ·
omne qd dicitur ds aut qd colitur	παντα · λεγομενον · θν · η · σεβασ‿μα ·
ita ut in templo di	ωστε · αυτον · εισ · τον · ναον · τȣ · θυ ·
sedeat osten	ινα[14] · θν · καθει‿σαι[15] · αποδικ‿νυ
5 dens se taqua ds sit · Non	οντα · εαυτον · οτι · εστιν · θσ · ου ·
retinetis qd cum adhuc	meministis μνημο‿νευεται · οτι · α · υτι ·
essem aput vos hæc dicebam vobis	ων · προσ · υμασ · ταυτα · ελεγον · υμι
6 et nunc quid detineat scitis ut	και · νυν · το · κατεχον · οι‿δαται · εισ

[1] αξειωση. [2] Κλησεωσ. [3] πληρωση. [4] αγαθοσυνησ. [5] Ερωτωμεν. [6] επαυτον. [7] Μητε. [8] πνσ μητε. [9] Μητε διεπιστολησ. [10] μηδενα. [11] *In marg.* discedite de anti χρα. [12] ανθρωποσ. [13] αντικειμενοσ. [14] ινα (ωσ above). [15] καθεσαι.

πολυφθηναι[1] · αυτον · εν · τω · εαυ	reveletur in suo
του · καιρω · Το · γαρ μυστεριων[2] ·	tempore · Nam mysterium
ηδη · ενεργιται · τησ · ανομιασ · μο	jam operatur iniquitatis · tan
νον · ο κατεχων · αρτει	tum ut qui tenet nunc · teneat
εωσαν · εκ μεσου · γενηται · κ(αι) · τοτε ·	donec demedio fiat · et tunc
απο · καλυφθη σεται · ο · ναμοσ[3] · ον ·	revelabitur ille iniquus · quem
ο κσ · ισ · αν ελοι · τω · πνι · τȣ · σωματοσ[4] ·	dns ih interficiet spu oris
αυτου · και · ταργεσει[5] · τη · επιφανι	sui · et destruet illustratio
α · τησ · παραυσιασ[6] · αυτου · Ου · εστιν ·	ne adventus sui · Cujus est
παρȣσία[7] · κατε νεργιαν · του · σατανα ·	adventus secundum operationem satanae
εν · παση · δυναμει · κ(αι) · ση μειοισ · και	in omni virtute et signis et prodi
τερασίν · ψευ δουσ · και · εν · παση · απα	giis mendatibus et in omni seductio
τη · αδικίασ · τοισ · απολλυμεοισ[8] ·	ne iniquitatis his qui pereunt
ανθων · την · αγαπην · τησ · αληθιασ ·	eo quod caritatem veritatis
ουκ · εξε δεξαντο · εισ το · σωθεναι[9] ·	non receperunt · ut salvi fierent ·
αυτουσ · και · δια τȣτο · πεμ πει · αυτοισ ·	et ideo mittet illis
οθσ · ενεργίαν · πλανεσ[10] · εισ το ·	ds operationem erroris ut
πιστευσαι · ψευδει[11] · ἵνα · κριθω	credant mendatio · utjudicen
σιν · απαντεσ · οι · με[12] · πιστευσαν	tur oms qui non credide
τεσ · τη · αληθία · αλλευ δοκεσαν ·	runt veritati · sed consense
τησ[13] · τη · αδικια ·	runt iniquitati ·
Ημεισ · δε · οφιλομεν · ευχαρεισ · τειν ·	Nos autem debemus gras agere
τω · θω · παντοτε · περι · υμων · α	do semper pro vobis fra
δελφοι · ηγαπη μενοι · απω[14] · κω · οτι ·	tres dilecti a dno · quod
δατο[15] · υμασ · οθσ · απαρχην · εισ ·	elegt nos ds primitias in
σωτηριαν[16] · εν · αγιασμω · πνσ ·	salutem in scificatione sps
αι · πιστι · αλεδιασ[17] · εισ · οι · κ(αι) · εκα	et fide veritatis · in qua et voca
λεσεν · υμασ · δια · τȣ · ευαγγελιου ·	vit nos perevangelium

ιλυφθηναι. [2] μυστηριον. [3] ανομοσ. [4] στοματοσ. [5] καταργησει. [6] παρουσιασ. [7] + η. (*ante* παρουσία). [8] απολλυμενοισ. [9] σωθηναι. [10] πλανησ. [11] + τω (*ante* ψευδει). [12] μη. [13] Αλλευδοκησαντεσ. [14] υπο (*pro* απω). [15] ἱλατο. [16] σωτηρεῖαν, *in marg.* σωτηρεια. [17] αληθιασ.

CAP. II.	nrm · inadquisitionem gloriae	ημων · εισ · περιποι_ησιν · δοξησ ·
v. 15	dni nri ihu xpi · Itaque	του · κυ · ημων · ιυ χρυ · αραουν ·
	fratres state et tenete	αδελφοι · στεκεται[1] · και · κρατειτε ·
	traditiones quas didicistis	τασ · παρα_δοσισ · ασ · εδι_δαχθητ
	sive perverbum · sive perepisto	ειτε · δια · λογου · ειτε · διεπιστο
16	lam nostram · Ipse autem dns nr	λησ · ημων · αυτοσ · δε · οκσ · ημων ·
	ihs xpc · et ds pater noster	ισ χρσ · ϗ οθσ · ο · πατηρ · ημων ·
	qui dilexit nos et dedit	ο · αγαπησασ · ημασ · και · δουσ ·
	consolationem aeternam et spem	παρα_κλησιν[2] · αιωνιον · και · ελπεί-
17	bonam ingratia · exhorte	δα · αγαθην · εν · χαρει · τει · παρα_
	tur corda vestra et confir	ση[3] · υμων · τασ · καρδιασ · ϗ στηρ
	met inomni sermone et opere bono ·	ξη · εν · παντι · λογω · και · εργω · αγ
CAP. III. 1	Decetero frs orate	π Ποι πον[4] · αδελφοι · προσευ_χεσθ
	pro nobis ut sermo dni	περι · ημων · ινα · ολογοσ · του · θυ -
	currat et clarificetur sicut	τρεχε[5] και · δοξασ θηται · καθοσ[6]
2	et apud vos · et utlibere	και · προσ · υμασ · και ινα · ρισθω
	mur ab inportunis et malis	μεν[7] · απο · των · ατοπων · ϗ · πονερο
	hominibus non enim omnium est	ανων · ου · γαρ · παντων · εστιν ·
3	fides · fidelis autem ds est qui confir	η · πιστισ · Πιστοσ · δε · οθσ · οσ ·
	mabit vos et custodiet a	σει · υμασ και · φυλαξει · απο · των
4	malo · Confidimus autem devobis	πονερου · Πεποι_δαμεν[9] · δε · εν -
	in dno · quo quaecepimus	κω · εφυμασ · οτι · α · παραγγελλ
	vobis et facitis et faci	μεν[10] · υμιν · και · εποιησαται · και -
5	etis · Dns autem dirigat cor	ποιειται · ο · δε · κσ[11] · κατευθυνη -
	da vestra in caritate	μων[12] · τασ · καρδιασ · εισ · την · α
	di et patientia xpi ·	του θυ · ϗ · εισ · την · υπομονην
		του · χρυ ·
6	Denuntiamus autem vobis frs	π Παραισ_γελλομεν[13] · δε · υμιν · αδε

[1] Στηκεται. [2] *In marg.* παρακλησισ. [3] παρακλησηε. [4] Λοιπον. [5] τρεχη. [6] δοξασθηται Καθωσ- [7] ρυσθωμεν. [8] πονηρων. [9] πονηρου Πεποιθαμεν. [10] παραγγελλομεν. [11] *In marg.* collecta. [12] ημων. [13] Παραιγγελλομεν.

III.	εν·ονοματι·κυ·ημων·ιυ·χρυ·	In nomine dni nri ihu xpi
	στελλεσθαι·υμασ·απο·παντοσ·α	utsubtrahatis vos abomni
	αδελφοι·ατακτοσ·περιπατουντεσ[1]·	fratre ambulante inordinate·
	και·μη·κατα·την·παραδοσιν·	et non secundum traditionem
v. 7	η·παρηλαβεται[2]·παρημων·αυτοι·	quam acceper anobis · Ipsi
	γαρ·οιδαται·πωσ·δει·μει_μεισ	enim scitis·quemadmodum oporteat
	θαι·ημασ·οτι·ουκ·ητακτεσα	imitari vos·qm non inquieti fui
8	μεν[3]·εν·υμιν·ουτε·δωρεαν·	mus inter vos · Neque gratis
	αρτον·εφαγομεν·παρατινοσ·αλλεν·	panem manducavimus ab aliquo sed in
	κοπο[4]·και·μοχ_θω·νυκτοσ·κ ημε	labore et fatigatione nocte et die
	ρασ·εργαζομενι[5]·προσ τομε[6] επι	operantes·ne quem vestrum
9	βαρησαι·τεινα·υμων·ουχ·οτι·ουκ·	gravaremus · Non quasi non
	εχομεν·εξουσιαν·αλλϊνα·εαυτουσ·	habuerimus potestatem sed ut nosmet
	τυπον·δομεν[7]·υμιν·εισ το_μει_μεισ	ipsos·formam daremus vobis ad imitan
10	θαι·ημασ·και·γαρ·οτε·ημεν·προσ	dos nos · Nam et cum essemus aput
	υμασ·τουτο·παρεγγελλομεν[8]·υμιν·	vos·hoc denuntiabamus vobis·
	οτι·ειτισ·ου·θελει·εργαζεσδαι·μεδε[9]·	quo siquis non vult operari·nec
11	εσθειετο[10]·ακου_ομεν·γαρ·τεινασ·πε	manducet · Audivimus enim quosdam
	ριπα_τουντασ·εν·υμιν·ατακτωσ[11]·	inter vos ambulare inquiete
	μεδεν[12]·εργαζομενουσ·αλλα·περι·	nihil operantes·sed curiose
12	εργαζομενουσ · Τοισ·δε·τοι·ουτοισ·	agentes · His autem qui ejusmodi sunt
	παραγγελλομεν·και·παρακαλουμεν·	denuntiamus et obsecramus
	εν κω ιυ χρω ϊνα μετα·ησυχΐασ·	in dno ihu xpo ut cum silentio
	εργαζομενοι·τον·εαυτον[13]·αρτον·	operantes·suum panem
|	αισθειωσειν · Ϋμεισ·δε·αδελφοι·	manducent · Vos autem frs noli
	μη·εκκακησεται·καλον·ποι ουντεσ·	te deficere bene facientes
	Ει·δε·τισ·ουχ·υπακουει·τω·	Quod siquis non oboedit ver
	λογω[14]·ημων·δι·επιστολησ·τουτον·	bo nostro per epistolam·hunc

[1] αδελφου ατακτωσ περιπατουντοσ. [2] παρελαβεται. [3] ητακτησαμεν. [4] κοπω.
[5] εργαζομενοι. [6] μη. [7] δωμεν. [8] παρηγγελλαμεν. [9] εργαζεσθαι Μηδε. [10] εσθειετω.
[11] *In marg.* contra inquietos. [12] Μηδεν. [13] εαυτον. [14] λογω.

F F

CAP. III.	notate·et ne commisceamini	σημει‿ουσθαι·𝔛 μη·συνα‿μιγ‿
v. 15	cum illo·ut con fundatur et no	νυσθαι·αυτω·ϊνα·εν·τραπη·𝔛·
	lite qsi inimicum existimare·sed	μη·ωσ·εκθρον·ηγεισθαι·αλλα·
16	corripite ut frem · Ipse autem	νϑθητειτε·οσ[1]·αδελφον · Αυτοσ·ι
	ds pacis det vobis pa	οθσ·τησ·ϋρηνησ[2]·δωη·υμιν·την·
	cem semper in omni loco	ϊρηνην·δια·παντοσ·εν·παντι·τοπ
17	dns cum omnibus vobis · Salu	οκσ·μετα·παντων·υμων · Ο ασ‿
	ta tio mea manu pauli	πασμοσ·τη·εμη·χιρι·παυλου·
	qd est signum in omni episto	ο·εστιν·σημειον·εν·παση·επιστο
18	la·ita scribo · Gratia	λη·ουτωσ γραφω · Η·χαρεισ·
	dni nri ihu xpi cum omnibus	του κυ ιυ χρυ μετα·παντων·
	vobis Amen	υμων · Αμην·
	EXPLICIT AD THESSALONIC·II·	Ετελεσθαι[3] προσ θεσσαλονι · Β[4]

Incipit ad timo theum · i ·

Αρχεται προσ τιμο θεον · α[5] ·

CAP. I. 1	Paulus apo	Παυλοσ απο
	stolus xpi ihu ·	στολοσ χρυ ιηυ ·
	secundum imperium di salvatoris	κατεπιτα‿γε[6]·θυ·σωτεροσ[7]·
	nri et xpi ihu spei	ημων·και·χρυ·ιυ τησ ελπει
2	nostræ·timotheo dilecto	δοσ·ημων·τιμοθεω·γνησειω·
	filio infide gratia misericordia	τεκνο[8]·εν·πιστι·χαρεισ·ελεοσ
	et pax a do patre et xpo ihu	ϊρηνη·αποθυ·πατροσ·και χρυ
3	dno nro · Sicut rogavi	του·κυ·ημων·καθωσ·παρεκα
	te ut remaneres ephesi	λεσα·σε·προσ·μει‿ναι·εν·εφεσ
	cum irem in macedoniam·	πορευομενοσ[9]·εισ·μακαι‿δονιαν
	ut denuntiares quibusdam ne aliter	ϊνα·παραγγελλησ[10]·τισιν·μη·ε·

[1] νουθετειτε ωσ. [2] ϊρηνησ. [3] Ετελεσθη. [4] II B. [5] I A. [6] επιταγην. [7] σωτηροσ. [8] τεκνω. [9] *In facsimili* πορευαμενοσ? [10] παραγγειλησ.

I. 4 διδασκαλειν · μηδε · προσ · εχειν ·
μυθοισ · και · γενεαλογειαισ · απε
ραντοισ · αι͜τινεσ · ζητησεισ · παρε
χουσιν · μαλλον · η ; οι͜κονομίαν · θ̅υ̅ ·
5 εν · πιστι · Το · δε · τελοσ · τησ · πα
ραγγελιασ · εστιν · αγαπησ · εκκαθα
ρασ · καρδιασ · ϗ συνι͜δησεοσ[1] ·
6 και · πιστεωσ · ανυποκριτου · ων · τινεσ ·
αστοχησαντεσ · εζετραπησαν[2] · εισ · ματ
7 αιω͜λογιαν · θελον͜τεσ · ειναι · νομο ·
διδασκαλοι · Μη · νο ουντεσ · μητε ·
α · λεγουσιν · μητε · περι τινον[3] ·
δια͜βαι βαι͜ουνται ·
8 Ο.ιδαμεν · δε · οτι · καλοσ · ονομοσ ·
εαν · τισ · αυτω · νομιμωσ · χρηται ·
9 ειδοσ[4] · τουτο · οτι · δι͜και͜ω · νομοσ · ȣκ ·
ειται · αλλανομοισ · τε ϗ · ανυπο
τακτοισ · ασεβεσιν · ϗ · αμαρτωλοισ ·
ϗ ανοσειοισ · και βεβηλοισ · πατρο
λωαισ · και · μητρολωαισ · αναροφο
10 νοισ[5] · πορνοισ · αρσενοκοι͜ταισ ·
ανδραποδιταισ · ψ̈ευσταισ · επι
ορκοισ · ϗ ειτι · ετερον · τη · ϋγει
εν͜νουση · διδασ καλια · αντι κειται ·
11 κατα · το · ευαγγελιον · τησ · δοξησ ·
του · μακαριου · θ̅υ̅ · Ο · επιστευ
12 θην · εγω · χαρειν · εχω · τω · εν · δυ
ναμω͜σαντι · μαι · χ̅ρ̅ω̅ · ι̅η̅υ̅ · τω · κ̅ω̅

docerent · neque intenderent
fabulis · et genealogiis · Intermi
natis · quae questiones praestant
magis quam aedificationem d̅i̅
quae est in fide · Finis autem prae
cepti est caritas · de corde pu
ro · et conscientia bona
et fide non ficta · A quibusdam
aberrantes · conversi sunt in vani
loquium volentes esse legis
doctores · Non intellegentes neque
quæ loquntur neque de quibus
affirmant ·
Scimus autem quia bona est lex
si quis ea legitime utatur ·
sciens hoc quia justo lex non est
posita · sed injustis · et non sub
ditis · impiis et peccatoribus
sceleratis · et contaminatis patri
cidis · et matricidis · homicidis ·
fornicariis · masculorum concubitoribus
plagiariis · p juriis mendatibus
et si quid aliud sane
doctrine adversatur quae
secundum evangelium est gloriae
beati d̅i̅ · q̅d̅ creditum est mihi ·
mihi · Gratias ago ei qui me
c̅ fortavit x̅p̅o̅ i̅h̅u̅ d̅n̅o̅

---

[1] συνδησεως : *in marg.* συνϊδησισ. [2] εξετραπησαν. [3] τινων. [4] Ειδωσ. [5] Αλλ. [6] ανδροφονοισ.

	Latin	Greek
CAP. I.	nro · quia fidelem me existimavit	ημων · οτι · πιστον · μαι · ηγησατο ·
v. 13	ponens in misterio qui prius	θεμενοσ · εισ · διακονίαν · το · προτε
	fui plasphemus et persecutor	ρον · οντα · βλασφημον · και · διωκ
	et contumeliosus · sed miseri	την · και · ϋβρεισ‿την · αλλα · ηλαι
	cordiam consecutus sum · quia ignorans ·	ηθην · Οτι · αγνον[1] · εποι‿ησα · εν ·
14	feci in incredulitate · Superabundavit autem	απιστια · Ϋπερ · επλεο‿νασεν · δε ·
	gratia dni nri cum	ηχαρεισ · του · κυ · ημων · μετα
	fide et dilectione quæ est in xpo	πιστεοσ[2] · και · αγαπεσ[3] · τησ · εν · χ
15	ihu · Fidelis sermo et omni accep	ιηυ · Πιστοσ · ολογοσ · και · πασεσ[4]
	tione dignus quia xpc ihc venit	δοξεσ[5] · αξιοσ · οτι · χρσ · ιησ · ελθε[6]
	in hunc mundum peccatores salvos	εισ · τον · κοσμον · αμαρτω‿λουσ ·
	facere · quorum primus ego sum ·	σωσαι · ων · πρωτο[7] · ειμι · εγω ·
16	sed ideo misericordiam consecutus sum	αλλα · δια · τουτο · ελαι‿ηθεν[8] ·
	ut in me primo ostenderet xpc	ϊνα · εν · εμοι · προτο[9] · ενδειξηται[10]
	ihc · omnem patientiam	ιησ · την · απασαν · μακροθυμιαν —
	ad informationem eorum qui	προσ · υποτυπωσιν · τον[11] ·
	credituri sunt illi	μελλον · των · πιστευ‿ειν · επαυτ
17	in vitam aeternam · Regi	εισ · ζωην · αιω‿νιον · Τω · δε · βα
	autem saeculorum inmortali	των · αιωνον · αφθαρτω ·
	invisibili · soli do	α · ορατω · α · θανατω · μονω · θω —
	honor et gloria · in sæcula	τει με[12] · και · δοξα · εισ · τουσ · α
	sæculorum Amen ·	των · αιωνων · Αμην
18	Hoc praeceptum com men	Ταυτην · την · απαγγελίαν · παρ
	do tibi fili timothee	τι θεμαι · σοι · τεκνον · τιμοθεε -
	secundum pcedentes inte pro	κατα · τασ · προ · αγουσασ · επι
	phetias · ut milites in illis	φητίασ · ϊνα · στρα‿τευη · εν · αυ
19	bonam militiam · habens fi	την · καλεν[13] στρατίαν · εχων ·
	dem · et bonam conscientiam · quam	τιν · και · αγαθην · συν‿ϊδησιν · ην —

[1] αγνων. [2] πιστεωσ. [3] αγαπησ. [4] πασησ. [5] αποδοχησ. [6] ηλθεν. [7] πρωτο...
[8] ελαιηθην. [9] πρωτω. [10] *In marg.* ενδιξεν. [11] των. [12] τειμη. [13] καλ...

CAP. I. τινεσ · απωσαμενοι · περι · την · πισ	quidam reppellentes · naufraga
v. 20 τῖν · εν · αναγισαν[1] · ων · εστιν · υμε	verunt circa fidem · ex quibus est
νεοσ · και · αλεξανδροσ · ουσ · παρε	υmeneus et alexander quos tra
δωκα · τω · σαταvα · ῖνα · πεδευθω	didi satanae · Ut discant
CAP. II. σιν · μη · πλασ φημιν[2] · Ταπακα‿λει[3] ·	non plasphemare · Obsecro
1 ουν · πρωτον · ποι‿εισθαι · δεεσεισ[4] ·	ergo primum fieri obsecrationes
προσευχασ · εντευξεισ · ευχαρισ	orationes · postulationes · gratia
τιασ · υπερ · παντον · ανθρω πον[5] ·	rum actiones · pro omnibus hominibus
2 υπερ · βασιλαιων · ꝁ παντων · των	pro regibus et omnibus
υπερ · οχε[6] οντων · ῖνα · ηρεμιον[7] ·	qui in sublimitate sunt, ut quietam
και · ησυχειον · βιον · διαγομην[8] ·	et tranquillam vitam agamus ·
εν · παση · ευσεβια · ꝁ · σεμνοτητι ·	in omni pietate · et castitate ·
3 τουτο · γαρ · καλον · ꝁ · αποδεκτον ·	hoc enim bonum est et acceptum
ενωπιον · του · σωτηροσ · ημων · θ̅υ̅ ·	coram salvatore nostro d̅o̅
4 οσ · παντασ · ανθροπουσ[9] · θελει · σω	qui omnes homines vult salvos fie
θηναι[10] · και · εισ · επιγνοσιν[11] · αληθῖ	ri et ad agnitionem verita
5 ασ · ελθειν · Εισ · γαρ · θ̅σ̅ · εισ · ꝁ μεσει	tis venire · Unus enim d̅s̅ unus et me
τησ · θ̅υ̅ · ꝁ ανθροπων · ανθροπωσ[12] ·	diator d̅i̅ et hominum · homo
6 χ̅ρ̅σ̅ · ι̅σ̅ · Ο · δουσ · εαυτον · αντιλυ	x̅p̅c̅ i̅h̅s̅ qui dedit redemtionem
τρον · υπερ , παντον[13] · ουτο · μαρτυ	semet ipsum pro omnibus testimoni
7 ριον · καιρουσ[14] · ιδει‿οισ · εδοτη[15] · εν · ω ·	um temporibus suis in quo
ετεθην · εγω · κηρυξ · και αποστολοσ ·	positus sum ego p̄dicator · et aposto
αλεδιαν[16] · λεγω · ου · ψευδομαι ·	lus · veritatem dico non mentior
διδασκαλοσ · εθνον[17] · εν · πιστι · ꝁ · αλη	doctor gentium in fide et verita
8 θε̂α · Θυλομαι · ουν · τυυσ · αναρασ,[18]	te · Volo ergo viros
προ σευχεσθαι · εν παντι · το‿πω ·	orare in omni loco
επαι ροντασ · οσι‿ουσ · χειρασ · χωρισ ·	levantes puras manus sine
9 οργησ · και · δια λογεισ‿μων · οσαυ	ira et disceptatione · Simi

[1] εναναγησαν. [2] βλασφημῖν. [3] Παρακαλει. [4] δεησεισ. [5] παντων ανθρωπων. [6] ὑπεροχη. [7] ηρεμιαν. [8] διαγωμεν. [9] ανθρωπουσ. [10] *In marg.* contra γοδδισκαλκον. [11] επιγνωσιν. [12] ανθρωπων. Ανθρωποσ. [13] παντων. [14] Καιροισ. [15] εδοθη. [16] Αληθιαν. [17] εθνων. [18] ανδρασ.

CAP. II. liter et mulieres in habitu
ornato · cum verecundia et sobri
etate ornantes se · Non
intortis crinibus aut auro aut
margaritis vel veste pretio
v. 10 sa · Sed quō decet mulieres pro
mittentes pietatem per ope
11 ra bona · Mulier in silentio
discat cum omni subjectione ·
12 docere autem mulieri non permit
to · Neque dominari in virum
13 sed esse in silentio · Adam enim pri
14 mus formatus est · deinde eva · et a
dam non est seductus · Mulier autem
seducta in prevaricatione
15 fuit · Salvabitur autem per filiorum
generationem · si permanse
rint in fide et dilectione et scī
ficatione cum sobrietate ·
f CAP. III. 1 Fidelis sermo si quis episcopatum
bonum opus deside
2 rat · Oportet autem episcopum sine
crimine esse · Unius uxoris
virum · Sobrium · prudentem · pudicum
ornatum · hospitalem · doctorem ·
3 Non vinolentum non percusso
rem · sed modestum · Non litigiosum
4 non cupidum · suae domui

τωσ[1] · και γυναικασ · εν · κατασ_τολη
κοσμειωσ · μετα · αιδουσ · κ̄ · σω
φροσυνησ · κοσμιν · εαυτασ · μη ·
εν πλεγμασιν · και · χρισειο[2] · η ·
μαργαρειταισ[3] · η · ϊμα_τεισμω · πολυ
τελει[4] · Αλλο · πρεπει · γυναξειν[5] · επ
αγcγελομεν_αισ · θε · σεβίαν[6] · δι · ερ
γων · αγαθων · Γυνη · εν ησυχία ·
μανθαναι · τω · εν · πασε[7] · υποτα_γη
διδασκειν · δε · γυναικαι[8] · ουκ · επι
τρεπω · ουδε · λυθεν · τειν · ανδρασ ·
αλλει_ναι · εν · εσιχία[9] · Αδαμ · γ–
πλασθε[10] · πρωτοσ · ειτα · ευα · και –
δαμ · ουκ · ηπατηθη · Η · δε · γυνη –
εξαπα_τεθεισα[11] · Εν · παρα_βασ–
γογονεν[12] · Cωθησεται · δε · δια · τη–
τεκνο_γονίασ[13] · εαν · μειν–
σειν · εν · πιστι · και · αγαπε[14] · και –
ασμω · μετα · σω φροσυνησ ·
Πιστοσ · ο · λογοσ · ειτισ · επισκο–
οραιγεται · καλου · εργου · επιθυ
μι · Δει · δετον επισκοπον[15] ανε–
λημπτον · ειναι · μιασ γυναι_κοσ –
ανδρα · νηφαλαιον · σωφρονα ·
κοσμιον · φυλοξενον[16] · διδακτι
κον · μη · παροι_νον · μη · πληκ
την · Αλλεπι ει_κην · αμαχον ·
α · φιλαργυρον · του · ϊδιου · οι_κου

[1] Ὡσαυτωσ. [2] χρυσειω. [3] μαργαργαρειταισ. [4] *In marg.* διασπολυτεσ. [5] γυναιξειν –
[6] επαγγελομεναισ θεοσεβίαν. [7] παση. [8] γυναικι. [9] ησυχία. [10] επλασθη. [11] εξαπατηθεισ–
[12] γεγονεν. [13] *In marg.* τεκνογονία. [14] αγαπη. [15] *In marg.* περι επισκοπου. [16] φιλοξενον –

III. καλωσ · προσ_ισταμενον · τεκνα ·	bene prepositum filios
εχοντα · εν · υπο_ταγη · μετα · πα	habentem subtitos cum om
v. 5 σησ · σεμνο_τητοσ · Ει · δε · τισ · του ·	ni castitate · Siquis autem
ιδιου · οικου · προσ_τηναι · ουκ · οιδεν ·	suae domui p̄ esse nescit
ποσ[1] · εκκλησιασ · θυ · επι_μελησεται ·	quo modo ecclesiæ d̄i diligentiam habebit
6 με[2] · νεο_φυτον · ινα · μη · τυφω_θεισ ·	non neophitum ne in superbiam elatus
εισ · κριμα · ενπεσε[3] · του · διαβολου ·	in juditium incidat diaboli ·
7 δει · δε · και · μαρτυριαν · εχειν · κα	oportet autem illum et testimonium habere
λην · απο · τω[4] · εξωθεν · ινα · μη ·	bonum · ab his qui foris sunt ut non
εισ · ονει_δεισμον · ενπεσε[5] · και · πα	in obprobrium incidat et la
γειδα · του · διαβολου · [6]	queum diaboli
8 Διακονουσ[7] · ωσαυτοσ[8] · σεμνουσ · μη ·	Diaconos similiter pudicos · non
διλογουσ · μη · ιονω[9] · πολλω · προσ	bilinges · non multo vino dedi
εχοντεσ · μη · αισχρο_κερ δεισ ·	tos · Nonturbe lucrum sectantes ·
9 εχοντασ · το · μυστηριον · τησ · πισ	habentes mysterium fi
τεοσ[10] · εν · καθαρα · συνιδησι ·	dei inconscientia pura
10 και · ουτοι · δεδοκειμαζεσθωσαν ·	et hiautem probentur
προτον[11] · ειτα · δια_κονει · τωσαν ·	primum · et sic ministrent
ανεν · κλητοιον · εχοντεσ ·	nullum crimen habentes ·
11 Γυναικασ[12] · ωσ · αυτοσ[13] · σεμ_νασ · μη ·	Mulieres similiter pudicas non
διαβολουσ · νη · φαλαιουσ · πιστασ ·	detrahentes · sobrias fideles in
12 εν · πασιν · Διακονοι · δε · εστωσαν · μιασ ·	omnibus Diaconi autem sint unius
γυναικοσ · ανδρεσ · τεκνων · καλων[14] ·	uxoris viri · qui filiis suis bene
προ ισταμενοι · και των · ιδιων · οικων ·	p̄sint · et domibus suis ·
Οι · γαρ · καλωσ · διακονησαν_τεσ ·	Qui enim bene ministraverint
βαθμον · εαυτοισ · καλον · περι	gradum sibi bonum adqui
ποι_ουνται · και · πολλην · παρρε	runt · et multam fiduci
σιαν[15] · εν · πιστι · την · εν · χρω · ιυ ·	am in fide quae est in x̄po īhu

[1] Πωσ. [2] Μη. [3] εν πεση. [4] των. [5] ενπεση. [6] v. 7 *habet ad calcem paginæ.*
[7] *In marg.* περι των διακονων. [8] ωσ αυτωσ. [9] οινω. [10] την πιστεωσ. [11] πρωτον.
[12] *In marg.* περι των γυναικων. [13] ωσαυτωσ. [14] καλωσ. [15] παρρησιαν.

CAP. III. v. 14	haec tibi scribo sperans me ve	ταυτα · σοι · γραφω · ελπειζο[1] · ελ
15	nire cito adte · Si autem tardavero	θειν · τα‿χειον · Εαν · βραδυνω ·
	ut scias quomodo oporteat te in domo	ϊνα · ιδησ · πωσ · δει · εν · οικω · θῡ ·
	dī conversari quæ est ecclesia	αναστρε‿φεσθαι · Η · τισ · εστιν · ε
	dī vivi columna	κλησια · θῡ · ζωντοσ · στυλοσ ·
16	et firmamentum veritatis · et	καὶ · αδραιωμα[2] · τησ · αληθιασ · και ·
	manifeste magnum est	ομο‿λογȣμενῶσ · μεγα · εστιν ·
	pietatis sacra mentum	το · τησ · ευσεβιασ · μιστεριον[3] ·
	quod manifestum est in carne	οσ̄ · εφανηρωθη[4] · εν · σαρκι · εδικαι
	justificatum est in spū apparuit ange ∫lis	ωθη · εν · πν̄ι · ωφθη · αγγελοισ ·
	p̄dicatum est gentibus · credi	εκηρυχθη · εν · εθνεσιν · πιστευ
	tum est in mundo · assumptum est in	θη · εν · κοσμω · ανελημφθη · εν ·
CAP. IV. 1	gloria · Sp̄s autem manifeste dicit	δοξη · Ο · δε · πν̄α · ρητωσ · λεγει
	quia in novissimis temporibus dis	οτι · εν · ϋστεροισ · και ροισ · Απ ‹
	cedent quidam a fide ·	τη‿σονται · τινεσ · τεσ · πιστεοσ
	attendentes spiritibus erro	πρωσ · εχοντεσ[6] · πνευμασιν · πλα
	ris · et doctrinis dæmo	νοισ · και · διδασκαλιαισ · δαι‿μο
2	niorum in hypocrisi loquentium	νιων · εν υποκρισι · ψευδο λο
	mendatium · et cauteriatam habentes	γον[7] · και · καυτηριασ μενων[8] · την
3	suam conscientiam · prohibentium	ϊδιαν · συν ϊδησιν · κωλυον‿των ·
	nubere · abstinere a cibis	γαμιν · απεχεσδαι[9] · βρωματων ·
	quos d̄s creavit · ad percipiendum	α · ο · θσ̄ · εκτεισεν · εισ μετα λημ
	cum gratiarum actione fide	ψειν · μετα ευχαριστιασ · τοισ –
	libus et his qui cognoverunt	πιστοισ · και · επι γνωκοσιν · την –
4	veritatem quia omnis creatura dī	αληδιαν[10] · οτι · παν · κτεισμα · θῡ –
	bona · et nihil rejiciendum	καλον · και · ουδεν · απο βλητον
	q̄d cum gratiarum actione percipi	μετευ‿χαριστῖασ · λαμβα‿νομε
5	tur · Sc̄ificatur enim per verbuın dī	νον · αγιαζεται · γαρ · δια · λογου –

[1] ελπειζω. [2] εδραιωμα. [3] μυστηριον. [4] εφανερωθη. [5] τησ πιστεωσ. [6] Προσ εχοντε-
[7] ψευδολογων. [8] κεκαυτηριασμενων. [9] απεχεσθαι. [10] αληθιαν.

μων εν χρω ιυ · Το · λοιπον · αδελ
φοι · οσα · εστειν · αληθη · οσα ·
σεμνα · οσα · δικαια · οσα · αγ_να · ο
σα · προσ φειλη · οσα · ευφημα ·
Ει τεισ · αρετη · και · ειτεισ · επαινοσ ·
επεισ · τημησ · ταυτα · λογει_ζεσθαι ·
α · και · εμαθαται[1] · και · παρελαβε
ται · και ηκου_σαται & ιδεται ·
εν · εμοι · Ταυτα πρασσεται · και
ο θσ τησ ϊρηνισ[2] · εσται · μεθυ_
μων · Εχαρην · δε · εν · κω · μεγα
λωσ · οτι · ηδη · ποτε · ανεθαλε
ται · του · υπερ · εμου · φρονειν ·
εφω · και · εφρονιται · Η και ρεισ_
θαι · δε · ουχ · οτι · καθυσ · τερεσιν[3] ·
λεγω · Εγο[4] · γαρ · εμαθον · ενοισ ·
ειμι · ανταρκησ · ειναι · Οιδα · και ·
ταπει_νουσθαι · οιδα · και · περισ_
σευειν · Εν · παντι · και · εν · πασιν ·
μεμυ · ημαι · και · χορτα_ζεσθαι ·
αι · πει_ναν · και · περισσευ ειν · και
υστε_ρεισθαι · παντα · ϊσχυω · εν · τω ·
· δυνα_μουν_τιμαι · χρυ · πλην ·
καλωσ · ποι_ησαται · συν κοι_νω
σαντεσ · τη · θλι_ψι · μου · Οιδα
· δε · και · υμεισ · φιλιππησει_οι ·
· εν · αρχη · του · ευαγγελιου ·
· εξηλθον · απο μακαι_δο_

vestras in xpo ihu · Decetero
frs quæcuque sunt vera quæ cumque
pudica quæ cumque justa quæcuque sca
quæ cumque amabilia quæ cuque bonæ famæ ·
Si qua virtus · si qua laus
disciplinæ · haec cogitate
quæ et didicistis et accepis
tis · et audistis et vidistis
in me · haec agite et
ds pacis erit vobis
cum · Gavisus sum autem in dno vehe
menter quo tandem aliquando reflo
ruistis pro me sentire
sicut et sentiebatis · Occupati
autem eratis · non quasi propter penuriam
dico · Ego enim didici in quibus
sum sufficiens esse · scio et
humiliari · scio et abunda
re · Ubique et in omnibus
institutus sum · et satiari ·
et esurire · et abundare · et
penuriam pati · Omnia possum in eo
qui me confortat · Verutamen
bene fecistis communican
tes tribulationi meae · Sci
tis autem et vos philippenses
quod in principio evangelii
quando profectus sum a macedo

1 εμαθεται. 2 ϊρηνησ. 3 συχ ουτι καθυστερησιν. 4 Εγω.

CAP. IV.[a] nia · nulla mihi eccle
sia communicavit · In oratione
dati et accepti · Nisi
v. 16 vos soli · quia et thesalo
nicam · et semel et bis
in usum mihi misis
17 tis · Non quia quæro da
tum · sed requiro fruc
tum abundantem in
18 ratione vestra · Habeo
autem omnia et abundo · re
pletus sum · Acceptis ab
epa frodito quae mi
sistis · odorem suavitatis
hostiam acceptam placen
19 tem do · Ds autem meus imple
at omne desiderium vestrum scdm
divitias suas in glo
20 ria in xpo ihu · do autem · et
patri nostro · gloria in
sæcula sæculorum Amen ·
21 Salutate omnem scm in xpo
ihu · Salutant vos qui mecum sunt
22 frs · Salutant vos
omnes sci maxime
autem qui de cæsaris domo sunt
23 Gratia dni nri ihu xpi cum
spiritu vestro · EXPLICIT
∫ AD PHILIPPENSES

νειασ · οτι · ουδεμια · μοι · εκκλη
σια · εκοι‿νωνησεν · εισ · λογον
δοσεωσ · και · λημ‿ψαιωσ · ειμη ·
υμεισ μονοι · οτι και εν · θεσα‿
λονι‿κη · και · απαξι · και · δ εισ
εισ · την · χριαν · μοι · επεμ‿ψα
ται · Ουχ · οτι · επιζετω[1] · το · δο
μα · αλλε‿πιζετω[2] · τον · καρ
πον · τον · πλεονα‿ζοντα · εισ ·
τον · λογον · υμων · απεχω ·
δε · παντα · και · περισσευω · πε
πληρωμαι · δεξαμενοσ · παρα ·
επα‿φροδιτου · τα · παρ ϋμων —
πεμφθεντα‿οσμην, ευωδει
ασ[3] · θυσιαν · δεκτην · ευαρεσ
τεν[4] · τω θω · Ο · δε · θσ · μου · πλη
ρωσε · πασαν · χριαν · υμων · κατα
του · πλουτοσ · αυτου · εν · δο
ξη · εν · χρω · ιυ · Τω · δε · θω · και ·
πατρι · ημων · η · δοξα · εισ · τουσ
αιωνασ · των · αιωνον[5] · αμην ·
Ασπασ‿θαι · παντα · αγιον · εν — χ
ιυ · ασπαζονται · υμασ · οι · συνε
μοι · αθελφοι[6] · ασπαζονται ·
παντεσ · οι · αγιοι · μαλλειστα —
δε · οι · εκ · τησ · και‿σαιροσ · οικ ·
Η · χαρεισ · του · κυ · ιυ · χυ · μετ
του · πνσ · υμων ; Ετελεσθη προ
∫ Φιλιππησιουσ

---

[1] επιζητω. [2] Αλλεπιζητω. [3] ευδωδειασ. [4] ευαρεστον. [5] αιωνων. [6] αδελφο —

Αρχεται προσ Κο	Incipit ad co
λοσσαισ ·	losenses ·
P. I. V. 1 Παυλοσ αποστο	Paulus aposto
λοσ χρυ · ιυ · δια · θεληματ	lus xpi ihu per voluntatem
τοσ · θυ · και · τιμοθεοσ · ο · αθελ	di · et timotheus fr
2 φοσ[1] · τοισ · εν · κολοσσαισ · αγιοισ · και	his qui sunt colosis · scis et fide
πιστοισ · αθελφοισ[2] · εν · χρω ιυ ·	libus frib · in xpo ihu
Χαρισ · υμιν · και · ϊρηνη · απο · θυ ·	Gratia vobis et pax a do
πατροσ · ημων · και · κυ · ιηυ · χρυ ·	patre nro · et dno ihu xpo ·
3 Ευχαρεισ · τουμεν · τω · θω · τω	Gratias agimus do et
πατρι · του · κυ · ημων · ιυ · χρυ ·	patri dni nri ihu xpi
παντοτε · ϋπερ · ϋμων · προσευ	semper pro vobis oran
4 χομενοι · ακουσαντεσ · την ·	tes audientes
πιστιν · υμων εν χρω ιυ · και	fidem vram in xpo ihu et
την · αγαπην · ην · εχεται · εισ · παν	dilectionem quam habetis in om
5 τασ · τουσ · αγιουσ · Δια · την · ελπι	nes scos propter spem
δα · την · αποκει_μενην · υμιν ·	quae reposita est vobis
εν · τοισ · ουρανοισ · ην · προ ηκου	in cælis quam audistis
σαται · εν · τω · λογω · τησ · αληθιασ ·	in verbo veritatis
6 του · ευαγγελιυ · του · πα_ρον_τοσ ·	evangelii qd pervenit
εισ · υμασ · καθωσ · και · εν · παντι ·	ad vos · Sicut et in univer
τω · κοσμω · και · εστιν · καπροφο	so mundo · et fructificat
ρουμενον[3] · και · αυξανομενον ·	et crescit ·
καθοσ[4] · και · εν · υμιν · αφημερασ ·	sicut in vobis ex ea die qua
ηκουσαται · και · επεγνοται[5] · την ·	audistis et cognovistis
χαριν · του · θυ · εν · αληθια · κα	gratiam di in veritate · Sicut
θωσ · μαθεται · απο επα_φρα · του_	didicistis ab epa phra

[1] αδελφοσ. [2] αδελφοισ. [3] καρποφορουμενον. [4] Καθωσ. [5] επεγνωται.

CAP. I.	carissimo conservo nro	αγαπητου · συνδυλουσ[1] · ημων ·
	qui est fidelis pro vobis · mi	οσ · εστιν · πιστοσ · υπερ · ημων · δια_
v. 8	nister xpi ihu · Qui etiam ma	κονοσ τȣ χρυ · Ο · και · δηλω
	nifestavit nobis dilectionem vram	σασ[2] · ημιν · την · υμων · αγαπεν[3] ·
9	in psiritu · Inde et nos	εν · πνι · Δια τουτο · ϗ · ημεισ ·
	ex qua die audivimus · Non	αφησ · ημερασ · ηκουσαμεν · ου
	cessamus pro vobis orantes	παυομαιδα[4] ϋπερ · ϋμων προσ_
	et postulantes	ευχομενοι · και αιτου_μενοι ·
	ut impleamini agnitio	ϊνα · πληρωθηται · την · επιγνω_
	ne voluntatis ejus · In om	σιν · του · θεληματοσ · αυτȣ · εν
	ni sapientia et intellectu spi	πασι[5] · σοφια · και συνεσι · πνευμα
10	ritali · ut ambuletis digne	τικη · περιπα_τεσαι[6] · αξιωσ · του ·
	do per omnia placentes · In om	κυ · εισ · πασαν · αρεσ_κίαν · εν · παν
	ni opere bono fructi fican	τι · εργω · αγαθω · καρπο_φορȣν
	tes et crescentes in sci	τεσ · και αυξανομενοι · τη · επι
11	entia di · In omni virtute	γνωσει · του · θυ · Εν · παση · δυνα
	confortati · secundum poten	μει · δυναμου_μενοι · κατα · το ·
	tiam claritatis ejus · In om	κρατοσ · τησ · δοξησ · αυτου · εισ -
	ni patientia et longanimi	πασαν · ϋπομονην · και · μα_κρο
12	tate cum gaudio · gratias	θυμίαν · μετα · χαρασ · ευχαρι
	agente do patri qui voca	στουν_τεσ · θω · τω · πρι · τω · κα
	vit nos in partem	λεσαντι · ημασ · εισ · την · μερει_
	sortis scorum in	δα · του · κληρου · των · αγιον[7] · εν -
13	lumine · Qui eripuit nos de	τω · φωτι · Οσ · ερυσατο[8] · ημασ
	potestate tene brarum	τησ · εξου_σίασ · του · σκο_τουσ -
	et transtulit in regnum	και · μετεσ_τησεν · εισ · την · βασ
	filii dilectionis suae ·	του · ϋιοϋ · τησ · αγαπησ · αυτου -
14	In quo habemus redemptionem	Εν · ω · εχομεν · την · απολυ_τρωσ

[1] συνδουλου. [2] δηλωσ : (ασ :) [3] αγαπην. [4] παυομαιθα. [5] παση. [6] περιπατησαι. [7] αγιων. [8] ερυσατο. [9] απολυτρωσιν.

ην·αφεσίν·των·αμαρτιων·ο[1]·	et remissionem peccatorum qui
στιν·εικων·τ8·θ̅ν̅·του·αορατου·	est imago d̅i̅ invisibilis
πρωτοκοσ[2]·πασησ·κτει_σεωσ·	primogenitus omnis creaturae·
Οτι·εν·αυτω·εκ τεισ_θη·τα·παντα·	Quia in ipso condita sunt omnia
εν·τοισ·ουρανοισ·και·τα·επι·τησ·	in cælis et in
γησ·τα·ορατα·και·τα·αορατα·	terra · Visibilia et invisibilia
ειτε·θρονοι·ειτε·κυρει_οτη	sive troni·sive dominationes
τεσ·ειτε·αρχαι·ειτε·εξουσειαι·	sive principatus sive po
τα·παντα·δι αυτου·χ̃ι·εισ·αυτον	testates·omnia per ipsum et in ipso
κεκ_τεισται·χ̃ι·αυτοσ·εστιν·προ·	creata sunt et ipse est ante
παντων·χ̃ι·παντα·αυτω·συν	omnes·et omnia in ipso con
εστη κην[3]·και·αυτοσ·εστιν·η·κεφα	stant·et ipse est ca
η·του·σωματοσ·τησ εκκλησίασ·	put corporis ecclesiae
·εστιν·αρχη πρωτο·τοκοσ·εκ·των·	qui est principium·primogenitus
κρων · ινα·γενεται[4]·εν·πασιν·	ex mortuis·ut sit in omnibus
υτοσ·πρωτευων·Οτι·εν·αυτω·	ipse primatem tenens qa in ipso
δοκησεν·παν·το·πληρομα[5]·	complacuit omnem plenitudi
τοι_κησαι·και διαυτ8·απο	nem habitare·et per eum recon
_ταλλαξαι[6]·τα·παντα·εισ·αυτον·	ciliare omnia in ipsum
ινοποιησασ·δια·του·αιματοσ·	pacificans per sanguinem
ν·σταυ_ρου·αυτου·Ειτε·τα·επι	crucis ejus sive quae in
·γησ·ειπε·τα·εν·τουσ[7]·ουρα	cælis sive quæ in terra
σ·και·υμασ ποτε·οντασ·	sunt·et vos cum essetis aliquan
ηλλοτριω·μενουσ[8]·και·εκθρ8σ·	do alienati et inimici
·διανοιασ·υμων εν τοισ	sensu vestro in
οισ·τοισ·πονεροισ[9]·Νυν·δε·	operibus malis · Nunc autem
ο καταλλα_γεντεσ·εν·τω·σω	re conciliavit incor po
τι·τησ·σαρκοσ·δια·τ8·θανα_	re carnis ejus per mortem

In marg. a̅g̅. [2] πρωτοτοκοσ. [3] συνεστηκεν. [4] γενηται. [5] πληρωμα. [6] αποκαλταλλαξαι. [7] τοισ. [8] απηλλοτριωμενουσ. [9] πονηροισ.

CAP. I.	exibere vos sanctos	του·παρασ_τησαι·ϋμασ·αγιουσ
	et immaculatos·et inreph̅ensibiles	και·αμω μουσ·και ανε κλητουσ
v. 23	coram ipso · Si tamen	κατενω_πειον·αυτου · Ει·γε·
	permanetis in fide funda	επι_μενεται·τη·πιστι·τεθεμε
	ti et stabiles et	λειω_μενοι·και·εδραιοι·και
	inmobiles a	μη μετα_κει_νου_μενοι·απο
	spe evangelii	τησ·ελπειδοσ·του·ευαγγελου[1]·
	quod audistis q̅d p̅dicatum	ου·ηκουσατε·του·κηρυχθεν
	est in universa creatura quæ sub	τοσ[2]·εν·πασε̣[3]κτισει·τη·υπου
	cælo est · Cujus factus sum ego	ρανον·Ου εγενομε̣ν[4]·εγω
24	paulus minister qui nunc gau	παυλοσ·δια_κονοσ·οσ νυν·χαι
	deo in passionibus pro	ρω·εν·τοισ·παθημασιν·ϋπερ·
	vobis·et adimpleo ea quæ de	υμων·και αναπληρω·τα·ϋσ
	sunt passionum	τε_ρηματα·των·θλι_ψαιων·τ
	x̅p̅i̅ in carne mea·pro	χ̅ρ̅υ̅·εν·σαρκι·μου·ϋπερ·του·
	corpore ejus quod est ec	σωματοσ·αυτου·ο, εστιν·η·ε
25	clesia · Cujus factus sum ego mi	κλησι̂α · Ησ·εγενο μην·εγω·
	nister secundum dispensatio	ακονοσ·κατα·την·οικονομι̂
	nem d̅i̅·quae data est mihi	αν·του θ̅υ̅·την·δοθεισαν·μοι
	in vos · Ut impleam verbum	εισ·υμασ·πληρωσαι·τον·λογ
26	d̅i̅ mysterium quo abscon	του θ̅υ̅·το·μυστηριον·το·απ
	ditum fuit a sae	κεκρυμμε_νον·απο·των·αιω
	culis et generationibus	νων·και απο·των·γενεων·
	Nunc autem manifestum est sc̅i̅s̅ ejus	Νυν[5]·δε·εφανερω_θη·τοισ·
27	apostolis·quibus vo lu	αποστολοισ·αυτου·οισ·ηθελ
	it d̅s̅ notas facere diviti	σεν·οθ̅σ·γνωρεισαι·το·πλου
	as gloriae sacra men	τοσ·τησ·δοξησ·του·μυστη
	ti d̅i̅ in gentibus	ριου·του·θ̅υ̅·εν·τοισ·εθ_νεσιν

[1] ευαγγελιου. [2] κυρυχθεντοσ. [3] παση. [4] εγενομην. [5] Μυν-

P. I. ο·εστιν·χρσ·εν·υμιν·η·ελπισ·
v. 28 τησ·δοξησ·ον·ημεισ·κα ταγ
γελλομεν·νουθετουντεσ·
παντα·ανον·κ)·διδασκοντεσ·
εν·παση·σοφια·πνευματι_κη·
ϊνα·παρασ_τησωμεν·παντα·ανων[1]·
29 τελιον·εν·χρω·εν,ο·και·κοπει
ω·αγωνειξομενοσ[2]·κατα·την·
ενεργîαν·αυτου·την·ενεργου
μενεν[3]·εν·εμοι·εν·δυναμει·
CAP. II. 1 θελω·γαρ·ϋμασ·ϊδεναι·η_λει
κον·αγονα[4]·εχω·περι·υμων
και των εν·λαο_δικια·

[5]

Vide p. 35. [R. B.]

quod est xpc in vobis spes
gloriae·quem nos adnun
tiamus corripientes·
omnem hominem·et docentes
in omni sapientia spiritali·
ut exibeamus omnem hominem
perfectum in xpo ihu·in quo et labo
ro certando·secundum
operationem ejus quam ope
ratur in me in virtute·
Volo enim vos scire qua lem
sollicitudinem habeo pro vobis
et pro his qui sunt laodiciae
et qui cuque non viderunt
faciem meam in carne·
2 ut con solentur corda
ipsorum·instructi in
caritate·et in omnes diviti
as plenitudinis in
tellectus·in agnitionem
mysterii di·patris xpi
3 ihu·in quo sunt omnes
thesauri sapientiæ et scien
4 tiae absconditi · Hoc autem
dico ut nemo vos decipi
at in sublimitate sermo
5 num · Nam et si corpore
absens sum sed spu vo

[1] ανων. [2] αγωνειζομενοσ. [3] ενεργουμενην. [4] αγωνα.

[5] *Hoc spatium prorsus vacuum est in Codice Boerneriano.*

CAP. II. biscum sum · gaudens et
videns ordinem vestrum
et firmamentum ejus
quae in xpo est fidei vestrae ·
v. 6 Sicut ergo accepistis xpm
ihm dnm nrum · In ipso
7 ambulate radicati · et
super aedificati in ipso
et confirmati fide · sicut
et didicistis abundantes
in illo in gratiarum actio
8 ne · Videte nequis vos
decipiat per philosophi
am · et inanem fallatiam
secundum traditionem
hominum · secundum ele
menta mundi et non
9 secundum xpm quia in ipso
habitat omnis plenitudo
10 divinitatis corporaliter et
estis inillo repleti
qui est caput omis principat'
11 et potestatis · In quo et circum
cisi estis circumcisione non manufacta
in expoliatione corporis
carnis · In circum cisione
12 xpi · Con sepulti ei
in baptismo · in quo et resur

κοσμου · και · ου ·
κατα · χν · οτι · εν · αυτω · κατοι
κει · παν · το · πληρομα[1] · τησ ·
θεοτητοσ · σωματικωσ · και
εσται · εν · αυτω · πεπληρωμε νοι ·
ο · εστιν · κεφαλη · πασεσ[2] · αρχησ ·
και εξουσιασ · εν, ω · περι ετμη
θηται[3] · περιτομη · αχειρο · ποιητω ·
εν · τη · απεκδυσι · του · σωματοσ ·
τησ · σαρκοσ · εν · τη · περιτομη ·
του · χρυ · Cυν ταφεντεσ · αυτω ·
εν · τω · βαπτισμω · εν · ω · και · συν

---

[1] πληρωμα. [2] πασησ. [3] περι τομη ετμηθηται.

IV. και · εν · τευξαιωσ · Ταυτα ·	et orationem · Haec
6 υποτι θεμενοσ · τοισ · αθελφοισ[1] ·	proponesis fratribus
καλοσ · εση · διακονοσ · χρι[2] · ιηυ ·	bonus eris minister xpi ihu
εν · τρεφομενοσ · τοισ · λωγοισ[3] · τησ ·	enutritus verbis
πιστεωσ · και · τησ · καλησ · διδασ	fidei · et bonae doctrinae
καλιασ · η ; παρη κολου θησασ ·	quam assecutus es ·
aniles	
7 Τουσ · δε · βαι βηλουσ · και · γραω	Ineptas autem et inanes
δεισ[4] · μυθουσ · π · ραι του[5] · γυμ	fabulas devita · ex
ναζε · δε · ση · αυτον[6] · προσ · ευσεβι	erce autem te ipsum ad pieta
8 αν · Η · γαρ · σωματικη · γυμνα	tem · Nam corporalis exerti
σια · προσ · ολιγον · μεν · εστιν · ωφε	tatio · ad modicum quidem uti
λιμοσ · η · δε · ευσεβια · προσ · παντα ·	lis est · pietas autem ad omnia
ωφελιμοσ · επαγγελιαν · εχουσα ·	utilis est · promissionem habens
ζωησ · τησ · νυν · και · τησ · μελλου	vitae quae est nunc · et futu
9 σησ · Πιστοσ · ο · λογοσ · και · πασησ ·	rae · Fidelis sermo et omni
10 απο δοχεσ · αξιωσ[7] · εισ · τουτο · γαρ ·	acceptione dignus · In hoc enim
και · κω πεωμεν[8] · και · αγωνιζο	laboramus · et maledicimur
μεδα[9] · οτι · ηλπικαμεν · επι · θυ[10] ·	quia speramus in dm
ζοντι[11] · οσ · εστιν · σωτηρ · παντων ·	vivum · qui est salvator omnium
11 ανων[12] · μαλλιστα · πιστων · παραγ	hominum maxime fidelium ·
γελαε · ταυτα · και · διδασ και ·	precipe haec et doce ·
12 Μηδεισ · σου · τησ · νεο τητοσ · κατα	Nemo adolescentiam tuam
φρονειτω · αλλα · τυποσ · γεινȣ ·	con temnat · Sed exemplum esto
τω · πιστων · εν · λογω · εν · αναστ	fidelium · in verbo · in cversati
τροφη · εν · αγαπη · εν · πιστι · εν	one · in caritate · In fide · In casti
13 αγνια · εωσ · ερχομαι · προσεχε ·	tate · dum venio attende
τη · αναγνωσι · τη · παρα κλησει ·	lectioni · exortationi
14 τη · διδασκαλια · Μη · αμε λει · τȣ ·	doctrinae · Noli neglegere

[1] αδελφοισ. [2] χρυ. [3] λογοισ. [4] και αιγραωδεισ. [5] παραιτου. [6] σεαυτον. [7] αποδοχησ αξιωοσ. [8] κοπειωμεν. [9] αγωνιζομεθα. [10] Θω. [11] ζωντι. [12] *In marg.* contra γοδδισκαλκον.

CAP. IV.	gratiam d̄ī quae inte est quæ data est	εν·σοι·χαρισματοσ·ο·εδοθη·σοι
	tibi per prophetam cum impositione	δια·προφητιασ·μετεπιθεσεωσ·
	manuum prespiterii·	των·χιρων·του·πρεσπυτεριου[1]·
v. 15	Haec meditare in his esto	Ταυτα·μελετα·εν·τουτοισ·ϊσθει·
	ut profectus tuus manifestus sit	ϊνα·σου·η̄·προκοπη·φανερα·η̄·πι
16	omnibus attende tibi et doc	σιν·επεχε·σεαυτω·και·τη·δι
	trinae·insta in illis·	δασκαλι͡α·επι·μεναι·αυτοισ·
	Hoc enim faciens·ette ipsum salvum	Τουτο·γαρ·ποιων·και·σεαυτον·
	facies·et eos qui te audiunt·	σωσισ·και·τουσ·ακȣοντασ·σου·
CAP. V. 1	Seniores ne increpaveris·sed	Πρεσβυτερω·μη·επιπλεξησ[2]·αλλ
	obscura ut patrem · Juvenes	παρα‿καλει·ωσ·πατερα · Νεω
2	ut fratres·anus	τερουσ·ωσ·αθελφουσ[3] · Πρεσβυ
	ut matres · Juvenculas	τερασ·ωσ·μητερασ · Νεοτε‿ρασ[4]
3	ut sorores in omni castitate	ωσ·αθελφασ[5]·εν·πασε[6]·αγνι͡α·χη
4	Viduas honora quæ vere viduæ sunt	τιμα·τασ·οντωσ·χηρασ·Ει·δε·
	siq autem vidua filios aut nepotes	τεισ·χηρα[7]·τεκνα·η·εκγονα·
	habet·discat primum	εχει·μανθανε‿τωσαν·πρωτον·
	domum suam regere·et mutu	τον·ϊδιον·οικον·ευσεβειν[8]·και
	am vicem reddere	αμοιβασ·αποδει‿δοναι·τοισ·
	parentibus hoc enim accep	προγονοισ · Τουτο·γαρ·εστιν·αι
	tum est coram d̄o·	δεκτον·ενωπιον·του·θ̄υ
5	Quæ autem vere vidua est et deso	Η·δε·οντωσ·χηρα·και·μεμο
	lata·sperat in d̄m·et	νωμενη·ηλπι͡κεν·επι·θ̄ν·και
	instat obsecrationibus et ora	προσ‿μενει·ταισ·δαι‿η‿σεσιν·κα
	tionibus nocte et nocte· (die)	ταισ·προ‿σευ‿χαρισ[9]·νυκτοσ·κα
6	Nam quae in deliciis est vivens	ημηρασ[10] · Η·δε·σπατα‿λωσα·ζ
7	mortua est·et hæc prae	τεθνηκεν·και·ταυτα·παραγ
	cipe ut in rep̄hensibiles IE	γελλαι·ϊνα·ανε πει‿λημπτοι·

[1] πρεσβυτεριου. [2] επιπληξησ. [3] αδελφουσ. [4] Νεωτερασ. [5] αδελφασ. [6] παση.
[7] Ḥ χηρα (*i.e.* H *vel* N. Matthaei). [8] *In marg.* phorphirii. [9] προσευχαισ. [10] ημερασ.

CAP. V. v. 8 ωσειν · Ει · δε · τισ · των · ϊδιων ·
και · μαλλειστα · οικιων · ου · προ
νοειται[1] · την · πιστιν · ηρνητε · και ·
9 εστιν · απισ_του · χειρων · Χηρα ·
κατα_λεγεσθω · μη · ελαττων
ετω̂ν · εξη_κον · τα · γεγον_υϊα ·
10 ενοσ · ανδροσ · γυνη · ενεργοισ ·
καλοισ · μαρτυρου_μενη · ει ·
ετεκνο_φορεσεν · Ει · εξενο δο
χησεν · ει · αγιων · ποδασ · ενει_
ψεν · Ει · θλιβομενοισ · επερκη_
σεν[2] · ει · παντι · εργω · αγαθω · επι
11 κολουθησεν · Νεωτερασ · δε ·
χερασ[3] · παραιτου · Οταν · γαρ ·
κατα_στρηνειασ · ουσ_ειν · του · $\overline{χυ}$ ·
12 γαμειν · θελουσιν · εχου_σαι · κρι
μα · οτι · την · πρω_την · πιστιν · ηθε
13 τησαν · αμα · δαι · και · αργαι · μαν
θανου_σιν · περι ερχομεναι · τασ ·
οικειασ[4] · Ου · μονον · δε · αργαι · αλλα
και · φλυαροι · και · περι_εργοι · λα
14 λουσαι · τα · μη · δεοντα · Βουλομαι ·
ουν · νεωτερασ · γαμειν · τεκνο_
γονι̂ν · οικοδεσπο_τεν[5] ·
Μηδεμιαν · αφορμην · δειδοναι ·
τω · αντικειμενω · λοιδορι̂ασ ·
15 χαρειν · Η · δε[6] γαρ · εξετραπεσαν[7]
16 τεινεσ · οπισω · τȣ · σατανα · Ει

sint · Si quis autem suorum
et maxime domesticorum · curam
non habet · fidem negavit et
est infideli deterior · Vidua
eligatur non minus sexagin
ta annorum · quaefuerit
unius viri uxor · In operibus
bonis · testimonium habens · si fi
lios educavit · Si hospitio re
cepit · si $\overline{\text{scorum}}$ pedes la
vit · Sitribulationem patientibus sub
ministravit · si omne opus bonum
subsecuta est · Adolescentiores
autem viduas devita · Cum enim
luxuriatæ fuerint · in $\overline{\text{xpo}}$
nubere volunt · habentes damna
tionem · quia primam fidem irri
tam fecerunt · Simul autem etociosæ
discunt circuire
domus · Non solum ociosæ · sed
et verbosae et curiosæ · loquen
tes quae non oportet · Volo
ergo juniores nubere · filios
procreare · matres familias esse ·
Nullam occasionem dare
adversario maledicti
gratia · Jam enim quaedam conver
sae sunt retro satanan · Si

[1] *In marg.* $\overline{μαρ}$ προνοια. [2] επηρκησεν. [3] χηρασ. [4] οικιασ. [5] Οικοδεσποτειν. [6] Ηδη. [7] εξετραπησαν.

	Latin	Greek
CAP. V.	quis fidelis habet viduas submi	τισ · πιστη · εχει · χερασ[1] · επαρικεισ
	nistret illis · et non gravetur	θω · αυταισ · και · μη · βαρεισ_θω ·
	ecclesia · utlhis quaevere vi	η · εκλησίασ[2] · ἵνα · ταισ · οντωσ ·
v. 17	duae sunt sufficiat · Qui bene	χηραισ · επαρκησει[3] · Οι · καλωσ ·
	praesunt presbiteri · dupli	προεστω_τησ[4] · πρεσβυτεροι · δι
	ci honore digni habeantur	πλησ · τιμησ · αξει_ουσ · θωσαν ·
	maxime quaelaborant in v̄bo	μαλλιστα · οικοπιωντωσ[5] · λογω ·
18	et doctrina · Dicit enim scri	και · διδασκαλία · λεγει · γαρ ·
	ptura · Non frenabis os bovi	ηγραφη · Βουν · αλοωντα · ου ·
	trituranti · dignus est enim ope	φ·μωσεισ · Αξειοσ[6] · γαρ · ο · εργα
	rárius mercede sua ·	τησ · του · μισθου · αυτου ·
19	Adversus presbiterum accusati	Κατα · πρεσβυτερου · κατηγο
	onem noli recipere · Nisi	ρίαν · μη · παρα_δεχου · εκτοσ · [exceptis]
	sub duobus aut tribus testi	ειμη · δυο · η · τριον[7] · μαρτυ [nisi]
20	bus · Peccantes autem	ρων · Τουσ · αμαρτα_νοντασ · δε ·
	coram omnibus argue	ενωπιον · παντων · ελεγχαι ·
	utetceteri timorem habe	ἵνα · και · οι · λοιποι · φοβον · εχω_
21	ant · Testor co	σειν · Δια · μαρτυρομαι · εν_
	ram d̄o et x̄p̄ō īh̄ū et	ωπιον · του · θ̅υ̅ · χ̅ · ι̅υ̅ · χ̅ρ̅υ̅[8] · και
	electis angelis	των · εκλεκτων · αγγελων ·
	ut haec custodias · sine	ἵνα · ταυτα · φυλαξησ · χωρισ ·
	p̄judicio nihil faciens	προ · κριματοσ · μηδεν · ποιων ·
22	in aliam partem declinando · Manus	κατα προσ · κλισιν · χειρασ ·
	cito nemini inposueris ·	ταχαιωσ · μηδενι · επιτι_θει ·
	Neque com̄unicaveris peccatis	μηδε · κοινωχει[9] · αμαρτειαισ ·
	alienis · te ipsum castum custodi ·	λοτρειαισ · σεαυτον · αγνων[10] · τηρει
23	Noli adhuc aquam bibere sed vino	Μη · κετει · ῡδρο · ποτει · αλλα · οινω
	modico utere · propter stoma	ολλιγω · χρωα · δια · τον · σ·τομα

[1] χηρασ. [2] εκκλησία. [3] επαρκεσει. [4] προεστωτεσ. [5] οικοπιωντεσ. [6] φιμωσεισ Αξειοσ p.m. [7] τριων. [8] χ̅ρ̅υ̅ ι̅υ̅. [9] κοινωνει. [10] αγνον.

P. V.	χον · σου · και · δια · τασ · πυκνασ ·	chum tuum · et frequentes
V. 24	σου · ασθενίασ · Τινων · ανων ·	tuas infirmitates · Quorundam ho
	αι · αμαρτιαι · προδηλοι · εισιν ·	minum peccata manifesta sunt
	προαγουσαι · εισ · κρισίν · τισε_ιν ·	pcedentia adjudicium quosdam
25	δε · και · επακολον_θουσιν · ωσ ·	autem et subsecuntur · Similiter
	αυτωσ · δε · και · τα · εργα · τα · καλα ·	autem et facta bona
	προ_δελα[1] · εισιν · ϗ · τα · αλλωσ ·	manifesta sunt · et quae alit
	εχοντα · κρυβηναι · ου · δυνα_	se habent · abscondi non pos
VI. 1	ται · ο σοι · εισειν · υπο · ζυγον ·	sunt · Quicunque sunt sub jugo
	δουλου · τουσ · ϊδει_ουσ · δεσπο_	servi · dominos suos
	τασ · πασησ · τιμησ · αξιουσ · ηγισ	omni honore dignos arbi
	θωσαν · ινα · μη · το · ονομα · του ·	trantur · Ne nomen
	θυ · και · η · δι_δασκαλία · βλασφη	dni et doctrina blasphema
2	μηται[2] · Οι · δε · πιστουσ · εχον ·	tur · Qui autem fideles ha
	τασ · δεσποτασ · μ(η[3])εκατα φρονει_	bent dominos non con
	τωσαν · οτι · αδελφοι · εισιν · αλλα ·	temnat · quia frs sunt sed
	μαλλον · δουλευ_ετωσαν ·	magis serviant
	οτι · πιστοι · εισιν · και · αγαπη_τοι ·	quia fideles sunt et dilecti ·
	οι · τησ · ευσεβίασ · αντιλαμβα	qui beneficii participes
	νομενοι[4] · Ταυτα · διδασκαι ·	sunt · haec doce
	και · παρακαλει · Ειτισ · ετερο ·	et exhortare · Siquis aliter
	δι_δασκαλει · και · μη · προσερχεται ·	docet et non adquiescit
	υγιαιν_νουσιν · λογοισ · τοισ · τȣ · κυ ·	sanis sermonibus dni
	ημων · ιυ · χρυ · και · τη · κατευσε	nri ihu xpi · et ei quæ secundum
4	βίαν · διδασκαλια · τετυφωται ·	pietatem est doctrinae · superbus
	μηδεν · επισταμενοσ[5] · αλλα · νο	nihil sciens sed lan
	σων · περι · ζητησει[6] · ϗ · λογομα	guens circa questiones · et pugnas
	χίασ · εξ · ων · γινεται · φθονοσ ·	verborum · ex quibus oriuntur · invidiae

[1] προδηλα. [2] βλασφημεται. [3] Μη. [4] *In marg.* φορφιριου.
[5] *In marg.* contra γοδδισκαλκον. Λογομαχῖα pugna verborum. Λογομαχοσ αγαν, etiam ευαγγελιον ελλινικον.
[6] ζητησεισ.

CAP. VI.	contentiones blasphemiæ suspitiones	ερεισ · βλασφημιαι · υπονοι ·
v. 5	male · Conflictationes hominum	αιπονηραι · διαπαρα_τριβαι · διεφ
	mente corruptorum ·	θαρμενων · ανων · τον · νουν ·
	et qui veritate privati sunt	και · απεστηρημενων[1] · τησ · αλη
	existimantium questum	θιασ · νομειζοντον[2] · πορεισμον ·
6	esse pietatem · Est autem	ειναι · την · ευσεβιαν · Εστιν · δε ·
	questus magnus pietas	πορισμοσ · μεγασ · η · ευσεβια · θυ
7	cum sufficientia · Nihil enim	μετα · αυταρκία[3] · ουδεν · γαρ ·
	intulimus in hunc mundum	εισνη_ηγκαμην[4] · εισ · τον · κοσμον ·
	haud dubium quia nec auferre qd	οτι · ουδε · εξενεγκειν · τι ·
8	possumus · Habentes autem ali	δυνα μεθα · εχοντεσ · δε · δια_
	menta et quibus tegamur · his	προφην · κ · σκεπακματα[5] · τουτοισ ·
9	contenti sumus · Nam qui vo	αρκεσ_θησομεθα · Οιδε · βουλο
	lunt divites fieri incidunt	μενοι · πλουτειν · εμπειπ_τουσιν ·
	intemptationem et laqueum	εισ · πιρασμον · και · παγιδα · του ·
	diaboli et desideria mul	διαβολου · κ · επιθυμιασ · πολ
	ta inutilia et nociva	λασ · ανοητου[6] · και · βλα_βερασ ·
	quaemergunt homines	αιτινεσ · βυθι_ζουσιν · τουσ · ανουσ
	in interitum et perditionem ·	εισ · ολεθρον · και · απωλίαν ·
10	Radix enim omnium malorum	Ρειζα · γαρ · παντων · των · κακων ·
	est cupiditas · quam quidem	εστιν · η · φιλαργυρια · εστινεσ[7] ·
	appetentes erraverunt	οργομενοι[8] · απεπλα_νηθη_σαν ·
	a fide · et inseruerunt	απο · τεσ[9] · πιστεωσ · κ · εαυτουσ ·
	se doloribus multis ·	inseruerunt περι · επιραν[10] · οδυναισ · πολλαισ ·
11	Tu autem o' homo di · haec	Cυ · δε · ω · ανθρωπε · του · θυ[11] · ταυτι
	fuge · sectare vero justitiam ·	φευγε · διωκαι · δε · δικαι · συνην[12] ·
	pietatem · fidem · caritatem · patienti	ευσεβιαν · πιστιν · αγαπην · υπομονη
12	am · mansuetudinem · Certa bonum	πραυπαθιαν · άγ · ωνειζου · τον · κα

---

[1] απεστερημενων. [2] Νομειζοντων. [3] αυταρκîασ. [4] εισηνëγκαμεν (ë ex correctione). [5] σκεπασματα : in marg. σκεπασματα. [6] ανοητουσ. [7] Ησ τινεσ. [8] ορεγομενοι. [9] τησ. [10] περιεπιραν. [11] In marg. μακ. [12] δικαιοσυνην.

λον · αγωνα · τησ πιστεωσ · επιλαβȣ ·
τησ · αιω͜νιου · ζωησ · εισεν · εκλα (η above εισεν)
θησ[1] · ϗ ομω͜λογησασ[2] · την · καλην ·
ομολογιαν[3] · ενωπιον · πολλον[4] ·
13 μαρτυρων · Παραγγελλον[5] · ενωπι
ον · του · θ̅υ̅ · του · ζω͜ογονȣντοσ · τα ·
παντα · ϗ · ι̅υ̅ · χ̅ρ̅υ̅ · του · μαρτυρη͜
σαντοσ · επιποντι · ου · πιλατȣ · την ·
14 καλην · ομολογιαν · Τη · ρησεσαι · την ·
εντολην · ασπειλον · ανεπιλημπτον ·
μεχρι · τησ · επιφανίασ · του · κ̅υ̅ · ημων ·
15 ι̅υ̅ · χ̅ρ̅υ̅ · ην · καιροισ · ϊδιοισ · δειξει ·
ο̅ μακαριοσ · ϗ · μονοσ · δυνασ · τησ ·
ο̅ βασιλευσ · των · βασιλευοντων ·
και · κ̅σ̅ · των · κυριευ͜οντων · Ο · μο
νοσ · εχων · αθανασίαν · φωσ · οικων ·
απροσϊτον · ον · ειδεν · αμων[6] · ουδεισ ·
ουδε · ϊδειν · δυναται · ωτιμη · κρα
τοσ · αιωνιον · αμην · Τοισ · πλου
τεσ͜οισ · εν · τω͜νυν · αιωνι · παραγγε
λλαι · μη · υψηλο · φρονιν · μηδε · ελ
πει͜ζειν[7] · επιπλουτου · αδηλο͜τητι ·
αλλεπι · θ̅ω̅ · τω · παρεχοντι · ημιν ·
πλȣσει͜ωσ · εισ · απολαυσιν · αγαθω͜
εργειν[8] · Πλουτει͜ζειν · εν,εργοισ · καλοισ ·
ευμετα͜δοτουσ · ειναι · κοινωνεικȣσ ·
αποθη͜σαυριζοντασ · εαυτοισ · θεμε
λιον · καλον · εισ · τον · μελλοντα · ϊνα ·

certamen fidei · apprehende
vitam aeternam · in qua vocatus
es et confessus bonam
confessionem · coram multis
testibus · Precipio tibi co
ram d̅o̅ · qui vivificat om
nia · et i̅h̅u̅ x̅p̅o̅ · quitestimonium
reddidit sub pontio pilato
bonam confessionem · utserves
mandatum sine macula inre̅phensi
bile · usque inadventum d̅n̅i̅ n̅r̅i̅
i̅h̅u̅ x̅p̅i̅ · quem suis temporibus osten
det beatus et solus potens
rex regum et
d̅n̅s̅ dominantium · Qui solus
habet inmortalitatem · lucem habi
tans inaccessibilem quem vidit nullus ho
minum · nec videre potest · cui honor et
imperium in scl̅a̅ amen · Diviti
bus hujus saeculi praeci
pe non sublime sapere · neque spe
rare in incerto divitiarum
sed in d̅n̅o̅ qui p̅stat nobis omnia
abunde ad fruendum · Bene
agere divites fieri in operibus bonis
facile tribuere · communicare
thesaurizare sibi fundamen
tum bonum in futurum · ut

[1] ηι εκληθησ. [2] ωμολογησασ. [3] *In marg.* ομολογια. [4] πολλων. [5] Παραγγελλων. [6] α̅ν̅ω̅ν̅. [7] ελπιζειν. [8] αγαθοεργειν.

CAP. VI. apphendant veram vitam·
v. 20 O timothee depositum custo
di · devitans profanas
vocum novitates·et oppositiones
21 falsi nominis scientiae·quam quidam
promittentes·circa fi
dem exciderunt · Gratia
tecum amen · EXPLICIT EPI
STOLA ADTIMOTHEUM·I·

επιλαβων_ται·τησ·οντωσ·ζωησ
Ω·τιμοθεε·την·παρα θεκεν·φυλ
ξων[1]·εκτρεπομενοσ·τασ·βηβελ
και_νο_φωνιασ[3]·και·αντι_θεσισ·
ψευδων·μου[4]·γνωσεωσ·Ην·τινεσ
επαγγελλομενοι·περι·την·
πιστιν·ηστοχησαν·η·χαρισ·με
θυμων · Επληρωθη·επι
στολη·προσ·τιμοθεον·α·

Incipit ad eundem · ii.

Αρχεται προσ · εαυτον[5]

CAP. I. 1 Paulus apo
stolus xpi ihu
pervoluntatem di secundum promis
sionem vitae quae est in xpo ihu·
2 Timotheo carissimo filio · Gratia
misericordia·pax a do patre et
3 xpo ihu dno nro · Gratias
ago do cui servio aprogenito
ribus inconscientia pura·
quam sine intmissione habeam tui
memoriam inorationibus meis
4 nocte ac die·desiderans te
videre memor lacrimarum
5 tuarum·utgaudio implear·recor
dationem·accipiens ejus fidei
quae inte est non ficta·quae et habitavit

ΠαυLοσ · απο
στολοσ · χρυ · ιηυ ·
δια·θεληματοσ·θυ·κατεπαγγε
λιαν·ζωησ·τησ·εν·χρω·ιηυ·
Τιμοθεω·αγαπητω·τεκνω·χαρι
ελαιοσ·ϊρηνη·απο τυ[6]·πατροσ·
χρυ·ιυ·τȣ·κυ·ημων·χαρειν·
εχω·τω·θω·ω·λατρευω·αποπρ
γονον[7]·εν·καθαρα·συν_ϊδησει·
ωσ·αδια λιπτον·εχω·την·περ
μνιαν·εν·ταισ·δεησαισιν·μου·
νυκτοσ·ϗ·ημερασ·επιποθω·εε
ϊδειν·με·μνημενοσ·σου·των·δα
κρυων[9]·ϊνα·χαρασ·πληρωθω·υ
μνησιν·λαβων·τησ·εν·σοι·αν·
κριτου·πιστεωσ · Η·τεισ·ενω

---

[1] o . . Ω τιμοθεε την. παραθηκην φυλαξον. [2] βεβηλουσ. [3] καινοφονιασ. [4] ψευδωνυμο
[5] αυτον. B II. [6] Θυ (pro τυ). [7] προγονων. [8] σε. [9] δακρυων.

I. πρωτον · εν · τη · μαμμη · σου · λοιδει ·	primum inavia tua loide ·
και · τη · μη_τρι · σου · ευνικη · Πεπεισ	et matre tua eunice · certus sum
v. 6 μαι · δε · οτι · και · εν · σοι · Δι · ην · αιτίαν ·	autem quod etinte · Propter quam causam
αναμει_μνησκω · σε · αναζωπυριν ·	admoneo te · utresuscites
το · χαρισμα · του · θυ · ο · εστιν · εν · σοι ·	gratiam di quae est inte
δια · τησ · επιθεσεωσ · των · χειρων ·	perimpositionem manuum mea
7 μου · ου · γαρ · εδωκεν · ημιν · ο · θσ ·	rum · Non enim dedit nobis ds
πνα · διλιασ · αλλα · δυναμαιωσ ·	spm timoris · sed virtutis et dilecti
και · αγαπησ · και · σω_φρονισ_μου ·	onis · et sobrietatis ·
8 Μη · ουν · επαισχυνθησ · το · μαρτυ	Noli itaque erubescere testimoni
ριον · του · κυ · ημων · μηδε · εμαι ·	um dni nri · Neque me
τον · δεσμιον · αυτου · αλλα · συν'	vinctum ejus · sed conlabora
κακο_παθησον · τω · ευαγγελιω · κα	evangelio · secundum
9 τα · δυναμιν · θυ · του · σω_σαντοσ ·	virtutem di qui nos liberavit ·
ημασ · και · καλεσαντασ · κλησῖ · αγια ·	et vocavit vocatione sua sca · non
ουκατα · τα · εργα · ημων · αλλα	secundum opera nostra · sed secun
καθ ἰδιαν · προθεσιν · και · χαριν ·	dum propositum suum et gratiam
την · δοθεισαν · ημιν · ην[1] · χρω · ιυ ·	quaedata est nobis · in xpo ihu
προχρονων · αιωνιων ·	ante tempora saecularia ·
10 Φανεροθεισαν[2] · δε · νυν · δια · τησ ·	Manifestata est autem nunc per in
επιφανιασ · του · σωτηροσ · ημων ·	luminationem salvatoris nostri
ιυ · χρυ · καταργησαντοσ · μεν · τον ·	ihu xpi · qui destruxit quidem
θανατον · φοτισαντοσ[3] · δε · ζωην ·	mortem · Illuminavit autem vitam
ϗ αφθαρσίαν · δια · του · ευαγγελι	et incorruptionem per evageli
11 ου · εισ · ο · ετεθην · εγω · κηριξ[4] · και ·	um · In quo positū sum ego pdicator
αποστολοσ · ϗ · διδασκαλοσ · εθ	et apostolus · et magister genti
12 νων · δι · ην · αιτίαν · και · ταυτα ·	um · Ob quam causam etiam haec
πασχω[5] · αλλουκ · επαισ_χυνομαι ·	patior · sed non confundor ·

[1] σ. [2] Φανερωθεισαν. [3] Φωτισαντοσ. [4] Κηρυξ. [5] *In marg.* πασχα.

CAP. I. Scio enim cui credidi et certus
sum · quia potens est
depositum meum servare in
v. 13 illum diem · formam
habe sanorum verbo
rum quae a me audisti infi
de etdilectione · in xpo ihu
14 Bonum depositum custodi
per spm scm · qui habitat
15 in nobis · scis hoc · qu(o)d aver
si sunt omnes qui sunt in
asia · ex quibus fygelus et hermo
16 genes · Det miam dns
onesi phori domui · quia sepe
me refrigeravit · et catenam
17 meam non erubuit · Sed cum ro
mam venisset · sollicite me quaesi
18 vit et invenit · Det illi
dns invenire miam adno in
illo die · et quanta ephesi
ministravit mihi melius tu
CAP. II. 1 nosti · Tu ergo fili mi confor
tare in gra quae est inxpo
2 ihu · et quae audisti ame per
multos testes · Haec commen
da fidelibus hominibus qui
idonei erunt et alios doce
3 re · labora sicut bo

Οιδα · γαρ · ω · πεπισ_τευκα · και · πε
πισμαι · οτι · δυνατοσ · εστιν · την ·
παραδεκην[1] · μου · φυλαξαι · εισ ·
εκεινην · την · ημεραν · Ποτυ_[2]
πουσιν · εχαι · ὑγειϲ · εμνον · των
λογων · ων · παρεμου · ηκουσασ · εν ·
πιστι · και · αγαπητη · εν · χρω · ιυ ·
Την · καλην · παραθηκην · φυλαξον ·
δια · πνσ · αγιου · ουτου · εν · οι_κουν
τοσ · εν · ημιν · οιδασ · τουτο · οτι ·
απεστραφησαν · μαι · παντεσ · οι · εν –
τη · ασια · ων · εστιν · φυγελοσ · ϗ · ερ
μ · γ ηνησ[3] · Δωη · ελαιοσ · ο κσ · τω
ονησει_φορου · οικω · οτι · πολλακισ ·
μαι · ανεψυξεν · και · την · αλυσιν ·
μου · ου κατα · ισχυνθη · Αλλα · γε
νομενοσ · εν · ρομη[4] · σπουδαιωσ · εζη
τησεν · μαι · και · ευρεν · Δωη · αυτω
ο κσ · ευριν · ελεοσ · παρα · κυ · εν · εκει
νη · τη · ημερα · και · οσα · εν · εφεσσω
διηκονησεν · Βελ_τειον · συ · γινωσ_
κισ[5] · συ · ουν · τεκνον · μου · εν · δυ
ναμου · εν · τη · χαριτι · τη · εν · χρω
ιυ · ϗ · ακουσασ · παρε · μου · δια ·
πολλων · μαρτυρων · Ταυτα · παρα
θου · πιστοισ · ανθρωποισ · οτινεσ[6]
ϊκανοι · εσονται · και · ετερουσ · δι
δαξαι · συνκα_κοπαθεσον[7] · ωσ · κα_

	Graece	Latine
P. II. v. 4	λοσ·στρατι_ωτησ·χρυ·ιηυ · Ουδεισ·	nus miles xpi ihu · Nemo
	στρατευομενοσ·τω·θω·εμπλεκε	militans do implicat se
	ται·ταισ·του·βιου·πραγματι_αισ·	negotiis saecularibus
	ϊνα·τω·σρατολογ_ησαντι[1]·αρεση·	utei placeat cui se probavit·
	[2]	
5	Εαν·δε·και·αθλη·τεισ·ου·στεφα	Nam et qui certat in agone
	νου_ται·εαν μη·νομειμωσ·αθλησῃ·	non coronatur·nisi legitime certaverit·
6	Τον·κοπειωντα·γεωργο̊ν[3]·δει·πρω	Laborantem agricolam oportet pri
	τον·των·καρπων·μετα·λαμβαν·	mum de fructibus percipere·
7	Νοει·ο·λεγω · Δωσει·γαρ·σοι·ο·κσ·	Intellege quaedico·dabit enim tibi
	συνεσειν·εν·πασιν·	dns in omnibus intellectum·
8	Μνημονευε·ιν·χρν·εγηγερμε	Memor esto ihm xpm resur
	νον·εκ·νεκρων·εκ·σπερματοσ·	rexisse amortuis ex semine
	δαδ·κατα·το·ευαγγελιον·μου·	dauid secundum evangelium meum
9	εν; ω·χ·κακο_παθω·μεχρι·δεσ_	in quo laboro usque ad vincula
	μων·ωσ·κακο·υργοσ[4]·αλλο·λο_	quasi male operans·sed ver
)	γοσ·του·θυ·ουδε·εται · Δια	bum di non est alligatum · Ideo
	τουτο·παντα·ϋπομενω·δια·τουσ·	omnia sustineo propter ele
	εκλεκτουσ·ϊνα·και·αυτοι·σωτη	ctos·Utetipsi salutem
	ριαν·τυχωσιν·τη εν·χρω·	consequantur quae est in xpo
	ιυ·μετα·δοξησ·αιωνειου·	ihu cum gloria caelesti·
1	Πιστοσ·ο·λογοσ·ει·γαρ·συνα_πεθα	Fidelis sermo·nam si conmortui
2	μεν·και·συν_ζωεομεν·ει·υπο	sumus et convivemus·si sustine
	μενομεν·	bimus·et cregnavimus·
	[5]	

[1] στρατολογησαντι. [2] Simile spatium in Cod. Boerner. [3] γεωργον. [4] Ωσ καὶ λουτρ κακουργοσ.
[5] Simile spatium in Cod. Boerner.

CAP. II.	Si non credimus	
v. 13	ille fidelis permanet·negare	εκεινοσ·πιστοσ·μενει·αρνησασθαι·
14	enim se ipsum non potest·haec	γαρ·εαυτον·ου·δυναται · Ταυτα·
	commone testificans	,,υπομειμνησκε·δι[1]·μαρτυρομενοσ·
	coram dō · Noli verbis con	εν^{ω}οπιον[2]·του·θ̅υ̅ · Μη·λογο_
	tendere · Inihilo enim utile est	μαχειν[3]·επ8δενει·γαρ·χρησειμον·
	nisi ad subversionem audien	επικατα·στροφη·των·ακουον
15	tium · Sollicite curā teipsum proba	των·σπου^{δ}τασον[4]·σεαυτον·δοκει_
	bilem exhibere dō·operarium	μον·παραστησαι·τω·θ̅ω̅·εργα_τηι
	inc̄fusibilem recte tractan	ανεπαισ_χυντον·ορθοτομουν_
16	tem verbum veritatis · Pro	τα·τον·λογον·τησ·αληθεiασ[5]·τασ
	fana autem et inaniloquia de	δε·βεβηλουσ·καινο_φωνiασ[6]·πε
	vita·multum enim profici	ρι·ιστασον[7] · Επιπλιον·γαρ·προκ
17	ent ad pietatem·et sermo eo	ψουσιν·ασεβιασ·ϗ·ο·λογοσ·αυ
	rum utcancer serpit·ex quibus	των·ωσ·γανγρα·ϊνα·νομην·εξει
	est hÿmeneus et filetus	ων·εστιν·Ϋμενεοσ·και·φυλητοσ[8]·
18	qui a veritate excide	οιτινεσ·περι·την·αλ^{η}εθiαν[9]·ησ_
	runt·dicentes resurrectionem	τοχησαν·λεγοντεσ·αναστασιν·
	jam factam·subverterunt	ηδη·γεγον·ειναι[10]·και·ανατρεπου_
19	quorundam fidem sed	σιν·την·πιστιν·τινων · Ο·μεν·
	firmum fundamentum dī stat	το·ισ_τεραιοσ·θεμελιοσ·του·θ̅υ̅·ε
	habens signaculum hoc·	τηκ^{ε}ην[11]·εχων·την·σφραγiδα·ταυ
	cognov̄ dn̄s qui sunt ejus·	την·εγνω·κ̅σ̅·τουσοντασ·αυτου·
	et discedat abiniquitate omis̄ qui	ϗ·αποστητω·απο αδικiασ[12]·πασ·
20	nominat nomen dn̄i · In ma	ονομαζων·το·ονομα · κ̅υ̅·εν·με_
	gna autem domo non solum sunt	γαλη·δε·οικια·ουκ·εστιν·μονον
	vasa aurea et argentea·sed	σ^{κ}τευη[13]·χρυσα·και·αργυρα·αλλα·
	et lignea et fictilia·et quaedam	και·ξυλεινα·ϗ·οστρακεινα·και

---

[1] δια. [2] ενωπιον. [3] *In marg.* λογομαχειν. [4] Cπουδασον. [5] *In marg.* Contra γoddiscaλκον. [6] *In marg.* α̅γ̅ κενοφωνia. [7] περι ιστασον. [8] φιλητοσ. [9] αληθiαν. [10] γεγον: εναι. [11] εστηκεν. [12] αδaικiασ. [13] σκευη.

II. α·μεν; εισ·τιμην·α·δε·εισ·ατι_	quidem in honorem quaedam autem in c̄
21 μίαν·εαν·ουν·τισ·εκκαθαρη·	tumeliam · Si quis ergo mundaverit
·σ	
εαυτον·αποτουτων·εσται·κευοσ[1]·	se ab istis·erit vas
ε	
εισ·τιμην·ηγιασμηνον[2]·ευχριστον·	in honore scīficatum et utile
τω·δεσποτη·προσ·παν·εργον·αγαθον·	dn̄o ad omne opus bonum
22 ητοι_μασμενον · Τασ·δε·νεω_τερί_	paratum · Juvenilia autem
κασ·επιθυμίασ·φευγε·διωκαι·δε·	desideria fuge · Sectare vero
δικαι_οσυνην·αγαπην·πιστίν·	justitiam·fidem·caritatem·
ϊρηνην·μετα·παντων·επικαλου	pacem·cum his qui invo
μενων·τον·κ̄ν·εκκαθαρασ·καρ	cant dn̄m decorde pu
23 διασ · Τασ·δε·μωρασ·και απαιδευ_	ro · Stultas autem et sine discipli
τουσ·ζητησεισ·παραιτου·ϊδιωσ[3]·	na questiones devita siens
24 οτι·γεννω_σειν·μαχασ · Δουλον·	quia generant lites · Servum
δε·κ̄υ·ουδει·μαχεσθαι·αλλανη_	autem dn̄i non oportet litigare·seman
πιον·ειναι·προσ·παντασ·διδακτι	suetum esse ad omnes·docibilem
25 κον·ανεξειλακον·συν·πριχοτητι·	patientem·cum modestia
παιδευοντα·τουσ·αντικιμενουσ·	corripientem eos qui resistunt veritati·
μηποτε·δωη·αυτοισ·ο θ̄σ·μετα	nequando det illis d̄s pæni
νοιαν·εισ·επιγνωσιν·αληθίασ·	tentiam ad cognoscendam veritatem·
26 και·ανανη_ψωσειν·εκ·τησ·του·	et resipiscant a diabo
διαβολου·παγειδοσ·εξωγρημε	li laqueis·a quo cap
νοι·υπαυτου·εκ·το·εκεινου[4]·θε_	ti tenentur ad ipsius vo
III. 1 λημα · Τουτο·δε·γινωσκεται·οτι·	luntatem · Hoc autem scito quod
εν·αισ_χαταισ·ημεραισ·εν·στησον	in novissimis diebus instabunt
2 ται·και_ροι·χαλεποι·εσονται·	tempora periculosa·et erunt
γαρ·οι·ανθρωποι·φιλαυτοι[5]·	homines se ipsos amantes·
φιλαργυροι·αλαζοντεσ·Ϋπερ_	cupidi·elati·super
η·	
ηφανοι·βλασφ·μοι[6]·γονευσιν[7]·	bi·parentibus nonoboedi

---

[1] σκευοσ. [2] ηγιασμενον. [3] *In marg.* εὐαγ. [4] εκεινον (ν above). [5] Φιλαυγοι. [6] Βλασφημοι. [7] *In marg.* ferγυc.

III. entes · Ingrati · scelesti ·
v. 3 sine affectione · sine pace · criminatores ·
incontinentes · inmites · sine benigni
4 tate · proditores · protervi · tumidi ·
voluptatum amatores magis
5 quam d̄ī · habentes speciem
quidem pietatis · Virtutem autem
ejus abnegantes · et hos
6 devita · Ex his enim
sunt qui penetrant do
mos et captivas ducunt
mulierculas · oneratas
peccatis · quaeducuntur va
7 riis desideriis · semper descen
tes · et numquam ad scienti
am veritatis pervenien
8 tes · Quem admodum autem iannes
et mambres restiterunt
moysi · ita et hi resistunt
veritati · homines
mente corrupti · repro
9 bi circa fidem sed ultra
non proficient · Insipien
tia enim eorum manifesta
erit omnibus sicut et illorum
10 fuit · Tu autem assecutus
es meam doctrinam institutionem
propositum · fidem · longanimi

απεθεισ[1] · αχαριστοι · ανοσει‿οι ·
αστοργοι · ασπονδοι · διαβολοι ·
ακρατεισ · ανημεροι · αφιλαγα
θοι[2] · προδοτοι[3] · προπετεισ · Τετυ
φωμενοι[4] · φιληδονοι · μαλλον ·
η φιλοθ̄ῡ οι[5] · εχοντεσ · μορφω
σιν · ευσεβîασ · την · δε · δυναμειν[6] ·
αυτησ · ηρνη‿μενοι · και · τουτουσ ·
αποτρεπου · εκ · τουτων[7] · γαρει‿
σ.[8]
σιν · οι · εν · δυνοντεσ · ει · τασ · οι
κîασ · και · αιχμα‿λωτιζον‿τεσ ·
γυναικαρια · σεσω‿ρευμενα ·
αμαρτειαισ · αγομενα · επιθυμι
αισ · ποικειλλισ[9] · παντοτε · μανθα
νοντα · και · μηδεποτε · εισ · επι
γνωσιν · αληθîασ · ελθειν · δυνᾱ‿
μενα · ον · προπον · δε · ϊαν‿νησ ·
και · μαμβρησ · αντεσ‿τησαν · τω ·
μωυσει · ουτωσ · και · αυτοι[10] · ανθει
στανται · τη · αληθîα · ανθρωποι ·
κατεφθαρμενοι · τον · νουν · α
δοκειμοι[11] · περι · την · πιστιν · αλλ
προκο‿ψουσειν · επιπλειον · η ·
γαρ · ανοια · αυτων · εκ‿δεμοσ[12] ·
εστιν · πασιν · ωσ · και · η · εκει‿νων
εγενετο[13] · Cυ · δε · ηκολουθη
σασ · μου · διδασκαλια · τη · αγωγη
τη · προθεσει · τη · πιστει · τη · μα

---

[1] απειθεισ. [2] *In marg.* φιλαγαθîα. [3] Προδοται. [4] Τετυφων̣μενοι. [5] *In marg.* φιλοθεοσ.
[6] – δε (*habet supra*). δυναμιν. [7] τουσ̣των. [8] εισ. [9] *In marg.* ευᾱγ.
[10] ουτοι (*pro* αυτοι). [11] Αδοκειμοι. [12] εκδημοσ. [13] ετενετο.

	Graece	Latine
II.	κροθυμια · τη · αγαπη · τη · υπο	tatem · dilectionem · patien
11	μονη · τοισ · διογμοισ[1] · τοισ · πα	tiam · persecutiones · passi
	θημασειν · οιαμοι[2] · εγενετο ·	ones · qualia mihi facta sunt
	εν · αντιοχεια[3] · εν · ϊκονειω · εν	antiochiae · iconio ·
	λυστροισ · οιουσ · δε · ιογμουσ[4] · υ	lystris · quales persecutiones su
	πηνιγκα · και · εκπατων[5] · με · ερ	stinui · et ex omnibus me eripu
12	ρυσατο · ο κσ · και · παν͜τεσ · δε ·	it dns · et omnes qui
	οι · θελοντεσ · ευσεβωσ · ζην · εν ·	volunt pie vivere in
3	χρω · ιυ · διωχ͜θησονται · πονη	xpo ihu persecutionem patiuntur ·
	ροι · δε · ανθρωποι · και · γονταισ[6] ·	mali autem homines et seductores
	προ · ιο͜ψουσειν · επι · το · χειρον ·	proficient in pejus ·
	πλανωντεσ · και · πλανομε	errantes et in errorem mit
14	νοι[7] · Cυ · δε · μενε · εν · οισ ·	tentes · Tu vero permane in his
	εμαθεσ · και · επιστωθεσ[8] · ει	quaedidicisti · et credita sunt tibi
	δωσ · παρα · τινων · ευαθησ[9] ·	sciens aquo didiceris ·
	και · οτι · απο · βρεφουσ · ϊερα · γραμ	et quia ab infantia sacras lit
	ματα · οιδασ · τα · δυναμενα ·	teras nosti quaete possunt
	σε · σοφεισαι · εισ · σωτηρίαν · δια ·	instruere ad salutem · per
	πιστεωσ · τησ · εν · χρω · ιυ · Πασα ·	fidem quae est in xpo ihu · Omnis
	γραφη · θεο͜πνευστοσ · και ·	scriptura divinitus inspirata
	ωφελειμοσ · προσ · διδασκαλιαν[10] ·	utilis est ad docendum
	προσ · ελεγμον · προσ · παι͜δίαν ·	adarguendum ad corrigendum ad rudi
	εν[11] · δικαιοσυνη · ϊνα · αρτει	endum injustitia · ut perfec
	οσ · η · υ · του · θυ · ανθρωποσ ·	tus sit homo di ·
	προσ · παν · εργον · αγαθον · εξ	ad omne opus bonum in
	ηργιμενοσ[12] ·	structus ·
1	Δια · μαρτυRομαι[13] · ενωπιον · του ·	Testificor coram
	θυ · χυ · χρω · ιυ · του · μελλοντεσ[14] ·	do et xpo ihu qui judica

[1] διωγμοισ. [2] Οια ἐμοι. [3] αντειοχεια (*marg.* αντιοχια). [4] δειωγμουσ. [5] εκ παντων. [6] γοηταισ. [7] πλανωμενοι. [8] επιστωθησ. [9] εμαθεσ. [10] *In marg.* ad erudiendum προσ επανορθωσιν. [11] + την (*ante* εν). [12] εξηρτιμενοσ. [13] Διαμαρτυρομαι. [14] μελλοντοσ.

I. 3 χρονων · αιωνιων · φανερω_	tempora saecularia manife
σεν[1] · δε · και_ροισ · ιδιοισ · τον · λο	stavit autem temporibus suis ver
γον · αυτου · ενκηρυγματι ·	bum suum in praedicatione
ο · επιστευθην · εγω · κατεπιζα	quae credita est mihi secun
γην[2] · του · σωτη^ρ^σοσ[3] · ημων · θ̅υ̅ ·	dum p̄ceptum salvatoris nostri d̄i
4 τειτω · γνησειω · τεκνω · κατα	tito dilecto filio secundum
κοινην · πιστιν · χαρισ · και · ῑ	communem fidem gr̄a · et pax
ρηνη · απο · θ̅υ̅ · πατροσ · και · κ̅υ̅ ·	a d̄o patre et d̄n̄o
ι̅η̅υ̅ χ̅ρ̅υ̅ του σωτηροσ · ημων ·	ι̅η̅υ̅ x̄p̄o salvatore nostro
5 ουτου[4] · χαρειν · απελειπον ·	hujus rei gratia reliqui
σε · εν · κρητη · ινα · τα · λειπον ·	te crate ut ea quae desunt
τα · δει_ορθωσησ · και · καταστη	corrigas et constitu
σεισ · κατα · πολειν · πρεσβυτε	as per civitates p̄sbite
ρουσ · ωσ · εγω · σοι · διεταξαμην ·	ros sicut ego tibi disposui
6 Επισ[5] · εστιν · ανεκκλ^η^ετοσ[6] · Μιάσ ·	Siquis sine crimine est unius
γυναικοσ · ανηρ · τεκνα[7] · εχων ·	ıxoris vir filios habens
πιστα · μη · εν · κατηγορια · ασω	fideles non in accusatione luxu
7 τίασ · η · ανυποτακτα · Δει ·	riae aut non subditos oportet
γαρ · τον · επισκοπον · αν^ε^ηγκλη	enim ep̄m sine crimi
τον[8] · ειναι · ωσ · θ̅υ̅ · οικονομον[9] ·	ne esse sicut d̄i dispensatorem
μη · λυ^θ^δαδην[10] · μη · οργειλον ·	non superbum n̄^n^ iracudum ·
μη · παροινον · μη · πληκτην ·	non vinolentum non percussorem
8 μη · αισχροκερδην · Αλλα · φι	n̄ turbis lucri cupidum sed hospita
λοξενον · φιλαγαθον · σωφρο	lem benignum sobri
να · [11] · δικαιον · οσειον · ενκρα	um · justum · sc̄m · continen
9 τη · αντεχομην[12] · του · κατα ·	tem amplectentem eum qui secundum
την · διδαχην · πιστου · λογου ·	doctrinam est fidelem sermonem
ινα · και · δυνατοσ · ή · και · πα	ut potens sit exhorta ·

[1] *In marg.* επ̲ι̲φανια. [2] κατεπιταγην. [3] σωτηροσ. [4] Τουτου. [5] Ει τισ. [6] ανεγκλητοσ.
[7] *In marg.* α̅γ̅α̅ν̅. [8] ανεγκλητον. [9] *In marg.* α̅γ. [10] λυθαδην. [11] Cωφρωνα. [12] αντεχομενον.

CAP. II.	placentes · non contra dicen	τουσ · ειναι · μη · αντι λεγον ·
v. 10	tes · non fraudentes	τασ · μη · δενοσ‿φιξομενουσ[1] ·
	sed in omnibus fidem bonam	αλλα · πασαν · εν · δικνυ‿μενοσ[2] ·
	ostendentes · Ut doctri	πιστιν · αγαθην[3] · ινα · την · διδασ
	nam salvatoris nostri	καλιαν · την · τουσωτηροσ · ημων ·
	ornent in omnibus	$\overline{θυ}$ · κοσμωσειν · εν · πασιν
11	Apparuit enim gratia $\overline{di}$	Επεφανη[4] · γαρ · η · χαρισ · του · $\overline{θυ}$
	salvatoris nostri omnibus homi	του · σωτιροσ[5] · ημων · πασιν · αν
12	nibus erudiens nos	θρωποισ · παιδευουσα · ημασ ·
	ut abnegantes impieta	ῑνα · αρνησαμενοι · την · ασεβεῖ
	tem et saecularia deside	αν · και · τασ · κοσμεικασ · επιθυμι
	ria · sobrie · et juste · et	ασ · σωφρονωσ[6] · και · δικαιωσ · και ·
	pie vivamus in hoc sae	ευσεβωσ · ζησωμεν · εν · τωνυν ·
13	cula · expectantes	αιωνει[7] · Προσ · δε · χομενοι · την –
	beatam spem et adven	μακαριαν · ελπειδα · και · επιφα
	tum gloriae magni	νιαν · τησ · δοξησ · του · μεγαλου –
	$\overline{di}$ · et salvatoris nostri $\overline{ιηυ}$ $\overline{xpi}$ ·	$\overline{θυ}$ και σωτηροσ · ημων · $\overline{χυ}$ $\overline{ιηυ}$
14	Qui dedit semetipsum pro nobis	Οσ · εδωκεν · εαυτον · ϋπερ · ημων –
	ut nos redimeret ab omni	ϊνα · λυτρωσηται · ημασ · απο · π[illegible]
	iniquitate · et mundaret	σησ · ανομιασ · ϗ · καθαρειση · ε
	sibi populum acceptabilem sec	αυτω · λαον · περι‿ουσειον · ζηλω ·
15	tatoreim bonum operum haec	την · καλων · εργων · ταυτα · λε
	loquere et exhortare · et argue	λει[8] · και · παρακαλει · και · ελεγχαι · —
	cum omnio imperio nemo	μετα · πασησ · επιταγησ[9] · μηδεισ ·
	te contemnat ·	σου · περι‿φρονειτω
CAP. III. 1	dmone illos principibus	πομειμνησ · και[10] · αυτουσ · αρ‿
	et potestatibus subditos esse	χαισ · εξουσιαισ · Υποτασσεσθαι ·
	dicto obedire ad omne o	και · πειθαργειν · προσ · παν · ερ‿

---

[1] μηδενοσ φιξομενουσ. [2] ενδικνυμενουσ. [3] *In marg.* αγαθα. [4] *In marg.* In nativitate christi. [5] σωτηροσ. [6] Cωφρονωσ. [7] αιωνει. [8] λαλει. [9] *In marg.* ευαγγελ. [10] Υπομειμνησ και.

CAP. IV.	turus est vivos ac mortuos	κριναι · ζωντασ · και · νεκρουσ ·
	et adventum ipsius · et	και · την · επιφανιαν · αυτου · και ·
v. 2	regnum ejus · p̄dica	την · βασιλιαν · αυτου · κηρυ
	verbum · insta	ξον · τον · λογον · επιστη_θει ·
	oportune importune · argue	ευκαιρωσ · ακαιρωσ · ελευξων[1] ·
	obsecra increpa	παρεκα_λεσον · επι_τιμησον ·
	in omni patientia et doctri	εν · παση · μακροθυμια · και · διδα
3	na · Erit enim tempus cum	χη · Εσται · γαρ · καιροσ · οτε ·
	sanam doctri	τησ · ϋγιενουσεσ[2] διδασκαλι_
	nam non sustinebunt · sed ad	ασ · ουκ · αναξονται[3] · αλλα · κα
	sua desideria coa	τα · τασ · ϊδιασ · επιθυμιασ · επι
	cervabunt sibi magi	σωρευσουσιν · εαυτοισ · διδασκα
	stros prurientes auri	λουσ · κνηθομενοι · την · ακο
4	bus · etaveritate quidem	ην · και · απο · μεν · τησ · αλθιασ[4] ·
	auditum avertent ad	την · ακοην · αποστρεψουσιν · επι
	fabulas autem convertentur ·	δε · τουσ · μυθουσ[5] · εκτραπη_σοντ
5	Tu vero vigila in omnibus la	Cυ · δε · νηφαι · εν · πασιν · και · κο
	bora · opus fac evan	παθεσον[6] · εργον · ποι_ησον · ευαγ
	gelistae · ministerium tuum	γελιστου · την · διακονιαν · σου ·
6	imple sobrius esto · Ego enim jam	πληποφορεσον[7] · Εγω · γαρ · ηδη
	delibor · et tempus meae reso	σπενδομαι · και · ο · καιροσ · τησ ·
7	lutionis instat · Bonum	λυσεωσ · μου · εφεστηκεν · Τον ·
	certamen certavi · cur	λον · αγωνα · ηγωνεισμαι · τον ·
	sum consummavi · fidem	δρομον · τετελεκα · την · πιστιν ·
8	servavi · In reliquo reposita est	τετηρηκαι[8] · Λοιπον · απο · και_
	mihi corona justitiae	μοι · ο · τησ · δικαιωσυνησ · στεφα
	quam reddet mihi dn̄s	νοσ[10] · ον · αποδοκαι[11] · μοι · ο κ̄σ ·
	in illa die justus	εν · εκεινη · τη · ημερα · οδικαιοσ ·

[1] Ελειξον. [2] ϋγιενουσησ. [3] ανεξονται. [4] αληθιασ. [5] *In marg.* Fabula μυθοσ inde dicitur liber μυθologiaru
[6] Καικοπαθησον. [7] πληροφορεσον. [8] Τετηρηκα. [9] αποκειται. [10] *In marg.* στεφανοσ. [11] αποδωσει

	Graece	Latine
V.	κριτησ · Ου · μονον · δε · εμοι ·	judex · Non solum autem mihi
	αλλα · και · πασιν · τοισ · ηγαπηκοσιν ·	sed et his qui diligunt
	την · επιφανιαν[1] · αυτου ·	adventum ejus ·
9	Σπου_δασον · ελθειν · προσ · με · τα	F estina ad me venire ci
10	χαιωσ · Δημασ · γαρ · μαι · ενκατε	to · Demas enim me dereli
	λει_πεν · αγαπησασ · τον · νυν · αιω	quit · diligens hoc saecu
	να · και · επορευθη · εισ · θεσσαλονικην ·	lum et abiit thesalonicam
	κρησκησ · εισ · γαλατιαν · τειτοσ · εισ ·	cresces in galatiam · titus in
11	δαλματιαν · λουκασ · εστιν · μονοσ ·	dalmatiam · lucas est mecum so
	μετεμου · Μαρκον · αναλαβων ·	lus · Marcum assume
	αγε · μετα · σεαυτου · εστιν · γαρ ·	et adduc tecum · est enim
	μι ευχρηστοσ · εισ · διακονιαν ·	mihi utilis in ministerium ·
12	Τυ_χεικον · δε · επεστειλα[2] · εισ ·	Tichicum autem mihi
13	εφεσσον · τον · φελονην · ον · απε	ephesum · penulam quēreli
	λειπον · εν · τρωαδει · παρακαρπο[3] ·	qui troade · apud carpum · ve
	ερχομενοσ · φερε · και · τα · βιβλια ·	niens aufer tecum · et libros
	μαλλιστα · τασ · μεμβρανασ ·	maxime membranas ·
14	Αλεξανδροσ · ο · χαλκευσ · Πολλα ·	Alexander aerarius multa mala
	μοι · κακα · ενεδεξατο[4] · αποδωσει ·	mihi ostendit · Reddet
	αυτω · ο κσ · κατα · τα · εργα · αυτου ·	ei dns secundum opera ejus ·
15	ον · και · συ · φυλασσου · λειαν · γαρ ·	quem ettu devita · Valde enim
	ανθεστη · τοισ · εμετεροισ[5] · λογοισ ·	restitit verbis nostris ·
16	Εν · τη · προστη[6] · μου · απολογια[7] · ου	In prima mea defensione ne
	δεισ · μοι · παραγενετο[8] · αλλα · παντεσ ·	mo mihi adfuit · sed omnes
	μαι · ενκατελειπον · Με[9] · αυ	me dereliquerunt non il
	τοισ · λογεισθει · η[10] ·	lis imputetur ·
17	Ο · δε · κσ · μοι · παρεστη · και · ενε_δυ	Dns autem assistit et conforta
	ναμωσεν · μαι · ινα · διεμου · το ·	vit me · utperme prae

[1] In marg. επιφανια. [2] Απεστειλα. [3] καρπω. [4] ενεδειξατο. [5] ημετεροισ. [6] πρωτη.
[7] In marg. απολογια. [8] παρεγενετο. [9] Μη. [10] λογεισθει η.

CAP. IV. dicatio impleatur·et audi	κηρυγμα·πληρωθη·και·ακου
ant omnes gentes·et libera	σωσῖν·παντα[1]·τα·εθνη·και·ερ
tus sum deorē leonis·	ρυσθην·εκ·στοματοσ·λεοντοσ·
v. 18 Liberavit me dns ab omni	Και·ερρυσατο·μαι·ο κσ·απο·παν
opere malo·et salvum faci	τοσ·εργου·υπονηρου·και·σω
et in regno suo	σει·εισ·την·βασιλιαν·εαυτου·
caelesti · Cui gloria in	την·ηπουρανιον · Ο[2]·δοξα·εισ·
saecula saeculorum amen·	τουσ·αιωνασ·των·αιωνων·αμην·
19 aluta priscam et aquilam·	Ασπασε·πρισκαν·και·ακυλαν·
et onesi phori domum·	και·τον·ονησιφορου·οικον·
20 Erastus remansit corintho trofimum	Ερασστοσ·εμεινεν·εν·κορινθω·τροφιμ—
autem reliqui mileti infirmum	δε·απελιπον·εν·μειλητω·ασθενουντα·
21 festina ante hiemem venire·	σπουδασον·προ·χειωνοσ[3]·ελθειν·
Salutat te eubulus et pudens et li	Ασπαζονται·σε·ευβουλοσ·κ πουδησ·κ
nos et claudia et frs oms·	νοσ·κ·κλαυδια·κ·οι·αδελφοι— —παντεσ
22 Dns ιhc xpc cum spu tuo · Gra vobiscum·	Ο κσ·μετα·του·πνσ·σου·Η·χ— —ρισ·μ
Explicit ad Timotheum·II·	Ετελεσθη[4]·προσ·τιμοθεον·Β—
Incipit ad titum·	**Αρχεται προσ τιτον** —·
CAP. I. 1 **Paulus**	**Παυλοσ**
servus di·	**δουλοσ · θυ ·**
apostolus autem ιhv	αποστολοσ·δε·ιηυ·
xpi secundum fidem	χρυ κατα·πιστιν·
electorum di et agnitionem	εκλεκτων·θυ·και επιγνοσιν[5]·—α
2 veritatis·quae secundum pietatem est	ληθιασ·τησ·κατα·ευσεβιαν·— εν
in spem vitae aeterne·quam promi	ελπιδει·ξωησ[6]·αιωνου·αν[7] επ—ηγ
sit qui n mentitur ds·ante	γειλατο·ο·αψευτοσ[8]·θσ·προ— ·

ις

[1] παντεσ παντα. [2] επουρανιον Ω. [3] χειμωνοσ. [4] Ετελεσ. [5] επιγνωσιν. [6] ζωησ. [7] Ην (pro αν). [8] αψευστοσ.

I. 3	χρονων · αιωνιων · φανερω_	tempora saecularia manife
	σεν[1] · δε · και_ροις · ιδιοις · τον · λο	stavit autem temporibus suis ver
	γον · αυτου · ενκηρυγματι ·	bum suum in praedicatione
	ο · επιστευθην · εγω · κατειπιζα	quae credita est mihi secun
	γην[2] · του · σωτησος[3] (ρ above) · ημων · θ̅υ̅ ·	dum p̄ceptum salvatoris nostri d̄i
4	τειτω · γνησειω · τεκνω · κατα	tito dilecto filio secundum
	κοινην · πιστιν · χαρις · και · ῑ	communem fidem gr̄a · et pax
	ρηνη · απο · θ̅υ̅ · πατρος · και · κ̅υ̅ ·	a d̄o patre et d̄n̄o
	ι̅η̅υ̅ χ̅ρ̅υ̅ του σωτηρος · ημων ·	ι̅η̅υ̅ x̄p̄o salvatore nostro
5	ουτου[4] · χαρειν · απελειπον ·	hujus rei gratia reliqui
	σε · εν · κρητη · ινα · τα · λειπον ·	te crǽte ut ea quae desunt
	τα · δει_ορθωσησ · και · καταστη	corrigas et constitu
	σεις · κατα · πολειν · πρεσβυτε	as per civitates p̄sbite
	ρους · ως · εγω · σοι · διεταξαμην ·	ros sicut ego tibi disposui
6	Επις[5] · εστιν · ανεκκλετος[6] (η above) · Μιάς ·	Siquis sine crimine est unius
	γυναικος · ανηρ · τεκνα[7] · εχων ·	uxoris vir filios habens
	πιστα · μη · εν · κατηγορια · ασω	fideles non in accusatione luxu
	τίας · η · ανυποτακτα · Δει ·	riae aut non subditos oportet
	γαρ · τον · επισκοπον · ανηγκλη (ε above)	enim ep̄m sine crimi
	τον[8] · ειναι · ως · θ̅υ̅ · οικονομον[9] ·	ne esse sicut d̄i dispensatorem
	μη · λυδαδην[10] (θ above) · μη · οργειλον ·	non superbum n̄ iracudum (n above) ·
	μη · παροινον · μη · πληκτην ·	non vinolentum non percussorem
	μη · αισχροκερδην · Αλλα · φι	n̄ turbis lucri cupidum sed hospita
	λοξενον · φιλαγαθον · σωφρο	lem benignum sobri
	να · [11] · δικαιον · οσειον · ενκρα	um · justum · scm̄ · continen
	τη · αντεχομην[12] · του · κατα ·	tem amplectentem eum qui secundum
	την · διδαχην · πιστου · λογου ·	doctrinam est fidelem sermonem
	ινα · και · δυνατος · ή · και · πα	ut potens sit exhorta ·

---

[1] *In marg.* επιφανια. [2] κατεπιταγην. [3] σωτηρος. [4] Τουτου. [5] Ει τις. [6] ανεγκλητος.
[7] *In marg.* αγαν. [8] ανεγκλητον. [9] *In marg.* αγ. [10] λυθαδην. [11] Σωφρωνα. [12] αντεχομενον.

	Latin	Greek
CAP. I.	li in doctrina	ρακαλιν·εν·τη·διδασκαλια·
	sana et eos qui contra	τη·υγει_εννουση·και·τ̇ου_σαν
v. 10	dicunt arguere·sunt	τιλεγοντασ·ελεγχειν·εισειν·
	enim multi et inoboedientes	γαρ·πολλοι·και·ανυπο_τακτοι·
	vaniloqui seducto	και·μαται_ολυγοι·και·φρεναπα
	i	
	res·maxime q decircumcisione sunt	ται·μαλλιστα·οι·εκ·περιτομησ·
11	quos oportet redargui·qui	ουσ·δει·επιστομιζιν·οιτινεσ·
	universas domos subvertunt	ολουσ·οικουσ[1]·ανατρεπουσιν·
	docentes quae non oportet	διδασκοντεσ · Α·μη·δει·
12	turpis lucri gratia · Dixit	αισχρου·κερδουσ·χαρειν·ειπεν·
		ω
	autem quidam ex illis proprius ipsorum pro	δε·τισ·εξαυτον[2]·ιδιοσ·προφη
	pheta · Cretenses semper m̄daces	τεσ[3]·κρηταισ_αει·ψευσται·κα
13	malæ bestiae·ventres pigri·	κα·θηρîα·γαστερεσ·αργαι·η·
	Testimonium hoc verum est	μαρτυρια·αυτη·εστιν·αληθησ·
	quam ob causam increpa illos	δι·ην·αιτειαν·ελεγχε·αυτουσ·
	dure·ut sani sint	αποτομωσ·ϊνα·ὑγει·ενωσειν·
14	in fide·non intendentes	εν·τη·πιστι·μη·προσ·εχοντεσ
	judaicis fabulis·et manda	ϊουδαικοισ·μυθοισ·και·ενταλ
	tis hominum aversantium	μασεîν·ανθρωπων·αποστρεφο
15	se a veritate · Omnia	μενων·την·αληθιαν · Παντα·
	munda mundis · Coinquina	καθαρα·τυισ·καθαροισ·τοισ·
	tis autem et infidelibus	μεμειαμενοισ·και·απιστοισ·
	nihil mundum·sed inquiina	ουδεν·καθαρον·αλλα μεμει_
	tæ sunt eorum et mens et	ανται·αντων·και·ονουσ·και·
		ο
16	conscientia · Confiteantur	η·συνϊδησεισ·θ̄ν·ομλογου_
	se nosse dm̄ factis autem	σειν[4]·ϊδεναι·τοισ·δε·εργοισ·
	negant cum sint abhomina	αρνουνται·βδελυκτοι
	biles et increduli·et ad om̄e	οντεσ·κα ·απιθεισ·και·προσ·
	f	

[1] ι ουκουσ. [2] αυτων. [3] προφητησ. [4] ομολογουσειν

I. παν · εργον · αγαθον · αδοκειμοι ·	opus bonum reprobi
II. 1 νδε; λαλει · απρεπει · τη · ΰ	Tu autem loquere quæ decet sa
γει · εννουση · διδασκαλια ·	nam doctrinam
2 Πρεσβυτασ · νη‿φαλει‿ουσ[2] · ειναι ·	Senes sobrios esse
σεμνουσ[3] · σωφρονασ · ϋγειεν ·	pudicos · prudentes · sanos
νοτασ · τη · πιστει · τη · αγαπη · τη ·	in fide · in dilectione et
3 υπομονη · Πρεσβυτειδασ · ωσ‿	patientia · Anus simili
αυτωσ · εν · κατα · σχηματι[4,5] · ϊερο‿	ter in habitu sancto
πρεπεισ · Μη · διαβολουσ · μη ·	non criminatrices non
οινω · πολλω · δε · δουλομενασ[6] ·	vino multo servientes
4 καλο · διδασκαλουσ · ΐνα · σωφρο	bene docentes · ut pudicitam
νιζουσειν[7] · Τασ · νεασ · φιλαν	doceant · Adolescentulas ut
δρουσ · ειναι · φιλο · τεκνουσ ·	viros suos ament filios diligant ·
σωφρονασ · αγνασ[8] · οικουργουσ ·	prudentes · castas · dom' curam habentes
αγαθασ · υπο · τασ · σομενασ · τοισ ·	benignas subditas
ιδιοισ · ανδρασιν · ΐνα · μη · ολσ	viris suis · ut non blasphe
γοσ · του · θυ · βλασφημηται ·	metur verbum di
Ουσ[9] · νεωτερουσ · ωσαυτωσ · παρα	Juvenes similiter horta
καλει · σω‿φρονιν · περιπαντα · σε	re ut sobrii sunt · In omnibus te
αυτον · παρεχομενοσ · τυπον ·	ipsum prebe exemplum
καλων · εργων · εν · τη · διδασκα	bonorum operum in doctri
λια · αφθονιαν · σεμνοτητα ·	na · In integritate · In gravitate ·
8 λογον · ϋγεινη[10] · ακαταγνωσ ·	verbum sanum in reprehen
τον · ινα · ο · εξεναντιασ ·	sibile · Ut is qui ex adverso est
εντραπη · μηδην[11] · εχων · λεγειν ·	vereatur nihil habens ma
περι · ημων · φαυλον ·	lum dicere denobis
9 Δουλουσ · ΐδειοισ[12] · δεσποταισ ·	servos dominis suis
υποτασ‿σεσθαι · εν · πασιν ευαρεσ‿	sub ditos esse · In omnibus ·

---

1 Cυ. 2 νηφαλαιουσ. 3 *In marg.* σεμνα. 4 Κατα στηματι. 5 *In marg.* σχημα B στημα. 6 δεδουλωμενασ. 7 σωφρονιζοισειν *p.m.* 8 *In marg.* αγνα αγαθα. 9 Τουσ. 10 ϋγειην. 11 Μηδεν. 12 δε‿ ΐδειοισ.

CAP. II.	placentes·non contra dicen	τουσ·ειναι·μη·αντι λεγον·
v. 10	tes·non fraudentes	τασ·μη·δενοσ͜φιξομενουσ[1]·
	sed in omnibus fidem bonam	αλλα·πασαν·εν·δικνυ͜μενοσ[2]·
	ostendentes · Ut doctri	πιστιν·αγαθην[3]·ινα·την·διδασ
	nam salvatoris nostri	καλιαν·την·τουσωτηροσ·ημων·
	ornent in omnibus	θ̅υ̅·κοσμωσειν·εν·πασιν
11	Apparuit enim gratia d̅i̅	Επεφανη[4]·γαρ·η·χαρισ·του·θ̅υ̅
	salvatoris nostri omnibus homi	του·σωτιροσ[5]·ημων·πασιν·αν
12	nibus erudiens nos	θρωποισ·παιδευουσα·ημασ·
	ut abnegantes impieta	ῑνα·αρνησαμενοι·την·ασεβεῖ
	tem et saecularia deside	αν·και·τασ·κοσμεικασ·επιθυμι
	ria·sobrie·et juste·et	ασ·σωφρονωσ[6]·και·δικαιωσ·και·
	pie vivamus in hoc sae	ευσεβωσ·ζησωμεν·εν·τωνυν·
13	cula·expectantes	αιωνει[7]·Προσ·δε·χομενοι·την·
	beatam spem et adven	μακαριαν·ελπειδα·και·επιφα
	tum gloriae magni	νιαν·τησ·δοξησ·του·μεγαλου·
	d̅i̅·et salvatoris nostri I̅H̅V̅ x̅p̅i̅·	θ̅υ̅ και σωτηροσ·ημων·χ̅υ̅ ι̅η̅υ̅
14	Qui dedit semetipsum pro nobis	Οσ·εδωκεν·εαυτον·ϋπερ·ημων·
	ut nos redimeret ab omni	ϊνα·λυτρωσηται·ημασ·απο·πα
	iniquitate·et mundaret	σησ·ανομιασ·ϗ·καθαρειση·ε
	sibi populum acceptabilem sec	αυτω·λαον·περι͜ουσειον·ζηλω·
15	tatoreim bonum operum haec	την·καλων·εργων · ταυτα·λε
	loquere et exhortare·et argue	λει[8]·και·παρακαλει·και·ελεγχαι [illegible]ι·
	cum omnio imperio nemo	μετα·πασησ·επιταγησ[9]·μηδεισ [illegible]σ·
	te contemnat·	σου·περι͜φρονειτω
CAP. III. 1	dmone illos principibus	πομειμνησ·και[10]·αυτουσ·αρ͜
	et potestatibus subditos esse	χαισ·εξουσιαισ·Υποτασσεσθαι·
	dicto obedire ad omne o	και·πειθαργειν·προσ·παν·ερ͜

---

[1] μηδενοσ φιξομενουσ. [2] ενδικνυμενουσ. [3] *In marg.* αγαθα. [4] *In marg.* In nativitate christi.
[5] σωτηροσ. [6] Cωφρονωσ. [7] αιωνει. [8] λαλει. [9] *In marg.* ευαγγελ̅. [10] Ϋπομειμνησ και.

· γον αγαθον · ετοιμουσ · ειναι ·	pus bonum paratos esse neminem
2 μη · βλασφημειν · αμαχουσ ·	neminem blasphemare non litigiosos
ειναι · επει εικεισ · πασαν · εν ·	esse · sed modestos · omnem osten
δι‿κνυμενουσ · πραοτητα ·	dentes mansuetudinem
προσ · παντασ · ανθρωπουσ ·	ad omnes homines ·
3 Ημεν · γαρ · ποτε · και · ημεισ · ανοητοι ·	Eramus enim et nos aliquando insipientes
απειθεισ · πλανωμενοι · δολευ	Increduli errantes servi
οντεσ[1] · επιθυμειαισ · και · η‿δο	entes desideriis · et volu
ναισ · ποικελαισ · εν · κακια · και ·	ptatibus variis · In malitia · et invi
φθονω · δια‿γοντεσ · οτοι · πητοι ·	dia agentes · odibiles ·
μισουντεσ · αλληλουσ ·	odientes · invicem ·
4 Οτε · δε · χρηστοτησ · και · ηφια	Cum autem benignitas et huma
ανθρωπῖα · επεφανη · σ(τ)ου[2] · σω	nitas apparuit salva
5 τηροσ · ημων · θ̅υ̅ · ουκ · εξ · ερ	toris n̅r̅i̅ d̅i̅ non ex operi
γων των[3] · δικαιοσυνη · α	bus justitiae · quae
εποι · ησαμεν · ημισ · αλλα · κατα ·	fecimus nos sed secundum
το ελεοσ · αυτου · εωσεν[4] ·	suam misericordiam salvos nos
ημασ · δια · λουτρου · παλιν · γε	fecit per lavacrum regenerati
νεσειασ · και ανακαινω‿σεωσ ·	onis et renovationis
6 δια · π̅ν̅σ̅ · αγιου · ουεξεχεν ·	s̅p̅s̅ s̅c̅i̅ quem effudit
εφ ημασ · πλουσειωσ · δια · ι̅υ̅ · χ̅ρ̅υ̅ ·	in nos abunde per i̅h̅m̅ x̅p̅m̅
7 του · σ(ω)τηροσ[5] · ημων · ινα · δικαι	salvatorem nostrum · ut justifi
ωθεντεσ · τη · εκεινου · χαριτη ·	cati gratia ipsius
κληρονομαι[6] · γενηθωμεν ·	heredes simus secun
καθελπιδα · ζωησ · αιωνιου ·	dum spem vitæ æternae ·
8 Πιστοσ · ο · λογωσ[7] · και · περι · του	Fidelis sermo · et de his
των · βουλομαι · σε · δια‿βεβαι	volo te confirma
ουσθαι · ινα φροντι‿ζωσειν ·	re · ut curent

---

[1] Δουλευοντεσ. [2] του. [3] + εν (post των). [4] εσωσεν. [5] σωτηροσ. [6] Κληρονομοι. [7] λογοσ.

v. 9	imperandi tibi quod ad rem pertinet	επιτασειν[1] · σοι · το · ανηκον · δια ·
	propter caritatem magis obse	την · αγαπην · μαλλον · παρακα
	cro · cum sis ut paulus	λω · τοι ουτοσ · ων · ωσ · παυλοσ ·
	senex · Nunc autem ut vinctus	πρεσβυτεσ[2] · Νυν · ει · δε · χ̅υ̅ · δεσμιος
10	ihu̅ xpi̅ · Obsecro te pro	ι̅υ̅ χ̅ρ̅υ̅ · Παρακαλω · σε · περι ·
	meo filio quem genui	του · εμου · τεκνου · ον · εγενησα[3] ·
	in vinculis onesimo · qui	εν · τοισ · δεσμοισ · ονησειμον ·
11	tibi aliquando inutilis fuit · Nunc autem	τον · ποτε ; σοι · αχρηστον · νυν , ει
	mihi et tibi utilis · quem	δε · και · σοι · και · εμοι · ευχρηστον ·
12	remisi · Tu autem illum	ον · ανεπεμψα · Cυ · δε · αυτον ·
	ut est viscera mea suscipe	τουτεστιν · τα · εμα · σπλανχνα ·
13	quem ego volueram mecum	ον · εγω · εβυλομην[4] · προσ · εμαυ
	deonere · Ut pro te	τον · κατεχειν · ἱνα · ὑπερ · σου ·
	mihi ministraret in vinculis	μοι · διακονη · εν · τοισ · δεσ_μοισ ·
14	evangelii · Sine consili	του · ευαγγελιου · Χωρεισ · δε ·
	o autem tuo nihil volui	τησ · γνωμησ[5] · ουδεν · ηθελησα ·
	facere · uti ne vel ut ex necessi	ποιησαι · ἱνα · μηωσ · καταναγ
	tate bonum tuum esset · sed	κην · το · αγαθον · σου · η · Αλλα ·
15	voluntarium · forsitan enim id	κατεκουσειον · Ταχα · γαρ · δια
	eo discessit ad horam	τουτο · εχωρισθη · προσ · ωραν ·
	ut aeternum illum reciperes	ἱνα · αιωνειον · αυτον · απεχησ ·
16	jam non ut servum · sed pro servo	ουκετει · ωσ · δουλον ·
	carissimum fratrem · maxime	αδελφον · αγαπητον · μαλλιστα ·
	mihi · quanto magis et tibi	εμοι · ποσω · δε · μαλλον · σοι ·
	et in carne et in dn̅o ·	και · εν · σαρκει · και · εν · κ̅ω̅ ·
17	Si ergo habes me socium · sus	ι[6] · ουν · με · εχεισ · κοινωννον · προσ
18	cipe illum sicut me · Si autem	λαβον · αυτον · ωσ · εμαι · Ειδε ·
	aliquid nocuit tibi · aut de	τι · ηδει_κησεν · σε · η · οφει_

[1] επιτασσειν. [2] πρεσβυτησ. [3] εγεννησα. [4] εβουλομην.
[5] + σησ (ante γνωμησ). [6] Ει.

	λειτει · τουτο · μοι · ελλοτα[1] ·	bet · hoc mihi imputa
	Εγω · παυλοσ · εγραψα · τη · εμη	Ego paulus scripsi mea
	χιρει · εγω · αποτεισω · ῑνα · μη ·	manu · Ego reddam · ut non
	λεγω · σοι · οτι · και · σε · αυτον ·	dicam tibi quod et te ipsum
20	μοι · προσοφιλεισ · ναι · αδελ	mihi debes · Ita fra
	φαι[2] · εγω · σοι[3] · οναιμην · εν ·	ter ego te fruar · in
	κ̄ω · αναπαυσον · μουτα ·	d̄no refice vis
	σπανχνα · εν · χ̄ρω ·	cera mea in x̄po ·
21		Confidens oboedientia tua
		scripsi tibi · Sciens quoniam et
	[4]	super id quod dico tibi
22		facies · Simul autem et pa
		ra mihi hospitum · Nam
	Folium ultimum deerat in Autographo.	spero per orationes vestras
23	[R. B.]	donari me vobis · Salutant
		te epaphras concaptivus
24		meus in x̄po īhu · Mar
		cus · Aristarchus · Demas ·
		et lucas · adjutores mei ·
25	[5]	Gratia d̄ni n̄ri īhu x̄pi
		cum s̄pu vestro Amen ;

[1] ελλογα. [2] αδελφε (η. αι) (*sic*). [3] σου. [4] Spatium vacuum habet Cod. Boernerianus. ad laudicenses incipit epistola.
[5] Ad finem : Προσ λαουδακησασ αρχεται επιστολη.

Addendum : p. 8. Rom. v. 16, ουχ (*pro* ουκ) Cod. Boerner.

Incipi Argumentum in epistolam ad hebreos

Inprimis dicendum est · cur apostolus
paulus In hac epistola scribendo
non servaverit morem suum · ut
vel vocabulum nominis sui · vel
ordinis scriberet dignitatem ·
Haec causa est · quod ad eos scribens
qui ex circumcisione crediderant ·
quasi gentium apostolus et non he
breorum · Sciens quoque eorum
superbiam · suamque humilitatem
ipse demonstrans · meritum oficii
sui noluit ante ferre · Nam simili
modo etiam iohannes apostolus
propter humilitatem In epistola sua ·
Nomen suum eadem ratione non p̄tulit ·
Hanc epistolam ergo fertur apostolum
adebreos conscriptam hebraica
lingua misisse · Cujus sensum
et ordinem retines (n) lucas evangeli
sta post discensum beati apostoli
pauli · greco sermone composuit ·

EXPLICIT ARGUMENTUM ;

INCIPIT IPSA EPISTOLA AD HEBREOS

I. 1 **Multifariā multisque modis olim d̄s loquens**
2 patribus In prophetis · Novissime di
istis · locutus est nobis in filio · quem con
stituit heredem universorum · per quem
3 fecit et saecula · Qui cum sit splendor
gloriae et figura substantiae ejus · portans
que omnia verbo virtutis suæ · purgationem
peccatorum faciens · sedet ad dexteram ma
4 jestatis in excelsis · Tanto melior angelis
effectus · quanto differentius prae illis · no
5 men hereditavit · Cui enim dixit aliquan
do angelorum · filius meus es tu ego hodie
genui te ? et rursum · Ego ero illi in patrem ·
6 et ipse erit mihi in filium · et cum iterum
Introducit promogenitum in orbem terræ ·
7 dicit et adorent eum omnes angeli d̄i · et ad
angelos quidem dicit · Qui facit angelos
suos sp̄s · et ministros suos flammam ig
8 nis · Ad filium autem · tronus tuus d̄s
in saeculum saeculi · Virga aequitatis
9 virga regni tui · Dilexisti justitiam
et odisti iniquitatem propterea
unxit te d̄s d̄s tuus oleo exultati
10 onis pre participibus tuis · Et tu

pio dne terram fundasti·
manuum tuarum sunt caeli·
bunt tu autem permanebis·
ut vestimentum veterescent·
amictum mutabis eos·
ɔuntur · Tu autem idem ipse es·
tui non deficient · Ad quem
m autem dixit aliquando·
extris meis·quo ad usque ponam
tuos scabellum pedum tuorum·
ɔmnes sunt amministratorii
ainisterium missi·propter eos
:ditatem capiunt salutis·
:ea abundantius oportet obser
ea quae audivimus ne forte
fluamus · Si enim qui per
dictus est sermo factus est fir
omnis praevaricatio et inoboe
accepit justam mercedis retribu
quomodo nos effugiemus si tan
glexerimus salutem · Quae cum
accepisset enarrari per dnm
qui audierunt · In nobis con
est·contestante do signis
:ntis·et variis virtutibus et
distributionibus secundum suam
tem·non enim angelis sub
orbem terrae futurum·

ver.
6 dequo loquimur · Testatus est
autem in quodam loco quidam
dicens · Quid est homo quod
memor es ejus aut filius hominis
7 quoniam visitas eum·minuisti
eum paulominis ab angelis gloria
et honore coronasti eum et con
stituisti eum super opera manuum
8 tuarum·omnia subjecisti sub pe
dibus ejus · In eo enim quod ei
omnia subjecit·nihil dimisit·
non subjectum ei · Nunc autem
9 necdum videmus omnia subjecta ei·eum
autem qui modico·quam angeli mino
ratus est · Videmus ihm propter pas
sionem mortis ejus·gloria et hono
re coronatum · Ut gratia di pro omni
10 bus gustaret mortem · Dicebat enim
eum propter quem omnia·et per omnia
qui multos filios in gloriam ad
duxerat·auctorem salutos eorum·
per passiones consummare·
11 Qui enim scificat·et qui scificatur
ex uno omnes · Propter quam cau
sam non confunditur fratres
12 eos vocare dicens·nuntiabo no
men tuum fratribus meis · In medio
13 ecclesiae laudabo te · Et iterum

ver.
Ego ero fidens in euum · et iterum ·
ecce ego et pueri mei · quos mihi
14 dedit ds · Quia ergo pueri com
municaverunt carni et sanguuini ·
et ipse similiter participavit his
dem · ut per mortem destrueret eum ·
qui habebat mortis imperium · Id est
15 diabolum · et liberaret eos qui timo
re mortis per totam vitam obnoxii erant
16 servituti · Nusquam enim angelos app
17 hendit · sed sem abrahæ apphendit Un
de debuit p omnia fratribus similari · ut mi
sercors fieret et fidelis pontifex ad
dm · ut propitiaret delicta populi ·
18 In eo enim in quo passus · ipse
temptatus · potens est et eis qui
temptatus auxiliari ·
III. 1 Unde fratres sci · vocationis cælestis
participes · considerate apostolum
et pontificem confessionis nostrae
2 ihm · qui fidelis est ei qui fecit illum ·
sicut et moyses in omni domo
3 illius · Amplioris enim gloriae
iste prae moyse dignus habitus
est · quanto ampliorem hono
rem habet domus qui fabri
4 cavit illam · omnis namque
domus fabricatur ab aliquo ·

ver.
qui autem omnia creavit ds est ·
5 et moyses quidem fidelis erat in tota
domo ejus tamquam famulus · In testi
monium eorum quae dicenda sunt ·
6 Xps vero tamquam filius in domo sua ·
quae domus sumus nos · si fiduciam et
gloriam spei usque ad finém
firmam retineamus ·
7 Quapropter sicut dicit sps scs · Hodie
8 si vocem ejus audieritis · nolite obdu
rare corda vestra · Sicut in exacerba
tione secundum diem temptationis
9 in deserto · Ubi temptaverunt me pa
tres vestri · probaverunt opera mea ·
10 Quadraginta annis · propter quod infen
sus generationi huic · et dixi semper
errant corde · Ipsi autem non cogno
11 verunt vias meas · sicut juravi in ira mea
12 si introibunt in requiem meam · Videte fra
tres ne forte sit in aliquo vrm cor malig
num incredulitatis discedendi
13 a do vivo · sed adhortamini vosmet
ipsos per singulos dies · donec
hodie cognominetur · ut non obdu
retur quis ex vobis fallatia peccati ·
14 Participes enim xpi · effecti
sumus · si tamen initium substan
tiae ejus usque adfinem

retineatis · Dum dicitur
vocem ejus audieritis · nolite
e corda vestra · quem admodum
exacerbatione · quidam enim
es exacerbaverunt sed non
qui profecti sunt ab egypto per
· quibus autem infensus est qua
annis · Nonne illis qui pec
t · quorum cadavera pro
unt in deserto · quibus autem ju
n intrare inrequem ipsius
illius qui increduli fuerunt
nus quia non potuerunt intro
ter incredulitatem · Timeamus
forte relicta pollititatione
ndi in requiem ejus existimetur
x vobis deesse ·
; nobis nuntiatum est quem
m et illis · sed non profuit illis
uditus · non am mixtis fidei
x his quae audierunt · Ingre
enim in requiem qui credimus
lmodum dixit · Sicut jura
mea · si introibunt in requiem
; quidem operibus ab institu
undi factis · dixit enim in
loco · de die septima sic
it d̄s die septima ab omnibus

ver.
5 operibus suis · et in isto rursum
si introibunt in requiem meam ·
6 Quō ergo super est quosdam in
troire in illam · et hi quibus
prioribus adnuntiatum est non
introierunt propter incredulita
7 tem · Iterum terminat diem
quendam hodie in david dicendo
post tantum temporis sicut supa ·
dictum est · hodie si vocem ejus audi
eritis nolite obdurare corda
8 vestra · Nam si eis jesus requiem
praestitisset · numquam de alia
9 loqueretur · sabbatismus populo
10 d̄i · Qui enim ingressus est in requiem
ejus · etiam ipse requievit ab ope
ribus suis · sicut a suis d̄s ·
11 estinemus ingredi ergo in illam re
quiem · Ut ne in id ipsum quis incidat
12 incredulitatis exemplum unius
enim est sermo d̄i et efficax et
penetrabilior omni gladio
ancipiti et pertingens usque ad divi
sionem animæ ac sp̄s · compagum
quoque et medullarum et discretor
cogitationum et intentionum
13 cordis et non est ulla creatura

ver.
invisibilis in conspectu ejus·omnia enim
nuda et aperta sunt oculis ejus
14 Ad quem nobis sermo·habentes
ergo pontificem magnum q[i] pene
travit caelos ih̄m filium d̄i·tene
amus confessionem ejus·
15 Non enim habemus pontificem qui non
possit compati infirmitatibus nostris
temptatum autem per omnia pro simili
tudine carnis absque peccato
16 deamus ergo cum fidutia ad
thronum gratiae·ut m̄iam consequa
mur·et gratiam inveniamus in
V. 1 auxilio oportuno · omnis namque
pontifex ex hominibus assumptus
pro hominibus constituitur in his quæ sunt
ad d̄m·ut offerat dona et sacri
2 ficia pro peccatis·qui c̄ dolore pos
sit his qui ignorant et errant q̄m
et ipse circum datus est infirmita
3 te·et propterea debet quem admo
dum et pro populo · Ita etiam
pro semet ipso offerre pro peccatis
4 Nec quis quam sumit sibi honorem
sed qui vocatur a d̄o tamquam
5 aaron · Sic et x̄ps non semet ipsum
clarificavit ut pontifex fieret
sed qui locutus est ad eum·filius

ver.
6 meus estu ego hodie genui te·quem
ad modum·et in alio loco dicit · Tues
sacerdos in aeternum secundum ordinem
7 melchisedech · Qui in diebus carnis
suae preces supplicationesque ad eum·
qui possit salvum illum a morte face
re·cum clamore valido et lacrimis
offerens·et exauditū est pro sua reverentia
8 t quidem cum esset filius d̄i didicet
ex his quæ passus est oboedientiam
9 et consummatus factus est omnibus ob
tem perantibus sibi causa salutis aeterne
10 appellatus a d̄o pontifex·juxta
11 ordinem melchisedehc · De quo gran
dis nobis sermo est·et in interp̄tabilis
addicendum·q̄m inbecillis facti estis
12 ad audiendum·et enim cum deb[r]etis
magistri esse propter tempus·rursum
indignetis ut vos doceamini quæ sint
elementa exordii sermonum d̄i
et facti estis quibus lacte opus sit
13 non solido cibo · Omnis enim qui lac
tis est particeps·expers sermonis justi
14 tiae·parvulus enim est · Perfectorum
autem est solidus cibus·eorum qui pro
consuetudine exercitatos habent sensus
ad discretionem boni ac mali
VI. 1 ua propter inter mittentes inchoa

xpi sermonem·ad perfectionem
r · Non rursum jacientes
ıentum poenitentiae ab operibus
s et fidei addm baptismatum
se · Inpositionis quoque manuum
rrectionis mortuorum et judicii
·et hoc faciemus si quidem
ıiserit ds·inpossibile est enim
semel sunt inluminati gustaverunt
lomum cæleste et participes
cti sps sci·gustaverunt nihil
di verbum virtutesque scli ven
prolapsi sunt renovari rursum
ıitentiam · Rursum crucifigen
et ipsis filium di et ostentui
s · Terra enim saepe venien
per se bibens imbrem et generans
oportunam illis a quibus
accipit benedictionem a do
ıs autem spinas ac tribulos reproba
ıaledicto proxima cujus consumma
onbustionem
ıs autem devobis dilectissimi
et viciniora saluti·tam
ı loquimur · Non enim injustus
bliviscatur operis vestri et dilec
uam ostendistis in nomine
ui ministrastis scis et ministra

ver.
11 tis cupimus autem unum quemque
vestrum eandem ostentare sollicitu
dinem·ad expletionem spei
12 usque in finem ut non segnes efficia
mini · Verum imitatores eorum
qui fide et patientia hereditabunt
13 promissiones · Abrahae namque
promittens ds·qm niminem habuit
per quem juraret majorem juravit
14 per semetipsum dicens · Nisi benedi
cens benedicam te et multiplicans
15 multiplicabo te·et sic longani
miter ferens·adeptus est repromissi
16 onem·homines enim per majorem
sibi jurant·et omnis controversi
ae eorum finis·ad confirmationem
17 est juramentum · In quo abundan
tius·ds volens ostendere pollici
tationes heredibus immobilitatem
consilii sui · Inter posuit jusjuran
18 dum·ut per duas res immobiles qui
bus inpossibile est mentiri dm
Fortissimum solatium habeamus qui
confugimus adtenendam propositam spem
19 quam sicut anchoram hebemus
animae tutam·ac firmam·et ince
dentem usque interiora velaminis
20 Ubi praecursor pro nobis introiit

ver.
ihs·secundum ordinem melchisedech
ponti fex factus in aeternum
VII. 1 ic enim melchisedech rex salem
sacerdos dī summi·qui obviavit
abrae·regresso acede regum et
2 benedixit ei·cui et decimas omnium
divisit abraham·primum quidem qui
interp̄tatur rex justitiæ·deinde
3 autem rex salem·q̄d[e] rex pacis sine
patre sine matre·sine genealogia
neque initium dierum neque vitæ finem
habens · Assimilatus autem filio dī ma
4 net sacerdos in perpetuum · Intue
mini autem quantus sit hic·cui et de
cimam dedit dep̄cipuis abraham pa
5 triarcha·et quidem de filiis leui
sacerdotium accipientes mandatum
habent decimas sumere A populo
secundum legem · Id est a fratribus suis
quā quam et ipsi exierunt delumbis
6 abrahae·cujus autem generatio non an
numeratur in eis · Decimas sumpsit
abraham et hunc qui habebat re
7 promissiones benedixit · Sine ulla autem
contradictione q̄d minus est a me
8 liore benedicitur·et hic quidem
decimas morientes homines accipi
unt · Ibi autem contestatus est·qui[a] vivit

ver.
9 et ut ita dictum sit per abraham et leui qui
10 decimas accepit decimatus est · Adhuc
enim in lumbis patris erat quando obvia
vit ei melchisedech·
11 i ergo consummatio per sacerdotum leuiticum
erat·populus enim sub ipso legem accepit
quid adhuc necessarium secundum ordinem
melchisedech · Alium surgere sacerdotem
12 et non secundum ordinem aaron dici·Trans
lato etenim sacerdotio·necesse est ut legis
13 translatio fiat · In quo enim hæc dicuntur
dealia tribu est·dequa nullus altari p̄sto
14 fuit · Manifestum est enim quod ex juda
ortus sit dn̄s noster·in qua tribu nihil de
15 sacerdotibus moyses locutus est et amplius
adhuc manifestum est·si secundum similita
dinem melchisedech exurgat alius sa
16 cerdos qui non secundum legem mandati
carnalis factus est sed secundum virtutem
17 vitae insolibis[u] · Contestatur enim
quō tues sacerdos in aeternum secundum
18 ordinem melchisedech · Reprobatio
quidem fit p̄cedentis mandati propter
19 infirmitatem ejus et inutilitatem nihil enim
ad perfectum ad duxit lex
Ntroducto vero melioris spei per quam
20 proximamus ad dm̄·et quantum est
21 non sine jure jurando · Alii quidem

re jurando sacerdotes facti sunt
em cum jure jurando per eum
cit ad illum · Juravit dn̄s et non
it eum tues sacerdos in aetn̄·
tum melioris testamenti sponsor
est ih̄c·et alii quidem plures
int sacerdotes · Id circo qd̄ morte
rentur permanere·Hic autem eo qd̄
in aeternum·sempiternum ha
cerdotium · Unde et salvare
etuum potest accedentes per
sum ad dm̄·semper vivens ad
llandum pro eis·Talis enim decebat
is esset pontifex·sc̄s·innocens·in
s·segregatus a peccatoribus et ex
cælis factus·qui non habet cot
ecessitatem quem ad modum sacer
rius pro suis delictis offerre·de
ro populo·hoc enim fecit semel se
lo · Lex enim constituit homines
tes·infirmitatem habentes sermo
jusjurandi qui post legem est fidelium
num·perfectum · Capitulum autem
a quaedicuntur·talem habemus
em·qui consedit in dextera se
gnitudinis in caelis sc̄orum mini
tabernaculi veri·qd̄ fixit dn̄s
homo · Omnis enim pontifex ad

ver.
offerenda munera et hostias consti
tuitur·unde necesse est·et hunc habere
4 aliquid qd̄ offerat · Si ergo esset super
terram nec esset sacerdos·cum essent qui
5 offerent secundum legem munera·qui
exemplari et umbrae deserviunt
caelestium · Sicut responsum est moy
si cum consummarent tabernaculum·
Vide inquit omnia facito secundum exemplar
6 qd̄ tibi ostensum est in monte · Nunc
autem melius sortitus est ministerium
quanto et melioris testamenti est me
diator·qd̄ in melioribus repromissioni
bus sc̄m est·
7 Nam si illud prius culpa vacasset·non
8 utique secundi locus inquireretur · Vitupe
rans enim eos dicit·ecce dies veniunt dic̄
dn̄s·et consummabo super domum isr̄l·
et super domum juda testamentum novum·
9 non secundum testamentum qd̄ feci patribus eorum·
In die qua apphendi manum illorum·
uteducerem eos deterra aegypti·
qm̄ ipsi non permanser̄ in testamento
meo et ego neglexi eos dicit dn̄s·
10 Quia hoc est testamentum qd̄ disponam
domui isr̄l p' dies illos dicit dn̄s·
Dando leges in mente eorum·et in cor
de eorum super scribam eas·etero

ver.
eis in dm·et ipsi erunt mihi
in populum·>
11 Et non docebit unusquisque proxi
mum suum·et unus quisque
frem suum·dicens·cognos
ce dm quo omnes scient me·
animo usque ad majorem eorum·
12 quia propitius ero iniquitatibus
eorum·et peccatorum eorum
13 jam non memorabor · Dicendo
autem novum inveteravit prius·
quod autem antiquatur et se
nescit·prope interitum est·>
IX. 1 Habuit quidem et prius justi
ficationes culturæ et scm
2 saecularae ·> Tabernaculum
enim factum est primum·
In quo inerant candelabra
et mensa·et propositio panum
3, 4 quod dicitur sca scorum·Aureum
habens turibulum·et archam
testamenti·circumtextam ex
omni parte auro·In quo urna
aurea habens manna·et virga
aaron quae fronduerat·et ta
5 bulæ testamenti ·> Superque eam
cherubim glae ob umbran
tia propitiatorium · de quibus

ver.
non est modo dicendum persingula
6 His vero ita compositis in priori qui
dem tabernaculo semper ntroibant sacerdo
tes·sacrificiorum officia consummantes·
7 In secundo autem·semel in anno solus pon
tifex·non sine sanguuine·quem offert
8 pro sua et pro populi ignorantia·Hoc sig
nificanté spu sco·nondum prolatam esse
sanctorum vitam·Adhuc priori tabernacu
9 lo habente statum quae parabola est
temporis instantis · Juxta quam mu
nera et ostiae offeruntur·quae non
possunt juxta conscientiam perfectum
10 facere servitutem·Solummodo in
cibis et in potibus et in variis baptis
matis et justitiis carnis·usque ad tempus
11 correctionis inpositis·Xpc autem assistens
pontifex futurorum bonorum per amplius
et perfectius·Tabernaculum non manu
factum·Id est nohujus creationis·
12 Neque per sanguinem hircorum·aut vitulorum·
sed proprium sanguinem introivit semel
in sca aeterna redemptione inventa·
13 Si enim sanguis hircorum · Aut taurorum
et cinis vitulæ aspersus inquinatos
scificat ad emundationem carnis·
14 quanto magis sangis xpi·qui per spm
scm semetipsum obtulit in macula

›·et emundavit cscientiam vestram
ribus mortuis ad serviendum do
·> Et ideo novi testamti me
est ut morte intercedente
mptionem earum prevarica
·quæ erant sub priori testa
promissionem accipiant qui voca
; hereditatis aeternæ · Ubi enim
entum·mors necesse est intercedat
ris · Testamentum enim in mortuis
natum est Aliquin·Nondum va
m vivit qui testatus est·Unde
m quidem sine sanguine dedi
est ·> Lecto enim omni mandato
moyse universo populo·>
iens sanguinem vitulorum et
um cum aqua et lana cocci
; ysopo·Ipsum quoque librum
nem populum aspexit dicens·
nguis testamenti quod manda
vos ds·Etiam tabernaculum
nia vasa ministerii sanguine
er aspersit·et omnia paene
guine mundantur secundum legem
sanguinis effusione non
issio·Non enim in manu
scis ihc introivit exempla
orum·Sed in ipsum cęlum ut appa

ver.
reat nc vultu di pro nobis·
25 Neque ut sepe offerat semetipsum
quem ad modum pontifex intrat·
in sca per singulos annos in sangui
26 ne alieno·Alioquin oporte
bat enim frequent pati ab ori
gine mundi ·> Nunc autem semel
in consummatione saeculorum·
Adtestitutionem peccati p hosti
27 am suam apparuit·et quem
ad modum statutum est hominibus
semel mori·post hoc autem judi
28 cium·sic et xpc semel oblatus
ad multorum exaurienda
peccata·Secundo sine peccato
apparuit exspectantibus se in sa
X. 1 lutem·Umbram enim futurorum
habens lex bonorum·Non ipsam
imaginem rerum·Per singulos
annos hisdem ipsis hostiis quas
offerunt indesinent numquam
Potest accedentes perfectos face
2 re Alioquin cessassent offer
re · Ideo qd nullam haberent
ultra conscientiam peccati cul
3 tores semel mundati · Sed in
ipsis commemoratio peccatorum
per singulos annos. fit·

ver.
4 inpossibile enim est sanguine tau
rorum et hircorum auferri peccata·
5 Ideo ingrediens mundum dicit·
hostiam etolationem noluisti·
6 corpus autem aptasti mihi · Holo
caustomata et pro peccato non tibi
7 placuit·tunc dixi ecce venio·
In capite libri scriptum est de me·
8 ut faciam ds voluntatem tuam·supe
rius dicens·quia hostias etobla
tiones etholocaustomata pro pecca
to noluisti·nec placita sunt tibi
quae secundum legem offeruntur·
9 Tunc dixi ecce venio ut faciam ds
voluntatem tuam·Aut fert pri
10 mum ut sequens statuat · In qua
voluntate scificati sumus per
oblationem corporis xpi ihu in se
11 mel·Et omnis quidem sacerdos pre
sto est cottidie ministrans eteasdem
sepàe offerens hostias quae num
quam possunt auferre peccata·
12 Hic autem unam pro peccatis offerens
hostiam in sempiternum sedet in
13 dextera di·e cetero exspectans
donec ponantur inimici ejus
14 scabellum pedum ejus · Una enim
oblatione consummavit·

ver.
15 in sempiternum scificatos·contestatur
autem nos et sps scs·post quam enim dixit·
16 Hoc autem testamtum qd testabor ad illos·
p' dies illos dicit dns·Dando leges
meas in cordibus eorum·et in mentem
17 eorum superscribam eam·et peccatorum eorum
et iniquitatum jam non recordabor
18 amplius·Ubi autem horum remissio·jam
19 non oblatio pro peccato ·> Habentes itaque
frs fiduciam in introitu scorum in san
20 guine xpi·quam initiavit nobis
veniam novam et viventem·Per velamen
21 ide carnem suam·et sacerdotem mag
22 num super domum di·Accedamus cum
vero corde in plenitudine fidei·
Aspersi corde a conscientia mala
23 et abluti corpus aqua munda·tene
amus spei nostrae confessionem indecli
nabilem·Fidelis enim est qui repromisit·
24 et consideremus invicem · In provocatione
25 caritatis·et bonorum operum non dese
rentes collectionem nostram sicut est con
suetudinem quibusdam sed consolantes
et tanto magis quanto videritis ad
26 propinquantem diem · Voluntariae
enim peccantibus nobis · P' acceptam
noticiam veritatis · Jam non relinqui
27 tur pro peccatis hostia · Terribilis

uedam expectatio judicii et
uulatio · quae consumptu
lversarios · Irritam quis fa
em moysi sine ulla miserati
duobus vel tribus testibus moritur ·
magis putatis deteriora mereri
· qui filium dī concalcaverit
inem testamenti pollutum duxe
10 scīficatus est · et spūi gra
tumeliam fecerit · Scimus
i dixit · mihi vindictā et ego
et iterum · Quia judabit
ulum suum · Horrendum est
in man' dī viventis ·
oramini autem pristinos dies · In
inluminati · magnum certamen
stis passionum · et in altero
obprobriis et tribulationibus
lum facti · In altero autem socii
nversantium effecti · Nam
is compassi estis · et rapinam
n vestrorum cum gaudio suscepis
gnoscentes vos habere melio
manentem substantiam · Nolite
mmittere confidentiam vestram ·
agnam habet remuneratio
'atientia enim vobis necessaria
oluntatem dī facientes repor

ver.
37 tetis promissionem · Adhuc enim
modicum quantulum cumque
qui venturus est veniet et non
38 tardabit · justus autem ms̄ ex
fide vivit · Quod si subtrax
erit se non placebit anime meæ ·
39 Nos autem non sumus subtractionis
in perditionem · sed fidei in ad
quisitionem animae ·
XI. 1 Est autem fides sperandarum sub
stantia rerum · argumentum non
2 apparentū · In hac enim testi
monium consecuti sunt seniores ·
3 Fide intellegimus apta esse sac̄la
verbo dī · ut ex invisibilibus
visibilia fierent ·
4 Fide plurimam hostiam abel
quam cain obtulit dō · per quam
téstimonium consecutus est esse
justus · testimonium perhibenti
muneribus ejus dō · et per illam de
functus adhuc loquitur ·
5 Fide énoch translatus est nevide
ret mortem · et non invenie
batur quia transtulit illum dn̄s
Ante translationem enim testimo
nium habuit placuisse dō ·
6 sine fide autem inpossibile est

ver.

placere dō · Credere enim opor
tet accedentem ad dm̄ · quia est ·
et inquirentibus se remunerator ·
7 fit · Fide noæ responso accep
to · de his quae adhuc non vide
bantur metuens aptavit archam in
salutem dom' suae · per quam dam
navit mundum · et justitiae
quae fidē est heres est constitutus ·
8 Fide qui vocatur abraham · Oboedivit
in locum exire · quem accepturus
erat in hereditatem · et exiit
9 nesciens quo iret · Fide mora
tus est in terra promissionis tamquam
in aliena · In casulis habitando
cum isaac et jacob · coheredibus repro
10 missionis ejusdem · Expectabat
enim fundamenta habentem civitatem
cujus artifex et conditor ds̄ ·
11 Fide etipsa sarra sterilis virtu
tem in conceptione seminis acce
pit · etiam pret̄ tempus aetatis ·
q̄m fidelem credidit esse qui promi
12 serat · propter q̄d et ab uno orti
sunt ei · et hoc emortuo tam
quam sidera celi in multitudinem
ut sicut arena quae est adoram
13 maris innumerabilis · Juxta

ver.

fidem defuncti sunt omnes isti · Non acce
tis repromissionibus · sed alonge eas aspi
cientes · etsalutantes · et confitentes ·
quia peregrini ethospites sunt super terram ·
14 Qui enim haec dicunt · significant se pa
15 triam inquirere · et siquidem illius me
minissent de qua exierunt · habe
16 bant utique tempus revertendi · Nunc
autem meliorem appetunt id est cęlestem ·
Ideo non confunditur ds̄ vocari ds̄ eorum ·
paravit enim illis civitatem ·
17 Fide obtulit abraham isahac cum tempta
retur · et unigenitum offerebat · qui sus
18 ceperat repromissiones ad quem dictum est ·
quia in isaac vocabitur tibi semen ·
19 Arbritrans quia et a mortuis suscitare
potens est ds̄ · Unde eum etin parabola
20 accepit · Fide et de futuris benedixit
21 isaac · jacob · et esau · Fidei jacob mo
riens singulos filiorum joseph benedixit ·
et adoravit super fastigium virgę ejus ·
22 Fide joseph moriens de profectione filio
rum isrl̄ memoratus est · et de ossibus
23 suis mandavit · Fide moyses natus
occultatus est mensibus tribus a parentibus
suis · eo q̄d vidissent eligantem infantem ·
24 et non timuer̄ regis edictum · Fide moy
ses grandis factus · negavit se esse filium

raonis·magis eligens affligi
pulo di·quam temporalis pec
ere ioiunditatem · Majores
estimans thesauro aegiptio
properium xpi · Aspiciebat enim
nerationem · Fide reliquit
n·non veritus animositatem regis·
lem enim tamquam videns susti

lebravit pascha·et sanguinis
m·nequi vastabat primitiva
eos·
nsierunt mare rubrum tamquam
am terram·qd experti aegiptii
sunt·
ri hiericho ruerunt circuitu
septem·
ab meritrix·non periit·cum
is·excipiens exploratores
e·Et quid adhuc dicam·
enim tempus me enarrantem
n·barach·samson·Ieptae·
t samuhel·et prophetis·
fidem vicerunt regna·opera
justitiam·adepti sunt repromissi
pturaverunt ora leonum·
runt impetum ignis · Effugerunt
adii·convaluerunt deinfir

ver.
mitate·fortes facti sunt in bello·
35 Castra verterunt exterorum Acce
perunt mulieres deresurrectione
mortuos suos · Alii autem distenti
sunt non suscipientes redemptio
nem utmeliorem invenirent re
36 surrectionem · Alii vero ludibria
et verbera experti·insuper et
vincula et carceres·
37 Lapidati sunt·secti sunt·temptati sunt·
inoccisione gladii mortui sunt·
Circuierunt in melotis in pelibus
caprinis · Egentes·angusti
38 ati·Afflicti·quibus dignus
non erat mundus · In solitu
dinibus errantes·in montibus et
in speluncis·et in cavernis
39 terrae · Et hi omnes testimonio
fidei probati inventi sunt·non acce
40 perunt repromissionem do pro nobis
aliquid melius providente·ut ne
sine nobis c summarentur·
XII. 1 Ideoque et nos tantam habentes in po
sitam nubem testium·deponentes
omne pondus·et circum stans
nos peccatum per pacientiam curra
2 mus propositum nobis certamen · Aspi
cientes in auctorem fidei·et con

M M

ver.
summatorem ihm · qui pro posito
sibi gaudio sustinuit crucem ·
Confessione contempta · atque
in dextera sedis di sedet ·
3 Recogitate enim eum · qui talem
sustinuit a peccatoribus adversus
semetipsum contradictionem
ut ne fati gemini animis
4 vestris deficientes · Nondum
usque ad sanginem restitistis ad
versus peccatum repugnantes ·
5 et obliti estis consolationis quae
vobis tamquam filiis loquitur
dicens · Fili mi noli neglege
re disciplinam dni · Neque fatige
ris dum ab eo argueris ·
6 Quem enim diligit dns castigat ·
flagellat omnem filium quem reci
7 pit · In disciplina perseverate ·
tamquam filiis vobis offert ds ·
Quis enim filius quem non corpit
8 pater ? qd si extra disciplinam
estis · cujus participes facti sunt
omnes · Ergo adulterini · et non
9 filii estis · Deinde · patres qui
dem carnis nostrae habuimus erudi
tores et reverebamur · Non mul
to magis obtemparabimus patri

ver.
10 spuum et vivemus · Et illi quidem
in tempore paucorum dierum secundum
voluntatem suam erudiebant nos ·
Hic autem ad id qd utile est · in recipien
11 do scificationem ejus · Omnis autem disci
plina in presenti quidem videtur ·
non esse gaudii sed meroris · Poste autem
pacatissimum exercitatis per eam reddit
12 justitiae · Propter qd remissas
manus · et dissoluta genua erigite
13 et gressus rectos facite pedibus vestris
ut non claudicans quis erret · magis
14 autem sanetur · Pacem sequimini
cum omnibus et scimonia sine
qua nemo videbit dnm ·
15 Contemplantes nequis desit gratie
di · Neque radix amaridinis sursum
germinans impediat · et per illam
16 inquinentur multi · Nequis fornica
tor aut profanus ut esau · qui propter unam
escam vendidit primitiva sua ·
17 Scitote enim qm et p'ea cupiens here
ditare benedictionem reprobatus est ·
Non enim invenit paenitentiae locum ·
quamquam cum lacrimis inquisisset
18 eam · Non enim accessistis adtracta
bilem · et accessibilem ignem etturbinem
19 et caliginem · et procellam · et tubae sonum ·

em verborum·quam qui audierunt
verunt se ne eis fieret verbum non H
ant qd dicebatur · Et si bestia
it montem lapidabitur · Et ita ter
erat qd videbatur · Moyses dixit·
itus sum·ettremibundus·sed acces
d syon montem·et civitatem di ·Vi
hierlm cælestem·et multorum milium
rum·frequentiam·et eclam primi
n qui conscripti sunt in celis·Et ju
omnium dm·et sps justorum perfec
·et testimenti novi·mediatorem dm
guinis sparsionem melius loquentem·
abel · Videte ne recusetis lo
m · Si enim illi non effugerunt
ntes eum·qui super terram
atur·multo magis nos·qui de celis
tem nobis avertimur·Cujus vox movit
tunc·modo autem·re· promittit dicens·
semel ego movebo·non solum terram·
celum·Quod autem adhuc semel dicit·
t mobilium translationem tamquam
m·utmaneant ea quae sunt in mobi
que regnum in mobile suscipientes
us gram per quam serviamus placentes
n metu et reverentia · Etenim
ter ignis consumens est · Caritas
tis maneat in vobis·

ver.
2 et hospitalē nolite oblivisci·
per hanc enim placuerunt quidam ange
3 lis hospicio receptis · Memento
te vinctorum tamquam simul
vincti·etlaborantium tamquam
etipsi in corpore morantes·
4 Honorabile conibium·etthorus
inmaculatû · Fornicatores
autem et adulteros judicabit ds·
5 Sint mores sine avaritia·
contenti psentibus ipse enim dixit·
Non te deseram·neque derelinquam·
6 Ita ut confidenter dicamus·dns
mihi adjutor est·non timebo quid
7 faciat homo mihi · Mementote
ppositorum vestrorum qui vobis
locuti s verbum di · Quorum
intuentes exitum conversatio
8 nis imitamini fidem · Ihs xps
heri et hodie ipse et in scla·
9 Doctrinis variis et peregrinis
nolite obduci · Optimum est enim
gra stabiliri cor · Non enim
escis quae non profuerunt ambulanti
10 bus in eis · Habemus altare de
quo hedere·non habent po
testatem·qui tabernaculo de
11 serviunt·quorum animalium

ver.
infertur sanguis pro peccato in sca·
per pontificem horum corpora·
12 cremantur·extra castra · Propter qd
et ihs·ut scificearct per suum sangui
nem populum·extra portam pas
13 sus est·Exeamus igitur ad eum ex
tra castra·inproperium ejus portantes·
14 Non enim habemus hic manentem civi
15 tatem·sed futurum inquirimus;· Perip
sum ergo offeramus hostiam laudis
semper do·idest fructum labiorum
16 confitentium nomini ejus · Beneficiæ
autem et communionis·nolite obli
cisci·talibus enim hostiis promeretur
17 ds · Obedite ppositis vestris·et
subjacete eis · Ipsi enim vigiliant
quasi rationem pro animabus vestris
*reddituri · Utcum gaudio hoc fa
ciant et non gementes · Hoc H
18 expedit vobis·orate pro nobis·
Confidimus enim quia bonam consci
entiam habemus in omnibus bene
19 volentes conversari · Amplius
autem depcor vos hoc facere · utqd
20 celerius restiatur vobis · Ds autem pacis
qui eduxit de mortuis pastorem
magnum ovium in sanguine in
testamenti aeterni·dnm nrm ihm

ver.
21 xpm aptet vos in omni bono·ut facia
tis voluntem ejû · faciens in vobis qd
placeat coram se·per ihm xpm·
cui est gla in saecla seculorum Amen·
22 Rogo autem vos frs·ut sufferatis verbum
solacii·et enim perpaucis scripsi vobis·
23 cognoscite fratrem nostrum timotheum·
dimissum cum quo et si celerius
videbo vos·
24 Salutate omnes ppositos vestros et omnes
scos
25 Sulutent vos deitalia frs gratia
cum omnibus vobis AMEN·

Post illam generalem baptismi
gram·et illud pretiosissimum marty
rii donum·quod sanguinis ablutio
ne conquiritur·multi sunt peniten
tiae fructus·per quos ad expiationem
criminum pervenitur; Non enim
tantum simplici illo penitentiae nomi
ne·salus aeterna repromittitur·de
qua beatus apls petrus; Penitemi
ni igitur et convertimini·ut deleantur ·inquit
vestra peccata; Et iohannes baptista·

lns; Pęnitentiam agite appro
enim regnum caelorum·sed etiam
tis affectum·peccatorum mo
ur; Caritas enim·operit
nem peccatorum; Similiter
elemosinarum fructum vulneribus
edela pstatur; Quia sicut aq^a
ignem·sic elemosina extin
tum; Ita et per lacrimarum
m·conquiritur ablutio delicto
vabo enim per singulas noctes
eum·lacrimis meis stratum
abo; Denique subjungit·osten
aniter eas fuisse profusas;
a me oms qui operamini ini
qm exaudivit dns vocem
; Nec non p criminum con
eorum abolitio conceditur;
·pronuntiabo adversus me in
meam dno·et tu remisisti impi
dis mei; Et iterum; Narra
tes tuas primus·ut
; Per afflictionem quoque
corporis·admissorum scelerum
imiliter obtinetur; Nam
t humilitatem meam et labo
·et dimitte omnia peccata
cipueque per emendationem

morum·auferte inquit malum
cogitationum vestrarum ab oculis
meis; Quiescite agere perverse·
discite bene facere; Quaerite
judicium·subvenite oppresso·
judicate pupillo·defendite vi
duam·et venite et arguite me
dicit dns; Etsi fuerint peccata
vestra ut coccinum·velut nix de
albabuntur; Si fuerint rubra quasi
vermiculus·velut lana erunt;
Interdum etiam intercessione scorum
impetratur venia delictorum;
Qui enim scit frem suum peccare
peccatum non ad mortem·petit et
dabit ei vitam ds peccanti non ad
mortem; Et iterum; Infirmatur
quis ex vobis·inducat pbros eclse
et orent super eum unguentes eum
oleo in nomine dni·et oratio fidei
salvabit infirmum·et alleva
bit eum dns; Et si in peccatis sit·
dimittentur ei; Nonnunquam
miae ac fidei merito labes exco
quitur vitiorum·secundum illud;
Permiam et fidem·purgantur
peccata; Per conversionem plerumque
ac salutem eorum·qui nris moni

tis ac praedicatione salvantur;
Qm qui converti fecerit peccatorem
ab errore viae suae salvat animam
ejus a morte·et cooperit multitudi
nem peccatorum; Perindulgentiam
nihilominus ac remissionem nostram
ad indulgentiam nostrorum facinorum
pervenitur; Si enim dimiseritis
hominibus peccata eorum·dimittet
et vobis pater vester caelestis delicta
vestra; Videtis ergo quantos miae
aditus patefecerit clementia sal
vatoris·utnemo salutem cupiens
desperatione frangatur·cum vide
at se tantis ad vitam remediis in
vitari; Si enim pro infirmitate car
nis afflictione jejuniorum·abolêre
te peccata non posse causaris·
nec potes dicere·genua mea in
firmata sunt a jejunio et caro mea
immutata est propter oleum·quia
cinerem tanquam panem mandu
cabam et potum meum cum fletu
miscebam·elemosynarū ea re
dime largitate · Indigenti si non
habes quod impertias·licet nullum
ab hoc opere necessitas inopiae·
ac paupertatis excludat·quan
doquidem et illius viduae duo tantum
æra·ingentibus divitum muneribus p fe
rantur·et pro calice aquae frigidae mer
cedem se redditurum dns repromittat·
certe absque illis morum poteris emen
datione purgari; Quod ·:ˢᵗ perfectionem
virtutum extinctione vitiorum om
nium non potes adipisci·sollicitudi
nem piam·erga utilitatem alienae sa
lutis impende; Si autem idoneum te
huic ministerio non esse conquíreris·
operire peccata poteris caritatis affe
ctu; In hoc quoque site fragilem fecerit
quaelibet mentis ignavia oratione
saltim atque intercessione scorum·remedia
vulneribus tuis humilitatis affectu
summissus implora; Postremo
quis est qui non possit suppliciter di
cere·peccatum meum cognitum tibi feci·
et injustitiam meam non operui·ut
per hanc confessionem·etiam illud
confidenter subjungere merea
tur·et tu remisisti impietatem cor
dis mei; Quod si verecundia re
trahente·revelare ea coram hominibus
erubescis·illi quem latere non possunt
confiteri ea jugi supplicatione n
desinas ac dicere; Iniquitatem meam

) et peccatum meum con
semper; Tibi soli peccavi et
m feci; Qui et absque ul
diae publicatione curare·
roperio peccata donare con
t istud quoque tam prom
nque subsidium · Aliud quoque
us·largita nobis est divina
samque remedii opem nro
bitrio·ut indulgentiam
celerum pro nostro p sumamus af
es ei; Dimitte nobis debi
cut et nos dimittimus debitoribus
uisquis igitur ad indulgen
n criminum desiderat
stis semetipsum aptare
rumentis·nec obdurati
icacia·a remedio salutari·
tae pietatis avertat;
i haec omnia fecerimus·n erunt
expiationem scelerum nostrorum·
itas dni clementiaque deleverit;
eligiosi conatus obsequia
nte a nobis oblata per
iguos parvosque conatus·
beralitate prosequitur dicens;
go sum·qui deleo iniquitates
er me·et peccatorum tuorum jam

non recordabor; Ad hunc ergo
quem pdiximus statum quisque con
scenderit·satisfactionis gram·coti
dianis jejuniis et mortificatione
cordis et corporis assequitur;
Quia sicut scriptum est·sine sanguinis
effusione non fit remissio; Nec
immerito; Caro enim et sanguis·
regnum di possidere non possunt;
Et ideo quisquis ab hujus sanguinis
effusione·gladium sps qd est verbum
di voluerit inhibere·absque dubio
illa hieremiae prophetae maledicti
one plectetur; Nam maledictus
inquit qui prohibet gladium suum
a sanguine · hic nanque est gladius·
qui illum noxium sanguinem
quo animatur materia peccatorum
salubriter fundens·quicquid
reppererit in membris nris carna
le·terrenumve·concretum·rese
cat et abscidit·ac mortificatos vi
tiis vivere do et spiritalibus facit
vigêre virtutibus · Etita jam
n recordatione veteris admissi
sed spe futurorum flere incipiet
gaudiorum · Nec tam depteritis
malis quam de futuris cogitas bonis·

non ex peccatorum maerore la
crimas·sed ex aeternae illius lae
titiae alacritate profundit·atque
obliviscens ea quae posteriora sunt·
id est carnalia vitia adea quae
in ante sunt extendetur·hoc est spirita
lia dona atque virtutes·

Ad calcem paginæ. Hic liber est monasterii Augié Majoris qui per dnm de Wild am Abbatem accomodatus fuit magistro Georgio Schoenlin de Schorndorff decretorum do canonico in Sindelfingen tempore basiliensis.

Primâ, ut videtur manu: Tu domine universorum qui nullam habes indigent

In libri operculo, ad initium, scripta sunt (post lineam erasam, antiquâ manu scrip Tempûs adhûc Veniet post.......)

Georgii Michaelis Wepferi Schaphusiani.

(*Aliâ manu:*) Jam Ludovici Christiani Miegii.

Emptus hic codex Richardo Bentleio A.D.ni MDCCXVIII. [*Bentleii manu.*]

Aliâ manu: Codex Augiensis (supposed to have been written in the ninth cent noted F in the second part of Wetstein's N. T. Vid. Marsh's Michaelis. Chap. VIII. Sect.

Aliâ manu: Wetstein's Prolegom. Vol. I. p. 153. Vol. II. p. 6. Monk's Life of Ben II. p. 121. Hunc codicem parvi æstimavit Wetstenius; plurimi Bentleius. vid. ejus not. ad init. Nov. Testamenti Oxon. 1675. 8vo (B. 17. 8 inscripti) quocum codicem con J. W[ordsworth]. 1839.

Item eâdem manu: This MS. is not written in Anglo-Saxon characters, as has described; but in the renovated minuscule of the Caroline period (Sæc IX vel X). J. O.

In operculo, ad finem voluminis, leguntur: Si Deus nobiscum quis contra nos.

Item Bentleii manu, Monasterium Augiae; in Belgis, ubi institutus est Goddeschal *et alia quædam, nullius frugis, variis manibus.*

ANNOTATIONES EDITORIS:

In quibus lectiones a secundâ et ab aliâ adhuc recentiore manu profectæ referuntur; atque de iis explicatur locis, quorum ratio dubia sit.

N.B.—Correctiones omnes interlineares, de quibus hic siletur, *secundæ* manûs esse mihi quidem videntur. Porro *p.m.* indicat lectionem primâ manu; *s.m.* secundâ manu; *r.m.* multo recentiore manu; *ras.* rasuram aliquam denotat; *eras.* verbum aut literam cui subjicitur eradi.

FOL.	PAG.	LIN.	
7	1	19	*ras.* inter δι et και.
„	2	3	ξ forsan rescript. super *ras.*
„	„	13	*ras.* post *et.*
„	„	19	*ras.* inter *ui* et *d.*
8	1	4	υ in δικαιυντα in ʊ mutatur, *s.m.*
„	„	12	*ras.* inter λυ et φθ.
„	„	17	ρ super π secund. *r.m.*
„	„	23	ε in αλλεν rescript. super *ras.*
„	2	8	*ras.* ad finem post σ.
„	„	15	*ex lege* ad finem *eras.*
9	1	24	γ ad finem mutatum?
„	2	2	σ *eras.* in μελλεισ.
„	„	10	δ *p.m.* in margine.
10	2	12	τιποσ *p.m.*?
11	1	26	[*Q*]*uid.* *Q* recentissimâ manu.
„	2	23	αιωται rescript.: sic l. 24 *autem.*
12	1	3	Annon potius legendum εφαπαζ?
„	2	11	*init.* α *s.m.*
„	„	19	*ras.* inter τη et δι.
„	„	20	δουλθιητε. ι super *ras.*[1]
13	1	7	*init.* η *s.m.*, at *A* in [*A*]*n* recentissimâ.
„	„	24	*init.* ω *s.m.*, at *I* in [*I*]*taque* recentissimâ.
			φ in αδελφοι *rescriptum*?
13	2	7	οτω · ο *eras.*
14	1	7	ω in marg. *p.m.* l. 16 σ in τησ *s.m.*?
„	2	12	ε ante Є rubro, *p.m.*
„	„	25	litera *eras.* ante *d̄n̄i.*
15	1	14	φ *eras.* in πεμφψασ.
„	„	17	ε in κατεκ. super α scriptum.
„	2	8	ρ in χ̄ρ̄υ, etiam l. 10 αυτου το μεν σωμα super *ras.*?
„	„	16	litera *eras.* ante *vivificavit.*
„	„	20	*init.* α *s.m.*
16	1	18	ιοτη · ι *eras.*
„	„	19	κατισεισ · α *eras.*
„	2	13	*init.* Ω *r.m.*
17	1	10	T *s.m.* sic etiam T l. 24.
„	„	11	*pro p.m.* at *præ r.m.*
„	2	10	verbum *eras.* ante *vita.*
„	„	19	*V* in [*V*]*eritatem* recentissimâ m.
18	1	9	αιωνασ: pro ι *p.m.* habet υ.
„	2	20	*t eras.* ante *uostendam*: *t* supra, *s.m.*[2]
„	„	26	*d̄r* pro *d̄s*, vix dubium. Vide tamen Fol. 126, p. 1, l. 26, *-tur*, vel *-tus*, et Cod. Boerner. 1 Cor. ii. 9, 10, facsimile apud Matthaei.

[1] "δουλευητε *p.m.*, δουλοιητε *s.m.* Corrigendo ex Є non tam O quam Θ per incuriam effectum est." Tischendorf. Anecdota Sacra et Profana, p. 211, cui assentior.

[2] l. 20 ενδειξομαι Tischendorf. Vide autem ξ l. 19.

FOL.	PAG.	LIN.	
19	1	5	*eras.* post *potesta.*
„	„	10	O : Θ *p.m.*: ib. l. 24 c in καλεσω: O *p.m.*
„	2	13	ω in σαβαωθ *rescriptum.*
„	„	18	*Q* in [Q]*uid*, *r.m.* at T. *s.m.*
„	„	24	Quid hic sibi velit ÷ parum intelligo, nisi sit signum omissionis. In Latinâ scripturâ denotat *est*. Vid. Cod. Boerner. Matthaei, p. 109.
20	1	6	*F* in [*F*]*ratres* recentissimè scriptum, et α in αδελφοι *s.m.* ut videtur.
„	2	27	*Q* in [*Q*]*uomodo* recentissimè.
21	1	3	*ras.* post *predican.*
„	„	8, 9	post νων l. 8 omnia super rasuram scripta sunt.
„	„	12	*ras.* inter *dit* et *aud.*
„	„	20	*S* in [*S*]*ed* recentissimè scriptum.
„	2	4	Addit margo post *credentem*, *r.m.* *Et contra dicentem.*
„	„	9	π secundum *s.m.* super lacunam in membranâ.
„	„	20	Litera *eras.* post *illi.*
22	1	11	/· ad calcem paginæ refert, ubi linea, in Græco omissa, suppletur.
23	2	17	*a* super *consequent·* *p.m.*
„	„	20	[*O*] recentissimè scriptum: sic etiam
24	1	4	*O* in [*O*]*bsecro.*
„	„	24	*ras.* ante *autem.*
„	„	26	/·/· superposita transpositionem indicant.
„	2	25	ϵ minusculum in ευλογειταε *s.m.* Sic Rom. xvi. 24.

FOL.	PAG.	LIN.	
25	1	25	Π in marg. *s.m.* at [*O*] *r.n*
26	1	19	Και *p.m.* super *ras.*
„	„	28	*I* in [*I*]*nfirmum* *r.m.*, at marg. *s.m.*
„	2	6	Hodie ϛ proculdubio: for *p.m.*
28	1	3	*D* in [*D*]*ebemus* *r.m.*, at marg. *s.m.*, ο exterior *p.*
„	2	20	π in marg. et *C* *s.m.*
„	„	24	ο in νου et μη super *rasuran*
„	„	26	ο supra *p.m.*? i.q. μεροσ?
„	„	28	*ras.* post τȢ.
29	2	2	| et ◡ recentissimè.
„	„	6	*fructus*, ut videtur, *p.m.*
„	„	7	*N* in [*N*]*unc* recentissimè.
„	„	10	P super αχ (*p.m.*?) non int
„	„	14	ι mutat. in τοισ: υ *p.m.*
„	„	24	π in marg. *s.m.*
30	1	1	α supra εν non intelligo. Fors
„	„	6	λημματοσ · χ̄ν · ῑυ · rescriptun videtur.
„	„	10	σ in marg. *s.m.* at [*C*] *r.m.* υ et νισ *ras.*
„	„	20	α in marg. *s.m.*
„	2	19	θ videtur esse rescriptum, *s*
31	1	6	*ras.* post χ̄ϛ.
„	„	11	π in marg. *s.m.*
32 } 33 }			*miserè maculata.*
32	1	23	*ut vos* super *ras.* scriptum: si πλουτι.
„	2	21	*ae secund.* ferè evanidum.
33	1	5	ϵ evanidum inter λ et ν.
„	2	9	*deêst in greco*, in marg. *s.m*

[1] Fol. 28, p. 2, l. 19. Mirè Tischendorf. Anecd. Sacr. et Prof. p. 215, *justitia* pro *virtute*.

OL.	PAG.	LIN.	
33	2	17	*o* in *ipso* rescriptum.
„	„	28	*te eras.* post *infirmita.*
34	1	14	[*sent* refert ad *crucifixis* l. 16.
„	„	19	*in cor homi* super *ras.* corde *p.m.*?
35	1	28	Litera *eras.* ante *uniuscujusque.*
„	2	10	οικει super *ras.* scriptum.
„	„	19	α·*eras.* super γρ in γεγ·ρπται: in marg. *s.m.*
36	1	5	Rescript. Græcè super *ras.* Forsan etiam ll. 3 et 4. ον tantum legibile ad finem l. 5, post λοιπον.
„	2	8	*ras.* post *spe.*
„	„	15	*usque in hanc horam et* super *ras.*: sic et
„	„	21—23	Græcè, Διω_κομε usque ad παρα καλθ. Ad fin. l. 21 legitur ν.
37	1	5	ακαλυ (sequente υ ?) super *ras.* Sic l. 12 Græcè.
„	„	14—25	Latinè, super *ras.* script. ut videtur.
„	„	24	*O* in [*O*]*mnino* recentissimâ manu.
„	2	5	Pro *jam s.m.* videtur legere *Etiam*; immo et *p.m.* ex vestigiis.
	1	5	*ni eras.* post *commisceami*; l. 18 οτι, l. 19 θσιν rescript.
	2	3	υ *secundum* in αυτου super *ras.*?
	„	12	*ju eras.* post *in*; sic l. 21 *b eras.* ad fin. post *e.*
	2	13	*s.m.* Lego *uualtit* seu *uualtet.* Procul dubio voluit scriptor per *waltet* Germanicè interpretari ἐξουσιάζει.
	2	9	*ras.* inter νη et σθω. νη rescript.
	„	16	ηθη certè rescript. Vid. Cod. Boern.
	1	9	C initio lineæ *eras.*
	„	21	η in σχημα rescript. super *ras.*

FOL.	PAG.	LIN.	
42	1	20	*ras.* post *idolothi.*
„	2	18	εοροκα *p.m.* ο *secundum* deletum, et α superimpositum *s.m.*
44	1	15	*pravi p.m.*: *p* in *b* mutatum forsan *p.m.*
„	2	8	*ras.* post *spirita.*
45	1	13	*ras.* inter *stis* et *sust.*
„	„	22	*ras.* post *quem*; sic l. 24 *ras.* post *quō.*
„	2	11	usque ad l. 22 Latinè, super *ras.* scriptum.
46	1	13	Græcè, rescript.: Latinè *ras.* post *judæ.*
„	„	14	*ras.* post *eccle.*
„	2	2	σ *prim.* in σευχομενοσ, item l. 5 in πασα mut. in ο, *r.m.*
„	„	10	ι in Ει rescript. super *ras.*
„	„	22	*prop*, *p* secundum semiscriptum.
47	1	9	α *prim.* in ατιμια recentissimâ manu.
„	2	16	Forsan *frangitur.*
48	1	2	πινηται το·ροι super *ras.* ut videtur.
49	1	8	*ras.* inter ο et πθσ.
„	„	20	*ras.* inter δε et ην.
„	2	6	*abandantiorem*: *a* secundum semieras.
„	„	12	*re*, l. 19 *qui*, l. 26 *ōms eras.* initio linearum.
„	„	25	*nūq̄d ōms* super *ras.* arctatur.
50	1	10	*et si eras.* initio: sic etiam l. 15 *nihil*, l. 26 *irrita*, l. 28 *gaudet.*
„	„	17	Vacua Græcè. Quatuor lineæ sequentes super *ras.* Græcè.
„	2	11	*lo eras.* initio; sic l. 12 *bam ut*, l. 16 *te*, l. 28 *pro.*
„	„	13, 14, 15	Latinè rescript. super *ras.*
„	„	18	*ras.* post *et*: l. 19 *cognitus sum* super *ras.*

FOL.	PAG.	LIN.	
50	2	21	*ras.* post *Sectami;* l. 22 *ni caritatem* super *ras.*
„	2	20	η·αφυμων super *ras.* rescript.
53	1	1	*ras.* ante *ste.*
„	„	3	*tit eras.* in fine; sic l. 16 *enim vobis*, l. 19 *dum*, l. 22 ad fin. *sus.*
„	„	20	Latinè, rescript. super *ras.* Sic forsan ll. 23–28.
„	2	1	*ras.* post *Novissi;* sic ad fin. ll. 24, 25, Latinè.
„	„	5	ειμι et l. 11 ασα forsan rescript. super *ras.*
54	1	7	λπ‿ι, l. 10 εκ, l. 11 δη, forsan rescript. super *ras.*
„	2	15	*quam abeo in xpo ihu, eras.*
„	„	27	ι in εγιρονται rescript. ut videtur.[1]
55	1	23	η in δοξη rescript. ut videtur.
„	2	26, 27	φ in φθαρτον et αφθαρσειαν super *ras.*
103	1	6	αμαρτιασ : σ *eras.*
„	2	5	πε in προπεμψηται fortasse mutatum.
104	1	9	ι in τοι *s.m.*, super *rasuram.*
„	„	10	κονιωντι *p.m.:* confer cap. xv. 58; 2 Cor. ii. 17.
„	2	2	ιυ: ι super *ras.* mutatum.
„	„	22	Post ησ·*ras.*
105	1	23	λπ in ηλπικαμεν super *ras.*?
„	2	11	*ras.* post η ad fin.?
„	„	14	εν τη ημερα κ.τ.λ. usque ad l. 23 βουλομε super *rasur.* rescriptum videtur. Non ita Latinè.
106	1	23	*Rasura* inter *i* et *cia.*
„	2	2	εδι super *ras.*

FOL.	PAG.	LIN.	
107	1	2	– *eras.* super θῡ.
„	„	9	*ras.* inter αμ·et βεῡ.
„	„	18	κ in ικανοσ super *ras.:* sic e αλλεξ, et l. 22 λαλ in λαλ
„	2	9	εποι in Πεποιθεσιν super scriptum.
„	„	19	*mortis*, *mo* mutatum *p.m.*
108	1	3	*ras.* post *cla*, sic et l. 19, p *velatum.*
„	„	16, 17	ημε ρασ τοαν super *ras.* re
„	2	7	τα·τησ rescript. super *ras.*,
„	„	25	ο·ειπων. l. 26, καρ *eras.* in fin.
109	1	2	χομεν·δε·Τον·θησαυρὸν·τ rescript. super *ras.* *p.m.*
„	2	17	κο in οικοδομην forsan re super *ras.:* sic et
„	„	19	αιωνι ut videtur.
„	„	20	ι prim. in *ingemiscimus*, script. super *ras.:* sic e
„	„	27	*o* in *exspoliari.*
110	1	7	μουμ super *ras.* scriptum:
„	„	13	μουμ, et l. 15 ι in ευαρεστο
„	„	9	*per speciem* forsan super *ra*
„	„	24	αι in ταισ rescript. videtu *ras.:* – super ταισ *eras.*
„	2	3	*ras.* post *sobrii.*
„	„	22	ν·εν rescript. super *ras.*?
56	1	1	Græcè rescript. videtur sup
„	„	5	Linea perpendicularis nov scripta. ω rescriptum vi Sic forte
„	„	9, 10	σωτηριασ·εβοη et δου.
„	„	15	Post ωσ *ras.*
„	„	17	Forsan εν non ειν.

[1] Fol. 55, pag. 1, l. 10. Tischendorf. (Anecd. Sacr. et Prof. p. 212), αλλα αλλη *p.m.* legendum censet persuasum est nihil nisi · (jam semi-erasum) inter αλλ‿ et αλλη intercedere.

.	PAG.	LIN.	
6	2		Membranæ scabrities speciem præbet correctionum in locis quibusdam. Forsan *ημων* l. 9: *η·τισ* l. 19: *μητα·ιδωλων* l. 23 mutantur.
„	„	16	*cum eras.* ad finem lineæ.
„	„	22	*infidele,* l. 25 *ds̄*, rescript. super *ras.*
„	„	23	*c eras.* ante *cum.*
„	„	25	*ν* prius in *νεν. eras.*
57	1	5	*θιγατερασ p.m.*
„	„	21	*ras.* post *omni.* Scabrities multa in hâc quoque paginâ.
58	2		Sic etiam in hâc paginâ: at l. 3 *μ* in *δυναμιν*: l. 11 *ε* in *θεληματοσ*: et l. 28 *φ* in *φερει* rescripta videntur.
9	1	9	*ras.* inter *ει* et *τισ* certè. Multa præterea scabrities.
„	„	21	*exortationem s.m.* at *exhrt. p.m.*
„	2	15	*ν? eras.* post *πεποιθησι.*
,	„	26	*υ eras.* ante *ημιν*, et *i* inter *d* et *anti.*
0	1	12	*s eras.* ante *substantia.*
,	2	14	*Οτι·η·διακο* forsan arctatum super *ras.*
1	1	2	*ανετ διητητο·p.m. ανεγ s.m.* Hic iterum scabrities, at
„	„	14	*νομ*, l. 16 *ω* in *ημων*, l. 25 *δι* forsan mutata.
„	„	15	*N* in [*N*]*am r.m.*: l. 23 *In obsequium* rescript.?
2	1	1—9	Latinè, rescriptæ videntur super *ras.*
,	2	„	Scabrities multa, nec quicquam videtur rescriptum.
'	„	5	*p eras.* in fine; sic et l. 26 *tres eras.*
3	1	5	*λ* in *κλιμασιν* forsan rescriptum: sic *quod* l. 7: ll. 16, 17 Lat.?

FOL.	PAG.	LIN.	
63	2	3	*s, eras.* ante *suf.*
„	„	22	*u* initio lineæ forsan *s.m.* additum.
„	„	24	*εναναγισα p.m.*
64	1	2	Post *ερη ras.* *η* legibile est.
„	„	27	*ι* in *δει mutatum,* ut videtur: *υ p.m.*
„	2	3	*ras.* inter *προ* et *αιτων.*
„	„	6, 7	Rescript. super *ras.* *οθσ̄ οιδεν αρπαγεντα.* Sic etiam Græcè, usque ad *σωματοσ*, l. 11.
„	„	17	*εμαυτοσ, σ eras.* et dubium.
„	„	21	*αι* rescript. Sic forsan *περβο* l. 24.
65	1	10	*εν* initio additum *p.m.* Latinè rescript. omnia hic *p.m.* Linea post l. 9 omissa in calce paginæ scribitur.
66	1	2	*θυμου p.m.*, at mutatum in *θυμοι.*
„	„	13	*bre p.m., ore s.m.?*
67	1	7	*ras.* inter *η* et *αγαπη.*
„	2	5	*σ* in *εισ* insertum, forsan *p.m.*: *cu eras.* post *sae.*
„	„	9	*χριστου* super *χαριτι* recentissimâ manu.
„	„	22	*ι* in *ανθρωποισ*, et
„	„	23	*σ* in *ηρεσκον* videntur rescripta super *ras.*
68	1	22	Pro *τουσ p.m.* *τοισ.*
„	„	24	*ras.* ante *sum:* plurima scabrities hoc in folio.
„	2	3	*υμην· p.m.*: in *υμιν* mutatum.
69	1	1	*a? eras.* ante *tem.*
„	„	2	*xpo ihu* et forsan alia rescript. super *ras.*
„	„	12	*ras.* post *vidis.*
„	„	16	*ε eras.* ante *εθνην.*
„	2	10	Latinè: super *ras.* rescript. arctâ manu.

FOL.	PAG.	LIN.	
69	2	22	ημσισ: σι super *ras.* mutatum?
70	2	5	ετα in Γινωσ‿κεται rescript. videtur: certe nota erasa est in margine. Cætera in hâc paginâ membranæ debentur, præter *ras.* post ερ l. 14, et forsan α in τα l. 9 rescript.
71	1	12	π π rescript.: forsan ρρ *p.m.* solitâ literarum confusione. In l. 8 φοι, l. 14 σιν, et si qua alia, ex scabritie oriuntur.
,,	,,	13	*ducit, p.m.* ut videtur.
,,	2	3	εστιν *s.m.*, at εετιν *p.m.*
,,	,,	21	*su? eras.* inter *di* et *estis.*
72	2	11	δθ·ομαι *p.m.* θ mutatum in ε, *s.m.*
73	1	4	ιδν super *ras.* scriptum.
,,	,,	12	εεχεν *p.m.* εσχεν *s.m.*
,,	,,	13	*ras.* post *de.*
,,	2	8	*ras.* post *scrip.*
74	1	7	εκτοΥ *s.m.*, εκτοι *p.m.*
,,	,,	8	*tum eras.* post *fermen.*
,,	,,	17	τιργηται, *p.m.*, ut videtur.
,,	2	5	γελεσηται *p.m.* τελ. *s.m.*
,,	,,	13	θ super *ras.* rescript.
,,	,,	21	*que eras.* post *conse.*
75	1	3	*a* in *balemus* semi-formatum.
76	1	2	*lestus eras.* post *mo.*
,,	,,	12—22	Latinè rescript. super *ras.*
,,	2	9	απολιτροσιν, ut videtur, *p.m.* } At υ malè format scriptor: vid. εγγυσ, Eph. II. 13.
77	1	9	αυτου *s.m.*, at αιτου *p.m.*?
,,	2	5, 6	ab εξου usque ad κυριο rescript. super *ras.*
,,	,,	24	*fillis* pene scriptum, *p.m.*
78	1	5	Forsan ηγαπισεν *p.m.*

FOL.	PAG.	LIN.	
78	1	15	εφημασ: η super *ras.* ι videtur.
,,	2	10	αι in αιματι forsan mutatı post *enim.*
,,	,,	20	εν·ενι· super *ras.* rescript. san Oτι l. 25.
,,	,,	28	Spatium inane ut nova in fol. 79 incipiat.
79	1	8	υ *eras.* inter μο et λογ.
,,	,,	15	τασ ut videtur, at ασ part
,,	2	11	του forsan rescript. super
80	2	10	κλησεωσ mutatum. Primo An male scriptum ε, ut επιθυμιασ, Eph. IV. 22.
,,	,,	19	δ, et forsan διδασ l. 28 su rescript.
81	1	23	ειτε in ποιειτε videtur super *ras.*, sic forsan *st*
,,	2	28	*i* in *di abo* mutatum: ab usque ad l. 26 Latinè su rescript.
82	1	4	δθναι: εθ mutatum videtur: At scabrities multa in p
,,	2	6	ι minusculum et > in οτι :
,,	,,	9	*i* super *xpo r.m.*
,,	,,	16	K in Kω rescriptum super
,,	,,	20	τηεισтιν *p.m.*, at τι·εστιν
,,	,,	25	υ in αυτων rescript. super ι
83	1	4	σ in χρσ mutat?
,,	,,	5	*bulet* super *ras.*
,,	,,	13	ι in εαυτοισ ex correction
,,	,,	18	παντωτε *p.m.* παντοτε *s.n* Post *nomi* sequitur *ne e*
,,	2	2	*d eras.* ante *diligite.*
,,	,,	14	*i* supra, *p.m.*
,,	,,	24	*o* in ανοσ, et

FOL.	PAG.	LIN.	
83	2	26	τη rescript. super *ras.*
84	1	12	μαχρωχρονειοσ *p.m.*, at ω mutatum in ο *s.m.*
„	2	5	οσ *forte* rescript.: sic l. 8 μου, l. 12 ναι.
	„	22	*ras.* inter τη·et ἡμερα.
	„	26	και·ενδυσαμενοι rescript. super *ras.*
	1	10	Latinè, rescripta super *ras.*, sic forsan *obsecrationem* l. 8.
	„	26	ο minusculum insertum ante ΛΗ *s.m.*
	1	8	√ et /· Græcè et Latinè ordinem mutatum indicant.
	„	17	*a* supra *men* forsan *r.m.*
	1	1	*ras.* post *gaudium* l. 1, *terre* l. 13, et *creda* l. 19.
	„	8	*ras.* inter ινα et ειτε. Verba forsan rescripta.
	„	13	υ in πτυρ. ex correctore? Cf. υ in θ̄υ, infra l. 17.
8	1	4	ε in με ex correctore: sic *forsan* l. 7 ων et ε sequens, et l. 20 εδρα.
„	„	12	*querela:* pro *r* *p.m.* habuit *l.*
„	„	15	In διεστ. pro σ *primo* fortasse fuit γ.
„	„	„	φ *eras.* ante φαι.
„	„	22	Pro ει· *p.m.* legitur εισ.
„	„	28	*s.* in marg. *p.m.*: sic et ε Græcè.
,	2	2	Suprascriptum: *cum cognovero* videtur esse ex correctore; *-overit* primo: *-tis* etiam Latinè ex correctione videtur.
	„	4	η in γνησιωσ, et l. 8 ε in δοκειμην mutata.
	„	19	Latinè, rescripta super *ras.* Hæc etiam correcta videntur: *fro* l. 16, *tiam* l. 27, *ego* l. 28.

FOL.	PAG.	LIN.	
89	1	1	Latinè, plane rescript. super *ras.* præter *eo*. Sic l. 3 *um*. Multa in hâc paginâ scabrities, hæc autem ex correctione orta esse videntur: l. 10 η in ρωση; l. 15 ται·τουσ·κ (procul dubio).; l. 18 η in τομη; forsan etiam l. 20 χ in χ̄ρω.
„	„	19	*ras.* post *servimus*, et l. 20 post *car, ne eras.*
„	2	15	σινην *p.m.* ut videtur. Confer autem Fol. 76, p. 2, l. 9 not.
90	1	1	ι in κατιληφοτα certè rescript. super *ras.*: sic forsan l. 2, σω; l. 12 ει; l. 15 *it*.
„	„	26	*l* super *savatorem* recentissimâ manu.
„	2	6	χαρισ tentatum *r.m.*
„	„	10	α in αυτο, l. 21 η in μηδεν, l. 23 εη mutata videntur.
„	„	18	χ et *g* in *p.m.*, ut videtur.
„	„	21	Forsan *sollititi* primo, at *-citi p.m.*
91	1	10	ησ ϊρηνι rescript. super *ras.*? Cætera Græcè membranæ sunt, nisi fortè εστειν, l. 2.
„	„	18	*h*? *eras.* ante *abunda*, et l. 24 *ras.* post *communican.*
„	2	8	*sed requiro fruc* rescript. super *ras.*
„	„	19	χρ rescriptum esse videtur.
92	1	4	χ̄ρυ·ῑυ·, et l. 13, *audientes* super *ras.* rescript.
„	2	7	ων ex correctione? sic l. 17 α secund. in κατα, l. 26 η in τησεν.
„	„	20	*gratias* rescript. *p.m.* super *ras.*; l. 22 *ras.* post *partem.*

FOL.	PAG.	LIN.	
93	1	9	ν in αυτον; l. 14 η in αρχη; l. 22 ε secund. in ειπε forsan rescripta.
,,	,,	28	*er* in *per* rescript. super *ras.* videtur.
,,	2		Hæc forsan ex correctore: l. 1 ι in αγιουσ (ε *p.m.*?); l. 3 ει in ειον et ε in γε; l. 15 σα; et l. 17 *ego*. *Ras.* post *sacramen* l. 27.
,,	,,	7	γελου: ι coalescit cum ο, forsan *p.m.*
94	1	20	Fortasse legendum *agnicionem*.
,,	,,	27	*nu* rescript.?
,,	,,	28	*ras.* post *vo*.
,,	2	18	ι in κατοι videtur esse mutatum.
,,	,,	22	*s* super *pat.* ex *s.m.*? Sic l. 26 *cisione*.
,,	,,	28	*babtismo p.m.*, *bap. s.m.* Sic *cibo s.m.*, at *cipo p.m.* Fol. 95, p. 1, l. 19.
95	1	3	ν prim. in νεκρων; l. 5, ρα et ν in παραπτωμασιν; l. 22, τω in μελλοντων rescripta videntur.
,,	,,	18	*ras.* inter αυτω et Mη.
,,	,,	23	*ducat eras.* post *se*.
,,	2	4	— (i.e. *m.*) super *conjunctionem* semi-deletum. Rescripta videntur, l. 5 ρη; l. 12 Græcè; l. 14 ν in φθεοραν; l. 21 ην in μονην.
,,	,,	26	Forsan legendum μετα.
96	1		Mutantur l. 7 ε in πλεον; l. 10 Διο; l. 12 οισ (ουσ? *p.m.*); l. 13 οτε et εζητε (ξ pro ζ *p.m.*); l. 18 ων; l. 20 εσθαι. *Ras.* post τον l. 23.
,,	2	2	*Ras.* post ελευτε. l. 5 *ergo* rescript. Hæc videntur rescripta super

FOL.	PAG.	LIN.	
			ras. l. 8 η in χρη; l. 23 υμιν; l. 26 μ in μοισ; l. 27 εν.
97	1	11	γονευσιν: pro υ forsan ι *p.m.* tamen Fol. 76, p. 2, l. 9. (l. 27, *p.m.* legit δουλειτε.
,,	,,	25	*Ras.* post *heredi*.
,,	2	4	*Ras.* post *presta*.
,,	,,		Rescript. l. 8 ε in εν secund. san l. 22 τυχ, et l. 24 ε in
98	1	2	Π super *ras.*; sic θ l. 7; η in πληρ. l. 18? Sic Latinè *ve* *nym* l. 26: nisi forte sit ı membranæ scabrities.
,,	2	1	*cta fu* rescript.? *Ras.* ante ı
,,	,,	2	Rescript. τοι: sic l. 6 π in β et σ in χαρισ, l. 11.
,,	,,	8	*Ras.* post *Salu*. Sic forte l. 5 *dici*.
,,	,,	16	C T rubro *eras.* lineâ rubrâ
,,	,,	19	Ÿ, et l. 23 ν in χων rescript. ı *ras.*
99	1	4	*mem.* primò, at *nem.* tamen ɟ
,,	,,	7	μονον et ει super *ras.*, sic f l. 11 εισ.
,,	,,	24	*enim de* certè rescript. super
,,	2	1	Post *expecta*, *re eras.*: l. 25 *onis sicut* rescript.
,,	,,	11	Rescript. οιδαται. Sic l. 1 ην; l. 23 η; l. 25 θ in κο l. 27 υ in μαρτυσ et υ et ι ζητουντεσ.
,,	,,	24	ποτε: ι coalescit cum ο. Fol. 93, p. 2, l. 7.
100	1	1	Primò *abi baliis*: *i* in *abi* m in *a*, *p.m.*

FOL.	PAG.	LIN.	
100	1	14	*Ras.* post *operan.* Cætera membranæ sunt.
„	2		Hæc forsan rescript.: l. 4 υ in θ̄υ et θαι; l. 6 θωσ primum; l. 17 και·η; l. 24 η in οργη.
101	1	5	ε? *eras.* ante ημασ.
„	„	8	ε in χησεωσ; l. 9 ν in θεν; l. 11 *V* forsan rescript.
„	„	18	*ras.* ante χ̄ρ̄υ; sic et l. 23 ante εισ.
„	2	10	θην rescript.? Sic l. 18 θα; l. 20 ση; l. 26, *ras*?
„	„	25	*d* mutat. *p.m.* (i inceptum pro *d*).
102	1	8	π̄ρ̄σ; l. 9 ουσια; l. 21 γαρ super scabritiem scripta.
„	„	12	π et *d. p.m.* l. 18 *ras.* post *quæ.*
„	2		Mutata videntur l. 3 δ et φ in αδελφον; l. 6 υ in τυρ (ι *p.m.*?): sic
„	„	16	αν; l. 21 φ; l. 25 σχ. Forsan autem membranæ sunt.
„	„	13	π in marg. *r.m.*? at l. 27 μ et *n* in marg. *p.m.*
„	„	15	*s* in *vos* rescriptum super *ras.*
111	1		Mutata videntur l. 7 ω in λογω; l. 8 ε in fine: sic
„	„	9	παρουσι; l. 10 η in ου·μη; l. 12 η in φονη. In l. 17 *ras.* inter νε et φαι.
„	„	23	π in marg. forsan *r.m.*? at δ *p.m.*
„	2	3	*dolor in* rescript.; l. 16 *ras.* post *carita.*
112	1	6	π et *r s.m.* nisi forte *r p.m.*
„	„	7	ατακτουσ·πα rescript. super *ras.*? Sic etiam l. 18, Latinè, excepto *solite.* Scripturæ prioris fragmenta extant.
„	1	18	ζβεν. Annon potius legendum ξβεν?

FOL.	PAG.	LIN.	
112	2	7	*i eras.* ante ih̄u; l. 26 ε *eras.* ante εν.
„	„	18	Ab υμιν usque ad l. 22 rescript. super *ras.* Græcè.
„	„	20	θ̄ω: Primò scriptum est θ̄ι.
113	1	12	υ in υμιν mutatum; sic et ε l. 20 fin. Sub calcem paginæ PA *p.m.* ut videtur: cf. fol. 127 *repetitum*, p. 2.
„	2	8	π et *r s.m.*, more solito.
„	„	13, 14	ηδε rescript. super *ras.* ambobus locis. Sic et l. 15 η et ε in τηκεν: l. 28 *s* in *tis.*
114	1	7	ο κ̄σ̄·ισ rescript. super *ras.* Sic l. 10 ε in κατε.
„	„	7	*u eras.* post *ih*; sic et l. 19 *runt* post *credide.*
„	„	22	Η in marg. *s.m.*: sic π p. 2, ll. 13, 28.
„	„	25	*elegt.* Primo videtur fuisse *elegit.*
„	2	3	A στ$^{\eta}$εκεται usque ad fin. l. 18 Græcè, omnia super *rasuram* rescripta *p.m.* Sic forsan l. 26 πομον.
115	1	2	α post παντοσ *eras.*: l. 7, ν *eras.* post ητακτ$^{\eta}$εσα.
„	„	5	A παρημων usque ad l. 15 ημασ omnia rescripta *p.m.*
„	2	13	ω super ·Π· dubium.
„	„	18	σ ad finem fortè rescript.
„	„	26	*e* videtur esse *erasum* ante *quibusdam.*
116	1	21	Atramentum evanidum in πορνοισ· αρσενοκοιταισ: attamen *p.m.*
„	„	26	*mihi erasum* post *est*: l. 27, *ras.* post *mihi.*

FOL.	PAG.	LIN.	
116	2	7	ηχαρεισ· rescript. super *ras.* Sic et l. 12 *facere.*
117	1	4	*n* in *discant* rescript.? Sic et l. 9 αι in βασιλαιων: sic forsan
„	„	12	η in παση : l. 18 ων in ανθροπων.
„	„	20	μαρτυ: ι *p.m.* Cf. autem Fol. 76, p. 2, l. 9.
„	2	7	σ *eras.* inter γ et γ.
„	„	17	*rint eras.* post *manse*; l. 20 *f* in marg. *s.m.* vel potius *r.m.*, et l. 21 *rat* post *deside*, *eras.*
„	„	17	τεκνο: κ mutatum a ν, quod videtur esse *p.m.*
118	1	8	ι *eras.* post κα. l. 16 *sc* mutatum, ut videtur.
„	„	26	*runt eras.* post *adqui.*
„	„	27	*am eras.* post *fiduci.*
„	2	2	ον videtur rescriptum.
„	„	9	$\overline{οσ}$ disertissimè.
„	„	18	h insertum *s.m.* ante υποκρισι ex Codice Boerneriano.
„	„	23	*libus eras.* post *fide.*
„	„	26	*Ras.* ante ουδεν.
119	1	12	A *pietas* usque ad *vitae* l. 14 proculdubio super *ras.* rescripta. ν in l. 13 mutatum?
„	2	3	πρεσπυ: pro υ *p.m.* habet ι: Sic l. 10 πρεσβυ, υ mutatum.
„	„	25	Secundum *nocte* lineâ deletum, *die* superpositum *p.m.* ρ secund. in προ‿σευ‿χαρισ lineâ suppositâ deletum *p.m.*
120	1	3	*e*? *eras.* post *et.* Sic et l. 9 φ *eras.* ante φορεσεν.
„	2	5	ο mutat. in τεροι? Sic l. 9 οω in αλοωντα: et l. 21 ησ in φυλαξησ. Nisi hæc membranæ sint vitia.
121	1	4	αι in προαγουσαι mutatum? Sic et l. 8 αι in κρυβηναι: l. 11 η in πασησ: l. 20 νομενοι: l. 23 γι in ὑγι: l. 27 σω et λογ. Forsan autem membranæ sunt.
„	„	9	*Ras.* inter ο et σοι.
„	2	25	Cυ·δε forsan rescript. super *ras.*
122	1	17	πρ in απροσῖτον ex correctione. l. 24 λ *p.m.* super πλ. l. 27 *thesaurizate.* *p.m.* ut videtur.
„	2	26	πιστεωσ: pro ε *p.m.* ι scribere volebat: Latinè *ficta*, *p.m.*
123	1	6	επιθεσεωσ: ε primum fortasse mutatum: pro π *p.m.* dedit γ.
„	„	8	$\overline{πνα}$ · διλιασ · haud dubito esse mutatum.
„	„	24	Post *evageli* eraditur *um.*
„	2		Mutari videntur a correctore l. 10 σ in τοσ: l. 14 *onesiph*: l. 17 *quæsi.*
124	1	11	υ in ευ mutatum? l. 17 τον, ο mutatum *p.m.*: l. 19 η et ε rescripta super *ras.*
„	„	17	*ctos eras.* post *ele.*
„	2	8	σπουγασον *p.m.* δ *s.m.* τ *r.m.*
„	„	„	linea recta partim *eras.* super *cura.*
125	1	2	*init.* *tu* in marg. *s.m.*? l. 27 *ras.* ante *elati.*
„	„	14	*seman* errore pro ſɔ (i.q. *sed*) *man.*
„	2	6	$\overline{θυ}$. $\overline{DY}$ *p.m.* l. 26 *Forsan* ετενετο legendum.
„	„	14	*descen*, *e* primum lineâ perpendiculari deletum.

[FOL.] PAG.	LIN.	
l	27	*R* Latinum inter Græca, ut *p.m.* Fol. 125, p. 2, l. 6, et *L* fol. 122, p. 2, l. 11.
2	23	γ in αγωνα videtur mutari super *ras.*
l	5	η in Δημασ forsan mutatum : sic et l. 22 σ in τοισ.
2	1 ad 15	Græcè, certè rescripta super *ras.* Sic *forsan* l. 23 ουδεν.
„	1	*ras.* ante *li*, nisi membranæ vitium sit. *Ras.* post *doctrina.*
„	„	*f* in calce paginæ parum intelligo.
2	4	*nam eras.* post *doctri.* Mutantur fortasse
„	2	ξ et ν : l. 5 ην in την : l. 16 οξ in δοξησ.
	2	*nemin* super *ras.* scriptum? Sic et l. 22 δικαι.
„	10	στοι. Forsan στοι *p.m.* l. 15 δικαιοσινη *p.m.*?
„	16	*ras.* ante αλλα.
2	12	*damnatur:* *t* errore pro *t*.
„	16	ϗ εκριτα *p.m.*?
	17	κ in και, et l. 18 ψ mutata.
	3	Δεσμεοισ *p.m.* ι insertum ante ο, ε *prim.* mutat.
	5	φ in φιλημονει super *ras.* l. 21 θο mutatum?
	25	*Rasura* post Διο.
	1	σου *p.m.* l. 5 pro χρ̄υ, *p.m.* habet χρ̄ι. Sic forsan υ in τουσ p. 1, l. 17. Hæc quoque mutantur : l. 7, σειμ : l. 10 π et ψ in ανεπεμψα : l. 15 υ in ευ : l. 18 τ in το.
	4	οτι·και·σε· super *ras.* l. 7 duæ

FOL.	PAG.	LIN.	
			literæ *eras.* ante μου : l. 13 *ras* ante *mihi.*
131	2	3	(col. 1) *Imprimis p.m.*
„	„	„	(col. 2) ᴍᴏᴅɪs super *ras.* : l. 26 Annon *partitipibus*?
132	1	12	(col. 1) *er* mutatum in *ministerium*? Sic l. 19 *dientia: ta* in *firmata*, l. 24.
„	„	6	(col. 2) fin. *a* abrasum : l. 21 *salutos p.m.*, *o* deletum per lineam perpendicularem *s.m.*?
„	2	11—13	(col. 1) ad *fieret* rescripta super *ras.*: l. 11 *n* ad finem *eras.*
133	2	6	(col. 1) *m* in *amus* forsan rescript. sic l. 9 *tem*?
„	„	14	(col. 1) Linea perpendicularis recentissimâ manu.
„	„	20	(col. 2) *dō p.m.* i. *s.m.* Lectiones mixtæ, ut supra, fol. 132, p. 1, col. 2, l. 21.
134	1	6	(col. 1) *s* in *res* et *ju* mutatum? l. 18 *herbem*, *p.m.*; *am s.m.* lectiones mixtæ: *am* post *oportun* rescript.
„	„	1	(col. 2) *tis* rescript? Sic et l. 23 *ti* in *Forti*?
„	2	20	(col. 2) *insolibis* correctio *p.m.* esse videtur.
135	2	4	(col. 1) *et* super *ras.* esse videtur.
„	„	27	(col. 1) *ras.* inter *ob* et *umb.* Cætera in hac paginâ membranæ sunt vitia : l. 3, col. 2, *i* in *introibant* vermiculis peresum.
136	1	22	(col. 1) *ras.* post *ministerii.*
„	„	9	(col. 2) *per hosti* super *ras.* rescript.

FOL.	PAG.	LIN.	
136	2	26	(col. 2) *P'* i.q. *Post*. Cf. Fol. 138, p. 2, col. 2, l. 22, &c.
137	1	7	(col. 1) *alcaverit* rescript. super *ras.* Sic et l. 9 *scificatus*: l. 18 *ob* *p.m.*, *b* mutato in *p* forsan *s.m.*
"	"	2	(col. 2) *ras.* ante *cumque.*
"	2	3	(col. 1) Pro·post *remunerator* *p.m.* scripsit ÷ (i.q. *est*).
"	"	13	(col. 1) *d* in *fide* mutatum, *p.m.*
"	"	9	(col. 2) *ras.* ante *appetunt.*
138	1	3	(col. 1) *ioi* planè: quamvis *o* vermiculis peresum.
"	"	5	(col. 2) *sus* rescript. super *ras.* Sic l. 12 *i* in *pelibus* mutatum.
"	"	19	(col. 2) *inventi sunt* lineâ transversâ deletum.
"	"	25	(col. 2) *omne.* Pro *n*, *p.m.* *f* scribere incipiebat.
139	1	2	(col. 1) H i.e. *enim*. Cf. p. 2, col. 1, l. 19. l. 28 *ras.* ante *maneat.*
139	1	23	(col. 2) *enim* lineâ transversâ deletum.
"	2	4	(col. 1) *scificet* primò scriptum: *t* in *a* mutatum.
"	"	"	(col. 2) *saecla*: *a* *eras.* l. 18 *baptismi* super *ras.*
"	"	19	(col. 2) *precios.* an *pretios.* dubium.
140	1	27	(col. 1) *dimitae* *p.m.*: *a* in *i* mutatum.
"	"	12	(col. 2) *intercessione* *p.m.*: – super *e* *eras.*
"	"	14	(col. 2) *frem*: *i* inceptum post *r*.
"	"	26	(col. 2) *fidem* rescriptum super *rasuram.*
141	1	9	(col. 1) Post *op* omnia maculâ obducta.

Hæc ferè sunt, ubi primæ manus lectio a correctoribus mutari vel suppleri videtur. Existunt porro loci haud pauci, quos enumerare supervacuum est, in quibus membranæ scabrities falsam correctionis speciem scripturæ intulerit.

Richardi Bentleii notulæ, in exemplari suo Novi Test. Oxonii, 1675, obiter scriptæ.

Hic liber collatus cum vetusto codice Paulinarum Epistolarum, Literis Capitalibus, sine accentibus, plus 800 annorum; descripto vero ex codice egregio, qualis nullus hodie extat. Porro is codex nunc [1718] est Richardi Bentleii. [Sic brevius ad Rom. I. 1.]

Rom. I. 1—III. 19. Variæ lectiones ex altero nostro Msto, ejusdem veteris exemplaris apographo.

Rom. VIII. 34. υπερει: videtur ortum ex duplici lectione περει ἡμων, ὑπερ ἡμων.

XI. 8. ἡμερασ και δαυιδ: linea videtur excidisse: imo margine habetur eadem manu.

XIV. 15, 20. απολλυειν, καταλυειν: Nota, in Lat. est noli *perdere*, noli *destruere*.

ib. 21. η σκαν. η ασθ. in quibusdam deest; nota ergo v. 13, η σκανδαλον.

1 Corinth. *initio*. Epae Pauli collatae ad vetustissimum MS. Codicem *nostrum*. Incipit cap. III. 19 Roman.

Ephes. III. 5. Confert Col. I. 26, [ubi pro ἁγιοισ legit αποστολοισ].

Phil. III. 6. ζηλοσ. Sic Clemens Romanus utitur.

1 Thess. II. 10. προσ: fortè erat πρ, ὡσ.

v. 3. MS ὡσπερ η ωδινεσ: lege ὡσπερει ωδ.

APPENDIX:

IN QUO EXHIBETUR COLLATIO PLENA ET ACCURATA

QUINQUAGINTA CODICUM,

DIVERSAS NOVI TESTAMENTI PARTES COMPLECTENTIUM,

AD EDITIONEM ELZEVERIANUM 1624

FIDELITER ELABORATA.

LOGUS LIBRORUM MANUSCRIPTORUM, QUORUM COLLATIO INFRA SUBJICITUR.

CONTINENT

. Coll. Cantab. B. x. 17.

m *v*) Cantab. Mm. 6. 9.

. Coll. Cantab. B. x. 16.

ıx Leicestrensis.

. Mus. Harleian. 5598.

ıgelistarium, Parham 18.

ıgelistarium, Parham 1.

ıgelistarium, Coll. Christi Cantab. . I. 8.

sem. z *bis* &c. *lectionem in* Pz *minimè constantem esse denotant.*

STOLORUM ET EPISTOLAS OLICAS CONTINENT

ɔeth 1182.

1183.

1184.

1185.

1255.

x Theodori.

x Wordsworth.

Mus. Butler 2.

„ Burnei. 48.

Coll. Cantab. B. x. 16.

Christi Cantab. F. I. 13.

x Leicestrensis.

Emmanuel. Cantab. I. 4. 35.

ab. Mm. 6. 9.

Mus. Add. 20003.

EPISTOLAS PAULINAS CONTINENT

a, b, c, d. iidem codices qui Act. Apost. exhibent.

e. Lambeth 1186.

f, g, h. iidem qui in Act. Apost.

j. Brit. Mus. Burnei. 18.

k, l, m, n, o. iidem qui in Act. Apost.

z. Evangelistarium: Coll. Christi Cantab. F. I. 8.

APOCALYPSIN CONTINENT

a. Lambeth 1186.

b. Brit. Mus. Butler 2.

c. „ Harleian. 5678.

d. „ „ 5778.

e. „ „ 5613.

f. Codex Leicestrensis.

g. Parham 17.

h. „ 2.

j. Brit. Mus. Add. 17469.

k Bodleian. Canonici Græci 34.

l. Brit. Mus. Harleian. 5537.

m. Mediomontanus 1461.

n. Bodleian. Barocc. 48.

N.B. + aliquid textui adjectum indicat, at – aliquid subtractum.

* literæ superpositum lectionem a *primâ manu* indicat, at ** lectionem a *secundâ manu*. ? lectionem indicat dubiam, subrasam, incertam.

SANCTI MATTHÆI EVANGELIUM.

Το κατα ματθαιον ἁγιον ευαγγελιον iv. ευαγγελιον κατα
APUT I. γεννεσεως iPz. υἱου *bis* P_2. 2. ἀβρααμ *passim* ivwH
γεννησεν *ubique in hoc capite* P. ἰσαακ *bis* w. εγενησε *tertium* i.
ιρᾶ z. 4. αμηναδαμ *bis* P_2. αμιναδαμ *bis* Hz. ἀασσων *prim.* w. 5
οζ *secund.* P_2. ὀβηδ *bis* P. ὀβηδ *prim.* P_2. ιεσσε P_2. ἰεσσαι
σολομῶνα ivwHz. σολομώνα P. σολομονα P_2. οριου w. 7. αβι
ιωσαφ *bis* z. ἰωραμ *bis* P_2. ὀζιαν iHP. 9. ὀζιας iwHP. αχατζ *bi*
rt. i. ιεζεκιαν P*. 10. μανασση H. μανασσὴς HP_2. την (*pro* τον
μμὼς *bis* w. –τον αμων· αμων δε εγεννησε P. 11. ἰεχωνιαν P.
w [*non* HPP_2]. 12. μετα δε *rescript. super rasur.* P. μετ
χωνιας P. 13. –δε *prim.* w*. ελιακιμ *prim.* P. *vv.* 13, 14. –τον α
γεννησε P. 14. σαδοκ *bis* P_2z. αχιμ *bis* vPP_2z. αχιμ δε εγενν
ılcem paginæ, deest in textu). 15. ματθᾶν z. εγενησε *tert.* P_2. 1
7. *init.* πασε ουν εγενιαιε P_2. οὐν P. γενεαι P. ἑως *bis* P_2. δεκατ
$_2$*. –και απο δαδ *usque ad* γενεαι ιδ i* (*habet marg. s. m.*). ἑως
ετοικησιας *bis* vw, *secund.* i. 18. γεννησης P. οὑτως P_2. ἠν
νηστευθησις P. μνιστευθεισης P_2. εὑρεθη PP_2. 19. ἰωσηφ (*sic*
καιως P_2*. ὧν w. ὡν P. παραδιγματισε w. παραδειγματησαι
ic v. 23) P. κατοναρ vPz. φαινεται P. φοβηθεῖς PP_2.
1. καλεσης P. ὀνομα (*sic v.* 23) P. 22. –το ρηθεν P_2* (*eâdem man*
á in v. 14). 23. ἑξει Pz. καλεσουσιν P. εστιν P. μεθερμηνονομει
ηνευωμενον P. 24. –ὁ *prim.* w. παρελαβεν iwH**P. 25. ἑω
H**P. εκαλεσεν wP. ὀνυμα HP.

CAP. II. 1. –δε HPz (*initio pericopes*). θηθλεεμ *hic tantum* v
m. ιλῆμ vw. 2. ἴδομεν v**P. ἠλθομεν wP. 3. –ὁ βασιλευς P
centi manu). 5. εμβηθλεεμ (*sic v.* 16) P. οὑτως ivwPz. οὑτως
si. ῆ (*pro* ει) P. ἡγεμωσιν P. 7. ἡκριβωσε i. ἡκριβωσεν wH**P.
πεν wHP. ἐπ' ἂν ivwH. ἐπᾶν Pz. εὑρητε P. 9. ιδον wP. ἑως P. +
ἦν P. 11. οἰκιαν wP. ειδον ivwHz, ἴδον P (*pro* εὑρον). 12. χρημ

P. κατ' ὄναρ (*sic vv.* 19, 22) H. κατοναρ (*sic vv.* 13, 19, 22)
13. −δε *et* των μαγων (*pro* αυτων) HPz (*init. peri.*). κατ' οναρ
θη iP. ησθη z. ἂν H. εἴπω P. +ὁ (*ante* ἡρωδης) z. *fin.* αυτω?
ιρελαβεν wH**P. αἴγυπτον w [*non v.* 13]. 15. ἦν w.
im. w. αἰγυπτου wP. 16. ενεπεχθη P. ανειλεν H**P.
υς w. κατοτερου P*. κατοτερω iP** *rubro.* ἠκριβωσε w
σεν P. 18. ῥαμᾶ w. ἠκουσθη wP. θρινος P. θρηνος *rescript.*
'argiorem in w. ὀδυρμος wHP. πολους i.* ραχιηλ P. ηθελεν
ισιν wHPz. 19. *Rasura in* P *inter* τελευτ *et* ησαντος
γυπτω w. 20. −πορευου *usque ad* μητερα αυτου *v.* 21, z*
n.). ιηλ (*sic v.* 21) v. την *secund. bis script.* P*. τεθνηκασιν
ιελαβεν wH**P. ἦλθεν w. ἦλθεν P. 22. χρηματησθεις P.
23. ναζαρεθ wH [*non* ivPz].
.. −δε ivw*. +ὁ (*ante* ιωαννης ὁ) Pz *semel.* 2. μετανοητε P.
ἤγγικεν P. 3. *init.* αυτος H. ἑτοιμασατε HP. 4. ειχεν
ν P. ἡ δε H. ἦν w. ἦν P. 5. και (*pro* τοτε) z *sem.*
+ἡ P (*an primâ manu?*), +πασα z *sem.* (*ante* ἱερουσολυμα).
−πασα *secund.* P**. περιχορος P. 6. ἐβαπτίζοντω̃ P.
ταμω (*post* ιορδανη) vw**Hz *bis.* 7. φαρισσαιων i. φαρισ-
αδδουκαιων και φαρισαιων z. 8. καρπον αξιον ivw*H [*non* z].
ιτι (*ante* πρα) z. ἀβρααμ *bis* ivwHz. 10. ἤδη H. 11. ὀπισω
25) i. −και πυρι ivHz. 12. ἁλωνα w. +μεν (*ante* σιτον) v.
+αυτου (*post* αποθηκην) vw**. 13. τω καιρω εκεινω (*pro* τοτε,
sic IV. 1). ἰορδανην w. 14. διεκολυεν H*?P. 15. ειπεν
αυτω (−προς) z. οὑτως ivwHPz. πρεπων v*?P. ἡμιν εστι v.
17) P. ιδεν P. ειδεν wz. καταβαινων P. ὡσεὶ P. 17. −ὁ

. ανηχθη ὁ ις vPz. −ὑπο του πνευματος P. 2. −και νυκτας
P* (*habet marg. s. m.*) z. επεινασεν wz. 3. γενονται iP.
. μονον P. 5. ειστησιν P. ἱστησιν vz. 6. +λεγει αυτω
πται) P*. *Ab* αυτου *usque ad* επι *super ras.* i. −και *secund.* v.
7. εφει P. λεγεγραπται P* (λε *eras.*). εκπειρασης v.
ιυτων *bis script.* H*. 9. συ (*pro* σοι) P. δοσω wP. προσ-
ιε z. 10. λεγ P*. +οπισω μου (*post* ὑπαγε) ivw**HPz (ὀπισω
ιννησης z. 11. ἴδοῦ *et* διήκουουν P. 12. −δε (*init. peri.*) Pz.
H*. καταλειπὼν i. καταλειπω̃ν P. καταλιπω̃ν z. ναζαρεθ

H. παραθαλασιαν P. ὁριοις v. νεφθαλιμ (*sic* v. 15) P. 16. ειδεν w. ἴδεν P. ιδε z. –καθημενοις v. 17. ἤρξατο HP. μετανωῆτε w. μετανοήτε P. ἤγγικεν P. ἠγγικεν wHz. 18. –δε (*init. peri.*) vPz. –ὁ ιησους iw. ειδεν iwH. ιδεν P. σιμονα w. αμφιβλιστρον z. ἦσαν w. ἦσαν HP. ἀλιεις (*sic v.* 19) HP. 19. ὀπισω wHP. ἀλυεις z. 20. και (*pro* οἱ δε) z. +αυτων (*post* δικτυα) w. ἠκολουθησαν iwHP. 21. ιδεν P. ειδε (–αλλους) z. –καταρτιζοντας τα δικτυα αυτων z. δυκτυα i*. 22. ἠκολουθησαν wP. 23. περιηγεν ὁ ις ὁλην την γαλιλαιαν Hz (*init. peri.*) *semel, at* περιειγεν z *semel*. 24. εξηλθεν Hz. –και βασανοις v. συνεχομενοις z *bis*. 25. ἠκολουθησαν wHP. τω ιυ (*pro* αυτῳ) HPz (*init. peri.*). ὀχλοι P. γαλλιλαιας P.

CAP. V. 1. ὀχλους P. ὀρος P. καθησαντος P. καθισαντος αυτου *rescript.* i. 5. κληρονομησουσιν wP. κληρονυμισουσι H. –την v. 8. ὀψονται HP. 10. ἐνεκεν wP. ὀτι αυτων *super rasur.* w. 11 ὅτ' ἂν iwH. εσται ὀτἂν ὀνειδησωσιν P. ὀνειδισωσιν w. ονειδισωσι και διωξωσιν ὑμας z. διωξουσιν P. εἶπωσιν P. ἐνεκεν wP. 12. *Post* χαιρε *rasura in* i (τε *omisso*). ἡμων (*pro* ὑμων *prim.*) w*. τω ουρανω z. οὑτως (*sic vv.* 16, 19, 47) ivwz. οὑτως H. –τους *secund.* w*. 13. ἀλας *et* ἀλισθησεται H. –δε H. ισχυι vz. ἐτι H. ειμι (*pro* ει μη) i. 15. επι (*pro* ὑπο) w. οικια wH. 16. οὑτως (*sic v.* 19) H. ὀρανοις w. 17. νομησητε iw. ἦλθον *bis* w. 19. ἐἂν H. αν (*pro* εαν) z*. διδαξει *bis* z, *prim.* v. ποιησει i*. ὀρανων w. 20. περισσευη P. ὑμων ἡ δικαιοσυνη ivw [*non* Pz]. πλεον iz. πλειων H. γραμματαιων P. φαρισσαιων i*. εισέλθηται P. 21. ἠκουσατε wP. [ερρεθη iz *passim*]. ερηθη w*P (*sic* P *vv.* 33, 38). ερρηθη vw**H. αρχεοις i. φονευσης i. 22. ὀργιζομενος w. εργαζομενος P. αυτῶ (*pro* αυτου *prim.*) w. *Post* αυτου *prim. in* P, *una linea eraditur, reliquâ versûs parte sub calcem paginæ positâ sec. man.* (μωραι P**). μορε w. γεεναν wz (*sic vv.* 29, 30, z). 23. οὖν P. προσφερεις HPz. επι τῶ H. και εκει iw [*non* z]. μνησθεις vwz. 24. τω (*pro* το) *bis* H, *secund.* z. διαλαγηθι H. διάλλάγηθη P. 25. ισθη iPz. ἢ (*pro* ει) z. ὀδῶ w. +σου (*post* αντιδικος) i. βληθησει P. 26. –αν w. οὖ (*pro* αν) z. κοδρατην w. 27. ἠκουσατε wHP. ερρηθη vwH. ερηθη P. –τοις αρχαιοις ivw [*non* Hz]. μοιχευσης i. μηχευσεις w. 28. εμβλεψας (*pro* βλεπων) i. τω (*pro* το) z. επιθημησαι w*. αυτην (*pro* αυτης) ivwHPz. ἤδη P. 29. –δε H*. ὀφθαλμος w. βαλαι i. εκβαλε P. απωληται (*sic v.* 30) vz. *Rasura in* H *ante* βληθη, *in* w *ante* γεενναν, *sic in v.* 30, *post* αυτην. vv. 29, 30. +την (*ante* γεενναν) wH. 30. *init.* και ἢ ει H. ὀλων H. 31. ερρηθη vw. –δε ὀτι z. –αν z. απολυσει iPz. αυτην z. 32. πας ὁ απολυων (*pro* ὁς αν απολυση) wHPz. περὶ ἐκτὸς (–λογου) P. γαμησει P. ὁ (*pro* ὁς εαν) z. αν (*pro* εαν) iw**

(−εαν w*). γαμησας (*pro* γαμηση) z. 33. −παλιν z. ἠκουσατε wHP. ερρηθη vwH. αρχαιοις H*. επιορκησεις H. −τῳ v. ὁρκους iv. τοις ὁρκοις P. 34. ὀμοσαι vwH. ὀμῶσαι P. ὀλος H. εστιν (*sic v.* 35 *bis*) HP. 36. ὀμος' w. ὀμωσεις P. ὀμοσης vH. δυνασε P. ἡ HP. μελενα P. 38. ἠκουσατε wP. ερρηθη vw. ὀφθαλμον wHP *bis*. ὀφθαλμου wP *bis*. ὀδοντ. *bis* wHP. −και οδοντα αντι οδοντος z. 39. *Eras. ante* μη *in* H. αντηστηναι P. ὅστις (*sic v.* 41) w. ὀτις H. ραπηζει P. ραπησει z. εις (*pro* επι) H. −σου vP. −σου σιαγονα z. 40. το (*pro* τῳ) P. χειτονα P. −σου z. *fin.* +σου Pz. 41. αν αγγαρευση w. αγγαρευση HP. 42. αἰτουντι w. αποστραφεις Pz. 43. ἠκουσατε wP. ερρηθη vw [*non* P]. 44. −εχθρους H*. τοις μισουσιν ivwHPz. επερεαζοντων Pz (+ὑμας P*, *at cœtera versûs desunt in* P* : *habet marg., ubi* διοκοντων P**). −και διωκοντων ὑμας z. 45. γεννησθε w. ὑπο (*pro* υιοι) z. +τοις (*ante* ουρανοις) iwH. ανατελει P. ανατελλη z. 46. αγαπησειτε H. αγαποντας w. εχητε z. ποιουσιν iwP. 47. φιλους (*pro* αδελφους) ivwHPz. οὑτως vPz, *at* το αυτο H. 48. εσεσθαι i. οὐν P. *fin.* εστιν wHPz.

CAP. VI. 1. εμπροσθε i**. 2. ὅτ' ἀν iHP *passim*. οὐν (*sic vv.* 8, 9) P. ποιεις i*P. +ὁτι (*ante* απεχουσι) P (−σιν P**). 4. ἡ wz. ἡ P. +σε (*post* βλεπων) P. −αυτος vPz. 5. πλατιῶν P. ἑστωτες wP. προσευχεσθε z. −αν vw*. φανωσιν P**. απεχουσιν (*sic* P *v.* 16) H**P. 6. ὀτ' ἀν wP. ταμειον vPz. κλησας i. θυρα (*pro* θυραν) z. 7. βατολογησετε P. εθνηκοι z. δοκουσιν H**. 8. ὁμοιωθηται P. οἶδεν P. υιδεν iwHz. +ὁ ουρανιος (*ante* ὡν) w**. ετησαι P. αἰτησαι w. 9. προσευχεσθαι w*P. ὀνομα P. 10. βασιλειας σου P. 12. ὀφειλ. *bis* wP. (ὀφιλημματα P). 13. εισενεγκεις H. πειρασμῶν P. δυναμεις P. [*Doxologiam habent* ivwHPz]. 14. −γαρ Pz (*init peri.*). 15. αφηται P. 16. ὅτ' ἀν H. αφανιζουσιν P. φανωσιν P. 17. ἀλειψαι v. 18. −εν τῳ φανερῳ iwHPz [*non* v]. 19. θησαυριζεται P. βρωσης (*sic v.* 20) P. αφανιζη z. διορυσουσιν (*sic v.* 20) P. κλεπτουσιν wP. 20. οὔτε *bis* P. οὐδε H. 22. ὀφθαλμος *bis* (*sic v.* 23) wP, *prim.* H. οὐν (*sic v.* 23) P. −ουν z. −ὁ *tertium* w. ἀπλους iH. ἡ wP. φωτινον iw. φωτηνον P. 23. ἡ w. εστιν wP. 24. οὐδεὶς P. ἡ γαρ w. ἕνα HP. μισησοι w. ἕτερον i. *Rasura in* w *post* αγαπησει. +του (*ante* ἑνος) z. ἑνος HP. ἑτερου iH. καταφρονισει H. δυνασθαι P. μαμωνᾶ ivwz. μαμωνὰ HP. 25. διατοῦτο ivz. ἡμων (*pro* ὑμων *prim.*) P. πυιητε i. μηδὲ vwPz *passim*. τι ὑμων *bis scr.* H*. ενδυσεσθε H*. πλειων H. εστιν P. 26. οὐχ' ivwHPz. ἡμεις (*pro* ὑμεις) w. 27. προσθηναι i*?w? Pz. πηχην w. ἑνα P. 28. αυξανη z. νιθει H. νηθη z. 29. σολωμων i. σολομῶν Pz. περιεβαλλετο wz.

30. ἴδε (*pro* εἰ δε) v. ὀντα P. αὔριον wH. ὀλιγοπιστοι wHP. 31. οὖν P. ἢ *bis* P. περιβαλλομεθα wz. περιβαλλωμεθα HP. 32. ταυτα γαρ παντα v. επιζητη z. οιδεν H *sem.* οἶδεν iH *sem.* P. οἶδε w. ειδε z. ἡμων (*pro* ὑμων) i. ὁ *secund.* H. ἀπαντων iH. 33. αυτου (*pro* του θῦ) v. 34. μεριμνησητε ivwH** *antiquâ manu.* αὔριον *bis* w. ἡ (*pro* ἡ *prim.*) H. +γαρ (*post* αρκετον) v.

CAP. VII. 2. κρινεται P. μετρητε z. μετριθησεται w. μετρηθησεται vH. [αντιμετ. iPz]. 3. −δε w*. τω (*pro* το *secund.*) z. το (*pro* τῳ *prim.*) P. ὀφθαλμω *bis* wHP. −σῳ w. 4. ἐκβαλῶ z. ὀφθαλμου wHP *bis.* ἡ (*pro* ἡ) w. 5. ὀφθαλμου *bis* wP. *fin.* σου z*, *at* αδελφου σου z**. 6. δοτε iz. τα ἅγια z. κυσιν P. μηδὲ *pass.* ivwPz. μήποτὲ P. κατατησωσιν w*. αυτοις (*pro* αυτους) P*? −εν τοις ποσιν αὔτων z. 7. αἰτήτε P *sem.* ζητειται P *sem.* εὑρισητε i. εὑρησετε HP *quater* z *sem.* κρουεται i. ανυγησεται P *sem.* 8. αἰτων w. ετων P *bis.* λαβανει w. λαμβανη P_2. εὑρησκει P *bis.* εὑρισκη P *sem.* εὑρισκει P *sem.* P_2z *sem.* το (*pro* τῳ) P_2. 9. ἢ P *sem.* −εστιν ivP *sem.* P* *sem.* z *sem.* εστι z** *sem.* ὁς (*pro* ὀν) v. αἰτηση w. αιτησει HP *sem.* 10. *init.* +ἢ w. ἰχθυν w. αἰτηση iw. αιτησει P *bis.* ὀφιν P *sem.* z. ὄφην P *sem.*, *at* ὀφην *sem.* 11. οὖν (*sic* v. 12) P *ter.* ὀντες HP *ter.* οἴδατάτε i. οἶδατε P *sem.*, *at* οἴδατε *bis.* δωματα i*z. δουναι P *sem.* πωσω P *sem.*, *at* ποσων *sem.* ἡμων (*pro* ὑμων *secund.*) Pz. ἐπ' ουρανιος (−εν τοις) P *sem.* αἰτουσιν w. 12. −ουν (*init. peri.*) v*Pz *sem.* οὖν P *sem.* εαν (*pro* αν) z *sem.* θεληται P *sem.*, *at* θελετε *sem.* ποιουσιν P *sem.* οὗτως ivwP *bis* z *bis.* ἡμεις (*pro* ὑμεις) w. και ὑμεις οὗτως H. ποιησατε P *sem.* οὕτως (*pro* οὗτος) iP *bis* z *bis.* 13. εισελθατε P *sem.* πλατεία z *sem.* εὑρυχωρος i (εὑρι i* ?) z *sem.* ευρυχορος P *sem.* −ἡ (*ante* απαγουσα) v. απωλιαν P *sem.* 14. *init.* [ὁτι i*H**]. τι i**vwH*z *bis.* τῆ στενῆ πυλη P *bis* (−ὁτι *et* ἡ). τεθλημενη iP *sem.* τεθλημμενη P *sem.* z *sem.* −την P* *sem.* ὀλιγοι iwHP *bis.* εὑρισκοντες P *sem.* 15. οἵτινες P *sem.* ἡμας z *sem.* εσωθεν μεν εισιν (−δε) P *sem.*, *at semel* εισιν *tantum.* ἅρπαγες HP *bis.* 16. −αυτων z *sem.* επιγνωσεσθαι H. ἢ P *bis.* σύκα ivPz *bis.* 17. οὗτως ivwHP *bis* z *bis.* δενδρων *prim.* z *sem. fin.* −ποιει *usque ad* καρπους πονηρους v. 18, v. 18. οὐδεδρον w. αγαθους (*pro* καλους) z. 19. ποιοῦν P. +το (*ante* πυρ) P*. 20. ἆράγε i. ἄραγε w. ἄράγε z. 21. *init.* −ου w. αλλα P*. 22. ερουσιν w. ὀνοματι *prim.* w, *tert.* H. επροφητευσαμεν z. −και τῳ σῳ ονοματι δαιμονια εξεβαλομεν v. 23. *init.* −και v*. +παντες (*post* εμου) H. 24. −ουν z (*init. peri.*). ποιων z. αυτω (*pro* αυτον) z. φρονημω z*. ὠκοδομησεν wH. ὠκοδομησην P. οἰκιαν wHP (*sic vv.* 25, 27 P).

25. ἦλθον w. ἦλθον P. προσεπεσαν vHPz [*non* iw]. οικια (*sic v.* 26) wH. επεσεν iwHP. 26. μη ποιων αυ *rescript.* P. ὁμοιωσω αυτω (*pro* ὁμοιωθησεται) z. ᾠκοδομησε w. 27. ἦλθον P. ἦν w, ἦν P. μεγαλη (*sic*) i. 28. ὀχλοι P. 29. ἦν H. αυτοις (*pro* αυτους) z. οὐχ' ivHPz. *fin.* + αυτων w.

Cap. VIII. 1. *init.* + και (— δε) z. ὀρους HP. ἠκολουθησαν wHP. ὀχλοι iHP. 2. προσελθων iPz. δυνασε μαι w. 3. ἥψατο w. — ὁ ιησους P. εκαθαρισθη P. 4. μήδενὶ iP. αλλ' iHPz. διξον H. πρόσένεγκαι P*. + σου (*post* δωρον) z. προσεταξεν wP. μωυσης w. 5. ελθοντι z (*init. peri.*). αυτω (*pro* τῳ ιυ) iv*w. ἑκατυνταρχος (*sic v.* 8 P) HP. 6. οἰκια wHP. δεινος w. 8. οὐκ H. στεγειν P. λογω ivwPz. 9. ὑπεξούσίαν P. ἐμ' αὐτὸν P. τουτω (*pro* τουτο) P: H *vice versâ.* 10. εθαυμασεν wH**P. ειπεν iwH**P. πιστην i. εἱρων P. 11. ἥξουσιν P. ανακληθησονται ivwPz. ἀβρααμ ivwHz. ἀβρααμ' P. ἰσαακ w. ϊσαακ' *et* ἰακὼβ' P. 12. εξοτερον i. ὀδοντων vwP. 13. — ὁ *prim.* z. ἑκατονταρχη ivwz. ἑκατονταρχη H. ἑκατουταρχω P*. *fin.* + και ὑποστρεψας ὁ ἑκατονταρχος εις τον οικον αυτου εν αυτη τη ὥρα εὗρεν τον παιδα ὑγιαινοντα w** *marg.* 14. οἰκιαν wHP. ειδεν w. ἴδεν P. 15. ἥψατο w. ἠγερθη wHP. *fin.* αυτω ivwz [*non* HP]. 16. ὀψιας iwH**P. εξεβαλεν H**P. εξεβαλον z. + τω (*ante* λογω) iP. 17. ανελαβεν wP. ελαβεν H**. εβαστασε (*omissis vv.* 18—22) v. 18. ὀχλους HP. περι ἑαυτων z [αὐτον iwHP]. 20. ἀλωπεκες v. αλοπικες P. φολεους Pz. εχουσιν wP. κλινει i. κλιναι Pz. 21. Ἑτερος H**. 22. ακολουθη HP. 23. — το (*init. peri.*) v *duobus locis* HP *sem.* z. ἠκολουθησαν wP *bis.* *In* v *post. v.* 23 *sequuntur vv.* 19—23. 24. ϊδοῦ P. κοιματων i*. εκαθευδεν wHP. 25. — αυτου ivwHPz. ἠγηραν P. απολυμεθα P. 26. δηλοὶ z. ὀλιγοπιστοι iwP. επετημησεν P. 28. γαδαρηνων w. γεργεσινων Pw** *marg.* [γεργεσηνων ivHz]. μηκέτι (*pro* μη) z. ὀδοὺ i. 29. εκραζον w. συ (*pro* σοι) z. ἦλθες wP. ὧδε wz [*non* ivP]. προκαιρου ivwHPz. βασανησαι P. *fin.* · *non* ; w. 30. *init.* ἦ w*. ἦν P. απ' αυτου P. — πολλων P* (*habet marg. s. m.*). βοσκομενων z. 31. εκβαλεις HPz. 32. — ὑπαγετε i*. ὁρμησεν P. ὥρμησεν z. — του v. κρυμνου w. κριμνου P. 33. ι *eras. in* και *secund.* P. 34. ϊδοῦ P. αυτου (*pro* τῳ ιυ) z. απαντησιν w. ἀπαντησιν P. ὁριων ivH.

Cap. IX. 1. + ὁ ις (*post* εμβας) v. — το HP *bis* z (*init. peri.*). διεπερασεν wH**P *bis.* ἦλθεν wP *bis.* 2. πιστην i. αυτου (*pro* αυτων) z. ειπεν wHP. αφεονται z. ἁμαρτιαις σου P. *fin.* — σου i* ? 3. γραμματαιων P. ἐν w. ἑαυτοις H. βλασφημη P. 4. ιδως w ? + αυτοις (*post* εἰπεν) w. ενθυμήσθε w. 5. — γαρ w. ευκοποτερον Pz. αφεονται z. σου (*pro* σοι) ivwz. ἢ P. εγειρε ivP [*non* z]. 6. ειδειτε P*. ιδειτε P**. ιδητε vz. ἆρον w. ἆρον iPz. οἰκον w. οἱ σου P. 7. ηγερθη και (pro εγερθεις) z. οἰκον HP. 8. – δε z. ὀχλοι P. 9. –εκειθεν Pz (init. peri.). ιδεν wP bis. ακολουθη HP. ηκολουθεισεν i. ἠκολουθησεν (sic fere vv. 19, 27) wHP. 10. οἰκεια w. οἰκια HP. 11. ιδοντες δε (–και) z. διατί (sic v. 14 w) wP. +και πινει (post εσθιει) w. 13. –δε H. ἐστε (pro εστιν) P. ἠλθον w. αλλα ivwHz. 14. προσηλθον τω ιυ H. νηστευουσιν wH. 15. εφοσον χρονον H. ὅτᾶν H. ὅτ' ᾶν i. ὀτ' ᾶν w. αρθη z. νηστευουσιν iw. 16. επιβλημμα z. ῥακκους z. εν (pro επι) H. ἱματ. H. αἱρει wHz. 17. οἶνον bis et οἶνος w. οἰνον νεον εις ασκους βαλλουσι καινους H. αμφοτεροι ivwHz. 18. +τις ivHPz sem., +εἱς w (post αρχων). αρχον P. προσελθων z. sem. προσελθων τω ιυ vHP. προσηλθε τω ιυ και z sem. (init. peri.). κε (loco ὀτι) P rescript. 19. ἠκολουθησεν H*. –σαν H**. 20. αἱμορρουσα w*. αἱμοροουσα P. ὀπισθεν HP. κραπεδου P*. 21. ελεγεν wH**P. ἑαυτη H. +ὀτι (ante εαν) w**. ἁψωμαι wH. ἁψομαι P. σωθησωμαι w. 22. στραφεῖς P. ειπεν wHP. θαρση v. πιστης i*P. σεσωκεν wH**P. 23. την κιαν w. οἰκιαν HP. αυλιτας z*. 24. απεθανεν wH**P. καθευδη Pz. κατεγελλων i*. κατεγελουν z. 25. ὀχλος P. εκρατησεν wH**P. ἡγερθη wHP. 26. εξηλθε δε (–και) v. αὑτη P. 27. init. αι i. ἠκολουθησαν H. υἱος wz [non i]. 28. +αυτω (post δε) P. οἰκιαν wHP. 29. ὀφθαλμων (sic v. 30 P) wHP. πιστην i*. 30. ενεβρημησατο P. μήδεἰς i. μήδεῖς P. 31. οἱ δε w. διεφημησαν iPz. 32. ἴδοῦ P. –ιδου v. 33. εξελθοντος (pro εκβληθεντος) z. ὀχλοι P. –ὀτι ivwHPz. εφωνη z. εν τω rescript. ιηλ marg. P, forsan primâ manu. 34. εκβαλει P. 35. πολης rescript. P. 36. Marg. init. +και πολλοὶ κολουθησαν αυτω w**. εσπλαγνισθη H. επ' αυτους H. ἠσαν wH. εσκυλμενοι ivw, σκυλμενοι z (pro εκλελυμενοι). [H cum Elzev.]. ερρημενοι i. –και ερριμμενοι z. ὡς (pro ὡσει) Hz. εχοντες w. 37. πολοις? i*. ὀλιγοι iwH. 38. εκβαλλη w.

CAP. X. 1. +ὁ ις (ante τους δωδ.) v (Scholz, at tantum rubro) H sem. –δωδεκα z bis. +κατα (ante πνευματων) vz sem. εκβαλεῖν P. θεραπεβειν w. 2. ταυτα εισι z bis. εστιν iw. εισι H. –ιακωβος ad fin. vers. z. 3. –ὁ του z sem. αλφεου? z sem. λεβαιος i. λιβαιος z sem. 4. κανιτης H. καναναιος z sem. και ιουδας ισκαριωθ ὁς και παρεδωκεν H. ισκαριωτης H**. –ὁ secund. ivHz bis. παραδιδους z bis. 5. –τους δωδεκα H sem. Pz. (vv. 2—4 omissis). οδων P. σαμαριτων H* sem. P. 6. πορευεσθαι i*. –μαλλον z. οἰκου P. 7. ἠγγηκεν P. 8. –νεκρους εγειρετε ivwHPz bis (z** habet semel post θεραπευετε). εκβαλετε P. δωτε P. 9. κτησησΤε w (Τ rubro). κτησασθε z. μὴδὲ bis ivwz (sic vv. 10, 14 passim). αργυριον H. 10. πειραν z. μὴδὲ ter H. μὴ (pro μηδε prim.) z. ῥαβδους ivw [non z]. +εστιν (post γαρ) H. του μισθου (*pro* της τροφης) wz. —εστιν Hz. 11. —εξετασατε z. ἄξιος H. εστιν w. 12. οἰκιαν wH. *fin.* +λεγοντες εἰρηνη τω οικω τοῦτω w** *marg.* H (ειρηνη *et* οἰκω H). 13. ει μεν εστιν (*pro* εαν μεν ῃ) z. ἡ wH. ἡ οἰκια w. εισελθετω z. εις (*pro* επ') z. ἡ (*pro* ἡ *secund.*) iwH. επιστραφειη z. 14. αν (*pro* εαν) H. +εξω (*post* εξερχομενοι) H. οἰκιας wH. ἡ H. εκτειναξατε v. 15. γομορας H. γομορρας z. 16. ἴδοῦ P. αποστελλῶ P. οὖν P. φρονημοι P. ὡσεὶ ὀφεις (—οἱ) P. ὡσεὶ (*pro* ὡς οἱ) v. οφης H*. 17. —δε z (*init. peri.*). παραδωσουσιν P. +εις συναγωγας και (*ante* εις συνεδρια) P. μαστηγωσουσιν i*P. 18. ἐνεκεν wHP. 19. ὅτ' ἂν i. ὁτ' ἂν w. ὅτ ἂν HP (*sic v.* 23). παραδιδωσιν i. παραδίδωσιν wP. παραδωσωσιν H**. παραδωσουσιν z. ἡ P. λαλησετε (*pro* λαλησητε) z. —δοθησεται *ad fin. vers.* vP* (*habet* P** *marg.*, *at* ἡμερα *pro* ὡρα). *fin.* λαλησητε iwP**z. 20. *init.* οὐ w. οἱ H. 21. αδελδελφον P. εξ ὑμων (*pro* αυτους) P. 22 ὀνομα P. 23. δηωκωσιν ? i*. —την i. —γαρ v. ἀν H. ἐλθῃ w. 24. +αυτου (*post* διδασκαλον) H. 25. γενητε w. τω δουλω (*pro* ὁ δουλος) H. —ει τον *usque ad v.* 28 μη ουν φοβησθε z. οἰκοδεσποτην H. επεκαλεσαν ivw. οικειακους iv. οἰκειακους wH. 26. —γαρ (*init. peri.*) z. συγκεκαλυμμενον z. απολυφθησεται w. 27. λεγων w. σκοτεια w. εἰπατε H. οὓς w. δοματων w. 28. φοβεισθε (*pro* φοβηθῆτε) iwz *sem.*, *at* φοβησθε z *sem.* αποκτενοντων ivHz *bis.* ἀπὸ κτεννόντων w. —και *secund.* z *sem.* +την (*ante* ψυχην) ivwz *sem.* +το (*ante* σωμα) ivz *sem.* [*non* wH]. εν γεεννη απολεσαι v. 29. πολειται; wH, απολειται z (*pro* πωλειται). της γης H. 30. αἱ H. ἠριθμηνται (—εισι) H. εισιν wz. 31. φοβησθε v. +αυτους (*post* φοβηθητε) wH. +γαρ (*post* πολλων) w. 32. —ουν (*init. peri.*) Pz. ὁμολογηση v. αυτου w* (*pro* εν αυτῳ, εν *supra* w**). +τοις (*ante* ουρανοις) w. 33. *Deest versus in* i. αρνησητε v. ορανοις w. 34. νομησητε w. ἦλθον *bis* w. βαλλεῖν *secund.* w. 36. +οἱ (*ante* εχθροι) i. οικειακοι ivH. οἰκειακοι w. 37. *init.* —ὁ v*. ἡ *bis* H *sem.* P. εστιν *bis* wH**P. 38. ακολουθῃ P*. ὀπισω wHP. εστιν wH *sem.* P. 39. απολεσῃ v. ἐνεκεν wH *sem.* +οὗτος (*ante* εὑρησει) z. εὑρισει w. εὑρησῃ v (*errat Scholz.*). 40. αποστιλαντα H *sem.* 41. ὀνομα *bis* H *sem.* 42. ποτησῃ i*. ἑνα H *sem.* ψυχρου' μονον w. ὁτι ου μη v. απολεσει i*.

CAP. XI. 1. συνετελεσεν H *sem.* μαθητας H*. τους δωδεκα μαθητας z. 2. —ὁ δε z, —δε *et* ὁ ιωαννης *ponitur post* δεσμωτηριω *in* P (*init. peri.*). δεσμοτηριω i. $\overline{\iota\upsilon}$ (*pro* $\overline{\chi\upsilon}$) Pz. 3. ἡ P. 4. ιωανη i. 5. αναβλεπουσιν wP. χολοι iP. περιπατουσιν wP. ακουουσιν wP. 7. ἠρξατο P. ὀχλοις wP. τοις οχλοις λεγειν z. [εξηλθετε P : *sic vv.* 8, 9]. θεασασθε iPz. 8. ἠμφιεσμενον P. ἴδοῦ (*sic v.* 10) P. οἰκοις P. βασιλειῶν ivwz. βασιλειων (*sic*) H.

9. −ὑμιν P**. περισσωτερον v. 10. εστιν HP. ἐγῶ ἀποστελλῶ P. κατασκευαση w. 11. εγειγερται z. εγγεννητοις (*pro* εν γεν.) P. μειζον *secund.* v. 12. −ἑως αρτι P. ἁρπαζουσιν P. 13. προυεφητευσαν v. 14. ἡ (*pro* ει) P. δεξασθε ivz. ἡλιας ivwP [*non* z]. 15. ὦτα v. ὥτα P. 16. −δε (*init. peri.*) z. παιδιοις ivwHz. ἀγοραις w. καθημενοις εν αγοραις z. ἑτεροις i*w. ἑτεροις vwHz. 17. ηὐλησαμεν w. ηὐλισαμεν z. ορχισασθε z. εκωψασθε ?z*. 18. ἦλθεν (*sic v.* 19) w. ηλθεν H. λεγουσιν w. ελεγον z. 19. οἰνοποτης wH. 20. ἠρξατο H *sem.* +ὁ ις (*ante* ὀνειδιζειν) wH. αἱ H. 21. χωραζειν v. χοραζειν w. χωραζην Hz. βηθσαϊδᾶ ivHz. βηδσαϊδαν w. οἱ (*pro* ει) z. σιδονι v**. σινδωνι w*. αἱ *bis* (*sic v.* 23) H. −εν ὑμιν z. +καθημεναι (*post* σπ.) H. 22. ἡ (*pro* ἦ) w : *sic v.* 24. 23. ἡ w, ἦ v (*pro* ἡ). ὑψωθης v. ὑψωθησα w*. +του (*ante* ἀδου) w. ἀδου H. καταβιβασθειση z. *Ras. post* εν *in* H. μεχρη w, *at* αχρι την σημερον z. 25. κε περ v. αυτα (*pro* ταυτα) H. 27. οὐδεῖς P. ει μι (*pro* ει μη) *bis* P. επιγεινωσκει *secund.* i. ὃ (*pro* ᾧ) z. ὁ ἐὰν P. βουλεται w*P. 28. κοποιωντες w. πε *eras. ante* κοπ. P. 29. ἀρατε H. ἐφ' ἡμας w. ἀπ' i. ἐμου P. εὑρησητε i. εὑρησετε P. 30. χς (*pro* χρηστος) P.

Cap. XII. 1. σαββασιν w*. ἠρξαντο H. ηρξατο z*. +τους (*ante* σταχυας) Hz. 2. φαρισσαιοι i*. +οὑτοι (*post* ιδου) v. +τι (*ante* ποιουσιν) z. +τω (*ante* σαββατω) z. 3. *init.* ὁ δε ις i. *Ras. inter* ανεγνω *et* τε H. εποιησεν w. ὁτε z. −αυτος vw* (*habent* w**i) z (επεινασε vz). 4. οἰκον H. ἐξ ὧν (*pro* εξον) z. ἦν w. ἦν z. ειμι w. ἱεροις (*non v.* 5) z. 5. +εν (*post* ὁτι) z. βεβηλουσιν w. ανετιοι i. εισιν w. 6. μειζον iwH. ὡδε wz. 7. ανετιους i. 8. −και ivw. εστιν ὁ υἱος του ανου και του σαββατου Hz. 9. ἦλθεν w. 10. ἦν w. +εκει (*post* ην) Hz. χειραν vH*. κατηγωρησωσιν H. 11. τις εστιν *rescript* ?z. ἐξει iwHz. ἐαν H. +τον (*ante* βοθ.) H. κρατηση wz. 12. μαλλον (*pro* ουν) H. σαββασιν w. καλοποιειν (*pro* καλως ποιειν) z. 13. σου την χειρα H. εξετεινεν w. απεκατεσταθη ivwz. 15. ανεχωρισεν i. ἠκολουθησαν wH *sem.* P. ὀχλοι P. 16. επετημησεν P. ποιησωσιν αυτον H *sem.* 18. ἴδου P *passim.* ηρετησα iz. ἡρετισα vwH. ἡρετησα P. ηὐδοκησεν P. −μου *tert.* v. επαγγελεῖ P. 19. ερησει z. 20. τυφωμενον w*. τυφομενων P. οὐ (*pro* αν) P. εκβαλει i*Pz. εκβαλλη H. 21. −εν ivwHPz. ὀνοματι iHP. ελπιουσιν wHPz. 22. τω καιρω εκεινω (*pro* τοτε) *et* τω ιυ (*pro* αυτω) z, *ut semper* (*e. g. v.* 38) *initio pericopes.* +και (*ante* τυφλος) H*. τον κωφον και τυφλον H. −και (*ante* λαλειν) Hz. 23. +ὁ χς (*post* εστιν) w** (*marg.*) Hz. 24. −τῳ H. 25. ιδως z. καθ' ἑαυτην *bis* iH. οἰκια wH. μερισθησα *secund.* H. 26. σατανὰς *et* σατανὰν z. 27. *init.* και εγω ει εν i. ει δε (−και) H. βεελζεεβουλ (*non v.* 24) i. εκβαλλοῦσιν i. εκβαλοῦσι H. εκβαλλουσιν w. διατοῦτο ivz *fere*. κριται εσονται ὑμων H. 28. εν πνι θυ εγω ivw. ἆρα iv. ἆρα w. *fin.* του θυ; z? 29. *init.* ἢ H. οικειαν *prim.*, *at* οικιαν *secund.* wH *bis*. διαρπᾶσαι iw, *at* ἁρπᾶσαι H. δισῃ H. δεισῃ z. *fin.* διαρπασῃ iwz. ἁρπασει H. 30. *init.* ὁ γαρ μη H. ὢν H *sem.* ὢν P. εστιν wHP. 31. διατοῦτο z. *Rasur. inter* ˢμαρ *et* τια *in* w. −ἡ δε του πνς iP* (*habet marg.* P**, *at* ειδε). 32. εαν (*pro* αν *prim.*) vwH**Pz [*non* i]. −αφεθησεται *usque ad* ἁγιου v*. του του ἁγιου w*. ουτε *bis* HP. εν τω αιωνι τουτω w. εν τω νυν αιωνι ivHz. 33. ἢ *bis* P. επιγινωσκεται P**. επιγινωσκετε z. 34. ὀντες P. περισευματος P. 35. −της καρδιας ivw*HPz (της καρδιας αυτου *bis in versu post* θησαυρου w** *marg.*). εκβαλει P *bis*. −τα (*ante* αγαθα) vwHP**z [*non* i]. +τα (*ante* πονηρα) P**. 36. ἐαν P. αποδωσουσιν wP. τουτου (*pro* αυτου) z. *Post* λογον *in* P *tres lineæ erasæ*. 37. δικαιωθησει P. δικαιωθεισῃ z. *fin.* κατακριθησῃ H. κατακριθησει P, *at* καταδικασθεισῃ z. 38. ειδειν i. 39. ζητει z*. ζητῃ z**. 40. ἦν w. ιωνας εν τῃ κοιλια ην z. +και (*post* εσται) vz. *Hic versus rescriptus usque ad v.* 41 κατακρινου *in* i. 41. μετενοησεν w*. ὡδε (*sic v.* 42 iz) iwz. 42. βασιλεισσα w. νωτου iz. ἦλθεν w. των της γης *rescript. super rasur. in* i. σολομωνος *prim.* z, *bis* vwH [−ωντος *bis* i]. −και ιδου πλειον σολομωνος z. 43. ὅτ' ἂν i. ὀτ' ἂν w. ὅτᾶν H. εκ (*pro* απο) z. οὐχευρισκῃ H. οὐχευρισκει z. 44. οικον w. ελθων iHz. εὑρ. H. +και (*ante* σεσαρωμενον) i. κοσμημενον w. 45. ἑπτα ἑτερα i. αυτου (*pro* ἑαυτου *secund.*) z. ελθοντα v. χειρωνα iz. +εν (*ante* τῃ γενεα) w. 46. ἡ (*pro* οἱ) w. εἱστηκησαν i*. εἱστηκησαν v. εἱστηκεισαν wH. 47. ειπεν (*sic v.* 48) iwH. ἑστηκασι i. εἱστηκεισαν w. ἑστηκασιν H. 48. −εισιν v. 49. −αυτου *secund.* z. 50. −γαρ αν z. ποιησει iz. αδελφοι (*pro* αδελφη) i. εστιν (*super rasur. in* i) ivwHz.

CAP. XIII. 1. −απο H. οικιας wH. 2. ὀχλοι H. εμβαντα εις το πλοιον και καθισαι i. καθισαι H. αἰγιαλον wH. ἤστηκει i. εἱστηκει wH. 3. ελαλει v. −πολλα v. σπειραι Hz. *fin.* του σπειραι τον σπορον αυτου i. 4. ὦ (*pro* ἁ) z. επεσεν wH. ἦλθεν w. ελθοντα (−και *tert.*) H. +του ουρανου (*post* τα πετεινα) wH. 5. ηχε i. ειχεν wH. εξανετειλεν wH. μη μη z. 7. ἀκανθαι H. απεπνηξαν i. 8. ὦ (*pro* ὃ) *ter* z (*sic v.* 23). ἑκατων i. ἑξηκοντα (*sic etiam* v *v.* 23) iwHz. ὁ *tertium* i. 9. ὦτα v *hic*, H. 10. +διδασκαλε (*ante* διατί) i. διά τι wH. τοις οχλοις (*pro* αυτοις) H. 11. γνωναι i. *fin.* δεδωται i. εν παραβολαις (*pro* ου δεδοται) H. 12. αν εχῃ (*pro* εχει *prim.*) z. 13. διατοῦτο z. λαλω αυτοις H. βλεπουσιν w. ακουῶντες i.

συνιουσιν w. ἱνα βλεποντες μη βλεπωσι et μη ακουωσι μηδε συνωσιν μηποτε επιστρεψωσι και τοτε πληρωθησεται (v. 14) H. συνιῶσι z. 14. –επ' ivwHz. ἡ λεγουσα του ἡσαιου z. –ἡ *secund.* ivH. ακοὴ z. ακουσητε vz. ακουσεται w. συνειτε z. βλεψητε vz. ιδειτε ?H*. 15. ὡσιν *bis* w, *prim.* H. ἡκουσαν H. τοις οφθαλμοις *bis* Hz. ὀφθαλμ. *bis* wH. +αυτων (*post* ωσιν) i. ακουσωσιν w. συνωσιν w. επιστρεψουσιν w. ιασομαι ivwHz. 16. –τα z. ὠτα wH. ακουουσι i. ακουουσιν Hz. 17. –πολλοι i. ἁ *prim.* H. ἀκουετε w. 18. σπειραντος H. 19. παντως z. συνιοντος z. ἀρπαζει i, *at* αιρει H. τον (*pro* το) z. 20. πετρωδει i. ευθεως H. δεχομενος και λαμβανον H. 21. εστιν ivH. εστιν· ειτα γενομενης (–δε) z. σκανδαλιζονται z. 22. ακανθα H*. αἰωνος w. απαπη w. συμπνηγει i. 23. επι την καλην γην z. οὑτος i. δει (*pro* δη) z. ἑκατῶν i. ἑξηκοντα H. *fin.* +προσθεσις i (*rubro*). +ὁ εχων ωτα ακουειν ακουετω iH (ὡτα H) z. 24. ὁμοιωθη iz. ὡμοιωθη v. 25. εν δε το iz. ἡλθεν w. εσπειρεν iwH. επεσπειρε z. ζηζανια (*sic vv.* 26, 27, 29, 30, 36, 38, 40) i. ἀναμέσον wz. 26. εποιησεν wH. 27. οἰκοδεσποτου wH. εσπειρες z. –σῳ H. *Rasura in* i *post* εχει. –τα vw [*habent* iHz]. 28. εποιησε v. λεγουσιν (*pro* ειπον) z. συλλεξομεν ivwHz. 29. οὒ z. τον σιτον ἁμα αυτοις i. 30. +ουν (*post* αφετε) Hz. αυξανεσθαι H. αυξανεσθε τα αμφοτερα z. –εν z. –τῳ ivH [*habet* z]. δεισατε z. –εις *prim.* H*. δεσμα z. προς τῶ z. συναγετε v. *fin.* +ὁ εχων ὦτα ακουειν ακουετω H. 31. ὁμοιωθη (*pro* ὁμοια εστιν) P *init. peri.* 32. εστιν *prim.* Hz *sem.*, *secund.* z *sem.* ὅτ' ἂν iH. –δε z *sem.* μειζων wHz *sem.* +παντων (*post* μειζων) wz *sem.* εστιν *secund.* wz *sem.* γινετε H. –και *ult.* H. *fin.* αυτων z *sem.* 33. +λεγων·(*ante* ὁμοια) wz *sem.* ἦν H. εκρυψεν ivz *sem.* [*at* ενεκρυψεν Hz *sem.*]. 34. ὀχλοις i. τους οχλους H*. –ουκ z. ελαλη i*. 36. ἡλθεν w. οἰκιαν wH (+αυτου H). 38. ἀγρος H. –οἱ *prim.* w*. 39. σπειρων z. +ἡ (*ante* συντελεια) i. 40. –ουν z. τα ζιζανια συλλεγετε H. καιεται ivwHz. αἰωνος z. 42. βαλλουσιν (*sic v.* 50) z. ὀδοντων (*sic v.* 50) ivwH. 43. ἡλιος i. ὡτα H. 44. α εστ *mutat. in* H. –τῳ i*Hz. εὑρων i. εκρυψεν iwH. –αυτου z *bis.* αγωραζει w. 45. ὁμοιωθη (*pro* ὁμοια ἐστιν) P *init. peri.* 46. *init.* οὒς P*, ὃν z *sem.* εὑρῶν P. ἓνα P. πολυτημον w. πεπρακεν wP. ειχεν iwHP. ἠγορασεν iwP. 47. σαγηνει v. βληθησα P. βληθεισα z. συναγαγοῦσα z. 48. *Rasura post* ὁτε *in* P. αναβηβασαντες iP. εις (*pro* επι) z. αἰγιαλον iwP. καθησαντες P. συνεεξαν P. 49. αφοριουσιν w. 52. διατοῦτο iz. τη βασιλεια (*pro* εις την βασιλειαν) w. οἰκοδεσποτη wP. 53. συνετελεσεν P. 54. ηλθεν *et* +και (*ante* εδιδασκεν) z *bis.* –αυτους *prim.* z *sem.*, *at* εδιδασκε τους οχλους *sem. init. peric.* τους εν *vix primâ manu in* i. εκπλησσεσθαι ivwH. τούτο

H. ἡ δυναμις i. αἱ (*sic v.* 56) H. 55. οὐχ' *prim.* vHz *sem.* ουχ (*pro* ουχι) z *sem.* λεγετε H. μαρια z *sem.* +λεγονται (*ante* ιακωβος) z *sem.* –και ιωσης v. ιωαννης (*pro* ιωσης) Hz *sem.* +ουχι προς ἡμας εισι; (*post* αδελφοι αυτου, *cœteris in versu omissis*) z *sem.* 56. οὐν τούτο H. ταυτα τουτω (–παντα) z *sem.* παντα ταυτα iwH. –ποθεν ην *ad fin. vers.* z *sem.* 57. ἑαυτω (*pro* αυτω) iz *sem.* ἑ (*pro* εστι) z* *sem.* προφητις i. πατριδη w. οἰκεια i. οἰκια w. –και εν τη οικια αυτου H* (*habet marg. antiquâ manu*). 58. –πολλας z *semel.*

CAP. XIV. 1. τω καιρω εκεινω (–εν) z *init. peri.* ἡκουσεν wH. 2. ειπεν iwH. βαπτισθης w. +γαρ (*ante* ηγερθη) z. ἡγερθη wH. διατοῦτο ivz. αἱ H. –εν z. 3. εδεισεν z. +τη (*ante* φυλ.) H. εις φυλακην z. 4. ελεγεν wz. –γαρ z. –ὁ H*z. εξεστιν wz. εχην w. 5. εφοβητω z. ὀχλον H. 6. γενομενων (*pro* αγομενων) z. ὠρχησατο H. ορχησατο z. ηρεσεν w. ἡρεσε H. 7. μεθ' ὁρκου i. ὡμολογησεν vz. αυτην z. δουναι αυτη w. αἰτησηται w. 8. προβιβασθησα i. –ὡδε Hz. ὧδε iv?w. 9. ὅρκους iv. εκελευσεν iw. 10. απεκεφαλησε i. απεκεφαλισεν w. 11. ἡνεχθη iw. 12. ἦραν (*sic v.* 20) w. +αυτου (*post* σωμα) i. 13. ακουσας δε (–και) Hz. εις πλοιον z. κατιδιαν (*sic v.* 23) ivz [*non* w]. ἰδιαν H. οἱ i. ἡκολουθησαν wH. πεζοι z. 14. εξελθον w*. ειδεν iw. ιδεν ὁ ις P, ειδεν ὁ ις z, *init. peric.* ὀχλον P. εσπλαγχνησθη P. επ' αυτοις ivwHPz. εθεραπευσεν wHP. 15. ὀψιας (*sic v.* 23) iwP (Ὁ *rubro* i). ἡδη P. ὀχλους HP. +κυκλω (*ante* κωμας) w**P*. αγωρασωσιν w. 17. *init.* οἱ w. εχωμεν i. ὡδε (*sic v.* 18) iwz. ὧδε P (*at* ὧδε *v.* 18). εἰ μὶ v. ἰχθυας (*sic v.* 19) w. 18. +ις (*post* ὁ δε) H. ειπεν wHP. φερεται P. 19. εκελευσας P*. ὀχλους P. ανακληθηναι iP, *at* αναπεσειν Hz. –και *secund.* ivwHP**z. ευλογησεν wHP. εδωκεν wHP. ὀχλοις P. 20. ἡραν P. περισευον i. κωφινους w. κωφηνους P. πληρης vz. 21. ἦσαν P. ὡσεὶ H. 22. ἡναγκασεν iwHP *bis* (Ἡ *rubro* i). –αὐτου i**HP *sem. tantum*, z *sem. tantum.* αυτους (*pro* αυτον) H*. οὗ wH. απολυσει iP *bis* z *sem.* ὀχλους P *bis.* 23. –και απολυσας τους οχλους P* (*habet marg., at* ὀχλους P**). ὀρος iP. κατίδιαν H. κατιδιαν z, *etiam* P *hoc loco* (*cf. v.* 13). ὀψιας H. ἦν (*sic v.* 24 *bis*) wP. 24. ἡδη P. ἦν H. κοιματων i. ὁ *mutatum in* P. 25. απηλθεν iwH**P. 26. επι της θαλασσης i. εστιν wH**P. 27. –ευθεως *usque ad* λεγων w* (*habet marg. s. m.*). φοβεισθαι w. 28. –αυτω wHz. ειπεν iwHP. ελθειν προς σε i. 30. εκραξεν wP. 31. ὀλιγοπιστε wHP. 32. εμβαντως αυτου z. 33. –εν τῳ πλοιῳ P* (*habet margo*). –τῳ w* (*habet marg.*). αυτο w. 34. ἠλθον wP. γενησαρετ iP (*sic* z *in v.* 35, *init. peric.*). γενησαρεθ Hz. 35. επιγνωντες i. –αυτον i.

ὁλην i. ηνεγκαν z. 36. και (*pro* ἱνα) H. ἁψωνται iwH. ὁσοι w. ἡψαντο H.

CAP. XV. 1. φαρισαῖοι w. 2. διὰ τί (*sic v.* 3) iwH. –σου v. παραβαινουσιν w. παραδωσιν (*sic vv.* 3 iw, 6 w) iw. νιπτωνται ?i*. ὁτ' ἀν iwH. +τον (*ante* αρτον) w. εσθιουσιν z. 3. αυτους H*. παραβαινετε, *rasurâ sequente in* i. των ανων (*pro* ὑμων) H. 4. –σου ivHz. τὴν *mutatum in* i. ἡ (*sic v.* 5 *bis* i) iH. 5. λεγεται i. αν (*pro* εαν) H. ὠφεληθης H. τιμησει H. 6. ἠκυρωσατε wH. παραθεσιν (*pro* παραδοσιν) z. 7. προεφυτευσε i. προεφητευσεν vwHz. 8. εγγιζη i*. χιλεσι i. χειλεσιν w. 9. διδασκωντες i. αυτων (*pro* ανθρωπων) z. 10. συνειτε z. 11. οὐ H. –τουτο v. 12. προσηλθον, *item* και ειπον (*init. peric.*) z. εσκανδαλισθησαν ακουσαντες τον λογον Hz. 13. ειπεν iwH. ἦν H. 14. αφεται w. –τυφλοι i. εμπεσουνται v. 16. *fin.* εστε· w*. 17. αφεδρονα w. 18. εξερχονται i. 19. λογισμοι z. 20. χερσιν w. –το δε ανιπτοις *ad fin. vers.* v*. 21. εισῆλθεν ὁ ις (*pro* ανεχωρησεν) Pz *init. peric.* μερει w. 22. ἰδοῦ P. ὁριων iv. υιος z. 23. λογω z. ἡρωτων wHP. αυτων (*pro* αυτον) z*. ὀπισθεν iHPz. 24. απεσταλη z. απολωλωτα P. οἰκου HP. 25. απελθουσα w. ἐξελθοῦσα H. προσεκυνησεν ivwHPz. 26. εστιν P. βαλλεῖν P. 27. ειπε z [ειπεν iwHP]. πιπτωντων P. 28. ὦ wP πιστης i*P. πιστι [σ *mut.*] H. θελης iP. ἠαθη H. 29. ηλθεν i. ἠλθεν w. ὀρος i. 30. +οἱ (*ante* οχλοι) i. χολους i. κωφους τυφλους w. κυλους z. 31. ὡσται i. βλεποντα H*. κωφους ακουοντας· αλαλους λαλουντας· Hz. κυλους ὑγιης z. 32. προσκαλεσαμενος ὁ ις z *init. peric.* ειπεν iHP. ειπεν αυτοις w. ὀχλον P. ἠδη P. ἡμεραι iwHPz [*non* v]. πρὸςμένουσιν P. εχωσιν w. τι *rescript. in* P. φαγωσιν wP. ὁδω i. 33. ὀχλον wP. 34. *init.* –και z. ἑπτα (*sic vv.* 36, 37) iP. ὀλιγα iwHP. ἰχθυδια (*sic* ἰχθυας *v.* 36) w. 35. εκελευσεν wHP. ὀχλοις P. 36. +δυο (*ante* ιχθυας) P*z. εκλασεν wHP. εδωκεν wH**P. ὀχλω (*sic v.* 39) P. τοις οχλοις H. 37. ἡραν wHP. περισευον i. πληρης vz. 38. ἡσαν wP. 39. ανεβη (A *rubro* i) ivwPz [*non* H]. ἦλθεν w. ἦλθεν P. ὁρια ivw. ὀρη P. μαγδαλὰν w. αμαγδαλα P. μαγδαλᾶ z.

CAP. XVI. 1. –οἱ H *sem.* z. +οἱ (*ante* σαδδουκαιοι) H *sem.* –πειραζοντες H *sem.* επηρωτων H *sem.* *fin.* αυτος ?H. 2. ὀψιας iwH. λεγεται vz. πυραζει vwH *sem.* z (*sic v.* 3, vH *sem.* z). 3. πρωϊας ivH *sem.* –ὑποκριται z. –μεν v. διακρινειν γινωσκετε H *sem.* *fin.* +γνωναι H *sem.* z. 4. επιζητη z. καταλειπων i. καταλοιπων w. απηλθεν iw. 5. λαβειν αρτους w. 8. –αυτοις w* (*habet marg.*). διαλογιζεσθαι i*. ὀλιγοπιστοι iwH. 9. οὐπω H. πεντακεσχιλιων i. –κοφινους z. 10. ποσους z. 11. αρτων iwz. +προσεχετε δε i**, +αλλα z (*post* προσεχειν). 12. *Deest versus in* v*. ειπεν wH. αλλα iwHz. −φαρισαιων και z. 13. −δε Pz *init. peric.* ἠρῶτα wHP. 14. ειπαν w. +αυτω (*post* ειπον) P. ἡλιαν vwP [*non* iHz]. ἑτεροι δε ἱερεμιαν H. ἢ ἕνα P. 15. λεγεται i. 16. ειπεν iwHPz. 17. προς αυτον H. ἰωνὰ P. απεκαλυψεν wHP. αλλα P*. 18. οἰκοδομησω wP. κατισχυσωσιν v. 19. δησεις P. ἐαν *secund.* H. λυσεις P. λελυμενων P*. 20. μήδενὶ w. μηδὲν z. −ις w [*habent* ivHz]. 21. −ηρξατο w* (*habet marg.*). εγερθυναι ?w. 22. −αυτον v. ηρξαντο w*. επιτημαν H. αυτον (*pro* αυτω) z. +και (*ante* λεγων) z. συ (*pro* σοι) H. οὐ H. 23. επιστραφεις w. ειπεν (*sic v.* 24) wH. ὀπισω iwH. −σκανδαλον μου ει z. 24. ἡτις θελη P *sem.* ὀπισω iwHP. απαρνισασθω H *sem.* ἑαυτου (*pro* αὐτου *secund.*) v. ακολουθητω vz. 25. εαν (*pro* αν) z. απολεση (*pro* -ει) i*z. ἑνεκεν H. εὑρησῃ z. 26. ὠφελειται wH. ανταλαγμα wHz. 27. δοξει z. ἑκαστω H. τα εργα (*pro* την πραξιν) z. 28. αμην αμην z. εισιν w. ὡδε z [*non* iwH]. ἑστηκοτων wz. τινὲς ὡδε ἑστοτες iv (ἑστωτες v). των ὡδε ἑστώτες H. γευσονται ivw.

CAP. XVII. 1. αυτον (*pro* αυτους) P*. ὀρος P. κατιδιαν (*sic v.* 19) ivPz [*non* w]. 2. μετεμορφωθει w. αυτον (*pro* αυτων) P*. ελαμψεν wH**Pz. ἡλιος H. εγενοντο wHPz. 3. ἴδοῦ (*sic v.* 5) P. ὠφθησαν wP. μωυσης wHz [*non* ivP]. ἡλιας vwP. συλαλουντες P. 4. ειπεν iwHP. −κε v*. ὡδε *bis* (*sic v.* 17) iwHz [*non* P]. εἱναι w. ποιησομεν z. συ (*pro* σοι) P. −και μωση μιαν z* (*habet marg.*). μωσει v. μωυσει w [*non* iH]. ἡλιαν μιαν w. ἡλια vP [*non* iHz]. 5. +δε (*post* ετι) P. νεφελῃ φωτεινῃ i. φωτινη P. οὗτος P. ηυδοκησα vH*. ηὐδοκησα P. 6. οἱ w. 7. φοβεισθαι w*. 8. ὀφθαλμους wHP. ἴδον P. ειμι P. 9. εκ (*pro* απο) ivwHz. ὀρους P. μήδενὶ iPz. μήδενι w. εἶπητε P. ὀραμα vw. ἕως σοῦ P. 10. −και z *init. peric.* ὀτι (*pro* τι ουν) z. −ουν H. ἡλιαν vwz [*non* iH]. 11. ἡλιας (*sic v.* 12) vw [*non* iz]. 12. −δε H. ἠλθεν wH. εγνωσαν z. αλλα w. ἠθελησαν iwH. οὑτως ivwHz. 14. προσηλθε τω ιυ (−αυτω) v. +τις (*post* ανος) ivPz *sem.* ανος τις προσηλθε τω ιυ H *sem. init. peric.* αυτον (*pro* αυτῳ *secund.*) ivwHPz *bis.* 15. −γαρ z *sem.* −και *tertium* P*. −το *secund.* z *sem.* 16. εδυνηθησαν w. −αυτον z *sem.* 17. ὦ i. ὦ v. ὦ H *sem.* P. ἑως *bis* H *sem.* −ἑως ποτε *usque ad* ανεξομαι ὑμων H *sem.* z *sem.* εσωμαι i*z *sem.* ανεξωμαι z *sem.* ἑως *secundum usque ad* επετιμησεν *v.* 18 *super rasuram in* i. ὡδε vH. ὧδε P. 19. προελθοντες w* (σ *insertum rubro*). πρὸσέλθώντες P. ειπον κατιδιαν z. διὰ τί iwP. ὑμεις (*pro* ἡμεις) iP. εδυνηθημεν w. *fin.* αυτω H. 20. απιστειαν P. +ὀτι (*ante* εαν) P**. εχειτε HP. τιστην i. ὀρει H. ὀρη P. μεταβηθη HP.

21. οὐκ H. ειμι H. 22. *fin.* +ἁμαρτωλων z. 23. αποκτενουσι w. 24. ελθωντων w. διδραγμα *bis* HP [*non* i]. τα διδραγματα *prim.* z, *at* τω διδραγμα *secund.* z*. +και (*ante* λεγει) i. 25. εισηλθον i. οἰκιαν wHP. λαμβανουσιν wP. τελει P. ἢ *bis* P. απο *secund.*, *rescript. in* i. 26. ἆράγε iv. 27. –την P*. βαλλε P. αναβαινοντα vHPz [*non* i]. –και (*ante* ανοιξας) z. εὑρησει P*.

CAP. XVIII. 1. τω ῑυ οἱ μαθηται αυτου Hz. λεγοντες αυτω z. ἆρα iv. ἆρα w. την̀ βασιλειαν H*. 2. αυτω (*pro* αυτο) iH*P. 3. –αμην λεγω ὑμιν v*. γενῆσθε P**. 4. ὁστις ουν *rescript. in* i. ὡστις οὖν P. ταπεινωσει ivHPz *bis.* ἑαὐτον H *sem.* ὡς w. οὐνων H *sem.* 5. δεξητε w. –ἐν wz. 6. ἑνα H. μῦλος vz. ὀνικος wH. εις (*pro* επι) ivw [*non* z]. 7. οὐαι H. διοῦ τα σκανδαλα H. *fin.* εισερχεται v. 8. ἠ (*pro* ει) iH. σκανδαλιζη i*. –εισελθειν v*. εις την ζωην εισελθειν v**w. ἢ ἢ v. κυλον z. –η δυο χειρας v*. 9. –ὁ w. ὀφθαλμ. w *bis.* +αυτον (*post* βαλε) z. εστιν Hz. γεεναν Hz. 10. ὁρατε H *sem.* ἑνος HP. ἀγγελοι z *sem.* διαπαντὸς ivwz *ter.* βλεπουσιν P. 11. ἠλθεν wP. –γαρ P*. +ζητησαι και (*ante* σωσαι) H** *manu antiquâ,* Pz *bis.* 12. ἑκατον iHP. αφης P. ἐνενηκοντὰ ἑνεα i. ἐνενηκονταεννεα v. ἐνενήκοντα ἐννέα wHPz (ἐνενίκ. P) *sic v.* 13. ὀρη P. πορευθης i. πλανομενον Pz. 13. εὑρεῖν αὐτῶ P. επ' αυτο iv. ἢ (*sic v.* 16) H. 14. εστιν wP. μου (*pro* ὑμων) z. +τοις (*ante* ουρανοις) iP. απωληται vz. εἱς P. 15. ἀμαρτηση H. ἀμαρτη z. –μονου P* (*habet marg.*). 16. +σου (*post* δε) P. παραλα H*. σεαυτου (*pro* σου) wL. ετη v. ἑνα ἢ P. ἢ *secund.* P. 17. τῆ (*pro* της) w*. τη εκκλησια (*pro* της εκκλησιας) P. ἐστωH. ὡσπε i*. εθνηκος i*Pz. 18. αμην αμην z *sem.* +γαρ (*post* αμην) P. αν (*pro* εαν) *bis* Lz, *prim.* wz. δεισητε z *sem.* δεδενα P*. –και ὁσα *ad fin. vers.* z *sem.* 19. +αμην (*post* παλιν) ivwLHz *bis* [*non* P]. +εξ (*ante* ὑμων) L. συμφωνησουσιν Hz *sem.* αἰτησωνται w. αιτησονται iPz *sem.* οὐνοις H *sem.* 20. ὁπου (*pro* οὑ) L, οὖ iH *sem.* εισιν HP. ἢ P. ὀνομα H *sem.* 21. –αυτῳ *prim.* i*. ειπεν iwLHz (+αυτω Hz). ἁμαρτηση vH. ὁ αδελφος μου εις εμε L. αφισω i. ἐπτακις i. 22. ἑβδομικοντακις i. ἑβδομηκοντακις wH. ἑπτα i. 23. διατοῦτο vL. ὁμοιωθη LP*z. ηθελησεν i. ἠθελησεν wHP. 24. ὀφειλετης iwH. ὀφιλετης P. 25. ὁ κς αυτου *super ras. in* i. ειχεν wH**P. 26. πεσῶν z. οὐν (*sic v.* 29) P. προσεκυνη P. –κε v*. αποδωσω σοι L. αποδοσω i*. 27. σπλαγχισθεις L. δανιον wLH. 28. ἑνα HP. ὁς *rescript. in* P. ὡφειλεν P. ἑκατον iHP. επνιγεν wH**P. επνηγε z. –μοι w. ειτι (*pro* ὁ,τι) ivwLHPz. οφειλης L. ὀφειληςwP. ὀφειλεις H. 29. συνλος P. ἀπαντα σοι αποδωσω L. –παντα ivHPz. σοι αποδωσω w.

30. ηθελησεν L. αλλα ivwLHPz. αυτον *bis script.* L. –αυτον z. ωφειλομενον i*. ὀφειλομενον (*sic v.* 34) wP. 31. γινομενα *prim.* z, *at* νομενα P*. απελθοντες L. εσαφησαν L. ἑαυτων ivwHP**, *at* αὑτων z. 32. προσκαλεσαμενος δε (–τοτε) w. ὀφειλην wP. αφηκασι (*pro* αφηκα σοι) z. *fin.* μοι (*pro* με) z. 33. καγω P*z. ἠλεησα wP. 34. οργισθης i*. ὀργισθεις H. –τοις L. βασανησταις P. 35. οὑτως ivwLHPz. –μου H*. ουρανιος w. [*nil omissum in his codicibus*].

CAP. XIX. 1. μετειρεν H. +της (*ante* γαλιλαιας) ivwLHz. ἠλθεν w. ὁρια iv. 2. ἠκολουθησαν wH. 3. –οἱ wH (φαρισαιοι τω ιυ H). αυτω (*pro* αυτον) L. –αυτῳ *secund.* wHP**. αἰτιαν (*sic v.* 10) w. 4. απ᾽ αρχης ὁ ποιησας L. απαρχην w. ἀπαρχης H. [ἀπ᾽ ἀρχῆς ivPz]. 5. ἑνεκεν wHP. καταληψει iLP. την μρα αυτου και τον πρα L. +αυτου (*post* πρα) iH** *antiquâ manu*, Pz. κολληθησεται vLH. προκολληθησεται w. γυναικη P. 6. οὐκ ἔτι iwHP [*non* vLz]. εισιν P. οὖν (*sic v.* 7) P. εζευξεν z. 7. –λεγουσιν αυτω P* (*habet marg.*). μωυσης w [*non* Lz]. 8. +ὁ ις (*ante* ὁτι) z. μωυσης wL [*non* z]. ἀπαρχῆς LP [*non* ivwHz]. οὑτως ivwLPz. οὑτως H. 9. –ὁτι v. απολυσει iP. –ει ivwH*Pz. παρεκτος λογου πορνειας (*pro* ει μη επι πορν.) L. –και ὁ απολελ. *ad fin. vers.* L. γαμων (*pro* γαμησας) w. 10. +αυτου (*post* γυναικος) w. 11. *init.* ὁ δε ις w. χορουσι i. χωρουσιν wP. 12. εισιν wP. οἱτινες *ter* w. +αυτων (*post* μρς) P**. εγενηθησαν iz. οὑτως ivwLHPz. +οἱ (*ante* εισιν *tert.*) L. ευνουχησαν iv?LPz. 13. και (*pro* τοτε) Hz. προσηνεχθησαν i. επιθη αυτοις (αυτω z) τας χειρας Hz. 14. ειπε v. κωλυσετε L*. κωλυσητε L**. 15. τας χειρας αυτοις Lz. 16. νεανισκος τις προσηλθεν (προσηλθε Hz) τω ιυ γονυπετων αυτον και λεγων HPz *init. peri.* αυτω ειπεν L. 17. +ις (*ante* ειπεν) v. ει μι i*w. –ὁ *secund.* P*. [*cætera cum Elzevir.* ivwLHPz]. ελθειν z. εις την ζωην εισελθειν w. 18. –ιησους z. ειπεν iwLHP. –το P**. φωνευσεις i. φονευσης P. κλεψης P. 19. –σου *prim.* ivHz [*non* L]. ἑαυτον wLPz [*non* ivH]. 20. ταυτα παντα ivL. *Rasura post* τι *in* w. ετη P. *fin.* στερω w*. 21. λεγει (*pro* εφη) L. θελης i. *Rasura post* ὑπαρχοντα *in* P. δως w. ἑξεις iwHPz. δευρω i*P. ακολουθη P. 22. απηλθεν wP. ἦν w. ἧν P. 23. ειπεν wHP. πλουσιος δυσκολως L. δυσκολος P. 24. εστιν P. διατρυμαλιας w. τρυπιματος P*. εισελθειν (*pro* διελθειν) vwL [*non* iPz]. ἡ P. πλουσιος L. των ουνων (*pro* του θυ) v. 25. –αυτου wL. ἆρα iv. ἆρα w. δυνατε iw. 26. λεγει (*pro* ειπεν) w. εστιν *prim.* wLP. –εστι *secund.* wL, *at* εστιν iHPz. 27. αποκριθεις δε (–τοτε) HPz (*init. peric.*). +κε (*ante* ιδου) iHPz. ἠκολουθησαμεν wP. ἆρα iw. *fin.* ὑμιν i*P. 28. –ὁ i. αυτω (*pro* αυτοις) H*.

[*Desunt puncta in* LPz, *cum Elzev.* i]. ὁτ' ἂν iwP. ὅτᾶν H. καθηση P. **καθησεσθε** LP. καθισεσθαι z. ευμεις ?L*. κριναντες i. φιλας z. τουτο (*pro* του) ιηλ L*. 29. ὀστις (*pro* ὁς) wL*. οικιαν w. οικιας HP. ἢ *quinquies* H, *sexies* P. ἐνεκεν wHP. ονοματος HP. ἑκατὸν ταπλασίονα w. **ἑκατὸνταπλασίονα** HP. ἑκατονταπλασίωνα z. 30. +οἱ (*ante* εσχατοι *secund.*) L.

Cap. XX. 1. ὡμοιωθη H, ὁμοιωθη P (−γαρ εστιν) *init. peric.* −γαρ z. **οἰκοδεσποτη** wP. τω πρωι w. 2. και συμφωνησας ivw**HP [*non* L], και **συνεφωνησε** z, (δε *omisso*). 3. −την ivwLHz. ἴδεν P. εν τη αγορα ἑστωτας L. ἑστωτας iwP. αγωρα P. 4. και εκεινοις ivLH. κακεινους P. ὑπαγεται P. +μου (*post* αμπελωνα) wL. ἢ w. 5. +την (*ante* ἑκτην) P. ἑκτην ὡραν και εννατην w. εννατην L [*non* vPz]. ἑνατην iH. ὡσαῦτως H. ὡσαῦτως P. 6. ἑνδεκατην wHP. εὑρεν P. ἀλλους w. ἑστωτας wP. ὡδε wL *ut videtur* ?z [*non* iP]. ἑστηκατε iwP. 7. οὐδεῖς P. +και (*ante* λεγει) z. +μου (*post* αμπελωνα) w. ὂ i. ἢ P. δι ον (*pro* δικαιον) L*. λιψεσθε P. δωσω ὑμιν (*pro* ληψεσθε) v. 8. ὀψιας iwP. κυρις v. αποδως i. 9. ελθοντες ουν (−και) L. ἑνδεκατην iwHP. ὡραν P. ἀναδηνάριον iwHPz. 10. και ελθοντες (−δε) L. ενομησαν iwHP. πλειον L. λιψονται P. ἀναδήναριον iLHP**z. 11. εγογγυζων i. οἰκοδεσποτου wHP. 12. ὡραν P. εποιησαν *secund.* P*. ἰσους w. αυτους ἡμιν L. βαστασασιν w*P. καυσωνα; vwz. 13. ἑνι P. ἑταιρε i. ἑτερε P. δηναριω i**. δηναριον w. συνεφωνησα σοι z. 14. ἆρον w. ἄρον Pz. *fin.* ὡσπερ και συ P. 15. ἢ *prim.* P. εξεστιν w. ὁ θελω ποιησαι L. ει (*pro* η *secund.*) ivLHPz. −ὁ *art.* w*. ὀφθαλμος wP. μου (*pro* σου) L. 16. −οἱ *prim.* i*? εισιν wP. ὀλιγοι iwP. 17. αναβαινον H. παραλαμβανει ὁ ις τους δωδεκα μαθητας αυτου z *init. peric.* παρελαβεν w. κατιδιαν ivz [*non* L]. και εν τη ὁδω ειπεν Lz. 18. κατακρίνουσιν L. 20. αἰτουσα iw. 21. ἐξευωνυμων vwLHz. ἐξευονυμων i (*sic v.* 23). +σου (*ante* εν τη βασ.) ivLHz. 22. οἴδατε (*sic v.* 25) vz. αἰτεισθε w. ποιειν (*pro* πιειν) i. μελω H**. πιειν (*pro* πινειν) z. η (*pro* και) iwLz (ἢ H) [*non* v]. 23. +ὁ ις (*ante* το μεν) L. +μου (*post* βαπτισμα) L. −ὁ εγω βαπτιζομαι L. −μου (*post* δεξιων) L. ἐξευωνυμων wLH. −και εξ ευωνυμων μου z. −μου *tert.* iw. ἐμῶν H. το δουναι i. +τουτο (*post* δουναι) w. ἀλλῦ H*. ἀλλῦς H**. ἡτοιμασται i. 24. ακουσαντες δε (−και) L. οἱ H. ἠγανακτησαν w. ἠγανακτισαν H. 25. −κατακυριευουσιν *ad* μεγαλοι v* *fin.*; w. 26. οὐχ' ivHz. −δε vw*L. γενεσθαι μεγας εν ὑμιν z. γενεσθαι μεγας v. εσται (*pro* εστω) iLH [*non* vz]. διακωνος i. 27. −εαν w. εσται (*pro* εστω) iwLH [*non* z]. 28. ἠλθεν w. ηλθεν διακονιθηναι H. 29. εκπορευομενου αυτου iv, *at* του ιῡ Pz *init. peric.* ἱεριχω ivwLz. ἵεριχῶ P. ἠκολουθησεν wHP. ὀχλος P. πολλυς i*. 30. ιησου (*pro* κ̄ε) L. υἱε vwLHPz. 31. *Deest versus in* P. *Rasura post* σι *in* σιωπησωσιν w. σιωπησωσι v. μειζων iLz. εκραυγαζον L. —λεγοντες z. κ̄ε ελεησον ἡμας L. υἱε vwHz [*non* L]. 32. αυτοις H**. ειπεν iwLHP. 33. ἱν w*. ανυχθωσιν i*. ανοιγωσιν L. ὑμων i*H. 34. σπλαγχνισθης i*. ἡψατο w. ομματων (*pro* οφθαλμων) L. ὀφθαλμ. *semel* wH, *bis* P. ἠκολουθησαν wHP.

CAP. XXI. 1. ἡγγησεν ὁ ῑς P *bis* z, *init. peric., at* ηγγισεν z. +ὁ ῑς *rubro post* ηγγισαν v**. ἡγγισαν i. εροσολυμα P* *sem.* ἠλθον w. ηλθεν iz. ἦλθεν P *bis.* βηθσφαγη και βηθανιαν L. βηθσφαγῆ ivwHP *sem.* z. βηθσφαγην P *sem.* ὀρος P *bis.* —ὁ ῑς HP *bis* z. —ὁ w*. απεστειλεν wHP *bis.* δυο των μαθητὼν αυτου L. 2. αυτους (*pro* αυτοις) P*. πορευεσθε L. κατεναντι L. εὑρησητε w. εὑρησεται P *sem.* εὑρησετε P *sem.* ὀνον (*sic v.* 7) HP *bis.* 3. ἐὰν P *sem.* τί· i. ,τί ερειτε L. —ὀτι w. αποστελλει ivP *sem.* z. αποστέλει LHP *sem.* [*cum Elzev.* w]. 4. ὀλον i. ὑπο (*pro* δια) L. 5. εἶπατε P *bis.* σιῶν P *sem.* +ὀτι (*ante* ιδου) z. ἴδου P *bis.* βασιλευσου z. ερχετε P *bis.* —και (*ante* πωλον) L. υἱῶν P *bis.* 6. θως προς H** *super ras.* προεταξεν L. 7. ἠγαγον iwHP *bis.* την (*pro* τον) L. ἐπ' (*pro* επανω *prim.*) L. αυτω (*pro* αυτων *prim.*) L. επεκαθισεν iLHz. εκαθησεν w. επεκαθησεν vP *bis.* 8. πλειστως P *sem., at* πληστος *sem.* ὀχλος P *bis.* αυτων (*pro* ἑαυτων) LP *bis.* τα ἱματια ἑαυτων z. —τα ἱματια v. 9. ὀχλοι (*sic v.* 11) HP *bis.* +αυτον (*post* προαγοντες) L. ακολουνούντες P* *sem.* ὡσάννὰ *bis* (*sic v.* 15) vwLHP *bis* z, [*non* i]. *In* P* *semel,* τω υἱω *ad fin. vers. rescript. post* ὡσαννὰ *secund., at eras.* 10. τι L. *fin.* οὑτως P *sem.* 11. ναζαρετ ivwLPz (ἀποναζ. iwL). [ναζαρεθ H.] 12. τω καιρω εκεινω (*pro* και) z *init. peric.* εξεβαλεν wH. πολουντας w. κολυβιστων Hz. κατεστρεψεν iw. πολουντων wH. 13. οἰκος *bis* w. 14. χωλοι και τυφλοι ivwHz (χολοι i, τοίφλοι H) [L *cum Elzev.*]. —εν τῳ ἱερῳ L. 15. οἱ γραμματεις και οἱ αρχιερεις L. —οἱ *secund.* w. εποιησεν wLHP *bis.* ἠγανακτησαν wHP *bis.* 16. +ουκ (*ante* ακουεις) vH. ουδε ποται P *sem.* ανεγνωται P *sem.* θυλαζοντων i. κατηρτησω iP *sem.* αἰνον vwHP *sem.* 17. καταλειπῶν P *sem.* βιθανιαν H. ηὑλισθη wHP *bis.* 18. παραγων H* *sem.* επαν H** *manu antiquâ.* +ὁ ῑς (*post* επαναγων) i*w** (*rubro*) z. επεινασεν wLH. επηνασε i*. 19. ἠλθεν w. ἐπ' (*pro* εν) H* *sem.* z. ειμι i. φυλα iH *sem.* μὴκέτι LHz *sem.,* μηκ' ἔτι iw. παρὰχρῆμα (*sic v.* 20) H *sem.* z *bis. fin.* συκῆ i. 20. +αυτου (*post* μαθηται) H *sem.* 21. πιστην i*H *sem.* —το z. ποιησητε H *sem.* z *bis.* 22. εαν (*pro* αν) ivwLH *sem.* ἂν H *sem.*

αιτησηται L. αἰτησητε w. *fin.* ὁτι ληψεσθαι i (ληψεσθε i**). 23. ελθοντος **αυτου** L. **ποια** ταυτα εξουσια (βα w**) w. η (*pro* και *tert.*) v. τι σοι w. **εδωκεν** wH. 24. **ερωτισω** i. **καγω** ὑμας w. ἑνα λογον z *sem.* ἑνα H *sem.* **και εγω** *secund.* L. 25. εστιν (*pro* ην) z *sem.* ἡ H *sem.* διελογηζοντο w. **διελογιζον** L. εν (*pro* παρ') z *sem.* ἑαυτοις H *sem.* ὑμιν (*pro* ἡμιν) w. διά **τί** wH [*non* Lz]. −ουν vz *sem.* 26. −ὡς L. 27. ὑμιν λεγων w. ὑμιν **λεγω** L. ποι L*. 28. −δε L. +τις (*post* ανος) w**LH* *sem.* z *bis.* ειχεν **w**H**** *sem.* προσελθον i. ειπεν iwLHz *bis.* −τεκνον z. −μου w. 29. **υπαγω κε και ουκ απηλθεν** (*pro* ου θελω *ad fin. vers.*) L. μεταμεληθῆς i. **απηλθεν** (*sic v.* 30) w. 30. προσελθων δε (−και) L. ἑτερω (*pro* δευτερῳ) **vwLH**** *sem.* z *semel tantum.* ειπε z. ὡσαύτως iH *sem.* ὡσαύτως H *sem.* **ου θελω·** ὑστερον δε μεταμεληθεις απηλθεν (*pro* εγω κε *ad fin. vers.*) L. **απηλθεν** H. 31. εποιησεν wH**. −αυτω L. εσχατος (*pro* πρωτος) L. **αἱ τελωναι** L*. οἱ πορναι (*sic v.* 32) w. 32. ἠλθεν wH *sem.* ηλθεν H *sem.* **ιωαννης** προς ὑμας z. ὁδω i. ωδω H *sem.* αἱ H *sem.* επορναι z. ουδε (*pro* **ου**) Lz. μεταμεληθητε L. *fin.* +εις (*supra* αυτω) w**. 33. −τις w*H *sem.* **ἠν** H *sem.* P *bis.* οἰκοδεσποτης wHP *bis.* ὡστις i. περιεθηκεν wLP. ὡρυξεν **wH** *sem.* P. −εν L. λινον P. ὠκοδομησεν wP. 34. ἠγγισεν wH *sem.* **ἠγγησεν** H *sem.* P. απεστειλεν wH**P. αυτων (*pro* αυτου) z. 35. −και **λαβοντες** *usque ad* αυτου L. λαβωντες H *sem.* εδηραν vPz *sem.* ελιθοβολισαν Lz *sem.* 36. −δουλους z *sem.* −αυτοις L. ὡσαύτως H *sem.* P. 37. απεστειλεν wH**P. απεστειλεν αυτοις (−προς) z *sem.* 38. κατασχῶμεν L. *fin.* αυτων L*. 39. −εξεβαλον *tantum* L. 40. ὅτ' ἀν iHP. ὁτ' ἀν w. **οὐν** P. ἐλθη w. ποιηση z. εκεινος w*. 41. −λεγουσιν αυτῳ L. απωλεσει i. εκδωσεται iwHP [*non* vLz *bis*]. αυτου (*pro* αυτῳ *secund.*) P*. 42. +ουν (*post* λεγει) z *sem.* ὃν H *sem.* απεδωκιμασαν w. οἰκοδομουντες wP. οὐτως z *sem.* γονιας i*P. αὐτη P. ἐστη w, εστν H* *sem.*, εστιν P (*pro* εστι). ὀφθαλμοις wHP. *fin.* ὑμων i**L. 43. διατοῦτο vLz *bis* [*non* i]. −ὀτι H. ἡμων i*w. εθνη i*z *sem.* ποιουντα z *sem.* 44. *init.* −και w. συνθλαστησεται w. ληκμησει i*. λικμισει H. λικμηση z. 45. φαρσαιοι w*. 46. ὀχλους wH.

CAP. XXII. 1. παλιν· vw. εν παραβολαις αυτοις L. 2. ὁμοιωθη LPz. ὡστις i. εποιησεν wP. 3. απεστειλεν wH**P. ηθελων i. εισελθειν z. 4. ἑτοιμα (*sic v.* 8) P. 5. ὁς μεν L. −τον P* (*habet marg.*). ὁς δε L. **επι** (*pro* εις *secund.*) L. εμπορειαν z. 7. και ακουσας ὁ βασιλευς εκεινος (−δε) **ivwHPz.** ὁ δε βασιλευς ακουσας L. ὠργισθη P. ὀργισθη z. απωλεσεν wH**P. φωνεις LP. ενεπρησεν wL. ενεπρισεν P. 8. δουλοις *super rasur.* i. ἑτοιμος H. καικλημενοι i**. κλημενοι i*. ἦσαν P. 9. οὐν P. εαν (*pro* αν) iw**LHP [*non* z]. εὑρητε (*sic v.* 10) P. 10. οὐς (*pro* ὁσους) v. επλεισθη L. +των (*ante* ανακειμενων) L. 11. ελθων z. βασιλευ w. θεασασθε H. –εκει z. 12. ἑταιρε iv? H. ἑτερε P. ὡδε ivwLz [*non* P]. εφημωθη LP. 13. ὁ βασιλευς ειπε L. δεισαντες z. χειρας και ποδας i [*non* vLPz]. –αρατε αυτον και L. ἀρατε w. εμβαλετε i. βαλετε vL. εκβαλατε z. ὀδοντων ivw?HP. 14. εισιν wP. ὀλιγοι wHP. 15. συμβουλιον ελαβον (εποιησαν H) οἱ φαρισαιοι HPz *bis, init. peric.* φαρισσαιοι i. παγιδευσουσιν z *sem.* 16. αποστελουσιν P. αυτον (*pro* αυτῳ) P*z *sem.* οἰδαμεν iH *sem.* P. οἴδαμεν v. αληθεις w*P. ἐναληθεία iw. ἐπ' αληθειας z *sem.* μελλη L, μελλει z *bis* [*cum Elzev.* iwHP]. ουδε (*pro* ου γαρ) z *sem. fin.* ανου w. 17. οὐν (*sic v.* 21) P. ὑμιν L. εξεστοι L. εξεστιν P. ἢ οὒ P. 18. ειπεν iwLHP. 19. επιδιξατε H* *sem. Rasura in* L *post* νομισμα. διναριον P. 20. +ὁ ιησους (*ante* τινος) L. αὑτη P. 22. ς *mutat. in* αφεντες H. 23. +οἱ (*ante* σαδδουκαιοι) L. –οἱ Hz *sem.* οἱ λεγουσιν (*pro* οἱ λεγοντες) z *sem.* 24. μωυσης wLH [*non* iz *sem.*]. αποθανει i*. +και (*ante* επιγαμβρευσει) L. επιγαμβρευση wz *bis.* τη γυναικι v. αναστηση z *bis.* εξαναστησει v. σπερμα (*pro* τεκνα) z *sem.* 25. ἠσαν wH. *Rasura in* i *post* δε. ουν (*pro* δε) v. ἑπτα iH *sem.* ετελευτησεν wLH. αφηκεν wH *sem.* 26. ἑως *et* ἑπτα H *sem.* 27. απεθανεν (–και w) wH** *sem.* 28. αναστασει ουν L. –ουν z *sem.* ἑπτα *hic* w. *fin.* +γυναικα z *sem.* 29. –αυτοις H *sem.* ιδοντες z *bis.* μηδὲ ivwLz *bis.* 30. οὑτε H. εγγαμισκονται L. –του LHz. εισιν εν τω ουρανω Lz. εισιν wH. 31. ἂν ἔγνωτε L. –ὑμιν wz, *at* ἡμιν H. 32. ἀβρααμ ivwL?Hz *bis.* –και ὁ θς ιακωβ L. +δε (*post* εστι) L. 33. –και z *sem.* 34. –ὁτι i*. εφιμωσεν i*wL. εφιμοσεν H *sem. Rasura in* L *post* συνη (ρ *erasum, teste Dobbin, non me*). ἐπιτο‿αυτὸ z *bis.* 35. νομικος τις προσηλθεν (θε H* *sem.* z) τω ιυ πειραζων αυτον (+και H *sem.* P**z) λεγων H *sem.* P*z, *init. peric.* λεγον w. 37. εφη (*pro* ειπεν) ivwHPz *bis.* –τῃ *prim.* ivLHPz *bis.* –τῃ *secund.* ivz. +και εν ὁλη τη ισχυι σου (*post* ψυχη σου) L. 38. αὑτη P. ἔστιν H** *sem.* P. εστιν ἡ μεγαλη και πρωτη L. 39. –δε z *sem.* ὁμοι L*. αὑτη vwLHz *bis.* αὑτῇ i. αὑτη P. ἀγαπησεις H *sem. fin.* ἑαυτον wLz *bis* [*non* ivHP]. 40. ὁλως w. 41. φαρησαιων P. φαρισεων z. 42. εστιν wLH** *sem.* P. 43. οὖν (*sic v.* 45) P. –δᾱδ w* (*habet marg. rubro*) P* (*habet marg.*). καλει αυτον L. 44. ἑως P. ὑποκατω (*pro* ὑποποδιον) L. 45. +εν πνι (*post* δᾱδ) wL. εστιν iwLH** *sem.* P.

46. ἠδυνατο i. ειδυνατο P. ἠδυνατο vz *bis* [*non* L]. –αυτῳ i*. αποκριθηναι αυτω wLz *sem.* οὐδε H *sem.* ετολμησεν wLP. οὐκέτι iwP.

CAP. XXIII. 1. ελαλησεν ὁ ι̅ς̅ LHP. ελαλησεν w. –και τοις μαθηταις αὐτου Pz *init. peric.* 2. καθεδρας μωυσεως L. εκαθησαν P. 3. οὖν P. εαν (*pro* αν) ivwLH *sem.* Pz *bis.* ἐαν H *sem.* ποιειται *prim.* w. λεγουσιν P. ποιουσιν·(*sic v.* 5) wP. 4. δεσμευουσιν wP. δε (*pro* γαρ) iw. επιτηθεασιν P. ὤμους P. οὐ H *sem.* θελουσιν wH** *sem.* P. κηνησαι P. 5. προς τω z *sem.* πλατυνουσιν P. γαρ (*pro* δε *secund.*) Lz *sem.* μεγαλυνουσιν P. 6. φιλουσιν H** *sem.* P. δε (*pro* τε) wL. φιλουντες (–τε) z. πρωτοκλησιαν ivLPz. 7. ἀσπασμους H. αγωραις P. καλεισθε i. καεισθαι P*. –ανων H* *sem.* ῥαμβι *bis* (*sic v.* 8) i. ῥαββεὶ *bis* (*sic v.* 8) L. ῥαββεῖ *bis* P. –ῥαββι *unum* z. 8. –μη L*. –ὑμεις δε *usque ad* ῥαββι P. –ὑμων ὁ καθηγητης *v.* 8 *usque ad* εἰς γαρ εστιν *v.* 9, v*. διδασκαλος (*pro* ὁ καθ.) H. –ὁ χ̅ς̅ w* (*habet marg.*). –παντες δε *ad fin. vers.*: *at addit ad finem v.* 9. H *duobus locis.* 9. ουρανιος (*pro* εν τοις ουρανοις) L. 10. μὴδὲ vwHPz *bis.* κληθηται L. ὑμων εἰς γαρ P. –ὑμων w. ὑμων *rescript.* i. –εστιν v. γαρ εστιν ὁ καθηγητης ὑμων Lz *sem.*, *at* εστιν ὑμων z *sem.* 11. εστω z. 12. ἑαυτὸν P. ταπειθωθησεται v. ὁ δε ταπεινων (*pro* και ὁστις ταπεινωσει) z. 13, 14. *Hos versus transferunt* ivwHz *bis* [*non* L]. 13. οὐαὶ ὑμειν P. –δε ivwLHPz *sem.* –γαρ z *sem.* και τους εισερχομενους αφιετε (οὐκ *supra* αφιετε *rubro*) i. 14. *init.* ουαι δε ivLH (οὐαι H *sem.*). οἰκιας wH *sem.* τινα (*pro* μακρα) z *sem.* διατοῦτο ivLz *bis.* ληψονται i. 15. περιαγεται L. +του (*ante* ποιησαι) L. ἐνα H. ὅτ' ἂν iH. ὁτ' ἂν w. ποιητε z *sem.* 16. μὶν i. ὀμοση *bis* iLHz *bis*, *secund.* v. ὀφειλει (*sic v.* 18) wH. 17. ἀγιαζων H. 18. αν (*pro* εαν) wLHz *bis.* ὀμοση *bis* LHz *bis*, *secund.* w, *prim.* v, *at secund.* ὠμωση [*non* i]. το (*pro* τῳ *tert.*) L. 19. +εστι (*post* γαρ) L. μειζων iwz *bis.* ἢ (*sic v.* 17 *sem.*) H. τῶ (*pro* το *tert.*) H *sem.* ἀγιαζων iw. 20. ὀμοσας ivwHLz *sem.* ὀμνυει iwLH. 21. ὀμοσας (*sic v.* 22) vLH *sem.* z *bis.* ὀμνυει (*sic v.* 22) wLH *sem.* z *bis.* κατοικησαντι vwHz *bis* [*non* L]. *fin.* εις αυτω z *sem.* 21, 22. *Deest ab* ομνυει *usque ad* ουρανῳ i. 22. αυτου (*pro* του θ̅υ̅) v. 23. +δε (*post* ουαι) H *sem.* ὀτι v. αποδεκατουται L. ιδιωσμον i. ἠδυόσμον w. ανιθον z *sem.* κυμηνον w* +και (*ante* την κρισιν) L. πιστην i. +γαρ i, +δε wHz *bis* (*ante* εδει). κακεινα w. κακεῖνα L. [κἀκεῖνα iz]. 24. κωνοπα v. 25. παροψῖδος (*sic v.* 26) z *bis.* +του πινακος (*post* παροψιδος) w. εξωθεν (*pro* εσωθεν) L. –εξ H. ἀρπαγης H *sem.* *fin.* αδικιας ivHz *bis* [*cum Elzev.* wL]. 26. καθαρησον i. εσωθεν (*pro* εντος) w. εντος (*pro* εκτος) z. αυτου (*pro* αυτων) L. 27. παρομοιαζεται L. παρ' ὁμοιαζετε z *sem.* κεκονιασμενοις L. οἱτινες w. μεν ἐξωθεν L. ὀστεων iw H *sem.* z *sem.* ὠστεων H *sem.* 28. οὑτως ivwH *sem.* z *bis* [*non* L]. οὕτως H *sem.* τοις ανοις δικαιοι *super rasur.* i. νηστευοντες (*pro* δικαιοι) v. −δε L. εστε μεστοι L. μεστοι *ad fin. vers. rescript.* i**. κρισεως (*pro* ὑποκ.) v. 29. οικοδομηται L. οἰκοδομειτε wH *sem.* οἰκοδομειται H *sem.* οἰκοδομῆτε z. κοσμειται L. 30. ημεθα *bis* ivLz *sem.*, *secund.* z *semel.* ἡμεν *prim.* wH *sem.*, *secund.* H *sem.* οὐκ H. αυτων κοινωνοι L. −εν *secund.* v. εν των H *sem.* 31. −εαυτοις L. ἑαυτους z *sem.* −ὁτι i* (*habet marg.*). +οἱ (*ante* υἱοι) i. 32. ἡμεις w. επληρωσατε z *sem.* 33. ὀφεις iH. γενηματα i. φυγετε Lz *sem.* 34. διατοῦτο vLz *bis.* ειδου L*. ἀποστέλω w. ἀποστελῶ z *sem.* −και *tert.* wL. 35. +αν (*post* ὁπως) iLz. ἐλθη w. −παν L. εκχυννομενον w. αἷματος H *sem.* −υἱου βαραχιου z. 36. ναι λεγω ὑμιν i** *rubro in marg.*: *deest in textu.* +ὁτι (*ante* ἡξει) ivwLHz *bis* (ἡξει i). παντα ταυτα ivw [*non* LHz *bis*]. 37. ἰλῆμ *bis* w, *secund.* H** *sem.* αποκτενοῦσα i. αποκτένουσα LH *sem.* z *bis.* αποκτεννουσα H *sem.* [αποκτειν. vw]. αποσταλμενους i. αὐτην ivwLH. ἠθελησα wH. ορνις επισυναγει L. επισυναγεῖν H *sem.* ὀρνις H *sem.* τας νοσσιας v. αυτης (*pro* ἑαυτης) z *sem.* ἑαὑτης H. επι (*pro* ὑπο) v. +αυτης (*post* πτερυγας) z. οὐκ H *sem.* 38. αφιετε wLz *sem.* −ὑμιν z *sem.* οἰκος w. 39. δε (*pro* γαρ) z *sem.* +ὁτι (*ante* ου μη) L. οὐ H *sem.* απαρτι iwL Hz *bis* [*non* v].

CAP. XXIV. 1. απο του ἱερου επορευετο L. +αυτω (*post* προσηλθον) i** w**Hz. οἰκοδομας wHP. 2. αποκριθεις (*pro* ις) L. ταυτα παντα iLHz. ὡδε w [*non* ivLPz]. οὐ H *sem.* −μη *secund.* ivLHPz [*non* w]. 3. +ιῦ (*post* αυτου) *rubro in* v. ὀρους iH *sem.* P *bis.* ελεων w. προσηλθων P *sem.* +αυτου (*post* μαθηται) H *sem.* z. κατιδιαν ivHP *bis* z [*non* wL]. 4. αποκριθης P *sem.* 5. το P *sem.* ὀνοματι HP *bis.* +ὁτι (*ante* εγω) H *sem.* πλανησουσι vLHz [*cum Elzev.* iwP *bis*]. 6. μελλησητε w. μελλησεται P *sem.* ακουην P *sem.* ουπως w*. οὔπω H *sem.* P *sem.* z, *at* οὐ P *sem.* εσται P *bis.* 7. ἐπέθνος w. −και λοιμοι P* (*habet marg.*). −και σεισμοι z. 8. ταυτα δε παντα Lz. ωδηνων i. ὠδινων wHP *sem.* ὠδηνων P *sem.* 9. παραδοσουσιν H *sem.* θλιψις H** *duobus locis.* θλιψεις z. μησουμενοι P *sem.* +των (*ante* εθνων) ivwLHP *bis* z. ὀνομα H *bis* P *bis.* 10. παραδωσουσιν wLH *sem.* P. μησισουσιν P. 11. πλανησουσιν wH *sem.* P. 13. *Ante v.* 10 *ponunt* H** *antiquâ manu et* P, *sed repetunt in loco suo.* −δε *init. peric.* z. ὑπομειναs H. +το (*ante* τελος) P* *sem.* οὗτος H *sem.* οὕτως P *bis.* 14. οἰκουμενη wHP. εθνεσιν z. ἡξει iwH *sem.* 15. ὅτ' ἂν iwH. ὅτᾶν P. [ὅταν Lz]. οὐν P. δε (*pro* ουν) z. ηδητε z*. ἑστως iwHP [*non*

Lz]. τωπω H sem. ἁγιω H sem. P. αναγινωσκον H sem. 16. εις (pro επι) H sem. H* sem. ορει w. ὀρη P. 17. init. +και i. ὁ δε επι του δοματος z sem. καταβαινετο P. καταβητω z sem. ἀραι w, ἄραι LPz bis (sic v. 18). −τι εκ της v. 17 usque ad αραι v. 18 H* sem. Habet marg., antiquâ manu. τα (pro τι) ivwLH** sem. H sem. Pz sem. [τι z sem.]. απο (pro εκ) z. οἰκιας wH sem. H** sem. P. 18. −τῳ z. ἀγρω H sem. (vv. 18, 19, 20 ad μη γε in H non p. m. sed antiquâ manu). επιστρεψατο P. +εις τα (ante οπισω) z. ὀπισωw H** sem. H sem. P. το ἱματιον wL. 19. εγγαστρι v. 20. προσευχεσθαι iz sem. ἡμων H*P. εν χειμωνος P. μὴδὲ ivwLPz bis. −εν iwLHz bis [non v]. 21. −τοτε z bis. θλιψεις i. θλιψης P. οἷα iLPz bis. γεγωνεν H sem. H** sem. απαρχης LHP [non ivwz bis]. οὐ secund. H. 22. −ει P*. εκολωβωθησαν v*. εκολοβοθησαν P. κολοβοθησονται αἱ ἡμ. P. αἱ secund. H sem. 23. ὑμων (pro ὑμιν) L. ἴδοῦ P. ὡδε bis wL?z bis [non iP]. ἢ HP. ὡδε secund. H sem. πιστευση P* +ται P**. 24. ψευδοχρηστοι L. δωσουσιν wP. αποπλανησαι z. 26. οὐν P. εστιν vwHLP. εξελθηται P. εξελθετε z sem., at εξελθατε sem. ταμιοις Pz sem. ταμιειοις H sem. z sem. πιστευσηται P. 27. −γαρ H** init. peric. φενεται P. −και secund. vwP [non iz bis]. 28. −γαρ (init. peric.) z sem. ἢ v. ἢ P. +και (ante οἱ) i**z ter. 29. σκοτησθησεται P. απω i. αἱ H. 30. τό (pro τοτε prim.) L*. τοται secund. P. κοψονται τοτε L. αἱ P. ὀψονται HP. Rasura in w ante μετα. πολησ H sem. z. 31. αποστελλεῖ w. αποστέλλει P. σαλπιγγος rescript. H sem. επισυναξουσιν w. επισυναξωσιν P. τεσαρων i. επακρων (pro απ᾽ ακ.) P. ἀπακρων Hz sem. ἑως H sem. P. των ουρανων ἑως των ακρων L. 32. μαθε z sem. ὅτ᾽ ἂν (sic etiam H v. 33) iw. ὀτ᾽ ἂν H sem. ὀτὰν P. −ηδη P. ιδη wz sem. ἠδη H sem. ιδητε ὁτι (pro ηδη) z sem. ὁ H sem. γενητε i. γεννηται H* sem. ἀπαλος γενηται z sem. ἀπαλος iwH sem. Pz sem. ἀπαλλος L. φυλα H sem. εκφυῆ wP. εκρυῆ v. γινωσκεται z sem. 33. οὑτως ivwLHPz bis. ὁτὰν H sem. ταυτα παντα ivLH sem. Pz bis. γινωσκεται wP. 32, 33 antiquâ, non primâ manu, rescript. in H. 34. +ὁτι (ante ου μη) L. οὐ H sem. αὐτη P bis. ἑως P sem. ταυτα παντα LP sem. z bis. −ταυτα H* sem. γενητε H sem. 35. παρελευσεται vz sem. παρελευσοντε H sem. παρευλευσεται P* sem. οἱ w. λογι i. παρελθωσιν iwLH** sem. H sem. P bis z sem. 36. −δε i** rubro Pz sem. (init. peric.). −της secund. ivwLHP sem. z sem. ὡρας H sem. οὐδεὶς P sem. at οὐδεῖς P sem. οἰδεν H sem. οὐδε H sem. −μου wLP. 37. −αἱ L. αἱ P. 38. ἦσαν w. ἥσαν P sem. τρωγωντες H sem. τρογοντες P. αχρις L. −ἡς L. εισηλθεν iwL.

ἤσηλθε H *sem.* εἰσῆλθεν P. κωβωτον P. 39. ἑως H *sem.* ἦλθεν wP. ἦρεν wH *sem.* P. ἄπαντας H. ηρε παντας v. 41. μυλω vw. αφιετε H *sem.* αφιθησεται P*. *fin.* +δυο επι κλινης μιας· εἰς παραλαμβανεται και εἰς αφιεται L. 42. γρηγορειται P *sem.*, *at* γρηγορητε *sem.* οὐν P *bis*, *at* —ουν *sem.* ὡρα H *sem.* P *sem.*, *at* ἡμερα L. ἡμων wP *sem.* 43. εκεινω P *ter.* γινωσκεται iH *sem.* P *bis.* ειδη L. ἠδη P *bis*, *at* ἠδη *sem.* ἤδη Hz. οικοδεσπωτης L*. οἰκοδεσποτης wP. ὡρ α (*sic: pro* φυλακη) L. —αν *prim.* P* *sem.* ἂν *prim.* w. οὐκ H *sem.* ειασεν wH** *sem.* H *sem.* P *sem.* ἴασεν P *bis.* διωρυγηναι z *sem.* οἰκιαν wHP *ter.* την οἰκιαν αυτου διορυγηναι P *sem.* 44. διατοῦτο ivLH *sem.* P *sem.* z *bis.* ἑτοιμοι iHP *ter.* ἡ H *sem.* ὡρα ἡ P *sem.* δοκηται P *sem.* 45. ἆρα iv. ἄρα w. φρονημος P *bis.* οικιας (*pro* θεραπειας) w*Lz (οἰκιας w*, θεραπειας *marg.*). θεραπιας iP *bis.* δουναι vLP *sem.* z. 46. εὑρηση P *sem.* *at* εὑρησει H *sem.* P *sem.* οὑτως ποιουντα Lz. οὑτως H *sem.* 47. πασιν P *sem.* πασιν αυτου τοις ὑπαρχουσιν w. 48. μου ὁ κς P. 49. αρξεται L. τυπτει L*, *at* δαιρειν z*. +αυτου (*post* συνδουλους) iLH** *sem.* z *semel tantum.* εσθιη v. εσθιει LHz *sem.* εσθειη P. τε (*pro* δε) i. πινη v. πινει LHPz *sem.* 50. ἥξει ivH *sem.* ἡ *secund.* w. ἡ *bis* H *sem.*, *prim.* H *sem.* ἡ *bis* P. 51. θεισῃ z. ὀδοντων wHP.

CAP. XXV. 1. ὡμοιωθη H *sem.* ὁμοιωθη P* *sem.*, *et bis iterum*, z *bis* (—τοτε, *init. peric.*). ὁμοιωθησεται i. αἰτινες P *sem.* εξηλθον (ον *mutat.*) H *sem.* ἀπαντησιν P *bis* z *sem.* 2. ἦσαν iwH. ἦσαν P *bis.* φρονημοι (*sic v.* 4.) P *sem.* +αἱ (*ante* πεντε *secund*) ivw**LHP *bis* z *ter.* (πενται *secund.* L). 3. —αἱτινες μωραι P* (*habet marg.*). αυτων (*pro* ἑαυτων *prim.*) ivwLHP *bis* z *ter.* μεθ ἑαυτων P *sem.* 4. αἱ δε H *sem.* P *sem.* ελαιων P* *sem.* αγγιοις wL** P *bis.* 6. +της (*ante* νυκτος) wz *sem.* ἴδοὺ P *bis.* εξερχεσθαι iP *sem.* ὡς (*pro* εις) i*? 7. ἠγερθησαν wH** *sem.* P *bis.* 8. αἱ *bis* H *sem.*, *sic v.* 11. φρονημοις P *sem.* ἑλαμπ. (*pro* αἱ λαμπ.) P *sem.* σβεννυνται P *bis.* 9. φρονημοι P *sem.* ου μη (*pro* ουκ) w*P *bis.* αρκεσει H *sem.* P *sem.* αρκεση *usque ad* ὑμιν *super rasur.* w**. ὑμιν (*pro* ἡμιν) L*. πορευεσθαι w. —δε *secund.* H *sem.* z [*non* ivLP]. πολουντας P *bis* z *sem.* (+ελαιον P* *sem.*). αγορασαται P *sem.*, *at rasura ante* τε *sem.* αγορασεται ἑαυτοις w. *fin.* αυταις P *sem.* 10. ἦλθεν P *sem.*, *at* ἦλθεν *sem.* —αἱ L. ἑτοιμοι iHP *sem.*, ἑαῖτυμοι P *sem.* 11. αἱ H *sem.* λυπαι H *sem.* P *bis.* 12. Ὁ H** *sem.* 13. γρηγοριτε P *sem.* οὖν P *bis.* οἶδατε P *sem.*, *at* οἶδατε *sem.* ὡραν P *sem.* την ὡραν ουδε την ἡμεραν v. —εν ἡ *ad fin. vers.* w* (*habet* w** *marg.*) [*habent* ivLHP *bis*]. 14. —γαρ z *sem.* (*non*

init. peric.). +τις (**post** ανος) vH *sem.* P *bis* z *sem.* αποδυμων w. εκαλεσεν wHP *bis.* **εδωκεν** z *sem.* 15. ὁ (*pro* ᾧ) *ter in* P *sem.* εδωκεν wH** *sem.* H *sem.* P *bis.* ὦ δὲ *bis* w. +δε (*ante* δυο) H *sem.* ἑκαστω H *sem.* δυναμην P *sem.* 16. πεντα *prim.* w. ηργασατο L. εκερδησεν (*pro* εποιησεν) L. 17. ὡσ αὔτως HP *sem.*, *at* ὡσαὔτος HP *sem.* +δε (*ante* και *prim.*) iz *sem.* −ὁ w*. εκερδησεν wH** *sem.* H *sem.* P *bis.* 18. +ταλαντον (*post* ἐν) P *sem.* ὠρυξεν P *sem.*, *at* ὀρυξεν *sem.* απεκρυψεν wH** *sem.* H *sem.* P *bis.* −του κῦ (*habet marg.*) P* *sem.* *fin.* αυτου *bis scriptum* P* *sem.* 19. πολυν χρονου L. πολυ z *sem.* του (*pro* των) L*. συνερει w*. λογον μετ' αυτων w. 20. ειπε (*pro* προσηνεγκεν *usque ad* λεγων) z *sem.* +αυτω (*post* προσηνεγκεν) P *sem.* ἴδε P *sem.* εκερδισα P *sem.* εν (*pro* επ') vP *bis* [*non v.* 22]. 21. −δε Hz *bis.* εὖ vH *sem.* (*sic v.* 23 H). ὀλιγα (*sic v.* 23) wHP *bis.* εις L, ἧς vwP *bis* z *sem.* *hic tantum* (*pro* ης : *sic* vPz *v.* 23). 22. −λαβων wL. ειπεν iwLHP *bis.* ἴδε i. 24. −ὁ i*. λαβων (*pro* ειληφως) z *sem.* ειπεν iwLHP *bis.* ανος ει z *bis.* εσπηρας i*. 25. φοβιθεις H *sem.* 26. ὀκνηρε wHP *bis.* +ει (*ante* ἠδης *sem.*, ιδεις *sem.*) P *bis.* ιδεις L. ιδης z. ὃ (*pro* ὀτι) L. θεριζων w. οὐκ *et* οὐ H* *sem.* 27. *init.* +και φοβηθεις απελθων H* *sem.* οὐν (*sic v.* 28) P *bis.* τραπεζηταις iLH *sem.* P *bis.* τραπεζειτας z *sem.* z** *sem.* (-ητας z* *sem.*) εγω ελθων i. εκομησαμην P *bis.* 28. το (*pro* τῳ) LH *sem.* P *sem.* 29. *init.* το (*pro* τῳ) P *sem.* −παντι H* *sem.* περισευθησεται H *sem.* P *sem.* δοκει εχειν (*pro* εχει) LH *sem.* P *sem.* z. *fin.* +ταυτα λεγων εφωνει· ὁ εχων ὠτα ακουειν ακουετω H *sem.* P *sem.* (*sic* i**Lz *sem. post v.* 30, *habent autem* ὠτα, εφωνη z, *et* i** *præponit* προσθεσις *additque* τελος *rubro*). 30. αχριον LP. εκβαλετε iv*H *sem.* P. εκβαλλεται w. βαλλεται L. εκβαλεται z *sem.* εξοτερον L. −ὁ *secund.* L. ὀδοντων vwH *sem.* P. 31. ὅτ' ἂν iwH *sem.* P *sem.*, ὀτ' ἂν H** *sem.* P *sem.* −δε P *sem.* (*mediâ pericopâ*), P *sem.* z *sem.* (*init. peric.*). ἐλθη w. −ἁγιοι w* [*non* L]. ἁγιοι H *sem.* ἀγγελοι z *sem.* καθησει LH *sem.* P *bis.* καθιση z *bis.* 32. συναχθησονται iwLH** *sem.* P *bis* z *sem.* αλληλων H *sem.* 33. στηση z *sem.* εριφηα P *sem.* εξευωνυμων (*sic v.* 41) ivLHP *bis* z *bis* (*sic* εκδεξιων *passim*). 34. κληρωνομησατε P *sem.* ἑτοιμασμενην P *bis*, ἡτοιμασμενην (*sic v.* 41) z. ἀποκαταβολῆς wL. 35. επινασα (*sic v.* 42) P. εποτησατε (*sic v.* 42) P *bis.* ἥμιν H *sem.* ἡμην (*sic vv.* 36, 43) P *bis* z. *fin.* μοι L*. 36. περιεβαλλετε z *sem.* ἠσθενησα HP *bis.* επισκεψασθε w. ἡμην H. ηλθατε LP *sem.* z *sem.* ἤλθατε P *sem.* ἤλθετε w. 37. ιδομεν (*sic vv.* 38, 39) LP *sem.* ιδωμεν (*sic vv.* 38, 39, 44) P *sem.* z *sem.* πινωντα iP *sem.* πεινουντα H* *sem.*, *at* πινουντα *sem.* εθρεψαμεν (α *dubium*) L. ἢ H *sem.* P *sem.* εποτησαμεν P *bis* z *sem.* επιτισαμεν L.

38. –δε wH *sem.* P. συνηγαγωμεν z *sem.* ἢ (*sic v.* 39) HP *bis.* περιεβαλλομεν P *sem.* περιεβαλωμεν z *sem.* 39. –δε w. ασθενὴν (*sic v.* 44) P *sem.* ἠλθομεν wP *sem.* ἠλθαμεν P *sem.* 40. αποκριθης P *sem.* ἐφόσον [*non* i] Lz. ἐφὁσον H *sem.* z *sem.* ἐνι H *sem.* P *bis.* τον αδελφον P* *sem.* 41. πορευεσθαι P* *sem.* ἐμου P *sem.* κατηρατημενοι i. κατηραμμενοι v. ἠτοιμασμενω P *sem.*, *at* ἠτοιμασμενον *sem.* 42. εποτησατε z *sem.* *fin.* μοι (*pro* με) L. 43. μοι (*pro* με *prim.*) L. περιεβαλλετε wP *bis.* οὐκ H *sem.* επεσκεψασθαι i*. 44. –αυτῳ ivwLHP *bis* z *bis.* ιδομεν L. πινωντα P *sem.* ἢ *quinquies* P *sem.*, *tert.* H *sem.* ξενων P *sem.* ***Rasura post*** **ου** ***in*** **w.** 45. αποκριθεισεται i. –αμην λεγω ὑμιν vz *sem.* αμιν ?L*. ἐνὶ HP *sem* τούτούτων L. +των αδελφων μου (*ante* των ελαχιστων) P*. –ουδε L. μοι w*. 46. οἱ H *sem.*

Cap. XXVI. 1. –παντας H. ειπεν iwHP. 2. οἶδατε i. οἶδατε vz *sem.* οἴδαται P *sem.*, *at* οἴδατε HP *sem.* γινετε P *sem.* παραδιδοτε L. παραδιδωται P *bis.* εις τῶ H *sem.* P *sem.* 3. –και οἱ· γραμματεις L. του λεγομενου του αρχιερεως w. 4. δολω κρατησωσιν ivwLHPz (κρατισ. P, -σωσι vz). αποκτεινωσι v. αποκτεινουσιν L. 5. ἑορτη H. θωρυβος H. 6. –δε P *sem.* z** (*init. peric.*). βιθανια L. οἰκια P *bis.* σημωνος P *sem.* 7. εχουσα αλαβαστρον μυρου L. –βαρυτιμου P *sem.* πολυτιμου w. κατεχεε (–επι) z *sem.* ***Duo verba erasa in*** **w** ***post*** **επι.** της κεφαλης LP *bis.* 8. –αυτου L. ἠγανακτησαν wHP *bis.* ηγανακτησιν (*sic*) L*. τη (*pro* τι) P *bis.* ἠ *mutatum in* L. απολεια wHz. απολια P *bis.* αὔτη (*sic vv.* 12, 13) HP *bis.* 9. εδυνατο w. ἠδυνατο H *sem.* P *bis* z. –το μυρον w [*non* iL]. +τοις (*ante* πτωχοις) wHP *bis* [*non* ivLz *bis*]. 11. τους πτωχους γαρ παντοτε ivLHP *bis* z *bis.* ου παν *super maculam in* L. οὐ H *sem.* 12. βαλλοῦσα P *sem.* αὔτη H *sem.* ενταφιασε P *sem.* 13. αν (*pro* εαν) L. –τουτο L. –λαληθησεται L. αὔτη HP, *at* αὐτὴ z *sem.* (*pro* αὔτη). 14. πορευθῢς i. πορευθης H *sem.* εἱς H. τον P *sem.* εισκαριωτης H. 15. ειπεν iwLHP *bis.* και εγω ivH *sem.* H** *sem.* z *sem.* ἑστησαν L. εστισαν P *sem.* αυτον (*pro* αυτῳ) P *sem.* 16. ἀποτότε wLP *bis.* ἐέζητει H* *sem.* εζητη wP *sem.* εζητουν P *sem.* ευκεριαν P *bis.* 17. αυτω οἱ μαθηται αυτου (*pro* τῳ ῑυ) P. –αυτῳ wL. ἑτοιμασομεν L. ἑτοιμασωμεν HP. 18. ὁ δε ιησους ειπεν αυτοις LP. οἱπαγετε H. πολην P. εστι ivH [*non* wL]. προσε L*. 19. προσεταξεν z. –αυτοις v. ἠτοιμασαν v. 20. ὀψιας iwHP. γεναμενης P. ἀνέ γεντο (*vix lego*) L. ανεκητο P. *fin.* +μαθητων w. 21. εστι οντων (*pro* εσθιοντων) L*? ετι οντων L**. λε (*pro* λεγω) L*. –ὁτι z. 22. λοιπουμενοι P. ἠρξαντο P. ειρξαντο z. εἱς (*pro* αυτῳ) L. 23. *init.* ὁ δε ιησους L. οὑτως P.

24. υπαγη P. καθως *super rasur.* i**. ουαι H. παραδιδωτε H. παραδιδωται P. ἦν w, ἦν P. η (*pro* ει) L. 25. ειπεν iwLHP. ραμβι i, ραββει P (*sic v.* 49). +ὁ ις (*ante* συ) v. 26. αυτων δε εσθιοντων L. ευχαριστησας (*pro* ευλογησας) ivwLHPz. εκλασεν wHP. δους (−και *ante* ειπεν) L. ειπεν iwLHPz. εστιν (*sic v.* 28) P. τῶ (*pro* το) i. 27. −το i*. ευχαρηστησας H. 28. −γαρ Hz. αἱμα H. κενης HP. εκχυννομενον w. εκχυνομενων L*. ἁμαρτιων H. 29. −ὁτι L. ἀπαρτι iwL*Pz. απαρτι οὐ μη πιω H. γενηματος ivwHP [*non* Lz]. ὅτ' ἂν i. ὁτ' ἂν w. ὅτἂν P. ὅτάν H. αὐτῶ HPz. πεινω L. καινον μεθ' ὑμων v. 30. ὁρος HP. −εις το ορος των ελ. v*. 31. σκανδαλισθησεσθαι P. −εν εμοι L. νυκτῆ P. διασκορπισθησονται iLH*. 33. απεκριθη δε ὁ πετρος και v. −και ivLHPz [*non* w]. +δε (*post* εγω) ivLHPz [*non* w]. σκανδαλισθησωμαι P. 34. αλεκτωρα HPz. φωνησε H. τρεις L. απαρνησει i. απαρνησαι L*P. απαρνησοι ?L**. 35. δεοιμι (*pro* δεη με) L. απαρνησωμαι iwLH. απαρνησομε z. δε (*pro* και) L. +δε (*post* ὁμοιως) ivwHPz. ειπαν L. 36. λεγωμενον H. γεθσημανεῖ iL [*non* HP]. γεθσημανι v. γεθσιμανῆ z. αυτοις (*pro* τοις μαθηταις) L. +αυτου (*post* μαθηταις) H. καθησατε LHP. ἑως σου P. ἑως H. αν (*pro* οὐ) wL. προσευξομαι vPz. εκει προσευξωμαι L. 37. ἡρξατο HP. αδειμονειν i. 38. +ὁ ις (*post* αυτοις) ivwHPz. ἑως HP. ὡδε wLz. 39. προσελθων ivw*LH*Pz. εστιν w. παρελθατο P. οὐχ' ivLPz. *fin.* σοι L. +*uno tenore* LHP *legunt* Luc. xxii, 43, 44 (=L** *marg.*). 40. +αναστας απο της προσευχης (*ante* ερχεται) ivHP [*non* L]. +παλιν (*post* ερχεται) H*. εὑρισκει P. +παλιν (*ante* καθευδοντας) H*. αυτοις (*pro* τῳ πετρῳ) wL. οὑτως; v. γρηγορεῖσαι z. 41. γρηγορηται ?L*. γρηγορειτε L**. γρηγορητε P. προσευχεσθαι L*P. ἡ H. ασθενεις z. 42. προσηυξατω P. +ὁ ιησους (*ante* λεγων) L. −ου L. το ποτηριον τουτο L. −το ποτηριον w* (*habet marg.*). −απ' εμου L. αὐτῶ HPz. 43. εὑρεν wLz. εὑρισκη P. −παλιν P. ἦσαν w. ἥσαν HP. ὀφθαλμοι P. βεβαρϋμενοι L. 44. −παλιν L. προσηυξατο παλιν w. προσηῦξατο P. ειπον z. 45. ερχετε P. −αυτου wL. καθευδεται z. −ιδου *usque ad* αγωμεν *v.* 46 P* (*habet* P** *marg. tantum* ϊδου ἡγγηκεν ἡ ὡρα· εγειρεσθαι αγωμεν). παραδιδοτε L*. παραδιδωται z. +των (*ante* ἁμαρτωλων) H*. 46. ἀγωμεν H. ἡγγικεν P. ηγγηκεν z. παραδειδους z. 47. ετη P. τουτου (*pro* αυτου) L. ἰδοὺ z. ηλθεν iH**. ἦλθεν P. −ηλθε w* (ἦλθεν w** *marg.*). ὀχλος P. 48. αυτων (*pro* αυτον *prim.*) P*?. εαν (*pro* αν) ivw. εστιν P. κρατισατε z. 49. προσὲ λθων (*literâ eras.*) P. ειπεν iwLHPz. 50. −ιησους z. ἑτερε P. ἐφ' ὁ ivwL [*non* z]. επεβαλλον P. προς (*pro* επι) z. εκρατισαν z. 51. ϊδοῦ P. τον (*pro* των) z. απεσπασεν wHP.

ὠτιον wP. 52. –σου w. την μαχαιραν σου L. μαχαιρα P, μαχαιρας z (*pro* μαχαιραν *secund.*). *fin.* αποθανουνται ivLHPz. 53. ἢ δοκῆς z. δυναμε wP. πλοιους ἢ z. ἢ H. λεγεωνας (ς *mutat.*) H. αγγελους w. 54. οὖν P. αἱ HP. οὐτως ivwLHPz. δη ?i*. 55. ὀχλοις HP. ἐπιληστὴν L. εξεληλυθατε v. εξηλθατε LP. μεταμαχαιρῶν w. με; *prim.* vw. καθήμεραν Pz [*cum Elzev.* ivwLH]. εκαθεζωμην P. εν τω ἱερω διδασκων w. εκρατισατε H. *fin.* μοι L*. 56. *Rasura in* i *post* Π *rubro in* παντες. 57. οἱ δε w. κρατισαντες H *sem.* +αυτον (*ante* προς) P *sem.* καϊφαν w. καϊαφα P *sem.* αρχιερεις (*pro* γραμματεις) z *sem.* 58. ηκολουθη iz *bis.* ἠκολουθη H *sem.* P *bis.* ἠκολουθει wH *sem.* –αυτῳ z *sem.* –απο H *sem.* απομακρυθεν LP *sem.* ἀπομακρωθεν P *sem.* εκαθιτο (*sic v.* 69) i*. εκαθητω (*sic v.* 69) P *bis.* ειδειν i*. 59. –και οἱ πρεσβυτεροι L. ὁλον το συνεδριον P *sem.* z *sem.* θανατωσωσιν LP *sem.* θανατωσουσιν αυτον iP *sem.* θανατωσωσιν αυτον vwHz *bis.* 60. οὐχ' *bis* vwz *bis.* ουχευρων *prim.* P**, *secund.* P *sem.* εὗρον *prim.* P *sem.* +ὑστερον δε προσελθοντες (*ante* και πολλων) w*. ψευδωμαρτυρων L*. προσελθωντων w. ελθοντων L. προσελθωντες P *sem.* [*omnia in* iH *cum Elzev.*]. 61. εἶπον *rescript.* z. *sem.* οὑτως P *sem.* ειπε (*pro* εφη) z *sem.* δυναμε z *sem.* οἰκοδομησαι wH *sem.* P *sem.* –αυτον L. 62. αποκρινει P *sem.* z *sem.* τή P* *sem.* οὐτι i*. σοι (*pro* σου) z *sem.* 63. –αποκριθεις L. ὁρκιζω w. ὀρκιζω L. εξωρκιζω P *sem.* ἢ (*pro* ει) P *sem.* 64. απεκριθη *ut videtur* (*pro* λεγει) i*. ἀπάρτι ivwLHP *bis* z *bis.* ὀψεσθαι P *sem.* ὀψεσθε HP *sem.* τον υἱον *bis scriptum* i*. εξερχομενον z *sem.* 65. διερρηξεν wHP *bis.* εβλασφημησεν wLH *sem.* H** *sem.* P *sem.* z *sem.* εβλασφημισεν P *sem.* ετη P *sem.* εχωμεν z. ἰδε z *sem.* ἠκουσατε wHP *bis.* *Rasura in* i *post* β *in* βλασ. 66. δοκη L. εστιν iwLHP *bis.* 67. εκολαφησαν v*P *bis* z *bis.* εραπησαν P *bis* z *sem.* εραπισαν z *sem.* 68. παισασε P *bis.* 69. –εξω z *sem.* μιᾶ z *sem.* σοῦ ἠσθα w. εισθα P *sem.* ἠσθα P *sem.* 70. ἠρνησατο P *bis.* ἐμπροσθεν H *sem.* αυτων (*pro* παντων) w. +αυτων (*ante* παντων) ivHP *bis* z *bis.* οἰδα P. 71. εξελθωντα P *sem.* ελθοντα z *sem.* ιδεν LP *bis* z *sem.* αυτω (*pro* αυτον *secund.*) P. αυτοις εκει· L. αυτοις· εκει ivHz *bis.* αυτοις εκει P (*sic*) *semel, at* + *interposito sem.* οὑτος H. ἦν P *bis.* 72. ἠρνησατο P *bis.* μετα w. μεθ' ὁρκου iv. +λεγων (*post* ὁρκου) z *sem.* οἶδα (*sic v.* 74) P *sem.* 73. –οἱ ἑστωτες P* *sem.* (*marg. habet*). ἑστωτες iwHP *sem.* δειλον P *bis.* 74. ἤρξατο H *sem.* P *bis.* ειρξατο w. καταθεματιζειν ivwLH*P *bis* z *bis.* ·ὀμνυειν wHP *bis.* αλεκτορ L*. εφωνησεν wH *sem.* H** *sem.* P *bis.* 75. –του *secund.* ivP *bis* (*at* ῑν P* *sem.*) [*non* wLH]. ειρηκωτος z *sem.* αλεκτορ L.

αλεκτωρα P *bis* z *sem.* απαρνησει με τρεις L. τρεις vP *sem.* εκλαυσεν wHP *sem.*, *at* εκλαψεν P *sem.*

CAP. XXVII. 1. –δε Pz* *sem.* εποιησαν (*pro* ελαβον) z *sem.* ὑπρεσβυτεροι P *sem.* αυτον θανατωσαι L. θανατωσουσιν L** *marg.* *fin.* αυτω z. 2. δισαντες L*P *sem.* –αυτον *prim.* P* *sem.* (*habet marg.*). ἡγεμονι i. ἡγεμωνι w*H. ἡγεμωνι z. ἡγεμωνη P *sem.* ἡγεμονη P *sem.* *et iterum* P** *rubro.* 3. –ὁ παραδιδους αυτον H** P *sem.* z *sem.* (*init. peric.*). αυτων w*. μεταμελιθεις i. απεστρεψαι L. απεστρεψεν wH**P *bis.* –τριακοντα z *sem.* αρχιερευσιν P *sem.* –τοις *secund.* z *sem.* γραμματευσι (*pro* πρεσβυτεροις) v. 4. οψη ivL*z *bis.* ὀψη P *bis.* 5. εις τον ναον L. ανεχωρησεν iwLHP *bis.* απηυξατο P *sem.* 6. αυτα (*pro* τα αργυρια) i. οὐκ z. εξεστιν P *bis.* γολγοθαν L*, κορβονᾶν ivL** *marg.* *fin.* εστιν iwHP *bis.* 7. τε (*pro* δε) P *sem.* ἠγορασαν wHP *bis* z *sem.* κεραμαιως P* *sem.* εἰς z *sem.* 8. δι' ὃ w. αἱματος H *sem.* ἑως H *sem.* την (*pro* της) z *sem.* 9. ἠρεμιου L. ἠερεμιου P *sem.* –ἱερεμιου z, *semel tantum.* προφ H* *sem.* ετημησαντο w*. 10. εβαλον (*pro* εδωκαν) L. εδωκα ?H* *sem.* H *sem.* συνεταξεν wP *bis.* +λεγει (*ante* κ̄ς) z *sem.* 11. ἑστη ?L. ἡγεμωνος H *sem.* επερωτησεν P *sem.* 12. Απο (*pro* ὑπο) w, A *rubro.* –των *secund.* i*wLz *sem.* 13. πιλᾶτος *ferè* in vH. οὐκ H *sem.* ποσσα P *sem.* καταμαρτυρουσιν; vwLHP *bis.* 14. ἐν H *sem.* ἡγεμωνα H *sem.* z* *sem.* 15. ειωθη vLHP *sem.* z *bis.* τω οχλω ἑνα Lz *bis.* ἑνα H. τω οχλω ἑνα H *sem.* P *bis.* ἤθελον P *bis.* 16. λεγωμενον H *sem.* βαρναβαν (*sic v.* 17) L*, ρρ L**. βαραβαν (*sic vv.* 17, 20, 21, 26) i. 17. συνηγμενον P *sem.* P* *sem.* οὐν P *bis.* δε (*pro* ουν) L. +τε (*post* τινα) w. ἢ H *sem.* P *bis.* 18. ἠδει H *sem.* ἠδη P *bis.* 19. απεστειλεν w H**P *bis.* μὴδὲν HP *bis* z *sem.* κατοναρ σημερον P *sem.* κατ' ὄναρ H *sem.* κατοναρ P *sem.* z *sem.* *et* z** [*non* ivwL]. 20. επισαν i. ὀχλους H *sem.* P *bis.* αἰτησονται iw. αιτισωνται H** *sem.* ετησονται P *sem.* βαραβαν (*sic vv.* 21, 26) L. απωλεσωσιν i, *at* αποκτεινωσιν P *sem.* 21. των *super ras.* H *sem.* 22. οὐν P *sem.* +ἡ (*ante* ῑν) H* *sem.* –ιησουν z *sem.* λεγουσι (–αυτῳ) w*L. σταυρωθητω *bis script.* w. 23. –ἡγεμων L. –λεγοντες w. 24. ὠφελει wH. οφελει L. ὀφελει P *bis.* απενηψατο L*P. +αυτου (*post* χειρας) z *sem.* ὀχλου H *sem.* P *sem.* αἱματος (*sic v.* 25) H *sem.* ὀψεσθε H *sem.* P *bis.* 25. ειπεν iwLHP *bis.* *fin.* ὑμων L*. 26. φραγελωσας iH *sem.* P *bis* z *bis.* φραγγελλωσας w. +αυτοις (*ante* ἱνα) P *sem.* 27. ἡγεμωνος iH *sem.* P *sem.* πρετοριον L. ὀλην i. 28. –αυτον H* *sem.* +τα ἱματια αυτου (*post* αυτον) P *sem.* χλαμιδα κοκκινην περιεθηκαν αυτῳ L. χλαμμυδα (*sic v* 31) H *sem.* κοκινην i*. 29. ἐξακανθων wL. εθηκαν wL.

της κεφαλης L. εν τη δεξια L. γουυπετουντες LP *sem.* z *sem.* γουυτησαντες w*. ενεπεζον LP *sem.* αυτον (*pro* αυτῳ) z *sem.* 30. –εις *secund.* z *sem.* 31. ενεπεξαν P *bis.* αυτον (*pro* αυτῳ) P *sem.* z *bis.* αυτου (*pro* αυτον *prim.*) L. χλαμηδα w. –αυτον *tert.* LP *sem.* 32. εὑρον P *sem.* κιριναιον i*. κυρηραιον v. κυριναιον P *sem.* z *bis.* ὀνοματι wHP *bis.* σιμονα P *sem.* τοτε (*pro* τουτον) z *sem.* ἠγγαρευσαν wHP *bis.* αρει i. ἀρη L. αρρη H* *sem.* 33. γολγοθαν i. γολγοθὰ wH *sem.* P *bis.* ὁ (*pro* ὁς) ivLHP *bis* z *bis.* εστιν P *bis.* [λεγομενος vLH *sem.* P *sem.*] *at* μεθερμηνευομενον H *sem.* P *sem.* z *sem. fin.* τοπον P* *sem.* 34. οινον L, ὀινον w (*pro* οξος). ὀξος H *sem.* P *bis.* μεμυγμενον i. μεμηγμενον P *sem.* οὐκ H *sem.* ηθελησε L. ηθελεν wH *sem.* P *bis.* 35. βάλοντες H** *sem.* P *sem.* βαλόντες H *sem.* δια (*pro* ὑπο) L. –ἱνα *ad fin. vers.* ivwHP *bis* z *bis* [*non* L]. κληρους L**. 36. ετερουν L. 37. αἰτιαν w. γεγραμενην i. –ιησους P *sem.* z *sem.* 38. εἱς *bis* H *sem.* και *mutatum* L. εξευωνυμων ivLHP *bis* z *bis. fin.* +Luc. XXIII. 39—43 *uno tenore* H *sem.* P *semel.* 39. οἱ δε w. αυτ̆ ον (*sic*) L. 40. λεγωντες P *sem.* ὁ H *sem.* καλυων H* *sem.* καταλυον P *sem.* οἰκοδομων wHP *bis.* +και ἡμας (*post* σεαυτον) z *sem.* υἱος, ὑ *mutat.* L. καταβηθη P *bis.* 41. –δε w*LH* *sem.* –και w. εμπεζοντες LH *sem.* P *sem.* *Rasura inter* εμπαιζοντ *et* εσ P *sem.* γραμματαιων wP *sem.* P** *sem.* –γραμματεων και z *sem.* –και πρεσβυτερων P* *semel* (*habet marg.*). πρεσβυτερον H *sem.* φαρισαιων (*pro* πρεσβυτερων) z *sem.* +και φαρισαιων (*ante* ελεγον) ivw [*non* L] HP *sem.* z *sem.* ελεγων H *sem.* 42. ἑαυτον H. σωσαι; vwLH?z *bis.* εστιν vwHP *bis.* πιστευσωμεν ἐπ' iwLH (-σομεν H *sem.*) P *bis* z *bis* [*at* –ἐπ' LP *sem.* z *sem.*]. +επ' (*ante* αυτω) v. 43. *init.* +ει P *sem.* –νυν wLz *bis.* +σωσατω αυτον (*ante* ει θελει) P *sem.* θελη z *sem.* ειπεν wHP *bis.* +του (*ante* θῦ) z *sem.* ῦς ειμι wP *sem.* 44. τοδ' αυτω P. λισται H *sem.* λησσται P *sem.* συνσταυρωθεντες L. ονειδιζον iLz *sem.* ὀνειδιζον P *sem.* ὠνειδιζον wHP *sem. fin.* αυτον ivwLHP *bis* z *bis.* 45. ἑκτης iwH *sem.* P *bis.* ἑως H *sem.* P *sem.* ἑως ὡρας εννατης *transfert* z *in locum ante* σκοτος. ἑνατης (*sic* iH *sem. v.* 46) i*. ενατης H *sem.* [εννατης vwLH *sem.* P *bis* z *bis: sic v.* 46]. 46. εβοησεν L. ἠλι ἠλι iwLHP *bis.* λειμᾶσαβαχθανί iHP *sem.* (-νῆ H, ἀβ. P), *at* λιμασάβαχθανι vP *sem.* λιμάσαβαχθανή w. λιμασάβαχθανει L. λημᾶσαβαχθανῆ z *bis.* τοῦτέστι vH *sem.* τουτέστι iLz *bis.* τουτέστιν wP *bis.* ἵνα τί iP *bis* z. εγκατελειπες iH *sem.* P *bis* z. 47. ἑστωτων iwH *sem.* P *bis.* ἠλιαν vwLH *sem.* P *bis* [*non* iz *bis*]. φωνὴν οὖτως P *sem.* φωνη wH *sem.* P *sem.* z. οὗτως i. οὗτος H *sem.* 48. εἶς ἐξ H *sem.* πληξας w*. οξου L. ὀξους H *sem.* P *bis.* εποτηζεν P *sem.* 49. ειπον (*pro* ελεγον) L.

ιεν P *sem.* εἰ H *sem.* ἡλιας vwLH *sem.* P *bis* [*non* iz *bis*]. σωσαι L.
·ον iH *sem.* P *bis.* σωσων z. 50. –παλιν z. αφηκεν wH**P *bis.*
ἰδοῦ P *bis.* εσχισθει i. επανωθεν (*pro* απο ανωθεν) L. ἑώς H. εσισθη
ἐ L*, ἐ i*P *sem.*, αἱ H *sem.* (*pro* αἱ). διεσχισθησαν z. 52. μνήμία P
. ανεωχθη w. ἡνεωχθησαν P *sem.* ἡνεωχθησαν z *bis.* ἁγιων H. ηγερ-
αν Lz *sem.* ἠγερθη iH *sem.* P *bis.* 53. εξελθωντες P *sem.* απο (*pro*
P *sem.* εισηλθον *mutat.* H *sem.* ἁγιαν H *sem.* ενεφανησθησαν P *sem.*
init. –ὁ H* *sem.* ἑκατονταρχος HP *bis.* μετ' αὐτοῦς P** *sem.* ἰδοντες
m. σισμον P *bis.* γινομενα P *sem.* ἦν w. ἦν P *bis.* οὑτως P.
ἠσαν wHP. –εκει z *bis* (*init. peric.*). +και (*ante* γυναικες) wz *sem.* και
αικες εκει H. –απο *prim.* w. απομακροθεν LPz *sem.* αἰτινες HP. ἠκολ-
ησαν wHP. διηκονουσαι w. 56. ἦν i. ἦν P. –ἡ του P**. ἰωσῆφ L**.
ητηρ *prim.* z *sem.* 57. Ὀψιας i (*rubro*) wP. ἠλθεν wP. τοῦνομα P.
θητευσαι L. εμαθητευσεν wH**P. 58. –τῳ w. ἠτησατο wP. τῶ
ο το) *bis* i. +ουν (*post* τοτε) P. *Rasura in* i *ad fin. vers.* 59. ενειλυσεν
αυτο σινδονη αυτω σινδονη L. αυτω i*HP. 60. –αυτο L. αυτῶ P.
υ L. ῶ (*pro* ὃ) z. –εν *secund.* P. προσκιλυσας L. μεγα L. μνημιου P.
ἦν w. ἦν P. 62. –δε wPz (*init. peric.* z). ἐπ' αὔριον ἥτις w. εστιν
*P. 63. ὁ πλανος εκεινος L. πλανος εκεινος (–ὁ) H. 64. οὐν P.
H. –της z. –νυκτος vw* [*habent* w** *marg.* iLHP]. ειπωσιν wHP. +ὁτι
te ηγερθη) z. ἠγερθη iwHP. χειρον L. 65. –δε vLHPz [*non* i].
ται w*H. κουστοδιαν L. οἰδατε HP. 66. ἠσφαλισαντο wH. ἠσφα-
αντο P. κουστοδιας L.

CAP. XXVIII. 1. Ὀψε (Ὀ *rubro* w) wP. –δε HPz *init. peric.* σαββατω
n. P. ἠλθεν iH**L. ἠλθεν wP. θεωρουσαι z. 2. ἰδοῦ w *passim.* ἴδοῦ P.
κυλησε L. απεκυλισεν H**P. +του μνημειου (*post* θυρας) H. 3. ἦν w.
?. ἰδεα w. ειδεα vz. ὡς w, ὡσῆ L, ὡσεἰ P (*pro* ὡσει). 4. εγενοντω P.
νωντο z*. ὡσοὶ L, ὡσεἰ P (*pro* ὡσει). 5. ειπεν iwHP. γυναιξιν iwHPz.
3ησθε L. οἰδα iHP. 6. εστι w. ὡδε iwLz [*non* vP]. ἠγερθη iwHPz.
εν iwLHPz. ὅπου i. 7. πορευθεισε ?w*. πορευθησαι LP. εἰπατε
v. 13) P. ἠγερθη iP. ὀψεσθε HP. ειπεν w. 8. απελθουσαι L.
μιου P. –αυτου L. 9. –ὡς δε *usque ad* μαθηταις αυτου L. –ὁ ivwH.
ιντησεν w. *fin.* αυτον P. 10. φοβησθε L. φοβεισθαι P. και εκει
Lz. ὀψονται P. 11. πορευωμενων P. ἴδοῦ τηνες P. κουστοδιας L.
ιγγειλαν w*. ἁπαντα wH. 13. ὑμων (*pro* ἡμων) i. κυμωμενων H.
ἡγεμωνος HP. πεισωμεν iLPz. αὐτῶν P. ποιησωμεν iwLHPz.
διεφημησθη L. –λογος H*? οὑτος H. 16. ἑνδεκα wH**P *bis.* επο-

ρευθησαν οἱ ἑνδεκα μαθηται (−δε) z *sem. init. peric.* γαλλιλαιαν i. ὀρος P. 17. ιδον L. αυτον (*pro* αυτῳ) P. 18. προσελθον i. 19. −ουν ivLHP**z *bis* [*habet* w: οὐν P*]. −τα H. ὀνομα HP. −του *tertium* i. ἁγιου H. 20. διδασκον (*cf. v.* 17) L*. -τες L**. ενετειλαμιν P. ἑως H.

SUBSCRIPTIONES CODICUM. ευαγγελιον κατα ματθαιον· στιχοι βχ́. i. ευαγγελιον κατα ματθαιον στιχοι δισχιλιοι ἑξακοσιοι· εξεδοθη δε ὑπ' αυτου μετα χρονους οκτω της του χῡ αναληψεως w *rubro*. *Nil habent* vL.

SANCTI MARCI EVANGELIUM.

[CAP. I. 1—16.]

Το κατα μαρκον ἁγιον ευαγγελιον iv. ευαγγελιον κατα μαρκον w *rubro*. εκ του κατα μαρκον ευαγγελιου L *rubro*.

CAP. I. 2. καθως (*pro* ὡς) w. ἐγῶ ἀποστελλῶ P. μου (*pro* σου *post* προσωπου) L*. ενπροσθεν σου w** *marg.* (*deest in* w*). 3. ἑτοιμασατε HP. +του (*ante* κ̄υ) v. 4. +ὁ (*ante* βαπτιζων) P. 5. εξεπορευοντο ivH* Pz. ενεπορευετο L. −ἡ w. ἡ H. ἱροσολυμιται w. ἱεροσολυμειται L. ἱεροσολυμηται iP. −και *tert.* L. −παντες L. +ποταμω (*post* ιορδανη) L. 6. ἦν P. +ὁ (*ante* ιωαννης) ivLHPz. οσφυν, υ *mutatum in* w. ὁσφυν H. ὡσφυν P. ὀσφῦν vz. μελη H*P. 7. εκηρυσσεν wP. −οπισω μου P. ὀπισω (*sic vv.* 17, 20) iwH. οὗ P. κηψας i. 8. −μεν L. ὑμας εβαπτισα L. −δε L. ὑμας βαπτισει L. 9. ἠλθεν wP. +ὁ (*ante* ι̅ς) iw**LHPz. *bis* [*non v*]. ναζαρετ ivL*?Pz *bis* [-εθ wL**H]. εις την γαλιλαιαν (*pro* της γαλιλαιας) P. εις τον ιορδανην ὑπο ιωαννου LP. 10. αναβαινον H. • εκ (*pro* απο) LPz. ειδεν wHz. ιδε L. ιδεν P. −το (*ante* π̄να) P. ὡς ivwH, ὡσεὶ P (*pro* ὡσει). καταβαινων P. εις (*pro* επ') L. 11. οὑτος εστιν (*pro* συ ει) P. σοι (*pro* ῳ) LH. ηυδοκησα vH. ηὐδοκησα P. 12. ευθεως w*Hz. εκβαλλει αυτον L. 13. ἦν *bis* (*sic v.* 22) w. −εν τῃ ερημῳ w* (*habet marg.*) L. +επι (*ante* ἡμέρας) L. τεσαρακοντα i. +και νυκτας μ̄ (*ante* πειραζομενος) w** *marg.* ἦν *secund.* H. −οἱ Hz. 14. −τον ivH. −ὁ ivwH*. −της βασιλειας L. 15. *init.* −και v. 16. και παραγων (*pro* περιπατων δε) L. ειδεν iH. +του (*ante* σιμωνα) L. του σιμωνος (*loco* αυτου) Lz (–του z). +του σιμωνος (*post* αυτου) ivwH. βαλλοντα H*. αμφιβαλλοντας vw*. αμφιβαλλοντας τα δικτυα εις την θαλασσαν (–αμφιβληστρον) L. αμφιβάλοντας αμφιβλιστρον z. ἦσαν wH. ἁλιεις (*sic v.* 17 wL) iwL. 17. γινεσθαι H*. –γενεσθαι L. ἁλειεις i. 18. –αυτων L. ἠκολουθησαν wH. 19. ὀλιγον wH. ιδεν L. ζεβαιδεου i. δυκτυα i. *fin.* +αυτων w. 20. +ευθυς (*ante* αφεντες) L. απηλθεν w. 21. καφαρναουμ L. –εισελθων H. εδιδασκεν εις την συναγωγην (–εισελθων) L. +την (*ante* συναγωγην) ivwHz. εδιδασκεν iwH. 22. οὐχ' ivwH. *fin.* +αυτων z. 23. τω καιρω εκεινω ανος τις εν τη συναγωγη των ιουδαιων Hz (*init. peric.*). ἦν w. ανεκραξεν w. 24. συ (*pro* σοι) z. ναζαρινε v. ναζωρινε L. ἦλθες w. οἶδα H. ἅγιος H. 25. φημωθητι L. 27. εξεθαμβηθησαν z. ἑαυτους ivwLz. ἑαυτους H. λεγωντας i. λεγοντες z. –τι εστι τουτο H. εστιν w. ἡ καινη διδαχη αὑτη L. διαδαχη w*. αὑτη ἡ καινη z. κατεξουσιαν wLH. πνευμασιν H. επιτασει H. 28. εξηλθεν iw. και εξηλθεν (–δε) Hz. –ευθυς v. +πανταχου (*post* ευθυς) L. 29. ευθυς L. εξελθων L. εισηλθον v. ἦλθεν w. ηλθεν L. ηλθεν ὁ ις (*init. peric.*) z. οικιαν w. 30. +του (*ante* σιμωνος) Lz. ευθυς L. 31. +και (*ante* κρατησας) L. 32. Ὀψιας (Ὁ *rubro* iH) iwH. ἥλιος iH. +παντες (*post* εφερον) L. 33. ην ἡ πολις ὁλη επισυνηγμενη H. ην ὁλη ἡ πολις επισυνηγμενη z. ην συνηγμενη L. ἦν w. 34. εθεραπευσεν wH. ποικιλοις L. εξεβαλλε v. εξεβαλεν wH. ηφιεν wLHz. ἤδεισαν w, *at* ἦσαν H* (δει *supra, rubro, antiquâ manu*). *fin.* +τον χν ειναι w**LH (–τον w**H). 35. εννυχα H. +και (*ante* αναστας) L. εξηλθεν wLH. +ὁ ις (*post* απηλθεν) ivPz *init. peric.* κακει iw [κάκει Lz]. 36. ὁ τε L, ὁ τε w (*pro* ὁ). σημων P. 37. εὑροντες P. ζητουσιν wLPz. –σε L, *at* σε ζητουσι [ν wPz] ivwHPz. 38. ερχομενας πολεις L. κωμοπολις P. και εκει ivwLHPz. ελυληθα i. εξεληλυθα w*, *at* εληλυθα w**LPz. 39. ἦν wP. εις τας συναγωγας wL. –τα H. 40. ὁ πεπρος (*sic*) L* (λ L**). –αυτον *secund.* L. –και *tert.* L*. λεγον αυτον z. [L *habet* ὁτι]. καθαρησαι P. 41. αυτον (*pro* αυτου) P. λεγων (*pro* και λεγει) L. 42. –ειποντος αυτου L. αυτου (αυ H**?) H. ἡ λεπρα απ' αυτου w. εκαθερισθη P. 43. εμβρυμησαμενος i. εμβρισαμενος L. εμβρημησαμενος αυτον P. εξεβαλεν αυτον ευθεως w. *fin.* αυτω L. 44. μηδενὶ iPz. μηδὲν ivz. –μηδεν LP. αλλα vw. αρχιερει L. πρὸσένεγκαι P. ἃ H. προσεταξεν wP. μωυσης w** [*non* iL]. 45. *Rasura in* w *inter* διαφη *et* μιζειν. μηκέτι i. ὥστε μηκέτι w. αλλα v. ἦν w. παντοθεν w*.

CAP. II. 1. εισηλθεν ὁ ις παλιν iv. εισηλθε (-εν w) παλιν wL. –παλιν *et* δι' ἡμερων HPz *init. peric.* καπερ *mutatum in* L: *cf.* I. 21. ἠκουσθη wHP.

οικον Pz. εστιν iwLPz. 2. ὥστε w. μηκέτι w. μὴκέτι Pz. μὴδὲ vLHPz. μὴδὲν i. ελαλη w. 3. φεροντες παραλυτικον L. αἱρομενον wLz. τεσαρων i. 4. αυτω προσεγγισαι w. αυτον (pro αυτῳ) P. ὄχλον P. ἦν wP. εξωρυξαντες LP. χαλωσιν P. κραβαττον iwLH [non v], κραβατον P (sic vv. 9, 11, 12). ἐφ' οὗ L. 5. και ιδων (–δε) L. πιστην iP. αφεονται P. σου (pro σοι) H*. αφεονται σου αἱ ἁμαρτιαι (–σοι) L. ἁμαρτιαις σου P. 6. ἦσαν P. τιναις P. γραμματαιων P. εκει' v. 7. οὕτω w. οὕτως οὗτος H. –οὕτως P. βλασφημειας i. ἁμαρτιαις w. 8. +αυτοι (post οὕτως) ivwLHPz (οὗτος P). –ειπεν αυτοις P* (habet marg.). αυτω (pro αυτοις) z. διάλογίζεσθαι P. 9. ευκοποτερον P. αφεονται LP. σου (pro σοι) ivwLHPz. ἢ P. εγειρε vLz [non iw]. εγηραι P. ἆρον w. τον κραβαττον σου (κραβατον P, κραββατον z) wLPz. περιπατι P. 10. ἴδητε P. επι της γης αφιεναι HP. ἁμαρτιας επι της γης w*z [i cum Elzev.]. 11. εγειρε ivwLz. εγηρε P. ἆρον w. οικον wP. 12. ἠγερθη wHP. ἆρας w. εξιστασθε z. ουδεποτε H. ειδωμεν L. ἴδομεν HP. εἴδωμεν z. 13. εξηλθεν wL. +ὁ ιησους (post εξηλθεν) L. επι (pro παρα) L*. 14. παραγων δε (–και) L. +ὁ ις (ante ειδε) ivPz [non L]. ειδεν ιακωβον (pro λευιν) L. ειδεν H. ιδεν wP. λευι w. λευειν P. τελωνειον L. ακολουθη P. ηκολου ησεν L. ἠκολουθησεν wHP. 15. –εν τῳ L. εν το i. ὀδω οικια L. οἰκια wHP. ἦσαν wHP (sic w v. 18). ἠκολουθησαν wHP. 16. ειδοντες L. –και ἁμαρτωλων L. fin. +ὁ διδασκαλος ὑμων L. 17. χριαν P. ἦλθων P. –εις μετανοιαν w* (habet marg. rubro). 18. ἦσαν H. φαρισαιοι (pro των φαρισαιων prim.) w*Lz. διὰτί iow. fin. νηστευουσιν ivwLH. 19. ὁ H. εστιν LH. ἑαυτον L. 20. ὅτ' ἂν iH. ὅτ' ἂν w. ἀρθη L. νηστευουσιν w. εκεινη τη ἡμερα wLz. 21. init. –και w*LHz. επιβλημμα z. ῥακκους wLz. επιραπτει wLH**z. –επι L. μηγε (pro μη) wH. αἱρει wLHz. –αυτου L. απ' αυτου το πληρωμα (pro το πληρωμα αυτου) w. +απο (post καινον) L. 22. οἶνον et οἶνος quater w. οἶνον prim. H. μηγε (pro μη) z. ρησει H*. –ὁ νεος L. απωλουνται v. αλλ' H. βλητεων H. 23. +παλιν (ante εγενετο) L. αυτον πορευεσθαι L. επορευετο ὁ ις Hz, init. peric. –εν iHPz. δια τον σποριμων εν τοις σαββασιν (των w**) w. σαββασιν P. ἤρξαντο P. οἱ μαθηται αυτου ηρξαντο L. ὁδοιπορουντες (pro ὁδον ποιειν) L. τειλλοντες z. 24. φαρισσαίοι P. Rasura post τι in w. ποιουσι w. +οἱ μαθηται σου (post ποιουσιν) L. –εν wL. εξεστιν wPz. 25. λεγει (pro αυτος ελεγεν) L. εποιησε (σε super lacunam) L. εποιησεν wHP. εσχεν wLHPz. επινασεν P. 26. οικον wHP. ἀβιαθαρ ?z. –του ivHP [non wLz]. ους i. +μονοις (ante τοις ἱερευσιν) L. –και εδωκε ad fin. vers. H. εδωκεν wP. ουσιν iwLz. οὖσιν P. 27. τῶ prim. P. οὐχ' ivwHPz sæpius.

CAP. III. 1. εισηλθεν wHP. ἦν w. ἦν P. εξηραμενην (sic v. 3) P. χειραν P. 2. —ει P*. σαββασιν αυτον θεραπευσει w. σαββασιν P. θεραπευσει i. κατηγορησουσιν v. κατηγωρησωσιν L. fin. αυτον H. 3. εχων P. εγειρε ivwLPz. 4. +τι w** supra εξεστι. εξεστιν εν τοις L. ἡ P. 5. μετ' ὀργης P. πορωσει iPz. πορρωσει H. —σου ivP. εξετεινεν wLP. απεκατεσταθη ivPz [non wH], at απεκτανθη L. —ὑγιης ὡς ἡ αλλη w* (habet marg. ὑγιεις w**). 6. εδιδουν (pro εποιουν) L, at εποιησαν Hz. απωλεσωσιν w. απολεσωσιν LH. 7. ανεχωρησεν wH. μετα των μαθητων αυτου ανεχωρησε L. παρα L, εις z (pro προς). ἠκολουθησεν w. ηκολουθησεν z. —και (ante απο secund.) L. 8. ιδουμαιας (δ mutatum) L. σιδονα LH. ακουοντες L. ὁσα i. εποιησεν w*. εποιη w**z. ἠλθον w. 9. ειπεν iwH. προσκαρτερει H. fin. +οἱ οχλοι L. 10. εθεραπευεν w. αυτω (pro αυτου) L. ἀψωνται iH. ἀπτωνται w. 11. —τα bis L. ὁτ' ἀν iH. ὁτ' ἀν w. εθεωρουν LH. αυτον εθεωρουν (pro αυτον) z. προσεπιπτον wLHz. εκραζον wLHz. λεγοντες LH*. fin. ὁ θς υἱος του θυ L. 12. φανερον αυτον ivwHz [non L]. ποιωσιν w*L (ποιησωσιν w**Hz). fin. +ὁτι ηδεισαν τον χν αυτον ειναι w** marg. 13. ανεβη ὁ ις z (init. peric.). ανεβη H. ὀρος H. +ὁ ις (post ορος) L. οὓς H. ηθελησεν L. 14. εποιησεν wH. +οὓς και αποστολους ωνομασεν (post δωδεκα) L. ὡσι v. ὡσιν w. αποστελλει v. αποστελει H. 15. εκβαλειν H. 16. init. +πρωτον σιμωνα L. επεθηκαν w. επεθηκεν ὀνομα τω σιμονι H. πετρον ?L*. 17. Rasur. inter τον et του H. —του secund. v. αυτου (pro του ιακωβου) L. ὀνοματα wH. βοανηργες wLz. 18. φιλιπον H*. βαρθολαμαιος L*. —και· βαρθολομαιον usque ad Θωμαν i. +τον τελωνην (post ματθαιον) L. —τον του z. θαδαιον H. 19. ἰουδαν L. ιουδαν bis scriptum z*. ισκαριωθ H. fin. τον οἰκον w. οἰκον H. 20. +ὁ (ante οχλος) w. ὀχλος H. ὡς (pro ὡστε) v. μηκετη (pro μη) H. δυνασθε L*. μηδὲ (pro μητε) wH sem. 21. εξεσταται L. 22. δαιμονων w*L. 23. σατανὰς σατανὰν z. εκβαλειν L. 24. αφ' (pro εφ') z. μερεισθη H. 25. Deest versus ob ὁμοιοτελ. in L. οικια prim. w, bis H. μεριθη H*. στηναι ἡ οἰκεια w*. 26. —ει v. 27. init. ουδεις δυναται (—ου) ivwHz. αλλ' ουδεις δυναται (—ου) L. οἰκιαν bis wH. διαρπᾶσαι iwHz. ἁρπασαι L. δειση z. fin. διαρπαση iwz [non L]. 28. τοις υἱοις των ανθρωπων τα ἁμαρτηματα Hz. +αἱ (ante βλασφημιαι) vLH (αἱ H) z. ὁσα LH*z. εαν H. 29. βλασφηση L*. βλασφημιση L**. εσται z [non L]. ἁμαρτιας (pro κρισεως) L. 31. init. και ερχονται (—ουν) L. οὐν H. +αυτου (post αδελφοι) w. ἡ μηρ αυτου και οἱ αδελφοι αυτου H. ἑστωτες iwH. [non z]. καλουντες (pro φωνουντες) L. 32. εκαθιτο i. εκαθηντο H. περι αυτον οχλος wLHz. και λεγουσιν (pro ειπον δε) L. +και αἱ αδελφαι σου (*ante* εξω) ivz [*non* wL]. ζητουσιν w. 33. και λεγει (*pro* λεγων) L. και (*pro* ἤ) z, *at* ἤ H. 34. τους κυκλω περι αυτον μαθητας καθημενους ειπεν L. ἰδοὺ wLz. 35. ποιησει i. αυτος (*pro* οὗτος) H. −μου *secund.* L. +μου (*post* μητηρ) v. *fin.* εστιν ivwHz.

Cap. IV. 1. παλιν δε (−και) L. συναγεται L. ὀχλος H. ὥστε (*sic vv.* 32, 37) w. −το wz. καθησθαι εις το πλοιον L. καθησθε H. καθεισθαι z. ἦν w. ἦσαν H. 2. αυτους (*pro* αυτοις) iHz. 3. σπειρον z. 4. ὦ z, ὁ ὃ (*pro* ὃ). επεσεν wH (επι *pro* παρα H). ὁδον i. ηλθεν wH. −του ουρανου ivwLH [*non* z]. 5. *init.* και Hz. αλλα (−δε) z. ἄλλα L. ὅπου i. ειχεν wH. εξανετειλεν wH, *at* εξεβλαστησε L. 7. *Bis script. in* v. επι (*pro* εις) z. απεπνιξαν H. εδωκεν wLH. 8. ἐν *ter* ivwHz [*non* L]. ἑξηκοντα wH. ἑκατον w. 9. −αυτοις ivwL [*non* z.] ὦτα vH. 10. ἠρωτησαν iwH. *fin.* επηρωτησαν αυτον οἱ μαθηται αυτου τις ἡ παραβολη αὕτη L. ηρωτησαν τον ιν οἱ μαθηται αυτου την παραβολην ταυτην z, *init. peric.* 11. λεγει z. γνων L. −γνωναι w* (*habet marg.*). τα μυστηρια Hz. −δε z. −τοις εξω H* (*habet antiquâ manu*). −τα w. 12. βλεπωντες Lz. βλεπωσιν w. ιδωσιν wL. ακουωντες i. ακουουσι i. ακουωσιν w. ακουσωσι H. συνιωσιν wL. σινιωσι z. επιστρεψωσιν w. αφεθησεται w. ἀφεθη L. 13. οὐκ' i. 14. +του θῦ (*post* λογον) z. 15. ὅτ' ἂν i (*sic v.* 16 H). ὅτ' ἂν w, *passim.* ὅταν H. ακουσωσι i. ευθυς LH (*sic vv.* 16, 17 H). σατανὰς z. αἱρει wL. ερει H. αἱρη z. εις αυτους (*pro* εν ταις καρδιαις αυτων) L. 16. −ὁμοιως L. ὁμοιως εισιν H. σπειρωμενοι (*sic v.* 18) z. +και (*ante* ευθεως) z. λαμβανουσι H. λαμβανωσιν z. −αυτον L. 17. εχουσιν w. εχωσι z. αὑτοις w*. γινομενης z. 18. −οὗτοι εισιν *prim.* L, *secundum* ivwHz. ακουσαντες L. 19. αἰωνος w. πορευομεναι Lz. 20. σπειροντες z. οἵτινες w. ακουωσι L. −τον L. ἐν *ter* ivwLHz. (−ἐν *secund.* w). ἑξηκοντα wz. ἑκατον w. 21. +ιδετε (*ante* μητι) L. ερχεται ὁ λυχνος H. −ὁ L. καιεται (*pro* ερχεται) L. μωδιον i. +ἵνα (*post* η) L. επι (*pro* ὑπο *secund.*) i. +τεθη (*post* κλινην) L. ὑπο (*pro* επι) L. *fin.* τεθη iL. 22. εστιν v. −τι wLz. εἰ μη ἵνα (*pro* ὁ εαν μη) L. −ὃ w. οὐδε H. αποκρυφον εγενετο z. ἐλθη w. ελθη εις φανερον H. 23. εχειν L. −ωτα L. ὦτα vwH. 24. −εν ᾧ *usque ad* μετρηθησεται ὑμιν L. +γαρ (*ante* μετρω) z. μετριτε i. μετριθησεται iw. 25. εαν (*pro* αν) i. εχει (*pro* εχῃ) iwz*. εχει γαρ (−αν) L. *fin.* +εν ᾧ μετρω μετρειτε μετρηθησεται ὑμιν και προστεθησεται ὑμιν L. 26. οὕτως H. ὥσπερ L, εαν H*, ὡς αν H** *antiquâ manu* (*pro* ὡς εαν). βαλη ανος z. βαλλει iL. −τον L. 27. καθευδει vL. εγειρεται vw*L. ἐγερεῖτε z. βλαστανει iv. μηκυνεται w*. *fin.* αυτον H*, αυτοις H**. 28. αυτοματι z. −γαρ z. +και (*post* χορτον) L.

σει i. πληρης z. σταχει L. 29. ὅτ' ἂν (*sic vv.* 31, 32) iH. εξαποστελ-
. παρεστη i. θερησμος z**. 30. και ελεγεν αυτοις πως ὁμοιωσω
ινι) L. ελεγεν iwH. ὁμοιωσω i. πως ὁμοιωσομεν (—τινι) H. τινι (*pro*
) LH. παραβολη αυτην θωμεν L. παραβαλομεν iHz. 31. *init.* παρα-
ομεν αυτην ὡς κοκκον L. κοκκον ivHz [*non* w]. ὡς (*pro* ὁς) L. σπαρει i.
κροτερος *ad fin. vers.* L. μικροτερον w*. μικροτερος εστιν παντων των
ρματων της γης z. 32. αναβαινη z. μειζων παντων των λαχανων Hz.
z. 33. —πολλαις iz. ελαλη (*sic v.* 34 i) iw. εδυναντο ivwL [*non* z].
αντο H. 34. κατίδιαν ivwL. +τον λογον (*ante* κατίδιαν) H. επελυεν iH.
λυεν w. επελυσε L. 35. ελεγεν L. ὀψιας i?w. διελθομεν iz.
αφιουσι *et* +και (*post* οχλον) L. ὀχλον H. ὡς H. ἠν *bis* (*sic v.* 38) w.
ια (*pro* πλοιαρια) iLHz. 37. λελαψ μεγαλη ανεμου L. λελαμψ i.
ιψ Hz. και τα κυματα (—δε) L. κοιματα i. επεβαλεν iz*. επιβαλλεν
ὡστε ηδη αυτο βυθιζεσθαι H. ἠδη i. 38. αυτος ην z. εν (*pro* επι
ι.) Lz. την πρυμνην i. εγειραντες αυτον λεγουσιν αυτο L. αυτο (*pro*
ν) H. μελλει iw*LH [*non* z]. απολυμεθα iw*. απολλοιμεθα z. 39. εγερ-
L. επετιμησεν w. ειπεν iwH. πεφημωσω i. γαλινη i. 40. οὑτως
οι εστε L. εσται i. οὑτως ivwHz. ουπω (*pro* πως ουκ) L. πιστην i.
αλληλους i. ἀρα iv. ἀρα w. εστι i. οἱ ανεμοι iv. ανμος H*. ὑπακουσιν
αυτω ὑπακουει L.

CAP. V. 1. ηλθεν iL. ἠλθον w** (ἠλθων w*?). ηλθεν ὁ ις z *init. peric.*
το z. —της θαλασσης L. γαδαρινων i. γεργεσηνων H [L *cum Elzev.*].
ξελθοντος αυτου LH. ὑπηντησεν L. 3. ὁς i. κατοικιαν z. μνημασιν
L**Hz. (-σιν z). οὑτε i. οὑτε H. ἀλυσεσιν (*sic v.* 4) iwH. +ουκετι (*ante*
ις) L. εδυνατο ivwLHz. δεισαι z. 4. α *mutat. in* αυτον H. πεδες iL**.
ες L*. παιδαις z*. διεσπασασθε i. *Rasura in* H *inter* διεσπασ *et* θαι.
τεις iwH. πεδαις (*pro* τας πεδας) z. συντρίφθαι z. ισχυεν αυτον wLHz.
σαι i. 5. διαπαντὸς iw. νυκτας z. εν τοις μνημασι (μνημειοις L, μνη-
ιν H) και εν τοις ορεσιν wLHz. μνημασι [*ordo cum Elzev.*] i. ἠν w.
γαζων L. κατακοπτον iH. 6. και ιδων το ιησουν (—δε) L. Ἰδων i.
μακρωθεν i. απομακροθεν L. —απο wHz. εδραμεν iw. *fin.* αυτον H.
πεν i. λεγει (*pro* ειπε) wHz. συ (*pro* σοι) i. ὁρκιζω ivwHz. 8. ελεγεν
απο (*pro* εκ) v. 9. επηρωτισεν i. ονομα σοι wLH (ὀν. H) z. +εστιν
e ονομα *prim.*) i. λεγει αυτω (*pro* απεκριθη λεγων) wLHz. —λεγων i.
εων z [L *cum Elzev.*]. ὀνομα H. +εστιν (*ante* ὁτι) L. 10. αποστειλη
ους iH. αποστειλη αυτον z. αποστεῖλλη αυτον w. 11. Ἠν H**. τω
iv. αγελη χοιρων μεγαλη προς το ορει L. —προσ τα ορη wHz, *at fin.*

+προς τω ορει wH (ὀρει H) z. 12. παρακαλεσαντες αυτον ειπον (−παντες οἱ δαιμονες λεγοντες) L. παρεκαλουν w. −παντες w. δεμονες H. 13. αυτους H. εθεως L*. −ὁ ις v. ὡρμησενiz. κρυμνουi. ἠσαν wH. επνηγοντοiHz. 14. init. και οἱ (−δε) LHz. αυτους (pro τους χοιρους) L. απηγγειλαν wHz. εξῆλθον w. ηλθον Hz. ειδειν i. 15. θεορουσι i. καθιμενον i. −και tertium iL. −και ἱματισμενον z. σοφρονουντα iH. 16. διηγισαντο δε (−και) iv (διηγη. v). 17. ηρξατο w*. ὁριων H. 18. εμβαινοντος wHz. αυτω (pro αυτον prim.) v. ἡνα H. μετ' αυτου η wLHz. 19. και (pro ὁ δε ις) wHz. και ὁ (−δε) L. οἰκον w. διαγγειλον L. αυτους (pro αυτοις) i. πεποιηκεν LH. πεποιηκε ivz. περιποιηκεν w*. ηλεησεν w. ἡλεησεν H. 20. απηλθεν wH. ηρξαντο w*. ἡρξατο H. ὁσα i. 21. +ηλθεν (post παλιν) L. προς (pro επ') L. ἦν w. 22. αρχησυναγωγων LHz. ὀνοματι wH. ιαιρος z*. προσπιπτει προς L. 23. −ὁτι L. εσχατος H. επιθεις z. χειρα αυτη (−τας) L. ἱνα (pro ὁπως) L. ζηση L. 24. απηλθεν wH. ηκολουν v. ἠκολουθει w. ἠκολουθη H sem. ἠκολουθησε τω ιυ ὀχλος H sem. ἠκολουθησαν τω ιυ ὀχλοι πολλοῖ P, ἠκολουθησεν τω ιυ z, init. peric. ὀχλος H. fin. αυτω z. 25. οὐσα wHP. ρυση vP. δωδεκα ετη L. 26. παρ' αυτης ivL [non z]. −παρ' H. παραυτης P. ὡφεληθεισα iw. ὀφεληθησα P. ὡφεληθησα z. 27. ὀχλω HP. εις τον οχλον L. ὀπισθεν wH. ὀπιθεν P. ἡψατο wH. +του κρασπεδου (post ἡψατο) Hz. ἱματιου i. 28. ελεγεν w. ελε P*. +εν ἑαυτη (post γαρ) iw. ἀψομαι LHP. ἁψωμαι wz. σωθησωμαι LP. 29. το (pro τῳ) P. ἰάται wP. ἰᾶται Lz. μαστηγος P. 30. επι (pro εν secund.) z. ὀχλω (sic v. 31) P. ελεγεν wLP*. λεγει P**. 33. φοβηθησα P. −και τρεμουσα H. ἴδυια P. τι (pro ὁ) z. επ' αυτην L. ἦλθεν w. ἦλθεν P. +εμπροσθεν παντων (ante πασαν) L. αιτιαν αυτης (pro αληθειαν) L. 34. init. ὁ δε ιησους Lz. +θαρσι (ante θυγατερ) P. πιστης P. σεσωκεν wHP. Post ειρηνην sic explicit pericope και ιαθη ἡ γυνη απο της ὡρας εκεινης H. ισθη z. 35. αρχησυναγωγου (sic vv. 36, 38) LH. απεθανεν w. −ετι H. σκυλλης L. σκυλεις z. 37. αυτω ουδενα H. οὐδ' ἑνα z. ακολουθησαι w. +του (ante ιακωβου) v. αυτου (pro ιακωβου) w*z. 38. ερχονται v. οἰκον wH. +και (ante κλαιοντας) wLHz [non iv]. αλλαλάζονται i. 39. κλαιοντες (pro και κλαιετε) H. 40. +ειδοτες ὁτι απεθανεν (ante ὁ δε) L. εκβαλλῶν w. παντας ivwLHz. ἦν (sic v. 42) w. fin. ανακημενον i*. κατακεκλιμενον L. 41. κρατεισας H. μεθ' ἑρμεινευομενον H. ταλειθά κουμεῖ L. κοὑμ z. εγειρε vwL [non iz]. 42. περιεπατη iw*. ἦν H. μεγαλει L. 43. διετειλατο v. διεστηλατο H. μηδεὶς iv. ειπεν iwH.

CAP. VI. 1. ἠλθεν wH sem. fin. ἑαυτου H sem. H** sem. 2. + οἱ (ante πολλοι) L. ακουσαντες vLH. τουτο (pro τουτῳ) L. −ὁτι ivLz. ἱνα (pro ὁτι)

w. −και *quart.* H. γινωνται wH. 3. οὐχ' ivwz. ὁ του τεκτωνος υἱος και
μαριασ L. +της (*ante* μαριας) H. ὁ αδελφος (−δε) z. ιωσητος (*pro* ιωση) L.
σιμονος w. αἱ H. ὡδε wz [*non* iL]. ὑμας w*. *fin.* ἑαυτω i. 4. ελεγεν
iwH. −αυτοις L. *Rasura inter* 'O *et* ι̅ς̅ *in* i. −ὁ ι̅ς̅ H. −ὁτι L. εστιν w. προ-
φητις i. ἀτιμος H. τη ἑαυτου πατριδι L. συγγενευσι iwL, *at* τη συγγενεια
αυτου z. οἰκια wH. *fin.* αὐτου (υ *mutat.*) v. 5. εδυνατο wH. οὐδὲμίαν
ivLz. οὒδὲμίαν w. ὀλιγοις wH. αρωστοις z*. εθεραπευσεν iwL. 6. εθαυ-
μαζεν wH**. περιηγεν ὁ ιησους L. περιῆγεν H. περιειγε z. περιηγαγεν
w*. κυκλω κωμας L. 7. −και προσκαλειται τους δωδεκα z *sem.*, *at* προσκαλε-
σαμενος ὁ ι̅ς̅ τους δωδεκα μαθητας αυτου ηρξατο Pz *sem.*, *init. peric.* ἡρξατο
wHP. αποστελλειν αυτους i. αποστελειν P. −των *bis* Lz *sem.* 8. παρηγ-
γελλεν iv. μὴδὲν iwz *sem.* αἰρωσιν vwHz *bis.* ἀρωσιν L. ερωσιν P. την
ὀδον i. μονην z *sem.* μη αρτον μη πηραν Pz *sem.* (*at* πειραν *cum* H, z *sem.*).
9. αλλα z *bis.* ενδυσησθε ivLP [*non* w]. ενδεδυσθαι Hz *bis.* 10. οἰκιαν wHP.
μενεται P. ἑως H. 11. *init.* και ὁς αν τοπος μη δεξηται L [*at* ακουσωσιν L].
εαν (*pro* αν) wHP. δεξονται HP. μήδέ ivwLPz *bis.* εισακουσωσιν H*. εκτει-
ναξατε HPz *sem.* ὑπὸκάτω wH. εστε Hz. ἢ *bis* P. και (*pro* ἢ *prim.*) z *sem.*
γομοροις i. πολη P. 12. εκηρυσσων H. μετανοησωσιν wLP. 13. εξεβαλον
i*z. ειληφον vwP. ἡλειφον H. εθεραπευοντο v. *fin.* +αυτους L. 14.
ἡκουσεν (ἡκ. z) ἡρωδης ὁ βασιλευς HPz. +την ακοην ιησου (*post* ἡρωδης) Lw**
(+και w** *marg.*) Pz (Pz *post* βασιλευς *init. peric.*). ὀνομα P. βαπτιστης L.
ἠγερθη P, *at* ανεστη w. διατοῦτο ivLz. αἱ δυναμεις ενεργουσιν iw (ενερργ. w*).
αἱ H. −εν P. 15. *init.* αλλοι δε wL. ἡλιας vwL [*non* iz]. −ὁτι ἡλιας εστιν
αλλοι δε ελεγον P. −δε vHz. −η ivwLHPz. 16. −ὁ w*z. απεκεφαλησα P.
−εστιν, αυτος L. εκ νεκρων ηγερθη L. +γαρ (*ante* ηγερθη) z. ἡγερθη wHP.
17. −ὁ L. εκρατησεν wH**P. και εβαλεν εις φυλακην (*pro* εν τῃ φυλακῃ) L.
−τῃ ivwHPz. φοῦ P** *marg. tantum.* 18. ελεγεν wH**P. εξεστιν wP.
συ (*pro* σοι) P. 19. ἡρωδιᾶς z. ενηχεν P. αυτου (*pro* αυτῳ) Pz. ἡθελεν P.
εδυνατο w. 20. εφοβητο P. ιδος P. ακουων H. +ἁ (*post* πολλα) L. εποιη
w*. ῒδεως P. ηκουεν iwH**z. ηκουσεν L. ἡκουεν P. 21. ευκερου P.
γενεθλιοις P*. εποιησεν L. μεγιστάσιν iwHP. μεγιστανοις z. −τοις
quart. i*. 22. −της *secund.* v. ωρχησαμενης v. ὀρχησαμενης P. αιτισον
P. αἰτησον z. αν (*pro* εαν, *sic v.* 23) L. ἐᾶν (*sic v.* 23) H. θελεις P.
αἰτησον με και δωσω σοι ὁ εαν θελης w. 23. ὡμωσεν P. ὡμοσεν z. αἰτησης
με w. −με LH*z. ἐᾶν αἰτησεις (−με) P. 24. ειπεν *bis* wHP, *prim.* i, *secund.*
Lz. αἰτησομαι wP. 25. ἡτησατο iwH. ἡτισατο P. ἐξαυτης vH. εξ αυ-
της L*. ἐξ αὐτῆς P. πινακη (*sic v.* 28) P. 26. ὁρκους iv*. ηθελεν H.

ἠθελησεν P. —αυτην L. ανταθετησαι L. 27. ὁ βασιλευς αποστειλας w. σπεκουλατορα i (εσπ. i*) vwLP [non Hz]. αχθηναι L (εχθηναι *Dobbin.*, *forsan verius*). αυτου την κεφαλην w. 28. απεκεφαλησεν iPz. ηνεγκεν H**. ἠνεγκεν P. 29. ἠλθον wP. ἠραν wLz. ἡραν P. εθαψαν (*pro* εθηκαν) i. αυτῶ (*pro* αυτο) LH. 30. συναγωνται H *sem.* —και (*ante* ὁσα *prim.*) vH *sem.* P**. και ὁσα εδιδαξαν και ὁσα εποιησαν w*. 31. +ὁ ιησους (*ante* δευτε) L. κατιδιαν (*sic v.* 32) ivL [*non* w]. ερειμον (*sic v.* 32) H. αναπαυσασθε L. ὁλιγον iwH. ἠσαν H. —οἱ *secund.* iw. ευκαιρουν ivLH. ηὐκαιρουν w. 32. απηλθεν iv. και απηλθεν εν τω πλοιω εις ερημον τοπον κατιδιαν L. εν πλοιω (—τῳ) H. 33. ιδον iLH. —οἱ οχλοι ivwH [*habet* L]. αυτους (*pro* αυτον *prim.*) w. —πολλοι L. προσηλθον αυτω (*pro* αυτους *secund.*) L. προηλθεν w*. συνεισηλθον L. —και συνηλθον προς αυτον H. 34. ιδεν L. ὁ ις ειδεν wH. —ὁ ιησους L. ὀχλον H. ἠσαν wH. ἠρξατο H. αυτους διδασκειν w. αυτοις (*pro* αυτους) z. 35. Ἡδη *prim.* H**. πολλης ὡρας z. πολλοῖς w. —αυτῳ wz. —αυτου L. +αυτω (*post* λεγουσιν) wL. ἠδη *secund.* iH. 36. ἑαυτους (*pro* ἑαυτοις) L. —γαρ z. εχωσιν z. 37. αυτους (*pro* αυτοις *prim.*) H. δωσωμεν αυτοις αυτοις φαγειν· ἱνα ἑκαστος βραχυ λαβη L. αγωρασωμεν H. δηναριων διακοσιων ivwLH (διακωσιων H) z. 38. —και γνοντες z. πωσους H. εχεται H. ιδεται H. λεγουσιν wLz (+αυτω Lz). ἰχθυας w. 39. ανακλιθηναι L. ανακληθηναι z. —συμποσια *prim.* L* ? (*marg.*). χλορω iL. 40. ανεπεσαν v. πετηκοντα w. πεντεικοντα H. 41. ἰχθυας *bis* w. ευλογησεν wLH. κατεκλασεν w. —αυτου H. εμερισεν w, *at* παρεθηκε z. πασιν wL. 42. —παντες H. 43. ἠραν wL. κωφινους v. κοφινων πληρωματα L. πληρης v?z. +δυο (*ante* ιχθυων) L. ἰχθυων w. 44. ἠσαν wH. —ὡσει ivwHLz. πεντακισχιλειοι w*. 45. ἠναγκασεν iwH. +αυτον (*post* προαγειν) Lz *bis.* βηθσαϊδα z *sem.* —προς βηθσαϊδαν z *sem.* (*init. peric.*). οὐ (*pro* αυτος) z *bis.* απολυσει wLH. τους οχλους Lz *bis.* ὀχλον H *sem.* 46. ὀρος i. πρὁσευξασθε H. 47. ὀψιας w. ἠν (*sic vv.* 48, 52) wH. μεσον (*pro* εν μεσῳ) z. θαλασης w*. —και αυτος μονος επι της γης z. ἠν *supra* μονος w**. 48. ιδεν L. ιδων H. εναντιος ὁ ανεμος i. εναντιως z. +σφοδρα (*post* αυτοις) L. ηθελεν wH. παρελθηναι i. *fin.* αυτοις H. 49. ειδοντες i. οἱδοντες L. επι της θαλασσης περιπατουντα z. *fin.* και απο του φοβου εκραξαν H. 50. ελαλησεν wH. —θαρσειτε v. ειμη μι H. φοβειϲθαι w. 51. αναβει w*. εθαυμαζων w*. 52. συνηκων z. αλλ᾽ ην (*pro* ην γαρ) H (ἠν H) z. αυτων ἡ καρδια ivwHz [*non* L]. πεπορωμενη iz. 53. ἠλθον w. απηλθον H. εις γην (—την) L. γεννησαρετ ivwH *sem.* z. γενησαρεθ L. προσωρμησθησαν i. 54. εξελθων ὁ ις εκ z *init. peric.* ευθυς L. *fin.* +οἱ ανδρες του τοπου L.

·εριδραμωντες i. περιεδραμον LH. +εις (*ante* ὁλην) L. ὁλιν H. +και
ηρξαντο) LH. ηρξατο H*z. –τοις L. κραβαττοις iwLH [*non* vz]. τοις
τους) H*. προσφερειν z. ἤκουον iH. εστιν iwHz [*non* L]. *fin.* +ὁ
56. εαν (*pro* αν *prim.*) z. ἂν *bis* H. εις (*pro* ἢ *prim.*) z. +εις (*ante*
ς *et* αγρους) v. πολις H**. ετιθεσαν H. κασπεδου w*. ἅψωνται w.
ται H. ἥπτωντο vz. ἥψαντο L. εσοζοντο iH. διεσωζοντο L.
;AP. VII. 2. χερσιν L. τοῦτἐστιν i. τοῦτέστιν w. τουτέστι L. τουτ-
vHz. +τους (*ante* αρτους) L. –εμεμψαντο z. 3. πυγμὴ wz. πιγμη
–τας z. εσθιουσιν (*sic vv.* 4, 5) wLH. +τον αρτον (*post* εσθιουσι) z.
ιωσιν? w*. 4. ἀπ' w. +κρατουντες την παραδοσιν των πρεσβυτερων
και αλλα) i. ἃ H. χαλκιῶν L. χαλκείων z. –και κλινων v. 5. επιτα
–αυτον L. +λεγοντες (*post* γραμματεις) L. διατί w. ου περιπατουσιν
θηται σου H. περιπατουσιν wL. παραδωσιν w*H *sem.* κοιναις χερσιν
οις L. –τον w. 6. καλος H. *sem.* προεφυτευσεν z. (Cη *marg.* L).
σιν wH *sem.* μετα απ' εμου L. 7. διδασκαλιαις z. +και (*ante* ενταλ-
L** *recenti manu.* 8. τας παραδοσεις i. παραδωσιν w*H. παρ' ὁμοια
ποιειτε πολλα w. ποιειται L*. 10. μωυσης wLHz [*non* i]. ειπεν
I. –σου *secund.* L. 11. ἣ (*sic v.* 12) H. +αυτου (*post* μρι) iw. κόρβαν z.
i. –ὁ *secundum* L. –εαν *secund.* v. οφεληθεις i. ωφεληθεις w. ὠφε-
L. 12. *init.* –και L. οὐκ ἔτι iw [οὐκέτι vLHz]. –αὐτου *bis* L. 13.
υντες iwz. παραδωσει ivwLz. ἢ iL. πολλα τοιαυτα L. –πολλα H.
ι (*pro* τοιαυτα) z. ποιειτε πολλα w. εποιειτε i. 14. *Ras. ante* ὀχλον
15. +το (*ante* εισπορευομενον) i. κοινωναι v. –απ' αυτου εκεινα H.
H. 16. ἤτις z. ὠτα v. 17. +τον (*ante* οικον) v. οἰκον w. 18.
ivwLHz. ουπω (*pro* ου *prim.*) H. δυνατε i. 19. αλλα L. εἰς
d. H. καθαριζων iL. και καθαριζει z. 20. ελεγεν iwH. –το i. εκπο-
ενον εκ του ανου i. κινει (*sic v.* 23) L. 21. πορνιαι L. 22. ασελγιαι
ασελγια H*. ὀφθαλμος wH. 23. ταυτα παντα z. –τα H*? εσοθεν
24. ἦλθεν P. ὁρια L. –και σιδωνος P *init. peric.* –και εισελθων εις την
z *init. peric.* –την ivwLHP. οἰκιαν wHP. οὐδ' ἕνα z. ηθελεν iwH.
σε L. ἠθελεν P. εδυνηθη w. ηδυνηθην Pz. 25. +ἡ (*ante* γυνη) L.
ο ἧς) P [*non* L]. ἧς z. ειχεν wP. –αυτης LP. εν πνι ακαθαρτω LP.
πεσεν iw. παρα (*pro* προς) z. προσεπεσεν αυτω (–προς τους ποδας
) LP. 26. *init.* ἠν iw. ἡ δε γυνη ην HPz (ἦν P). ελλινης i. ἑλληνις
συραφοινικησα i. συρα· φοινικισσα v. συροφοινικισσα wz. συραφοι-
τα LH. συροφοινικησα P. το γενει i. ἠρωτα iwHP. εκβαλλει iw.
λη vHPz. της θυγατρος αυτης εκβαλλη (–εκ) L. –εκ P. 27. οὐ H.

εστιν iP. εστι καλον Hz. τοις κυναριοις βαλειν H. 28. λεγουσα (*pro* και λεγει αυτῳ) LP. –ναι LP. –γαρ LHP. ὑποκάτω wLz. εσθιουσιν LHP. εσθιῃ z. ψυχιων i. παιδαριων P. 29. διατοῦτον L. εξελυληθεν i. εξεληλυθεν w. εξεληλυθη P. 30. οἰκον P. εὑρεν w. εὑρεν iP. εξεληλυθῶς z. *Post* αυτης *sic explicit* H: εὑρεν και το παιδιον βεβλημενον επι την κλινην και το δαιμονιον εξεληλυθος. 31. *init.* –και i. +ὁ ιησους (*post* εξελθων) ivLz. ὁριων *bis* vL, *prim.* iH. σινδωνος L*. ἠλθεν wP. ηλθεν H. ηλθεν εις (*pro* προς) L. θαλασαν w*. γαλλιλαιας P. ἀναμέσον vLHPz. ἀναμέσων iw. 32. κοφον iP. μογγιλαλον ivLz. μογγιλαλων P. επιθει i. +επ' (*ante* αυτω) z. την την v. χειραν z. 33. επιλαβομενος H*Pz. εκ (*pro* απο) P. ὀχλου HP. κατιδιαν ivLPz. κατ' ἰδιαν H. εβαλεν iwHP. επεβαλε L. ὠτα wHP. πτυσας εις τα ωτα αυτου και ἠψατο L. ἠψατο i. γλωττης H. 34. εστεναξεν wP. ανεστεναξε L. εφαθα P. εφφαθᾶ z. εστιν wP. 35. διηνυχθησαν z. ελαλη P. +ευλογων τον θν̄ (*post* ελαλει) H*, *at eras. et* ορθως *in locum suffect.* H**. 36. *init.* και διεστηλατο w. αυτους i, αυτος w (*pro* αυτοις *prim.*). μὴδενὶ iPz. μαλον i. 37. ὑπερ· περισως L*. ὑπὲρπερισσῶς z. εξεπληττοντο L. πεποιηκεν iwHPz. κουειν w*. αλλαλους i.

Cap. VIII. 1. παλιν πολλου (*pro* παμπολλου) L. παμπολου iw*. πολλου Hz. φαγωσιν (*sic v.* 2, wL) iwL. –ὁ ιησους wz. 2. σπλαχνιζομαι i. χλον i. ηδι i. ἠδη w. ἡμεραι ivwHz [*non* L]. προσμενουσιν w. εχωσι v*. εχουσιν w. 3. αυτοις i. νηστις H. +του (*ante* οικον) L. οἰκον w. ὁδω w. απομακροθεν LH. ἡκουσι i. ἡκουσιν w. ἡκασιν LH. ἡκασι z. 4. δυνησηται L. –ὡδε L. ὡδε vwz [*non* i]. αρτον iHz. ερημιαις w. 5. αρτους εχετε z. 6. παρηγγειλεν w. ἑπτα (*sic v.* 8) H. εκλασεν wH. παραθωσιν w. παρατιθωσιν Lz. 7. ειχεν i. +και (*ante* ιχθυδια) z. ὀλιγα iw. +αυτα LHz, +ταυτα w (*ante* ευλογησας). ειπεν iwH. παραθηναι iv [*non* L]. παρατιθεναι H. παρατεθηναι z. *fin.* τω οχλω (*pro* και αυτα) z. 8. +παντες (*post* εχορτασθησαν) w. ἠραν wL. *fin.* +πληρεις L. 9. ἠσαν w. –οἱ φαγοντες H. ὡσεὶ z. 10. εμβας ευθυς wLH (ευθεως w). –το L. ἠλθεν w. μαγδαλα (*pro* δαλμανουθα) L. δαλμανουθᾶ z. 11. ηλθον H. ηρξᾶτο (*i.e.* αυτο?) w. συζητουντες (*pro* συζητειν αυτῳ ζητουντες) L. εκ (*pro* απο) L. 12. ου (*pro* ει) L. *fin.* τῆ γενεὰ αὕτη σημεῖον v. 13. παλιν εμβας L. –παλιν i. –το *prim.* iz. εις το πλοιον απηλθε παλιν (–εμβας *et* εις το περαν) H. 14. +οἱ μαθηται αυτου (*post* επελαθοντο) w**L. αρτους λαβειν L. +τους (*ante* αρτους) v. ἑνα μονον εχοντες αρτον (–και ει μη *et* ουκ) L. ἑνα H. 15. διεστειλατο Lz. +και (*ante* βλεπετε) L. +απο (*ante* της ζυμης *secund.*) L. *fin.* των ἡρωδιανων L. 17. ὁ δε ις̄ γνους (–και) H. +εν ἑαυτοις ολιγοπιστοι (*post* διαλογιζεσθε) LH (ὀλ. H). ου (*pro* ουπω) z. πεπορωμενην iz. 18. ὀφθαλμους wH. ὠτα vwH. *fin.*· *non*; z. 18, 19. *Jungunt* μνημονευετε ὁτε ivwL (ὁτι vL). 19. +οὑς (*ante* εκλασα) L. +και (*ante* ποσους) Hz. −πληρεις L. πληρης vz. κλασματων πληρις H. ἡρατε (*sic v.* 20 z) Lz. 20. +αρτους (*post* ἑπτα) Lz. εις τους ἑπτα εις H. −τους *secund.* z. 21. λεγει wz [*non* L]. ουπω (*pro* πως ου) wH (οὑπω H). ουν ουπω (*pro* ου) L. 22. ερχονται L. βηθσαϊδα vLHz. ἁψηται i. 23. [του τυφλου *habet* L]. αυτους (*pro* αυτον *prim.*) H*? +και (*ante* επιθεις) L. επειρωτα H. ετι (*pro* ει τι) i. 24. ελεγεν wH. λεγει L. −ὁτι Hz. −ὁρω Hz. ὡρω i. 25. επεθηκεν wH. εθηκε z. ὀφθαλμους wH. αναβλεψεi, βλεψαι H (*pro* αναβλεψαι). αναβλεψαι και διεβλεψεν και απεκατεσταθη και ενεβλεπε τηλαυγως ἁπαντα L. απεκατεσταθη ivz [*non* wH]. ανεβλεψαι i, ενεβλεπε v, ανεβλεψε z (*pro* ενεβλεψε). ενεβλεψεν wH. ἁπαντας H. 26. απεστηλεν w. −τον vz. *Post* λεγων *legit* L, ὑπαγε εις τον οικον σου· και εαν εις την κωμην εισελθης μηδενι ειπης μήδέ εν τη κωμη L. μήδε *prim.*, μήδε *sec.* H. μήδὲ *prim.* i, *bis* vwz. 27. καισαριαςi. 28. +αυτω λεγοντες οἱ μεν (*post* απεκριθησαν) L. αλλοι δε ἡλιαν (−και) L. ἡλιαν vH *etiam* P [*non* iwz]. και αλλοι (−δε) L. ἑνα HP. 29. λεγεται w. λεγε P*. −δε *secund.* w. −ὁ *prim.* Hz. ειπεν (*pro* λεγει *secund.*) P. *fin.* +ὁ υἱος του θῦ του ζωντος L. 30. μήδενὶ iP. λεγουσι i. λεγουσιν w. λεγωσιν LP*. *fin.* +ὁτι αυτος εστιν ὁ χ̅ς̅ H. 31. +απο τοτε (*ante* ηρξατο) L. ἡρξατο P. αυτοις (*pro* αυτους) z. ὑπο (*pro* απο) w. +των (*ante* αρχιερεων) ivHPz (*et ante* γραμματεων ivHP** *marg.*). των αρχιερεων και πρεσβυτερων και των γραμματεων L. −και μετα *ad fin. vers.* H*, *habet marg. antiquâ manu.* τη τριτη ἡμερα (−μετα) L. *fin.* εγερθηναι (*pro* αναστηναι) z. 32. ελαλη i*. επιτημαν H. 33. *init.* ὁ δε ι̅ς̅ w. ειδων i. επετημησε i. επετιμησεν wH. ὀπισω wH. 34. ειτις (*pro* ὁστις) L. θελη i*P. ὀπισω wHP. ακολουθειν (*pro* ελθειν) ivHPz *bis.* απαρνισασθω i. ακολουθητω P. 35. −γαρ P. εαν (*pro* αν *prim.*) w. θελει vw*P. απωλεση *bis* i. απολεση (*pro* -σει) z *sem.* ὡς δ' αν P. απολεσει (*pro* -ση) HPz *sem.* την ἑαυτου ψυχην *secund.* ivwL [*non prim.*] HP *sem.* z *ter.* (ἑαὑτου P). ἑνεκεν HP *sem.* −οὑτος w*. οὑτος i. οὑτως P. 36. ὀφελησει P. α̅ν̅ο̅ς̅ v*L. +του (*ante* α̅ν̅ο̅υ̅) w. ζημειωθη w. 37. ἡ P. δωση P. ανταλαγμα wLHP. 38. εαν HP [ἀν iL]. επεσχυνθη iP *sem.* μυχαλλιδι H. ὁτ' ἀν iwHP [*non* z]. ελθη w. −τη (*ante* δοξη) v*?

Cap. IX. 1. εισιν wH**P. ὡδε vz. ἑστηκοτων iHP. οἱτινες iw. γευσονται LP [*non* vH]. ἑως P. ιδωσιν wH**. εληλυθεια L. εληλυθαν P**. δυναμη P. 2. −τον *secund. et tert.* i [*non* wL]. −τον *tert.* v. αναφαιρει i.

ὑψιλον i. κατιδιαν ivL. και εν τω προσευχεσθαι αυτους μετεμορφωθη ὁ ιησους L. ἐμπροσθεν i. 3. εγενοντο wL. –στιλβοντα w*. ὡσει iw. χειων w. κναφευς w. +οὑτως (ante λευκάναι) L. 4. +ιδου (ante ωφθη) L. ὡφθη w. ἡλιας vwL [non i]. μωση i. μωυσει w. ἠσαν w. 5. ελεγε L. ῥαμβι i. ὡδε w [non iL]. θελεις ποιησωμεν (–και) L. μωυσει wL. ἡλια wL. ἡλιαν v*. 6. ἠδει wL. λαλησει ivwL. 7. +ιδου (ante εγενετο) L. αυτους (pro αυτοις) L. ἠλθεν w. φωνη ηλθεν L. –λεγουσα iv*w. 8. ευθεως (pro εξαπινα) L. ουδενα ουκετι i. οὐκ ἔτι w solus. ιδον (sic v. 9) w. 9. εκ (pro απο) i. μηδενὶ i. ἁ ειδον εξηγησωνται L. ὅτ' ἂν i. ὁτ' ἂν w. 10. init. οἱ δε (pro και) L. +οἱ μαθηται (post εκρατησαν) L, (post ἑαυτους) z, init. peric. ἑαυτους H. ζητουντες H*. εστιν wL. ὁταν (pro το) L. fin. αναστη L. 11. επηρωτησαν Lz. πως ουν (pro ὁτι) L. ἡλιαν (sic vv. 12, 13) ivL [non z]. διελθειν (pro δει ελθειν) H. 12. ἡλιας w [non vv. 11, 13]. καθως (pro και πως) w. εξουθενωθη L. 13. –και prim. Lz. +ηδει (ante εληλυθεν) w** marg. εληλυθεν iwHL. εποιησαντο L. +εν (ante αυτω) w. ὡς (pro ὁσα) z. ἠθελησαν w. καθῶς wL. fin. περι αυτου L. επαυτο H*. 14. +αυτου (post μαθητας) L. ιδεν w. πολυν οχλον H. ὀχλον z. +τους (ante γραμματεις) L. συζυτουντας i. συζητουντες αυτον (pro αυτοις) z. 15. ευθυς L. ιδοντες LH. εξεθαμβηθησαν LHz. ἠσπαζοντο wH. 16. επηρωτησεν w. συ ζητειτε (συ mutat. w**) w. συζυτειτε (cf. v. 14) L. fin. αὑτους ivwLz. ἑαυτους H. 17. εκ του οχλου εἱς L. ειπεν (sic vv. 21, 39) iwL (+αυτοις L). ἠνεγκα P. 18. init. και bis script. P. εαν (pro αν) w. –αν z. –αυτον prim. i. ῥισσει v. ρησει LP. ὀδοντας vwPz. –αυτου L. ξηρενεται P. αὐτῷ (pro αυτο) Pz. εκβαλλωσιν wPz. 19. init. ὁ δε αποκριθεις λεγει αυτοις w. και αποκριθεις ὁ ιησους (–δε et αυτῳ) L. ὠ wHPz. +και διεστραμμενη (ante ἑως prim.) L. ανεξωμαι L. 20. ἠνεγκαν HP. εσπαραξε το παιδιον (pro αυτον) L. πεσον P. 21. επηρωτησεν wP**. +λεγων (ante ποσος) L. ειπεν HPz. 22. –και secund. L. +το (ante πυρ) ivHPz [non L]. εβαλεν iwH**P. εβαλλεν z. +τα (ante ὑδατα) v. απολεσει HP. σπλαγχνισθης i*. σπλαγχνησθεις P. 23. –το w*L. πίστευσαι L. 24. ελεγεν wHPz. ειπεν (pro ελεγε) L. απιστεια P. 25. επισυνεχει i*. +ὁ (ante οχλος) iwLHP [non z]. επετιμησεν wHP. των (pro τῳ prim.) L*. αὐτὸ (pro αυτῳ) i. τω $\overline{\pi\nu\iota}$ τω αλαλω P* (τω $\overline{\pi\nu\alpha}$ το αλαλον P**). μηκέτι iwPz. μηκέτι H. εισελθεις w. 26. και πολλασπα ρ P** (super rasur. rescript.). εξηλθεν iwLHP. ὡστε w. 27. –αυτον prim. L. +αυτου (post χειρος) L. ἠγειρεν P. 28. init. και εισελθοντος αυτου εις οικον προσηλθον αυτω οἱ μαθηται αυτου κατιδιαν· και επηρωτησαν αυτον λεγοντες, ὁτι L.

ra i. οἰκον wHPz (+τον z). κατιδιαν ivHP [*non* wz]. διάτί (*pro* ὅτι)
οὐκ' P. εκβαλλεῖν P. 29. δυνατε P. 30. γαλλιλαιας P. 31.
κεν wHP. παραδοθησεται L. *fin.* εγερθησεται L. 32. οἰγνοουν i.
υν w. ερωτησαι L. 33. ειλθεν i*. εισηλθεν L. ἠλθεν HP. οἰκια
ἐπηρῶτα z *passim.* ὁδω w. *fin.* διελογισθη προς ἑαυτους L. 34.
ιχθησαν v. μειζω i. τις αυτων μειζων ειη L. 35. καθησας P. εφων-
ιP. 36. αυτῶ (*pro* αυτο *prim.*) P. –εν μεσω αυτων P* (*habet marg.*).
αλησαμενος αυτον P. 37. αν (*pro* εαν *prim.*) L, *at* ἐ ἂν H. εκ (*pro* ἐν)
ιπι τω ονοματι *usque ad* δεξηται z. εν (*pro* επι) L. επι το i. ονοματι
ι. 38, 39, 41) P. ὡς (*pro* ὁς *secund.*) P. μονον αλλα και L. 38. και
ιθεις (*pro* απεκριθη) L. –δε Lz. –ὁ ivwL [*non* z]. ιαννης i. ειπεν (*pro*
) L. εἶδομεν i. ιδομεν wP [*non* L]. –εν ivw. επι (*pro* εν) z. ονοματι
εκβαλλων τα δαιμονια z. ακυλουθη *prim.* P. –και εκωλυσαμεν *ad fin.*
P* (*habet marg. cursivâ manu*). –ὁτι ουκ ακολουθει ἡμιν L. 39. –ιη-
ι. ειπεν LHP. κολυετε P. ουδ' εἱς z. ποιηση ?v*. εν (*pro* επι) L.
ττιν *bis* wPP₂. ὑμων *bis* ivwPz, *prim.* H. [ἡμων *bis* LP₂]. 41. πο-
H. ποτησει P. επι (*pro* εν) L. –τῳ ivwHP₂. –μου w*. κυ (*pro* μου)
εσται P. απολεσει P. 42. εαν (*pro* αν) ivwz, *at* ἂ H*. +τουτων (*post*
) Hz. εἱς z. περικειτε H. μυλωνικος λιθος L. 43. *Rasura in* w
σκανδαλι *et* ζη. σκανδαλιζει H. εστιν (*sic v.* 45) iwH. –σοι L. καλον
(+σε L**) L. κυλον H*z. –τας v. –την (*ante* γεεναν) H. 44. σκω-
c i. 45. +γαρ (*post* καλον) w. εστιν σε (–σοι) wL. σοι εστιν vHz.
λθειν v. –τους Hz. εχοντας L*. –την (*ante* γεενναν) L. *vv.* 47, 48
t *in* v*. 47. ὀφθαλμ. *bis* w. εκβαλλε w. –σοι εστι L. +σε (*post* εισελ-
L. ἠ τους δυο H. απελθειν (*pro* βληθηναι) H. 48. οὐ *secund.* H.
λισθησεται *bis* wHz. ἀπασα ?H*. ἀλι wH. –ἀλι z. 50. +γαρ (*post*
) L. ἀλας *ter* w, *prim. et secund.* H. γαρ (*pro* δε) L. ἐν τινι L.
ητε L. αρτυθησεται z. +ὑμεις ουν (*ante* εχετε) L. αυτοις (*pro*
ις) iz.

ΑΡ. X. 1. και εκειθεν L. ερχετε i. ὁρια vwL [*non* i]. –δια του LH.
ου w. συμπορευεται ὀχλος (–παλιν *prim.*) L. ὀχλοι H. ειωθη z.
ι iwL. επηρωτων (*sic v.* 10) H. 3. —α τι ὑμιν *v.* 3 *usque ad* ειπεν
v. 5 *in* v*. μωυσης wLHz (*sic v.* 4 w). 4. επετρεψεν iv**wL.
εψε μωυσης Hz. 5. εγραψε (–ὑμιν) vL. επετρεψεν (*pro* εγραψεν) z.
ησεως H. και *bis script.* i. *fin.* +και ειπεν LH. 7. ἑνεκεν w. κατα-
ἀνος H. +αυτου (*post* μρα) wz. 8. ὡστε w. οὐκ ἔτι w [οὐκέτι ivL].
pro ουκετι) z. σαρξ μια ivwLHz. 9. ὁ (*pro* ὃ) z. εζευξεν z. 10. οἰκια

w. εις την οικιαν H. τουτου (*pro* του αυτου) H. −περι του αυτου z. 11. εαν ανηρ (−ὁς) L. αν H. 12. και γυνη εαν εξελθη απο ανδρος και γαμηση αλλον μοιχαται (*sic*) L. απολυσασα (−και *secund.*) H. ἀνδρα H *sem.* −αὐτης H. γαμηση (*pro* γαμηθῃ) z. 13. αυτων ἁψηται H. 14. ηγανακτησεν iwH (ἡγ. wH). και επιτιμησας αυτοις ειπεν L. −και (*ante* μη) ivwL [*non* z]. των γαρ των L*. 15. *init.* μην i. +το (*ante* παιδιον) H. 16. ενεγκαλισαμενος L. τιθων L. εὐλογεῖ i. εὐλόγει vwL. ευλογησεν z. κατηυλογει· τιθεις τας χειρας επαυτα (−αυτα *tert.*) H. 17. ιδου τις πλουσιος προσδραμων (−εἱς) wL. (προσδραμον w). εἱς H. γονυπετων L. ἐπηρῶτα z *passim.* +λεγων (*ante* διδασκαλε) L. αἰωνιον w. 18. −αυτῳ H. 19. οἰδας iLH. μοιχευσεις, φονευσεις, κλευσεις, ψευδομαρτυρησεις *et* αποστερισεις z. −μη αποστερησῃς vwL (*habet* L** *marg.*). 20. −αυτῳ w. −διδασκαλε w*z (*habet* w** *marg.*). *fin.* +τι ετι ὑστερω wL. 21. −ις w*. ἠγαπησεν wH. λεγει (*pro* ειπεν) L. +ει θελεις τελειος ειναι (*ante* ἐν σοι) wL, (*ante* ὑπαγε) H. σε (*pro* σοι) wH**z. δως i. διαδος L. −τοις ivwLHz. ἐξης i. ἕξεις wHz. δεῦρω i. ἀρας w. *fin.* +σου Hz, *at* και ἀρας τον σταυρον σου δευρο ακολουθει μοι L. 22. +τουτω (*post* επι) L. απηλθεν w. λοιπουμενος w. ἦν w. κτιματα i. 23. χριματα i. 24. ειπεν (*pro* λεγει) z. −τεκνα ivw. δυσκολως z. εστιν iL. −τοις *secund.* ivwHz. εισελθειν εις την βασιλειαν του θῦ L. 25. ευκοποτερον z. εστιν w. τρυπηματος βελονης (*pro* τρυμαλιας ῥαφιδος) L. τρϊμαλιας i. −της *bis* wLHz. εισελθειν (*pro* διελθειν) ivH [*non* wLz]. ἡ H *sem.* −η πλουσιον *ad fin. vers.* i. πλουσιος L. 26. α αυτους H* *sem.*, αυτους z (*pro* ἑαυτους). δαναται w. 27. −δε H *sem.* +αυτοις (*post* λεγει) z. +μεν (*ante* ανοις) L. +τουτο (*ante* αδυνατον) L. αλλα (−ου) v*. οὐ H *sem.* −τῳ *prim.* ivLHz [*non* w]. −τῳ *secund.* i. −παντα γαρ *ad fin. vers.* L. −εστι H. 28. *init.* −και ivw*LH. +δε (*post* ηρξατο) w*. −ἡμεις z. ἠκολουθησαμεν wH. 29. και αποκριθεις (−δε) ivL. +γαρ (*post* αμην) z *semel.* οἰκιαν wH. γυνακα H*. ἡ τεκνα w. ἑνεκεν wH. +ἑνεκεν (*ante* του ευαγγελιου) ivwLHz. 30. ἑκατονταπλασιωνα z *sem.* οἰκιας w. +και πρα (*ante* και μρα) wH. μρα wHz *sem.* [*non* L]. 31. ελευσονται (*pro* εσονται) v. −οἱ vwHz [*non* iL]. 32. ἠσαν w. ἠν w. +αυτον (*ante* εφοβουντο) L. −και ακολουθουντες εφοβουντο v. +ὁ ις (*post* παλιν) i*v. ὁ ις (*pro* παλιν) z *initio peric.* ἠρξατο H. ἠρξατω P. μελοντα P. συμβενειν P. 33. ϊδοῦ P. αναβαινωμεν z. παραδιδοται H. αρχιερευσιν w. −τοις *secund.* ivwHPz [*non* L]. γραμματευσιν w. παραδοσουσιν L. εθνεσιν wLPz. 34. εμπεξουσιν LP. αυτων (*pro* αυτον *prim.*) L*. αυτον (*pro* αυτῳ) *bis* P, *prim.* z, *secund.* L. *fin.* εγερθησεται i. 35. προπορευονται H*. −οἱ iwHP. θελωμεν iw. αν σε (*pro* εαν) L. +σε (*ante* αἰτη-

ϖ. ποιησεις Pz. 36. ποιησω (−με) L. 37. ἐξευωνυμων (*sic v.* 40
:) ivwLHPz. καθησωμεν P. βασιλεια της δοξης (*pro* δοξῃ) L
ποκριθεις (*ante* ειπεν) L. οὐκ H. αἰτεισθε w. αιτεισθαι P. ποιειν i.
και) L. —*a* βαπτισθηναι *v.* 38 *usque ad* βαπτιζομαι *v.* 39 *in* v*.
. δε *ad* δυναμεθα v**. ισμα ὁ εγω βα *in marg. rescript.* i. *fin.* βαπ-
μαι L*. βαπτισθησεσθαι P. 40. καθησαι P. −μου *secund.* ivwLHPz.
ται i. ἡτοίμασθαι L. 41. ἤρξαντο wHP. 42. κ̅σ̅ (*pro* ι̅ς̅) L. +ουκ
δατε, *non interrogativè*) L. οἶδατε i. οἶδατε w. οἶδατε P. ἀρχεῖν i.
σιν L. κατεξουσιεζουσιν ?P*. 43. [οὐχ' *ferè omnes, non* H]. οὕτως
?z. ὡς (*pro* ὃς) P. ἐὰν z, *at* αν L. μεγας γενεσθαι L. εστω (*pro*
:cund.) L [*non v.* 44]. ὑμων διακονος ivwLHP**z (ἡμων P*). 44. εαν
) ivwLHz. ὡς ἐὰν P. 45. ηλθεν wHP. 46. ἱεριχῶ *bis* wL, *prim.* i,
z. +ὁ wH, +ιδου ὁ L (*ante* υἱος). βαρτιμαῖος iL. −ὁ (*ante* τυφλος) H.
:αντο w*. ιησου υἱος δ̅α̅δ̅ (−ὁ) L. υἱε (*pro* ὁ υἱος) Hz. 48. *Deest
in* i* (*habet marg.*). +ιησου (ante υἱε) L. 49. φωνησατε αυτον H.
ρο αυτον) L. θαρσων εγειρου L. εγειρε ivw [*non* z]. φωνη wL*z.
οβαλλων z. ἱματιον i. αναπηδησας (*pro* αναστας) z. ηλθεν wH.
: λεγει αυτω w. σοι θελεις ποιησω wH. ῥαββουνι ivwH. ῥαβουνι L.
:*. 52. και ὁ ι̅ς̅ (−δε) H. λεγει (*pro* ειπεν) w. πιστης i. σεσωκεν
νεβλεψεν iw. ηκολουθη i. ἠκολουθει w. ἠκολουθησεν z. αυτω (*pro*
Lz.

P. XI. 1. ηγγισαν L. ἱεροσολυμα L. ηγγιζεν ὁ ι̅ς̅ εις ἰλ̅η̅μ̅ και ηλθεν
it. peric.). βηθσφαγὴ iw. βηθσφαγῆ vHz. βηφαγη L. ὀρος H.
ante αποστελλει) z. απεστειλε iv. 2. λεγων (*pro* και λεγει) L.
ε H. +ουπω (*ante* ουδεις) w, (*post* ανθρωπων) L. κεκαθικεν iH.
εν v (-κε v) wLz. +και (*ante* λυσαντες) L. 3. εἴπη *et* εἴπατε i. ποιητε
ungit w τουτο ειπατε). λυετε τον πωλον (*pro* ποιειτε τουτο) L. απο-
ι ivLHz [*non* w] (+παλιν Hz). ὡδε wz [*non* iLH]. 4. ουν (*pro* δε)
ον ivwL [*non* z]. 5. τινες δε (−και) L. ἑστηκοτων iwH. ποιητε w.
ο τον) L. 6. καθῶς i. +αυτοις (*post* ενετειλατο) L. *fin.* αυτον L**,
'L* (*pro* αυτους). 7. αγουσι L. ἤγαγον H. αυτοις (*pro* αυτῳ *prim.*)
. εν τη ὁδω *prim.* L*, *bis* vw. −δε *secund.* w. στειβαδας iv. στιβαδας
εστρωννυον i*L. 9. ὡσάννὰ (*sic* iwz *v.* 10) iwHz. ὡσαννᾶ (*at* ὡσάννᾶ
ι. ὡσάνὰ (*sic v.* 10) L. +τω ὑψιστω (*post* ὡσάνὰ) L. ὀνοματι (*sic*
H. 10. *init.* +και w. −εν ονοματι κ̅υ̅ L. 11. ὁ ι̅ς̅ εις ἱεροσολυ [μα
H. −και *secund.* L. περιβλεψαμμενος L. ὀψιας wH. ἡμερας (*pro*
. *fin.* +μαθητων Hz *sem.* +αυτου z *sem.* 12. ἐπ' αὔριον w. εξελθων-

των H*. −αυτων L. επεινασεν wLH. 13. συκὴν (*sic ferè vv.* 20, 21) iLH. +μιαν (*post* συκην) w. απομακροθεν LH. εχουσα w. φῦλλα *bis* L. +εις αυτην (*post* ηλθεν) L. ἆρα iv. ἆρά τι εὑρηση w. τι εὑρησει H. εν αυτη (*pro* επ' αυτην) v. +μονον (*post* φῦλλα *secund.*) L. ἦν w. 14. *init.* μη (*pro* και) L. −ο ῑς wLHz. μὴκέτι i. μὴκέτι w. μηδεις (*pro* ουδεις) ivwLHz. φαγη L. ἠκουον wH. 15. +παλιν (*ante* εἰς ἵερ) H. εἰσηλθεν H. ελθων iz. ἠρξατο H. εκβαλειν i*H. πολουντας H*. +τους (*ante* αγοραζοντας) wH. +εξεχεεν (*post* κολλυβιστων) L. πολουντων w. κατεστρεψεν iwLH. 16. διενεγκει z. 17. εδιδασκεν w. και ελεγεν (*pro* λεγων) L. ὁτι (*pro* ου) L, *at* οὑ H. −ὁτι vL. οἰκος *prim.* i, *bis* w, *secund.* H. εθνεσι v. αυτον εποιησατε wHz [*non* L]. 18. ἠκουσαν H. αρχιερεις *rescript. in* i. οἱ αρχιερεις και οἱ γραμματεις w. +και οἱ φαρισαίοι (*post* γραμ.) H. −οἱ *secund.* v. φαρισαιοι (*pro* αρχιερεις) z. απολεσωσιν ivwLHz. −αυτον *secund.* w* (*habet margo*). πας γαρ (−ὁτι) L. 19. ὁτ' ἂν w, ὁταν z (*pro* ὁτε). ὀψε H. εγινετο vL. εξεπορευοντο w. 20. παραπορευομενοι πρωι H. ιδου wL. εξηραμενην wL*. 21. ἀναμνησθῆς H. τω ιῡ (*pro* αυτῳ) z. −ραββι z. ἰδε H. συκὴ z. ἦν i. ἦν w. κατηρασσω H*. εξηραται L. 22. +ὁ (*ante* ῑς) ivwL. +ει (*ante* εχετε) L. 23. ὡς (*pro* ὁς) P. εαν (*pro* αν) Lz. ειπει w*. εἶπη *bis* P. ὀρει H *sem.* ὀρη P. το ορει τούτο P_2. βληθηθητι P. πιστευσητε L. πιστευσει H *sem.* −ὁτι *secund.* P_2* (*at* ὅτι *supra* αλλα P_2**). ὃ (*pro* ἁ) z, *at* ἇ H *sem.* ἑαν H *sem.*, ἂν *sem.* 24. διατοῦτο vLz. εαν (*pro* αν) w. αἰτεισθε w. αιτεισθαι P. αιτησθε HP_2. 25. ὅτ' ἂν iH. ὁτ' ἂν w. ὅταν PP_2. στικητε P. στηκετε vLz. ἡμων (*pro* ὑμων *prim.*) i*. αφησει v, αφηση P (*pro* αφῃ). −ὑμιν v. 26. *Deest in* v, *at* v** *ad calcem habet* λεγω δε ὑμιν *addito Matth.* vii. 7, 8 (*v.* 8 εὑρησκει). αφηετε P_2. +ὑμιν (*post* αφησει) L. 28. η τις (*pro* και τις) H. δεδωκεν iL. εδωκε την εξουσιαν ταυτην Hz. *fin.* ποιεις w. 29. και εγω ὑμας i. κἀγω ὑμας w. και εγω vL. ἑνα H. −και ερω *usque ad fin. v.* 30 L. 30. ἦν w. ἢ H. 31. διελογιζοντο wLz. λογιζοντο H*. τι ειπωμεν (*pro* λεγοντες) L. +ὁτι (*ante* εξ) L. +ἡμιν (*post* ερει) L. διατί vw. −ουν z. 32. αλλα H. −αλλ' z. −εαν ivwH. ουνων (*pro* ανων) L. φοβουμεθα L. ἁπαντες H. −οντως H. οντως ὁτι L. ἦν w. 33. τω ιησου λεγουσιν L. λεγουσιν H. αποκριθεις ὁ ιησους wL.

CAP. XII. 1. λαλειν (*pro* λεγειν) L. ἀνος τις εφυτευσεν αμπελωνα L. περιεθῦκε i. περιεθηκεν w. ὡρυξεν wH. ωκοδομισε i. ωκοδωμησεν w*. οἰκοδυμησε L. ὡκοδομησε H. πῦργον iLz. εξεδωτο iv. απεδημησεν iwLH. 2. απεστειλεν (*sic vv.* 4, 5, 6) w. +εν (*ante* τω καιρω) L**. δουλον τω καιρω w. 3. και (*pro* οἱ δε) H. εδηραν v. 4. λιθοβολισαντες iLH. εκεφαλεωσαν

H. ητιμωμενον wH. 5. απεστειλεν LH. ἀπέκτεινεν L *apud Tregelles.*, *cf. autem* VI. 27 *supra, et Prolegomena.* δερόντες w. δαιροντες L. οὓς μεν δαιροντες οὓς δε Hz (δεροντες H). αποκτενοντες ivLz. αποκτεννοντες w. αποκτεννυντες H. 6. *init.* ὕστερον δε ετι (−ουν) L. +τον (*ante* αγαπητον) L. εσχατον προς αυτους wLHz. 7. +θεασαμενοι αυτον ερχομενον προς αυτους (*ante* ειπον) LH (ἑαυτους H) z. −προς ἑαυτους Lz. 8. λαβοντες απεκτειναν αυτον H. +αυτον (*post* απεκτειναν) z. +αυτον (*ante* εξω) wHz. εξεβαλον εξω του αμπελωνος και απεκτειναν L. 9. +τουτους H, +εκεινους z (*post* γεωργους). 10. εγεννηθη z. 11. εστιν ivw. εστη H. ὀφθαλμοις w. *fin.* ὑμων z. 12. ειπεν iwLH. ἀ Ἀπηλθον (A *rubro*) w. 13. αποστελλουσιν w. +εκ (*post* τινας) L. *fin.* λογον L*. 14. ηρξαντο ερωταν αυτον εν δολω λεγοντες (*pro* λεγουσιν αυτω) L. οἴδαμεν iH. μελλει iw*Lz [*non* vH]. επαληθειας (*sic v.* 32 iwLP) iv [*non* Lz]. ἐπαλ. H. +ειπε ουν ἡμιν (*ante* εξεστι) H (ειπον H) z. δουναι κινσον καισαρι Hz (κηνσον H). ἤ *prim.* H. οὔ w. 15. ὁ δε ιησους ιδων (*pro* ειδως) L. +ὑποκριται (*post* πειραζετε) L. ἴδω L. 16. ἤνεγκαν w. −ἡ v**. εἰκων L. εικον z. −αυτῳ vLHz. 17. +ουν (*post* αποδοτε) L. 18. οἵτινες iw. −λεγουσιν L. αναστασις ουκ εστιν L. επηρωτων Hz. 19. μωυσης wLHz [*non* iv]. ὑμιν L. −ὅτι L. ἐαν w. καταλειπη ivLH. καταλειπει z. εξαναστησει Lz. −αυτου *secund.* v. 20. −ουν ivwL [*non* z]. ἦσαν wH. +παρ' ἡμιν (*post* ησαν) L. ελαβεν iw. γυναῖ L. αποθνισκων i. αφηκεν iH. ἀφηκεν w. 21. ελαβε και (*pro* ελαβεν αυτην και) z. απεθανεν (*sic v.* 22 w) iwLH. +ουκ (*ante* αφηκε) z. αφηκεν w. ὡσαυτως w. ὡσαυτως *cum sequent.* L. ὡσαύτως H. 22. −ελαβον αυτην L. οὐκ H. αφηκεν w. εσχατον wL (+δε w*L). και ἡ γυνη απεθανεν L. 23. ὅταν ουν αναστωσιν εν τη αναστασει L. −ουν iv. ὅτ' ἂν (*sic v.* 25) wH. αναστωσιν w. 24. αποκριθεις δε (−και) L. διατοῦτο ivwL [*non* z]. μὴδὲ ivwLz. 25. ὅτ' ἂν (*non v.* 23) i. οὐτε *bis* H. εκγαμισκονται i. γαμιζονται Hz. ἦσιν (*pro* εισιν) H. −οἱ vw. θῦ (*pro* οἱ) L. 26. +της αναστασεως (*post* δε) L. ανεγνωται L. μωυσεως wHz [*non* ivL]. του (*pro* της) ivLHz. πως (*pro* ὡς) z. +ειμι (*post* εγω) v. ὁ ὁ θσ̄ i. ἀβρααμ ivwL?Hz. ἰσαακ wL?. 27. −ὁ v (εστι) w. ὁ θς̄ θς̄ νεκρων iL. −θς̄ (*ante* ζωντων) vwLHz. πολλω z*. 28. τις (*pro* εἷς) Pz *init. peric.* −των H*. γραμματεον ?H*. αυτου συζητουντων των σαδδουκαιων μετ' αυτου Hz. ιδων (*pro* ειδως) LHz. απεκριθη αυτοις L. εστιν iwLP. −πασων L, *at* παντων ivwHPz. ντολη v. 29. ειπεν (*pro* απεκριθη) L. παντων ivwLHPz. −των wz. εντολη w. +εστιν (*post* εντολων) L (*sic*). +και (*post* ἡμων) i. *fin.* εστιν iwLP. 30. −και εξ ὁλης της ψυχης σου vw*. +παντων (*ante* εντολη) w. 31. αὕτη P, ταυτη L (*pro* αὐτη). ἑαυτον wLHz. μειζω i. *fin.* εστιν ivwLPz. 32. ειπες P. εστιν ὁ θ̄ς iL. εστιν *prim.* (–θεος) w*Pz. –θεος H. +θ̄ς (*post* αλλος) P**. 33. ὁλης *tert.* i. –της *quart.* P. πληον P. εστιν LP. ολοκαυτοματων i. –των *secund.* ivwHPz [*non* L]. 34. ειδως v. –αυτον *prim.* Hz. –απο v*. οὐδεῖς *passim* P. οὐκ ἐτι iwP. –ουκετι z. ετολμα ουκετι L. επηρωτησαι w. επερωταν L. 35. ελεγεν wHP. –ὁ *secund.* w. +ὁ (*ante* υἱος) L. εστιν wP. δᾱδ εστιν LHz. 36. –γαρ L. –τῳ *bis* ivwLHz. [ἁ H**] γιω H. π̄ν̄ι ἁ [γιω P**] P. λεγει (*pro* ειπεν *secund.*) ivwHz. *In* P λεγει *eraditur rubro ante* ειπεν. –ὁ i. ἑως P. 37. οὐν P. πως (*pro* ποθεν) L. εστιν iwLHPz. πολλυς z. ὀχλος (*non* i *v.* 41) iHP. ηκουε i. ἠκουεν wH. λεγων *eras. ante* ἡδεως L. 38. –εν i. IN (*pro* εν *secund.*) H*? εντολαις (*pro* εν στολαις) L. 39. πρωτοκαθεδριαις L. πρωτοκλησιας iL. 40. *init.* οἱ L. –οικιας των i. οἰκιας w. +και ορφανων (*post* χηρων) L. μακρᾶ vw. οὗτοι z, *at* οἱτινες L. ληψωνται v. κρίμα vz. 41. ἑστως (*pro* καθισας) L. απεναντι Hz. γαζοφυλακειου Hz. εβαλε L*, εβαλλε L** (*pro* βαλλει). +τον (*ante* χαλκον) L. γαζοφυλακειον (*sic v.* 43 ivLHz) ivHz. εβαλον w. 42. εβαλεν wH. εβαλλε L. δυο λεπτα v. εστιν w. κοδραντῖς i. κοδραντος w. 43. τοις μαθηταις L. ειπεν (*pro* λεγει) wHz. ἡ πτωχη αὐτη Hz. *Rasura post* πλειο *in* i. εβαλε Hz. βεβληκεν L. βαλλοντων i**vwLHz. 44. περισευματος H. περισσευματος z. αυτοις (*pro* αὐτοις) w *alii.* εβαλλον z. ὑστερισεως w. εβαλλεν L**.

CAP. XIII. 1. +εκ (*post* εἰς) L. οἰκοδομαι (*sic v.* 2, wH) iwH. 2. αποκριθεις ὁ ιησους wL. τας οικοδομας τας μεγαλας L. +αμην λεγω σοι (*ante* ου μη *prim.*) L. +ὡδε (*post* αφεθη) Hz. επι λιθον wLHz [*non* iv]. καταλυθησεται L. 3. καθιμενου i. επηρωτα L. κατιδιαν ivz. κατ' ἰδιαν H. και ιωαννης και ιακωβος L. 4. *init.* ειπον ὑμιν L. ὁτ' ἀν i, ὁτ' ἀν w (*sic vv.* 7, 11, 14, 28, 29). ὁτᾶν H, *at* ὁτ' ἀν *v.* 7. μελλει L. ταυτα παντα wLHz. 5. και αποκριθεις ὁ ιησους ηρξατο αυτοις λεγειν (–δε) L. ηρξατο λεγειν αυτοις H (ἠρξατο H) z. 6. ὀνοματι wH. +ὁ χ̄ς (*post* ειμι) L. 7. ακουσετε L. ακουας (*pro* ακοας) w. θροησθε v. οὑτω Hz. 8. επ' εθνος wL. –και εσονται σεισμοι κατα τοπους i. αρχη wHz. ωδηνων i. ὠδινων w. ταυτα δε παντα αρχαι ωδινων L. 9. τε (*pro* δε) L. –δε *init. peric.* z. παραδωσουσιν w. και εν ταις συναγωγαις αυτων δαρησεσθε· Hz. *Jungunt* συναγωγας *cum* δαρησεσθε vL (δερησ ?L). και επι *bis script.* i*. +δε (*post* ἡγεμονων) w. ἑνεκεν H. 10. *Deest in* Hz. 11. ὁτᾶν H, *sic v.* 29: ὁτ' ἀν *vv.* 14, 28. αγωσιν wL. μεριμνατε vHz [*non* L]. +πως η (*ante* τι) L. λαλησετε (*pro* λαλησητε) v. –μηδε μελετατε L. μήδὲ (*sic v.* 15) ivwHz. εκεινο (*pro* τουτο) L. οὐ H

εις εστε Hz. 13. +των εθνων (*post* παντων) i. 14. −δε z *init. peric.*
ητε H. ειδητε z. −της ερημωσεως L. στηκον (*pro* ἑστως) L. ἑστῶς i.
τὸς v. ἑστῶς z. ἑστος w. ἑστὼς H. οὐ *bis script.* i. οὐ (*pro* ου) H, *sic v.*
bis. ἡ (*pro* οἱ) i. ουδαιΑ (Α *rubro*) w*. −εις τα ορη v. 15. −δε iv. οἰκιαν
H. μήδέ L. ἄραι Lz. ἀραι w. τίz. οἰκιας wz. 16. ὀπισωi H. πισω L.
αι iz. ἆραι w. 17. οὐαι H. εγγαστρι vz. 18. γενητε wz. ταυτα
το ἡ φυγη ὑμων) L. 19. θλιψεις L*. οἷα i. οἷα w. οἷα z. γεγονεν
z. απαρχης iHz. ουδ' (*pro* και) L. 20. ει μι i. ὁ θ̄ς (*pro* κ̄ς) L.
λοβωσεν *bis* w. +εκεινάς (*post* ἡμερας) L. οὐκ H. δια δε (−αλλα) L.
. −η LHz. πιστευσετε i. πιστευετε LHz. 22. ψευδοχρηστοι L*.
ησουσι (*pro* δωσουσι) L. σιμεια i. 23. προηρηκα i*. ἀπαντα wHz.
. −αλλ' (*init. peric.*) z. μεραις H. των ἡμερων εκεινων (*pro* εκεινην) L.
οτησθησεται i. 25. αστεραις i. +εκ (*post* αστερες) vL. εσονται εκ του
ανου πιπτοντες wHz. 26. ὀψονται z. νεφελες i. νεφελη L. δυναμεως
ι δοξης πολλης wL. 27. τεσαρων i. +της (*ante* γης) wLHz. ακρων (*pro*
ρου *sec.*) v. +του (*ante* ουρανου) wLHz. 28. μαθε z. ηδη ὁ κλάδος αυτης wL.
η w. γενητε ἀπαλος w. ὁ κλαδος ηδη γενηται ἀπαλος Hz. ἀπαλος i. ἐκφυῆ
γινωσκεται w. εγυς i. *fin.* εστι w. 29. *Deest ab initio versûs usque ad*
τιν i. οὑτως vwLHz. ιδητε ταυτα wLHz (ειδητε z). 30. παρελθοι i.
ς αν (*pro* μεχρις οὐ) L. ταυτα παντα L. 31. παρελευσεται ivHz. εμοι
γοι (−μου) H. *fin.* παρελθωσιν iv*wL, *at* παρελευσονται Hz. 32. η (*pro*
) vwHz [*non* iL]. −της *secund.* ivL [*non* wz]. οὐδεῖς εἶδεν i. −οἱ *secund.* vH.
ανοις i. 33. +δε και (*post* βλεπετε) L. προσευχεσθαι z *sem.* οἶδατε P.
. ὥσπερ γαρ (*pro* ὡς) L. ἀφεὶς P. οἰκιαν (*sic v.* 35) wHPz *sem.* ἑκαστω
ἑκαστου P. θυρορω P. γρηγορει P. 35. οὐν P. οἶδατε (*non v.* 33)
sem. ὀψε iwP. ἢ *ter* P. −η μεσονυκτιου z *sem.* αλεκτροφωνιας L. πρωι
36. −μη P. εξεφνης P. εὑρη P. 37. ὃ (*pro* ἃ) wHz *sem.* −πασι
γω P.

CAP. XIV. 1. ἦν w. +και οἱ φαρισαιοι (*post* γραμματεις) z *sem. initio peric.*
ν Lz *sem.* *vv.* 1, 2, *desunt in* P. 2. −εν v. 3. ὀντος HP. −τῃ P. οἰκια HP.
ακειμενου v**. +τε (*post* κατακειμενου) z *sem.* ηλθεν wHP. προσηλθεν αυτω
ο ηλθε) L. πολυτιμου (*pro* πολυτελους) LPz *sem.* τον (*pro* το) iwz. 4.
αν w. εισαν P. +των μαθητων (*post* τινες) L. αγανακτωντες L. −και H.
ολια P. 5. εδυνατο w. ἠδυνατο P. +το μυρον (*post* τουτο) wHz *sem.* πρα-
αι το μυρον τουτο L. διναριων L*P. −τοις z *sem.* ενεβριμῶντω P. 6.
τους αυτη v. καλον γαρ εργον L. ηργασατο H*L. *fin.* εν εμοι ivwLHz
n. 7. ὁτ' ἂν iH, ὅτᾶν P, ὁτ' ἂν w (*sic v.* 25). θελετε z *sem.* αυτοις (*pro*

αυτους) LH. 8. εσχεν ivwHPz [*non* L]. –αὐτη L. αὐΤη (T *rubro, super rasur.*)i. αὔτηP. αὐτῆ z *sem.* εποιησεν iv*wLHPz. προελαβενwHP. τῶ σωμα w. το σωμα μου H. 9. +δε (*post* αμην) ivw. εαν (*pro* αν) ivHPz *sem.* –τουτο L. 10. *init.* και ιδου L. –ὁ *bis* vL, *prim.* wz. ἰοῦδας L. +ὁ (*ante* εἱς) z *sem.* απηλθεν wL. αυτον παραδω L. 11. επηγγηλαντο i. αργυρια v**wHz *sem.* εζητηw. αυτον ευκαιρως z *sem.* 12. θελῃς i. ἑτοιμασομεν L. 13. των μαθητων αυτου δυο L. +εισελθοντων ὑμων εις την πολιν (*ante* απαντησει) L. βασταζοντα z. +και (*ante* ακολουθησατε) L. 14. αν (*pro* εαν) w. εισελθοι i. οἰκοδεσποτη w. +μου (*post* καταλυμα) LHz. φαγομαι L. 15. δειξη L. ανογεον i. ανογαιον w. ανωγαιον z [vLH *cum Elzev.*: αναγεον L *apud Tregelles:* cf. xii. 5, *supra*]. –μεγα H. εστρωμμενον i. ἑτοιμασατε H. *fin.* ὑμιν v. 16. ἠλθον w. ἡτοιμασαν *dub.* i. 17. ὀψιας iwH. 18. –αυτων Hz. παραδοσει z. *fin.* μετ' εμε z. 19. λυπεισθε H. λεγιν H. καθεῖς H. καθεἱς iz. +ειμι (*post* εγω) L. 20. *Rasura inter* εμβα *et* πτομενος w. τρυβλιων H. 21. καθῶς w. οὐαι H. ἦν w. εγενηθη L. 22. –ὁ ις w. τον αρτον vL (+και L). εκλασεν iwH. εδιδου τοις μαθηταις (–αυτοις) L. ειπεν iwLHz. –φαγετε wHz [*non* L]. 23. –το vz. 24. αἷμα H. ὑπερ (*pro* περι) L. εκχυννομενον w. *fin.* +εις αφεσιν ἁμαρτιων L. 25. +δε (*post* αμην) iv. οὐκέτι wz [*non* iL]. γενηματος ivwLH [*non* z]. ὅταν H. αὐτῶ (*pro* αυτο) H. 26. ὀρος H. 27. +ὑμεις (*post* παντες) L. –εν *secund.* L. –εν εμοι εν τῃ νυκτι ταυτῃ i. διασκορπισθησονται iH. τα προβατα διασκορπισθησεται L. *fin.* +της ποιμνης w. 29. ετρος H. αποκριθεις λεγει (*pro* εφη) L. και *super rasur.* H. ει και L. +εν σοι (*ante* αλλ') w**. αλ' z. οὐκ wH. 30. +συ (*ante* σημερον) ivwLHz. –εν L. –η LH. δῦς ?i. –δις H. αλεκτορα τρις (δις L**) L. απαρνησει (–με) L*. 31. *init.* ὁ δε πετρος Lz. μαλλον περισσως ελεγεν ὁτι (*sic*) L. ελεγεν w. *Jungunt* vz μαλλον *cum sequent.* δεη με L. συν σοι αποθανειν i. σοι (*pro* σε) z. *Omittit versum* H. 32. οὑ H. γεθσημανει iL (*ut videtur mihi et Dobbinio;* γεθσημανῆ *Tregelles.*) H. γεθσημανι vw. ὡδε z *solus.* +αν απελθων (*post* ἑως) L. προσευξομαι ivHz. 33. παραλαμβανη z. –τον *secund.* ivHz. –και ιωαννην i. +τον (*ante* ιωαννην) wL. μετ' αὐτου L. εκθαμβεισθε H. αδημονην H. 34. *init.* τοτε (*pro* και) L. λεγειν ivz. ὡδε w *solus.* 35. προσελθων ivLz [*non* w]. προσελθον H. +επι προσωπον (*post* επεσεν) LHz. επι την γην L. εστιν H. εστιν ἱνα (*pro* εστι) L. 36. ἀβᾶ ὁ πηρ μου παντα σοι δυνατα εστιν L. παρενεγκαι wz. απ' εμου το ποτηριον w. τουτο απ' εμου L. ουχ ὡς (*pro* ου τι) L. οὐτι H. αλλ' ὡς L, αλλ' ειτι H, αλλ' εἶτι z (*pro* αλλα τι). 37. καθευδης ?w*. ισχυσατε LHz. γρηγορεισε z. 38. ασθενεις H. 39.

πελθων παλιν ηυξατο L. 40. ἠσαν w. βεβαρυμενοι i. καταβαρυνομενοι Lz. αυτω τι L. αποκριθωσιν ivwL. αποκριθωσιν αυτω z. 40, 41. —α αλιν v. 40 *usque ad* ερχεται v. 41 H. 41. −το *secund.* Hz. +το τελος post απεχει) w** *marg.* L. ἠλθεν wH. παραδιδοτε vH. −τας wL. −των L. 2. ηγγικεν iwLHz. 43. −ευθεως L. παραγινετε vH. ιουδα H*. +ὁ σκαριωτης (*post* ιουδας) wHz. ὠν i. ὠν L. −ων wHz. −πολυς L. +απεσταλ-ενοι (*ante* παρα) Hz. −των (*ante* γραμματεων) wLHz. −των (*ante* πρεσβυ-ερων) LH. 44. δεδοκει H. συσημον H. εστιν iLH. απαγετε L. +αυτον ante ασφαλως) i. 45. +αυτω (*post* λεγει) iv. χαιρε (*pro* ῥαββι *prim.*) L, pro ῥαββι *secund.*) v, +χαιρε (*ante* ῥαββι *prim.*) Hz. κατεφιλισεν H. 46. πεβαλων H. επέβαλλον z. επ' αυτων H*. τας χειρας αυτων επ' αυτον w. τας χειρας αυτω (−επ' αυτον *et* αυτων) L. 47. −την H. επεσε iL. επαισεν v. ωτηον ?w*. ὠτιον H. 48. −ὁ ις v. λῃστιν H. εξηλθατε iL. ἐξῆλ-θετε Hz. 49. καθήμεραν i. καθημεραν z. προς ὑμας ημην H (ημιν H) z. αι H. *fin.* +των προφητων L. 50. τοτε οἱ μαθηται αφεντες αυτον ἁπαντες φυγον (*sic*) L. εφυγον παντες Hz. 51. ηκολουθησεν ivLz. Ἠκολουθησεν H *rubro*) wH. γυμνος (*pro* επι γυμνου) L. *Post* γυμνος *habet* L οἱ δε νεανισ-κοι εκρατησαν αυτον (−και). 52. καταλειπων H. σινδωνα (*non v.* 51) i. 53. +καϊαφαν (*post* αρχιερεα) wL. −αυτῳ L. −και οἱ πρεσβυτεροι z. *fin.* οἱ γραμματεις και οἱ πρεσβυτεροι w. 54. απομακροθεν wL. ἠκολουθησεν w. κολουθει L. ἠκολουθη H. ἠν w. συνκαθημενος w. +αυτου (*post* ὑπηρετων, −και *sequens*) L. θερμενομενος iL. +το (*ante* φως) ivwLHz. 55. ὁλον i. ὑχ' ivwz. ηὑρισκον v. −και ουχ εὑρισκον H. 56. ψευδομαρτυρουν w*. ται iwL?. ἴσαι z. —α και ισαι v. 56. *usque ad* κατ' αυτου v. 57 *in* v*. αἱ H. −αυτων (*post* μαρτυριαι) L. 57. αλλοι δε (*pro* και τινες) L. ἠκουσαμεν wH**. −ὁτι ἡμεις ηκουσαμεν αυτου λεγοντος H*, *habet antiquâ manu ad calcem paginæ, at* ἠκουσαμεν H**, λεγοντες *mutatum.* 58. οἰκοδομησω wH. 59. ὑδ' wL. ἴση ἠν w. 60. −το ivwL [*non* z]. επηρωτησεν w. επηρωτα (*sic* z . 61) Hz. 61. *init.* +ις (*post* ὁ δε) w** *marg.* +και (*ante* παλιν) L. +εκ δευ-τερου (*ante* και λεγει) L. +ει (*ante* συ) v. +του θυ (*post* υς) w. 62. *init.* Ὁ *deest in* i. αποκριθεις ειπεν αυτω· συ ειπας ὁτι εγω ειμι L. ὀψεσθε iH. εκ δεξιων καθημενον ivwLHz. επι (*pro* μετα) Hz. 63. εχωμεν LHz. 64. ηκουσατε wH. +παντως (*post* ηκουσατε) z, *at* πάντος την βλασφημιαν H. +αυτου (*post* βλασφημιας) z, *at* την βλασφημιαν του στοματος αυτου L. δοκει (*pro* φαινεται) H. και (*pro* οἱ δε) L. ὁ δε z. 65. αυτον (*pro* αυτῳ *prim.*) w. περικαλυπτιν H. προσωσωπον L. −αυτῳ *secund.* L. +ἡμιν χε τις εστιν ὁ παισας σε (*post* προφητευσον) w** *marg.* LHz (νυν *pro* ἡμιν L, −χε Hz, εστι w**). *fin.* εβαλον iwHz, *at* ελαμβανον L. 66. ὀντος H. −κατω L. κατω εν τη αυλη Hz. παιδίσκῶν v. παιδίσκων wz. 67. αυτον (*pro* τον πετρον) L. θερμενομενον L. −ιυ i. του ιυ του ναζαρηνου H. ιυ του ναζαρινου z. *fin.* ἠσθα wH, *at* εἶς (*sic*) L. 68. ηρνισατο H. +αυτον (*post* ηρνησατο) w. ουτε (*pro* ουδε) iL. επισταμε H. εις την εξω προαυλιον (*sic*) L. εφωνησεν (*sic etiam* LHz, *v.* 72) iwHz. 69. παρεστωσιν w. +και (*ante* οὗτος) L. *fin.* ηρνητο ?i*. ηρνησατο L. 70. ειπον αυτω (*pro* ελεγον τῷ πετρῳ) H. εἰ; *prim.* L. εἶ *secund.* z. 71. ὀμνυειν iwL. ὀμνύναι v. ὀμυναι H. ὀμνῦναι z. 72. +ευθεως (*ante* εκ δευτερου) L. ὁ Ὁ πετρος (Ὁ *rubro*) i. αναμνησθεις L. το ῥημα ὁ (ὡς *pro* ὁ w) ivwHz [*non* L]. ειπε H. αλεκτωρα i. δῆς H. απαρνησει z. επιβαλῶν w. εκλαιεν iwLHz.

Cap. XV. 1. επι τῶ vwP. γραμματαιων HP. κατα του ιυ και δησαντες αυτον z *sem.* απηγαγον (*pro* απηνεγκαν) H *sem.* +αυτον (*post* παρεδωκαν) L. 2. +λεγων (*ante* συ) L. 3. αυτω L, αυτον H (*pro* αυτου). *fin.* +αυτος δε ουδεν απεκρινατο LHz *sem. tantum.* (∴ v**). 4. πιλᾶτος (*sic ferè vv.* 5, 9, 12, 14, 15, 43, 44, *et v.* 2, vwH) ivwH. επηρωτα LHz *sem.* αποκρινει iz *sem.* ουδεν αποκρινη (−ουκ) P. 5. ιησους δε (−ὁ) z *sem.* οὐκέτι wz [*non* LP]. απεκρινατο L. 6. ἑορτην H. ειωθει ὁ ἡγεμων απολυειν L. ἑνα HP. ὃν αν (*pro* ὀνπερ) L. ἠτουντο wHP. 7. ἦν w. ἦν P. +τοτε (*post* δε) L. βαραβᾶς i. βαραββᾶς (*sic v.* 15) P. στασιαστῶν L. δεδεμενων P. οἱτινες w. εν *mutat.* H. 8. ὀχλος ἡρξατο P. αἱτεισθαι w. αιτεισθε H. καθῶς w. εποιη i. 9. −ὁ δε πιλατος *usque ad* αυτοις P. 10. επεγινωσκεν w. επεγινωσκε z *sem.* εγινωσκεν P, *at* ηδει L. παρεδωκησαν i. παρεδεδωκεισαν w. παρεδωκαν LP. παρεδωκεισαν H. 11. ανεσσεισαν i. απεσεισαν P. ὀχλον (*sic v.* 15) P. βαραβᾶν iL. απολυσει HP. 12. παλιν αποκριθεις w. οὐν P. −θελετε L. −ὀν λεγετε L. +τον (*ante* βασιλεα) LHz *sem.* τον (*pro* των) i. 13. +λεγοντες (*post* εκραξαν) wz *sem.* εκραζον ανασειομενοι ὑπο των αρχιερεων και ελεγον L. 14. εποιησε κακον Hz *sem.* εποιησε v. περισσως εκραζον wLz *sem.* εκραζον P. 15. +ελεγεν αυτοις (*ante* βουλομενος) L (...*recenti manu*). παρεδωκεν i*wP. φραγελωσας ivP. φραγγελλωσας z *sem.*, *at* φραγγελωσας *sem.* *Rasura in* H *inter* στ *et* αυρ. 16. τον ιυ (*pro* αυτον) Pz *init. peric.* εσω (−εσω H) εις την αυλην LHP (+του καϊαφα HP). εστιν H** *sem.* P. πραιτοριου i. −την H *sem.* 17. ενδιδυσκουσιν L. +χλαμυδα κοκκινην και (*ante* πορφυραν) L. περιτιθουσιν L. 18. ἤρξαντο H *sem.* P. ασπαζεσθε H *sem.* +και λεγειν (*ante* χαιρε) w** *marg.* ὁ βασιλευς ivwLHPz. αυτων (*pro* των) L*. 19. ετοιπτον H *sem.* αυτον (*pro* αυτῳ *prim.*) P *bis*, z *sem.* τυθεντες z *sem.* γωνατα HP. προσέκυνουν (ου *mut.*) H

m. *fin.* αυτον v. 20. *init.* —και L. ενεπεξαν HP. αυτον (*pro* αυτῳ) z
m. αυτω (*pro* αυτον *prim.*) z *sem.* +την χλαμυδα και (*ante* την πορφυραν)
ἱματια (*non v.* 24) z *sem.* —τα ιδια z *sem.* ἱνα H *sem.* σταυρωσουσιν Lz
m. 21. αγγαρευουσιν H *sem.* εγγαρευουσιν P. σιμονα P. κηρυναιον L.
ριναιον HPz. ἀρη L. 22. αγουσιν (*pro* φερουσιν) L. εις τον (*pro* επι)
γολγοθᾶ iwH *sem.* P. εστιν P. μεθ' ἑρμηνευομενον wz (*sic. v.* 34 wz
m.). μεθερμινευομενον H. 23. εδιδου wz *sem. tantum.* αυτον H* *sem.*
ιειν iz* *sem.* εσμυρνησμενον P. οἱνον HP. οὐκ H. ελαβεν iwLH *sem.* Pz
m. 24. διαμεριζονται ivwHz. διεμεριζοντο L. διέμερισαυτο P. βάλον-
ες H *sem* P. αρει i. —τις τι αρη z *sem.* 25. ἦν w, ἦν P (*sic v.* 26). τριτη
ρα wz *sem.* ὁτε (*pro* και) L. 26. αἰτιας w. —επιγεγραμμενη i. γεγραμμενη
[** *sem.* 27. σταυρουσιν wHP. ἑνα *bis* HP. ἐξευωνυμωνi LHPz. —αυτου v.
8. *Deest versus in* HPz *sem.* [*habent* ivwL]. 29. αυτον (*pro* αυτων) H *sem.*
ὰ ivLz. οὐα wH *sem.* καταλυον P. οἰκοδομων wHPz? *sem.* 30. καταβηθη P.
ταβηθι z. 31. —δε v*wLHPz *sem.* [*non* i]. εμπεζοντες H *sem.* —προς αλλη-
ους L. αληλους w. γραμματαιων Pz. ἑαὐτον H. σωσαι ; vLH?z. 31, 32.
ungunt wz *sem.* σωσαι ὁ χ̅ς̅ (—ὁ χ̅ς̅ z) ὁ βασιλευς ι̅η̅λ̅ ; (—του). 32. —του
rim. L. —ἱνα ιδωμεν i. +αυτω (*post* πιστευσωμεν) iv**LHP, *at* +εις αυτον z.
ειδιζον w. ὠνειδιζον H. 33. και γενομενης (—δε) L. ἑκτης wH. ἑως
ρας H *sem.* ενατης (*sic v.* 34) wLH [*non* ivz]. 34. και τη ενατη ὡρα L.
εβοησεν H *sem.* ἐλωῒ *bis* L. λειμασαβαχθανι i. λειμᾶς ἀβαχθανί v.
μᾶς ἀβαχθανί (*sic*) L. λειμὰς ἀβαχθανεῖ H *sem.* λημᾶσαβαχθανῆ z *sem.* λῖμα
H *sem.* z *sem.* εστιν H** *sem.* —μου *prim.* wLz *sem.* [εγκ] ατελειπες w
γκ *deest ob lacunam*). 35. παρεστωτων z *sem.* +ὁτι (*ante* ιδου) wHz *sem.*
ε Lz *sem.* ἡλιαν (*sic v.* 36) ivLH [*non* wz]. φωνη H *sem.* 36. *init.* και
αμοντες εγεμισαν (—εἱς) L. ὀξους H. και περιθεντες (—τε) L. εποτηζεν
[*sem.* λεγον H *sem.* εποτιζον, λεγοντες, αφες, ἡλιας σῶσον και καθελειν
αφες H. 37. φωνη μεγαλη z *sem.* εξεπνευσεν iwLHz *sem.* 38.
ισθη H *sem.* απανωθεν ἑως κατωθεν (...*s. m.*) L. ἑως H *sem.* 39. —ὁ
rim. L*. κεντηριων L. εξεναντιας ivwLHz *sem.* οὑτως H *sem.* εξεπνευσε
sem. οὑτος H *sem.* +του (*ante* θ̅υ̅) L. θ̅υ̅ ην w. 40. ἡσαν wH *sem.*
ακρωθεν i. απομακροθεν L. αἱς H. ἦν (*sic* w *vv.* 41, 43, 46, *non* 42) wH
em. —και *secund.* iLH *sem.* z *sem.* —ἡ του wLz *sem.* ιωσητος L. 41. ὁτε H
em. ηκολουθησαν v. ἡκολουθουν wH. —και διηκονουν αυτῳ iH *sem.* z *sem.*
i H. 42. ὀψιας i*w. επι (*pro* επει) i. ην (*pro* εστι) v. πρ̊Caββατον
i.e. πρὸς, *sequente* C *rubro*) i. 43. *init.* ελθων wLHPz (*init. peric.*) [*non* i]. —ὁ
sem. αριμαθιας L. ευσχημω w. ευσχημον P *sem.* ἦν P *sem.*, *at* ἦν *sem.* εισηλθεν

wHP —εισηλθε z *sem.* ητισατο i. ἠτησατο wHP. 44. εἰ H *sem.* ηδη P *sem.*, *at* ιδει L. τεθνηκεν iwLHP. κεντηριωνα L. κεντυριονα P* *sem.* επερωτησεν Lz *sem.* ἠ παλε (*pro* ει παλαι) z *ambobus locis.* παλε H *sem.* απεθανεν iwLHP. 45. κεντηριωνος L. εδορησατο w. —τῳ P*, *supra* P**. του ιυ (*pro* τῳ ιωσηφ) z *sem.* 46. αγωρασας H *sem.* σηνδονα P *sem.* ενειλησεν wH** *bis*, P *sem.* ενειλυσε L. την σινδονα z *sem.*, *at* σινδονη Lz *sem.* εθηκεν L. μνημιω P *sem.* ὡ (*pro* ὁ) z *sem.* ἠν P. εν τη πετρα L. προσεκυλισεν wH *sem.* προσεκυλησε L. προσεκυλησεν P *sem.*, *at* προσκυλησεν P* *sem.* τη θυρα z *sem.* μνημιου P *sem.* 47. μαγδαλινη (*sic* XVI. 1 ivw; *v.* 40, XVI. 9 v) ivw. ιακωβου και ιωσητος μηρ (*pro* ιωση) L. +ἡ (*ante* ιωση) H, *at* ἰωση H *sem.* τεθειται wLP *sem.* τεθηται z.

CAP. XVI. 1. —και *initio* P *sem.* z *sem.* —ἡ του ivLPz. —του *secund.* H. ἠγορασαν wP. ἵνα P. ἀλειψωσιν v. αλειψωσι LHz. του ιυ (*pro* αυτον) LHPz. 2. σαββατου w. +των (*ante* σαββατων) L. +ετι (*ante* ανατειλαντος) w. ἡλιου H. 3. αποκυλυσει L. απο (*pro* εκ) L. 4. αποκεκυλυσται L. ἠν wP. 5. ιδου wP. 6. *Rasura in* P *post* λεγει. εκθαμβεισθαι ?L*. εκθαμβησθε iP. ναζωρηνου L. ναζαρινον Pz *sem.* εσταυρωμενον ; w. ἠγερθη wP. ὡδε z *solus.* ἴδε i. 7. αλλα w. ὀψεσθε w. 8. —ταχυ iwLHPz [*non* v]. ειχεν wH. 9. *init.* ναστας (A *rubro omisso, hic tantum in Evangeliis*) L. +ο ις *post* δε *rubro* v**w**. ὁ ις (*pro* δε) LHPz *initio peric.* σαββατων iwH Pz. σαβαατων ?L*. εφανει i. μαγδαλινη P. ἀφεὶς H. εκβεβληκη ἑπτα P. 10. απελθουσα (*pro* πορευθεισα) w. πορευθησα P. απηγγηλε (*non v.* 13) i. απηγγειλεν wP. γινομενοις L. πενθουσιν w. κλαιουσιν wz. 11. ἠπιστησαν wHP. ηπιστεισαν L. 12. ἑτερα i. 13. λυποις i. 14. +δε (*post* ὑστερον) w. ἑνδεκα wHP. ωνειδησε i. ωνειδισεν w. ὀνειδησεν P. απιστειαν iP. κληροκαρδιαν w*. σκληρωκαρδιαν P. εγειγερμενον iLPz (+εκ νεκρων L). 15. πᾶση iw. κτησι P. 17. σημεία wz. ὀνοματι HP. εκβαλλοῦσιν w. εκβαλοῦσιν P. γλῶσσαις i. λαλησουσιν wP. 18. ὀφεις HP. ἀρουσι ?L. αρουσιν wP. ποιωσιν iL. βλαψη vwLHPz [*non* i]. επιθησουσιν w*P. καλος P. ἐξουσιν iHPz. 19. οὐν P. +ις (*post* κς) w*. λαλεῖσαι H. τους ουρανους L. εκαθησεν P. 20. πάντα χῡ (*sic*) L. του (*pro* των) w. *fin.* +αμην ivwLHPz.

SUBSCRIPT: *Nil habent* vwL. ευαγγελιον κατα μαρκον στιχων B̅C̅ i *rubro.*

SANCTI LUCÆ EVANGELIUM.

Το *κατα λουκαν ἁγιον ευαγγελιον* iv. *ευαγγελιον κατα λουκαν* w. *εκ του*
ατα λουκαν ευαγγελιον L.

Cap. I. 1. Επει *δή περ* L. *πληροφορημενων* P. −*εν* Pz. 2. *παρεδωκαν*
*. *παρεδωσαν* Pz. *απαρχης* iLP. *αππτοπται* P. 3. *εδοξεν* P (*rasur. in*
ne versûs). 4. *ασφαλιαν* P. 5. *ὀνοματι* wP. *ὀνομα* HP. *ἐλισαβετ* iL
ion v. 7). *ἐλισαβετ'* w. 6. *ἥσαν* (*sic v.* 7) P. *αμφωτεροι* P. *δικαιωμα-*
ν P. 7. *καθὅτι* iH. *καθ' ὅτι* wP. −*ἡ* Lz. *ἦν prim.* HP, *secund.* w (*ἦν*
cund. P). 8. *ἐφ' ἡμεριας* HP**. *εναντιον* wLHP. 9. *ἱερατιας* L.
ρατίας P*. *ελαχεν* wH**, *at ελαβεν* P. *θυμιᾶσαι* ivwz. +*και* (*ante εισελ-*
ον) P. 10. *ην του λαου* vHPz (*ἦν* P). *της ὡρας* L. 11. *ὡφθη* w. −*κυ̅* ?i*.
·τῶς iP. *ἑστὼς* w. 12. *επεσεν* v. 13. *ειπεν* wHP. *δι' ὅτι* w. *διὅτι* P.
τήκουσθη P. *δεησης* P*. *ἐλισαβετ* L. *ὀνομα* wHP. *αυτω*? (*pro αυτου*)
. 14. *χαρασσοι* P. *αγαλλιασεις* P. *εν* (*pro επι*) L. *γενεσει* w. *χαρισ-*
ται P. 15. −*του* wHPz [*non* i]. *θυ̅* (*pro κυ̅*) L. *οἰνον* wHP. *πιει* iP.
'. *ἡλιοῦ* iwLP [*ἡλιου* vz]. +*των* (*ante πρων̅*) w*. *ανων* (*pro πατερων*) L.
ριθεις H. *φρονισει* H. *ἑτοιμᾶσαι* iv. *ἑτοιμασαι* P. +*τω* (*ante κω̅*) w.
ιτασκευασμενον iLHPz. 18. *ειπεν* wHP. 19. *γαβ̃ιηλ* (*sic v.* 26) w.
ιρεστικως i. *παρεστηκος* P. *απεσταλειν* i. 20. *ϊδοῦ* (*sic vv.* 31, 36, 38,
ł, 48) P. *οἱτινες* w. 21. *ἦν* (*sic v.* 22) w. *ἦν* P. 22. *ἐδυνατο* w.
ὶυνατο P. −*αυτοις* L. *ὀπτασιαν* wLP. *ἦν* P. *διεμενεν* wH**. *διεμεινεν* P.
3. *επληρωθησαν* i. *λειτουργειας* vw. *οἴκον* P. 24. *τας ἡμερας ταυτας* L.
ισαβετ' i *fere.* *ἐλισαβετ* L. *ἐλισσαβετ* P *sem.*, *at ἐλισαβετ' sem. et ελισα-*
ετ sem. *ζαχαριου* (*pro αυτου*) P *bis* z *sem. init. peric.* *περιεκριβεν* L*.
5. *οὑτως* ivwLHPz. *πεποικεν* P. *εφιδεν* L. *αφαιλειν* z *ambobus locis.*
ειδος P. 26. *ἑκτω* P. *απεσταλει* P. −*ὁ* L. *αρχαγγελος* z. *απο θυ̅* (−*του*)
. *ἡ* iP. *ὀνομα* Pz. *ναζαρετ'* iP. *ναζαρετ* vwz [-*εθ* LH]. 27. *μεμνησ-*
ευμενην (*ην mutat.*) i. *ὀνομα bis* P (*sic v.* 31), *prim.* z. −*ιωσηφ usque ad*
ομα secund. w* (*habet marg.* w**). *ἐξ οἰκου* P. 28. *προς αυτην ὁ αγγελος*
. *ειπεν* iwLH. *ειπεν προς αυτην* P. *κεχαριτομενη* i. *κεχαρητωμενη* z.

γυναιξι L. 29. παταπος w. ει (*pro* ειη) L. ἀσπασμος H. οὑτως P. 30. ειπαν αυτη ὁ αγγελος L. προς αυτην (*pro* αυτῃ) z. εὑρες P. —τῳ z. 31. συλληψει vLP. τεξει vLP. 32. +γαρ (*post* οὑτος) v**. 33. οικον w. —οικον P. 34. ειπεν (*sic v.* 38) wHP. +μοι (*post* εσται) v**LHz. 35. ἀγγελος ?L. δι' ὁ w. γενωμενον w. γεννομενον L. γενομενον P. 36. ἐλισαβεθ L* (-ετ L**). ἡ συγγενισου i. συγγενις L. αὐτῆ iLz, αὐτη w, αὔτη P (*pro* αὐτῄ). γηρει ivwLHPz. ἐκτος (*non v.* 26 w) wP. αὔτη (*pro* αυτῃ) i. 37. αδυνατησῃ L. 38. ἡ H. 39. και αναστασα w. —δε wHPz *init. peric.* αναστας L. ὀρεινην w. ὀρηνην P. ἰοῦδα vLP. 40. εισ-ἔλθεν ?w. οἰκον P. ἠσπασατο wLH. εισπασατο P. ἐλισαβετ (*sic v.* 41 *bis*) L. 41. ἤκουσεν wP. ηκουσε τον ασπασμον της μαριας ἡ ἐλισαβετ L. ἀσπασμον της μον της H*. ἐλισαβε P*. εσκιρτησεν wH**P. 42. εφωνησεν P, *at* ανεβοησε L. γυναιξιν wP. 43. ἐλθῃ w. ἡ μηρ του κυ μου ελθῃ z. 44. ἀσπασμου H. ὠτα wP. εσκιρτησε το βρεφος εν αγαλλιασει ivwLHPz (εσκιρτησεν wHP). 46. ειπεν wHP. μεγαλυνη P. 47. ἠγαλλιασε iH. ἠγαλλιασεν wP. ηγαλλιαασε z. 48. μακαριουσιν wP. αἱ γενεαι P. 49. εποιησεν (η *super rasur.* w) wP. μεγαλια P. ὀνομα P. 50. εις γενεαν και γενεαν iL. 51. Εποιησεν w. 52. καθειλεν w. ὑψωσεν w. 53. —και πλουτουντας *ad fin. vers.* w* (*habet marg.* w**, *at* εξαπεστειλεν καινους). 54. ελ (*pro* ελεους) v. 55. ελαλησεν w. ἀβρααμ ivwL. ἑως αἰωνος (*pro* εις τον αιωνα) L. 56. εμεινεν wH**P. —ὡσει L. ὡσεί P. οἰκον wP. 57. της δε ἐλισαβετ L. ἐλισσαβετ P. +και (*post* χρονος) L. 58. ἤκουσαν P. συγγενης ?i*. αυτης *prim.* (η *mutat.*) L. εμεγαλυνεν wHP. συνεχαιρεν P. συνεχαιρων H. *fin.* συναιχερεν αυτης L. 59. ὀγδοη wH. τη ἡμερα τῃ ογδοη L. ἠλθεν w*. ἠλθον w**P. αυτον i, αυτῶ LHP (*pro* αυτο). το ὀνοματι wP. ὀνοματι H. 60. αποκριθησα P. 61. οὐδεὶς P. εκ της συγγενειας w. συγγενια P. το ὀνοματι P. ὀνοματι wH. 62. θελει i. θελῃ P. *fin.* αυτο LP. 63. αἰτησας w. αιτισας H*. εγραψεν wP. —εστι v*. εστιν wP. ὀνομα HP. 64. παραχρῆμα iwz. ελαλῃ iw*. 65. εγενετο δε (—και) w. περιοἰκουντας P. αυτου (*pro* αυτους) w. ορηνῃ i. ὀρεινῃ wH. ὀρηνῃ P. ὀρεινῄ z. διέλαλητο P. 66. ακουοντες P. ἆρα v. ἀρα wL. ἦν w. ἦν P. *fin.* μετ' αυτων L. —και χειρ *ad fin. vers.* H*: *habet marg. antiquâ manu.* 67. επροφητευσεν w. προεφητευσεν P. 68. εποιησεν wHP. —αὐτου ?i*. 69. ηγειρεν w. —τῳ L. οἰκω w. 70. καθῶς i. ελαλησεν w. —των *secund.* L. αιωνος (αι *supra rasur.*) w. 73. ὀρκον iv. ωμοσεν w. ὡμοσε L. ἀβρααμ ivwL. 74. —των L. —ἡμων L. 76. ὑψιτου v. κληθησει P. προπροσωπου H. ἑτοιμασαι P. ἑτοιμᾶσαι vHz.

. ἀφεσει L. ἡμων (*pro* αυτων) v. 78. σπλαχνα i. οἱς v. 79. ἐπι-
:ναι vL. κατευθῦναι ivL. κατευθῆναι w. ὀδον ?i. 80. ηὔξανεν wP.
ξανε ?L. ηυξανεν H. εκραταιουτω P. ἦν wPz*. ἑως P.
CAP. II. 1. –εγενετο δε HPz. εξηλθεν wH**P. απογραψασθαι L.
ουμενην wHP. 2. *Jungunt* vH ,πρωτη εγενετο. ἡγεμονευοντος i. κυρι-
ν LHPz. 4. ναζαρετ i (-τ' iP) vwPz (*sic vv.* 39, 51 : *at* LH *cum Elzev.*).
ϑλεεμ P. οἰκου P. 5. απογραψαι P (C *supra* ψ *p. m.*?). συμμαριαμ' P.
τω w *alii.* γυναικη οὐση P. εγγυω vz. 7. ἐτεκεν w. ετεκεν H**P.
:κλινεν P. διότι wP. ἦν P. 8. ποιμαῖνες L. ἠσαν P. εν τη αυτη
ρα L. 9. ἴδου (*sic vv.* 10, 25, 34) P. αυτοις (*pro* αυτους) z. –φοβον με-
ν P* (*habet* P** *uncial.*). 10. ἡτις i. 11. εστιν w*P. 12. εὑρησεται
. εὑρησεται P. εσπαργανομενον iLP. –τη ivwLHz [*non* P]. 13. εξεφνης
αἰνουντων (*sic v.* 20) w. 15. απηλθεν L*. οἱ αγγελοι εις τον ουρανον L.
ιτους (*pro* αλληλους) L. διελθομεν iLz. +εις (*post* ἑως) v. βιθλεεμ P.
γονως wP. εγνωρησεν P. 16. απηλθον σπεῦσαντες i. εὗρον L.
. διέγνωρησαν P. –τουτου iv. 18. οἱ i. εθαυμαζον v. παρα (*pro* ὑπο) z.
. μαρια i. παντας L. συμβάλουσα i. 20. ὑπεστρεψαν ivwHPz. οἱπε-
ρεψαν L. οἱς H *sem.* ἠκουσαν H *sem.* P. ιδον wLP. καθῶς w. ελαληθει
21. +αἱ (*ante* ἡμεραι) LPz. ωκτω i. ὀκτω wP (Ὀ *rubro* w). αυτον
ro το παιδιον) w. –και *secund.* L. ὀνομα P. συλλυφθηναι i. 22. αυτων
ο αυτης) ivwL [*non habent* HPz]. μωυσεως wL [*non* i]. ανοιγαγον w.
οσολυμα w. ἑροσολυμα P. 23. καθῶς i. +τω (*ante* νομω) v. διανοιγων
P. 24. τρυγωνων P. ἡ LP. νεοσοῦς P. 25. ἦν *prim.* wP* (ἡ P**).
ρουσαλημ L*. ἰλημ H. ὀνομα HP. ευσεβης w, ευσεβεις P (*pro* ευλα-
ς). ην ἁγιον iLHPz (ἦν P) [*non* v]. *fin.* επ' αυτω. v. 26. ἦν P. κεχρισ-
τισμενον L. *Rasura post* ἁγιου H. ιδειν (*pro* ιδη) wL (–η L), ιδει P (–η,
P** *uncial.* ει *supra*). 27. ἠλθεν P. εισαγειν Lz. γωνεις w. ιθισμενον
ἠθησμενον P. 28. αυτον (*pro* αυτο) LPz. αγγαλας v. –αυτου w* (*habet*
rg. w**). ευλογησεν HP. ειπεν iwLHP. 30. ιδον wP. 32. πῶς L*
ως L**). καιλα δοξαν L (.. L**). 33. ἦν w. ἦν P. +Ὁ (*ante* ιωσηφ) w
bro. ἰωσηφ H. 34. ηὐλογησεν P. ειπεν wHP. 36. ἦν P. προφητης
ετη ἑπτα μετα ανδρος w. μετα ανδρος ετη ἑπτα LP (ἑπτα P). 37.
t. και αὐτὴ ivHz, *at* αὐτῆ LP (*spiritu eraso in* P). ογδοηκοντατεσαρων i.
δοηκοντα wP. ἡ w. ἡ z. ηφιστατο z. δενησεσιν P. νυκταν LP*z.
. –αὐτη w. τῆ τῆ (*pro* αυτη τη) P*. ανθομολογειτο iz. ανθομολογητω P.
αλη w*P. πασιν P. –εν w. ἰηλμ v. ἰλημ H. 39. –τα wL. ἑαυτων
LH**. 40. ηυξανεν wH**. ηὔξανε L. ηὔξανεν P. εκραταιουτω P *sem.*

εκρατεοῦτω P *sem.* σοφια P *sem.* ἦν P. *fin.* αυτω v**LP* *sem.* P *sem.* z.
41. πορευοντο L*. κατετος ivLP. 42. αναβαινοντων w. 43. +ὁ (*ante* ιησους) iL. 44. νομησαντες P. ἠλθον P. ὁδον (ὁ *mutat.*) P. συγγενευσι i. συγγενευσιν LP. −εν *tert.* wL. 45. εὑρωντες i. εὑροντες P. αναζητουντες L. 46. εὗρον P. 47. επι τη συνεσει και ταις αποκρισεσιν αυτου παντες οἱ ακουοντες αυτου L. 48. ειπεν iwLHPz. οὗτως H. μηρ (*pro* πηρ) P. και εγω οδυνομενοι ζητουμεν σε L. ὀδυνωμενοι iwH. ὀδυνομενοι P. 49. ειπε δε (−και) L. ειπεν wHP. ιδητε L. ειδητε P. με ειναι; L. 50. ελαλη P. 51. ἠλθεν P. ἦν w. ἦν P. ὑποτασομενος i. ἡ δε μηρ (−και) ivLHPz (Ἡ *rubro* i). τα ῥηματα ἀπαντα w. αυ *in* ταυτα *mutat. in* P. 52. προεκοπτεν wH**Pz.

CAP. III. 1. Ενετει (−δε) iP (ετι P). −δε *prim* Hz. πεντεκαὶδεκάτω iP. πέντε καὶ δεκάτω w. τῆβερίου P. πηλατου P. ἡρωδου της γαλιλαιας w. γαλλιλαιας P*. ἰτουραιας w. ἡτουραιας P. τετραχωνιτιδος L. τραχωνιτηδος P. αβιλινης ivwz. αβυλινης P. 2. επι αρχιερεως ivwLHPz. −θῡ? i*. κῡ (*pro* θῡ) P. −του iwHPz. −υἱου i* (*supra* i**). 3. ἦλθεν P. ἰορδανου (*sic* iv. 1) w. 4. ἑτοιμασατε HP. 5. φαραξ iL*Pz. ὁρος wLP. −και βουνος P. αἱ τραχιαι P. ὁδους H. λιας Pz. λεῖας L. 6. ὁψεται wP. 7. ελεγε δε (−ουν) Lz. οὗν (*sic vv.* 8, 10, *non* 9) P. ὀχλοις P. 8. ἀβρααμ *bis* ivwLHz, *prim.* P. 9. ἠδη HP. −ἡ i. ποιοῦν w. ποιοῦν P. +το (*ante* πυρ) L. 10. επηρωτουν (*non v.* 14) L. ὀχλοι P. −ουν z. ποιησωμεν (*sic vv.* 12, 14) iwLPz [*non* vH]. 11. ελεγεν L. μεταδιδοτω P. ποιητω L. 12. ἦλθον P. +ὑπ' αυτου (*post* βαπτισθηναι) iw. −και *secund.* L*. 13. ειπεν (*sic v.* 14, wHP) wLHP. μηδὲν ivPz. πρασσεται P. 14. τι ποιησωμεν και ἡμεις L. μηδένα HPz. διασησητε i. μηδὲ ivwLPz. ὀψονιοις w. ὀψονιοις L. ὀψωνιοις P. 15. προσδικωντος L. πρὸσδοκόντος P. −και w. −αὐτων ?i*. −του *secund.* LH*?P. μήποτὲ P. εἶ (*pro* ειη) L. 16. −ὁ L. ἀπασιν Pz. ἀπασι *cum præced.* H. ὑμας βαπτιζω εν ὑδατι L. +κυψας (*ante* λυσαι) L. 17. πτῦον ivz. ἀλωνα wP, *at* ανωλα L. +μεν (*ante* σιτον) L. εχυρον i. 18. οὗν P. αλλα L*, *at* ἑτερα L** *marg.* ἑτερα H. ευαγγελιζετο v. 19. Ἡρωδης v. −φιλιππου iv*Lz [*non* wH]. εποιησεν w. 20. προσεθηκεν w. πασιν L. −τῃ iv*wH. 21. −δε Lz *init. peric.* μετα το βαπτισθηναι (*pro* εν τῳ βαπτισθηναι) z. 22. *Rasura in* w *ante* ἁγιον. φωνη w*. ουρανων iL. +προς αυτον (*post* γενεσθαι) iL. λεγουσα w. ευδοκησα iwLz *sem.* [*non* vH]. 23. ουν (*pro* ην) L. ἦν H. −ὁ ις i. αρχομενος ειναι ὡς ετων λ' L. ἑτων w. ων *cum præcedent.* iv. −ων L. ὦν i. ἡλει iL. ἡλι vz. 24. ματθα v. ματθαν LHz. λευει L. μελχει iL. ιωαννα iH. ιαννναι L. ιωνα z. 25. ματθαιου v. ἀμως z. εσλειμ v, εσσαι L, εσλιμ Hz (*pro* εσλι). αγγαι i. 26.

·L. ματθιου L. μαθθαθιου H. μαθθαδιου z. σεεμει ivL. ιωσηχ LHz.
LH. ιωαδα z. 27. ιωαναν ivH. ιωανναν L. ιωναναν z. ρησσα ?L
ροζοβαβελ Lz. νηρει iL. του νηρι του σαλαθιηλ z. 28. μελχει iL.
i. αδδει v. ελωδαμ v. ελμωδα L. ελμοδαμ z. ἡρ L. 29. ιησου
ιωση) L. ελεαζερ L. ιωρεμ L. ιωρημ i*v. ιωρι H. –του ελιεζερ του
μ z. μαστθα L*, ματτθα L**. ματταθ wz. ματθαθ H. 29, 31.
nt omnia in L ab του λευι v. 29, usque ad ματταθα v. 31. 30. ιωαναν
ιωνα Hz. ελειακειμ i. ελιακιμ Hz. 32. ἰεσσαι L. ιωβηδ L. ὠβηδ z.
wL. σαλμαν ?L. –του ναασσων z. 33. αμιναδαμ LHz. του αδμιν·
αρηι (loco του αραμ) L. +του ιωραμ (post αραμ) Hz. εσρωμ vwL. ερωμ
φανες L. ἰοῦδα L. 34. ιακωβου z. ἰσαακ w. ἀβρααμ ivwLHz.
α LHz [non iw]. 35. σερουχ ivwLHz. ῥαγαβ ?w. ραγαμ L** (ρεγαυ
. φαλεγ ivwHL. εφερ L. ἔβερ H. 36. μαϊναν L** marg. (at καϊναν
λαμαχ L. 37. ματουσαλα w. ιαρεθ w. μελελεηλ L. 38. ἐνως w.
CAP. IV. 1. πληρης πνς ἁγιου iwz. ἁσιου ?L*. ἠγετο H. 2. +ουδε
, (post ουδεν) iL. συντελεσθησων i. αυτω ?H. επεινασεν iwLH**z.
α οἱ λιθοι οὗτοι αρτοι γενωνται H. 4. απεκριθη δε αυτω ὁ ιησους λεγων
+ὁ (ante ις) i. προς αυτον ὁ ις (–λεγων) H. –ὁτι L. –ὁ ivLHz [non w].
πορευομενω δια στοματος (ante θῦ) w** marg. Hz. 5. ἀναγὼν v*. ὀρος
+λιαν (post ὑψηλον) L. οἰκουμενης wH. 6. δοσω i. ἀπασαν H. πα-
δονται i. αν (pro εαν) i. ἐαν (sic v. 7) H. διδομι i. 7. +πεσων (post
i. προσκυνησις z. εμου iv. εστω i. σοι (pro σου) z. πασα ivwLHz.
ιπεν αυτω vw. ὁ ιησους ειπεν αυτω iLH. ὀπισω wH. –γαρ vw. κν του
ου προσκυνησεις iLHz. 9. ηγαγε δε (–και) i. Ἡγαγεν H**. εἰς ?L.
σολυμα Hz. ἐστησεν L. –ὁ ivwLHz. βαλλε z. –εντευθεν iv. κατω
υθεν L. 10. –αὐτου L. 11. –ὁτι iv. αρουσιν w. 12. κς (pro ις) L.
ηται w*. εμπειρασεις L. 13. απεστει H. αχρη w*. 14. –ὁ vwH. –ὁ ις
n. κς (pro ις) L. εξηλθεν wLz. εξ (pro καθ') L. καθολης iHz sem. 15.
α (pro ὑπο) vw. 16. init. –και w. ἠλθεν P. +ὁ ις (post ηλθεν) iv rubro z
peric. –την prim. i. ναζαρετ' i. ναζαρετθ P. ναζαρετ vwz [ναζαρεθ
]. ὁπου (pro οὑ) L. ἠν P. ανατεθραμμενος L. εισηλθεν wP. ειωθως
αυτου (pro αυτῳ) L*. 17. του προφητου ἠσαϊου L. ανοιξας (pro
πτ.) v*. εὑρεν w. εὑρεν P. ὀπου (pro οὑ) L. οὗ ἦν P. 18. εἱνεκεν i.
εν w. εἱνεκεν vLH. οὗ ἠνεγκεν P. ἠνεκεν z. εχρισεν wP. ευαγγελι-
θαι ivwLHz. ευαγγελισασθε P. απεσταλκεν wP. τη καρδια P. –ιασα-
ι usque ad καρδιαν L. κηρῦξαι (sic v. 19) i. αἰχμαλωτοις w. αιχμαλοτοις
τεθραμμενους w. τεθρασμενους P. 19. ἐνιαυτον w. 20. εκαθισεν

iwLz. εκαθησεν P. οἱ οφθαλμοι εν τη συναγωγη i. ησαν οἱ οφθαλμοι vw (ἤσαν w). ὀφθαλμοι ἤσαν P. *fin.* εις αυτον L. 21. ἤρξατο P. αὔτη P. *fin.* ὥσιν ἡμων P. 22. εν (*pro* επι) L. εν (*pro* εκ) L*. ουχ' ivwHz. ουχ ὁ υἱος εστιν ιωσηφ οὗτος ;L. 23. ειπεν (*sic v.* 24 wLHPz) wHPz. παντες L* (παντως L**?). παντος HP. ἠκουσαμεν wP. εις (*pro* εν *prim.*) L. –τη *prim.* iwLH. [ὧδε *omnes*]. πατριδη (*sic v.* 24) P. πατριδου L. 24. οὐδεῖς (*sic v.* 27) P. 25. επαληθειας vP. –δε v*. +ὅτι (*ante* πολλλαι L** *sic*) iv**L. ἤσαν H *sem.* P. ἡλιοῦ iwLP. [ἠλιου vz]. ὁ H *sem.* ἐτη H *sem.* ὀς (*pro* ὡς) LP*. μεγαλη L. 26. οὐδεμίαν vwH *sem.* z. ἡλιας iwLP [*non* vz]. ἀρεπτα i. σαρεφθα vL. αρεφ [θα P**] P. αραφθα H *sem.* σαραφθα H *sem.* σαραπτα z. σιδωνιας vH *sem.* Pz. σιδονιας L. 27. ἤσαν P. εν τω ιηλ επι ἐλισσαιου του προφητου L. εκαθερεῖσθη P. ναιμαν wL. ναιεμαν H. 28. πλησθησαν i. επλεισθησαν P. ἀπαντες i. ακουωντες i. 29. εξεβαλλον P. ἤγαγον HP. –της *secund.* ivwHPz, *at* του L. οφρῦος i. ὀφρυος wHPz. ὀρους P. ωκοδομητο αυτων L. ὠκοδομητο P. ὥστε (*pro* εις το) L. κατακρημνῆσαι iLz. κατακριμνησαι (–το P*) P. 30. διαμέσου i. 31. ηλθεν H. +ὁ ις (*post* κατηλθεν) v. ἠν HP. αυτοις (*pro* αυτους) iP. σαββασιν iLPz. 32. ἦν (*sic v.* 33) P. 33. ανεκραξεν wH**P. φωνην μεγαλην P. 34. ἐά P. συ (*pro* σοι) P. ναζαρινε L. ναρηνε P. ἦλθες i. ἦλθες P. οἰδα iP. ἀγιος H. 35. φημωθητι iLPz. απ' (*pro* εξ) L. –το *secund.* iwP [*non* vLz]. μηδὲν iHPz. 36. –εν z. πνευμασιν P. 38. απο (*pro* εκ) L. +ὁ ις (*post* συναγωγης) v. ὁ ις ηλθεν (*pro* εισηλθεν) w. ηλθεν ὁ ις z *init. peric.* οἰκιαν wH. –ἡ ivwLHz. ἠρωτησαν iwH. 39. επετιμησεν w. αναστας w. 40. [δυνοντος vL]. ἠλιου v. ὀσοι w. ποικιλοις L. ουδε (*pro* ὁ δε) L. ἐνι ἐκαστω H. επιτεθεις z. επιτιθεις LH. εθεραπευεν v**. 41. κραυγαζοντα iLHz. *fin.* αυτον τον χν ειναι L. 42. επορευετο iw. επεζητουν iLHz. 43. +ις (*ante* ειπε) i. ειπεν wHz. ἑτεραις H. επι τουτο απεσταλην L. 44. εις τας συναγωγας LHz. ιουδαιας (*pro* γαλιλαιας) z.

CAP. V. 1. ἐστως HP. +ὁ ις (*post* ἐστως) v *rubro.* γεννησαρεθ L. γενησαρετ HP *semel.* *In* P** *semel legitur* γεννησαρετ ιδεν δυο πλοια ἑστῶτα παρα την λιμνην, *deest p. m.* 2. *init.* –και P**z *init. peric.* ιδεν wLP. ειδεν H**z. ἐστωτα iw. ἀλιεις HP. 3. πλυων H. ἠν P. ἠρωτησεν iwHPz. αυτων (*pro* αυτον) i. ὀλιγον iwHP. καθησας P. απο (*pro* εκ) L. ὀχλους P. 4. ειπεν wHPz. ἀγραν (*sic v.* 9) H. 5. διόλης i. διὄλης w. ελαβωμεν L. το ρηματι wP. χαλασωμεν w. δηκτυον H. 6. συνεκλυσαν i. συνεκλησαν P. πληθος ιχθυων ivwLHPz (ἰχθυων w). *fin.* +ὥστε μη δυνασθαι αναγαγειν αυτο i. 7. τους (*pro* του) P**. ελθοντος v. ἦλθον P. αμφοτεροι L

ε w. *βυθηζεσθαι* P. 8. +ὁ (*ante* σιμων) L. −πετρος L. προσεπεσεν
. γονασιν ιυ (−του) ivwHPz (γονασι w, γωνασιν P, *cum Elzev.* L). ἐμου
9. περιέχεν L. εν (*pro* επι) w. ἰχθυων w. 10. ἠσαν wP. ειπεν
Pz. 11. ἠκολουθησαν wP. 12. − εν τῳ L. πληρεις wHz. 13.
ιτο w. αυτο αυτου H*. λεγων (*pro* ειπων) L. τελω ?L*. απηλθεν
ϊπρα L. ἠ H. 14. μήδενὶ ivLH, *at* μήδὲν z. ἀλλ' iL. σεαυτω (*pro* σε-
ον) L. προσενεγκαι i. προσεταξεν w. μωϋσης wLz [*non* iv]. 15. −δε L.
ιura *in* w *inter* συνηρχ *et* οντο. −ὑπ' αυτου L. ασθενιων H*. 16. ὑπο-
ων i. ερημαις L*. 17. +ὁ ις (*ante* ην) i, (*post* διδασκων) v. ἦν *bis* P.
ι μια των συναγωγων (*post* διδασκων) L. ἠσαν *bis* P. νομωδιδασκαλοι H.
[. συνεληλυθοτες L. ἰλημ H. 18. κληνης iP. +της (*ante* κλινης) w.
r. ἦν P. παραλυτικος H. θηναι P. *fin.* αυτων L. 19. εὑρωντες i.
ντες H. εὑρωντες P. −δια *prim.* ivwPz. ποθεν (*pro* δια ποιας) LH.
ον P. εμπροσθε i*. 20. +ὁ ιησους (*post* ιδων) L. ειπε τω παραλυτικω
υτῳ) i. αφαιωνται P [*non* L], *rasur. in* i *inter* αφε *et* ωνται. αἱ (*sic v.*
H. 21. ἠρξαντο P. διαλογιζεσθε z. +αυτων (*post* γραμματεις) i. ει μι
. 22. γνους H. ειπεν iwHPz. διαλογιζεσθαι wP. 23. ευκοποτερον i.
ιωνται iP [*non* L]. εγειρε (*sic v.* 24) ivwLP. 24. ιδητε L. Επι
nutat.) L. ὁ υἱος του ανου εξουσιαν εχει w. −επι της γης P (P** *habet in*
rg.). ειπεν wHPz. παραλυτικω L. ἀρας w. οἶκον (*sic v.* 25) P. 25.
των (*pro* αυτων) L. εφ' ὃ vwHz. 26. ἀπαντας H. *Deest in* L *ab initio*
ue ad τον θν. λεγόντες w. ιδομεν wP. ειδωμεν L. ειδομεν ?z. 27.
αταῦτα L. εξηλθεν iwL (+ὁ ιησους L). παραγων ὁ ις εθεασατο Pz.
ιτο L, *at* ιδεν w (*pro* εθεασατο). ὀνοματι wP. λευι v. λευεῖν P. επι
w. το τελωνεῖν L. λεγει (*pro* ειπεν) LH. ακολουθη P. 28. καταλει-
ν iP. καταλοιπων w. ἀπαντα HP *sem.* ἠκολοῦθει L. ἠκολουθησεν wHP.
εποιησεν wHP. −ὁ ivwLHPz. λευεις P. τῳ οἶκω (*pro* τη οικια) w.
α HP. εν τη οικια αυτου, αυτω v. ἦν w. ἦν P. ὀχλος P. τελονων P
ι. πολυς τελωνων L. −πολυς v. ἠσαν P. κάταυτον (*pro* μετ' αυτων) L.
εγγογγυζον L*H**. φαρισσαῖοι P *sem.* διὰ τὶ (*sic v.* 33 w) vwHPz [*non*
|. +των (*ante* τελωνων) ivwLHz. εσθηετε P *sem.* 31. αποκριθεις δε
ιαι) H. ειπεν wHP. εχωσιν L. ισχυοντες (*pro* ὑγιαινοντες) L. οἱ *secund.*
κακων L*. εχωντες L. 32. καλεσε L*. 33. +οἱ δε ειπον αυτω (*post*
του) L. αυτω (*pro* προς αυτον) H. διὰ τὶ H. νηστευουσιν wH. νηστευ-
ττι L. συ εσθιουσιν H. 34. *init.* ὁ δε ιησους LHz. ειπεν wHz. εστιν
35. −και L. ὅτ' ἂν i. ὀτ' ἂν w. ὅτ' ἀν H. ὅτᾶν z. +και (*ante* τοτε) L.
στευουσιν wz. νηστευσωσιν L. 36. ελεγεν wH. αυτοις (*pro* προς

αυτους) L. επιβλυμα *prim.* wL. +απο (*ante* ἱματιου) L. κενου *prim.* L*. επι ἱματιου παλαιου z. σχισει Hz. συμφωνη ?w*. +το (*ante* επιβλημα *secund.*) iLHz. −επιβλημα *secund.* vw. 37. επιβαλλει H. οἰνον w. παλεους w. ριξει v. ὁ οἰνος ὁ νεος wH. ὁ οἰνος ὁ νεος z. 38. αλλ' iwL. οἰνον iH. −καινους v. συντυρουνται L. 39. ουδ' εἰς L. ποιων i. πιων L. εστι v.

CAP. VI. 1. −δευτεροπρωτω LPz. (τοις σαββασιν HP, τοις σαββασι z, *initio pericopes*). −των w. σπορηματων L. ετειλον L. ισθιον P. ἡσθιον Hz. χερσιν ivwLHPz. 2. εξεστιν w*P. −ποιειν εν L. −εν v*. σαββασιν iLPz. 3. ὁ ιησους ειπε προς αυτους iwL (ειπεν w). εποιησεν wP. ὁποτε v, *at* ὁτε L. ὀντες P. −οντες L. 4. πως L, ὡς P (*pro* ὡς). οἰκον P. τον αρτον L. ελαβεν P. −ελαβε και wLH. εφαγεν wP. εδωκεν wP. εξεστιν P, *at* ἑστι L. ει μι iH. μονοις L*. μονον Pz. τοις ἱερεις L. 6. −εγενετο *usque ad* διδασκειν HPz. −και *prim.* v. −και εν L. συναγωγειν L. ἠν ανος εκει w. ἠν *bis* P. *Rasura ante* χειρ *in* w. 7. παρετηρουντο w. και παρετηρουντο (−δε) L. −αυτον vwHPz [*non* iL]. −εν w. θεραπευει w. θεραπευση z. +αυτον (*post* θεραπευσει) L. εὑρωσιν P. +κατ' (*ante* αυτου) w. 8. ἠδη P. ειπεν wHPz. ειπε δε (−και) L. εξηραμμενην w. χειραν z. εγειρε ivwLP. στιθη P. ἑστη (*sic v.* 17) vL. 9. ειπε δε (−ουν) L. οὐν P. προς αυτους ὁ ις w. ὑμασ· τι iwLHPz [*non* v]. εξεστιν wP. ἠ *bis* P. *fin.* αποκτειναι ivwHPz [*non* L]. +οἱ δε εσιωπουν iw** *marg.* (εσιωπων w**). 10. +μετ' οργης (*ante* ειπε) L. ειπεν αυτω (*pro* τῳ ανῳ) vwHPz. οὑτως iw. −οὑτω HPz. εποιησε v, εξετεινεν L (*pro* εποιησεν οὑτω). απεκατεσταθη ivLPz [*non* wH]. −ὑγιης w* [*non* L]. ὑγιεις P. 11. ελαλουν w*. ποιησιαν i. ποιησει w. ποιησαιεν L. 12. εξελθειν αυτον (*pro* εξηλθεν) i. 13. προσεφωνησεν w. επ' (*pro* απ') z. ὠνομασεν w. ὠνομασεν Lz. ὠνομασε H. 14. −σιμωνα ὀν και ωνομασε L. ὠνομασε wH. ονομασε z. +και (*ante* ιακωβον) wL. *fin.* +και ιωαννην *iterum* L. 15. ματθαιαν L. θωμαν και ιακωβον L. −τον του L. αλφεου v. 16. *init.* +και L. ἰουδαν *bis* L. 17. μεταβας εκειθεν (*pro* καταβας) L. πεδεινου HPz. ὀχλος (*sic v.* 19 P) H *sem.* P. +των (*ante* μαθητων) H* *sem.* +και περαιας (*post* ἰλημ) H* *sem.* z *sem.* ἰλημ H *sem.* σιδονος (σινονος ?L*) L. ἠλθον P. 18. ὀχλουμενοι H *sem.* P *sem.* z. απο (*pro* ὑπο) vH *sem.* H** *sem.* Pz. *fin.* +ἀπαντες L. 19. ἀπτεσθαι wH *sem.* P. ἰατω P *sem.* z. 20. ελεγεν iwLHPz *sem.*, *at* ειπεν z *sem.* +τω πνι (*post* πτωχοι) iLz *sem.* *fin.* των ουνων (*pro* του θυ) wLz *sem.* z* *sem.* 21. +αυτοι (*ante* χορτασθησεσθε) z *sem.* χορτασθησονται L. 22. ὀτ' ἀν *bis* iH. ὀτ' ἀν *bis* (*sic v.* 26) w. ὀτἀν *bis* P. μισησουσιν i. αφορησωσιν P. ονειδισωσιν wP.

νειδισωσι H. ονειδισωσιν z sem. εκβαλλωσι wLHz sem. εκβαλλωσιν P. νομα P. ἑνεκα P. 23. χαρητε ivwLHPz. ἰδοῦ P. –γαρ prim. w. –ὁ L. τοις ουνοις L. και (pro κατα) ivL (sic v. 26, i): at κατα τα αυτα z sem. fin. μων (pro αυτων) z sem. 24. οὐαῖ (sic vv. 25, 26) w. ἡμιν (pro ὑμιν) L. πεχεται L. 25. –ὑμιν bis iL. +νυν (post εμπεπλησμενοι) iL. 26. –ὑμιν vwHz. ὅτἂν z sem. ὅτ' ἀν H. –ὑμας Lz sem. ειποσιν ὑμας z sem. ειπωσιν vH. –παντες iv. κατα τα αυτα wHz. καταταῦτα L. –γαρ H. fin. ὑμων pro αυτων) L. 27. αλλα vwLHz [non i]. 28. –ευλογειτε usque ad και i. μας (pro ὑμιν) wL. –και vLHz. επιρεαζοντων iH. επερεαζοντων L. επειεαζοντων z. fin. +και διωκοντων ὑμας L. 29. σοι (pro σε) L. σιαγωνα z. τρεψον αυτω (pro παρεχε) L. τη αλλη ?H*. αἱροντος w. αἱροντος (sic . 30) Lz. 30. –δε w. αἰτουντι w. απαιτη ivL. 32. ἡ (pro ει) H. στιν (sic ferè vv. 33, 34, 36) ivwLH**Pz. αγαπωσιν iwLH**Pz. 33. αγαθοποιειτε ivP. χαρις ὑμιν εστιν P. –οἱ vH*. αὐτῶ (pro αυτο) P. ποιουσιν wLPz. 34. δανειζετε iwPz. δανειζεται L. απολαβην i. –οἱ vwH. ἁμαρτωλους (pro -οις) H. απολαυωσιν P. ἴσα iwL. ἰσα v. 35. δανιζετε H. ηδὲν ivPz, μηδένα w. εστε (pro εσται) L. –του ivwHPz [non L]. χς H, ρηστος P (pro χρηστος). 36. οὖν P. οἰκτιρμ. bis wP. –και iP. ἡμων (pro μων) L**, forsan L* (+ὁ ουρανιος L). εστιν H. 37. και tert. in L bis criptum. 38. διδωτε L. πεπισμενον z. –και secund. L. εσαλευμενον H*. -και tert. L. ὑπερέκχυννομενον w. –και ὑπερεκχυνομενον H* (habet marg. antiquâ manu). δις (pro εις) L*. –γαρ L. μετρητε LH. αντιμετριθησεται iw. 39. ειπεν wHz, at ελεγε L. +και (ante παραβολην) L. δυνατε L. ὁδηγειν i. ουχ οἱ (pro ουχι) L. εμπεσουνται εις βοθυνον L. 40. –αὐτου prim. L. 41. –δε prim. w. τῶ (pro το secund.) w. –δε secund. z. ὀφθαλμω prim. H, secund. w. την δε εν τω σω οφθαλμον δοκον (–ιδιω) L sic. 42. ἀφες i. εκβαλῶ L. εκβαλλω z. –το secund. L. ὀφθαλμ. quater w, quart. H. δοκων prim. L*. μη (pro ου) L. βλεπον ?H*. εκβαλλε z. εκβαλλεῖν z. εκβαλειν transfert L ad fin. versûs. εκ του οφθαλμου (pro το εν τω οφθαλμω secund.) i. 43. οὐ H. ποιοῦν prim. w. +παλιν (post ουδε) L. 44. ἑκαστον H. γινωσκετε v. συλεγουσι H. σύκα ivwLHz. εκ βατων σταφυλην τρυγωσιν Hz. σταφυλας τρυγωσιν L. 45. εκ (pro της prim.) z. –της καρδιας αυτου secund. L. –του (ante περισσευματος) w*Hz. –της (ante καρδιας tert.) w*H. fin. –αυτου iHz. 46. –δε init. peric. z. καλειται L. λαλειτε (pro καλειτε) z. ἁ H. 47. Rasura inter μου et των w. ὁμοιος (sic v. 49, non 48) w. ὁμοιος εστιν L. 48. οἰκοδομουντι (sic v. 49 w) wH. οἰκιαν (sic v. 49) wH. +και (ante εσκαψε) Hz. εσκαψεν wH. εσκαψαι L. εβαθυνεν wL. εθηκεν wH. προσερριξεν (*non v.* 49) z. οἰκια wH. ισχυσεν w. 49. οἰκοδομουντι L. ἦ i. ἡ LHz. ευθυς Hz. συνεπεσεν LHz. επεσεν iw. ρῆμα w*. οἰκιας w.

Cap. VII. 1. επειδη επληρωσεν (−δε) w. επληρωσεν ὁ ιησους L. επληρωσεν H. ταυτα (*pro* αὐτου) L. +ο ι̅ς̅ (*post* εισηλθεν) v. 2. ἑκατονταρχου (*sic v.* 6) HP. εμελλε iwz [*non* vL]. εμελλεν P. ἠμελλε [ν H**] H. ἦν w. ἦν P. εντημος P. 3. απεστειλεν wH**P. αυτους (*pro* αυτον *prim.*) v*. −προς αυτον L. ερωτωντες αυτον (ο *mutat.*) P. 4. αυτου (*pro* τον ι̅ν̅) z. ηρωτων (*pro* παρεκαλουν) L. +αυτω (*post* λεγοντες) iw. παρεξεις i. παρεξη vw. ὥπερ ἕξει (*pro* ᾧ παρεξει) P. *fin.* τοῦτω z. 5. ὠκοδομησεν HP. 6. ἡδη P, *at* ειδη L. οὐ H. απεχοντος *bis script.* v. −απο L. οἰκιας wHP. επεμψεν wH**Pz, *at* απεστειλε L. λεγον z. προς αυτον (*pro* αυτῳ) L. σκυλου Pz. εἰμι H. μου ὑπο την στεγην ivLz [*non* HP]. 7. δι' ὃ w. ἠξιωσα wP. αλλ' ivwHPz. +μονον (*post* αλλα) L. λογον LP*. 8. −τασσομενος L. ταττομενος z. εμαυτου L. τουτο (*pro* τουτῳ) i. τουτω (*pro* τουτο) P. 9. εθαυμασε (−αυτον) v. ὀχλω P. ειπεν ivwLHPz. +αμην (*ante* λεγω) LH. ὀτι ουτε i, ουτε H, οὐτε P (*pro* ουδε). 10. εις τον οικον οἱ πεμφθεντες w. οἰκον P. −εις τον οικον v. 11. τω (*pro* τῃ) ivL. ἑξῆς iw. επορευθη ὁ ιησους L. +ὁ ι̅ς̅ (*post* επορευετο) ivw** *rubro* z. ναυι L. ναειν P. ναην z. −αυτῳ L. οἰκανοι L*, ἱκανοι wz (*non v.* 12). ὀχλος (*sic v.* 12) P. 12. ὠς δε ηγγισεν τη πυλη w** *marg.* (*deest in* w*). ηγγιζε L. ηγγισεν H**. ἠγγησεν P*. παλη L*. −και *prim.* v. τεθνηκος i. τεθνικως P. αὐτῇ iH*z, αὐτὴ vH**, αὐτῆ L, αὕτη P (*pro* αὐτη). [w *cum Elzev.*]. ἱκανος H. −ην ivwHPz. 13. ι̅ς̅ (*pro* κ̅ς̅) i. επ' αυτην wL. 14. ἡψατο iw. ἑστησαν vL. ειπεν wLHPz. συ (*pro* σοι) iL. +αναστας (*post* λεγω) L. 15. ανεκαθησεν LHP. ὁ w. ἡρξατο HP. 16. ελαβεν wH**P. παντας ivwLHPz. εγειγερται z. −ὁ θ̅ς̅ L. *fin.* +εις αγαθον iwL. 17. του ι̅υ̅ (*pro* οὑτος *et* περι αυτου) z *init. peric.* 18. +τω (*ante* ιωαννη) i. ἰωαννην w. +περι αυτου (*post* ιωαννη) L. +και (*ante* περι) L. των εργων αυτου (*pro* τουτων) Hz *init. peric.* *fin.* ἰωαννης *hic* w. 19. επεμψεν wz. κ̅ν̅ αυτου (*pro* ιησουν) L. ἢ H *sem.* ἑτερον H *sem.*, ἑτερον z (*pro* αλλον). 20. *Deest versus in* v*. βαπτῆστῆς w. βαπτισθεις L*. ἢ H *sem.* ἑτερον (*pro* αλλον) H *sem.* προσδοκομεν H* *sem.* 21. *init.* εν εκεινη τη ἡμερα (−δε) L. εκεινη (*pro* αυτῃ δε) H *sem.* εθεραπευσεν wH *sem.* z. +και ασθενειων (*post* πονηρων) z. −πολλοις H *sem.* −το iv*wL. του (*pro* το) z. 22. ιδετε wz. ἠκουσατε wH *sem.* ηκουσετε z. ἁ ακουετε και βλεπετε (βλεβετε L*) L. −ὁτι LH *sem.* z. +και (*ante* χωλοι) Lz. περιπατουσιν wLz. και κωφοι ακουωσιν L. ακουουσιν H *sem.* z. +και (*ante* πτωχοι) L. 23. ἐαν H. 24. απελθοντες z. μαθητων (*pro* αγγελων) wz. τοις οχλοις (−προς) ivHz. εξηλθετε (*sic v.* 25) w. εξηλθατε (*sic vv.* 25, 26) L. εξεληλυθα H*. 25. εξῆλθατε z *hic.* ἐξῆλθετε *hic* H. *Rasura in* w *inter* μαλακι *et* οις. ἠμφιέσμενον w. διαγοντες (*pro* ὑπαρχοντες) w. 26. και (*pro* ναι) z. περισσωτερον v. περισοτερον H. 27. +γαρ (*post* οὑτος) iv**Lz. εστιν wLz. 28. δε (*pro* γαρ) L. −γαρ z. εκ γεννητης L. −προφητης iw. +μου (*post* θῦ) L. *fin.* εστιν iwLHz. 29. +ὁ (*ante* ακουσας) i. τω βαπτισματι H. 30. ἠθετησαν w. ἠθετισαν L. αυτους w* (ἑ w**). −μη v. 31. −ειπε δε ὁ κς ivwL. ειπεν ὁ κς (−δε) z *init. peric.* −ουν z. ὁμοιοι *hic* i. 32. ὅμοι L. αγρω (*pro* αγορᾳ) z. λεγοντες (*pro* και λεγουσιν) L. ηυλισαμεν ivz. ηὑλησαμεν wH. οὑκ' *prim.* i. οὑκ H. ορχησασθε vLz. εθρηνισαμεν L. εκκοψασθε (*pro* εκλαυσατε) L. ουκεκεκλαυσατε i. 33. εληλυθεν wHz. −γαρ Hz. βαπτισθῆς w. μηττε *prim.* L*?. −αρτον L. −οινον L. οἰνον H. *fin.* εχειν L*. 34. *Pro* ιδου *habet* L δαιμονιον εχει και. +εστι (*ante* φαγος) L. οινοπωτης w. φιλος τελωνων ivwLHz. 35. −παντων i. απο παντων των τεκνων αυτης L. 36. ἠρωτα wHP. (−δε *et* αυτον, +τον ιν *ante* ἱνα, Pz *init. peric.*). αυτων (*pro* αυτον) L. φαγει P. οἱκιαν (*sic v.* 37) wH. τον οικον L. οἱκειαν (*sic v.* 37) P*. ανεκληθη ivP. 37. ἴδου P. *Rasura in* P *post* πο. γυνη τις ἠν εν τη πολει ἁμαρτωλος L. ἡτις wH. ἡτι z. ἠν P. +και (*ante* επιγνουσα) wLH, *at* επιγνους w. κομησασα P. 38. −ποδας *prim.* v*. του ιυ (*pro* αυτου *prim.*) w. οπισω παρα τους ποδας αυτου z. ὀπισω wHP. −κλαιουσα v*. κλεουσα v**. ἠρξατο P. δακρυσιν iwLHPz. θριξιν P. εξεμασσεν iw**H. εξεμασεν w*P. εξεμασε L. κατεφιλη v. ἠλειφε iz. ηλειφεν w. ειληφεν P. το μυρο ?L*. 39. ἑαυτω H. −λεγων L. −ει P. ἠν HP. +ὁ (*ante* προφητης) P*. εγινωσκε (−αν) L. ἡτις H. ἁπτεται wHP. *fin.* εστιν iwLHPz. 40. αποκριθεις δε (−και) H. ειπεν wHPz. τί ειπειν; w. φησιν wPz. 41. χρεοφειλεται ivwHP. ἦσαν P. δανησται P. ωφειλεν wz. οφειλε L. ὀφειλεν P. +δηναρια (*ante* πεντηκοντα) L. 42. −δε w. −αυτων *prim.* i. αμφοτερους ?L*. οὑν P. αυτον (*pro* αυτων *secund.*) i. −αυτων *secund.* L. εἶπε (*pro* ειπὲ) L, πλειονα z. −αυτον i. αυτων (*pro* αυτον) L. 43. −ὁτι P*. ὁ (*pro* ῳ) LP*. +ις (*post* ὁ δε) i. 44. −σου i. οἱκιαν wH. αὑτη (*sic v.* 45) P. εβρεξεν w. εβρεξαι L. εξεβρεξεν P. θριξιν wP. −της κεφαλης w. εξεμαξεν iwPz. 45. εισηλθεν iLz (εισῆλθον P). διελειπε ivL. διελειπεν wP. 46. οὑκ' ειληφας P. ἠλειψε [ν P] τους ποδας μου ivHP. ηλειψεν wL?. ἠλειψε *hic* z. 47. *init.* οὑ iHP. αφεονται (*sic v.* 48) L. αφαιονται (*sic v.* 48) P. αυτης αἱ ἁμαρτιαι wL. −αἱ *secund.* L. ἠγαπησεν wP. ἠγαπησε H. ὁ (*pro* ῳ) P. ὀλιγον *bis* iwP, *secund.* H. *fin.* αγαπατε L. 48. ειπεν (*sic v.* 50) wHPz. 49. ἠρξαντο P.

αυτοις (*pro* εν ἑαυτοις) L* (*marg. cum Elzev.*). εστιν οὑτος L. αφειησιν i.
50. πιστης iP. σεσωκεν iwP.

CAP. VIII. 1. διοδευε i, διωδευεν w, διοδευεν L, *at* επορευετο H. κωμην
και πολιν v. 2. +νοσων και μαστιγων και (*post* απο) H** *antiquâ manu*, z.
−καλουμενη i. μαγδαλινη v. 3. σουσανα i. αἱτεραι L*. αἱτινες H.
αυτοις (*pro* αυτῳ) vLH. εκ (*pro* απο) wL. 4. *init.* συνελθοντος L. ειπεν
w. 5. −του w. ἑαυτου iv. ὁ μὲν v. επεσεν wHP. *Linea post* κατεπα-
τηθη *eras. in* P. *fin.* αυτω P*. 6. ἡγμαδα P. ἰκμαδα z. 7. επεσε H*. −εν
(*at* ˝μέσω *sic*) L. συμφυῆσαι z. *fin.* αυτον i. 8. και τερον H. εις (*pro* επι)
ivwLHPz. −την *prim.* P*. *Rasura in* w *post* την *secund.* εποιησεν wH**P.
ἑκατονταπλασιονα HP. −ταυτα λεγων *ad fin. vers.* LHPz. 9. επηρωτουν L.
−ειη P. αὕτη P. 10. +αυτοις (*post* ειπεν) iL. +λαλω (*post* παραβολαις) i.
βλεπωσιν LP. +ακουσωσι και (*post* ακουοντες) L. +ακουσωσι μὴδὲ (*ante* συνιω-
σιν) i, *omisso* μη. συνίωσιν v. συνιωσι L. 11. *init.* εστιν wH**P. αὕτη P.
12. αἱρει wLz. 13. ὅτ' ἂν iH. ὁτ' ἂν w. ὁτᾶν P. ακουσωσιν wP. εχω-
σιν P. +και (*ante* προσκαιρον) i. κερον P. πιστευουσιν H**P. κερω i. 14.
εμπεσων i. πεσων L*. ακουοντες wP. συμπνηγονται i. συγπνιγονται L*.
τελεσφορουσιν iwLPz. 15. οἱτινες w. ακουοντες L. κατεχουσι τον λογον v.
κατεχουσιν wP. καρπον φερουσιν L. *fin.* +πολλη L. +ταυτα λεγων εφωνει
ὁ εχων ωτα (ὠτα H) ακουειν ακουετω w** (*marg. rubro*) LHP. 16. οὐδεὶς P.
−δε vwPz *init. peric.* ἁψας HP. σκευη L. ἢ P. ὑπὸκάτω wHz. −αλλ'
usque ad επιτιθησιν H*P* (την λυχνιαν H** *uncial. marg.*, λυχνιαν P** *marg.
cursivâ manu*). την λυχνιαν (*pro* λυχνιας) w. επιτιθησι v. τιθησιν (*pro*
επιτιθησιν) L. εισπωρευομενοι ? w*. βλεπουσιν P. 17. *init.* οὐ H. εστιν P.
+τι (*ante* κρυπτον) i. +μη (*ante* γνωσθησεται) P. φως (*pro* φανερον *secund.*)
z. ἐλθη w. 18. οὐν P. +και προστεθησεται ὑμιν τοις ακουουσιν (*post* ακου-
ετε) L. εχει *bis* P. εανχη (*pro* αν εχη) L. εαν (*pro* αν *secund.*) LHP, *bis* v
(ἐαν H) z. −ὃ z. δοκη (η *dubium*) L. 19. +αυτου (*post* μηρ) LHP. ουκ-
εδυναντο w. ὀυκ' ἠδυναντο P. ὀχλον P. 20. απηγγελλη i. απαγγελλει δε
(−και) L. απαγγελλει z. ἑστηκασιν iwP. 21. ειπεν (*sic v.* 22) wHPz. +ἡ
(*ante* μηρ) L. +οἱ (*ante* αδελφοι) L. οὑτοι H. *fin.* −αυτον w. 22. εγενετο
δε (−και) iwL. ανεβη v**wLHP [*non* iz]. +ὁ ις (*ante* εις πλοιον) ivP *init.
peric.* +το (*ante* πλοιον) L. λυμνης L*. 23. αφυπνωσεν iwLPz. λελαψ
iHP. λαῖλαψ w. λυμνην L*. συνεκινδυνευον L. 24. και προσελθοντες
(−δε) w. −επιστατα *secund.* w**P. απολυμεθα P. επετιμησεν P. επαυ-
σατο vw. γαλινη iP. *fin.* +μεγαλη iw. 25. ειπεν wHP. και ειπεν
(−δε) z. −εστιν *prim.* w. πιστης P. −λεγοντες v. προς αλληλους λεγοντες i.

α ivwHz. εστιν οὗτος L. επιτασει P. 26. καταπλευσαντες L. γαδαρι-
ν ειτις L. αντιπερα ivwL. γαληλαιας ?L*. 27. π̓ὶ i. ἠπηντησεν L.
ρ L. –τις H*. ειχεν wHP. οὐκ' *prim.* P. ενεδυδυσκετο L. οικεδεδυσκετο
οἰκια wP. εις οικιαν L. μνημασι v. 28. –δε P*. ανακηρυξας L. ειπεν
'LHPz (*sic v.* 30 *præter* i). –ιησου iL. 29. παρηγγελλεν iw. παρηγγελ-
ι v. παρηγγειλεν H**P. ἁλυσεσι iH. ἁλυσεσιν P. πεδες iL. παιδαις w.
αιδες P*. διαρρησων i. ελαυνετο L. ἠλαυνετο wPz. –του *secund.* L. 30.
ηρωτησεν HP. ὀνομα HP. πολλα δαιμονια L. εισηλθον iw. 31. παρε-
λουν L. –μη P. επιταξει w*HP. 32. ἦν P. κει H. χυρων P. βοσκο-
νη wL. ὀρει HP. επιτρεψει wH. αυτους (*pro* L* αυτοις *prim.*) L**.
ελθειν L. 33. εισηλθον i?vwPz. ὡρμησεν iw. ὡρμησε πασα ἡ αγελη
ων χοιρων L. κριμνου i*P. κρυμνου wL. λημνην ?v. απεπνιγει i*. 34.
οντες i. ιδωντες z. γεγονος wL. γενομενον vP. γεγεννημενον H. –απελ-
οντες iwLHPz. πολην P. 35. γεγονως iz. ἦλθον P. ἤλθον z. εὗρον P.
ἐληλυθη (*sic v.* 38) P. σοφρονουντα H. 36, 37. *Desunt in* HPz. 36.
αυτοις και L. ιδοτες i. –και οἱ ιδοντες v. 37. ἡρωτησεν w. ηρωτησεν L.
της περιχωρου v. γεσινῶν (*sic, pro* γαδαρηνων) L. συνηχοντο i. 38. τα
ιμονια εξεληλυθει L. εξεληλυθη i. εξεληλυθε v. απελυσεν wHP. 39.
κον P. εποιησεν *prim.* wHP. απηλθεν wHP. απηλθον L. καθοληv LP.
ρυσσον H. 40. ὑπεδεξατο L** (*s. m. ut videtur*). υτὸν v. ἦσαν w. 41.
ηλθεν i*. ανος (*pro* ανηρ) H (+τις H) Pz *init. peric.* ὦ ὀνομα HP. ιαηρος
. ϊαΐρος P. οὗτος (*pro* αυτος) L. ὑπηρχεν wLHPz. οἰκον HP. 42.
w. ἦν P. ὡσει w. ἐτων (*sic v.* 43) w. αὐτῇ i, αὐτὴ L, αὔτη P (*pro* αὕτη).
χλοι (*sic v.* 45) P. συνεθλιβον L. 43. οὖσα HP. ρυση H. αἱματος (*sic*
44) H. ιατροις (–εις) ivwLHPz. ισχυσε παρ' (*pro* ὑπ') L. ὑπ' i. 44.
ισθεν iHP. ἥψατο ὀπισθεν w. κραπεδου P*. παραχρῆμα (*sic v.* 55, *non*
7) i. ἐστη L, *at* εστι H. ρυσης P. 45. ὁ ις *rescript. in* P. ἁψαμενος *bis*
HPz?. συν αυτω (*pro* μετ' αυτου) Lz. –και οἱ μετ' αυτου w (*habet* w**
arg.). συνεχουσιν wP. αποθλιβουσιν P. 46. απ' εμου εξελθουσαν v. *fin.*
ιοῦ P. 47. οὐκ H. ελαθεν wHP. ηλθεν wH. ἠλθεν P. ἦν wP. αἰτιαν
. ἡψατο ?w. –αυτῳ *secund.* w*L. ἑως (*pro* και ὡς) L. παραχρῆμα (*sic* H
ι *v.* 55) Hz. 48. *init.* ὁ δε ις i. πιστης P. σεσωκεν wH**P. 49. ερχε-
ι H. αρχησυναγωγου LHP. –αυτῳ i. σκυλου P. 50. –λεγων i. 51.
it. ελθων ivwLHPz. οἰκιαν wHP. αφηκε τινα εισελθειν συν αυτω (–ουδενα)
. ειμι H. ιωαννην και ιακωβον vwLHPz [*non* i]. 52. ε *mutat. in* εκοπτον-
ο L. +ις (*post* ὁ δε) P. ειπεν wLHPz. οὐκ H. ου γαρ απεθανε το κορασιον
. καθευδη P. 54. παντας εξω w. εφωνησεν HP. 55. επεστρεψεν

wHP. διεταξε δοθηναι αυτη iL. διεταξατο αυτην (*pro* αυτῃ) z. 56. μήδενὶ iwPz.

CAP. IX. 1. *init.* και προσκαλεσαμενος P *sem.* z *sem.* (—δε, +ὁ ις *init. peric.* P *bis* z *sem.*). —δωδεκα Hz *sem.* αποστολους (*pro* μαθητας αυτου) iL. —μαθητας αυτου wP *sem.* αυτους (*pro* αυτοις) i. 2. επεστειλεν ?L*· αυτοις (*pro* αυτους) H. κηρυσσιν P *sem.* ειασθαι i. ιασθε z. 3. ειπεν wHPz. μήδὲν iwHPz. αἱρετε wP *sem.* z. αιρεται L*P *sem.* —την LP *sem.* ραβδον LP *sem.* ραβδου P *sem.* (*sic*). πειραν HP *sem.* χειτωνας P. εχην i. 4. ἦν wPz. ἦν H. —αν v*. οἰκειαν P *sem.* P* *sem.* οἰκιαν H. εξερχεσθαι H. 5. εαν (*pro* αν) vLHP *sem.* P** *sem.* z. δεξονται iL*HP. δεχονται w. +απο της οικιας η (*post* εξερχομενοι) L. —απο *secund.* P** *duobus locis.* αποτειναξατε iv. επ' αυτοις Pz. αυτοις (—επ') L. 6. διήρχοντο P. 7. ἤκουσεν wH. γενομενα iL. —ὑπ' αυτου L. εγειγερται i, ηγερθη L. +των (*ante* νεκρων) LHz. 8. αλλοι (*pro* ὑπο τινων) L. ἠλιας iL. εφανει i. —εἱς L. τις (*pro* εἱς) Hz. 9. ειπεν δε (—και) L. —ὁ ivwHz. απεκεφαλησα Lz. οὑτος H. ταυτα (*pro* τοιαυτα) L. ειδειν i. 10. τω ιησου (*pro* αυτῳ) L. ὑπεχωρισε i. ὑπεχωρησεν w. —ὑπεχωρησε L. κατιδιαν ivz [*non* wL]. —πολεως καλουμενης βηθσαιδα L. βἱθσαϊδαν i. βηθσαϊδαν v. 11. γνωντες iz. ἠκολουθησαν wH. αποδεξαμενος iL. +τα (*ante* περι) iL. —του θῦ z. τους δε χρειαν (—και) L. θεραπιας i. ιασατο LHz. 12. πορευθεντες (*pro* απελθοντες) LHz*. —τους L. ὡδε Hz. ἐν H. 13. ειπεν (*sic vv.* 14, 20 *bis*) wHz. —ἡμιν L. +ει μη (*ante* πλειον) L. πλοιον (*pro* πλειον) z. ιχθυες δυο ivwLHz (ἰχθ. w). τοι (*pro* τι) L. ὑμεις w*. —τουτον H* (*habet marg. antiquâ manu*) z. 14. ανδρες ὡσει i. 15. οὑτως ivwLz. οὗτως H. κατεκλιναν L. παντας v. ἁπαντας H. 16. ἰχθυας w. ηυλογησεν Hz. κατεκλασεν wL. +αυτου (*post* μαθηταις) iL. παρατεθηναι L. παραθηναι Hz. 17. παντες και εχορτασθησαν L. περισσευμα L. κλασματα H. δωδεκα κοφινοι i. 18. κατὰ μόνας iv. +αυτου (*post* μαθηται) iLHz. αυτου L, αυτοις H* (*pro* αυτους). ὀχλοι H. 19. ἠλιαν iL [*non* vwz]. +ἑτεροι δε ἱερεμιαν (*post* ἠλιαν) L. ἑτεροι (*pro* αλλοι *secund.*) H. —ὁτι L. προφητις ?i*. 20. λεγεται w. —ὁ iL. ειπεν *secund.* L, *bis* H. 21. —αυτοις L. παρηγγειλεν LH. μήδενὶ iz. λεγειν (*pro* ειπειν) vLHz. παρηγγειλεν αυτοις μηδενι λεγειν τουτο w. 22. αρχιερεων και πρεσβυτερων L. *fin.* αναστηναι wL*. —και τη τριτῃ ἡμερᾳ εγερθηναι i. 23. ελεγεν w. θελη P. ὀπισω wHP. ερχεσθαι (*pro* ελθειν) vwLHz. αρνησασθω w*. ἑαυτου H. —καθ' ἡμεραν iP [*non* vwLz]. ακολουθητω LHP. *fin.* μου z. 24. εαν (*pro* αν *prim.*) ivw. ἀν *prim.* L. θελει iwL. απολεση (*pro* -ει) iv*. δὰν i. απολεσει (*pro* -ῃ) LP. ἑνεκεν HP. δἰ εμε (*pro* ἑνεκεν

υ) L. αυτος (*pro* οὑτος) vw. 25. ὠφελειται wH. ὀφελειται L. ὀφε-
ρει P. –δε P. ἤ P, ἡ z *at* ὑ L (*pro* ἢ). ζημειωθεις i. 26. εαν (*pro* αν)
Lz. ὁτ' ἂν w. ὀτᾶν P. ὅτ' ἂν Hz. ἐλθη w. –αὐτου και i*. 27.
ηθως *cum sequent.* v. +ὁτι (*ante* εισι) iw. εισιν wHP. –τινες v. ὡδε Hz.
·ωτων iLz. ἑστωτων wHP. οἱτινες (*pro* οἳ) w. γευσωνται vwHz. ειδωσι
ιδωσιν P. 28. –δε L. ὡς (*pro* ὡσει) L. ὠκτῶ i. ὀκτῶ w. –τον ivwL.
ωβον και ιωαννην i *solus.* (+και *ante* ανεβη Pz *init. peric.*). ὀρος P. 29.
ς P. –ἑτερον και ὁ ἱματισμος αυτου P. λευκον P. εξαστραπτον H. 30.
ῦ *passim* P (ι *mutat. in* L). αυτου (*pro* αυτῳ) L** *marg.* οἱτινες w.
ιν HP. μωυσης iwLz [*non* vHP]. ἠλιας ivwLP [*non* Hz]. 31. *init.* οἱ
HPz [*non* v]. ωφθεντες i. ὀφθεντες P (+αυτω v**HPz). +και (*ante*
ιγον) v**HP. +δε (*post* ελεγον) L. ἦν w. ἦν LH. εμελλεν wHP. πλη-
ν z. ϊελημ P. 32. ἠσαν HP. βεβαρυμενοι iL. ιδον wP. 33. ειπε
HP) πετρος (–ὁ) ivHPz. +παντοτε (*ante* ὡδε) HP. ὧδε wz. –και *secund.*
IPz. τρεις σκηνας LHPz. συ (*pro* σοι) LP. μιαν μωση iHPz. μιαν μωσει
μιαν μωυσει (ει *mutat.*) w. ἠλια iw [*non* z]. ἠλιαν P. μιαν ηλια και
ιν μωσει L. τι (*pro* ὃ) Hz. –μη ειδως ὁ λεγει P. 34. εισελθειν εκεινους
Pz. 35. +εν ὡ ηυδοκησα (*post* αγαπητος) HPz (ὧ H, ηὐδ. HP). 36. εὑρεθη
–ὁ ivw. και *secund. mutat. in* L. εσηγησαν P. ἑωρακασι w. ἑωρακαν
37. –εν iL. ἑξης iw. κατελθωντων w, *at* καταβαινοντων L. –αυτων
ὀρους P. ὀχλος (*sic v.* 38) P. 38. εβοησε L. ανεβοησεν P. ἐπιβλέ-
ψαι vw*H (ἐπίβλεψαι w**). μονογεννῆς P. μοι εστιν Pz. εστιν w. 39.
εφνης i. εξαφνης ?L. κραζει και ρησει και σπαρασει i. συντριβων iHz.
. εκβαλωσιν ivwHP [*non* Lz]. αυτῶ (*sic v.* 47) i. εδυνηθησαν w. οὐκ'
υνηθησαν P. 41. ὦ wP. εσωμαι i. προς ὑμας εσωμαι L. ἑως ποτε (*pro*
ι *secund.*) wLHz. ανεξωμαι L. τον υἱον σου ὡδε ivwLHPz. 42. ερριξεν
at ερριψεν v, ερρηψεν H**. συνεταραξεν z. +αυτον (*post* συνεσπαραξεν) iw.
·ετιμησεν P. *Ras. in* H *post* ακαθαρτω. 43. εξεπλήσσον L. μεγαλιοτητι
. αυτου L* (*pro* του θῦ, *quod habet* L** *marg.*). εποιει L. ειπεν w. τοις
υτου μαθηταις H. 45. οἱγνοουν w. ἠγνοουν Hz. ἦν w. παρακεκαλῦμ-
νον (ῦμμ *rescript.*) i. παρ' (*pro* απ') L. αισθονται i. εσθοντε ?L. αυτον
ro αυτο) L. επερωτησαι w. αυτον ερωτησαι L. 46. εισηλθεν wH. 47.
δως (*pro* ιδων) w. παιδιον Hz. ἑστησεν L. αυτω (*pro* αυτο) iL. παρε-
τῶ iL. 48. αν (*pro* εαν) *bis* L. ἐὰν *prim.* w, *bis* z. +εμε ? (*ante* δεξηται
im.) H*. τουτο τον H*. δεχεται (*pro* δεξηται *secund.*) L. δεξηται L,
χηται z (*pro* δεχεται *secund.*). ὑπαρχον L. εστιν ὁ H, εστι z (*pro* εσται).
). ὁ w. –ὁ L. ιδομεν iwH. ιδωμεν L. ειδωμεν z *sem.* εν (*pro* επι) LHz.

ὀνοματι wH *sem.* —τα ivwLHz. —μεθ' *semel tantum* z. ἡμιν (*pro* μεθ'. ἡμων) L,
at ὑμων z. 50. ειπεν wHz. αυτους Lz *sem.* +ου γαρ εστι καθ' ὑμων (*post*
κωλυετε) H *bis* z (οὐ *et* εστιν H *sem.*). εστιν *prim.* iH. ὑμων (*pro* ἡμων) *bis*
vwHz, *at* καθ' ὑμων μεθ' ἡμων ὑπερ ἡμων (*sic*) L. 51. —δε L (*sic* z *sem. init.*
peric.). εστηριξεν wL. εστηρισε το προσωπον αυτου Hz *sem.* ἰλημ (*sic*
v. 53) H. 52. απεστηλεν w. προπροσώπου ivL. ἑαυτου L**. εις πολιν
σαμαριτων εισηλθον L. —εισηλθον i. πολιν (*pro* κωμην) ivz *sem.* σαμαριτῶν i.
ἑτοιμᾶσαι ivwz. ἑτοιμασαι H. 53. ἦν w. 54. ειδόντες i. θελης i*. εἰ-
πωμεν i. ειπομεν z. απ' ουρανου (—του) Hz *sem.* καταναλωσαι i. αυτοις
(*pro* αυτους) z. ἡλιας iL [*non* wz]. εποιησεν wLHz. 55, 56. *Desunt*
omnia præter και επορευθησαν *ad fin. vers.* 56 *in* z *sem.*, *sic in* H *post* επετι-
μησεν αυτους. 55. +ὁ ις (*post* δε) iw. αυτους (*pro* αυτοις) H. οἴδατ L.
ποιου iw**z *sem.* —ὑμεις iL. ὑμεις ;w. 56. —γαρ iLz. ηλθεν w. 57.
και (*pro* εγενετο δε) L. ὁδω w. ειπεν (*sic vv.* 59 *bis*, 60, 61, 62) wHPz [*non*
L]. σου z (*cf. v.* 23). εαν (*pro* αν) wLPz [*non* i]. 58. κς (*pro* ις) L. αἱ
P. φολεους P. εχουσιν LPz. κατασκηνωσης P. κλινει i. κλῖναι L. 59.
ακολουθη P. απελθειν πρωτον τον πρα μου θαψαι w. απελθειν L. —πρωτον
vL. 60. —θαψαι τους ἑαυτων νεκρους L. ἑαύτων P. διαγγελε iLHP.
61. επιταξασθαι v. οἰκον iP. 62. ὁ ις προς αυτον vwLHz [*non* i]. οὐδεις
H. οὐδεῖς P. ἐπιβαλῶν P. αρωτρον i. ἐπάροτρον L. στραφεις (*pro*
βλεπων) z. ὀπισω wHP [*non* i].

CAP. X. 1. ἑβδομηκοντα H. +μαθητας (*post* ἑβδομηκοντα) Hz *sem.* ανα
δυο δυο vwL. εκ των μαθητων αυτου δυο Pz *sem. init. peric.* οὗ P. ημελλεν
iLz *sem.* ἡμελλεν P. διερχεσθαι L. 2. ελεγε δε (—ουν) Lz *sem.* οὐν *bis*
P. ὀλιγοι iwHP. δεηθηται H*. εκβαλη iHz *sem.* αν εκβαλη v. εκβαλει P.
αν εκβαλλει w [*cum Elzev.* z *sem.*]. αμπελωνα (*pro* θερισμον) i. 3. αποστέλω
w. αποστελλῶ P. 'E ἐν w ('E *rubro*). 4. βασταζητε z *sem.* βαλλαντιον
wLz** *sem.* βαλαντια z *sem.* πειραν H. μὴδὲ ivwz, μὴδε H, *at* μητε L.
μὴδένα iHz. ὁδον w. 5. ἦν (*sic vv.* 8, 10 w) wz *sem.* δὰν (*sic v.* 10, *non*
8 i) iz *sem.* δᾶν z *bis.* οἰκιαν wHz *sem.* πολιν εισελθητε εις οικιαν L. πρω-
τον, λεγετε w. ειρηνην εν (*pro* ειρηνη) L. οἰκω H. 6. —μεν ivw*LHz.
ἦ wz *sem.* ἦ H. εἶ L. —ὁ ivwLHz. επαυτον επαναπαυσεται L. επανα-
παυσετε H. προς (*pro* εφ') L. ανακαμψη H. επανακαμψει z *sem.* 7. —τη
H* (*habet antiquâ manu*). οἰκι : *ter.* wH. —τα L. παρ' αυτον L. —ὁ z *sem.*
εστιν vwLz. —εστι H. μεταβενετε H. εξ οικιαν εις L. 8. εις ἡν *rescript.*
L. ἣν ἂν H. ἣν δὰν P. —δ' vLHz. εισερχεσθε v. δεχονται iLH*P.
9. ἠγγικεν H. ἡ βασιλεια του θυ εφ' ὑμας i. 10. οἰκιαν (*pro* πολιν) H.

εισερχεσθεi, at εισελθητε L. δεχονται iL. δεξωνται H. πλατει H. 11. —τον secund. P. κωλλυθεντα L. ὑμιν (pro ἡμιν) LP. απο (pro εκ) z. ἡμων (pro ὑμων) v. +εις τους ποδας ἡμων (ante απομασσ.) vwLHz. απομασσωμεθα L. ἠγγικεν P. 12. —δε vwLPz sem. σοδωμοις L. ανεκτοτερον εσται εν τη ἡμερα εκεινη L. —η τη πολει εκεινη L. 13. οὐαι secund. i, bis w. ουαι secund. H. Οὐαι prim. H**. χῶραζείν v. χοραζειν w. χώραζῆν L. βηθσαϊδαν (ut videtur) i. βιθσαϊδᾶν L. τηρω (non v. 14) L. σιδωνη L. εγενηθησαν L. αἱ δυναμης αἱ H. γινωμεναι L. γινομεναι H. σαπκω L*?. καθημενοι Hz. 14. σιδονη L. εν ἡμερα κρισεως L. 15. ἡ (pro ἡ) L. ὑψωθησα iL. +του (ante ἀδου) Hz. καταβηβασθηση i. καταβιβασθῆσα L. καταβασθειση z. 16. init. +και ελεγεν αυτοις H, in transitu. ὑμων ακουων w. ἡμων ?L*. —εμε prim. i*. αθετη ultim. P. 17. +μαθηται (ante μετα) i. μετα χαρας οἱ ἑβδομηκοντα wH sem. ἑβδομηκοντα P sem., at ἑβδυμικοντα sem. ὑμιν v*P sem. ὀνοματι H sem. P. 18. ειπεν wHP. πεσωντα i. 19. ἴδου διδωμη P sem. (μ mutat. in διδωμι L). ὀφεων P. εχρου H* sem. ου mutat. P sem. αδικηση vwLHPz ter [non iz sem.]. 20. πλιν P sem. τούτο P sem. χερετε prim. P sem. ὑμων (pro ὑμιν) L. ὑποτασεται P sem. —ὑμιν usque ad ονοματα P sem. —μαλλον ivwLHP bis z. ὀνοματα H sem. P. εγραφει P sem. 21. ταυτη (pro αυτη) P sem. +δε (post αυτη) i. ἠγαλλιασατο iwHP sem. ἠγαλλιασατω P bis. ὁ ις τω πνι i. Rasura in w post πνι. αυτα (pro ταυτα) P sem. 22. init. +και στραφεις προς τους μαθητας αυτου (—αυτου v) ειπε ivw** (ειπεν w**) [non L]. ειπεν ὁ κς z init. peric. μοι παρεδοθη ivLH (παρεδωθη H) z sem. μοι παραδεδοται w. επιγινωσκει Hz. τις εστιν ὁ πηρ ειμι ὁ υἱος· και τις εστιν ὁ υἱος ειμι ὁ πηρ i. +ουδεις γινωσκει (post πηρ secund.) L. ὧ (pro ᾧ) L. βουλεται L. 23. κατιδιαν ivLHz. κατίδιαν w. ειπεν wLHz. ὀφθ. H. 24. ἠθελησαν wH. ειδειν i. +ειδον ουδε (ante ηκουσαν) L. 25. τις προσηλθε [ν P] τω ιυ πειραζων Pz init. peric. πειραζων H. 26. init. ὁ δε ιησους L. ειπεν (sic vv. 28, 29, 40) wHPz. 27. απησεις L. ἐξόλης quater i. —και εξ ὁλης της ισχυος σου v. ἑαυτον vwLP [non iHz]. 28. ὀρθος H. ὀρθως P. απεκριθεις wHP. τουτω P. σωζει (pro ζηση) Pz. 29. εστιν wP. 30. ὁ δε ιησους εφη (—ὑπολαβων et ειπεν) L. ἴλημ HP. ἱεριχω ivwLz (ἱ w). εκδησαντες i. εἱμήθανή P. 31. αντιπαρηλθε L. αντηπαρηλθεν P. 32. —ελθων w. +αυτον (post ιδων) iwP. αντιπαρηλθε iv. 33. σαμαρειτις w*H*z. σαμαριτης L. +εν τη ὁδω εκεινη (ante ηλθε) i*. ηλθεν w. ἦλθεν P. 34. κατεδυσε iL. κατεδησεν P. οἰνον HP. επιβηβασας P. ἤγαγεν P. —αυτον secund. v. επιμεληθη L. 35. αὐριον wLz? εκβαλῶν P. εδωκεν wH**P. δεδωκε z. το (pro τῳ prim.) L. τουτου (pro αυτου) v. ὅτι vHP.

+δ' (*ante* αν) w. προσδαπανισης i. προσδαπανησεις P. επαρερχεσθαι w. μοι (*pro* με) LP. 36. οὖν (*sic vv.* 37, 40) P. πλησιον δοκει σοι vwLHPz [*non* i]. ληστας *rescript. super rasur.* P. 37. ειπε δε (–ουν) iL. σοι H. 38. –και L. ηλθεν i. +ὁ ις (*post* εισηλθεν) v. ὀνοματι wHP. οἰκον P. 39. ἦν P. *Pro* ἥ L *habet* ἥ, z ἥ. παρακαθησασα iP. παρακαθησα L. ηκουεν w. ἠκουεν H**P. των λογων i. 40. πολην i. ειπεν vLH. μελλει iz [*non* vwLH]. μονη L. εγκατελιπε v. κατελειπεν wP**. εγκατελειπεν P*. κατελειπε Lz. κατελιπεν H**. εἶπε (*pro* εἰπὲ) L. μη (*pro* μοι) L. συναντιλαβητε v*LP. συναυτηλαβηται H. 41. ὁ ις ειπεν αυτη iwL. τιρβαζη i. τυρβαζεις L. 42. ἑνος P. εστιν w*P. χρια P*. γαρ (*pro* δε *secund.*) L. αφερεθησεται P. ἀπαυτῆς i.

CAP. XI. 1. προσευχωμενον L. επαυγατο L. ειπεν (*sic vv.* 2, 5, 28, 39, 46) wHz *sem.* ὑμας (*pro* ἡμας) i. προσευχεσθε P₂. –και (*post* καθως) LP. εδιδαξεν wH** *sem.* P. 2. ειπεν LH *sem.* PP₂. ὅτ' ἂν (*sic vv.* 21, 34, 36 i) iH. ὁτ' ἂν wP₂ [*non* z]. +δε (*post* ὅτἂν) P. προσευχεσθε iP. προσευχεσθαι L. ἁγιασθητω H. ὀνομα P. βασιλειασσου P₂. –της L. 3. το (*pro* τον *secund.*) w. –το P. καθημεραν i. *Rasura in* P₂ *inter* το *et* μεραν (η *eras*?). καθἡμεραν H *sem.* Pz. 4. ἡμων (*pro* ἡμιν *prim.*) P*. ἁμαρτιας H *sem.* ἡ [μων P**] P. +και (*ante* αυτοι) P. αφιομεν iv. αφιωμεν P. +τω (*ante* οφειλοντι) Pz. (ὀφιλοντι P). ὀφειλοντι H. ἡμων (*pro* ἡμιν *secund.*) L*. –και (*ante* μη) P. εισενεγκεις H *sem.* πειρασμῶν P. –ἡμας *secund.* z *sem.* 5. ειπεν H *sem.* ἐξ' z *sem.* ἐξει iH *sem.* z. πορευεται z *sem.* ερει (*pro* ειπῃ). wLz *sem.* τρις (*pro* τρεις) L. 6. ἐπεὶ δὴ i. μοι (*pro* μου) Lz *sem.* –μου vHz *sem.* [*non* i]. ἐξοδου i, *sic passim.* 7. ειπεν (*pro* ειπῃ) L. κοποις z *sem.* +γαρ (*post* ηδη) L. κεκλυσθαι L. –μου i. 8. +δε (*post* λεγω) w**z. μῖν H* *sem.* δοσει *bis* z *sem.* φιλος L. ανεδειαν i. αναιδιαν H* *sem.* ὁσον ivLz [*non* wH]. +αν z *sem. ante* χρηζη z. 9. αιτητε P. ἡμιν *secund.* P*. εὑρησητε iL. εὑρησετε P. εὑρησεται z *sem.* –κρουετε *ad fin. vers.* v*. ανοιχθησεται (*sic v.* 10 iwz *sem.*) i *solus.* 10. αἰτων (*sic* w *vv.* 11, 13, *non* 9) wP. λαμβανη z *sem.* εὑρισκει P. εὑρησει L*. εὑρησκει L**. ανοιχθησεται H. 11. +εξ (*ante* ὑμων) iwLH** *sem.* z *sem.* αιτηση z *sem.* επιδωση *prim.* L. επιδοση *bis* z. –ει και ιχθυν *ad fin. vers.* L. η (*pro* ει) ivwHPz (ἡ P, –και vz *sem.*). ιχθυως P. ὀφιν H *sem.* P. 12. *init.* ἡ P. –η z. –εαν L. αν z* *sem.* αιτηση ivHz. αἰτηση w. ὁ ὢν (*pro* ωον) P. ὠον z *sem.* επιδωση L. επιδοση z. 13. οὖν P. οντες ivw, ὀντες P (*pro* ὑπαρχοντες). οἰδατε P. δοματα αγαθα ivwLHPz (δωματα iv*LP). διδωναι P. πῶσω P. ὁ πηρ ὑμων ὁ ουρανιος z *sem.* +ὑμων (*post* πηρ) Hz *sem.* ξ (*pro* εξ) L. δοσει *z sem.* —πνα i*. πνα ἁγιον *super ras.* H *sem.* αγαθον (*pro* ἁγιον) z *sem.* 14. ἦν *prim.*, ἦν *secund.* H. εκβαλων z. αὐτῶ L. και εγενετο (—δε) L. εκβληθεντος και (*pro* εξελθοντος) L. εθαυμαζον Hz. οἱ ὀχλοι H. 15. +τω (*ante* αρχοντι) iwLHz. *fin.* +και αποκριθεις ειπεν πως δυναται σατανας σαταναν εκβαλλειν w. 16. ἑτεροι H. εξ ουνου εζητουν αυτω (—παρ') L. 17. τα διανοηματα αυτων w. διαμερισθεισα *mutat. in* i. μερισθεισα z. ἐποικον wH. 18. σατανὰς iz. εμερισθη i. λεγεται i. εκ (*pro* εν) L. εκβαλειν i. —με L. με εκβαλεῖν H. με εκβαλλειν z. 19. —*ab initio usque ad* δαιμονια L. εκβαλω iH. οἱ H. —οἱ z. εκβαλοῦσι iH. εκβαλλωσι v. εκβαλλουσιν wLz. αυτοι ὑμων εσονται κριται i. αυτοι κριται ὑμων wLHz. ἐσωνται H. 20. *init.* ει δε εγω i. +εγω (*ante* εκβαλλω) L. εκβαλλονται (*pro* εκβαλλω τα) z. ἄρα ivwz. 21. ὅτ' ἂν (*sic ferè vv.* 24, 34, 36) wH. καθοπλησμενος i. καθωπλησμενος H. καθοπλισμενος z. φυλασσει i. βλεπει (*pro* φυλασσῃ) L. +φυλασσων (*post* αυλην) L. εστιν w. 22. ἐπ' ἂν i, ἐπ ἂν vz (*sic v.* 34 *etiam* w). απελθων i. νικησει i. νηκηση L*. +και (*ante* την πανοπλιαν) L. αἱρει wLHz. επεποιθη iLz. σκυλλα i, *at* σκευη w. διαδιδοσιν z. 23. ὢν wH. ὤν z.. εστιν wH *sem.* z. *Totus versus in* L *ita legitur:* ὁ μη ων μετ' αυτου σκορπιζει. 24. +δε (*post* ὅτ' ἂν) i. ακαθαρτον H. ἀνυδρων w. ζητων L. εὑρισκων iLz. οἶκον H. 25. *init.* ελθων iwLHz. +σχολαζοντα (*ante* σεσαρωμενον) iL —και *secund.* i. κεκεκοσμημενον v. κοσμημενον w*H*. 26. μεθ' ἑαυτου ἑτερα πνατα πονηροτερα ἑαυτου ἑπτα L. ελθοντα v. 27. εγινετο L. εκ του οχλου φωνην w. ὀχλου P. μαστοῖ P. 28. ειπεν wHP. —γε w* (w** *supra*). των (*pro* του) i*. *fin.* —αυτον w*. 29. επαθροιζομενων των οχλων z (—δε) *init. peric.* ἠρξατο H. +γενεα (*ante* πονηρα) LHz. εστιν wLz. ζητει wz. αὐτὴ (*pro* αὐτῇ) L. ιωνὰ i. ιωνᾶ L. 30. ἰωναί L. νηνευιταις i. οὐτος L. *fin.* +σημειον z. 31. βασιλεισσα i. νωτου i. —των *prim.* L. σολομονος *prim.* i. σολομωνος *bis* v, *prim.* L, *secund.* iH [*cum Elzev.* wz]. —και ιδου πλειον σολομωντος L. ὡδε (*sic v.* 32) wz [*non* iL]. 32. νινευιται iwL. αναστησετε L*. μετενωησαν i. ιωᾶναί *prim.* (—και) L*. ἰωνὰ *secund.* i. 33. —δε iv*w. ῞Αψας (῞Α *rubro*) w*. κρυπτον H**z. οὐδε H. μωδιον i. —ουδε ὑπο τον μοδιον L. αλλ' ivwHz [*non* L]. οἱ w. βλεπουσιν iz *sem.* βλεπωσι το φως (*pro* φεγγος) L. 34. —ὁ *secund.* w. ὀφθαλμος *secund.* w, *bis* H. οὐν H. ἁπλους ει i. ἁπλος L. ἠ *bis* wH. —και *prim.* iLz. φωτινον (*sic v.* 36 i *bis*, w *prim.*, L *secund.*) iL. εσται (*pro* εστιν *secund.*) w. ἐπ' ἂν z. ει (*pro* ἠ *secund.*) iL. *fin.* +εστι i, εσται w. 36. εχων i. φωτινον *prim.* w. μερος τι wL. ὁς (*pro* ὡς) i. φωτιζει iLz. 37. *init.* εν δε το i. +αυτον ταυτα (*post* λαλησαι) iLHz.

Ἠρωτα (Ἡ *rubro*) w. ἐρώτα L. ἠρῶτα z. –τις L. αριστησει LHz. *fin.* και εισελθων (–δε) εις την οικιαν φαρισαιου ανεκλιθη L. 38. προτερον L. –προ L, *at* πρω H. 39. ειπεν Hz. καθαριζεται L. του ποτηριου ἡμων (*loco* ὑμων) L. ἁρπαγης H. 40. οὐχ ivwHz. εποιησεν vwLHz. 41. αινοντα z. ἁπαντα Hz. ὑμιν ἁπαντα καθαρα εσται L. ἐσται H. εσται z. 42. αλλα vL. οὐαῖ (*sic vv.* 44, 46, 47, 52 *non* 43) w. οὐαι (*sic sem.* 43, 44, 46) H. φαρισαῖοις (*sic v.* 43 i) iz. αποδεκατουται H. ἡδυοσμον v. +και το ανηθον (*post* ἡδυοσμον) L. πυγανον L. παρερχεσθαι LH. κρισην i. +δε (*ante* εδει) wLHz [*non* v]. ἐδει H. ποιειν i. αφειναι v*. 43. +και την πρωτοκλισιαν εν τοις δειπνοις (*post* συναγωγαις) L. ἀσπασμους H *sem.* 44. ἡμιν L*. εσται iz *sem.* αδειλα i. ἀδηλα wH *sem.* –οἱ *secund.* ivwLHz. ἐπ' ἄνω v. 45. –και L. ὑμας ? H* *sem.* ἡμας H *sem.* 46. ειπεν vLHz. +και (*post* ὑμιν) H *sem.* τοις ανοις H *sem.* +βαρεα και (*post* φορτια) H *sem.* ἑν H *sem.* οὑ H *sem.* προσψαυεται L. 47. οὐαῖ *P.* οἰκοδομειτε (*sic v.* 48) w. οικοδομειται L*. μνημια *P.* 48. ἆρα ivPz. ὁτι (*pro* και) L. ἡμων (*pro* ὑμων) *P.* +οἱ δε πρες ὑμων (*ante* ὁτι αυτοι) L*. –αυτους *P.* *fin.* τους ταφους αυτων οικοδομειτε L. 49. διατοῦτο (*sic v.* 19) vwLPz [*non* i]. –και *prim.* i. αποστελλῶ i. –και *tert.* wL. αποκτενουσιν z. εκδιωκουσιν L. 50. εκδικηθη (*pro* εκζητηθη, *non v.* 51) *P.* αἱμα H. εκχυννομενον wH. εκκεχυμενον L. –απο της γενεας ταυτης (*spatio quodam relicto*) L. 51. +του δικαιου (*post* αβελ) iw. απολλομενου v. απολωμενου z. απολελῦμενου L. *Ras. in* H *ante* θυσιασ. οἶκου w*P.* +'τι (*ante* εκζητηθησεται) L. 52. εἰραται z. +και (*ante* αυτοι) L. εἰσῆλθετε wH. εισηλθατε L. 53. –λεγοντος *usque ad* προς αυτους L (*incipit* και ηρξαντο L). προς αυτους ταυτα z. +ενωπιον παντος του λαου (*ante* ηρξαντο) i. –ενεχειν και w* (*habet marg.* ενεχειν w**). συνεχειν (*pro* ενεχειν) v. συμβαλλειν αυτω (*pro* αποστοματιζειν αυτον) L. 54. –και ivwLz. –τι i [*non* Lz]. τι θηρευσαι w. κατηγορησουσιν L. –ἱνα κατηγορησωσιν αυτου i.

CAP. XII. 1. επισυναχθησων iz. ὡστε w, ὡς (*pro* ὡστε) z. +δε (*post* ηρξατο) L. πρωτον *cum præcedent.* vwz [*non* iL]. ἑαυτους (*pro* ἑαυτοις) i. 2. –δε LPz *init. peric.* εστι συγκεκαλυμμενον i. συγκεκαλυμενον H. 3. σκοτεια iwP. +αει (*ante* ειπατε) L. ακουσθησεται, σθ *mutat. in* P. οὗς wL. ταμιειοις w. ταμιοις P. δοματων LP. 4. *In* L λεγω *in textu illegibile, habet* L** *marg., sic* περι *et v.* 6 του θῦ. φοβηθήτε P. αποκτενοντων ivw LHPz. τι περισσον i. τι περισσοτερον L. 5. ἡμιν (*pro* ὑμιν *prim.*) L. φοβηθεῖτε (*pro* φοβηθῆτε) v*. φοβηθεῖτε (*pro* φοβηθῆτε· φοβήθητε) L. φοβηθῆτε (*pro* φοβήθητε *prim., non secund.*) w. φοβηθήτε (*pro* φοβήθητε

n.) wP [cum Elzev. H]. —εξουσιαν εχοντα i. εχοντα εξουσιαν wLPz.
ἀλλεῖν w. 6. πωλειτε i. πωλουνται L. πολειτε P. ασαριων P. επιλε-
μενου iL*. 7. αἱ HP. αριθμηνται w. ἠρυθμηνται L. ἠριθμηνται P.
P. φοβῆσθε z. fin. +ὑμεις wLHP. 8. ὁμολογησει (pro -ση) P.
λογηση (pro -σει) iLH. ἑαυτον (pro εν αυτῳ) L. αγγελω P*. 9.
ιρνησαμενος L. εμπροσθεν (pro ενωπιον prim.) w. 10. το πνα το ἁγιον
11. ὅτ' ἂν iH (sic w vv. 54, 55, non iz). ὁτ' ἂν w. ὅτάν P. εισφε-
ιν i. προσφερουσιν w. εις (pro επι) L. μεριμνησητε L. a pro ἢ prim.
ἢ bis P. απολογησεσθε vH*. απολογισησθε z. 12. δη (pro δει) P.
ειπεν (sic vv. 15, 16, 18, 20, 22, 41, 42) w. ὀχλου H. την κληρονομιαν
τ' εμου Hz. 14. —ανθρωπε L. κατεστησεν wH. ἡ H. κριτην η δικασ-
(—μεριστην) L. fin. ἡμας w. 15. ειπεν (sic v. 13) Hz. ὁρατε H.
λασεσθε H. πασης (pro της) iwLHz [non v]. οὐκ' z. περισευειν H.
ιν transfertur in w in locum post ουκ. αυτω (pro αυτου prim) v. 16.
φορησεν w. ηφωρισεν (vel -εισεν?) L. 17. συναξαι L. 18. —και ειπε i.
εν (sic v. 20) HPz. μειζωνας P. οἰκοδομησω wP. γενηματα ivHPz.
σιτον (pro τα γεννηματα) L. τα αγαθα μου και τα γενηματα μου w.
ἀγαθα H. +και (post πιε) L. 20. αφρον wLH [non ivPz]. απετουσιν
απαιτουσιν απο σου την ψυχην σου L. τινη P. 21. οὑτος L. —ὁ L.
σαυριζον L. +εν (ante ἑαυτω) i. fin. +ταυτα λεγων εφωνει (-νη w**P)
χων ωτα (ὠτα w**P) ακουειν ακουετω ivw**LHPz. 22. διατοῦτο iLz.
γω ὑμιν LHz. —ὑμων w. μηδὲ ivwLz. +ὑμων (post σωματι) LHz. 23.
t. +ουχι Hz. +γαρ (ante ψυχη) L. τω (pro το) w. 24. εστιν w. τα-
ιον L. ὁ δε θς (—και) L. αυτα L. 25. ἐξ z. προσθηναι ivHz. ἑνα H.
οὔτε L. 27. νηθι i. +ὁτι (ante ουδε secund.) iL. 28. init. ἴδε (pro ει δε) v.
αγρου (—εν) Hz. σημερον εν τω αγρω w. του αγρου σημερον εν αγρω
α L. αὑριον wHL? οὑτος αμφιεννυσιν L. αμφιεννυσιν H. ὀλιγοπιστοι
29. φαγησθε L. και (pro η) Hz. ποιητε ?w*. 30. επιζητουσιν L.
εν H. χριζετε i. χρηζητε w. fin. +ἁπαντων Lz. 31. init. λην initio
εæ i. +πρωτον (post ζητειτε) L. —παντα vHz. 32. ηὐδοκησεν P sem.
πωλυσατε L. πολησαται P sem. βαλλαντια wLz [non H]. ανεκληπτον
em. z. —εν z. οὐκ' P sem. διαφθηρει iP sem. 35. ἐστωσαν z. αἱ οσφυες
ν ivw. καιομεναι ?L*. κεομενοι P sem. 36. ὅμοι L. αυτων (pro ἑαυ-
) L. αναλυση i. 37. εὑρησει P. περισωσεται i*H*?. ανακληνεῖ P sem.
κονῆσαι z. 38. —ελθῃ prim. i. ἐλθῃ w. —φυλακῃ prim. i. η (pro και
und.) i. +εαν (ante εν τη τριτη) w. και ελθων (pro ελθῃ και) w. εὑρη P.
ει z. οὑτως ivwLHPz. —εισιν i. οὑτοι (pro εκεινοι) v. 39. ειδει v.

ἤδη w. ἤδει P sem. ιδη P sem. φυλακη (pro ὥρᾳ) H. οἰκοδεσποτης wP. εγρηγορισεν i. –αν secund. iwLH*. αφηκεν wP. την οικιαν iP sem. (οἰκιαν P), at οἶκον P sem. 40. οὖν P. ἑτοιμοι P. ἣ P sem. δοκειται i. 41. –κυριε L. ὑμας i. 42. και ειπεν (–δε) L. ις (pro κς prim.) iL. ἆρα ivz. εσται iw. οἰκονομος wH. ὁ (pro και) v. +αυτου (post κς secund.) iz. θεραπιας i. –αὐτου i. +αυτοις (post διδοναι) L. –το L. 43. εὑρισει L. εὑρησει H. οὑτως ποιουντα LHz. 45. ειπει w. +κακος (ante δουλος) L. μου ὁ κς ελθειν w. τὲ iLz. –τε w. 46. ἣ prim. ἣ secund. H. οὐ H. ὡ (pro ὥρᾳ) L. Rasura in w inter ουπ (sic) et γινωσκει. ὑποκριτων (pro απιστων) H. 47. αυτου (pro ἑαυτου) vwLz [non i]. –ἑτοιμασας μηδε L. ἑτοιμασας H. η (pro μηδε) i. μὴδὲ vHz. δαρρησεται (sic v. 48) z. 48. –δε z sem. initio peric. ἀξια H. ὀλιγας iwH. εδωθη H sem. παρεθετο H sem z. παρευθετο H sem. αιτησωσιν i, at ζητησουσιν v. 49. ἠλθον H. επι (pro εις) wLHz. ἰδιανηφθη L. 50. βαπτισθειναι H. συνεχωμαι w. οὗ iH, at ὁτου wL. 51. αλλα (pro αλλ' η) L. 52. ἑνι H. τινι (pro ἑνι) z. διαμερισμενοι iw. τρις (pro τρεις) LH. δυσιν w. τρισιν wLz. 53. init. +και L. διαμερισθησονται Hz. επι (pro εφ') ivHz [non L]. εφ' υω πηρ w. 54. ελεγεν w. ὀχλοις H. ὅτ ἂν H hic. ειδητε z. –την L. ανατελουσαν L. +ὁτι (ante ομβρος) iwL. οὑτως ivwHz. οὗτος L. 55. λεγεται w. καυσον εστι z. fin. +οὑτως i, οὗτος L. 56. του ουρανου και της γης iwHz. οιδετε? (οι mutat.) L. οἰδατε H. δοκιμαζεται H. 57. διακρινεται Hz*, διακρινετε z**. 58. ὑπαρχοντα L, επαρχοντος z (pro επ' αρχοντα). κατασυρει συ σε προς τον κρητην L παραδωσει L. πρακτωρι wz. βαλη ivwz. βαλλει L. βαλεῖ H. 59. εξελθεις H. ἕωσοῦ H alii. τον (pro το) ivw [non z]. αποδωσης L.

CAP. XIII. 1. ηλθον τινες (–δε) H. –εν L. απαγγελοντες wHP. εμηξε i*. το αἱματι πηλάτος εμιξεν P. πιλᾶτος iwH. εμιξεν wL. 2. αποκριθεις δε (–και) HP. οὑτοι οἱ γαλιλαιοι L. γαλιλαῖ H. ταυτα (pro τοιαυτα) i. +τα (ante τοιαυτα) L. 3. ἑαν P. μετανοησητε iLHz, μετανοειτε vP (sic v. 5). παντως (non v. 5) vP*. ὡσαὑτως P, at ὁμοιως L. απολεισθαι L. 4. init. ει (pro η) L. ἣ P. ὀκτῶ (sic i vv. 11, 16) iHz. ὀκτὼ (sic vv. 11, 16) w. ὀκτῶ P. σιλωαμ' P. οὗτοι iH, οὗτοι P, at αυτοι wL (pro οὗτοι). ὀφειλεται wP. ὀφειλετε H. +τους (ante ανθρωπους) L. –εν secund. iP. ιλημ H. 5. αλλα w**. ἑαν H. 6. ελεγεν wHP. την παραβολην ταυτην w. συκὴν iLHz. τις ειχεν iw. ειχεν P. ηλθεν wH. ἦλθεν P. ζητων καρπον ivwL HPz. –εν αυτῃ w*. εν ἑαυτῃ v. οὐχ' (sic etiam P v. 7) ivwHz. εἱρεν P. 7. ειπεν wLHPz. μ mutat. in αμπελουργον L. +αφ' οὗ (post ετη) L. –εν H. αυτη (pro τῃ συκῃ ταυτῃ) i. εγκοψον ουν L. ἱνα (–τι) P. ἵνατί z. καταργη vLH*P. καταργης z. 8. ειπεν (*pro* λεγει) z. ἐτος w. βαλλω i. βαλῶ L. κοπριαν iv*w. κοπρον L. κόπρια Hz [P *cum Elzev.*]. 9. ποιησει iP. *Post* καρπον *legit* L εις το μελλον δε εἶ μή ποιηση (*sic*) εκκοψον αυτην. εις το μελλον· ει δε μηγε i. εκκοψης z. *fin.* + ταυτα λεγων εφωνει ὁ εχων ωτα (ὦτα P) ακουειν ακουετω HP. 10. ἦν (*non v.* 11 *bis*) w. ἦν P. +ὁ ις (*post* διδασκων) v. −εν *secund.* L. σαββασιν v*LPz. αββασι H*. 11. ἰδου (*sic v.* 16) P. ἦν *prim.*, ἦν *secund.* P. ασθενιας (*sic v.* 12 iP* *sem.* P *sem.*) P* *sem.* P *sem.* ἐτη L. ετι H. ὀκτῶ HP. δυνομενη P *sem.* εις το παντελες ανακυψαι L. 12. προσεφωνησεν wLH**P *sem.* P** *sem.* γῦναι iLz. +απο (*post* απολελυσαι) wP. 13. παράχρῆμα i. παραχρειμα P *sem.* ιαθη (*pro* ανωρθωθη) i. ανορθωθη LPz. εδοξαζεν wH**P. 14. αρχησυναγωγος LP. το σαββατον L. ελεγεν wH**P. ὀχλω HP. δη (*pro* δει) H*?P *sem.* αυταις (*pro* ταυταις) wL. ταυτες P. οὖν (*sic v.* 15, P *sem.*) P. ερχωμενοι ?L. θεραπευεσθαι P* *sem.* 15. −ουν P *sem.* δε (*pro* ουν) L. −αυτῳ L. ιησους (*pro* κς) iL. ὑποκριται ivwLH*P [*non* z]. ἑκαστος H. ἢ P. ὀνον HP. τον ονον αυτου η τουν βουν L. −απο της φατνης L. 16. +την (*ante* θυγατερα) P* *sem.* θυγατεραν iLP *sem.* z [*non* vH]. ἀβρααμ ivwL?Hz. ἀβρααμ' P. οὖσαν P. ἦν (*pro* ἣν) wL (*sic* w, v. 21), *at* ἣν H. εδυσεν L. σατανὰς iz. δεκα (*a mutat.*) P *sem.* ὀκτῶ P. −ετη (ετι i**) i*. εδη w*P. 17. καταισχυνοντο L. κατήσχυνοντο P *sem.* −πας P *sem.* λαος (*pro* οχλος) i. ὀχλος P *sem.* εχερεν P *sem.* πασιν P. γενομενοις v. 18. ελεγεν w. ελεγεν ουν (−δε) L. +ὁμοιωματι (*ante* ὁμοιωσω) L. ὁμοιωσω i. 19. *init.* ὡμοιωθη ἡ βασιλεια των ουρανων HPz *init. peric.* εστιν w. σιναπεος w. συναπεως L*. ὁν (*pro* ὁ) ivwLHPz. ἑαυτον L*, αυτου wP (*pro* ἑαυτου). ηυξησεν wH**. ηὔξησεν P. κατεσκηνουν L. 20. *init.* −και ivwHPz. παλην P. ειπεν wHPz. 21. ὅμοια z. εστιν wP. εκρυψεν ivwz [*non* LP]. ἀλεύρους· ἅτα P. ἑως P. εζημωθη L. 22. πολις P. κωμας και πολεις L.ποριαν v. εν (*pro* εις) wL. ἰλημ H. 23. ειπεν *bis* wPz. ὀλιγοι iwPz. ει (*pro* οἱ) i. σωζωμενοι L. *fin.* ειπεν (−προς αυτους) L. 24. αγωνιζεσθαι L*. 25. εαν ελθη (*pro* αν εγερθῃ) L. οἰκοδεσποτης P. αποκλεισει i. αποκλησει P. θυρα *bis* i. αρξεσθε L. ἑστάναι iw. ἑστᾶναι v. ἑστᾶναι HP. στάναι L. οἶδα (*sic* 27) w. −και αποκριθεις ερει ὑμιν P* (*habet* P** *marg.*). οὐκ' οἶδα (*sic v.* 27) P. 26. *Deest hic versus usque ad v.* 27 ποθεν εστε *in* i. αρξησθε vwLHP. εφαγωμεν P. επιωμεν P. 27. εσται P. αποχωρειτε (*pro* αποστητε) P. ἐμου P. −οἱ vH. 28. ὀδοντων wHP. ὅτ' ἂν wH. ὀτ' ἂν P. ὀψησθε iwHP. οψεσθε L. ἀβρααμ ivwLH [*non* P]. −ὑμας δε *usque ad fin. v.* 29 L. 29. −απο *secund.* ivwHP. ανακληθησονται ivwP. 30. εισιν *bis* w. 31. ταυτη (*pro* αυτῃ) w. ὡρα (*pro* ἡμερᾳ) L. προσηλθ H*. –αυτῳ H. μελλει (*pro* θελει) H. 32. –αυτοις w. ἀλωπεκι vwH. ταυτα (*pro* ταυτῃ) z. εκβαλω i. αὐριον (*sic etiam* H *v.* 33) wz. –και τῃ τριτῃ *usque ad* αυριον *v.* 33 L. 33. –τῃ z. ερχομενῃ iL. 34. –ἡ L. αποκτεννουσα H*. αποκτενουσα H**z*. ει *in* αποκτεινουσα *mutat. in* i [vwL *cum Elzev.*]. αποσταλμενους i. αὐτην ivwLH. ἠθελησα w. επισυνᾶξαι i. ορνεις L. τα ἑαυτης νοσσια vw. νοσιαν H*. 35. ἰδου H. αφιετε z. οικος w. –ερημος w*L (*habet* w** *marg.*). λεγω δε (–αμην) ivwLHz. ιδητε με w. ειδητε με L. –με z. ειδητε z. ἡξει i. ἡξῃ v. ἡξει H. –εως αν ἡξῃ w* (απαρτι ἑως αν ἡξει w** *marg.*). ειπητε μοι (–ἡξῃ ὁτε) L.

CAP. XIV. 1. –και L. –εν τῳ L. εισελθειν L. –αυτον L. οἰκον HP. των φαρισαιων· των αρχοντων v. ἠσαν w. ἡσαν HP. 2. ἴδοῦ P. ἠν wP. ὑδροπικος L. ὑδροπικως P. 3. ειπεν (*sic vv.* 5, 19, 20, 21, 25) wHP. νομικρους P*. εξεστιν H**. +η ου (*post* θεραπευειν) L. 4. +αυτου (*post* επιλαβομενος) L. –αυτον L. απελυσεν i*wLP. 5. –αποκριθεις wL. ειπεν L. ειπε [ν w] προς αυτους iw. ὀρος L, ῡς HP (*pro* ονος). ἡ P, *at* υιος η βους η ονος i [*non habet* z]. πεσειται wL. –και *secund.* L. οὐκ' P. –εν wL. 6. αποκριθηναι i. 7. ελεγεν wH**P. πρωτοκλησιας (*sic* ivLP *v.* 8 πρωτοκλησιαν) ivLHP. προτοκλισιας w. εξελεγχοντο L. 8. ὅτᾶν (*sic v.* 10 *bis* H; *non* i *vv.* 10 *prim.*, 13) iH. ὅτ' ᾶν (*sic vv.* 10 *bis*, 12, 13) w. ὀτ' ᾶν (*sic v.* 10) P. κληθῇς v. κλιθῃς w*. κληθεις (*pro* κληθῃς *et iterum pro* κατακλιθῃς) P. κατακληθῃς vw. μήποτὲ P. εντιμωτερος vL. εντημωτερος (–σου) P. ἠ wP, ει L (*pro* ῃ). 9. ὡσσε (*pro* ὁ σε) L. ερῃ H. τοτον *prim.* w. μετα vLH* P. 10. πορευθυς L. αναπεσε iwLH [*non* v]. αναπεσαι P. ὅτ' ᾶν *secund.* (*sic* iH *v.* 12) i. ἐλθῃ w. κεκληκος i. –σε L. ειποι L. ειπει vP. προσαναβηθη P. δοξαν i*. +παντων (*post* ενωπιον) iL. ανακειμενων w. 11. ὁ δε ταπεινων ἑαυτων (–και) L. –και ὁ ταπεινων *ad fin. vers.* v. 12. και ελεγε (–δε) z. ελεγεν wH. ποιῃ v. δυπνον *hic* i. φωνῃ z. μήδὲ *ter* ivwz, *bis* L. μήδε *ter* H. –μηδε τους αδελφους σου L. συγγενης i*. γειτωνας i. τους γειτονας σου τους πλουσιους L. αντικαλεσουσι σε L. αντικαλεσωσιν H. ανταποδωμα vz. 13. αλλα Hz. ὅτᾶν H. ποιεις LH. χολους L. 14. εστιν (*pro* εσῃ) z. και (*pro* ὁτι) L*. δε (*pro* γαρ) L. 15. μακαριον ὁστις φαγητε L. αριστον wLHz [*non* i]. των ουνων (*pro* του θῡ) L. 16. εποιησεν wP. μεγαν LH*z. εκαλεσεν wP. 17. απεστειλεν P. κεκλημενεις w. ερχεσθαι iw. ἠδη wHP. ἠδει z. ερχεσθε ὁτι ηδη *bis script.* L (ἑρ. *secund.* L). ἑτοιμα HP. εστιν LP. 18. ἠρξαντο HP. παρετίσθαι H. παρετεισθαι P. παραιτεισθε vz. ἠγορασα (*sic v.* 19 Hz) wHPz. αναγκειν H. ειδειν i. εχω (*pro* εχε) L. 19. ἑτερος (*sic v.* 20) H. ειπεν (*sic v.* 20 L, *vv.* 20, 21 HPz) LHPz. ἠγωρασα P. πεν H*. δοκιμᾶσαι i*vz. –με L. 20. ἑτερος *hic* i. διατοῦτο vwLz [*non* i]. 21. παραγεναμενος L. –εκεινος wL. απηγγηλε i. απηγγειλεν wP. ἑαυτου L. οργισθης i. οἰκοδεσποτης wP. χολους i. –και χωλους L. +τους (*ante* τυφλους) L. και τυφλους και χωλους w. ὧδε z *solus* (ὥδε P). 22. προσεταξας L. εστιν iwLPz. 23. γεμησθη iP. γεμιστῇ w. μου ὁ οικος w. οἰκος P. 24. οὐδεῖς P *pass.* γευσηται iP. γευσετε H. *fin.* +πολλοι γαρ εισι (ν P) κλητοι, ὀλιγοι (ὀλ. LHz) δε εκλεκτοι iv**w**LHPz. 25. τω ιυ (*pro* αυτῳ) v. ὀχλοι H. ειπεν Hz. 26. αυτου (*pro* ἑαυτου *prim.*) ivwL. –και την γυναικα *usque ad* αδελφας i. ἀαδελφας w. ἑτι H. ἑαυτου *secund.* w, *bis* H. την ψυχην αυτου L. ειναι μαθητης iwL [*non* v]. 27. *Deest in* L. ὁστις w. βαστασει z. ἑαυτου iH. ακολουθει (*pro* ερχεται) w. ὀπισω wH. ειναι μου iHz. 28. +ὁ (*ante* θελων) v. πῦργον ivz *ferè*. οἰκοδομησαι (*sic* w *v.* 30) wH. καθησας ψιφιζει H. εις (*pro* προς) ivL. ἀπαρτισμον w. 29. μηπω τεθεντος L. *Rasura ante* θεντος *in* i. θεμελιου L. –και i. ισχυσαντος Hz. αρξονται iLz. αυτω εμπαιζειν wHz. αυτον (*pro* αυτῳ) L. 30. οὑτος H. ἠρξατο H. 31. *init.* ει (*pro* η) L. ἢ H. καθησας LH, *at* πρωτον καθισας Hz. ἐνδεκα (*pro* εν δεκα) L. χιλιᾶσιν v. ὑπαντησαι L**. απαντησαι εν δεκα χιλιασιν i. εἰκοσι v. χιλιαδῶν iL. προς i, ὑπ' v (*pro* επ'). *fin.* αυτω L. 32. ἑτι H. πορρω αυτου ivwHz [*non* L]. οντως w*. πρεσβιαν H. εις (*pro* προς) w. 33. οὑτος L. ἐξ' w. ὑπαρχουσιν ἑαυτου v. ὑπαρχουσιν αυτου w. ἑαυτου H. ειναι μου Hz. 34. +ουν (*post* καλον) L. ἀλας *bis* wH. +και (*post* εαν δε) Hz. μαρανθη L. αρτιθησεσθε L**, αρθηθησεσθε L*. οὑτε *prim.* οὑτε *secund.* H. +την (*ante* γην) L. εστι i. βάλουσιν i. βαλλοῦσιν αυτω L. ὠτα wH.

Cap. XV. 1. ἠσαν wH. αυτω εγγιζοντες wL. 2. οἱ γραμματεις και οἱ φαρισαιοι iL. οὑτος H. ἁματωλους L*. *fin.* αυτους z. 3. ειπεν wHPz (*sic vv.* 17, 21, 22, 29 *et v.* 11 w). –λεγων L. 4. –ανθρωπος i. εξ αυτων ἐν L. ἐξ' w. ουχι (*pro* ου) LH. καταλιπει vz. ἐνενηκοντα εννεα (*sic v.* 7 iLz) i. ἐνενηκονταεννεα (*sic v.* 7) v. ἐνενηκοντα ἐννεα (*sic v.* 7 wH) Hz. ἐνενηκονενεννεα (+προβατα) L*. ἐνενικοντα ἐννεα w. τω H. απωλωλος (*sic v.* 6 v*) v. απολολως L. +οὑ (*post* ἑως) Lz. εὑρη w. εὑρει αυτῶ L. 5. επιτηθησιν H. ὡμους Hz. αυτου vwLz [*non* i]. ἑαυτου H. 6. οἰκον H. συγκαλειται iL. συγχαρηται L*?. εὑρον (*sic v.* 9) H. προσωπονβατον L*. –μου z. 7. οὑτως (*sic v.* 10) ivwHz. οὑτος (*sic v.* 10) L. εστιν (*pro* εσται) z. ἑνι ἁμαρτωλω (*sic v.* 10) H. ἦ z. δικαιων z. εχουσιν H. 8. ἢ H. δραγμας w*. δραγχμας L. εχουσα δραγμας i. απολεσει H. δραγμην i [*non* w]. δραγχμην L. ουχ L. οὐχι H. ἀπτει iwH. σαρει iL. οἰκιαν w. ἑως H. –ὁτου L. εὑρη H. 9. υ *in* εὑρουσα *mutat. in* L. εὑρουσα H. συγκαλει vwz [*non* L]. γιτονας i. εὑρον w. δραγμην i. δραγχμην L. ἡν w. ἡν H. απολεσα iLH. 10. οὑτως H. εσται (*pro* γινεται) L. +εν ουνω (*ante* ενωπιον) L. αγελων v. 11. –ειπε δε L. ειχεν wH**P. 12. νεοτερος (*sic v.* 13) P. επιβαλον i. οὑσιας ?w. διηλεν iH. 13. πολας i. συννγαγων P*. κακει L. διεσκορπισεν wLH**P. ασωτος iHP. 14. λοιμος L*. ἡρξατω P. ὑστερησθαι L. 15. εκολληθει i. εκολλυθη L. ἑνι HP. πολητων P. 16. επεθυμη γεμησαι P. χορτασθηναι (*pro* γεμισαι την κοιλιαν αυτου) L. εισθιον L. ἡσθιον Pz.• και *secund. bis script.* z. οὐδεὶς P *passim.* +τις (*post* ουδεις) L. 17. εφη (*pro* ειπε) L. πῶς οἱ (*pro* ποσοι) iwLP. περισευουσιν P. λοιμω (*cf. v.* 14) L*. απολλημαι L. απολυμαι P. 18. ερωτω (*pro* ερω) L. 19. –και vw*P. οὐκἐτι (*sic v.* 21) iwPz [*non* LH]. ἑνα P. μισθιον P. 20. ηλθεν wH**. ἡλθεν P. αυτου (*pro* ἑαυτου) ivwLz. ιδεν wP. ευσπλαχνισθη P. επεσεν iwLz. κατεφηλησεν P. 21. –και *secund.* w*. ει μη (*pro* ειμι) L. 22. –την *prim.* w*. χειραν P. *fin.* +αυτου iwL. 23. –τον μοσχον w* (*habet marg.* w**). 24. ὁ υἱος μου οὑτος L. μου ὁ υἱος w. ἡν *bis* P. ανεζησεν ivwLHP**. –και *secund.* ivwL. απολωλος (*sic v.* 32 iLPz) ivw*LPz. –ην *secund.* L. ηὑρεθη P. ἡρξαντο P. 25. ἡν w. ἡν P. ηγγιζε L. ηγγισεν τηι οἰκιαι ηκουσεν w. ηγγισεν H**. ἡγγησεν P. οἰκια P. ἡκουσεν H**. ἡκουσε H*P. χωρων ?H*. 26. ἑνα P. τινα (*pro* τι) i. +αν (*ante* ειη) L. *fin.* τουτο w. 27. ἡκει iH. εικει P. απελαβε z. 28. ὡργισθη LP. οὖν P. παρεκαλη w*. 29. +αυτου (*post* πρι) L. τῶς αὗτα H. ουδεπο z. ημοι L*. 30. ὁ *prim.* w. οὑτως P. καταφαγῶν iz. ἡλθεν P. 31. +πηρ (*ante* ειπεν) L. μετεμου *mutat.* P. 32. δει (*pro* δε) L. –και χαρηναι w* (*habet marg.* w**). εδη P. +και αγαλλιασθηναι (*post* εδει) w. ἡν *prim.* P. ανεζησεν wLH**P. –και *tert.* iL. ἡν *secund.* wP. –ην *secund.* L. ηὑρεθη H. εὑρεθη P.

CAP. XVI. 1. ελεγεν w. –και *prim.* L. –αυτου L. οἰκονομον wH. διεβληθει L. ὡς H. 2. –αυτον L. τουτω w. οἰκονομιας (*sic v.* 4) wH. –σου *secund.* w. δυνησει i. δυνει L. δυνη z. 3. ειπεν (*sic vv.* 7, 24, 25, 27, 31) wHz. η *in* ποιησω *mutat.* i. –μου z. αφερειται i. οἰκονομιαν H. αφαιρειται με της οἰκονομιας (–απ' εμου) w. απο σου (*pro* απ' εμου) v. αἰσχυνομαι H. 4. ὁτ' ἀν H. ὁτ' ἀν w. αποσταθω L. +εκ (*ante* της οικονομιας) Lz. δεξονται iL. *fin.* ἑαυτων z. 5. ἑνα ἑκαστον H. χρεωφιλετων i. χρεοφειλετων v. χρεὀφειλετων w. αυτου (*pro* ἑαυτου) ivw*L. ἑαυτου H. ειπεν wH, ειπεν αυτων v (*pro* ελεγε). –τῳ πρωτῳ H. ωφειλεις i. οφειλης

on v. 7) L. ὀφειλεις (sic v. 7) wH. +συ (ante τω κ̄ω) iz. 6. ἑκατον βα-
ιυς καδδους H*. καδους (pro βατους) z. ελαιω L. ὁ δε (pro και prim.) L.
ἑτερω H. ειπεν L. συτων (pro σιτου) L*, at σιτους H*. –και prim. L.
ιδοηκοντα wH. 8. οἰκονομον wH. φρονημοτεροι z. γεννεαν ?H*. εισιν
Lz. 9. +ὑμιν (ante ἑαυτοις) i. ἑαυτους H*z. μαμονᾶ (sic v. 11, non 13)
ὅτ' ἂν iwH. εκλειπητε ivz. εκλειπη (sic) L. δεξονται iLz. ἡμας (pro
ας) w. fin. κηνας L. 10. εστιν bis wLP. 11. οὖν (sic v. 27) P. μα-
ινᾶ i. εγινεσθε (sic v. 12) L. πιστευση LP. 12. ὑμων (pro ὑμιν) L.
. οὐδεῖς P. ικετις i. οἰκετης wP. ἢ bis HP. ἑνα P. μὴσήσει P. ἑνος P.
. ἤκουον w. ἤκουων P. παντα ταυτα w. –παντα H. –και prim. i. οντες
ro ὑπαρχοντες) L. 15. εσται i. ἑστε vH. ὑψῖλον P. αυτου (pro του
) P. fin. –εστιν w*H (habet marg. w**). 16. μεχρι (pro ἑως) L. ἀπο-
ιτε Hz. +τις (post πας) L. 17. ευκοποτερον i. –δε iL. εστιν LH. ἢ H.
α κεραια z. κερεαν L. 18. Ὁ H**. γαμῶν bis i. ἑτεραν H. μοιχαται
ro μοιχευει prim.) w. –πας secund. L. απολελυμμενην z. 19. –δε Pz
it. peric. ἦν (non v. 20) wP. ενεδυδυσκετο L*. ενεδιδισκετο L**. καθη-
ραν i. καθήμεραν HPz. 20. ἦν P. ὀνοματι P. ἡλκομενος i. εἰκομενος
ἡλκωμενος H. εἰλκομενος P. εἰλκωμενος vz. 21. +και ουδεις εδιδου
ιτω (post πλουσιου) L. απελιχον ivL (forsan υ pro ι in i). ἑλκη iP. 22.
δε L. ὑπο των rescript. in P. –του iwHz. ἀβρααμ (sic vv. 23, 24, 25, 29,
) at non 25 in i) ivwLHz. (ἀβρααμ' ferè P). απεθανεν wHP. 23. ἀδει z.
φθαλμους wP. ἀπομακρόθεν L. 24. ειπεν (sic vv. 25, 27, 31 wHPz) wLHPz.
ιταψηξη w. καταψυξει L. μου την γλωσσαν P. ὠδυνωμαι L. ὀδυνωμε P.
λογη HP. 25. +αυτω (ante αβρααμ) i. –συ prim. LP. –δε (post νυν) v.
δε ivLHz, ὧδε wP (pro ὁδε). ὀδυνᾶσαι wHz. ὠδυνάσαι L. ὀδυνᾶσε P.
. πάσιν P. +τε (post ἡμων) i. ενθεν διαβηναι (–εντευθεν) L. ενθεν iHP,
ιπροσθεν z (pro εντευθεν) [vw cum Elzev.]. δυνονται L. μὴδὲ ivwLHPz.
ιας (pro ἡμας) iP**. –προς ἡμας P*. 27. σε ουν L. οἰκον HP. 28.
αμαρτυρεται L. αυτους (pro αυτοις) z. ἐλθωσιν ?w. 29. +δε (post λεγει)
rz. εχουσιν P. μωυσεα w. 30. αλλα L. εκ (pro απο) v. +των (ante
κρων) i. +αναστη και (ante πορευθη) L. μετανοησωσιν iv. 31. μωυσεως w.
των L. οὐκ' P. απο (pro εκ) L. +των (ante νεκρων) LP. πιστησονται i.
ιστησωνται L. πισθησονται H. πιστευθησεται P.

Cap. XVII. 1. ελεγε δε και (ελεγεν, –και H) προς τους μαθητας αυτου
[z init. peric. –τους w. +αυτου (post μαθητας) L. ανενσκτον i*. ἐστι H.
του (ante μη) ivwLHz. διελθειν L. πλην ουαι (–δε) L. οὐαῖ w. 2. λυ-
ειτελει H. λιθος μυλικος L*Hz (μηλικος L**, pro μυλος ονικος). ερρυπται L.

ἐρριπται H. ἢ *et* ἑνα H. ἑνα *bis script. in* L. 3. ἑαυτοις H**P. ἁμαρτηση L. ἁμαρτη (*sic v.* 4) H. εις (σ *mutat.*) L. −εις σε w*. εἰσε H. αυτον (*pro* αυτῳ *prim.*) z. +μεν (*ante* μετανο.) H. μετανωηση P. αφες (σ *mutat.*) H. 4. ἑπτακις *prim.* L*?HP. ἁμαρτησει i. αναστηση (*pro* ἁμαρτηση) L. +εαν (*ante* ἑπτακις *secund.*) w. ἑπτακης *secund.* P. επιστρεψει LP. −επι σε ivw LHP. προς (*pro* επι) Hz. αφεισεις L. αφη *rescript.* z. 6. ειπεν (*sic v.* 22) wHP. εχετε ivw?L. εχεται P. κοκκω i. σιναπεος w. ελεγεται P. εκριζωθητε L*. 7. ἐξ' w. αροτριουντα i. ἢ P. ποιμενοντα iL*P. εισελθοντα LP. +αυτω (*post* ερει) L. ευθεως *cum sequent.* v. αναπεσε vw. αναπεσον H. ανεπεσεν P. 8. ἑτοιμασον P. διακονη P. +αν (*post* ἑως) wP. μεταταῦτα LH. 9. εκεινω τω δουλω w. εποιησεν wP. +παντα (*post* εποιησε) L. διατεταγμενα (*non v.* 10) i. −αυτῳ ivwHP [*non* L]. 10. οὑτως ivwLHP. ὁτ' ἂν iw. ὁτᾶν H. ὁτ' ἂν P. ποιησετε w*. ποιησηται L*. ποιηση τα παντα P*, *at* παντα ποιησηται P**. λεγεται L. −ὁτι *prim.* vw. αχρειοι δουλοι LH. οφειλομεν v. ὡφειλομεν w. οφειλωμεν L. ὀφελομεν P*, ὀφειλομεν P**. 11. διαμέσου i. ανα μεσον L. σαμαριας iL. 12. ὑπηντησαν L. 13. ἠραν HP. 14. +αυτους (*post* ιδων) L. ἑαυτοις (*pro* ἑαυτους) iP. αρχουσι (*pro* ἱερευσι) i. ἱερευσιν wLHP (ῑ HP). εκαθερισθησαν (*sic* H*, *non* iP *v.* 17) iP. 15. εἶς P. ἐξ' P. ιανθη L*. ὑπεστρεψεν wP. 16. επεσε (−επι προσωπον) L. ἦν P. σαμαριτης L. 17. +οὑτοι (*post* δεκα) w. −δε *secund.* w*. 18. οὐχ' ivwP. αλογενης P. 19. πιστης P. σεσωκεν wP. 20. επερωτιθεις i. επηρωτηθεις z. τινων (*pro* των) i. απεκριθει L. 21. οἱ δε (*pro* ουδε) L. ὡδε (*sic* z *v.* 23) Hz. −η L. 22. ειπεν Hz. επιθυμησεται iz. του επιθυμησαι ὑμας (*pro* ὁτε επιθυμησετε) L. 23. +εαν (*ante* ερουσιν) i. −η wLHz. +ὁ $\overline{\chi\varsigma}$ (*post* εκει) ivw. −απελθητε μηδε L. μὴδὲ ivwz. διωξετε iL. 24. −ἡ *secund.* LHz. ὑπο τον ουρανον *prim.* w. ὑπ' ουρανων *bis* z, *at* L *habet* ὑπο των ἐπ' $\overline{\text{ουνων}}$ *pro* εκ της *usque ad* ουρανον *secund.* [*vix* απ' *pro* επ']. −και ivwLHz. 25. −πολλα L. πολλα παθειν αυτον w. 26. −του *prim.* vwLHz. ταις προ του κατακλυσμου (*post* ἡμεραις *prim.*: −του νωε *ad fin. vers.*) i. −και *secund.* L. τη ἡμερα *secund.* L. +του (*ante* υἱου) vw LHz. 27. εγαμιζοντο iL*. (εγ *rescript.* H). εισηλθεν wH. ἦλθεν και ηλθε (−ὁ) L. ηρεν (*pro* απωλεσεν) i. απωλεσε παντας v. 28. καθως (*pro* και ὡς) ω *mutato in* L. ἠγοραζον w. επουλουν L. ὠκοδομουν w. 29. −ἡ δε z. ἧ (*non v.* 30) iH. εξηλθεν w. εβρεξεν w. θειον και πυρ w*L (w**β, α). εξ (*pro* απ') L. απολεσεν iz. απωλεσε παντας v. ἁπαντας H. 30. τα αυτα wHz. 31. απο (*pro* επι) L. οἰκια wH. αυτου (*pro* αυτα) L*. −ὁ L. −τῳ L. ὁμοιως *repetitum pro* εις τα L. ὀπισω wH. 32. μνημονευετε (ν *mutat.*)

33. ζητησει i. απολεση iz, απολεσαι H (pro απολεσει). ὁς δ᾽ αν (–και, pro εαν secund.) L. απολεσει (pro απολεση) w*. ἐνεκεν εμου ζωοποιηση ro ζωογονησει) i. fin. απολεση την ψυχην αυτου σωσει αυτην L. 34. δυο ονται wLHz [non v]. κινης i. –ὁ prim. ivwHz. παραλαμβανεται w. παραφθησεται (non v. 35) L. 35. ἐπιτοαυτο iv. –ἡ prim. ivwHz, secund. v. ἡ ἑτερα (–και) L, at και ὁ ἑτερος H*. 36. Deest versus in vw*H*? (certè bet antiqua manus) L. –εσονται iHz. –ὁ prim. iw**Hz. 37. πτωμα (pro ιμα) v?w**L. επισυναχθησονται z. +και (ante οἱ) w**. fin. ἐτρι w*. εκει ι οἱ αετοι συναχθησονται L.

Cap. XVIII. 1. –και L. +αυτους (post προσευχεσθαι) vwL. εγκακειν w. κακειν L. 2. –τις z. της? (pro τις) i*. ἠν P. τινη i, τῆ P (pro τινι). ιλη H*. 3. –τις vwLHPz [non i]. ἠν P. ἠρχετο P. 4. ηθελεν vwL. ἐλησεν P. χρονων w*. 5. δε (pro γε) P**. +μη (ante παρεχειν) v. με ro μοι) L. κοπους iL (forsan P*). χηρα iz. ὑποπιαζη ivPz [wH cum lzev.]. fin. ὑποπιαζει μαι L. 6. ειπεν (sic ferè vv. 9, 19, 21, 24, 27, 28, l, 41) wHPz. 7. ποιηση vLHPz. μακροθυμει w*. 7, 8. Post νυκτος L abet · ναι λεγω μακροθυμων (μ mutato) επ᾽ αυτους ποιησει (–ὁτι). 8. ἀρα H. εὑρησει H. 9. –και prim. vwL. των πεποιθοτων L. εισιν w, at οἱ ἰν L. 11. σταθης H*. προσηυξατο w. πρόσηὕχετο P. οὐκ᾽ P. λοι (pro ιποι) L. ἁρπαγες HP. ἠ P. ὁ τελωνης οὗτος w. 12. δῆς P. τω (pro ου) i*. σαββατου w*. 13. init. ὁ δε τελωνης (–και) L. απο μακροθεν w. ακρῶθεν P. ἑστως iwPz. ἤθελεν i. αδελφθαλμους w. ὀφθαλμους P. επαει (επ mutat.) P. ετυπτε (–εις) w. ἱλασθητι i. 14. +δε i, +γαρ z (post εγω). +ὁτι (ante κατεβη) w. δεδικαιομενος P. οἰκον wP. +γαρ (post η) wHPz [non L] (ἠ wP). ἑαὑτον prim. P, at ἑαυτην v. 15. –δε z init. peric. αυτῳ w*. –τα L. βρεφοι L. ἁπτεται L. ἁπτεται H. και ιδοντες (–δε) [. +αυτου (post μαθηται) w. επετιμουν L. 16. λεγει L*, ελεγεν L** (pro πεν). κωλυεται w. κολυετε H*. αυτων H. 17. αν (pro εαν) LH. 3. ἀνος τις προσῆλθεν τω ιυ πειραζων αυτον και λεγων HP init. peric. προσλθε [ν H**] H. επηρωτησεν αυτον τις L. επηρωτησεν w. αιωνηον P. 9. οὐδεῖς P. ει μι P. εἱς ὁ θς τας rescript. super ras. P. 20. οἱδας iP. ωνευσης P*. κλεψεις w*. ψευδομαρτυρησεις w. –σου secund. iw. 21. ειπεν ic vv. 24, 27, 31 L) v*L. παντα ταυτα w. 22. –ταυτα L. ἐτι H. λιπει . ἐξεις iwP. δευρω ακολουθη P. 23. ἠν wP. 24. –αυτον H* (habet arg. manu antiquâ). χρημα L. των ουρανων (pro του θῡ) w. 25. ευκοπωτερον iP. –γαρ L. εστιν LP. καμηλον (λ mutat.) L. τριμαλιας L, at ρυπηματος H. βελωνης (pro ῥαφιδος) L. διελθειν (pro εισελθειν prim.) P.

ἠ P. —η πλουσιον L* (*illeg.? habet* L** *marg.*). 26. λεγουσιν αυτω οἱ μαθη-
ται αυτου z *init. peric.* υσαντες και *rescript.* P (*forsan* —και P*). 27. *init.*
ὁ δε ις i. τα παρα ανοις αδυνατα L. *fin.* παρα τω θω εστιν Hz. 28. —ὁ
ivw [*non* z]. αφεντες παντα τα ιδια (—και) L. ηκολουθησωμεν i. ἠκολου-
θησαμεν wH. 29. *init.* —Ὁ i. αμην αμην z. οικιαν w. οικιας L. +η
αδελφας (*post* αδελφους) i*. ἠ *ter* H. 30. λαβη i. απολαυει (*i. e.* -βει) L.
31. αναβαινωμεν Lz. τελειωθησεται Hz. ὑπο (*pro* δια) L*. περι του υἱου
(*pro* τῳ υἱῳ) iL. 32. εμπεχθησεται L. 33. τη τριτη ἡμερα vL. 34.
τοῦτω L*. ἠν H. κεκαλυμμενον ὑπ' (*pro* επ') z. 35. εν τη ἱεριχῶ L.
ἱεριχῶ iw. ἱεριχὼ v. ἵεριχῶ HP. τιφλος i. *Rasura in* H *ante* τις.
προσαῖτων P. 36. ὀχλου HP. επυνθανετο (υν *mutat.*) L. +αν (*ante* ειη)
iwL. ει (*pro* ειη) P. *fin.* ταυτα L. 37. ναζωρεος P. 38. εβοησεν wP.
—ιησου iw*. 39. παραγοντες w. επετιμουν L. σιγηση (*pro* σιωπηση) i.
σιωπησει P. μαλον i. εκραζε λεγων (*pro* εκραζεν) v. +ιησου (*ante* υἱε) L.
40. εγγιζοντος L. εγγησαντος P. +ὁ ιησους (*post* αυτον *secund.*) L. 41.
θελης i*?P. 42. αναβλεψων w*. πιστης P. σεσωκεν wH**P. 43. πα-
ρὰχρῆμα (*sic* i, XIX. 11) iwH. ανεβλεψεν wLH**P. ἠκολουθει w. ἠκολου-
θη P. οχλος (*pro* λαος) iL. —ιδων w. αἱνον w. *fin.* τον θν L*.

CAP. XIX. 1. διηρχετω P. ἱεριχῶ i. ἱεριχῶ w. ἱεριχὼ vL. ἵεριχῶ HP.
2. ἴδοῦ P. ὀνοματι wP. οὑτος (*pro* αυτος) L. ἠν (*sic v.* 3) *bis* P. αρχη-
τελωνης LP. αυτος (*pro* οὑτος) w*L. οὑτως P. —ην *secund.* w*L. ἠν w**.
3. ειδειν i. εστιν wLH**P. οὐκ' ἠδυνατο P. εδυνατο w. ὀχλου P. 4.
προδραμῶν iw. προσδραμὼν v. δραμων L. πρὸσδραμὼν P. συκομωραιαν
iwP. συκομοραιαν vz. σιμοραιαν L. συκομωρεαν H. ειδη Lz. —δι' iwH*z
[*non* vLP]. εμελλεν w. εμελλε z. ημελον L. ημελλεν H. ἠμελλεν P.
5. ἠλθεν P. ηλθεν L. ιδεν w. ειπεν (*sic vv.* 8, 9, 11, 13, 15, 19, w, *et ferè*
Pz) wHPz. σπεῦσας (*sic v.* 6) i. καταβηθη P. οἰκω P. 7. +αυτον (*post*
ιδοντες) vw. παντες ivPz. οἱ φαρισαιοι (*pro* ἁπαντες) L. διεγογγιζον wL.
διέγογγυζων P. εισηλθεν wH**P (εισῄ. P). 8. σταθης P. +ὁ (*ante* ζακχαι-
ος) P. ιησουν (*pro* κν) iwL. τα ἡμισυ iL. μοι (*pro* μου) Hz. διδωμει L.
ἡτινος P. εσηκοφαντησα w. εσυκοφαντισα P. αποδιδωμη P. αποδιδομι z.
9. —προς w. οἰκω P. εγενετω P. καθ' ὅτι i. καθὅτι H. καθ ὅτι z.
ἀβρααμ ivwLHz [*non* P]. εστι L. 10. ηλθεν w. ἠλθεν P. ζητεισαι i.
ζητησε P. απωλωλος w*. 11. ακουωντων i. —αυτων L. παραβολην ειπεν
L. 12. —ειπεν ουν i. 13. —δε L. αυτου (*pro* ἑαυτου) Hz. μνὰς i** *et*
i *vv.* 16 *bis*, 18, 20, 24, 25, w *v.* 24, L *vv.* 16, 18, 24. ειπεν (*sic vv.* 15, 19)
H. εν ὡ wHz, ὡς L (*pro* ἑως). ερχωμαι w*. 14. ὀπισω wH. θελωμεν

15. εν το H. εκεινους (*pro* τουτους) i. εδωκεν wL. ἱνα *repetit. in*
g. ob lacunam L. επιγνω Hz. 16. +ιδου (*post* κε) i. μνασσου (*sic vv.*
20) i. προσηργασατο i*. 17. εὖ w. δουλε αγαθε L. −ὁτι L. εχω H*.
ἠλθεν H. μνασσου *hic tantum* v. εποιησεν w. 19. τοῦτο i. πολεω
ιutat.] H, *sic v.* 17. 20. +ὁ (*ante* ἑτερος) L. ἑτερος H. ηλθεν w.
'Hz. 21. αἱρεις z. *fin.* +και συναγεις ὁθεν ου διεσκορπισας iLHz.
−δε iLHz. +ὁ κς αυτου (*post* αυτω) L. ειδεις iL. ἠδεις z. ὁτι H. ανος
τηρος ειμι εγω Hz. αἱρων wz. *fin.* +και συναγων ὁθεν (ὁ L) ου διεσκορ-
ɪ LHz [*non* i]. 23. *init.* −και L. διατί w. −την vwL [*non* iz]. ελθων
L. *fin.* αυτω L. 24. δωτε vw*z. τω εχοντι τας δεκα μνας L. 25.
st versus in L. ειπεν (*pro* ειπον) H. 26. ἡμιν w*. −ὁτι Hz. +και περισ-
θησεται (*post* δοθησεται) w** *marg.* L. δοκει εχειν (*pro* εχει) L. ἀρθησε-
i. 27. τουτους (*pro* εκεινους) vw. θελοντας L. επ' αυτων L. ὡδε Hz.
ασφαξετε L. +αυτους (*post* κατασφαξατε) Hz. 28. πορευαιτω L*,
ευετω L**. 29. βηθσφαγῆ i. βησφαγῆ (σ *rubro*) w. βηθσφαγεῖ L.
'σφαγῆ vHz. βιθανιαν L. −το καλουμενον wL. +των (*ante* ελαιων) wL.
στειλεν w. 30. λεγων (*pro* ειπων) L. απεναντι L. εκπορευομενοι H.
ησητε L. εὑρησετε H. πωποτε ανων ουδεις L. ουδης H. εκαθισεν v*w
z. −αυτον i. αγαγετε αυτον w. 31. διατί iLz. 32—34 *desunt in* i.
απελθωντες w. *Rasura post* οἱ H. *fin.* +ἑστωτα τον πωλον H (ἑστωτα
z. 33. λυωντων z. των (*pro* τον *prim.*) L. 34. +ὁτι (*post* ειπον) wL
35. ἠγαγον H. επιριψαντες i. επιρρηψαντες L. αυτων (*pro* ἑαυτων)
36. ἑαυτων wz. ἑαυτων τα ἱματια H. 37. εγγιζοντος (ζ *mutat.*) L,
mutat.) H. −ηδη z *sem. init. peric.* ὁρους H. ἠρξατο (*sic v.* 45) i. ηρξατο
z. ἀπαν H. +αυτου (*post* μαθητων) v. −ὡν L. ὧν H. ιδων w*, ιδον
'. +γινομενων (*post* ειδον) L. 38. ἐρ (*sic, pro* ερχομενος) L. 39. ειπον
ω απο του οχλου (−προς) L. αυτον (ν *mutat.*) H *sem.* 40. −ὁτι L.
οι H *sem.* κεκραξωνται L. και κραξουσιν H *sem.* 41. ηγγιζεν L. ἠγ-
εν w. εκλαιεν L*. επ' αυτην wL. 42. −σου *prim.* z. σοι (*pro* σου
ınd.) L. εκριβει L. +των (*ante* οφθαλμων) i. ὀφθαλμων wH. 43. ἠ-
α[ιε]πι (ιε *super rasur.*) H. περιβαλλοῦσιν w. περιβάλλουσιν z. σοι
ο σου) z. περὶκυκλώσουσιν w. συναξουσιν w. συναξωσι L. σοι (*pro* σε
.) i. 44. εκδαφιουσι i. ενδαφιουσιν w. σοι (*pro* σε) L** (*supra: an*
n.?). λιθον (*pro* λιθῳ) w. 45. εκβαλειν i*. πολουντας iz. −εν αυτῳ L.
+ὁτι (*post* γεγραπται) wHz. και εσται ὁ οικος μου οικος προσευχης
στιν) L. κληθησεται (*pro* εστιν) v, *at* εστι H. σπηλαιων H. 47. −το
καθημεραν ivLH. καθἡμεραν z. 48. οὐχ' ivwz. εὑρισκων i. εὑρισκον

H. −το L. ποιησουσιν Hz. ἁπας γαρ ὁ λαος i. ὁ γαρ λαος L. ἁπας H. ακουειν iL.

CAP. XX. 1. −εν τῳ ἱερῳ w. ευαγγιλιζομενου w. ἱερεις ivwHz. οἱ γραμματεις και οἱ αρχιερεις L. 2. ειπαν L. της L*. σου (*pro* σοι) z. 3. ὁ δε αποκριθεις ειπεν (−προς αυτους) L. ειπεν (*sic vv.* 13, 17, 23, 41, *et* 19, 45 w) wHz. +ὁ ις w** *rubro, supra* προς αυτους. επερωτησω v. καγω ὑμας wL. λογον ἑνα w. −ἑνα L. ἑνα H. 5. συνελογ. (λ H**) H. ἑαυτους H. −ὁτι i. διατί ivLHz. −ουν ivL. *fin.* αυτο iz. 6. καταλιθαση i. πεπισμενος iL. γεγονεναι (*pro* ειναι) L. 7. +το (*ante* ποθεν) L. 8. λαλω (*pro* λεγω) H. 9. −τις vw. εξεδωτο v. απεδημησεν w. 10. +τω (*ante* καιρω) Hz. απεστειλεν wH. δωσει L, δωσουσιν Hz (*pro* δωσιν). απεστειλαν (*pro* εξαπεστειλαν) w. 11. +αυτοις (*ante* πεμψαι) Hz. 12. κακεινον (*pro* και τουτον) w. τραυματησαντες i. εξεπεμψαν (*pro* εξεβαλον) L. 13. ἰσως iw. ισος z. 14. διελογισαντο w. ἑαυτους H. −δευτε w* (*habet marg.*). γενειται H. 15. −αυτοις H*. 16. εκεινους (*pro* τουτους) L. αλλους z. ειπαν Hz. 17. ειπεν L. −ουν i*. −τουτο w*. κ *in* οικο *mutat.* w. 18. εις (*pro* επ') i. πεσοι L. λικμηση i. λυκμισει L. 19. εζητουν Hz. οἱ γραμματεις και οἱ αρχιερεις w. +και οἱ πρεσβυτεροι (*post* αρχιερεις) L. επιβαλλειν w. την χειρα w. −τον λαον i. −γαρ i. ειπε την παραβολην ταυτην L. *fin.* τας παραβολας ελεγεν (−ταυτην *et* ειπε) Hz *init. peric.* 20. *Ita legitur in* z *sem.* οἱ δε αρχιερεις και οἱ φαρισαιοι απεστειλαν προς αυτον λεγοντες συμβουλιον ελαβον ὁπως αυτον παγιδευσωσιν εν λογω και παρατηρησαντες *init. peric.* εκκαθετους L. επιλαβονται i. λογου i. τον (*pro* το) L. −τῃ *secund.* Hz. ἡγεμωνος i. 21. επερωτησαν (*non v.* 27) w. λεγον z *sem.* οἰδαμεν i. οἶδαμεν vw. ὀρθως iH. επαληθειας ivH [*non* Lz]. 22. ἡμας (*pro* ἡμιν) L. καισαρος L**. 24. δειξατε LHz. +οἱ δε εδειξαν· και ειπε (*ante* τινος) L. αποκριθεντος L. ειπον (ο *mutat.*) L. 25. ειπε προς αυτους L. τοινυν αποδοτε L. υ *in* θῡ *mutat.* L. 26. οὐκ H. ισχυσεν z. επιλάβεσθαι i. 27. παρελθοντες ?L*. σαδουκκαιων L. οἱ λεγοντες μη ειναι αναστασιν Hz. επηρωτουν L. 28. μωυσης iwLHz [*non* v]. ὑμιν (*pro* ἡμιν) L*. αποθανει *prim.* i*. γυναικαι *prim.* L. αποθανει *secund.* L, *at* ἢ *habet* i. εξαναστησει Lz. 30. *init.* −και L. +αυτην (*post* ελαβεν) H. οὑτος H. απεθανε H*. 31. ὡσαυτως· ὡσαυτως ivHz. −και *tert.* ivHz. κατελειπον i. 32. −δε vL. απεθανεν w. και ἡ γυνη απεθανεν Hz. 33. αναστασει ουν Hz. εσται i, γυνεται z (*pro* γινεται). 34. −οἱ z. εκγαμιζονται (*sic v.* 35 wLH) wLHz. 35. −και z. των (*pro* της εκ) v. γαμιζονται z. εκγαμιζονται v. 36. −γαρ *prim.* v. εισαγγελοι iL. ἰσαγγελοι w. εισιν *prim.* wL. −εισι *secund.* vw. +και (*ante* της αναστ.) H. 37. μωυσης wHz [*non* ivL]. ἀβρααμ ivwLHz. ἰσαακ w. –και τον θ̅ν̅ ισαακ i* (*habet marg.*). 38. εστιν w. 39. γραμματαιων (*sic v.* 46) w. 40. οὐκέτι vLH. ετολμουν L. αυτον επερωταν i. 41. λεγουσιν w. +τινες (*ante* τον χ̅ν̅) vw. L *legit:* πως λεγουσιν οἱ γραμματεις ὁτι ὁ χ̅ς̅ υἱος δ̅α̅δ̅ εστιν. 42. +των (*ante* ψαλμων) LHz. 43. ἑως H. 44. αυτον κ̅ν̅ wH. αυτου υἱος w. 45. +αυτου (*post* ακουοντος) i*. 46. περιπατην P. εν στολαις περιπατειν L. ἀσπασμους H. πρωτοκαθεδριαις iL. προκαθεδριας P. πρωτοκλισιαις i. πρωτοκλησιαις L. πρωτοκλησιας vP. ταις (*pro* τοις) i. 47. *init.* οἱ κατεσθιοντες i. κατεσθιουσιν P. οἰκιας wP. προφασηz*. μακρᾶ vwz. προσευχομενοι L. οὑτο v. λειψονται H. κρῖμα iwL.

CAP. XXI. 1. ιδεν (*sic v.* 2 wP) w. ειδεν (*sic v.* 2 Hz) HP. βαλοντας P*. τα δωρα *rescript. in* i. γαζοφυλακειον ivPz. εις το γαζοφυλακειον τα δωρα αυτων L. 2. τινα και iLP. –και vwHz. πενηχραν iP. βαλλουσα P. 3. αὐτη ἡ πτωχη iL. αὐτη (*non v.* 4) P. πλιον P. εβαλλεν P. 4. αυτοι (*pro* οὑτοι) L. –του L. περισσευματος L. αυτων (*pro* αὐτοις) L. εβαλλον P. παντα L. εβαλεν iwLHPz. *fin.* +ταυτα λεγων εφωνει (εφωνη w**P) ὁ εχων ωτα (ὠτα iw**, ὀτα P) ακουειν ακουετω iw**LHPz. +ὁ εχων ὠτα ακουειν ακουετω v**. 5. αναθυμασι L. καὶ κόσμηται i. ειπεν (*sic v.* 8 wLHz, *v.* 29 wHz) wLHz. 6. παντα (*pro* ταυτα) ἁ H. λιθον ὡδε (*pro* λιθῳ) L. σαλευθησεται (*pro* καταλυθησεται) L. 7. ὀτ' ἀν (*sic ferè vv.* 9, 20, 30, 31) iwH [ὀταν z]. μελλει wL. γενεσθαι L. 8. πλανηθηται P *sem.* ελευσοντε P. εν τω ονοματι w. ονομαπι HP. ηγγικεν iwLHz *sem.* ἠγγικεν P. οὐν (*sic vv.* 14, 36) P. πλανηθητε H**, πλανηθηται P (*pro* πορευθητε). ὀπισω wHP. –πολλοι *v.* 8 *usque ad* αυτοις *v.* 10 z *sem.* 9. ὀτ' ἀν P. ακουσηται P. πτωηθητε iP. οὐκ' P. 10. +γαρ (*post* εγερθησεται) Hz (*initio clausulæ*). *fin.* βασιλεια z. 11. –και λιμοι L. μεγαλα απ' ο̅υ̅ν̅ο̅υ̅ εσονται L. 12. HPz *initio peric* προσεχετε απο των α̅ν̅ω̅ν̅· επιβαλοῦσι [ν P] γαρ. παντων ivwL. ἐπῖβαλλοῦσι w. διωξουσιν LP. παραδίδοντες L. αγωμενους P. ἑνεκεν P. ονοματος wP. 14. θετε w. θεσθαι Lz*. ἡμων i. 15. ἡ P, ῆ z (*pro* ῆ). δυνησωνται P. ἀντ' εἰπεῖν iv. ειπειν z. η (*pro* ουδε) wL**. αντιστηναι ουδε αντειπειν?L*. 16. παραδοθησεσθαι L*. –και *prim.* L. και συγγενων και φιλὼν και αδελφων ivHPz [*non* wL]. ἐξ' w. 17. εσεσθαι L*. δια το ονομα μου ὑπο παντων w. ονομα P. 18. απο (*pro* εκ) L. απολυται L. απολειται P. απωληται vz. 19. ὑπομονὴ i. κτισασθε iP. κτησεσθε H. *fin.* ἡμων iw. 20. ὀτ ἀν H. –δε z *init. peric.* ειδητε z. την ἰλ̅η̅μ̅ ὑπο στρατοπεδων i. ερημωσης w. 21. ἰουδαῖα z. ορει w*?. ὀρη H. εκχωρητωσαν ivHz. εκκεχωρητωσαν L. εν αυτη (*pro* εις αυτην) i. 22. ἡμερα H*.

αὐταί L. αὗται H. εισιν wL. πλησθηναι ivw. πληρωθῆν L. 23. οὐαὶ w. τᾶς (*pro* ταις *tert.*) L. +τοτε (*ante* αναγκη) Hz. ὀργῇ z. −εν *tert.* wLHz. 24. στωματι ?L*. αἰχμαλωτισθησονται w. αχρις οὗ πληρωθωσιν L. 25. και ε[σται v**] και v. ηχους wL (L *mutat.* ?). ἠχουσης HPz *sem.* 26. ἀπό-ψυχῶν τῶν *sic* L. αποψυχωντων P*. οἰκουμενη wHP. 27. ὀψονται iHP. *Rasura* [ν ?] *post* νεφελη *in* w. 28. δἰ ὅτι w. 29. ιδε v. συκὴν iwLz. παν τα δενδρα H*. 30. −ὅταν προβαλωσιν i. προβαλλωσιν Lz. ἤδη *prim.* wH. εφ' (*pro* αφ') i. απ' αυτων L. −ηδη *secund.* ivw. *Rasur. ante* το H. το θερος εγγυς L. 31. οὕτως iwLHz [*non* v]. ὅτ ἂν H. ειδητε z. +παντα (*ante* γινομενα) L. 32. αμην αμην L. γενεᾶ Lz. −αν z. +ταυτα (*ante* παντα) L. 33. *init.* −ὁ L. παρελευσεται iw. οἱ H *sem.* οὐ H *sem.* παρ-ελθωσιν vwLHPz. 34. −δε L. αυτοις iz. μήποτὲ P. βαρυθωσιν i. βαρηθωσιν vwPz [L *cum Elzev.*]. αἱ καρδιαι ὑμων L. κρεπαλη vP. εφνιδιος iP. αἰφνιδιως w. αιφνηδιως L. αἰφνιδιως H. εφνιδιως z. −ἡ v. 35. παγεις L. παγης P. ελευσεται LH*. κατοικουντας L. προσωπον (οσω *mutat.*) L. της γης πασης w (β, α w**). 36. −ταυτα ivwHPz. γενεσθαι L. 37. ἦν w. ην διδασκων (διδασκον z) ὁ ις εν τω ιερω τας ἡμερας Hz *init. peric.* ερχομενος i*. ηὐλιζετο w. προς (*pro* εις) iHz. ὀρος H. ἐλαιών (*sic* xxii. 39 v) vw. 38. ορθριζε i. ωρθριζεν w. οθριζε L. ορει (*pro* ἱερῳ) Hz. *Post hunc versum* L *habet* JOHANN. VII. 53—VIII. 11, *initio lineæ* (*quod necesse fuit*) *at uno prorsus tenore. Sequitur Cap.* XXII. *eâdem lineâ : videas lectiones varias apud Johann. in loco.*

CAP. XXII. 1. ηγγιζεν wz *sem.* (−δε z *sem.*). ἤγγιζεν H. ἑορτη H. −ἡ λεγομενη πασχα v. 2. οἱ *secund.* H. ανελωσι τον ιν Hz *sem.* 3. εισ-ηλθεν wH. −ὁ ivwLH** *sem.* z *sem.* σατανὰς (*sic v.* 31) z *sem.* +ὁ καλου (*post* σατανᾶς) L*. −εις ιουδαν L. καλουμενον Lz *sem.* ὀντα H (*a s. m.* H *sem.*) z *sem.* 4. συνελαλησεν w. αρχιερευσιν L. +και γραμματευσι (*post* αρχιερευσι) H *sem.* z *sem.* −τοις *secund.* ivwLH *sem.* z *sem.* ὁπως (*pro* το πως) L. αυτοις παραδω αυτον w. 5. εχαρισαν i. αυτον (*pro* αυτῳ) z *sem.* αργυρια wLHz [*non* iv]. 6. −και εξωμολογησε H* *sem.* εξομολογησε ivLz *sem.* εξομολογησεν wH**. εξωμολογησεν H *sem.* z *sem.* ευκεριαν L*. −αυτοις z *sem.* ἀτερ z *sem.* ὀχλου H. −ατερ οχλου L. 7. ἦλθεν wH** *sem.* Ἦλθον H* *sem.* ηλθεν H *sem.* −εν z *sem.* δει L. θυεσθε H *bis.* 8. απεστειλεν w. ἑτοιμασαιτε L*. ἑτοιμα-σατε (*sic* H *v.* 9) Hz *sem.* φαγομεν z *sem.* ἱνα φαγωμεν το πασχα L. 9. οἱ w. +ἱνα (*post* θελεις) L. *fin.* +σοι z *sem.* 10. συναντηση L. ὑπαντησει z *sem.* ἡμιν (*pro* ὑμιν) w*. κεραμειον L. βασταζοντος L. +και (*ante* ακο-λουθησατε) i. οἰκιαν wH. +εαν (*post* οὗ) w. εις ἣν (*pro* οὗ) z *sem.* 11.

ικοδεσποτη w. οἰκωδεσποτη H. οἰκιας wHz* sem. καταλυμμα L. 12.
ειξη Lz sem. αναγαιον i. ανογαιον w. ανωγεων L. ανωγαιον vHz (Hz
em., cum Elzev. semel). εστρωμμενον i. +ἑτοιμον (ante εκει) L. ἑτοιμασατε
L. 13. +οἱ απεσταλμενοι (ante εὑρον) w**. εὑρον H sem. ειρηκει L.
ιπεν (pro ειρηκεν) z sem. +ὁ ις (post αυτοις) i. +αυτω (post ἡτοιμασαν) L.
4. ανεπεσεν wLH. 15. ειπεν (sic vv. 17, 31, 34, 52, 56, 60, 67) wH sem. z.
ιπεν αυτοις (−προς) H sem. επεθυμισα i. επιθυμησα w. επεθυμησαν L.
πεθυμια επεθ. H sem. 16. οὐκ ἔτι iwz sem. [non vL]. −ουκετι z sem. απ'
pro εξ) L. αυτω (pro εξ αυτου) z sem. ἑως H sem. −του θῦ v. 17. +το
ante ποτηριον) iwH*. −ποτηριον v. ειπεν (sic vv. 34, 56) LH. fin. εις
αυτους vwL. ἑαυτοις H. 18. +απο του νυν (post πιω) v (ἀ Ἀπο v) wz sem.
γενηματος iv (−του v*) LHz sem. [non w]. ἑως H sem. οὑ (pro ὁτου) z sem.
λθη w. 19. λαβον H sem. ἀρτον H sem. εκλασεν w. −εκλασε και z sem.
υτους H* sem. H sem. 20. και το ποτηριον ὡσαυτως z sem. ὡσαὑτως H
em., ὡσαὑτος sem. δειπνησε H sem. εμω αἱματι (−μου) L. αἱματι ?z sem.
κχυννομενον w. 21. −ιδου Lz sem. ἡ w. 22. ὁτι (pro και) z sem. Rasura
n w post μεν [μεντοι ?]. ὁρισμενον z sem. κατα το ὁρισμενον πορευεται LH
em. z sem. οὐαῖ iw. ὐυαι H sem. παραδιδωται H sem. 23. ἤρξατο H*
em. ἑαυτους H sem. ἆρα ivwz sem. ἦ (pro ειη) z sem. τοῦτον i. τουτο ὁ
μελλων H sem., τούτο ὁ μελλον sem. μελλων τουτο z sem. πρασσειν μελλων
L. 24. φιλονικια iH sem. z sem. ἑαυτοις Lz sem. μειζον L. 25. init. ὁ
sic v. 26 sem.) w. ὁ δε ις Hz sem. κατακυριευουσιν L. κυριευσουσιν z. 26.
οὐχ' ivH sem. z. οὑτως H sem. ὑμειν w. γενεστω L*. γινεσθω Hz sem.
−ὁ secund. L. ὁ ult. H sem. 27. +εστιν (post μειζων) Lz sem. ἡ ὁ H.
οὐχ' w. −ὁ tert. L. −δε H* sem., habet rubro. μεσος ὑμων ειμι (−εν) z sem.
28. εσται H sem. z sem. 29. διατιθεμε Hz sem. ὑμας (pro ὑμιν) H sem.
ις (pro πατηρ) L. βασιλειαν ὁ πηρ μου z sem. 30. ἐσθιῄ τέ καί πίνη μετ'
μου L (sic). εσθιηται H sem. −εν τη βασιλειᾳ μου iH. καθισεσθε ivwHz.
αθησεσθε επι θρονους δωδεκα L. κρινωντές H*. 31. ειπεν (sic vv. 34,
52, 56, 60, 67) H. ι in ιδου in marg. L. ἡμας (pro ὑμας) z sem. σινιᾶσαι
vz (ν mutat. in L). 32. −δε z sem. εκλιπη w. εκλειπι H sem. εκλειπει
sem. στηρισον w*, at τηρησον z sem. fin. −σου z sem. 33. ειπε (−αυτῳ)
sem. ἑτοιμος H sem. 34. οὐ H sem. −μη prim. z sem. φωνηση vH. ἑως
οὑ w, ἑως Lz sem., πριν ἡ H sem., πρινι z sem. (pro πριν η). τρεῖς iv. με απαρ-
νηση μη ειδεναι L. απαρνησει wz. εναι με super rasur. in w. με ειδεναι
(−μη) z sem. 35. πεστειλα v. απεσστειλα H sem. ἀτερ iL. βαλλαντιου
vLz sem. πειρας z sem. μἢ τινος ὑστερηθητε z sem. και ειπον (−οἱ δε) i.

οἱ w. ουθενος ivwH sem. οὐθενος H sem. οὐθ' ἑνος Lz sem. 35, 36. οἱ δε εἰπον αλλα νυν (cæteris omissis) z sem. 36. ειπε δε (pro ειπεν ουν) Lz sem. βαλλαντιον wLz sem. ἀρατω L. πειραν z sem. πωλησει iLHz sem. πωλησῃ v. πωλισατω z sem. αγορασει ivLHz sem. αγορ., ο mutat. in w. αγορασατο z sem. 37. –ετι z sem. –το prim. z sem. περιεμου i. 38. ὡδε H sem. z. εστιν wL. 39. εξελθων (λθ mutat.) w. επορευετο Hz duobus locis. το καλουμενον (pro των) i. ἠκολουθησαν wHsem. ἠκολουθουν H sem. –και secund. Lz sem. 40. εμπεσειν (pro εισελθειν) L. πεισρασμον L. 41. –απ' v. ὡς ἡ (pro ὡσει) L. βολιν H. θῆς H. 42. παρενεγκαι wL. παρενεγκιν H. τουτο το ποτηριον Hz. –μη L*. γινεσθω vwz. 43, 44. Desunt in L*Hz sem., at LPz sem. habent inter vv. 39 et 40 Matth. xxvi, uno prorsus tenore. In v v. 43 obelo notatur s. m. 43. ὡφθη wP. απο του ουρανου L. ενισχυον P. 44. ἱδρως iv. ἱδρῶς w. ιδρος z. ὡσεί P. αἱματος H. 45. +και (ante ελθων) v. –αὐτου ivwLHz. κοιμωμενους αυτους L. 46. ειπε cum hiatu H, sic vv. 48, 51. καθευδεται L*. 47. –δε wL. ἰδοῦ w. ὀχλος H. ἰουδας L. προηγεν (pro προηρχετο) LHz. αυτους (pro αυτων) ivwLz, at αυτοις H. ηγγισεν w. fin. αυτῶ (pro αυτον) L. +τουτο γαρ σημειον δεδωκει αυτοις, ὁν αν φιλησω αυτος εστιν ivw**LHz (εδωδοκει αυτοις σημειον w**, δεδωκεν L, φιλισω w**, εστι H). 48. ιοῦδα L. 49. οἱ w. παταξωμεν Hz. –εν z. 50. –τις L. του αρχιερεως τον δουλον L. το οὖς αυτου L. οὖς w. 51. ἑασατε?L. εατε· ἑως τουτου; v. ἁψαμενος iwHz. ὡτιου H. 52. προς (pro επ') ivH (+οχλους ante προς H). ληστιν H. εξηλθετε wH. εξηλθατε L. 53. καθημεραν iL. ὀντος H. εν τω ἱερω μεθ' ὑμων οὐκ H. +και (ante ουκ) z. αλλα iHz. εστιν ὑμων wHz. σκοτους; v. 54. –δε w. –αυτον secund. w. την οἰκιαν w. οἰκον H. ἠκολουθει w. αυτω απομακροθεν L. ἠκολουθη αυτω απο μακροθεν H. 55. ἁψαντων wHz. πυραν Hz. συνκαθισαντων LH. εκαθιτο i. εκαθητω H. 56. ἰδουσα (I rubro) i. ατενησας i. ειπεν v. 57. –αυτον prim. vwHz. γῦναι vz. 58. εφη (pro ειπεν) wL. 59. διάστασϊς i. ισχυριζετο L. επαληθιας H. οὗτος H. ἦν w. γαλλιλαιος i. 60. παραχρῆμα Hz. του πετρου (pro αυτου) w. –ὁ secund. ivwLHz. 61. $\overline{ις}$ (pro $\overline{κς}$) z. ενεβλεψεν w. επεβλεψε L. ανεβλεψε H*z. πετρος (π mutat.) L. $\overline{ιυ}$ (pro $\overline{κυ}$) z. αλεκτωρα w. +σημερον (ante φωνησαι) L, (post φωνησαι) w. τρεις iH. 62. –εξω H. –ὁ πετρος w. εκλαυσεν w. 63., init. και non p. m. in H. αυτον (pro τον $\overline{ιν}$) w. –δεροντες L. 64. –ετυπτον αυτου το προσωπον· και w* (habet marg. w**). ηρωτων L. –αυτον secund. w. –προφητευσον w. fin. παισασε i. 65. αυτον, ελεγον (pro ελεγον εις αυτον) i. 66. πρωϊ (pro ἡμερα) L. –τε ivHPz sem. τέ z

sem. +οἱ (ante γραμματεις) v. απηγαγον LP. τον ιν̄ (pro αυτον) z init.
generic. αυτων (pro ἑαυτων) ivwPz sem. 67. ειπεν P. −ὑμιν z. εἶπω P.
68. ἐρωτησω i. επερωτησω ὑμας L. ἢ HP. απολυσετε L. 69. του θῡ
της δυναμεως L. 70. ουν (pro δε prim.) wLz. οὖν P. −ουν in loco suo L.
-ὁ prim. P. −προς αυτους P. 71. ε in ετι mutat. w. χρεῖαν i. εχωμεν
μαρτυρων L. ηκουσατε w. ἠκουσαμεν HP.

CAP. XXIII. 1. ανασταντες ἅπαν HP. αναστας z sem. −αυτων L. ηγα-
γον ivLz sem. ἤγαγον w (rubro) P. απηγαγον Hz sem. προς (pro επι) P.
εις τον πηλάτον i. πιλᾶτον (sic ferè vv. 3, 4, 6, 12, 13, 20, 24) wH. 2.
ηρξαντο P. και ηρξαντο (−δε) Hz sem. κατ' ἠγορειν αυτον H. λεγοντος
L*. εὗρομεν i. εὕρομεν HP. +ἡμων (post εθνος) ivwLz sem. κολυοντα H.
φορον wz sem. λεγον L. αὐτον P. 3. πηλάτος (sic vv. 4, 6 tantum) i.
φει i. 4. πιλᾶτος ferè, v alii. ειπεν (sic vv. 14, 22, 28, 46) wHPz. ὀχ-
λους P. +ὅτι (ante ουδεν) Hz sem. εὑρισκω P. αἴτιον Hz sem. αιτιαν L.
5. ενισχυον L. ανασιει H. ανασειη z sem. οχλον (pro λαον) v. καθὅλης
vz sem. καθόλης z sem. γαλλιλαιας (sic vv. 6 bis, 49, 55, xxiv. 6) i. −αρξαμενος
απο της γαλιλαιας L. αἵωσώδε P. ὥδε z. 6. γαλιλαια H*. −ὁ Pz sem.
εστιν wHPz. 7. εξουσιας (ουσι mutat.) P. ὄντα HP. ἱλ̄ημοις w. 8. ιδον
H. εχαρει P. λεγων (pro λιαν) L. ἦν HP. εξ ἱκανου χρονου θελων L.
εξ ἱκανου θελων Hz sem. ἱκανου v. +χρονου (post ικανου) iwz sem. δια τοῦ P.
ακουην H. +αυτον (post ακουειν) Hz sem. −πολλα w. περι αυτου πολλα L.
ἤλπιζεν wP. ηλπιζεν H. απ' (pro ὑπ') i. γενομενον L**. 9. επηρωτησεν
P. επηρῶτα z. fin. −αυτῳ z sem. αυτον Hz sem. 10. ειστηκησαν i. εἱσ-
τηκεισαν wLHP. 11. εξουθενισας L. +και (ante ὁ ἡρωδης) L. εμπεξας P**.
περιβαλλὼν w. περιβαλῶν P. −αυτον secund. H. αυτω (pro αυτον secund.)
wL. ἐσθητα ivwPz. λαμπρᾶ H*. αυτον tert. (ον mutat.) L. −τῳ w*z sem.
12. ὁ τε ἡρωδης και ὁ πιλατος Hz sem. −ὁ secund. iLPz sem. ὡρα (pro ἡμερᾳ)
Hz sem. προυπῆρχον wz sem. πρὸσυπήρχον P. ὄντες HP. 13. προσ-
καλεσαμενος v. 14. Rasura in w inter προ et σ. ἑαυτους z sem. πρὸσ-
ενεγκατε P. −τουτον i. διαστρεφοντα L. ἴδου (sic vv. 15, 29) P. εὑρων P.
αυτω (pro τῳ ανθρωπῳ τουτῳ) L. αιτιαν v. αἴτιον (sic v. 22) w. ὧν H.
κατηγορειται L. 15. οὐδε H. ανεπεμψε γαρ αυτον προς ἡμας wLz sem. (at
ανεπεμψεν w, ὑμας L). οὐδεν H. fin. +εν (ante αυτω) vLHP. 16. οὖν (sic
vv. 20, 22) P. 17. Deest versus in w*z sem. αναγκη z sem. αυτοις απο-
λυειν L. απολυσαι P. ἑόρτην w**. ἑορτην H. ἑνα P. 18. −δε LP.
παμπληθεῖ ivz sem. πανπληθεῖ Hz sem. πανπληθῆ L. παμπλήθη P. αἴρε
vLP. αἰρε wHz. −τον ivwHPz. βαραβᾶν L solus. 19. ἦν P. βεβλημε-

νον L. βεβλημμενος P. +την (*ante* φυλακην) z *sem.* 20. προσεφωνησεν wP. +προς αυτους (*post* προσεφωνησε) L. θελον z *sem.* 22. κακον (ν *mutat.*) v. οὗτος i. +γαρ (*post* ουδεν) L. αἴτιον P, *at* αξιον z *sem.* εὕρων εν ἑαυτῶ P. 23. επεκηντο P. αἰτουμενοι w. κατἴσχυον w. αἱ HP. 24. επεκρινεν wP. ὑπεκρινε z *sem.* τῶ L. αιτιμα P. 25. απελυσεν wP. −αυτοις iP [*non* vwz]. +τον βαραββαν Lz *sem.* (βαραβαν L, *ante* τον δια). −την L. ἤτουντο wP. +φραγγελωσας (*ante* παρεδωκε) L. παρεδωκεν v*wHP. το (*pro* τῳ) P. 26. −τινος P. σιμωνα τινα κυρηναιον (−του) ερχομενου L *sic.* κυριναιου Pz *sem.* −του *prim.* ivwLHPz. ερχομενον ?H*. αυτον (*pro* αυτῳ) P. φερειν (ε *mutat.*) i. ὄπισθεν P *at* ὄπισω H, οπισω z *sem.* 27. ἠκολουθει wH. ἠκολουθη P. ἠκολουθη z *sem.* −δε z *sem.* πληθος πολυ L. −αἳ L. αἱ H. 28. προς αυταις P. ειπεν L. θυγατερ" (*i. e.* αις) i. ἰλημ (ι *mutat.*) w. ἰλημ H. ἴλημ' P. ἐφ ἑαὐταις P. 29. −ιδου L. ελευσονται L. ερουσιν wLP. μακαρίαι iLPz *sem.* αἱ P. +αἱ L, +αἱ P (*ante* κοιλιαι). εγενησαν L*. μασθοι i. μαστοἳ P. 30. ορεσιν wL. ὄρεσιν P. ὑμας (*pro* ἡμας *prim.*) i*P, (*pro* ἡμας *secund.*) z *sem.* 31. οἱ (*pro* ει) z *sem.* ξυλα ?L. ξυρῳ i. τη (*pro* τι) H. γινεται i. 32. *Deest in* H *sem.* z *sem.* ηγωντο w*. ἤγοντο συν τω ιυ (−δε) Pz *init. peric.* (ηγοντο z). −δε H *sem.* ηγοντο δε συν τω ιησου (το *mutat.*) L. ἑτεροι H *sem.* ανερεθηναι iH *sem.* 33. απηλθεν z *sem.* ηλθον L. λεγομενον (*pro* καλουμενον) v. κρανιου Pz *sem.* αυτον εσταυρωσαν L. +δυο (*ante* κακουργους) P. ὃν *prim.* P. −εκ L. δεζιων P. ἐξαριστερων iwHPz *sem.*, *at* ἐξευωνυμων L. −και τους κακουργους *ad fin. vers.* 43, z *sem.* 34. ειπεν (*pro* ελεγε) wz *sem.*, ειπε z *sem.* ελεγεν LH**P. οὐ H. οιδασιν H**. οἰδασιν P. ποιουσιν wLHPz *sem.* ἱματι L. εβαλλον i. 35. εἰστηκει iwHP. θεόρων H. εξεμυκτηριζων z *sem.* +αυτον (*post* εξεμυκτηριζον δε) L. αρχιερεις (*pro* αρχοντες) w. −συν αυτοις L. σεσωκεν wz *sem.* εσωσεν LP. ἑαυτον H. ἑ αὐτον ου δυναται σωσαι P** *super ras.* (*pro* σωσατω ἑαυτον). οὗτος P. *fin.* ὁ υἱος του θῦ ὁ εκλεκτος L. 36. ενεπεζον L. αυτον (*pro* αυτῳ *prim.*) L. −αυτῳ *prim.* Hz *sem.* ὄξος HP. 37. +ὁ χ̄ς (*post* εἶ) L. ὠ (*pro* ὁ) i*. 38. ἦν P. ἡ (*pro* και *prim.*) z *sem.* −και *prim.* v. +ἡ (*ante* επιγραφη) H. επ' αυτω γεγραμμενη L. ἑλληνικοις HP. και ἑβραϊκοις και ρωμαϊκοις P. ἑβραικοις iH. −και ἑβραικοις L*. οὗτως P. 39. εἱς H. κρεμασθεντων (κ *rubro super rasur.*) w. −κρεμασθεντων z *sem.* εβλασφημη wLz *sem.* αυτω (*pro* αυτον) Lz *sem.* εἱ H, εἶ P (*pro* εἰ). 40. ἑτερος H. αυτον (*pro* αυτῳ) iwL. −λεγων z *sem.* ουδεν φοβη σοι τον Lz *sem.* φοβει v. (39—42 *inter Matth.* xxvii. 38 *et* 39 *uno tenore in* P). 41. *Jungit* i δικαιως αξια. −γαρ iz *sem.* ὧν H *sem.* ὧν P *sem.* ὃν P *sem.* απολαμβανωμεν LH *sem.* οὗτος H. οὐδεν

H *sem.* επραξεν wLH *sem.* P. 42. ελεγεν wH *sem.* H** *sem.* P. —κε w* (*supra* w**). ὅτ' ἂν iwH. ὁτ' ἀν P *sem. at* ὁτἀν *sem.* [ὅταν z]. ἐλθης (η *mutat.*) w. βασιλειασσου H* *sem.* 43. αμην αμην P. 44. ʽΗν (H *rubro*) w. ἦν Pz *sem.* ὡς ἡ (*pro* ὡσει) LP. ἑκτη HP. ἑως H. ενατης wH. 45. ἡλιος H *sem.* του ἡλιου εκλειποντος (*pro* και ὁ ἡλιος εσκοτισθη) H *sem.* (εκλίποντος H) z *sem.* 46. ειπεν LHPz *sem.* παρατιθεμαι wH *sem.* z *sem.* παρατιθημι z *sem.* τουτο (*pro* ταυτα) wLPz *sem.* 47. ἑκατονταρχος H *sem.* P. γενωμενον L. εδοξασεν wH *sem.* H** *sem.* οντος iz *sem.* ὀντος P. ὀντως Hz *sem.* ἦν P. 48. ὀχλοι P. και θεωρουντες (—επι) την θεωριαν ταυτην· θεωρουντες τα γινομενα (*post* οχλοι) L. +και (*ante* θεωρουντες) z *sem.* +τον σεισμον και (*post* θεωρουντες) H *sem.* αυτων (*pro* ἑαυτων) LPz *sem.* στηθει i. στιθη z *sem.* 49. εἱστηκεισαν ivwHPz *sem.* εἱστηκησαν z *sem.* μακρωθεν P. αἱ H, *passim.* συνακολουθησαι H* *sem.* —αυτῳ i. 50. ὀνοματι wH. βουλευτῆς iw. +και (*ante* ανηρ *secund.*) Hz. 51. συγκαταθεμένος i, συγκατατιθεμενος L. οὑς L, ὡς H (*pro* ὁς). ὁς και αυτος προσεδεχετο (—και *sem.*) vw. —και *secund.* L. —και αυτος L. 52. αυτος (*pro* οὑτος) L. ἡτησατο wHz. 53. —αυτο *prim.* L. ενετυλιξε (—αυτο *secund.*) Hz. σινδωνι z. αυτω (*pro* αυτο *secund.*) L. +εν (*ante* σινδονι) v. σινδονη L. +καθαρα (*post* σινδον.) w** *marg.* L. —αυτο *tert.* L. μνημειω v. ὦ (*pro* οὑ) Hz. ουδεις ουδεπω wLHz. *fin.* +και πρὸσέκυλησε ληθον επι την θυραν του μνημειου w** *marg.* [*nil additum in* iL]. 54. +ἡ (*ante* ἡμερα) L. ἡμερα z. —και *secund.* iwHz. απεφωσκεν w. επεφωσκεν LH. 55. —και *prim.* ivw. αἱ (*pro* και *prim.*) LHz (αἱ H). αἱτινες H. ἡσαν wH. εθεωρουν L. *fin.* του ι̅υ̅ (*pro* αυτου) v. 56. ἡτοιμασαν z. μῦρα z. —μεν Hz.

CAP. XXIV. 1. —δε w*HPz *init. peric.* βαθεως ivwHPz. ἦλθον w. ἤλθον P. +γυναικες (*post* ηλθον) iHPz. ἃ P. τινεσυν P. τιναις z. 2. εὑρον P. μνημιου P. 3. οὐχ' ivPz. 4. και εγενετο εν τω διαπορισθαι αυτας περι τουτου i** *marg. rubro* (—i*). ἴδοῦ P. ανδρες δυο ivwLHPz. επεσθησαν i. ἐσθησεσιν iwz. αισθησεσιν vP. 5. κλινουσων P. τα προσωπα w. ειπεν HP*. 6. ὧδε z *solus.* —αλλ' ηγερθη P*. ἡγερθη iHP** *marg.* ἡμιν iHP. ὢν L. 7. οὑτως (*pro* ὁτι) L. παραδωθηναι H. —ανθρωπων P. 9. μνημιου P. παντα ταυτα ivw [*non* Hz]. ἑνδεκα wHP. πασιν HP. 10. *init.* ἦν L. —ησαν δε iHPz. ἤσαν w. μαγδαλινη v. —και μαρια ιακωβου z. +ἡ (*ante* ιακωβου) ivw. αἱ HP. λυπαὶς συν αυτοις P*. —αἱ i*wHPz. αἱ i** *rubro.* 11. ὡσει P. λυρος i. ἡπιστουν wHP. 12. —δε P *bis* z *sem. init. peric.* μνημιον P *sem.* προσκυμψας P* (μ *eras.*). ὀθονια wH *sem.* P *bis.* —μονα L. *Jungunt* απηλθε προς ἑαυτον LH *sem.* z *duobus locis.* απηλθεν wH *sem.* P *bis.* θαυμαζον P. γεγονως wL*. 13. ἦσαν HP. ὡρα (*pro* ἡμέρᾳ) z. κομην (*non v.* 28) i. ἑξηκοντα wHPz [*non* i]. ιλ̄ημ (*sic v.* 33, *non vv.* 47, 49, 52 w) wH. ἡ LHP. 14. ὡμιλουν ivz. ὁμιλουν P. 15. ὡμιλειν i. ὁμιλειν z. εγγησας z*. 16. ὁ (*pro* οἱ) w*. ὀφθαλμοι (*sic v.* 31 P) wP. 17. ειπεν (*sic vv.* 18, 25 wHP, 44 wP) wHPz. ενπεριπατουντες v. [L *in hoc vers. cum Elzev.*]. 18. αποκριθεις (ι *prim. mutat.*) L. εἰς εξ αυτων ὦ ονοματι (–ὁ) L. ὀνομα HP. –εν *prim.* ivwHPz [*non* L]. 19. ὡς (*pro* ὅς) wz [*non* iL]. 20. τὲ iwLPz. αυτον παρεδωκαν wL. οἱ *prim.* H. ὑμων iz. κριμαν i. κρῖμα w *alii.* 21. ελπιζομεν wL. ἠλπιζομεν P. μελλον P. αλλαγε (α *secund. mut.*) v. συμπασι [ν P**] vP. τριτην (η *mutat.*) L. –ταυτην P*? αγη L. 22. τιναις P*. ἐξ' vz. εξεστισαν P. ὑμας i. γενωμεναι L*. ορθριναι w. ὀρθριαι H. 23. εὑρουσαι P. ἦλθον P. ὀπτασιαν iwLH. ἑωρακεναι P. αἳ (*pro* οἳ) L. λεγουσαι L. αυτον (α *mutat.*) L. ζειν P. 24. και απηλ. *rescript.* P. εὑρον P. οὑτως ivwHz. οὗτος L*. οὗτως P. αἱ P. ιδον wP**. 25. ὦ wP. ὦ z. 27. μωυσεως w*. διερμηνευεν iLHP. *fin.* ἑαυτου ivwHz [*non* L]. 28. ειγγυσαν L. ἤγγησαν P. προσέποιητω i. προσέποιῆτο P. πορροτερω v. 29. μεῖναι (*mutat., pro* μεινον) L. ἑσπεραν HP. εστιν LP. κεκληκεν LP. εισηλθεν wP**. 30. εν τοi. κατακληθηναι LPz. ευλογησεν wLP. 32. ουχ L. ἦν P. ελαλη w*P. 33. ὡρα P. εὑρον P. ἑνδεκα wHP. τοις (*pro* τους *secund.*) P. 34. ἠγερθη iwHP. ὀντως H. οντος P. ὠφθη wH. 35. –ὡς w*. 36. λεγοντων (*pro* λαλουντων) L. αναστας ὁ ῑς̄ εκ νεκρων Pz *init. peric.* ἑστη L, *at* εστι P *sem.* 37. πτωηθεντες iL*P. +οἱ μαθηται (*ante* εδοκουν) L. εδωκουν P. 38. διατί wP [*non* ivL]. λογισμοι v. 39. ειδετε *prim.* L. ψηλαφησετε LP*. ὀστεα wHP. οὐκ' P. 40. εδειξεν ivw. 41. θαυμαζωντων P*. βρωσιμων H. 42. αυτον (*pro* αυτῳ) P. ιχθῦος i. ἰχθυος (ι *mutat.*) w. ὀπτου wHP. μελισιου iP. [vwLz *cum Elzev.*]. κιριου i. κηριου wL. 43. λαβῶν w. αυτον i. εφαγε v. *fin.* +και τα επιλοιπα εδωκεν αυτοις vw. 44. ειπεν H. οὗτοι i. +μου (*post* λογοι) w. ὦν w. ἡμιν (*pro* ὑμιν) vL*. ὧν συν ἡμιν P. μωυσεως w. *fin.* ; w. 46. οὑτως *bis* ivwHz (P *prim.*). οὗτος *bis* L. οὗτος *secund.* P. 47. το P. ὀνοματι HP. ιλ̄ημ (*sic v.* 49) H. 49. εγω ιδου w. αποστελλῶ P. ἡμας (*pro* ὑμας) w. καθησατε LP. δυναμην P. ἑξύψους i. 50. εξηγαγεν wHP. βυθανιαν w. 51. αυτοις (*pro* αυτους) P. 52. *Rasura in* w *inter* προσκυνη *et* σαντες. *Duo lineæ erasæ post* μετα *in* P. 53. ἦσαν P. ἦσαν Hz. διαπαντὸς wP [*non* i]. Ἱερω (Ἱ *rubro*) w. αἰνουντες w.

SUBSCRIPT: iw *rubro* ευαγγελιον κατα λουκαν στιχων β̄ω̄, +εξεδοθη δε μετα χρονους ῑε̄ της χ̄ῡ αναληψεως w. τελος συν θω̄ του κατα λουκαν ἁγιου εναγγελιου v *rubro.* *Nihil habet* L.

SANCTI JOHANNIS EVANGELIUM.

Το κατα ιωαννην ἁγιον ευαγγελιον iv. ευαγγελιον κατα ιωαννην w.
ναγγελιον εκ του κατα ιωαννην L *rubro*.

CAP. I. 1. Ἐναρχῇ (*sic v.* 2) iP. ἦν *ter* (*sic vv.* 2, 15 *bis*, 28, 40, 41, 45)
'. 2. οὗτος (*sic v.* 7 i) iH. 3. χορις P. 5. σκοτεια *bis* i, *prim.* L. αυτω
z. κατελαβε L*. 7. πιστευσουσιν H. 8. ἱνα P. μαρησῃ i. 9. παν^τ
ι (*sic*). 10. οὐκ' (*sic vv.* 13, 20, 21, 27 *pass.*) P. 11. ηλθεν wLP. 12.
λαβον w. αυτου (υ *mutat.*) P. 13. εγενηθησαν iL*z. 15. μαρτυρι i**
ubro (*deest in* i*). κεκραγεν wP. οὗτος P. ὀπισω (*sic v.* 30 w, 27 P) wP.
-ὁ (*ante* ερχομενος) v. εμπροσθε (*sic v.* 27) z. 16. χαρητος i. 17. μωυσ-
ως w. ἡ *prim.* H. 18. οὐδεὶς P. ἑωρακεν wP. ποποτε P. μογενῆς P*.
ν w. ὢν P. –του πατρος L. 19. αὕτη P. ὅτε (O *rubro*) w. +προς αυτον
post λευιτας) wLP (*vix* P*). 20. *init.* –και ὡμολογησε z *sem.* ὡμολογησε
. ὁμολογησε *prim.* z *sem.* ὁμολογησεν *bis* wP, *secund.* z *sem.* ἠρνησατο
sequuntur lineæ duo erasæ) P. *Secundo loco,* ὡμολογησεν v. ὁμολογησε H.
1. ἠρωτησαν (*sic v.* 25) iwHPz *sem.* ἡλιας (*sic v.* 25 iLP) ivLP [*non* wz].
πεκριθη (*pro* λεγει) L. –ὁ L. λεγει ουκ ειμι (*pro* απέκριθη ου) L. 22.
-τι λεγεις περι σεαυτου i. σεαὐτου w [L *cum Elzev.*]. 23. *init.* ὁ δε εφη
ι. –εγω vL. 24. φαρισσαιων (*sic* III. 1) z *sem.* 25. αυτὸ' P (*sic*). ὁ P.
ὗτε *bis* P. 26. –ὁ z *sem.* +μεν (*post* εγω, *sic*) L. ὕδασι z *sem.* ἑστηκεν
z *sem.* εστικεν P. 27. *Rasura post* οὐ P. ουκ ειμι εγω L. –εγω z. *fin.*
-εκεινος ὑμας βαπτισει εν πνι ἁγιω και πυρι iv. 28. +μεν (*post* ταυτα) w.
ηθανια ivHPz. βηθαβαρὰ w. βηθεβαρα (*sic*) L. –ην L*. 29. ἐπαὔριον
ic vv. 35, 44) w. –ὁ ιωαννης w. αἴρων Lz *sem.* ερων P. 30. εστιν wHP.
ὑμιν (*post* ειπον) L. ὀπισω P *sem.* εμπροσθε L. ἦν P. 31. ειδειν L*.
δην P. διατοῦτο ivLz *sem.* ἦλθον P. –τῳ *secund.* L. 32. +ὁ (*ante* ιωαννης)
z. καταβαινων P. (*pro* ὡσει) ivH. ἐξ' P. 33. οιδειν L. ειδην P.
ι (μ *mutat.*) L. ειδοις L, ἴδεις P (*pro* ιδῃς). μενων Pz *sem.* 34. ἑορακα i.
ορακα P. +αυτον (*post* ἑωρακα) v. μεμαρτυρικα P. 35. εἱστηκει ivwHP
em. ἵστηκει P *sem.* –ὁ z. 37. ἠκ [ουσαν P**] HP. αυτω (*pro* αυτου) L.

ạụṭ λαλουντος L. ἠκολουθησαν wHP. 39. λεγουσιν (*pro* ειπον) P. ἑρμη-νευομενον διδασκαλε *rescript.* i. ἑρμηνευομενον H. μεθέρμινευομενον P. 40. +οὖν (*post* ηλθον) P**. ιδον wP. εκεινην τ̣ην ἡμεραν L. –δε ivwLHPz. 41. +ὁ (*ante* ανδρεας) z. εἷς P. 42. εὑρισκει (*sic vv.* 44, 46) P. πρωτον wL. εὑρικαμεν (*sic v.* 46) i. εὑρηκαμεν P. μεσιαν ivwLHPz. μεθερμινευο-μενον P. –ὁ (*ante* $\overline{χς}$) ivwLHPz. 43. ἤγαγεν HP. –δε i*vwLHPz. ειπεν wLHP. ιωνα; Lz. κληθησει P. κληθεισῃ z. ἑρμηνευετε H. ἑρμηνευεται P. 44. [*cum Elzev.* ivLz]. Ἠθελησεν (Ἠ *rubro* w) wHP. –ὁ $\overline{ις}$ *in loco*, +ὁ $\overline{ις}$ (*ante* ακολουθει) wH. ακολουθῃ P. 45. –ὁ Lz. φιλιππος H* *sem.* βιθσαΐδα P. ανδρεα L. 46. εὑρισκει H. ν̈αθανιηλ *mutat.* L. εγραψεν wP. μωυσης w. εὑρικαμεν P. –του wz. ναζαρετ (*sic v.* 47) ivz [*non* wHP]. να̣̈ ναζαρεθ L*. 47. ναθαηλ' (*sic v.* 48, *non vv.* 46, 49, 50) P. ἐρχου H. 48. ιδεν w. ϊσραϊλιτης P. εστιν wLHPz *sem.* 49. –ὁ ivwHPz *sem.* ὀντα H. συκῆν ivLz *sem.* ιδον (*sic v.* 51 w) iw. 50. ειπεν (*pro* λεγει) z *sem.* ῥαββι Pz *sem.* *fin.*; L. 51. +ὁ (*ante* ιησους) LH. σε (*pro* σοι) i. σοι ειπον L. –ειπον σοι z *sem.* ὑποκάτω z. πιστευησ̣ιz *sem.* z* *sem.* μειζων Pz *sem.* ὀψῃ ivw. ὀψει P [L *cum Elzev.*]. 52. –*unum* αμην Lz. ἀπάρτι ivLHz [*non* w]. απαρτει P. ὀψεσθε H *sem.*

Cap. II. 1. τη τριτη ἡμερα L. ἦν (*sic v.* 13, *passim*) P. 2. –και *prim.* v. 3. –και z. οἶνου P. εχουσιν wLP. 4. *init.* +και wL. συ (*pro* σοι) LPz. γῦναι i**z. οὔπω HP. ἥκει ivH. 5. ὅτι vLP. λεγει HP. ἡμιν H. +ποιειν (*ante* ποιησατε) z. ποησατε i. 6. ἦσαν P. ὑδριαι (*non v.* 7) i. –λιθιναι H*. λιθηναι iH**P. ἐξ P. κειμεναι ἐξ L. τῶν (*pro* τον) w. χορουσαι i. μετριτας iP. ἢ P. 7. γεμησατε ivz. ὑιδριας L (ὑ *forsan s. m.*). ὑδριας H. εγεμησαν ivPz. ἑως P. ἀνω w. 8. κ̤άν τλησατε L (*sic*). φερεται z. αρχητρικλινω (*sic v.* 9 *bis*) P. οἱ δε (*pro* και *tert.*) wz. 9. γεγεννημενον H*. ηδη i. ειδει P. οἴδησαν L. ἤδεισαν P. ἠντληκοτες P. φωνῃ w*Pz. τονυμφιον v. 10. οἰνον *bis* P. τιθησιν iLP. ὅτάν i. ὅτ' ἀν w. μεθυσθωσιν P. –τοτε z. +δε (*post* συ) L. τετηρικας H*. οἶνον *secund.* w *hic tantum.* 11. εποιησεν wLP. –την *prim.* w. εφανερωσεν wHP. 12. μετατοῦτο L. ηλθεν ὁ $\overline{ις}$ (*pro* κατεβη) Pz *init. peric.* και οἱ μαθηται αυτου και οἱ αδελφοι αυτου w. –και οἱ μαθηται αυτου v. εγγυς εμεινεν (*pro* εκει εμειναν) i. οὐ H. 13. ἦν P. +το (*ante* ἱεροσολυμα) w. ὁ $\overline{ις}$ εις ἱεροσο-λυμα (ἱ *deest* P*) HPz. –ὁ ιησους L. 14. εὗρεν P. πολουντας P. ποας (*pro* βοας) L*?. 15. φραγελιον v. φραγγελλιον w [*non* iP]. σφραγελιον L. σχυνιων P. εξεβαλον z. κολυββιστων L. εξεχεεν wP. *fin.* ανεστρεψεν w, *at* κἄτορθωσε L*, κατεστρε̈ψε L** *marg.* 16. πολουσιν P. +και (*ante* μη)

[. ποιῆτε iLP. 17. καταφαγεται ivwHP [*non* Lz]. 18. −ουν L.
(*sic v.* 22) P. οἱ H. 19. −ὁ i?vw*HPz. 20. ουδαιοι w (Ἰ w**). αρά
marg. L. ὠκοδομηθη wHP. οὗτος P. εγειρης z. 21. ελεγεν wP [L
n *Elzev.*]. 22. ἠγερθη iwHP. +των (*ante* νεκρων) z. −αυτου i. ελεγε
[z. −αυτοις ivLHPz [*non* w]. το (*pro* τῳ) wz*?. +αυτοις (*post* ειπεν) i*L.
sura in P *inter* ι *et* C (IC). 23. +τοις (*ante* ἱεροσολυμοις) ivwL. το
ηχα (−εν *secund.*) L. −αυτου *secund.* v. 24. −ὁ ις i*. επιστευσεν ?w*.
-ὸν (*pro* ἑαυτον) v*. παντα ivL. 25. χρεῖαν i. εγινωσκεν wL.

CAP. III. 1. ἦν (*sic vv.* 23 *bis*, 24, 26) P. −ην δε z *init. peric.* νικωδης *hic*
itum L. αρχον P. 2. οὗτος P. ἦλθεν wP. νυκτος προς τον ιν z. αυτον
ο τον ιν) w. ῥαββεῖ (*sic v.* 26) P. τοιαυτα (*pro* ταυτα) v. −τα L. ει
ο ἦ) i. ἐὰν μὴ ἦ H. 3. −ὁ vwP. ειδειν ?w*. 4. ὢν P. γενηθηναι
und. i, *prim.* H*. 5. −ὁ ivwHPz [*non* L]. +και ειπεν αυτω (*ante* αμην)
. −αμην *unum* z. οὐ H. 6. γεγεννημενον *bis* ivwLH, *prim.* P, *secund.* z
ιννωμενον *prim.* z, γεγεν ν P, *rasurâ inter* ν *et* ν). εστιν *bis* wLP, *prim.* H.
init. +και v*L. δη (*pro* δει, *sic vv.* 14, 30) z. ἡμας LP. 8. πνῆ z.
υτου i*. κουεις L. οὐκ H. οὗτος L, οὕτως HP. εστιν wLP. γεγενημε-
L. 9. δῆ (*pro* δυναται) i. 10. −ὁ *prim.* ivwHPz [*non* L]. ου γινωσ-
ι ταυτα w. 11. ἑορακαμεν w*?P. +και (*ante* μαρτυρουμεν) z. 12. ἡμιν
ο ὑμιν *prim.*) i. −και L. ουπω (*pro* ου) ?w*. ουκ επιστευσατε (*pro*
πιστευετε) v. −ὑμιν *secund.* iv. ουρανια v. *fin.* πιστευσητε ivLH**Pz.
ιτευσησε w. 13. −και P *sem.* z *sem. init. peric.* οὐδεῖς P *sem.* −ὁ *prim.*
sem. ὢν w. ὢν P. 14. *init.* −και i* (*supra rubro*). μωυσης w *solus.*
ωσεν wP *sem.* ὀφην P. οὕτως H *sem.* δη (*pro* δει) P *sem.* z *sem.* 15.
ολληται (*sic v.* 16) L. απωληται (*sic v.* 16) z. εχει (*sic v.* 16 *etiam* w)
.HPz. 16. οὕτως ivwLHPz. −γαρ H *sem.* Pz *init. peric.* ἠγαπησεν (*sic*
19) iwH *sem.* P (Ἡ w *rubro*). ὥστε w. μογενη w*. μονογ⁝⁝ογενη P *sem.*
+ουχ (*ante* ἱνα *prim.*) L. 18. *init.* +πας z. ἠδη P. −μη *secund.* L.
μα P. 19. +αυτον (*post* ἠγαπησαν) P. το σκοτος μαλλον ἢ H. αυτων
ηρα wLz. 20. −γαρ iw. ελεχθη P. αυτου τα εργα iw. 21. ερχετε P.
εργα αυτου (φανερωθη *super rasur.?*) L. +τω (*ante* θῶ) vwLP. εργασμενα
22. μεταταῦτα L. διετριβεν wP. 23. αἰνῶν LPz. εκγης (*pro*
γυς) L. σαλημ vLHz [*non* iw]. τοὺς ἀλειμ P. παρεγενοντο iLPz (+οἱ
δαιοι z). 24. ουπω wL. εν τη φυλακη z. 25. εγενετο w (νε w**?).
ζητησεις P. ιουδαιου vwHP [Lz *cum Elzev.*]. περι καθαρισμου μετα
δαιου i. 26. ὡς σὺ μεμαρτυρικας P. οὗτος P. 27. +ἀφ᾽ ἑαυτου (*ante*
εν) L. ἦ H. +ανωθεν (*ante* εκ) L. 28. −μοι ivwP [*non* Lz]. *Rasura*

inter μαρτυρει *et* ται *in* P. 29. ν̣ῦμνυμφιος P. ἑστηκως wH. ἑστικῶς P. χαρὰ *prim.* iLH. νιμφιου *secund.* L*. αὐτη P. 30. ελατουσθαι P. 31. αἵνωθεν ?L. ὢν w. ὢν P. απο (*pro* εκ *prim.*) L. −εκ της γης *secund.* P* (*super rasur.* P**). εστιν *ter* wL. εστι *prim.* z (−ὁ ων *ad fin. vers.* z). · *fin.* εστι ivH. 32. ἑορακε iH. ἑωρακεν vw. ἑῶρακε [νP**] P. ἤκουσε [νP**] P. ηκουσεν εκεινο (*pro* τουτο) L. μαρτυρειαν P. 33. αυ *in* αυτου *mutat. in* P. εσφραγησεν Pz. αληθεις P. 36. απιστων (*pro* απειθων) L. +την (*ante* ζωην *secund.*) ivL. ἡ w. μένει v*.

CAP. IV. 1. ις (*pro* κς) i. +ὁ (*ante* ιησους) L. ι *in* ποι *et* ν *in* ιωαν *mutat. in* L. 2. +ὁ (*ante* ιησους) L. αυτος ις w. οἱ w. 3. αφηκεν w. +γην (*post* ιουδαιαν) L. απηλθεν (−παλιν) ivw [*non* L]. 5. +ὁ ις (*post* ουν) i*v, *sic* P (−ουν) *init. peric.* [z *hiat usque ad v.* 46]. πολην (*sic v.* 8) P. σαμαριας (*sic v.* 7) P. λεγομενη L. συχαρ ivwHP [*non* L]. ὢ (*pro* ὃ) L. 6. ἦν *bis* P (*sic v.* 46). −ουν L. οὖν (*sic vv.* 9, 11, 28, 30, 40, 52, *non* 33 P) HP. κεκοπικως L. απο (*pro* εκ) L. ὀδυποριας P. −οὑτως L. ὡς ἡ LP. ἑκτη wHP. 7. −ὁ w. δως (*sic v.* 10) P. 8. απεληλυθασιν L. απεληλυθησαν ivHP. αγωρασωσι i. αγορασωσιν wLP. 9. −ουν w. σαμαρειτης L. σαμαριτης P. ὢν P. αἰτεις w. η *in* ουσης *mutat.* w. οὔσης H. οὐ H. συχρωνται i*. +οἱ (*ante* ιουδαιοι) vH. σαμαριταις ?L. 10. +ὁ (*ante* ιησους) L. οιδης ?L. ὁ w. ποιειν ?w*. ἤτησας P. −αν *secund.* w*L. συ (*pro* σοι) P. 11. εστιν HP. 12. ἡ (*pro* ει) iL. πρς *mutat. in* P. δεδωκεν L. +τουτο (*post* φρεαρ) L. επιεν wLHP. 13. −ὁ *prim.* ivwHP. διψηση ?i*. 14. πιῇ w. πιει L. δοσω *prim.* P. διψησει LP. −ου μη διψηση *usque ad* δωσω αυτῳ i. αλλ H. ὅ *mutat.* ? *in* L. +εγω (*ante* δωσω *secund.*) L. −εν P. ἀλλομενου ivwP. ἁλομενου L. 15. μήδὲ ivwLP. ερχομαι ivLP. 16. σου τον ανδρα L. 17. +αυτω (*post* ειπεν) ivw. 18. εστιν wHP. ηρηκας i*. 20. εν τω ορει τουτω ivwLH. ἐν τω ὀρει τουτω P. λεγεται wP. 21. πιστευε μοι λεγοντι L. οὔτε *prim.* P. ὀρει P. προκυνησετε w. προσκυνησουσι L. προσκυνησεται P. 22. προσκυνητε i. οἴδαμεν P. +εγενετο και (*post* ιουδαιων) L. 23. ὡρα P. προσκυνησουσιν wHP. (κ *in* προσκ *mutat. in* L). +μου (*post* πρι) L. 24. −πνα *usque ad* αυτον L. προσκυουντας v. 25. οιδαμεν L. μεσιας ivLHP [*non* w]. χ *in* ερχεται *mutat. in* L. ὅτ' ἂν iwH. ἐλθη w. ὑμιν iP. +τα (*ante* παντα) L. 27. τοῦτο iL. ἦλθων P. εθαυμαζον w. οὐδεῖς P. ειπεν (*sic* 29, 39 wHP) vwLHP. ἦ P. 28. ἡ γυνη την ὑδριαν αυτης P. 29. ειδετε L. οὗτος P (οὗτος *vv.* 42, 47). 30. −ουν ivwH. 31. *init.* εν δε το iP. ἠρωτουν (*non v.* 40) L. ἠρωτων (*sic v.* 40) wHP. +αυτου (*post* μαθηται) i. ῥαββει P. 32. ἦν w. 33. προς αλληλους

ιθηται L. ἠνεγκεν P. 34. ποιησω w. 35. οὐχ' (*sic v.* 38) ivwHP.
ται P. -ετι iwL. ετη P. τετραμηνος i?vwLHP. εστιν vwP. +εγω
ε λεγω) i. ὀφθαλμους wHP. εισιν wHP. ἠδη P. 36. χαιρει iLP.
τοῦτο i. -ὁ *secund.* vw. 38. κεκοπιακασιν LP. αὐτόν (*pro* αυτων) LH.
+εξ αυτων (*post* αυτον) L. των λογων L. 40. ἠλθον P. 41. +εις αυτον
t επιστευσαν) L. 42. γυναικῆ P. οὐκέτι iwP. +παρ' αυτου (*post* ακηκοα-
L. εγνωκαμεν (*pro* οιδαμεν) w. οἴδαμεν H. -αληθως w* (*marg.* w**).
ιabet ὁ χς]. 43. -και απηλθεν L. 44. -ὁ vw. *Rasura in* L, *inter* προφ
ης. 45. αυτων L*? (*pro* αυτου). ἑορακοτες i. ὁσα (*pro* ἁ) L. εποιησεση-
L. 46. ηλθε παλιν ὁ ις (-ουν) i. παλιν ὁ ιησους vwL. κανὰ iwL. εποι-
w. βασιλεικος (*non v.* 49) i. οὗ P. ἠσθενη w*. ἠσθενει P. 47. οὑτος iHP.
(*ante* ις) P. ἡκει ivwHz. απο (*pro* εκ) L. απηλθεν wP, *at* ηλθε L.
τα iwHP. ἠρῶτα z. -αυτον *secund.* L. παιδα (*pro* υιον) i. τον υν
ιυ P. εμελλεν w. ειμελλε L. ἠμελλεν P [iv *cum Elzev.*]. αποθνισκειν i.
ιδηται L. πιστευσηται L*. *fin.*; v. 49. καταβηθη P. τον υἱον (*pro*
ταιδιον) L. 50. σο (*pro* σου) i. ζει P. ὦ (*pro* ᾧ) P. -αυτῳ *secund.* vw*.
(*ante* ις *secund.*) ivwLHz (ι *mutat.* ?L). επορευθη L. 51. ἠδη P. κατα-
οντος P*. οἱ H. ἠπηντησαν L. αυτον (*pro* αυτῳ) P. ανηγγειλαν w.
(*pro* παις) wL. 52. επυνθανετο L. εποιθανετο P. δε (*pro* ουν) L.
ὡραν παρ' αυτων wL. ὡραν *bis* P. κομψωτερον L. εσχεν H**P. -ὁτι i.
θες L. ἑβδομην wP. 53. +αυτου (*post* πηρ) L. -εν ῃ L. ἡ H. οἱκια
ὁλη H. 54. +δε (*post* τουτο) L. 'γαλϊλαίαν *sic* i.

CAP. V. 1. μεταταῦτα (*sic v.* 14) i. +ἡ (*ante* ἑορτη) ivw [*non* L]. -ὁ w.
-εστι δε εν τοις ἱεροσολυμοις L. εστιν wH. ἑστη P. ἑβραιστη iP.
αϊστη v. βιθεσδα iL. βηθεσδᾶ z. *Rasura in* P *inter* δ *et* α. 3. ταυ-
L*. χολων iL. 4. *Obelo notat rubro* w. +κυ (*post* γαρ) wL. ελουετο
ο κατεβαινεν) w. εταρασσετο το vH. εταρασσεν P* [iwLz *cum Elzev.*].
(*sic vv.* 10, 12, 18, 19) P. ενβᾶς P. εγενετο iLHz [*non* v]. εγεινετο P.
ν (*pro* δηποτε) w. κατηχετο i. κατειχε v. 5. +και (*post* τριακοντα)
P. ὠκτῶ i. ὀκτῶ HP. τρϊακονταοκτὼ w**z. 6. πολλυν z. ἠδη P.
εἶς P. 7. +ναι (*ante* κε) vz. ανπον ?L*. ὁτ' ἂν iw. ὅτἂν P. βαλλει i.
ιη vwHz. βαλει L. -εγω L. *fin.* +εγω δε ασθενων πορευομαι L. 8.
ιρε ivwLP (+και w) [*non* z]. αρων P. κραβαττον (*sic vv.* 9, 10, 11, 12,
ι. 12 κραβατον w*) iwH [*non* vPz]. κραββαττον (*sic vv.* 9, 10, 11, 12) L.
+εγερθεις (*ante* ἠρε) L. ἠρεν w. ἧρεν P. ἧν (*sic v.* 35) P. ἦν z. 10.
ι. το τεθεραπευμενον L. +και (*ante* ουκ) L. εξεστιν P. ἆρε i. *fin.* +σου
z. 11. *init.* +ὁ δε w. 12. ἠρωτησαν iwP. -ὁ ανθρωπος i. 13. οἶδει L.

ὀχλου H. οντως iz. 14. εὑρισκει P. ὑγιεῖς i. μὴκέτι iwLP [*non* z]. σοι τι ivPz [*non* L]. γενητε i. 15. ανηγγειλεν wP. απηγγειλε Lz. 16. διατοῦτο (*sic v.* 18 *etiam* z) ivLz. οἱ ιουδαιοι τον ιησουν L. —και εζητουν αυτον αποκτειναι L. επιει i. *fin.* +τα ιαματα iv. 18. διὰ τούτο P. —αυτον P* (*habet marg.*). οὐ H. ελυεν wP. τω (*pro* το) P. ελεγεν wP. ἶσον w. ἱσων P. ἶσον vz (ι *eraditur in* i). ἑαὐτον L. ἑαὐτον P. 19. +του ανου (*post* υἱος) L. αφ' ἑαυτου ποιειν L. βλεπει i. ποιοῦντα w. ποιει (*pro* ποιῇ) iwP. τα γαρ εργα ἁ ἐκεινος ποιει (—αν) z. *fin.* ποιη ?L*. 20. —γαρ z. πιει i. μειζωνα iwP. θαυμαζεται L. θαυμαζετε P. 21. *Rasura in* i *ante* οὑτως. οὑτως ivwLHz. οὑτος P. 22. *init.* ου (*pro* ουδε) i*. κρινεῖ w. οὐδ' ἑνα z. δεδωκεν wHPz. αυτω (*pro* τῳ υἱῳ) z. 23. τιμώσιν *bis* P. 24. *Bis scriptus hic versus in* i. των λογων i (των L*?). ακουον P *sem.* 25. εσται (*pro* εστιν) L. ακουσωσι Lz. υἱ *in* υἱου *mutat. in* w. ανου (*pro* θυ̅) wz. ζησουσιν z. 26. οὗτος L. εδωκεν wP. 27. +του (*ante* ανου) v. *fin.* εστιν wP. —εστι (*nullo puncto ad fin. vers.*) L. 28. θαυμαζητε H. ερχετε i. 30. *init.* οὐ H. εμη (η *mutat.*) w. εστι L. —πατρος w. 31. +γαρ (*post* εαν) i. ἐμ' αὐτου w. αληθεῖς P. 32. οἶδα i. οἶδατε P. +αυτου (*post* μαρτυρια) i. ἦν wH. μεμαρτυρηκε L, μαρτυρειτε z (*pro* μαρτυρει). 33. και *rescript.* P. μεμαρτυρηκεν wH. μεμαρτυρικεν P. 34. περι (*pro* παρα) L. λαμβανω την μαρτυριαν z. ὑμει L. 35. ἦν P. ἠθελησατε iwHP. αγαλλιαθηναι ivwHz [*non* L]. αγαλληαθηναι P. 36. μειζον L. μειζων Pz. εδωκεν wP. δεδωκε Lz. τελεσω L. ἁ H. —εγω *secund.* z. +και (*ante* ὁτι) L. απεσταλκεν wHP. 37. μεμαρτυρικε i. μεμαρτυρηκεν wH. μεμαρτυρικεν P. φωνης i. πωποτε ακηκοατε iwL. πῶποτε z. ἑωρακατε H. 38. απεσταλκεν H. τουτον iLP, τουτου z (*pro* τουτῳ). 39. δοκῆτε L. αἰκειναι (*pro* και εκειναι) z. 40. +αιωνιον (*post* ζωην) L. εχειτε P. 41. ανου iw. 42. ὁτϊ (ϊ *mutat.*) w. ἔχεχετε w. *fin.* αυτοις v. 43. ὀνοματι *prim.* P. ἐλθη w. *fin.* λειψεσθαι P* (-ε P**). 44. δυνασθαι P. παρ' vL. ανων (*pro* αλληλων) iH. λαμβανωντες P*. —την *secund.* L. οὐ H. 45. δοκῆτε LP. κατηγορεισω P. πρα ;vwz. μωυσης w. 46. μωσει iv** LHPz. μωυσει w. επιστευσατε (*pro* επιστευετε *secund.*) i. 47. ρημασιν P. *fin.* πιστευσητε (*pro* πιστευσετε) iLz [*non* vP].

Cap. VI. 1. +δε (*post* μετα) L. απηλ L, *at* ηλθεν z. —της θαλασσης H. —της γαλιλαιας iH. γαλλιλαιας P. 2. ηκολουθη δε (—και) L. ἠκολουθει H. ἠκολουθη wP. ηκολουθησαν z. ὀχλος P. ἑωρουν P, *at* εθεωρουν Lz. —αυτου iwL. 3. ανηλθεν ουν (—δε) L. εκαθεζετο L. 4. +οἱ (*post* των) w. 5. *Hiat* z *usque ad v.* 14. —ουν P *init. peric.* τους οφθαλμους ὁ ιησους wL.

ὀφθαλμους wHP. πολλυς ὀχλος P. προς αυτον ερχεται w. αγορασωμεν ivwL. αγωρασωμεν P. ἵνα P. οὑτοι H. 6. ειπεν w*, *at* ελεγεν w**HP. ῄδει i. οιδει L. ἡδη P. ημελλε iv**. μελλε v*. εμελλεν w. ημελλεν H. ἠμελλεν P. 7. απεκριθει L. +ὁ (*ante* φιλιππος) v**. ἑκαστος H. ἑκαστον P. –αυτων wL. 8. αυτον (*pro* αυτῳ) P. –αυτου w*. –ὁ L. 9. εστιν wHP. –ἐν wL. ὠδε v. ὡδε (*sic v.* 25) P *solus*. ὁς (*pro* ὁ) P. ὀψαρια iP. ὀψορια w. 10. ειπεν (*sic v.* 35 w) wHP. ε (*pro* δε) v*. ἠν P. πολλυς P. ανεπεσαν vLHP. –ουν P. +ανθρωποι (*ante* ανδρες) w*. των αριθμων LP. 11. ελαβεν wHP. και λαβων (–δε) L. +εις τας χειρας (*post* ὁ ις) P** *marg.* εδωκε L. διεδωκεν HP. –τοις μαθηταις οἱ δε μαθηται w* (*habet marg.*). ὀψαριων wP. ὁσον ὁσον i*. ὁσων L. ἠθελον P. 12. σιναγαγετε L*. περισευσαντα P. απωλνηται v. αποllηται L. απωλειται P. 13. οὐν (*sic vv.* 14, 15, 19, 24, 30 *bis*, 32, 41, 42, 43, 52, 53, 62**, 68, *non vv.* 28, 67) P. εγεμησαν iP. κωφινους v. κωφηνους P. σκλασ H**. επερισσευσεν wH. περιεσευσαν P. 14. οἱ w. οἱ ουν οἱ L. εποιησεν wHP. σημειων P* *sem.* 15. ὁ ουν ιησους L. γνοὺς iv. +οἱ οχλοι (*post* ερχεσθαι) i. ἁρπαζειν (ν *mutat.*) w. ἁρπαζειν HP. ποιησωσι (–αυτον *secund.*) z. ανεχωρησεν wLHP. –παλιν LHPz [*non* iw]. ὁρος P. 16. ὀψια iwP. οψιας z*. εις (*pro* επι) L. θαλασαν H. 17. αναβαντες w. εμβαντος z. +εις το (*ante* περαν) L. σκοτεια iP. ἠδη P. ουπω (*pro* ουκ) L. εληλυθη iw*P. *fin.* +εις το πλοιον iw. 18. ἡτε w. –μεγαλου i*L. διεγειρετο L. 19. εληλακοτος Lz. ὡσει (*pro* ὡς) i, *at* ὡ P*. θεωρουσιν P. γενομενου L. γενομενον HP. –και *secund.* L. 20. λεγει αυτοις ὁ ις (–ὁ δε) v. φοβησθε i*. φοβεισθαι w. 21. ἠθελον P. αυτον λαβειν L. εγενετο το πλοιον L. την γην L. ἠν w. 22. ἐπ' αὑριον w. –ὁ *secund.* v. ἑστηκὼς wH. ἑστηκος P*. ἑστως z. ιδον w. ειδων P*. αλλο πλοιαριον L. αλλω P*. ἠν P. εκεινω w**P. ὀν (*pro* ὁ) w**L*. εκεινο εις ὁ ενεβησαν οἱ μαθηται αυτου *deest in* w* (*habet* w** *marg.*). ανεβησαν z. του ιησου (*pro* αυτου *prim.*) L. συνησηλθε i*. συνεισηλθεν w. –ὁ ις i. πλοιον (*pro* πλοιαριον *secund.*) wL. –αλλα μονοι *ad fin. vers.* z. 23. ἠλθεν wH. ἦλθεν P. ηλθον z. +της (*ante* τιβεριαδος) iP**. ευχαρηστησαντος ?w*. ιυ (*pro* κυ) vw. –ευχαριστησαντος του κυριου L*. 24. ιδεν w. +ὁ (*ante* ιησους) L. ελαβον αυτοι τα πλοιαρια (*pro* ενεβησαν και αυτοι εις τα πλοια) L. ανεβησαν z. –και *prim.* ivwHPz. ἦλθον P. *fin.* αυτον (*pro* τον ιν) w. 25. εὑροντες P. ῥαββεῖ P. ὧδε z. 26. ειπε v. οὐχ' (*sic ferè vv.* 38, 42, 46) ivwPz. ιδετε iwPz. ι *mutat. in* ὁτι *secund.* w. 27. απολλημενην L. –την βρωσιν *secund.* vL. ἠν H. ἠν P. δωση ὑμιν L. δ *in* δωσει *mutat.* w. τουτο (*pro* τουτον) L. εσφραγησεν P. 28. ποιησομεν L.

ποιουμεν z. εργαζομεθα i. 29. –ὁ ivw*HPz. εστιν w*P. +ἁπαντες (*post* ἱνα) L. 30. *init.* λεγουσιν αυτω οἱ ιουδαιοι H *sem.* (*init. peric.*). –συ iLz. ειδωμεν L. ἴδομεν P. πιστευσομεν L. *fin.* εργαζ (η *eras.*) v. 31. ὑμων (*pro* ἡμων) wL*. εφαγον το μαννα iL. μανα P. εστιν P. ἀρτον i. δεδωκεν L. 32. –αμην *semel* L. μωυσης w. εδωκεν i. –τον *prim.* i. *Post* τον αρτον *prim. desunt omnia in* L *præter* τον αληθινον. –αλλ᾽ ὁ πηρ *usque ad* ουρανου *secund.* z. ουρανον *secund.* v. 33. καταβαινον (*sic v.* 50) H* *semel* z. (κ *mutat. in* L). διδους ζωην w. 35. ειπεν w. ειπεν ουν (–δε) L. πεινασει P. πιστευον H. διψησει HP. πωποτε z. 36. ἑορακατε H. οὐ H. 37. ὡ (*pro* ὁ) i *hic.* διδωσιν wH. με (*pro* εμε) wP**. ἡξει iv. εμε (*pro* με) v. εκβαλλω L. 38. απο (*pro* εκ) L. 39. εστιν HPz*. δεδωκεν wHP. απωλεσω iz*. αλλ᾽ iLP**. αυτον (*pro* αυτο) iHz. –εν iv [*non* L]. 40. γαρ (*pro* δε) wL. –δε Pz *init. peric.* εστιν P. +πρς (*ante* ἱνα) LP. εχει iLPz. εγω αναστησω αυτον i. +εν (*ante* τη εσχατη) iwL [*non* vP]. *fin.*; w. 41. *Partim rescript. in* i. εγγογιζον (*non v.* 61) L. οἱ *sæpe* H. ιουδαιοι z** *super rasur.* –περι αυτου L. ε *in* εγω *mutat.* L. ὁ εκ του ουρανου καταβας L. 42. οὑτος *prim.* H, *bis* P. –ιησους iw. οὑ HP. οἰδαμεν w. οἴδαμεν P. –ουν v. –οὑτος *secund.* iL. –ὁτι L. κατεβηκα z. 43. –ουν wL. ἱνατί γογγιζετε (–μη) L. 44. ἑλκυση ivH. ἑλκυσει L. ἑλκυσει P. +εν (*ante* τη εσχατη) ivwLPz. 45. προφηταις i. –του *prim.* ivwL. –ουν L. ακουων v. 46. ὁ ὡν w. ἑωρακεν w. 49. ἡμων LP. μανα L. 50. ἐξ z. φαγει (*sic v.* 51) P. αποθανει i*. 51. ἡ εμη (*pro* μου) L. ἠν z. 52. ὑν (*pro* ουν) w*. οἱ w. οἱ ιουδαιοι προς αλληλους L. την σαρκα δουναι ἡμιν L. ὑμιν i. 53. –ουν v. ποιητε i. πιετε Lz. *fin.* ἑαυτοις HP *sæpe.* 54. τρογων (*sic v.* 57) P. κἀγω w. –εγω P. +εν (*ante* τη εσχατη) vwLz [*non* iP]. 55. –γαρ w. αληθης *bis* iw, *prim. tantum* L. 57. απεστειλεν wHP. απεσταλκε L. *Rasura in* w *inter* ὁ *et* ζων. ζησει w. ζηση L. *fin.* διεμοῦ H. 58. ἡμων P (η *et* υ *ambo formantur in* L). ζησει ivHz. ζησετε w. 60. ὁ λογος οὑτος w. οὑτως P. ακουειν αυτου L. 61. εγνω (*pro* ειδως) L. ουν (*pro* δε) Lz. γογγυζουσιν wP. +και (*ante* ειπεν) L. 62. –ουν P* (οὐν P**). θεωρειτε ivP. ἠν P. πρωτερον P. 63. εστιν *prim.* H, *ter* P. σαρξ P. οὐκ᾽ i. οφελει ουδενα L. ἁ H. λελαληκα wL. 64. ἠδη P. οἱ (*pro* οἱ) w. ἐξ i. ἐξαρχῆς L *solus.* 65. ελεγεν wP. διατοῦτο (*sic* VII. 22 vLz) ivLz. –ὁτι w. οὐδεῖς i *hic.* ἠ H. 66. +ουν (*ante* πολλοι) L. των μαθητων αυτου απηλθον wL (μ *eras. in* L *ante* αυτου). απηλθων P (+εκ ?P*). ὀπισω HP. οὐκ ἐτι iP [*non* vwLHz]. 67. +μαθηταις (*post* δωδεκα) L. ὑπαειν P. 68. –ουν iwLz. απελευσωμεθα P. ῥημα P*. 70. –απεκριθη αυτοις ὁ ις (ειπε

:n *eras.*) i. −ὁ ις v. αυτω (*pro* αυτοις) L. ἀγω L. ἐξ w. 71. ελεγεν
ἰοῦδαν L. σιμονος i. αποκαριωτου (*pro* ισκαριωτου) L. εμελλεν w.
λε παραδιδοναι αυτον L. εἷς v. ὢν w. −εκ v.
CAP. VII. 1. και μετα ταυτα περιεπατει ὁ ις iwL. −και *et* μετα ταυτα Pz
peric. ι *in* ις *mutat* P. οὐ H. αυτον οἱ ιουδαιοι εζητουν i. *Verbum eras.*
αποκτειναι P. 2. ἦν (*sic vv.* 12, 39) P. 3. −αυτου P* (*habet* P**
r.). μεταβηθη P. +συ (*ante* ποιεις) i. *fin.* ποιης z. 4. τι εν κρυπτω w.
ιρρησια αυτος L. σεαυτὸν P *passim.* 5. ου (*pro* ουδε) L. 6. εγει v*.
ι H. ἡμετερος i*. ἑτοιμος P. 8. αναβηται P. ἑορτην *bis* (*sic vv.* 11,
1. −ταυτην *prim.* w*. ουπω αναβαιν *rescript.* i. ουκ (*pro* ουπω *prim.*)
ου) [*non* vLz]. οὔπω *prim.* H. καταβαινω (*pro* αναβαινω) P. −εις την
ην ταυτην *secund.* L. ὁ εμος καιρος L. οὔπω *secund.* P. 9. *init.* ταῦ z.
νP. αυτος (*pro* αυτοις) w. 10. Ὡς *rubro* i. εις την ἑορτην, τοτε και
ς ανεβη w. 11. οἱ ουν οἱ wz. ιου *mutat.* P. −εν τῃ ἑορτῃ L. 12.
.υς i. −δε ivwHPz [*non* L]. −ελεγον *secund.* L. οὐ *rescript.* i. ουχι w.
οχλους L. οχλ *rescript.* P. 13. μεντοιγε z. 14. −ηδη δε Pz *init.*
. μεσαζουσης L. −ὁ ις i*. −εις το ἱερον P* (*habet supra*). εδιδασκεν
IP. 15. οὗτος H. οὑτως P. ειδε i. οἱδεν wH**. οἱδεν P. μαθηκως w.
+ουν (*post* απεκριθη) ivwLHP (οὖν P) z. −αυτοις iw, *at* +αυτοις (*post* ειπεν) i.
γνωσετε H. προτερον L. εις (*pro* η) L. ἡ P. ἐμ' αὐτοῦ P *pass.*
λω z. 18. ἑαύτου w. οὗτος (*sic vv.* 25, 26, 46 *bis*) P. αληθεις P.
ι *prim.* LP. 19. μωυσης w. ἡμιν (*pro* ὑμιν) L. αποκτιναι P. 20.
ριθησαν ουν οἱ ιουδαιοι και ειπαν αυτω w. ειπεν vLHP. τισε i. απο-
αι P. 21. −ὁ ivLHPz [*non* w]. 22. μωυσης wL. οὐχ' (*sic ferè vv.*
4, 35, 36) ivwHPz. μωυσεως (*sic v.* 23) wL. εστι i. περιτεμνεται iP.
i [*non* P]. 23. ὁλον iP. εποιησα ὑγιη L. 24. κρινατε (*pro* κρινετε)
25. ελεγουν i. ἱεροσολυμητων ivwLP. οὐχ' w. 26. −και *prim.* iwL.
ι ? w*. αυτον (*pro* αυτῳ) P. λεγουσιν iwL. −αληθως *secund.* w*L. −ὁ
fin. · v*. 27. ὅτ' ἂν wHP. ερχηται vwH [*non* iLP]. ερχητε z.
στι H. 28. εκραζον z. ὁ ις διδασκων εν τω ἱερω i. ὁ ιησους εν τω ἱερω
κων L. οἶδατε *secund.* w, *at* οἰδατε P. ἐμ' αὐτοῦ P. 29. −δε ivLPz
w]. καγω (*pro* εγω δε) H. οἶδα P. 30. πιᾶσαι (*sic v.* 44, ivz) iv.
. εξηλθεν εκ της χειρος αυτων (*post* πιασαι) L. οὐδεὶς P. χειραν L.
ι γαρ (−ὁτι) L. οὔπω wP. εληλυθη iP. ὡρα P. 31. εκ του οχλου
νw) πολλοι (−δε) wL (ποιλλοι L). −ὁτι L. ὅτ' ἂν iw. μη (*pro* μητι) i**w..
ντων i*wL. ποιηση ivL. *fin.* ποιει ; L. εποιησε v. 32. *init.* +και L.
ν (*post* ηκουσαν) iw. γογγιζοντος L. οἱ αρχιερεις και οἱ φαρισαιοι wL.

ὑπηρετας οἱ φαρισαιοι και οἱ αρχιερεις iv. *ὑ in ὑπηρετας mutat.* L. 33. –αυτοις vwL. χρονον μικρον L. 34. ζητειτε L. +με (*post* εὑρησετε) w. εγω ειμι L. εισελθειν w. 35. αυτους (*pro* ἑαυτους) L. εὑρησωμεν w. 36. ὁ λογος οὑτος wL. ειπεν (*sic v.* 39 wLP) wL. ζητειτε L. εγω ειμι L. –ὑμεις L. οὑ w. 37. –δε P, –εν δε z, *init. peric.* ἑορτης H. εἰστηκει ivwHP. εκραξεν wP. εκραζε L. 38. ῥευσουσιν ivL. ρευσουσιν wHPz. 39. ειπεν H. ὁ (*pro* οὑ) z, *forsan* P*. ημελλον ivLH. ἡμελλον P. ημελλ (*ultimâ syllabâ erasâ*) z. οὑπω HP. ἠν H. –ἁγιον w. –ὁ (*ante* ις) ivwLHPz. οὑδεπω H. 40. οὑν (*sic vv.* 43, 45, 47) P. ὀχλου HP. +αυτου (*post* λογον) iP**. των λογων wH (+αυτου w). οὑτος H. 41. +δε (*post* αλλοι *prim.*) L. +ὁτι (*ante* οὑτος) L. –δε ivwLHP. –οὑτος εστιν ὁ χς· αλλοι δε ελεγον z. ερχεται ὁ χς w. 42. –του L. ἠν P. 43. ὀχλω H. 44. ἡθελον P. εξ αυτων ηθελον z. οὑδεὶς w, οὑδεὶς P. ἐπέβαλλεν P. 45. ἠλθον P. οἱ H. –εκεινοι w*. διατί ivLz. δίατί w. οὑκ H. ἠγαγετε P. 46. +αυτοις (*post* απεκριθησαν) P. +προς τους αρχιερεις και φαρισαιους (*post* ὑπηρεται) L. –ὁ L. 47. –ουν i. –αυτοις L. 48. –εκ *prim.* L. ἠ P. 49. ὁ *prim.* w. ὀχλος P. –οὑτος L. επικαταρρατοι L. εισιν wLP. 50. νικοδιμος P. προς αυτον νυκτος w. +το προτερον (*ante* εἱς) L. ὤν w. ὢν P. · ἐξ P. 51. κρινη z. πρωτον iwL. ποιη ;z. 52. ειπαν w. ειδε L. εγειγερται iz. εγειρεται w.

Cap. VII. 53—VIII. 11. *Habent* ivw *nullo suspicionis vestigio* (i, πβ *in textu,* περι της μοιχαλιδος *ad calcem rubro:* v *habet,* ι περι της μοιχαλιδος *ad caput paginæ rubro; in* vw *deest pericope Ammoniana, at* w *habet rubro* εις τας ἑορ. πελαγιου και μαριας και ευδοκιας και θεωδωρας. *In* L, *prorsus omittitur hoc loco, nullo spatio interposito; at legitur ad fin. Lucæ* xxi (*notat in marg. manus planè recens*). *In* HP *semel* z *semel deest omnino quamvis in mediâ pericopâ; at* P *habet* viii. 3—11 της ἁγιας θεοδωρας (*Sept.* 18), *et* z viii. 1—11 του πελαγιου και εις λοιπας ἁγ.

Cap. VII. 53. απηλθεν (*pro* επορευθη) L. τα ιδια (*pro* τον οικον) L. VIII. 1. και ὁ ιησους (–δε) L. επορευθη ὁ ις (–δε) z *init. peric.* προς (*pro* εις) i. 2. +βαθεος (*post* παλιν) w** *marg.* ηλθεν (*pro* παρεγενετο) L. –προς αυτον vw. –και πας ὁ λαος *ad fin. vers.* Lz. 3. ξ αρ. *marg.* i *rubro.* Αγουσιν (Α *rubro*) w. και προσηνεγκαν αυτω (*pro* αγουσι δε) L. –δε P *init. peric.* –προς αυτον LPz. επι (*pro* εν *prim.*) iLPz [*non* w]. μοιχειαν L. μοιχια P. καταληφθεισαν vw. κατηλημμενην P. +τω (*ante* μεσω) iL. 4. ειπον (*pro* λεγουσιν) iL. τω ιυ (*pro* αυτῳ) P. +πειραζοντες (*ante* διδασκαλε) vw. αὑτη P. ειληπται iL. κατεληφθη vw. κατηληπται Pz*?. κατειληπται z**. ἐπ' αὐτοφορῳ iwz. επαυτοφορω vL. ἐπ' αὐτωφορω P. 5. +ἡμων (*post* νομω) iw**z. και εν τω νομω ἡμων (−δε) P. μωυσης w. −ἡμιν iPz. ἡμιν μωσης L. ἐνετείλάτω P. λιθαζειν iLz. λιθαζεσθαι P. οὖν P. *fin.* +περι αυτης iL. 6. ειπον (*pro* ελεγον) Pz. εκπειραζοντες Pz. −αυτον P* (*habet marg.* P**). σχωσι i. κατηγοριαν κατ' αυτου iL. σχωσι [ν P] κατηγοριαν Pz. κατακυψας v*. κάτοκυψας v**. εγραψεν L. *fin.* +μη προσποιουμενος vw. 7. ανεκυψε [ν Pz] και ειπεν (λεγει z) αυτοις (−προς) iPz. ειπεν w. αναβλεψας ειπεν αυτοις (−ανακυψας *et* προς) L. αναμαρτιτος P. ἡμων (*pro* ὑμων) w. επαυτη τον λιθον i. ἐπ' αυτην τον λιθον vw. −τον L. επ' αυτη λιθον P. βαλετω επ' αυτην L. βαλλετω w. βαλετω λιθον επ' αυτην z. 9. −οἱ δε *usque ad* ελεγχομενοι (*incipit* και εξηλθον εἷς καθείς) L. −και ὑπο *usque ad* ελεγχομενοι P. +ιδιας (*ante* συνειδησεως) z. καθεῖς ivw. καθεῖς Pz. −ἑως των εσχατων vw* (*habet marg.* w**) P. κατεληφθη i*Pz*. −μονος iLPz. *fin.* ουσα (*pro* ἑστωσα) ivwLPz (οὖσα w). 10. αναβλεψας (*pro* ανακυψας) L. −και μηδενα *usque ad* γυναικος LPz (*habent* Lz ειδεν αυτην και ειπεν). −αυτῃ L. γυναι (−ἡ) iLPz (γῦναι iz). −ἡ γυνη vw. −εκεινοι iLPz. −οἱ κατηγοροι σου P. οὐδεῖς (*sic v.* 11) P. 11. *init.* ει δε P. ὁ δε ι̅ς̅ ειπεν αυτῃ i. ειπεν *bis* wP. −αυτῃ vwz. και ὁ ιησους ειπεν αυτη (−δε) L. κρινῶ vw. −και L. +απο του νυν (*ante* μηκετι) iPz. μὴκέτι iwPz.

Cap. VIII. 12. αυτοις ὁ ι̅ς̅ ivwHPz. ελαλησεν wHP. παλιν ουν αυτοις ελαλησεν ὁ ιησους L. ακολουθον i. περιπατηση vwHz. σκοτεια iwLP. ἑξει H. ἑξη z. 13. οὖν (*sic vv.* 12, 19, 22, 24, 25, 28, 36, 38, 41, 42, 52, 57, 59, *non* 48) P. μαρτυρεις; vwLz. αληθεις *hic* z. 14. +ὁ (*ante* ιησους) L. οἶδα (*sic v.* 37) i. −δε vw. −ὑμεις δε *ad fin. vers.* LHP*z. οἴδατε P**. ερχομε P**. η που (*pro* και που *secund.*) iwP** (ἡ P**). 15. ουδ' ἑνα z. 16. −δε i. δε εγω κρινω L. −ὁτι μονος *ad fin. v.* 17, L. +εγω (*ante* αλλ') H. 18. *Rescript. super rasur.* P*. 19. εκεινος (*pro* ὁ π̅η̅ρ̅ σου) P. −ὁ *secund.* ivwHPz. οὐτε *bis* H. ειδειτε *prim.* iL. ειδητε *bis* v. ιδητε *bis* z. οιδατε *secund.* L. ἠδειτε P. 20. −τα ῥηματα z. −ὁ ι̅ς̅ w*. γαζωφυλακιω w*H. γαζοφυλακειω vz. επηασεν ?w*. οὐπω H. εληλυθη iw*z. 21. ζητειτε L. αποθανεισθαι P. +και (*ante* ὁπου) i. ὑπαγω εγω *secund.* z. 22. *init.* +και L. +αυτω (*post* ουν) z. ιδαιοι L. αυτον (*pro* ἑαυτον) L. ὁπου P. 23. ελεγεν (*pro* ειπεν) L. εσται P*. τω ανω L. *fin.* τουτου του κοσμου L. 24. αποθανεισθαι *prim.* wP*. −μη w* (*supra* w**). εαν γαρ μη πις *super rasur.* P. +μοι (*post* πιστευσητε) L. 25. −και *prim.* L. ὁτι ivwLHPz. 26. ὁ w. αλληθης P. εστιν vwLHP. ἡκουσα wHP. λαλω (*pro* λεγω) iwL. 27. +ουν (*ante* ὁτι) L. 28. −ουν i. ι̅ς̅ (ι *mutat.*) w. ὁτ' ἀν (*sic v.* 44 i, ὅτᾶν w) iw. ὀτᾶν H. εδιδαξεν wH**P. –μου L. οὑτως (*pro* ταυτα) H. *fin.* ποιω L*H, λαλω L** *supra.* 29. –με L. αφηκεν wHP. –ὁ πατηρ L. +μου (*post* πηρ) i. 31. εληλυθοτας (*pro* πεπιστευκοτας) H. μαθητε w. 32. *Rasura post* και *prim.* w. ελευθερωση v*L. 33. +και ειπον (*post* απεκ.) H. +οἱ ιουδαιοι (*ante* σπερμα) iLP** *marg.* ἀβρααμ (*sic vv.* 37, 39 *ter*, 40, 52, 53, 56, 57, 58) ivwLH [*non* P]. +και (*ante* πως) L. –ὀτι L. 34. –αμην αμην λεγω ὑμιν ὀτι i. εστιν HP. 35. οὐ H. μενεῖ *bis* i. οἰκια P. 36. –ουν L. ελευθερωσει P. ὀντως iH. οντος L. 37. οἶδα wH. 38. *init.* εγω δε ἃ (*pro* ὃ) L. ἑωρακα wP. –ουν i. ἃ (*pro* ὃ *secund.*) wL. ηκουσατε (*pro* ἑωρακατε) iwL. του πρς *secund.* w. ἡμων (*pro* ὑμων) w*. *fin.* ποιητε ?i*. 39. αυτω και ειπον L. εστιν wLHP. τεκνον P*. ἠτε vw. εποιητε?w*. –αν HP. –τα εργα *ad fin. vers.* L. 40. ανος L. λελαληκα ὑμιν L. ἤκουσα wHP. του πρς μου (*pro* του θῦ) L. εποιησε L. 41. ποιητε v*. τε τα εργα *in marg.* i, *vix prim. manu.* πορνειας (α *mutat.*) L. πορνιας H. γεγενημεθα vwL. ἑνα P. 42. –ουν w. ἦν (*sic v.* 44) P. ἠγαπάτε i. ἠγαπατε wH *sem.* P. ἂν H *sem.* ἡκω ivwHP *sem.* ου (*pro* ουδε) L. απεστειλεν wLHP. 43. διὰ τί (*sic ferè v.* 46) vwP [*non* L]. τον εμον λογον L. 44. +του (*ante* πρς *prim.*) ivwLP. +ὑμων iP** (*post* πρς *prim.*, υ *vel* η *eras. in* i). ενθυμησεις i. ανθρωποκτονως w. ἀπαρχῆς iLH. ἀπάρχῆς P. οὐκ ἑστηκεν iw L**P. (οὐκεσ. w, οὐκ' P *bis*, *sic vv.* 49, 55). ἑστηκαν?L*. αληθεια ουκ εστιν v. ὅτ' ἂν H. λαλει (*pro* λαλῃ) iHP. εστιν *secund.* wLHP (*jungunt cum sequent.* wLH). +καθως (*post* εστιν *secund.*) P** *marg.*, *at eras.* 46. *Deest versus in* v. ἐξ' wP. –δε w*L. +την (*ante* αληθειαν) L. διὰ τί H. 47. ὢν w. ὢν P. διατοῦτο ivL. διὰ τούτο P. 48. –ουν LH. λεγωμεν i. ὑμεις wL. σαμαρειτις HP. +ὀτι (*ante* δαιμονιον) L. 49. απεκριθη ὁ ιησους και ειπεν L. +και ειπεν αυτοις (*post* ις) v. 50. –δε L. 51. ἀ'Αμὴν (A *rubro*) v. 'Εἂν ('Ε *rubro*) i. τηρησει (*sic v.* 52) P. θεωρησει HP. 52. απεθανεν (*sic etiam* P, *v.* 53) wH. –μου i. γευσηται iwHP [*non* v]. γευσητε L. θανατον w. αιωνα; v. 53. ἠ (*pro* ει) L. +του (*ante* ἀβρααμ) L. απεθανεν P. –συ *secund.* w*. 54. +ὁ (*ante* ιησους) L. –εγω i. δοξασω L. ἐμαυτὸν w. λεγεται P. ἡμων (*pro* ὑμων) vwL*HP [*non* i]. εστιν wLHP. 55. οἶδα *secund.* w. οἶδα *tert.* iw (*prim. et secund.* P). οἶδα *prim. et tert.* H. οὐκ H. εσωμαι P. ὀμοιως P. 56. ἡμων P*?. ἠγαλλιασατο iwHP. ειδη (*pro* ιδῃ) L. ἡμε *rescript.* i. ιδε i, ειδεν H**, ιδεν wH*P (*pro* ειδε). εχαρην LP*. 57. ουδαιοι (*sic* IX. 22) w*. πεντικοντα H. οὐπω P. ἑωρακας HP. 58. +ουν (*post* ειπεν) iL. γενέσθε L. 59. ἠραν wP. βαλλωσιν LP. βαλουσιν ?H*. εκριβη i. εκριβει L. εξηλθεν απ' αυτων δια μεσου εκ του ἱερου (–διελθων) L. διέλθὼν w. διαμέσου i.

CAP. IX. [*A capite* VIII. 29 *usque ad* X. 1, z *hiat omnino*]. 1. −και P
it. peric. +ὁ ις (*post* παραγων) v. ιδεν iw. γεννητης vwP. γενετής L.
ἠρωτησαν wHP. ῥαββεῖ P. τι (*pro* τις) L. ἡμαρτεν· L. οὗτος ἢ P.
+αυτοις (*post* απεκριθη) i. −ὁ vwLHP [*non* i]. οὔτε *prim.* P, *secund.* i.
τε *secund.* P. 4. ερχετε νυξ' P. οὐδεὶς wP. δυνατε P. 5. ὅτ' ἂν wH.
' ἂν P. ῳ̃ i. ὦ vw. 6. επτυσεν wHP. εποιησεν (*sic vv.* 11, 26) wHP.
ρισματος i. επεχρησε (*sic v.* 11) i. επεχρισεν (*sic v.* 11 wH**) wLH**P.
τον πηλον L. ὀφθαλμους (*sic vv.* 11, (14 w), 15, 17, 21, 26, 30, 32, *non*
10) wP. 7. εις τον σιλωαμ την κολυμβῆθραν L. ἑρμηνευεται P. οὖν (*sic*
. 8, 10, 12, 15, 16, 18, 19, 24, 25) P. ηλθεν wH**P. 8. +προσαῖτης
post τυφλος) w, +και προσαίτης (*ante* ελεγον) L. ἦν (*sic vv.* 14, 16, 24, 33)
οὐχ' ivwHP. 9. οὗτος P. +δε (*post* εκεινος) vwLP. 10. ἠνεωχθησαν i.
εωχθησαν vP. σου (*pro* σοι) ivwLHP. 11. επεχρησεν P. ὀφθαλμους H
passim. ειπεν *secund.* (*sic vv.* 36, 37) wHP. ὕπαγε νιψαι εις την κολυμβηθ-
ν του σιλωαμ (−και) iwL. −δε w. 12. *Rasura inter* ειπον *et* ουν w. +αυτοις
post λεγει) L. οἶδα i. 13. φρισαιους L. 14. ηνεωξεν i. 15. ηρωτησαν
ἠρωτων w. ἠρωτησαν P. −και *prim.* L. επεθηκε [ν wH**] μου επι (−επι
) τους οφθαλμους [ὀφθ. wHP] ivwLHP. 16. εστιν vwHP. εκ (*pro*
παρα) v. −του w*LP. +δε (*post* αλλοι) L. 17. λεγουσιν wLH**P (+ουν L).
εωξε i. ανεωξεν w. ἠνοιξεν P. 18. −ουν L. ἦν P. ἕως P. ὁτου H.
ωνης P**, γωνῆς ?P*. 19. ἠρωτησαν wHP. 20. +δε (*post* απεκριθησαν)
HP [*non* wL]. −αυτοις L. οἴδαμεν H. οἶδαμεν (*sic v.* 21 *prim.*) P. ὑμων
*. 21. ἢ P. ἠνοιξεν P. οἶδαμεν *secund.* (*sic* P *vv.* 24, 29) vP. +δε (*post*
τος) w. ἡλικιαν (*sic v.* 23) v. περι ἑαυτου iwH [αὑτου vL]. 22. τοις
δαιοις P*. ἤδη P. συνετιθοντο L. ὁμολογηση αυτον wL** (ὠμολ. L*).
ολογησει P. ἀπὸσυνάγως P. 23. διατοῦτο ivwL. ειπον οἱ γονεις αυτου
ηλῐκιαν w (*sic*). 24. ἁμαρτωλος i. 25. −ουν iw. −και ειπεν w* (*habet*
** *marg.*). οἶδα *secund.* i. ὢν P. 26. ουν (*pro* δε) wL. ανεωξεν w.
οιξεν H**. ἠνοιξεν P. 27. ἤδη P. οὐκ' ἠκουσατε P. επιστευσατε (*pro*
ουσατε) L. μὴ *interrogativè* P. μαθηται αυτου ivP. −αυτου L. 28.
ιδορησαν P*. −ουν ivwHP [*non* L]. ειπαν P. μωυσεως w. 29. μωσει ivL.
ωυσει (ει *mutat.*) w [*non* P]. 30. τούτο HP. εστι *prim.* L. οὐκ' P.
τιν *secund.* HP. ανεωξεν P. 31. οἴδαμεν P. γαρ (*pro* δε) L. ἁμαρτω-
ν P. ἢ i, ἢ P (*pro* ῆ). του θυ̅ (*pro* αυτου) L. ποιει ivL*P. 32. οὐκ'
ουσθη P. ὅτι H. ηνοιξεν wLH**. ἠνοιξεν P. +τους (*ante* οφθαλμους) L.
3. ἡ (*pro* ει) H. ειμι P. οὗτος iH. οὗτος P. εδυνατο w. οὐκ' ἠδυνατο P.
4. ἁμαρτιαις i. ἐναμαρτιαις (*cf. v.* 23) w. διδασκης P. εξεβαλλον P.

35. ἠκουσεν P. +ουν (*ante* ὁ) L. εὑρῶν P**, εὑρον P*?. 36. ειπεν vL. +και
(*ante* τις) ivw**LHP. εστιν wHP. 37. ἑωρακας P. 38. *Rasura in* P
inter εφ *et* η. 39. κρῖμα w. βλεπωσιν wLH**P. γενονται i. γενησονται
L. 40. ἠκουσαν HP. ὑμεις P. 41. *init.* +και L. ἦτε i. ουκ αν ουκ
ειχεται (*sic*) i. −αν wL. βλεπωμεν iP. ει (*pro* ἡ) i. −ουν wL. οὖν P.
ἡμων (*pro* ὑμων) P.

Cap. X. 1. αβλην P *semel*, αλην P* *sem.* (αυλην P**). αλαχοθεν iP *sem.*
z. εστιν wP. λιστης z. 2. αμην αμην λεγω ὑμιν ὁ εισερχομενος (−δε) P
sem. init. peric. εστιν LP. −των προβατων P *sem.* 3. *init.* τοῦτο iP *sem.*
θυρορως P *sem.* κατ ὀνομα P *sem.*, κατονομα *sem.*, κατὀνομα *sem.*, κατὄνομα z.
4. ὅτ' ἂν δε (−και) w. ὅτ' ἂν i. ὁτ' ἂν P *sem.*, ὅτ ἂν HP *sem.* [ὅταν P *sem.* z].
εκβαλλη i. εκβαλλει LP *sem.* εκβαλει P *bis.* ακολυθη P *sem.* οἰδασιν P.
5. ακολουθησουσιν iHz. οὐκ' οἴδασιν P *bis.* οἴδασιν P *sem.* 6. ελαλησεν
(*pro* ειπεν) i. ὁ ῑς *transfert* P *sem. ad fin. versûs.* εγινωσκον L. ἦ L, ἦν P
sem. (*sic v.* 22), ἦν P *sem.* (*pro* ἦν). ελαλη P *sem.* *fin.* +ὁ ιησους LH (*cf.* P).
7. −ειπεν *usque ad* ὁ ῑς P *sem.* οὖν (*sic vv.* 19, 24, 31) P *sem.* αυτοις παλιν
w. −παλιν L. −αυτοις P* *sem.* −ὁτι wH. 8. ηλθον προ εμου ivwL. −προ
εμου HP* *sem.* P *sem.* z. ἦλθον P. εισιν H** P *sem.* ἦσαν (*pro* εισι) P *sem.*
ἠκουσαν P *sem.* αυτω L*, αυτον P* *sem.* (*pro* αυτων). 9. εισελθοι L. ελθει
(εις *eras.*) *P*. εὑρησει P. εὑρηση z. 10. κλεψει *P*. θυσει *P*. εχωσιν *bis*
H. περισσοτερον L. *fin.* εχωσι v. 11. τιθησιν (σ *mutat.*) w. 12. ὁ δε
μισθωτος L. μισθοτος *P*. ὢν z. εστι (*pro* εισι) w*L. εισιν *P*. αφιεισι i.
αφιησιν *P*. ἁρπαζει H*P*. +και σκορπιζει αυτα (*ante* και σκορπιζει) L*. *fin.*
−τα προβατα w. 13. εστιν *P*. μελλει iL*P*z [*non* w]. 14. ἑμα H. γινωσ-
κωμαι z*. 15. τιθησιν L, τιθημοι *P*. 16. δει με wL. ακουσωσι ivLz.
ακουσουσιν H. ακουσωσιν *P*. εἶς *P*. 17. διατοῦτο ivL. διὰ τούτω P.
18. αἱρει L. τίιθημι P. θηναι iw*?P. 20. ἐξ P. μενεται iP. μαινετε w.
21. +δε (*post* αλλοι) L. +ὁτι (*ante* ταυτα) L. τα ῥηματα ταυτα v. εστιν
H**P. ὀφθαλμους wP. ανοιξαι L. *fin.*· v*. 22. −δε Pz (*non init. peric.*
P *sem.*). −τοις ivwLHPz. −και w* (*supra* w**). 23. −του ivwLHPz.
σολομωνος ivLPz [*non* w]. 24. αυτω (*pro* αυτον) z. ἑως P *sem.* ἡμων
mutat. P *sem.* ερεις P *sem.* αἱρεις Lz. σοι (*pro* συ) P *sem.* 25. +μοι (*post*
πιστευετε) L. ἃ H. −εγω P* *sem.* ὀνοματι HP *sem.* 26. ὁτι ουκ εστε
(−γαρ) L. ειπων P *sem.* −καθως ειπον ὑμιν w* (εἶπον w** *marg.*). 27.
ακουουσιν L. ακολουθουσιν wP. 28. ζωὴν P *sem.* απολονται L?P *bis.* απω-
λονται L?P *sem.* απωλωνται z. οὐχ' ivwHP *bis* z. ἁρπασει wHP *bis.* +του
πρ̄ς (*post* χειρος) L* *vel potius* L** (*deletum*) P *sem.* 29. δεδωκεν wH**P.

τα (*post* μοι) iL. εστιν wH**P. οὐδεὶς P *bis*. ἁρπαζειν HP *bis*. ἁρπα-
αυτα L. 31. –παλιν LP. οἱ ιουδαιοι λιθους L. 32. εργα καλα w.
ων (*pro* εργον) wP. και δια ποιων εργων (–αυτων) L. 33. –λεγοντες
–συ w* (*supra* w**). ὧν P. ἑαυτον L. 34. εστιν H**P. ειπον iL
35. ειπεν wLHP. 36. *init.* ὃν w. ἡγιασεν wH**P*, ἡγαπσεν P**.
ν LH. 37. μη (*pro* ου) L. 38. ου (*pro* μη) L. πιστευετε (*pro* πισ-
ητε) iLP, (*pro* πιστευσατε) w. +μου (*post* εργοις) i. πιστευσηται (*pro*
τε) L*. 39. –ουν v. –ουν παλιν i*?z *init. peric.* –παλιν L. αυτον παλιν
+οἱ ιουδαιοι (*ante* πιασαι) L. πιᾶσαι ivz. 40. απηλθεν vw. –παλιν v.
προτερου L. 41. –μεν L. εποιησε[ν w] σημειον iwLz. ουδε ἐν L. ὁσα
. περι τουτω z. 42. πολλοι επιστευσαν z. εις αυτον εκει wLz.
CAP. XI. 1. ἠν H. ἦν (*sic vv.* 2, 6, 18, 30, 38, 41) P. –δε Pz *init. peric.*
ασθενων *mutat.* L. –εκ της κωμης μαριας z. 2. αληψασα w*P. ἑαυτης
z. ησθενησεν L*. ἠσθενει H. ἠσθενη P. 3. οὖν (*sic vv.* 6, 12, 14,
17, 20, 21, 31, 32, 33, 41, 45, 53, 54) P. αἱ H. +αυτου (*post* αδελφαι)
φλεις w*. εφηλεις P*. φηλεις P**. 4. ἡ ασθενεια αυτου (–αὐτη) L.
ενια P*. εστιν wHP. *fin.* αυτων L. 5. ἠγαπα [ν P*] wHP. μαρθα H*.
μαριαν και την αδελφην αυτης μαρθαν L. 6. ἧκου L*. ἠκουσεν HP.
ενη H*. εμειναν P*. 7. επιτα μετα τουτω P. μετατοῦτο L. +αυτου
st μαθηταις) iwL. παλιν εις την ιουδαιαν L. 8. ῥαββει P. νυν εζητουν
i rescript. i. ε *mutat. in* εζητουν w. οἱ ιουδαιοι λιθασαι iL. λιθᾶσαι iz.
ισε P. –οἱ *secund.* z. 9. –ὁ ivwLHPz. ὧραι ivwLz. ὡραι εισι wLHz
ι i]. ὡραι εισιν P. περιπατει (*sic v.* 10 iLHP) iv*LHP. 10. –τῃ w.
η P*. 11. ταυτα δε ειπων και P. –ειπεν*. ειπεν (*sic vv.* 34, 41 wLH)
Hz. ὑμων (*pro* ἡμων) z. καὶ κοίμηται (*sic v.* 12) P. ἀλλᾶ L. –ἱνα i.
γνησω iLz. 12. αυτω οἱ μαθηται (–αυτου) w. 13. ειρηκη P. 14.
ις P* (*supra* P**). απεθανεν wLH**Pz. 15. πιστευσηται P. ειμην i.
α ivwHPz [*non* L]. 16. συν τοις μαθηταις (*pro* τοις συμμαθηταις) L.
θανομεν P. *fin.* συν αυτω w. 17. +εις βηθανιαν (*ante* εὑρεν) i. εὑρεν P.
P. –ηδη z. ηδη ἡμερας L. 18. βιθανια H. ἀποσταδίων iHPz. 19.
i. εληλυθησαν iw*L. εληλυθασιν P. παραμυθησονται iHP. παραμηθη-
ται: L. +και (*post* αυτας) H*. αδελφω v*. 20. ἡ H. –ὁ ivwLHP [*non* z].
pro ις) z. ἠπηντησεν L*. αυτον (*pro* αυτῳ) i, *non v.* 30. οἰκω HP.
–ἡ ivLHP [*non* wz]. εἰς L, ἧς vPz (*pro* ης). ὧδε P. ὧδε z *solus* (*non*
2). απεθανεν (*pro* ετεθνηκει) w. ετεθνηκη Pz. 22. οἰδα (*sic v.* 24) iP.
w. αἰτησῃ w. αἰτῆσοι L. αιτησει H. ετησῃ P. δώσωσοι σοι L. 24.
(*ante* μαρθα) wP. αναστηστησεται P*. αναστασῃ w*. αισχατῃ H.

25. λεγει (*pro* ειπεν) L. +ουν (*post* ειπεν) z. ειμη P. −ἡ *secund.* H. −και αποθανη *v.* 25 *usque ad* πιστευων εις εμε *v.* 26, iw* (*habet marg.* w**). 26. αποθανει iL. 27. σοι (*pro* συ) P. −κοσμον L*. ερχομενον ?L*. 28. απηλθεν wH**P. εφωνησεν wP. απηλθεν εφωνησε δε και L. παρεστη z. φωνη L*Pz. *fin.* σαι (*pro* σε) H. 29. +δε (*ante* ὡς) L. ἠκουσεν P. ερχετε P. 30. οὔπω P. εληλυθη iPz*. προς (*pro* εις) L. ἦν wz. επι του τοπου L. 31. οἱ ουν οἱ ἰδαιοι w. οἰκια wH. παραμοιθουμενοι P. αυτη (*pro* αυτην) i**. μαριὰν (*sic v.* 28) w*. ταχεος z. εξηλθε H*. ἠκολουθησαν wHP. αυτην (*pro* αυτη) P. ὑπαγη P. κλαυσει LHP. 32. *init.* ει (*pro* ἡ) P. ἠλθεν P. ἦν P. −ὁ w. αυτου εις τους ποδας ivwLP. ἧς vwP. ὧδε v. ὁ αδελφος μου ουκ αν απεθανεν i. ἂν w. απεθανεν wH**P. απεθανεν ὁ αδελφος μου L. 33. ιδεν wP. συνεληλυθοτας v. ενεβριμισατο L. *fin.* αυτον P. 34. ειπεν P (*cf. v.* 11). τεθηκατε ivwLPz. ειδε L. 35. *init.* +και L. 36. αυτοις (*pro* ουν) L. −ουν P. 37. ελεγον (*pro* ειπον) w. εἶπων H. εδυνατο w. ἠδυνατο P. οὑτος H. ὀφθαλμους wHP. τοῦφλοῦ P*. οὕτως P. αποθανει L. 38. δε (*pro* ουν) i. −ουν LP. εμβριμουμενος L. ερχετε P. −επ' v. *fin.* επ' αυτο iH. 39. −ὁ w (*mutat.* P). αυτω (ω *mutat.*) w. αδελφη i. τετελευτηκοτος (*pro* τεθνηκοτος) w. ἠδη P. ιδε (*forsan* ιδη, *pro* ηδη) L. ὀζει wHP. ωζη z. τεταρτεως (εως γαρ *rescript.*) P. *fin.* εστιν wLH**P. 40. αυτη (η *mutat.*) i. −ὁτι L. οψη ivLz. ὀψη wP. ὀψει H. δυναμιν (*pro* δοξαν) i. 41. ἠραν wH**P. τεθνηκος (*sic v.* 44, XII. 1, i) iP. −ὁ τεθνηκως κειμενος w* (*habet marg.* w**). −δε L. ἦρεν *hic* w. ἥρεν H**P. +αυτου L, +εις τον ουρανον w (*post* οφθαλμους). ὀφθαλμους wHP. πεν (*pro* ειπεν) P*. ἠκουσας wHP. 42. γαρ (*pro* δε) i. κἀγω (−δε) L. οιδειν L. ἠδειν P. ὀχλον P. 43. φωνῇ iLHPz. εκραυγασεν wLHP. 44. τεθνηκῶς w. τας χειρας και τους ποδας L. κυριαις L. κηριαις P. 45. οὐν H. −οἱ v. ελθωντες P. ἃ P. 46. ἐξ ἀυτόν L. +αρχιερεις και (*ante* φαρισαιους) L. ὁσα w, ὅ L (*pro* ἅ). 47. δε (*pro* ουν) L. πρεσβυτεροι (*pro* φαρισαιοι) L +κατα του ιησου (*post* συνεδριον) LP (−ουν P *init. peric.*). λεγοντες (*pro* και ελεγον) L. ὁ ανος οὗτος H. 48. οὑτως ivwHL**. οὗτος L*P. πιστευσωσιν iLP. −οἱ L. −και *tert.* i*w. 49. εἷς P. ἐξ' P. καὶ ἄφας L*. ὢν P. ἐνιαυτου (*sic v.* 51 wH) w. οὐκ' οἴδατε P. 50. λογιζεσθε L. ὑμιν iv. ἵνα P. ἀνος H. αποθανει LHP. απωληται v. απολειται LHP. 51. ἀφ' ἑαυτου P. αλλ' P. ὢν P. ημελλεν L. −ὁ ivwH [*non* L]. αποθνισκειν i. 52. οὐχ' ivwP. διασκορπισμενα v. −τα διεσκορπισμενα L. συναγει i. συναγαγει LHP. 53. εβουλευσαντο L. αποκτεινουσιν L. 54. οὐκέτι vLH. περιέπατῆ w*. τη ιουδαιαις w*. αλλ' P. −εκειθεν H. −την L. ἐφραιμ w. και

ει L. διετριβεν wHP. 55. −προ v*. −προ του πασχα L. προτου i.
νισωσιν i. 56. ἑστηκοτες w. ἑστηκοτας (ας?) εν τω ἱερω L. ἡμιν ?L*.
θη w. 57. −και *prim.* ivwL. εντολας i. εστιν w. μηνυσει v.

CAP. XII. 1. −ὁ ουν ις L*Pz. ἠλθεν P. +ιησους (*post* ηλθεν) LPz *init.*
ric. ἠν (*sic vv.* 2, 6, 16) P. τεθνηκος iP (θ *mutat. in* L). ἠγειρεν (*sic vv.*
17) P. *fin.* +ὁ ις w. 2. οὐν (*sic vv.* 3, 4, 7, 9, 17, 19, 21, 28, 29, 35) P.
ει δειπνον L. −και ἡ μαρθα διηκονει i*. διηκονη i**. διείκονει P. εἰς (*non*
4) HP. ανακειμενων συν ivwLHPz. 3. ἡλειψε i. ηλειψεν wH. ἡλειψεν
εξαιμαξε i. εξεμαξεν wHP. ταις θριξειν εξεμαξεν τας ἑαυτης τους ποδας
c) L. +ὁλη (*post* οικια) L. ὀσμης H. ὠσμης P. 4. [*cum Elzev.* ivL].
ουδας z. σιμων H**. σημων ὁ (*pro* σιμωνος) P. *Rasura in* z *post* σιμω (ο
itur). παραδιδωναι P. 5. διὰ τί wHP [*non* L]. διακοσιων L. εδωθη P.
ειπεν (*sic ferè v.* 38) wHP. τουτω L. οὐχ' ivwPz. περη L*. εμελλεν
LH [*non* w, z *dubium*]. ειχεν wLHP. βαλομενα z. 7. +αυτοις (*post*
ν) L. +ἱνα (*ante* εις) w. τηρηση w. *fin.* αὐτῷ P. 9. +ὁτι (*post* ουν) L.
λος (*sic* P *vv.* 12, 17, 18, 29, 34 *sem.*) HP. εστιν vwLHP. ἠγειρεν (*sic v.*
) H. 11. αυτων P*. ὑπήγον iw. ὑπηγων L. ὑπηγοντο z. επιστευσαν
επιστευων H. 12. +ουν (*post* τη) w** *marg.* ἐπ' αὐριον w. −ὁ *secund.*
wz. 13. φυνικων P. απαντησιν w. συναντησιν L. ἀπαντησιν P. +λε-
ντες (*post* εκραζον) w. ὠσάννὰ iwPz [*non* LH]. ὠσάννᾶ v. ευλογημενος
mutat.) L. −ὁ ερχομενος P. −ὁ *secund.* ivwLHPz. 14. εὑρον P. −ὁ v*.
αριον wHPz. εκαθησεν P. επ' αυτω wPz. 15. ἴδοῦ *pass.* P. βασιλευσου
πωλου w. πολου L. ὀνου P. 16. −αυτου w*. *Rasura in* w *post* τὸ.
πρῶτον ivLz. πρωτερον P. αλλωτε ?P*. −ὁ vwH. 17. εμαρτυρι P.
ων z *init. peric.* −ὁ *prim.* z *sem.* ὢν H *sem.* ὤν P. ὀτε (*pro* ὁτι) iLHPz
on w]. ἠγειρεν H *sem.* 18. διατοῦτο (*sic ferè vv.* 27, 39) ivLz, *at* διὰ το
sem. −και i. απηντησεν L*?. −ὁ L. ηκουσεν v*. ηκουσαν w. ἠκουσαν
sem. P. ἠκουσεν H *sem.* αυτον (ο *mut.*) H *sem.* ηκουσαν αυτον πεποιη-
ναι το σημειον τουτο (τουτον L*) L. σημειων P*. *In* z ὁτι ηκουσε *super*
sur. recenti manu: θεωρουντ *marg. s. m.:* τοῦτων αὐπερ πεποιη *ut videtur,*
per rasur. 19. οἱ H *sem.* ἑαὐτους H *sem.* ὀτι (υ *pro* τ L*) L. οὐκ'
θελειτε P. ωφελει i. ὀφελειται L*. ωφεληται z. +ὁλος (*post* κοσμος) v.
ηλθεν ὁλος ὀπισω αυτου (ὀπ *pro* απ L*) L. ὀπισω wHP. 20. Ἥσαν (H
bro) i. ἤσαν H *sem.* P. −ἑλληνες εκ L. ἑλληνες P. ἑλληνες τινες z. +εις
οσολυμα (*ante* ἱνα) i. προσκυνησουσιν Pz. ἑορτη H *sem.* 21. οὗτοι H *sem.*
ων L. προσειχον (*pro* προσηλθον) L. γαλιλαιας (ας *mutat.*) L. ἠρωτων
HP. ειπον αυτω (*pro* ηρωτων αυτον) L. θελωμεν iLz. 22. φιλλιππος

prim. L*. λεγουσιν wH *sem.* P. λέ L. 23. −ιησους v. απεκριθη λεγων αυτοις L. αὐ[τοῖς *rubro*] i. 24. ἐαν *bis* H *sem.* αποθανει *prim.* iL*P *sem.* (*rasura inter* ν *et* η *in* w). αποθαθανη H* *sem.* φερη z *sem.* 25. φειλων P *sem.* απολεση Lz *sem.* −τουτω w*. τουτο w**z *sem.* εν τω κοσμω τουτω *rescript.* z *sem.* 26. τις εμοι διακονη *prim.* L, *at* διακονει L*. διακονει *bis* iP. τις διακονη *prim.* w. ακολουθητω wLP *bis* z. −και *tert.* L. τιμηση iL, *at* τηρηση z *sem.* αυτων P* *sem.* ?. *fin.* +μου L. 27. εἶπω H *sem.* P. ὡρ. *bis* P *sem.* −αλλὰ z *sem.* ἦλθον H *sem.* P *sem.* 28. +ἅγιε (*post* περ) iw. ὀνομα HPz *sem.* ἦλθεν w. ἦλθεν P *sem.* φωνῆ iz *sem.* 29. *init.* ὁ H. ὁ ουν ὁ L. ὀχλος P. ἑστηκως iL. εστὼς v. ἑστηκως w. ἑστὼς H *sem.* ἑστῶς P. ἑστῶς z *sem.* −και L. ελεγεν wHP *sem.*, ελεγον P *sem.* z *sem.* (*pro* ελεγε). βροντῆ z *sem.* *Rasura post* αλλοι P *sem.* +ὅτι (*ante* αγγελος) L. 30. −ὁ vwLHP *sem.* z [*non* i]. ἡ φωνη αὐτη iz *sem.* αὐτη P *sem.* 31. εστιν Pz *sem.* −νυν ὁ αρχων του κοσμου τουτου LP* *sem.* 32. και εγω L. ἑλκυσω ivwz *sem.* [*non* HP]. ἑλκυσωσι L. 33. ελεγεν wH** *bis* P. εμελλεν wH** *sem.* ἠμελλεν H *sem.* P. [ἠμελλεν iLH* *sem.* z]. αποθνισκειν i. 34. ὀχλος P. ἠκουσαμεν wHP. −εκ του νομου i. εις τον αιωνα μενει L. μαινει P *sem.* λεγεις συ w. −ὅτι *secund.* i*vHPz [*non* L]. −τις εστιν *ad fin. vers.* v*Lz *sem.* −οὑτος v**P *sem.* 35. χρονον μικρον L. εν ὑμιν (*pro* μεθ' ὑμων) wL. εστιν wLPz *bis.* ὡς (*pro* ἑως) w. μεθ' ὑμων εστι (*pro* εχετε) v. εχητε z *sem.* (*sic v.* 36 z *bis*). +ἡ (*ante* σκοτια) w. σκοτεια *bis* (*sic v.* 46) iLP. οιδεν wH** *sem.* P. ὑπαγη P *sem.* z *sem.* 36. ἕΩς (Ω *rubro*) w. εκριβη L. 37. σιμεια P. οὐκ H *sem.* −ουκ *usque ad* ἱνα *v.* 38 P*. επιστευσαν LP**. 38. ἳνα *iterum eras.* P**. του προφητου ἠσαϊου v. −του προφητου LP. πληρωθη του προφητου z *sem.* ειπεν LH. επιστευσεν iwHP. βραχιον P. 39. εδυναντο w. οὐκ' ἠδυναντο P. οὐκ *rescript.* z *sem.* 40. ὀφθαλμ. *bis* wP, *prim.* H *sem.*; *bis* H *sem.* επηρωσεν w. επορωσεν L. πεπορωκεν z *sem.* πεπορρωκεν z *sem.* αυτον (*pro* αυτων *secund.*) i. ιδωσιν H** *sem.* P. +και τοις ωσιν ακουσωσιν (*post* οφθαλμοις) L. νοησουσι L. νοησωσιν H** *sem.* P. τη καρδια συνωσι (*pro* νοησωσι) w. επιστρεψωσι w. επιστρεψουσι L. επιστραφωσιν H** *sem.* Pz *sem.* ιασομαι iwLz [*non* HP]. 41. ὁτι (*pro* ὁτε) z *sem.* ιδε H *sem.* ιδεν wH *sem.* P. του θεαυ (*pro* αυτου *prim.*) L. ελαλησεν wHP. −και ελαλησε *usque ad* του θῦ *v.* 43 (*cf.* L) i. 42. οὐχ' vHPz. ὁμολογουν L*Pz *sem.* γενονται P. 43. ἠγαπησαν wHPz *sem.* μαλλον (*pro* γαρ) L. μαλλον ὑπερ (*pro* μαλλον ηπερ) L. ἡπερ HP. ειπερ z. του *mutat.* P. 44. *init.* +ὁ L. εκραζε και ελεγεν (*pro* ειπεν) L. εκραξεν wHP. 45. με (*pro* εμε) i. αποστειλαντα (*pro* πεμψαντα) L. *fin.* −με H *sem.* 47. ακουη v.

ακουσει P. της φωνης (*pro* των ρηματων) L. πιστευσει P. φυλαξη (*pro* πιστευση) wL. σῶσω z *tribus locis*. 48. λαμβανη z *sem*. κρίνει v*. κρινη z *sem*. *v*. 48. *usque ad* αιωνιος εστιν *v*. 50 *deest in* H. 49. εξ εμαυτου εγω vz. ἀπ' (*pro* εξ) L. εδωκεν w. δεδωκεν z *sem*. δεδωκε Lz *sem*. *fin*. και τι ειπω η τι λαλησω i. είπω z *sem*. 50. οἶδα i. εστιν αιωνιος L. εστι v. εγω λαλω Lz. ειρηκεν wH *sem*. ενετειλατο (*pro* ειρηκε) L. οὕτως ivwH *sem*. z. οὗτος L.

CAP. XIII. 1. –δε *init. peric*. Hz. εωρτης H. ιδως H. ηλθεν (*pro* εληλυθεν) wLHz. –αυτου v. του (*pro* τουτου) L. ἠγαπησεν wH. 2. διπνου H*. ἤδη z. –ιουδα L*. ἰοῦδα (*non v*. 26) i. 3. +δε (*post* ειδως) iLH *sem*. P *sem*. +του (*ante* θυ̅) P *sem*. θυ̅ *mutat*. L. εξηλθεν wLHP** *sem*. P *sem*. z. –τον w. ὑπαγη P *sem*. 4. εγειραιτε H *sem*. τιθησει P. τιθησιν H**z. ἱματια v. διελζωσεν v*. ἑαυτον H *sem*. 5. ἠτα P *sem*. εἶτα z *sem*. λαβων ὕδωρ βαλλει L. νηπτηρα iPz. ἤρξατο H *sem*. P *sem*. εκμασσει L. εκμασσην H*? *sem*. P *sem*. εκμασιν z *sem*. ὃ (*pro* ᾧ) Pz *sem*. ἦν P. 6. οὖν (*sic vv*. 12 *sem*. 14) P. +τον (*ante* σιμωνα) L. 7. +ὁ (*ante* ις̅) iw. –αυτῳ P *sem*. οἶδας w. οἴδας P *sem*. γνωσει i*LPz. μεταταῦτα iLH *sem*. μεταταύτα H *sem*. 8. +ὁ (*ante* πετρος) LHP *sem*. z *sem*. νιψεις w*Pz *sem*. μου νιψης τους ποδας L. –ὁ vwz *sem*. 9. –μου wLP *sem*. 10. λελουσμενος L. οὐ H. χριαν iP. εχη P *sem*. ει μη wL, ἠ̂ H *sem*. Pz *sem*., ει z *sem*. (*pro* ἠ̂). –αλλ' *prim*. L. αλλα ? H* *sem*. εστιν H**Pz *sem*. εσται Pz. οὐχι (*non v*. 11) wH *sem*. 11, ἤδει H *sem*. ἤδη P. ηδη z *sem*. παραδιδουντα Pz *sem*. διατοῦτο iwLz *sem*. ουχ οἱ (*pro* ουχι) L. εσται z *sem*. 12. [–ουν, ενιψεν ὁ ις̅, των μαθητων αυτου (*pro* αυτων) P *sem*. z *sem*. *init. peric*.]. ἐνιψὲν w. ενιψεν HP. ενιψεν αυτων τους ποδας L. [αυ H**]τῶν H. ελαβεν wH**P. ἱματι L. αὐτου (ου *mutat*.) P *sem*. γινωσκεται z *sem*. 13. –με L*. ὁ κς̅ και ὁ διδασκαλος vLz *sem*. καλος HP *sem*. z. λεγεται ειμη z *sem*. 14. *init*. Oἰ (O *rubro*) i. τους ποδας ὑμων w. +ουν (*post* ὑμεις) z *sem*. ὀφειλετε wH. ὀφιλετε P. ὀφειλεται z *sem*. νιπτην P* *sem*. 15. ὑποδιγμα P. δεδωκα iwLPz *sem*. –εγω iv. επεποιηκα v. πεποιηκα L. *fin*. ποιειτε i*z. 16. εστιν wH** *sem*. H *sem*. Pz *sem*. μεῖζων *duobus locis* vz *sem*. οὐδε P *sem*. 17. οἴδαται P *sem*. οἶδατε P *sem*. ειδατε z. εσται iP *sem*. z *sem*. ποιειτε i*z. 18. [*Non habent Evangelistaria vv*. 18—30]. +γαρ (*ante* οιδα) wL. –την L. 19. ἀπάρτι (*sic* xiv. 7, vwL) ivwL. ὅτ' ἂν iw. γενητε L. 20. –αμην *unum* v. αν (*pro* εαν) iw*. λαμανει *prim*. i. 21. –τῳ πνευματι i. εμαρτυρησεν wL. –ὅτι i. 22. +αυτου (*post* μαθηται) L. απορουντες L. 23. +εκ (*post* εις) wL. ἠγαπα w. –ὁ ιησους L. 24. –ουν L, *at* οὖν w. πύθεσθαι iL. 25. *αναπεσων* w. *ουν* (*pro* *δε*) L. +*ουτως* i, +*ουτος* v (*post* *εκεινος*). 26. *αποκρινεται αυτω ὁ ιησους και λεγει αυτω* L. *εστι*, i. *εμβαψας* (*pro* *βαψας*) w, *at* *βαψας* (*pro* *εμβαψας*) L *sic*. *ἰουδα τω* (−*σιμωνος*) L. 27. *σατανὰς* i. *ταχειον* v. 29. −*ὁ* L. *ἰοῦδας* iL. 30. −*εκεινος* L. *εξηλθεν* *ευθεως* vL, *et* *εξηλθεν* vL *v.* 31, *cætera cum Elzev.* L. 30, 31. *Jungunt* *ην δε νυξ ὁτε εξηλθε* (−*ουν*) ivw. 32. *init.* *εἰ* w. −*ὁ* *secund.* P. *δοξαση* *bis* i. *αυτω* (*pro* *ἑαυτῳ*) z. *ευθεις* iw*?. 33. *ζητειτε* (*pro* *ζητησετε*) L. *ζητησετε με και ουχ' εὑρησετε και* (*loco* *ὁτι*) i. −*εγω* i. *εγω ὑπαγω* vwLz. *δυνασθαι* L*. 34. *διδομι* L. *ἀγαπάτε* *prim.* iw. −*καθως* *ad fin. vers.* iL*. *ἠγαπησα* wHP. 35. *τοῦτο* i. *γνωσοντε* H. *εσται* Pz*. *ἀγαπην* H. *εχετε* iP. *εχειτε* H*. *αγαπατε αλληλους* (*pro* *αγαπην εχητε εν αλληλοις*) Lz. 36. −*ὁ* v. +*εγω* (*ante* *ὑπαγω*) iv**LH *manu antiquâ* z, (*post* *ὑπαγω*) w, (*supra* *ὑπαγω*) P**. *με* (*pro* *μοι* *prim.*) w. *ακολουθησαι αρτι* (−*νυν*) i. −*νυν* P. *ακολουθησης* (*pro* -*σεις*) z. −*μοι* *secund.* w** (*super rasur.: habuit* w* *ut videtur*). 37. −*ὁ* ivwH**P [*non* Lz]. −*κε̄* P*?. *διὰ τί* wHP. *δυναμε* P. *νυν ακολουθησαι* (−*αρτι*) v. 38. *αποκρινεται* L. −*αυτῳ* wL. −*ὁ* w. *φωνηση* vw Hz [*non* iL]. *τρις απαρνησει με* L *sic*. *απαρνησει* P. *τρεις* P**.

CAP. XIV. 1. *ταρασεσθω* HP *bis*. *πιτευετε* *secund.* H *sem.* 2. *οἰκια* wH *sem.* P. +*ὁτι* (*ante* *πορευομαι*) vwL. *ἑτοιμασω* w. *ἑτοιμασαι* P. *ἑτοιμᾶσαι* vHz *sem.* *ὑμιν τοπον* P *sem.* 3. −*ab initio usque ad* *τοπον* w*LP* *sem.* −*και* *secund.* ivw**HPz *sem.* *ἑτοιμασαι* P *sem.* *ἑτοιμᾶσαι* z *sem.* *τοπον ὑμιν* z *sem.* *ερχωμαι* i. *παραλειψομαι* P *sem.*, *at* *παραληψωμαι* *sem.* *ἐμαυτὸν* w. +*εκει* (*post* *εγω*) vw. *fin.* *ἡτε* vwP. 4. −*εγω* L. *ὑπαγω εγω* H. *οἰδατε* *bis* P *bis*, *prim.* H *sem.* 5. *οἴδαμεν* P. *ὁδον* H *sem.* *ἴδεναι* P *sem.* 6. −*ἡ* *secund.* z *sem.* *οὐδεῖς* P *sem.* *ειμι* (*pro* *ει μη*) P *sem.* 7. *εγνωκητε* *bis* iz *sem.* *εμε* z *sem.* *ἀπάρτι* HPz. 9. −*ὁ* w. *ἑωρακας* (*pro* *εγνωκας*) z *sem.* *φιλιππε*; vwH *sem.* P *sem.* *ἑωρακῶς* P *sem.* *ἑωρακεν* wP *sem.* *ἑωρακε* H. +*και* (*post* *ἑωρακεν*) P *sem.* *σοι* (*pro* *συ*) L. *διξον* P* *sem.* 10. *εστιν* ivwLH *sem.* H** *sem.* P. −*ὑμιν* L *bis*. *ὑμην* P *sem.* *ἐμαῦτοῦ* w. *οὐ* H *sem.* *μαινων* P. 11. −*εστιν* ivwLH *bis* P *sem.* z. *ταυτα* (*pro* *αυτα*) z *sem.* *Post* *εμοι* *in* L *repetitur* *τα ῥηματα κ.τ.λ.* *v.* 10, *usque ad* *εν εμοι εστιν* *v.* 11 (−*ὑμιν* *v.* 10). −*μη* L*. 12. −*και μειζονα τουτων ποιησει* P* *sem.* *μειζωνα* w*P *sem.* P** *sem.* −*μου* wL. 13. *ὅτι* ivLHP, *εἰτι* z *sem.*, *at* *εἰτι* *sem.* *αἰτησητε* (*sic* *v.* 14) w. *αιτησηται* LH *sem.* *αἰτησειτε* H *sem.* *εαν̕ αιτησατε* z *sem.* *ὀνοματι* (*sic* *v.* 14 HP *sem.*) H *sem.* P. *τουτω* P *sem.* 14. +*με* (*post* *αἰτησητε*) H *sem.* P *sem.* 15. *αγαπάτε* i. *μου* (*pro* *τας εμας*) iP *bis*. −*εμας* P* *sem.* (*habet marg.* P**). *τηρησητε* L*z. 16. −*εγω* z *sem.* *μενει* ivLP *sem.* z *sem.* *μαινει* P

m. μενεῖ P sem. μεθ rescript. P sem. 17. ὁ ὁ H sem. δυνατε L*. αυτω
rim. secund. et forsan tert.) L. –ουδε γινωσκει αυτο z sem. –ὑμεις δε γινωσκετε
το P* sem. z sem. (γηνωσκετε αυτω P** marg.). Rasura post γινωσκετε P
m., at θεωρειτε z sem. –αυτο tert. P sem. παρ' ὑμων z sem. fin. εστιν L.
3. αφισω H sem. ὀρφανους P. 19. εμε (pro με prim.) v. οὐκέτι vLH sem.
z. οὐκέτι H sem. ζησεσθαι P. 20. –ὑμεις H* sem. –μου z. και εγω
ro καγω) H sem. P. 21. –ὁ δε αγαπων με P* sem. (habet P** marg.).
γω (pro και εγω) i. εμφανησω P. αυτο (pro αυτῷ) P sem. εμ' αὐτον P
m. fin. αυτον εμαυτω i. εμαυτω H*. 22. Deest versus in P sem. ουδας i.
ῦδας L. οὐχ' ivwHP sem. z. +και (ante τι) ivwLHP sem. z. ἑαυτον (pro
αυτον) L*. 23. Incipit P sem. και εαν τις. –ὁ prim. ivwHP sem. z. αυ-
ης (pro αυτῷ prim.) H*. ἀγαπᾷ i. τηρηση ivLHz. αγαπηση Pz. ελευσ-
μεθα P sem. z, ελευσομηθα ?P* sem., at πορευσομεθα L (pro ελευσομεθα).
ησωμεν iwH*Pz. ποιησομεθα L. 24. –πατρος L. 25. fin. παρ' ἡμων
νων (ἡμιν μενον L*) L. 26. πεμψη L*. ὀνοματι wHP. ὁσα (pro ἁ) i.
asura post ἁ (αν?) in w. ειπω w. 27. εἰρηνην prim. rescript. z sem. ἀφι-
ιην P sem. οὐ rescript. z sem. –διδωσιν i*. ὑμην tert. P sem. ταρασεσθω
*P sem. μὴδε i. μὴδὲ vwLP bis z. δειλιᾶτο z sem. 28. ἠκουσατε wP.
εγω P sem. +εγω (ante ερχομαι) L. ἠγαπάτε i. ἠγαπατε wH sem. P sem.
απατε LP sem. z. –ειπον secund. w. εγω (pro ειπον secund.) L. +εγω
nte ειπον secund.) H* sem. +μου (post π̄ρ̄α) L. μειζον z sem. fin. εστιν wL
P. 29. πρὶν i. προ του (pro πριν) L. ὁτ' ἀν i. ὅτ' ἀν wH. ὅτὰν
γενητε L. πιστευσηται P*. 30. οὐκέτι vLHP sem. z. ερχετε H sem.
γαρ L. ὁ αρχων του κοσμου L. –τουτου ivwLHPz sem. [habet z sem.].
χων z sem. εὑρησει (pro ουκ εχει) w. Rasura in P sem. inter ου et κεχει.
. +μου (post π̄ρ̄α) z. οὑτως ivwHPz sem. οὗτως z sem. rescript. οὗτος L*.
ομεν L. ἀγωμεν H.

Cap. XV. 1. η prim. rescript. i, at ει (pro ἡ prim.) P sem. αληθινη P
m. εστιν wLP. 2. +ουν (post παν prim.) P sem. –μη P* sem. αἱρει H
m. z sem. αὐτῶ prim. P sem. –και παν usque ad καθαιρει αυτο L. τον
ro το) wz. φερων bis P bis, secund. wP sem. καθερει w*P sem. πλιονα P
m. πλειωνα P sem. z sem. φερει LPz* duobus locis. 3. ἠδει H sem. ἠδη
+δε (post ηδη) z sem. εσται P sem. 4. ἡμιν vel ὑμιν pro εμοι prim. P*
m., at rasura post ενε P semel. ἡμιν L*. +γαρ (post καθως) L. οὐ H sem.
νατε H sem. P bis. φερει εν ἑαύτω (pro αφ' ἑαυτου) L. ἀφ' ἑαυτου P sem.
τος ?L*. οὗτος H sem. και (pro ουδε) P sem. –μη secund. P sem. fin. εαν
ιοι μη μεινητε (–εν) z sem. 5. μαινων P bis. ουτως P sem. πολυ z sem.

χωρεις P *sem.* οὐ H *sem.* δυνατε L. δυνασθαι P. 6. μητης P *sem.* μεινει P *sem.* ἐμοι P *sem.* ἡμιν *forsan pro* εμοι L*. εκβληθη P* *sem.* z *sem.* αυτο (*pro* αυτα) iw, *at* αὐτῶ L. +το (*ante* πυρ) ivwLHPz. βαλλουσιν wH** *sem.* P. βαλλουσι ναι L*. καιετε w. κεεται P *bis.* 7. ἐὰν P *sem.* +μη (*ante* μεινητε) L. θελετε i. θεληται P *bis.* αἰτησεσθε w. αἰτησασθε H* *sem.* P *sem.* z *sem.* αἰτησαισθε H** *sem.* αιτισεσθε H *sem.* αἰτησασθε z *sem.* γενησετε z *sem.* *Sic legitur in* L, και τα ῥηματα τα εμα ου (*mutat.*) μενεῖ εν ὑμιν· ἐαν δε μενητε εν εμοι μηνει· και ὁ εαν θελητε γενησεται ὑμιν (–αιτησεσθε και). 8. τουτο H. δοξασθη i. πολυν καρπον v. γενησθε wP *sem.* μοι (*pro* εμοι) P *sem.* 9. ἠγαπησεν wP. Ἠγαπησε H**. ἠγαπησα (*sic v.* 12 iwHP) wHP. μειναται P *sem.* 10. τας *prim. mutat.* L. τηρησετε P* (-ητε P** *rubro*). μενητε w*z. μενῶ vP *sem.* εαν (*pro* εν *secund.*) L*. 11. λελαληκα (αλη *mutat.*) P *sem.* ἡ (*pro* μεινη) w. μενη P *sem.* 12. αὐτη HP. +δε (*post* αὐτη) L. ἀγαπάτε (*sic v.* 17) i. ἠγαπησαι i. 13. μειζο L. μειζωνα P. οὐδεῖς (*sic v.* 24) P. 14. ποιειτε i*P. ἁ (*pro* ὁσα) vLz. –εγω z. εντελλωμαι L. εντελομαι P *sem.* 15. οὐκ ἔτι iP [*non* vz]. οἰδεν wH**P. οἰδε z. τη (*pro* τι) H. ὁ κ̄ς αυτου z. –δε L. ἃ H. ἠκουσα HP *sem.* εγνωρησα P. 16. οὐχ' ivwHPz. εξελεξασθαι P *sem.* ἐγω H. +εκ του κοσμου (*ante* και εθηκα) z. μεινη w. μένει LHP *sem.* μενεῖ P *sem.* ὅτι ivHP. και ὁτι L, και ειτι z (*pro* ἱνα ὁ,τι). αἰτησητε w. ετησητε P *sem.* –τον π̄ρα iL. ὀνοματι (*sic v* 21 HP) wHP. δωη ὑμιν (η ὑ *rescript.* i) iv. δωσει w**HP** *sem.* z. δωη P *sem.* δωει P* *sem.* *Loco* δῳ ὑμιν *habet* L τουτο ποιησω· ἱνα δοξασθη ὁ π̄ηρ εν τω υἱω. 17. εντελλωμαι P *sem.* *at* εντελομαι *bis.* εντελλομε *sem.* 18. μιση (*sic v.* 19) z *sem.* μεμησηκεν i*. 19. ἦτε P *sem.* ειτε P *sem.* εφιλη ivP *sem.* z. εξεξαμην (ξ *et* μ *rescript.*) i*. διατοῦτο ivLz. 20. οὐ P *sem.* οὐκ' P *sem.* εστιν wHP (*sequitur rasura in* w). μειζον L. μιζων z *sem.* *fin.* τηρησωσιν Pz *sem.* 21. ποιησωσιν P. ποιησω z *sem.* –ὁτι ουκ οιδασι *ad fin. vers.* v*. οἶδασι iv**. οἴδασι H. οὐκ' οἰδασιν P *sem.* οἴδασιν P *sem.* 22. ἦλθον P *sem.* εχουσιν wL*P. εχωσιν L**. 24. εποιησεν (*pro* πεποιηκεν) wL. ἑωρακασιν wP *sem.* ἑωρακασιν (*sequitur linea erasa*) P *sem.* ἑορακασι H. μεμισηκασιν i. –και μεμισηκασι P* *sem.*, *at* μεμησικασιν P**, μεμησηκασιν P* *sem.* 26. ὅτ' ἂν iwH *sem.* ὅτᾶν H *sem.* ὁτᾶν P. ἐλθη w. ὃν P *sem.* ὑμῆ ?P *sem.* +μου (*pro* π̄ρς *prim.*) w. *Rasura in* w *post* π̄να. μαρτυρηση vz *sem.* 27. ἀπαρχῆς LH *sem.* P *sem.* z *sem.* [*non* ivH *sem.*] *fin.* εστιν (*pro* εστε) i. εσται P *sem.*

Cap. XVI. 1. σκανδαλισθητε (λι *mutat.*) w. 2. ποιησων L. ποιησωσιν P *sem.* z *sem.* ερχετε P *sem.* z *sem.* ὡρα P *bis.* αποκτινας H* *sem.* λατρεῖαν i.

εια w. 3. ποιησωσιν z sem. −ὑμιν ivwHP sem. P* sem. z. οὐδε H sem.
ι P sem. ὅτ' ἀν (sic vv. 13, 21 bis w, 21 bis i) wH sem. ὅτ ἀν H sem.
ἀν P sem., sic v. 21 sem. (at ὀτὰν vv. 13, 21 bis). ἐλθη (sic v. 13) w.
ων (post ὡρα) w. αυτων μνημονευσητε L. μνημονευετε iP sem. μνημο-
ται P sem. −ὑμιν tert. L. ἐξαρχῆς iwHP sem. ἡμην H sem. P. 5.
πρα (post προς) L. ουδεις H sem. οὐδεὶς (sic v. 22) P. ἐξ vP sem. z
με ερωτα L. ὑπαγης H sem. 6. ὀτι w. ἡμων (pro ὑμων) P sem.
ιν λεγω w. −ὑμιν secund. H sem. +εγω (post γαρ) ivwLHP. εγω (pro
z. −δε L. Post ὑμας prim. eraditur in P sem. εαν δε πορευθω ὁ παρα-
ος ουκ ελευσεται προς ὑμας. 8. ελεγξη z sem. −περι tert. L*. 10.
δε δικαιοσυνης L. πορευομαι i*v (γρ. ὑπαγω i** marg.). ου (pro ουκ ετι)
οὐκέτι (sic vv. 21, 25) vLH (non v. 21 H sem.) z. 11. κεκρειται w.
ετη P. και (pro ετι) rescript. z sem. λαλειν (γρ. λεγειν i** marg: cf.
) i*. λεγειν (ει mutat.) w. οὐ H. δυνασθαι P. 13. ὅτ' ἀν (sic v. 21
I. ὁ παρακλητος (pro εκεινος) H sem. ὁδηγησει i. ὡδηγηση L. ὁδη-
z. ὅσα w. εαν (pro αν) w. λαλησῃ secund. Pz sem. ερχωμενα w*.
γελῆ (non vv. 14, 15) z sem. 14. και (pro ὁτι) L. ληψετε P. 15.
ντα in w post παντα. διατοῦτο ivwLz sem. λαμβανει vLHPz [non i].
γελη L*. 16. ὀψεσθε (sic ferè H vv. 17, 19, et P v. 17 bis, 19 sem.)
em. ὄψεσθαι P sem. +και (ante ὁτι) L. −εγω iwLHP sem. z. −τον L.
Deest versus in L. ειπον (ει mutat.) H sem. οὖν (sic vv. 18, 19, 22) P.
(sic v. 15 P) wP. ὑμιν (pro ἡμιν) z sem. +ὁτι (ante μικρον prim.) z.
sem. και και οψεσθε i. οψεσθαι (sic v. 19) z. −εγω wz sem. ὑπαγω
z sem. 18. τι εστι τουτο L. −τι prim. z. −ὃ λεγει L. +ἡμιν (post
ι) v. οὐκ H sem. οἶδαμεν vP sem. οἴδαμεν P sem. λαλῆ P sem. 19.
pro ουν) w. ὁτι H sem. ἡθελον H sem. P. ημελλον (pro ηθελον) L.
(pro ειπεν) L. ζητητε P sem. ὀψεσθαι P sem. 20. −αμην unum L.
θρηνησετε P sem. θρηνησεται P sem. χαρησεσθε L, χαρησετε H sem.
χαρησεται). λυπηθησεσθαι P sem. ἡ w. 21. τικτει z sem. εχη P sem.
ι. z** sem. −ὁτι ηλθεν ἡ ὡρα αυτης z sem. ἤλθεν P sem. της (pro αυτης)
ἡ (sic) P* sem. γεννησει P. οὐκέτι H sem. εγενηθη w. 22. μεν (pro
L. −ουν z sem. −νυν P sem. −μεν νυν z sem. [non L]. ἐξετε w. ὀψομαι
m. P. χαρισεται P. αἰρη P sem. αἰρει H sem. z. 23. −αμην unum z
ὁ εαν (pro ὁσα αν) w. αἰτησητε w. Rasura in P sem. post αιτησετε
ὀνοματι (sic vv. 24, H sem. P, 26 H sem. P sem.) HP. δωσω P sem. vv. 23,
−δωσει ὑμιν v. 23 usque ad ονοματι μοὐ v. 24, z sem. 24. αρτη P sem.
P. ἠτησατε P, αιτησασθε z (pro ητησατε). αἰτειτε w. αιτειται P sem.

ἡ P *sem.*, ἡ vP *sem.*, ἡ H *sem.* (*pro* ἡ). *fin.* +εν ὑμιν i. 25. λελαλη [κα P**] P*. −αλλ' *prim.* L. οὐκέτι H *sem.* P *sem.* ἀπαγγελῶ w. 26. αἰτησεσθε w. αιτησασθε P *sem.* ερωτισω H *sem.* 27. πεφηλεικατε P. απο (*pro* παρα) H* *sem.* πρς (*pro* θῦ) z *sem.* *fin.* +και ἡκω L. *vv.* 27, 28. εξηλθον *unum omissum in* w (*præcedente brevi rasurâ*). 28. +δε (*post* εξηλθον) z *sem.* −παλιν αφιημι τον κοσμον z *sem.* πορευσομαι z *sem.* 29. −αυτῳ w* (*habet* w** *marg.*). οἱ μαθητ P** *marg.* ἴδε P *sem.* νὺν *ferè* P (*sic vv.* 30, 32). οὐδέμίαν vwP *sem.* z [*non* i]. 30. εγνωκαμεν (*pro* οιδαμεν) L. οἴδαμεν w. οἴδαμεν P *sem.* οἰδας *hic* iP. τούτο P. τοῦτω z. *fin.* εληλυθας LH *sem.* 32. ἴδοὺ P. ιδεια w*. ἑκαστος H. αφειτε L. οὐκ' P. +μου (*post* πηρ) iL. εστιν wLH *sem.* P. 33. −εν *prim.* P*. εχειτε w, εχετε P *sem.* (*pro* εχητε). θλιψην P. εχετε (*pro* ἕξετε) vwH *sem.* Pz [*non* iL]. νενικηκα εγω z *sem.*

CAP. XVII. 1. επαρας iLH *sem.* P *sem.* z *sem.* *initio peric.* *Rasura in* v *post* επηρε. επηρεν wH *sem.* ὀφθαλμους wH *sem.* P *sem.* επηρεν την φωνην (*pro* τους οφθαλμους) P *sem.* −αὐτου z *sem.* −και *secund.* iLH *sem.* P *sem.* z *sem.* ειπεν wHP. −εληλυθεν ἡ ὡρα z *sem.* δοξασει i*wP *sem.* 2. −αυτῳ *prim.* L. εδωκας (*pro* δεδωκας) vH. δωσει ivwLH *sem.* Pz. αυτης (*pro* αυτοις) i*. 3. αὕτη P *sem.* γινωσκωσιν wP. γινωσκουσι z *sem.* αληθινον μονον L. 4. τελειωσας (*pro* ετελειωσα) w. εδωκας w. 5. ἡ i. −ἡ L*. −ειναι i. 6. ὀνομα (*sic v.* 26) H *sem.* P. οὓς P *sem.* εδωκας (*pro* δεδωκας) *bis* w. ἦσαν w. ἦσαν H *sem.* P *sem.* εισαν P *sem.* μου (*pro* σου *secund.*) v. τετηρηκασιν wL (*sic*) H** *sem.* P *sem.* τετηρικασιν P *sem.* 7. εγνωσαν vwLz *sem.* [εγνωκαν iHPz *sem.*]. σοι (*pro* σου) L. 8. ὁσα εδωκας (*pro* ἁ δεδωκας) w. εδωκας P *sem.* σοι (*pro* συ) P *sem.* 9. αυτον (*pro* αυτων) L*z *sem.* (*sic* z *sem. v.* 20). εισιν wLH *sem.* P. 10. εστιν wLH *sem.* P. −και τα σα εμα P* *sem.* δεδοξασμε H *sem.* P *sem.* 11. οὐκέτι vLHP *sem.* z. εν τω κοσμω ειμι w. οὗτοι (*sic v.* 25) i. σοι (*pro* εν τῳ κοσμῳ *secund.*) i. εισιν wLP. ὀνοματι HP (*sic v.* 12 H *sem. at* P *bis tantum*). ὧ iwH *sem.* P *sem.*, ὡ P *sem.*, ὁ H *sem.* z *sem.* (*pro* οὓς, Lz *sem. cum Elzev.*). ὦσιν (*sic v.* 19 v) ivP *sem.* +και (*post* καθως) LH *sem.* *fin.* +ἐν εσμεν iP** *marg.* 12. ἡμην Pz *sem.* οὓς H *sem.* οὐδεὶς P *bis.* ουδις z *sem.* ἐξ' P *sem.* απολετο iH *sem.* P *sem.* ειμι H *sem.* P *bis.* απολειας iH *sem.* P *sem.* z *sem.* απολιας P *sem.* πληρωθη ἡ γραφη P *sem.* 13. εχωσιν H *sem.* P. *fin.* ἑαυτοις iw [*non* vH *sem.* P]. επ' αυτοις L**. 14. εμησισει P *sem.* ὀυκ' *bis* P *sem.* −καθως *ad fin. versûs* LP* *sem.* (*habet* P** *marg.*). εκ του κοσμου ουκ ειμι i. 15. τηρησεις P *sem.* 16. οὐκ' *bis* P *sem.*: *secund.* P *sem.* εισιν wLP. κἀγω L. 17. ἁγιασον H *sem.* εστιν wP. 18. καθως συ πατερ εμε απε (*eras.*) απεστειλας H *sem.* *init. peric.* 19. ἁγιαζω H *sem.*

m. ἐμ' αὐτὸν wP *sem.* ὤσιν και αυτοι w. ωσι και αυτοι ὑγιασμενοι L.
ν P *sem.*, ὦσιν *sem.* 20. +παντων (*post* περι *secund.*) w. πιστευοντων
LHPz. 21. ωσιν ἡγιασμενοι εν αληθεια (*pro* ωσι καθως *usque ad* ἐν ωσιν)
m. ὦσι (*sic vv.* 23, 24) i. ωσιν *prim.* wL *at* ὦσιν (*sic v.* 22) vP *sem.*
ν *secund.* i (*sic v.* 22) w. ὦσιν *prim.* (*sic vv.* 22, 23, 24) P *sem. at secund.*
ν. +και (*post* ἵνα *secund.*) P *sem.* πιστευσει P *sem.* σοι (*pro* συ) z *sem.*
ἣν H *sem.* ἣν εδωκας w. εδωκα w. ἡμοις i. –ἡμεις P* *sem.* 23. *init.*
ω z *sem.* ὦσι vH *sem.* τετελιωμενοι P *sem.* –και (*ante* ἵνα *secund.*) L.
υσκει iw*P. ἠγαπησας *bis* (*sic ferè vv.* 24, 26) iwHP. 24. οὓς H *sem.*
κας (*pro* δεδωκας) w. ὤσιν μετ' ἐμου H *sem.* ὤσιν P *sem.* και εκεινοι
ν w. θεωρωσιν P. –μετ' εμου ἵνα θεωρωσι z *sem.* εμιν P *sem.* ἣν iwP
. ἣν δεδοκας H *sem.* δεδωκας (*pro* εδωκας) iLH *sem.* Pz. προκαταβολῆς
I *sem.* P *sem.* 25. –και οὗτοι εγνωσαν L. αυτοι (*pro* οὗτοι) P *sem.*
ὄνομα H *sem.* P *sem.* ἵνα H *sem.* ἣν (*pro* ἣν) wP *sem.* ειη i, ῇ w, ῇ P
., εἶ P *sem.* z *sem.* (*pro* ῇ).

CAP. XVIII. 1. εξηλθεν wH**P. ἣν (*sic vv.* 10, 13 *bis*, 14, 15, 16, 18
nd., 25, 28, 30, 40) P. 2. ἤδει P. ηδη z. ἰοῦδας (*sic vv.* 3, 5) L. +και
t συνηχθη) ivH. εκει ὁ ις P. 3. οὖν *semel et vicies in capite* P. +ὅλην
st λαβων) L. σπηραν L*. ὅπλων z. 4. ὁ δε ιησους ιδων (–ουν) L. 5.
ε ειπον (*pro* απεκριθησαν αυτῳ) i. –ὁ ις H*. ἱστηκει i**. ἵστηκει P.
ηκει vwH. 6. οὖν *mutat.* L. +ὁ ις (*post* αυτοις) i. –ὅτι w. απηλθεν v.
τω HP. 7. επηρωτησεν αυτους L. αυτοις (*pro* αυτους) ivwH*z. επ-
τησεν wP. 8. +αυτοις (*post* απεκριθη) iL. –ὁ vwHPz. ζητῆτε i. 9.
ιν z. δέκάς L, εδωκας w (*pro* δεδωκας). 10. εἵλκυσεν iHP. ἥλκυσεν L.
τε. i. επαισεν w. επεσεν HP. ὠτιον P. ἣν (*sic vv.* 25, 40) w. ὄνομα
. +εκεινω (*ante* μαλχος) H*P. 11. –ουν z. –σου ivwH [*non* L]. +αυτης
st θηκην) LPz. δεδωκεν wHP. +μου (*post* πηρ) L. ποίῳ L. *fin.* αὐτῶ P.
init. ἡ οὖν H. ει (*pro* ἡ) z. συνελαβοντο z. εδεισαν Pz. 13. ηγαγον L.
γασι z. –αυτον vHz. ἣν *semel* w. ἐνιαυτου w. 14. ἑνα P. αποθανειν
ο απολεσθαι) L. 15. *init.* ηκολουθη τω, σιμων L* (*sic*). ἠκωλουθει w.
λουθει H. ἠκολουθη P. ηκολουθη z. αυτω (*pro* τῳ ιυ) v. ὁ δε αλλος μαθη-
(–εκεινος) i. συνεισηλθεν wH**. συνησηλθεν P. 16. εἱστηκει (*cf. v.* 5)
HP. την θυρα w. τη θυρα [ν *rubro*] P. την θυραν Lz. εισηλθεν (*pro*
λθεν) L*. εκεινος (*pro* ὁ αλλος) L. ειπεν (*sic vv.* 29, 32) wHP. εισηγεν wH**P. 17. οὐκ' (*sic v.* 28 P**) P. 18. εἱστηκησαν i. εἱστηκεισαν
HP. ουν (*pro* δε *prim.* ?) z. ανθρακειαν P*. εθερμενοντο (*at* θερμαινο-
ς) P. γαρ (*pro* δε *secund.*) L. +και (*ante* ὁ πετρος) L. ἑστως wHP.

θερμενομενος H. 19. ἠρωτησε i. ἠρωτησεν wH**P. −περι *secund.* L. 20. −ὁ v. −εδιδαξα εν τη (*habet recentissima manus*) L *sic.* −τη ivwHP [*non* z]. παντοτε ivHz, παντες wLP (*pro* παντοθεν). 21. ερωτησον L. ακηκοωτας L. οὗτοι i. οἴδασιν iL**P (οἴ L*). 22. −δε vL. εἷς P. ἑστηκως L. εδωκεν wHP. οὕτως v. οὗτος L*. αποκρινει ivwLPz (αποκρίνε L, *teste Dobbinio, et forsan verè*). 23. ὁ δε ιησους ειπεν αυτω (−απεκριθη) L. μαρτυρισον P. μαρτυρησων z. ει *secund. mutat.* P. δαιρεις z. 24. απεστειλε δε (−ουν) L. −ουν ivwHPz. 25. ἑστὼς wz. ἑστῶς P. εἶπων P. +ουν (*post* ηρνησατο) iw**HPz [*non* L]. ἠρνησατο P. 26. απεκοψεν wH**P. ὠτιον wP. ιδων i. ιδον wz. ἴδον P. κειπω H. 27. ὁ πετρος ηρνησατο L. ἠρνισατο P. −ὁ iw*. 28. αγουσι (−ουν) iLP *sem. init. peric.* z *bis.* −ουν HP *sem.* πρετωριον *prim.* L*. −ην δε *usque ad* πραιτωριον *secund.* P* *sem.* ἦν w. ἦν P** *sem.* P *sem.* πρωι vLHP *sem.* P** *sem.* z. εισηλθον (ει *mutat.*) L. εἰσῆλθον P *sem.* πρετωριον *secund.* L. φαγωσιν wP. 29. πιλᾶτος (*sic quinquies Cap.* xviii, *duodecies* xix) iw (*sic ferè* vH). +εξω (*post* πιλατος) w, (*ante* και ειπε) L. φερητε z. 31. −ουν *prim.* v. λαββετε v. −αυτον *secund.* i. δε (*pro* ουν *secund.*) w. −οἱ v. ὑμιν (*pro* ἡμιν) i. 32. ειπεν LHP (*sic v.* 29 HP). εμελλεν w, ὦ ημελλον L. ἠμελλεν HP, (*pro* ημελλεν). αποθνισκειν i. 33. παλιν ὁ πιλατος εις το πρετωριον L. εφωνησεν wHP. 34. απεκρινατο (−αυτῳ) w. σοι (*pro* συ) L. αλλος wz. ἢ αλλοις σε P. ειπεν w. ειπε z. 35. +αυτω (*post* απεκριθη) i. μήτὶ P. σοι (*pro* σε) w. 36. −ὁ ivwHPz [*non* L]. +και λεγει αυτω (*ante* ἡ βασιλεια) z. ἡ (*pro* ει) P. ἦν P. οἱ εμοι ηγωνιζοντο αν L. ηγονιζοντο i. ἠγωνιζοντο wH. ἠγονιζοντο P. παραδω L. παραδωθω H. −νυν δε *ad fin. vers.* v*. 37. ὀυκοῦν w. οὐκ' οὖν P. οὐκοῦν vz. σοι (*pro* συ *prim.*) P. −ὁ *secund.* ivw*Hz [*non* L]. −εγω *prim.* L. γεγεννημαι vLz. −εις τον κοσμον i. ὧν P. αλληθειας P. 38. τουτω (*pro* τοῦτο) L. παλην w. εξηλθεν wH**P. οὐδὲμίαν (*sic* xix. 4 vwz, *v.* 11 vz) ivwPz. δεμίαν *sic* L. αἰτιαν (*non* xix. 4) w. +θανατου (*post* αιτιαν) L. εὑρισκω HP. 39. εστιν wP. ἡμιν (*pro* ὑμιν *prim.*) i. −ἱνα ἑνα ὑμιν P. ὑμων (*pro* ὑμιν *secund.*) v. απολυσω ὑμιν *bis* w, *secund.* Lz. ἑν (*pro* εν) P. −ἱνα ἑνα ὑμιν απολυσω z. βουλεσθαι P. −ουν z. +ἱνα (*post* ουν) w. 40. −παλιν wLz. −παντες i. βαραβᾶν L *solus.* βαραβᾶς L.

Cap. XIX. 1. οὖν *semel et vicies in hoc capite* P. εμαστιγωσεν wLHP. *fin.* +αυτον P**. 2. ἐξακανθων i. επι την κεφαλην w. αυτω (*pro* αυτου) z (*mutat. in* L). 3. *init.* + και ηρχοντο προς αυτον vwL. εδιδου z. αυτον (*pro* αυτῳ) H*. 4. και εξηλθεν (−ουν) w. −παλιν εξω i. ὁ πιλᾶτος παλιν εξω v. ὁ πιλατος εξω L. −εξω *prim.* z. αυτον ὑμιν z. οὐδὲμίαν αιτιαν εν

τῳ i. −ουδεμιαν L. αἰτιαν (*non v.* 6) P. εὑρισκω (*non v.* 6) P. ουχ εὑρισ-
αιτιαν L. 5. ἐξῆλθεν P. −ουν H. εξω ὁ ις w. ακανθηνον L. ἀκανθινον
ἱματιον *hic* i. 6. ιδον wP *sem.* z. φαρισαιοι z *mediâ pericopâ, at*
ρεσβυτεροι P *sem.* z *sem. init. peric.* (*pro* ὑπηρεται). +των ιουδαιων (*post*
ηρεται) L. αρον αρον σταυρωσον αυτον P *sem.* z *sem. init. peric.* +αυτον
ost σταυρωσον *secund.*) ivwLHP *sem.* z. πηλατος P *sem.* οὐχ' vPz. αιτειαν
sem. 7. +και ειπον (*post* ιουδαιοι) L. ὀφειλει wHP. ἑαυτον H. θῦ υἱον
HPz. υἱον θῦ ἑαυτον L. −του ivwLPz. 8. ὡς (*pro* ὀτε) L. ηκουσε
υτον τον λογον ὁ πιλατος L. Ἤκουσεν H**. εἴκουσεν P. τον λογον
υτον P. +δε (*post* μαλλον) L. εφοβηθην P. 9. *init.* παλιν ὁ πιλατος
γει τω ιυ (*vv.* 7, 8 *omissis*) P *sem.* z *sem.* εἰσῆλθεν P *sem.* πρετωριον L.
ησους z. 10. −ουν LH *sem.* H* *sem.* ὁ πι *marg.* P* *sem.* −εμοι ου λαλεις;
in loco. οὐκ' P *sem.* οἰδας iP *sem.* οἴδας P *sem.* *fin.* +και εμοι ου λαλεις; L.
. −ὁ *prim.* ivwHPz *sem.* [*non* Lz *sem.*]. +και ειπεν αυτω (*post* ις) LP**
rg. εχεις (*pro* ειχες) wPz. οὐδεμίαν iz. κατ' εμου εξουσιαν οὐδεμίαν w.
(*sic* P *vv.* 14, 19 *sem.*, 20 *prim. sem, bis sem.*, 23, 31 *bis sem.*, *secund. sem.*,
, 42) P *sem.*, *at* ἦν (*sic* P *vv.* 19 *sem.*, 20 *secund. sem.*, 31 *prim. sem.*) P *sem.*
(*pro* σοι *prim.*) P *sem.* δεδωμενον P *sem.* διατοῦτο ivLz. μειζωνα v.
ιζον' L. μειζον P *sem.* μειζων z. 12. +ουν (*post* τουτου) w** *supra* L.
ολυσαι αυτον ὁ πιλατος w. ὁ πιλατος απολυσαι εζητει τον ιησουν (−αυτον) L.
δε H. οὐν (*pro* δε) P. εκραυγαζων i. εκραυγαζον LP. εκραυγασαν w. ἦν
ἦ z (*pro* ει). ἑαυτον (*pro* αὑτον) ivwLPz. καισαρει P. 13. *init.* τοτε
ν ὁ πιλατος H *sem.* P *sem.* z *sem.* τουτων των λογων ivH. τον λογον του-
ν w. ἤγαγεν HP. εκαθησεν P. −του w. βιματος P *sem.* λιθωστρωτον
. λιθοστροτον P *sem.* ομενον λι *marg.* P** *semel.* ἑβραϊστη iP *sem.*
βραϊστι H *sem.* P *sem.* γαβαθα iH *sem.* P *sem.* z. γαββαδα w. γαβαθθα
sem. γαββαθᾶ (β *secund. mutat.*) L. 14. [*cum Elzev.* i]. παρασκευῒ P.
wLz, ἦν P, (*pro* δε *secund.*). ὡς (*pro* ὡσει) v. ὡς ἑκτη w. ὡσεὶ ἑκτη H
m. P. 15. εκραυγαζον w. εκραζων P *sem.* +λεγοντες (*ante* αρον) LH *sem.*
sem. z *sem.* ἆρον *bis* w. ἄρον *bis* P. σταυρῶσω P *sem.* +ουν (*post* απεκρι-
σαν) L. ει μι P *sem.* 16. παρεδωκαν z. αυ[τοις P**] P *sem.* *Post*
ρωθῆ *legit* L: οἱ δε παραλαβοντες αυτον επεθηκαν αυτω τον στρον' *v.* 17.
ι βασταζων αυτον εξηλθεν κ.τ.λ. παραλαβοντες H *sem.* P *sem.* z *sem.* παρε-
ιβων P *sem.* ηγαγον ivwz *sem.* ἤγαγον P *sem.* ἤγαγον εις το πραιτωριον
-και) H *bis* P *sem.* z *sem.* (ηγαγον z). 17. βασταζον H *sem.* P *sem.* z. ἑαυτω
ν σταυρον (−αὑτου) wz *sem.* ἑαυτου vH *sem.* z *sem.* ἑαυτου H *sem.* εις τοπον
ρο εις τον) iv. ὃ (*pro* ὃς) vH *sem.* H** *sem.* P *sem.* z *sem.* ἑβραϊστι H *sem.*

ἑβραϊστη iP. ἑβραϊστη z. 19. εγραψεν wH**P. τιτλον L. επεθηκεν iwP *sem.* +ἑβραϊστι ἑλληνιστι ῥωμαϊστι (*post* γεγραμμενον) L. −ιησους ὁ ναζωραιος L. ἰουδαιων H *sem.* 20. −*ab initio usque ad* ιουδαιων L. −ουν i. ὁ τοπος της πολεως ivwHPz [*non* L]. −και ην γεγραμμενον *ad fin. vers.* L. ἑβραϊστη iP *sem.* ἑβραϊστι H *sem.* P *sem.* ἑλληνιστη i. ἑλληνηστι H *sem.* P *sem.* ἑλληνηστῆ P *sem.* ῥωμαϊστη iP *sem.* 21. ελεγουν P *sem.* −των ιουδαιων *prim.* i? ἰουδαιων *secund.* H. ειπεν (*sic v.* 30 wHP) wLHP. εγω (*pro* των ιουδαιων *tert.*) i. 23. λαβων (*pro* ελαβον) L. −και *prim.* L. ἑκαστω HP. στρατιωτι P. *Post* μερος *legit* L τον δε χιτωνα επει ην αραφος εκ κ.τ.λ. χιτονα H. χιτον HP. αραφος ivwHPz. 24. −ουν L. λαχομεν i. ἡ *secund.* P. ἑαυτοις H. εβαλλον iP. 25. εἱστηκεισαν ivHP *bis.* εἱστηκησαν wP *bis.* −δε Pz *init. peric.* −του ιυ H* *sem.* αυτου *secund.* (ου *mutat.*) P *sem.* κλοπᾶ vwLH *bis* (κλωπα *bis*) P *bis* z. του κλοπα *v.* 25 *usque ad* οὐν ἰδων *v.* 26 *rescript. super rasur.* P *sem.* μαγδαλινη vH *sem.* 26. ιδως i. ἴδων P *sem.* −παρεστωτα i. ἠγαπα iwHP. γῦναι z. ἴδε ivH *ter* P *bis* z *sem.* [*non* wLH *sem.*]. ἴδου P *sem.* −ὁ υἱος σου *v.* 26 *usque ad* ιδου *v.* 27, z* *sem.* 27. ἡμερας (*pro* ὡρας) LH** *bis* Pz. ὁ μαθητης αυτην wH *ter* z *sem.* [*non* ivLH *sem.* Pz *sem.*]. +εκεινος (*post* μαθητης) H *sem.* P *sem.* z *sem.* 28. μετατοῦτο Lz *sem.* ἴδως H** *sem.* P *sem.* ιδων vLH *sem.* P *sem.* z *sem.* ηδη παντα wz *sem.* (ἤδη w). ἤδη H *sem.* −ηδη H *sem.* P *bis* z *bis.* +περι αυτου (*post* τετελεσται) H *sem.* P *sem.* z *sem.* πληρωθη (*pro* τελειωθῃ) L. 29. +μετα χολης (*post* οξους) L. *Rasuræ in* i *inter* οξους *secund.*, και ὑσσωπω (πω *mutat.*), περιθεντες *et* προς. ὀξους *bis* HP. περιθαντες ?z *sem.* το στοματι HP. 30. δε (*pro* ουν) wz *sem.* οὐν H *sem.* ελαβεν wH** *sem.* H *sem.* P. ελαβεν ὁ ιησους το οξος μετα χολης L. ὀξος wHP. τετελεστε P. κλῖνας i. παρεδωκεν wH** *sem.* H *sem.* P. το *secund. mutat.* H? *sem.* 31. Οι (Ο *rubro*) w. οἱουδαιοι P *sem.* ιουδαιοι (ι *prim. mutat.*) L. οὐν H *sem.* ἐπεῖ i *at* επι P *bis.* παρασκευῖ P. *Transfert* L επει παρασκευη ην *in locum ante* ἱνα μη μεινη. ἠν *secund.* H *sem.* −ἡ vP *bis* z *bis.* του σαββατου εκεινη L. εκεινου vwHPz *sem.* [*cum Elzev.* iz *bis*]. ἠρωτησαν iwH *sem.* P. ἵνα H *sem.* 32. ἦλθον P *sem.* ἦλθον P *sem.* +αυτου (*post* κατεαξαν) H* *sem.* σκελει *hic tantum* i*. 33. ιδον wPz *sem.* ἤδη H *bis* P. οὐ H *sem.* 34. εἱς H *bis.* λογη i. εξελθων λογχη την πλευραν αυτου L. ἐνυξεν w. ενυξεν LH**Pz *sem.* ευθεως iLHPz *bis* [*non* wz *sem.*]. αἱμα H *bis.* 35. ἑωρακὼς iP *sem.* ἑορακὼς P *sem.* εορακὼς P *sem.* ἑωρακὼς H *bis* P *sem.* μεμαρτυρηκεν wLH *bis* H** *sem.* P *sem.* z. μεμαρτυρικεν P *bis.* εστιν αυτου vH *bis* [*non* L]. εστιν ἡ μαρτυρια αυτου H *sem.* Pz *sem.* ειδεν (*pro* οιδεν) L. οἱδεν HP. αληθειαν (*pro* αληθη) P *duobus locis.* +και (*post* ἱνα) wLz.

z* *sem.* πιστευσηται P *sem.* 36. ὀστουν H *sem.* Pz. οὐ H *sem.*
**] P *sem.* +απ' (*ante* αυτου) LH *sem.* P *sem.* 37. ἑτερα H. ὀψονται
38. μεταταῦτα (−δε) i. −δε *prim.* vw. ἠρωτησε i. ἠρωτησεν wHP.
im. iwLHz. αριμαθιας w. ὢν w, ὢν P. −κεκρυμμενος *usque ad* ιησου
l. L. καὶ κρυμμένος P. διὰ τῶν H. .αυτου (*pro* του ιυ *secund.*) H.
(*sic* wH *v.* 39, *at* ἦλθεν P) wHP. ηρεν wH. ἦρεν P. 39. −και *prim.* v.
uος P. τὸ πρωτον vw, τῶ πρῶτον P, πρῶτον (−το) z. νυκτος προσ-
τον ιησουν προτερον L. φερον L* (ω *recenti manu*). σμιγμα i. μῖγμα w.
ια P. αλωης L*. ὡς (*pro* ὡσει) vwH [*non* L]. ὡσεὶ λητρας P. ἑκατον HP.
ὐτῷ H. εδεισαν z. +εν (*ante* οθονιοις) ivHz [*non* wL]. ἐνοθωνιοις P.
ης w. −των L. −εθος P. εστιν HP. ἰουδαιοις (*sic v.* 42) H. 41.
prim. L. μνημιον καὶνὸν P. κενον L. ουδεποτε i. οὐδεῖς P. 42.
ι παρασκευειν H. μνημίον (*sic*) P. −ὀτι εγγυς ην το μνημειον z. των
τον) w. *fin.* αυτον τον ιησουν L.

AP. XX. 1. −δε HPz *init. peric.* μαγδαλινη (*sic v.* 18 v) iv. ερχετε
. 6) P. σκοτειας i. ετη v. εις το μνημειον, σκοτειας ετι ουσης L.
ον P. απο (*pro* εκ) L. 2. οὖν *novies in hoc capite* P. σιμονα i. ὂν
ἦραν P. οὐκ' P. οιδα i. οἶδα P. οἶδαμεν vz. 3. εξηλθεν (ν *mutat.*)
ὁ *secund.* z* (*supra* z**). ἤρχοντο P. προς (*pro* εις) z. 4. προεδραμεν
. ταχειον i. ηλθεν w. ἦλθεν P, *at* εισηλθεν H. 5. *Deest in* L *v.* 5 *et*
ιsque ad εις το μνημειον. ὀθονια (*sic vv.* 6, 7) wP. οὐ H. εἰσῆλθεν
. 6) P. εισηλθε z. 6. σιμον P. 7. ἦν wH. ἦν P. μετα τα των L.
νν H. εντετίλυγμενον L*. ἑνα P. 8. εισηλθεν wHP. −ὁ *prim.* z (*habet*
ι *manus, non eadem quæ in v.* 3). ιδεν wHP. ιδε z. ειδον και επιστευ-
ι. 9. ἠδεισαν P. 10. απηλθων P*. *Rasura post* παλιν *in* i. 11.
ιPz *init. peric.* εἰστηκει ivwHP. προς τω μνημειω vw. προς το μνη-
ι. εκλαιεν vwHP. 12. Ἑνα *prim.* (ϵ *mutat.*) L. την κεφαλην P**
. ἑνα *secund.* P. τῶ σωμα P. 13. αυτῃ (η *mutat.*) i. γῦναι (*sic v.*
ι. +τινα ζητεις (*post* κλαιεις) L. ἦραν HP. οὐκ' οἶδα P. 14. *init.*
w. ὀπισω wHP. ἑστωτα wHP. ηδη P. −ὁ ivwLHPz. εστιν (*sic v.*
LHP) vwLHP. 15. εθηκας αυτον ivwLHPz. 16. μαριαμ w*. στρα-
i. εκεινη στραφεισα L. αυτῳ (ω *mutat.*) i. +ἑβραϊστι (*ante* ῥαββουνι)
ῥαβουνι LPz [*non* iwH]. 17. ἁπτου wHP. οὐπω P. −και (*ante* θν
.) w* (*supra rubro.*). 18. απαγγελουσα HP. ἑωρακεν wH. ἑορακεν P.
υτοις (*pro* αυτῃ) L. 19. −ουν LHPz *init. peric.* ὀψιας wP. κεκλυσ-
ι (*non v.* 26) i. ὀπου P. ἦσαν w. +αυτου (*post* μαθηται) w. των φοβων
ἑστη (*sic v.* 26) vL. 20. οὖν (*sic vv.* 21, 25, 30) P. 21. απεσταλκεν

wP. αποστελλω (*pro* πεμπω) w. 22. ενεφυσησεν wP. 23. ἂν *prim.* i. αφιεται L* (ν *insertum supra et in marg.* L**). κρατειτε z. καὶ κράτυνται? καὶ κράτηνται i (*forsan*) wHP (*rasura in* P *ante* τηνται). κεκρατειντai z. 24. δυδυμος L*, δυδιμος L**. δηδυμος P. οὐκ' ἦν P. ἦλθεν w. 25. ελεγεν w. ἑωρακεν w*. ἑωρακαμεν H. ἑορακαμεν P. ειδω L. βαλλω *bis* i, *secund.* P (βαλλο *prim.* P). —και βαλω *usque ad* ἥλων L. —των ἥλων *secund.* v*. ὑλων v**. 26. ὠκτῶ i. ὀκτω wHP. ἥσαν P. —αυτου L. +ὁ (*ante* Θωμας) L. +ουν (*ante* ὁ ις) H. λεγει αυτοις (*pro* ειπεν) i. 27. ὧδε wz. ὧδε P [ὥδε iL]. εἶδε L*. 28. *init.* —και L. απεκριθει ?L*. —ὁ *prim.* ivwLHPz. —αυτῳ v. 29. ειπεν δε (*pro* λεγει) L. ἑωρακας P. —Θωμα ivwLHPz. πεπιστευκας ; vwL. 30. —αὐτου w. ἃ P. εστιν wH**Pz. 31. πιστευσηται P*. —ὁτι *usque ad* θῦ i. —ὁ *prim.* vwLHPz. και ἱνα πιστευοντες *bis scriptum* L* (*secund. eras.*). + αιωνιον (*post* ζωην) L.

CAP. XXI. 1. μεταταῦτα iL. εφανερωσεν *bis* wHP. (—μετα ταυτα *et* παλιν HPz *init. peric.*). ὁ ιησους παλιν L. +αυτου (*post* μαθηταις) iLHPz. (+εγερθεις εκ νεκρων LHPz). —της *secund.* v. εφανερωσεν δε οὗτος ?L*. 2. ἦσαν w. ἥσαν (*sic* P *v.* 8) HP. διδιμος L. ἀποκανᾶ L. κανὰ wz. +υἱοι (*post* οἱ) P*z. 3. ἁλιευειν wHPz. +ουν (*post* εξηλθον) iz. ενεβησαν ivwLHP**z. —ευθυς L. εποιασαν (*non v.* 10) w. 4. —ηδη LH. ἤδη P. γινομενης w. ἑστη iL, *at* εστι H. —ὁ w. επι (*pro* εις) iH. αἰγιαλον wz. ἤδεισαν wHP. +αυτου (*post* μαθηται) L. εστιν LHP. 5. —ουν iH. οὐν (*sic vv.* 6, 7 *bis,* 9, 13, 23) P. μήτὶ P. εχητε i. οὖ P. 6. βαλλετε H. μερει i. —το L. εὑρησητε L. εὑρησεται H. εὑρησεται P. εβαλλον HP. οὐκέτι vLHz. ἑλκῦσαι ivL. ἑλκυσαι αυτο w. αυτω ἑλκυσαι HP. ισχὺον w. ἰχθυων (*sic* w *v.* 8, *non* 11) wH. 7. —ὃν ηγαπα ὁ ις H. ἠγαπα wP. ὁ ις τω πετρω *in marg.* i. εστιν *prim.* v, *bis* wLHP. ἦν P. ἑαὑτον H. 8. ἦλθον (ο *mutat.*) L, ἦλθον P. εισαν. H. αποπυχων L*. σηροντες L*. 9. *Rasura post* γην *in* w. ὀψαριον iwHP (*sic vv.* 10 wHP, 13 wP). 10. *init.* +και P. ὧν P. 11. ἥλκυσε i*? εἱλκυσεν w. εἱλκυσε H. εἱλκυσεν P. δυκτυον *prim.* i. εις την γην w. την γην L. μεστῶν iP. ἑκατον HP. πεντίκοντατριῶν w. ὀντων P. 12. οὐδεῖς P. ἐξετᾶσαι z. ιδοτες i. ϊδωτες P. 14. τουτον w*. τοῦτω ειδει L*. ἤδη P. εφανερωσεν ἑαυτον HP *quater initio pericop.* (*cum Elzev. semel, in mediâ pericopâ*) z *duobus locis.* —αὐτου w. 15. και (*pro* ὁτε ουν ηριστησαν, *et* —ὁ ις) Pz *init. peric.* σιμονι i. οἶδας (*sic vv.* 16, 17) i. 16. οἶδας (*sic v.* 17) P. ποιμενε i. ποιμαιναι P. [L *cum Elzev.*: *errant Millius, Wetstenius*]. 17. ἰωανᾶ *hic tantum* L. ελυπη L. οἴδας w. 18. Ὅτι (O *rubro*) i. εἶ L, εἶς P, ἧς vz (*pro* ἧς). εζωνοιες ἑαὑτον P. περιὲπάτης P.

ηθελες P. ὅτ' ἂν iwH. γειρασης P. αλλοσε w*. *Rasuræ in* w *inter* ζωση, και, *et* εισυ (υ *recenti manu*). εισυ w, ἧσοι L, οἰσει P, οιση z (*pro* οισει). 19. —δε L. ειπεν (*sic v.* 20) wLHP. τον θῦν *mutat. in* L. τουτω *secund.* i. ακολουθη (*sic v.* 22) P. 20. —δε w*. ἠγαπα iwHP. ακολουντα w*. τω στιθος P. 21. οὗτος v. 22. ερχωμαι i, ερχομε P (*non v.* 23 P). τις L*. 23. αποθνισκει *bis* iP. αποθνησκη w* (*prim., et forsan secund.*). —αυτῳ L. μενην ἑως ἑρχομαι H. 24. τουτου (*pro* τουτων) v. +ὁ (*ante* και γραψας) L. οἰδαμεν P. αληθεις P. 25. εστιν wH** *sem.* H *sem.* P. ἁ (*pro* ὁσα) v. ἁτινα H *sem* P. γραφητε vLP *sem.* z. καθέν L. καθὲν HPz. ουδ' wL. οὐδε H *sem.* οἶμε P *sem.* οἶμαι P *sem.*

SUBSCRIPT: ευαγγελιον κατα ιω στ^χ βγ. i. τελος *rubro* w, *post quod legit*

ἡ τετρας των μαθητων του λογου
εκχει το ρευμα των αειρρυτων λογων·
τοινυν ὁ διψων μη κατοκνει του πινειν,
ψυχην καταρδων και ποτιζων τας φρενας.

Nil habent vL: z *ita explicit*, Δοξα τω λογω τω δοντι τελος· αμην+.

ACTA APOSTOLORUM.

[CAP. I. 1—10.]

INSCRIPTIONES: *initio.* Λουκα bo, +ευαγγελιστου b, +πραξαποστολος συν θῶ των ἁγιων αποστολων· Λουκα του ευαγγελιστου d, +αἱ (*ante* πραξεις) gh. —ἁγιων mp. αρχη συν θεω πραξαποστολος f, *cum Elz.* ak.

CAP. I. 1. ὦ p. 3. ἑαυτον p. τεσσερακοντα *hic* p. οπτανομενος km. λεγον a. 4. συναυλιζομενος b**cd*em. παρηγγελλεν bd. ἰερος. p. κουσατε a. ἣν ηκουσατε k. 5. βαπτισθησεσθαι a*. εν πνι βαπτισθησεσθε p. πολας a. —ου μετα πολλας ταυτας ἡμερας k. 6. επηρωτον d. ει *illeg.* m. 7. εἶπεν mp. εστιν p. ἣ p. ὁ k. 8. ληψεσθαι m. δυναμιν, o. και εσεσθε *illeg.* in m. ἰλημ (*sic vv.* 12 *bis*, 19) p. —εν *secund.* ahp. πᾶσι p. 9. απεντων m. —βλεποντων m. ὀφθαλμων kp. *fin.* —αυτων a*. 10. αισθητι d.

εσθισεσι λευκαις p. 11. ειπαν p. ἑστηκατε m?p. βλεποντες dgkop. εμβλεποντες (*sic*) e. —ὁ ῑς *usque ad* οὑτως m. —ὁ *prim.* ah. αναληφθης ἀφ᾽ p. οὑτος ?l*. οὑτω ?p. +παλιν (*post* ελευσεται) d. εθεασασθαι e. 12. εν ταις ἡμεραις εκειναις (*pro* τοτε) c. +οἱ αποστολοι (*post* ὑπεστρεψαν) cm. ἱλη̄μ *bis* k. ὁρους p. ὡ (*pro* ὅ) o. σαβατου a*. εχων eko. 13. εις το ὑπερ. ανεβ. p. ἡσαν k. —και (*ante* ιωαννης) ah. και ιωαννης και ιακωβος p. βαρθομαιος k*. +ὁ του (*ante* αλφαιου) d. 14. ἡσαν *hic* p. —τῃ *secund.* m. —και τῃ δεησει p. γυναιξιν p. μαριαμ p. 15. αυταις (*pro* ταυταις) m. +αδελφοι (*ante* ὀνοματων) k. ἡν τε ὀχλος ὀνομ. p. ἐπιτοαυτὸ (*sic* II. 1, IV. 26) k. ἑκατον p. εικοσι fmp. εἰκοσι o. 16. ταυτην *bis scriptum* k*. —ταυτην p. προειπεν op. ἰοῡδα m. περὶοῡδα p. 17. καταριθμημενος c. κατηρηθμημενος k. εν (*pro* συν) p. ελαχεν op. 18. οὐν p. —του abc defghklm [*non* o] p. πρινης ae. ελακισε abcegh. ελακησεν p. σπλαγνα k. 19. χοριον d. εκεινω a*d. αχελδαμαχ p. τοῡτέστιν p. 20. ἐν *prim.* k. αυτων (*pro* αυτου *prim.*). m*op. ηρημωμενη p. λαβετω ἑτερος p. 21. οὐν kp. δει ουν *super rasuram in* h. συνελη λυθοτων o. —εν *secund.* p. εισηλθεν op. —ὁ e. 22. αχρι (*pro* ἑως) p. συν ἡμιν γενεσθαι kmp. ἑνα p. 23. ἑστησαν mp. επικαλουμενον c. βαρσαββαν bfgp. 24. ειπαν p. —συ o. ὁν (ὡν f) εξελεξω εκ τουτων των δυο ἑνα abcdefghlmop. ὁν εξελεξω εκ των δυο τουτων ἑνα k. 25. ἑνα *cum hoc versu jungit* d. αφ᾽ (*pro* εξ) p. ἰοῡδας m. 26. αυτοις (*pro* αυτων) p. ἐπεσεν p. εκληρος *vel* ενκλ. m* (*pro* ὁ κλ.). συνκατεψιφησθη p. ἑνδεκα p.

CAP. II. 1. —και c. πεντικοστης a. ἡσαν (*sic v.* 2) k. παντες cdp. +οἱ αποστολοι (*ante* ὁμοθυμ.) cdkm. ὁμου (*pro* ὁμοθ.) p. 2. ἀφνω p. ἠχος p. οἰκον k. 3. ὡφθησαν kp. εκαθισεν mo. και εκαθισεν (—τε) p. *fin.* ἑκαστον αὐτὸν p. τουτων b. 4. παντες p. ἑτεραις p. αποφθεγγεσθαι αυτοις p. 5. των ουρανων c. των ουρανου m. 6. γεναμενης m. συνηλθεν p. ἡκουον k. ηκουεν εἰς ἑκαστος p. —εἱς e. +αυτων (*post* ἑκαστος) c. 7. —παντες *prim.* aefhlmo. —προς αλληλους p. ουχ᾽ p. εισιν abdfghklmo. εισιν· οὑτοι p. 8. ακουωμεν a*. ἑκαστος p. εγενηθημεν f*kp. 9. μιδοι k. οἱ p. καπαδοκιαν m*. 10. αἰγυπτον k. λῐβυης k. κηρηνην m*. κυρινην p. 11. αρραβες kl. 12. αλληλοις (*pro* αλλος προς k) *k.* θελει (—αν) p. 13. ἑτεροι p. διαχλευαζοντες achkp. εισιν mop. 14. —σταθεις *usque ad* ἑνδεκα c*. +ὁ (*ante* πετρος) p. ἕνδεκα kp. επηρεν mp. επεφθεγξατο ab**h. +οὑτως (*ante* ανδρες) l. +οἱ (*ante* ιουδαιοι) e?. οἱ p. ἰλημ παντες p. γνωστων c. ἑστω p. 15. ἑστιν p. 16. εστιν p. 17. ἑσται (*sic v.* 21) p. προφητευσουσισιν m. ἡμων (*pro* ὑμων *prim. et secund.*) a*. αἱ p. θυγατεραις abel.

—και οἱ νεανισκοι ὑμων d*. ὀψονται p. ενυπνιοις f. εν ὑπνιοις kp. ενυπνασθησονται d*. 18. δουλοις c. εν *bis script. in* m. μος (*pro* μου *tertio*) c. προφητευσουσιν mp. προφυτευσουσι g. 19. —τῳ d. ἄνω kp. —ανω m. ἀτμῖδα m. 20. —ἡ p. μεγαλη m. 21. ὀνομα p. 22. νδρες m. ακουσαται a. αποδεδειγμενον απο του θῦ mp. απο του θῦ *bis scriptum in* c. αποδεδειμενον c. ἡμας (*pro* ὑμας) ck. εποιησεν ὁ θς̄ δι' αυτου dl. εποιησεν p. —και *ultimum* mp. οἰδατε p. 23. ὡρισμενη p. προσγνωσει c. ενδοτον ?m*. —λαβοντες p. χειρος p. ανειλατε dp. 24. ανεστησεν εκ νεκρων d. ανεστησεν mp. ὠδῖνας k. ὠδίνας mp, *at* οδυνας ac. καθ' ὅτι m. καθὅτι p. 25. ενοπιον c. διαπαντὸς hlmp *passim.* 26. διατοῦτο klmp *alii.* ηυφρανθη m. ηὐφρανθη p. ἡ *bis* p. ἡγαλλ. k. 27. ἀδην bfk?op. ἀδην c. 28. ὀδοὺς p. ευφροσυνην m. 29. εξῶν cp. ἡμας (*pro* ὑμας) c. —και *prim.* d. ετελευτησεν p. ἀχρι p. 30. οὐν p. ὀρκω ὠμοσας o. ὀσφυος p. *Rasura inter* αν *et* αστησειν *in* k. αναστησει c. —το κατα σαρκα αναστησειν τον χν̄ p. +τε (*post* καθισαι) fk. τον θρονον p. 31. προειδων ce. ελαλησεν p. ουτε (*pro* ου) p. κατεληφθη ace. ουκ εγκατελειφθη dfk. εγκατελιφθη p. —ἡ ψυχη αυτου p. ἀδην bk?op. ουτε (*pro* ουδε) p. ειδεν mp. 32. μαρτυρες εσμεν c. 33. ουν δεξια c. του πνευματος του ἀγιου cp. εξεχεεν p. τουτων (*pro* τουτο) c. —νυν p. ἡμεις e. βλεπεται p. +τε (*ante* και) c. ακουεται p. 34. ὁ αυτος g. 36. +ὁ (*ante* οικος) c. ισρ. (σ *mutatum?*) m. +και (*ante* κυριον) abcdefghklmop. ὁ θεος αυτον cm. εποιησεν m. εποιησεν ὁ θς̄ p. 37. ακουσατες m*. κατηνυγησαν την καρδιαν p. ειποντες (—τε) l. δε (*pro* τε) p. ποιησωμεν ahkp. 38. *init.* ειπε δε πετρος ah. ειπε e, εφησε l (*pro* εφη). —εφη p. +φησὶν (*post* μετανοησατε) p. ἑκαστος p. ὀνοματι p. των ἀμαρτιων ὑμων p. 39. *init.* ἡμιν e. προσκαλεσητε a. προκαλεσηται c. 40. ἑτεροις p. —τε c. δε (*pro* τε) k. πλειουσι c. διεμαρτυρατο ahp. +αυτους (*post* παρεκαλει) p. γεᾶς p. 41. οἱ p. οὑν p. —ασμενως p. +εν (*ante* τη ἡμ.) p. ὡς (*pro* ὡσει) l. τρισχιλιοι m. 42. προσκατερουντες h. —και (*post* κοινωνια) p. ἀρτου p. 43. πασα ψυχη c. πᾶσι p. +μεγας (*post* φοβος) c. —τε m. δε (*pro* τε) p. *fin.* εγενετο ce. εγινοντο l. ἐγινετο p. 44. *init.* +και p. αντες m. πιτευοντες c. πιστευσαντες f. 45. —τα p. πασιν mp. —καθοτι *ad fin. vers.* m. ἀν p. ειχεν p. 46. καθημεραν fghlp (*sic etiam* kmo *in v.* 47; III. 2). ὁμοθυμαδῶν cp. ἱερω p. —τε *secund.* p. —αρτον k. 47. ἐχοντες p. προσετιθη p. ἡμερας c. +εν (*ante* τη εκκλησια) k. —τῃ εκκλησιᾳ (*jungens* καθημεραν *cum* ἐπὶ τὸ ἀυτὸ) p.

Cap. III. 1. επιτοαυτο (*sic* II. 44 &c.) ho**. —δε (πετρος δε m**p) mp. ἰωαννης p. ἱερον (*sic v.* 2 *bis*) p. ενατην ab**ghlm [*non* kp]. 2. της (*pro*

τις) c. κοιλοιας *k*. επι (*pro* προς) p. πυλην (*pro* θυραν) bo. ελεημοσυνη
c. 3. –ὀς *usque ad* ἱερον p: ιδον τε τον πετρ. και ιω. p** *marg.* μελοντας c.
ἠρωτα kp. –λαβειν acefghklm [*non* p]. 4. αυτο (*pro* αυτον) a. ειπεν ck*
mp. ειπον e. ἠς (*pro* εις) c. 5. επιχεν ?c. αυτων (*pro* αυτοις) k. 6.
ειπεν mp. οὐχ' p. ὑπαρχει k. ἐχω p. ὀνοματι p. εγυρε ?c. εγειρε m.
ἐγειρε p. περιπατη?e. 7. κρατησας (*pro* πιασας) k. –δεξιας e. ηγειρεν m.
ηγειρεν αυτον p. αἱ βασεις αυτου p. 8. ἐστη p. περιεπατη c. εισηλθεν cp.
περιπατων εις το ἱερον k. *Rasur. ante* περιπατων *in* l. –και *quartum* k.
ἀλλομενος fkop. αινων (*sic v.* 9) k. αἰνὸν *hic* p. 9. ειδε (–αυτον) e. ειδε
(ειδεν p) πας ὁ λαος αυτον cp. 10. επεγινωσκε l. δε (*pro* τε) p. αυτος
(*pro* οὗτος) gp. ὡραῖα p. *fin.* αυτο c. 11. αυτου (*loco* του ιαθεντος χωλου)
cp. –τον c. +τον (*ante* ιωαννην) mp. συνεδραμεν ep. συνεδραμον k. πας ὁ
λαος προς αυτους p. σωλομωντος a*. σολομωνος c [*non* mp]. 12. +ὁ (*ante*
πετρος) kop (ὁ p). ἀνδρες p. τοῦτο m*p. ἠ *prim.* p. πεποιηκοσιν m. –τον
p. 13. ἀβρααμ (*sic etiam* bmo *v.* 25) bhklo, *passim.* ι̅υ̅ (*pro* ι̅υ̅) p. ἡμεις e.
+μεν (*post* ὑμεις) abcdfghklop [*non* m]. –αυτον p. –αυτον κατα *usque ad*
δικαιον *v.* 14, a. 14. ηρνησασθαι d. 15. εσμεν μαρτυρες e. 16. –επι p.
ὀνομ. *bis* p. –τουτον *usque ad* ονομα αυτου m. οἶδατε k. οἶδατε p. εστερε-
ωσεν p. ὁλοκληριαν p. ἀπεναντι p. *fin.* ἡμων a*. 17. οἶδα p. ἀγνοιαν kp.
18. προκατηγγειλεν p. –αὐτου p. χρηστον p. +αυτου (*post* χ̅ν̅) cp. οὕτως
abcefghklop. οὕτος dm. 19. οὖν p. εξαλιφθηναι k. ἀν p. ἐλθωσι k.
ελθωσιν p. –του km. 20. προκεχειρισμενον (*pro* προκεκηρ.) abcdefghk
(–τον k) lmop. υἱον (*pro* ὑμιν) m. χ̅ν̅ ι̅ν̅ acghl [*non* m]. 21. δεξασθε km.
ἀχρι p. χρονον m. –παντων *prim.* b*e, *secund.* op. +των (*ante* ἁγιων) adfg
hklmop. +των (*ante* απ') c. των απ' αιωνος προφητων k. απαιωνος αυτου
προφητων p. 22. μωϋσης abdgh*lop. –γαρ b*op. –προς τους π̅ρ̅α̅ς̅ p.
προ (*prim.*) m. +ἡμων (*post* π̅ρ̅α̅ς̅) def. αναστησει p. ἡμων (*pro* ὑμων) *bis* a,
pro primo bcefhlo. ακουσεσθαι a**m. ἀν p. λαλησει cep. *fin.* ἡμας a.
23. ἐσται p. εαν (*pro* αν) bcdefglmop. εισακουση bo. 24. καθεξεις e.
καθὲξης p. κατηγγειλαν cdefgklmp. *fin.* αυτας m. 25. +οἱ (*ante* υιοι) b**
cek*k*p. διεθετω p. –τους d. ὑμων (*pro* ἡμων) km*p. +εν (*ante* τῳ σπερ-
ματι) abcdefgh*k*lmop. ενευλογιθησονται d. ευλογηθησονται e. 26.
–ι̅ν̅ p. +και ἁγιαζοντα (*post* ευλογουντα) k *et k*. επιστρεφειν l. ἑκαστον
p. +ὑμων (*ante* απο) k.

CAP. IV. 1. των b*, αυτον a (*pro* αυτων). +τα ῥηματα ταυτα (*post* λαον)
c. ἱεροις d. ἱερεις *et* ἱερου p. 2. καταγγελειν dk. των (*pro* την εκ) acdf
ghlmo** [*non* p]. 3. επεβαλλον m. +αυτους k, +αυτοις m (*post* εθεντο).

αὔριον (*sic v.* 5) k, αιωνιον m (*pro* αυριον). ἑσπερα p. ἤδη k. 4. τον (*pro* των *prim.*) m. −ὡσει p. 5. +τους (*ante* πρεσβυτ.) bceop, *et ante* γραμματ. bcop. εν (*pro* εις) bhkop. 6. αννας ὁ αρχιερευς και καϊαφας και ἰωάννης και αλεξανδρος p. ἦσαν kp. ἱερατικου m*. 7. −τῷ abc**dfghklmo [*non* p]. ἡ p. ὀνοματι p. 8. ειπεν mp. 9. εἰ k. επ' m. 10. ενωποιονe. ὑγιὴς k. 11. ὁ ἐξου. k. εξουδενωθεις c. αφ' (*pro* ὑφ') o. οικοδομων c. οικονομουντων e. οἰκοδ. k. −γενομενος k*? (*habet k*). 12. ἀλλω k. −ἡ fk*. ουδε (*pro* ουτε) abhko. ἑτερον εστιν achm (εστι cm). −ὑπο τον ουρανον bcglmo. διδομενον d. τοις (*pro* εν *secund.*) c**. 13. +οἱ ιουδαιοι (*post* δε) dm. εισιν m. αγραμματι d. ται (*pro* τε) a**. 14. τε (*pro* δε) c. θεωρουντες (*pro* βλεποντες) bo. ἑσ-τωτα ko. −τον *secund.* h. 15. −δε c. εξω του συνεδριου αυτους c. συνε-βαλλον abdefghk**lmo. +τε (*ante* προς) e. 16. ποιησωμεν km. *Rasur. ante* ἀνοις *in* k. γεγονεν em. ἰλημ *super ras.* o**. +ὡς (*ante* ου) k. αρνεισ-θαι c. 17. απειλησομεθα bdek**o. μηκέτι *et* μηδενὶ k. *fin.* ανω ahl. 18. παρηγγειλεν?m*. −αυτοις k. τοκαθόλου h. −μη φθεγγεσθαι e. μηδὲ klmo. 19. ειπον προς αυτους ck. ενωπιον *bis script. in* m. μαλον k*. 20. ειδωμεν af. +ἁ (*ante* ηκου.) ah. ἥκουσ. k. 21. προάπειλησαμενοι a. προσαπειλησα-μενου l*. μη (*pro* μηδεν) k. κολασονται abcdefghklmo. γεγονωτι?m*. 22. ὁ ανθρωπος τεσσαρακοντα c. εγενετο k. 23. −δε e*. +οἱ αποστολοι (*ante* ηλθον) f. ανηγγειλαν ah. 24. −*ab initio usque ad* ειπον a* (*habet marg.*). ηραν φωνην ὁμοθυμαδον m. +την (*ante* φωνην) c. +ει (*post* συ) k*? *k*. −και (*post* γην) o. θάλ. k*. 25. *init.* ὁ δια του πατρος ἡμων εν δαδ (*sic*) k*k*. −του acdghkm [*non* o]. 26. επιτοαυτο h. τω αυτω e. *fin.* αυτων l*. 27. −γαρ b*. επαληθειας h. +εν τη πολει ταυτη (*ante* επι) bcdegko. εχρησας a. πιλᾶτος k. 28. βουλλη b*. προωρησε a. 29. τανῦν hkm. +δε (*post* νυν) o. ἐπίδε m. δουλοισου k. −πασης g. πασις d. 30. εκτει-νην e. −σε ef. ὀνοματος k *passim.* 31. εσεισθη k. ἦσαν k. 32. ουδε εἰς abdfghkmo. ουδεις el. αυτων (*pro* αυτῳ) b**fgkl*m. 33. δυναμει μεγαλη ach. απεδιδου m. οἱ αποστολοι το μαρτυριον aghko. −της αναστασεως m. ιῦ χῦ (*pro* του κῦ ιῦ) e. ην μεγαλη k. 34. ην (*pro* ὑπηρχεν) ah. οικειων em. ὑπηρχων (*sic*) e. 35. καθο g. καθ' ὅ m. −αν m. καθοτις (−τι αν) l. 36. απο (*pro* ὑπο) adghlm. μεθερμηνευομενος a. −μεθερμηνευομενον c**. λεβιτης *k*. 37. αυτου d*f*m. τω (*sic*) e.

Cap. V. 1. ονοματι ανανιας bcm [*non* o]. σαπφειρα ab**ghl [*non* km] o. σαπφειρει e. 2. συνειδιας e. τι μερος l. εθηκε παρα τους ποδας των αποσ-τολων g. εθηκε f. 3. +ὁ (*ante* πετρος) bm. +προς αυτον (*post* πετρος) c. ες (*pro* σε) m. +σε (*post* νοσφισασθαι) abefghm [*non* o]. *Rasur. post* τιμης *in* d. 4. μενων eh*. +εν (*ante* σοι) e. εμεινε e. επι (*pro* εν *prim.*) c. ὑπηρχεν km. 5. +ὁ (*ante* ανανιας) abdfghkmo. −ταυτα k. 6. ενεγκαντες f. 7. *Rasur. post* γυνη *in* k. εισηλθε k. 8. −αυτη b*. προς αυτην em. πετρος προς αυτην (−ὁ) d. ειπεν m. 9. +του (*ante* κῡ) k. το ἁγιον (*pro* κῡ) e. −σου o. 10. παραχρῆμα *hic* o. 12. εγενετο h [εγινετο ce]. +μεγαλα (*post* τερατα) k. πολλα εν τω λαω mo. −πολλα k. ἡσαν k *passim.* παντες l. +του (*ante* σολομ.) cko. σολομωνος abcd*efghlm [*non* ko]. 13. *fin.* ὁ θς̄ λαος (*sic*) a. 15. και εις (*pro* κατα) k. κληνων e. κραβατων c. +του (*ante* πετρου) abh. επισκιασει m. 16. συνηρχοντο d. −και *prim.* c. ἱλῆμ (−εις) k. +τους (*ante* ασθενεις) m. ὀχλουμενους k. και (*pro* οἱτινες) ah. 17. οὐσα k. ερεσις c. αἱρεσις o. σαδουκαιων m*. 18. επεβαλλον c. τηρηση ?k*. 19. τες (*pro* τε) c. ειπεν m. 20. τω λαω εν τω ἱερω g. 21. +οἱ αποστολοι (*post* εισηλθον) m. −εις το ἱερον e. αραρχιερευς k. συνεκαλεσαντο f. απεστιλαν *k*. 22. παραγενομενοι ὑπηρεται ah. *Rasur. inter* παρ *et* αγενομενοι *in* d. ουχ' dko. απηγειλαν h. 23. εὑρωμεν *bis* c. −εξω abcdefghklmo. ἑστωτας ko. προς c, επι m (*pro* προ). ουδενα εσω o. 24. −ἱερευς και (*sic*) e. στρατιγος k (*sic v.* 26 k*). 25. −λεγων abcdfghk lmo. ἑστωτες ko. 26. ηγαγον l. εφοβουντων a. λιθασθωσιν d*. 27. ἑστησαν m. *Rasur. post* συνεδριω *in* d. 28. το (*pro* τῳ) c. τουτο (*pro* τουτῳ) a. ἡμων (*pro* ὑμων) c. επαναγαγειν m. ὑμας (*pro* ἡμας) e. 29. −ὁ abcdfghklmo. θω̄ δει m. 30. −ἡμων k. +τον παιδα αυτου e, +τον ο (*ante* ιν̄). +μεν (*post* ὑμεις) f. διεχειρησασθε em. δε ἐχειρισασθαι κρεμμασαντε c. 31. πατερα (*pro* σωτηρα) m. 32. −αυτου gh, *at* αυτο c, αυτο m. −δε m. ὁ θς̄ εδωκε k. 33. *init.* O οἱ d. ακουοντες ch. +ταις καρδιαις αυτων (*post* διεπριοντο) f. επεβουλευσαντο b. εβουλοντο el. εβουλευσαντο k. 34. γαμαλιηλ *mutat. in* o. τους αποστολους βραχυ τι deo (βραχυτητι *pro* βραχυ τι o). 35. ειπεν m. δε (*pro* τε) k. ἰσραηλιται o. αυτοις (*pro* ἑαυτοις) m. *Rasur. post* ανοις *in* k. 36. των ἡμερων τουτων m. λεγον c. +μεγαν (*post* ἑαυτον) ko. προσεκληθη a*gl. προσεκλιθη a**bdhm. προσεκοληθη c. προσεκολλιθη e. +ὁ (*ante* αριθμος) k. ανδρων αριθμος m. ὡς a, ὡς h (*pro* ὡσει). επηθοντο e. 37. τουτο (*pro* τουτον) k. ἰου̃δας m. γαλλιλαιος c. απεστησεν ἱκανον λαον k. ὀπισω k. απολετο a. απωλετο e. 38. ταν̃υν hkm. ανθρωπον *prim.* c. ἑαυτους (*pro* αυτους) f. −αὑτη abcfghl. καταλυθῆσετε k. 39. η (*pro* ει) e. εστιν; k. εστι o. δυνησεσθε ahk. 40. πεισθησαν l. δηραντες ab**g**ho. 41. κατηξιωθησαν (κατιξ. a) ὑπερ του ονοματος adhm. του χῡ aehm, του κῡ ιῡ bfgl**, ιῡ ko (*pro* αυτου). 42. *Versus deest in* c. −και *prim.* am. κατοῖκον m. *fin.* τον χν̄ ιν̄ adhmo. τον τον κν̄ ιν̄ (−χν̄) k.

CAP. VI. 1. –εν δε ταις ἡμεραις ταυταις c. πληθηνουντων k. γογυσμος
ἑλληνηστων c. 2. εστι καταλιποντας ἡμας k. το λογον m. 3.
κεψασθαι d. πληρει c. πληρης k. καταστησομεν abc (*tacitè*) dfghklmo
e]. 4. προσκαρτερουντες c. προσκαρτερησωμεν elm. 5. ἠρεσεν k.
ῃς cdfkl*m. πληρεις e. προχωρον l. νικανωρα e. αντιοχια c. 6.
ι (*post* οὓς) l. ἑστησαν (*sic v.* 13) l. 7. ηὐξανε k. επληθυναιτο c. δε
τε) o. ιουδαιων (*pro* ἱερεων) eo. ὑπηκουε g. πηστει c. 8. πληρεις e.
τος (*pro* πιστεως) k. εν τω λαω μεγαλα o. *fin.* +δια του ὀνοματος του
χῡ k. 9. των λεγομενων k. συζητουντας ?m*. 10. ισχυσαν f.
ια d*. ελαλη ?k*. 11. ὑπεβαλλον e. –ὁτι d. προς ? (*pro* εις) k*.
ιην b** (*rubro*) efklo. 12. –τους *secund.* k. γραμματοις k. +αυτον
ηγαγον) e. 13. μαρτυρες a*. +ὁτι (*post* λεγοντας) d. παυετε f.
υτου abcefhlo. κατα του τοπου τουτου του ἁγιου και του νομου λαλων
ιτα βλασφημα k. 14. –γαρ e. –οὑτος c. –τουτον c**. εθει e. ἁπερ
εν d. ὑμιν (*pro* ἡμιν) klo. μωσης acfhm. 15. παντες c. –οἱ k. κα-
νοι c.

CAP. VII. 1. ἆρα hk. οὗτος a. 2. ὠφθη k. ἀβρααμ *passim* dhklmo.
ἡ hlm. κατοικισαι m. εις (*pro* εν *secund.*) o. χαρᾶ m*, χαρρᾶ m**. 3.
ω e. ἦν k *passim.* 4. της (*pro* γης) m* (γῆς *supra*, m**). κατωκισεν m.
κατωκησεν *in* k αυτον εις την γην ταυτην εις ἡν ὑ *eras.* εις (*pro* εν) efmo.
κειθεν eglm. μετωκησεν cekmo. –αυτον e. *fin.* κατεικειτε e. 5. ου δε-
ν l. επηγγειλατου m. δουναι αυτω bcefglmo. δουναι αυτην εις κατα-
ιν αυτω ahk. (κατάσχε a). 6. αυτω (*pro* οὑτως) k. +αυτω (*post* οὑτως) b.
παροικονκον m. αυτω (*pro* αυτο) e. κακοσουσιν m. 6, 7. –και κακωσ-
ν *usque ad* εθνος a. 7. *init.* το δε (–και) e. +εκεινο (*post* εθνος) m. +και
ε ᾧ) a. ὁ (*pro* ᾧ) cg. δουλευσωσιν m. μεταταῦτα hlm. 8. οὑτος elo.
νησεν o. ισαακ *prim.* k. –τῃ ἡμερᾳ b*. –ὁ *bis* k. 9. *Jungunt* hlm ζηλω-
ες τον ιωσηφ. +αυτον (*post* απεδοντο) c. αἰγυπτον k. 10. εξειλατο
εναντι φαραω̄ k. αἰγυπτου (*sic vv.* 11, 12, 15, 17, 22, 24, 28, 34, 39,
k. +εφ' (*ante* ὁλον) g. οἶκον k. 11. ἐφ' k. ηὑρισκον k. 14. +ὁ (*ante*
φ) m. ιακωβ τον πατερα αυτου ahm. –την o. –αὐτου *secund.* be (?) fg
ἑβδομηκονταπεντε (-ται m) ψυχαις afhm. ἑβδομηκοντα και πεντε
αις c. ἑβδομήκοντα πέντε k. ἑβδομήκονταπέντε o. *fin.* +μετετεθησαν
υχεμ και ετελευτησεν αυτος και οἱ πρες ἡμων o. 16. εισυχεμ k. ᾧ (*pro*
glm. ὠνησατο k. ἀβρααμ (*sic v.* 17) klo. εμμωρ ach. εμορ efl. ἑμμορ
εμμορτοῦ, (*sic*) m. 17. ηγγιζεν (*sic*) e. ηγγισεν m. ὡμοσεν p.
ξησεν b*. ηὐξησεν k. επληθυνετο ?e. 18. ἄχριςοῦ g. ἑτερος p. +επ'

αιγυπτον (*post* ἑτερος) o. 19. εκακωσεν p. τα βρεφη αυτων εκθετα mp. ἠαὐτων (*pro* αὐτων) a*. 20. εγενηθη km. μωϋσης abcefhk**lop [*non* m]. αστειως p. ανεστραφη m*. οἰκω p. −αὐτου abefghlmp. 21. εκτεθεντος δε αυτου p. τουτον (*pro* αυτον *prim.*) o. ανειλατο f*p. −αυτον *secund.* acehko, *tertium* c. 22. επεδευθη e. μωϋσης abcefghklop. και ην (*pro* ην δε) e. τε (*pro* δε) l. −εν *secund.* abefhop. εργοις και εν λογοις c. ἐν λογω και εν εργω k. *fin.* +αυτου ep. 24. τινὰ hklm. τινᾶν p. ἠμυνατο k. 25. ενομιζεν p. διδωσι [-σιν p] σωτηριαν αυτοις mp. 26. τε (*pro* δε) abcefghklm op. συνηλλασσεν o. συνηλλασεν p. −ὑμεις p. 27. τω (*pro* τον) k. τουτον (*pro* αυτον) ah. ἡμων m**p. 28. −σu p. 29. εφυγεν p. μωυσης elop. τουτο p. 30. ὠφθη k. ὁρους p. −κ̄υ p. 31. ὁ p. μωυσης cefgklop. εθαυμασεν ιδων k. εθαυμαζεν p. εθαυμαζε bfglm. ὁραμα ko. −αυτου o. −προς αυτον p. 32. ἀβρααμ klmo. −ὁ θ̄ς *secund.* k, *tert.* kp, *quart.* p. μωυσης aefghklop. 33. ειπεν p. +εκ (*ante* των ποδων) k. τος (*pro* τοπος) m. εφ (*pro* εν) p. ἑστηκας ko. 34. +του (*ante* εξελεσθαι) ef. δευρω e. αποστελλῶ a. αποστειλω ćp. 35. μωσην b*c**m. ηρνησατο b. ειρνησατο p. +εφ' ἡμας ko, +εφ' ἡμων p (*post* δικαστην). αρχηγον (*pro* αρχοντα *secund.*) ah. +και (*ante* αρχοντα *secund.*) p. απεσταλκε (-εν p) συν (*pro* εν) cp. ὀφθεντος k. ωφθεντος hm. 36. *init.* οὑτως m. οὑτος p. −γῃ b*m. αιγυπτω hk (αἰγ. k) lop. τη αιγυπτω m. 37. εστι afho. −ὁ *prim.* ab**cef ho. μωσης b*m. ὃ εἶπας p. −κ̄σ p. −ὑμων *prim.* p. ἡμων (*pro* ὑμων *prim.*) acfghklo [*non* m]. −αυτου ακουσεσθε afghlmp [*non* o]. 38. εστι e. αυτου (*sic*) e. ὀρει p. −ἡμων e. λογον (*pro* λογια) elm. *fin.* ὑμιν k. 39. ὑμων (*pro* ἡμων) ckop. αλλα ko [*non* p]. απεστραφησαν m (επεσ. *Dobbin.*, *vix rectè*). τη καρδια abcefghklmo [*non* p]. 40. μωυσης ab**cefghklop. οἴδαμεν p. 41. ανηνεγκαν co. ηὐφραινοντο k. εφραινοντο p. 42. εστρεψαι f. ἐστρεψεν p. αυτοις (*pro* αυτους) p. εν τη ερημω ετη τεσσαρακοντα ah. οἶκος p. 43. αστρων ?l*. −θ̄υ b*. ἡμων a*l. ρεφαν g. ρεφφαν hkl. ρεφφα o. ρεμφᾶ p. *Post quod rasura est in* b. ἡμας a*. 44. *init.* ἡ p. ἧν (*pro* ἦν) mp. −εν *prim.* abcefghk*lmop. −ἡμων km, *at* ὑμων go. τω μωση ὁ λαλων m. μωσει b*. μωυσει b**. μωυση acefghklop. 45. ἣν και εἰσηγαγον k. ὑμων (*pro* ἡμων *prim.*) k. ὀν (*pro* ὠν) o. 46. εὑρεν *et* εὑρειν p. ἠτησατο k. 47. ὠκοδομησεν k. οἰκῶν (ο *supra p. m.* ?) p. 48. −οὐχ' a. ουχ m *alii.* −ναοις p. κατεικει k. +και (*post* καθως) o. 49. +εστιν (*post* θρονος) *k.* οἶκον p. οικοδομησεται a*mp. −κ̄ς b?. ἢ p. *fin.* +εστιν *k.* 50. εποιησεν p. παντα ταυτα lm. 51. ταις καρδιαις c. +ὑμων (*post* καρδια) o. ὠσιν p. −και τοις ωσιν f. αντιπιπτεται *k.* +και (*post* ὡς) o. 52. [τ] ων l*.

p. προδοτε p*. φωνεις p. *fin.* εγενεσθε kp. 53. ελαβεται k. ελαβε
54. +ὑμων (*ante* αυτων) m*. +αυτων (*post* ὀδοντας) k. ὀδοντας kp.
+στεφανος (*ante* πληρης) e, *at* στεφανος δε ὑπαρχων o. +πιστεως και
ost πληρης) o. ειδεν mp. +την (*ante* δοξαν) l*. ἑστωτα (*sic v.* 56 *præter* p)
p. ἐκδεξιῶν (*sic v.* 56) h. 56. ἰδου θεορω k. διηνοιγμενους p. ἑστωτα
δεξιων m. 57. φωνὴν μεγαλη p. συνεσχων k. ὠτα p. αυτον (*pro*
των) a*. 58. ἐκβαλλόντες m. +αυτον (*ante* εξω) k. −αὐτων ab*fghlm.
ου (*ante* καλουμενου) fh. 59. $\overline{\chi\epsilon}$ (*pro* $\overline{\iota\upsilon}$) k*? +$\overline{\chi\epsilon}$ (*post* $\overline{\iota\upsilon}$) d. ιουσου m.
τε (*pro* δε) e. εκραξεν p. στησεις dk?. ἁμαρτιαν p. εκυμηθη ?d*.
ιμηθει ?g.

CAP. VIII. 1. *Jungunt* o *alii* σαυλος *usque ad* αυτου *cum cap.* VII. ἦν p.
ν *secund.* m. ἱεροσ. p. και παντες (−τε) ko. δε (*pro* τε) abdefghlmp.
ας g. σαμαριας ?a*. 2. συνεκομισαντο bo. συνεκομησαν k. εποιησαν
3. ελυμενετο e. οἰκους kp. 4. οἱ p. οὐν p. διασπαραντες ?m*.
τὲ (*pro* δε) p*. +την (*ante* πολιν) m. εκυρησεν m*. εκυρησσεν m**. 6.
(*pro* τε) ahp. −του f. δια το (*pro* εν τῳ) d. ἁ p. 7. πολλοι p. −των o.
ματα d. φωνη μεγαλη abfghklmop. εξηρχοντο kp. εξειρχετο o. −και m.
ιοι a. 8. εγενετο δε (−και) p. πολλῆ χαρᾶ (−μεγαλη) p. 9. ὀνοματι p.
ττανων p. 10. προσηχον e. −παντες abdefghlmo [*non* p]. ἡ *secund.* k.
αλουμενη (*ante* μεγαλη) p. 11. προσηχον e. τε (*pro* δε) e. τω ep.
νου p. μαγιαις f. εξιστακεναι kmo. 12. −τα (*ante* περι) p. ὀνομ. p.
ου *tertium* abdefhklmop. 13. επιστευσεν mp. ἦν p. δυναμεις και σημεια
μεγαλα o *at cæteri* −μεγαλας) γινομενα abdefghlo [*non* kmp]. 14. −οἱ
ἀποστολοι p. σαμαρια l*. εξαπεστειλαν k. −τον *secund.* op. ἰωαν.
15. οἵτινες k. προσηυξατο a. πρόσηὔξαντο (υ *p. m.* ?) p. λαβωσιν p.
οὐπω k. ουδεπω p. ἦν p. επιπτωκος a*. βαπτισμενοι k. ησαν (*pro*
ηρχον) e. ὑπηρχον p. ὀνομα dp. $\overline{\chi\upsilon}$ (*pro* κυριου) adefghl [*non* p]. 17.
τιθεσαν op. 18. *init.* ιδων (*pro* θεασαμενος) b*dkop. −ὁ k. αποστολον
19. αν (*pro* εαν) ab**ghlmo. λαμβανει ae*?km. 20. ειπεν p. εἰη k.
λειαν p. 21. οὐκέστιν p. μερος l. επι (*pro* εν) a. ει (*pro* η) e.
ντιων a. εναντιον hp. 22. $\overline{\kappa\upsilon}$ (*pro* $\overline{\theta\upsilon}$) kop. ἆρα kp. σου ? (*pro* σοι) l*.
σαι (*pro* σε) k. ὀντα p. 24. −ὁ g. ειπεν mp. $\overline{\theta\nu}$ (*pro* $\overline{\kappa\nu}$) kmo.
λθοι e. εμοι (*pro* εμε) e. ὧν k. ηρηκατε m. 25. διαμαρτυρομενοι dflo.
στρεφον p. ἱεροσολυμα ckop. *Rasura in* k *inter* ευη *et* γγ. ευηγγελι-
το p. 26. ελαλησεν p. −επι p. ἱερουσ. p. −εστιν p. 27. *init.* −και m.
ιοψ k. βασιλικης m. βασιλεισσης (−της) p. αἰθιοπων k. εληλυθη ag*.
ι p. 28. ὑποστρεφῶν (ω *p. m.* ?) p. εν τω ἁρματι (*pro* επι του ἁρματος)

-ι) m. —και *secund.* acef. ανεγινωσκεν mp. ἡσαιαν τον προ-
). ειπεν p. τῶ πνα aep*. το φιλιππω k. προσεχε (*pro*
ματι b*. *fin.* τουτου c. 30. προσδραμων (*sic*) ce. τε (*pro*
k. —γε cd. ἁ p. 31. *init.* και (*pro* ὁ δε) h. ειπεν mp.
ιοι a. ει (*pro* εαν) k. ὁδηγηση mp. παρεκαλεσεν mp. παρα-
καθησαι ep. 32. ἡ p. αὕτη p. σφαγειν a. κειραντος fkl*
ιφονος d*. οὑτος (*pro* οὑτως) fm**o. ανοιγι m. ανοιγη g*.
) *cum præcedentibus* εν τη ταπεινωσει αυτου. αἱρεται km.
ων ανομιων a*. 34. ειπεν mp. προφητις d*. τουτω (*pro*
35. —ὁ c. 36. ἡλθον p. τῶ a, το m (*pro* τι *prim.*). +το
υνουχος) k. βαπτισθηναι με c. 37. *Deest versus in* abcdfg
) (*pro* ὁ φιλιππος) e. +σου (*post* καρδιας) e. —τον *secund.* e.
). στηναι το *super ras. in* o. εις το ὑδωρ αμφοτερα ck.
39. απο (*pro* εκ) cfo. ἡρπασεν d. ἡρπασε mo. ἡρπασεν p.
cef. οὐκέτι αυτον ειδεν (—ουκ) k. οὐκ ἔτι m. 40. ευρεθη
αζωτον m. καισαριαν *hic* p.

. —ετι l. φωνου k. 2. ητοισατο e. ἡτησατο k. ἑαν p.
της ὁδου p. δεδεγμενους m. αγαγει f. ιλημ op. 3. *init.* εν
p. το p. +αυτον (*post* πορευεσθαι) c. εγενετω e. εξεφνης e.
αι) p. περιηστραψεν abcdefhklop. αυτον περιηστραψε mp.
. —του c. 4. ηκουσεν p. σαυλε σαυλε l. 5. *init.* ειπεν p.
ιπεν p* (ειπε p**). προς αυτον (*pro* ειπεν) o. 5, 6. *Desunt*
ον σοι *usque ad* προς αυτον *v.* 6, *ubi habent* αλλα (αλλ᾽ mo)
bcdefghklmop. πολην k. +εκει (*ante* λαληθησεται) c. ὁτι
ε k. 7. ειστηκησαν e. εἱστηκεισαν k?m?o. εἱστησαν p.
ακουσαντες f. μηδεν k. ακουοντες δε της φωνης μηδένα θεωρ.
8. ἡγερθη k. —ὁ b*p. ηνεωγμενων p. τε (*pro* δε *secund.*)
ὁφθαλμων (*sic v.* 18) kp. εβλεπεν mp. εισηεσαν c, ηγαγον
ν). +αυτον (*post* εισηγαγον) o. 9. ἡν (*sic v.* 10) p. βλεπων
ν p. ειπε κυριος προς αυτον (—ὁ) e. ὁραματι (*sic v.* 12) o.
κς m. 11. ειπε (*pro* κυριος) e. *Rasura ante* αναστας *in* l.
ι kp (*sic vv.* 10, 14 p). ταρεσα m. ταρσεαν p*. 12. ειδεν
ιδεν p. —εν ὁραματι p. ανανιαν ονοματι ahmp (ὀνομ. p).
χειρας (*ut videtur*) p. 13. —ὁ abcde?fghklmop. +αυτω
ι. ἡκουσα (*pro* ακηκοα) ἀπο p. τοις ἁγιοις σου εποιησεν m.
ιησεν (—σου) p. 14. ὡδε (*sic v.* 21) klmp. 15. ειπεν p.
στι μοι cm. ἐστιν μοι p. βαστᾶσαι o. ὀνομα (*sic v.* 16) p.

ωποιον e. +τὲ (*post* εθνων) p. −τε m. 16. ὑπεδειξω a. δειξω c. δη (*pro*
ι) f*?. αὐτον ?k. 17. *init.* απηλθεν p. τοτε εγερθεις ανανιας απηλθε
-δε) c. οἰκιαν kp. ειπεν p. σαυλε l. απεσταλκεν p. −ιησους bdeghklm
ιον op]. ὀφθεισσει (−σοι) k. οφθησσοι p. αναβλεψεις e. πλησθεις cf.
3. *init.* −και (*jungens* ευθεως *cum v.* 17) f. απεπεσαν p. αυτου απο των
φθαλμων m. ὡς (*pro* ὡσει) p. ανεβλεψεν mp. −παραχρημα degl*mp.
αρὰχρῆμα o. 19. τροφης g. ενισχυσε co. −ὁ σαυλος cp. +οντων (*ante* εν)
1 (ὀντων d) gkmo. δαμασκων p. 20. εκηρυσσεν p. $\overline{ιν}$ (*pro* χριστου) achp.
1. −οἱ ακουοντες d. +αυτου (*post* ακουοντες) o. ὅτος p. ἰλημ p. ὀνομα p.
δε op. εληλυθεν abcdefghklmp. ἱνα p. αγαγει e. απαγαγη g. 22.
τὸς p. 23. επληρουνται k. ικαναι ('ι *rubro* l) lp. −οἱ m. 24. παυλω?p*.
αρετυρουν a. παρετηρουντο δε και (−τε) p. ἡμερας p. −τε *secund.* dfk.
ελωσιν mp. 25. οἱ μαθηται αυτου mp (*in* p αυτου *primò scriptum judice*
ischendorf.). +αυτου (*post* μαθηται) b. τοιχους c. δια του τειχους καθηκαν
p (+αυτον p). 26. *init.* γενομενος l. −ὁ σαυλος p. εν (*pro* εις) bcehklm.
$\overline{ημ}$ p. επειραζεν p. *Rasura in* b *post* πιστευοντες. εστιν p. 27. +της
ειρος (*ante* ηγαγε) e. ηγαγεν p. αυτους (*pro* τους) p*. ειδεν ap. εν το d.
ονοματι dp (*sic v.* 28 p). −του mo. +$\overline{κυ}$ (*ante* $\overline{ιυ}$) ae**hk. 28. *Versus deest*
ι e. μετ' αυτου m. −και εκπορευομενος bdflmo. εκπορευομενος και εισ-
ορευομενον p. εις (*pro* εν *prim.*) bcdfgklmop. ἰλῆμ p. −και *tert.* p. −του
ι. −κυριου ah. −$\overline{ιυ}$ p. 29. ἑλληνιστᾶς p. ανελειν αυτον ahmp. 30. επι-
γνοντες p. −αυτον *primum* e, *secund.* a**h. +νυκτος (*post* καισαρειαν) c. 31.
μεν ουν εκκλησια p. οὐδαιας p. γαληλαιας o. ειχεν p. οἰκοδ. k. οικοδο-
μουμενη p. πορευομενη p. −του *prim.* kp*. επληθυνετο p. 32. διαπάντων
λυδαν m [*non v.* 38]. 33. εὑρεν p. ὀνοματι αινεαν km** (ὀν. m) p.
ονοματι ενεαν m*. αἰνεαν (*non v.* 34) p. ἐτων ὀκτω k. ὀκτων p. κατακει-
μενον a*. κραβατω m. κραβαττου p. 34. −αυτῳ c. −ιησους bc. −ὁ *secund.*
σεαὐτῳ p. 35. λυδαν m*. ασσαρωνα ab**ghlo. σαρωναν b*c (*tacitè*)
p. σαρωνᾶ d. αΣαρωνα e. ασσαρωναν f. [σαρωνα m]. οἱτινες k. 36.
ιοππη p. ἠν p. ὀνοματι p. ταβηθα (*sic v.* 40 *præter* p) adefghkp [*non* m].
ερμηνευομενη l. αὐτη p. πληρεις c. πληρης ην m. εργων αγαθων m. 37. −δε
+τω (*ante* ὑπερωω) aho. εθηκαν αυτην p. 38. λυδδας p. ἡ ιοπη m.
δυο ανδρας abdfghlo [*non* kmp]. ὀκνησαι kp (*evanidum : forsan* ὀκνησης :
ischend. ὀκνησῃς). ἑως αυτων διελθειν c. *fin.* ἡμων (*pro* αυτων) p. 39.
ὁ (*ante* πετρος) co. περιεστησαν αυτον (*pro* παρεστησαν αυτῳ) c. αἱ p.
ποδεικνυμεναι k. ἱματια p. οὐσα k. 40. −εξω e. παντας εξω m. +και (*ante*
εις) p. σωματι e. ειπεν mp. διηνοιξε k. ηνοιξεν p. ὀφθαλους d*. ὀφθ. p.

ανεκαθισεν mp. 41. *τε* (*pro δε prim.*) c. *και φωνησας* (–*δε*) c. –*φωνησας usque ad τας χηρας* e. +*και* (*ante παρεστησεν*) e. *χειρας* (*pro χηρας*) g*m. 42. *ἰοππης* (*sic v.* 43; x 23 *tantum*) k. *επιστευσαν πολλοι* mp. *εις* (*pro επι*) h. 43. *ηκανας* e. –*αυτον* b. *αυτον ἡμερας ἱκανας μειναι* ahp (*ἱκανας* p). *ἰοππη* p. *τηνι* p. *βυρση* c*.

CAP. X. 1. –*ην* p. –*εν* k. *ἑκατονταρχης* (*sic v.* 22) p. *σπειρας* ab**g h*lo [*non* mp]. *ιτταλικης* c. *ἱταλικης* k. 2. *κ̅ν̅* (*pro θ̅ν̅*) p. *οἴκω* p. –*τε* p. *διάπαντός* m*o. 3. * εραματι* a. *ὁραματι* k. *περι* (*pro ὡσει*) cd. +*περι* (*post ὡσει*) ko. *ὥσπερὶ* (*sic*) p. *ενατην* abghklm [*non* o] p. –*του* l. *αυτον* (*pro αυτῳ*) e. 4. –*και primum* e. *ειπεν prim.* m, *bis* p. *ἐστιν* p. *αἱ prim.* p. –*αἱ secund.* ad*mp. *λεημοσυναι* e (*sic* e *v.* 31) k. +*σου* (*post μνημοσυνον*) c. *εμπροσθεν* p. 5. *μεταπεμψον* g. *ανδρας εις ιοππην* mp (*ἰοπ.* p). +*τινα* (*post σιμωνα*) p. *επικαλειτε* p. *fin. τον επικαλουμενον πετρον* (*pro ὁς επικ. πετρ.*) bcdefgklmo [*non* hp]. 6. *init. και αυτος εστι ξενιζομενος παρα σιμωνα τινα βυρσεα* c. *οὑτως* m, *οὑτος* p (*pro οὑτος prim.*). *σιμωνι τινι* m. *ὡς ἐστιν* p. *οἰκια* k. –*οὑτος λαλησει ad fin. vers.* abcdefghklmop. 7. –*ὁ secund.* gm. *αυτω* (*pro τῳ κορνηλιῳ*) p. *οἰκετων* kp (–*αὑτου* p). *των οικετων αυτου δυο* l. *στρατιοτην* k. *τον* (*pro των secund.*) d. 8. *αυτης* (*pro αυτοις*) b. *ἀπαντα αυτοις* p. *παντα* c. *απεστειλλεν* e. *αυτοις* (*pro αυτους*) m. –*την* cf. 9. *ἐπ' αὑριον* k. *ὁδοιπορουντων* p. +*αυτων* (*ante εκεινων*) c. *αυτων* (*pro εκεινων*) dkop. *προσεγγιζοντων* c. *εγγιζωντων* e. *ἐγγιζοντων* p. *προσευξασθε* k. *ἑκτην* p. 10. *προσπινος* p. *ηθελεν* p. *αυτων* (*pro εκεινων*) p. *εγενετο* dp, *επεσεν* l (*pro επεπεσεν*). 11. *Ordo in* c *est ανεῳγμενον και τεσσαρσιν αρχαις δεδεμενον σκευος τι ὡς οθονην μεγαλην καταβαινον* (–*επ' αυτον*) *και καθιεμ.* –*επ' αυτον* p. *τί* hm. *ὀθονην* k. *τερσασιν* a. *καθΐμενον* ?b*. *καθημενον* m. *την γην* p. 12. *ᾧ ὑπηρχε rescript. in* h. *ὑπηρχεν* p. *και τα ἑρπετα και τα θηρια* m. *Transferunt* op *της γης in locum post ἑρπετα, at in* p –*και τα θηρια, et* –*τα ante ἑρπ. et ante πετεινα.* 14. *ειπεν* mp. *μήδαμῶς* kmp. *κυνον ἢ* p. 15. *προς αυτον εκ δευτερου* eg. *εκαθερισε* mp (-*εν* p). *κυνου* p. 16. *τρεις* dh*p. *ευθυς* (*pro παλιν*) p. –*το σκευος* e. 17. *αυτω* (*pro ἑαυτῳ*) k. *ἀν* p. *ὁραμα* km (*sic v.* 19 m). *ὦ* (*pro ὁ*) a. *τουτο* (*pro ὃ ειδε*) c. *ειδεν* mp. –*και* p. *δυο* (*pro οἱ prim.*) l. *ὑπο* (*pro απο*) ab**cghop. *οἰκιαν* kp. +*του* (*ante σιμωνος*) cp. –*σιμωνος* k. *απεστησαν* k. 18. *φωνισαντες* p. 19. *διενθυμουμενου* acdefghklmop. *ειπε το πνευμα αυτω* mp (-*πεν* p). –*τρεις* abcdghklmo [*non* p]. *ζητουντες* ?p*, *ζητουνταις* p**. 20. *αλλ'* bcl. *καταβηθη* d. *μήδὲν* kop. *ὁτι* (*pro διοτι*) hp. –*εγω* p. 21. +*ὁ* (*ante πετρος*) bdo. –*τους απεσταλμενους usque ad αυτον* bcdeghklop.

κορνηλιου fm. −απο του κορνηλιου προς αυτον a. −προς αυτον m. ειπε
ς αυτους f. −ιδου c. ἐγω p. τί (*pro* τις) m. 22. ειπαν p. +ὁ (*ante*
τοντ.) km. ἑκατονταρχυς c*. −τε c. −ολου e. −αγιου ah [*non* mp]. ἁγιου
γελου o. οἰκον p. −και ακουσαι *ad fin. vers.* m. ῥήματος? k*. 23. προσ-
εσαμενος o. οὐν p. αυτοις (*pro* αυτους) e. εξενισεν mp. +αναστας (*post*
υριον) cdkm, (*ante* εξηλθε) op (-θεν p). −ὁ πετρος dp. εξηλθεν a. −της
defghklmop. ἰωππης p. εν ιοππη m. 24. *init.* τη δε (−και) p. εισηλ-
p *at* συνηλθον m. −την m. *Rasura in* k *ante et post* κ *in* καισαρειαν.
. συγκενεις a. −αὐτου p. −τους *secund.* e. 25. ὡς ? p. +του (*ante*
λθειν) abc (ελθειν cl) defh [*non* k] lmop. +αυτου (*post* ποδας) ego. 26.
ιρε e. ηγειρεν αυτον acdfhkmp (ἠγ. p). και γαρ εγω (*pro* κἀγω) ck.
εγω p. 27. εισηλθεν mo (+εις τον οικον o) p. εὑρισκει συνεληλυθοτα p.
ως (*ante* πολλους) c. 28. εφησε (−τε) o. επιστασθαι kmp. ἡ *bis* p.
σερχεσθε g. αλλοφυλλω d. −ὁ θεος *ad fin. versûs* c*. καμοι επεδειξε
θς) o. μοι (*pro* εμοι) p. εδειξεν mp. μηδένα km. κυνον p. 29.
ιτηρρητως ? c. αναντιρητως ἦλθον p. μεταπεμφθῆς k. οὐν p. λογο e.
επεμψασθαι k. μεταπεμψασθαι p. 30. −ὁ k. +και (*ante* μεχρι) c.
ρη p. ἡμην kp. −νηστευων και p. ενατην abcghklmp [*non* o]. −ὥραν p.
ι p. ἐστη mp. ἐνεσθῆτι k. 31. φησὶν kp. φησί· hlm. αἱ προσευχαι
εισηκουσθησαν c. ἡ δεησις σου (*pro* σου ἡ προσευχη) e. και (*pro* και
*. και αἱλεημοσυναι p. ανεβησαν (*pro* εμνησθησαν) c. 32. οὐν p.
τηνp. μετακαλεσε k. οἰκια p. +τινος (*ante* βυρσεως) e. παρα-
νομενος l*. −ὁς παραγενομενος λαλησει σοι p. 33. ἐξαύτης (*sic* xi. 11
) klmop. οὐν *bis* p. παραγεναμενος p. διατεταγμενα o. −του *secund* p.
κυριου (*pro* θῦ) c. 34. +ὁ (*ante* πετρος) l. +αυτου (*post* στομα) dko.
ληθειας hp. οὐκέστιν p. προσοποληπτης a. 35. −εν ek*. εθνη dekp.
ουμενος p. +και εργαζομενος αυτον (*ante* και εργαζομενος) f. δεκτος (κ
atum) d. εστιν αυτω m. *fin.* εστιν p. 36. *init.* τον γαρ λογον αυτου
ν) c. −ὃν p. οὑτος p. εστιν a*p. 37. οἰδατε p. γεγονος c. κατ᾽
c. καθόλης p. βαπτησμα ? g*. +ὁ (*ante* ιωαννης) c. ἰωάννης p. 38.
ιρετ abdfghlop [-εθ km]. ὃς (*pro* ὡς) m. εχρησεν ? g*. +εν (*ante* πνι)
ιωμενος p. ἦν p. 39. μαρτυρες εσμεν c*. −εσμεν p. ὧν k. εποιησε
−τε c. ἱεροσολυμοις k. +και (*post* ὃν) abcdefghklmop. ανειλαν p. 40.
ρεν εκ νεκρων d. ἤγειρεν p. +εν (*post* ηγειρεν) m. αυτω (*pro* αυτον) o.
ανει c. 41. μαρτυσιν p. οἵτινες (*sic* v. 47; xi. 20) k. προκεχειροτονη-
νοις d. +των (*ante* νεκρων) b. 42. κηρυσσειν k. κηρυξε p*. οὑτος (*pro*
ς) k. 43. *init.* τουτο m*o. ἁμαρτιων p. ὀνοματος p. 44. +δε (*post*

ετι) befgo. επεπεσεν (το πνα το in o super ras.) op. 45. −οἱ c?. συνεισῆλθον o. του πνευματος του ἁγιου c. 46. ἠκουον p. −ὁ p. 47. δυναται κωλῦσαι p. ελαχον ?c. ὡς (pro καθως) achkp. 48. προσεταξεν p. δε (pro τε) dp. −τε l*. το (pro τῳ) d*. εν τω ὀνοματι του κυ ιυ χυ βαπτισθηναι p (at του κυ eras.). +ιῦ (post κυ) ah. ιυ χυ (pro του κυ) cdk. ἠρωτησαν k.

Cap. XI. 2. ὁτε k. ὁτε δε (−και) p. ἰλημ' p. 3. εισηλθες προς ανδρας ακροβυστιαν εχοντας ahp (at εισηλθεν p). εισηλθε και συνεφαγεν c. συνεφαγεν p. 4. −ὁ p. 5. ημιν (sic v. 11) k. ἡμην p. +τη (ante πολει) c. ἰοππη p. ὁραμα kp. καταβαῖνων a. τί h. ·σκευος τί καταβαινων p. οθονην f. ὀθονην k. 6. ἦν k. της γης transferunt dg [non p hic] in locum post θηρια. ἑρπατα b. ἑρπετα p. 7. +και (ante φωνης) op. λεγουση h. λεγουσις p. 8. −παν cop. κυνον ἢ p. ουδεποτε transferunt co in locum post ὁτι. 9. −μοι p. εκ δευτερου φωνη ah. +λεγουσα (post ουρανου) gk. εκαθαρε l. εκαθέρισεν (α p.m?) p. κυνου p. 10. ἐπιτρίς h. τρεῖς p. απεσπασθη c. ανεσπασθη παλιν ἀπαντα p. 11. τρεις ανδρες εξαυτης b. εις (pro επι) b. οἰκιαν p. ἡμην p. αποσταλμενοι ko. 12. ειπον p. το πνα μοι p. μὴδὲν (sic v. 19) kp. διακριναντα p. ἠλθον p. οἱ ἐξοὶ p. οἰκον p. fin. +τουτου l. 13. απηγγειλεν p. δε (pro τε) ahp. ειδεν p. +του θῦ (post αγγελον) o. οἰκω p. −αυτῳ p. −ανδρας ahp. μεταπεμψε p*. 14. −ὁ p*. οἰκος kp. 15. init. εν δε το h*?k. επεσε a. επεπεσεν p. εν αρχη εφ' ἡμας e. 16. εμνησθη k. +του (ante κυ) acfhklop. +ὁτι (ante ιωαννης) aeh. ἰωαννης p. βαπτισθησεσθαι kp. 17. ἰσιν k. ἰσην p. δεδωκεν o. −και b*. −χριστον ah. −δε ahkop. −τις p. ἥμιν (pro ημην) k. ἡμην p. κωλῦσαι hk. 18. ἡσυχασαν p. εδοξασαν chp. ἆράγε l. ἆρα (−γε) kp. ἄράγε o. εδωκε την μετανοιαν c. εις ζωην εδωκεν p. 19. οἱ k. οὖν p. μὴδενὶ o. μονοις c. +τοις (ante ιουδαιοις) k. 20. κυριναιοι c. συνελθοντες a. ελθοντες op. ἑλληνας (pro ἑλληνιστας) c. και προς τους ἑλληνιστας p. 21. ἦν p. +του ιασθαι αυτους (ante πολυς) e. +ὁ (ante πιστευσας) p. επιστρεψε b*. 22. ἠκουσθη k. ὠτα kp. −της a, +ουσης (ante εν) ck (οὖσης k) p. ἱεροσολυμοις k. ἰλημ p. +τα (ante περι) k. βαρ a. −διελθειν p. 23. παρεκαλη ak. προσμενην ?p*. 24. ὀχλ. ἱκαν. (sic v. 26) p. 25. εξηλθεν p. θε (pro δε) a. +τον (ante σαυλον) e. ευρον e. εὑρῶν p. −αυτον bis ahp, primum c, secundum dfko. αντιοχειαν (sic) e. 26. αυτοις (pro αυτους) cp. ἐνιαυτον k. −εν primum abcdeghl [non kp]. χρηματεῖσαι p. χρηστιανους p. 27. αυταις (pro ταυταις) c. −δε e. 28. εἷς p. ὀνομαπι kp. εσημα νεν p. −μεγαν e. μεγαλην p. εσεσθαι eras. post μεγαν a. −μελλειν fl. οἰκουμενην ὁστις k. οστης e. ἥτις p. −και p. −καισαρος p. 29. ευπορειτο abegkl [*non* o]. ηὐπορειτο p. ὥρισαν fp. ἑκαστος p. αὐτὸν ?p*. 30. −προς l* (*habet margo* l**).

Cap. XII. 1. ὁ βασιλευς ἡρωδης c*p. ὁ βασιλευς *super ras.* o. 2. αν-ειλεν p. +και (*post* δε) g. μαχαιρη p. 3. ιδων δε (−και) p. εστιν p. συ-λαβειν k*. +αἱ (*ante* ἡμεραι) ab**defghkl** [*non* o] p. 4. τεσσαρσιν p. φυλαττειν g. βουλωμενος d*. αγαγειν e. 5. εκτενεις p. γενομενη ep. γινομενης k. περι (*pro* ὑπερ) op. 6. ημελλεν lp. ημελλε c. πρὸ ἀγαγεῖν αυτον p. εμελλε προαγειν αυτον ahko (προαγαγειν a, προσαγειν o). προ-αγειν αυτον c. ἡρωδης (*sic vv.* 11, 19) p. νυκτῆ p. ἦν p. ἁλυσεσι (*non v.* 7) k. ἁλυσεσιν δυσιν p. −τε e. 7. εξεπεσων h*. εξεπεσαν p. +παρα-χρημα (*ante* εξεπεσον) c. απο (*pro* εκ) ck. 8. ειπεν p. δε (*pro* τε) ac. προς αυτον ὁ αγγελος b. περιζωσε ?k*. ζωσαι ap. ὑποδυσαι e. εποιησεν p. οὑτως bcefghklo. οὑτος p. ἱματιον p. ακολουθη k. 9. ἠκολουθει k. −αυτῳ p. γενομενον bc. γινομενον e. εστιν το γενομενον p. παρα c, ὑπο el (*pro* δια). +ὁτι (*ante* ὁραμα) e. ὁραμα k. 10. −δε p. +την (*ante* πρω-την) a. επι την πολην (*pro* εις) p. ἡτις p. ηνοιγη ap. ἠνοιχθη k. 11. εν ἑαυτω γενομενος acp. ειπεν p. οἰδα p. εξαπεστειλεν ap. ὁ θς (*pro* κς) a. +ὁ (*ante* κς) c. εξειλατο μαι p. 12. *init.* συνιδον f. δε (*pro* τε) akop. +ὁ πετρος (*ante* ηλθεν) f. οἰκιαν k. +της (*ante* μαριας) p. επιλεγομενου k. οὗ p. ἠσαν kp. ἱκανοι p. συνηθρισμενοι e. συνηγμενοι g. +αδελφοι (*post* συνηθροισμενοι) a. 13. κρουσαντὲς (*forsan* ο *p. m.*) p. αυτου (*pro* του πε-τρου) p. θυρα c. προσηλθεν p. ὀνοματι k. 14. ηνυξε k. ονοιξε h. ηνοιξεν p. +αυτῳ (*ante* τον πυλωνα) c. ἑστάναι hl. ἑστᾶναι k. ἑστάναι op. 15. *init.* οἱ p. ειπαν p. μαινει ?a*. ἡ p. οὑτὸς (ω *forsan p. m.*) p. οἱ δὲ *bis* kl. 16. επεμενεν ep. 17. −αυτοις *prim.* e, *at* αυτους gl. σηγαν p. εξηγησατο c*. −αυτοις *secund.* ap. εξηγαγεν αυτον p. *Transfert* c αυτον *in locum post* φυλακης. απο (*pro* εκ) eg. ειπεν τὲ (*pro* δε) p. +αυτοις (*ante* απαγγειλατε) a. ἑτερον p. 18. ενομενης h. ἠν p. ἆρα kp. 19. τε (*pro* δε) a. εὑρων p. −την aep. εις την καισαρειαν *cum sequent.* lo. 20. ἠν p. −ὁ ab*ko. ὁ ἡρωδης (*sic*) c. −ὁ ἡρωδης p. σιδυνιοις ef. τε (*pro* δε *secund.*) ch. ησαν (*pro* παρησαν) c. αυτου (*pro* του βασιλεως) o. ἡτουντο k. τρεφεσθε k. αυτους (*pro* αυτων την χωραν) a. βασιλεικης e. 21. −ὁ a. ενδυσαμενος ὁ ἡρωδης eo. −και (*ante* καθησας) p. 22. επεφωνη o. φωνη θυ befglo. φωνη κυριου (*non* θυ) c. 23. παρὰ χρῆμα o. αυτον επαταξεν c. −ων e. ἀνθῶν p. εδωκεν eop. −την bcfghklo [*non* p]. 24. ηὔξανεν p. 25. παυλος e. απο (*pro* εξ) bco, *at* εις klp. ἱ ελημ p. +εις αντιοχειαν (*post*

Cap. XIII. 1. ἤσαν p. −τινες ap. αντειοχεια e. αντιοχειαν f. οὖσαν k.
επικαλουμενος o. κυριναιος p. μαναϊν bd. μανναην o. 2. νιστευοντων p.
ειπεν τῷ p. αφορησατε dp. −τε bcdefghl. −τον secund. acp** (τον eras.
p. m. judice Tischendorf.). 3. αυτοις τας χειρας bko. 4. init. Οὗτοι l,
αυτοι ap. −ουν hp. εκπεφθεντες p. ὑπο του ἁγιου πνευματος ap. κατεῖλθον
p. −την prim. aop. σελευκιαν d. κἀκειθεν (pro εκειθεν τε) c. κἀκειθεν δε
(−τε) e. δε (pro τε) bdfglop. −την secund. aeop. 5. γενομενὸ (sic) p.
σαλαμηνι e. σαλαμινη p. κατηγγελον ceg*kp. τὲ (pro δε) p. 6. διελ-
θοντων e. −δε c?. +ὁλην (ante την νησον) kp. εὑρον p. +ανδρα kp, +εκει
ανδρα o (ante τινα). ὀνομα (sic v. 8) p. βαρισηουν ab**defghklp. 7. σερ-
γιο p. −παυλῳ l. 8. −αυτοις e. οὑτως acdfghlo. οὗτος kp. μερμηνευε-
ται p. τον ανθυπατον διαστρεψαι c. 9. πλησθῆς p. −και secund. cfp.
10. ειπε o. ὦ p. πανη c. πανσει k. διαστρεφον a. 11. −του abcdefgh
klop. +και (post τυφλος) o. τε (pro δε) p. επεσεν p. −αχλυς και d. 12.
γεγονως ep. −επι f. εκπληττομενος ab**ghk. εκπλησομενος d*. 13.
παμφου a. −τον cp. ειλθον p. παμφιλιας k*. +ὁ (ante αποχωρησας) a.
αποχωρισας c. 14. ελθοντες p. παρεγένον a. παραγενοντο k. πισιδειας c.
εκαθησαν p. 15. προς αυτους οἱ αρχισυναγωγοι ah. ει τις εστιν ap. εν
ὑμιν λογος acp. ἡμιν d*. παρακλησεσεως d. λεγεται d. 16. +σιγαν
(post χειρι) k. 17. −ισραηλ bcdefhklo [non p]. αιγυπτου abc**dp. αἰ-
γυπτω k. βραχιωνος ef. βραχειονος p. ὑψιλου d. 18. τεσσαρακοντα ἔτη
χρονων p. ετροποφορησεν (πο secund. manu) l. 19. init. −και p. καθελων
usque ad κατε[κληρο] rescript. in l. ἑπτα p. χαναν d*. κατεκληρονομησεν
bcd** (-ισεν d*) efgklp [non o]. κατεκληρονομη h* (-μει h**). αυτης (pro
αυτοις) d. −αυτοις p. τον γην d. 20. −και μετα ταυτα c*p. μεταταῦτα
l. ·ὡς p. πεντικοντα p. +·και μετα ταυτα (ante εδωκεν) p. εδωκεν kp. −τον
p. 21. ητησαν a*. ητοισαντο e. ἠτησαντο kp. βασελεα d. βασιλεαν
(non v. 22) p. −ὁ θεος e. βενιαμην k. βενιαμεῖμ p. τεσαρακοντα ?d. 22.
ειπεν p. μαρτυρισας k. ιεσαι bd. ἰεσσαὶ k. 23. ηγαγε (pro ηγειρε) bgl.
ἤγαγεν (pro ηγειρε τῳ ιηλ) p. σωτηριαν (pro σωτηρα ιν) bdfghl [non p].
−ιν (σρα cum sequent.) o. 24. προκυρυξαντος d. ιωανου d. προπροσωπου
hlp. προσωπω (−προ) o. βαπτισ d*. −παντι et λαῳ defghlo. 25. −δε
a*. −ὁ alp. ελεγεν τι μαι p. ὑπονοειται d. μετ' εμε ερχεται c. εμου (pro
εμε) h. +αυτου (post ποδων) a. 26. ἀβρααμ hklo. ἡμιν (pro ὑμιν) bis p,
secund. c. +οὑτος (post λογος) d. εξαπεσταλη ahp. 26. −εν bdehkp [non o].
+την (ante ἰλημ) e. ἰλημ (sic v. 31) p. τουτων e. πασαν (pro παν) o.
αναγηνωσκομενας d. 28. μηδὲμίαν hl. μὴδὲμίαν ko. μὴδεμίαν p. αἰτιαν k.

ρουτες p. ητοισαντο e. ἠτησαντο k. 29. πανταabcdfghklop. 31. ὡφθη k.
ις (pro τοις) d. αυ [τω] d*. +νυν akp, +αχρι νυν c (post οἵτινες). οἵτινες k.
τιν αυτου μαρτυρες a. 32. ὑμιν (pro ὑμας) dgo. −ὑμας e. γεγενημενην f.
πεπληρωκεν dp. εκπεπληρωκεν ὁ θς k. 33. −τῳ prim. e. γεγραπται
ο δευτερω aep. εν τω δευτερω ψαλμω o. γεγεννηκα (sic) ce. γεγεννηκα p.
ι. μηκέτι kp. +αυτον (post μελλοντα) k. εις διαφθοραν ὑποστρεφειν e.
ποστρεφην p. Rasura post οὕτως in k. αυτω (pro ὑμιν) o. 35. διότι p*.
ι, 37. ειδεν p. 37. −ὁ θς p. οιδε (non v. 36) ef. 38. ἐστω p. −ανδρες c.
' αυτου (pro δια τουτου) d. ἡμιν (pro ὑμιν secund.) c. ἀφεσις k. αφε d*.
ιαρτιων p. καταγγελεται cep. 39. ὤν k. −τῳ hp. μωϋσεος adhl. μω-
εως p. πηστευωνd*. 40. οὖν p. ελθη d. εις (pro εφ') c "et in fine versûs
guntur:" Sanderson. ὑΰμας a. 41. οἱ p. +και εμβλεψατε k, +και επι-
λεψατε o (post καταφρονηται). +και επιβλεψατε (post θαυμασατε) a. και
ιβλεψατε και θαυμαζετε (sic) c. θαυμασετε l. αφανισθηται p. εργαζομαι
γω kp. −εγω h*?. −εργον secund. bcdfghklo [non p]. ὃ (pro ᾧ) abefgkop.
διηγειται fk. διηγηται o. 42. αυτων (pro εκ της συναγωγης των Ιουδαιων)
). +αυτων (ante εκ) beko. συναγωγεις d. −των ιουδαιων k. −τα εθνη ackop.
λληθεναι l*. λαληθειναι l**. αὐτοις p, cæteri. fin. −ταυτα el. 43. ληθεισης
. λυθησης e.. ηκουλουθησαν d*. −τῳ prim. d*, secund. b. οἵτινες k. −αυτοις
cdefghlo. αυτοις (pro αυτους) p. προσμενειν αυτους h. προσμενειν (pro
ιμενειν) cdkop. 44. init. τη d. τε (pro δε) cdefghkl [non p]. πολης p*.
ον λογων d. fin. κῦ (pro θῦ) ap. 45. −δε lp. −του c. λαλουμενοις (pro
εγομενοις) p. −αντιλεγοντες και adep. 46. τε (pro δε prim.) op. −ὁ secund. c.
παν p. −ην o. επει (pro επειδη) p. αποθεῖσθε k. αυτους (pro ἑαυτους) a*.
ς τα εθνη rescript. l**. 47. οὕτως eko [non bhl]. οὕτως p. ἡμιν εντεταλται
. εντεταλκεν e. εντελλεται p. τεθηκα e. −σε secund. a. ἕωσχάτου k.
8. εχαιρε efgklo. εδοξαζε eg. θεον (pro λογον του κυριου) c. +τω λογω
ου θῦ (post επιστευσαν) c. 49. και διεφερετο (−δε) a. κυριω ?c. θῦ (pro
ῦ) k. καθ' (pro δι) ak. 50. οιουδαιοι d. παρωξυναν (pro παρωτρυναν) p.
-και prim. p. επειγειραν e. −του secund. ackp. 51. οἱ δε (sic v. 52, XIV.
) p. εκτειναξαμενοι ck. +απο (ante των ποδων) cdg. −αὐτων akp. ἰκονιον
sic XVI. 2, non XIV. 19, 21) k. 52. τε (pro δε) a.

CAP. XIV. 1. κατατοαυτὸ h. καΚα (Κ rubro) o. −αυτους a. −και
αλησαι usque ad ιουδαιων a. καιλησαι f*. οὕτως p. ἑλληνων πολλυ p.
λῆθος πολυ aek. 2. απειθησαντες aop. απιθουντες e. +διωγμον (post
πηγειραν) c. 3. ἱκανον p. οὖν p. −και prim. cdefghklo. διδοντος p.
νεσθαι ce [sic]. 4. −της πολεως a. −ιουδαιοις οἱ δε συν τοις d. 5. ὁρμη

kp. —τε c. —αὐτων o. ὑβρῖσαι p. 6. συνειδόντες p. λυκαυνυας e. +και (*ante* λυστραν) d. περιχορον d. 7. εναγγελιζομενοι ησαν cp (ἠσαν p). 8. —αδυνατος τοις ποσιν c. +ετι (*ante* εκ) c. —ὑπαρχων cp, *at* ων a. περιεπατησεν ap. περιπεπατηκει b**cefghklo. 9. *init.* και αυτος c. οὗτος ηκουσεν p. ηκουσε bce. *Rasura in* k *post* λα. εχει πιστιν akp. 10. ειπεν p. —τῃ kp. +σοι λεγω εν τω ονοματι του κυ ιυ χυ (*post* φωνη) aeo (—του κυ e). αναστιθη e. +και στηθι (*ante* επι) e. ορθως e. ὀρθος p. ἡλλατο bghkl**o. ἡλλατο ac. ἡλατο ep. 11. *init.* οἱ δε οἱ ὀχλοι k. ὀχλοι p. ὁ (*pro* ὃ) p. —ὁ (*ante* παυλος) c. αυτων την φωνην o. λυκαονιστι *cum præcedent.* ho. λυκαονιστη p. ὡμοιοθεντες k. +τοις (*ante* ανοις) l. εφ' (*pro* προς) l. 12. δε (*pro* τε) abg. —μεν p. διαν op. σαυλον l. ἑρμὴν p. επει (*pro* επειδη) k. ἠν p. —ὁ c. ἡγουμενος p. 13. τε (*pro* δε) ac. τοτε ὁ ἱρευς (—δε) p. του οντος διος c. ὀντος πρωτων πυλων της πολεως p. —αυτων ap. +αυτοις (*ante* επι) c. του πυλωνος l. ηθελον lp, *at* ημελε e. 14. εξεπηδησαν acp. ὀχλον p. 15. ποιειται k*. ὁμοιωπαθης p. —ὑμιν c. ὑμιν εσμεν fho. των ματαιων τουτων c. θν̄ ζωντα (—τον *bis*) akp. εποιησεν p. 16. παροχημεναις c. ειασιν e. ειασεν p. αὑτων p, *omnes, passim.* 17. —γε ap*. αμαρτυρων p. αυτον (*pro* ἑαυτον) c. ποιων (*pro* αφηκεν αγαθοποιων) e. αγαθουργων ap. οὐρανοθεν k. ουνονθεν *sic* (—ἡμιν) p. ὑμιν (*pro* ἡμιν) bcefghklmo. διδους ὑετους akp. +τε (*ante* τροφης) l. *fin.* ὑμων (*pro* ἡμων) bcfklop. 18. ειποντες (*pro* λεγοντες) c. *fin.* +αλλα πορευεσθαι ἑκαστον (ἑκαστον p) εις τα ιδια kmp. 19. *init.* διατριβοντων δε αυτων και διδασκοντων επηλθον (—δε) απο abfkmop (επηλθαν p). *Item post* ιουδαιοι *legunt* akmp και διαλεγομενων αυτων παρρησια ανεπεισαν (επεισαν k) τους οχλους. *Post* οχλους *legunt* akmop αποστηναι απ' αυτων· λεγοντες ὁτι ουδεν αληθες λεγουσιν αλλα παντα (ἀλλ' ἁπαντα p, —παντα o) ψευδονται και λιθασαντες κ.τ.λ. (*Pergit* k και πεισαντες τους οχλους και λιθασαντες). *In* a* *desunt* εσυρον *usque ad* αυτον (*habet marg. sec. manu*). εσυραν bho [*non* p]. νομησαντες c. νομιζοντες p. *fin.* τεθνηκεναι akp. 20. *Rasura in* k *post* δε. των μαθητων αυτου chkm**p. αυτων em*. εν τη πολει c. εξηλθεν akp. +ὁ παυλος (*post* εξηλθεν) a. εκ δερβην συν τω βαρναβα e. δερβιν p. 21. ευαγγελιζομενοι a. ἱκανους p. —την *secund.* h. +εις (*ante* ικονιον) ap, (*ante* αντιοχειαν) amp. ἰκονιον p. 22. +και (*ante* παρακαλουντες) ac. επιμενειν a. ενμενην p. πιστη e. θληψεων p. 23. χειροτονισαντες p. κατ' εκκλησιαν πρεσβυτερους a (κατα a) kmp. +και (*ante* προσευξαμενοι) cf (προσηυξ. c). νηστειας a. νιστειων p. *fin.* και πεπιστευκασι ce (—και e). 24. πησιδιαν k*. +την (*ante* παμφυλιαν) p. 25. εις την περγην του λογου του κῡ p. +κῡ (*post* λογου) k. αταλειαν fk*.

ισαν p. παρεδεδομενοι b. παραδεδεμενοι m. 27. συναγοντες p. απηγ-
ιν k. ανηγγειλαν m. ανηγγελον p. ὁ θς εποιησε ac. οτε (pro ὁτι) b.
εν p. εθνεσιν p. 28. διετριψαν c. —εκει p. —ουκ p. ὀλιγον p. γον
escript. in l**. ταις k.

CAP. XV. 1. ἐαν μη περιτμηθητε p. το (pro τῳ) c. μωυσεος afgh**l.
ως cmo. +τω (ante μωϋσεως) p. περισωθηναι m. 2. δε (pro ουν) abkp.
(post ουν) g. ενστασεως l. ζητησεως (pro συζητησεως) abcdefghklmop
ης p*. αναβαινην p. —εις b*c. ἰλημ p. 3. διήρχοντο την τε p. +την
σαμαρειαν) bdfmo. 4. γενομενοι l. ε (pro δε) l*. ἰεροσολυμα παρε-
σαν p. ἰεροσολυμα k. προσεδεχθησαν k. +δε (ante ὑπο) a*. και των
τολων bis script. o*. απηγγειλαν b. εποιησεν μεταυτων ὁ θς p. fin.
ὁτι ηνοιξε τοις εθνεσι θυραν πιστεως abdefg. 5. αἱρεσεως op. πρεσ-
ρων (pro φαρισαιων) m. πεπιστευκοτων bl**o. περιτεμνεσθαι k. πα-
γελειν b*m. μωυσεος adfg. μωσεως bcehlo. 6. τε (pro δε) dp.
ματος (pro λογου) c. περι του λογου τουτου ιδειν e. 7. τὲ (pro δε) p.
σεως acp. ειπεν mp. εν ἡμιν εξελεξατο ὁ θς akp, εν ἡμιν ὁ θς c, at ὑμιν
ἡμιν) hkop. —εν ἡμιν m. —του prim. m*. τον λογον τα εθνη· e. Jungit
ι ευαγγελιου cum sequent. 8. δος αυτοις a** marg. —δους αυτοις a*e.
: f. —αυτοις secund. p. 9. ουθεν bgklm. διεκρινεν emp. αυτο̈ν prim.
rsan p. m.) p. 10. οὐν p. πειραζεται d. επιθηναι c. επιτιθειναι m.
ηλον p**. οὐτε prim. p. ουτε ἡμεις ουτε οἱ πατερες ἡμων c. 11. αλλ'
ο αλλα) c. δι p. +του (ante κῡ) abdfghklmop. —χριστου bcdefghklop
st m]. πιστευομεν p. —καθ' k. 12. εσιγησαν c. εσηγησε o. εσιγη-
. ἁπαν fm. το πληθος ἁπαν a*. ηκουε m. εξηγουμενου p. ὁ θς
σε k. —εν τοις εθνεσι e. εθνεσιν p. 13. σηγησαι e. 14. συμεω̃ν k.
ος a. επισκεψατο k, at εξελεξατο c*. —επι p. ὀνοματι (sic vv. 17, 26)
15. τουτο (pro τουτῳ) o. 16. μεταταῦτα lm. ανοιδομησω prim. k.
σκαμμενα b*. κατεσκαμενα m. αυτοις (pro αυτης) o. +καθως αἱ ἡμεραι
ιωνος (ante και ανορθωσω) o. 17. —αν ak. εκζητησωσην e. καταλιποι
οἱ καταλυποι p. εφ' οὑ a. fin. παντα ταυτα efgl. —παντα mp. Jungit
17, 18 usque ad αιωνος. 18. init. ἁ εστι γνωστα αυτω απ' αιωνος a:
α versûs desunt in ap. +γαρ (post γνωστα) ck. εστι mutat in b, εισι o.
ταρενοχλην dk. προς (pro επι) c. 20. init. αλλ' cdmop. επιστηλαι k.
χεσθαι (cf. v. 29) m*. —απο p. αλγισματων d. ἀλιγισματων m. ε.δο-
ε. +τε (ante και της) e. —και του secund. d* (d** habet και). και του
τος και του πνικτου και της πορνειας a. —του bis p. fin. +και ὁσα αν μη
σιν αυτοις γινεσθαι ἑτεροις μη ποιειν abeo. 21. μωυσης abcdfklmop.

τους κηρυσσοντας αυτον κατα πολιν εχει m. εχειν k. 22. εδοξεν p. εκλεξαμενοις ad*. −τῷ bdfghklmo [non p]. +τω (ante βαρναβα) ac. καλουμενον p. βαρσαββαν bemp. ἡγουμενους p. συν (pro εν) c*. 23. χειρων l. −και οἱ (ante αδελφοι) p. −την h. εν κῶ (pro εξ εθνων) g. 24. ἠκουσαμεν k. ὑμων (pro ἡμων) m*. εξ (pro εξελθοντες) a*. λογους d*. λογοις cum sequent. hmo. ἡμων (pro ὑμων) ek. −λεγοντες usque ad τον νομον p. διεστηλαμεθα e. διαστειλαμεθα p. 25. εκλεξαμενοις acdhkmop. ἡμας (pro ὑμας) d. αγαπιτοις e. ὑμων (pro ἡμων) km*?. 26. παραδεδωκῶσι f. τας ἑαυτων ψυχας a*. ἑαυτων a**bo. −του ονοματος a. 27. απεσταλκεν o. απαγγελοντας amp. απαγγελλοντες ?f*. −τα m. 28. εδοξεν p. εδοξεν ουν (−γαρ) k. τω π̅ν̅ι̅ τω ἁγιω kp. ὑμιν (pro ἡμιν) p. μὴδὲν kop. πλειον a. τουτων των επαναγκες amp. −τουτων c. 29. απεσχεσθαι cum præced. m. πνικτων hic p. +και ὁσα μη θελετε (θελητε e) ἑαυτοις γινεσθαι ἑτεροις μη ποιειν (post πορνειας) ae. αυτους (pro ἑαυτους) o*. πραξατε ?l*. 30. κατηλθον ap. συναγαγὼντες p. 31. εχαρισαν e. 32. τε (pro δε) abcde? (tacitè) fghklm op. εστηριξαν l. επεστηρηξαν p. 33. αποστειλαντας αυτους (pro αποστυλους) ap. 34. Deest versus in cdghlm [non o] p. σιλαν (−τῳ) k. αυτοθι aef. 35. τον λογον του κ̅υ̅ μετα και ἑτερων πολλων g. ἑτερων p. 36. ειπεν p. προς βαρναβαν ὁ (−ὁ p) παυλος mp. −δη c. επισκεψομεθα c. τους (pro ἡμων) c. −ἡμων ap. πολιν πασαν km. θ̅ῡ (pro κ̅ῡ) l. εχουσιν mp. 37. εβουλετο acep. συμπαρλαβειν f*. λαβειν και (pro συμπαραλαβειν) c. +και (ante τον ιωαν.) p. −τον prim. achk. +και (ante ιωαννην) hk. επικαλουμενον cdkp. 38. ἠξιου k. συμπαραλαμβανειν acp. 39. δε (pro ουν) p. χωρισαι c. χωρισθηναι h. 40. +τον (ante σιλαν) m. εξηλθεν emp. κ̅ῡ (pro θ̅ῡ) p. 41. −την συριαν και κιλικιαν e. επιστηριζωντες d. εκκλησειας ?k*.

CAP. XVI. 1. κατηντησεν p. +και (post δε) am. +εις (ante λυστραν) cp. ἡν p. ὀνοματι (sic v. 14) kp. −τινος akp. ἑλληνος p. 2. των ελλυστροις p. +εν (ante ικονιω) m. ἰκονιω k. 3. ἠθελισεν k. ελαβε και (pro λαβων) c. λαβον ?d*. ὀντας p. τω τοπω εκεινω m. ηδεσαν h. τον π̅ρ̅α̅ αυτου ἁπαντες c. ἁπαντες (παντες m, ἁπαντες p) ὁτι ἑλλην (ἑλλην p) ὁ π̅η̅ρ̅ αυτου ὑπηρχεν amp. 4. παρεδιδοσαν p. αυταις a. κεκρυμμενα cmp. κεκρυμενα f. −των secund. ap. ἱεροσολυμοις ap. 5. αἱ μεν ουν αἱ p. επερισσευοντο a. επερισευον e. καθημεραν afgh [non lmop]. 6. διηλθον acdekmp. τέ (pro δε) m. −την secund. p. 7. +δε (post ελθοντες) ab*dkmp. εις (pro κατα secund.) cekmp. βυθινιὰν m. πορευθῆναι mp. −και ουκ ειασεν ad fin. vers. a. fin. +ι̅υ̅ mp*. 8. τρωαδαν p. 9. ὁραμα m. εφανη (pro ωφθη) c. τω παυλω ωφθη mp. παῦλω kp passim. μακεδων ην a. μακεδων τις ην mp (τις' p). ἑστως o. +και (*ante* παρακαλων) aep. −και *secund.* e. +την (*ante* μακεδονιαν) h. βοηθισον c. 10. ὁραμα km. εξητησαμεν m*. −την akp. εις την μακεδονιαν εξελθειν c. προσκεκληκεν l. θ̅ς̅ (*pro* κ̅ς̅) alp. ευαγγελισασθαι αυτους ὁ κ̅ς̅ m. ευαγγελιζεσθαι l. *fin.* αυτοις dk. 11. δε (*pro* ουν) mp. −της cmp. +την (*ante* σαμοθρακην) h. σάμον θράκην p. δε (*pro* τε) abckmop. 12. κακειθεν (−τε) amp. εστιν p. δε (*pro* τε) c. ἥτις (*at* ἡμεν) k. −της μεριδος c. −της *secund.* amp. κωλωνεια akp*. κολωνεια bcdeghp**. *Jungunt* πολις κολωνεια klmo. ἡμεν p. τη αυτη (*pro* ταυτῃ τῃ) bo. αὐτη (*pro* ταυτῃ) cdefghlm [*non* p]. 13. δε (*pro* τε) aco. πυλης (*pro* πολεως) ap. +τον (*ante* ποταμου) l. ενομιζομεν προσευχην (−οὐ) p. ευχη m. καθησαντες m. γυναιξιν mp. 14. πορφυροπολις aeflm. πορφυρόπωλης k. ηκουσεν ack. ηνοιξε c. διηνοιξεν p. προσεχην p. 15. +αυτη (*post* εβαπτισθη) dh. +πας (*ante* ὁ οικος) a. οἰκος *et* οἰκον p. παρεκαλει ael. παρεκαλεσεν mp. κεκρινατε k. εκρινατε o. μοι *vel* μαι (*pro* με) m*. τω κω̅ πιστην f. ειναι τω κω ck. −τῳ κ̅ῳ̅ l. εν τω οικω (*pro* εις τον οικον) g*. μενετε p. 16. πορευομενον d*. +την (*ante* προσευχην) p. παιδισκη b*p. τι να εχουσα p. πνεμα d. πυθωνα p. ὑπαντησαι p. ἀπαντησαι k. ἡτις p. παρηχε e. παρειχεν mp. αυτοις (*pro* αὐτης) e. 17. αὐτη παρακολουθησασα p. τω σιλα (*pro* ἡμιν) h. εκραξε c. εκραζεν p. καταγγελουσιν mp. ἡμιν (*pro* ὑμιν) c (*tacitè*) de (*tacitè*) fghklmp [*non* abo]. 18. εποιη g*. ειπεν mp. παραγγελω ap. −τῳ *secund.* ckp. 19. εἰδόντες *et* ἰ p. −τον *secund.* l. εἰλκυσαν p. 20. αυτοις (*pro* αυτους) c. στρατιγοις e. ειπαν p. 21. καταγγελουσιν b*mop. +ἡμιν (*ante* εθη) c. εθει e. ποιειν ουδε παραδεχεσθαι ck. οὐσιν k?. ουσιν mp. 22. συναπεστη p*. −ὁ ahk. στρατιγοι e. περιρὴξαντες p. 23. δε (*pro* τε) p. εβαλλον dh*. δεσμωφυλακι e. 24. παραγγελειαν p. λαβων amp. ησφαλησατο e. εισφαλισατο αυτων p. εν τω ξυλω a*. 25. +ὁ (*ante* παυλος) bo. και επηκροωντο (−δε) c. επικροωντο g*km*?p. δεσμοιοι e. 26. σαλευθῦναι k. ηνεωχθησαν m. ηνοιχθησαν p. δε (*pro* τε) ac*hkmp. αἱ p. ανειθη ab*ckl*o [*non* p]. 27. *Rasura post* ιδων *in* a. +την (*ante* μαχαιραν) p*. ημελλεν p. αυτον (*pro* ἑαυτον) m. ανερειν p*. 28. εφωνησεν p. ὁ παυλος φωνη μεγαλη k. μὴδὲν ko. πραξεις kl. ἑαυτω a. σέαυτον p. 29. αἰτησας k. εισεπηδησεν fp. ὑπαρχων (*pro* γενομενος) ck**. προσεπεσεν p. 30. προσαγαγων cl*p. τη (*pro* τι) e. 31. ειπαν p. −χ̅ν̅ p. σωθησει e. −ὁ b. +πας (*ante* ὁ οικος) ag. οἰκος (*non* v. 34) kp. 32. συμπᾶσι (*pro* και πασι) p. οἰκια kp. *fin.* κῡ συν παση τη οικια αυτου a. 33. +και ἡμων (*ante* ελουσεν) d** *marg.* +αυτους (*post* ελουσεν) k. +και (*ante* αυτος) o. υἱοι (*pro* οἱ) m. ἁπαντες c. 34. αναγαγωντες (−τε) b. αναγαγον m. −αὐτου cp. γαγων *usque ad* θηκε *rescript. in* l**. παρεθηκε, π *mutato in* m. παρεθηκεν p. ηγαλλιατο beghmo [*non* p]. ἠγαλλιατο dk. πανοικη h*. 35. απεσταλκασιν c. στρατιγοι eg*. ῥάβδοχους k. 36. απηγγειλεν kp. δεσμοφυξαξ p*. −τουτους a. απεστειλαν p. στρατιγοι e. απολυθηται p. πορευεσθαι dk. 37. −εφη p. δηραντες b**fghk. δεῖραντες p. ἡμας *prim. super* ras. o. ανους· op. εβαλλον g*. −ἡμας *secund.* d. εκβαλοῦσιν cm*. οὐ k. αλλ' m. −ἡμας *tertium* ghl. εξαγαγετωσαν ἡμας aek. 38. απηγγειλαν ab*? cmop. ανηγγηλαν e. οἱ ῥαβδουχοι τοις στρατηγοις a. στρατιγοις e. −τα ρηματα a. εφοβηθησαν δε (−και) ahmp (*in* p τε *eras. ante* δε). εισιν mp. 39. ἠρωτων k. +απο (*ante* της πολεως) k. απελθειν α[πο a**] της πολεως ap. 40. απο (*pro* εκ) ah. προς (*pro* εις) abcdfghklmop. τους αδελφους (*pro* αυτους) p.

CAP. XVII. 1. +οἱ αποστολοι (*post* δε) m. +την (*ante* απολλωνιαν) ap. απολωνιαν e. απωλλωνιαν k. θεσαλονικην d*k. −ἡ p. 2. τω (*pro* το) cp*. εισηλθεν km. εισηλθον p. διελεχθη c. διελεξατο p. 3. +αυτοις (*post* παρατιθεμενος) bg*?ko. εδει τον χ̅ν̅ m. οὑτος εστιν χ̅ς̅ ι̅ς̅ (−ὁ) p. ιησους ὁ χριστος cfh. καταγγελω kp. 4. −εξ αυτων a. επιστευσαν (*pro* επεισθησαν) c. προεκληρωθησαν m. δε (*pro* τε *prim.*) p. και ἑλληνων p. πολλν o*. πληθος πολυ achkmp. 5. *init.* προσλαβομενοι δε οἱ ιουδαιοι οἱ απειθουντες (−ζηλωσαντες *et* και) b [οἱ απειθουντες ιουδαιοι bo, απιθουντες e] defg hl [*non* ackm] o. οἱ ιουδαιοι και προσλαβομενοι οἱ απειθουντες των αγορ. c. οἱ ιουδαιοι οἱ απειθουντες am. −απειθουντες p. ιδαιοι p. −και προσλαβομενοι m. αγορεων k. ανδρας τινας ahkp. ὀχλοποιησαντες kp. +κατ' αυτων (*post* πολιν) a. και επισταντες (−τε) akmp. οικια kp. +του (*ante* ιασονος) a. ιασωνος dehklm [*non* p]. προαγαγειν abekop. προσαγαγειν c. 6. εὑροντες p. εσυραν ab. −τον p. ιασωνα dehkl. πολυταρχας h*. βοωντας e. −οἱ c. οἰκουμενην kp. ·οὑτοι και p. ενταυτα (*pro* ενθαδε) e. 7. ἰασων p. οὑτοι p. −δογματων k. πρασσουσι abcdefghklo. πραττουσιν m. πρασσουσιν p. ἑτερον λεγοντες acfhkp (ἑτερ. p). 8. ὀχλον p. 9. ἱκανον p. ιασωνος dehkl. λυπων p. 10. −της am. −δια της νυκτος p. εξεπεμψα (*lacuna post* α) p. δε (*pro* τε) p*. βερροιαν b**c** eghkl. απηεσαν των ιουδαιων bcdefghlo [*non* p]. 11. ἠσαν k. +οἱ (*ante* ευγενεστεροι) mo. θεσαλονικη d*. −το ahp. τοκαθημεραν g. καθημεραν akp. ταυθ' οὑτως εχοι m. εχει cl. 12. *init.* ολλοι l*. −ουν a*. οὐν (*sic v.* 17) p. ἑλληνων d*. ἑλλήδων p. και των ευσχημονων ανδρων l*. ολιγων c*. 13. βερροια b**c** eghkl. κατηγγελει a. κατηγγελλη dfhkp. ὁ λογος του κ̅υ̅ ὑπο του παυλου (−θ̅υ̅) e. +και ταρασσοντες (*post* σαλευοντες) acmp. 14. −δε p*. −τοτε c.

εξαπεστειλλαν e. —ὡς b*co. ἑως (*pro* ὡς) p. ὑπεμειναν aep. ὑπεμεινε c. επεμειναν m. τε (*pro* δε *secund.*) cmp. —ὁ *secund.* o. 15. καθιστοντες e. ἀποκαθιστάνοντες p. ηλθον (*pro* ηγαγον αυτον) a. —αυτον *prim.* cmp. ἀθηνων k. —τον *secund.* bo. +τον (*ante* τιμοθεον) ep. ἱν' m. ἐλθωσιν k*. ελθωσιν p. 16. ἀθηναις k. αθην'' (*i.e.* ες) p. του παυλου αυτους a*. —αυτους e. παροξυνετο c. ἑαυτω (*pro* αυτῳ) abdo. θεωρουντος akp. οὐσαν kp. 17. των ιουδαιων (*pro* τοις ιουδαιοις και) e. —και τοις σεβομενοις a. —και *secund.* k. παρατυγχανοντας *mutatum in* e, *at illegibile.* 18. *init.* τινες δε και abdeghlmop. επικουριων ckp; —των *secund.* acdlop. στοικων acfk [*non* p]. —φιλοσοφων b*?. συνεβαλον abcd*fghm [*non* op]. ἀν p. θελει c. καταγγελευς ειναι δοκει c. +αυτου (*post* αναστασιν) a. ευηγγελιζετο αυτοις acfkmp. —αυτοις bdghlo. 19. τε (*pro* δε) p. αυτον (*pro* αυτου) adk. ηγαγον επι τον αρειον παγον c. +ου (*ante* δυναμεθα) b*cgo. ἡ καινη αὑτη ἡ p. λεγομενη (*pro* λαλουμενη) p. 20. εισφε *usque ad* τας *rescript. in* h. εισφειρεις m. βουλωμεθαγ οὖν (γ *eras.*) p. τινα (*pro* τι αν) ap. θελει p. ταυτα θελη c. θελει d. 21. ἑτερον ηὐκαιρουν p. ηυκαιρουν c. ἡ p. 22. εν μεσου p. καταπάντα hk. 23. —γαρ a*. εὑρον p. επεγεγραπτω h. ἀγνως τω θῶ m. ὁ (*pro* ὃν) p. οἰν p. καταγγελω p. 24. οὑτος p. ὑπαρχων κς akmp. 25. ουδ' m. ανθρωπινων ap. θεραπευετε m. αυτοις *vel* αυτους (*pro* αυτος) b*?. πασιν p. πνοην και ζωην κατα παντα c. *fin.* και πνοην κατα παντα abdefghklmo. 25, 26. πνοην · και παντα εποιησεν τε (—τα) p. 26. δε (*pro* τε) m. —αἱματος ep. γενος (*pro* εθνος) ac. παντος προσωπου (—το) p. τεταγμενους a. προστεταγμενους cdeghlmop. —τας c**. ὀρεθεσιας p. +αυτων (*post* ὀροθεσιας) a*. κατοικείας p. 27. θν (*pro* κυριον) adp. ἆρα k. ἆράγε p. —γε *prim.* ek. ψηλαφησαιεν a. ψηλαφειάν p. εὑροιαν k. εὑροιεν p. —τοι bcdefghklmop. ουκαμαρτυρον (*loco* ου) p*. αφ' (*pro* απο) am. ἑνος ἑκαστου p. ὑμων (*pro* ἡμων) km. *fin.* απεχοντα a. 28. ειρηκασιν m. τουτου (*pro* του) el**. 29. αργυριω ?k*. 30. ἀγνοιας k. τὰ νῦν klo. παραγγελει e. πασι τοις ανοις k, (*rasura ante* πασι). 31. καθοτι ac, ὀτι ο (*pro* διοτι). ἑστησεν am. κριναι a. οἰκουμενην k. 32. —ακουσαντες δε αναστασιν νεκρων e. περι τουτου παλιν a. 33. ουτος e. 34. +ην (*post* εν οἱς) fk. ὀνοματι (*sic* XVIII. 2; *non* vv. 7, 24) k. θαμαρις a. *fin.* ἑτεροι πολλοι συν αυτω k.

CAP. XVIII. 1. —δε a. ηλθον a*. 2. εὑρον eg*. ακυλλαν gm. ἰταλιας k. πρισκιλαν a. πρισκυλλαν km*. προστεταχεναι ad. τεταχεναι fkm. ιδιους (*pro* ιουδαιους) m. απο (*pro* εκ) abdgkmo. 3. εμεινε ac?d. εμεινεν m. ηργαζετο k. ἡσαν k. τη τεχνη cgl. 4. *Rasura ante* συναγωγης *in* k. επειθεν m. ται (*pro* τε) f. 5. −της hk. ὁτι (*pro* ὁ,τε) o. συνηχετο f. λογω (*pro* πνευματι) c. +ειναι (*ante* τον χν) abd (−τον d) ko. 6. αντιτασομενων k. εκτειναξαμενος c. +αυτου (*post* εκτιναξαμενος) am. +αυτου bo, +ἑαυτων k (*post* ἱματια). τας κεφαλας h. 7. εισηλθεν a. οἰκιαν (*non v.* 8) k. ἡκια k*. −ην a*. εν τη συναγωγη συνομορουσα (*sic*) e. 8. ρισπος o. επιστευσεν m. παντι (*pro* ὁλῳ) m. ακουσαντες cm. επιστευσαν c. 9. εν νυκτι δι' ὁραματος am (ὁρ. m). εν ὁραματι της νυκτος c. 10. επιθησαι ?f*. μοι πολυς εστιν m. 11. δε (*pro* τε) acm, *at* ται k. ἐνιαυτον k. διδασκον d*. 12. αχαϊκης k. οἱ ιουδαιοι ὁμοθυμαδον g. −ὁμοθυμαδον c. −οἱ m. οἱ οἱουδαιοι d. −αυτον l. 13. αναπειθει οὑτος ahk. αναπιθει e. 14. γαλιων (*non v.* 12) o. −ουν abco. −ην dm. ην *transfertur in locum post* ραδιουργημα *in* f. ω ἰουδαιοι η ῥαδιουργημα πονηρον k. *fin.* ὑμιν (*pro* ὑμων) d. 15. ζητηματα ac. ζητηματων (*pro* ονοματων) k. οψεσθαι em. ὀψεσθε k. −εγω b*o. 17. −οἱ ἑλληνες e*. ἀρχησυναγωγον km (ἀρχ. m). ἐτυπτον k. εμελλε τω γαλλιωνι a. γαλιωνι o. ημελλεν c. εμελλεν defgklm. 18. προσμηνας e. ηκανας e. τοις αδελφοις *cum præcedent.* ak. +αυτοις (*post* αποταξαμενος) a. πρισκιλα d*. πρισκυλλα e. προσκιλλα ?m*. εν κεγχρεαις την κεφαλην am. κεγχεαις b*. κεχρεαις c. 19. κατηντισε c. κατηντησαν k. και εκεινους bdefglmo. κακει κατελιπεν αυτους (*pro* κακεινους κατελιπεν αυτου) k. διελεξατο a. διειλεχθη c. διέλεγετο k. 20. αυτον (*pro* αυτων) bdg**km**o. −παρ' αυτοις c. 21. αλλα bcfgko. αποταξαμενος a. επεταξατο m. αὑτοῦς ?k. +και (*ante* ειπων) a. +ὁτι (*ante* δει) g. −δει με *usque ad* ἱεροσολυμα a. παντος f. ποιη m. −δε a. −του a. −και (*ante* ανηχθη) a. ανηχθησαν e. 22. +την (*ante* καισαρειαν) c. +ὁ παυλος (*ante* αναβας) m. τους αδελφους (*pro* την εκκλησιαν) a. 23. εξηλθεν m. −καθεξης e. 24. δε *mutatum in* g. ἀπολλῶς m. 25. −ην m. τον λογον (*pro* την ὁδον) abo. −του *prim.* k. ιῡ (*pro* κῡ *secund.*) ach. επισταμενος *ad fin. vers. transfert.* k *in locum post* κῡ *primum.* 26. *init.* οὑτως m. −τε f. αυτον (*pro* αυτου) m. −αυτου *usque ad* προσελαβοντο a* (*habet marg.*). ακυλλας k. *fin.* τον λογον του θῡ a. την ὁδον του θῡ ckm. κῡ (*pro* θῡ) g. 27. ελθειν (*pro* διελθειν) c. προπεμψαμενοι (*pro* προτρεψ.) g. προτρεψαμενοί αδ. o. +και (*ante* παραγενομενος) c?. −δια της χαριτος c. −της k. 28. ευτονω m. διακατηλλεχετο e. διακτηλεγχετο m.

Cap. XIX. 1. ἀπολλῶ km. +τη (*ante* κορινθω) bo. παῦλω k. κατελθειν abo. ευρον e. 2. πιστευσαντες ελαβετε k. οὐδε k. ἠκουσαμεν k. 3. *init.* οἱ δε ειπεν αυτοις k. ειπεν m. δε (*pro* τε) a. ειπεν ουν (*pro* ειπε τε) c. −προς αυτους ach. −ουν o*. ει δε (*pro* οἱ δε) k. βαπτισμα ιωαννου m.

+ὁ (*ante* παυλος) a. —μεν a. εβαπτισεν km. τω λαω *cum præcedent.* h.
' αυτων g*. πιστευσωσιν m. τοῦτεστιν k. 5. +αυτου (*ante* εβαπτισθη-
) e. 6. +επ' (*ante* αυτοις) k. —τας cm. —τε m. δε (*pro* τε) o. εφη-
ον a*. 7. δωδεκα akm. 8. μεινας o. τρεις' *cum præcedent.* m. 9.
ληρουντο k. ἠπειθουν k. +παντος (*post* ενωπιον) bo. αφορισε h. +το
te καθ') c. καθημεραν fghm. 10. εγινετο c. θῡ (*pro* κῡ) c. —ιησου ack.
δε (*pro* τε) ah. ὁ θ̅ς εποιει m. 12. αποφερεσθαι a. σιμικινθηα e.
ιμῑ *rescript. in* h. απαλλασεσθαι h*o. απαλλαττεσθαι k. πνεματα (*sic v.*
d. εκπορευεσθαι (*pro* εξερχεσθαι) acdk. —απ' αυτων *secund.* acdk. 13.
(*pro* απο) acm. —τα *primum* k. ι̅υ̅ χ̅υ̅ (*pro* κ̅υ̅ ι̅υ̅) k. εξορκιζομεν ao.
ιζωμεν ck. ὁρκιζομεν h. ὑμιν (*pro* ὑμας) f. —ὁ cm. 14. τινας m. —υἱοι
υἱοι *transfert* a *in locum post* ἑπτα. —οἱ a. 15. πνεμα d. +ποτε (*post*
υμα) c. ειπεν αυτοις (*pro* ειπε) acm. +μεν (*ante* ι̅υ̅) c. επισταμε k.
ιλον (—τον) *rescript.* o**. 16. επιλαβομενος (*pro* εφαλλ.) a. —επ' αυτους
ὁ ανθρωπος επ' αυτους cm. —και *secund.* ac. κατεκυριευσεν a. κατακυρι-
αν dfghkm. αμφοτερων c, αυτον d (*pro* αυτων *prim.*). +και (*ante* ισχυσε)
κατισχυσε c. ενισχυσε e. ισχυσεν m. εκφευγειν c. 17. γνωστον
νετο bdmo. πασι (πασιν h) γνωστον ah. ελλησιν e. κατοικουσιν o.
ην c. επεπεσεν e. του *ante* κ̅υ̅ *forsan s. m. in* o. 18. πιστευοντων c.
εξομολογουμενοι αναγγελλοντες e. αναγγελοντες b*. απαγγελλοντες g.
Deest in m *ab initio usque ad* πραξαντων. εργα (*pro* περιεργα) d.
ντων ενωπιον ?k**. συνεψηφησαν g*k. συνεψηφισαντο hm. ευρων e.
ργυριου ?h*. αργυριον m. μυριαδες k. 20. οὑτως ck. οὑτω o. κατα-
ιτος hk. θῡ (*pro* κῡ) k. 21. επληρουτο k. διέλθειν k. μακεδωνιαν ?g*.
ην (*ante* αχαΐαν) abdo. πορευθηναι k. ἱεροσολυμα ck. μετα τω k*. ἰδειν
22. —την *prim.* bkmo, *at* τη a*. αυτων (*sic*) e. 23. +δε (*ante* ουκ)
24. ὀνοματι k. ἀργυροὺς ἀρτεμηδος k. +της (*ante* αρτεμιδος) o.
οηχετο e. ουκ ολιγην εργασιαν km. 25. οὑτος (*pro* οὑς) c. +ὑμεις (*ante*
στασθε) f. επιστασθαι k. ὑμων a, ἡμιν cd (*pro* ἡμων). εστιν m. 26.
ης (*ante* εφεσου) am. —της (*ante* ασιας) m. +ανθρωπων (*ante* γινομενοι)
c. 27. το μερος κινδυνευει ἡμιν c. ἡμιν κινδυνευει m. ἱερον αρτεμιδος
;o. ἱερον αρτεμηδος e. ουθεν df. λογισθηναι εις ουδεν k. λογι-
ναι e. μελλει ae. —τε ae. δε (*pro* τε) bdfghkmo. —και (*post* τε) c.
; μεγαλειοτητος ac. μεγαλιοτητα k. μεγαλοτητα m. ἡ οικουμενη και ἡ
α a*. ἡ ασια ὁλη m. —ἡ *secund.* k*m. οἰκουμενη k. σεβετε ?g*. 28.
ηρης c. εκραξαν k. 29. +της (*ante* συγχυσεως) abcdfghmo. δε (*pro*
m. μακεδονιας d. —του abcdfghkmo. 30. του παυλου δε k. παυλου δε

(−του) m. −βουλομενου o. 31. ἀσιαρχων k (*hic tantum*). αυτον (*pro* ἑαυτου) c. 32. ἄλλότι ho. ἄλλότι m. +ὁλη (*post* εκκλησια) fk. ἕνεκεν k. συνεληλυθησαν g*. 33. συνεβιβασαν a. προβαλοντων b**c (*tacitè*) e (*tacitè*) gmo. αυτο ν b (*ras. ante* ν). ουν (*pro* δε *secund.*) k. απολογισασθαι k* (*notat margo* k**, γρ. και γεισθαι). 34. επιγνοντες cdefghkm [*non* bo]. −μια c. +δε (*post* ὡς) o. δυο ὡρας bmo. 35. κατασεισας (*pro* καταστειλας) c. τον σχλον ὁ γραμματευς m. ανθρωπων ackm. νεοκορον ac (?). οὖσαν k. −θεας c. 36. αναντηρρητων c. ἀναντιρή (*sic*) m. τουτων οντων bo. −εστιν k. μὴδὲν ko. πρασσειν abcdefghko. 37. ἡγαγετε k. οὖθ' *prim.* m. ἱεροσυλλους d. +οντας (*post* ἱεροσυλους) c. ουτε *secund.* c. θεον b**de fghkm [*non* o]. ἡμων (*pro* ὑμων) bfo. 38. +ὁ (*ante* δημητριος) c. εχουσι προς τινα λογον abcdefghkmo. +και (*ante* εγκαλειτωσαν) c. 39. περαιτερω (*pro* περι ἑτερων) d. επιζητειται cdo. ζητειτε a. ενομω d. 40. στασεως, o. +γενομενης (*post* σημερον) k. μὴδενὸς αἰτιου k. +ου (*ante* δυνησομεθα) bcefghmo (δυναμεθα c). δουναι bdeg. λογον δουναι o. +περι (*ante* της συστροφης) dkm.

Cap. XX. 1. μετα (μ *s. m.*) d. μεταστειλαμενος a, μεταπεμψαμενος m (*pro* προσκαλεσ.). και παρακαλεσας ασπασαμενος τε (*pro* και ασπασαμενος) acm. πορευθειναι d. −την abckmo. 2. ελαδα e. 3. επιβουλης αυτω ak. επι (*pro* εις) a. ὑπὸστρέψαι k. 4. συνηπετο e. δ' m. −αυτῳ b*o. σωσιπατρος c. +πυρου a, +πυρρου bm, +ποιρρου o (*post* σωπατρος). βερροιαιος ab**efghk. βηροιαιος m. θεσαλονικεων b*d*. θεσσαλονικαιων h*. θελασσονικεων ?m. σεκουνδος m. δερβαιος· *cum* γαϊος *jungit* m. ασιανι b*. τροφημος d*e. 5. +δε (*post* οὑτοι) ac. προσελθοντες fgkm. 6. −τας d*. ἀζυμων k. ἠλθομεν k. αχρι d. και (*pro* οὗ) c. 7. −τῃ k. ἡμων (*pro* των μαθητων) a*c. −του abcdefghkmo. αυτους ?o*. μελλον m*, μελλοντες m**. αχρι (*pro* μεχρι) ak. 8. ημεν (*pro* ησαν *secund.*) abdefghmo. +μεν (*post* ησαν *secund.*) k. 9. καθεζομενος a. νεανισκος c. ευτυχος ονοματι a*. βαθυ cf. −κατενεχθεις απο του ὑπνου a*. ὑπο (*pro* απο *prim.*) bo. επεπεσεν c. 10. συμπαραλαβων ek. +αυτον (*ante* ειπε) a. ειπεν m. θορυβεισθαι dk*. μετ' (*pro* εν) c. 11. εφικανον m. ουτος e. 12. τε (*pro* δε) c. 13. ελθοντες c. προσελθοντες efghkmo. εἰς (*pro* επι) d. πλειον (*pro* πλοιον) a. επι (*pro* εις) a. ασον b*fk (*sic etiam v.* 14 *ras. ante* α *in* b*). θάσσον o (*vid.* b). αναλαμβανην d. οὕτως b*chkm. οὕτο d. οὑτος o. διατεταγμενος ην am. διὰτεταγμένον k. παιζευειν f. 14. ασσων m* (*vid. v.* 13). θασον o. ἠλθομεν k. μιτυλινην dk*. 15. κἀκει (*pro* κακειθεν) c. κανηντησαμεν m*. σσαμον ?m. −και μειναντες εν τρωγυλλιῳ a. τρογυλλιω b.

ωγυλιω h. τρογγυλιω cefgk. τρογγυλλιω l. τρογυλιω mo. τη δε
χομενη a. τη ερχομενη m. ἠλθομεν k. 16. κεκρικει a. χρονοτροβησα
. ειη (*pro* ην) a. ἱλημ ac. 17. εκλησιας a. 18. +της (*ante* πρωτης
mo. −ἀφ' h. ὠς (*pro* πως) c. 19. δουλευων *cum præced.* m. +μεθ' ὑμων
nte μετα) c. επιβολαις m. 20. *init.* +και bo. 21. διαμαρτυραμενος m
λησιν m. −τον *prim.* dhk. −την (*post* πιστιν) a. *fin.* −χριστον bcegh
. δεδεμενος εγω ak. συναντισοντα e. συναντησαντα l*m. συμβησομενα a
. +μοι (*post* πνευμα) c. διαμαρτυρετε b*. διαμεμαρτυρηται c. +μοι (*ant*
γον) abdekm (+με o). λεγων fk?l*m*. και θλιψεις με ack. 24. ουδ
ς k. +τουτων (*ante* λογον) k. ποιουμε f. −μου *prim.* c. ὡστε (*pro* ὡς
do. τετελειωσαι o. −μου *secund.* m. ἠν k. παρελαβον bcko. +χυ (*pos*
a. 25. −ιδου l. οιδα εγω m. οὐκέτι (*sic v.* 38) o. οψεσθαι k. προσ
ον e. παντες ὑμεις k. διῆλθον k. το ευαγγελιον (*pro* την βασιλειαν) a
του θυ c. 26. διοτι g. +και (*post* διο) f. ὑμων c, ἡμιν m* (*pro* ὑμιν). εγ
θαρος a**. −εγω c. +ειμι (*ante* απο) ac. *fin.* +ὑμων adel. 27. *Trans*
t ὑμιν m *in locum ultimum.* 28. προσεχεται d. −ουν o. αυτοις l* (ἑαυτοι
). κυ (*pro* θυ) a, *at* του κυ και θυ bdfghklmo. του αἱματος του ιδιου acm
. −τουτο a. ἄφιξην k. μετα την αφιξιν μου εισελευσονται eg (εισηλ. e)
. −αυτων *prim.* e. ὀπισω k. 31. νουθετων μετα δακρυων c. *fin.* +ὑμω
cdko. 32. τὰ νῦν lo. τω θω αδελφοι c. +ὑμας (*post* δυναμενω) abc
ικοδομησαι d. ἡμιν ?h*. 33. +τουτων (*ante* επεθυμησα) d. 34. −δ
cdefghklmo. ὑπηρετισαν c. χεῖραις fk. 35. *init.* +και bo. ουτω
lefghlmo [*non* k]. κοποιωντας k. δει· αντιλαμβανεσθε m. τον λογον ad*
k. του λογου h. ειπεν m. μαλλον διδοναι bcdfghkl [*non* mo]. 36. −αι
ν f. πασι d. 37. εγενετο δε κλαυθμος ἱκανος c. κλαυθμος εγενετο ahkm
αχηλοι m. −του c. 38. ὀδυνωμενοι k. −δε b*.

CAP. XXI. 1. του αχθηναι (*pro* αναχθηναι) d. αποσπασθεντες ab. ἠλ
ομεν d. ἠλθομεν k. κω abcdefghko. κών lm. ἑξῆς k. +τα (*ante* παταρ
o. 2. διαπερὸν ak, *at* διαπορευομενον c. 3. αναφαναντες a**bc (*tacitè*)
acitè) o. −και *prim.* km. καταλειποντες h*. +την (*ante* συριαν) b. εκ
ro εκεισε) d. το πλοιον ην c. 4. ανευροντες δε (−και) am. εὑροντες b**
τους bcdefghklo. αυτοις (*pro* αυτου) k. οἵτινες ελεγον τω παυλω l
ροσολυμα ak. 5. εξαρτησαι g. +τα (*post* γονατα) m. αἰγιαλον l
ροσευξομεθα k. προσευξαμεθα m. 5, 6. προσευξαμενοι ησπασαμεθα (−κα
d (απησπασαμεθα d). 6. +και (*post* αλληλους) ad. ανεβημεν acd. εν
ημεν k. τε c, *at* μεν k** *rubro in marg.* (*pro* δε). 7. απο τυρου cu
ræcedent. lm. επεμειναμεν k. 8. ἐπ' αὔριον k. −οἱ περι τον παυλον cehl

ἤλθομεν k, ηλθον glm. –του *secund.* bcdefghklmo. ὄντος d. +διακονων (*post* ἑπτα) d*. –ἐκ των ἑπτα *usque ad* τουτῳ δε *v.* 9, m. 9. *init.* τουτο e. ἦσαν k. τεσσαρες παρθενοι akm. 10. –ἡμων k. κατηλθεν m. ὀνοματι k. 11. –και *secund.* e. –τε abcmo. ἑαυτου abco. –τας d, *mutat in* m. τους ποδας και τας χειρας a**befghklo. ειπεν k*m. –το ἁγιον a* (*habet marg.*). –ἡ ζωνη a* (*habet marg.*). +ἡ (*ante* αὐτη) c. οὑτως cefghklm [*non* d] o. οἱ εν ἰλ̄η̄μ̄ ιουδαιοι bo. ἰουδαιοι m. εχθρων (*pro* εθνων) a. 12. ἠκουσαμεν k. εις ἱερουσαλημ αυτον e. 13. *init.* +τοτε m. –δε e. τε (*pro* δε) dfghklm. +και ειπε (*post* παυλος) abdko (ειπεν bo). ποιητε e. συνθριπτοντες c. –εις ἱερουσαλημ ab*ko. ἱερουσασαλημ d. ἑτοιμως εχω εις ἰλ̄η̄μ̄ f. ἑτοιμως εχω *transfert* c *ad finem versûs.* 14. πειθομενοι e. τε (*pro* δε) c. ἡσυχασαν l*. +ὅτι (*post* ειποντες) o. του κ̄ῡ το θελημα m. γινεσθω fgmo. 15. παρασκευασαμενοι a. επισκευασαμενοι bdfghklmo. αναιβαινομεν ko*?. ἱεροσολυμα a. 16. απο καισαρειας και των μαθητων m. μνασω g. μνασσωνι k. 17. ἰλ̄η̄μ̄ c. ασμενος e. απεδεξαντο ak. 18. επαυριον (*pro* επιουσῃ) a. εις (*pro* προς) c. δε (*pro* τε) m. οἱ πρεσβυτεροι παρεγενοντο ab. +προς αυτον (*ante* οἱ πρεσβ.) e*?. *fin.* +προς αυτον a. 19. –ἐν h. –δια l. 20. ακουοντες k. θ̄ν̄ (*pro* κυριον) adefgko. ειποντες (*pro* ειπον τε) ceghm. Δε (*pro* τε) l, Δ *rubro.* εν τοις ιουδαιοις (*pro* ιουδαιων) a. ὑπαρχουσιν k*m. 21. μωσεος adfhl. μωϋσεως cm. εθη e?o. περιτεμνειν (ειν *mutat.*) b. μηδε (*sic v.* 25 μηδὲν ko) hklmo. εθνεσι ?g*. 22. δη (*pro* δει) o. συνελθειν πληθος adk. 23. εκ ἡμιν (*sic*) c. 24. *init.* τουτοις c. ἁγνισθητι km (*sic* k *v.* 26 ἁγνισθεις, *at* ἁγνισμου). δαπανισον f. αυτους (*pro* αυτοις *secund.*) a. ξυρησονται ckl. ξυρισονται o. τας κεφαλας ab*eo. γνωσονται adm. +περι (*ante* ὧν) ae. εστι d. φυλασσων τον νομον acm. 25. –των k. ἡμῆς ?m. απεστειλαμεν l. *Rasura in* o *inter* επε *et* στειλαμεν. αλλα (*pro* ει μη) a. –αυτους *secund.* a. –τε c *at* τη m*. ηδωλοθυτον e. –το *secund.* ac. +το (*ante* πνικτον) lm. 26. παραλαβων ὁ παυλος bdflo. ανθρωπους (*pro* ανδρας) c. ερχομενη m. εισηεις το k. διαγγελων k*m*o. ἑωσοῦ gh. προσενεχθῇ a. προσηεχθη d*. –ἡ g. 27. ημελλον chm. Α῾ι l (Α *rubro*). τελειουσθαι c. θεασαμενοι αυτον οἱ απο της ασιας ιουδαιοι c. λαον (*pro* οχλον) c. επεβαλλον b*o. επ' αυτον τας χειρας achkm (αυτους k). 28. βοηθειται k. –και του νομου a* (*habet marg.*). νομου (*iterum pro* τοπου) f, *ob sphalma.* –τουτου ho. απανταχη a. πανταχη bco. –τε m. κεκοινω κε bl (*ras. inter* ω *et* κε). κεκοινωνηκεν o. 29. ἦσαν k. ἑωρακοτες defghklm. τροφημον h*. 30. εκηνηθε e. τον παυλον d. ἥλκον f. 31. τε (*pro* δε) a. αὑτων (*pro* αυτον) em*. της *bis script. in* m. σπειρας abceghо. +ἡ (*ante* ἰλ̄η̄μ̄) dfh. 31, 32. *Deest* της σπειρης

ιe ad παραλαβων in k. 32. ἐξ αὐτῆς lmo. 33. –τοτε bdefghklo. +δε
ιt εγγισας) iidem codices. αυτον (pro αυτου) ?d. Ὑπελαβετο k (Ὑ rubro).
3αλετο m. ἁλυσεσι k. δυσιν m. –αν a. 34. επιβοων sic m. επεβοων c,
πεφωνουν a, επεφονουν k. δυναμενου δε αυτου m. εκελευσαν m. αυτον
σθαι km. 35. εγινετο o. αυτον βασταζεσθαι a**. αυτον bis scriptum
. 36. ἡκολουθει k. ηκολουθη m. οχλου (pro λαου) c. κραζοντες abd
(sequitur rasura in a). κραζων ef. αἶρε ko. 37. δε (pro τε) abchko.
σθαι k. εις την παρεμβολην εισαγεσθαι ach. ειπε (pro λεγει) m. τις
ɔ τι) m. . –τι dfghl. προσε e. ελληνιστη e. ἐλληνηστι m. 38. ἆρα
ι. αιγυπτυος d. αἰγυπτιος k. αναστατωστας h*. 39. εγω μεν usque
ταρσευς b** marg. rescript. (defuit aliquid in textu). –μεν k. ταρσιυς ?k.
γενει (pro της κιλικιας) l. –δε secund. e. τε (pro δε) c, sic. επιστρεψον
με (pro μοι) k. 40. επιστρεψαντος m. ἑστως o. τω[ν mutat.] g.
ιτου (post χειρι) a. τον λαον ck. γενομενης σιγης a. προσεφωνει egh.
CAP. XXII. 1. ἡμας (pro ὑμας) ?d*. νυνι bcdeghklmo. 2. προσεφω-
εν abcko. ἡσυχιαν super ras. in o. φησί k. 3. –μεν a. γεγενημενος o.
: ch*. +δε (post πεπαιδευμενος) km. κατ' ἀκρίβειαν m. τω πατροω (-ρωω
') νομω k. –του θῦ c. ὑμεις εστε σημερον παντες c. 4. ὁδον k. μεχρι c,
k (pro αχρι). +τε (post δεσμευων) c. 5. μοι μαρτυρει m. ἁπαν k.
'σβυτερειον l*. –παρ' ὡν a*. εκεισαι de. 6. πορευομενω μοι c. πορευ-
ω o. περιηστραψαι ?c. περὶήστραψε k. περίάστράψας m. 7. επεσα
ι. επεπεσον o. σαυλε σαυλε l. 8. ειπεν m. δε (pro τε) abo. 9. της
νης δε f. 10. –κυριος k. –σοι prim. g, at σο k*. –παντων k. 11. εισ-
lον ceg. 12. ευλαβης (pro ευσεβης) abcegko. –των k. +εν δαμασκω (ante
ιαιων) abcehklmo. 13. σαυλε l. και εγω a. 14. ειπεν abfgklmo. +μοι
st ειπε) c. προεχειρησατο k. φωνης m. –του kl. 15. εσυ e. αυτο a*,
·ου c, αυτω cum rasura k. +τε (post ὡν) bco. 16. μελεις o. βαπτισε
αυτου (pro του κ̅υ̅) ac. fin. +ι̅υ̅ k. 17. ὑποστρεφοντι k. επιστρεψ-
·ι m. προσευχομενω e. –μου e. μοι (pro μου) c. μοι (pro με) a** marg.
–εν l. απο (pro εξ) k. –την a. 19. και εγω c. ημιν (non v. 20) k.
ρων b**gh. κατατατας k. εις (pro επι) h. 20. πρωτομαρτυρος ackm.
εστως k. αναιρεση k. –και quartum bceflo. φυλαττων m. +τε (post
λασσων) c. fin. αυτων ?m*. 21. –προς με k. εξαποστελλω e. 22.
υτου c. του λογου τουτου a*ckm. αυτων την φωνην m. αἶρε k. καθηκει
καθηκεν bcfghklmo. ζειν e. 23. κραζοντων ceglo, at πειραζοντων k.
τι πλειον (post αυτων) aek (αυτον e). ῥιπτοντων abo. κονιορτων e. 24.
χιλιαρχος εισαγεσθαι αυτον akm. ὁ χιλιαρχος αγεσθαι αυτον h. ὁ χιλιαρ-

χος αγειν αυτον e. —αυτου *prim.* c. εισαγεσθαι c. ειπε δε (*pro* ειπων) k. εταζεσθαι m. αυτον ανεταζεσθαι bo. ἰν' m. αἰτιαν k. κατεφωνουν c. 25. προετειναν abcegh [f *dubium*, klmo *cum Elz.*]. τοις ἱμασιν αυτον c. εφεστωτα abko. 26. τω χιλιαρχω ανηγγειλεν (—λεγων) c. τω χιλιαρχω απηγγειλε ahkm. εστιν m. 27. λεγε μοι συ· ῥωμαιος ει; f. —εἰ acfm. συ; a. 28. δε (*pro* τε) ack. εκτισαμην k. γεγενημαι em*. 29. επιγνους ὁτι ῥώμαιος εστιν εφοβηθη k. εστιν m. *fin.* δεδωκως a**mo. 30. τε επιουσῃ (*pro* δε επαυριον) c. ἐπἰγνώναι k. κατηγορειτω c. ὑπο (*pro* παρα) abcfhko. αυτων (*pro* αυτον) m*. —απο των δεσμων a. εκελευσε συνελθειν abkmo. συνεισελθειν c. παν (*pro* ὁλον) achkm. —αυτων ack. —και *tert.* o. κατεγων b*.

CAP. XXIII. 1. τω συνεδριω ὁ παυλος a. —ὁ c. αγαθη συνειδησει k. συνηδεισει e. συνηδησει m. πολιτευομαι o. της ἡμερας ταυτης cm. ὡρας (*pro* ἡμερας) a. 2. εκελευσε a, προσεταξε l (*pro* επεταξε). τοις παρεστωσιν αυτω επεταξε c. 3. ειπεν m. 5. δε (*pro* τε) c. αρχιερευς εστι a*. +ὁτι (*ante* αρχοντα) k. 6. φαρισαιων το δε ἑτερον σαδδουκαιων ah. σαδουκαιων m*. —νεκρων e. 7. ειποντος (*pro* λαλησαντος) abko. επεσε (*pro* εγενετο) c. των σαδδουκαιων και των φαρισαιων cgm (φαρισσ. c), *at* —των *secund.* be kmo. 8. —μεν o. λεγουσιν mo. μὴδὲ *prim.* mo. μητε (*pro* μηδε) achkl. μὴδὲ (*pro* μητε) bo. 9. μεγλη c. τινες των γραμματεων (*pro* οἱ γραμματεις) acm (φαρισαιων γραμματεων m). —οἱ f. τινες (*pro* οἱ) k. ουθεν c. ευρισκομεν p. ἢ p. +εν αυτω (*ante* μη) c. —μη θεομαχωμεν p. 10. φοβηθεις (*pro* ευλαβηθεις) acp. εκελευσεν p. καταβηναι και (*pro* καταβαν) bcefghklmo. καταβαν (κατ *forsan. s. m.*) p. ἁρπασαι p. δε (*pro* τε) p. —τε m. +αυτων (*post* τε) l. 11. ειπεν bmop (+αυτω bo). —παυλε a. ἰλημ p. οὑτως cfgkl [*non* dm] op. 12. τε (*pro* δε) c. οἱ ιουδαιοι (*pro* τινες των ιουδαιων) c, *sic* ap (—οἱ a) συστροφην *præposito*. συστροφην τινες των ιουδαιων km. ανεθεμετησαν c. ἑαυτοις g. —λεγοντες abcho. ποιειν (*pro* πιειν) dkm (*sic* k, *v.* 21). ἕωσοῦ (*sic v.* 21) h. ανελωσι (*pro* αποκτ.) h. αποκτεινωσιν p. 13. την συνομωσιαν ταυτην m*. συνωμωσιαν c*m**. συνομοσιαν aep. ποιησαμενοι ap. ποιησαντες eg. —πεποιηκοτες o. 14. οἵτινες (*non v.* 21) k. αρχιερευσιν p. ειπαν p. ανεθεματησαμεν c. αναθεματισαμεν k. ἑαυτοις g. μὴθενὸς k. ἕωσοῦ gh. αποκτεινομεν c. 15. οὐν p. ἡμεις (*pro* ὑμεις) o. εμφανησατε m. +ὁλω (*ante* τω συνεδριω) c. πως (*pro* ὁπως) f**. —αυριον ap. αὐριον k. καταγαγει e. καταγαγη αυτον aghkmp. εις (*pro* προς) p. ἡμας (*pro* ὑμας) eg. μελλοντες p. διαναγινωσκειν b. ακριβεστερον διαγινωσκειν clm. ἑτοιμοι εσμεν προ του εγγισαι αυτον e. ἐγγισαι p. αυτω (*pro* αυτον *secund.*)k. ἑτοιμοι p. —του (*ante* ανελειν) ag [*non* p]. 16. το ενεδρον bde (*tacitè*) fghlmo [*non* ackp]. εισελθον d. απηγγελε d. απηγγειλεν p. 17. ἑνα p. ἑκατοντ. p. ειπεν (*pro* εφη) p. απαγε p. απαγγειλαι τι kp. αναγγειλαι l. 18. ὁ μεν οὐν p. ἡγαγεν p. φησὶν hlmo. —ὁ (*ante* δεσμιος) p*?. ἡρωτησεν p. ἡρωτησε k. τον νεανιαν τουτον bco. νεανισκον aegp. +ὡς (*ante* εχοντα) l. 19. Τουτου (*pro* αυτου) p*. κατιδιαν fhklp. απαγγειλε p*. 20. ειπεν p. —οἱ aklo. τον παυλον καταγαγης εις το συνεδριον amp. καταγαγης αὐριον τον παυλον εις το συνεδριον k. καταγαγης τον παυλον εις το συνεδριον c. +αυτων (*post* συνεδριον) f. καταγαγεις e. μελλοντα am. μελλον b*, *at* μελλων op. μελλοντων efgk. 21. οὐν (*sic vv.* 22, 31) p. πησθεις e. πεισθεις fk. πισθεῖς p. ενεδρευουσιν p. —αυτον *prim.* a. ανεθεματησαν c. ενεθεματισαν k. μη (*pro* μητε *prim.*) m. ἑωσοῦ g. εισιν ἑτοιμοι amp (ἑτοι m, ἑτοιμοι p). 22. απελυσεν p. νεανισκον a. +αυτον (*ante* μηδενι) p. μὴδενὶ kp. εκλαλεισαι p. ενεμφανισας e. 23. τινας δυο p. ἑκατοντ. p. ἑτοιμασατε p. +ενοπλους (*post* στρατιοτας) k. ἱππεις ἑβδομηκοντα p. εις καισαρειαν (*pro* ἑως καισαρειας) c. 24. επιβαντες (τον παυλον *cum sequent.*) l. διασωσωσιν m. διασώσῑ o. φιληκα abcdfko [*non* hlp]. φιλικα em. 25. περιεχουσα f. εχουσαν acp. 26. φιληκι abdfko. φιλικι cem. 27. ανε^αι^ρεισθαι (αι *p. m.*?) p. εξειλαμην p. —αυτον adp. ῥωμαιως p*. εστιν mp. 28. επιγνωναι ackp. αυτον (*pro* αυτῳ) e. —κατηγαγον *ad fin. vers.* p. —αυτον k. 29. —ὁν εὑρον *usque ad* αυτων c. και εὑρων (*pro* ὁν εὑρον) e. εὑ̃ρων ?k*. μὴδὲν kp. —δε beghop. ἣ p. δεσμιῶν ?k*. εχοντα εγκλημα abklmop (εγκλιμα p). 30. μηνυθησης e. προς (*pro* εις) hm*. —μελλειν ap. —ὑπο των ιουδαιων acp. ἐξ αὐτῆς klmo, *at* εξ αυτων acp. επεψα p. +δε (*post* παραγγειλας) k. τα προς αυτον επι σου ειπειν (*pro* λεγειν) c. —επι σου p. ἐρρωσο p. 31. ειγαγον k. +αυτον (*post* ηγαγον) e. —της p. 32. ἑασαντες p. ἱππεις p. συν αυτω πορευεσθαι m. απερχεσθαι (*pro* πορευ.) ep. 33. ελθοντες c. —την *prim.* a. αναδοσαντες kl*?. τω ἡγεμονι την επιστολην m. ἡγεμονη ?d*. ἡγεμονι p. —και *secund.* a*. 34. —ὁ ἡγεμων p. επερωτισας k. επηρωτησας m. εστιν mp. πειθομενος f. εκ (*pro* απο) a*. κιλιας b*. 35. παραγενωνται fp. κελευσας (*pro* εκελευσε τε) ckp. εκελευσεν m. αυτον *transferunt* ckp *in locum post* φυλασσεσθαι. πραιτοριω m. —του abdefgklo [*non* mp]. ἡρωδου p. φυλασεσθαι g. φυλαττεσθαι em*.

CAP. XXIV. 1. μερας d*. —των ckmp. +τινων (*post* πρεσβυτερων) ckmp. τερτυλου el. ητινες e. εφανησαν l*. ενεφανησαν ch**m. ανεφανισαν k. ἡγεμονι p. 2. τερτυλος el. 3. διορθωματων p. +τινων (*post* κατορθωματων) f. γενομενων c. γιγνωμενων m. εθνη k. παντι (*pro* παντη) dfk.

φιληξ abdefko. φιλιξ cm. ευχαριστειας g*kp. 4. πλεον h. κοπτω m.
—σε *secund.* em. επιεικια eg. 5. *init.* εὑρομεν eo. εὑροντες p. —γαρ e.
λυμῶν p. κοινουντα d*. στασεις p. +κατοικουσι (*ante* κατα) g. οἰκουμενην
kp. προστατην o. τω ναζωραιων a*. αἱρεσεως p. 6. ἱερον p. επειραζε c.
επειρασεν mp. επηρασε o. —και *tertium* g**. εβουληθημεν (*forsan* ηβου., *pro*
ηθελησαμεν) m. εβουληθημεν ανελειν (*pro* ηθελ. κρινειν) f. κριναι abeg**kmo.
7. βια πολλη (—μετα) g**. αφιλετο (*pro* απηγαγε) g**. απηγαγεν αυτον
εκ των χειρων ἡμων m. *In* dg*hlp *desunt omnia ab* και κατα τον ἡμετερον *v.* 6
usque ad επι σε, *v.* 8. *In* f *inter* χιλιαρχος *v.* 7 *et* παρ' οὑ *v.* 8 *sic legitur,*
ἡρπασεν αυτον εκ των χειρων ἡμων πεμψας προς σε· (*desunt cætera*). 8.
+και (*post* κελευσας) ag**. —αυτου *prim.* ao. επι σου ερχεσθαι m. —επι σε
g**. προς (*pro* επι) a. σου (*pro* σε) cko. ὡν (*pro* οὑ) bm*o [*non* p]. +και
(*ante* δυνηση) g**. γνωναι c. +και (*ante* ἡμεις) e. 9. συνεπεθεντο acdfghk
lmp. —οἱ kl. ιδαιοι p. 10. τε (*pro* δε) a*cp. αυτου (*pro* αυτω) b*. ἡγε-
μονος p. λαλειν (*pro* λεγειν) c. ὀντα p. κρητην f. +δικαιον (*post* κριτην)
cehk. εθνη ?h*. ευθυμως cdp. 11. επιγνωναι bckop. εισιν p. —η abcdfg
hklmop. δωδεκα cmp. προσκυνησω p. εις (*pro* εν) a**dp. ἰλημ p. 12.
ἱερω εὑρον p. ἡ p. ουτε (*pro* η) c. εποστασιαν (αποσ. p**) p. +του (*ante*
οχλου) l. ὀχλου kp. οὑτε *secund.*, *at* ουδε *pro tertio* p. 13. *init.* ουδε p.
+με (*post* παραστησαι) c (*tacitè*) fglm [*non* aekop]. νυν δυνανται περι ὡν blo.
+σοι (*post* δυνανται) a**degkmp. νυν περι ὡν νυνι c. νυνι dmp. —νυν k.
κατηγορουσιν p. *Cum Elzev.* a. 14. ἡν (*sic v.* 15) k. αἱρεσιν gp. —οὑτω
a. οὑτως cfgklmop. +τοις (*ante* εν τοις προφηταις) bcekmop. —εν adfghl
15. +δε (*ante* εχων) c. —εις τον θεον c. προς (*pro* εις) a. εκδεχονται c.
—νεκρων kp. 16. τε m, και bdkop (*pro* δε). +και (*ante* αυτος) cgm. εχων
abcefghklmo [*non* p]. +τε (*post* προς) bdhlo. διαπαντος προς τε τον θεον
και προς τους ανθρωπους c. διαπαντως e. διάπαντὸς kop. 17. *init.* +και a.
—δε a. *Transfert* c παρεγενομην *ad finem versûs, at* mp *in locum post* μου.
+εν ἰλημ (*post* παρεγενομην) g**. ελεημοσυνας παρεγενομην a**. ελεημοσυνην
k. ποιησον e. 18. εν αἱς b*cop. ηὑρον c. εὑρον p. εν τω ἱερω ἡγνισμε-
νον d. ἱερω p. ὀχλου p. ουτε (*pro* ουδε) c. τινες των απο της ασιας
ιουδαιων bco. [των (*pro* δε) c]. —δε e, [*vid. Mill.*, ak *cum Elzev.*]. +των f,
+δε των m, +δε p (*ante* απο). 19. δει bfgklmo [εδει cep, *vid. Mill.*]. Βα-
ρειναι (Β *rubro*) k. ἐχοιεν προς εμε p. 20. ἡ p. +και (*ante* αυτοι) c. αυτον
(*pro* αυτοι) k. —ει bdefghklmop. —εν εμοι p. μοι (*pro* μου) o. 21. ἡ p.
φωνης ταυτης ck. εκεκραξα abdmop. εν αυτοις ἑστως ckmp (ἑστῶς k).
ἑστως o. σημερον κρινομαι a*c. κρινωμε ?d*. αφ' e, εφ' mp (*pro* ὑφ').

—ακουσας δε ταυτα cp. ανεβαλλετο δε ὁ φιλιξ αυτους c. ανεβαλετο δε ·οις ὁ φήλιξ p. φιληξ abdfko. φιλιξ em. ανεβαλλετο deg. αυ (rasurâ uente) d. ὁδου εἶπας p. +ὁτι (ante ὁταν) c. ὁ χιλιαρχος λυσιας cm. κα-3ει ?m*. διαγνωσωμαι k. ἡμας g*. 23. —τε prim. b*cop. ἑκατονταρ-p. αυτον (pro τον παυλον) ckp. δε (pro τε secund.) m. μὴδένα k. τον ·ν d. ὑπηρετεισθαι bo. ὑπερετην p. —η προσερχεσθαι p. και (pro η) a. τινας ἡμερας c. φιληξ abfko. φιλιξ cem. φιλης d. +ιδια (ante γυναικι) τη ιδια γυναικι (—αὐτου) abkmo. —αὐτου prim. cefghl. οὖσα m*. οὐσῃ +παρ' (ante αυτου) c. —εις m. +ιν (post χν) defghlmp. 25. του μελλον-· κριματος (—του) m. —εσεσθαι p. φιληξ abcdfko. φιλιξ em. τον νυν m. ιν p. λαβων abdekop. μεταπεμψομαι (pro μετακαλ.) c. 26. ἁμα p. ε abcdefghklmop. —και prim. bco. +και (post ὁτι) ck. αυτω δοθησιται c. πως λυσῃ αυτον p. απολυση ae. πικνοτερον e. —αυτον secund. hl. ωμει-e. 27. πληρωθησης ek. ελαβεν p. φιληξ bis abcdfko. φιλιξ e bis, m sel. θελον d*. δε (pro τε) bcdeghkl**op**. χαριν c. χαριτα p. κα-θέσθαι χαριν k. —ὁ φηλιξ secund. m. κατελειπεν p.

CAP. XXV. 1. +δε (ante ουν) d*. —ουν a*. οὐν (sic v. 4, non 5) p. την αρχιαν p. 2. ανεφανησαν m. τε (pro δε) kp. οἱ αρχιερεις cdp. +τε ost ὁ) a. της πολεως (pro των ιουδαιων) p. 3. αἰτουμενοι kp. παρ' (pro τ') e. ἱεροσολυμα k. ενεδρον c. αναιλειν e. 4. εις καισαρειαν p. ταχε 5. init. ει (pro οἱ) mo. εν ὑμιν φησι δυνατοι mp (φησὶν p). φησὶν εν ιν k. —τουτῳ dp. +ατοπον (post εστιν) beo, at acdg**mp ante κατηγορει-σαν. κατηγωρειτωσαν f. 6. +ου (ante πλειους) a**bdemop [non hk]. κτω (ante η δεκα) amp (ὀκτῶ p). καισαριαν p. +και (ante τη επαυριον) c. 9ησας k*. βιματος d. εκελευσεν p. 7. του (pro αυτου) d*. παρεστησαν d. ·υτον beo, +αυτω p (post περιεστησαν). καταβαντες gk. —καταβεβηκοτες e. δαιοι p. αιτιαματα πολλα και βαρεα g. αιτιωματα a**dfmp (αἰτ. p). αιτη-ατα h. αἰτιαματα k. καταφεροντες (—κατα του παυλου) p. αλλ' (pro ἁ) ισχιον e. 8. του παυλου απολογουμενου (pro αυτου) cmp. —ουτε εις · νομον των ιουδαιων ad. οὐτε secund. et tert. p. —το e. ἱερον p. ἡμαρτεν ἡμαρτον p. 9. φηστος ουν (—ὁ et δε) k. θελων τοις ιουδαιοις ckmp. ·εν mp. κριθηναι e. κριθειναι p. επι dp. ὑπ' (pro επ') bgho. 10. ·εν p. —ὁ f. Ponit m ἑστως post παυλος. ἑστὼς kop. μαι (pro με) p. : (pro ουδεν) c. ἠδικησα k. ηδικικως (—ὡς) p. γινωσκεις cd*. 11. ουν ·ο γαρ) dkp (οὐν p). αδικον (pro αδικω) k. του (pro το) eflmo. Rasur. d post ει δε. κατηγορουσιν m**p. μου (pro με) m. δυνατε p. επικεκλη-: k. 12. συνλαλησας p. —συλλαλησας ?e. συμβολιον ep. επικεκλησαι, o.

καιρα *secund.* p. πορευσει f. 13. *init.* μερων d*. −τινων ck. αγριπας *hic tantum* m. αΑγριππας (A *rubro*) d. κατιντησαν p. ασπασαμενοι k*l* (*vel* ωμενοι l*?) m. 14. ὡς p. διετριβεν dfgkl (*jungit cum* ὁ φηστος kl). ανεθεντο (*at* λεγων) k. −τα k*?. εστιν p. καταλελημμενος l*p. φιληκοι abdfko [*non* lp]. φιλικος cem. 15. −μου fm. ενεφανησαν m. +του λαου (*post* πρεσβυτεροι) a*. αἰτουμενοι k. 16. ῥωμαιους m. τινι (*pro* τινα) o. −εις απωλειαν cp. πρινὴ hl. πρινῆ p. εχει b*cdefk. ἔχοι p. 17. οὐν (*sic v.* 23) p. ενθαδε αυτων c. ουδεμιαν g. μὴδὲμίαν lo. μηδὲμίαν p. μὴδεμίαν αναβολην k. ἐξῆς kmp, *forsan* h*. 18. οὐν (*pro* οὐ) p. οὐδὲμίαν klop. αἰτιαν k. εφερον cp. ὧν k. ὡν εγω ὑπενοουν mp. *fin.* +πονηραν ckm, +πονιρων p. 19. −περι της ιδιας *usque ad* και a. ιδειας ?d*. δεισιδαιμαινιας m. ελεγεν (*pro* εφασκεν) c. 20. δ' m. −εις *prim.* bdeflop. −περι cm. τουτων (*pro* τουτου) cmp. περι την τουτων ζητησιν (−εις) hk. πορευθηναι d. ἱεροσολυμα ckmp. κακεισε m. τουτου (*pro* τουτων) d. 21. *init.* ου (*pro* του) e. επικαλουμενου k. αυτον τηρεισθαι c. ἕωσοῦ gh. αναπεμψω ckmp. εις (*pro* προς) k. +τον (*ante* καισαρα) m. 22. ειπεν (*pro* εφη) a. ηβουλομην c. αὐριον k. ακοῦσαι ? (*pro* ακουσῃ) m*. 23. δε (*pro* ουν) a. −και εισελθοντων k. −τοις *prim.* ckp. +τοις (*ante* ανδρασι) e. ἀνδρᾶσι p. κατεξοχην fmp. −ουσι p. της πολεως οὐσι k. τοις (*pro* της *secund.*) e. −και *ultim.* p. 24. φησὶν hlo. ἀγριππα *hic* p. τουτον; a. τουτου (*pro* οὐ) a. ἁπαν ckp. ἐν p. βοωντες p. αυτον ζην a*bkmop. μὴκέτι kmp. *fin.*; l. 25. λαβομενος a. κατελαβομην p. μὴδὲν p. −αυτον *prim.* p. αυτον αξιον θανατου g. πεπραχεναι αυτον θανατου c. −και p. −αυτον *secund.* p. 26. οὖν (*pro* οὐ) m. −τι *prim.* m, *at* τις p*. +μου (*post* κυριω) e. +και (*post* διο) g. προσηγαγον l. αγριππα βασιλευ g. *fin.* ἐχω τῇ γραψω p. 27. δοκει μοι c. ειναι μοι δοκει m. δεσμιον πεμποντα l.. αἰτιας k. σημᾶναι chklmop. σιμαναι f.

Cap. XXVI. 1. ἀγριππας (*sic v.* 2) p. +ὁ βασιλευς (*post* δε) ad. επιτετραπται bcop. επιτρεπαιτε k. περι (*pro* ὑπερ) p. λαλειν περι σεαυτου (*pro* ὑπερ σεαυτου λεγειν) c. σέαυτὸν k. σὲ αὐτὸν p.. τας χειρας c. εκτεινας την χειρα απελογειτο kmp. (απελογεῖτῶ p, ο *forsan p. m.*). 2. ἡγειμαι f. ἥγημαι k. ἐμαυτον p. επι σου μελλων απολογεισθαι abcdefghk lo. ·επι p. επι σου μελλων (μελλω p) σημερον απολογεισθαι mp. +τη (*ante* σημερον) g. 3. σὲ παντων ειδὼς οντα τῶν (αβγδε, m**) m. ὀντα p. ιουδαιων df. ηθων afgm. ἤθων d. ἐθῶν k. −σου ekp. 4. −μεν ουν c. −μεν k. οὐν (*sic vv.* 9, 22) p. −την *secund.* m. ἀπαρχῆς hkmp. εθη e, εθνη p (*pro* εθνει). ἐν *secund.* p. ἴσασι k. ἴσασιν p. −οἱ dkmp. 5. −με c. ἐαν p.

ιβεστεραν bgo. αἱρεσιν p. 6. εις (pro προς) dp. +ἡμων (post πατερας) dmop. γενομενης επαγγελειας c. ἑστηκα ko. κριναμενος p. 7. δωδεκαλλον m. εκτενια ghlm. ἡμερα k. +και (ante περι) d. −των abcdefghk ›p. ὑπο ιουδαιων transfert a** in locum post εγκαλουμαι. ὑπο ιουδαιων σιλευ αγριππα dkmp (−αγριππα p). 7, 8. Uno tenore p. 8. τι cum ruent. hlmp. κρινετε o. εν (pro παρ᾽) k. ἡμιν (pro ὑμιν) ce. 9. ὀνομα +του (ante ιυ) o. εναντια πολλα a*. πράξαι hmo. 10. init. ὁ omnes. ·ε (post πολλους) p. +εν (ante φυλακαις) bekmop (εφυλακαις p*). λαβων ιυσιαν l. δε (pro τε) a**c. 11. κατασπασας (pro κατα πασας) m. ἠναγζον k. περισσοτερως bdo. εμμενομενος efk*m. και ἑως (pro ἑως και) a. . −και prim. c. −την abchko. μετα (pro μετ᾽) c. −παρα cp. 13. μεστης e. κα (pro κατα) a*. ειδον κατα την ὁδον e. +αγριππα (post βασιλευ) περιλαμψαντα mp, at περιαστραψαν a. 14. τε (pro δε) cp. −ἡμων d. ι (pro εις) ep. φωνης λαλουσης a. φωνης λεγουσης προς με (−λαλουσαν και) m. λεγουσαν (pro λαλουσαν) p. −και λεγουσαν bop. λεγουσης a. οαιδι p. σαυλε σαυλε l. 15. ειπα (pro ειπον) klp. +κς (ante ειπεν) kmp. ‹ ναζωραιος (post ις) m. διωκες ?c. 16. αλλ᾽ abo. ες (pro σε) m. ειδες ωφθησομαι h. ὀφθησομαι p. 17. +εκ (ante των εθνων) klp. −νυν ce. ω (pro νυν) abdfghklmop. ἐξαποστελῶ σε mp. ἀποστελῶ ag. ἀποστελῶ cdk. αποστελλῶ σε f. 18. ανοιξε f. ὀφθαλμους kp. αποστρεψαι bce ›p. ὑποστρεψαι l. +απο (ante της εξουσιας) ac. ἁμαρτιων p. 19. απειs k. ὀπτασιας d. ὀπτασια kmp. 20. +τε (post πρωτον) p. +τοις εν c, ·ν k (ante ἱεροσολυμοις). απαγγελλω bcdefhklo [non p]. απαγγελλων gm. ι τον θεον επιστρεφειν e. +ζωντα (ante θεον) m. πραττοντας m. 21. ·κα kp (ἐ rubro k). ἑνεκεν τουτου bo. με eras. post συλλ. et denuo ·iptum ante συλλ. a**. ιουδαιοι με (−οἱ) mp. συλλαβομενοι οἱ ιουδαιοι a. ιουδαιοι συλλαβομενοι με οντα εν c. +οντα (ante εν) mp (ὀντα p). ἱερω p. . −της prim. m. ὑπο c, απο p (pro παρα). ἑστηκα kop (·ἑστ. p). μαρρομενος bcdhklmop. εξωθεν (pro εκτος) c. προελαλησαν c. μωυσης abcd nop. 23. μελλειν m*p. καταγγελειν kp. +τε (ante λαω) bhklop. νεσιν dmp. 24. φησὶ kp, at ειπε c. μαινειν p*. μαινει p**. γραμμτα b. . init. ὁ δε παυλος dp. φησιν κρατηστε p. αλλα abcdfgklmop. φθεγμαι a*co. 26. λανθανει m. −τι a. −ου prim. abceop. ουδεν πειθομαι m. ντων ουθεν πειθομαι p. ουδε (pro ου secund.) m. −εστιν fghl. εν γωνια ντο (delet a**) πεπραγμενον τουτο εστι a. εν γωνια εστι m. 27. οἰδα p. . −εφη p. ποιησαι (pro γενεσθαι) p. 29. −ειπεν p. ευξαμην c*lp. ξαμην f. ἀν p. ὀλιγω p. πολω d*. μεγαλω (pro πολλῳ) kp. εν πολλῶ και εν ὀλιγω (αβ, m**) m. σημερον *cum sequent.* lp. και εγω (*pro* καγω) c. 30. –και ταυτα ειποντος αυτου cp. –και *prim.* k. +δε c, +τε p (*post* ανεστη). ἡγεμων p. οἱ (*pro* ἡ) m*. +παντες (*ante* οἱ) a. 31. αναχωρισαντες p. εκαλουν m. –ὁτι m. αξιον θανατου c. θανατου η (ἠ p) δεσμων αξιον τι kp. η δεσμων αξιον τι πραττειν ὁ m. 32. ἀπολέλυσθαι m. ηδυνατο ackm (ἠδ. k). αἰδυνατο p. μι (*pro* μη) e. απεκεκλητο ?m.

CAP. XXVII. 1. τους περι τον παυλον (*pro* ἡμας) m. ἰταλιαν (*sic v.* 6) k. παρεδιδου a. –τε c. –ἑτερους cp* (ἑτ. p**). ἑκατονταρχω c*gk?. ἑκατονταρχη m. ἑκατονταρχη p. ονοματι p. σπειρας begho [*non* klmp]. 2. *Rasur. in* g *inter* επι *et* βαντες. +εν (*ante* πλοιω) c. αδραμυτηνω adekl. αδραμητινω c. ατραμητινω g. ατραμυτηνω b*o. ατραμυτινω b**h. [mp *cum Elzev.*]. μελλοντι abcdop. αποπλειν h. πλεειν επι c. +εις (*post* πλειν) ap. ὀντως p. θεσσαλονικεος d*. *fin.* θεσσαλονικεων τε αρισταρχος και σεκουνδος c. 3. δε (*pro* τε *prim.*) kmp. ἑτερα p. φιλανος d. φιλανθρωπος m. –ὁ a. χρησαμενος τω παυλω a. επετρεψαι d. επετρεψεν p. +τους (*ante* φιλους) abdfghklmp. –προς φιλους o. πορευθεντι p. 4. +εις (*ante* την κυπρον) k. ειναι τους ανεμους m. εναντιους ειναι o. 5. τότε mo *alii.* –την a. διαστρεψαντες (*pro* διαπλευσαντες) k. +δι' ἡμερων δεκαπεντε (*ante* κατηλθομεν) c. κατηχθημεν bdho. σμυρναν m, μυραν p (*pro* μυρα). 6. κἀκειθεν l. κακεισε m. εὑρων p. ἑκατονταρχης p. αλεξανδρηνον abdklo [*non* p]. πλεων f. –την bchklo. ανεβιβασεν acdflo. ενεβιβασαν m. ενεβηβασεν p. *fin.* αυτον ?l*. 7. *init.* –εν bo. εκειναις (*pro* ἱκαναις) *sic* p. βραδιπλοουντες c. ουκ εωντος (*pro* μη προσεωντος) bo (εωντας b). κριτην kp (*hic*). 8. παραγενομενοι (*pro* παραλεγομενοι) c. ἠλθομεν k. πολις εστι a*. πολις ην a**. λασαιεα e. λασαῖα l. λασεα mp. 9. ἱκανου p. ὀντος p. ἠδη *prim.* k. του πλοος επισφαλους c. ηδη και την νηστειαν a. –ηδη *secund.* k. των ιουδαιων λεγεσθαι ηδη (*sic*) c. 10. μεθ m. ὑβρεως πολλης και ζημιας l. ὑβρεως p. φορτιου ac**defgklmp [*non* bo]. 11. ἑκατονταρχης bdfglmop [*non* k, ἑκατ. p]. κυβερνιτη f. ναυκληρω p. μαλλον επειθετο kmp. ἠ p. –του p. 12. ανευθυτου m. οἱ m. πλειονες p. αχθηναι a. εκειθεν (*pro* κἀκειθεν) bcehkop [*abhinc hiat* e]. ὀπως (*pro* ειπως) k. δυναιτο b*. φινικα d*. κριτης b*km. λυβα ?k*. 13. ὑποπλευσαντος k. νωτου p. ἆσσον, agh, ἄσσον, fop, ἄσον k [lm *cum Elzev.*]. κριτην b*k. 14. εβαλεν p. καλουμε m. εὑροκλύδων kmo. εὑρο κλυδων p. 15. επιδιδοντες f. +τω πλεοντι και συστειλαντες τα ἱστια (*ante* εφερομεθα) c. 16. νησιδιον g. νησσιων m. ὑπεκδραμοντες a. περιδραμοντες k. κλαυδαν c*. κλαυδα p. ισχυσαμεν μολις mp. ἰσχυσαμεν k. περικρατης d. 17. ἁραντες m. βοηθειας cp. ὑποζωννυντες f. ὑποζωννῦντες hk. πλειον k.

πως (*pro* μη) k. συρτην acdfgk?h*lmo*. εκπεσωσιν mp. εμπεσωσϊ bo.
3. ἐξῆς kp. ἐπιουντο k. 19. +ἡμερα (*post* τριτη) bo. ερριψαν b (*super*
rasur. a) op. *fin.* +εις θαλασσαν c. 20. αστερων g. επιφαινοτων b*.
ιφαινομενων c. επιφανεντων l, *at* επιφεροντων m*. πλειους c (*ut videtur*)
περιῄρειτο p. ελπις πασα kmp. +ἡ (*ante* ελπις) a. 21. τε (*pro* δε) cp.
λειους (*sic*) c. ἡμων (*pro* αυτων) c. ὦ kp. −της d. κριτης k. ὕβρην h*.
2. τὰ νῦν lop. ουδεμιας bcmo. οὐδεμία klp. ἐσται p. ἡμων (*pro* ὑμων) g.
3. παρεστι m. ταυτη τη νυκτι abcdfghklmop. *Transfert* m αγγελος
locum post λατρευω. κῦ (*pro* του θῦ) p. οὗ p. −και l. 25. οὕτως p.
ιλαται a*. 27. τέσσαρες (-ρας p) καὶ δεκάτη (*sic v.* 33 kp) kmp. εγενετο
ξ c. επεγενετο p. προαγειν b*o, προσεγγιζειν c (*pro* προσαγειν). αυ-
κς τινα k. αὐτοις hlmp *alii.* 28. βολησαντες *bis* g, m *prim.* εὑρον p.
εὑρον ὀργ. *usque ad* παλιν βολισαντες c. −βραχυ δε *usque ad* οργυιας k (*habet*
** *in marg.*). οργιας *bis* a, d *prim.*, *at* οργυας *bis* b*, *prim.* o. ὀργῦας *bis* p.
κοσι m. διαστυντες h. −και παλιν βολισαντες a*l. λυσαντες (*pro* βολισαν-
τες *secund.*) m. *fin.* ουργυιας πεντεκαιδεκα c. 29. δε (*pro* τε) cp. μηπου cp.
τα (*pro* εις) cp. βραχεις (*pro* τραχεις) c. εκπεσωμεν abghklmo [*non* p].
ομηνης c. ηὐχοντο kp. 30. εκφυγειν c. −εκ *secund.* a*. πρωρης d. αγκυρας
λλοντων mp. εκτεινειν αγκυρας k. 31. *init.* ειπεν δε p. ἑκατονταρχω ck.
ατ. p. ἐαν p. εν τω πλοιω μεινωσιν ch. ου δυνασθε σωθηναι c. δυνασθαι
ο. 32. απεκοψαν οἱ στρατιωται cm. −οἱ στρατιωται p. 33. *init.* χρι l.
ιελλεν cl. ἡμερα ἠμελλεν p. γενεσθαι bco. γιγνεσθαι m. ἁπαντας p.
ταλαβειν ἁπαντας l. τεσσαρας και δεκατην p. ἡμεραν σημερον ck. μηδὲν
ο. μηδενος l. 34. μεταλαβειν bdhkop. +τινος (*ante* τροφης) c. ἡμετερας
ι. οὐδὲνὸς k. ἀπο (*pro* εκ) p. απολειται (*pro* πεσειται) mp. 35. +τε
post ευχαριστησας *ut videtur legendum*) k. ηυχαριστησε lm. ηὐχαριστησεν
36. προσελαμβανον c. 37. *init.* ημεθα p. πασαι ψυχαι εν τω πλοιω
-αἱ) kmp (ἁπασαι m). διακοσιοι a. ἑβδομικονταεξ d. ἑβδομήκοντα ἓξ k*.
βδομήκονταὲξ o. Cοϛ p (σοζ *Tischendorf., vix rectè*). −ἓξ m. 38. +της
ante τροφης) dglm. εκβαλομενοι a. 39. ὑπενοουν hkm. αἰγιαλον (*sic v.*
) k. εβουλευοντο k. εβουλοντο p. δυνατον (*pro* δυναιντο) abcdfghklm**o.
. −τας a* (*prim.?*). ἁμα· *cum præcedent.* p. πιδαλιων d. αρτεμωνα ab**
dfglm** [*non* ko] p. τη γη προσπνεουση (*pro* τη πνεουση) c. κατηλθον bo,
τηγον g (*pro* κατειχον). 41. επεκιλαν p. ναυ ab*o. −μεν a*. ερρεισασα
εμενεν ch. διελυετο bmo. απο (*pro* ὑπο) k. 42. στατιωτων d*.
σμιους h. αποκτεινωσιν p. εγκολυμβησας g. διαφυγη abcdfghlop [*non* k].
3. ἑκατονταρχης dmp (ἑκατ. p). εκολυσεν b*. βουλευματος af. εκελευσεν p.

δε (*pro* τε) cp. της γης c. 44. τους (*pro* οὓς *prim.*) c. οὕτως *rescript. in* h.

CAP. XXVIII. 1. +οἱ περι τον παυλον εκ του πλοος (*ante* τοτε) bgkmo (+τουτου o) [*non* p]. επεγνωμεν c*p. μελητη o. 2. τε (*pro* δε) cp. −ἡμιν m. ἁψαντες c. ἀψαντες p. αναψαντας ?m. προσανελαμβανον c. υἱετον m. ἐφεστωτα k. ψῦχος o. 3. +τε (*post* φρυγανων) p ("*ex incuriâ pro* τι" Tischend.). απο (*pro* εκ) bckop. διεξελθουσα adfgklo [*non* p]. καθηψατο bho. ενηψε c. καθηψεν p. 4. δ' m. το θηριον κρεμαμενον p. −εκ *prim.* c. προς αλληλους ελεγον cmp. πάντος p. διασωθητε k. ἡ k. 5. οὒν p. αποτιναξαμενος bdghklo. αποτειναξαμενος c. ἀπὸτηναξάμενος p. επασχεν c. πονηρον (*pro* κακον) c. 6. πιπρασθαι o*. ἢ p. +αυτον (*ante* αφνω) m. επιπολυ h. αυτον ? (*pro* αυτων) h*. προσδοκοντων fkp. θεωρησαντων c. θεωμενων l. μὴδὲν kop. *Rasura in* k *post* μὴδὲν, *item inter* ατο *et* πον. αυτω (*pro* εις αυτον) d. εις αυτο γιγνομενον m. μεταβαλομενοι bcp. αυτον θν̄ ackm. αυτον ειναι θν̄ p. 7. τοπο̄υ (ω *p. m.* ?) p. εκεινων p. ὑπηρχον k. ὀνοματι kp. ποπλοιω (*non* v. 8) k. πουπλιω p. −τρεις ἡμερας a. ἡμερας τρεις ckm. 8. −του a. πουπλιου p. πυρετος d*. δυσεντεριω m. −συνεχομενον a. επευξαμενος a. +και (*ante* επιθεις) ak. +τε (*post* επιθεις) m. ἰασατο p. 9. δε (*pro* ουν) cgkp. ουν γε *rescript. in* h. λυποι p. οἱ εν τη νησω εχοντες ασθενειας kmp. 10. +οσον χρονον επεδημουμεν (*post* ἡμας) c. ἐπέντο p*. 11. ηχθημεν ab*klmo. αλεξανδρηνω abdko. αλεξανδρειν ω̄ (*forsan* ω̃ν) p. παρασιμω f. διοσκοροις bp**. 12. συρρακουσας a. απεμειναμεν ?k*. 13. ἡς (*pro* εις) m. ῥιγιον d. ρηγειον ?h*. ἡλθομεν (*sic vv.* 14, 16) k. ἦλθον m*. ποτιωλους ?p*. 14. εὑροντες αδελφοις p. παρ' (*pro* επ') dm*p. επιμειναντες c. μειναντες l. ἑπτα *rescript. in* h. ἑπτα p. −την abcko. (ηλθομεν εις ρωμην bko). οὑτως ηλθομεν εις την ῥωμην p. 15. ακουσαντες οἱ αδελφοι a. ηλθον p (*sic*). συναντησιν g. ἀπαντησιν k. ἡμω̃ν (*pro* ἡμιν) cdgkop. αχρι p. απιου a. ελαβεν p. 16. εισηλθομεν dmp. +την (*ante* ρωμην) c. −ὁ ἑκατον. *usque ad* στρατοπεδαρχη (επετραπη τω παῡλω *sequente*, δε *omisso*) p. παραδεδωκεν m. τοις (*pro* τους) l*. στρατοπεδαρχω g*k?lm. επετραπει f. καθ' *rescript. in* h. συν τὸ p. φυλαττοντι m. αυτω (*pro* αυτον) k. στρατιωτι p. 17. μεθ' m. ἡμερας (ἡ *rescript.*) o. αυτον (*pro* τον παυλον) kp. ὀντας p. ειπεν (*pro* ελεγε) p. εγω ανδρες αδελφοι cp. πραξας (*pro* ποιησας) p. ἢ (*sic* v. 21) p. εθνεσι b*d*. εθεσιν p. δεσμιως h*. εν ἰλημ (*pro* εξ ἱεροσολυμων) c. 18. οἵτινες ?k. +πολλα (*post* οἱτινες) c. ηβουλοντο m. εβουλοντω p. απολυειν d. μὴδεμίαν αἰτιαν k. μὴδεμίαν l. μὴδὲμίαν op. 19. −των c. *Rasura in* k *inter* ιουδ *et* αιων. +και επικραζοντων αιρε τον εχθρον ἡμων (*post* ιουδαιων) c.

ναγκασθην k. ηνεγκασθην p. κατηγορειν p. *fin.* +αλλ' ἱνα λυτρωσομαι ην ψυχην μου εκ θανατου c. 20. οὐν p. αἰτιαν k. ἑνεκα d. ἑνεκεν kp. λυσιν kp. περικειμε (αι *forsan p. m.*) p. 21. ειπαν p. ουδε (*pro* ουτε rim.) p*, *at* ου a*. παραγενωμενος h*. –τις k. ελαλησεν mp. –τι l. ονηρον περι σου h. 22. ακουσαι παρα σου bdo. –μεν bo. –γαρ a*. αἱρεσ-ως p. ἡμιν εστιν km. ὑμιν εστιν p. 23. ηλθον (*pro* ἡκον) kp. εις την ενιαν προς αυτον k. εξεθετο a. διαμαρτυρουμενος p. και πειθων (–τε) d. ειθον fp. –τα acp. –του *secund.* k. ιυ (ι *mutat.*) o. μωυσεος dhl. μωυσεως ἑσπερας p. 24. επειθοντω p. ἠπιστουν k. 25. ὀντες p. ἐν p. λος (ω *p. m.?*) p. ελαλη a, η *mutatum.* ελαλησεν p. ἠσαϊου p. –του ροφητου a*. ὑμων (*pro* ἡμων) kp. 26. *init.* λεγων f. ειπον (*pro* ειπε) bdfghk?lmop. ακουσητε ab*mp. συνειτε p. –και βλεποντες βλεψετε p. λεψητε m. 27. ἡ p. ωσιν αυτων (*pro* ωσι) bdo (ὡσιν d). ὠσι k. ὡσιν ις p. ἠκουσαν k. τοις οφθαλμοις (*pro* τους οφθαλμους) o. ὀφθαλμ. *bis* p. καμμισαν ?b*. εκαμυσαν d. *Rasura inter* εκαμ *et* σαν *in* k (εκαμμΰσαν k**). ωσιν p. ὀφθαλμοις *et* ὡσιν k. ακουσωσιν mp. συνωσιν p. επιστρεψουσιν p. ισομαι g*l. ιασωμε p. 28. οὐν p. ὑμιν εστω mp. +τουτο (*post* απεσταλη) p. –και do. 29. *Deest versus in* p. εχον m. 30. επεμεινεν ουν (*pro* μεινε δε) c. ενεμεινεν p. –ὁ παυλος cp. ὁλην p. ἰδιω kp. εις (*pro* προς) m*. *fin.* +ιουδαιους τε και ἑλληνας c. 31. διδασκον d*. –χριστου c. ·πασης c. *fin.* +αμην c.

SUBSCRIPT: *Nil habent* dgklm. *Silet* c. *Hiat* e. πραξεις των αποστο-λων p. *In* a *sequuntur quinque paginæ* πραξεις των ἁγιων αποστολων *com-lectentes.* τελος των πραξεων bo (*rubro*). τελος των πραξεων των ἁγιων ποστολων f (*rubro*). *Cum Elzev.* h.

EPISTOLÆ CATHOLICÆ.

S. JACOBI EPISTOLA: επιστολη καθολικη ιακωβου a (*rubro*) c. γραμμα ρος ἑβραιους ιακωβου αδελφοθεου f. ιακωβου καθολικη επιστολη gh. καθολικη πιστολη ιακωβου j. επιστολη ιακωβου καθολικη ko. ιακωβου αποστολου πιστολη καθολικη l. επιστολη του ἁγιου αποστολου ιακωβου καθολικη m. *Nil habent* bd. *Hiant in Epist. Cath.* ep.

CAP. I. 1. +πρς (*post* θῦ) a. 3. −ὑμων a. 5. αἰτειτω (*sic v.* 6) k. −θῦ j. ουκ (*pro* μη) dfhjlm. ωνειδιζοντος f. ὀνειδιζοντος k. 6. μηδὲν ko. +ὁτι ληψεται (*post* διακρινομενος *prim.*) a. εοικεν c. ἐοικε jko. κλυδονι h*. 7. ὁ k. 10. παρηλευσεται? m. 11. εν (*pro* συν) c. −αυτου *prim.* a. εξεπεσεν m. −και *tertium* c. οὑτως acdfghklmo. 12. ὑπομενεῖ fjl. ὑπομενῆ m. ὁτι k. −ὁ κυριος a*. 13. μηδεὶς k. πειραζο ενος d. ὑπο (*pro* απο) a. −του abcdfghjklmo. 14. ἰδιας k. 15. *Rasura in* d *inter* τι *et* κτει. 17. παρα (*pro* απο) b*ko. εστι (*pro* ενι) b*cdo. *fin.* +ουδε μεχρι ὑπονοιας τινος ὑποβολη αποσκιασμτος c. 18. +γαρ (*post* βουληθεις) g. εποιησεν (*pro* απεκυησεν) ac*. +πρωτους και τιμιωτατους της ὁρωμενης κτισεως (*ante* απαρχην) c. κτησματων k. 19. +και (*ante* βραδυς *prim.*) g. 20. ουκ εργαζεται l*m. 21. ρὑπαρειαν k. πραοτητι k. *fin.* ἡμων (*pro* ὑμων) dfk. 22. −δε k. νομου (*pro* λογου) c. +του (*ante* λογου) m. ακροαται μονον a. *fin.* ἑαυτοις d. 23. νομου (*pro* λογου) b**h. εστιν m. οὑτως (*pro* οὑτος) m. ἐοικεν jko. εσωπτρω ? b*. 24. κατενοησεν αυτον (−γαρ) a. απεληλυθεν m. απεληλυθη k. 25. −τον j*. οὑτως (*pro* οὑτος *prim.*) g. γινομενος m*. −οὑτος *secund.* l. 26. *init.* ει δε τις m. πιστος (*pro* θρησκος) b*o. +την (*ante* γλωσσαν) o. ἑαυτου (*pro* αὑτου *prim.*) c. αλλα bdfgjklo [*non* m]. ἑαυτου (*pro* αὑτου *secund.*) k. 27. *init.* θρησκια f. θυσια (*post* θρησκεια) a. −τῳ bcdfghjklmo. −και *secund.* g. επισκεπτεσθε m**o. θλιψη k*. +και (*ante* ασπιλον) lm?.

CAP. II. 1. εχητε d. της δοξης του κ̄υ ἡμων ῑυ χ̄υ ac. 2. −την c. *Rasura in* k *ante* συναγωγην. εισελθοι (*pro* εισελθῃ *secund.*) m. ἐνεσθῆτι ρὑπαρὰ k. 3. *init.* επιβλεψητε δε (−και) ac (τε c). την λαμπραν εσθητα ach (εσθητε a). −αυτῳ acj. ὧδε ak *prim.*, jl *bis*, o *secund.* −συ (*ante* στηθι) a. κάθο *secund.* m. −ὧδε *secund.* ac. επι (*pro* ὑπο) acd. 4. *init.* −και ab**ch. διέκριθητε d. *Rasura in* k *inter* δι *et* εκρι. εγενεσθαι o. διάλογισμῶν m. 5. μου αγαπ^β^ητοι αδε^α^λφοι (β, α, a**) a. μου αδελφοι οἱ αγαπητοι c. −τουτου abcdfghj klmo. οἱς (*pro* ἡς) o. 6. ἡτοιμασατε ag*ho. ἡτιμασατε m. ουχι ac. ὑπλούσιοι (*pro* οἱ πλουσιοι) m. 7. και (*pro* ουκ) c. κληθεν ac. ἡμας (*pro* ὑμας) c. 8. *init.* Οἱ (*pro* ει, Ο *rubro*) k. ἑαυτον bcdfjklmo**, ἑαυτους a (*pro* σεαυτον). ποιητε k. 9. ερζαζεσθε m*. 10. τον νομον ὁλον m. πληρωσει (*pro* τηρησει) ac. ἐν, ἑνὶ (*pro* εν ἑνι) m. 11. μη φονευσης ειπε και ου μοιχευσεις a. "φονευσης *pro* μοιχευσης, *et vice versâ*" c. μὴ χεύσης f. μοιχευσεις *et* φονευσεις (*pro* -ης) k. οἱ (*pro* ει) m. −δε *prim.* ?a. μοιχευσης (*pro* -εις) ch*. 12. οὑτως *bis* acdfghklo, *at prim.* m. μελλοντας m. κρινεσθε m**. 13. ανιλεως b*l**. ανελεος cgjkl*mo. ανηλεος h. ανελεως f. ελεον *bis* bo, *at secund.* b**dfhklm.

ται abcdfghjklmo. 14. λεγει c. σχη ac, εχει d*fhl (*pro* εχῃ). δυνατε k. ῃ a*. 15. –δε dm. ὑπαρχουσι f. ὑπαρχουσιν m. ὑπαρχωσιν η (*pro* και) d. πομενοι m. ἐφ' ἡμερου f. 16. *init.* και ειπη (–δε) d. της? (*pro* τις) m*. ων (*pro* ὑμων) a. ὑπεγετε ?j. χορτασθητε o. τα του σωματος επιτηδεια m. . οὑτως adfghklmo. απεχη εργα (*pro* μη εργα εχῃ) c. εχη εργα abdmo. ει f. κατα αυτην?a*. 18. –εχω m. χωρις (*pro* εκ *prim.*) am. –σου *secund.* . σοι δειξω acjm. δειξον (*pro* δειξω) d. –μου *secund.* ac. την πιστιν μου εκ ων εργων μου o*. 19. –ὁ lm. εἰς θς̄ (–ὁ) ac. εστιν m. +και (*ante* καλως) φριττουσι ab*l. φρισσουσιν m. φριττουσιν o. 20. –των k. 21. βρααμ (*sic v.* 23) ahjklmo. ὑμων (*pro* ἡμων) k. ανενεγκας (*sic*) c. αλλ' εγκας m. ἰσαακ k. 22. συνηργει *usque ad* αυτου *super rasuram in* g. αυτου a, +αυτων αυτου c (*post* εργων). 23. επιστευσεν ἀβρααμ (–δε) a. δε c. δουλος (*pro* φιλος) ac*. *fin* ; l. 24. ὁρατε ; οὑτως (*pro* τοινυν ὁτι) –τοινυν cd. +ουκ (*ante* εξ εργων) f. 25. κατασκοπους (*pro* αγγελους) dg. εν (*ante* ἑτερα) d. ἐκβαλουσα k. 26. +του (*ante* πνς̄) m. οὑτως dfghkl o. –των a. *fin.* εστιν km.

CAP. III. 1. γινεσθαι c*k. –ὁτι b*. μεῖζων d. λειψομεθα f. 2. πται- ι c. δυναμενος ach. *fin.* +αυτου k. +και ὁλων (*eras.*) o. 3. *init.* ἴδε ιcdghjk. εἰδέ lm. –ἰδοὺ o. το στομα (*pro* τα στοματα) cj. +αυτων (*post* ·οματα) b**. *fin.* μεταμεν f. 4. τηληκαυτα ?d*. ανεμων σκληρων abch o. πιδαλιου d. ὁρμη ko. ευθηνουντος c. ιθυνοντος h. βουλοιτο a. 5. τως cfghklmo, *at* ὡσαύτος d. ὀλιγον (*non* IV. 14) k. 6. –οὑτως c. –και λογιζουσα *usque ad* γενεσεως b*. 7. –τε *prim.* k. +και (*ante* ἑρπετων) c. τε *secund.* ac. δεδαμασται και δαμαζεται bo. 8. δαμασαι ανθρωπων acm. μασαι; h. κατασχετον k. θανατηφορου ιου l. 9. το θῡ m. καθομοιωσιν ι. του θεου c (*sic*). *fin.* γεγενημενους d. 10. κατάρα ; j. –ου b*. +αγαπητοι οst αδελφοι μου) fg. οὑτως fghklmo. 11. ὁπης k. το πικρον και το γλυκυ ι. 12. σύκα hlo. –οὑτως c. οὔτε μία c, οὐδὲμία hjklo. ου a** *marg.* ἁλυ- ν k. –και m. 13. ειτις (*pro* τις) fk. πραοτητι k. 14. ταις καρδιαις bjo. υχασθε am. 15. ἡ σοφια αὑτη ac. –ἡ k. 17. ειρηνηκη m. –και *secund.* 18. –της acdhk. δικαισυνης k.

CAP. IV. 1. +ειρηνη (*ante* πολεμοι) a*, *eras. rubro.* +ποθεν (*ante* μαχαι) acm. ιων (*pro* ὑμων *prim.*) m*. 2. και ουκ εχετε (*pro* ουκ εχετε δε) ab**cfgkl**. δε b*dhjl*mo. αἰτεισθε k. αιτειν καλως (*pro* αιτεισθαι ὑμας) c. 3. +δε οst αιτειτε) dm. αιτειτε (*pro* αιτεισθε) m. 4. ὡς (*pro* ὁς) o. εαν (*pro* αν) ι. –ουν acfkl. εστιν (*pro* καθισταται) l. 5. *init.* ει (*pro* η) k. +ὑμων (*post* θονον) k. λεγει προς φθονον, h. προς φθονον ; j [m *cum Elzev.*]. *fin.*

ὑμιν c. 6. −διο λεγει a*. κς̅ (*pro* ὁ θς̅) fl. 7. ὑποταγηται k. κω̅ (*pro* θω̅) g. +δε (*post* αντιστητε) abcdglmo (ἀντιστῆτε m). εκφευξεται l. 8. ὑμων (*pro* ὑμιν) a. ἁγιασατε ac. 9. ταλαιπορησατε k. γελος k. μετατραπητω a. μετατραπειτω c. μεταστραφειτω j*. καταστραφητω o. εις κατηφειαν ἡ χαρα a. 10. −του ac. *fin.* ἡμας j. 11. καταλαλητε (*pro* καταλαλειτε) d. καταλειτε j*. +γαρ (*ante* καταλαλων) ach. η (*pro* και *prim.*) cjo. κρινον dk. φον αυτου κατα *rescript. super. ras. in* b. νομον (*pro* νομου *prim.*) d. κρινης (*pro* κρινεις) k. ουκετι (*pro* ουκ) m. 12. +και (+ὁ j) κριτης (*post* νομοθετης) abghjmo [*non* kl]. απωλεσαι f. +δε (*post* συ) dfjklmo. ὁ κρινων (−ει) m. κρινης ?g*. *fin.* ὁ κρινων τον πλησιον (*pro* ὁς κρινεις τον ἑτερον) ac. 13. ἀγε (*non* v. 1) k. και (*pro* η) abc (*tacitè*) dfghjklmo [*cætera cum Elzev.* dl]. πορευσωμεθα ab*fhjkmo [*non* c]. ποιησωμεν abfghjkmo [c *silet*]. ἐνιαυτον k. εμπορευσωμεθα ab*fghjkmo [c *silet*]. κερδησωμεν abfghjkmo [c *silet*]. 14. τα (*pro* το) ac. αὐριον k. −γαρ *prim.* c. ἡμων (*pro* ὑμων) ah. ατμης ?b*. εστε d, εσται fgjkm. −δε ach. +και (*post* δε) bdfgjkmo. 15. λεγει b*. αν (*pro* εαν) b. θελη ad. θελει c. θελησει f. ζησομεν cdkl. ποιησωμεν abfghjmo [*non* k]. 16. νυνι m. επι (*pro* εν) ac. αλαζονιαις ch*k. ὑμων; j. +ουν ac, +γαρ d (*post* πασα). 17. ποιειν καλον c.

CAP. V. 1. ὀλολυζοντες jko. ται (*pro* ταις) b*. 2. σεσηπεν m. ἱματια m. σιτοβρωτα m. 3. ἰος k. εστι (*pro* εσται) g. *Rasura in* b *ante* ὡς. ὡς πυρ *cum sequent. in* ko. +ταις (*ante* εσχαταις) j. 4. −και h. θερησαντων k. 5. +και (*ante* εθρεψατε) k. ἡμων (*pro* ὑμων) k. 5, 6. *Jungit* m σφαγης κατεδικασατε. 7. χυ̅ (*pro* κυριου) hk. +γαρ (*post* ιδου) j. αυτον (*pro* αυτῳ) cfghkl. −αν djkl. λαβοι c. και τον προϊμον (−ὑετον) m. 8. παρρουσια k. +ἡμων (*ante* ηγγικε) ac. ηγγικεν km. 9. στεναζητε d. στεναξετε m. αδελφοι (+μου d) κατ᾽ αλληλων acdm. κριθητε abcdfghjklmo. +ὁ (*ante* κριτης) abcdfghjklmo. ἑστηκε a. ἑστηκεν jko. 10. αδελφοι μου (−μου ach) της κακοπαθειας abcdfghjklmo. +εν (*ante* τω ονοματι) ahl**m. το ὀνοματι (*rasura ante* μ) d. ὀνοματι k. +του (*ante* κυριου) alm. 11. ὑπομειναντας a. ἠκουσατε k. +του (*ante* κυ̅) a. ιδετε jkm. πολυευσπλαγχνος acdfg**. εστι bdfghjklm (*silet* c, εστι· *tantum* o). −ὁ κυριος abcdfghjklmo. οἰκτειρμων d. οἰκτιρμων k. 12. −δε l. ὀμνυητε d. ἡτω k. οὐ οὐ k. εις ὑποκρισιν (*pro* ὑπο κρισιν) abc (*tacitè*) dfghjklmo (ὑποκρησιν o). πεσηται m. 13. ψαλετω b*d*mo. 14. προσευξασθωσαν (ξ *mutatum*) m. αυτω (*pro* αυτον *prim.*) m. αληψαντες f. −αυτον *secund.* a. −του f. 15. προσευχη (*pro* ευχη) bo. ἡ πεποιηκῶς k. αφεθησονται jm. 16. εξομολογεισθαι k. +ουν (*ante* αλληλοις) acg. τας ἁμαρτιας ὑμων (*pro* τα παραπτωματα) acd

(−ὑμων d). −πολυ *ad fin. vers.* j. +γαρ (*post* πολυ) d. 17. ἠλιας dk? [*non* mo]. ὁμοιοπαθεις a. ὁμοιωπαθης o. ἱνα μη βρεξῃ (−του) c*. +ετι (*ante* ενιαυτους) b**. ἐνιαυτους k. ἐξ *super rasuram* a. 18. −ὁ k. εδωκεν m. 19. +μου (*post* αδελφοι) abcdmo. +της ὁδου (*post* απο) dj. −και a*. επιστρεψητε (−τις) c. επιστρεψει fhm. 20. γινωσκετε cm. *fin.* +αμην c.

SUBSCRIPT.: *Nil habent* abcdfgjkmo. τελος h. *Hiat* l.

S. PETRI EPISTOLA PRIMA.

[CAP. I. 1—25].

Πετρος ιουδαιοις ταδε πρωτα τεθεσπικε πιστοις f *rubro*. πετρου καθολικη ᾱ επιστολη h. πετρου επιστολη πρωτη jkmo.

CAP. I. 1. −χριστου a. +και (*ante* ασιας) c. βῦνιας m. 2. −πνευματος k. ῥατισμον m. 3. μων a. ελεος αυτου achm. ἡμας (*pro* ὑμας) abc (*tacitè*) df ghjkmo. δια αναστασεως a**. 4. αμηαντον?m*. ἀμαραντον k. −και αμαραντον o. +τοις (*ante* ουρανοις) ac. *fin.* ὑμας abdfghjklmo. 6. ὀλιγον k. −εστι c. λυπηθεντας dfjk?m. 7. δοκιμον a. πολυτιμοτερον bdjkmo. εὑρεθειη a. δοξαν και τιμην acdhm. +εις (*ante* δοξαν) fgj. 8. ιδοτες b*. ιδοντες jo. +και (*post* αγαπατε) g. 9. ελεος (*pro* τελος) l. 10. −σωτηριας o. εξερευνησαν km. −οἱ c. ὑπερ (*pro* περι) c (*post* −οἱ). ἡμας (*pro* ὑμας) aj. 11. η *mutatum in* h. εδηλουτο εν αυτοις το π̄ν̄α του χ̄ῡ m. *Rasura in* k *inter* προ *et* μαρτ. μεταταῦτα m. 12. επεκαλυφθη k. οὐχ᾽ ἑαυτοις k. ὑμιν (*pro* ἡμιν) acfghjkm. ανηγγελει νυν a. ανηγγελλει c. ανηγγελλη fm. απηγγελη g. εξ (*pro* απ᾽) k. επιθυμουσι k. 13. νηφοντες τελειως, hklmo. 14. −ταις m*?. ἀγνοια k. 16. +ὁτι (*ante* ἁγιοι) m. εσεσθε ad, γινεσθε b**hjkm (*pro* γενεσθε). κἀγω k. 18. εκ τη m. πατροπαραδοτου αναστροφης am. 19. +τω (*ante* τιμιω) m. *Rasura in* b *inter* a *et* μωμου. 20. −προ b*. εσχατου d. ἡμερων (*pro* χρονων) m. *fin.* ἡμας k. 21. δι᾽ αυτου πι *et* δοντα *in* h *super rasur. rescript.* +τον (*ante* θεον *prim.*) d. πιστην d*. −ὑμων o. 22. ανυποκριτοι k. αγαπωμεν τε (*pro* αγαπησατε) a. 23. αναγενομενοι m. αλλ᾽ m. 24. −ὡς *prim.* a. αυτης (*pro* ανθρωπου) a. −αυτου ac. επεσε k. εξεπεσεν m. 25. εις τον *rescript. in* g.

CAP. II. 1. και παντα δολον *bis script. in* o*. καταλαλιᾶς m. 2. +και
(*ante* αδολον) adg. αξιωθητε (*pro* αυξηθητε) m. *fin.* +εις σωτηριαν abghjmo
[*non* k]. 3. $\overline{χs}$ (*pro* χρηστος) dfm. 4. +ὡς (*ante* λιθον) b**. αποδεδο-
κισμασμενον k. αποδεδοκισμενον m. παρα θω̄ δε k. ελεκτον m. 5. εποι-
κοδομεισθε bdo. οἰκοδομεισθε k. θυσιας πνευματικας cg. 6. διοτι (*pro*
διο και) acdfghjklmo. –και *prim.* b. –τῃ k. ἡ γραφη (–εν) adh. ακρογοn-
αιον c. εκλεκτον ακρογωνιαιον m. πιστευον d*. επ' αυτον d. 7. πιστευ-
οσιν m. απιστουσι (*pro* απειθουσι) a. λιθος (*pro* λιθον) c. απεδωκιμασαν k.
–οὑτος *usque ad* γωνιας c. λιθον (*pro* λιθος) km. προσκοματος dh. 8.
ὁσοι (*pro* οἳ) am. *fin.* εις ἡν παρεσκευασαν ἑαυτους ταξιν και ετεθησαν (*pro*
εις ὁ και ετεθησαν) a. 9. *init.* ἡμεις m. αγαθον (*pro* θαυμαστον) c*. 10.
οἳ *bis* m. 11. +του κοσμου τουτου (*post* παρεπιδημους) a. απεχεσθε c**fh
j*o. 12. *init.* παρακαλω δε και τουτο· την εν τοις εθνεσιν ὑμων αναστροφην
εχειν καλην a. εχοντες καλην εν τοις εθνεσιν bcdfghjklo. καταλαλωσιν cfgjm.
αγαθων (*pro* καλων) d. +ὑμων (*post* καλων) a. εποπτευοντες ajm. δοξαζωσι
g. 13. –ουν m. κτησει a. κτιση ?b*. κτισει ανθρωπινη m. –δια m*
(*habet marg.* m**). 14. –μεν dgklm. 15. οὑτος m* *vel* m**. +ὑμας (*ante*
φιμουν) bmo (φημουν o). 16. επικαλυμα d*o. +του (*ante* θῡ) f. *vv.* 16, 17.
θῡ δουλοι παντας τιμησατε *jungit* m. 17. αγαπησατε ghklm. 18. ὑπο-
τασομενοι d*. +ητε (*ante* εν) a. δεσποτες k. επιεικεσι f. –και *secund.* m.
κολιοις m. 19. +παρα τω θω̄ aco, +παρα θωι· εις τουτο γαρ και εκληθητε j
(*post* χαρις). συνηδησιν ?g*. αγαθην (*pro* θῡ) abco. λυπας τις a. 20.
+κακοποιουντες (*ante* κολαφιζομενοι) m*. κολαζομενοι a. ὑπομενετε *prim.*
ac, *bis* mo. +γαρ (*ante* χαρις) k. +τω (*ante* θω̄) acdhkm. 21. +και (*post*
γαρ) bfho. +ὁ (*ante* $\overline{χs}$) o. ὑπερ ἡμων, ὑμιν (*pro* ὑπερ ὑμων, ὑμιν) afhjlo, *et*
ἡμων ἡμιν d [*cum Elzev.* ckm]. ἰν' m. επακολουθησετε c. 23. λοιδωρου-
μενος ?g*. αντελειδορει k. 24. ανηνεγκεν αυτος m. ηνεγκεν c. του ξυλου
k. οὑ (υ *mutatum*) g. –αυτου *secund.* ab*cdmo. 25. *Rasura inter* H *et*
τε *in* h. ἡτε km?. πλανομενα ko. επεστρεψατε a. επιστρεψατε c. *fin.*
ἡμων cd*g*hjlm*.

CAP. III. 1. Ὀὁμοιως (Ὀ *rubro*) d. +και (*post* ὁμοιως) b. –και a. οἱτινες
(*pro* ειτινες) ac. ει και τινες bmo. απειθωσι m. κερδηθησονται b**cdfhklm.
2. εποπτευοντες a. ἁγνην k. 3. εκ πλοκης go, εν πλοκαις j (*pro* εμπλοκης).
4. πραεως cfm. –πνευματος o. 5. οὑτως h [*non* dklmo]. εις (*pro* επι) acd.
–τον bdmo. *Rasura in* k *inter* ι *et* διοις. 6. σᾶρα a. ὑπηκουε m.
ἁβρααμ ahklmo. εγεννηθητε acfklm. εγενηθη o. πτοουμεναι (*pro* φοβου-
μεναι) a. μηδὲμίαν hjo. μὴδὲμίαν kl. 7. γυναικιω f. γηναικειω k. και

ὡς g. ὡς και συγ *super ras.* b**. κληρονομοι c. συγκληρονομοις mo. +ποικιλης (*ante* χαριτος) ac. +και (*ante* ζωης) k. ζωσης bflo (*rasura in* b *post* ω). ενκοπτεσθαι c. εγκοπτεσθαι djkl. 8. +παντες (*ante* συμπαθεις) k. ταπεινοφρονες (*pro* φιλοφρονες) acdgj. 9. +τινα (*post* λοιδοριαν) ac. λοιδορειας ?m*. κληρομησητε k. 10. ἡμερας ιδειν ach. παυσασθω bo. γλωτταν o. —αὐτου *secund.* a. 11. +δε (*ante* απο) acm. +το (*ante* αγαθον) k. 12. —οἱ abdfghklmo. ὠτα k. *In* εις m, *vix* σ *p. m.* *fin.* +του εξολοθρευσαι αυτους εκ γης a. 13. κακασων m. ζηλωται (*pro* μιμηται) acd. 14. οἱ (*pro* ει) f. πασχετε ac. πασχητε fkm. μὴδὲ hklmo. και ου μη (*pro* μηδε) ac. 15. χ̄ν (*pro* θεον) ac. ἁγιασαντες m. 'Ετοιμοι ('Ε *rubro*) l. —δε *secund.* abco. —παντι g*. αἰτουντι k. ὑμιν (*pro* ὑμας) f. ἡμιν (*pro* ὑμιν) c. +αλλα (*ante* μετα) ac. πραοτητος ack. 16. καταλαλεισθε ac. καταλαλουσιν b**dfh. καταλουσιν (*sic Jac.* IV. 11) j. —ὑμων ὡς κακοποιων ac. την εν χ̄ω αγαθην abco. τη αγαθη εν χ̄ω αναστροφη h. 17. —θελει l. θελοι abcdfghjkmo. 18. ὑπερ (*pro* περι) k. +ὑπερ ὑμων abo, +ὑπερ ἡμων c, (*post* ἁμαρτιων). απεθανε (*pro* επαθε) ak. επαθεν m. ἱν' m. ὑμας (*pro* ἡμας) abjmo. προσαγαγει f. π̄ρι (*pro* θεῳ) bo. —τῳ (*ante* πνευματι) abcdf hjklmo [*non* g]. 19. τω ἀδη (*pro* φυλακῃ) c. πνευμασιν m. 20. ὁτι (*pro* ὁτε) a. απεξεδεχετο (*pro* ἁπαξ εξεδεχετο) abcdfghjkl (*forsan* αποξ l) o. ἁπαξ εδεχετο m. ἠν ὀλιγαι k. τουτο εστιν m. ὀκτω k. *Rasura in* b *post* οκτω. 21. ὃ (*pro* ᾧ) acm. ὡ αντιτυπον νυν και ἡμας (ὑμας bo) σωζει bdfg hjklo (*at* ὃ fhjk). ὑμας (*pro* ἡμας) cm. —νυν a. αποθεσιν h*. δια l. 22. εις ουρανον (*sic*) c. ουρανους d. —αυτῳ k, *at* αυτο m.

CAP. IV. 1. ὑμων (*pro* ἡμων) bmo. ἡμεις (*pro* ὑμεις) k. τοιαύτην (*pro* αυτην) d. ὁπλισασθε o. —εν acdhl. +απο (*post* πεπαυται) b**g. ἁμαρτιαις ?b*. 2. +του (*ante* θ̄υ) a**c. —εν b*. 3. ὑμιν (*pro* ἡμιν) abcho. —ἡμιν d. παρεληλυθος f. —του βιου ah. του βιου ὁ παρεληλυθως χρονος m. βουλημα (*pro* θελημα) adj. κατειργᾶσθαι a. οινοφλυγιαις επιθυμιαις j*l. κωμαις ?k*. ειδωλολατριαις ab**cdfghjlmo. 4. ἡμων (*pro* ὑμων) c. +αυτοις (*ante* εις) ac. ασωτειας m. 5. αποδωσουσιν h*. κρινοντι (*pro* εχοντι κριναι) a. 6. —και νεκροις a*. κριθῶσι (*sic*) c. ανθρωπον g. 7. ηγγικεν m. —τας b*cdjko. προσεχας m. 8. διαρκη (*pro* εκτενη) c. —ἡ cdjklo. καλυπτει acho. 9. γογγυσμου abd. 10. καθο c. αυτον ?k. οἰκονομοι km. 11. ὡς (*pro* ἡς) b*dfjlmo. χορηγιαν (*pro* ἡς χορηγει ὁ θ̄ς) ac. εν πασιν ὁ θ̄ς δοξαζηται ac. παση m. —ὁ *secund.* h. —εστιν dkl. —των αιωνων achm. 12. —μη l*. δοκιμασια (*pro* πυρωσει) c. γινωμενη f. ὑμων (*pro* ὑμιν *secund.*) m. 13. καθο abc (*tacitè*) dfghjklmo. παθεσι (*pro* παθημασι) c. παθημασιν m. 14. *init.*

αλλ' ει και a. –εν l. +τω (*ante* ονοματι) bgo. κ̅υ̅ (*pro* χ̅υ̅) k. το της δοξης και δυναμεως του θ̅υ̅ ονομα και πνευμα ac. +και δυναμεως (*post* δοξης) gk. –το *secund.* d. αναπεπαυται bdfghko. επαναπαυεται c. –κατα μεν αυτους *ad fin. vers.* acd. βλασφημειτε o*. 15. *init.* μη τις γαρ ac. *Rasura in* b *inter* π *et* ασχετω. +η λοιδορος (*post* φονευς) m. κακουργος ac. αλλοτριεπισκοπος d. αλλοτριος ἐπισκοπος m. 16. ονοματι (*pro* μερει) m. 17. –ὁ cdj. ου (*pro* ὁ) l*. –του (*ante* θ̅υ̅ *prim.*) m* (*habet marg.*). ὑμων (*pro* ἡμων) cjm. αποιθουντων k. 18. ὁ *prim.* k. ὁ ἁμαρτωλος και ασεβης a. ασεβεις k. +ὁ (*ante* ἁμαρτωλος) l. 19. –ὡς d. παρατιθεσθωσαν b*. ἑαυτων ψυχας m. αυτων (*pro* ἑαυτων) abcdfghjklo. αγαθοποϊα a*. αγαθοποϊαις b*do.

CAP. V. 1. +ουν (*ante* τους εν) o. ουν (*pro* τους) a. –τους c. παρακαλω εν ὑμιν ac. ὡς (*pro* ὁ *prim.*) afj. –του j*. μελλουσης (ο *eras.*) b. 2. επισκοπευοντες ac. αναγκαστικως l. +κατα θ̅ν̅ am, +και κατα θ̅ν̅ bo (*post* ἑκουσιως). μηδὲ klmo. μη (*pro* μηδε) c**. *fin.* μακροθυμως m. 3. *init.* μηδὲ g. μηδὲ hl. μηδ' kmo. 4. αρχηποιμενος d*. στεφανον της δοξης m. 5. ὁμοιως m. +δε και οἱ ac, +δε οἱ bo, +και οἱ m (*ante* νεωτεροι). +τοις (*ante* πρεσβυτεροις) g. ὑποταγωμεν (*pro* ὑποτασσομενοι) c. εγκοβωσασθε b*. εγκολπωσασθε cf. εγκωμβωσασθε l*. εγκοβωσασθαι m*. 6. –ουν a. ὑ m. ἡμας ?m*. ὑψωση ὑμας acd. ὑψωσει km*o. *fin.* +εν τω μελλοντι αιωνι (*sic*) c. 7. επιρρηψαντες m. εις (*pro* επ') ac. μελλει cfjkmo. ὑπερ (*pro* περι) achk. –ὁτι αυτῳ μελει περι ὑμων d. 8. –ὁτι bdfgjklo. ἡμων (*pro* ὑμων) cd. λεον d. ὁρυομενος k. ὡρυομενος j. ὡρυωμενος m. περιερχεται (*pro* περιπατει) ach. καταπιειν τινα m. καταπιει jkl. καταπιειν ch. καταπιη ?d*. 9. +ὁτι (*post* ειδοτες) ac. –τα a*. –ὑμων a*. αδελφοτητι ὑμων a**cm. επιτελεισθε a*. 10. ὑμας (*pro* ἡμας) abdfhjlmo. +ζωην (*post* αιωνιον) a*. –ιησου ac. ολιγα ac. ὀλιγον (*sic v.* 12) k. καταρτισει d. –ὑμας a. στηρηξαι h*. στηριξει (j**), σθενωσει, θεμελιωσει b*dfjklmo. 11. το κρατος και ἡ δοξα ac*m. –και το jl. 12. ἡμιν (*pro* ὑμιν) f. αδελφου του πιστου ac*. αλη η (*sic*) b*. στητε j. ἑστηκατε o. 13. –ἡ l*. ρωμη (*pro* βαβυλωνι) c. βαβὐλῶνη f. 14. ἁγιω (*pro* αγαπης) d.

SUBSCRIPT.: *Nil habent* abcdgklmo. εγραφη (εγγραφη h) απο ῥωμης f *rubro* h. +στιχοι $\overline{\text{cλβ}}$ h. ἡ πρωτη πετρου επιστολη εγραφη απο ῥωμης j *rubro.*

S. PETRI EPISTOLA SECUNDA.

[Capp. I. 1—II. 2].

Δευτερα ταυτα παλιν θεοκηρυκων οχ' αριστου· Πετρου καθολικη β' f.
ετρου β̄ καθολικη επιστολη h. Πετρου επιστολη δευτερα jlmo (δευτερη o).
πιστολη πετρου δευτερα k.

Cap. I. 1. σιμων a*clm. λαχουση o. −του k. −ἡμων *secund.* abc (*tacitè*)
fghjklmo. ιῡ χῡ χαρις *rescript. in* l. 2. −του θεου και ac. εν επιγνωσει
ν κῡ και θῡ ἡμων (−ιησου) j. του κῡ ἡμων ιῡ χῡ ac. +χῡ (*ante* ιυ) dg**.
ιο *cum Elzev.*]. 3. +τα (*ante* παντα) c. ὑμιν (*pro* ἡμιν) k. αυτου δυ-
μεως a. ιδια δοξη και αρετη ac. −δια *secund.* acl. [m *cum Elzev.*]. 4. δι' ὁν
ro ὡν) j. τα τιμια και μεγιστα ἡμιν ac. τα τιμια ἡμιν και μεγιστα bdfghjk
. και τιμια ἡμιν m. ενταλματα (*pro* επαγγελματα) j. διατουτω m. −θειας
' (*habet marg. p. m.*). −εν *secund.* j. της εν τω κοσμω επιθυμιας και φθορας
. 5. δε τουτο acdh. −πασαν ac. παρεισενεγκοντες a. επιχωρηγησατε f.
εγκρατειαν (γκ *mutatum*) b. [7. φιλαδελφιαν *omnes*]. 8. +εν (*ante* ὑμιν)
9. μυωπαζων *pro* μυωταζων c (*sic*). −αὑτου a. ἁμαρτηματων d. 10.
ἱνα δια των καλων εργων (*post* σπουδασατε) ac. βαιβαιαν m. ποιησθε a,
κεισθε c (*pro* ποιεισθαι). 11. οὑτως b*cfgklmo [*non* h]. χορηγηθησεται o.
ἡ b*. +ἡ (*post* εισοδος) bg. −και σωτηρος ak. 12. αει ὑμας bdfghjlmo
on k]. ὑπομιμνησκειν ὑμας αει ac. 13. εφοσον fjh. εν τω σκηνωματι
ντω o. 14. ταχεινη c. σωματος (*pro* σκηνωματος) bo. 15. σπουδασατε
σπουδαζω m. −και a. ἑκαστωτε km. +ταυτα και (*ante* μετα) ac. 16.
εξακολουθησαντες o. εξακουλουθησαντες d. ἡμιν (*pro* ὑμιν) c. εγνωρισα
(*pro* εγνωρισαμεν) m. +τε (*post* δυναμιν) m. εσοπται m. 17. +του
nte θῡ) ac. +και (*ante* πρς) bo. ενεχθησης h*. εν ὡ (*pro* εις ὁν) al. −εγω
. ηυδοκησα ?m. 18. ἠκουσαμεν k. ἐνεχθῆσαν f. 19. εχωμεν d. ἕωσοῦ
+ἡ (*ante* ἡμερα) m. διαυγασει a. φωσσφορος k. ἑωσφορος a. ανατειλει
n*. 20. γραφη προφητειας a. γραφεισα (*pro* γραφης) j. 21. ἠνεχθη
προφητεια ποτε acm. αλλα gj. απο (*pro* οἱ ἁγιοι) a. −οἱ bcdfghjklmo.

Cap. II. 1. +εκεινω (*post* λαω) a. +τε (*post* επαγοντες) j*. αυτοις am,
υτους o (*pro* ἑαυτοις). ταχεινην c. 2. αυτω (*pro* αυτων) o. ασελγει-
s (*pro* απωλειαις) abcdfghjklmo. ἁς (*pro* οὑς) h. λασμηθησεται (β *eras.*) a.

3. ὑμας λογοις a. εμπορευσονται ὑμας m. ου καταργη m. νυσταξει hjklmo. 4. παρεδωκε k. τηρουμενους acdfghjklmno (n *ut videtur*). 5. αρχεου b*. αλλα gjl. δικαιωσυνης g*. εφυλαξεν kmn. κατακλισμον ?h*. ασεβων κατακλυσμον κοσμω k. κοσμου κατα (*pro* κοσμῳ) a. 6. ασεβεσι (*pro* ασεβειν) a. 8. βλεματι k*. 9. οἶδε km? οιδεν n. πειρασμων ῥυσασθαι m. πειρασμων ah. 10. ὀπισω k. πορευομενους εν επιθυμια μιασμου k. επιθυμιαις a. μιασμον πορνευομενους m. 10, 11. *Jungunt* dj βλασφημουντες ὁπου. 11. ισχυει jm. −παρα κυριῳ ad. 12. γεγεννημενα (γενημενα m, γεγενημενα dh) φυσικα adhm. γεγενημενα bcfgjklno (n *ut videtur*). ει (*pro* εις) k. ἁλωσιν h. ἁλοσιν n. βλασφημουντας m. *In* j *rasura inter* καταφθαρ *et* σονται. 13. −εν *secund.* a. κατευωχουμενοι ὑμῶν c. συνευοχουμενοι m. +εν (*ante* ὑμιν) a. 14. ὀφθαλμους k. μεσθους m. ακαταπαυστου bk [*non* o]. −και ακαταπαυστους ἁμαρτιας d. γεγυμνασμενην καρδιαν a*. πλεονεξιας cdghklmno. 15. −την abcdfghjklmno. ὀδω k. βααλ m. ἠγαπησεν k. ηγεπησεν ?m. 16. ελεγχον c. ειχεν ?b*. +ὁ (*post* αφωνον) c. +τε (*post* εκωλυσε) a. 17. εισιν d. +και (*ante* νεφελαι) j**. και ὁμιχλη (*pro* νεφελαι) m. λελαπος n. ελαυνομενη m. ὁ k. αιωνας d. 18. φθεγξαμενοι ?l*. ενεπιθυμιες k. −εν *secund.* bc (*tacitè*) fgjklmn. ασελγειας (*pro* εν ασελγειαις) adho. ολιγον (*pro* οντως) a, *at* οντας k. 19. επαγγελομενοι k. δεδηλωται ?o*. 20. *init.* οἱ (*pro* ει) ac. μυασματα f. +ἡμων (*post* κῡ) adf, *at* (*post* σωτηρος) g. του σ̅ρ̅ς̅ και κ̅υ̅ o. −και σωτηρος f. −δε a*. γεγονε (−αυτοις) o. 21. κρειττων n. ἡν k. αυτοις ην m. επιγνωκεναι n. +εις τα οπισω (*ante* επιστρεψαι) a, (*post* επιστρεψαι) j. απο (*pro* εκ) a. παραδοθησης k*. παραδοθησεις n. 22. −αληθους k. τον ιδιον εμετον (*non* εξεραμα) a. εξερεμα ? (*cf.* v. 15) m. κυλισμον a.

CAP. III. 1. ἤδη k. +την (*ante* επιστολην) bco. 2. ὑμων (*pro* ἡμων) bcdfghlmno [*non* k]. 3. *init.* τουτον h*o*. ελευσομαι m. εσχατων adhkl. εμπεκται n. επιθυμιας αυτων bcdfghjklm*no. −αυτων a*. 4. αυτων (*pro* αυτου) c. ἀφῆς h. +ἡμων (*post* π̅ρ̅ε̅ς̅) a. οὑτως cfklno [*non* hm]. απαρχης m. 5. ἠσαν k. εμπαλαι m?. −δι' hk. συνεστωτα h. *fin.* το του θῡ λογιον o. 6. ὁν (*pro* ὡν) m. κατακλησθεις m. 7. *init.* Ει (Ε *rubro*) l. οἶδε m. αυτου a**bcdfghjklmno. εισιν m. τυρουμενοι k. ασεβων *dubium in* c. αασεβων a. 8. τουτω (*pro* τουτο) c, *at* ἐν δε τουτω gm. −παρα a*. 9. βραδυνη cn*. −ὁ hjn. ὑμας (*pro* ἡμας) m, *at* δι' ἡμας a, ἐφ' ὑμας c (*pro* εις ἡμας). απωλεσθαι fk. 10. ἡξει n. −ἡ kl. ἧν (*pro* κ̅υ̅) m. −εν νυκτι k. −οἱ adhjklm. + μεν (*post* ουρανοι) dj. +ἡ (*ante* γη) m. −εργα a. καταησεται m. 11. −ουν παντων a. ἁπαντων g. +οὑτως (*ante* λυομενων) am. ὑμας ὑπαρχειν d. ἡμας (*pro* ὑμας) cjk*?. 12. +τους (*ante* προσδοκωντας) m. κῡ (*pro* θεου) d. +οἱ (*ante* ουρανοι) dk. −και στοιχεια καυσουμενα τηκεται a. 13. αυτου επαγγελμα f. προσδοκωμεν αυτου k. ενοικει a. 14. δι' ὁ n *pass.* αμωμοι d. −αυτῳ cj. εὑρεθεντες k* (*at* -ηναι *videtur esse p. m.*). 15. ἡγεισθαι dkm. −και *secund.* j. αδελφος ἡμων ao (ὑμων ο *primò*). δοθεισαν αυτω abdmo (δοθησαν d*). 16. αυτοις (*pro* αυταις) l. αἱς (*pro* οἱς) adjm [*non* hklno]. εισι (*pro* εστι) cdhl. αστηρηκτοι h*. στρεβλωσουσιν d. 17. −αγαπητοι a. γινωσκοντες m. φυλασσεσθαι d*. φυλασεσθε g. στηργμου d. 18. αυξανοιτε bo. αυξανητε c?h. −δε a. +του (*post* χαριτι) a*. πιστει (*pro* γνωσει) m. +και θῡ πρς (*post* χῡ) a. ᾧ (*pro* αυτῳ) a. −και (*ante* νυν) n. ἡμερας a. −αμην o.

SUBSCRIPT.: *Nil habent* abcdfglmo. τελος hk. επιστολη πετρου β' n.

S. JOHANNIS EPISTOLA PRIMA.

[CAP. I. 1—10].

Βροντης υἱος ιωαννης ταδε χριστιανοισιν f. καθολικη ᾱ επιστολη ιωαννου h. ιωαννου επιστολη πρωτη jlmo. επιστολη ιωαννου πρωτη k. ιω̄ του αποστολου και ευαγγελιστου επιστολη ᾱ. n.

CAP. I. 1. ἦν kn. ἀπαρχης (*sic* II. 7 *bis*, 13, 14, 24 *bis*, III. 8, 11) hm (*non* m *in* II. 7, 14). ἑωρακαμεν k. ὀφθαλμοις k. ἁ (*pro* ὁ *quart.*) n. ἐψηλαφησαν k. εψηλαφισαν m**. 2. απαγγελομεν a*. ἡτις k. εφαρεωθη *secund.* h*. 3. +και (*ante* απαγγελλομεν) k. −δε a*. −μετα (*ante* του υἱου) m. 4. ἡμων (*pro* ὑμων) bfghklmno [*non* c]. 5. εστιν αὑτη acfg hklmn. αγγελια cdfghjkln. απαγγελλομεν a. αναγγελομεν d. −ὁ k. ουκ εστιν εν αυτω m. οὐδὲμία jklo. 6. ειπομεν o. εχωμεν f. περιπατουμεν c. −ψευδομεθα *usque ad* περιπατωμεν *v.* 7, m. 7. ὁ (*pro* ὡς) m. −χριστου a. καθαρισει bo. ὑμας (*pro* ἡμας) a. 8. ε (*pro* εαν) b*. −ἡ l. αληθει n*. +του θῡ (*post* αληθεια) a. εν ἡμιν ουκ εστιν adjm*. 9. +δε (*post* εαν) c. −και *prim.* m. +ἡμων aj, +πασας j* (*post* ἁμαρτιας *secund.*). καθαρησῃ d. 10. οὐχ' klnò. ψεῦστην n. ποιουμεν (*sic*) c. εν ἡμιν ουκ εστι a.

CAP. II. 1. ἁμαρτανητε a. 2. +ἡμετερων (*ante* ἁμαρτιων) d. −δε g. του κοσμου ὁλου m. 4. +ὁτι (*ante* εγνωκα) aj. ὁ λεγων ὁτι εγνω ὁ λεγων ὁτι εγνωκα d. εστιν (*pro* εστι) m. αυτω (*pro* τουτῳ) g. −ἡ o. 5. τηρει c. τηρησῃ j. ἡ αγαπη του θῦ εν τουτω m. 6. ὀφειλει k. −οὑτως d. οὑτω gj. 7. −αδελφοι j (*rubro tantum* a, *init. peric.*). αγαπητοι (*pro* αδελφοι) d. +ὁ εστιν αληθες εν αυτω (*post* ὑμιν) m*. αλλα c. εχετε a*k. ἠκουσατε (*sic vv.* 18, 24 *bis*) k. −απ᾽ αρχης *secund.* dj. 8. ὁτι (*pro* ὃ) l. ἡμιν (*pro* ὑμιν *secund.*) cm. ἠδη k. 9. *Deest hic versus et v.* 10 *usque ad* μενει *in* j. ἀρτι k. 10. ουκ εστιν εν αυτω j. 11. μισον m. εστιν m. εἶδε (*pro* οιδε) h. ποῦ lmn, *alii.* ὀφθ. (*sic v.* 16) k. 12. αφεονται n. ὑμων (*pro* ὑμιν *secund.*) ac?jkm. ναὶ (*pro* αἱ) o. 13. ἀπ᾽ k. νικηκατε m*. νενηκηκατε o*. εγραψα (*pro* γραφω *tert.*) ajo. 15. μὴδὲ hklmno. −τῳ lm. *Transfert* m ουκ εστιν *ad fin. vers.* θῦ (*pro* πατρος) d. 16. τῷ (*pro* το) hn. −τῳ a. −ἡ επιθυμια της σαρκος και o. αλαζονια bh*n. αλαζωνια k. *fin.* εστιν mn. 18. εστιν (*pro* εστι) fmn. αντιχρηστοι d*m. 19. ηλθον (*pro* εξηλθον) c. ἠσαν *bis* k. οὐκ k. ει γαρ εξ ἡμων ησαν a. φανερωθη a. εισιν (−παντες a) an. 20. χαρισματα (*pro* χρισμα) j. 21. ἔγρα m. *fin.* εστιν mn. 22. ψεῦστης (*cf.* I. 10) n. οησους m*. αντιχρηστος m. −ὁ αρνουμενος τον π̄ρα και τον υἱον πας a. 23. *fin.* +ὁ ὁμολογων τον υἱον και τον π̄ρα εχει ab**j [*cum Elzev.* dfghklmno]. 24. −ουν a. +και (*ante* εαν) c. +δε (*post* εαν) g. π̄νι (*pro* π̄ρι) m. εν τω π̄ρι και εν τω υἱω ch. 25. ὑμιν m*. −την *prim.* bo. 26. πλανοντων a*fjkmno*. 27. χρῖσμα *bis* n. μενετω (*pro* μενει) ad**. μεντω εν ὑμιν d*. μενετω εν ὑμιν m. χριαν n. διδασκει (*pro* -σκῃ) cdfm*n. −αλλ᾽ ὡς *usque ad* ὑμας o. αυτου (*pro* αυτο) k. διδασκῃ (*pro* -σκει) k. μενετε (*pro* μενεῖτε) ad. 28. −και νυν τεκνια μενετε εν αυτῳ am. +μου (*post* τεκνια) bl. ἱν᾽ j. ὅτ᾽ ἂν n. εαν (*pro* ὁταν) d. σχωμεν παρησιαν d. εχομεν n. ενσχυθωμεν m. παρ᾽ (*pro* απ᾽) a. 29. ιδητε b*fgmno. οιδατε c. ηδητε (*sic*) j. εστιν m. +και (*ante* πας) ad. −την a. γεγενηται ajklm.

CAP. III. 1. εδωκεν cd. ὑμιν (*pro* ἡμιν) m*. +και εσμεν (*post* κληθωμεν) a. διατοῦτο (*sic* 3 *Johan.* 10) hklmn *alii.* ὑμας (*pro* ἡμας) b*fgklmno. εγνων a*, εγνωκεν ?b*, *vel* εγνωτε *cum* o (*pro* εγνω). 2. θῦ τεκνα m. εσωμεθα *prim.* f. οἶδαμεν kn. αυτου (*pro* αυτῳ) l. οψωμεθα b*fm. ὀψομεθα k. *fin.* εστιν (*sic vv.* 3, 5, 7, 15) m. 3. εν (*pro* επ᾽) m. αυτον (*pro* ἑαυτον) m*o. ἀγνος (*at* ἀγνιζει) k. 4. −την *prim.* m. 5. ἀρῃ m. *fin.* εστιν n. 6. οὐχ᾽ *bis* kln. +και (*ante* πας *secund.*) h. εγνω ag. 7. *fin.* εστι bo. 8. *init.* ὁ δε ποιων k. 9. γεγενημενος jo. +το (*ante* σπερμα) c. δυνατε b*.

τι (*post* ὅτι *secund.*) m. γεγενηται jo. 10. +την (*ante* δικαιοσυνην) cfgkm. ἀδελφον a. 11. επαγγελια an. ἠκουσατε k. 12. καθῶς m. καην n*. 3. θαυμαζητε b*dm** (-ται m*). –μου dm. ἡμας (*pro* ὑμας) j. 14. *init.* μεις o. +δε (*ante* μη) l. +αυτου (*ante* μενει) acm. μενεῖ d. 15. –πας *rim.* c. ἀάδελφον d. εστιν m. +ουκ (*ante* οιδατε) m [*non interrogativè*]. αυτω abdfghjklno (αὐτω m). 16. εγνωμεν c. αγα m. τεθεικεν την ψυχὴν αυτου m (γαβ, m**). –αυτου n. εθηκεν n. ὀφειλομεν k. τας ψυχας υπερ των αδελφων c. 17. εχει dfk. θεωρει a*ch*km. μενεῖ dfj. 18. μου ad. μηδὲ klmno. +τη (*ante* γλωσση) abcfghjklmo [*non* n]. γλωσσει . +εν (*ante* εργω) abghklmo [*non* n]. 19. αλλ' εκ τουτου a. –και *prim.* . γνωσομεθα aj. πεισωμεν ah. 20. ἡ καρδια καταγινωσκη ἡμων b. καταγινωσκει fkn. –ὁτι *secund.* d. –εστιν k. γινωσκη (*pro* γινωσκει) m. 21. ων (*pro* ἡμων *prim.*) c. καταγινωσκει cfk. 22. αν (*pro* εαν) am. λαβανομεν h. λαμβανωμεν km. απ' (*pro* παρ') a. 23. πιστευωμεν afl. πιστευομεν c. –τῳ ονοματι, *at* τω υἱω *et* χριστω d. –ἡμιν bcdfghjklo. 24. και *tert.* cgh. εν ἡμιν μενει c. *fin.* εδωκεν ἡμιν abdmo. δεδωκεν f.

CAP. IV. 1. αγαπητοι μη *in* d* *ante* εκ του πνος *cap.* III, *v.* 24 *p. m:* a, d**. πιστευητε b*mo. εστι m, *at rasura in* a *inter* ε *et* στιν. εξεληλυθεισαν l. 2. γινωσκομεν a. γινωσκεται bcdfghjkmo. *fin.* εστιν (*sic vv.* 3 *prim.*, 16, 17) m. οὐκ' ο** *super* εστι, *at incipit v.* 3 και τουτο. 3. –τον cdghl. –χριστον a. –εκ k. –το df. κος (*pro* κοσμῳ) m. ἤδη k. 4. τεκνα m. ἡ k. 5. *Rasura in* k *ante* εισι. εισιν m. +και (*ante* δια) a. διατοῦτο n. λαλουσιν m. 6. αληθειας *eras. ante* πλανης *in* a. 7. γεγενηται jl*. . –ὁ μη αγαπων ουκ εγνω τον θν̄ d. ἐκ ἔγνωκε (*pro* εγνω) m. 10. ἠγαπησαμεν k. +πρωτος (*post* αυτος) f: *cf v.* 19. ἠγαπησεν (*sic vv.* 11, 19) k. λασμον k. 11. ὁ θσ̄ οὑτως a. ηγαπησεν ἡμας ὁ θς̄ o. ὀφειλομεν k. 12. *n.* εν ἡμιν τετελειωμενη εστιν am. 13. εδωκεν c. 15. εαν (*pro* αν) ak. *n.* και αυτος και εν αυτω (*pro* και αυτος εν τῳ θῳ̄) a, *και posteriore rubro raso.* –και αυτος εν τῳ θῳ̄ (*deest v.* 16) o. 16. –και ὁ θς̄ εν αυτῳ a*. *fin.* -μενει b*fgjklm. 17. τετελειται f. εχομεν cf. εν τουτω τω κοσμω a. 8. ἡ αγαπη ἡ τελεια m. 19. +ουν (*post* ἡμεις) gkm. τον θν̄ (*pro* αυτον) cd. πρωτον a. 20. *init.* +αγαπητοι f. αγαπα (*pro* αγαπω) c. μισει dfghlm. –αὐτου *secund.* m. ἑωρακεν ου (*pro* ἑωρακε πως) a. ἑωρακεν *bis* k*. υνατε k.

CAP. V. 1. ὁ χς̄ εστιν bo (εστι o). γεγενηται d*jk*lm*. +αυτον (*post* γεννησαντα) a. το (*pro* τον *secund.*) m. 2. ποιωμεν (*pro* τηρωμεν) adg. τηρουμεν m*o (*sic v.* 3 o*). 3. –αἱ f. 4. γεγενημενον jlo. ὑμων (*pro* ἡμων) bklo. 5. +δε (*post* τις) ac. −εστιν (*prim.*) j**. 6. αἱμτος b. +και πνς (*post* αἱματος) a. −ὁ *secund.* acdghjklmo. αλλα και (*pro* αλλ᾽) bo. +εν (*ante* τω αἱματι) jk. αλλ᾽ εν τω αἱματι και εν τω ὑδατι m*. 7. *init.* +οἱ (*ante* τρεις *prim.*) a. 7, 8. *Desunt omnia ab* εν τῳ ουρανῳ *v.* 7, *usque ad* εν τῃ γῃ *v.* 8 *in* abcdfghjklm (*hiat* n) o. 8. −και (*ante* το ὑδωρ) a. 9. *init.* εις (*pro* ει) o. λαμβανωμεν h*k*. μειζω g*. αὐτή (*pro* αὕτη) o. *fin.* αὐτου (ου *mutatum*) k. 10. +του θυ̅ (*post* μαρτυριαν *prim.*) b**d. αυτω (*pro* ἑαυτῳ) dfgjkl. υἱω (*pro* θεῳ) b**cdk. ουκ επιστευσεν (*pro* ου πεπιστευκεν) d. μεμαρτυρηκε (−ὁ θς̅) dj. 11. δεδωκεν al. ὁ θς̅ ἡμιν hm. 12. +του θυ̅ (*post* υἱον *prim.*) a. +και (*post* εχει *prim.*) a. −την *prim.* k. +αιωνιον (*post* ζωην *prim.*) k. τον υἱον (*pro* την ζωην *secund.*) m. 13. −του υἱου *prim.* j. τοῦ θυ̅ τοῦ υἱου ἵνα (αβγ m**, *cf.* III. 16) m. −ἱνα ειδητε *ad fin. vers.* c. αιωνιον εχετε abd (-ειον ?d*) fghjklo. 14. −τι m. αἱτωμεθα (*non v.* 15) k. του θυ̅ (*pro* αυτου) b**. 15. ακουῃ g. εαν (*pro* αν) acdfghkl. τωμεθα a. αἱτηματα *et* ἡτηκαμεν k. 16. την (*pro* μη *prim.*) d. αἱτησει k. −αυτῳ a. τω ἁμαρτανοντι a. ἁμαρτανουσιν o. εστιν ἁμαρτια *usque ad* εκεινης *super rasur. in* b. εστιν ἁμαρ[τιαν k**] k. +τις (*ante* ερωτηση) d. 17. εστιν *prim.* fm. εστι και (*pro* εστιν και) c *sic.* 18. γεγενημενος j*. 19. +δε (*post* οιδαμεν) c. −του a*. επι (*pro* εν) m. 20. *init.* και οιδαμεν ad. −δε adj. εδωκεν ac [*non* m]. ἐξουσιαν *eras. ante* διανοιαν *in* j. γινωσκομεν cg*. +θν̅ (*post* αληθινον) ad. −εν *prim.* o. αληθηνω ?k*. −εν τῳ *secund.* a**. χυ̅ l. −ἡ bdjo. +ἡ (*ante* αιωνιος) cfghklm. *fin.* και ζωη ἡ αιωνιος ab**. 21. φυλαξετε d. αυτους a*. ἑαυτα cm. −αμην d.

SUBSCRIPT.: *Nil habent* abcdgklmo. απο εφεσου f. τελος της α̅ ιωαν. επιστ. ἡτις εγραφη απο εφεσου j *rubro.* τελος. στ^x σολ̅. h.

S. JOHANNIS EPISTOLA SECUNDA.

Θειος ιωαννης ταδε δευτερα τοις προτεροισιν f *rubro.* ιωαννου καθολικη επιστολη δευτερα h. επιστολη ιωαννου δευτερα k. ιωαννου επιστολη καθολικη β′ l. ιωαννου επιστολη κα [*hiat*] m. ιω επιστολη, δευτερη o.

VERS. 1. –'Oj (*abscissum*). +τη (*post* εκλεκτη) m. κυρια (*nomen pro-*
rium; *sic v*. 5) jk. –εν b*. 2. οὖσαν (*pro* μενουσαν) d. ὑμιν (*pro* ἡμιν) cj.
ιων (*pro* ἡμων) acj. εστιν (*pro* εσται) m. 3. ἡμων g*kl [*non* c]. χαρᾶ
ro χαρις) o. απο (*pro* παρα *prim.*) c. θῦ και πατρος l. –παρα *secund.* f.
υ ιυ (–κυ) d. αυτου (*pro* του πατρος) f. *vv.* 3, 4. –και αγαπῃ *usque ad*
αληθειᾳ j. 4. εχαρη a. –λιαν o. περιπατουντα l. *Rasura ante* καθως
a. ελαβωμεν f. 5. οὐχῶς j. καινην γραφων (γραφω d*) σοι dm. γρα-
ω c *tacitè*. αλλ' acjo. ἣν *mutat. in* b. εχομεν ab*chjkl**o. ηχομεν f.
ταρχης (*sic v*. 6) ahm. 6. κατὰς o*. εντολη *super rasur. in* b. ἡ εντολη
τιν m. +ἵνα (*ante* καθως, *etiam ante* εν) m. οικουσατε a. ἠκουσατε k.
ριπατειτε o. 7. εξηλθον (*pro* εισηλθον) d. +ει τις ουκ ὁμολογει ιν χν εν
ρκι (*ante* οὗτος) g. –ὁ *secund.* k. αντιχρηστος m. 8. απολεσητε dfj
ιον m]. ειργασασθε dfj. +καλα (*ante* αλλα) f. απολαβητε dfj. απολαβο-
ν k. 9. παραμενων (*pro* μενων *prim.*) o. θῦ (*pro* χῦ *prim.*) k. –θῦ ουκ
ει' ὁ μενων εν τῃ διδαχῃ του χῦ a*b*o. +δε (*ante* μενων *secundum*) h. μενον
cund. m. και τον υἱον και πρα m. *fin.* ουκ εχει o, *cf.* 1 Jo. IV. 2. 10.
ν διδαχην ταυτην m. οικιαν (ο *mutat.*) m. *fin.* λεγητε d. λεγεται k*.
.. λεγων γαρ m. –αυτῳ kl. 12. εχω o. γραφειν ὑμιν bjo. γραψαι g.
ουληθην abghlmo. –αλλα d. αλλ' ahjm. +γαρ (*post* ελπιζω) d. γενεσθαι
ro ελθειν) d. χαρις? (*pro* χαρα) l*. ὑμων (*pro* ἡμων) c. 13. εκλετης k.
αμην d.

SUBSCRIPT.: *Nil habent* abcdfgjklmo. τελος· στ^x λ̄. h.

S. JOHANNIS EPISTOLA TERTIA.

Αλλα παλιν τριτα ταυτα περικλυτος ιωαννης f. ιωαννου τριτη επιστολη
επιστολη τριτη ιωαννου καθολικη k. ιωαννου επιστολη καθολικη γ' l.
αννου καθολικη τριτη m. επιστολη ιωαννου καθολικη γ' o.

VERS. 1. Γ[αιω *abscissum*] j. αγαϊω m. 3. εχαριν k. –γαρ d. 4.
υτης (*pro* τουτων) d. χαραν ταυτης ουκ εχω m. τα εμα τεκνα ακουω d.

5. −*ειs secund.* d. 7. −*αυτου* ac (*tacitè*) dfhjkl [*non* bo]. *παρα* (*pro απο*)
d. 8. *γινομεθα* c. *γενωμεθα* f*. 9. +*αν* (*post εγραψα*) d. 10. *διατοῦτο*
klm. *ἐλθω* k. *ποιη* d*. *επεδεχεται* m. *βολομενους* a. −*εκ* bh. 11. −*δε*
bcdfgjklo. 12. −*και οιδατε* a. *οιδαμεν* b**ch. *οιδας* dg. *αληθης εστιν ἡ*
μαρτυρια ἡμων (*ἡμων rescript.*) m. 13. *γραψαι σοι* (*pro γραφειν*) m. *οὐ*
k. *μελλανος* g*. *γραψαι σοι* d. *fin. γραφειν* m. 14. *ἐλπιζω* k. *σε*
ιδειν m. 15. *ειρηνην* a. *αδελφοι* (*pro φιλοι*) dm. *κατονομα* gh.

SUBSCRIPT.: *τελος* h, *cæteri nil.*

S. JUDÆ EPISTOLA.

Αλλος αδελφοθεος ταδ' ιουδας ευσεβεεσσιν f. *ιουδα καθολικη επιστολη* ho. *επιστολη ιουδα αδελφου ιακωβου* k. *ιουδα επιστολη καθολικη* lm. *Hiat* j *in hâc epistolâ.*

VERS. 1. *ἰοῦδας* m. *χυ ιυ* bcdklo. 2. *πληθυνθειη* (*η prim. mutat.*) g.
3. +*ὑμων* (*ante σωτηριας*) m. *ω in επαγωνιζεσθαι eras. in* g. *παραδοθησι*
?g*. 4. *ανοι bis script.* a*. −*θεον* b*do [*non* hklm]. 5. *ἡμας* (*pro ὑμας*
prim.) ak. −*ὑμας secund.* cd. *αἰγυπτου* k. *τοδεύτερον* h. 6. *δε* (*pro τε*) f.
αλλ' ahkm. *οἰκητηριον* k. 7. *ὁμοιον* k. *εκπορνευσασαι τροπον* k. *ὀπισω* k.
αιωνιου, ho. 8. *μιαινουσιν* k. *δοξας* (*a mutat.*) l. 9. *μωϋσεος* d. *ετολμη*
σεν a. *ὑπενεγκειν* bco. *επιτιμησοισαι κς* d. [*επιτιμήσαι* hklo *alii: Elzev.*
malè]. 10. −*ὁσα prim.* k. −*ζωα* c. 11. *απολογια* (*pro αντιλογιᾳ*) h.
12. *ὁ φοβος* (*pro αφοβως*) k. *ποιμενοντες* f. *παραφερομεναι* abcdfghlo.
φερομεναι k. *φθινοπορινα* acd*k. *φθηνοπωρινα* o. +*και* (*ante εκριζωθεντα*)
bko. 13. −*θαλασσης* c. *αστεραις* a. *πλανητε* f. *πλανῖται* l. *εις αιωνας*
a. −*τον* acdfhk. 14. *ἁγιαις μυριασιν* abcdfghklo (*ἁγιαις* ac, *μυριᾶσιν* k).
15. *ελεγξαι* abdfghklo. −*αυτων prim.* b*do. *ὧ* (*pro ὧν prim.*) a. *ἠσεβησαν*
k. 16. *γογγισται* k. *ἑαυτων* (*pro αυτων prim.*) acdfghl (*ἑαυτων* a).
ὑπερογγα ?k. 18. *επ' εσχατων των χρονων* g. *τους* (*pro τας*) c. *επιθυμιας*
ἑαυτων f. 19. −*ἑαυτους* ac (*tacitè*) fhkl [*non* do]. 20. *εποικοδομουντες*
ἑαυτους τη ἁγιωτατη ὑμων πιστει d. *επικοδομουντες* k. *ἁγιω·* k. 22.

ελεητε ?o*. 23. –εν φοβῳ d. –του acghkl. ἁρπαζοντες k. +οὑς δε ελεγχεται εν φοβω (*ante* μισουντες) k. εσπιλομενον g. 24. αυτους (*pro* ὑμας) abc (*tacitè*) ghlo. +και ασπιλους (*post* απταιστους) k. κατ' ἐνωπιον lo. –αμωμους k. 25. θω̄ σοφω o. +δια ιῡ χῡ του κῡ ἡμων (*ante* δοξα) k. –και *prim. et tert.* k. μεγαλοσυνη ak. –και *secund.* c. +προ παντος του αιωνος (*post* εξουσια) d.

Subscript.: *Nil habent* abcdgklo. τελος h. τελος συν θω̄ ἁγιω των πραξεων και των επιστολων των ἁγιων αποστολων ὡν και του ιουδα τετελειωται δια στιχων ξή. αμην. f *rubro.*

SANCTI PAULI EPISTOLÆ. AD ROMANOS.

[Cap. I. 1—28.]

Προς ῥωμαιους επιστολη h. προς ῥωμαιους παυλου επιστολη k. επιστολη παυλου προς ῥωμαιους l. παυλου αποστολου επιστολη προς ῥωμαιους m. προς ῥωμαιους no.

Cap. I. 1. αφορισμενος n. 5. –αυτου c. 6. ἡμεις (*pro* ὑμεις) k. 7. ουσιν k. 8. –μου a**. –δια ιῡ χῡ c. χω̄ o. περι (*pro* ὑπερ) o. καταγγελλετε n. 9. μοι (*pro* μου *prim.*) b*o [*non* m]. ὡ k. διαλειπτως m. 10. δεομενος *cum sequentibus in* no. ὁπως (*pro* ει πως) o. ευωδοθησομαι k. –του g. ελθειν k. εφ' (*pro* προς) l. 11. ὑμιν χαρισμα m. στηρηχθηναι n. *vv.* 11, 12. –ὑμας· τουτο δε εστι συμπαρακληθηναι ao. 12. –δια της εν αλληλοις πιστεως m. 13. –δε k* (*supra, init. peric.*). εκωλυθειν n. τινα καρπον abcdfghklmno. –και *secund.* lo. 14. ὀφειλετης ειμη k. 15. οὑτως acfgk lmno [*non* h]. +εν (*ante* ὑμιν) b*o. 16. θῡ *super rasur. in* h. 17. πιστεως, o *alii.* 18. αδικεια n. 19. *init.* το γαρ γνωστον (–διοτι) bo. ἑαυτοις (*pro* εν αυτοις) h*. ὁ θς̄ γαρ m. 20. κτησεως n*. ποιημασιν f. 21. γνωντες m. οὐχ' kno. ηυχαριστησαν cdklmn [*non* o]. –εν τοις διαλογισμοις αυτων d. 23. ηλλαξαντο cghk. ανοῡ φθαρτου l. ἑρπετων n. 25. μετηλλαξαν k. 26. διατοῦτο *pass.* klmn. θηλιαι n. 27. –τε a*bho. δε (*pro* τε) dl. –οἱ k. αρρενες *prim.* abdfghklmno. +εις την (*post* χρησιν) k. –εν *prim.* h. –εν τῃ ορεξει αυτων n. αρενες *secund.* b*. –εν ἑαυτοις a*. 28.

εχει m. 29. +ακαθαρσια (*post* αδικια) m. κακια πορνεια πονηρια πλεονεξια d. 30. ψιθιριστας ?h*. *Post* ψιθυριστας *in* a *duo verba erasa.* εφερευτας παθων o. 32. +τα (*ante* αυτα) k. συνευδοκουσιν m. +μη (*ante* πρασσουσιν) n**. *fin.* πρασσουσιν mno. πραττουσι h.

CAP. II. 1. ὦ (*non* v. 3) k. +κριματι (*ante* κρινεις) m. κατακρινης k. 2. γαρ (*pro* δε) m. εστιν n. −τα m. 3. λογιζει n. εκφευξει k. 4. τον πλουτον a. χριστοτητος k. *fin.* ·*non*; *in* h (*sic v.* 27). 5. σκηροτητα d*. +και (*ante* δικαιοκρισιας) abcdfghklmno. −του h. 6. −τα l. 7. ζητουσιν mn. 8. *init.* της (*pro* τοις) m. ερηθειας f. −και *prim.* d. −δε *secund.* a*. οργη και θυμος m. 9. θλιψεις k. ανθρωθου m. του κατεργαζομενους o. ιουδαιω m. ἑλληνι m. ἑλληνις ?n. 10. τε (*pro* δε *prim.*) d. ἑλληνη d*. 11. εστιν k*. 12. ἡμαρτον *prim.* m. 13. −τῳ k* (*supra* k**). 14. ὅτ' ἂν f. ὁτ' ἂν n. −γαρ a. +τα (*ante* εθνη) k. ποιει n. 15. οἱτινες k. συμμαρτυρουσης d*. 16. κρίνει l. *Rasura in* c *post* κατα. −μου m. 17. *init.* εἰδὲ d**. ἴδε klmno. επονομαζη k. καυχασε c. 19. ὀδηγων m*. 20. εν των νομω l. 21. +τον (*ante* ἑτερον) n. κλεπτην (*pro* κλεπτειν) c. *In vv.* 21, 22, · *mutatum quater in*; n**. 22. μοιχευσης (*pro* μοιχευειν) o. 23. ατημαζεις n*. 24. εθνεσιν m. 25. −γαρ dm. ὠφελεῖ k. πρασσεις f. 26. ὁταν (*pro* εαν) d. ἡ k. τα δικαιω *rescript. in* b. 27. *Non interrogative* hko *alii.* 29. κριπτω b*. −ὁ *secund.* b*o. ἐπαινος k. −του a.

CAP. III. 1. −ἡ c. 2. πολλη (*pro* πολυ) c. 3. ἡ (*pro* ει, *sic v.* 5) n [*malè Mill.* ἦ]. ἡπιστισαν k*. ἡπιστησαν k**n. ἡπιστασαν ?m*. καταργηση b*o. 4. γενεσθω c. αληθεις d. δικαιωθεὶς fo. δικαιωθῇς n. νικησεις n. 5. −ἡ a*. συνιστησιν mn. +ουν (*post* τι) f. 7. δε (*pro* γαρ) d. αληθα ?c. ψευματι o. επεριεσσευσεν o. ἁμαρτλος c. 8. −και *secund.* a. ποιησομεν m. ἐλθη k. +εφ' ἡμας (*post* ελθη) m. τἀγαθὰ k*. αγαθα· n. *fin.* εστιν mn. 9. προσεχωμεθα k*. παντα (*pro* παντας) n. 10. −ὁτι achl. ουδεις (*pro* ουδε εἰς) l. 11. συνιὼν l. *Post* συνιων *desunt omnia in* n. 12. ἁμα n. ἠχρειωθησαν k. ηχριωθησαν m. εστιν *bis* n. πιῶν b*. 13. λαρυξ adk. χηλη ?g*. 14. ἀρὰς k. 15. ὀξεις k. 16. συντριμα dm. αυτων (ων *mutat.*) g. 17. ὁδον (*non v.* 16) k. 18. ὀφθαλμων k. 19. ὁσσα ?m. λεγει ὁ νομος b. 20. δι' ὅτι n *passim* o. ἐξ' ἐρχων o. −νομου *prim.* c. ενωπιον αυτου πασα σαρξ g. του θεου (*pro* αυτου) adk. 21. νυν k. −και m. 25. αἱματι αυτου m. δειξιν a*. παρεσνεσιν k. −δια την παρεσιν *v.* 25 *usque ad* δικαιοσυνης αὐτου *v.* 26 b* (*habet marg. rubro*) o. 26. *fin.* ιυ̅ (*pro* ιησου) bdfgmo. 27. *init.* πως (*pro* που) o. −ἡ k. πιου k*. *Post* εργων *in* n*·, *at in* n**;. 28. νομου (*pro* εργων) f*. 29. *init.* −η n.

ιωνων abo. —δε k. *Post* εθνων *prim.* · n*,; n** (*cf. v.* 27). 30. ὁ θς̄ εἱς k.
l. γοῦν (*pro* ουν) l. —της k. —νομον ουν καταργουμεν δια της πιστεως d.

CAP. IV. 1. *init.* τι ερουμεν ουν a. ἀβρααμ (*sic vv.* 2, 3, 9, 12, 13, 16)
ıklmo. *fin.* σαρκα· l. 2. εχη ?g*. 3. επιστευσεν (—δε) b*o. τω θῶ
βρααμ m. 4. —δε a*. —το abcdfghklmno. ὀφειλημα k. 5. —μη n*
abet marg.). 6. +ὁ (*ante* δᾱδ) g. δικαιοσυνη c (*sic*). 7. αφειθησαν ach.
φηθησαν k. απεκαλυφθησαν klo. 8. λογησηται g*o. λογισεται n. 9.
και k. —επι την *secund.* a. ἡ πιστις τω ἀβρααμ k. 10. —οντι a* (*habet
arg.*). οντη n*. —ουκ εν περιτομῃ *usque ad v.* 11 εν τῃ ακροβυστιᾳ m.
ουκ εν περιτομῃ *ad fin. vers.* n. 11. σφραγίδα cko. —τῃ bco. πιστευσ-
ντων (*cf. v.* 24) l. +περιτομην (*post* λογισθηναι) m** *manu recenti.* —και
cund. a. *fin.* εις δικαιοσυνην (—την) d. 12. οὐκ' n. ου τοις (*pro* τοις ουκ)
n. τυχουσι (*pro* στοιχουσι) lm. —τῃ m. της πιστεως της εν (+τη a**bgko)
ιροβυστια abcfghklno (επι *pro* εν g). 13. το (*pro* τῷ *secund.*) h. ειναι αυτον
—του d. —δια *secund.* a*c. +και (*ante* πιστεως) c. 14. +και (*post* γαρ) a
script. κληρομοι a*. κεκαινωται f. κεκενωτε n. 16. διατοῦτο ln *passim.*
ο (*pro* τῳ *secund. et tert.*) m, (*pro secund.*) n. —του dh. 17. πολλων πατερα
ι. *Rasura in* h *inter* τεθει *et* κα. λαλουντος (*pro* καλουντος) l*. ὀντα *secund.*
. 18. επιστευσε o. τω? (*pro* τό *prim.*) l*. —οὑτως o*. το σπερμα (*sic*)
fin. —σου o. 19. ασθενησης m. κατενοησαι d. ἠδη k. 20. ενδυναμωθη
ι. 21. πληροφοριθεῖς k. 24. —δι' n. μελλη ?m*. πιστευσασιν l.
5. ἠγερθη kn. δικαιοσυνην (*pro* δικαιωσιν) a.

CAP. V. 1. δικαιοθεντες b*. εχωμεν fh*m [*non* klno]. 2. —την *prim.*
*. χαραν (*pro* χαριν) d*, *at* χαρν m. ἑστηκαμεν ko. καυχομεθα c. —επ'
ιπιδι *v.* 2 *usque ad* καυχωμεθα *v.* 3, k. 3. +ἡμων (*post* θλιψις) c. 4.
δε ἡ δοκιμη k. 5. καταισχυνη co. κακαταισχυνει k. κατ' αἰσχυνει n.
ει (*pro* ετι) h. καιρῶν fz. απεθαθανε b. απεθανεν (*sic v.* 8) m. 7.
τοθανειτε c*. —και m. 9. —εν b. σωθησωμεθα g*z (*sic v.* 10, z). *fin.* +της
ιλλουσης b** (*marg. recenti manu*). 10. *init.* οἱ (*pro* ει) dg*m* (O *rubro*
). 11. καυχωμεθα bhm. καυχομεθα cd. 12. διατοῦτο *passim* lmn.
θανατου (*ante* ανου) m. εισηλθεν m. δι' ῆλθεν n. 13. +τω (*ante* κοσμω)
ι. ελλογειτω f. εκλλογεῖται m. οντως h*. 14. απο αδ *super rasur.*
ιo. μωϋσεος afgh*l. μωϋσεως h**kmn. 15. οὐχ k. οὐχ' (*sic v.* 16 no)
ιo. οὑτως (*sic vv.* 18, 19, 21) cfgklmno (*non* m *vv.* 18, 19). χαρς (*pro*
αρις) m, *cf. v.* 2. —τῇ cmn. πολους k. επερισσευσεν mn. 16. οὐχ m *alii.*
δι' ?l*. ἁμαρτισαντος d. 17. ἐνNος (N *rubro*) *prim.* d. περισσιαν k.
τη (*ante* ζωη) k. βασιλευουσι o. 18. ἆρα mn. το παραπτωμα (*pro*

παραπτωματος) m. το δικαιωμα (*pro* δικαιωματος) m. 19. *Duo vel tria verba amissa in* d *ante* ανου. κατεσταθημεν m. −της *secund.* m. 20. παρ' εισηλθεν n. ἁμαρτημα (*pro* παραπτωμα) bo. ὑπερεπεριεσσευσεν k. 21. βασιλευσει cl*o. +της (*ante* δικαιοσυνης) ko. −εις ζωην g*? (*habet margo*).

CAP. VI. 1. −ουν k. επιμενωμεν b*mo. επιμενομεν dn. επιμεινωμεν k. 3. εις χριστον εβαπτισθημεν (−ιησουν) a. ιν χν o. 4. −τον k* (*supra* k**). ἠγερθη kn. οὑτως (*sic vv.* 11, 19) cgklmn (h *in v.* 11, o *in vv.* 4, 11). 5. ὁμοιωματι k. 6. μὴκέτι kn. 8. συζησωμεν k. συνζησομεν n. 9. +ὁ (*ante* χριστος) k. οὐκέτι *bis* fhln, *secund.* m. οὐκέτι *bis* ko, *prim.* m. 10. ὃ (*pro* ὁ) *bis* bc (*tacitè*) dfghlmno, *secund.* k. απεθανεν *bis* n. τη ἁμαρτια, k. ἐφάπαξ k. ἐφ' ἅπαξ mn. 11. ἡμεις (*pro* ὑμεις) k. 12. ἡμων f**. 13. μηδὲ hklmno. παριστανητε a*. παραστανετε k. βελη (*pro* μελη *prim.*) m (*sic v.* 19). −εκ k. 14, 15. ὑπο k. 15. ἁμαρτησωμεν cmn. ἁμαρτισομεν k. *Deest versus in* o, *præter* μη γενοιτο. 16. ἡτοι k. 17. ἡτε (*sic v.* 20 *bis*) k. ἠντε m. 18. −δε m. 19. ἡμων (*pro* ὑμων *prim.*) a. −ὡσπερ γαρ παρεστησατε τα μελη ὑμων a* (*habet margo, at legit* ἡμων *p. m.*; ὑμων *s. m.*). −τῃ ακαθαρσιᾳ *usque ad* δουλα m. 20. τη ἁμαρτια l. 21. ἐπ' αἰσχυνεσθε n. *Nullum interrogationis signum in* ln. 22. *init.* νυν cl. δουλωθεντες (*ultimo* ε *mutato*) l. τη δικαιοσυνη (*pro* τῳ θῳ) l. 23. ὀψωνια k. ἁμαρας k*. *fin.* ὑμων m.

CAP. VII. 1. −η d. +τοις (*post* αδελφοι *rubro*) a *rubro*. −γαρ a. γινωσκουσιν Ὁι γαρ (O *rubro*) k. 2. ανδρη ?b*. +αυτης (*post* ανηρ) d. +του νομου (*post* απο) abc (*tacitè*) dfghklmno. 3. ἆρα k. ἄρα n. μιχαλις c. 4. ἡμεις (*pro* ὑμεις) a*. γενέσθε m. +ανδρι (*ante* ἑτερω) bcfo, (*post* ἑτερω) g. 5. ἠμεν k. ὑμων (*pro* ἡμων) c. 6. αποθανοντες abc (*tacitè*) dfghklmno. 7. +ὁτι (*post* ερουμεν) fk. 8. κατηργασατο d. −κατειργασατο *usque ad* εντολης *v.* 9 m* (*habet margo recens, at* −ποτε). 10. −μοι a*. −ἡ *secund.* m*. 13. αλλ' akm. 14. οἶδαμεν k. οἴδαμεν n. γαρ *super rasur.* d. σαρκινος b*o *soli.* 15. ποιω (*pro* πρασσω) m. ὢ (*pro* ὃ *tert.*) n*. μησω n. μισ *rescript. super rasur.* d. τοῦτω *secund.* k. πρασσω (*pro* ποιω) m. 16. +εγω (*post* θελω) m. εμφημι k. 17. νυν n. οὐκέτι lmn. το a*, αυτω g* n* (*pro* αυτο). οἰκουσα (*sic v.* 20) k. 18. τοῦτέστιν kn. οὐχ' *passim* klno. 19. −ου γαρ ὁ θελω ποιω αγαθον k. +τουτο (*ante* ποιω) c. −κακον c. 20. −ου a*. −εγω *prim.* bo. εγω ου θελω τοῦτω k. οὐκέτι dglmn. −εγω *secund.* o. αυτω g*. 21. ἆρα (*sic v.* 25) n. −τον k*. −τον νομον f. ποιειν εμοι l. 23. τε (*pro* δε) a*. −νομῳ του o. αἰχμαλωτιζοντα k. +εν (*post* με) b*ckmno. 25. τω νοϊ μου m**, *recenti manu.* νομον (*pro* νομῳ *prim.*) g.

CAP. VIII. 1. ἀρα (*sic v.* 12, n) kn. 2. της ζ *super rasur. in* o. ἠλευθερωσε dk. ἠλευθερωσεν n. 3. —γαρ a*. ησθενει kn. αυτου (*pro* ἑαυτου) a*. κατεκρινεν n. 5. *Deest versus in* k, *præter* τα του πνς. 6. ειρηνη *mutat. in* g. 7. ου (*pro* ουδε) m. δυνανται m**, *at deest v.* 8 *in* m (*habet recens margo*). 9. οὐκ' *prim.* kn. οἰκει (*non v.* 11) k. θῦ (*pro* χριστου) b*o. ουκ εχει χῦ m. οὐκέστιν n. 10. δια (*pro* δι') dgn. δια την ἁμαρτιαν m. και δικαιοσυνη (*pro* δια δικαιοσυνην) bo. 11. +τον (*ante* ιν) o. ἡμων (*pro* ὑμων) d. το ενοικουν αυτου πνευμα bc (*tacitè*) fghklno [*cum Elzev.* dm]. ἡμιν (*pro* ὑμιν *secund.*) c. 12. ὀφειλεται k. τη (*pro* του) m. 13. μελλεται o. ει δε *bis scriptum* l*. ζησεσθαι kn. 15. ελαβεται *bis* n. ἀβᾶ m. 16. συνμαρτυρεῖ n, *sic v.* 17 σύνκληρονομοι. 17. συμπασχωμεν b*. συμπαχωμεν m. σύνδοξασθῶμεν n. 19. κτησεως n (*sic* κτησις *vv.* 20, 21, 22, *non* 39). πιστεως (*pro* κτισεως) m. την αποκαλυψιν των υἱων *mutat. in* g. εκδεχεται a. 20. οὐχ m *alii.* 21. επ' ελπιδι *cum præcedentibus in* bc (*tacitè*) dghklmno. αὐτῇ o. δουλιας kn*. *Rasura ante* φθορας *in* k. 22. οἴδαμεν n. στεναζει l*. συνωδινη k. 23. +οἱ (*ante* την απαρχην) bco. ἀπ' ἀρχην m. —του πνς o*. συστεναζομεν f. υἱοθεσιας k. εκδεχομενοι a*. 24. οὐκέστιν n. 26. ὡσαύτὸς d. συναντιλαμβανηται a*. τη ασθενεια m. προσευξομεθα abcdfghklmno. καθ' ὃ l. καθ ὃ no. οὐκ' n *ferè.* αλλα al. αυτῶ (*pro* αυτο) d. —το (*ante* πνα *secund.*) k. ὑπερεντυχανει k. στελαγμοις m. 27. ευρενων m. οιδεν n. ἡμων (*pro* ἁγιων) k. 28. —δε a. +το (*ante* αγαθον) afk. —τοις κατα *ad fin. vers.* a. οὐσιν k. 29. *init.* οὓς γαρ (—ὅτι) a. προωρισεν n. συμορφους d. —του υἱου c. προτοτοκον n. 30. προωρισεν m. εκαλεσεν *prim.* lm. οὓς δε (*pro* και οὓς) clm. —εδικαιωσεν· οὓς δε εδικαιωσε τουτους και c. —εδικαιωσεν· οὓς δε d* (*habet marg.*). εδικαιωσε *prim.* k. 32. —παντων fo. χαρησηται h. χαρησεται cfm. 34. —και *prim.* gkl, *secund.* bco. εκδεξιων a. —του o. —ὁς *secund.* l. 35. χωριση c. χαρισει (ει *mutatum?*) m. θῦ (*pro* χῦ) a*. η λιμος η διωγμος dk. 36. ἑνεκεν mn. 37. πασι τουτοις c. 38. επεισμαι (π *rubro* k**) k. +ουτε εξουσιαι (*post* αρχαι) fn. *Transfert* m ουτε δυναμεις *in fin. vers.* 39. τι (*pro* τις) m. ἑτέρα k.

CAP. IX. 1. συμαρτυρουσης d*. συνμαρτυρουσης n. 2. μοι λυπη o. λιπη m*. ὀδυνη k. —μου c. 3. ευχομην ckln. —του al. συγκαινων d. +των (*ante* κατα) a**. 4. οἱτινες k. οθεσια (*pro* υἱοθ.) b*. διαθῆ o. —αἱ *secund.* (*at in marg. forsan p. m.*) n. 5. ἐξ kno. ὧν (*pro* ὢν) k. ευλογητος, l. 6. οὐχ' klno *pass.* εκ *in* εκπεπτωκεν *mutat. in* g. 7. ἀβρααμ klmo. ισαακ (*non v.* 10) k. κληρωθησεται l. 8. τοῦτεστιν k *pass.* τοῦτ' ἔστιν mn.

+ὀτι (*ante* ου) m. −του m. −τα *secund.* k. επαγγελειας (*sic v.* 9) n. 10. ὀὐ k. ῥέβεκα k*. ρεβεκκαν m. 11. μὴδὲ klmo. φαυλον (*pro* κακον) m. ἡνικα (*pro* ἱνα) n. προθεσις του θῡ abcdfghklmno. μενει kn. οὐκ' n. −εξ n. 12. ερρεθη bdfhkno [*non* lm]. ερηθη c. ελασσωνι n*o*. 13. +ὀτι (*post* γεγραπται) f. ἠγαπησα k. ἱσαυ m. ἡσαυ hkln *alii.* 15. μωϋση abfhkl mno. μωϋσει cd. μωσει g. −και οικτειρησω *ad fin. vers.* n. οικτηρωσω ?g*. οἰκτειρησω k. *fin.* οἰκτειρω k. οικτειρησω m. 16. *init.* ἀρ' gn. ἆρα k. −θελοντος *usque ad* ελεουντος a. 17. εξήγειράσαι (*pro* -ρά σε) f. ενδειξομαι cl*. διαγγελλει b*. διαγγειλη m. διαγγελεῖ fo. 18. ἄρα k. ἆρα n. αν θελη (*pro* θελει *prim.*) g. θελη (*pro* θελει *secund.*) gk. 19. μοι ουν m. ὀτι (*pro* ετι) d. το (*pro* τῷ) c. +γαρ (*ante* βουλήματι) abc (*tacitè*) dfghklmno. ανθεστηκεν mno. 20. ὦ k. ω ανε μεν ουνγε m. 21. ὀ μὲν *et* ὀ δὲ o. 22. −δε o. ηνεγκεν (*sic*) c. κατηρτησμενα d*. 23. *init.* −και m. σκευει f. 24. μονων d. +ουκ (*post* μονον) g. 25. ωσε b*. ωσιε dn. ώσηε k. οὐκ' n. ἠγαπημενην *secund.* k. 26. ερρεθη dfhkl**n [*non* mo]. ερηθη c. εὑρεθη ?l*. ὀ (*pro* ου) m*. 27. ἠσαιας m *hoc loco.* ἦ (*pro* ῃ) k. ὡσει (*pro* ὡς η) ac. καταλειμα k*. κατελειμμα ?m. 29. προηρηκεν m. εγκατελει[πεν] n. [πεν *abscissum*]. γομορα b*c. ὡμοιωθημεν n. 30. κατελαβεν n. δικαισυνην *secund.* (*sic* x. 3 *primo loco*) h*. 31. διωκον d. δικαιοσυνην (*pro* νομον δικαιοσυνης *prim.* ?) k. −εις νομον δικαιοσυνης o. εφθασεν mn. 32. οὐκ' (*sic* x. 14 *bis*, 19) n. ἐπιστεως (κ *supra* k**) k. αλλα (−ὡς) a. προσεκοψε l. προεκοψαν o. −γαρ a*. 33. προσκοματος b*. κατ' αἰσχυνθησεται n. *Desunt omnia in* o *usque ad* προσκομματος.

CAP. X. 1. αδελφοι *rubro* a (*init. peric.*). −τον b. *fin.* ἡ σωτηρια (−εις) m. 3. −ιδιαν a*. ζητουντες δικαιοσυνην m. 5. μωϋσης bcfkmo. −γαρ a. −την *secund.* o. ταυτα m* (αυτα m** *marg.*). 6. οὑτως cgklmno. +τη (*ante* καρδια) ac (*tacitè*) dfghklmno. τουτέστι ghl (*sic vv.* 7, 8). τοῦτέστι k (*sic vv.* 7, 8, *etiam* n). τοῦτέστιν n. τουτέστϊν o. *Rasura ante* χ̄ν *in* g. καταγεῖν b*. 7. ἀβυσον d. [τοῦτ' ἔστι (*sic v.* 6) m]. τουτέστϊ (*sic v.* 8) o. −εκ νεκρων d. 8. −εστιν εν *usque ad* το ῥημα d. τουτέστι m. 9. εν το d. +και εν τη καρδια σου (*ante* κ̄ν) o. πιστευσεις m. ηγειρεν αυτον bko (ἠγειρεν k). 10. στομα n. 11. εις αυτον (*pro* επ' αυτῷ) l. 12. *Rasura ante* αυτον *in* a. 13. −αν ak*. εαν (*pro* αν) lm. 14. επικαλεσωνται a. πιστευουσιν g. ακουσονται d, ακουσωσι m, ακουσουσιν n (*pro* ακουσουσι). 15. κηρυξωσιν a. ακουσωσιν (*pro* κηρυξουσιν) c. αποσταλῶσοι d. αποσταλωσιν mn. *Omnia post* ποδες *rescript. super rasur. in* b. 16. οὐ k. −γαρ l*. επιστευσαν (*pro* τις επιστευσε) m. 17. ἆρα mn (+ουν m). +του (*ante* θ̄ῡ) a. 18. λογω (*pro* λεγω) n. *οἰκουμενης* k. 19. *μη* $\overline{ιηλ}$ *ουκ εγνω* dm. *ου εγνω* o. *μωϋσης* abc dfg*klmo [*non* hn]. +*γαρ* (*post εγω*) m. ` *εθνη prim.* fkm. *ἐπ' bis* m. *παρ-ωργιω* o. 20. *εὑρεθην* m. −*μη prim.* o. *επερωτωσιν* kmn.

CAP. XI. 1. *ἀπωσάτω* (*non v.* 2) o. −*εγω* o. *ἀβρααμ* klo *alii* [*non* mn]. *βενιαμειν* m. 2. *ἢ rubro* g** (*deest in* g*). *ἡλια* hkl [*non* no]. *ἰλια* (*cf.* IX. 13) m. *fin.* λεγω b*. 3. *ὑπελῆφθην* o. *fin.* +*λαβειν αυτην* n. 4. *χρησμος* (*pro χρηματισμος*) b*o. *κατελειπον* n. +*το* (*ante γονυ*) o. [*τη βααλ omnes*]. 5. *Ὀυτως* (*Ὀ rubro*) l. 6. *οὐκέτι quater* lmn. 7. +*ὁ* (*ante* $\overline{ιηλ}$) bo. *τουτο* (*pro τουτου*) abcfkl*mno. *fin.* *επορευθησαν* c. *επερωθησαν* ?m. 8. *ὀφθαλ-μους* (*non v.* 10) k. *ὠτα* k. *αχρι* (*pro ἑως*) c. −*ἡμερας* a. 9. +*ενωπιον αυτων* (*post αυτων*) k. *αυτοποδομα* c. *ανταποδωμα* n. 10. *διάπαντὸς* o. *συγκαψον* b*dfkl*?m**. *συνκαψον* m*. *συνκαμψον* n. 11. *επτεσαν* n. *πεσωσιν* m. *τα αυτων παραπτωματα* b*o. *τυ* (*pro τῳ*) c. 12. *το prim. mutatum in* k. *αυτου* (*pro αυτων prim.*) b. *κοσμου usque ad μαλλον rescript. super rasur. in* b. *ἡττημα* kn. *Nullum interrogationis signum in* l. 13. *ἐφόσον* fgh. −*μεν* a*. −*εγω* n. *διδασκαλος* (*pro αποστολος*) d*. 15. *init.* *ἡ* (*pro ει*) fn. *πλουτος* (*pro καταλλαγη*) c. *καταλαγη* d*m. *προληψις* k*. 16. *ἡ απαρχη* (*sic*) c. −*ἡ prim.* f. *οἱ κλαδοι rescript. in* b. 17. −*δε secund.* k. *ὧν* k. *ενεκενρισθης* b*. *ποιοτητος* dm*. *εγενου και της πιοτιτος της ελαιας* k. 18. *ἡ* k. 19. −*οἱ* adfghklmn [*non* bo]. *ενκεντρισθῶ* d. *εγκε-τρισθω* k. 20. *απιστεια* (*non v.* 23) k. *πιστι* d. *ἑστηκας* kno. *ὑψηλοφρονη* d*. 21. *ὁ* $\overline{θς}$ *et κατα φυσιν rescript. in* b. −*κατα φυσιν* o. *φεισεται* abcd fghklmno. 22. *ἴδε* klmo. *ἴδε* n. −*δε* k* (*supra* k**). 23. *init.* *κἀκεινοι* cdk [*non* m]. *απιστεια* dn. *ὁ* $\overline{θς}$ *εστι* ahkl. *Rasura in* h *inter εγκ et εντρισαι*. 24. *ενεγκεντρισθης* km. *καλίελαιον* d. *αυτοι* (*pro οὑτοι*) d. *εγκετρισθησονται* m*. 25. *ου θελω δε* (−*γαρ*) m. −*αδελφοι* g. *μῦ* (*μεν p. m ?*) *in μυστηριον* m. *φρονημοι* cn. *ἄχρισοῦ* g. 26. *οὑτως* (*sic v.* 31) cgklno [*non* m, *at in v.* 31]. *ἥξει* n. *αποστρεψη* a. *ασεβεις* o. *εξ* (*pro απο*) d. *ασεβειας απο ιακωβ rescript. in* f. 27. *ἑμου* k. *ὅτ' ἂν* n. 28. *ἡμας* (*pro ὑμας*) g. 29. *του θῦ και ἡ κλησις* m. 30. *ποτε και ὑμεις* bo. −*και* d. *ἐπειθήσατω* k. *ἠλεηθητε* k. *ελεηθητε* ?m. 31. *ἠπειθησαν* k. *ὑμετερω* abc (*tacitè*) dfghklm**no. *ελεηθωσιν* m. 33. *ὦ* k. *ὦ* lo. *και σοφιας θῦ και γνωσεως* a. *ανεξηρευνητα* a. 35. *ανταποδωθησεται* a.

CAP. XII. 1. −*ὑμας* h. *οἰκτιρμων* k. −*ὑμων secund.* c. 2. −*μη* d*. *σχηματιζεσθε* d*. *συσχηματιζεσθαι* gkn [*non* m]. *μεταμορφουσθαι* cgko*? [*non* m]. *ανακενωσει* ao. −*το tert.* l*. *το ευαρεστον* (−*και*) m. 3. +*του θῦ* (*post χαριτος*) dfm. *παρὸ* ghm. −*αλλα φρονειν εις το σωφρονειν* ab* (b** *habet in marg.*). εμετρισε k. εμερισεν o. 5. *init.* +και (*post* οὕτως) dm. καθεὶς abdfghkmo [*non* l]. καθ᾽ εἷς n. 6. ὑμιν (*pro* ἡμιν) dk. 7. ὁ διακονιῶν (*pro* διακονιαν) m. διδασκον d*. 9. *fin.* το αγαθον c. 11. ὀκνηροι kn. 12. [κω̃ *omnes*]. θλιψι ?m. 14. ευλογητε *prim.* n. καταράσθε k. 16. γινεσθαι d. φρονημοι cn. 17. *init.* +και d. μὴδενὶ ko. 18. *Totus versus deest in* a *præter* ειρηνευοντες. ἐξ᾽ ἡμων o. −ανθρωπων c. 19. ἑαυτους μη d*. αδελφοι (*pro* αγαπητοι) k. εμη (*pro* εμοι) h. 20. *init.* αλλ᾽ εαν (−ουν) m. πινα n. ψωμισον m*. −γαρ a* (*bis scriptum* a**). σωρευσης a.

CAP. XIII. 1. ὑποτασεσθω m. ὑπο (*pro* απο) abcdfghklmno. +του (*ante* θῡ *prim.*) ck. οὖσαι k. −του lm. εισι τεταγμεναι k. 3. φοβεισθε mo. τη εξουσια k. ἐξεις k. *fin.* ἐξαυτῆς n. 4. *init.* −θῡ *usque ad* αγαθον c. εστιν (−σοι) b*o. ποιεις cdn. εσται (*pro* εστιν *secund.*) m. εις οργην εκδικος bcfkno (· *post* οργην kn). −τῳ m. 5. αναγκῃ ὑποτασσεσθε m. ὑποτασσεσθαι abc (*tacitè*) dfghklno. συνηδησιν n. 6. διατοῦτο lmn. 7. ὀφειλας k. −το *prim.* k. −τῳ τον φοβον τον φοβον n* (*habet marg. p. m.?*). −την τιμην *secund.* k* (*marg. habet*). 8. μὴδὲνὶ μὴδὲν ὀφειλετε k. μὴδενὶ μὴδὲν no. οφειλοντες c. αληλους αγαπαν m* (αλληλους m**). πεπληρωκεν dmn. 9. −ου ψευδομαρτυρησεις cgl [*habent* dfhkmno]. ἡτις (*pro* ειτις) l εν τω λογω τουτω dm. *fin.* σαυτον g*, σεαυτον bcdho [*non* klmn]. 10. το n. ου κατεργαζεται bf. 11. ὑμας (*pro* ἡμας) d, *at* ηδη ὑμας m. ἠδη k. −γαρ a. Ὑμων (*pro* ἡμων, Ὑ *rubro*) k. −η (*ante* ὁτε) a*. 12. ὁπλα ho (*at super ras. in* o). 13. κωμαις m*. μεθες k. 14. −χριστον ck. ποιησθαι k.

CAP. XIV. 1. −δε l. δικρισεις k*, κρισεις dl (*pro* διακρισεις). λογισμων kmo. 2. φαγη c. 3. μη εσθιοντα *bis script.* b*. −μη *prim.* h*. μι (*pro* μη *secund.*) n. ὁ μη ἐσθιον k. +μη (*ante* εσθιοντα *secund.*) o. 4. κρινον d*. οἰκετην k. οικετιν n. γαρ (*pro* δε) o. 5. ἡμεραν, ὁς δε κρινει πασαν ἡμεραν *rescript. in* b. παρημεραν h. +την (*post* πασαν) a. +δε l, +δ᾽ m (*post* ἑκαστος). πληροφορεισθω (φορεισ *rescript.*) h. 6. +ου (*ante* φρονει *prim.*) k*. +και (*ante* ὁ εσθιων) abcdfghklmno. και ευχαριστει (*pro* ευχαριστει γαρ) c. 8. *init.* εαν γαρ τε b*. εσμεν (*pro* ζωμεν *secund.*) c. αποθνησκομεν a*, αποθσωμεν b*, (απθνησκωμεν *sic* c), αποθανωμεν lo, αποθανομεν n (*pro* αποθνησκωμεν *prim.*). αποθνησκωμεν [μεν d**] (*pro* αποθνησκομεν) d*k. αποθνησκομεν (*pro* αποθνησκωμεν *secund.*) fm*n. 9. −και *prim.* acg. απεθανεν o. εζησεν (*pro* ανεζησεν) abcdfghklmno. κυριευσει n. 11. +ἐπ᾽ ουρανιων και επιγειων και καταχθονιων (*post* γονυ) *marg.* n**. εξομολογησηται m*. 12. ἆρα kmn.

13. *Hic versus in* g *rescriptus in marg.* μήκέτι kmn. κρινομεν m*. τῶ (*pro* το) f. προσκωμ[μα d**] d*. εις (*pro* η) b*mno. 14. πεπεισμε n. χῶ (*pro* κῷ) bkmno. αυτου (*pro* ἑαυτου) abcfghklno. το (*pro* τι) n. ἐκεῖνω n, *at* εκεινο gl. 15. *init.* ει γαρ (−δε) dm. οὐκέτι lno, οὐκέ m. περιπατης d. απολυε ah*kmn** (*marg. forsan p. m.*) o, απωλλυε f, *at* καταλυε n*. απεθανεν mn. 17. εστι k. βασια (λ *supra*) k*. πῶσις k. −και ειρηνη b* (*bis habet* b**). 18. κῶ k, θῶ n (*pro* χῷ). χῶ (*pro* θῷ) n. 19. ἆρα n. διωκομεν ao. οιδομης d*. οἰκοδομης k. 20. ἑνεκεν n. προσκοματος d*. 21. τῶ (*pro* το) cf. κρεας m. μηδὲ *bis* hlmno, k *sem.* (και *pro* μηδὲ *prim.* k). ποειν ?m*. οἰνον k. 22. +δε (*post* συ) m. σεαυτον cgklno. κρινω a*. 23. γαρ (*pro* δε *secund.*) bo. το (*pro* ὃ) m. οὐκ' n. *fin.* εστι abdfghklno [*non* m]. *Addunt* abcdf* (=f** *marg.*) ghklmno, *Cap.* XVI. 25—27 *ad finem hujus capitis.* *Cap.* XIV *non legitur in* e, *at hi versus desiderantur in cap.* XVI.

CAP. XV. 1. Ὀφειλομεν (Ὁ *rubro*) k. Ὀφειλωμεν (Ὁ *rubro*) m. −δε b*o. 2. −γαρ abcdfghklmno. ὑμων (*pro* ἡμων) abcfglmo. το (*pro* τῳ) m. οἰκοδομην k. 3. οὐχ' klno. επεπεσαν g* (*forsan* επεπεσων g*) lmn. εις (*pro* επ') n. 4. προέγραφη *prim.* h, *at in* l *mutatum.* +παντα (*ante* εις) m. +δια (*ante* της παρακλησεως) bdfgn [*non* o]. −των γραφων *usque ad* της παρακλησεως *v.* 5 *in* o. εχομεν afn. 5. δοη n. φρονει o. ιησουν χν m. 6. δοξαζηται a*. −θεον και a*. 7. πρόσλαμβάνεσθαι k*n. ὑμας (*pro* ἡμας) bcgl**mno. +του (*ante* θῦ) m. 8. χν ιν acdfghklmn [*non* bo]. γενεσθαι c. γεγεννησθαι k. επαγγελειας n. 9. διατοῦτο kln. εθνεσιν m. +κυριε (*post* εθνεσι) ch. το ὀνοματι d. 11. −και *secund.* acn. 12. ἠσαΐας m. ἰέσσαι k. αρχην d. εθνει (*pro* εθνη) f. εθνη επ' αυτω m. *fin.* ελπιουσι +και εσται ἡ αναπαυσις αυτου τιμη d. 13. πληρῶσαι kmno. ἡμας (*pro* ὑμας *prim.*) n*. −χαρας και m. ευφροσυνης (*pro* ειρηνης) a. *Rasura ante* ειρηνης *in* d. 14. ἡμων (*pro* ὑμων) a*. αγαθοσυνης kmn. +της (*ante* γνωσεως) kn. αλλους (*pro* αλληλους) abcdf?ghklmno. 15. ὑπαναμιμνησκων o. 16. μαι (*pro* με) d. χῦ ιησου m. 17. +την (*ante* καυχησιν) m. +τον (*ante* θῦ) acdfghkl mno. 18. *init.* οὐ k. τι λαλειν m. ουκ ειργασατο g. ἐμοῦ k. +των (*ante* εθνων) d. +εν (*ante* λογω) f. 19. ἁγιου (*pro* θῦ) cm. μη (*pro* με) o. ἰλ-λυρικοῦ k. −του *secund.* k. 20. οὕτως cgklmno. −δε n* (*habet supra*). φιλοτιμουμενου l*. ευαγγελισασθαι n. ὠνομασθη kn. επι a. οἰκοδομω k. 21. οψονται *transfert* m *ad initium versûs.* ανηγγελει a. ανηγγελλη chk** o. ανηγελλη k*. ὀψονται k. συνησουσιν m. 22. δι' ὃ n. 23. μήκέτι kn. κλημασι m. ἐπὶ πόθω o. εχω (*pro* εχων *secund.*) mo. ἱκανων (*pro* πολλων) m. ἐτῶν k. 24. πορευομαι a*b*cfm*n. ισπανιαν adf. ἱσπανιαν (non v. 28) k. εις (pro προς) l. δε (pro γαρ) a**. θεασασθαι usque ad πρωτον rescript. in b. ἠφ᾽ (pro ὑφ᾽) d. επλησθω m*. 26. ηυδοκησαν (sic v. 27) m. 27. ὀφειλεται k. +εν (ante τοις πνευματικοις) d. ὀφειλουσι k. κοινωνησαι (pro λειτουργησαι) m. 28. —την m. ισπανιαν adf. σπανειαν hic n. 29. ὁ (pro ὁτι) k. 30. αδελφοι rubro initio versûs in a. +του ονοματος (ante του κυ) a. πρς (pro πνς) k. συναγωνιζασθε c. συναγωνισασθε fg**. συναγωνιζεσθαι l. τε̃ς (pro ταις) k. +ὑμων (post προσευχαις) n**. 31. —ἡ secund. b*hm. ,γενηται dubium in c. τοις ἁγιοις γενηται m. 32. ἐλθω k. συναναπαυσομαι b*cfk.

CAP. XVI. 1. συνιστημ d* (addit αι d**). υνιστημι (cf. xv. 1) m. ἡμιν ?k. ὑμων (pro ἡμων) k. οὐσαν k. κεγχρέαις l*. 2. προσδεξησθε αυτην d. χρηζει a. +παραστηναι (ante και γαρ) g. αὐτὴ gm, αὐτῆ k, αὔτη n (pro αὐτη). προστατης h*m. fin. εμου αυτου dm. 3. πρισκαν dghmn [non fklo]. αγκυλαν ?k. 4. ἑαυτὸν (pro ἑαυτων) c. 5. —ασπασασθε ad fin. vers. a. ἐπαινετὸν klm. 6. ειτις (pro ἡτις) k. ὑμας (pro ἡμας) dgh. 7. οἷ (pro οἱ) lmo alii. —και (ante προ) n. 8. κω mutatum in m. 9. εις χω a. κυριω (pro χῳ) cm. 10. ἀπελλῆν (ην mutatum) g. απελλὴν kln. 11. ἡρωδιωνα abc (tacitè) dfhklmno. ἡρωδιανα ?g. τῶν ἀρκισσου o. 12. Ασπασασθε περσιδα incipit versum in c: prior pars versûs deest. ἡ (pro ἡτις) m. ασπασασθε περσιδα usque ad fin. vers. transfert f in locum post v. 13. 13. Deest versus in d. ρούφον k. 14. ἑρμην πατροβαν ἑρμαν m. ἑρμᾶν no. ἑρμὴν n. —αδελφους a. 15. —και tert. c. ὀλυμπᾶν k. 16. init. ἀσπάσθε k. +πασαι (post εκκλησιαι) m. fin. θυ (pro χυ) a**k. 17. ποιουντας και τα σκανδαλα παρα την διδαχην ἡν ὑμεις ἐμαθετε n. εκλινατε b*. εκκλινετε m. 18. —ιησου em. αυτων (pro ἑαυτων) a*. εξαπατωσιν e. 19. ακοη ει ? (pro ὑπακοη εις) b*. ακοη o. το εφ᾽ ὑμιν συνχαιρω (—ουν) m. —το prim. d. ὑμων (pro ὑμιν) k. ὑμιν σοφὺ (pro ὑμας σοφους) n. —μεν o. —ειναι h. 20. fin. —αμην bc (tacitè) defgklmno. 21. ασπαζεται m. Rasura in b inter συγγε et νεις. συγγενης ?m*. 22. —εγω m. 23. Rasura in l inter ξεν et ος. ὁλης της εκκλησιας m. οἰκονομος k. 24. —ἡμων m. ἡμων (pro ὑμων) h. 25—27. Confer cap. XIV. ad fin.: m addit in margine, recenti manu "ex fraude Marcionis, ut vult Hieronymus." 25. ἡμας m. και bis script. b*. κηρηγμα d. —αιωνιοις f. σεσιγημενον o. 26. —δε b*o. 27. αἰώνας ko passim.

SUBSCRIPT.: +ἡ (ante προς) ak. —προς ῥωμαιους m. —της (post φοιβης) k. —της εν κεγχρεαις εκκλησιας abdefkmn. fin. +στιχοι ͅκ e. +στιχ᾽ ἀκ᾽. n.

αναγνωσματα(?) πεντε· κεφαλαια ιθ̄. μαρτυριαι μ̄? (*ras.*) στιχοι ϡκ̄ k. *Silet* *Habent* df τελος της προς ρωμαιους επιστολης· εγραφη (+δε d) απο κορινθου α φοιβης (φοιμης d) της (−της f) διακονου. *Habet* h εγραφη δια φοιβης απο ρινθου στ^x ϡκ̄. *Nil legunt* gl. εγραφη απο κορινθου o.

AD CORINTHIOS EPISTOLA PRIMA.

[CAPP. I. 1—II. 7.]

Προς κορινθιους ᾱ επιστολη hn. προς κορινθιους επιστολη πρωτη k. προς ρινθιους πρωτη lo (πρωτης o). προς κορινθιους m.

CAP. I. 1. χ̄ῡ ιησου m. 2. ουσ̄η k. πασιν e. υμων (*pro* ημων *secund.*) h. παντωτε c. περ (*pro* περι) k. 5. επλουτησθητε m. 6. θ̄ῡ (*pro* χ̄ῡ) n. ϐαιβαιωθη d. 7. υστερησθαι de. 8. ανεκλητους f. 9. διακονιαν (*pro* ινωνιαν) l. 10. αδελφοι παρακαλω υμας (−δε) a. η̊ ko. η̊τε k. σχηματα *pro* σχισματα) m. αυτων (*pro* αυτῳ) o. 11. −γαρ a*. −μοι k. εισιν m. k. +μου (*post* θ̄ῳ̄) dg. 15. εβαπτισθητε am. 16. ει *mutatum in* m. 7. απεσταλκε c. απεστειλεν n. αλλ' (*sic*) c. *Rasura in* k *inter* στρ *et* ς. 3. −γαρ b*. −ὁ *secund.* a*. απολυμενοις m*. εστιν *prim.* b, *secund.* o, *bis* . 19. −γαρ k. ἀπολλῶ ckmn. 20. σύζητης mo. αιαιωνος k. −τουτου *cund.* a. 21. επηδη (*non v.* 22) k. *Linea in* e *erasa ante* ουκ εγνω. δοκησεν (*cf. Rom.* xv. 26, 27) m. ευδοκισεν n. πιστευωντας d. 22. επιτουσι (*pro* αιτουσι) a. αιτουσιν em. αἰτουσι k. 23. ἐσταυρωμενον (*sic* . 2) m. εθνεσι (*pro* ἐλλησι) m. 24. −τε k. 25. ισχυρωτερον m. *fin.* τιν bm. −εστι o. 26. −αδελφοι (*habet rubro, initio peric.*) a*. σαρκα; n. πολλοι ευγενεις; ου πολλοι δυνατοι; a. δυνατοι; o. ευγενεις; kno. ευγενεις *ubium in* c. 27. καταισχυνη τους σοφους k. −τους σοφους *usque ad* ἱνα *cund.* m. 28. αγεννη b*dko. *Duo verba erasa in* l *post* κοσμου. εξουθεομενα a. 29. ἱνα (*pro* ὁπως) bo. +αν (*post* ὁπως) a. καυχησηται ac (*tacitè*) efghklm [*non* bo]. καυχησητε n. του θ̄ῡ (*pro* αυτου) abcdefghklmno. 30. γεννηθη kn. σοφια ἡμιν m.

CAP. II. 1. σριον k, μυστηριον n (*pro* μαρτυριον). 2. τι ειδεναι (−του) m. 3. κἀγὼ akm. ασθενια k. προμω ?m. 4. πειθοῖ b*eo. ανοις (*pro* νθρωπινης) m. −λογοις a. λογου k. −και *tert.* c. 5. ἡμων c. −ἡ̊ cm. υναμη n. 6. ν (*pro* εν) d. τελιοις k. 7. θ̄ῡ σοφιαν akm. αποκεκριμμενην

h. αποκεκρυμενην m*. προωρησεν n. 8. εγνωκαν? (*pro* εγνωσαν) e*.
9. οιδε b*cf. ειδεν emn. οὖς kn. ηκουσεν em. ἡτοιμασεν m. 10. γαρ
(*pro* δε) m. απεκαλυψεν ὁ θς̄ am. 11. οὑτως clno. εγνωκεν (*pro* οιδεν
secund.) adm. ει *secund. in* m *mutatum.* 12. +το (*ante* του κοσμου) egn.
−του *secund. et tert.* k. ιδωμεν dm. ιδομεν n. εκ (*pro* ὑπο) k. *fin.* ὑμιν c.
13. διδακτικοις *bis* b*o, *prim.* l*. ανθρωπινοις f. 14. −του θῡ b*o. εστιν e.
16. ὁ σύνμβιβασει (*sic* III. 1. ὡσσαρκικοις) m.

CAP. III. 1. κάγω am. ἠδυνηθην n. ὑμιν λαλησαι abcefghlno [*non* km].
2. −και m. οὔπω k. εδυνασθε befghlmo. ἠδυνασθαι k. ἠδυνασθε n. ουδε
(*pro* ουτε) cdf, *at* οὐδε k. −αλλ' ουτε *ad fin. vers.* m. 3. ουπω? (*pro* ὁπου)
l*. ερεις en. −και διχοστασιαι a. ου (*pro* ουχι) bk. −και *tert.* o. 4. ὅτ' ἂν
n. λεγει dfk?n. εγω δε (*pro* ἑτερος δε· εγω) c. −εγω *secund.* m. +δε (*ante*
απολλω) bo. ἀπολλῶ km. 5. −ουν d. τις ουν εστιν απολλω· τις δε εστι
παυλος m. +και (*ante* απολλως) o. ἢ k. 6. ὁ δε θς̄ (−αλλ') f. ηὔξανεν k.
7. οὐτε *bis* k. *Rasura ante* φυτευων *in* a. 8. −ιδιον *prim.* bo. 9. οἰ-
κοδομη k. οικοδομημα m. 10. θεμελειον *hoc loco* n. τεθηκα fn. εθηκα m*.
−ἑκαστος *ad fin. vers.* m. ἐπ' οἰκοδομει (*sic v.* 12) n. 11. θηναι ?e*. −ὁ abc
defghklmno. 13. +αυτο (*post* πυρ) m. 14. ἐπ' οἰκοδομησε n. εποικοδο-
μησεν o. 15. κατακαϊσεται k. ζημειωθησεται o. οὑτω eh, *at* οὗτος n. 16.
εν ὑμιν οικει· m. οἰκει k. 18. μηδεὶς k. 19. −τῳ b*o. εστιν m. 20.
ανων (*pro* σοφων) k. 21. μηδεὶς ko. ἐνοις (*pro* εν ανθρωποις) k. εστι g.
22. ἐνεστωτα ?m.

CAP. IV. 1. 'Υμας ('Υ *rubro*) d. οικονομους (*sic v.* 2) k. 2. ζητειτε fgn.
3. εἶς m. ἡμων (*pro* ὑμων) o. −η c. 4. ἐμαυτῷ n. 5. προκαιροῦ mn.
ἐλθη (*sic v.* 21) k. −και *prim.* ck. ἐπαινος k. −του (*ante* θῡ) l. 6. *init.*
αὗτα o. ἀπολλῶ mn. ὑμιν (*pro* ἡμιν) l. ἡμιν (*pro* ὑμιν) c, *sic.* +μη (*ante*
φυσιουσθε) b**ehn, *at* φυσιουσθαι n. 7. −και k. καυχᾶσε c. καυχαυσαι e.
8. ἠδη *bis* k. καικορεσμενοι m*. κεκορισμενοι n. επλουτισατε gk. ὤφελον
l. −και οφελον γε εβασιλευσατε mn. 9. ἐπὶ θανατίους f. εγεννηθημεν d.
κοσμω· lm. 10. ἡμεις (*pro* ὑμεις) *prim.* k, *ter* l*. φρονημοι cn. 11. γυμ-
νιτευομεν aghm. 12. χερσιν m. λοιδωρουμενοι m. ἀνεχομεθα ?k. 13.
ὡσπερεί καθάρματα m. ὡς περὶ καθάρματα n. 14. ταυτα γραφω k. 16.
γινεσθαι a*dm.* 17. διατοῦτο klmn. 'Ως (*pro* ὁς *prim.*) o *rubro.* εστιν e.
μου τεκνον m. αναμιμνησει a*. +ιυ̅ (*post* χριστω) bmo. 18. −δε d**.
19. θελησει f. τον πεφυσιωμενον hm.

CAP. V. 1. πορνεια; *bis* k. *fin.* ; l. 2. *Rasura ante* ἱνα *in* a. αρθη am.
fin. πραξας m. *Non interrogativè in* l. 3. −γαρ o. −ὡς *prim.* m. ηδη k.

ͅτως cgklno [non m]. 4. ημων (pro υμων) o. 5. ολεθρον kn. fin. κυ ιων ιησου χυ m. 6. fin. ζυμη vel ζυμει m. 7. –ουν l. –ινα ητε usque ad ζυμοι d* (habet margo recenti manu). υμων (pro ημων secund.) g. ετυθη bc (tacitè) dfghklmno [hiat e]. 8. ἑορταζομεν d. μηδὲ klmo. εἰλικρινειας εἰλικρινιας lo. 9. συναναμιγνυσθε (cf. v. 11) ko. 10. +και (ante ἁρ-αξιν) m. ειδωλολατρης a*, post quod desunt omnia usque ad η λοιδορος v. 11 ιabet a** in marg.). ειδολολατραις d*. ωφειλετε cn. οφειλεται d. ἄρα þειλετε k. ἄρα n. 11. νυν d** et d antiquior kn. αναμιγνυσθαι d* ːcentior, at συναναμιγνησθαι d antiquior. συναναμιγνυσθε k. ὀνομαζομενος ἡ (pro ᾖ) b*c (tacitè) d (semel tantum, recenti manu) hlmn**o. ειδολολα-ͻης d*. η ειδωλολατρης η πλεονεκτης m. μεθυσσος c. μεθος m. μηδὲ hklno. ηδε συνεσθειειν m*. 12. –τι γαρ usque ad κρινειν b* (habet marg. rubro). ȝ. εσω o*. κρινεῖ abdfghklo [non m]. κρίνεῖ n. εξαῖρεῖται a* (-τε a**). ἀρεῖται b*fo. εξαρατε (–και) dm.

CAP. VI. 1. +εξ (ante υμων) a*dm. υμων (ων mutat. cf. v. 5) b. κρι-σθε n. 2. init. +η am. κρινοῦσιν e. κρίνουσι· m. –ει k*. 3. μητοιγε –βιωτικα d. 4. καθεζετε a. 5. υμων (pro υμιν prim.) gko, in b ω as. ενι (pro εστιν) abcdefghlno, at ἐνι k. [cum Elzev. m]. ουδε εἱς σοφος n. ανακριναι n. 7. –ουν a. ἡττημα kn. –εν abcdefghklmno. αδικεισθαι supra) o*. αδικεισθε (pro αποστερεισθε) n. 8. αλλ' hkln. fin. ; o. 9. βασιλειαν m. –ου o*. κληρονομησουσιν mn. αρσενοκοιτε n. 10. ουτε λεονεκται ουτε κλεπται bcdefghln [non m] o. –ουτε κλεπται k. ου (pro τε tert.) a. μεθυσσοι c. ουτε (pro ου prim.) k. –ου ultimum l*. κληρονο-ισουσιν emn. 11. αλλ' ter a. αλλα ter bno. αλλ' secund. hm. αλλ' rt. c [kl cum Elzev.]. –του κυ l. +ἡμων (post κυ) m. +χυ (post ιυ) lm. ȝ. βρωμασι o. θε (pro δε prim.) m*. fin. το σωματι e. 14. ηγειρεν m. ιας (pro υμας) abc (tacitè) defghklmno. εξεγειρεῖ m. –δια m. 15. ἄρα *e**gk, ἀρα d [non almno] (pro αρας). μελη πορνης g. 16. –ἡ a**bcdef ɩlno [non m]. 17. εστιν mn. fin. ; k. 18. φεύγε o. fin. ἁμαρτανη (errat Millius). 19. τα σωματα cdfgmn. +θυ (post ναος) m*. ὃ (pro οὗ) 20. ἠγορασθητε kn.

CAP. VII. 1. οὑ (pro ὧν) o. ανων (sic v. 26 b*) b. ἁπτεσθε k. ἁπτεσ-ιι n. 2. εχετω γυναικα g. 3. ὀφειλομενην k. 4. ιδιου (υ mutat.) b. ἡ secund. k. 5. αποστερειτε (στ mutatum) b. αποστερητε d. +ουν nte αλληλους) m. σχολασητε a*. ἐπιτοαυτὸ kn. συνερχησθε bdefgklm › [συνερχεσθε c]. ημας (pro υμας) a*o. 7. δε (pro γαρ) d. –και ag. ἐμ' ᾽τὸν n. εχει χαρισμα m. απο (pro εκ) m. +του (ante θυ) c. 8. ταις (*pro* τοις) cko. μηνωσιν n. +οὑτως (*ante* ὡς) m. εγω (*pro* κἀγω) a. 9. γαμειτωσαν f. κρειττον am. −εστι c. πυρουσθε d. 10. παραγγελω n. 11. καταλλαγειτω c. καταλαγητω d. 12. λεγω εγω m. ἀπιστον ?m. οἰκειν (*non v.* 13) k. 13. ειτις b*hk. οὑτος (*pro* αυτος) m. *fin.* αυτην ?o*, τον ανδρα m (*pro* αυτον). 14. επειδη (*pro* επει) a*. ἆρα kn. εστιν *bis* m. 15. −ἡ m. −ἡ k*. εν δε εν ειρηνη o. βεβληκεν (*pro* κεκληκεν) m. 16. γῦναι kn. ἀν ἐρεῖ εἰ (*pro* ανερ ει) m. 17. −ει μη k. ὁ θς εμερισεν k. ὁ κς κεκληκεν k. *In* m θς *et* κς *transponuntur.* οὑτως *bis* cgklmno. 18. επισπαστω c. κεκληται τις (*pro* τις εκληθη *secund.*) am. 19. εστιν *bis* mn. 20. +δε (*post* ἑκαστος) n. κλησῃ ak*. ἡ k. 21. μελλετω d. χρῆσε m. 22. ε (*pro* εν) b*. επελευθερος ?b*. +δε (*post* ὁμοιως) l. χριστου εστι c. 23. ἠγορασθητε k. γινεσθαι m*o. 24. −αδελφοι a* (*habet rubro init. peric.*). −τῳ abcdfghlmno [*non* k]. θεου c. 25. −των m. ἠλεημενος k. 26. ὑπαρχων, o. ἐνεστωσαν a. +τω (*ante* ανθρωπω) c. 27. δεδεσε cn. 28. γαμησης (*pro* γημης) m. +μη (*ante* γημη) k. ἡμαρτεν kmn. ἐξουσιν kn. 29. −ὁτι abc (*tacitè*) fgkmno. εστι, το λοιπον a*. συνεσταλμενος εστι το λοιπον· m. εστι· ἱνα o. [*cum Elzev. dispungunt* bdeghkln]. −το n* (*habet supra et in marg.* n**). +οἱ (*ante* εχοντες *prim.*) abc (*tacitè*) defghklmno. ωσιν mn. 30. ὡς μη χαιροντες *bis script. in* o. 31. του *rescript. in* n. 32. −δε o. *Rasura inter* κῡ *et* πως *in* k. 33. −δε m. −του a*. 34. +και (*post* μεμερισται) abcdefghklmno. ἡ (*pro* ἡ) k. −και (*post* ἁγια) m. +τω (*ante* σωματι) am. +τω (*ante* πνευματι) am. ἡ δε k. 35. συμφερων ?k*. επιβαλλω b*o. ευπαρεδρον m. απαρεδρον o. 36. ἑαυτου (*pro* αὑτου) c. ἡ n. ὑπεραμος b*. ὀφειλει k. οφειλι b*. γενεσθαι a. ποιητω c. γαμητωσαν n. 37. ἑστηκεν ἑδραιος kno. εν τη καρδια (+αυτου dm) ἑδραιος adm (ἑδρ. ad). εχει *mutat. in* k. εν τη ιδια καρδια (−αυτου a) am. −του *secund.* cd. 38. −ὡστε *usque ad* καλως ποιει bd (*habet* b** *in marg.*). +την ἑαυτου παρθενον (*post* εκγαμιζων *prim.*) m. ποιησει *bis* m. και ὁ (*pro* ὁ δε) m. κρειττον m. 39. γυνι n. +και (*ante* κοιμηθη) abefhlo [*non* kmn]. −αυτης *secund.* bc defghklno [*non* m]. ὡ n. γαμϊθηναι k. 40. μακαριωρα a*. οὑτως cgklm no. γαρ (*pro* δε *secund.*) m.

CAP. VIII. 1. −δε a*. φυσιῶ d. οἰκοδομει (*sic v.* 10) k. 2. −δε a. ειτις δε m. ειναι a*, εγνωκεναι m (*pro* ειδεναι). −ουδεπω m. εγνωκεν en, *at* εγνω am. 4. +δε (*post* περι) e. −ουν e. 5. εἶπέρ n. −της fgklmn. 7. γαρ (*pro* δε) m. συνηδησει m*. ἑως αρτι του ειδωλου m. −ὡς cd. εσθιουσιν e. οὖσα k. 8. −δε k* (d *rubro, init. peric.*). ὑμας (*pro* ἡμας) cklm. περισσευωμεν d. 9. αὐτῆ m. 10. ειδωλιω hkmn. καθημενον (*pro* κατακειμενον) l. ουτως m*. ασθενης οὖσα (*pro* ασθενους οντος) k. 11. απολλυται a. *In* m αδελφος *transfertur in locum post* γνωσει. –ση o. ὀν (ν *mutatum*) l. +ὁ (*ante* χριστος) d. 12. οὕτως cgklmno. 13. δι' ὅπερ e. δι' ὁπερ n.

CAP. IX. 1. ουκ ειμι ελευθερος ουκ ειμι αποστολος m. –χριστον a. ἑορακα e. ἑωρακα n. οὖ (*pro* οὐ) m. 2. οὐκ εἰμὶ hm *passim*. –γαρ a*. επιστολης (*pro* αποστολης) m. 3. εμοι (*pro* εμη) g*. *Rasura inter* απο *et* λογια *in* b. ανακρινουσι k. εστιν αὐτη m. 4. μὴ *interrogativè* (*sic vv.* 5, 8, 9, *passim*) lno. ποιειν km. 5. –και *prim.* a**. 6. εργαζεσθε n. 7. ὀψωνιοις k. οψονιοις m*. ποιμαινη ?k. 8. λεγω (*pro* λαλω) f. 9. τω νομω μωσεως f. μωϋσεος gl. μωϋσεως k. φημωσεις m. ἀλοουντα a [kmn *cum Elzev. vv.* 9, 10]. ἀλοωντα begho [*non v.* 10 bo]. μελλει a*ck. 10. ὑμας (*pro* ἡμας *prim.*) m*. ἡμας (*pro* ὑμας) c *sic*. οφειλει επελπιδι m. ὀφειλει k. ἀλοων aefgh [*non* m]. –αυτου c. 11. ὑμων (*pro* ὑμιν) a. πνευτικα και m. μεγα· ει ἡμων ὑμων m. θερισωμεν cm. 12. οἱ (*pro* ει) m. ὑμων εξουσιας m. ἡμων (*pro* ὑμων) bk**n*o. εκκοπην ab*fgko. συνεκκοπην m. 13. εσθιουσι o. +και (*ante* οἱ *secund.*) a. +προσεδρευοντες (*ante* συμμεριζονται) m*. 14. οὕτως (*sic vv.* 15, 24, 26 *bis*) cglno [*non* km]. –το b (*mutat. in* a). καταγγελουσιν a. 15. ου κεχρημαι ουδενι m. τουτων εχρησαμην c. οὕτως (*sic v.* 24 : *non v.* 26 *bis* h) hkm. –μου b. κενωσει k. 16. ευαγγελιζομαι *bis* f, *prim.* k, *secund.* m. 17. +ουκ (*ante* εχω) b*mo. οἰκονομιαν k. 18. μου (*pro* μοι) n. –του χριστου a. 19. –γαρ (*initio pericopes*, d**? *rubro*) ad*. ὦ e*, ὢν k, ὦν n (*pro* ὢν : *v.* 21 ὢν k). 20. –και m [*cætera cum Elzev.*]. 21. θῦ dm. αλλα m. ενομος (*pro* εννομος) bk*. χῦ dm. 22. ασθενεveis o. κερδανω m. *fin.* δωσω o. 23. παντα (*pro* τουτο) m. +μου (*ante* ἱνα) m. 24. *fin.* καταλαβοιτε m*. 25. –ουν k. 26. οὕτως *bis* km (*cf v.* 14). κ (*pro* ουκ) k*. δαιρων b**fgh. 27. αλλα m. ὑποπιαζω ab*cfg**no. ὑποπιεζω el*m [hk *cum Elzev.*]. γενομαι c.

CAP. X. 1. γαρ (*pro* δε) a (δε *rubro* d). αδελφοι αγνοειν k. ὑμων? (*pro* ἡμων) c. ἡσαν k. 2. μωϋσην abcfghklmo [*non* n]. 3. *Deest versus usque ad* εφαγον *in* a* (*habet marg.*). 4. επιον m*, *at* επινον m** (*recenti manu, pro* επιον). ακολουθησης k. ἦν n. 5. –γαρ o. 6. ἡμων *vel* ὑμων *dubium in* k (*cf. v.* 13). –μη o*. επεθυμητας n. εκεινοι o. 7. μη (*pro* μηδε) bo. μηδὲ (*sic etiam* o *vv.* 8, 9, 10) hklmn [*non v.* 8 n]. ειδωλολατρας γινεσθαι ck. οἱ δωλολατραι γινεσθαι m*. ὡσπερ (*pro* ὡς) abcfghlmno [*non* k]. εκαθησεν d. 8. πορνευσωμεν m. επεσαν lm. εικοσιτεσσαρες m. 9. –και *prim.* amn. εξεπειρασαν am. 10. γογγυζητε d. –και *prim.* adm. ηὑτων c. ὀλοθρευτου do *tantum*. 11. παντα δε ταυτα τυπικως συνεβαινεν d. ει (*pro* εις) k.

τελει d. 12. ὁ k. ἑστάναι ko. ἑστᾶναι n. 13. ἡμας (*pro* ὑμας *prim.*) m. ου κατειληφεν a. δυνατος (*pro* πιστος) ch. πειρασθηναι ὑμας m. ποιῆσαι n. −ὑμας *tert.* (*non secund. ut vult Millius*) n, *at* ἡμας k*. 14. δι' ὅπερ n, *at* διο o. αδελφοι (*pro* αγαπητοι) d. ειδωλολατριας abcdfgh**lo. ειδωλολατρεας k. 15. φρονημοις n. +ὑμιν (*ante* λεγω) c. ὑμας b*. 16. εστιν *prim.* g*kno. αυτου (*pro* του χυ *secund.*) n. 18. θυσιας *illegib. in* c. *fin.* εισιν m. 19. +οὐχ' (*ante* ὅτι *prim.*) k. *Transfert* m ειδωλον *et* ειδωλοθυτον. 20. θυουσι m. δαιμονιοις και ου θῶ θυουσιν m. δαιμονων c. 21. +και (*ante* ου *secund.*) a*. δυνασθαι *secund.* k. −ου δυνασθε τραπεζης *ad fin. vers.* m. 22. ισχυρωτεροι (*cf.* I. 25) m. 23. *init.* αυτα k*. εξεστι *prim.* m. οὐ *bis* k. οἰκοδομει k. 24. μηδεὶς (*sic vv.* 25, 27) kno (*non* 27 *in* o). αυτου ?o*. +και (*post* αλλα) bego. 25. μακελω b*. ἀνακρινοντες (*non v.* 27) k. 26. του κυ γαρ a. 27. πορευθηναι a. πορευεσθε m. 28. *Deest versus in* k *usque ad* συνειδησιν (*marg.* k** *habet: at* εστιν [*sic* m], εσθιεται, μυνησαντα). δε *rubro tantum* d. Ἡμιν (Ἡ *rubro*) o. 29. −δε m. εμαυτου (*pro* ἑαυτου) m. −του l. κρινετε n. 30. −δε abcdefghklmno. *Rasura in* b *post* οὐ. 31. −ειτε τι ποιειτε d. 32. και ιουδαιοις γινεσθε m. ἑλλησιν m. 33. παντάπασιν m. ἑαυτου (*pro* εμαυτου) ac. συμφερων d. σωθωσιν mn.

CAP. XI. 1. μιμητε n. γινεσθαι k. 2. −αδελφοι a. −και o. παρεδωκα o. παραδωσεις cg*l*. 3. εστιν emo. −κεφαλη δε γυναικος ὁ ανηρ a* (*habet margo*). +του (*ante* χυ) m. 4. +καλυμμα (*post* προφητευων) bo, (*ante* εχων) h** (*marg.*). *Desunt omnia ab* αὐτου *v.* 4 *usque ad* κεφαλην *v.* 5 *in* o. 5. ακαταλυπτω m. κατ' αἰσχυνει (*non v.* 4) n. αυτης ab*dg**ho. ἐν γαρ και το αυτο εστι a. εξηρημενη d. 6. κειρεσθω a. κειρεσθαι ach. κυρασθαι l. −η ξυρασθαι m. ξηρασθαι ?e*. 7. −γαρ k. ωφειλη ? (*sic v.* 10) g*. *fin.* εστι o. 9. εκτισται d. *fin.* αρνδρα k. 10. διατοῦτο (*sic v.* 30, *etiam* m) l. οφειλη o. ἡ γυνη οφειλει m. −εχειν c. 11. πλην ουτε γυνη χωρις ανδρος ουτε ανηρ χωρις γυναικος εν κω dm. 12. οὑτως cklmo. εκ (*pro* δια) f. 13. εστιν (*sic v.* 14) m. 14. οὐδε k. ἡ φυσις αυτη am. κωμᾶ h*l. −αυτῳ l*. 15. κωμᾶ l. εστι h. κωμη k. αυτη δεδοται adm. −αυτῃ *secund.* efhl. 16. −αἱ d. 17. παραγγελων d. −το *prim.* l. αλλα m. ἡτον d. ἡττον k. συνερχεσθαι ?o*. 18. −τῃ acdefklmo. ὑπαρχην d. 19. γαι (*pro* γαρ) m. εν ὑμιν αἱρεσεις fh. και ἱνα και m*. ἱνα και m**. 20. −ὑμων m*. επιτοαυτο k. 21. πινα m. 22. καταισχυνεται o. ειπω ὑμιν m. εν τουτω; *cum præcedentibus jungunt* c (*tacitè*) ghklo. 23. γαρ *rubro tantum* d (*sic v.* 31). δε (*pro* γαρ) o. −ὁ (*ante* κς) k. +χς (*post* ις) gl**. ἡ o. 24. ειπεν em. ἡμων (*pro* ὑμων) l*. ποιητε k*. 25. αἱμω (*pro* εμῳ) d. ονοματι (*pro* αἱματι) k. αἱατι μου (−εμῳ) m. −ὁσακις αν πινητε adm. 26. ὡσακις m. εαν (pro αν rim.) a. −τουτο c. χυ (pro κυ) k. καταγγελετε a. ἄχρισοῦ g. −οὐ d. ιθη (sic v. 34) k. 27. εσθιει m. −τουτον o. ποτηριον του κυ αναξιως του ι e. ἐνοχος k. +του (ante αἱματος) a**bcefglmo [non k]. 29. Rasura in post αναξιως. 30. διατοῦτο k alii. 31. εκρινομεν a**m. ου γαρ (pro ικ αν) o. εκρινωμεθα d. 32. +του (ante κυ) m. παιδευωμεθα d. 33. δεχεσθαι o*. 34. πινα m*. διαταξωμαι m.

CAP. XII. 1. [π]ερι m* (π m**). θελομεν c. ἀγνοειν k. 2. +ὁτε (post τι) acefghko [non d]. ὁτε (pro ὁτι) m. ἡτε k. ἡγησθε b*o. ανηγεσθε ιl forsan ενηγεσθε m. επαγομενοι l* (forsan m). 3. δυνατε k. 4. εισιν ic v. 5) m. 5. −ὁ k. 6. εισιν· και ὁ αυτος θς ενεργων (−δε, εστι et ὁ) m. ριστος (pro εστι) c. πασι o. 7. −δε m (rubro d). Desunt omnia in o ab φανερωσις v. 7 usque ad διδοται v. 8. 9. −αλλῳ δε ad fin. versûs cm. ἑνι ιro αυτῳ secund.) a. 10. προφητειαι h. −δε quartum l. −αλλῳ δε ἑρμηνεια λωσσων dk. 11. Legitur versus in g rescript. super rasur. 12. −γαρ a ubro d). ενεστιν (pro ἐν εστιν prim.) m. μελλη prim. m. πολλα εχει m. δε a*. −του ἑνος d. ὁντα f. οὑτως cklo. 13. ἑνη d. ἑνι k. οἱτε (pro τε secund.) m. ει (pro ειτε quart.) a*. −εις secund. d. πομα (pro πνευμα) gl. 14. μελλος m. 15, 16. fin. · non; in hkl. 16. οὖς k. Versus eest in o. 16, 17. ὀφθαλμος (non v. 21) k. 17. +ακοη (ante οφθαλμος) *. οσφρισις d. ὀσφρησις k. 18. νῦν l. −αυτων m. Rasura ante καθως ι a. ἠθελησεν k. 21. −δε dm. +ὁ (ante οφθαλμος) abcdfgklm. ειπην d. οσιν h*m. 22. ασθενεσθερα ?f. εστιν m. 23. δο ουμεν a*. ατιμοτερα deghklo. τιθεμεν o*. περισσοτεραν ευσχημοσυνην a. 24. −εχει a*. λλα begmo. συνεκερασεν e. το (pro τῳ) m. 25. σχισματα abcdegk. ερι μνωσιν e. 26. πασχη d, συμπασχει h** (pro πασχει). μελλος prim. m. υμπασχη bchklo. δοξαζηται c. συγχαιρη bdhlo. συνχαιρει m. fin. μελει f. 7. −δε a*h (rubro d). 28. +και (ante τριτον) m. δυναμης d. επειτα (pro τα) a. 30. λαλουσιν m, at λαλωσι c. −μη παντες διερμηνευουσι; d. διερ- ηνευουσιν m. 31. ζηλουται ko**. μειζονα (pro κρειττονα) m. καθυπερ- ολὴν gm. fin. δεικνυμοι k.

CAP. XIII. 1. ἠχων k. αλαλαζων d. 2. ειδω (pro ιδῶ) c (sic). πασαν rim. (ασ mutat.) a. −ὡστε m. μεθισταναι m. ουθεν abc (tacitè) efghklo non dm]. 3. ψωμισω abc (tacitè) defghklmo. μου τα ὑπαρχοντα c. μοι pro μου prim.) l. καυθησομαι b**cdfhk [non lm]. ὠφελουμαι k. 4. −ἡ γαπη tertium a. περπερευεται (περευ mutat.) a. 5. ζηλει l**. 6. +επι nte τη αληθεια) c. 8. παυσωνται c. 9. δε (pro γαρ) abcdefghklo. 10.

ἐλθη k. 11. ὁτε *prim.* ?g. ἡμιν k. ελαλουν ὡς νηπιος m. ὡς νηπιος εφρονουν ὡς νηπιος ελαλουν ck. 12. βλεποιμεν m. +ὡς (*post* αρτι *prim.*) bgo. ἐσοπτρου k. εσοπρου l. +και (*post* εσοπτρου) f. *Rasura in* g *post* καθως. 13. −ἡ l.

CAP. XIV. 2. γλωσσαις bo. −τῳ l. 3. οἰκοδομὴν (*sic vv.* 5, 26, *non* 12) k. 4. οἰκοδομη *prim.* k*. −ὁ δε προφητευων *ad fin. vers.* km. προφυτευων g. 5. −λαλειν k*. κρεισσω (*sic, pro* μειζων) m. διερμηνευει abdfghklo. διερμενευει (+ἡ) c. −ἡ f. 6. αδελφοι *rubro, init. peric. in* ad (*sic v.* 20). ἐλθω k. ὠφελησω k. −ἡ *prim.* c. αποκαλυψη h*. −εν (*ante* διδαχη) b. 7. ἀψυχα k. διδῶ abcdeghklmo. 8. σαλπιγξ φωνην d. φωνη m*. 9. οὑτως cglmo. ὑμεις *dubium in* c. γλωσης e. γνωσθησετε m. 10. τυχη bo. +τω (*ante* κοσμω) bo. −αυτων d. +εστιν (*ante* αφωνον) c. 11. ιδω am. −και ὁ λαλων εν εμοι βαρβαρος a* (*habet marg.*). 12. οὑτως cklmo. επιζηλωται (*pro* επει ζηλωται) m. 14. προσευχομαι fg*. εστιν m: μενει (*pro* εστι) c. 15. −εστι a*. το πνι *prim.* ?b. το νοϊ *prim.* d. −ψαλω *ad fin. vers.* d. +τω (*ante* νοϊ *secund.*) abc (*tacitè*) efghklmo. 16. ευλογης b*o. ευλογησεις ck. ευχαριστεια co. οιδεν ef. οἰδεν m. 17. −γαρ o. ευχαριστης cd αλλα l. 18. λαλω (*pro* λαλων) c. 19. τω νοϊ (−δια) m. −λογους *secund.* c. 20. αδελΦφοι (Φ *rubro*) k. γινεσθαι ?m*. νηπιαζεται k*. φρεσιν *bis* e, *at* φραισι *secund.* f. 21. ἑτερωγλωσσοις k*. ουδε a. 22. −εις o. 23. συνεισελθη o. ἐπὶτὸαυτὸ k. πανταις m. λαλωσι m. ἰδιωται (*non v.* 24) k. 24. −δε *prim.* d*. ἀπιστος k. 25. *init.* −και m. οὑτως *bis* cklo, *prim.* gh, *secund.* m. φανερα *non p. m. in* o. οὑτος (*pro* οὑτω *secund.*) g. απαγγελων d. −ὁ l*. −οντως k. οντως ὁ θς h. *fin.* εν ἡμιν εστιν m. εστιν ce. 26. αδελφοι *rubro in* d. αδελφοι εστιν m. συνεισερχησθε o. −ὑμων a. −διδαχην εχει k. +προφητειαν εχει (*ante* γλωσσαν) f. αποκαλυψιν εχει γλωσσαν εχει d. −αποκαλυψιν εχει m. γινεσθω abcdefghklmo. 27. πλειον a*c. ἀναμέρος klm. −και *secund.* a**. 28. −δε *prim.* a*. ἡ k. λαλητω g*. 29. +η (*ante* δυο) a. λαλητωσαν g*k. −οἱ l*. αλλο o. 31. καθένα l. καθὲν ἁπαντες (*pro* καθ' ἑνα παντες) g. πα^βντες καθένα h* (βα, h**). μανθανωσιν em. 33. ακαταστασιας *dub. in* c. αλλα egk. +και (*post* ὡς) f. −των ἁγιων o*. *fin.* +διδασκω bo. 34. επιτετραπται (ι *prim. mutat.*) e. αυτοις (*pro* αυταις) em. 35. εθελουσιν m. εννοικια (*pro* εν οικω) b. +τω (*ante* οικω) k. οικια o. εσχρον o. γυναιξι λαλειν εν εκκλησια m. 36. κατηντισεν c. 37. +δε (*post* ει) eg. −ἡ l*. −του abcdefghklmo. εντολαι εισιν m. 39. +μου (*post* αδελφοι) cgmo. κωλυητε d. μη κωλυετε γλωσσαις m. 40. +δε (*post* παντα) am. επιστημονως (*pro* ευσχημονως) bo.

CAP. XV. 1. αδελφοι γνωριζω δε ὑμιν a*d (αδελφοι et δε rubro in d:
uente αδελφοι nigro). +μου (post ευαγγελιον) a. ἑστηκατε ko. 2. ζω-
τθε m*. ἠ (pro ει secund.) m. 3. −ἡμων a*. 4. τη ἡμερα τη τριτη m.
ατα τας γραφας b*o. 5. ὠφθη (sic vv. 6, 7, 8) k. επειτα (pro ειτα) m.
init. ειτα a. ἐπάνω k. ἐφ ἅπαξ o. πλειονες km. μενωσιν c. ἄρτι k.
ε f*. 7. επειτα (pro ειτα) aceg. 8. ὡσπερεί τῳ a. ὡσπερεί τω bgho.
περιττω k. ὡσπερείτωι l (τ deest p. m.). ὡσπερί τῶ m. 9. δι' ὅτι e.
. με (pro εμε) h. καινη c*. παντων αυτων a. εκοιπιασα k*. +μονος (post
ε εγω δε) a. 11. οὑτως bis cgklmo. κηρυσωμεν m. επιστευσαμεν o.
. χ̅ν̅ o. λεγουσιν k. λεγουσιν εν ὑμιν τινες a. 13. −ει δε αναστασις
ρων ουκ εστιν ad. 14. εγειγερται o. ἄρα (sic v. 15) k. +και (post αρα)
**lm (αρακη e). κενὶ k. −δε secund. a*m. fin. ἡμων l. 15. εὑρισκωμεθα
αρα (pro δε) m. ηγειρεν bis e. εγηρονται k. 16. χ̅ς̅ εγηγερται super
rur. in g. 17. ὁτι (pro ετι) m. 19. εις χ̅ν̅ (pro εν χ̅ω̅) k. εν χ̅ω̅ ηλπικοτες
ιεν m. ανων bis scriptum in m. 22. και (pro γαρ) o. οὑτως cklo.
−δε h. ἀπ' ἀρχη o. +του (ante χ̅υ̅) abcdefghklmo. παρρουσια k. 25.
ρισοῦ g. −αν a**. ανσθη? (pro αν θη) d. ταυς (pro τους prim.) m*. 27.
ιονότι fk. 28. −ὁταν usque ad τα παντα prim. m. ὑποταγησσεται m.
. fin. πασιν abdefghklmo. 29. ποιησωσιν m. ὁλος d. +αυτων (ante των
ρων secund.) m. αυτων (pro των νεκρων secund.) ad. 30. κινδυνεβομεν d.
. καθημεραν fgh. ἡμετεραν akm (prima litera eras. in h). [cum Elzev.
o]. +αδελφοι (ante ἠν) m. 32. πιομεν m*. αὑριον k. 33. χρηστα ab
efghklmo. [λακωνικη παροιμια· ※ μενανδρου κωμωδιογραφου γνωμη, e marg.].
. −γαρ k. τινες θ̅υ̅ a. τινες εχουσιν m. εχωσι a*. εχουσιν c. ὑμων
ro ὑμιν) bgko. fin. λαλω (pro λεγω) km. 36. αφρων m. ζωοποιηται k*.
οποιειτε o. 37. −το prim. b*o. τῶ σωμα k. κοκον k. τυχη c. τυχει f.
διδωσιν αυτω bdmo. ἡθελησε k. ηθελησεν m. 39. −ἡ αυτη σαρξ k.
αρξ tert. abcdefghklmo. −αλλη δε σαρξ κτηνων km. Post κτηνων in a
ba quatuor eras. αλλοι δε ἰχθυων k. fin. πετεινων a. 40. Tria verba
ısa ante επουρανια in b. 41. αστερων (pro αστερος) h. 42. οὑτως (sic
45, etiam m) cgklo. 43. ενατιμια; k. δοξει f. 44. −εστι σωμα ad fin.
s. k. 47. +της (ante γης) m. 49. χοϊκου super rasur. in b. φορεσωμεν
efhklmo. 50. δυνατε k. κληρομει k. 51. δε (pro μεν) k. κοιμησομεθα
52. ὀφθαλμου k. 53. τουτον prim. k. In g vv. 53, 54 super rasur.
cript. 54. ενδυσητε prim. b*o. ενδυσεται (prim.) ἀάφθ. k*. νίκος (sic
55, 57, at non m v. 57) klm. 55. σε (pro σου prim.) m. ἅδη m. νεικος
56. −δε prim. l. 57. τω θ̅ω̅ δε o. δοντι abdlo. νίκος n. 58. αγα-
τοι μου αδελφοι b. ἑδραιοι k. αμετακινοιτοι e. εις το εργω k. εστιν bn.

CAP. XVI. 1. ευλογιας k** *marg.* l*. ούτως cgklmno. ποιειτε (*pro* ποιησατε) c. 2. σαββατω (*cf.* xiv. 5) m. ότι hmn. ευοδουται h. ὅτ' ἂν (*sic vv.* 3, 5, 12) n. ἐλθω (*sic v.* 12 *bis*) k. ευλογιαι l*. γινονται a*c*dm. 3. +προς ὑμας (*post* παραγενωμαι) bo. δι' επιστολων *cum sequent. in* n. τουτοις o. 4. δε *rubro* d. ἢ k. αξιον η am. πορευθηναι c. πορεβεσθαι d. *fin.* πορευονται b*. 5. δε (*pro* γαρ) m. 6. τυχων e*. ἵν' bo. προπεμψηται c*. πορευσωμαι b*o. πορευομαι fk. 7. αρτι ὑμας k. επιτρεπει cfk**. επιτρεψη dm. 8. ἐπιμένω mn. πεντικοστης d. 9. ανεωγεν n. +οἱ (*ante* αντικειμενοι) d. 10. βλεπεται ?k*. +του (*ante* κῡ) m. κἀγω n. 12. ἀπολλῶ n. ευκαιριση dk. 13. στηκητε b*. στηκτε c. 15. οἰκιαν k. +και φουρτουρνατου και ἀχαϊκου (*post* στεφανα)a. *fin.* αὐτους m. 16. ὑποτασησθε g. κοποιωντι k. 17. κα του (*pro* και *prim.*) m. φορτουρνατου e. φορτουνατου m. ἡμων a, ὑμετερον m (*pro* ὑμων). 18. ανεπαυσαντο m. εμον (*pro* εμοι) c *sic.* επεγινωσκεται m. 19. –ασπαζονται *usque ad* ασιας am. ασπαζεται (*pro* ασπαζονται *secund.*) c. πολλα εν κῶ a. πρισκϋλλα m*. κατοῖκον mn. 20. ασπαζεσθε (*pro* -σασθε) bo. 21. εμη *mutat. in* g. 22. +ἡμων (*post* κῡ) abcdfhkl [*non* m] o. μαρὰ, ναθὰ e. ·μαραναθά fghklo [n *cum Elzev: at in marg. forsan p. m.* τη συρων φωνη μηνευει ὁ κς ηλθεν]. 23. +ἡμων (*post* κῡ) bfkmo. –ιῡ χῡ l. –χῡ n. 24. –εν χῷ ιῡ m.

SUBSCRIPT.: +ἡ (*ante* προς) ak. –προς κορινθιους πρωτη bmo. φιλιππων a, ασιας bo, εφεσου dh (*pro* φιλιππων). του φορτουνατου m. φορτουρνατου e. *fin.* +στι^{x}. ωο gn. +αναγν. ε̄. κε. θ. μαρτυριαι ιζ. στιχ ωο. k. *Nil in* l: *silet* c. τελος της προς κοριν. ᾱ επιστολης ἥτις εγραφη κ.τ.λ. d. εγραφη απο εφεσου δια στεφανα φουρτουνατου αχαϊκου και τιμοθεου. στ^{x} ωο. h.

AD CORINTHIOS SECUNDA.

[CAP. I. 1—4.]

Προς κορινθιους β̄ επιστολη του ἁγιου αποστολου παυλου h. επιστολη (–επιστολη mno) προς κορινθιους δευτερα (β̄, lno) klmno. *Hiat* d.

CAP. I. 1. –του θῡ k. πασι τοις ἁγιοις g. οὖσιν k. ουσι o. 3. –ευλογητος *usque ad* ιῡ χῡ m. οἰκτιρμων k. πῆρ (*pro* θς̄ *secund.*) m. 4. εν (*pro* επι) ln. –ἡμων εις το *usque ad* θλιψει f. δυνασθε m. τοις (*pro* τους) c.

ʳ (*pro* ἧς) m. 5. παθήτα m. οὕτως cgklno. +και (*ante* δια) m. +του
st δια) abcefghklmno. εις ἡμας (*pro* ἡμων) l. 6. ουν (*pro* δε) k. +πολλη
st ὑπομονη) bgo. αυτου (*pro* αυτων) bcgko. ειτε παρακαλουμεθα *usque*
σωτηριας *ponit* m *ante* της ενεργουμενης. και ἡ ελπις ἡμων (ὑμων o) βε-
α ὑπερ ὑμων (ἡμων ao*) *transferunt* abcefghklno *in locum post* πασχομεν.
ἡμων m*. 7. −ὁτι k. οὕτως cgklmno. 8. ἀγνοειν k. περι (*pro*
ρ *prim.*) bm**o. καθυπερβολην gh. εβαρυνθημεν o. ὑπερ δυναμιν
ιρηθημεν m. +την (*ante* δυναμιν) o. ἡμας (*pro* ὑμας *secund.*) c *sic.* 9.
ι. αλλ' am. πεποιθῶτες c. ὡμεν k. εγειραντι b*l*o. 10. τηλλικουτου
ἡμας (*pro* ὑμας) c *sic.* +και (*post* ὁν) m. −ετι hk. 11. ὑμων (*pro* ἡμων
m.) e**. +το (*post* ἱνα) m. εις *bis script. in* c. *fin.* ὑπερ ὑμων ce**fghlmn
ν b) o. 12. ´−ἡμων *prim.* m*. εστιν mn. μαρτυρι b*. ἁγιοτητι (*pro*
λοτητι) m. ειλικρινια el*o. εἰλικρινεια fgn (*sic* II. 17 gn). +του (*ante* θυ̅
m.) am. +και (*ante* ουκ) am. +τη (*ante* σαρκικη) o. σαρκικῆ k. χαρι m,
υματι c (*pro* χαριτι). +του (*ante* θυ̅ *secund.*) lm. ἀνεστράφη μέν m.
επιγινωσκεται k. −η και επιγινωσκετε o*. 14. ἡμεις (*pro* ὑμεις) k.
ου m. +ἡμων (*post* κυ̅) m. *fin.* +χυ̅ bmo. 15. ελθειν προτερον προς
ς a. ελθειν προς ὑμας το προτερον bcdefgklno. προτερον προς ὑμας
ειν m. τοπροτερον h. +και (*post* ἱνα) k. 16. ελθειν (*pro* διελθειν) abo.
ς *bis script. in* l. αφ' (*pro* ὑφ') blo. ἡμων (*pro* ὑμων *secund.*) d. 17.
ιλομενος achmo. ἆρα hln. βουλομαι *prim.* m. ἧ k. εμου bo, ἐμοι k
ο εμοι). οὖ οὖ· k. οὖ οὖ; l. 18. −ὁτι ὁ λογος (*habet marg. p. m.?*) n.
ς (*pro* ὑμας) a*m. οὖ (*sic v.* 19) k. 19. ὁ του θυ̅ γαρ m. ἐμου k.
+του (*ante* θυ̅) fo. διο και δι' αυτου (*pro* και εν αυτῳ) m. 21. δε *rubro*
ὑμας συν ἡμιν ado. ἡμιν b*. ὑμιν, ι *rescript. in* l. +ὁ (*ante* θς̅) l**. 22.
. −ὁ aemo. διδους g. αραβωνα m. 23. μαρτυραν επικαλουμαι τον θν̅ n.
ἐτι ko. ἠλθον k. 24. της πιστεως ὑμων a. χαριτος (*pro* χαρας) m.
ν (*pro* ὑμων *secund.*) k. ἑστηκατε do, *at* ἑστηκαμεν e.

CAP. II. 1. γαρ (*pro* δε) m. ἑμαυτω n. του (*pro* το) b*co. εν λυπη
ς ὑμας ελθειν abcdefghklmno. 3. εγρα m. +επι λυπην (*post* λυπην) a.
ο (*pro* εχω) ad. πεπειθως f. ἡμας (*pro* ὑμας) a. 4. αλλ' ἱνα την αγαπην
αλλ' ἱνα γνωτε την αγαπην l. ἧν k. 5. λε *prim. dub. in* n. αλλα abc
ghklmno. −μη l*. 6. το τοιουτον o*. 7. χαρησασθαι ὑμας k. 8. *Hic*
sus rescriptus in b, *secundâ manu* (*primâ manu amittitur*). δι' ὅ e. 9.
ιτην (*pro* δοκιμην) a*. −ει b*. 10. *init.* ει (*pro* ὧ) f. καγω (*pro* και εγω)
. ὡ κεχαρισμαι ειτι κεχαρισμαι m. ὡ κεχαρισμαι *forsan sec. manu in* g.
ὠτοῦ ?d. 12. −δε l*. εσχικα k. το (*pro* τῳ *secund.*) fl*mn. τίτόν

(*pro* τιτον του) m. 14. δε *rubro* d. θριαβευοντι m*. εν χω̄ ιησου (—τῳ) m. την (*mutat.*) ὀσμην b. ἡμων k. 15. σωζομενης d. απολυμενοις m. 16. +εκ (*ante* θανατου *et* ζωης) m. 17. λοιποι (*pro* πολλοι) defghln [*non* kmo]. ειλικρινιας e. κατ' ἐνωπιον elo. κατεναντι θῡ (—του) m. —του *secundum* a. θ *mutatum in* θῡ *tertio apud* n. λαλουμεν εν χω̄ n*.

CAP. III. 1. αρχωμεθα g*. ἀρχομεθα ?m. ἁλιν l*. ἑαυτοις n*. η (*pro* ει) afm. χριζομεν h*. ὡσπερ m. ἐξ' ὑμων k. 2. —ἡ b *ut videtur*. ὑμων (*pro* ἡμων *secund.*) bko. 3. —εγγεγραμμενη a* (*in marg.* a** και γεγραμμενη). γεγραμμενη bo. αλλ' εν πνι m. λιθενες k. αλλ' εν adfklmno. καρδιαις adfhlno [*non* k]. 4. δε *rubro* d (*sic* ουν v. 12). 5. ἱκανὴ d. αφ' ἑαυτων εσμεν m. λογιζεσθαι ln. 6. αποκτενει acghkm*no. αποκτεννει ef lm**. 7. *init.* ἡ (*pro* ει) m. εγγραμμασιν o**. μωϋσεως bekmn. μωϋσεος dfghlo. 9. τῆ (*pro* ἡ *prim.*) a. ποσω (*pro* πολλῳ) c. περισσευσει ko. 10. ου δεδοξασται abcdefgklmno. εἰνεκεν gm. ἑνεκεν k. ὑπερβαλουσης m*. 12. +την (*ante* τοιαυτην) o. 13. μωϋσης ab**cdefghklmno. —το *prim.* n* (*habet marg. p. m., ut in* I. 18). αυτου (*pro* ἑαυτου) acdm. ἐνάτενισαι g. 14. —αλλ' επωρωθη τα νοηματα αυτων c. επωρωθησαν ?g*. αχρη f. —της *prim.* a*f*. +ἡμερας (*post* σημερον) m. ὅτι (*non* ὅ, τι) ghlmno. εν χω̄ ιησου καταργηται m. *In vv.* 14, 15 *deest in* k *ab* το αυτο καλυμμα *v.* 14 *usque ad* σημερον *v.* 15. 15. αναγινωσκηται cm. μωϋσης ab*efgklmno. εις (*pro* επι) m. 16. —αν k. επιστρεψει k. 17. —το *secund.* k.

CAP. IV. 1. διατοῦτο lmn. ταυτης ?m. ἠλεηθημεν kn. ὀκ n. εγκακουμεν (*cf v.* 16) m. 2. *init.* αλλα cdefghkln [*non* o]. μὴδὲ hklmno. καρδιας (*pro* αληθειας) m. ανθρωπου c. 3. —και o. εστιν *bis* en, *prim.* m. απολυμμενοις l. απολλυμμ̈ενοις o*. *fin.* καλυμμενον b*. 4. ετυφλωσεν e. διαυγασαι d. αυτους (*pro* αυτοις) a. *fin.* +του αορατου aflm. 5. —κυριον d. *fin.* χῡ (*pro* ιν) d. 6. —ὁ *prim.* n. ὑμων (*pro* ἡμων) c. —της δοξης a. χ̄υ ῑυ a*. 7. ἧ k. 8. οὐ (*sic v.* 9, οὐκ *secund.*) k. ου *secund.* o*. εξαπορουμενοι d. 9. εγκαταλιπομενοι c. 10. —ἡμων o. 11. *init.* ει k. —και a. 13. δε *rubro* d. αυτο το πνευμα d. δι' ὃ n (*sic* v. 9), *at* διὸ *v.* 16. 14. +δι' (*ante* ἡμας) k. +του (*ante* ιῡ) g. +χῡ (*post* ιῡ) bo. εξεγερει abfo. *fin.* ἡμιν (*pro* ὑμιν) gmo. 15. ἡμας k*m. ευχαριστειαν kmo. περισσευη bdo. 16. ουγκ (*pro* ουκ) m. εγκακουμεν em. εἰ k. φθειρεται a**d. εσω (*pro* εσωθεν) dm (+ἡμων m). 17. δε (*pro* γαρ) c. παρ' αὐτικα f. καθυπερβολην h.

CAP. V. 1. δε (*pro* γαρ) c. γαρ *rubro* d. οἰκια k. κατοικια o. οἰκοδομην εχομεν εκ θῡ k. οἰκιαν (*sic v.* 2) k. 2. επενδῦσα m. 4. —οἱ m. +τουτω (*post* σκηνει) d. εφ' ὡ (*pro Millii* επειδη) c. ὡν (*pro* ῳ) e. ενδυσασθαι (*pro* εκδυ-

ασθαι) fl*o. 5. +εις (ante τουτο) m. +και χρισας ἡμας (post θς̄) k.
ιδους a. αραβωνα mo. 6. θαρουντες (non v. 8) k. 7. εἰδους ?k. 8. −δε
*do. −εκ a**. απο (pro εκ) m. −τον a. 9. φιλοτιμωμεθα m. ειναι αυτω
. 10. 'Υμας (Υ rubro) o. δει φανερωθηναι k. κομισητε f. κομησηται g*
no*. −προς ἁ επραξεν (sic) n. φαυλον (pro κακον) dm. 11. φανερωμεθα m.
μων o. φανερωσθαι m*. 12. συνιστανωμεν f. αλλ' a. καυχησεως (pro
αυχηματος) n. εχηται k. καυχομενους c. fin. και μη εν καρδια m. 13.
ιτι (pro ειτε prim.) k. ὑμιν mutat. in e. 14. Super rasur. hic versus in g.
5. −ει deln. +χ̄ς (ante ὑπερ secund.) a. Ππαντων secund. (Π rubro) a.
-αρα οἱ παντες usque ad απεθανεν o. μὴκ̀ετι e. μὴκέτι kn. αυτοις (pro
αυτοις) l. παντων (pro αυτων) afhln. +παντων (post αυτων) b**. γερθεντι
. 16. init. ὡστε και ὑμεις m. οὐκ̀ετι e. οὐκέτι hklmn. γινωσκωμεν h.
7. +ανακαινιζεσθε (post κτισις) a. τα παντα καινα bdfko. 18. −δια c.
αταλαγης d. 19. +ὁ (ante θς̄) b*o. ην· εν n. καταλασσων efh*k.
αταλσων n. καταλλασσον d*. θεμενος abc (tacitè) defghklmno. −εν secund.
hl*n. 20. καταλλαγῆτε m. 21. εποιησαν k. γενωμεθα ab**defgklmno.
νομεθα b*c. θῡ δικαιοσυνη d. θῡ (υ mutatum) b.

CAP. VI. 1. δε rubro d. −και abkmo. καινον k*. δεξασθε n. 2. διο
εγει (−γαρ) m. 3. μὴδεμίαν klo. μὴδεμίαν m. μωθη f. fin. +ἡμων d. 4.
υνιστοντες f. +εν διωγμοις (post αναγκαις) a. στενενοχωριαις n. 5. νηστεια
. 6. ἀγνοτητι no. χριστοτητι k. ἀγαπη k. 7. ὀπλων o. +των (ante
ριστερων) bgo. 8. ευφημιας και δυσφημιας m. 9, 10. ὡς λυπουμενοι αει δε
αιροντες, ὡς παιδευομενοι και μη θανατουμενοι a*. 10. μὴδὲν kn. +τα
ante παντα) dl. 11. ὑμων (pro ἡμων prim.) o. ανεωγεν n. +γαρ (ante
ιρδια) k. πεπλατυνται ago. πεπλατηνται m*. 12. στενοχωρησθε secund. ?b*,
t στενοχωρεισθαι prim. c*. ὑμιν (pro ἡμιν) ac. −δε al. fin. ἡμων b*o. 13.
n. ἡμεις b*k*. 14. +δικαιο (post γαρ) a*, eras. rubro. η τις κοινωνια (−δε)
m. προσκοτος k. 15. προσφωνησις m. βελιαρ abc (tacitè) defghklno.
ελιαν m. 16. μετα (pro Millii μετ') c. γαρ rubro d. −γαρ o. −ὁτι m.
εν o. μου (pro μοι) m. 17. δι' ὁ n. αφωρισθητε fmo. ἁπτεσθε k.
πτησθε m. ἁπτεσθαι o*. 18. παντοκρατορ f.

CAP. VII. 2. συγχωρησατε a**. χωρισατε o**. ουδενα ἡδικησαμεν bis
script. d*. ἡδικησαμεν k. 3. οὐ k. +μου (post κατακρισιν) o. αποθανειν cf.
υναποθανην d. 4. ὑπερπερισσευμαι de. πᾶσι k. fin. ὑμων (pro ἡμων) bco.
. οὐδὲμίαν klmno. ανεσιν εσχηκεν d. ανεσι m. εξοθεν n. 6. −ὁ θεος a.
, 7. παρρουσια k. 7. παρεκληθην m. εφ' ὑμὴν ?b*. διαγγελλων a.
παγγελλων k. οδυρμων m. τον εμον ὀδυρμον (pro ὑμων) k. −με m.

8. μεταμεμεληmαι a, μεταμελλομαι dk (*pro* μεταμελομαι). μεταμελομην?b*. 9. μηδενη d. ζημειωθητε m. 10. γαρ *rubro* d. εργαζεται *prim.* m. 11. ἡμας (*pro* ὑμας) a. ποσιν k. κατηργασατο k*m. +εν (*ante* ὑμιν) cd (ὑμηνd*). –αλλα φοβον αλλα επιποθησιν b* (*habet marg.*). αλλ' *quartum* ah. αλλα *sextum* abdfmo. ἀγνους km?o. 12. ἀρα n. ἑνεκεν *ter* adfk. +αλλ' (*ante* ουδε) m. αλλα bo. εινεκα (*pro* εινεκεν *tertium*) l. ὑμων την ὑπερ ἡμων abc (*sic*) efghklmno. ἡμας (*pro* ὑμας) c. 13. διατοῦτο lmn. επι τη παρακλησει δε ὑμων περισσοτερως μαλλον d. –δε e. εν (*pro* επι) m. αναπεπαυτε n. 14. αυτου b*. οὑτως gkmo. ὑμων (*pro* ἡμων) c. προς τιτον (*pro* επι τιτου) m. +εν (*ante* αληθεια *secund.*) g. 15. ἡμας (*pro* ὑμας) m*. αναμημνησκομενου h*. αναμιμνησκομενος kl*. 16. –ουν abc (*tacitè*) defghklno [*non* m]. θαρω d*. –εν *secund.* al.

CAP. VIII. 1. γνωριζω ch. –δε m (*rubro* d). –ὑμιν a*. –αδελφοι a. 2. χαριτος (*pro* χαρας) l: *errat Millius.* καταβάθος k. βαθος o. ὁ καταβαθος (*non* ἡ) d. ἁπλοτητος k, χρηστοτητος m (*pro* ἁπλοτητος). 3. αυθερεται f. 4. δεομενος d. ὑμων b*o. –δεξασθαι ἡμας ab*defglmno [*non* k]. –ἡμας (δεξασθαι *post* κοινωνιαν *locato*) c. 6. ὡστε (*pro* εις το) d. ὑμας (*pro* ἡμας) a. τῖτον no. οὑτως cgklno. επιτελεσει cn. –και *secund.* ck. +εις (*ante* την χαριν) a. 7. αλλα k. πεIισσευετε (I *rubro*) g. παση (η *mutat.*) b. εξ ἡμων ἐν ὑμιν abm. εξ ὑμων εν ὑμιν no. *fin.* περισσευεται c. 8. ὑμετερας a* (*vel* a**) bc (*tacitè*) defghk**lmno. 9. ἡμας (*pro* ὑμας) akl*mo. ὤν k. ἡμεις (*pro* ὑμεις) ab. –ὑμεις c. *fin.* πλουτησωμεν ab*. πλουτισητε g*. 10. ἡμιν (*pro* ὑμιν) o. συμφερον ὑμιν c. –το *prim.* b*o. περισυ c. περυσι (υ *mutat.*) d. ἀποπέρυσι h. 11. επιτελεσατε (ατε *mutat.*) b*. οὑτως ckln o [*non* m]. του (*pro* το *secund.*) k. 12. ἡ (*pro* ει) b. καθ' ὃ *bis* eln, *secund.* m. καθ ὃ *bis* f. αν εχει (*pro* εαν εχῃ) f. 13. ανεσης k. θλιψης k. –αλλ' n. ·*post* καιρω n. 14. –γενηται *prim.* a. ἰσοτης k. 15. ὧ (*pro* ὁ) *bis* f, ὃ m *prim.*, *et forsan secund.* επλεονασεν m. –ὁ *secund.* bg*hko. τὸλίγον m. ὀλιγον n. ηλατονησε d. ηλαττονησεν mn. 16. δε *rubro* d. δοντι deln. –την k. αυτην (ην *mutat.*) b. ἡμων o. 17. σπουδεοτερος f. εξηλθεν n. 18. αυτω (*pro* μετ' αυτου) m. τον αδελφον μετ' αυτου c. ἐπαινος k. 19. χειροτονιθεις k. +εγενετο (*post* ἡμων *prim.*, *quod p. m. videtur deesse*) b. εν (*pro* συν) dm. ὑφ' *bis scriptum in* m. ὑφ' ὑμων b**l. –αυτου d. αυτην (*pro* αυτου) a. *fin.* ἡμων (*pro* ὑμων) abcefghklmno. 20. ὑμας (*pro* ἡμας) bghmo. ἁδροτητι hk. ὑμων (*pro* ἡμων) c. 21. προνοουμεν γαρ (*pro* προνοουμενοι) f. +γαρ (*post* προνοουμενοι) m. +του (*ante* κῦ) k. +των (*ante* ανων) al. [παροιμιων σολομωνος e *marg.*]. 22. νυν c. –πολυ a. προς (*pro* εις) c. 24. ενδειξασθαι k. –και *secund.* abcdefghklmno.

CAP. IX. 1. εστιν e. 2. ἡμων (*pro* ὑμων *prim.*) m. +λεγων (*post* μακεδοσι) m. περισυ c. –εξ a. ηρεθισε k. 3. ἡ *eras. post* ὑπερ *in* f. μερη fk*. +αλλ' (*ante* ἱνα *secund.*) m. ἠτε k. 4. ἐλθωσι k. απαρασκευαστους m. λεγομεν k. ταυτης (*pro* ταυτῃ) a. 5. –ουν a* (*habet marg.*). ἡγησαμην no. προελθωσι προς (*pro* εις) m. προκαταρτησωσι ckn*. προεπηγγελμενην d. κατηγγελμενην k. ἡμων (*pro* ὑμων) e. ταυτην *cum præcedentibus* n. –ὡσπερ l. ὡς (*pro* ὡσπερ) acdefghkmno. 6. –τουτο δε a, *at* αδελφοι (*pro* τουτο δε) m. 7. –καθως o. 8. +εστιν (*post* δε) bo. αυταρκιαν f. –πασαν αυταρκειαν εχοντες k. 9. εδωκεν eo. 10. επιχωρηγων mo. σπειραντι m. βρωσιν, hk *at* · ln. χορηγησει m. χωρηγῆσαι f. χορηγῆσαι lo. πληθυνεῖ m. πληθῆναι f. αυξησει m. αυξῆσαι lo [*verba cum Elzev.* n]. γενηματα abdefghlmno. 11. ἁπλοτητα d (*etiam* k *v.* 13). ἡτι m. ὑμων (*pro* ἡμων) ac. 12. λειτουργειας km. πρὸς αναπληρουσα e. 13. ἁπλοτητι k. –ὑμων m. διακονιας (*pro* κοινωνιας) l. 14. ἡμας (*pro* ὑμας) m. *fin.* ἡμιν m*. 15. –δε a. ἀάνεκδιηγητω a. ανεκδιηγειτω f.

CAP. X. 1. *init.* +και b*o. επιεικειας (*sic*) c. θαρρων d. 2. παρον fl. ἡ n. +επι τισι (*post* λογιζομαι) a*, *eras. rubro.* 4. στρατιᾶς emn, στρατίας l*. τω θω̄ προς *super rasur. rescript. in* h. οχυρωματων kn. 5. αιχμαλωτευοντες e. αἰχμαλωτιζοντες k. 6. εκδηκησαι? g*. +πασαν παραβασιν και (*post* εκδικησαι) a. ὅτ' ἂν n. 7. βλεπετε· lo. παλιν λογιζεσθω d. οὑτως cklno [*non* m]. 8. –τε d. –και *prim.* c. περισσον k. –τι m. καυχησομαι cfk. ἡμων (*pro* ἡμιν) o. οἰκοδομην k. καταίσχυνθησομαι d². 9. +δε (*post* ἱνα) afm. 10. βαρει o. 11. τουτο ὁ λογ. o. οιαι o. ἐπιστολων k. απωντες d². το εργον d². 12. τολμων m. κριναι (*pro* εγκριναι) n. ἐπ' αὑτους (*pro* ἑαυτους *secund.*) o. αλλ' am. ἑαυτοις ἑαυτους *secund.* m. συνιᾶσιν m. 13. ουκ (*pro* ουχι) cd'm, *at* οὐκ' (*sic v.* 15) k. εμερησεν ? g*, *at* εμετρησεν a. *fin.* ἡμων (*pro* ὑμων) d². 14. ἡμας (*pro* ὑμας) d². –γαρ *secund.* d'. ἡμων (*pro* ὑμων) d'd². 15. καυχομενος d'd². –δε cln. αυξομενης h. ἡμων (*pro* ὑμων) d. –εν ὑμιν k. 16. ὑπερεπεκεινα o. –ὑμων c. ευαγγελισασθαι (*pro* καυχησασθαι) m. 17. καυχομενος c. 18. –ὁ *prim.* a*. ἑαυτῶν n. συνισταν d. συνισταμων m. εστιν d.

CAP. XI. 1. Ὀφελον (Ὀ *rubro*) k. ωφελον mn. ανειχεσθε abc (*tacitè*) efghkln**o. ανεχεσθαι d. ανεχεσθε mn*. –μικρον d. –τι abc (*tacitè*) defg hklmo [*habet* n]. τη αφροσυνη bc (*tacitè*) efghklmno (–της n). 2. ζηλω θῡ m. ἡρμοσαμην k. ἑνὶ k. –παρθενον ἁγνην o. –ἁγνην d. κω̄ d, θω̄ m (*pro* χριστῳ). 3. ποτε (*pro* πως) a. –ὁ cd. εὑαν ho. εξηπατησεν ευαν m. οὑτως cgklno [*non* m]. φθαρει d. +και της ἁγνοτητος (*post* ἁπλοτητος) a.

—τον d. *fin.* ἁπλοτητος της εν $\overline{χω}$ k. 4. λαμβανεται d. ἑτερον ευαγγελιον c. εδεξασθαι c*. ανειχεσθε b*efgo. ἠνειχεσθε k. ἄν εἴχεσθε (*sic*) m [n *cum Elzev.*]. 5. μηδὲν ko. 6. +ειμι (*post* ιδιωτης) d. οὐ k. αναγνωσει o. 7. ἐμ' αὐτὸν n, *at* ἑαυτον h (*pro* εμαυτον). —το b*. *Deest; ad finem in* l. 8. εσηλησα d. ὀψωνιον k. οψονιον m. ἡμας (*pro* ὑμας) l. *fin.* ουθενος m. ου κατεναρκησεν ὑμων ἡ καρδια (—ουδενος) d. 9. +μου (*post* αδελφοι) m. απο (α *mutat.*) l. μακεδονιαν d*. αβαρει k. —ὑμιν m* (*at habet* m** *post* εμαυτον). ἑαυτον (*pro* εμαυτον) bo. ετηρησα εμαυτον d. ετηρησα και τηρησω εμαυτον g. 10. —εις εμε a* (*habet marg.*). φραγΐσεται k. σφραγισεται d. [φραγήσεται c]. κλημασι fmn. 11. διατί· ko. 12. *fin.* ὑμεις d. 13. ψευδ' ἀποστολοι n. εργαται· o. μετασχιματιζομενοι d. 14. θαυμα a. μετασχιματιζεται d. 15. —οἱ d. —τα a*. 16. —με *prim.* m. κἀν n. ἀάφρονα *secund.* b. δεξασθαι o*. κάγω μικρον τι abcdefghklmno. καυχησομαι d*. 17. κατα $\overline{κυ}$ λαλω ad, *at* κατα $\overline{ανον}$ λαλω m. 18. καυχησωμαι g*m. 19. φρονημοι c. ανεχεσθαι (*non v.* 20) k. 20. επαιρετε m. εις προσωπον ὑμας mo. δαιρει b**fgh. 21. ὑμεις (*pro* ἡμεις) d. ἠσθενησαμεν k. ησθενηκαμεν m. 22. εισιν *prim.* m. ἀβρααμ hklmno. 23. λεγω (*pro* λαλω) e. ὕπερ hkl**o, *at* ειπερ d. 24. παραμίαν hkm. 25. εραβδισθην acdfkmno. ελιθαστην d. εναβαγησα d. βϊθω ?k. 26. —κινδυνοις ληστων κινδυνοις εκ γενους a. —κινδυνοις εκ γενους κινδυνοις εξ εθνων d. κινδυνοις εξ εθνων· κινδυνοις ληστων· κινδυνοις εκ γενους k. ερημιαις bo. 27. διψη g**l. ψυχω o. γυμνωτητι ?n*. 28. ἐπιστασις k. καθημεραν fgh. καθήμεραν m. 30. καυχασθε o. τὰς (*pro* τα της) k. 31. —ἡμων eghlmn. —$\overline{χυ}$ m. ὢν k. 32. την πολιν (πολλην m*) δαμασκηνων am. δαμασκον (*pro* δαμασκηνων) d.

CAP. XII. 1. δει ου συμφερειμι d. δει; e, δει fgmo, δει· n, δῆ, k (*pro* δη) [l *cum Elzev.*]. ὀπτασιας kn. 2. ἐτῶν k. —του d. οἶδεν (*sic v.* 3) k. +ανθρωπον (*post* τον τοιουτον) bo. 3. —του d. 4. ἡρπαγει d. ανθρωπων b. 5. εἱμὶ d. ασθενιαις dk. 6. θελω m. τις *super rasur. in* m. λογησηται h*k. λογισητε o. —τι m. 7. αποκλυψεων m. ὑπεαιρωμαι ? *prim.* c. ὑπερερωμαι *prim.* k. ὑπεραιρομαι *bis* dm, *secund.* k. εδοθει k. σκωλοψ dm*. σατὰν h**kln. κολαφιζει df. 8. τρεὶς d. 9. ἥδιστα (*non v.* 15) k. επισκηνῶσει d. επισκηνώσει f. 10. δι' ὃ n. ἐναναγκες k. +και (*post* διωγμοις) a. στενοχωριες k. ὅτ' ἂν n. 11. καυχομενος d. ηναγκασετε d. ἠναγκασατε k. ωφελον b*l**. οφειλον d. ουθεν (*sic*) c. ουδενος (*pro* ουδεν *prim.*) g. τον (*pro* των) m. ὑπερλίαν m. *vv.* 11, 12. ει δε και ουδεν ειμι αλλα τα (—μεν) m. 12. μεντοι (*pro* μεν) ac. +γαρ (*ante* σημεια) bo. των αποστολων a*. κατηργασθη d. —εν ὑμιν o. —εν *tertium* a. +τε (*post* σημειοις) a.

vv. 12, 13. κατειργασθη *usque ad* εκκλησιας *rescript. super rasur. in* b. 13. εστι dm. ἡττηθητε ko. εγω αυτος m. +δε (*post* χαρισασθε) d. 14. +τουτο (*post* τριτον) abcdmo. εχω ἑτοιμως c. +χαρισασθε δε μοι την αδικιαν ταυτην (*post* ὑμων *prim.*) d. αλλα *prim.* adefkmn. οφειλη g*. ὀφειλωσι k. γονευσι (*sic*) c. 15. δαπανηθησομαι m. αγαπῶ b*d. 16. γαρ (*pro* δε) d. −ου a* (*habet marg.*). κατεναρκησα (*pro* κατεβαρησα) a. αλλα am. 17. ὂν (*pro* ὧν) g. απεστειλα m. 18. τῖτον *et* τῖτος n. συνεπεστειλα ?m. του *bis script. in* c. μητε (*pro* μη τι) d. ἡμας (*pro* ὑμας) c. ἰχνεσι k. ιχνεσιν m. 19. κατ' ἐνωπιον hlno. κατεναντι θῶ (−του) m. του *at non* θῦ *legitur in* k. χῦ (*pro* θῦ) d. οἰκοδομης (*sic* XIII. 10) k. 20. *init.* φουμαι o. δε (*pro* γαρ) m. οιος (*pro* οιον) d. ερις bdfghk. ερυθιαι d. εριθιαι e. ἐρίθειαι klo. φυσιωσεις· εριθειαι· καταλαλιαι· ψιθυρισμοι k. ακαταστασια a. 21. ταπεινωσει c?dfgkn. +με (*ante* ὁ θς) d. προημαρκοτων a*. προημαρτικοτων a**. ἡμαρτηκοτων l. −μη *secund.* b*. −και μη μετανοησαντων d. πονηρια (*pro* πορνειᾳ) f. ασελγια m [*cætera cum Elzev.*].

CAP. XIII. 1. *init.* +ιδου abcdfo. το (*pro* τουτο) e*. δυο και τριων μαρτυρων a. 2. +γαρ (*post* προειρηκα) o. γραφωνοις m*. προημαρτηκοσιν e. ἡμαρτηκοσι l. πασι d. −ὁτι m. ἐλθω k. +τινος (*ante* ου φεισομαι) a. 3. +δε (*post* επει) d. −εις k*. οὐκ k. δυναται d. δυνατοι g. 4. −ει l*. +και (*post* ει) g. αλλεξῆ εκ m. −και (*ante* ἡμεις) abc (*tacitè*) dehklmno. ασθενωμεν d. εις ὑμας εκ δυναμεως θῦ g. ἡμας (*pro* ὑμας) cd. 5. πειραζεται o*. εἰ (*pro* ἢ) o. εστι do. τοι (*pro* τι) m. +ἆρα (*ante* αδοκιμοι) d. 6. γνωσεσθαι f. γνωζεσθε m*. 7. ευχομεθα m. μηδεν κακον bo. μήδὲν ko. μηθεν m. ὑμεις (*pro* ἡμεις *prim.*) dm. −ἡμεις δοκιμοι φανωμεν αλλ' ἱνα a. τω καλον ?e*. ποιειτε d. ὡμεν k. 8. −αλλ' ὑπερ της αληθειας d. αλλ' ὑπερ της *bis script. in* o. 9. χαιρωμεν f. ὅτ' ἂν n, *at* ὁτι d. ἡτε k. καταρτησιν df. 10. διατοῦτο lmn. μη παρων c. μη παρων μη m. χρησομαι cdk*. ὁ κ̅ς̅ εδωκε μοι a**m. εδωκεν n. −ὁ c. 11. *init.* +το f. καταρτιζεσθαι k. ειρηνεβετε d. +της (*ante* ειρηνης) adfhk. της ειρηνης και της αγαπης m. 12. ασπασασθε (σασθε *mutat.*) b. ασπαζεσθε ko. φιληματι ἁγιω egmn. φιληματι αγαπης (*pro* ἁγιῳ) f. 13. +ἡμων (*post* κῦ) ghkmo. −χῦ k**. +και π̅ρ̅ς̅ (*post* θῦ) dn**. +ειη (*ante* μετα) f.

SUBSCRIPT.: −προς κορινθιους δευτερα bkmo. +επιστολη (*ante* β̅) g. γρα k. −της μακεδονιας abfgkmno. *Silent* ce, *nil habet* l. *Rubro in* d *tantum* τελος της προς κορινθιους β̅ επιστολης· εγραφη απο φιλιππων. εγραφη απο φιλιππων δια τιτου βαρναβα και λουκα· h. *fin.* +στ^χ φς̅ gh. +αναγν. δ̅,

AD GALATAS EPISTOLA.

[Capp. I. 1—II. 9.]

Προς γαλατας επιστολη του ἁγιου αποστολου παυλου h. (+παυλου k) επιστολη προς γαλατας kl. προς γαλατας mno.

Cap. I. 1. δι' ανθρωπων b*co. 2. της γαλατιαις g. 3. χα ις d*. ἀΑπο (A *rubro*) a. −ἡμων al. πρς ἡμων και κῡ ιῡ χῡ d [*non* m]. 4. περι (*pro* ὑπερ) acefmn. +αυτων (*ante* ἡμων *prim.*) d*. εξελειται ὑμας d. ενεστοτος d. −αιωνος e*. πονηρου αιωνος k. +του (*ante* πονηρου) a*. 5. −των αιωνων d. 6. οὑτως cfgklmno. +του (*ante* χῡ) l. 7. οἱ (*pro* ει) d. 8. ὑμεις (*pro* ἡμεις) d. *Rasura in* d *post* αγγελος. ευαγγελιζητε a. ευαγγελιζεται ckn. εβαγγελιζεται d. ὑμας (*pro* ὑμιν *prim.*) fl. παρὸ (*sic v.* 9) ghmo. ευηγγελισαμην f. *vv.* 8, 9. −ὑμιν παρ' ὁ *usque ad* ευαγγελιζεται d* (*habet marg.*). 9. προειρηκα k. ἀρτι (*non v.* 10) k. ὑμιν (*pro* ὑμας) bd**o. 10. αρεσκειν ανοις bo. 11. δε *rubro* d. −αδελφοι a (*habet rubro, initio peric.*). *Rasura in* d *post* αδελφοι. εμου *rescript.* o (ἡμων *p. m.*?). εστιν en. 12. ουδε (*pro* ουτε) m. διδαχθην m. δια a**. −ιῡ h. 13. Ἀκουσατε (Ἀ *rubro*) l. καθυπερβολὴν hm. 14. παραδωσεων e*f. 15. αφωρισας mn. +με (*post* καλεσας) eg. −αὑτου d. 16. ευαγγελιζομαι cfk. −και a*. 17. απηλθον (*pro* ανηλθον) a. απολους k*. αλλα abcefghklmno. προς (*pro* εις *secund.*) d. αρραβιαν g. 18. τρια ετη abo. απηλθον ?e*. εις ἱεροσολυμα *bis script.* a*. επεπειμεινα m*. 21. ὁτι (*pro* επειτα) b*o. κλημματα dfm. −και της κιλικιας d*. 22. ημιν k. της εκκλησιας της ιουδαιας της εν χῡ d. 23. ακουσαντες bo. ἠσαν k. ὑμας (*pro* ἡμας) d. ευαγγελιζετα ?g. επορθη d.

Cap. II. 1. +και (*ante* συμπαραλαβων) d. τῑτον (*sic v.* 3, *passim*) no. 2. *init.* +και k. ανεβη h*. εθνεσιν ekm. κατιδιαν ghm [*non* klno]. δοκουσιν d*m. καινον mn. 3. ἡναγκασθη k. 4. ὑμων (*pro* ἡμων) d. εχωμεν ?d*. καταδουλωσωνται (*sic*) c. 5. ηξαμεν d*. ἡξαμεν n. διαμεινει k. *fin.* ἡμας d* m. 6. ἠσαν k. +δε (*ante* θς) d. ανου θς m. οἱ k. 7. τοὐναντίον k. ειδοτες f. ιδοτες mn. τω ? (*pro* το) o*. 8. −της o. κάμοι afkm. 9. γνωντες d*. δοθει[σαν n**] n*. +εις τα εθνη (*ante* ιακωβος) k.

+και (*ante* κοινωνιας) l*. κοινωνειας k*. +μεν (*post* ἡμεις) abd**fho. περιμην k*. 10. μονων k. μνημονευομεν d*. 11. ηλθεν e, ἠλθε k. αυτου (*pro* αυτῳ) h. αντεστιν ek. κατεγνωσμενως d. ἠν k. 12. γαρ του m. εθνων, m. ὑπεστελε d*. ὑπεστελλεν m. ὑπεστελλε ἑαυτον και αφωριζεν f. ηφωριζεν a. αφοριζεν d*h. αυτον (*pro* ἑαυτον) do*. 13. συνυπαχθηναι a. τη ὑποκρισει αυτων bmo. 14. ιδου m. ορθοποδουσιν d*. εθνηκως ζεις f. εθνικως και ουχ ιουδαικως ζῃς m. –και a. –ουκ *secund.* cd*, *at* ουχι d**l. πως (*pro* τι) m. 15. ἁμαρτλοι c. 16. +ουν (*post* ειδοτες) f. αν (*pro* εαν) d*. ιυ χυ (–εις) a*. –ιυ d* (*habet marg.*) l. δι᾽ ὅτι n. ουκ εξ εργων νομου δικαιωθησεται a. εξ εργων νομου οὐ δικαιωθησεται m. 17. *init.* οἱ (*pro* ει) a*c. δικαιωθηναι ζητουντες c. ἄρα hko. 18. –ταυτα k. οἰκοδομω k. 20. οὐκέτι ehlmn. δε (*pro* δ᾽, *sic*) c. ἡμας (*pro* με) d. *fin.* ἡμων (*pro* εμου) d. 21. ἡ (*pro* ει) d. δικαιωσυνη e. ἆρα k?. ἆρα mn.

CAP. III. 1. ὦ k. εβασκηνε ab* (εβασκηνεν b**o) cghklo [*non* n]. εβασκανεν d*. οφθαλμοις d. 3. επιτελεισθαι d*. 4. επαθατε m. 5. επιχωρηγων o. 6. ἀβρααμ (*sic vv.* 7, 8, 9, 14, 16, 18, 29) fhklmo, n *hic et in v.* 18. επιστευσεν e. *fin.* ; k. 7. γινωσκεται k. 8. τα εθνη δικαιοι m. ενευλογηθησονται abc (*tacitè*) defgklmo. 9. –οἱ d. 10. ὁσι m. εισιν *bis* mo. –ὑπο καταραν εισι d*. +ὁτι (*ante* γεγραπται) a. –επικαταρατος *usque ad* εμμενει a. εμμενη d. –εν *prim.* m. 11. δῆλον ὅτι k. 13. γεννωμενος d. κρεμμαμενος f. 14. γενησεται o. ευλογιαν (*pro* επαγγελιαν) k. πρς (*pro* πνς) o. λαβομεν d. λαβω k. 15. αδελφοι *rubro, init. peric. in* a. κεκηρωμενην d. διατασσεται d*. 16. ερρεθησαν cefh. ερεθησαν d. –ου (λεγει· *cum præced.*) o. –ὡς *prim.* b*. *fin.* εστιν ὁ χς n. 17. προκεκηρωμενην d. τετρακοσια και τριακοντα ετη am. γεγονος e*. γεγωνως k. ακηροι d. ακυρη m. 18. οὐκέτι lmn. εχαρισατο a. 19. ἄχρισοῦ g. οὗ k. ἐλθη k. ὃ (*pro* ᾧ) b**cdghk. επηγγειλατο a. επηγγελτο d. –δι᾽ k. δὲ (*pro* δι᾽) n. διαταγης δι᾽ αγγελου d. 20. –ὁ δε θς εἱς εστιν d* (*habet marg.*). 21. ὀντως n. εκ νομου αν (–ην) a. 22. συνεκλησεν df. ὑφαμαρτιαν m. δοθει d. πιστευουσιν d*km. 23. *init.* προ δε του g. –δε (*init. peric.*) ad*. γαρ (*pro* δε) k. συγκεκλεισμενει k. κρισιν (*pro* πιστιν *secund.*) d. 25. οὐκέτι lmo. 26. ιυ χυ (–εν) a. 27. εναπτισθημεν d*. 28. αρσε f. –εστε a. –ιησου c. 29. ἡμεις d*. ἆρα n.

CAP. IV. 1. γαρ (*pro* δε) d. –χρονον d. –ὁ k. διαφερη δουλος d. ὣν k. 2. ἀλλ᾽ ahk. εστιν m. οἰκονομους k. 3. οὑτως cfgklmno [*non* ah]. ἥμεν *bis* k, *prim.* n. στοιχια d. 4. ηλθεν e. ἠλθε k. γεννωμενον (*pro* γενομενον *prim.*) adefg, *at* γενωμενον k*. 5. νομων ?m*. απολαβομεν d. 6. ὁτε (*pro* ὅτι) m. –αυτου k. ἡμων (*pro* υμων) cln. ἀββά mn. 7. οὐκέτι hlmo. εἶ k. αλλα bgno. κεκληρονομος (*pro* και κληρονομος) d. +ιῡ (*ante* χῡ) dk. 8. –αλλα (*init. peric.*) a* (αλλ' a**). ὅτε (*pro* τοτε) a. +τον (*ante* θῡ) d. φυσει μη οὖσι k. –μη o. 9. +μαλλον (*ante* γνοντες) m. γνωντες d. στοιχια d. στοχεια m. δουλεβειν d. 10. παρατηρεισθαι m. κερους n. ἐνιαυτους k. *fin.* ; ek. 12. γινεσθαι m. επει (*pro* ὅτι) d. 13. –της a. 14. –μου *prim.* m. εξεπτησατε d. εξεπτυσαπτε m. 15. –ην mo. ὀφθαλμους k. εξωρυξαντες d. ἂν, k. ἂν, o. 16. *Non interrogativè* k. 17. *init.* ζηλουσι γαρ f. αλλ' dgk. ἐκκλεισαι k. ὑμας (*pro* ἡμας) abc (*tacitè*) defghklmno. ζηλουται d. ζηλῶτε l**. ζηλωται m. 18. –δε h. τω (*pro* το) f. εν καλου d. παρὴν ἐμὲ (*pro* παρειναι με) d. 19. ωδυνω d. ὠδίνω (*non v.* 27) k. ἄχρισοῦ g. μεχρις m. +ὁ (*ante* χς̄) l. *fin.* ἡμιν m*. 20. –δε a. 22. –ὅτι ac. ἀβρααμ hklmo. 23. γεγενηται m*. δι' επαγγελιας (–της) b*o. 24. αληγορουμενα dfm. εισι δυο (–αι) abdefghklmno. –αἱ (*sic*) c. δουλιαν γενωσα d. 25. δε (*pro* γαρ) m. σινὰ (*sic v.* 24 k) kl. ὄρος m. αρραβια g. συστοιχοῖ f. δουλεβη d. 27. –ἡ ου τικτουσα ῥηξον και βοησον d. οδινουσα f. 28. Ὑμεις (Υ *rubro*) ko. –δε a. αδελφοι *initio, rubro,* a. α ελφοι d*. *Rasura in* a *inter* ισα A *et* κ. 29. ὡς (*pro* ὥσπερ) m. εδιωκεν e. οὕτως cklno [*non* m]. 30. λεγη d. εκβαλλε n. –μη m. κληρονομησει k*mn. *Rasura ante* ελευθερας *in* a. 31. +της (*ante* παιδισκης) d.

CAP. V. 1. –ουν ἧ m. ἧ o. ὑμας (*pro* ἡμας) c. ηλευθερωσεν dn. ἠλευθερωσε k. ελευθερωσεν m. [*non* ουν *post* στηκετε *in* m]. δουλιας d. ενεχεσθαι k. ανεχεσθε l?m. 2. ἴδε blmno. ἴδε k. +μη (*post* εαν) f. περιτεμησθεn*. ἡμας m*. ωφεληση d. 3. –παλιν a. περιτεμνωμενω ah*. ὀφειλετης k. εστι d. *fin.* πληρωσαι (*pro* ποιησαι) b*o. 4. δικαιουσθαι k*. εξεπεσετε ab**cdefghkm [*cum Elzev.* lno]. 5. ὑμεις d. 6. ενεργουμενης d. 7. ενεκοψε abcdfghklmno. ενεκοψεν e. 8. –ἡ d. ὑπομονη d, πλησμονη o (*pro* πεισμονη). 9. *fin.* ζυμει ?m*. 10. φρονησατε d. φρονησεται o*. κρίμα fklmo *passim.* εαν (*pro* αν) bo. *fin.* ἧ k. 11. –εγω δε o. αδελφοι *rubro* (*init. peric.*) a. –ετι *prim.* f, *at rescript. in* b. διωκωμεν d. ἆρα (*ad fin.* ;) m. 12. ωφελον ln. –και b*o. 13. αδελφοι *cum sequent.* m. +ὑμων (*post* ελευθεριαν) m. δουλεβετε d. 14. πεπληρωται m. σεαυτον bc ghno. 15. +τε (*ante* και) c. ὑπ' agm. 16. περιπατῆτε f. 17. δε (*pro* γαρ) d. επιθυμη d. αλληλοις αντικειται m. αντικεινται cdgk. εαν (*pro* αν) a. –ταυτα *secund.* a. ποιητε ταυτα m. 18. αγεσθαι o*. 19. εστιν *prim.* e. μοιχεῖα fk. ἀσελγεία m. 20. ειδωλολατρια a**bcdfghklo.

ιαρμακιαι d. φαρμακεῖαι l. εχθρα b*. ερις bfghko. –ζηλοι *usque ad* αἱ-
ρεσεις a. εριθιαι e. ἐρίθειαι fklmo. αἱρεσεις k. 21. κώμοι f. κωμαι m*.
ιοια k. προεῖπον ek. κληρονομησουσι ao. 22. αγαθοσυνη dm (υν *in* m
mutat.). 23. εστιν dn. 24. *init.* ει (*pro* οἱ) dm. –την a*?. τὴν σαρκα
οῦ χῦ εσταυρῶσαν (αβγδ m**) m. ταις (*pro* τοις) d. παθημασιν m. 25. +δε
post ει) m. στοιχουμεν e. 26. γενωμεθα acg*km. γενομεθα d. προσ-
αλουμενοι a*cdf. αλληλους cdkl, *at* αλληλοιυς a (*pro* αλληλοις).

Cap. VI. 1. –και *prim.* o. προσλειφθῇ d. ανος ὑμων ἐν τινι m. πει-
ασθεὶς d. 3. οκει d. μὴδὲν kno. φρεναπατα ἑαυτον m. φρενατα h*.
. αὐτου adm. ἕξει το καυχημα k. ἤξει (*pro* ἑξει) d. 5. γαρ *rescript. in*
, *at* δε (*pro* γαρ) o. φορτειον d. 6. κατοιχουμενος f. κατοιχουντι f*.
. μυκτηριζετε d. –γαρ f. αν (*pro* εαν) m. +ὁ (*ante* ανος) d. ἑκαστος (*pro*
νθρωπος) bo. θερισῃ d. 8. ὁ *prim.* k. αυτου a*. θερισῃ *bis* d. 9. εγ-
ακωμεν m. θερισωμεν dh*km. εκκλυωμενοι d. 10. ἆρα m. εργαζομεθα
dmn. εις (*pro* προς *prim.*) c. οικιους g*. οἰκειους k. οικους o*. 11.
οικιλοις ὑμων (*pro* πηλικοις ὑμιν) d. *fin.* ; l. 12. εμπροσωπησαι d. –οὑτοι
ἡμας (*pro* ὑμας) a. +ιησου (*post* χῦ) m. διωκονται adfkm. 13.
, (*pro* ουδε) a*. περιτετμημενοι abcefgkmno. ἡμας (*pro* ὑμας) a. ἡ-
ετερα do. καυχησονται cd. 14. –δε z (*init. peric.*). [15. μωϋσεως
ποκρυφοι e *marg.*]. 16. στοιχισουσιν d. *Duo verba erasa post* ιηλ *in* d.
7. μὴδεὶς knz. –εγω k* (*habet* k** *marg.*). 18. –ἡμῶν m. –χριστου e.

Subscript.: *init.* +ἡ a. –προς γαλατας bmo. +δε (*ante* απο) b. *fin.*
στχ σιγ n (*vid. Mill.*). *Nil in* l. d *habet rubro* τελος της επιστολης προς
αλατας: h εγραφη απο ῥωμης· στχ τϟβ. k *tantum* αναγ. β, κεφ. ιβ, μαρτ. ια,
τ. τκ.

AD EPHESIOS EPISTOLA.

[Cap. I. 1—3].

Τοις εφεσιοις μυσταις ταυτα διδασκαλος εσθλος f. προς εφεσιους επιστολη
ου ἁγιου αποστολου παυλου h. προς εφεσιους επιστολη k. επιστολη προς
φεσιους l. προς εφεσιους mno.

Cap. I. 1. οὖσι k. –και m. *fin.* –ιησου d. 2. ἡμων (ἡ *mutat.*) m. 3.
ευλογητος *usque ad* ιυ χυ o. ὑμας (*pro* ἡμας) cd. εν χριστω (*cf. Millium*) c.

4. ὑμας (*pro* ἡμας *prim.*) d. προκαταβολῆς mo. −ἡμας *secund.* d. −και k. κατ᾽ ἐνώπιον lno. του θῡ (*pro* αυτου) k. 5. προωρησας d. −χριστου c. δια ιυ χυ o. αὐτον hklo *alii.* 6. −εις επαινον δοξης της χαριτος αὐτου ab* (*habet* b** *marg.*). ἐπαινον *hoc loco* k. εχαρισεν d. ἠγαπημενω k. 10. οικονομιαν m*. οἰκονομιαν k. ανακεφαλαιωσας l. −τῳ d. τα επι τοις ουρανοις (−τε) acdehln. −τε *tantum* bfgko [m *cum Elzev.*]. −γης a*. 11. *init.* εν αυτω *cum præcedentibus in* n. προωρισθεντος d, προωρισθεντες m. +την (*ante* προθεσιν) l. παντας (*pro* τα παντα) d. −κατα την βουλην *ad fin. vers.* m. 12. −εις *secund.* o. −της abcdefgklmno. πρὸσήλπικοτας d. 13. ἡμεις (*pro* ὑμεις) efg*hklno. ἡμων (*pro* ὑμων) ad. των ἁγιων (*pro* τῳ ἁγιῳ) c. 14. *init.* ὁστις αραβων (−εστιν) d. αραβων m. 15. διατοῦτο lmn. και την εις παντας τους ἁγιους αγαπην m. και την εις παντας αγαπην τους ἁγιους n* (n** *marg. cum Elzev.*). 16. *init.* +αδελφοι (*init. peric.*) k. παβομαι d. ἡμων (*pro* ὑμων *prim.*) d. −ὑμων *secund.* m. +παντοτε (*post* ποιουμενος) bo. 17. −ἡμων g. δωει d. δοη n. 18. ὀφθαλμους k. του (*pro* της *prim.*) m*. καρδιας (*pro* διανοιας) abcefghklmno [*non* d]. 19. ὑμας (*pro* ἡμας) dm. πιστευσαντας g. 20. +των (*ante* νεκρων) bdeghlno [*non* k]. +αυτον (*post* εκαθισεν) d. 21. ὑπὲρ ἄνω kln. −και κυριοτητος a. ὀνοματος ὀνομαζομενον k. ωνομαζομενου d. 22. εδωκεν n. 23. εστιν e. τῶ σωμα k. +τα (*ante* παντα) abcdfghklmno. εν παση πληρωμενου m.

Cap. II. 1. ἡμας (*pro* ὑμας) ade*. παραπτωμασιν dm. *fin.* +ὑμων m. 2. πνς᾽ l. 3. αἰς (*pro* οἰς) a. −παντες a. τε (*pro* ποτε) f. ποιουντας ?m. +ἡμων (*post* διανοιων) k. φυσει τεκνα m. −ὡς d*. 4. αυτου ευσπλαγχνιαν (*pro* αγαπην αυτου) n. ἧν k. ἠγαπησεν kn. 5. παραπτωμασιν εζωοποιησεν d. συνεζωοποιησεν e. σεσωσμεναι ?m*. 6. συνεκαθησεν m. ἐπ᾽ οὐρανοις (*sic.* I. 3, III. 10) n. 7. ὑπερβάλοντα m. 8. ἡμων (*pro* ὑμων) d. +αλλ᾽ εκ (*ante* θῡ) d. 9. *init.* +και m. −εξ m. 10. −γαρ a. επ᾽ acgkm. προητιμασεν m. αυτω (*pro* αυτοις) d. 11. δὶ ὃ n. μνημονεβετε d. ἡμεις (*pro* ὑμεις) k. ποτε ὑμεις m. +τη (*ante* σαρκι *prim.*) b*o. *fin.* αχειροποιητου k. 12. χορις d. απηλλωτριωμενοι mo. επαγγελειας d. των επαγγελιων της διαθηκης bo. 13. νυν m. εγεννηθητε fk. εγενηθητε εγγυς m. 14. μεσοτυχον dm*n. 15. κτηση a. κτισει ck*. αὐτω (*pro* ἑαυτω) m. 16. αποκαταλλαξει dm*?n. *fin.* +στρῶ a* (*eras. rubro*). 17. ειρηνη o. ἡμιν (*pro* ὑμιν) acdfh. 18. −οἱ am. 19. ἄρα m. οὐκ ἔτι ko. συμπολῖται bo. οἰκειοι k. 20. οντως emn. ακρογωνιαιου c (*sic*). ακρογονιαιου m. −ιησου m. 21. −ἡ abcdefghklmno. οἰκοδομη k. αὖξη d. αὖξη f. αὖξει k.

Cap. III. 1. *init.* τουτο d. +ὁ (*ante* παυλος) d. ιυ᾽ n. −ιησου o.

2. ἠκουσατε k. οἰκονομιαν k. 3. εγνωρισεν n. 4. αναγινωσκωντες h*. ευαγγελιω (*pro* μυστηριῳ) k. 5. –εν *prim.* abcefghklmno [*hiat* d]. αποκαλυφθη (υ *mutat.*) h. +ἁγιω (*ante* πνι) g. *fin.* +ἁγιω abco. 6. συμμετωχα m. συνμετοχα n. 7. +εγω (*ante* διακονος) g. δοθησαν f. 8. ελαχιστωτερω k*. –των abcefghklmno. ἁγιω e. –αὐτη n. –εν o. εθνεσι· m. 9. οικονομια (*pro* κοινωνια) abcfghk**lmno. κονομια k*. αποκεκεκρυμμενου c. κτησαντι f. 10. γνωσθῆ hl. –εν τοις επουρανιοις c. ἐπούρανοις k. πολλη ποικιλοσοφια m. πολυποικιλλος ?o. 11. αιωνιων k. +τω (*ante* χῶ) m. 12. ειχομεν o. πεποιθεισῃ f. 13. δι' ὃ n. αἰτουμαι (*sic v.* 20) k. εγκακειν m. ἡμων (*pro* ὑμων *prim.*) c. ειτις (*pro* ἡτις) k. ἥτίς ἐστιν ἡ δοξα n. *fin.* ἡμων (*pro* ὑμων) fm. 14. το πνα (*pro* τον πρα) m. –χριστου o. 15. ουρανω cg. +της (*ante* γης) b. 16. δῶ m. 17. κατοικισαι m. –δια της πιστεως c. 18. ερριζομένοι k. πλᾶτος k. +το (*ante* μηκος) l. και ὑψος και βαθος m. 19. *Prior pars versûs rescripta in* b *super rasur.* αγαπην της γνωσεως a. 20. και (*pro* δε) k. ὑπερεκπερισσοῦ hl. ὑπερέκπερισσοῦ k. 21. κλησια a.

CAP. IV. 2. ταπεινωφροσυνης ?g*m*. 3. ἑνοτητα (*non v.* 13) k. αγαπης *ante* ειρηνης *eras. rubro in* a. 4. –και *secund.* k. *fin.* ἡμων o. 6. επι (*pro* εν) m. ἡμιν (*pro* ὑμιν) abcefghlmno [*non* k: *hiat* d]. 7. –δε a*. ὑμων (*pro* ἡμων) k, *at* ἡμων (*sic*) c. –ἡ k. 8. δι' ὃ (*sic v.* 25) n. ηχμαλωτευσας a* (ῃ a) c. ἠχμαλωτευσας k. δωματα km. 9. –και m. 10. εστιν e. εστι. και ὁ αναβας h. ὑπὲρ ἄνω kln. –παντων a*. 13. καταντησομεν abghkl. ἠλικιας k. 14. μὴκέτι (*sic v.* 17, *at* μὴκέτι *v.* 28) k. μὴκέτι m (*at v.* 28 μηκέτι). μὴκέτι (*sic v.* 28, *at* μὴκέτι *v.* 17) n. ὡμεν k. κλυδονιζομενοι o*. +τη (*ante* πανουργια) a. μεθοδιαν emn. 16. συναρμολογουμενων m*. ἀφης b*kn. ἀφης· a. ενεργειαν· no. –εν μετρῳ c. κατα μερος m*. κατα μερους m**. –του σωματος h. ποιειται του σωματος c. αὐτου (*pro* ἑαυτου) am. 17. +του (*ante* μηκετι) f. καθα k. –τα a*. 18. εσκτισμενοι b*. ζω *super rasur. in* o?. οὐσαν k. την καρδιας h. 19. αυτους (*pro* ἑαυτους) a. +και (*ante* εις) b*. πασης ακαθαρσιας m. *Rasura in* k *inter* πλε *et* ονεξια. 20. οὐχ' klno. *Rasura post* εμαθετε *in* k. 21. ἠκουσατε k. 22. αγαπης (*pro* απατης) o. 23. ανανεουσθε km. 24. ενδυσασθε km. –τον *secund.* k. 25. +την (*ante* αληθειαν) b*ko. *Silet* c *in hoc versu.* 26. *fin.* ἡμων e. 27. μηδὲ cf, μὴδὲ ghklmno (*pro* μητε). διδωτε o. τοπω k. 28. μὴ κέτι e. +ιδιαις (*ante* χερσιν) af. ταις ιδιαις χερσι το αγαθον m. εχει f. 29. οἰκοδομην k. ακουουσιν mo. 31. και οργη και θυμος m. βλασφημιαι ?m. 32. –δε k. +εαν τις προς τινα εχει μομφην (*ante* καθως) f. +τω (*ante* χῶ) k. *fin.* ἡμιν abcefgklno [*non* m].

CAP. V. 1. μι *in* μιμηται *mutat. in* m. –του o. 2. ηγαπησεν (*sic v.* 25) k. υμας m. ημων k, *at* υμων m. 3. –πασα m. και (*pro* η) blo. μηδὲ hk lmo. μηδε n. ονομαζεσθω k. +εν (*ante* αγιοις) l*. 4. η (*pro* και *secund.*) c. και (*pro* η) c. ευτραπελεια m. ανικοντα k. μαλον ευχαριστεια k. 5. ιστε (*pro* εστε) h. χῡ, και a. 6. μηδεὶς k. ερχετε k. 8. ητε k. 9. +αγιου (*ante* πνευματος) a** *rubro.* αγαθοσυνη m. –και δι o. 11. ακαθαρτοις bo, ατακτοις n* (*pro* ακαρποις). ελλεγχετε (*sic v.* 13) k. 13. φωτος, hko. φωτος *cum sequent.* l. φανερουνται cm. 14. δι᾽ ὃ n. εγειρε en. 15. κριβως k*. 16. εισιν em. 17. διατοῦτο klmn. 18. ασωτηα ? h*. +μαλλον (*post* αλλα) m. 19. ωδες b*k. αδοντες k. –και ψαλλοντες m. 20. –ευχαριστουντες o. πρι και θω m. 21. *init.* +και n. υποτασσομενον m*. χῡ (*pro* θεου) cfkm. 23. –ὁ *prim.* acefghkmn. κεφαλη εστι m. +εστι (*ante* της εκκλησιας) g [*habet* m και *secund.*]. 24. ουτως gklmno. *fin.* πατι m. 25. αρδρες k. αυτων m**. 26. ιν᾽ c. εαυτην h. +και (*ante* καθαρισας) h. +εν k, +αυτην n* (*post* καθαρισας). 27. εαυτην (*pro* αυτην) m*. *Jungunt* lno ενδοξον την εκκλησιαν. ριτιδα c. ἢ k. 28. οφειλουσιν k. 29. αλλα abehl no. αλλα τρεφει g. χς (*pro* κς) b*kmo. 30. οστεων k. 31. τη γυναικι (–προς) m. –γυναικα n* (*habet* n** *in marg.*): *in textu* ιδιαν *erasum in loco.* 32. –εις *secund.* bghko. 33. καθένα fg. φοβειται b. φοβητε fo.

CAP. VI. 2. +σου (*post* μρα) m. 4. εκτρεφετε k. +τα τεκνα (*post* εκτρεφετε) a*. παιδια b*. 5. τοις κατασαρκα κυριοις m. +υμων (*post* κυριοις) n*. –της ab*ckno. 6. οφθαλμοδουλιαν b*efhmn. ανθρωποπαρεσκοι m. –του *prim.* ln*. ποιουν *rescript. in* o. *Jungunt* kno εκ ψυχης *cum v.* 7. 7. +ὡς (*post* δουλευοντες) bcl**mo. 8. –ὃ gk*. αν (*pro* εαν) a. –εαν τι n* (*habet marg.: forsan p. m: sic v.* 6). της (*pro* τι) k. εκαστος ὁ εαν (–τι) m. ποιησει c. κομιειτε k. 9. ταυτα (*pro* τα αυτα) c. απειλην (ει *mutat.*) k. οτι και αυτων και υμων m. –ὁ ab**. εστιν *bis* a. εστιν εν (*pro* εστι παρ᾽) b mo. 10. αδελφοι μου *rubro, init. peric.* a. –κῳ και εν τῳ a* (*habet marg.*). 11. *Post* ενδυσασθε *in* n *rasura:* ουν n**. δυνασθε k. μεθοδιας em. 12. υμιν (*pro* ημιν) ac. σαρκαν m. κοσμοκρα (*sic*) c. τους του αιωνος του *rescript. super rasur. in* l. επουνιοις ko. επ᾽ ουνιοις n. 13. διατοῦτο klmn. 14. ημων (*pro* υμων) km*. 15. υποδυσαμενοι ac?kmno. 16. εν (*pro* επι) m. 17. δεξασθαι abcefghlmn?o [*non* k]. 18. αγριπνουντες ? m. καρτερησει o. υπερ (*pro* περι) m. –των g. 19. περι (*pro* υπερ) ag*?. δοθῇ abcefghklmno. *Jungunt* εν παρρησια *cum sequent.* hkm. λαλησαι (*pro* γνωρισαι) m. 20. παρρησιασομαι cf. μαι (*pro* με) f. 21. ειδειτε a. διειδητε ? m. υμεις *mutat. in* m. γνωρισει υμιν m. τυχηκος o. 22. παρακαλεσει co. 23. –χῡ m. 24. αγαποντων fk.

SUBSCRIPT.: +ἡ (*ante* προς) a. −προς εφεσιους bko. *fin.* +στιχ^ω. τιβ n. *Cum Elzev.* m. εγραφη απο ῥωμης δια τυχικου. στ^χ τιβ h. *Nil habet* l. *fin.* +αναγνωσ. β. κεφ. ι. μαρτ. ϛ. στ^χ. τιβ k.

AD PHILIPPENSES EPISTOLA.

[CAPP. I. 1—II. 2.]

Ταυτ' αγορευει παυλος φιλιππησιοισιν f. επιστολη προς φιλιππησιους l. προς φιλιππησιους (φιλίππίσιους m) hkmno (+επιστολη hk).

CAP. I. 1. οὖσιν k. 3. ἡμων m*. 4. *Jungit* k παντοτε *cum v.* 3. +τη (*ante* δεησει) cm. +μου (*ante* ποιουμενος) ck. 5. +της (*ante* πρωτης) km. 6. πειποιθως k. ἐνάρξαμενος e. αχρι a*. χυ ιυ cekn. 7. εστιν m. εμοι δικαιον m. +εν (*ante* τη απολογια) abcefghklmno [*hiat* d]. μοι (*pro* μου *secund.*) kl. 8. επιποθων e. επιθω o*. χῡ ιησου m. 9. τουτω (*pro* τουτο) l. −ετι m. περισσευση km. ενεπιγνωση k. εν (*pro* και *tert.*) c. 10. δοξαζειν m. −ὑμας m. ἡτε k. εἰλικρινεις gn. 11. καρπον *et* τον fmn. χῡ ιησου m. 12. −αδελφοι a* (*habet rubro, init. peric.*). 13. −εν χῷ a*. πασιν m. 14. αφοβως *dubium in* c. +του θῡ (*ante* λογον) f, (*post* λογον) km. λαβειν (*pro* λαλειν) m. *vv.* 15, 16. −κηρυσσουσιν *usque ad* χῡ c. 16. εριθιας e. καταγγελουσιν b*m*. οὐχ' klno. οἰομενοι n. οἰομενος o. θλιψεσιν m. *vv.* 16, 17 *sic leguntur in* km: οἱ μεν εξ αγαπης *ad fin. versûs* 17, *sequente v.* 16, οἱ δε ἐξεριθειας *ad fin. vers.* 18. +ὁτι (*ante* παντι) c. +εν (*ante* αληθεια) m. χαρισομαι h*. 19. δε (*pro* γαρ) mo. αποβησετε k. επιχωρηγιας h*n. 20. καραδοκιαν h. ἀπὸκαρδοκιαν k*. ἐν *secund.* k. νυν και o. μεγαλυνθησετε k. θανατον k. 21. θανειν l. 22. εργου και τι αἱ *rescript. in* h. αἱρησομαι kn. 23. δε (*pro* γαρ *prim.*) abcefghklmno. −γαρ *secund.* abc (*tacitè*) eghklmno [*habet* f]. 24. −εν cko. 26. *fin.* ἡμας m*. 27. μονον· *cum præced. in* o. *Rasura ante* ευαγγελιου *in* a. πολιτευεσθαι d. *Rasura in* k *inter* εἶ *et* τε *prim.* +και (*ante* μια) l. ψυχη· h. 28. πυρομενοι m. απο (*pro* ὑπο) k. −μεν εστιν o. 30. οἱον g. ειδετε abcefghklo [*cum Elzev.* dmn].

CAP. II. 1. τις acdfgkln, τι behmo (*pro* τινα). οἰκτιρμοι k. 2. αυτου (*pro* αυτο) o. φρονειτε adk. συμψυχοι (o *mutat.*) m. το ἐν φρονουντες *cum sequent. in* m. 3. μὴδὲν ko. κατ' lmn. εριθιαν de. μήδέ (*pro* η) m. +κατα (*ante* κενοδοξιαν) m. παντας (*pro* αλληλους) c. 4. σκοπουντες c. σκοπεῖτω k. –και o. το (*pro* τα *secund.*) ahln. +των (*ante* ἑτερων) b*cko. 5. –γαρ km. 6. οὐχ' ἁρπαγμον n. τω?m*. ἴσα hmn. ἴσα k. 7. ὁματι o. 8. ὑπηκος m. 9. δι' ὃ n. 10. καμψει a²cd. ἐπ' ουνιων n. 11. γλωσα m. εξομολογησεται a²dekm. +εἰς (*ante* κυριος) b*o. 12. +και (*ante* νυν) c. –νυν fk. πολω d*. κατεργαζεσθαι m*. 14. ποιειται d. γογγυσμου bc, οργης f, οργεῖς d (*pro* γογγυσμων). 15. *Rasura in* k *ante et post* ε *in* ακεραιοι. σκολιας γενεας k. φαινεσθαι bd. φοστηρες d. 16. καῦχημα k. +και (*post* εμοι) m. καινον *bis* d. 17. λειτουργειας d. λειτουργεια o. 18. ἡμεις· (*pro* ὑμεις) a. 19. ταχεος d. εμψυχω d. 20. ουδεν d*. *In* k *linea post* γαρ *eraditur: legas autem* αυτων ζητουσιν ου τα χριστου, ε *v.* 21. ἰσοψυχον k. τα περι ὑμων γνησιως a. 21. –οἱ d. –του aceklmo. 22. πηρ f. 23. *init.* τουτο o. ὑμων (*pro* εμε) k. ἐξ αὐτης efgklmno. 24. εποιθα l*. 25. ἡγησαμην o. 26. επει (*pro* επειδη) c. ποθων bo. επιποθω (ν *eras.*) d* (–ην), *at* +ἦν (*post* επιποθω) d**. –ην m*. +ιδειν (*post* ὑμας) ab**flmn. δι' ὅτι n. ἠκουσατε k. ἠσθενησε (*non v.* 27) k, ησθενησεν mn. 27. ησθενησεν emo. θανατου l. αλλα *bis* cen. ἠλεησεν k, ελεησεν m, *ante* αυτον *prim.* κἀμε a. λυπην (*pro* λυπη) defghl*mn [*non* ako]. 28. σπουδαιωτερως f. , *ante* παλιν k. αλυπωτερος dkm*n. ὦ k. 29. εχεται d. 30. ηγγισεν e. ἤγγισε k. αναπληρωσει d. πληρωση hln. εμε (*pro* με) bco. λειτουργειας g*.

CAP. III. 1. +ουν (*post* λοιπον) f. αδελφοι *rubro* (*init. peric.*) a. εγραφειν d. οκνηρρον a*. οκνηρος d. +το (*ante* ασφαλες) dhkmn. αφελες o. 2. +δη (*post* βλεπετε) d. 3. εσμετ d. θῡ (*pro* θῳ) abcdefghklmno. πεποιθωτες d. *Rasura in* a *post* πε. 4. εχω k. +και (*post* εχων) o. –και (*ante* εν *prim.*) ano. αλλος δοκει a. αλλως m. 5. περιτομῆ f [*non* aeghklmno]. ὀκταημερος k. βενιαμην dh*. βενειαμειν m*. 6. ζηλον (ζη *mutat.*) m. 7. μη (*pro* μοι) l. μοι ην bco. ἦν k. –τον k. 8. μὲν οὖν ln. –γε acdefghl n [*non* ko]. ιῡ χῡ bfo. ὧν (*pro* ὁν) d. τα *mutat. in* g. –τα o. εζημειωθην o. 9. –εμην o. εν (*pro* εκ *prim.*) d. +του (*ante* νομου) c. +ιυ (*ante* χῡ) c. 10. του γνωναι αυτον *cum præcedent.* aghlmno. δυναμην d*. 11. ὁπως (*pro* ει πως) o. 12. ἤδη *bis* k. –και *secund.* l*. κατελειφθην n. –του acf. ιῡ χῡ a. 13. ουπω b**cgh, οὔπω k (*pro* ου). ου λογιζομαι εμαυτον n*. 14. των (*pro* τα) c. οπισθεν bco, ὀπισω k. σκοπων f. κατασκοπων m. διωκων k. ἀνω k. 15. *init.* ὁσιοι d. φρονουμεν n. 16. το αυτο φρονειν, τω αυτω κανονι στοιχειν m. 17. συμμιται (*sequente rasurâ*) d. συμμιμηται k. συμμι-

μητε h. *οὕτως* fklno [*non* adhm]. *οὕτω* g. *fin.* *ἡμων* o*?. 18. *περιτουσιν* a*. *νυνι* m. *τους σταυρους* o. 19. *οἱ* k. 20. *init.* *ὑμων* c. *ὁ Ρανοις* (P *rubro*) k. *ἐκ ἐξ οὗ* k. 21. *μετασχηματησει* k. *της ταπεινωσεως usque ad σωματι bis script. in* c. *γενεσθε* k. *αυτω* (*pro αυτο*) o. *συμμορφος* d. *δυνασθε* d. *αυτω* (*pro ἑαυτῳ*) b*fko.

CAP. IV. 1. *οὕτως* cfklmno. 2. *ευωδιαν* k. *συντυχειν* dm [*cum Elzev.* aeflno. *Silet* c]. 3. *init.* *ναι* (*pro και*) abcdefgklmno. *γνησιε συζυγε* co. *πρόσλαμβανου* d. —*και* (*ante κλημεντος*) a. 4. +*και* (*ante παλιν*) bo. 5. *ὑμιν* m. *γνωσθειτω* m. 6. *μὴδὲν* ko. *ευχαριστειας* ckmo. *ετηματα* d. *αἰτηματα* k. 7. —*ἡ prim.* a*. 8. —*αδελφοι* c. *ὁσα ἁγνα ὁσα δικαια* m. *ἡτις* (*pro ειτις*) *bis* d. *λογιζεσθαι* k. 9. —*και prim.* a. *ιδετε* dhmn. *πρασεται* d. 10. *εχαριν* dh*k. *ἠδη* k. *ανεθαλλετε* d. *φρονειτε* (*pro εφρονειτε*) d. *ἠκαιρεισθαι* d. *ἠκαὶρεῖσθαι* k*. *ηκαιρεισθε rescriptum in* l. *ηυκαιρεισθε* o. 11. *οὐχ'* (*sic v.* 17) klno. —*ειμι* o. *αυταρκις* dn. 12. *και* (*pro δε*) acghklmno. *χορταζεσθε* o*. *πεινην* e. 13. *δυναμουντι* m. 14. +*και ὑμεις* (*post πλην*) f. *συγκοινωνουντες* l. 15. *init.* *ἰδατε* (*o eras.*) d**. —*δε* fm. *ἡμεις prim.* k*. *φιλιπησιοι* d. *οὐδὲμία* klo. *εκοινωνισεν* d. *δωσεως* g*. 17. —*το* g. *δωμα* h*. *ἐπιζητω secund.* k. 18. *Επεχω* (*Ε rubro*) d. *επαφροδητου* d*. *περι* (*pro παρ'*) c. 19. *πληρώσαι* bcg. *πληρῶσαι* mo. *τον* m [*το* m**?]. *δοξει* f. 20. —*ἡ* kn. *αἰώνας* ko *sæpe.* 21. *συνεργοι* (*pro συν εμοι*) o. 22. —*οἱ prim.* n. *μαλλιστα* d. *καισσαρος* c. *οἰκιας* k. 23. —*ἡμων* bceghmno [*non* k].

SUBSCRIPT.: *init.* +*ἡ* a. —*εγραφη ad fin.* b. *δια* g. *fin.* +*στι*[xx]. $\overline{\text{CH}}$ n. +*αναγν.* $\overline{\beta}$, *κεφ.* $\overline{\zeta}$, *στ.* $\overline{\text{CH}}$, k. *Nil habet* l: *cum Elzev.* d, *at εγραφη απο ῥωμης δια* (*δι'* h) *επαφροδιτου* hkmo.

AD COLOSSENSES.

[CAP. I. 2.]

Ἡ *προς κολασσαεις επιστολη· ταυτα διδασκαλιη κολασσαευσι παρα παυλου* f. *προς κολασσαεις* (?) *επιστολη του ἁγιου αποστολου παυλου* h. *επιστολη προς κολασσαεις* kl. *προς κολασσαεις* bo. *προς κολασαεις* m. *προς κολοσσαεις* n.

CAP. I. 2. *κολασσαις* abc (*tacitè*) d**g [*non ita in titulo* g] hklmo [*non*

efn]. κολασαις d*. −και κυ ιυ χυ dk. 3. ὑπερ (*pro* περι) m. 4. ακουοντες f.
+την (*ante* εν) mo. ἡν εχετε (*pro* την *tert.*) amo. 6. παροντας b. −και
prim. f. −και *secund.* k. εστιν n. +και αυξανομενον (*post* καρποφορουμενον)
ahmo. ἠκουσατε (*sic vv.* 9, 23) k. 7. επαφρᾶ (ᾶ *mutat.*) k. επαφρᾶ l.
εφρᾶ m. ὑμων (*pro* ἡμων) m*. ἡμων (*pro* ὑμων) a*. 8. ὑμιν την ἡμων l, *et*
ὑμιν (*pro* ἡμιν) n. 9. διατοῦτο lmno. αφεὶς d. περι (*pro* ὑπερ) d. αἰτου-
μενοι k. τη επιγνωσει mo. 10. ἡμας (*pro* ὑμας) e*. −ὑμας m. 12. ευχα-
ριστουμεν o. +θῶ και (*ante* πρι) bgko. τω θω πρι m. ὑμας (*pro* ἡμας) a.
την μεριδα (*sic*) c. των ἁγιων (ω *duobus mutatis*) m. 13. ὑμας (*pro* ἡμας) e.
της αγαπης του υἱου k, *super rasur.* 14. −δια του αἱματος αυτου delmno.
15. +της (*ante* κτισεως) fln. 16. −τα *secund.* m. −και *prim.* b*. ὁρατα a.
αορατα k (*pro* ὁρατα). τα αορατα και τα ὁρατα m. εις αυτον και δι' αυτον
m. εκτιστε d. 17. συνεστηκεν mn. 18. ὃ (*pro* ὅς) m. +ἡ (*ante* αρχη) b.
Rasura post πρωτοτοκος *in* a. αυτος εν πασι d. ε[ν] a*. αυτοις (*pro* αυτῳ
secund.) b*. προτευων n. 19. ηυδοκησε o. 20. −δι' αυτου *secund.* f. −τα
ultim. o. επι (*pro* εν) dghln. 21. απηλλοτριομενους c. απηλλωτριωμενους
dmn*. 22. +αυτου (*post* θανατου) ab**chk. κατ' ἐνωπιον fn. 23. ἑδραιοι
kn. −και *secund.* k. −τῃ (*ante* κτισει) mo. κτησει o*. ὑπ' ουρανον (−τον) a.
των ουρανον h*. των ουρανων k. 24. παθημασιν aeflmn. −μου *prim.* acefl
mn. −ὑπερ *prim.* m*. αναπληρω k. θληψεων d. −ὃ m. ὅς (*pro* ὃ) o. −ἡ d.
25. οἰκονομιαν k. οικονομομιαν a. 26. αποκεκρυμενον m*. ὃ νυν (*pro* νυνι δε)
km. εφανε ρωθη (ε *secund. mutat.*) g. 27. ἠθελησεν k. τι το (*pro* τις ὁ) ac
deglmn [*non* ko]. 28. −παντα ανθρωπον *secund.* f. −εν παση σοφια ἱνα πα-
ραστησωμεν παντα ανθρωπον ad. −ιυ h. 29. −και dl. κοποιω g*k. αγων-
ζομενος k. *fin.* +θυ d.

Cap. II. 1. δε (*pro* γαρ) m. +και (*post* γαρ) b*. −εχω a. τω εν m.
λαοδικια dfk. ἑορακασι den. 2. −της πληροφοριας l. −του *secund.* d. −και
(*ante* του χυ) b*o. −και πρς και του χυ m [*cum Elzev.* ln]. 3. σὶ (*pro* εισι)
n*. 4. ὑμας μηδεις (−μη τις) m. 5. ἡμιν (*pro* ὑμιν) o. 7. ερριζομενοι f.
ἐποἰκοδομουμε d. βεβεβαιουμενοι m. −εν *secund.* k. −εν αυτῃ m. 8. *init.*
+αδελφοι bo. συλλαγωγων kl. *fin.* +ιυ f. 9. πλῆρωμα k. 11. −των
ἁμαρτιων f. 12. −των adfklm. 13. ἡμας (*pro* ὑμας) b. −εν fghkm. παραπ-
τωμασιν m. −ὑμων k. +ἡμας aegl**m, +ὑμας dfhkl*no (*post* συνεζωοποιησεν).
συνεζωωποιησεν f [*errant Steph.* 3, *Elzev.*]. εν (*pro* συν) dm. χαρισά m.
ἡμιν (*pro* ὑμιν) a**bfghklno [*non* c]. 14. ἦν k. ὑμιν m*. ηρεν abcfghk.
16. τις ουν m. Ἡμας (Ἡ *rubro*) l. −εν *prim. et secund.* l. −εν *secund.* ad.
ποση d. νεομηνιας l. σαββατου l. σαββατω m. 17. −του abcdefghklno

[*non* m]. 18. μηδεὶς kmn. θελλων m. ·θελων n. ἑορακενden (n *habet* μη). ενμβατευων m. απο (*pro* ὑπο) d. 19. ἀφων abkno. αὔξει *et* αὔξησιν k. αυξη m. 20. –ουν dk. –τῳ abcdefghlmno [*habet* k]. στιχειων d*. δογματιζησθε ?b*. 21. μη (*pro* μηδε) *prim.* o, *secund.* a. μηδὲ *bis* hklm, *prim.* n, *secund.* o. θηγης k. 22. +τας (*ante* διδασκαλιας) bc. 23. εχοντα μεν m. μη (*pro* μεν) a. εθελοθρησκια egl. ταπειφροσυνη a. αφειδεια fgk. της σαρκος (*sic*) c.

CAP. III. 1. εστιν ὁ $\overline{\chi\varsigma}$ m. +ὁ (*ante* εν δεξια) n. 2. –της a. 3. *Rasura post* γαρ *in* a. –τῳ *secund.* delno. 4. ὅτ' ἂν n *passim.* +δε (*post* ὁταν) b**. ὑμων (*pro* ἡμων) k. και τοτε και m (... m**). ὁτε (*pro* τοτε) o. ἡμεις (*pro* ὑμεις) ao. δοξει d. 5. πορνιαν d*. +ασελγειαν (*post* παθος) o. ειτις (*pro* ἡτις) m. ειδωλολατρια abd**fghl. ειδολολατρια d*. 6. ερχετε k. 7. ηὑμεις (*sic*) d. 8. *Rasura ante* κακιαν *in* b. –κακιαν c. 9. –εις a*. 10. κατεικόνα hmo. κτησαντος dk. αυτον (*sic*) c. 11. οὐκ' ἔν n* (ἔνι n**). –τα l. *fin.* $\overline{\chi\varsigma}$ n** (*forsan* $\overline{\theta\varsigma}$ n*). 12. +οἱ ? (*post* ὡς) a* *eras.* –του c. ἠγαπημενοι k. οικτιρμου aelilmno. οἰκτιρμου k. χρηστωτητα d. ταπειφροσυνην (*cf.* II. 23) a. 13. +εν (*ante* αυτοις o*) o. τινα (*pro* τις) l. εχη προς τινα b [*non* o]. εχει cfk. εχητε l. ἡμιν (*pro* ὑμιν) akn. οὑτως cgklno [*non* hm]. *fin.* ἡμεις ?k*. 14. –της l. τελειωτητος d. 15. –ἡ a*d. $\chi\bar{\upsilon}$ (*pro* $\theta\bar{\upsilon}$) m. βραβετω c. 16. $\theta\bar{\upsilon}$ (*pro* $\chi\bar{\upsilon}$) ko. ενοικητω g*. ενηκειτω o*. ἑαυτοις m**, *at* αυτοις m*. –ἑαυτους o. ὠδαις kn. –εν χαριτι d. ευχαριστια (*pro* χαριτι) a. εν χαριτι *cum præcedent.* hkmno. ἀδοντες k. +και ψαλοντες (*post* αδοντες) f. ταις καρδιαις b*. αδοντες εν τω $\kappa\bar{\omega}$ ὑμων τω $\kappa\bar{\omega}$ ταις καρδιαις ὑμων τω $\kappa\bar{\omega}$ m (... m**). 17. ὁτι hklo. εαν (*pro* αν) o. –εν *secund.* ack. +του (*ante* $\kappa\bar{\upsilon}$) acg. 18. –ιδιοις cd*ek. ὡ (*pro* ὡς) m. $\dot{\epsilon}\kappa\bar{\omega}$ e. 19. πικραινεσθαι d. 20. καταπάντα (*sic v.* 22) hkm. ευαρεστον εστιν m. εν (*pro* τῳ) befglmn [*non* k]. 21. παροργιζετε (*pro* εριθιζετε) m. τεκνα (εκ *mutat.*) n. θυμωσιν k. 22. –κατα παντα d. οφθαλμοδουλιαις b**cefln. ὀφθαλμοδουλειαι k. ανθρωποπαρεσκοι m. απλωτητι (*sic*) d. καρδιας (ας *mutat.*) m. 23. ὁτι klmno [*non* h]. αν (*pro* εαν) a*dfm. εργαζομενοι n* (*marg. p.m.* ? *cum Elzev.*). +δουλευοντες (*post* $\kappa\bar{\omega}$) o. 24. ληψεσθε ab*cfghkm. απολη‌ψασθε d. απυληψεσθε ? (απο *illegibile*) n. ανταποδωσιν d. +ὑμων (*post* κληρονομιας) m. –$\chi\bar{\omega}$ m. 25. κομιειτε b. κομισεται dm. κομισηται k. ἠδικησε k. ηδικησεν m.

CAP. IV. 1. ἰσοτητα k. παρεχετε b*f. παρεσθε k*. παρεσχεσθε m. ουρανω m. *fin.* +και προσωποληψια ουκ εστιν εν αυτω o. 2. χαριστια n*. 3. αρα (*pro* ἁμα) m. ἱν' c. ανοιξει k. θυρα m*. διὸ gklmo. 4. αυτω e*. 5. +παση (*ante* σοφια) m. περιπαΤτειτε (T *rubro*) a. *fin.* +ὁτι αἱ ἡμεραι πονηραι εισιν o. 6. ἀλλατι m. ἠρτημενος k*, ἠρτυμενος k**. ὑμας πως δει d. ἐνι dk. 7. τυχηκος d. 8. επεμψα (ψ *mutat.*) m. γνωτε m. ἡμων (*pro* ὑμων *prim.*) m. παρακαλεσει f. καρκαρδιας h*. και παρακαλεση *usque ad* ονησιμω *v.* 9 *desunt in* b* (*habet* b** *marg.*). 9. ὀνησιμω k. –και c. +τω (*ante* αγαπητω) m. γνωριζουσι m. ταδε (*pro* τα ὡδε) l*. ὡδε fghl**mo. 10. ασπαζετε ?g*. –ὁ *prim.* d. σὑναἰχμαλωτος m. ελθει d. ἐλθη k. 12. +ιησου (*post* χυ̅) m. ητε (*pro* στητε) cgl**. –του k. *fin.* χυ̅ (*pro* θυ̅) l. 13. –ὑπερ ὑμων m. 14. –ὁ αγαπητος d. 15. ασπασασθαι h*. λαοδικια g*. 16. ὅτ' ἂν n *pass.* ὑμων (*pro* ὑμιν) k. +αὐτη (*post* επιστολη) m. λαοδικαιων fgn. –και την εκ λαοδικειας m. λαοδικεας c. *Ad* λαοδικεῖας *apponit* e *in marg.* την προς τιμοθεον πρωτην λεγει. –και (*ante* ὑμεις) o. 17. *init.* και πατε m. δικονιαν k. 18. –μου b**. ηὑμων (*cf.* III. 7) d.

SUBSCRIPT.: ἡ προς κολασσαεις a. –προς κολοσσαεις bhkmo. κολασαεις d*. κολασσαεις d**fg. +και τιμοθεου (*post* τυχικου) m. ὀνισημου k. *fin.* +στιχων CH n. +αναγν. β̅, κεφ. ῑ, στ[x] C̅H̅ k. *Nil habet* l.

AD THESSALONICENSES PRIMA.

[CAP. I. 1—8.]

Θετταλικοις πολιταις ταδε κῆρυξ ουρανοφοιτης f. επιστολη προς θεσσαλονικεις ά l. προς θεσσαλονικεις επιστολη πρωτη hk (ά h). προς θεσαλονικεις πρωτη m*. πρωτη επιστολη g. προς θεσσαλονικεις ά n. επιστολη παυλου προς θεσσαλονικεις πρωτη o.

CAP. I. 1. και τιμοθεος και σιλουανος a. +ἡμων (*post* πρ̅ι̅) m. χυ̅ (*pro* χυ̅) d. –ἡμων l. 2. ευχαριστωμεν l*. περι παντων ὑμων παντοτε a. πανπαντων m. –μνειαν ὑμων *ad fin. vers.* c. ποιουμενος d. 3. +και (*post* ὑπομονης) k. εμπροσθε dk. 4. –αδελφοι a*. ἠγαπημενοι kl** (*rubro*). +του (*ante* θυ̅) bkmo. θυ̅, την a [*non* hklmno]. 5. εγεννηθει d. μονω cdk. –εν *tert.* cel no. πληφορια a*. +ὁτι (*ante* οἱοι, *at* οἱοι *vix primâ manu*) m. –εν *quintum* f. 6. –και *secund.* b*. 7. –τη *secund.* cghmo. +εν (*ante* τη αχαΐα) k. 8. –γαρ k. εξηκηται e**. +εν τη (*ante* αχαΐα) abdeghln [*non* m] (+τη *tantum* fko). αλλ' (–και) m. ὑμας (*pro* ἡμας) o. εχει b*. εχειν ὑμας c, *at* εχειν ἡμας m. τί no. 9. ὑμων (*pro* ἡμων) ahkno. απαγγελουσιν dhl*o (-οῦσιν o). εσχομεν abcdefghklmno. επι (*pro* απο) m. 10. ἠγειρεν k, γει *mutat. in* g. +των (*ante* νεκρων) abcdefghklmno. ῥυωμενον n*.

CAP. II. 1. –αυτοι γαρ b. +δε (*post* οιδατε) b**. αδελφοι *in* a *ponitur rubro ante* οιδατε. κενϊ d. 2. –και *prim.* abcdefghklmno. +π̄ρι (*post* θω̄) a. 3. οὐδ᾽ m. 4. –καθως c. οὕτως cgklmno. οὐχ᾽ klnó. ου τοις (*pro* ουχ ὡς) m. –τῳ (*ante* θω̄) b. 5. κολακιας df. –εν *secund.* a. 6. –ουτε ζητουντες εξ ανθρωπων δοξαν (*habet marg.*) b*. οὔτε *secund.* k. απο (*pro* απ᾽) abcdefghklno. 7. *init.* –αλλ᾽ a. ἤπιοι ko, *at* νηπιοι am. θαλπει df km. 8. ἱμηρομενοι c. ὁμειρομενοι demn. ὁμηρομενοι ὑμας (*pro* ὑμων) k. ὁμηρωμενοι f. χ̄υ (*pro* θ̄υ) o. δι᾽ ὅτι n, *at* διο d*. ἡμων (*pro* ἡμιν) agm. *fin.* εγενηθητε am. 9. *initio* αδελφοι *rubro*, a. των κοπων bcl. ὑμων (*pro* ἡμων) f. των μοχθων bcl. –γαρ *secund.* dk. βαρησαι d. ὑμας (*pro* τινα ὑμων) l. –εις c. χ̄υ (*pro* θ̄υ) o. 10. +γαρ (*post* ὑμεις) m. και αμεμπτως και δικαιως b. εγεννηθημεν *ut videtur* m (*cf.* v. 14). 11. εις (*pro* ὡς *prim.*) o. 12. μαρτυρομενοι bcdefgkl**no [*non* m]. περιπατειν km. ἡμας (*pro* ὑμας *prim.*) g*. χ̄υ (*pro* θ̄υ) bc. 13. διατοῦτο klmno. 14. αδελφοι μου μιμηται εγενηθητε a. ιμηται d*. εγενηθηται h. εγεννηθητε mo*?. τα αυτα (*pro* ταυτὰ) abcdefghklmno. συμφιλετων ?h*. 15. των αποκτειναντων τον κ̄ν ῑν (–και) b. ἡμας *bis scriptum* b* [ἡμας c]. εναντιον dm. 17. *init.* ὑμεις (Ὑ *rubro*) d. απορφανισθεντες abc (*tacitè*) defghklmno. ὑμιν (*pro* ὑμων *secund.*) n. επι ? (*pro* εν) l*. 18. *init.* δι᾽ ὃ (*sic* III. 1) n. διοτι m. ἠθελησαμεν k. εισελθειν d. 19. ὑμῖς f, *at* ἡμεις l. εμπροσθε (*cf.* I. 3, III. 9, 13) dk. +θ̄υ και (*ante* κ̄υ) o. –χ̄υ dehl. *v.* 20 *ante* εμπροσθεν *locat* m. 20. ὑμων c.

CAP. III. 1. +και (*post* διο) a. μὴκέτι (*cf v.* 5) k, *at* οὐκ ἔτι n. καταληφθηναι o. 2. ἡμας (*pro* ὑμας *prim.*) a. –ὑμας *secund.* m. ἡμων (*pro* ὑμων) c. 3. *init.* τον ?b*, του l, το b**defghkmno. μὴδένα km*. 4. ἡμεν k. πρωελεγομεν f. θλιβεσθε k. ειδετε c, ὕδατε d (*pro* οιδατε). 5. διατοῦτο (*sic v.* 7) klmno. και εγω c. μὴκέτι kn. την ὑμων πιστιν m. +και την αγαπην (*post* πιστιν) b. γενητε k. κοπως d. *fin.* ὑμων (*pro* ἡμων) k. 6. ὑμας (*pro* ἡμας *prim.*) k. –την *secund.* c. εχεται d. παντοτε *cum sequent.* n. –καθαπερ και ἡμεις ὑμας b*. *fin.* ὑμεις m*. 7. *init.* διὰ του d*. ὑμας (*pro* ὑμιν) d. πασῖ d. αναγκη και θλιψει m. ὑμων (*pro* ἡμων) b*. 8. στηκετε ab*dfgklmno. 9. ανταποδουναι τω θω̄ a*k. ὑπερ (*pro* περι) ck. εν (*pro* επι) m. εμπροσθε dk. –ἡμων a. 10. νυκτος και ἡμερας· *cum præced.* o. ὑπερεκπερισσοῦ l. καταρτησαι d. *fin.* · n. 11. ὑμων (*pro* ἡμων *prim.*) d*. −ὁ *secund.* k. εις (*pro* προς) b. 12. −δε m. περισσεῦσαι kl* mo. καπερ d*. 13. ἡμων (*pro* ὑμων) e. εμπροσθε dk. παρρουσια k*. −ἡμων *secund.* g. −ιῡ χῡ m. −χῡ dln. *fin.* +αμην m.

CAP. IV. 1. −το *prim.* bdeflmno [*habet* k]. λοιπων b*. −ουν d*km. αδελφοι *rubro* a. ερωτω a*. +ἱνα (*ante* καθως *prim.*) m. −ὑμας *secund.* a*. ἡμας (*pro* ὑμας *secund.*) b*. +τω (*ante* θῶ) m. +καθως και περιπατειτε (*post* θῶ)m. *fin.* περισσευσητε k. 2. δεδωκαμεν m. εν κῶ (*pro* δια του κῡ) m. *fin.* +χῡ a. 3. +το (*ante* θελημα) c. −του l. ἅγιασμος k. απεχεσθε dk. 4. +εν (*ante* τιμη) d. 5. παθη cf. ατιμιας (*pro* επιθυμιας) ah. −και a*. +λοιπα (*ante* εθνη) k. −τον n. 6. ὑπερβενειν d*. [τῶ hkno *alii*]. δι' ὅτι n. θεος (*pro* κυριος) c. −και *secund.* c. προειπομεν abcdefghklm [*non* no]. διεμαρτυρομεθα defl*mn [*non* k]. διαμαρτυρομεθα o. 7. ἐπ' m. ἐν k. 8. τοιγαροῦν kn. αθετη d. −και o. αυτου το πνευμα c. ὑμας (*pro* ἡμας) abdefghklmno. 9. εχομεν b. γραφεσθαι (*pro* γραφειν) c. ἡμιν (*pro* ὑμιν) o. −ὑμεις hm. αΑγαπαν (A *rubro*) g. 10. −γαρ a*. 11. και φιλοτιμεισθαι· *cum v.* 10 *in* ekno. −και *tert.* o. −ιδιαις k. χερσι (−ὑμων) m. +και (*post* καθως) m. 12. περιπατειτε adk. ενευσχημονως m. μηδενῶς d. μηδένος k. −χρειαν o. 13. θελομεν abcefghklmno. αδελφοι (−δε) *initio peric. in* a². αγνωειν a². κοιμωμενων en. λυπεισθε b*c. λοιπεισθε d. *Verbum erasum post* καθως *in* d. 14. οὑτως cklno [*non* bhm]. ἑξει m. 15. λεγωμεν a². ὑμεις (*pro* ἡμεις) a²m. περιλοιπομενοι d. κῡ *mutat. in* m. κοιθεντες k*. 16. ἑ (*pro* εν) m* *semel.* −οἱ νεκροι m. πρωτος ?d*. 17. οἱ ζωντες ἡμεις n. ἀπαντησιν g. εις απαντησιν του κῡ *bis script.* o. οὑτως cgklmno [*non* bdh]. 18. −ὡστε a*. παρακαλειται e. −τουτοις a* (*init. peric.*). *fin.* +του πν̄ς g.

CAP. V. 1. χρονον d. −και d. καιρον d. δελφοι m. 2. γαρ (*pro* και) c (*sic*). 3. ὅτ' ἂν n. εφνιδιος dn. αιφνηδιος m. αἱφνιδιος k. εφιστατε k. επισταται m. +ὁ (*ante* ολεθρος) a**. +γαρ (*post* ὡσπερ) c. ωδινη m. −εν l*. εγγαστρι no. 4. οὑκέτι (*pro* ουκ) o. −ἡ c. 5. +γαρ (*post* παντες) cm. 6. ἆρα kmo. −και *prim.* b. λοποι m*. −ὡς και οἱ λοιποι f. −γρηγορωμεν και f. 7. καθευδουσιν h*mo. *fin.* μεθυσιν d*. 8. *init.* ὑμεις a. +υἱοι (*ante* ἡμερας) b, *at* (*post* οντες) af. νηφομεν m. 9. ὁ θς̄ ἡμας m. 10. ὑμων m. ἡτε (*pro* ει τε *prim.*) d. γρηγορουμεν bcgho. καθευδομεν bcfghklmo. 11. δι' ὃ n. οἱκοδομειτε k. εποιειτε d. 12. κοπιόντας o. ε κῶ e* (*sic Col.* III. 18; 2 *Tim.* I. 17). 13. ἡγεισθε bdefgklm. ὑπερεκπερισσοῦ hl. αυτοις (*pro* ἑαυτοις) ab*dlno. 14. −δε a. παραμυθησθε ?f*. παραμυθεισθαι o**. ὀλιγοψυχους k. ανεχεσθε a. αντεχεσθαι d. αντεσχεσθε m. 15. −τινι a*g. —αλλα o. —και *prim.* m. 18. ευχαριστητε f. +εστιν (*post* θῡ) m. —ιησου d. προς (*pro* εις) c. ἡμας (*pro* ὑμας) do. 19. σβεννητε h. σβεννυται l*m*. 21. +δε (*post* παντα) ab**dehlmno. δοκιμαζοντες abcfgkl**o. δοκημαζετε ?d*. 22. απεχεσθαι m. 23. ἡμας (*pro* ὑμας) e*. κω̄ ὑμων ?o. 24. παρακαλων m. ποιησαι a. *fin.* +την ελπιδα ὑμων βεβαιαν a. 25. *Jungit* k αδελφοι *cum v.* 24. +και (*ante* περι) m. 27. ὁρκιζω hko. αναγνωρισθηναι a. 28. —αμην o.

SUBSCRIPT.: *init.* +ἡ a. —προς θεσσαλονικεις πρωτη bhkm. *fin.* +στ^{x} ρϟγ hn. *fin.* +αναγ. ᾱ, κεφ. ζ̄, στ^{x} σ̄ k. *Nil habent* lo: *cum Elzev.* d.

AD THESSALONICENSES SECUNDA.

[CAPP. I. 3—II. 3.]

Ανδρασι θεσσαλιης ταδε δευτερα ουρανιος φως f. προς θεσσαλονικεις δευτερα επιστολη h. ἡ προς θεσσαλονικῆς β̄ επιστολη k. προς θεσσαλονικεις επιστολη β̄ l. προς (θεσσαλονεϊκεις m) θεσσαλονικεις δευτερα (β̄ n) mn. προς θεσσαλονικεις β̄ επιστολη παυλου o.

CAP. I. 3. ὀφειλομεν k. ἑκαστου o. αλληλους d*. 4. ὑμας (*pro* ἡμας) n. αυτους ἡμας m. +της (*ante* πιστεως) af. ἡμων (*pro* ὑμων *secund.*) dm. —ὑμων *secund.* c. θληψεσιν d. ἁς (*pro* αἱς) g**. ανεχεσθαι c*. 5. ενδειγματι της διακρισεως (*marg. p. m.* γρ̄. δικαι) n. δικαιοκρισιας bk. +και (*ante* ὑμας) b [*non* o]. ἡμας (*pro* ὑμας) a. —εις το καταξιωθηναι *usque ad* θῡ n. —και o. 7. αποκαλυψη n. μετα *secund.* m. δυναμαιως d**. ,αυτου *cum sequent.* o. 8. εκδηκησιν d*. +του (*ante* θῡ) abfg. —ἡμων k. —χριστου bdeklno. 9. —του b*. ἀποδόξης (—της) k. 10. ὅτ' ἂν n. ὅτἂν *hic* o. ἐλθη k. —ὁταν ελθη *usque ad* ἁγιοις αὐτου a* (*habet marg.*). —εν *secund.* m. πασιν d. πιστευσασιν bcdeghklmno. ὑμων εφ' ἡμας c. 11. εις ὁ κ *super rasur. in* b. αξιωσαι ?d*. ὑμων (*pro* ἡμων) emn. πληρωσαι ?d. πληρωσει o. αγαθοσυνης dmo. 12. ὃ (*pro* ὁπως) d. —ἡμων *prim.* k. —χῡ *prim.* adegklmno.

CAP. II. 1. ρωτωμεν (*cf.* 1 *Thess.* v. 1) m. ἡμας (*pro* ὑμας) a. περι (*pro* ὑπερ) b. *fin.* ἐπ' αὐτῶ o. 2. ἡμας (*pro* ὑμας) al. θροεισθε cfm. μη (*pro* μητε *quart.*) k*. *fin.* κῡ (*pro* χῡ) mo. 3. *init.* μητι g*. μηδένα ko.

ἐλθῃ k. πρώτων ?d*. απεκαλυφθη ?e*. απωλειας (*sic*) c. απολειας o. 4. ὥτε o. −αυτον a*. ὡς *eras. in* h?. καθησαι d*. ἀποδεικνῦντα hno, αποδεικνυοντα m. 5. μνημονευεται d. −ετι a. 6. οἴδατε o. +ἡμας (*ante* αυτον) a*. αυτου (*pro* ἑαυτου) ckm. 7. ἤδη k. κατεχον o. αρτι· n. 8. ὃν o. την επιφανειαν f. 10. *init.* −και n. απατει f. τοποις (*pro* τοις) o. αδικιας (*pro* αληθειας) c. εδεξατο c. 11. διατοῦτο lmno. 12. −εν dhm. εν τη αδικια *post rasur. in* b. 13. οφειλομεν μεις (−δε *init. peric.*) a. −δε k. ὀφειλομεν ko**. −αδελφοι (*sed rubro, initio versûs*) a. ἠγαπημενοι k. +του (*ante* κῡ) m. εἵλετο k. εἵλατο ?m (*vix legibile*). ἡμας (*pro* ὑμας) l. ἀπαρχῆς hm. 14. +και (*post* ὃ) m. 15. ἆρα ko**. παραδωσεις d. παραδοσις o. επιστολων k. 16. −ὁ *prim.* m*? −ιησους χ̅ς̅ *usque ad* π̅η̅ρ̅ ἡμων f. ι̅ς̅ χ̅ς̅ και *eras. in* k. ὑμας (*pro* ἡμας) c. 17. παρακαλέ m. ἡμων (*pro* ὑμων) o. −ὑμας m. εργω και λογω cm. −και εργῳ d.

CAP. III. 1. αδελφοι προσευχεσθε fo (-θαι o). θ̅ῡ (*pro* κ̅ῡ) k. τρεχει f. 2. ρυσθῶ k. 3. +και (*post* ὃς) m. 4. εφ' ηὑμας d. −και ποιησετε l*n. *fin.* ποιησηται c. ποιησεται o. 5. +την (*ante* ὑπομονην) abcdefghklmno. 6. −αδελφοι (*habet rubro, initio peric.*) a. −παραδοσιν ἡν m. ἣν o. παρελαβον abcdefghklmno. 8. αρτου d. ελαβομεν (*pro* εφαγομεν) delno. ἡμερ m. τινας (*pro* τινα) l. 9. οὐχότι f. οὐχ' kln, *et* οὐκ' n (*sic* οὐχ' *v.* 14, *passim*). τυπων o. 10. ἡμεν k. παρηγγελομεν a. μηδὲ hklmo. 11. ατακτος d*. μηδὲν ko *alii.* εν ὑμιν ατακτως περιπατουντας m. +και (*post* αλλα) g. −αλλα περιεργαζομενους dl. 12. −ἡμων c. ἑαυτον (*pro* ἑαυτων) f. 13. εκκακισητε καλον ποιουντες c. εγκακησητε m. καλλοποιουντες f. το[ν *eras.*] καλον ποιουντες h. 14. ὑμων (*pro* ἡμων) b*m. ·δια της επιστολης *cum sequent.* o. σημειουσθαι d. συναναμιγνυσθαι o. 15. αδελφος d. 16. θ̅ς̅ (*pro* κ̅ς̅ *prim.*) dfg. διαπαντὸς hklmno. *fin.* ἡμων o. 17. οὑτως cklmno [*non* dh]. 18. −ι̅ῡ χ̅ῡ l.

SUBSCRIPT.: *init.* +ἡ a. −προς θεσσαλονικεις δευτερα bfhk. *Habet* b *rubro* εγραφη απο ρωμης· η και απο αθηνων γραφου. +επιστολη (*post* δευτερα) g. ρωμης (*pro* αθηνων) fgh. *Nil habent* lo, *cum Elzev.* dm. *fin.* +στι^{χ} ρ̅ς̅ hn. +αναγ. ᾱ, κεφ. ς̅, στ^{χ} ρ̅ς̅ k.

AD TIMOTHEUM PRIMA.

[Capp. I. 1—II. 8.]

Τιμοθεω ἑταιρω παυλος διελεξατο ταυτα f. προς τιμοθεον πρωτη (ᾱ no) hmno. +επιστολη h. προς τιμοθεον επιστολη πρωτη k. επιστολη προς τιμοθεον πρωτη l.

Cap. I. 1. πρ̅ς̅ (pro σωτηρος) b*. του σωτηρος ἡμων θῡ m. χ̅υ̅ ι̅υ̅ n. 2. +τη (ante πιστει) k. +και (post ι̅υ̅) k. fin. και κ̅ῡ ιησου χ̅ῡ του σωτηρος ἡμων m. 3. παρεκαλεσα (α tert. mutat.) l. παραγγελης b*. ἑτερωδιδασκαλειν do. 4. μὴδὲ klmno. παρεχουσαι m*. οικονομιαν (pro οικοδομιαν) abc (tacitè) defghklmno. 5. παραγγελειας (sic v. 18) o. συνοιδησεως ?k*. συνηδησεως o. 7. διδασκαλοι a*h. λεγουσιν m. 8. +τεκνον τιμοθεε (post ὁτι) o. 9. ασεβεσει ?m*. ασεβεσιν n. πατραλοιαις aben. πατρολωαις dfhkl. πατραλοιας c. πατρολοαις m. πατριλοιαις o. μητραλοιαις abce. μητρολωαις dfghklo. μητρολοαις m. μητρολοιαις n. 10. πορνοι k. −ψευσταις (at rasura) o. −τι m. ὑγιαίνοῦσι d. ὑγειαινουση n. 11. −δοξης τ̣ϱυ a*. ὦ c, οὗ d (pro ὃ). 12. θ̅ω̅ ι̅υ̅ χ̅ω̅ (pro χ̅ῳ̅ ι̅υ̅) o. 13. ποτε (pro προτερον) m. πρωτερον n. αλλα abcdefghklmno. ἠλεηθην (sic v. 16 o) ko. απιστεια d. 14. ὑπερέπλεονασεν d. +ιησου χριστου (post ἡμων: "reliqua postea desunt") c. −της k. 15. ιησους χριστος ck. εν κοσμω (pro εις τον κοσμον) c. 16. διατοῦτο lmn. πρωτον a*cmo. ενδειξητε χ̅ς̅ ι̅ς̅ k. −χ̅ς̅ l. ἁπασαν d. ἀπασαν m. 17. σο (cf. 2 Thess. II. 17, III. 8, infra IV. 7) m.· −και cdefglno. 18. τεκνον τιμοθεε rubro, initio versûs et peric. in a. παρατιθεμαις (αις mutat.) b. σε (pro σοι) m. σοι (pro σε) o. στρατευει f. −εν αυταις k. 19. πιστην d. οἱτινες (pro ἥν τινες) m. ἧν k. ἥν o. ενεναγησαν m. 20. ὑμαιναιος k. παρεδωκε d.

Cap. II. 1. init. +τεκνον τιμοθεε (sic v. 5 init.) o. init. +αδελφοι m. ποιησθαι e. εντευξεις k. ευχαριστειας cdk. 2. −ὑπερ βασιλεων και παντων a*. −εν prim. k. ὀντων o. ἠρεμον kmno. −βιον k. σεμνωτητι d. 3. −καλον και ?l*. −καλον o. ἀποδεκτὸν mn. 4. θελη k. 5. ι̅ς̅ χ̅ς̅ bf. 6. ἰδιοις (non III. 4, 5, &c.) k. μαρτυριον· καιροις h. 7. κῆρυξ lmn. +γαρ (post αληθειαν) d. −εν χριστῳ cn. 8. προσευχαισθαι d. ὁσιας g**k. −και o.

διαλογισμων ac. 9. ὡσαύτως e. ὡσαύτος o. κοσμια c. αἰδοὺς k. ἐδοὺς o. σοφροσυνης do. ·κοσμειν n. κοσμὴν o. 10. ὡς (*pro* ὃ) d. επαγγελομεναις a. 11. μαθανετο o. 12. –δε k. διδασκειν δε γυναικι m. οὐδε (ου *mutat.*) m. 13. εὕα kl. 14. ἠπατηθη o. δη ?m*. εξαπατηθεισα c. γεγονεν dmno. 15. –δε a*. μεινωνωσιν ?n. σοφροσυνης o.

CAP. III. 1. *init.* +τεκνον τιμοθεε (*sic v.* 13, IV. 9, V. 17, VI. 17, *init.*) o. ει τι o. επισκοπος k. ὀρεγεται ko. 2. επισκοπ a*. ανεπιληπτον m. νηφαλειον m. νηφαλεον aefn. νηφαλαιον do [k *cum Elzev.*]. [τον επισκοπον. (*sic*): *at* νηφαλιον c]. σοφρονα d. 3. –μη αισχροκερδη n. +μη πλεονεκτην (*post* αισχροκερδη) o. επιεικει d. αφιλαργυρος d**. 5. προστειναι k. δυναται *eras. rubro inter* ου *et* κ *in* ουκ, a. οιδεν emno. ειδε (*pro* οιδε) h. επιμελησηται d. 6. εμπεσει o. 7. εχην καλην k. εξωθε k. ὀνειδισμον ko. 8. ὡσσαυτως b*. ὡσαύτως (*sic v.* 11) o. μη *prim.* (μ d**) d. διαλογους (*pro* διλογους) m. –μη οινω πολλω προσεχοντας (*habet marg.*) b*. αισχροκερδεις *mutat. in* d. *vv.* 8, 9. –μη αισχροκερδεις εχοντας o. 9. αναστασεως (*pro* πιστεως) o. 10. ανεκλητοι a. 11. μη *eras. ante* νηφαλιους *in* l. νηφαλεας a. νηφαλαιους df. νηφαλεους el*mno [*sic Millius, et in v.* 2: *at* νηφαλιους c]. πασιν d*?mo. 12. *Rasura in* d *post* διακον. ,ανδρες *cum sequent.* m. προισταμεμενοι d. οικον o. 13. ἑι (*pro* οἱ, ἑ *rubro*) k. διαονησαντες ?m*. 14. γραφων k. ελπιζω h*m. ταχειον o. 15. +και (*ante* βραδυνω) n. ἱν' ιδης m. –δει d. ζωντος· lmn (*etiam* · *in fine versûs* mn). στῦλος hn. ἑδραιωμα ako. 16. *init.* +ὁ o. ὁμολογουμενος d*. ·ὁ θς m [θς *disertè* abdefghklno: *silet* c]. εφανερωθει d.

CAP. IV. 1. *init.* τωι e. ῥητος d. +απο (*ante* της πιστεως) a. πλανης (*pro* πλανοις) acfhkmo. διδασκαλιας m. 2. εν ὑποκρισει· *cum præcedent.* m. καικαυστηριασμενων d. κεκαυτηριασμενω h*. κεκαυστηριασμενων mo. 3. κωλοιοντων d. εκτησεν d*. ευχαριστειας cd*k. 4. μετ' m. ευχαριστειας cdk. *Post* ευχαριστιας m *habet* τοις πιστοις *v.* 3 *usque ad* μετ' ευχαριστιας *v.* 4. λαβανομεν o. 6. ὑποθεμενος o. καλως dk*. χυ ιυ egm. εκτρεφομενος c. τη καλη διδασκαλια d. –καλης k. 7. γραωδης o. γυμνα m. σεαὐτην o. 8. ὀλιγον ko. ωφεληθμος *bis* c, *secund.* df. ὠφελιμος *bis* k, *prim.* n. εστιν ωφεληθμος *secund.* fk (ὠφελιμος k). επαγγελιας deghlmno. 10. τουτω d. κοποιωμεν k. ωνειδιζομεθα f. ὀνειδιζομεθα ko. αγωνιζομεθα (*pro* ονειδιζομεθα) c. ζοντι o. μαλλιστα.a*. +δε (*ante* πιστων) ack. 11. παραγγελε a*lm*n. δηδασκε ?e*. 12. μηδείς k. καταφρονητω h*. καταφρονηται o. γενοῦ df. ἀγνεια (*sic* v. 2) k. 13. ερχωμαι e. διδασκαλεια ?m*. 14. αμελη k. δι' (*pro* μετα) c. πρεσβυτερου m. 15. ἡσθη ?d*, ἠσθα k (*pro* ισθι). ἢ k. πᾶσι af. 16. προσεχε (*pro* επεχε) a. –επεχε *usque ad* διδασκαλιᾳ c. σεαυτῷ mo. –τῃ o. ακοοντας h.

CAP. V. 1. επιπληξεις cf. νεότερους d. –ὡς *secund.* n*. 2. ἁγνει n*. 3. *Rasura in* k *inter* ὄντ *et* ως. 4. *init.* ἡ (*pro* ει) o. οικον· m. αμυβας d. αποδιδονε n. εστιν aefghkln. –καλον και acefghkln [*non* mo]. 5. ὀντως (*sic v.* 16) k. +μη (*ante* χηρα) o. μεμωνωμενη h*m*?. ἠλπικεν k. 6. τεθνηκεν dmno. 7. ὡσιν k. 8. οἰκειων k. προνοειται k. ἠρνηται o. 9. ἐξηκοντα ko. ἐξηκοντα ετων l. 10. ἐργοις e. καλλοις m. η (*pro* ει *secund.*) o. επηκολουθησεν mn. επικολουθησε ko (-σεν o). 11. *init.* τέρας o. –δε (*init. peric.*) dh. ὅτ' ἂν no. καταστρινιασωσι d. 12. πιστην dk. την πιστιν την πρωτην o. ἠθετησαν ko. 13. μανθανουσαι· l. οικειας do. οἰκιας k. 14. γαρ (*pro* ουν) a*. τας νεοτερας m. +χηρας (*ante* γαμειν) acf. οἰκοδεσποτειν k. μὴδεμίαν kl. μήδεμίαν m*. μηδὲμίαν n. λοιδωριας dh*. 15. ηδει d. ἠδη k. ὀπισω k. 16. ειτεις ?m*. –εχει n* (*habet marg., forsan p. m.*). επαρκεσει d. –μη e*. οντες m, οὑτως o (*pro* οντως). 17. οἱ *bis* o. μαλλιστα d*o. κοποιωντες k. διδασκαλεια o. 18. αλοουντα a. ἀλοωντα befghl. μη (*pro* ου) o. φιμωσης c. φημωσεις ?e*. ου φημωσεις βουν ἀλοωντα m. μὴσθου o*. 19. καταδεχου o. 20. εχωσιν m. 21. μαρτυρομαι a*. +ἡμων (*post* κῦ) l. μὴδὲν kn. μηδὲ l*o. προσκλησιν abdefgklmno. 22. μὴδενὶ kno. επιτιθε m. μὴδὲ klmno. 23. μὴκέτι km. μὴκέτι n. ὑδρωποτει m. ὑδροποτη o. οἰνω o. ὀλιγω ko. πικνας dm*?. 24. –ανθρωπων mn. –αἱ ἁμαρτιαι o. επακολουθουσαι a. επακουλουθουσι ?d*. 25. ὡσαύτως o. τα εργα τα καλα m. καλλα d. εισι (*pro* εστι) cko. εστιν m. –τα *secund.* l* *ut videtur.* κριβηναι h. δυνανται abcdfhlno [*non* km].

CAP. VI. 1. δουλειας (*pro* δουλοι) b*k. οικιους (*pro* ιδιους) o. βλασφημειται ac. 2. εχοντας km (*vid.* m *v.* 11). καταφρονητωσαν o. εισι *prim.* k. –ὁτι αδελφοι εισιν c. –ὁτι αδελφοι *usque ad* δουλευετωσαν n. –ταυτα o. 3. προσερχηται n. –ἡμων a*. διδασκαλεια k. 4. *Rasura in* k *inter* τετυφ *et* ωται. προστετυφλωται (–μηδεν) o. μὴδὲν k. –ὑπονοιαι πονηραι c. ὑπονναι e. ὑπονιαι g*. 5. διαπαρατριβαι aefghkmno. δια, παρατριβαι c. διατριβαι dl [b *cum Elzev.*]. 6. δε πορισμος (*sic*) c. ευταρκιας (*cf.* I. 19) m. αυταρκιας o. 7. εισενεγκαμεν b*fo. δηλονότι fgklo. ουδεν (*pro* ουδε) o. τὶ lmno. +νυν (*post* τὶ) o. 8. *Rasura in* k *post* και. τουτους n*. αρκεσθησωμεθα dn. 9. [*Post* παγιδα *in* m, *recenti manu, marg.* του διαβολου. χρυσ. γρ.] –και *secund.* k. ὀλεθρον ko. απολειαν o. 10. ὀρεγομενοι ko. επλανηθησαν c. περιεσπειραν o. ὀδυναις ko. 11. –δε *prim.* (*habet rubro, initio perio.*) a*. ὦ (*sic v.* 20) k. του *bis script.* in n. φαυγε m. τεκνον τιμοθεε διωκε (−δε) z. −δε *secund.* o. δικαιδικαισυνην o. 12. καλλον d. ἡν k. −και *prim.* abcefgk [*non* o]. εκληθεις o. ὁμολογησας cdo. ενωποιων (*sic v.* 13) d. ενωπιων o*. 13. ῑυ χ̄υ knz. 14. τηρήσαι k. −σε z. επιφανιας k*. 15. δειξη ck. 16. ιδεν d. −και (*ante* κρατος) nz. 17. παραγγελε b*do. μὴδὲ klmo. ελπικεναι dmo. *Rasura in* k *post* επι. παντα πλουσιως abcdefghklno. τα παντα πλουσιως m. −εις απολαυσιν (*habet marg.*) a*. 18. κοινωνηκους ?g*. 19. αποθησαυριζωντας d. ἑαυτους o. επιλαβονται cd*o. +οντως (*ante* ζωης) m. 20. παραθηκην acdehmn [*cum Elzev.* bklo]. εκτρεπωμενος d. ψευδωνυμου (*sic*) c. ψευδονιμου d. ψευδονυμου o. γνωσεως (ε *mutat.*) m. 21. επαγγελομενοι ad*. ἠστοχησαν ko.

SUBSCRIPT.: *init.* +ἡ ak. −πρωτη a. +επιστολη (*post* πρωτη) k. λαδικιας o. ἡτι k. +της (*ante* φρυγιας) g. καπατιανης (*pro* πακατιανης) egk [*non* n] o. *fin.* +ιδου δη και ἡ εκ λαοδικειας a. *fin.* +στιχ. σ̄λ no. +αναγν. μια, κεφ. ῑη, μαρτ. β̄. στ^χ. σ̄λ̄γ k. εγραφη απο λαοδικειας μητροπολεως φρυγιας της καπατιανης· στ^χ c̄λ h. *Cum Elzev.* d. *Nil habent* blm.

AD TIMOTHEUM SECUNDA.

[CAP. I. 1—12.]

Και ταυτα προς τιμοθεον παυλοιο εφετμαι f. προς τιμοθεον δευτερα (β̄ n, δευτερις o) hkmno. +επιστολη hk. προς τιμοθεον επιστολη β̄ l.

CAP. I. 1. χ̄υ ῑυ (*ante* δια) degn. επαγγελιας (−ζωης) o. 2. *fin.* και κ̄υ ιησου χ̄υ του κ̄υ ἡμων km. 3. αδιαληπτον km. ·νυκτος και ἡμερας *cum sequent.* m. 4. σε *eras.* ?b. μεμνημενων o. 5. ενωκησεν o. λωΐδη d. +εν (*ante* τη μ̄ρ̄ι) fk. ευνεικη abcghkl. ευνηκη f. πεπεισμε (*non v.* 12) ko. −ὁτι και o. 6. αἰτιαν (*sic v.* 12) k. αιτιαναμιμ. m. αναμνησκω b*. ὑπομιμνησκω c. αναμιμνησκον o. χ̄υ n* (θ̄υ *supra, forsan p. m.*). *fin.* σου (*pro* μου) o. 7. δουλιας d. φρονισμου d*. σοφρονισμου o. 8. επαισχυνθεὶς d. μὴδὲ klmno. συγκάκακοπαθησον (*sic*) d. το (*pro* τῳ) o. 9. +ἡμας (*post* καλεσαντος) k. κατα ιδιαν bk. ἰδιαν n. −εν χ̄ῳ ῑυ h. 10. φανερωθησαν dk. +νυν (*ante* ζωην) o. 11. κῆρυξ *passim* lm. −και *secund.* cd. 12. πασχων (−αλλ') o. οὐκ k. ὁ (*pro* ᾧ) c. εστιν n. παρακαταθηκην bgk. −μου ak. την παραθηκην μου δυνατος εστι c [*errat Millius de* n]. 13. ὑγειαινοντων n. λογου a*dk*. ἐμου (*sic* II. 2)k. ἠκουσας k. 14. *init.* +τεκνον τιμοθεε o. παραθηκην acdehlmno [*non* bk]. κατοικουντος c. *fin.* ὑμιν g*n. 15. οιδα n. −παντες a. φυγελος cemn. φρυγελλος l. φύλλος ?o*. ἑρμογενης o. 16. ονησηφορου n. ὀνησιφορου o. πολλακης d. ανεψυξεν mn. ἀλυσιν n. επαισχυνθη cdfk*mo. 17. παραγενομενος d. ερωμη e. σπουδεοτερον o. εξεζητησε l. εξητησε m. εζητησεν o. εὑρεν emno. 18. δωει (*non v.* 16, &c.) k. εὑρειν ὁ κς b. εὑρειν n. ελεον en. διηκονησεν n. +μοι (*post* διηκονησε) m.

CAP. II. 1. +τεκνον τιμοθεε (*post* τεκνον μου) o; *sic v.* 11 *init.*; *v.* 22 *ante* διωκε (−δε *secund.*). 2. ηκουσαν d**?. ἠκουσας k. οἰκανοι k. ἱκανοι n. 3. χῡ ιησου m. −ιῡ n* (*supra p. m.?*). 4. πραγματιαις dgh. το (*pro* τῳ) d. αρεσει cd. αρεσκη m*. 5. αθλει ?c. +δε (*post* εαν *secund.*) o. *fin.* αθλησει ck*. 6. δῆ d. καρπον d*. τον καρπον km*o. 7. πασιν mno. 10. διατοῦτο hlmo [*non* kn]. −παντα a*. 11. +και πασης αποδοχης αξιος (*post* λογος) a. +και (*post* γαρ) m. συναπεθανωμεν o. συζησωμεν m*o. 12. ει ὑπομενομεν και συμβασιλευσομεν *bis script.* b*. ὑπομενωμεν co. κἀκεῖνος n. 13. +γαρ (*post* αρνησασθαι) eglm. 14. *init.* αυτα d. ὑπομιμνηκε l*. χῡ a, θῡ bcm (*pro* κυριου). μηδε (*pro* μη) c. λογωμαχειν ?n*. 15. ἑαυτον dk. 16. βῐβλους (*pro* βεβ.) κενοφονιας προϊστασο o. περιηστασο d. περιστασο m. περιΐστασο n. ἀσεβειας n. 17. γαγραινα d*. ἑξη k*. ἑξει n. εστι k. ὑμαιναιος dk*. υμυναιος ?o. 18. ἠστοχησαν fko. ἠδη k. ανατρεπουσιν n. 19. *init.* ου (*pro* ὁ) m. ·ἑστηκεν kn. ·ἑστηκεν o. φραγῖδα a*. σφραγίδα hklmno. −ὁ *secund.* am. ὀνομαζων m. +του (*ante* χυ) c. κυ (*pro* χυ) abdfghklmno. 20. οικεια d. οἰκια k. εστιν m**n. μονα m. αργυρα και χρυσα m. −και (*post* αλλα) a*. οστρακεινα d. ὀστρακϊνα ko. 21. αὐτον n* (ἑ *supra*). −και f. ἠτοιμασμενον n. 22. −δε *secund.* a*. 23. γενωσι d*m*. 24. ἡπιον fkmno. *Rasura inter* διδα *et* κτικον *in* a. 25. +κς (*ante* ὁ θς) k. 26. ανανηψασιν k. ανανιψωσιν no. παγῖδος k*m.

CAP. III. 1. *init.* +τεκνον τιμοθεε (−δε) o; *sic v.* 10 *init.* (−συ δε); *v.* 14 *init.* (−συ δε). 2. αχρηστοι (*pro* αχαριστοι) m. 3. ακρατεις· ανημεροι· αστοργοι· ασπονδοι· διαβολοι· αφιλαγαθοι· k. ασπονδοι αστοργοι m. 4. τετυφλομενοι (*cf.* 1 Tim. VI. 4) o. φιληδωνοι k. 5. τουτουτους m. 6. −οἱ o. ενδυοντες h. οικειας d. οἰκιας k. αιχμαλωτιζοντες ab*cdfh. αἰχμαλωτιζοντες k. αιχμαλωτευον m. −τα bceghklmn. −αγομενα επιθυμιαις ποικιλαις (*habet marg.*) b*. αγομενοι o. 7. μαθανοντες o. μὴδέποτε km. γνωσιν n. δυναμενα ελθειν m. δυναμενοι o. 8. ἰαννὴς mn. ἰαμβρής mo. ἰαμβρὴς n. μωϋσῆ abdefghkn. μωσει clm. μωϋσεα o. οὑτω dhm [*non* lno].

ανθισταται (ι *prim. mutat.*) d. 9. οὐ k. προκοψουσιν (*sic*) c. ανοι m*. 10. +τεκνον τιμοθεε (*post* συ δε) m. προθεση g. 11. ἰκονιω no. ερυσατο d. 12. ἡ (*pro* οἱ) o. ζην ευσεβως m. 13. −δε d. χειρος d. πλανοντες o. πλανομενοι eo. 14. μεναι d. +οἷς (*ante* επιστευθης) b**h (επιστωθης b*?h). επιστοθης o. 15. −και a*. εκ (*pro* απο) b. σαι d. +της (*ante* πιστεως) m. 16. γραφη, l. ὀφελιμος d. ,και ωφελιμος· hn. ὠφελιμος· k, ὀφελημος· o. [*puncta desunt in* m]. +εστι (*post* ωφελιμος) f. ελεχον d*. παιδιαν do. δικαιοσυνην h*. 17. ει (*pro* ῃ) dk. εξηρτημενος cno.

CAP. IV. 1. γουν (*pro* ουν) c. −του *secund.* f. [*cum Elzev.* abklno]. κριναι b. −και την βασιλειαν αυτου (*habet marg.*) d*. 2. επιστηθη d*. παρακαλεσον επιτιμησον m. *Ad fin. verbum eras. in* a. 3. κατα τας ιδιας επιθυμιας gm. επισωρευσουσιν ἑαυτοις m. επισωρευουσι o. 4. επιστρεψουσιν m*. 5. +τεκνον τιμοθεε (*ante* νηφε) m. νύφε o*. παση d. 6. γαρ *super rasur. in* b. ἡδη k. σπενδωμαι h*. +μου (*post* αναλυσεως, −εμης) m. εφεστηκεν mn. 7. τον καλον αγωνα m. ηγονισμαι c. ηγωνισμαι fk. ἠγωνισμαι o. 8. −ὁ *secund.* d*k. −δε a. ἠγαπηκοσι kn. 9. *init.* +τεκνον τιμοθεε o. ταχεως προς με k. 10. εγκατελειπεν o. επορευθει d. εις *prim. mutat. in* m. κρισκης ab**cdfghkln [*non* m]. γαλατειαν k. τῖτος o. δελματιαν no. 11. αγαγε df. εστιν *secund.* n. 12. τυχικου b*. 13. φαιλονην begl*o. φαιλωνην f. φελωνην mn. [*cum Elzev.* ck]. απεστειλα m, απελειπον o (*pro* απελιπον). τρωαδη c. −παρα καρπῳ a. +δε (*post* μαλιστα) km. βεμβρανας m (μεμβρ *mutat. in* e). 14. κακα μοι m. αποδωσει m. −ὁ *secund.* bk. 15. ἡμητεροις c. λογος e*. 16. παρεγενετο k. 17. μου (*pro* μοι) o. ενεδυναμωσεν o. το κηρυγμα δι' εμου o. πληρωθη (*pro* πληροφορηθῃ) k. ερυσθην m. 18. ῥυσαι τὸ (*pro* ῥυσεται) c. εκ (*pro* απο) l. σωσοι c. σωση n. αυτω (*pro* ῳ) k. 19. πρισκιλαν a. πρισκιλλαν bl**o**. πρικιλλαν f. ὀνησιφορου ko. ονησηφορου n. 20. +δε (*post* εραστος) m. −δε ao. μηλιτω o. ἀσθενουντα n. 21. σπουδης l*o. −και λινος c. −και κλαυδια και οἱ o.

SUBSCRIPT.: *init.* +ἡ a. ἡ δε δευτερα ἡ προς αυτον τον τιμοθεον k. επισκοπον πρωτον a. −πρωτον eno. −της εφεσιων *usque ad* χειροτονηθεντα fk. ὁτι k. +ῥωμης (*ante* νερωνι) aefno (+ῥωμαιων k). *fin.* +αναγν. ᾱ. κεφ. θ̄. μαρτ. ᾱ. k. +στ[xx] $\overline{\text{ροβ}}$ kno. προς τιμ. β. επιστ. εγραφη απο ῥωμης *tantum* g: εγραφη απο ῥωμης στ[x] $\overline{\text{ροβ}}$ *tantum* h. *Hiat* d, *nil habent* blm.

AD TITUM.

[CAPP. I. 1—II. 15.]

Ταυτα παραιφασις εστι φιλω τιτω παρα παυλου f. προς τιτον επιστολη του ἁγιου αποστολου παυλου h. προς τιτον klmno, +επιστολη kl, +παυλου k.

CAP. I. 1. −δε o. 2. −επ' cm. επιγγειλατο k. επηγγειλετο *ut videtur* m. Αιωνιων (Αι *mutat.*) h. 3. εφανερωσεν o. ὡ (*pro* ὃ) ck. 4. +ἡμων (*post* κυ) k. 5. −τα o. καταλειποντα o. καταστησας a*. καταστησεις a**c. −ὡς l*. 6. ἡτις (*pro* ει τις) k. −τεκνα εχων πιστα c. τακνα ?m. εχων (ων *mutat.*) l. ασωτειας cn. +απιστειας (*post* ·ασωτιας) k. 7. οἰκονομον k. αυθαδει o. οργιλοι g. ὀργιλον hl. 8. εγκρατει o. 9. −την abmo. ἡ k, ει o (*pro* ἠ). −και *prim.* l. τη ὑγιαινουση διδασκαλια m. ὑγειαινουση n. 10. +και (*ante* πολλοι) d. −και *prim.* ak. +και (*ante* ματαιολογοι) ac. 11. οἰκους k. ανατρεπουσιν mno. 12. ειπεν d*emno [e *habet in marg.* επιμενιδου κρητος μαντεως χρη +σα ος +ᾱ, *sic*]. ιδιος αυτων προφητης *bis script.* m*. ἰδιος n. −κακα θηρια k. γαστεραις f. 13. αἰτειαν k. αἰτιαν n. ὑγειάινωσιν n. ὑγιαινουσιν o. −τῃ d*. 15. μεμιαμενοις df. 16. +μη (*post* αρνουνται) m. βδελλυκτοι d. βδελοικτοι o.

CAP. II. 1. ὑγιαινουση (η *mutat.*) dk (ὑγιαινοῦσῐ k**). ὑγειαινουση n. *fin.* πιστει και διδασκαλεια o. 2. πρεσβυτερους o. νηφαλεους ab*?elmn. νηφαλαιους dfo [*cum Elzev.* k]. ὑγειαινοντας n. 3. +δε (*post* πρεσβυτιδας) m. ὡσαύτως o. +σεμνας (*post* ὡσαυτως) b**. ἱεροπρεπει m. δεδουλωμενους l*. 4. σοφρονιζουσι o. 5. ἁγνας kn. οἰκουρους k. ὑπωτασσομενας ?g*. ὑποτασομενας k. βλασφημειται cdfm*. 6. νεότερους d. ὡσαύτος o. 7. παντας ἑαυτον m*n. αδιαφοριαν h. +ἁγνειαν (*post* σεμνοτητα) h** *marg.* *fin.* +αφθαρσιαν abc (*tacitè*) defghklmno. 8. ὑγιᾶ e. ὑγειη n. ἐξεναντιας bghklmno. μὴδὲν ko. ἡμων (*pro* ὑμων) abcdefgklmno. λεγειν περι ἡμων m. 9. δεσποτες b*?d. ὑποτασεσθαι dko. *Jungit* k ὑποτασεσθαι εν πασιν. 10. πασαν πιστιν m. ·αγαθους· k. *fin.* ἐπᾶσι k. 11. −γαρ a**mo. 12. εὐσεβως n. 13. σωτηρες ?m. 14. ἑαυτον (*pro* ἑαυτῳ) f. 15. αὖτα d. λαλεῖ o. παρακαλεῖ o. μὴδεὶς k. σε ?l*. *fin.* καταφρονειτω ceglo [*non* k].

Cap. III. 1. ὑποτασεσθαι dm*. ὑποτάτάσεσθαι o. ἑτοιμους ?o. 2. μὴδένα k. 3. ηπεν o. πλανομενοι cd*o. κακακια m. *fin.* αλλους a*. 4. −ἡ *secund.* (*habet marg.*) a*. 5. ἐσωςεν m. παλινγενεσιας n. πᾶλινγγενεσίας o. *Rasura post* παλι *in* k. ανακαινισεως a*. ανακενωσεως g*o. 6. εξεχεθην m. ἡμας o. 7. γενομεθα o. 8. βουλωμαι d. φροντισωσι m. προϊσταται m. προΐστασθαι (*sic v.* 14) n. πεπηστευκοτες k*. οἱ πε *rescript. in* n. −τα m. −καλα (*habet* τα) k. ωφελημα cdfkno. 9. και γενεαλογιας (*sic*) c. ερις bcgk. περῐΐστασο (ῐ ΐ *mutat.*) l. περιΐστασο n. 10. +δευτ (*post* αἱρετικον) m*. παρετου d. παρ᾽αιτοῦ n. 11. ἁμαρτανη k, *at* ἁμαρτιαν o. ὡν m. ὧν n. ὧν ko. 12. ὅτᾶν n. ῞Οτ᾽ ἂν o. +δε (*post* ὁταν) k. πεμπω d. ἀρτεμὰν l. κεκρινα k. παραχειμᾶσαι kn. 13. ἀπολλῶ hkm. μὴδὲν k. *fin.* λιπη bg**m, *at* λυπη f, λοιπη o. 14. ὑμετεροι c. καλλων d*. εργω b*. εναντιας (*pro* αναγκαιας) o. 15. ασπαζοντε d*. ἀσπασαι k. +του θῦ (*post* χαρις) n** *in marg.* ηὑμων d, *at* ἡμων g*.

Subscript.: *init.* +ἡ a. −της *prim.* g. −πρωτον o. ἀρχ ἐπισκοπον o. −επισκοπον χειροτονηθεντα g. χειροτονηθεντος a. νικοπολεος d. *fin.* +στιχ ϛζ n. *In* bh *tantum* εγραφη απο νικοπολεως, +της μακεδονιας b, *at* +στχ ϛζ h. *Nil habent* klm.

AD PHILEMONA.

[v. 1—11.]

Παυλος επιστελλει ταδε βεβαια φιλημονι πιστω f. επιστολη προς φιλημονα kl. προς φιλημονα hmno. +επιστολη h. +του ἁγιου αποστολου ὀνησιμου o.

Vers. 1. ιῦ χῦ adfhk [*non* mo]. φιλημωνι m. 2. απφια (π *mutat.*) k. αρχιππο d. συστρατηωτη d*. *Rasura in* k *inter* και *et* τη κατ᾽. κατ᾽ οἶκον o. 3. ἡμιν (*pro* ὑμιν) g*. *fin.* χῶ d. 4–9. *Desunt in* o *ob* ὁμοιοτελ. 4. παντοτε, h. −σου c. 5. ακουω b*. την πιστιν και την αγαπην m. 6. +εργου (*ante* αγαθου) b**cegl**, *at post* αγαθου k. ἡμιν (*pro* ὑμιν) abdefgkln. 7. *init.* χαριν bc (*tacitè*) defghklmn. −γαρ dlm. πολλην εχομεν m, *at* πολλην εχω a. 8. διὸ n. εχων εν χῶ παρρησιαν d. παρρησιαν εν χῶ l. εχων παρρησιαν a*. επιτασσει l*. ανεικον d. 9. δια την αγαπην· *cum præcedent.* m. χῦ ιησου m. *fin.* ; n. 10. δε (*pro* σε) a. +εγω (*post* ὀν) m. 11.

αχριστον d*o. +και (*post* δε) b. επεμψα d. 12. σπλαγχα o. *Transfert* m προσλαβου *in locum ante* αυτον. 13. εβουλομην προς εμαυτον *bis script. in* o. διακονει c. 14. ἠθελησα ko. κατ' (*pro* κατα *prim.*) cm. ἑκουσιον n. 15. διατοῦτο hklmo [*non* n]. εχωρησθη d. απεχεις a*. επεχης n. 16. οὐκ ἔτι ko. αλλα m. +ὡς (*ante* ὑπερ) do. μαλλιστα o. ποσον (−δε) d. −δε o*. −σαρκι και εν b*. 17. με (*pro* εμε *prim.*) bcdeghklmno. 18. *init.* ἡ δε τι d. ἠδικησεν do. εἰ δ' ἔτι n. ηδικησεν (−σε) n. ὀφειλει o. ελλογη d. 19. +δε (*post* εγω) m. −σοι k. προσοφιλεις k. προσοφειλης o. 20. σοι ὀναιμην (*pro* σου) o. ωναιμην n. σου (*pro* μου) m. −μου o. −εν κυριῳ *secund.* cd. *fin.* χῶ (*pro* κῷ *secund.*) am. 21. +σοι (*post* λεγω) l. 22. ἁμα ko. +και (*post* ὁτι) dno. ευχων (*pro* προσευχων) cdl*. 23. ασπαζεται m. συνεχμαλωτος d. 25. χῡ *eras. in* h*, μετα *superascripto.*

Subscript. : *init.* +ἡ a. −προς φιλημονα hkm. εγραφει n. δι' ghm. ὀνησιμου o. −οικετου dh. οἰκετου k. *fin.* +στˣ λζ̄ no, +αναγν. ᾱ, κε. β̄, στˣ μς̄ k. *Nil habet* l, *at* b *legit* προς φιλημονα και απφιαν δεσποτας ονησιμου και προς αρχιππον διακονον της εν κολασσ" εκκλη. εγραφη κ.τ.λ.

AD HEBRÆOS.

[Cap. i. 1—9].

Παυλος αποστολος ἑβραιοις ταδε συγγενεεσσιν f. (+ἡ a) προς ἑβραιους επιστολη (ἐπιστολῆς o) aghko, +παυλου ako, +του ἁγιου (+αποστολου h) παυλου gh. (+επιστολη l) προς ἑβραιους lmn.

Cap. I. 1. πατρασιν (ατρα *mutat.*) g. εσχατου abdefgkmn**o [*non* l]. αισχατου hn*. ἡμιν (*sic*) c. 2. κληρονομων d. εποιησε τους αιωνας m. 3. ὧν k. φερον d. τέ m, *passim.* δυναμαιως d**. ποιουμενος o*. των ἁμαρτιων ἡμων ποιησαμενος m. εκαθησεν do. +του θρονου (*post* δεξια) d. 4. τοσουτο m*. κρειττω cl. κρειττον k. κριττω o. ὁσο m**. +και (*post* ὁσω) k. ειληφεν a, κεκληρονομικεν o (*pro* κεκληρονομηκεν). 5. ειπεν de. των αγγελων ποτε o. υς̄ o. ἔστέ m. 6. ὅτᾶν n. ὅτ' ἂν o. εισαγαγει o. πρωτοτοκον o. οἰκουμενην k. λεγη n. προσκηνησατωσαν d. −αυτῳ o. 8. ῡν̄ o. 9. ἠγαπησας kno. εμησησας d*. διατοῦτο hlm [*non* no]. εχρισεν no. σαι (*pro* σε) d. ὁ θς· ὁ θς ὁ θς σου (*sic*) n. 10. καταρχας fhlmno. εισιν (ισ *mutat.*) b. 11. διαμενης d. 12. ἑλιξης d. ἑλιξεις fklno. ἑλλιξεις m. ἀλαγησονται d* (ἀλλ...d**). *Rasura in* g *post* ει. εκλειψουσιν mno. 13. ειρηκεν dmo. εκδεξιων σου h. —σου *prim.* m.

CAP. II. 1. διατοῦτο hklm [*non* no]. ακουσθησι k. ακουσθεισιν mn. παραρύωμεν n. 2. ενδικον ελαβεν m. ελαβεν *bis script. in* l. 3. εκφευξωμεθα d. αμελισαντες d. καλεισθαι m, λαλεινσθαι o (*pro* λαλεισθαι). ὑπο του κυ (*etiam in Hypothesi, ubi* δια *pro sequente* ὑπο) m. ακουοντων a. 4. Νυνεπιμαρτυρουντος (N *rubro*) d. —τε ghk. τερασιν n. δυναμεσιν n. θελησεν k. 5. ὑπεταξεν d. οὐκουμενην k. 6. διεμαρτυρετο o. πο (*pro* που) d. μιμνησκει cdno. υς n. επισκεπτει n (επι *mutat. in* b). 7. ἠλαττωσας ko. αυτω (*pro* αυτον *prim.*) o. —και *secund.* b**. —και κατεστησας *ad fin. vers.* acdefghkln. 8. ὑπεταξεν o. ὑπὸ κάτω n. το (*pro* τῳ) fk. αυτω (*pro* αυτῳ *secund.*) m. ανυποτακτο d. οὔπω k. 9. *init.* ον d. αγγελλους m*. ἡλαττομενον f. ἡλαττωμενον ko. ὅπως n. 10. επρεπεν o. ὧν (*pro* ὃν) do. —επρεπε γαρ αυτῳ (*incipit* δι᾽ ὧν) d. ζωης (*pro* σωτηριας) a. 11. *init.* ὅτε γαρ ὁ a. ῞Οτε (Ο *rubro* ko) kmo *alii*, ῞Οτε (Ο *rubro*) l. —γαρ o. ἁγιαζωμενοι d. αἰτιαν n. οὐκ᾽ *passim* n. 12. ἀπαγγελλῶ m. 13. ἰδοὺ ?n. 14. κεκοινωνηκεν αἱματος και σαρκος m. μετεσχες o. καταργησει d. 15. απαλλαξει ?k*. διαπαντὸς lm**. ζειν k. ησαν k. 16. ἀβρααμ hklmo *alii* [*non* dn]. —αλλα σπερματος αβρααμ επιλαμβανεται a* (*habet minio*). 17. ὀθεν (*sic* III. 1) n, *at* ὀται o. —ωφειλε κατα παντα o. ωφειλεν en. οφειλε m. καταπάντα hkm. ὁμοιωθηναι n. ελεημον d. γενητε k. εις τω k*. ἱλασκεσθαι o. 18. πειραζωμενοις d.

CAP. III. 1. ουρανιου a. ιν χν abcdefghklmno. 2. μωϋσης abcefghkl mno. *fin.* οὐτου d. 3. οὗτος δοξης m. μωϋσην abcefghlno [*non* km]. ἠξιωται ko. καθόσον ghm [*non* k]. +αυτου (*post* οικου) a*. 4. +ἄνωθεν (*ante* ὑπο) o. ὁ (*sequente ras.*) δὲ o. 5. μωϋσης bcd**efghklno [*non* m]. πιστως d. 6. υς o. του οικου (*pro* τον οικον) d. οἰκον n. +ὁ (*ante* οικος) o. μεν (*pro* εσμεν) l. βεβαῖαν (*sic v.* 14) n. βεβαί o. 7. διὸ (*sic v.* 10) n. το ἁγιον πνα k. —το ἁγιον a*. 8. σκληρυνετε a. σκληρυνηται d. σκληρηνητε m. —ὡς m. 9. τεσσαράκον o. 10. —διο a*k. προσωχθησα cdfk*n. *Jungit* k προσωχθησα *cum v.* 9. ειπα ack. πλανων m*. 11. ωμωσα hm*. ὡμοσα (*sic v.* 18) k. καταπαυσσιν b*. 12. αδελφοι βλεπετε (*init. peric.*) a. βλεπεται d. +μου (*post* αδελφοι) c. ἔντινι m. 13. παραλεῖτε o. ἑκαστιν k. ἄχρισοῦ g. καληται e*. σκληρηνθη m*. εξ ὑμων τις abcde fghklno [*non* m]. μαρτιας k*. 14. του χυ γεγοναμεν m. 15. —αυτου n.

—ὡς a*. 16. *init.* ινες d*. τίνες o. ·αλλ'hl [*puncta in* m *cum Elzev. v.* 16; *vv.* 16—18, *non interrogativè in* mno]. αἰγυπτου k. μωϋσεος abfghlo. μωυσεως kn. 17. γαρ (*pro* δε) c. προσωχθησε cdfmno. ἁμαρτισασιν o. επεσον abfgk [*non* no]. 18. ωμοσεν b. ωμωσε fo. εισελευεσθαι g*. εἰμὴ k. απειθησασιν mo. 19. ἠδυνηθησαν o. ηδυνηθησαν (ηθ *mutat.*) m. δια fhmno.

CAP. IV. 1. *init.* +αδελφοι o. +ου δυνηθωμεν (*ante* δοκη) o. δοκει dghk mn. 2. *Post* ωφελησεν *rasura in* a. οφελησεν mo. —μη g* *ut videtur.* συγκεκραμενους abcfghl**o. συγκεκραμμενους dkl*n. συγκεκερασμενους m. 3. εισερχωμεθα m*. καθῶς (*sic ferè v.* 7, v. 3, 6) no. ωμωσα d. ώμοσα o. —ει o. τι (*pro* τοι) b*. γεννηθεντων mo. 4. ἑβδομης k. οὑτως cghklmno. —και no. ἑβδομη n. —παντων o. 5. —ει do. 6. —ουν a*. εις αυτην εισελθειν g. —εις αυτην c. ευηγγελισθεντες o. δια a. διαπαθειαν d. 7. ὁριζει f. ·λεγων, h. —μετα τοσουτον *usque ad* σημερον *secund.* k. ακουσηται d. σκληρυνηται d. *fin.* ἡμων d. 8. αυτος (*pro* αυτους) acdk. +ὁ (*ante* ις̅) f. +ὁ του ναυϊ (*post* ις̅) o. μεταταῦτα mo. 9. ἆρα o. απολιπεται c. απολειπο' k. *Rasura in* k *inter* σαββα *et* τισμος. 10. ἰδιων n. 11. πεσει f. *fin.* απαθειας o. 12. *init.* Των (T *rubro, cf.* II. 4) d. διικνουμενος n. μεχρι (*pro* αχρι) o. —τε *prim.* bd*k. ἁρμων ko. 13. εστιν n. +εν (*ante* τοις οφθαλμοις) a. ὀφθαλμοις ko. 14. —ουν a*. μεγα b*. 15. ἀσθενειαις n. πεπειραμενον abc (*tacitè*) dfghklmno [*hiat* e]. ὁμοιωτητα d. ἁμαρτιας n. 16. προσερχομεθα a*cdgkl*o. —ουν ?a*. λαβομεν o. ελαιον dk*. ελεος g**. εὑρωμεν n, *at* ἑρομεν c. —εις ευκαιρον f.

CAP. V. 1. *init.* ας l*. προσφερει do. 2. μετριωπαθειν b*. αγνωουσι d. πλανομενοις m. περικειτε k. ἀσθενειαν n. *fin.* περικείμε νῦν ἀσθενεία o. 3. διαταύτην m. ὀφειλει (*sic v.* 12) k. +και (*ante* περι *prim.*) c. οὑτως cgkl no [*non* dhm]. του (*pro* ἑαυτου) a*. 4. —και *prim.* a*. λαμβανει τίς m. —την g*. αλλ' fgn. —ὁ *bis* bdhklmo. —του n. —ὁ *secund.* acfgn. 5. οὑτως b** (*marg.*) cklmno [*non* dh]. ἑαυτω m. γεννηθηναι kno. αρχιερεα ; n. γεγεννηκα m. 6. σοι (*pro* συ) o. *Post hunc vers.* a *habet plura verba erasa* (*lego* γονατε *ad fin.*). 7. —τε o. 8. ὢν (*pro* ὢν) k. εμαθων o. επαθεν mn. 9. πασι τοις ὑπακουουσιν αυτω m. αἴτιος gn. 10. —του a. +εις τον αιωνα (*post* αρχιερευς) m. μελχιδεκ b. 11. δυσσερμηνευτος d. νοθροι d. 12. ωφειλοντες d. ὀφειλοντες ko. εχεται m. —της αρχης cd. 13. +και (*ante* δικαιοσυνης) o. εστιν mn. 14. ἐξην f. ἐξιν kn. ἐσθητηρια ko.

CAP. VI. 1. διὸ n. —της c. τελειωτητα φερομεθα o. νεκρων, o. *fin.* θῡ d. 2. βαπτισμὸν d, βαπτισμοι n. 3. *Deest versus in* m. *init.* και τοῦ o.

ποιησωμεν dlno. επιτρεπει cdfh. –ὁ a*. 4. γεννηθεντας fkmo. 5. *init.* –και d. δυναμις o. 6. ανακαινιζει c. 7. ἡ n. ποιουσα h. πολλακις τον επ᾽ αυτης b. ἐπαυτης g. ἑαυτης (*pro* ἐπ᾽ αυτης) o. πολλακεις d. ερχομενον πολλακις m. εκεινους o. –και *secund.* cd. γεωργειτε o. μεταλαμβανεν k. –του d. 9. –αγαπητοι f. κρειτονα a**. κρεισσονα bfln. κρισσονα o. –ει d. οὑτως cgklmno. 10. του εργου *forsan deest in* m*. ενεδειξασθαι d. εἰσέδειξασθαι (*pro* ἡς ενεδειξασθε) o. 11. +αυτου (*post* αυτην) o. –αχρι τελους m. 12. –δε o. τὸν (*pro* των) o. 13. –γαρ o. ἀβρααμ hkmo *alii* [*non* ln]. επαγγελλομενος o. ειχεν m. μειζωνος d. ὀμοσαι ko. ὡμοσε (*sic v.* 16 ὀμνυουσι ko) k. ἑαυτον d. 14. –λεγων o. ἡμιν (*pro* η μην) o. ἦ (*pro* ἦ) fklm. ἡμὴν n. ευλογῶ (*pro* ευλογησω) k. 15. οὑτως cgklmno. 16. ὀμνυουσιν (*non v.* 13) n. αυτης (*pro* αυτοις) f. περας, m. ὁ ὀρκος no. 17. +κλητοις (*ante* κληρονομοις) m. ὀρκω no (*at* ω *mutat. in* m). 18. αμεταθετον d* εχομεν kmn*?. καταφευγόντες c. καταφυγῶντες d. καταφεύγοντες o. τοις (*pro* της) o. 19. –τε c. 20. +ἡμων (*post* προδρομος) k. ὑμων (*pro* ἡμων) m.

Cap. VII. 1. Οὗτος n [*Elzev.* Οὗτος *errore*]. μελχϊσεδεκ (χϊ *mutat.*) l. +του (*ante* ὑψιστου) abc (*tacitè*) dfghklmno. συναντισας o. ἀβρααμ (*sic vv.* 2, 4, 5, 6, 9) hklmo [*non* dn]. 2. *init.* +και ευλογηθεις ὑπ᾽ αυτου o. –δε cd. εστιν amn. 3. αφωμοιωμενος (*sic*) c. μενων a*. 4. θεωρειται f. πιλικος οὗτως d. ὁ (*pro* ᾧ) m. –αβρααμ c. εδωκεν ἀβρααμ m. δεδωκεν a. ακροθηνιων dmn. 5. ἱερατιαν g*k. τοῦτέστι o *alii.* εξεληλυθοτα m. 6. εκ τουτων (*pro* εξ αυτων) c. –εξ αυτων δεδεκατωκε τον d. ἀβρααμ; m. επαγγελειας d. ευλογηκεν mno (*at* αδελφοι *sequente in* o, *init. v.* 7). 7. Ππασης (Π *rubro*) a. κρειτονος d*. κριττονος o. ευλογητε o. 8. ὡδε gkln [*non* ho]. λαμβανουσι b. λαμβαννουσιν o. 9. δι᾽ cm. ἀβραμ m. απολαμβανων n. λαμβανον o. δεδεκατωτε do. 10. ὀσφυι o. 11. *init.* ει *eras. in* n. τελειοσις m. ἱεροσυνης (*sic v.* 12, *non vv.* 14, 24) k. επ᾽ αυτῃς m. επ᾽ αυτην ko. ἐνομοθετητο k. *fin. non interrogativè in* n. 12. μετατιθεμενος g. εξαναγκης gkn. 13. μετέσχε k, μετεσχηκε a, μετεσχηκεν o (*pro* προσεσχηκε). 14. ἰοῦδα m. ἰουδα (*non* viii. 8) n. μωϋσης abcdfghklmno. ελαλησεν bmn. 15. ὀμοιωτητα d. ανιστατε k. 16. σαρκινης a*fhln [*non* ko]. σαρκηνης d. 17. –συ m. +ει (*post* συ) bo. ἱερὲ b. *Rasura in* g *inter* κατα *et* την. 18. –μεν ?o*. εντωλης o. ἀσθενες n. ανοφελες do. 19. ἐπεισαγωγῆ l. 20. καθόσον ghmn. ὀρκωμοσιας kn. 21. ὀρκωμοσιας *prim.* kn. –εισιν *usque ad* ὀρκωμοσιας *secund.* n* (*habet marg.*). οἱ δὲ (*pro* ὁ δε) o. μεθ᾽ ὀρκωμοσιας km. τον λογον τον (*pro* του λεγοντος) o. ὡμοσε k.

23. εισιν m. κολυεσθαι o. 24. διαμενειν (-το) m. εχειν o. 25. ὁθεν (*sic* VIII. 3) n. δυναται ?m*. προσευχομενους (*pro* προσερ.) o. ετυγχανειν o. 26. *init.* +αδελφοι *rubro* o. ουτος γαρ *super rasur. in* h. ὑμιν (*pro* ἡμιν) k. —των *prim.* a*. ανων (*pro* ουρανων) a. 27. οὐκ (*sic* VIII. 2, 7, 9 *passim*) n. καθημεραν gh [*non* km]. ὑπο (*pro* ὑπερ) c. ἰδιων n. ἁμαρτηματων g. ἐπειτα o. ἐφαπαξ k. ἐφάπαξ o. 28. αρχιερεας l. ἀσθενειαν n. ὁρκωμοσιας n.

CAP. VIII. 1. μεγαλοσυνης ?m*. τοις *mutat. in* m. ουρανιοις m. 2. επιξεν o. 3. προφερειν m. τοιουτον (*pro* και τουτον) a, (*pro* τουτον) o. προσενεγκει fo. προσενεγκοι h. 4. ἦν *bis* k. +της (*ante* γης) c. αρχιερευς (*pro* ἱερευς) m. 5. καθω ?f. καθῶς n *pass.* κεχριματιστε o. μωϋσης abcf ghklno [*non* m : *hiant* de]. μελλων *super rasur. in* m. ὁρᾶ n. ὥρα o. ποιησεις abcfghklmno. 6. διαμφορωτερας k. τετυχηκε ab*. λειτουργειας mo. ὁσον l. —και m. κρειττωσιν c*. νενομοθετητε o. 7. εκεινη (ει *mutat.*) b. εζητειτω f. εξητειτο m. 8. —ισραηλ και επι τον οικον a* (*notatum minio*). ἰοῦδα mo. 9. +μου (*ante* της χειρος) abc (*tacitè*) fghkl m**no (m** *recenti manu*). αἰγυπτου k. την διαθηκην (*pro* εν τη διαθηκῃ) h. ἡμελησα k** (-ισα ?k*). ἡμελησα o. 10. —αὐτη b*. διαθηκη (κη *mutat.*) m. ἦν o. —τῳ o. της ἡμερας εκεινης o. —την fko. καρδιαν g. —και επι καρδιας αυτων o. 11. διδαξωσιν (*sic*) c. ἑκαστος *prim.* o. πολιτην (*pro* πλησιον) bgklmno. —αυτων *prim.* lo. 12. ὁτι ἱλεως *usque ad* ἁμαρτιων αυτων *deest in* m. ἰλεος fn. αυτου (*pro* αυτων *tertio*) m. 13. πεπαλαιωκεν o.

CAP. IX. 1. ηχεν a². ειχεν m. —μεν ὀυν και a². —και a*b*k. —σκηνη hln* (*habet recens margo*). εκεινη (*pro* σκηνη) m. δικαιωμα o. τότε mn. 2. ἧτε (*pro* ἡτε) o. ἁγία (*non v.* 3) m. [*Silet* c, *cum Elzev.* aa²hklo]. 4. παντοθε k. χρυσιω (ω *mutat.*) an. εχουσα *secund. bis script.* m. μανα m*. —ἡ (*ante* βλαστησασα) m. 5. ὑπὲρ ἄνω k. ὑπὲρ ἄνω l*n. ὑπερανων m. ὑπεράνω o. χερουβειμ m. χερουββιμ ?o. οὐκ *pass.* n. εστιν a². νυν ουκ εστι κατα μερος λεγειν a. 6. οὑτως cgklmno. κατασκευασμενων b?fm. κατασκευασμενον o. διὰ παντὸς n [*non* klmo]. τελουντες l. 7. ἐνιαυτου k. αγνωηματων a²o. 8. μηποτε b*. +της (*ante* σκηνης) m. 9. +καθεστηκε f, +καθεστηκεν mo (*post* ενεστηκοτα). ὃν (ὧν b*?) b**. προπεμπονται (*pro* προσφερονται) o. συνηδησιν o. 10. βρωμασιν n. πομασιν n. βαπτισμους f. κεροῦ o. διορθωσεω b*. 11. —δε o. παραγεναμενος m. μειζωνος f. τελεωτερας c. τελειωτερας fhm. 12. δια (*pro* δι᾽) k. ταυρων (*pro* τραγων) c. ἐφ᾽ ἅπαξ kn. εὑραμενος abc (*tacitè*) dfghklmo. εὑραμενος n. 13. αἱ (*pro* αἷμα) m. τραγων και ταυρων n. δαμαλαιως f. δαμαλεος k. 14. ἁγιου (*pro* αιωνιου) abfh. +ἁγιου (*ante* αιωνιου) k. ἀμωμον k. καθαρισει a. ἡμων (*pro* ὑμων) h. 15. διατοῦτο hlmo [*non* kn].

καινης διαθηκης m. *εν* (*pro* *επι*) b. *κεκληρωμενοι* (*pro* *κεκλημενοι*) kl. 16. *ὁπου* n. *αναγκη* (*κ* *mutat.*) m. *διατιθεμενου* df. 17. *διαθήκαρ* o*. *ισχϋ* g. *ὁ* k. 18. *ουδε* achko. *εγκαικαινισται* c*. 19. *λαληθησης* k. +*τον* (*ante* *νομον*) gk. *μωϋσεος* afhlo. *μωσεως* bcdegk [*non* mn]. −*των* a. −*και* *τραγων* k. +*και* (*ante* *ὑδατος*) a. *μεθ'* *ὑδατος* m. *ὑσσοπου* o. *εραντισε* d*f. 20. *λεγω* b*. (*λ* *mutat. in* m). *ἡμας* a. 21. *σκευει* o. *λειτουργειας* dk*?. *το* *αἱματι* *ὁμοιος* *εραντισεν* o. *εραντισε* f. *ερραντισεν* mn. 22. *εννm*. *τα* (*pro* *κατα*) o. *αἱματος* *ἐκχυσιας* l*. *ουχινεται* m. 23. *των* *mutat. in* m. *των* *οὐνοῖ* m. *θαριζεσθαι* f. *επουρανα* b*. *κρειττωσι* g*. *fin.* *ταυτα* l*. *ας* *in* *ταυτας* *mutat. in* m. 24. *προσηλθεν* *ἁγια* m. *αντιπυπα* m*. *αληθηνων* d*. 25. *ουδε* a. *εισερχεται* *dubium in* c. *εισσερχεται* o. +*των* *ἁγιων* (*post* *ἁγια*) km. 26. *πολλακις* *αυτον* n. *νυνι* m. −*δε* a. *πεφανερωτε* d. 27. *καθόσον* cfghkm [*non* ln]. *το* *θανειν* (*pro* *αποθανειν*) l. 28. +*και* (*post* *οὑτως*) acd efghklmno (*οὑτω* cdeghkm). *ὀφθησεται* ko. *αυτων* (*pro* *αυτον*) d. +*δια* *πιστεως* (*post* *απεκδεχομενοις*) m. *δια* *πιστεως* (*loco* *εις* *secund.*) o (*sic*).

Cap. X. 1. −*ὁ* *νομος* k. *ου* *κατα* (*pro* *ουκ* *αυτην*) m. −*αυταις* a*cdln. *αυτων* (*pro* *αυταις*) m. *αἱς* (*pro* *ἁς*) k. *διηνεκαις* o. −*δυναται* k. *δυνανται* a** b*dfl*mno. *προσευχομενους* (*cf.* vii. 25) o. 2. +*ουκ* (*ante* *αν*) bdefghklm no [*non* c]. *καν* (*pro* *αν*) c [*cum* *Elzev.* a: *non* *interrogativè* hklmno]. *επαυσατο* b. *μὴδὲμίαν* kl. *μηδὲμίαν* n. *ετι* *εχειν* a. +*των* (*ante* *ἁμαρτιων*) a. *λατρεύονο*. *κεκαθαρισμενους* m. 3. *fin.* +*γινεται* o. 4. *τραγων* *και* *ταυρων* m. 5. *δι'* *ὁ* n. *καταρτισω* m. *κατηρτησω* o. 6. *ὀλωκαυτωματα* d. *ὀλοκαυτωματα* (*sic* *v.* 8) n. *ἁμαρτιας* (*sic* *v.* 8) n. *ηὐδοκησας* (*sic* *v.* 8 m) mo. 7. *ἡκω* n, *at* *οἴκω* (*non* *v.* 9) k. *το* *θελημα* *σου* *ὁ* *θς̄* (*sic* *v.* 9, b) bk. −*ὁ* *θς̄* f. +*μου* (*post* *θς̄*) e. 8. −*και* *tert.* (*non* *v.* 6) n. *περὶαμαρτίας* (*non* *v.* 18) h. *ουτε* (*pro* *ουδε*) a. *αἱτινες* *bis script.* m. −*τον* m. 9. *ἡκω* n. *τοῦτο* (*pro* *του*) m. +*μου* (*post* *θς̄*) g. *στησει* c. 10. *ἡαγιασμενοι* o*. +*οἱ* (*ante* *δια*) a**bc (*tacitè*) defghlmno [*non* k]. −*του* *secund.* abcdefghklmno. −*χῡ* n. *ἐφ'* *ἁπαξ* g*k. *ἐφάπαξ* o. 11. −*μεν* k. *αρχιερευς* (*pro* *ἱερευς*) ab*fgkm [*non* o]. *ἀρχιερευς* d. *ἑστηκε* kmno. *καθημεραν* ghlmn [*non* ko]. *ου* a*, *ουδεπω* b* (*pro* *ουδεποτε*). 12. *οὑτος* (*pro* *αυτος*) k. *εκαθησεν* d. 13. *ὑπὸπόδιον* n *more suo.* 14. *διnεκες* h. *ἁγιαζομενους* o. 15. *δε* *ἡμιν* *mutat. in* f. *ειρηκεναι* (*pro* *προειρηκεναι*) c. 16. *αὑτη* (*η* *mutat.*) m. *ἣν* k. 17. *init.* +*ὑστερον* *λεγει* bfkl m [*non* o]. +*ὑπεροῦ* *λεγει* c. −*και* *prim.* f. +*επι* (*ante* *των* *ανομιων*) a*. −*αυτων* *secund.* m. +*ουκετι* *προσφο* (*ante* *ου* *μη*) a*: *eras. rubro.* *μνισθω* k. +*αυτων* (*ante* *ετι*) o. 18. *ουκετι* glmn [*non* ko]. 19. −*αδελφοι* (*habent* *rubro, init. peric.*) ao. *αδελφοι* *εχοντες* (−*ουν*) z *init. peric.* +*του* (*ante* ιν) z. 20. ενεκαινησεν d. εκαινισεν f. —ὁδον f. διαυτου (*pro* δια του) o. τοῦτέστι k. τουτέστιν nz. τοῦτέστιν o. 21. οἰκον k. 22. προσερχομεθα cdghkoz. —εν πληροφορια *usque ad* καρδιας *secund.* z. ερραντισμενοι m. 23. λελουμεναι ?k*. —το z*. τω σωματι a*o. τω σωμα d. κατεχομεν cmoz. —γαρ a. 24. —και κατανοωμεν (*in marg. rubro*) a. παροξυσμων m. 25. εγκαταλιποντες clz. εγκαταλειπόντες o. επεισυναγωγην k. +την (*ante* ἑαυτων) z. καθος f. καθῶς n. τισην d. τοσουτο d. τοσουτον z. ὁσον cz. βλεπεται d. 26. ἑκουσιως no. της αληθειας την επιγνωσιν a. οὐκέτι ghlmnz [*non* ko]. ἁμαρτιας a. 27. κατεσθιειν m. εσθιει n. μελλοντος c*. μελλοντας d. μελλô z. 28. αθετισας f. +γαρ (*ante* τις) g. μωϋσεως demno. μωϋσεος fhl [k *cum Elzev.*]. οἰκτιρμων k. τρισιν n. αποθνησκειν z. 29. ποσον z. δοκειται d. αξιωθησετε k. τιμοριας c. 31. χειρας (ει *mutat.*) b. 32. αναμιμνησκεσθαι d*. —δε a. +ὑμων (*post* ἡμερας) m. 33. ὀνειδισμοις o. θληψεσι df*. θλιψεσιν m. 34. δεσμιοις (—μου) h. εν τοις δεσμοις m (*tantum in Hypothesi, non in textu*). σὐνέπαθησαται d. ἁρπαγην no. ὑμιν (*pro* ὑμων) l. εδεξασθε bc. πρὸσέδεξασθαι d. προσδεξασθε mo. —εν *prim.* abcfhlmno [*non* k]. 35. αποβαληται d**. αποβαλλητε f. ἡυμων d. μισθαποδωσιαν d. μεγαλην μισθαποδοσιαν m. 36. ὑπομωνης ?m*. εχεται d. κομισησθαι d. 37. ἡξει n. 38. ὑποστειλητε fkm. ὑποστηλειται d. ὑποστηληται o. ευδοκη ?k*. ευδοκειται ?l*. 39. *init.* +και d. απολειας o.

CAP. XI. 1. εστιν n. ετι (*pro* εστι) o. πραγματων· hm. —ου o. 3. εκ των μη φαινομενων a** *supra*. γεγονεναι *dubium in* c. 4. πλειωνα o. δικαιος ειναι b. αυτου· του θῦ n. —και l*. δι' αυτην ?h*. *fin.* λαλει a** [*cum Elzev.* lmn *cæteri*]. λαλειται (λ *prim. rescript.*) b. λαλεινται (*cf.* II. 3) o. 5. ἰδειν n. εὑρισκετο n. διότι μετετεθηκεν d. δι' ὅτι (*sic v.* 23) o. ευαρεστηκεναι o. 6. πιστευσας m. —γαρ o. +πρωτον (*post* δει) ab. —τῳ k. εστιν mn. εκζητουσι d. +εξ (*ante* αυτον) o. 7. βλεπωμενων dh. κατεσκευασαι d. κατεσκευασεν e. τοις (*pro* της) f. —και της κατα πιστιν *ad fin. vers.* h. 8. καλουΜενος (Μ *rubro, altero* μ *eraso*) g. ἀβρααμ hkmo (*sic vv.* 9, 17 mo; ἀβρ. ln). εμελλεν a. ημελλεν dmn. εμελλε bcefgk. εξηλθεν n. *fin.* εχεται c. απερχηται o. 9. +ἀβρααμ (*post* παρωκησεν) mo. —την a*b*cdeghk [*non* mno]. σκηνêς k*. 10. ἡς n. δημηουργος d. 11. +στειρα ουσα f, +ἡ στειρα m (*post* σαρρα). +στειρα οὑσα (*post* δυναμιν) k. ελαβεν mn (+εις το τεκνωσαι m). ἡληκιας f. ἐτεκεν k. ἡγισατο d. 12. διὸ n. εγγεννηθησαν k. καθῶς mn. +και (*post* καθως) o. ὡς ἡ (*pro* ὡσει) abdefghklmno. 13. —αυτας d. ιδοντες αυτας k. +τας επαγγελιας ιδοντες (*post* ιδοντες) o. —και πεισθεντες abdefghklmno. *Rasura in* k *inter* παρεπιδημ *et* οι. 14. *Rasura in* k *ante* εμφανιζουσιν. +και (*post* ὅτι) m. επιζητουσιν dmn. 15. οἱ (*pro* ει) k. εμνημονεβου d. εφ' h, εξ m (*pro* αφ'). εξηλθεν o. 16. νυν abcfhklmno. ὀρεγονται ko. τοῦτέστιν ko. διὸ n. +και (*post* διο) o. ἡτοιμασε n. αυτους (*pro* αυτοις) o. 17. προσενινοχεν d. προσσενηνοχεν k. ἀβρααμ kl *alii*. ἰσαακ (*sic vv.* 18, 20) n. προσηφερεν d. αναδεξαμενος (ξ *mutat.*) g. 18. ελαληθει d. −ὅτι a*. ἰσαακ *hic tantum* k. κ *in* κληθησεται *mutat. in* m. 19. ὁ θς εγερει (−δυνατος) o. ὅθεν n. εκομησατο d*. 20. +και (*ante* περι) b*m. ηυλογησεν (*non v.* 21) m. ἰσαυ k [ἡσαυ dhlmno]. ἰακωβ? (*sic v.* 21) n. 21. ἰωσηφ (*sic v.* 22) n. ευλογησεν emn. προσεκοινησεν n. ῥβδου m. 22. εμνημονευσαι d. εμνημονευσεν mn. ὀστεων ko. 23. μωυσης (*sic v.* 24 *omnes*) abcdefghklmno. εκριβη c. −και d. 24. φαραῶ no. 25. ἐλλομενοι f. ἑλομενος o. 26. μειζωνα o. ἡγισαμενος d. αιγυπτου (*pro* εν αιγυπτῳ) ehn, *at* τον αιγυπτου θησαυρον f. αἰγυπτω (*sic vv.* 27, 29 k) kmo. θησαυρὸν o. ονειδεισμον d. 27. πιστι h. +μωυσης (*post* πιστει) a*. κατελειπεν do. φοβηθης o. βασιλεος (*mutat.*) d. εκαρτερησεν m. 28. προτοτοκα k. θηγει c. θηγη m. θιγη τα προτοτοκα o. 29. πειραν (ει *mut.*) h. −οἱ b*. αἰγυπτιοι o. κατεποντισθησαν (*pro* κατεποθησαν) k. 30. τειχη (*pro* τειχει) c (*sic*). ἱεριχῶ ko [ἱεριχὼ hlm]. επεσον m. κυκλωθεντας d. 31. απειθησασιν df. ὑποδεξαμενη cdf. 32. −τι k*. επιληψει d. επιληψη k. −γαρ b*. δηγουμενον b. +αλλων (*ante* προφητων) m. 33. *init.* οἱ k, *at* οἱ ἁγιοι παντες a*o, *init. peric.* (οἱ ‖ οἱ a). κατηγονισαντο o. εἰργασαντο k. 34. μαχειρας (*mutat.*) m. εγεννηθησαν o. ισχυροι· h. 35. αυτῶν (*sic*) h. κριττονος d. κρειττονως o. 36. εμπεγμων o. −δε *secund.* m. 37. *Rescript. super rasur. in* b επρισθησαν επειρασθησαν εν φονω μαχαιρας. αἰγιοις o. κακοχουμενοι dm. 38. πλανομενοι ko. ὡρεσι d. σπ *mutat. in* m. ὀπαις ko. 39. μαρτυριθεντες o. −της m. 40. του θυ περι ἡμων· *cum præcedentibus jungit* m. τελεωθωσι d. τελειωθωσιν mo.

Cap. XII. 1. εχωντες o. −ἡμιν *prim.* o. τρεχομεν cdfo. −τον h. 2. *Rasura in* k *ante* αισχυνης. κεκαθηκεν ado. κεκαθικε bf. κεκαθικεν ceghklm [*hiat* n]. 3. αναλογησασθε cf. αναλογισασθαι m. ὑπομενηκοτα m. ἁμαρτωλων b. −ὑμων a*m. 4. +γαρ (*post* ουπω) o. αντεκατεστητε dklm. αντεκατε (*sic*) o. προς την ἁμαρτιαν αντικυτεστητε c. ἁμαρτι b*. της ἁμαρτιας m*. αναγωνιζομενοι b*. αγωνιζομενοι m. 5. εκλελυσθε a*. ἡμιν (*pro* ὑμιν) o. −ὡς m. διαλεγετε k. −μου am. ολιγορη k. ὀλιγωρει o. παιδιας d. μὴδὲ hklmo. 6. Ὃν o. μαστιγει m. παραδεχηται (*dubium*) c. 7. *init.* εις (*pro* ει) l*mo. ει σπαιδειαν ?e. παιδιαν dfo. ὑπομενεται d. ἡμιν

d. ὐ (*pro* ου) o. 8. εσται παιδιας d. γεγονασιν e. ἆρα o. *fin.* και ουχ υιοι εστε m. 9. –πατερας a. ενετρεπομεθα abc (*tacitè*) defghklmo. ὑποταγησωμεθα d. πρων̄ dk, πνικῶν o (*pro* πνων̄). –και *secund.* o. ζησωμεν dm. 10. ὀλιγας ko. τα (*pro* το *prim.*) d. οἱ δε (*pro* ὁ δε *cf.* VII. 21) ko. ἁγιωτητος df. 11. παιδια o. δε *secund. bis script.* o. ειρηνηκον d. αυτοις (*pro* αυτης) g. γεγυμνασμενος d*. 12. *Rasura in* b *inter* παρει *et* μενας. ανορθωσατο k. 13. +τας (*ante* τροχιας) m. χολον o. ιαθηναι o. 14. *init.* +αδελφοι m. οὐ (*pro* οὐ) m. ὀψετε k. 15. πικρά l*. φυουσαι g. δι᾽ αὐτης (*pro* δια ταυτης) k. μιανθωσιν o. 16. ἠσαυ b**dhklmo. πρωτοτοκεια d. 17. ἰστε ko. εὑρεν mo. εζητησας o. 18. ψυλαφωμενω d. ψηλαφομενω fhlo. ορει ψηλαφωμενω m. 19. ἠχῷ m. φωνῇ km. ακουοντες l. 20. θηγη fm. λιθοβολιθησεται m. –η βολιδι κατατοξευθησεται abcdefghjklm. 20, 21. και οὑτως η βολιδι κατατοξευθησεται· φοβερον o. 21. οὑτως klm. μωϋσης a bcdefghjklmo. εμφοβος fk. 22. *Rasura in* k *inter* ι *et* λημ̄. μυριᾶσιν o. 23. πανηγυρει· *cum præcedent.* abdhjklmo. απογεγραμμενων εν ουρανοις m. –θῳ̄ b**. 24. *init.* –και l*. κρειττον abcdefghjklmo. λαλουντα k. το (*pro* τον) b**hj [*non* dklm]. 25. οἱ (*pro* ει) m. –της abcdefghjklmo. παραιτησαμενοι τον επι γης m. παραιτησαμενον o. ουρανου bcdfhjkl. 26. εσαλευσεν mo*. *Rasura in* d *post* μονον. [αγγαι^ϑ j *marg. rubro*]. 28. *init.* +αδελφοι o. παραλαβοντες o. εχομεν acde**fkm. λατρευομεν abcdeghjk mo. ευχαριστως (*pro* ευαρεστως) f. αἰδοῦς k. 29. θς̄ *mutat. in* d. καταναλισκων d. καταναλσκον o*.

CAP. XIII. 2. επιλανθανεσθαι do. +τους (*ante* αγγελους) ?k*. 3. μνησκεσθε d*. +δε (*post* μιμνησκεσθε) h. κακουχουμενον c. κακοχουμενων (*cf.* XI. 37) dm. 4. ε (*pro* εν) m. πᾶση d. πασιν o. κὴ ἡ (*pro* και ἡ: ἡ *mutat.*) m. 5. ουδε μη (–ου) m. εγκαταλειπω cdfkmo. 6. θαρουντας dk. ποισει a*. μοι *bis script.* d*. 7. ὑμων (*pro* ἡμων) c (*sic*). οἰτινες k. ἡμιν (*pro* ὑμιν) c. –ὑμιν o. της ανα *vix p. m. in* a. στροφης m*. την εκβασιν της αναστροφης *rescript. super rasur.* b**. μιμεισθαι o. *fin. Unum verbum erasum in* k. 8. –και *prim.* m. 9. πικιλαις d. παραφερεσθε abcfhjkm** [*non* o]. παραφερεσθαι m*. 10. εχωμεν h. 11. –εις τα ἁγια δια του αρχιερεως c. καιεται k. κατα (*pro* κατακαιεται) m. κεεται o. 12. +ὁ (*ante* ις̄) ho. τον λαον δια του ιδιου αἱματος g. οικειου (*pro* ιδιου) k. επαθεν d*emo. 13. εξερχομεθα k. ὀνειδισμον k. ονειδεισμον o. 14. εχωμεν f. ὡδε gl [*non* hkmo]. 15. αναφερομεν b*cdmo. διὰ παντὸς o *alii.* –τουτεστι a. καρπῶν f. 16. μὶ επιλανθανασθε c. επιθανεσθε o*. 17. ἡγουμενης d. ὑπηκετε d. ἡμων (*pro* ὑμων *secund.*) k. αποδοσοντες o. ποιωσιν m. ἀλυσι-

γαρ o. 18. προσευχεσθαι cd. *Rasura in* k *inter* συνειδη *et*
). εχωμεν h. εν πασι· hk *at* εν πασι καλως, o. 19. ταχειον
·ω̂ m. 20. −τον *prim.* m. *fin.* +χ̅ν̅ f. 21. ποιειν (*pro*
ιν (*pro* ὑμιν) defgk. αυτου *secund. bis script. in* m. −των
ουν (*pro* δε) m. απεστειλα ab*. 23. γινωσκεται d. +ἡμων
n. απολελυμενων m. αν *vel* εν (*pro* εαν) m. ταχειον d.
ερχητε dk. ὀψομαι ko, *at* οψυμον c. 24. ἡγουμαινους c.
·o) a. −της b*. ιταλειας a. ἰταλιας kmo.

init. +ἡ ak. −προς ἑβραιους bghj. −της bhjk. ἰταλιας ko.
at ψ̅γ̅ o, ψ̅ν̅ +δοξα τω παντοκρατορι θω̅· αμην j. *fin.* +αναγν.
τ. λ̅. στ^{x} ψ̅γ̅ k. *Nil habent* lm. *Cum Elzev. prorsus* d.

S. JOHANNIS APOCALYPSIS.

[CAP. I. 1—5].

ικαλυψις adg. +του ἁγιου (*ante* ιωαννου) bcn. αποκαλυψις
τολου ιωαννου του θεολογου και ευαγγελιστου e *rubro.* απο-
ιου ιω̅ του αποστολου και ευαγγ. θεολογου h *rubro.* αποκα-
υ και ενδοξου αποστολου και ευαγγελιστου ιωαννου του θεο-
ατμω τη νησω εθεασατο l *rubro.* αποκαλυψις του ἁγιου ιω̅
ἢν ειδεν εν πατμω m *rubro.* *Cum Elzeviro* fj. *Nil habet* k.
ἐσημανεν g. δι' αγγελου (−του) n. 2. εμαρτυρησεν adlm.
ὁσα τε g. −τε abcdefhjklmn. ειδεν adfgm. οιδα (*pro* ειδε) e.
*. *fin.* +και ἁτινα εισι (εισιν l) και ἁ (ἁτινα n. −ἁ l). χρη
ταυτα hln. 3. *init.* +και k. μακαριον ?f*. τους *bis script.*
(*post* προφητειας) l. +οἱ (*ante* τηρουντες) g. *vv.* 3, 4 *uno*
εστι ταις ἑπτα (−ιωαννης). 4. ἰωαννης (*sic v.* 9, *non v.* 1) g.
ἁ *erasâ*) d. εἱρηνη g. −ταις εν τῃ ασιᾳ k. κ̅υ̅ c, θ̅υ̅ abdefgjk
m.). −του *prim.* hln. ὢν l. ὁ ἦν amn. ἦν g (*non v.* 8). −ὁ
ς (*non v.* 8). −εστιν abcdefgjkm, *at* εστι n. ἐνωπιον g. *fin.*
ου) n. 5. −ὁ *secund.* j. ὁς μαρτυς πιστος εστιν (*pro* ὁ μαρ-
υτοτοκος l. −εκ abcdefgjklmn [*non* h]. αγαπωντι abcdefgjkl

[*non* hn], *at* ὁς ἠγαπησεν (*pro* τῳ αγ.) m. ελουσεν m. λυσαντι n. εκ (*pro* απο *secund.*) n*. ἁμαρτιων g. *Ante* λουσαντι *inserit* l λυσαντι και των της ἁμαρτιας κιλιδων λουσαντι τη εκχυσει του ζωοποιου αἱματος και ὑδατος και ποιησαντι ἡμας βασιλειον ἱερατευμα και. 6. εποιησεν g. ποιησαντι f. ἡμιν (*pro* ἡμας) c. βασιλειαν (*pro* βασιλεις και) abcdeghjklm [n *cum Elzev.*]. βασιλειον ἱερατευμα (−και) f. −και το κρατος j. αἰωνας (*sic v.* 18 *bis, at hic* αἰωνων) g. −των αιωνων jn. 7. ὀψεται *et* ὀφθαλμος g. αυτων (*pro* αυτου *prim.*) n. +ὁ (*ante* οφθαλμος) m. αὐτον *secund.* g. κοψωνται f. ἑπαὐτον g. 8. αλφα abcdfghjkmn [*non* e]. ὦ g. [ω abcf, *alii*]. −αρχη και τελος abcd efghjkl [m *cum Elzev.*]. ἡ αρχη και το τελος n. κς̅ ὁ θς̅ (*pro* ὁ κυριος) abce fghjklmn [*hiat* d]. και ὁ ὢν l. ὁ ἦν amn. −και *quartum* f. +και (*ante* ὁ παντοκρατωρ) b. −ὁ *ultim.* n. 9. −και *prim.* abcd?efghjklmn. ἡμων (*pro* ὑμων) n. κοινωνος abcdeghjkl [*non* fmn]. −εν τῃ *secund.* abcefghjkmn [*non* l: *hiat* d]. ὑπομονῄ m. εν χω̅ ιυ̅ (*pro* ιυ̅ χυ̅ *prim.*) abcdefghjklm [*non* n]. −δια *secund.* cmn. *fin.* −χυ̅ n. 10. −εν *secund.* n. ἠκουσα g. ὀπισω gm. φωνην οπισω μου abcdefghjklm (−μου f). οπισω μου φωνην σαλπιγγος μεγάλην (−ὡς) n (*falsò Wetst.*). 11. λαλουσης (*pro* λεγουσης) ?g. −λεγουσης l. −εγω ειμι *usque ad* εσχατος και abcdefghjkmn, *at* l *legit* εγω αλφα και το ω̅· πρωτος και ὁ εσχατος· ὁ βλ. ἁ (*pro* ὁ) m. βλεπης g. +ἑπτα (*ante* εκκλησιαις) abcdefgh jklmn. −ταις εν ασιᾳ abcdefghjklmn. ἐφεσον g. −και (*post* εφεσον) bn. σμυρνην e. μυραν g*. μυρναν g**. θυατειραν dfm. και *bis script. post* θυατειρα g. −και εις σαρδεις j* (*habet supra, recenti manu*). εἰς *quintum* h. και εις *bis script. post* σαρδεις g. φιλαδέλφιαν akln. φιλαδελφους d. λαοδικιαν d*n. 12. *init.* εκει (*pro* και) c. +εκει (*ante* επεστρεψα) abdeghjkl [*non* fmn]. −την f. ελαλει abcefhjkmn. ελαλη d. ἐλαλη g. ελαλησεν l*. ιδον fl. χρυσους k. 13. *init.* ὁ (*pro* και) k. −ἑπτα n. +των χρυσων (*post* λυχνιων) m. υἱον bcdflmn [*non* ek]. ποδυρη f. εν (*pro* προς) m. μασθοις ejl. μαζοις hn. ζωννην e. 14. κεφαλη g. τριχαις b. και ὡς aekm, ὡς bcdfgjl (*pro* ὡσει, *Elzev.* hn). ἐριον g. ερειον l. +και το ενδυμα αυτου (*ante* λευκον) j. −λευκον d. λευκον *cum sequent.* f. +και (*ante* ὡς χιων) d. ὁ χιων (*pro* ὡς χιων) k. χιον n. −ὡς (*ante* φλοξ) n. φλογξ l. 15. *init.* −και l. χαλκῶ λιβάνω l. −ὡς εν καμινῳ πεπυρωμενοι j. φωνῆ *secund.* n. 16. ειχεν (*pro* εχων) m. χειρι αυτου cfhm. −χειρι gn. ἀστερας k. ὀξεια gk. ὀψις g. −ὁ j. φαινη k. 17. ιδον l. επεσον abefkn. ἐπεσον g [επεσα cdhjlm]. εθηκε abcefjk [*non* n]. εθηκεν dl*m. −χειρα abcdefgjklm [*non* hn]. −μοι abcdefghjklmn. −ὁ *ultim.* k. 18. εἰμὶ gj *alii.* −των αιωνων αμην j. τας (−τας k) κλειδας (κλεις hlm) του θανατου και του ἀδου abcdefghjklm (ἅδου ak, αἵδου g, ᾅδου hj) *at* n *cum Elzev.* 19. +ουν (*post* γραψον) abcd?efghklmn [*non* j]. ιδες (*sic v.* 20) l. εἰσὶ ghjl** (εἰσὶν l*). γενεσθαι bc?fhn? —γινεσθαι k. μετα ταυτα *cum sequent.* f. μεταταῦτα hl. 20. —τας *prim.* aegk. και των ἑπτα λυχνιων (—τας χρυσας) j. +ταυτα εστιν (*post* χρυσας) b. ἄγγελοι *et* εισι *bis* g. εισι των ἑπτα εκκλησιων j. εισιν *prim.* fl*m (*post quod desunt omnia ad fin. capitis in* f). —και *secund.* k. αἱ λυχνιαι αἱ ἑπτα abcegk. —ἃς ειδες bcegjkl m. ἑπτα *ultim.* gj. *fin.* και αἱ λυχνιαι αἱ ἑπτα εκκλησιαι εισι jl (εισιν l*). και αἱ ἑπτα λυχνιαι αἱ (ι *insertum*) ἑπτα εκκλησιαι εισιν m. *fin.* εισιν n, *cætera in versu prorsus cum Elzev.*

CAP. II. 1. *Linea inter Capp.* I *et* II *erasa in* l. εν εφεσω (*pro* εφεσινης) abcd?efgh? (*rasur. post* εφεσω h) jk (εν νεφεσω k) lmn. *Jungit* e γραψον τάδε. γραψον εκκλησιας k. +κυριος (*post* λεγει) km. +χειρι (*post* δεξια) m. —αυτου c. —ἑπτα *secund.* j. λυχνων f. 2. *init.* ὡν ειδα (*pro* οιδα) n. ἐργα g. —και τον κοπον σου ek. —σου *secund.* hn. δυνει l. κακα c. επειρασας abcde fhjklmn. ἐπειρασας g. τους λεγοντας ἑαυτους αποστολους ειναι abcdef (αποστολου f) ghjklmn. εισιν dfl*m. 3. *Transferunt* abcdefgjkm [*non* ln] και εβαστασας *in locum post* εχεις (εχειν k). +με (*post* εβαστασας) l. —και *tert.* abcdefghjklmn. —δια c. ὀνομα g. —κεκοπιακας abcdefhjklmn. *fin.* και ουκ εκοπιασας abcdefghjklmn. 4. αλλα abcdfghjlm [*non* en]. 5. ὁθεν (*pro* ποθεν) bn. πεπτωκας abcdefgjkm [*non* hln : πεΠπτωκας j, Π *rubro*]. —σοι h. μετανοησεις jl. 6. μισης g. 7. οὖ (*pro* οὖς) f. νικουντι l. —αυτῳ h. *fin.* εν τω παραδεισω (παραδισω k) του θῦ μου (—μεσῳ του) abcdefgjkl [*non* hmn]. *fin.* +μου fhm. 8. *init.* —και m. της εν σμυρνη εκκλησιας (εκκλισιας b) ab cdefhjklm. της σμυρναιων εκκλησιας n. ὁ εν σμυρΝνηι (Ν *rubro*) g. —ὁ *secund.* ch. +ὁ πρωτος των νεκρων (*post* εσχατος) f. —ὃς abegjk [*non* lmn]. *fin.* και εζησε πρωτος n. 9. —την *secund.* n. πτωχιαν j. αλλα πλουσιος ει (—δε) abcdefghjklmn. +σου (*post* βλασφημιαν) m. +εκ (*ante* των λεγοντων) abcdefgjklm [*non* hn]. ἑαυτους ιουδαιους ειναι n. αυτους (*pro* ἑαυτους) c. 10. μη (*pro* μηδεν) g. μὴδὲν jklmn. ὦ (*pro* ἃ) n, *errat Wetst.* μελλει e. παθειν abcdefgjk [*non* hlmn : *at* πειθανειν k, *p. m. eras.*]. +δη (*post* ιδου) abc deghj [*non* fl]. βαλλειν aem. ὁ διαβολος εξ ὑμων abcdefhjlmn. ὁ διαβολος βαλειν ἐξ ὑμων g. φυλακην (ην *mutatum*) g. ἐξητε d. ἐξεται e. ἐξετε lm n. ἡμερας abcdefgjk [*non* hlmn]. 11. οὖς (*et in v.* 17) n. ακουσατῳ j. λεγει το π̅ν̅α̅ c. αδικιθη ek. του δευτερου θανατου n. 12. *Hic versus et deinceps usque ad* και γνωσονται *v.* 23 *prorsus omittit* k, *nullo omissionis vestigio.* 13. —ὁπου *prim.* f. —και (*post* πιστιν μου) abcdef (*etiam* —μου f) ghjlmn. +μου (*post* ἡμεραις) g. —εν (*ante* αἱς) abcd?efgj. αντεῖπας j. +και (*post* αντιπας) m. +μου (*ante* ὁς) f. −ὁς cm. παρ' ἡμιν e. παρ' ὑμων g. *fin.* ὁ σατανας κατοικει abcdefghjlmn. 14. αλλα abcdfgj. ὀλιγα gln. −εκει j. βααμ (*pro* βαλααμ) g*. εδιδαξε abcefghjl. εδιδαξεν dm. εδιδασκε n. βαλααμ bfg*, βαλαακ cg** (*pro* βαλακ). +και (*ante* φαγειν) abcdefgjlm. ειδωλωθυτα c*. 15. ου (*pro* συ) f. −των abcdefm [*non* ln]. ὁμοιως (*pro* ὁ μισω) abcdefghjlmn (*cum sequent.* f). 16. +ουν (*post* μετανοησον) abcdegjl m [*non* fn]. −σοι f. σου m. *fin.* +και εν τη απειλη ἡ φιλανια l. 17. λεγει το πνα c. νικοντι dl. των νικολαϊ τω νικωντι (*pro* τῳ νικωντι) f. −φαγειν απο abcdegj [*habent* hln]. του φαγειν μανα f* (−απο του: *at* μαννα f**). του μαννα φαγειν (−απο) m. κεκρυμενου n. *Transfert* j και δωσω αυτω του μαννα του κεκρυμμενου *in locum post* λαμβανων. κενον g. −ὃ n. οιδεν (*pro* εγνω) abcdefghjlmn. λαμβανον g. 18. τοις (*pro* της) cn. θυατηροις ab. θυατειρη djl. θυατειρα f. θυγατεροις n. κς (*pro* υἱος) f. ὀφθαλμους g. χαλκῷ λιβάνῳ l. 19. και την πιστιν και την αγαπην και την διακονιαν g. και την πιστιν και την διακονιαν abcdefhjlmn. −και (*ante* τα εσχατα) abcdef ghjlmn. 20. αλλα abdgjm [*non* celn]. −ολιγα abcdefghjlm. πολλα (*pro* ολιγα) n. ἀφεὶς abcefhjmn, ἀφεῖς dl, αφιης g (*pro* εᾳς). +σου (*post* γυναικα) abcdefghjmn [*non* l]. ιεζαβελ abcdeghjln (*errat Wetst. de* n). ἰεζαβελ fm. ἡ λεγει (*pro* την λεγουσαν) abcdefghjmn (*at* ἥ dn, ἥ m). ἥ λεγει αυτην l. προφητην h*lm. και διδασκει και πλανα τους εμους δουλους abcdefghjlmn. *fin.* φαγειν ειδωλοθυτα abcdefghjlmn (εἰδωλ. g). 21. αυτην (*pro* αυτῃ) g. *fin.* ἱνα μετανοηση (μετανοησηι g, μετανοησει l) και ου θελει (θελοι l) μετανοησαι εκ της πορνειας αυτης abcdefghjlmn. 22. −εγω abcd?efghjlmn. κλινην (ην *mutatum*) g. μοιχευσαντας f. *fin.* αυτης (*pro* αυτων) abcefghlm (*hiat* d). 23. −εν f. −αἱ k. εκκλησι f. εκλησιαι g*. −εγω k. νεφρον n* (-ους *recentissimè*). 24. −δε c. εγω (*pro* λεγω) j. τοις (*pro* και *prim.*) abcd (*teste Mill.*) efghjlmn. −και *prim.* k. θυατηροις bln. θυατειραις f. −και *secund.* abcdefghjklmn. ὁσοι (*pro* οἱτινες) n. βαθεα abcdfghjklm [*non* n]. βαθυτερα e. βαλλω abcdegjklm [*non* f]. ουκ αλλ εφ' (*pro* ου βαλω εφ') n* *ut videtur.* ἡμας (*pro* ὑμας) k. αλλω l. 25. [εχετε c: *errat Paulus*]. αχρι f. ἄχρισοῦ h. ἥξω n. ανοιξω (*pro* αν ἡξω) abdefgjk [*non* hlmn]. 26. *init.* −και kl. τελων (*pro* τηρων) k. *Rasura post* τα *in* h. 27. σιδηρω n. +ἀ (*ante* ὡς *prim.*) d. κεραμεικα bce. συντριβησεται abcdefghjkmn [*non* l]. εἴληφα n. απο (*pro* παρα) n. 28. πρώινον f. 29. οὖς k *passim.* οὖς n *passim.*

CAP. III. 1. τοις (*pro* της) e. +κυριος (*ante* ὁ εχων) m. −ἑπτα *prim.* n. −του θῦ b. τα εργα σου j. ἑργα k. −το (*ante* ονομα) abcdefghjklmn. και ζης (*pro* ὁτι ζης) abcdefgjk [*non* hlmn, *errat Wetst. de* n]. −και *ultim.* f.

2. στηρισον a*cdgh**. τηρησον (*pro* στηριξον) bekn. στηρησον h*. στηρηζων l [m *cum Elzev.*]. εμελλε αποβαλλειν a. εμελλες (ημελλες bj) αποβαλλειν bcdefgjk (−ά f). εμελλες αποβαλειν h. ημελλεν αποθανειν l. εμελλον αποθανειν m. εμελλον αποθνησκειν n. −πεπληρωμενα b. *fin.* +μου abcdefghjkl mn. 3. −ουν f. εἴληφας και ἤκουσας· τηρει (−και) n. −και ηκουσας και τηρει abcdefgjk [*habent* hlm]. γρηγορησεις l. ἥξει *prim.* f. ἥξω *bis* n. −επι σε *prim.* n. γνωση bdefgjkm [*non* n]. γνωσει l. ποῖαν df. ἥξα *secund.* g. 4. *init.* αλλ' ολιγα (ὀλιγα lm) εχεις ονοματα (ὀνο. g) abdeghjlm. αλλ' (αλλα f) ολιγα ονοματα εχεις cfk. αλλ' ἔχεις ὀλιγα ον. n. −και *prim.* abcdefghj klmn. αἳ k, οἳ n (*pro* ἃ). αυτων τα ἱματια αυτων n. ἱματια l. περιπατησουσιν dfl*mn. λευκαις e. εἰσίν fh. 5. οὕτως ah. περιβαλλεῖται m. −εκ της βιβλου *usque ad* ονομα αυτου n. του (*pro* της *prim.*) k. εν βιβλω της ζωης ταυτης (*ut videtur*) g. ὁμολογησω abcdefghjklm. −και *ultim.* l. ενωπιον *secund.* h*?. 7. φιλαδελφια acklmn. κ̅ς̅ ὁ ἅγιος και αληθινος (−ὁ *secund.*) m. −ὁ *tert.* n. κλειν abcdeghjkl [*non* fmn]. ἁδου (*pro* δαβιδ) l*. *fin.* και ουδεις κλεισει (κλειση el) αυτην ει μη ὁ ανοιγων (+και κλειων l) και ουδεις (οὐδεὶς g) ανοιξει (ανοιξη el) abd? (*teste Mill.*) efghjkl. κλεισει και κλειων m. και ουδεις κλειων και ὁ κλειων και ουδεις ανοιγων n (*malè Wetst.*). *fin.* ανοιξει c (*cætera cum Elzev.*). 8. οδου (*pro* ιδου) f*. +σοι (*post* δεδωκα) m. σοι ενωπιον n. θυραν ενωπιον σου g. ηνεωγμενην cm. ἣν (*pro* και *prim.*) abcd (*Mill.*) efghjlmn. μακραν f. τα ἐργα (*pro* τον λογον) g. 9. διδομι l. διδωμοι n. ἥξουσι bcn. ἥξωσιν dl*m. ἥξωσι f, *at* αξωσι k. προσκυνησουσιν bc. ενωπιον *bis scriptum* f. αυτων ποδων k*. γνωση f. −εγω abcdefghjkm [*non* n]. ἠγαπισα g. ἠγαπησας σε kn (n *tamen habet* εγω). 10. σου (*pro* μου) k. της της γης h. 11. −ιδου abcdefghjklm [*non* n]. +σοι (*ante* ταχυ) c. ταχει f*. μηδεὶς mn. *fin.* ἱνα μη λαβη τις ταχυ τον στεφανον σου l. 12. ναω abcdefhjlmn, *at* ὀνοματι g (*pro* λαῳ), πιο *eras. ante* ναω k. −μου *prim.* e. −και εξω *usque ad* του θ̅ῡ μου *tert.* j. ἐτη (*pro* ετι) g. εξελθει k. εξελθω n. −επ' αυτον n. θ̅ῡ ? (*pro* θ̅ῡ *tert.*) f*. −μου *tert.* f. ἣ dgl, ἡ fm (*pro* ἣ). ἡ καταβαινουσα n. απο του ουρανου (*pro* εκ) abcdegklm. −απο *sequens* bl. −μου *ultimum* abcdefgjkl. 13. *fin.* +του θ̅ῡ n. 14. της εν λαοδικεια (λαοδικια bl) εκκλησιας abcdefghjklmn (−εκκλησιας g). ὁ (*pro* και *secund.*) fln. απαρχη (*pro* αρχη) n. πιστεως (*pro* κτισεως) b. 15. −ὁτι n. −ουτε *prim.* c*. ὀφελον gm. ωφελον k. οφελος l. ης (*pro* ειης) abcdefg (ἧς g) hjlm, *at* ἧς ὁ ζεστος (−η) n. *Jungit* k οὕτως· *cum præcedent.* 16. ἧς (*pro* ει) m. ου (ουτε n) ζεστος ουτε ψυχρος abcdefghjklmn. εμμεσαι k. εμαισε l. ἐμεσαι m. 17. −ὁτι *secund.* abdefhjkl [*non* cgmn]. πεπλουτικα l. ειδας k.

—ει k. ταλαιπορος l. +ὁ (*ante* ελεεινος) abcdejkl (ελεϊνος l) m [*non* fghn]. και γυμνος και τυφλος dl. 18. συμβουλευσω n. αγορασω k. χρυσιον παρ' εμου abdefghkl [*non* n]. —παρ' εμου cjm. πλουτισεις l. ἱματια l. περιβαλλη fmn. περιβαλει l. φανη f. αισχυνηι g, ασχημοσυνη l (*pro* αισχυνη). κολλυριον bcdfjlm. κουλουριον en [gk *cum Elzev.*]. ἱνα εγχριση abc [d *illeg.*] efgjkm, ἔγχρισαι l [*malè Mill.*] n, (*pro* εγχρισον). εγχρισον επι h. *fin.* βλεπεις l, *at* κλεπτης n ("*non serio scriptum*" *Wetst.*). 19. ελέῶ? (*pro* ελεγχω) k. ζηλευε abefgjkm [*non* ln]. ζηλου c. —ουν ln. 20. ἑστηκα cjkl mn. +ουν (*post* εαν) n. +και (*ante* εισελευσομαι) abcdefghjkm [*non* ln]. μετ' αυτον (*pro* μετ' αυτου) f*. 21. εκαθησα f. —εν τῳ θρονῳ μου n. 22. οὖς n, *semper nisi* II. 7.

CAP. IV. 1. μεταταῦτα h *alii* (*sic* fh *ad fin. vers.*). με (*pro* μετα) f*. ειδον fl [*initio capitis* περι της ὁραθεισης θυρας εν τω ουρανω l *rubro*]. ανεωγμενη abdefghjklmn. —ἡ *prim.* j. πρωτη k. ἠκουσα mn. λεγουσης a, λαλουσα k (*pro* λαλουσης). λεγων abcdefgjkm, και λεγουσης l (*pro* λεγουσα). ὡδε bdhjmn [*non* cf], *at* ῳδε e. δειξωσι (*pro* δειξω σοι) n*. σε (*pro* σοι) b*. *fin.* μετα ταυτα *cum sequent.* k. 2. *init.* —και abcdefgjk [*non* hlmn]. επι τον θρονον abcdefgjklm [*non* hn]. 3. —και ὁ καθημενος ην abcdefghjkmn [*non* l]. —ην l. ὑασπιδι e. σαρδιω abcdefghjklmn. ἴρις fghjlm *alii*, *at* ιερεις n (*pro* ἶρις). κυκλωθεν b*l. ὁμοιοι (*pro* ὁμοια) n. *fin.* ὁμοιως ὁρασις σμαραγδινων (σμαργαγδινων k) abdegjk [*non* ch: beg *jungunt cum v.* 4]. ὁμοιως ὁρασεις σμαραγδων f. σμαραγδω m. 4. *init.* —και abdefgjk [*non* lmn]. κυκλωθεν l. κυκλω n. εικοσιτεσσαρις *bis in versu* j. κδ *bis* ak, *prim.* g, *secund.* m. εικοσιτεσσαρες (—και) bcdefh. θρονους εικοσιτεσσαρες (—και) m. —τους θρονους ειδον g. —ειδον bcdefjklmn [*habet* h]. τους εικοσιτεσσαρας (—και) bcd efg. ὁ κδ n*, οἱ κδ πρεσβυτεροι καθημενοι n** *recenti manu*, *at* πρεσβυτερος καθημενος n*. —εν n. ἱματιοις l. —εσχον abcdefghjklmn. 5. εξεπορευοντο l. φωναι και αστραπαι και βρονται e. και φωναι και βρονται abcdfghjklmn. ἑπτα *bis in versu* g. καιομεναι πυρος g. εκκαιομεναι k. +αυτου (*ante* αἱ) abc deghjklmn. ἃ (*pro* αἱ) b. αυτου· και (*pro* αἱ εισι) f. εισιν ἑπτα (—τα) abc deghjklm [*non* n]. 6. +ὡς (*ante* θαλασσα) acdefghjklmn [*non* b: +αυτου *ante* ὡς l]. ὑαληνη g. ὑελινη j. ὑαλενη n. ὁμοιω d. κρυσταλω e. —και κυκλῳ του θρονου ekn. κυκλωθεν d. ζωα τεσσαρα n. γεμωντα l. οφθαλμους n. ὀπισθεν g, *at* οπισω k. 7. το πρωτον το ζωον b. τῶ πρωτον ζωον n. λεωντι l. ζωιον *secund. et tert.* (*sic v.* 8) g. εχων ln (—το *sequens* l). εχον προσωπον ανθρωπου (—το *et* ὡς) abcefgjkm [*non* hln: d *illeg.*]. —ζωον (*post* τεταρτον) abcefgjkm [*non* hln]. αἰτω n. πετομενω abefhjkm [cln *cum Elzev.*]. πετωμενωι g. 8. +τα (*ante* τεσσαρα) acefghlmn. ἓν καθ' ἓν (*pro* ἐν καθ' ἑαυτο) abcefghjklmn (d *illeg.*: καθ glm, καθὲν hjn). +αυτων (*post* καθ' ἓν) hlmn. −ειχον c. εχων aklm. εχον befghj. εχει n. (+ἑστως *ante* εχων m). ἐξ πτερυγας f. [δ πτερυγας n *apud Wetst. falsò*]. κυκλωθεν ln. −και εσωθεν kn. +εξωθεν και (*loco* και *ante* εσωθεν) f. γεμουσιν abcefghj klmn [d *illeg.*:]. νυκτα n. λεγοντες bcfgjklmn. ἁγιος *nonies* ahjkm, *octies* e. σαβαωθ (*pro* ὁ θς̄) ln. ὁ ἦν amn. ὁ ων και ὁ ην bc. ὁ ὁ ων n. ὢν l. 9. ὀτ' ἂν l. ὅτ' ἂν m. δωσι abc (*malè Paulus*) d??eghjkm. δωσωσι fl [n *cum Elzev.*]. +τεσσαρα (*ante* ζωα) m. ευχαριστειαν gn. +και προσκυνησωσι (*ante* τω ζωντι) ag. το ζωντι l. *fin.* +αμην g*. 10. −πεσουνται *usque ad* αιωνων a. κδ̄ ghkl. ἡ οἱ κδ̄ n. εικοσιτεσσαρες (−και) bcdefjm. προσκυνησουσιν dfl*. −και προσκυνησουσι e* (*habet marg.*). ὁ και βαλλουσι n. βαλλουσι m. βαλουσιν d. −ενωπιον του θρονου g. 11. ὁ κς̄ και ὁ θς̄ ἡμων ὁ ἁγιος (*pro* κυριε) abc (−ὁ *secund.* c) defghjkm (*at* ουρανιος *pro* ἁγιος k). +ὁ θς̄ ἡμων (*post* κυριε) ln. +και (*post* λαβειν) n. και την *erasum ante* δυναμιν k. +και (*ante* ὁτι) f. κτισας k. −τα (*ante* παντα) abcdefgjklm [*non* n]. ησαν (*pro* εισι) abcdegjk, *at* ουκ ησαν f, εισιν l*, ἐισι l**m.

CAP. V. 1. *init.* −και n. ιδον fl. −επι *prim.* n². τον θρονον n². γεγραμενον h. εξωθεν (*pro* οπισθεν) abcdeghjklmnn² [*non* f]. κατεσφιγμενον g. σφραγίσιν defjklnn² (*sic passim, at non* j *v.* 9). 2. ιδον fl. +αλλον (*ante* αγγελον) m. κηρυσοντα f*. +εν (*ante* φωνη) abcdefgjkln² [*non* hmn]. −εστιν hn². αξιος εστιν abcdefgjklmn. φραγιδας a. σφραγίδας fhkl *passim.* 3. εδυνατο abcdehjkm. ἠδυνατο g [*cum Elzev.* flnn²]. +ανω (*post* ουρανω) abcd efg (ανωι g) jkl [*non* mn]. ουτε (*pro* ουδε) *ter* acdefgjkm, *bis* bn², *tertium* l [n *cum Elzev.*]. +κατω (*post* επι της γης) b. −ουδε ὑποκατω της γης b. ὑπὸ κάτω cfjm (*sic* b *v.* 13). −ουδε βλεπειν αυτο n². 4. *Versus deest in* k. −εγω n². πολυ abcdefghjlmnn². −αξιος c. εὑρεθη αξιος n². −και αναγνωναι abcdefgjlmnn² [*non* h]. ουδε (*pro* ουτε) n. 5. −ὁ ων fn². −ων abcdeghjkl mn. −εκ n². ιουδα φυλης c. +του (*ante* δᾱδ) kn. ὁ ανοιγων (*pro* ανοιξαι) abcdefgjkm. −λυσαι abcdefghjklmnn². −ἑπτα n. +δι' (*ante* αυτου) g. 6. ιδον f. ιδων l. −και ιδου abcdefghjkln [*non* m]. ζῶων l. ἑστηκος dgk. εστηκῶς l. ἑστηκως mn. −ὡς cg. εσφραγισμενον cl. εχων ln. −και (*ante* οφθαλμοὺς) f. ἃ abcdefghkln, ἁτινα j (*pro* οἵ). εισιν dl*. πνευματα του θῡ αποστελλομενα (−τα) abcdefghjkm. πνευματα του θῡ τα αποστελλωμενα l. πνευματα του θῡ n. 7. ηλθεν adl*m. ειληφεν abcdefhjkl*mn. −το βιβλιον abcdefghjkmn [*non* l]. *fin.* +του θῡ n. 8. ελαβεν ad. οἱ *mutat. in* f. κδ̄ adghjk (−οἱ k) l. ἡ οἱ κδ̄ (ἡ *pro* και) n. επεσαν l. εχοντες εκ της κιθαρας φιαλας χρυσας k. κιθαραν abcdfgjmn [*non* l]. χρϊστας (*pro* χρυσας) n. μεστας (*pro* γεμουσας) l. αἵ εισι προσευχων (–αἱ) adel (εισιν l*, *non* των προσευχων dl). αἵ εισι προσευχαι (–αἱ) bcfgjkm [h *cum Elzev.*]. 9. ἀδουσιν f. ᾀδουσιν h. αδουσι καινην ωδην m. ὠἱδην g. εσφαγεις l. ἡμας τω θω̄ clm. ὀνοματι (*pro* αἱματι) g*. –πασης m. φυλακης d, φϊλης k (*pro* φυλης). –και *ultim.* f. 10. αυτους (*pro* ἡμας) abcdefghjklmn. –ἡμων c*. βασιλευουσιν abefgln. βασιλευσουσιν cdhjkm. 11. ιδον fl. ἡκουσα n. +ὡς (*ante* φωνην) abcdeghjklm [*non* n]. πολλων αγγελων g. αγγελλων m. –πολλων l. κυκλω (*pro* κυκλοθεν) abcdefghjlmn. κυκλου k. +αυτου (*post* θρονου) n. 12. λεγοντων gj. εστιν dl*. +του (*ante* πλουτον) abcdefjklm [*non* n]. –και πλουτον g. +την (*ante* σοφιαν) bk. σοφι g. 13. και *prim. bis script.* f. –εστιν *prim.* abcdefgjkl [*non* hmn]. εν ουρανω και επι γης n. επι της γης abcdefghjklm. –και ὑποκατω της γης fg. ὑπὸκάτω m. –επι (*ante* της θαλασσης) k. –ἁ abcdefgjkl. ὁσα (*pro* ἁ) m. –ἁ εστι n. εστιν *secund.* dfl*. +και (*post* τα εν αυτοις) fn. παντας (*pro* παντα,) abdehjln [*non* cfkm]. +και (*ante* ηκουσα) km. ἡκουσα n. λεγοντων m. επι τω θρονω acdefklm (*non* bn, –τω k). *fin.* +αμην acdefghjkn [*non* lm]. 14. –και τα τεσσαρα ζωα ελεγον αμην g. λεγοντα το (*pro* ελεγον) abcdefhjk (–το fk; n *cum Elzev.*). ελεγον το αμην l. ελεγεν το αμην m. –εικοσιτεσσαρες abcdefghjklmn. επεσον abcefghjkn [επεσαν dlm]. –ζωντι εις τους αιωνας των αιωνων abcdefghjklmn.

Cap. VI. 1. ιδον fl. ὁτι (*pro* ὁτε) abcdefghjkm [*non* ln]. ηνοιξεν dl*m. ἡνοιξε (*sic vv.* 3, 7, 9, 12). –εκ *prim.* fh. +ἑπτα (*ante* σφραγιδων) abdefg (ἑπτα g) hjklm [*non* cn]. –και (*ante* ηκουσα) l. ἡκουσα (*sic vv.* 3, 6, 7) n. –ἑνος g. –ζωων f. λεγοντος (ος *mutatum*) f. φωνῆ alm. φωνὴ bdefghj [c *cum Elzev.*]. λεγοντος ερχου ὡς φωνὴ βροντης n. ιδε (*pro* βλεπε) abcd efgjklm. –και βλεπε hn. 2. –και ειδον abcdefgjkm [*non* hln]. ιδον l. ἱππος k (*sic vv.* 5, 8) n (*sic vv.* 4, 5, 8). επ' αυτον abcdefghjklmn. εχον g. εξηλθεν dl*. νικησει n. 3. ηνοιξεν dm. ηνυξε l. ηνοιγε k. δευτερα e. σφραγίδα dln *alii, passim* (*sic* m *v.* 7). την σφραγῖδα την δευτεραν m. ζῶιου (*sic v.* 5) g. –και βλεπε acdefghjkln. ιδε (*pro* βλεπε) bm. 4. *init.* και ειδον· και ιδου εξηλθεν m. πυρος b*cdefglmn [*non* hjk]. επ' αυτον abcdf ghjln. επ' αυτου e [*cum Elzev.* km]. εδωθη *prim.* ln. –αυτῳ *secund.* c. εκ (*pro* απο) abcdefghjkmn. –απο l. –και (*ante* ἱνα) abcdefghjkln [*non* m]. *Verbum erasum ante* αλληλους *in* j. σφαξωσιν dfl*m. κατασφαξωσι n. 5. ὁτι g**, ὁτη k (*pro* ὁτε). ηνοιξεν dm. την σφραγιδα την τριτην abcdefghjk lm. και ἡκουσα ανεωγμενης της τριτης σφραγιδος (–ὁτε) n. ιδε (*pro* βλεπε) abcdefgjkm. –και βλεπε bln (*errat Wetst. de* n). –και ειδον abcefgjkm [*non* hn], *at* ἰδου l. επ' αυτον abcdefghjklmn. 6. ζωίων g. χοίνιξ jn. διναριου *prim.* f*, *secund.* gl. –δηναριου *secund.* f. τον ελαιον f. ελεον l. αδικησεις kln?. 7. ηνοιξεν d. –φωνην abcdefgjklm [*non* hn]. λεγοντος abcdefghjklmn. ἰδε (*pro* βλεπε) abcdefgjkm. –και βλεπε hln. 8. –και ειδον acdefgjkm [*non* bhn]. ἰδον (*sic v.* 9) l. λευκος (*pro* χλωρος) g. χλορος k. –ὁ (*ante* θανατος) gh. αἴδης g. ᾄδης h. ηκολουθει abcdefg (ἠκολ. g) jkm. ηκολουθη l [*cum Elzev.* hn]. αυτω (*pro* μετ' αυτου) abcdefgkm (*sic* j** *marg. at* hj*ln *cum Elzev.*). εδοθει g. εδωθη l. αυτω (*pro* αυτοις) abcdefghjklm [*non* n]. επι το τεταρτον (+μερος n) της γης· αποκτειναι abcdefghjklmn. –εν (*ante* λιμω) k. –εν (*ante* θανατω) j. 9. ηνοιξεν dm. την σφραγιδα την πεμπτην f. πεπτην g. +και (*ante* ἰδον) f. ἰδον fl. ὑπὸ κάτω fjm. +των ανων (*post* ψυχας) h. εσφραγισμενων (*pro* εσφαγμενων) l. +του αρνιου abcdefghjkl [*non* n], +ιῦ χῦ m (*post* μαρτυριαν). ἦχον g. 10. εκραξαν φωνην μεγαλην abc (εκραζον c) de (φωνη μεγαλη ehjl) fghjklm. φωνὴ n. λεγοντος n. –και *secund.* m. –ὁ *tert.* abcegjkln [*non* m]. ὁ αληθινος και ἅγιος f. ὑμων f*n. εκ (*pro* απο) abcdefghjkm. απο (*pro* επι) n. 11. εδοθη abcdefghjkl (εδωθη l*) mn. αυτοις ἑκαστω fhlm, αυτοις abcdegjk, ἑκαστω αυτων n (*pro* ἑκαστοις). στολη λευκη abcdefghjklmn. ερεθη k. ερρηθη m. ερριθη n. αναπαυσονται dkln. αναπνευσωνται f**. ετη χρονων (*pro* ετι χρονον) m. χρονων n. –μικρον abcdefghjklm [*non* n]. ἑως πληρωσωσι (–οὗ) abc (πληρωσουσι cg) de (πληρωθωσι e) fgh (ἕωσοῦ h) jkl (πληρωσωσιν l*) m, *at* ἑως οὗ πληρώσουσι n. δουλοι (*pro* συνδουλοι) k. –και (*ante* οἱ αδελφοι) b. –οἱ αδελφοι αυτων k. +και (*ante* οἱ μελλοντες) abcdefgj [*non* hmn]. αποκτενεσθαι bcdeghklmn. αποκτεννεσθαι a [fj *cum Elzev.*]. –και *ultim.* e. 12. –ειδον aegk. ἰδον fl. +και (*ante* ὅτε) fh. ηνοιξεν d. ἤνοιξεν m. –και *secund.* a**. –ἰδου abcdefghjklmn. εγενετο μεγας c. μεγας *bis script.* e. μελας εγενετο (*pro* εγενετο μελας) abcdefghjklm (*non* n, *at* μεγας m). σκακκος f. +ὁλη (*ante* σεληνη) abcdefgj kln (*non* hm, *at* ὁλε k). εις (*pro* ὡς *secund.*) ek. αἱμα n. 13. επεσον abce fghjkmn [*non* l, d *illeg.*]. συκὴ cf**k. αποβαλλει n. βαλουσα abcdegkl. βαλλουσα jm. ὀλυνθους g. αυτηνς e. απο (*pro* ὑπο) c** *marg.* f. ανεμου μεγαλου abcdefgjklm [*non* n]. σειομενου d. σειωμενη l. 14. +ὁ (*ante* ουρανος) abcdefghjlmn. –ουρανος k. ἑλισσομενος ae (d *Mill.*) k. ἑλισσομενον fh. ἑλισσομενος bcgj (ν^{0} gj). εἰλισσομενος d *me judice.* ἑλισσομενον lm. εἰλισσομενος n. ὁρος gk. –αὐτων c. εσαλευθησαν (*pro* εκινηθησαν) g. 15. *Hiat* d *usque ad* VIII. 1. μεγιστάνες cefghjklmn. και οἱ χιλιαρχοι και οἱ πλουσιοι abcefghjklmn. ισχυροι (*pro* δυνατοι) abcefg (–οἱ g) hjklmn. –πας *secund.* abcefgjklm [*non* hn]. ὁρεων (*sic* ὀρεσι *v.* 16) gk. ὡρεων n. 16.

λεγουσιν l*. ορεσιν l*. πεσατε ln. ὑμας (pro ἡμας) bis e. κρυψετε e*
(rasura post κρυψατε in l). επι τω θρονω abcf**gkm. –και ultim. m. 17.
init. ὁτε n. τῇ μεγαλη f. fin. στηναι m.

Cap. VII. 1. τουτο (pro ταυτα) abcefhjklm [non gn]. ιδον (sic v. 2) fl.
τεσσαρεις prim. l. ἑστωτας gln. ἐπι prim. g, at ὑπο (pro επι prim.) e.
κεφαλης (pro γης prim.) m. κρατουντας usque ad της γης deest in g*,
insertum s. m. inter sequentia. +και (ante κρατουντας) bn. πεσηι g, πνευση
m (pro πνεῃ). +ὁ (ante ανεμος) afgk. μητι (pro μητε secund.) c*. τι (pro
παν) abcefgjklm [non hn]. 2. αναβαινοντα abcefghjklmn. +της (ante
ανατολης) k. φωνῇ n. εδωθη l. –αυτοις n. +τε (post αδικησαι) k. 3. –μη
αδικησητε usque ad θαλασσαν c. αδικισειτε l. μητι (pro μητε prim.) n.
ἄχρισοῦ h. αν (pro οὐ) n. σφραγισομεν c. –ἡμων gn. μετοπων mn. 4.
ἠκουσα n. –τον αριθμον g. τῶν ἀριθμῶν ln. –ρμδ χιλιαδες εσφραγισμενοι ae
gkn (at n in fine vers. χιλιαδων ρμδ habet). ἑκατοντεσσαρακοντεσσαρες b.
ἑκατονκαιτεσσαρακοντα c. ἑκατον τεσσαρακοντα και τεσσαρες f. ἑκατον
και τεσσαρακοντα (+και j) τεσσαρες (τεσσαρεις l) hjlm. εσφραγισμενων (pro
εσφραγισμενοι) bcfjlm. +των (ante υἱων) eh*. 5. ἰοῦδα l alii. εσφραγισ-
μεναι abcegj, εσφραγισμενων fkl (pro εσφραγισμενοι prim.: cum Elzev. mn).
Deest εσφραγισμενοι alibi in vv. 5, 6, 7, 8, præter ultimum in v. 8 in abefgh
jkm. l habet εσφραγισμενων pro -μενοι ter in v. 5, prorsus omittit in vv. 6,
7, usque ad v. 8 ultim.: n habet -μενοι primo et secundo loco in v. 5, prorsus
omittit reliquis locis usque ad v. 8 ultim. +και (ante εκ φυλης ρουβιν) l.
ῥουβιν abfgjln (l forsan ῥουβιμ: errat Wetst. de n). ῥουβειν c. ῥουβειμ ehm.
ῥουβεν k. δωδεκα passim bcefm. 6. init. +και l. –και φυλης ασηρ ιβ
χιλιαδες εσφρ. m. νεφθαλιμ af**. νεφθαλημ bf*k. εκ φυλης νεφθαλειμ $\overline{ιβ}$
χιλιαδες bis script. in n. –εκ φυλης μανασση ιβ χιλιαδες εσφ. k. 7. –εκ
φυλης συμεων ιβ χιλ. εσφ. m. –εκ φυλης λευι ιβ χιλ. εσφ. n. ισσαχαρ aekl.
ισαχαρ bcfhjmn. ἰσαχαρ g [ισασχαρ Elzev.]. fin. χιλιαδας m. 8. ζαβου-
λῶν fl. ζαβουλον k. χιλιαδας prim. m. –εκ φυλης ιωσηφ $\overline{ιβ}$ χιλ. εσφρ. f,
quam clausulam post εκ φυλης βενιαμιν κ. τ. λ. postponit n. fin. εσφραγισ-
μεναι abcegjkl [non fhmn]. 9. μεταταῦτα fh. –ειδον k. ιδον fl. ὀχλος
g. –αυτον abceghjklmn [non f]. εδυνατο abcehjl [non fmn]. ἠδυνατο g.
δυναται k. και λαων και φυλων e. –και (ante γλωσσων) f. ἑστωτα a.
ἑστωτας bcefm. ἑστωτας gkln. –ενωπιον secund. e. περιβεβλημενους abc
efklm [non n]. περιβεβλημενας g. φοινικας abcefghjkn [non m]. 10.
κραζουσι abcefghjkln. κραξουσι m. +κραυγη και (ante φωνη) n. $\overline{σρι}$ f.
των (pro τῳ θῷ) k. επι τω θρονω abcefghkmn [non l]. το αρνιον k. 11.

+ἁγιοι (ante αγγελοι) n. ειστηκεισαν abcefhjk. ειστηκεισαν gl*mn. ειστηκησαν l**. ζῳων g. +αυτου (post θρονου secund.) abcefjklm [non ghn]. επι τα προσωπα abcefghjklmn. 12. ἀμην prim. k. —ἡ ευλογια ad fin. versûs n (errore citat Wetst.). —ἡ (ante ευχαριστια) k. —ἡ (ante ισχυς) g. —των αιωνων m. 13. απεκριθει k. ὁτι (pro ουτοι) ek. τας λευκας στολας n. εισιν fl*. ποτε (pro ποθεν) e. 14. ειπον (pro ειρηκα) abcefghjklm [non n]. +μου (post κυριε) abcefghjklmn (συ μου n). ειπεν afgkl*mn (—μοι n). +ὁτι (ante ουτοι) e. επλατυναν (pro επλυναν) abegjk (non cflmn). —στολας αυτων secund. abcefgjklm, at αυτας legit h. και ελευκαναν τας στολας αυτων και ελευκαναν αυτας (sic) n. 15. init. +και n. διατοῦτο fhjkl. θρωνου prim. g. —του θῡ k. τουτω (pro αυτου) c. σκηνωση l. κατασκηνωσει n. επι τω θρονω abcfghkl [non n]. 16. διψασουσιν e. ουδε μη διψησωσιν f. —ετι secund. m. ουδ' ου μη (pro ουδε μη) abceghjklm [non n] (ουδε k). ουδε secund. (δ mutat.) f. ὁ ἡλιος επ' αυτους c. το (pro παν) c. 17. ἀνάμεσον f. ἀναμέσον ghkln. ποιμαινει abcegh** (supra) jkm [cum Elzev. fln, l malè Mill.]. ὁδηγει abcegh**jkm [non fn]. ὁδιγει l. αυτο (pro αυτους secund.) n. ζωης (pro ζωσας) abcefghjklmn. —παν n. παντα τα δακρυα f. εκ (pro απο) abc ehjklm [non fn].

CAP. VIII. 1. —ὁτε k. ηνοιξεν a. ἡνοιξε mn. σφραγίδα fm alii. ἑβδόμην g. +και (ante εγενετο) km. ἡμωρον j. ἡμυωριον k. 2. ιδον fl. ἑπτα semel g. +του θρονου (ante του θῡ) n. ἑστηκασιν dfl*. ἑστηκασι gn. εδοθη aghm. εδοθει k. εδωθησαν l. αυτη (pro αυτοις) e. fin. +ἱνα σαλπισωσι g. 3. ηλθεν adl*m. εξηλθε f. εσταθην f. επι του θυσιαστηριου prim. abcefgh jklmn. εδωθη l. επεδοθη n (malè Wetst.). δωσει beghmn, δωσι d, δω f (pro δωσῃ: kl cum Elzev.). 4. —του prim. j. των αγγελων f*. 5. ηλειφεν e. ειληφεν n. το (pro τον) l. εγεμησεν fkl. αυτο (pro αυτον) l. —φωναι και j. βρονται και φωναι abcdefgkm [non hn]. και αστραπαι και βρονται l. 6. +οἱ (ante αγγελοι) k. +οἱ (ante εχοντες) abcdefghjklmn. —ἑπτα secund. ej. ἡτιμασαν f*. ἡτοιμασαν l. επ' αυτους (pro ἑαυτους) f. σαλπισωσιν cdfl*m. 7. —αγγελος abcdefghjlm [non kn]. εσαλπισεν dfl*m. εσαλπησε k*?. μεμηγμενη l. μεμϋγμενα m. +εν (ante αἱματι) abcdefghjklmn. εβληθησαν m. της γης (pro των δενδρων) fj, at +και το τριτον της γης κατεκαη (post εις την γην) abcdeghkln [non m: post κατεκαῃ prim. explicit versus in k]. κατεκαει ter l. ὁ χορτος ὁ χλωρος bl. χλορος n. 8. —ὁ g. εσαλπισεν df l*m. +εγενετο (ante ὡς ὁρος) g. ὁρος gk. —πυρι abcdefghjkl [non mn]. καιομενος n. +και (ante εβληθη) g. —το n. +μερος (post τριτον, sic v. 9 primo loco) m. αἱμα n. 9. απεθανεν dl*m. —των secund. abcdefghjkln [non m].

διεφθαρησαν hn. διεφθαρει l. 10. –ὁ g. εσαλπισεν dfl*m. πιγας g. +των (*ante* ὑδατων) abcdefghjklmn. 11. *Incipit versus in* k εις αψινθον. ὀνομα g. ελεγετο l. +ὁ (*ante* αψινθος) abcdeghjmn [*non* fl, *errat Mill. de* l: *at* ἀψινθος abcjm]. εγενετο (*pro* γινεται) abcdefghjlmn (–το *sequens* n). ἀψινθον abcj. αψινθιον dln. +των (*ante* ανθρωπων) abcdefghjklmn. απο (*pro* εκ) e. 12. εσαλπισεν dfgl*m. επλη f. επλιγει l. και εσκοτισθη (*pro* ἱνα σκοτισθῃ) m. ουκ εφαινεν (*pro* μη φαινῃ) m [*cætera in* m *cum Elzev.*]. *fin.* και το τριτον αυτων (αυτοις b, αυτης cdfl, –αυτης g) μη φανη (φανει l, ἱνα μη φαινη n) ·ἡ ἡμερα (+αυτης n, –ἡ k) και ἡ νυξ ὁμοιως (*pro* και ἡ ἡμερα *ad fin. vers.*) abcdefgkln [h *cum Elzev.*]. και μη φανη ἡ ἡμερα και ἡ νυξ ὁμοιως (–το τριτον αυτης *ultim.*) j. 13. ιδον fl. –και (*ante* ἠκουσα) n. ἑνος g. αετου (*pro* αγγελου) abcdefghjkm [*non* ln]. πετομενου abcdefghjkl**mn. μεσουρανιματι jl. +τω (*ante* μεσουρανηματι) n. +τρις hn, +τρεις l (*post* μεγαλη.). οὐαὶ *ter* g. οὐαῖ *ter* l. τους κατοικουντας abcdefgjkm [*non* hln]. φανων ?n. μελοντων f.

CAP. IX. 1. εσαλπισεν dfl*m. ιδον fl. πεπτωκοτα εκ του ουρανου eg. προς την γην e. επι της γης j. εδωθη (*sic vv.* 3, 5) l. κλεῖς j. 2. –και ηνοιξε το φρεαρ της αβυσσου abcdefgjk [*non* hlmn]. ηνοιξεν m. ἠνοιξε n. –εκ του φρεατος ὡς καπνος m. καιομενης (*pro* μεγαλης) abcdefg (καὶ ὁμενης g) hjklm [*non* n]. εσκοτωθη f. ἡ σεληνη *eras. ante* ὁ αηρ *in* e. αειρ l. 3. αυτοις (*pro* αυταις) l (*sic v.* 5, *at non v.* 4). εξουσιαν (*pro* εξουσια) f. εξουσιαν εχουσιν g. 4. ερρηθη m. ερριθη n. αυτοις (*pro* αυταις) fm (*non v.* 5). αδικησωσιν l*. χλορον k. –μονους abcdefgjklmn [*non* h]. –του θεου n. μετοπων kn. *fin.* –αὐτων n. 5. αδικησωσιν (*pro* αποκτεινωσιν) g. αυτους (*forsan* αυτας *p. m.*) f. βασανισθωσιν dgn. βασανησωσιν (ν *secund. eras.*) l. βανισθωσι k. σκορπιπιου ?g*. +ὡς (*ante* ὁταν) n. ὅτᾶν m. πεση (*pro* παισῃ) bklm, *at* πληξη h** *quasi glossa supra verbum.* 6. –και εν ταις ἡμεραις ταυταις l. ζητουσιν dh. –τον k. και ου μη εὑρησουσιν abcdefghjklmn (εὑρησο σιν a, εὑρησωσιν f, εὑρησουσιν g, εὑρωσιν mn). απ᾽ αυτων ὁ θανατος abcdefgh jkm. ὁ θανατος αυτων (–απ᾽) n. επιθυμησουσι (ν *eras.*) τον θανατον και φευξεται απ᾽ αυτων l. 7. δα *eras. ante* ακριδων k. ὁμοιωτατα e. ἱπποις g *sæpe.* ἡπποις n. ἡτοιμασμενοις kl. χρυσοι (*pro* ὁμοιοι χρυσῳ) abcdefghjkl [*non* mn]. –ὡς *prim.* n. ὡσπερ (*pro* ὡς *secund.*) k. 8. τριχα *secund.* n. ὀδοντες n. 9. –*ab initio vers. usque ad* σιδηρους g. ειχων l*. –ὡς θωρακας aek. ἁρματων l. –ἱππων e. ἱππου n. 10. ὁμοιοις f. –ην lmn. και (*pro* ην) abcdefghjk. ταις ουρας d. εξουσιαν εχουσι (εχουσιν gn) του (–του n) αδικησαι (*pro* και ἡ εξουσια αυτων αδικησαι) abcdefghjkn. –και (*ante* ἡ εξουσια)

m. του (*loco* και ἡ εξουσια αυτων) l. 11. *init.* εχουσαι βασιλεα επ' αυτων αγγελον (–και *et* τον) abcdeghjkl (*at* επ' αυτους τον αγ. l; αγγελου k). εχουσαι επ' αυτων (–και) f. και εχουσι βασιλεα επ' αυτον αγγελον m. επ' αυτων n [*cætera in* n *cum Elzev.*]. ἑβραιστῆ g. ἑβραϊστι l. αββααδδων a. αββαδων bcen. αβααδδων d. αβλαδδων f. αββααδων gm. αββαδδων h. αββαιαδῶν k (*sic p. m.*). αβααδδ l, *malè Mill.* εν δε (*pro* και εν) abcdefghj klmn. εχη l. εχων απολυων k. 12. οὐαι *prim.* g. οὐαῖ *bis* l. παρηλθεν (*pro* απηλθεν) n. ερχεται abcdefghjkl [*non* mn]. ετι δυο ουαι ουαι f. –ετι j. δευτερα (*pro* ετι δυο) l. ουαι δυο n. μετα ταυτα *cum vers.* 13 *jungunt* abcdefghjkl [*non* mn: και μετα ταυτα f, μεταταῦτα h]. 13. *init.* –και f. ἐκτος k. εσαλπισεν dfl*m. ἡκουσα n. μιαν φωνην εκ του θυσιαστηριου ενωπιον του θῦ (*desunt cætera*) f. μεγαλην (*pro* μιαν) m. εκ των κερατων κεκραγοτος (–τεσσαρων) n. –του (*ante* ενωπιον) n. 14. λεγοντος abcdefgjk [*non* hlmn, *errat Wetst. de* n]. ὁ εχων abcdefghjkln, τω εχοντι m (*pro* ὁς ειχε). λῦσον fj. λυσων k. τεσσαρεις (*sic v.* 15) l. τεσσαρες m. ανεμους (*pro* αγγελους) k. εν (*pro* επι) l. 15. ελυσαν j. ανεμοι (*pro* αγγελοι) k. –οἱ *secund.* k. ἡτοιμασμενοι j. προἡτοιμασμενη n, *malè Wetst.* +εις την (*ante* ἡμεραν) abcde (+οἱ *ante* εις e) fgjklm. +την (*ante* ἡμεραν) hn. –και μηνα k. μηνα και και a. ἐνίαὐτόν f. ενιαυτον kl. αποκτεινωσιν dl*. +μερος (*post* τριτον) n. 16. +των (*ante* στρατευματων) abcdefghjklmn. ἱππου (*pro* ἱππικου) adeghjkm [*non* cl: ἱππου g]. των ἱππων (*pro* του ἱππικου) b. ἱππικου n. –δυο abdefghjklm [*non* n]. δις c. –και *secund.* abcdefghjklmn. ἡκουσα n. των αριθμων m. 17. ιδου fl. ἱππικους f. ἱππους n. ὁρασηι g. ὑάκινθινους a. ὑακινθυνους d. οιακινθινους l. ὑακινθους n. ἱππων (*sic v.* 19) n. –των (*ante* στοματων) l. εκπορευονται e. εκπορευσαι k. –και *ultim.* n. 18. απο (*pro* ὑπο) abcdefghjklmn. +πληγων (*ante* τουτων) abcdefghjklmn. απεκτανθη j. απο (*pro* εκ *prim.*) abcdefgjklm [*non* n: και απο f]. *Post* πυρος *tria verba erasa in* l. –εκ *secund. et tert.* abdefghjklmn. τουτου (*pro* του *ultim.*) m. –εκπορευομενου l. των εκπορευομενων n. του στοματος g. 19. *init.* ἡ γαρ εξουσια των ἱππων (–αυτων) abcdefghjklmn. εστι (*pro* εισιν) ab cd (*Mill.*) efghjklmn (εστιν fl*). +και εν ταις ουραις αυτων (*ante* αἱ γαρ ουραι) abcdefghjklmn (*at* των ἱππων *pro* αυτων e, και γαρ *pro* αἱ γαρ *sequent.* m). οφεων abcdegjklm [*non* hn]. αδικουσιν fl*mn. 20. –οἱ k. ου (*pro* ουτε *prim.*) abcdeghjklmn (*at* ουδε f). προσκυνησουσιν l*. δαιμωνια l. +τα (*ante* ειδωλα) abcdefghjklmn. –τα (*ante* αργυρα) c. –και τα χαλκα abcdegjkl [*habent* fhmn, *errat Wetst. de* n]. ταλυθινα f. οὔτε g *ter.* δυνανται lmn. ουτε περιπατειν *bis script.* k. 21. φώνων k. φαρμακων abcfgm [*non* ehjn].

φαρμακιων l, *malè Mill.* –ουτε εκ των φαρμακειων αυτων dk. –ουτε εκ της πορνειας *ad fin. vers.* l. κλεμμακων k. –αὐτων *ultim.* f.

CAP. X. 1. ιδον fl. αγγελον αλλον l. –αλλον abcdefghjkn [*non* m]. +και (*ante* περιβεβλημενον) n. κεφαλην (*pro* νεφελην) k. +ἡ (*ante* ἶρις) abc defghjm [*non* kl, *at* ἵρις l. ἵρις dfghjm]. ἔρϊν n. εκ (*pro* επι) d. +αυτου (*post* κεφαλης) abcdefghjklmn. ὑποδες (*pro* οἱ ποδες) g. –οἱ k. στῦλοι h. 2. εχων (*pro* ειχεν) abcdefgjkm [*non* hln]. βιβλιδαριον fhln. βιβλιον abcd egjkm. ηνεωγμενον cl. ἠνεωγμενον m. εθηκεν adl*. της θαλασσης abcdef ghjklmn. το δε ευωνυμον k. της γης acefghjklmn [*non* b]. 3. εκραξεν *prim.* l*. εκραζε k. φωνην μεγαλην d. –αἱ (*ante* ἑπτα) l. *fin.* ταις ἑαυτων φωναις l. φωνᾶς ?d. *vv.* 3, 4. –τας ἑαυτων φωνας και ὁτε ελαλησαν αἱ ἑπτα φωναι ben. 4. –αἱ *prim.* k*. –τας φωνας ἑαυτων abcdefghjkln. τας ἑαυτων φωνας m. ημελλον bfj [*non* den *alii*]. εμελλων l. ἠκουσα n. –μοι abcd efghjklmn. σφραγησον l. αυτα (*pro* ταυτα) abcdefgjklmn. γραψεις kln, *at* h και μετα ταυτα γραφεις h. 5. ιδον fl. –ἑστωτα c*jk. ἑστωτα ln. ηρεν adl*m. χειραν k*. +την δεξιαν (*ante* εις) abcdefghjklmn, *at* επι (*pro* εις) f. 6. –εν (*post* ωμοσεν) abdefgjkm [*habent* cln: *at* ωμοσε bdefgjk, ὀμωσεν l, ωμωσε m, ωμωσεν n]. ὃ (*pro* ὁς) m. εκτισεν adm. εκτησε n. –και τα εν αυτῳ n. –και (*ante* την γην *et* την θαλασσαν) e. αυτοις (*pro* αυτῃ *prim.*) n. –και την θαλασσαν και τα εν αυτῃ ck. *fin.* οὐκετι (οὐκ ἔτι adlmn) εσται ab cdefhjklmn. οὐκ ἑτι εσται g. 7. αλλ' abcdeghjklmn. ὅτ' ἂν dlm. μελλει cklmn. μεληι g. –και bh. ετελεσθη abcdefgjkm, τελεσθει l (*pro* τελεσθῃ *Elzev.* hn). ὃ (*pro* ὡς) hn. ευηγγελισεν d. ευαγγελισαι f. ευηγγελησε g. ευηγγελισατο hn. ευαγγελισε k. *fin.* τους δουλους αυτου τους προφητας abc def (αυτου δουλους f, *malè Mill.*:) ghk (–αυτου k) lm. τοις δουλοις αυτου j. τοις αυτου δουλοις n. 8. *init.* και ηκουσα φωνην εκ του ουρανου παλιν λαλουσαν και λεγουσαν μετ' εμου l. ἦν g. ἠκουσα gn. λαλουσαν f. –και (*ante* λεγουσα) n. λεγουσαν f. +και (*ante* λαβε) c. βιβλιδαριον abcdehjklmn. βιβλιον f. ανεωγμενον abdefghjkln [*non* m]. –εν c. +του (*ante* αγγελου) abcefghjklmn. ἑστωτος kln. –της *ultim.* k. 9. απηλθεν ?d. απηλθα j. δουναι (*pro* δος) abcdefgjklm [*non* hn]. βιβλιδαριον abcdef (βϊ *mutat.* f) ghjklmn. αυτῷ e, αὐτῶ l (*pro* αυτο). ποικρανει l. –εσται c. ἑσται n. γλυκω ?g*. 10. βιβλιον abcegjklm. βιβλιδαριον dfhn. εγενετο (*pro* ην) m. επι (*pro* εν) n. –ὡς n. μελϋ n. γλυκαζων (*pro* γλυκυ) l. –ὁτε εφαγον αυτο m. εποικρανθη l. 11. λεγουσι (*pro* λεγει) abd (λεγουσιν d) efgjkm [*non* chn]. δευτε (*pro* δει σε) e. προφητευσαι παλιν j. λαου g, λαους m, πολλοις j (*pro* λαοις). +επι (*ante* εθνεσι) abdefghjklmn [*non* c: εθνεσιν adfkl*]. –και (*ante* γλωσσαις) n. γλῶσσαις m. βασιλευσιν l*.

Cap. XI. 1. εδωθη (*sic v.* 2) l. −και ὁ αγγελος ἑιστηκει abc (*habet* και c) degjkln (*at* και φωνη λεγουσα n). ἑιστηκει ὁ αγγελος fhm (ἑιστηκει m). εγειρε adfklm. μετρησαι gl (−και *ante* μετρησαι l). μετρισον n. λαον (*pro* ναου) e. −εν c*. 2. εξοθεν f, εσωθεν m (*pro* εξωθεν). εξωθεν (*pro* εξω) fh mn. μετρηση k. μετρησεις l. μετρισης n. +αυτη (*ante* εδοθη) e. εθνεσιν dfl*m. πατησουσιν dl*m. +και (*ante* δυο) abcdegjkl [*non* f]. μβ hn. 3. μαρτυσιν f. −χιλιας διακοσιας (*sic* xii. 6) e. χιλιες? ἑξηκοντα πεντε (−διακοσιας) f. δυακοσιας k. ἑξηκοντα l. μσξ n. περιβεβλημενους hln. 4. εἰσὶν fgjl. ελαιαι (ε *mutat.*) f. ἐλαιαι k. +αἱ (*ante* δυο *secund.*) abcdefghjklmn. −αἱ (*post* λυχνιαι) cfglm, *at* οἱ b. κῡ (*pro* θῡ) abcdefghjklm [*non* n]. +επι (*ante* της γης) n. ἑστωτες abcfm. ἑστωτες dk. ἑστωσαι gln [e *cum Elzev.*]. 5. ἡτις αυτης (*pro* ει τις αυτους) e. θελει αυτους *prim.* m. θελει αδικησαι αυτους *prim.* f. αυτους θελει αυτους αδικησαι *prim.* k. θελει *bis* abcdefghjk mn [*non* l]. εκπορευσεται f. απο (*pro* εκ) j. εξωθεν (*pro* εχθρους) n. θελει αυτους *secund.* (*rasura post* θελει *in* a) abcdefghjklmn. αποκτειναι (*pro* αδικησαι *secund.*) n. οὑτως bcdfhjmn [*non* egk], *at* οὑτος l. αυτους (*pro* αυτον) m. 6. εχουσι (εχουσιν l*) τον ουρανον εξουσιαν κλεισαι (κλυσαι l) abcdegkl m [*non* hn]. των ουρανον κλεισαι f. τον ουρανον κλεισαι j. ὑετος βρεχει k. ὑετος (ὑετους j) βρεχη (βρεχει n) τας ἡμερας της προφητειας αυτων (−εν) abc defg (αυτων της προφητειας g) hjklmn. εχουσι *secund.* c. −των n. −παση πληγη g. +εν (*ante* παση πληγη) hn. την γην ὁσακις εαν θελησωσιν εν παση πληγη abcdefjm (θελωσιν fj). ὡσακις εαν θελησωσι(ν *eras.*) εν παση πληγη l, *at* ὡσακις εαν ελθωσιν εν παση πληγη k. 7. −και ὁταν τελεσωσι g. ὁτ' ἀν lm. τελεσωσιν kl. αναβαινων l. μετ' αυτων πολεμον abcdefghjlmn. ποιησουσιν αυτων πολεμον k. νικηση l. αποκτεινει n. −και αποκτενει αυτους jm. 8. το πτωμα abcdefgjkl [*non* m]. +εασει (*post* τα πτωματα αυτων) n. πλατειας d. +της (*ante* πολεως) abcdefghjklmn. +αταφα (*post* μεγαλης) n. ἡτις g. σοδομαι e. αἰγυπτος g. −και *ultim.* flm. αυτων (*pro* ἡμων) abcdefgh jklmn. 9. βλεπουσιν abcdefghjklmn. και εθνων και γλωσσων e. το πτωμα (*pro* τα πτωματα *prim.*) abcdefjklm (f *in sequent. cum Elzev.: malè Mill.*). −και (*ante* ἡμισυ) abcdefhjklm [*non* gn]. *Post* ἡμισυ *explicit versus in* k. το σωμα (*pro* τα πτωματα *secund.*) f. αφησουσιν fl*. αφιασι g. και τα στοματα αυτων ουκ αφιουσι τιθηναι n. *fin.* μνημα abcdefghjlmn. 10. επι την γην m, την γην n (*pro* επι της γης *prim.*). χαιρουσιν abcdefghjklmn. εν (*pro* επ') n. ευφραινονται gn [f *cum Elzev.: falsò Mill.*]. δωσουσιν (*pro* πεμψουσιν) abcdefjkm, *at* πεμπουσιν n. [αλληλοις n, *errat Wetst.*]. −οὑτοι m. εβασανησαν kl. αυτους (*pro* τους) n. 11. −τας hn. τρεις ἡμισυ ἡμερας (−και) f.

τρεις και ἡμισυ ἡμερας n. ἡμησυ g. –ζωης εκ του d (*Mill. errat*) ζωῆ n. αυτοις (*pro* επ' αυτους) l. εις (*pro* επ') abcdefjkm [*non* h], *at* εν αυτοις gn** (*deest in* n*). και *tert. bis script.* j*. ἑστησαν f. ἑαυτων (*pro* αὐτων) g. ὑπο τους ποδας αυτων k. επεσε μεγας n (*errat Wetst.*). επεπεσεν d (*Mill.*) hl. 12. ηκουσα abcd (*Mill.*) efghjklmn (ἠκουσα n). φωνης μεγαλης ghn. λεγουσης ghn. –αυτοις n, *at* αυτους (*pro* αυτοις) c*. ὡδε hjmn. ῳ̑δε k [ὡδε fgl *alii*]. –τῃ n. εθεωρουν j. 13. *init.* –και abcdefjk [*habent* ghlmn]. ἡμερα (*pro* ὡρᾳ) abcd (*Mill.*) efhjklmn [*non* g]. επεσεν adfl*m. λοι [ποι f**] f*. εν φοβω f. γενομενοι (*pro* εγενοντο και) n. 14. *init.* +και b. –ἡ *prim.* m. οὐαῖ *prim.* l. παρηλθεν (*pro* απηλθεν) n. ἡ ουαι ἡ τριτη ιδου abcdefhjkm [*non* g]. ιδου ἡ τριτη ουαι n. –ἡ *tert.* g. απηλθε[ν *eras.*] και ἡ ουαι ἡ τριτη l (–ιδου, *errat Mill.*). –ταχυ m. 15. –ὁ k. εσαλπισεν dfl*m. λεγοντες adfk. εγενετο ἡ βασιλεια abcdefghjkmn [*non* l]. –του κοσμου n. ὑμων (*pro* ἡμων) e. ἡμων του χῡ (–και *et* αυτου) n. βασιλευει fmn. 16. κδ̄ aghkln. –και *secund.* bcdefjm. –οἱ *secund.* fgl. +του θρονου (*post* ενωπιον) abcdefjlm [*non* ghn]. αυτου (*pro* του θῡ) c. ˙οἱ καθηνται (*pro* καθημενοι) abcdejkm [*non* n], *at* καθηνται *sine* οἱ g. +οἱ (*ante* καθημενοι) f (*errat Mill.*). θρουνους ?a*. επι του θρονου j. επεσον abcefg (+και *ante* επεσον g) hkmn [*non* djl]. –και *ultim.* m. 17. +ἡμων (*post* θς̄) n. ὢν l. ὁ ἠν mn. –και ὁ ερχομενος abcdefjklm [*non* ghn]. 18. οργισθησαν bn. ὠργισθησαν g. ὀργῆ n. καιρος (ι *mutat.*) f. εθνων (*pro* νεκρων) k. +του (*ante* κριθηναι) d, *errat Mill.* –τοις δουλοις σου f. –και (*ante* τοις φοβουμενοις) n. βουλομενοις (*pro* φοβουμενοις) k. διαφθειραντας hlm. 19. ηνοιχθη abcdejk [*non* flm]. ἡγοιγη gn. +ὁ (*post* θῡ) fgm. του κῡ acdefhjk, κῡ l, του θῡ b (*pro* αυτου *prim.*: *cum Elzev.* gmn). και βρονται και φωναι fjmn. –και φωναι c. σεισμοι m. –και σεισμος abcdefhjkl [*non* gn].

CAP. XII. 1. σῆμεῖον n. ωθη k*. γυνη (υ *mutat.*) b. ἡλιον g. –ἡ j. ὑποκάτω f*m. *fin.* δι' αστερων ιβ̄ n. 2. γαγαστρι f. +και (*ante* κραζει) g. εκραζεν abcdhj. εκραξεν e (*malè Griesb.*) fkl (*malè Mill.*) m [*non* gn]. ὠδινουσα g. +του (*ante* τεκειν) g. 3. αλλον f. αλλω j. πυρος μεγας abcdefjkl. πυρος gmn [*non* h]. δεκα κερατα n. δωδεκα (*pro* δεκα) k. αυτων (*pro* αυτου) m. ἑπτα διαδηματα abcdefghjkl (*errat Mill.*) mn. 4. εβαλλεν f. δρακον g. ἑστηκεν dgklmn. ἑστη f. +αυτων (*post* γυναικος) n. τικτειν h. ὅτᾶν m. τεκει l. καταφαγει l. *fin.* +αυτο (, *post* αυτης) m. 5. αρσενα g. μελει k. ποιμενειν bgk. –εν gjn. σιδηρῶ n. ἡρπαγη b. ἡρπαγη cegh. ἡρπασθη kn. *Rasura ante* σθη (–ἡρπα) d. –αυτης n. +προς (*ante* τον θρονον) abcdefghjklmn. 6. εχῃ l. +εκει (*post* εχει) abcdeghjklmn [*non* f]. ὑπο [illegible] abcd [illegible] abcdefhjklm [illegible] abcdefghjklmn [illegible] abcdefghjklmn [illegible] abcdefghijklmn [illegible] τῃ γῃ και τῃ θαλασσῃ abcdefhjklm [illegible] dl*m. [illegible] 14. [illegible] aυτου (pro αετου του k. [illegible] b*, πετησαι k, [illegible] (pro πετηται, ὁπως τρεφηται (pro ὁπου τρεφεται acdef τρ[illegible] f, male Walt., hjklm [non bgn]. ειμισυ g. 15. ὑπερεβαλεν ὁ οφις l [illegible] (ὀπισω g, της γυναικος abcdefghjklmn. [illegible] αυτην (pro ταυτην) abcdefghjkmn [non l]. ποταμοφορητον [illegible]. [illegible] ποταμοφορητη τόν ποιηση (sic) k. ποιησει l. 16. εβο[illegible] k* [illegible]. γη, prim. g. γη bis j. ἡνοιξεν n. ηνοιξε (— ἡ γη) n [illegible] f κατεπιεν adl*. ανεβαλεν f. 17. οργισθη l. + [illegible] [illegible] ad ανεβαλεν [illegible] v. 16 legit f post γυναικι. απηλθεν dlm. + [illegible] g [illegible] αυτου e, και της k sic (pro αυτης). ιῡ abcefghjmn, του ιῡ d (Mill.) l, [illegible] k (pro του ιῡ χῡ). 18. εσταθη m. ἀμμον l.

Cap. XIII. 1. ιδον fl. αναβαινων l. εχων cdkl. εχοντα n. κερατα [illegible] abcdefghjklmn. αυτων (pro αυτου prim.) l. επι τῃ [illegible] d. [illegible] abcdefhjklm. ὀνομα g. 2. ὃν (pro ὃ) l*. — ὃ n. ιδον f. [illegible] g. [illegible] mn. παρδαλου k. παρδαλι l. αρκου ab*cdfjl m**n [illegible] b**chkm*]. ἀρκτου g. λεοντων f. λεοντος l*. [illegible] n — και εξουσιαν μεγαλην aek. — και ultim. l. 3. — ειδον abcdefhjklmn [non g]. + εκ (post μιαν) abcdefghjklmn. ὡσει (pro ὡς) abcd fhjklm [non egn]. [illegible] b. εσφαγμενη h. εσφραγισμενην αθανατω

—(—εας) k. και εθαυμασθη εν ὁλη τη γη n. επι (*pro* οπισω) f. ὀπισω g. 4.
— τω δρακοντι τω δεδωκοτι την εξουσιαν (—ὸς) abcdfghjklmn (*at* τω δοντι f, ὀτι
εδωκε g, ὀτι εδωκεν m, ὀτε εδωκε n, την ουσιαν k). —τον δρακοντα *usque ad*
προσεκυνησαν e. το θηριον (*pro* τῳ θηριῳ *prim.*) n, *vid. v.* 2. τω θηριω (*pro*
το θηριον) abcdefghjklmn. +και (*ante* τις *secund.*) fghmn. δυνατος (*pro*
δυναται) abcdefhkl [*non* gjmn]. *fin.* αυτο (*pro* μετ' αυτου) j. 5. —και εδοθη
usque ad βλασφημιας c. εδωθη *bis* l. μεγα k. βλασφημιαν adefhjkl [*non*
bg]. βλασφημα mn. —πολεμον gn. πολεμησαι (*pro* πολεμον ποιησαι) f.
τεσσαρακοντα πεντε δυο (πεντε *eras.*) c. +και (*ante* δυο) g. $\overline{\mu\beta}$ n. α *ante* δυο
mutat. in a. 6. ηνοιξεν dl. ἡνοιξε n. —το *prim.* ade. —εις βλασφημιαν
usque ad ονομα αυτοὺ n. βλασφημιας gm. —και *ultim.* b*cdefghjkl. αρχαις
(*pro* τῳ ουρανῳ) c. κατοικουν̀τας (*pro* σκηνουντας) b. 7. εδωθη *bis* l. +εξου-
σια (*post* εδοθη αυτω *prim.*) b. —και εδοθη *usque ad* νικησαι αυτους f. ποιη-
σαι πολεμον abcdeghjkln [*non* m]. +και λαον (*post* φυλην) abcdefgjklmn.
8. αυτον (*pro* αυτῳ) abcdfjkn [*non* gm]. —επι g. ὡ (*pro* ὡν) d. ουτε (*pro*
ου) adejk. το ονομα abcdefhjklm [*non* gn]. +αυτων (*post* ονοματα) g. τω
βιβλιω abcdefghjklmn. +του (*ante* εσφαγμενου) abcdefghjklmn. 9. εχηl. οὑς
k. οὑς n. 10. *init.* ειτις εχει αιχμαλωσιαν (,j) ὑπαγει (—συναγει εις αιχμαλω-
σιαν) ab*cdehjk (b** *cum Elzev.*, τὶς *pro* ειτις k). —συναγει εις αιχμαλωσιαν f
(*malè Mill. Wetst.*). —αιχμαλωσιαν συναγει gn. αιχμαλωτιζει (*pro* αιχμαλω-
σιαν συναγει) l. ει τις εις αιχμαλωσιαν επαγει ες αιχμαλωσιαν ὑπαγει (*sic*) m.
—αποκτενεῖ abcdefjk [*non* hl]. αποκτεννει g. αποκτένει m. αποκτεινει n.
—εν μαχαιρᾳ *secund.* abcdefjk [*non* ghlmn]. αποκτανθῆναι f*. ὦδε hjmn
[*non* fg]. ἐστὶν j. ὑπομονῆ n. θλιψις (*pro* πιστις) j. 11. ιδον fl. αλλον l*.
αναβαινων l. εκβαινον c. ειχεν adkl*m. —δυο abcdejk [*non* fghlmn]. +τω
(*ante* αρνιω) l. —ὡς δρακων n. 12. του $\hat{\alpha}$ g. πασαν του πρωτου θηριου c.
του θηριου του πρωτου f. τω θηριω τω πρωτω gm. ποιειν *prim.* j. ποιησει
bis m. εποιει abcdefhjl [*non* gn], εποιη k (*pro* ποιει *secund.*). τους εν αυτη
(αυτω e) κατοικουντας (κατοικουν d) abcdeghjklmn. προσκυνησωσιν ad. προσ-
κυνησουσι fkl* (ν *eras*). ὡ (*pro* οὑ) k. πασα γη (*pro* πληγη) k. *fin.* —αυ-
του f. 13. εποιει (*pro* ποιει) c. και ποιησει μεγαλα σημεια m. και πυρ
ἱνα εκ του ουρανου καταβαινη (καταβαινει kl) επι την γην (—ποιῃ) abcdefh**
jkl (—και f, την γης f, *rescript. in* h). ποιει (*pro* ποιῃ) g. ἐέκ g. —εις την γην g.
ἱνα και πυρ εκ του ουρανου καταβηναι εις (—ποιῃ) m. ἱνα (—και) εν πλανη
ποιει· πυρ εκ του ουρανου καταβαινειν εις n. 14. +τους εμους (*post* πλανα)
abcdehjk [*non* fglmn]. κατοικατοικουντας j. εδωθη (*sic v.* 15 l) ln. λεγον
bfg. το θηριον (*pro* τω θηριω f**) f*. ὁς (*pro* ὁ) mn, *cætera cum Elzev.*

ειχε (*pro* εχει) fgh. —την f. +απο (*post* πληγην) f. εζησεν fgm (*cum sequentibus jungit* g). *fin.* ὃ (ὦ l) ειχε (ειχεν adl, +την l) πληγην και εζησεν απο της μαχαιρας abcdejkl. 15. πνευμα δουναι abcdehjklm [*non* fgn]. —ἱνα και λαλησῃ ἡ εικων του θηριου cf. λαλησει gkl (—και *secund.* gl). ἡι εικων g. —ἱνα και λαλησῃ *usque ad* την εικονα του θηριου n. ποιησει fgk. εαν (*pro* αν) abdefhjklm. —αν cg. προσκυνησωσιν ah. προσκυνησουσι cfl* (ν *eras.* l). τη εικονι abcdefghjkm. —ἱνα *secund.* abcefjkmn (d *illeg.*), *at transferunt* gl *in locum ante* ὁσοι. αποκτανθωσιν dl*. αποκτανθηναι f. 16. —και τους ελευθερους και τους δουλους k. δωσωσιν ajkln. δωσουσιν bce. δωσιν fhm (d *illeg.*). λαβωσι τω χαραγμα αυτου (*pro* δωσῃ αυτοις χαρ.) g. χαραγματα abcdefhl [*non* jkmn]. —της *prim.* abcdejk [*non* fglmn, *errat Wetst. de* n]. της δεξιας αυτων j. το μετωπον abcd (*Mill. omittit in loc., sed habet in Proleg.* § 1489) efgklm [*non* j]. των μετοπων (—αυτων) n. 17. *init.* —και hn. μηδεὶς (*pro* μητις) m. δυναται bcfln. ἀγορᾶσαι n. πολησαι l. πωλησαι η αγορᾶσαι ετι m. ει *mutat.* f. η (*pro* ει) k. —η (*ante* το ονομα) abcefghjklmn (d *illeg.*). 18. ὡδε hl** *rubro* mn [*non* f]. ὡδὲ g. ὦ δὲ j, *at* οὐδε e. —τον *prim.* abcefghjkl [*non* m]. εστιν· ὁ εχων ουν (*pro* νουν) n. ψιφησατω ln. το ονομα (*pro* τον αριθμον) f. εστιν *secund.* g. —και (*post* εστιν *secund.*) abcdefjklm [*non* gn]. του θηριου (*pro* αυτου) c. +εστιν (*post* αυτου) ghn. ἑξακοσια gl. ἑξακοσια e. +ἑξηκοντα ἑξ egl. χξϛ hj. χξσ n. χμϛ *seu forsan* χρϛ d.

CAP. XIV. 1. ιδου fl. ἰδοῦ g. το θηριον *eras. ante* το αρνιον c. +το (*ante* αρνιον) abcefgjklm (d *illeg. : cum Elzev.* hn). ἑστηκεν c. ἑστηκος dk. ἑστως gn. ἑστηκῶς l. ἑστηκὼς m. ὁρος g. +αριθμος (*post* μετ᾽ αυτου) abce jlm (d *illeg.*). ρμδ afhkmn. τεσσαρακοντεσσαρες (*sic* VII. 4) b. τεσαρακοντα τεσσαρες c*. ἑκατὸνσαρακοντατέσσαρις (*sic* v. 3) l. +αἱ (*ante* εχουσαι) f. +το ονομα αυτου και (*post* εχουσαι) abcdefghjmn (ὀνομα *bis* g). το ονομα αυτου και του πατρος αυτου kl, *errat Mill.* —αυτου (*post* πατρος) e. εγγεγραμμενον e. μετοπων kn. 2. ἡκουσα *bis* n. —και ὡς φωνην βροντης μεγαλης n. και ἡ φωνη ἡν ηκουσα ὡς κιθαρωδων (*pro* και φωνην ηκουσα κιθαρωδων) abcd (*Mill.*) efghjklm. +ὡς (*ante* κιθαρωδων) n, *cætera cum Elzev.* 3. αδουσι f*. ᾳδουσιν h. ἀδουσιν n. —ὡς abcdefhjklm [*non* gn]. ωιδην *prim.* g. ὡδην *bis* k. —ενωπιον του θρονου και j. ἐνωπιον *prim.* k. ζωιων g. ουδε εἰς abcde. εδυνατο acdehjkln (f *dubium*). ἠδυνατο g. —αἱ aln. ρμδ adfhjkmn. ἑκατὸνσαρακοντατέσσαρις l. ηγορασαμενοι k. ἡγορασμενοι n. 4. *init.* οὑτοι εισιν *usque ad* παρθενοι γαρ εισιν *transfert* j *in locum post* ὑπαγη. εἰσὶν *prim.* g, *bis* j. οἱ (*pro* οἳ) k. —εισιν *secund.* (οὑτοι *cum præcedentibus*) g.

—εισιν *tert.* n (*malè Wetst.* εισιν *prim.*). ακολοθουντες n. ακολουθουντας ?f. εαν (*pro* αν) abcdefjkl [*non* gmn]. ὑπαγει lmn. οἱτοι ἠγορασθησαν g. +ὑπο ιυ̅ (*ante* ηγορασθησαν) abcdefhjkl [*non* gmn]. 5. *init.* και ουχ (ουκ l) εὑρεθη εν τω στοματι αυτων ψευδος (*pro* δολος) abcdefjkl, *etiam* ψευδος (*pro* δολος) ghn. οὐχ' jkn. αμωμητοι γαρ εισι (ν *eras.*) l, *etiam* εισι bcegh. —ενωπιον του θρονου του θυ̅ abcdefghjkln. 6. ιδον fl. —αλλον abcdefjkln [*non* gh]. πετομενον abcefghjk (d *illeg.*, *non* ln). μεσουρανιματι gl (ου *mutat. in* f). +ερχομενον (*post* αιωνιον) n. ευαγγελισασθαι hn. ευαγγελησαι l. καθημενους (*pro* κατοικουντας) abcdeghkl [*non* fn], *at* τοις καθημενοις j. +επι (*ante* παν) abcdefghjkl [*non* n]. 7. λεγων abcdefghjkln. εν φωνη μεγαλη λεγων l. κυ̅ (*pro* θυ̅) abcdefjkl [*non* ghn]. δοξαν αυτω n. ὁτε (*pro* ὁτι) n. +αυτω (*post* προσκυνησατε) l. αυτον τον ποιησαντα (*pro* τῳ ποιησαντι) abcdefjkn [*non* ghl]. +την (*ante* θαλασσαν) abcdefhjkln [*non* g, l *habet* και]. τας πηγας των ὑδατων f. 8. +δευτερος (*post* αλλος) abcdejkl, (*post* αγγελος) hn (*errat Wetst. de* n). δευτερος (*pro* αγγελος) g. [f *cum Elzev.*]. ηκολουθησεν dl*. —επεσεν abcefjk. —επεσε dl [*habent* ghn]. βαβυλων abcdefghjkln. —ἡ πολις abcdefghjkln. μεγαλη g. —ὁτι abcefhjkln (d *illeg.*), *at* ἡ (*pro* ὁτι) g. —του θυμου h. ταυτης (*pro* αὐτης) aekl. πεποτηκε fjl. +τα (*ante* εθνη) abcd?efgh jl [*non* k]. ἡς πεποτικε τα εθνη παντα n. 9. *init.* και αλλος αγγελος τριτος abcdeghjkln (—και b, τριτον ?l*). αλλος (*pro* τριτος) f. ὁτι (*pro* ει τις) k. προσκυνει το θηριον abcdehjkln. προσκυνει το ποτηριον f. προσκυνηι τωι θηριωι g. τηι εικονι g. εικονη l. —και (*ante* λαμβανει) f. +το (*ante* χαραγμα) gn. μετοπου n. —αὐτου (*post* μετωπου) f. 10. πιετε f. αυτου (*pro* του θυ̅) f. εκ του ποτηριου (*pro* εν τῳ ποτηριῳ) l. βασανισθησονται d (*Mill.*) f. —των (*ante* ἁγιων) f. αγγελων ἁγιων (—των) g. 11. αυτου (*pro* αυτων) l. εις αιωνας αιωνων αναβαινει abcdefghjkln (αἰωνας αἰωνων g, αιωνα αιωνων fl, αιωνα αιωνος n, *errat Wetst.*). τωι θηριωι και τηι εικονι αυτου g, *at* τη εικονη *tantum* l. 12. *init.* ἡ δε ὑπομονη των ἁγιων εστιν· ὡδε n. ὡδε *bis* h, *semel* j. +ἡ (*ante* ὑπομονη) abcdefghjkl. ἑστὶ g. —ὡδε *secund.* abcd?efgjk. των τηρουντων g. +του (*ante* ιυ̅) h. *fin.* +χυ̅ n. 13. ἠκουσα n. φωνην b. λεγουσαν b. —μοι abcdefgjkl [*non* hn]. —γραψον c. απο αρτι (*cætera cum Elzev.*) n. απαρτι λεγει ναι το πνα abcdefhjkl (*non* g; και *pro* ναι k: απαρτι· hj; λεγει· af; *reliqui legunt uno tenore*). +το ἁγιον (*post* πνα) g. αναπαυσονται kln. απο των εργων (*pro* εκ των κοπων) f. γαρ (*pro* δε) g. 14. *Ab initio versûs usque ad* λευκη *bis scriptum in* h*. ιδον fl. νεφαλην n, κεφαλην f (*pro* νεφελην). καθημενον bcdefgh*kmn. [a *cum Elzev.*]. ὁμοιον abcdef gh*kn [*non* l]. υιον bcdfk [*non* ael]. ανω (*pro* υἱῳ ανθρωπου) j. υἱῶν n.

+ὁ (*ante* εχων) k, *at* εχοντα egn. την κεφαλην (*pro* της κεφαλης) abdekn. ὀξυ (*sic vv.* 17, 18 *bis*) g. οξυν n. 15. αγγελος αλλος c. εξηλθεν κραζων (−εκ του ναου) e. ουρανου (*pro* ναου) ln (*non v.* 17). φωνη μεγαλη abcdef ghjklmn.. επι την νεφελην n. τον δρεπανον σου θερισον (−και) c. τον δρεπανον (*non v.* 16) k. ὁτε (*pro* ὁτι *prim.*) n. ηλθεν (−σοι) abcdefghjk mn (ηλθεν σοι l*, εξηλθεν m). −του (*ante* θερισαι) bcdfjlmn [*non* aeh]. εξιρανθη l. 16. εβαλεν λαβεν (λαβεν *eras.*) k. τη νεφελη abdfl. της νεφελης j. εξηρανθη (*pro* εθερισθη) n. επι της γης m. *fin.* γῆ j. 17. *Hiat* a. *Deest versus in* f. αγγελος αλλος m. −του *secund.* l. −αυτος k. δρεπανα οξυ n. 18. εχον e. εφωνησεν εν (*pro* εφωνησε) bcdefklm (*non* ghjn : φωνησεν l). φωνη (*pro* κραυγῃ) cg. −τῳ (*ante* εχοντι) c, *at* το g. το *prim. mutatum in* f. −λεγων f. +σου (*post* δρεπανον *secund.*) e. +λεγων (*ante* και τρυγησον) m. βοτανας b, βοτρϋς n (*pro* βοτρυας). ὁτε (*pro* ὁτι) n, *cf. v.* 15. ηκμασεν ἡ σταφυλη της γης (−αυτης) bcdefjkm [*non* n]. ηγμασαν? αἱ σταφυλαι της γης (−αυτης) l. 19. εξεβαλεν (*pro* εβαλεν *prim.*) bcdejklm. επι της γης (*pro* εις την γην) j. ετρυγησεν dlm. απελον b. *fin.* εις την ληνον του θυμου του θῦ τον μεγαν bcdefhjk (gln *cum Elzev.* τον *pro* την bjk, τον θυμον b). την ληνον την μεγαλην του θυμου του θῦ m. 20. ὁ ληνος jk. εξωθεν bcdefghjklm [*non* n]. εξηλθεν bcefghjklmn (*hiat* d). αἱμα n. εκ του ληνου k (*non* j). χαληνων n. ἱππων n. ἑξακοσιων g. α͞χ dfjn.

CAP. XV. 1. ιδον (*sic vv.* 2, 5) fl. θαυμασιον f. ἑπτα πληγας cn (ζ n). ταυταις (*pro* αυταις) n. 2. ὑελινην *prim.* c, *bis* ghk (ὑεληνην *prim.* g*), *secund.* l. ὑελλινην *bis* ej. εκ της εικονος και εκ του θηριου αυτου bcdefgjk (*non* hlmn, *at* −εκ *secund.* kl). −εκ του χαραγματος αυτου bcdef (*habet* f και, *malè Mill.*) ghjkl. +και (*ante* εκ του αριθμου) mn. ἑστωτας gkln. +την μεμιγμενην πυρι (*ante* εχοντας) m. +τας (*ante* κιθαρας) bdejlm [*non* kn]. 3. ᾀδουσιν dl* (ᾳδουσι h). −την ωδην μωσεως δουλου του θῦ και d. μωυσεος behj. μωυσεως cf klm [gn *cum Elzev.*]. +του (*ante* δουλου) hn. −την *secund.* e. ωιδην *secund.* g, *at* φωνην *pro* ωδην *secund.* m. λεγοντας f. αλιθηναι g. βασιλευ (−ὁ) ek. εθνων bcdefhjklmn, αἰωνων g (*pro* ἁγιων). 4. τις σε ου φοβηθη (−μη) g. −σε κυριε f. κ͞ς? (*pro* κ͞ε) n. και τις ου δοξασει g. δοξασει mn. ἁγιος (*pro* ὁσιος) bcdefghjklm [*non* n]. +ει (*post* ἁγιος) gh. παντες (*pro* παντα τα εθνη) cefjklm [*non* n, *hiat* d]. −τα εθνη g. ἡξουσιν l*m. ἡξουσι n. −και *secund.* k. +κ͞ε (*ante* ὁτι *tert.*) g. 5. *init.* −και b. μεταταῦτα fh. −ιδου bcefghjklmn (*hiat* d). ηνοιγει c. η *prim. mutat. in* f. ἠνοιγη gmn. −του μαρτυριου c. 6. εκ του ναου οἱ εχοντες τας ἑπτα πληγας b. −εχοντες *usque ad* εκ του ναου e. +οἱ (*ante* εχοντες) cfghjklmn. −ἑπτα *secund.* h. ουρανου (*pro* ναου) h. −εκ *του ναου* cdfjkm. +*οἱ ησαν* (*ante ενδεδυμενοι*) bcdefhjklm (*non* gn). *λινουν* fj, *at ληνον* l. *λῖνον* hm. −*και λαμπρον* b, *at* −*και tantum* cdefghjklmn. *περιζωσμενοι* k. −*περι* c. *επι* (*pro περι*) n. *στῆθι* l. *ζωνναs* e. *ζῶγαs χρυσάs* m. 7. −*ἐν* l. *εδωκεν* dm. *ξυλοις* (*pro ἑπτα αγγελοις*) n. *φυαλας* mn. −*του prim. et secund.* n. −*του tert.* k. *fin.* +*αμην* n. 8. *εγενετος* (*pro εγεμισθη*) k. +*του* b, +*εκ του* adefjkm (*ante καπνου*). *εκ του καπνου ὁ ναος* c. [gn *cum Elzev.*]. *Ante και ουδεις legit* n *και τις ενεγκει τον θυμον αυτου*; *εδυνατο* abcdejkl [*non* fhmn]. *ἠδυνατο* g. *ελθειν* lm. −*ἑπτα secund.* hn.

CAP. XVI. 1. *ἠκουσα* (*sic v.* 7) n. *μεγαλης φωνης* bcdfgj [*non* klmn]. −*εκ του ναου* abcdefjkl [*non* ghn]. −*τοις* l. −*και secund.* hln. *εκκεχετε* f, *ut videtur.* *φυαλας* mn (*sic* mn *ferè, at non* m *vv.* 2, 3, 4, 8, 10, 17). +*ἑπτα* (*ante φιαλας*) abcdefgjklm (*non* hn: ζ g). *fin. επι την γην* n. 2. +*αγγελος* (*post πρωτος*) mn. *εξεχεεν* adl. *την φυαλην επι την γην αυτου* n (*errat Wetst.*). *εις* (*pro επι*) abcefgjklm [*non* hn, d *illeg.*]. *ἑλκος* l. *επι* (*pro εις*) a *ut videtur* bcefgjklm (d *Mill.: at non* hn). *του θηριου το χαραγμα* l. *τους προσκυνουντας τη εικονι αυτου* abcdefghjklmn (−*τους* eln, *οικονι* k). 3. −*αγγελος* g. *εξεχεεν* dl*. *φυαλην* (*sic vv.* 4, 8, 10, 12) n. *αἱμα* (*non vv.* 4, 6 *bis*) n. *ὡς αἱμα νεκρου* l. −*ζωσα* abcdefjkm (*non* hln). *ζωης* g. +*των* (*post απεθανε*) g. *εν τη θαλασση απεθανεν* n. 4. −*αγγελος* abcdefgjkl [*non* hm]. *εξεχεεν* dl*. *εξεχε* f*. *επι* (*pro εις*) c *bis*, −*εις secund.* gh. *εγενοντο* g. 5. *ἠκουσα* mn (*non v.* 7 m). +*του επι* (*post αγγελου*) g. −*κυριε* abcdefghjklmn. −*εἶ* l. *ὢν* l. *ὃς ἦν* adefk. *ὁ ἦν* mn. −*και ὁ* adefjklm, −*και* bchn, −*ὁ* g (*ante ὁσιος*). 6. *εδωκας αυτοις αἱμα ποιεινf.* *ποιειν* k. −*γαρ* abcdefghjklmn. *εισιν* dfl*mn. *εἰσί* g. 7. −*αλλου εκ* abcdefghjklmn. −*και ultim.* f. *δικαιοι* l. 8. −*αγγελος* adefgjkl [*non* hn]. *εξεχεεν* dl*. *εδωθη* l. *καυματησαι* l. *εν πυρι τους ανους* abcejklm (*hiat* d). 9. *καυματι μεγαλω* n. +*οἱ ανοι* abcdefhjklm [*non* g], +*εις* n (*ante το ονομα*). *κατα του ὀνοματος* g. +*την* (*ante εξουσιαν*) h. *ἐξουσιαν* j. *αυτας* (*pro ταυτας*) f. −*και ultim.* n. 10. *πτεμπτος* b. −*αγγελος* abcdefgjkl [*non* hmn]. *εξεχεεν* dl*. *εσκοτισμενη* en. *εσκοτομενη* k. *εμασσωντο* abdfghk [*non* cejmn]. *εμασοντο* l. *χλωσσας* c*. *γλωσας* f*. 11. *εβλασφημισαν* ?g. −*και εκ των ἑλκων αυτων* m. *ἑλκων* k. *εκ τα ἑλκει* l. 12. −*αγγελος* abcdefgjkl [*non* hmn]. *εξεχεεν αυτου την φιαλην* bd?fjl. *φυαλην* mn. −*τον* (*ante ευφρατην*) abc(*hiat* d) ehjkl [*non* fgmn]. *ἑτοιμασθει* lm. *ανατολης* abcde?fgjklm [*non* hn]. 13. *ιδου* fl. *ακαθαρτα τρια ὡς βατραχοι* (−*ὁμοια*) abcdefghjklmn (*τρια ακαθαρτα* ghln, *βατραχους* j). *fin.* +*εκπορευθεντα* n. 14. *εισιν* dl. *δαιμονιων* abcdefgjklm [*non* hn]. +*ακαθαρτων* (*post δαιμονιων*) g. *εκπορευεσθαι* (*pro ἁ εκπορευεται*) g. +*και* (*post ἁ*) n.

εκπορευονται l, *malè Mill.* —της γης και abcdefghjklmn. οἰκουμενης gj. +του (*ante* πολεμον) abcdefghjklmn. —εκεινης fg (της μεγαλης ἡμερας g). —του *ultim.* c. παντοκρατωρος ln. 15. [f *cum Elzev.* ιδου, *malè Mill.*]. τιμων (*pro* τηρων) a. ἱματια l. περιπατει kln. βλεπουσι n. ασθ. *eras. in* c *ante* ασχημοσυνην, *at* αισχυνην el. 16. —τον *bis* f. ἐβραϊστει l. μαγεδων abcd ejk. ἀρμαγεδων gm. ἁρμαγεδων hl. μαγιδων n (*Wetst. etiam* μαγεδων *malè*), *at* μακεδδων f. 17. ἑβδημος g. —αγγελος abcdefgjkl [*non* hmn]. εξεχεεν adl*. κεφαλην (*pro* φιαλην) n. επι (*pro* εις) abdegjklm [*non* cfhn]. εξηλθεν dl. φωνῇ f. εκ (*pro* απο *prim.*) g. —του ναου n. —του ουρανου fg. —απο *secund.* fk. τουτου (*pro* του *ultim.*) k. και απο του θρονου του θῦ b. γεγονεν adfkl*m. 18. +ευθεως (*ante* εγενοντο *prim.*) b. αστραπαι και βρονται και φωναι abcdefghjkl (*malè Mill.*) mn, *at* αστραπη n, και φωναι και βρονται gn. —εγενετο *prim.* abcdejklm [*non* fghn]. ἀφοῦ h. εγενοντο οἱ α̅ν̅ο̅ι̅ c. —οἱ fg. —επι της γης fl. οὕτως gjn [*non* bfhklm]. 19. —ἡ *secund.* c. —αἱ n. επεσαν dh**jln. —και *tert.* c. μεγαλη *secund.* g. +του (*ante* δουναι) n. —το (*ante* ποτηριον) g. —της οργης f. 20. +ἡ (*ante* νησος) m. εφυγεν fl*m. ὀρη gk. +και (*post* ορη) n. οὐχ' jln. 21. χαλασσα *prim.* g. +ἡ (*ante* μεγαλη) n. ταλαντιαῖα djkl. ταλαντιεα f. προς (*pro* επι τους) n. —τον θεον b. επι της πληγης f*. αὐτη bcjln. αυτου e, αὐτῇ f (*pro* αυτης): ghkm *cum Elzev.*

Cap. XVII. 1. ηλθε l**. τις (*pro* εἱς) l. —εκ gn. —ἑπτα *prim.* c. φυαλας n. ελαλησεν dl*. —μοι abcdefghjklm [*non* n]. δεῦρω n. δειξωσι (—σοι) n. κρίμα fghm. πορνειας (*pro* πορνης) d. —των (*ante* ὑδατων *et* πολλων) gmn. 2. αἱ βασιλεις e. εμεθυσαν l. οἱ κατοικουντες την γην εκ του οινου της πορνειας αυτης abcdefghjklmn. 3. απονεγκεμενοι (—με) k. απηνεγκεν d. απεινεγκεν (ν *eras.*) l. μοι (*pro* με) be. +την (*ante* ερημον) c. ερρημον n. +τοπον (*post* ερημον) g. —εν abejk. ιδον l, *non* f *hoc loco*. γυναιον n. +το (*ante* κοκκινον) abejk. γεμων l. ονοματα abdef (*Mill.* τα ον. dfl *falsò*) jkl [*non* chmn: ὀνοματα g]. βλασφημειας g*. εχων lmn. 4. ην (*pro* ἡ *secund.*) abcdefghjklmn. πορφυρουν (πορφυραν hk?n) και κοκκινον abcdefghjklmn. —και *tert.* abcdefghjkmn. κεχρυσομενη k. περικεχρυσωμενη m. χρυσιω ab cdefjklm [*non* ghn]. μαργαριτοις k. εχουσαι n. ποτηριον χρυσουν abcdfg jklm [*non* hn: +το *ante* ποτ. f]. ποτερον (—χρυσουν) e. γεμων b*f?l. γεμουσα k. *fin.* και τα ακαθαρτα της πορνειας της γης abcdefghjklmn (αυτης *pro* της γης c*ghlmn). 5. μετοπον ln?. —ονομα j. πορνη *eras. in* e *ante* μητηρ. ἡμων (*pro* ἡ μητηρ) k. πόρνων aehkl [*non* bcdfgmn]. *fin.* αυτης (*pro* της γης) n, *sequente spatio vacuo*. 6. ιδον f, ιδων l (*pro* ειδον). —την m.

—εκ *prim.* abdefjk. —και *secund.* abdejkm. —εκ *secund.* ch. +του (*ante* ιῦ) g. —ιδων e*, *at* ειδων l*. —αυτην f. 7. ειπεν adl*m. διὰ τί g. ερω σοι abcde gjklm [*non* fh]. 8. *init.* +το abcdefghjlm (Ττο g, Τ *rubro*). ιδες l [*non* f]. εστιν *prim.* adfl*m. την γην (*pro* επι της γης) abefjkm. το ονομα επι του βιβλιου abdefjklm (*non* c, *at* τα ονοματα l). το ὀνομα εν τω βιβλιω g. *Jungunt* απο καταβολης κοσμου *cum* βλεποντων bc. βλεποντων abcd?efgjkl m [*non* h]. *fin.* ὁτι ην το θηριον και ουκ εστι abcdefjklm (gh *cum Elzev.*, d *partim illeg.*, *at* εστιν dl*m, εσται b). *vv.* 8, 9. *Jungunt* και παρεσται ὡδε abefjk, *at* και παρεσται· ὡδε cdghlm. 9. ὡδε bhjm. και (*pro* αἱ) g. ἑπτα ορη εισιν abcdeghjklm (ὀρη gk). —ἑπτα *secund.* f. επανω (*pro* επ᾽) f. 10. εισιν ἑπτα abcdefjklm [*non* gh]. επεσον abcefgh**kl (*malè Mill.*) m [επεσαν dh*j]. —και *secund.* abcdefghjklm (ὁ δε εἱς h). —ὁ (*ante* αλλος) c. οὐπω (*sic* v. 12 g) gm. ηλθεν adfgh*kl*m. ὁτ᾽ ἂν l. ὁτᾶν m. ὀλιγον l. δει αυτον abcdejklm [*non* fgh]. ειναι *eras. in* e *ante* μειναι. 11. ὁ ἦν a. —και *secund.* g. εστιν d *bis* (*tert. illeg.* d) fl* *ter*, m *secund.* οὑτος (*pro* αυτος) abdegjklm [*non* cfh]. ἐστί *secund.* h. —εστι *tert.* k. 12. ※a *in marg.* δα (*pro* τα) f*. ιδες l. —ουπω k. αλλα fg. λαμβανουσιν dm. 13. εχουσι γνωμην abcdefjl m [*non* gh]. εχουσι γυναικα την δυναμιν (—γνωμην *et* και) k. —την *bis* f. —την *secund.* acgkl [*hiat* d]. αὑτων abcdefghjklm. διδοασιν abcdefghjkm. διδωασιν l. 14. ἀρνιου g, *at* αρκιου k. πολεμησουσιν dfl*. πολεμισουσιν g. νικησῃ l. αυτοις (*pro* αυτους) m. εστιν dfl*. βασιλεις (*pro* βασιλευς) k. αυτοι (*pro* αυτου) f. —κλητοι και d. και πιστοι και εκλεκτοι m. 15. —ἁ k. οιδας (*pro* ειδες) l. +και ἡ γυνη (*ante* οὑ) c. εισιν fl*m. οχλοι *et* εθνη *transfert* m. 16. ιδες l. και (*pro* επι) abcdefghjklm. μισησουσιν l*. μισησωσι m. ειρημωμενην f. εἱρημωμενην g. ερημωμενην j. ποιησωσιν d *prim.* m *bis.* —και γυμνην cj. +ποιησουσιν αυτην (*post* γυμνην) abdefhklm [*non* g]. —σαρκας k. φαγωνται ehm. κατακαυσωσι πυρι (—εν) m. 17. κς̄ (*pro* θς̄) f. γνωμην μιαν abcdefhjkl [*non* g]. γνωμην αυτων (*pro* μιαν γνωμην) m. +αυτων (*post* γνωμην *secund.*) g. αυτου (*pro* αυτων *secund.*) f. *fin.* τελεσθωσιν οἱ λογοι του θεου abcdefghjklm (d *malè Mill.*, τελεσθησονται h). 18. ιδες l. —εστιν a. μεγαλῃ g. —ἡ (*ante* εχουσα) bg. μη εχουσαν (*pro* ἡ εχουσα) f. +επι (*ante* της γης) abd (*Mill.*) ekl [c *cum Elzev.*].

CAP. XVIII. 1. *init.* —και abcdefgjk [*non* hlm]. μεταταῦτα fh. ιδον f. ἴδων l. +αλλον (*ante* αγγελον) abdeghjklm [*non* f], *at post* αγγελον c. γυνη (*pro* γη) d. απο (*pro* εκ *secund.*) b. 2. ισχυραν φωνην aek (εκραξε k), ισχυρα φωνη bcdfgjlm, εν ισχυρα φωνη h (*pro* εν ισχυι, φωνῃ μεγαλῃ). επεσεν *bis* lm. —επεσεν abcejk. —επεσε df [*habent* gh]. +ἡ (*ante* βαβυλων) f.

–ἡ μεγαλη e. εγενετετο g. κατοικητηριον f. +των (*ante* δαιμονων) c. δαιμονιων g. –και φυλακη παντος ορνεου ακαθαρτου *ad fin. versus* cfl. +δαιμονιου (*post* πνς) l. 3. εκ του θυμου του οινου hm. πεπωκασι acd (*Mill.*) km. πεπτωκασι bdefg**l (ν *eras. in* l, *errat Mill. de* dfl). πεπτωσι g*. πεποκασι j. [h *cum Elzev.*]. στρηνου b. επλουτισαν e. 4. εξελθε abcdefjklm [*non* h]. εξελθετέξ g. ἐξ h [*habet* εξ αυτης f]. –ινα *prim.* b. συγκοινωνησητε g. συγκοινωνησηται fk. και εκ των πληγων αυτης ἱνα μη λαβητε abcdefghjklm (–αυτης j, –μη k, λαβειτε l, λαθητε b). 5. εκολληθησαν (*pro* ηκολουθησαν) abcdefghjklm. αἱ ἁμαρτιαι αυτης ek. +αυτης adehjkm, +αυτοις b (*post* εμνημονευσεν). *Jungunt* τα αδικηκατα αυτης *cum versu sequent.* adekm. 6. *init.* αποδοτε αυτη ὡς και αυτη διπλα τα εργα αυτης (*cæteris usque ad* εργα αυτης *omissis*) m. αποδωτε l. αὔτη (*pro* αυτη) g. απεδωκε (–ὑμιν) abdefgjkl [*non* ch], *at* απεδωκεν dfl*. διπλωσατε τα διπλα ὡς και αυτη (αυτοι f). και (–και f) κατα τα εργα abdefjk [*non* ch]. διπλασατε διπλα (–αυτη) g. +αυτης (*post* ποτηριω) abdefjklm [*non* gh]. +εν (*ante* ῳ) c. ὁ ejl, ὡς m (*pro* ῳ). εκερασεν dl*m. εκεκρασε k. 7. *init.* ὡς (*pro* ὁσα) m. αυτην (*pro* ἑαυτην) abejkl [*non* dm]. εστρηνιασεν dfl*m. –και πενθος *prim.* h. +ὁτι (*ante* καθημαι) cghj. ὁτι καθως ad (*errat Mill.*) e (*errat Griesb.*) k, ὁτι ειμι καθως b (*pro* καθημαι). ὁτι εγω καθημαι m. +ὡς (*ante* βασιλισσα) j. βασιλισα k. βασιλεισσα l. 8. διατοῦτο ghjlm. –εν ek* (η *in loco* k*, *at* εν k** *supra*). ἡξουσιν clm. –και *prim.* abdejkm. λοιμος k. –κς g. –ὁ θς ck. κρινας abdeg ?hjklm [*non* c]. 9. *init.* και κλαυσουσι και κοψονται επ' αυτην (–αυτην *prim.*) abdeghjklm (επ' αυτη gj). και κοψονται και κλαυσουσι επ' αυτην c. κλαυσουσιν fl*. η *eras. in* h *inter* γης *et* οἱ. ὅτ' ἂν l. ὅτἂν m. βλεπουσι k. 10. ἀπομακρόθεν (*sic vv.* 15, 17) h. μακρῶθεν ἑστηκῶτες l. ἑστωτες g. ἑστηκοτες m. αυτων (*pro* αυτης) c. οὐαῖ οὐαὶ l. οὐαὶ *ter* m. –ἡ πολις ἡ μεγαλη *vel* –ουαι ουαι *vel* –βαβυλων *ob spatium* d (*illeg.*). +ἡ (*ante* βαβυλων) m. –εν abcdeghjklm. μιαν ὡραν g. κρίσις *omnes*. 11. κλαυσουσι (ν *eras.* l) και πενθησουσιν abceklm. κλαυσουσιν επ' αυτη και πενθησουσιν ὁτι j. πενθησουσιν d (*miserè mutilum: legere videtur* και πενθησουσιν επ' αυτη και οἱ εμποροι της γης και κλαυσουσι: *cf. Mill.*). επ' αυτης m. αυτης (*pro* αυτων) cm. αγορασει k*. +και (*post* αγοραζει) l. οὐκέτι *cum sequent.* abcegjklm (οὐκ ἔτι g, Ὁ οὐκ ἔτι m, Ο *rubro*). 12. αργυριου b. ἀργυροῦ f. μαργαριτων gm. βυσσινου abcdef**gjlm [*non* h]. βυσινου f*. βισσινου k. πορφυρου abcd (*Mill.*) ehjk [*non* gm]. συρικου bc. σιρικου l. θεϊνου e. σηδηρου g. 13. κινναμωμον abcej**l. κινναμωμον g. κιναμωμον k [m *cum Elzev.*]. +και αμωμον (*ante* και θυμιαματα) cm. θυμιαματων b. θυμιαμα g.

μυρων b. μῦρον hj. —και οινον abejkl. και ελαιον και οινον cf. ελεον l. και σεμιδαλιν και οινον και ελαιον m. σεμιδαλι g. και (+τα k) προβατα και κτηνη abcdefjklm [*non* gh]. ἱππους g. ραίδων bcghjl [*non* a, d *illeg.*]. ῥέδων m. —και σωματων b. —και *ultim.* m. 14. ὁ[πωρα] f. πόρα g. ὀπῶρα j. ὀπωρα klm (+σου m). σου της επιθυμιας της ψυχης g. ψυχης ισου (*pro* της ψυχης σου) k. συνάπηλθεν (*pro* σου απηλθεν) l. —και παντα τα λιπαρα *usque ad* απο σου *secund.* j. λειπαρα l. +σου (*post* λιπαρα) g. απωλετο abcefgk, απωλοντο d (*ut videtur*) hlm (*pro* απηλθεν *secund.*). οὐκ ἔτι gm. εὕρης c. εὑρησεις h. ευρεις l. *fin.* αυτα ου μη εὕρης abdefjl. ου μη αυτα εὕρης g. και οικετας ου μη εὕρης (—ουκετι) k. *fin.* +ουτε ψυχας ανθρωπων του λοιπου εμπορευση c. *Jungit* m *vv.* 14, 15, *legens* αυτα ου μη εὑρησουσιν οἱ εμποροι. 15. ἑμποροι l. μακρωθεν l. +και (*ante* κλαιοντες) abcdefjkl [*non* ghm]. —και (*ante* πενθουντες) k. 16. *init.* —και abcdj. —ουαι *unum* abdejk. οὐαι g. οὐαὶ *ter* m. βυσσον abejkl [*non* cdm]. πορφυραν bm. κεχρυσωμενη χρυσιω (—εν) abcdegjklm (κεχρυσωιμενη g). κεχρυσωμενη *tantum* h. μαργαριτηι g. μαργαριτες k. ηριμωθη e. ἠρημωθη m. —ὁ g. 17. ὁ επι τοπον πλεων (*pro* επι των πλοιων ὁ ὁμιλος) abdefgjklm. πλεων επι των πλοιων (—ὁ ὁμιλος) c. ὁ επι των πλοιων πλεων (—ὁ ὁμιλος) h. απομακροθεν f. μακρῶθεν l. ἑστησαν fj. 18. εκραξαν gm. εκραζων (*sic v.* 19) l. κα *eras. ante* πυρωσεως k. λεποντες a*k*, βλεποντες a**bcdeghjk**l?m (*pro* ὁρωντες). ὁμοιαι g. 19. επεβαλλον g, *at* εβαλλον e. +τον (*ante* χουν) ek. και πενθουντες και πενθουσιν e. +και (*ante* λεγοντες) abcdehjkl [*non* gm]. —ουαι *unum* eg. οὐαὶ *ter* m. μεγαλη g. ἐν ᾗ l. +τα (*ante* πλοια) abdefghjkl [*non* m]. τιμιωτητος l. ετι (*pro* ὁτι) k. ειρημωθη l. ἠρημωθη m. 20. επ' αυτη abcd (*Mill.*) eghjl, *at* εν αυτη k. +και οἱ (*ante* αποστολοι) abcdeghjklm. εκρινε (—ὁ θς) k. 21. *Rasura in* g *inter* ῃ *et* ρεν. μῦλον c. —οὑτως h. *Jungit* c λεγων οὑτως·. ὁρμηματι lm. μεγαλι a. εστι ? (*pro* ετι) k. *fin.* +εν αυτη f *apud Mill.* (ῃ *tantum nunc extat ante* και φωνη). 22. αυλιτων l. σαλπιγγων m. ακουση *vel* ακουστη (*pro* ακουσθῃ *prim.*) f. ακουστη σοι (—εν *prim.*) k. *Transfert* l *ad fin. vers.* και πας τεχνιτης *usque ad* εν σοι ετι *secund.*, *legens* εὑρεθει: *malè Mill.* —εν *secund.* k*. φανη c, ακουσθει l (*pro* ακουσθῃ *secund.*). —και φωνη μυλου *ad fin. vers.* aekm (*omittit* m* *usque ad* και φωνην νυμφιου sic *v.* 23). 23. φανει l. νυμφις g. —εν σοι *secund.* j. —ὁτι *prim.* abejk. —οἱ *prim.* g. —ησαν b. μεγιστάνες ceghj. μεγισταναις l. μεγιστάνοι m. φαρμακια lm. επλανησας m. 24. αἱματα a?bcdefghjklm. εὑρεθησαν l (f *apud Millium*).

Cap. XIX. 1. *init.* −και abcef (*ex notâ marginali*) gjklm [*non* h, *hiat* d). μεταταῦτα hl. −ὡς l. φωνην μεγαλην οχλου πολλου abcdefgjklm [*non* h, *qui legit* εν τω ουρανω *cum sequent.*]. λεγοντων abceghjklm. λέ[γουσαν *Mill.*] d. −και ἡ τιμη d *Mill.* *fin.* και ἡ δυναμις και ἡ δοξα του θῦ ἡμων (−και ἡ τιμη *et* κῷ) abceghjkl. και ἡ δυναμις και ἡ δυναμις και δοξα του θῦ ἡμων m. 2. αληθηναι g. δικαιοι l. εκρινεν dl*. πολιν (*pro* πορνην) f. διεφθειρε abce hjk [*non* gm]. διεφθειρεν d?l*. +κς̄ (*ante* εξεδικησε) g. εξεδικησεν dl*. −της (*ante* χειρος) abcdefghjklm. 3. −και k. δυο (*pro* δευτερον) e. εκ δευτερου ειρηκαν m. ειρηκεν ac?ehjkl. ειρηκασιν bg (d *illeg.*). −ὁ b. ανεβαινεν m. 4. επεσαν hj, *forsan* d [*non* f]. οἱ πρεσβυτεροι επεσαν l. οἱ εικοσιτεσσαρες πρεσβυτεροι bf (οἱ *supra, vix primâ manu*, f). κδ̄ agjkl. −και *secund.* cdehm. −τα k. δ̄ ζωῖα g. επι τω θρονω acdefgklm [*non* hj]. −αμην l. 5. απο (*pro* εκ) bdegjklm [*non* h]. εξηλθεν dl*. οὐνου εξηλθε *tantum manet in* f. +αἰνειτε (*ante* παντες) g. −και *tert.* bcdeghjkl. −οἱ *ultim.* l. 6. −ὡς *prim.* cd (*ut videtur, Mill.*) m. −ὡς *secund.* b. −ὡς φωνην οχλου πολλου και k. πολων j. λεγοντες bdefjkl [*non* gm]. λεγοντας h. εβασιλευσεν dl*. −κς̄ d. +ἡμων (*post* θς̄) bcdef (ʿμων f) hjklm [*non* g]. 7. αγαλλιωμεν gm. −την j*m. −αυτου l. ἡτοιμασεν k. 8. εδωθη l. περιβαλληται dfkm. περιβεβληται c. λαμπρον και καθαρον bcdefghjlm (−και gl). *fin.* των ἁγιων εστι bcdeghj klm (εστιν dl*), *sic* f (δικαιωματα των *tantum extat*). 9. εις εις (*pro* οἱ εις) e, *priore* εις *eraso.* τον δειπνον jm. +και δη γε και απιοντες ὡς δει (*post* κεκλημενοι) c. τον δειπνον του γαμου βεβλημενοι (−εις *et* του αρνιου *et* κεκλημενοι) k. −και λεγει μοι *secund.* k. *fin.* του θῦ αληθινοι εισι gk. του θῦ εισι bcdefjlm (εισιν fl*). 10. επεσα bh*jlm [*non* cefg, *hiat* d]. του αγγελου (*pro* αυτου) g. +ποιησης (*post* ὁρα μη) g. −του (*ante* ιῦ *prim.*) bceghjklm (*hiat* d). *Jungit* c ιῦ *cum* τω θῶ. −του (*ante* ιῦ *secund.*) g. θῦ (*pro* ιῦ *secund.*) k. εστιν dl*. 11. ιδου l. −καλουμενος c. δικαιωσυνει g. κρινεῖ m. 12. −ὡς bcehjkl [*habent* gm, *hiat* d]. εχων ονοματα γεγραμμενα και (+εχων b) ονομα γεγραμμενον bdeghjkm (ὀνομ. *bis* g). οὐδ' εἷς d. ειδεν (*pro* οιδεν) k. 13. ἱματιον gl. βεβλημενον ἱματιον (−βεβαμμενον αἱματι) k. +πορφυρουν (*post* ἱματιον) b. ερραντισμενον (*pro* βεβαμμενον) gm. +εν (*ante* αἱματι) c. κεκληται bdegjkm. 14. των ουρανων (*pro* τα εν τῳ ουρανῳ) d. −τα *secund.* cjlm. −τῳ g. ἠκολουθει g. ηκολουθη αυτοις (*pro* αυτῳ) k. επι bcdehjkm [*non* g]. ἱπποις k. −και *secund.* bcdhjkm. λευκοβυσσινον καθαρον (−και) g. καθαρον λευκον (−και) l. 15. +διστομος (*ante* οξεια) bcdeghjklm. ὀξεια gl. −ἱνα l. παταξη bcdghjm. παταξει el. +παντα (*ante* τα εθνη) j. πατη l. λοινον k. του θυμου του οινου g. −και (*ante* της οργης) bcdehjklm. −του *ultim.* e. παντοκρατωρος l. 16. ἱματιον k. μετωπον (*pro* ἱματιον) g. +αυτου (*post* ἱματιον) m. −το *secund.* bcdeghjklm. 17. ιδον l. −ένα bcdejk [*habent* ghlm]. +αλλον (*post* ἑνα) m. ἑστωιτα g. ἑστωτα kl. ἡ Ἡλιω (Ἡ *rubro* g). εκραξεν εν bej (ξ *dub. in* j) klm [*non* cg, d *illeg.*]. εκραζε g. πασιν d. −πασι g. πετομενοις beghjm [*non* ckl, d *illeg.*]. μεσουρανιματι l. συναχθητε (*pro* και συναγεσθε) bcdeghjklm. *fin.* εις τον δειπνον τον μεγαν του θῦ bcdeghjklm (*at* το δειπνον jl, το μεγα deghjl, τον μεγα k). 18. χιλιαρχῶν m. +τας (*ante* σαρκας *quint.*) ek. +τε (*post* ελευθερων) bcdeghjklm (τὲ jl). −και (*ante* μικρων) k. +τε (*post* μικρων) bcehjkl [*non* gm, *vix* d]. +των (*ante* μεγαλων) g. 19. ιδον l. θηριων c*. αυτου (*pro* αυτων) c. +τον (*ante* πολεμον) dekl. ποιησαι πολεμον συνηγμενα g. 20. μετ᾽ αυτου (*pro* μετα τουτου) h. ὁ μετ᾽ αυτου ψευδοπροφητης bcdegjklm. επλανησεν l*. −τῳ (*ante* θειω) beghjkl [*habet* m, *forsan* d]. 21. +αυτου (*post* ῥομφαια) g. π *eras. ante* καθημενου *in* k. εξελθουσῃ (*pro* εκπορευομενῃ) bcdeghjklm. *fin.* αυτου (*pro* αυτων) m.

Cap. XX. 1. ιδον l. κλειν bcdeghjkm [*non* l]. ἁλυσιν l. 2. εκρατησεν dl*. εκρατη g*. εστιν dl*. εστιν ὁ διαβολος j. +ὁ (*ante* σατανας) chjm. +ὁ πλανων την οικουμενην ὁλην (*post* σατανας) bdehjklm (−ὁλην e). 3. θαλασσαν (*pro* αβυσσον) k. εκλεισε (−αυτον) bcdeghjklm (εκλεισεν d). πλανα bcdehjklm. ετι τα εθνη bcdeghjklm. τελεσθωσι b. τελεσθηναι j. τελεσθει l. ετι (*pro* ετη) l. −και (*post* ετη) bdegjl [*non* h]. +δε (*post* μετα) e. μεταταῦτα h. κατα δε ταυτα (*pro* και μετα ταυτα) k. −δει l. λυθηναι αυτον bdegjklm [*non* h]. 4. ιδον l. εκαθησαν kl. εδοθη κριμα b. κρίμα glm *passim.* εδωθη l. +ειδον (*ante* τας ψυχας) g. πεπελεκημενων b. προσεκυνουν το θηριον ουδε την εικονα αυτου bdjkm (προσεκυνησαν jkm, *forsan* d). ουδε (*pro* ουτε) egl. ελαβων l. +του θηριου (*post* χαραγμα) g. των μετωπων bl. −αὐτων *prim.* bcdegjklm. −επι (*ante* την χειρα) g. τας χειρας b. −τα (*ante* χιλια) h. 5. *Deest versus usque ad* χιλια ετη *in* bdejkl. και οἱ λοιποι (−δε) cgh. εζησαν αχρι (*pro* ανεζησαν ἑως) cghm. +ὁτι (*ante* αὑτη) l. 6. *init.* +και e. −μακαριος *usque ad* τῃ πρωτῃ k. πι τοῦτον *sic* e. ὁ δευτερος θανατος bcdeghjklm. εχη l. βασιλευσουσιν dl*. μετα ταυτα τα b, μετα ταυτα dj (*pro* μετ᾽ αυτου). 7. ὅτ᾽ ἂν m. μετα (*pro* ὁταν τελεσθῃ) bejl. *At* k *legit vv.* 6, 7: βασιλευσουσι· και μετα ταυτα χιλια ετη λυθησεται κ. τ. λ., *omissis cæteris.* 8. −τα *prim.* b, *secund.* em. τεσσαρσιν l*. γονιαις g. γωδ᾽ d. μαγως e. μαγωδ d *Mill.* (δ *evanidum*). +και (*ante* συναγαγειν) c. +τον (*ante* πολεμον) bdeghjklm. ὧν (*pro* ὤν) l. +αυτων (*post* αριθμος) bdegklm [*non* h]. ὡσει (*pro* ὡς ἡ) bejl [*non* m, *hiat* d]. ὁ (*pro* ἡ) k. 9. εκυκλευσαν bdehk [*non* jm]. +και την πολιν των ἁγιων (*post* ἁγιων) j. ἠγαπημενην g. εκ του ουρανου απο του θεου bcdehjkm [*non* gl]. 10. +του (*ante* θειου) glm (και *omittit* l). +και (*post* ὁπου) bcdeghjklm. −και (*post* θηριον) l. νυκτας m. −των (*ante* αιωνων) e. 11. ιδον (*sic v.* 12) l. μεγαν λευκον bdeghjklm. επ' αυτον bcdehjklm [*non* g]. οὐ απο του προσωπου αυτου g. ὁ ουρανος και ἡ γη h. −ὁ (*ante* ουρανος) k. ὁ m. οὐχ' jklm (*sic v.* 15, *passim*). 12. −μικρους και μεγαλους bdejk. τους μεγαλους και τους μικρους hm. τους μεγαλους και τους μικρους τους νεκρους l. ἑστωτας τους μικρους και τους μεγαλους c. −ἑστωτας k. ἑστωτας l. θρονου (*pro* θῦ) bcdehjlm. και βιβλιον (βιβλια ekm) ηνοιξαν (ηνοιχθησαν m) και αλλο βιβλιον ηνεωχθη (ηνοιχθη em, ανεωχθη j) bdejkm [*non* l: *errat Mill. de* dl]. ανεωχθησαν· και αλλο βιβλιον ανεωχθη h. ηνοιχθησαν και αλλο βιβλιον ὁ εστι της ζωης ηνεωχθη c. αλλο βιβλιον l. ὁ εστιν ἡ ζωη l. εστιν d. 13. τους νεκρους τους εν αυτη bcdejklm [*non* h]. εδωκε (*pro* εδωκαν) l. τους νεκρους τους (−τους k) εν αυτοις bcdejkm [*non* h]. τους ἑαυτου νεκρους l. *fin.* αυτου (*pro* αυτων) cdejkl. 14. −ὁ *prim.* b. −οὑτος εστιν ὁ δευτερος θανατος bcj. οὑτος ὁ θανατος ὁ δευτερος εστιν dlm (−εστιν l). οὑτος ὁ δευτερος εστιν (−θανατος) e. οὑτος εστιν ὁ θανατος ὁ δευτερος h. οὑτος ὁ δευτερος εν τη λιμνη του πυρος (−εστιν *et* θανατος) k. *fin.* +ἡ λιμνη του πυρος dehlm. 15. ουκ εὑρεθη l. εν τω βιβλιω bcdejkm [*non* hl].

CAP. XXI. 1. ιδον (*sic v.* 2) l. −καινον k. −πρωτη e. παρηλθεν l*, *at* απηλθον bdej, απηλθε ckm [h *cum Elzev.*]. 2. −εγω ιωαννης bcdehjklm. *Transferunt* bcdehjklm ειδον *in locum post* καινην. εκ του ουρανου απο του θῦ bcdejklm [*non* h]. 3. ἰδου (*sic v.* 5) k. σκηνωση l. λαος bcdehjklm. αυτης (*pro* αυτου) e. −αυτου l. −ὁ (*ante* θς̄ *prim.*) k. μετ' αυτων εσται bdejklm [*non* h]. *fin.* −θεος αυτων bdehklm. 4. απ' αυτων bd?ejm, εξ αυτων k (*pro* ὁ θς̄). −ὁ θς̄ chl. −ουτε πενθος *usque ad* εσται ετι km. *fin.* απηλθε c. απηλθεν be jk [d *illeg.*, hl *cum Elzev.*]. *Jungunt vv.* 4, 5 be. 5. *init.* −και bej. επι τω θρονω bcdejkl [*non* h]. εν τω θρονω m. παντα καινα bcdejkl. ποιω παντα hm. ποιησω k. −μοι bdejklm. −ὁτι b. *fin.* εισί h. πιστοι και αληθινοι του θεου εισι (εισιν dl*) bdejkl (*malè Mill. de* dl) m. *fin.* +του θῦ c. 6. ειπεν dl*. γεγονα cdehjklm. −εγω ειμι bdehjk. −ειμι clm. αλφα bcdhkm [*non* e]. +και (*ante* ἡ αρχη) bdejkl, *at* αρχη και τελος ch, *sine articulis.* διψοντι kl (*etiam* και *pro* εγω k). +αυτω (*post* δωσω) bcdejm. −εκ της πηγης *usque ad* ὁ νικων *v.* 7, k (*jungens* δωσω αυτω ταυτα). −της ζωης bhm. 7. δωσω αυτω (*pro* κληρονομησει) bcdejkm. ταυτα (*pro* παντα) bcdhjkm. κληρονομηση ταυτα (−παντα) l. +ὁ (*ante* θς̄) k. −ὁ *secund.* cehjlm. μου υἱος (−ὁ) bdk (εμου k). 8. *init.* τοις δε δειλοις bcdehjklm. +και ἁμαρτωλοις (*post* απιστοις) bcdehjklm.

εβδελλυγμενοις d. φαρμακοῖς bcdehjm. φαρμάκοις kl. ειδωλατραις k. λημνῃ j. καιωμενη l. *fin.* ὅ εστιν ὁ θανατος ὁ δευτερος bcdehjklm. 9. ηλθεν (−προς με) bc (η *mutat. in* c) dehjklm. +εκ (*post* εἰς) bcdehjkl. ὁ πρωτος (*pro* εἰς) m. −ἑπτα *secund.* h. −τας (*ante* γεμουσας) bcdehjk [*non* lm]. εχουσας (*pro* γεμουσας) m. −των (*post* γεμουσας) bcdejk [*non* lm]. ελαλησεν dl*. δεῦρω l. την γυναικα την νυμφην του αρνιου bcdehjkl. την νυμφην την γυναικα του αρνιου m. 10. *init.* απηνεγκεν εν πνι (−και *et* με) k. απηνεγκεν d. απεινεγκε[ν *eras.*] l. επι ορος m. εδειξεν dl*. −την μεγαλην bdejklm [*non* h]. και *pro* την *ante* ἁγιαν c, *at* τη m*. −απο του θυ b. απο του ουρανου εκ του θυ c. εκ του θυ dejkm. 11. −εχουσαν την δοξαν του θυ και k. −και *prim.* bcdehj. τιμιω b. −ὡς λιθῳ l. ϋασπιδι e. κρυσταλιζοντι dejkm. 12. −εχουσαν *usque ad* ὑψηλον k. εχουσα (*pro* εχουσαν) *bis* bcdehj [*non* m: *prim.* l, *secund.* k]. −τε bcd?ehjlm. ὑψιλον e. πυλεωνας c. ταις (*pro* τοις) m. δεκαδυο (*pro* δωδεκα *secund.*) bdjklm [*non* e]. ὀνοματα j. +ονοματα (*post* εστιν) bcdejkl [*non* h]. εστι τα ονοματα m. του (*pro* των υἱων) b. −των (*ante* υἱων) cejkm [d *illeg.*: *non* hl]. 13. απο ανατολων...και απο δυσμων... και απο βορρα...και απο νοτου b. απο ανατολων...και απο βορρα...και απο δυσμων (−απο νοτου) c. απο ανατολων...και απο βορρα...και απο νοτου... και απο δυσμων dehjl (*lineâ ante* και απο νοτου *erasâ in* l). απο ανατολων... και απο νοτου...και απο βορρα...και απο δυσμων k. πυλωνας *prim. secund. et tert.* l. 14. εχων jkl. −και εν αυτοις l, *malè Mill.* και επ' αυτων δωδεκα ονοματα των δωδεκα απ. bcdehjk. 15. λάλῶν h. ειχεν dl*. +μετρον (*ante* καλαμον) bdehjl, *at* μετρον καλαμον c. μετρησει l. −και το τειχος αυτης bde hjkl (−*etiam* αυτης *ante* και το τειχος d). 16. −το *prim.* k. −τοσουτον εστι bcdehjkl.† −και *tert.* bcdehjkl. +αυτης (*post* πλατος) l. εμετρησεν d. +εν (*ante* τω καλαμω) c. δεκαδυο (*pro* δωδεκα) bcdejk [*non* h]. +δωδεκα (*post* χιλιαδων) bcdehjk. ἶσα cejk. *fin.* εστιν l*. 17. −εμετρησε bcdejk [*habent* hl]. ρμδ dhjkl. μετρος e. 18. ενδωμησις j. εκδομησις k. ϋασπις (*sic v.* 19) e. ὁμοιον bcdehjk. ὁμοιω l. ὑελω bhk. ὑελλω ej. 19. *init.* −και bcdejk [*non* h]. κεκοσμημενῳ k. −ὁ (*ante* πρωτος) c. σαπφηρος l. χαλκιδων ek. λυχνιτης (*pro* χαλκηδων) j. 20. σαρδωνυξ ce [d *illeg.*, *non* hjl]. σαρδιον bc dejk [*non* hl]. βηρυλλιος cl. βηριλλος e. κηρυλλος k. ενατος bdhj [*non* cek]. ἑνατος l. τὸ πάζιον d. χρυσοπασος ejk. χρυσοπασσος j. χρυσοπρασσος l. ἑνδεκατος kl. αμεθυσος bcehjl [*non* dk]. 21. ἀναεἰς h. πυλων (*pro* πυλωνων) j. ἦν (*pro* ἦν) l. ἐξ k. ὑελος bdhkl. ὑελλος ej [*non* c]. *fin.* διαυγης (*pro* διαφανης) bcdehjkl. 22. ειχεν (*pro* ειδον) ek [ειδον l, *hoc*

† ἐστι ὅσον Elzev., quod addas locis supra citatis p. lxxx.

loco]. εστιν d. -εστι l*. 23. *init.* -και k. +αὐτη (*post* πολις) j. ου χρειαν ουκ εχει (ου *vix p. m.*) k. εχη l. ἱνα φαινωσιν· αὐτὴ γαρ ἡ δοξα (-εν) bdejl [h *cum Elzev.*]. ἱνα φαινοι· αὐτῇ γαρ ἡ δοξα k. -εν c. εφωτησεν l. λιχνος k. 24. *init.* και περιπατησουσι[ν *eras.* l] τα εθνη δια του φωτος αυτης (-των σωζομενων) bcdehjkl. φερουσιν l*. *fin.* φερουσιν αυτω δοξαν και τιμην των εθνων εις αυτην bcdejk [hl *cum Elzev.*]. 26. οισουσιν d. ισουσι k. -των εθνων k. *fin.* +ἱνα εισελθωσι(ν d) bcdejk [*non* hl: *jungit* e *verba cum* εις αυτην]. 27. ουκ (*pro* ου μη) k. κοινον (*pro* κοινουν) bcdehjkl. ὁ ποιων (*pro* ποιουν) bdejkl [*non* ch]. εγγεγραμμενοι c.

CAP. XXII. 1. εδειξεν dl*. -καθαρον bdejk. ποταμον καθαρον chl (ποταμῶν l). ὡσει (*pro* ὡς) c. κρυσταλον e. *Jungunt* bcjkl [*non* dh] και του αρνιου *cum sequentibus, puncto post* πλατειας αυτης *posito.* 2. εκειθεν (*pro* εντευθεν *secund.*) bcdejkl [*non* h]. ξυλα e. ποιουντα e. -ἑνα bcdehl. και κατα μηνα αποδιδους ἑκαστον καρπον αυτου (-ἑνα *et* τον) k. αποδιδουν ἑκαστον b. αποδιδους ἑκαστος d. αποδιδοντα ἑκαστον καρπον (-τον) e, *qui deinceps hiat.* αποδιδους ἑκαστον jl. αποδιδους h. φυλα h. *fin.* καταγγελλεται εις θεραπειαν των ψυχων των εθνων (των ψυχων *eras.*) c. 3. καταθεμα bcdhjkl. εκει (*pro* ετι) hl. του θ̄υ (*pro* αυτου) l. λατρευουσιν dk. 4. -αυτου *prim.* k. 5. -εκει bdjk [*non* hl]. και ου χρεια λυχνου (-εχουσι) bdjkl. -και (*ante* φωτος) j. -ἡλιου bdjkl [*non* h]. φωτιεῖ bdhjkl [c *cum Elzev. in hoc versu*]. 6. λεγει (*pro* ειπε) bdhjkl. αληθηνοι k. π̄νων των (*pro* ἁγιων) bcdhjkl. απεστειλεν d. -δειξαι τοις δουλοις αυτου bdj, *at* j *habet* γνωρισαι σοι *in loco. Transfert* k δειξαι τοις δουλοις αυτου *ad fin. vers.* 7. *init.* +και bdjkl [*non* h]. -ιδου ερχομαι ταχυ k. 8. κἀγω bdhjk [*non* l]. ὁ ακουων και βλεπων ταυτα bdhjkl. ὁ βλεπων και ακουων ταυτα c. ειδον (*pro* εβλεψα) bdjkl (+και ὁτε *ante* ειδον djl, *at* ιδον l). δεικνυντος hjl. 9. -γαρ bcdhjkl. +εγω (*post* ειμι) c. εἰμὶ jl *alii.* -και (*ante* των τηρουντων) bch. -τῳ θ̄ῳ *usque ad* βιβλιου τουτου *v.* 10, k. 10. σφραγισεις l. ὁ καιρος γαρ (-ὁτι) bcdjkl. 11. -και ὁ ῥυπων ῥυπωσατω ετι j. και ὁ ῥυπαρος ῥυπαρευθητω ετι bcdhkl. δικαιοσυνην ποιησατω (*pro* δικαιωθητω) bcdhjkl (ποιητω l). 12. *init.* -και bcdhjkl. +μακαριος ὁ τηρων τους λογους της προφητειας του βιβλιου τουτου (*post* ταχυ) l. θυμος (*pro* μισθος) k. -μου c. εσται αυτου bhjk [*non* l, d *illeg.*]. *fin.* +ὁ μισθος j. 13. -ειμι bc (*forsan* d) hjkl. αλφα bcdhjl [ω *omnes:* ā k]. ὁ πρωτος και ὁ εσχατος ἡ αρχη και το τελος bdjkl. -ὁ *secund.* h. -ὁ *bis* d *apud Mill.*: (*illeg.*). 14. οἱ πλυναντες τας στολας αυτων (*pro* οἱ ποιουντες τας εντολας αυτου) l. +του θ̄υ (*ante* ἱνα) k. εισελθωσι c. 15. -δε bchjk?l [*vix* d]. κῦνες j. φαρμάκοι l. -οἱ (*ante* ειδωλολατραι) c. -ὁ bdhjk [*non* l]. ὁ ποιων και φιλων c. 16. *—*επι c. ἡ ῥιζα δᾱδ και το γενος b. *—*του chjk. +και (*ante* ὁ αστηρ) l. *fin.* ὁ πρωινος (*pro* και ορθρινος) bhjkl (ὁ *vel* και *deletum in* k). ὁ πρωινος ὁ λαμπρος cd (d *ut videtur:* ὁ πρωινος *tantum apud Mill.*). 17. ερχου (*pro* ελθε) *bis* bcdhjkl. ὑπατω (*pro* ειπατω) k. ερχεσθω (*pro* ελθετω) bcdhjkl. *—*και (*ante* ὁ θελων) bchjkl. λαβετω ὑδωρ (*—*το) bcdh jkl. 18. μαρτυρω εγω (*pro* συμμαρτυρουμαι γαρ) bcdhjkl (μαρτυρομαι c, μαρτυρω j). +τω (*ante* ακουοντι) bcjkl [*non* dh]. *—*τις k. επιθη επ' αυτα επιθησαι bcdhjkl (*at* επιθει l; αυτῳ k; επιθησει cl; αι *in* επιθησαι, *quod legerat Mill. in* d, *periit omnino*). επ' αυτον ὁ θς̄ h. +ἑπτα (*ante* πληγας) ch. +τω (*ante* βιβλιω) bcdhjkl. 19. αφελη απο των λογων της προφητειας του βιβλιου τουτου αφελοι b. αφελη απο των λογων του βιβλιου της προφητειας ταυτης αφελεῖ cde*hjkl (*at secundo loco* αφελοι dh, αφελη e*k, αφελαι j). του ξυλου (*pro* βιβλου *secund.*) bcd (*teste Mill.*) e*hjkl. *—*και *ultim.* bce*hjkl. +τω (*ante* βιβλιω) bce*hjkl. 20. *—*ναι *secund.* c. και (*pro* ναι *secund.*) l. *fin.* +χε̄ bc. 21. *—*κυριου ἡμων ιῡ c. *—*ἡμων bhjkl. των ἁγιων (*pro* ὑμων) bchjkl.

SUBSCRIPT.: *Hiant* adefgmn. *Nihil habent* bhjl. *Nihil ad rem.* c. τελος της του ἁγιου ιωαννου του θεολογου θειας αποκαλυψεως k.

Sequuntur lectiones Codicis Leicestrensis (f), *apud Millium, Jacksonium, et Wetstenium servatæ, quarum vestigia pauca in deperditarum schedarum fragmento hodie extant. Vid. supra p.* xlii.

APOC. CAP. XVIII. 7. ὁτι καθιω. 8. ὡρα (*pro* ἡμερᾳ). κρινας. 9. κλαυσουσι και (*—*αυτην). *—*επ' αυτῃ. *fin.* αυτων. 10. *—*εν. 11. κλαυσουσι και πενθησουσιν. 12. βυσσινου και πορφυρου. 13. κιναμωμου. θυμιαματος. *—*και οινον. προβατα και κτηνη. και ῥεδιων. και ψυχων. 14. *—*τα *prim.* λαμπρα απωλετο απο σου. αυτα ου μη εὑρης. 15. και κλαιοντες. 16. *init.* *—*και. *—*ουαι *semel.* βυσσον. *—*εν. χρυσιω. 17. ὁ επι τοπον πλεων. 18. βλεποντες. 19. τα πλοια. 20. επ' αυτη. και οἱ ἁγιοι και οἱ αποστολοι. 21. θαλασσαν μεγαν. *fin.* +εν αυτη. 22. *—*εν σοι ετι *prim. usque ad* εν σοι ετι *secund.* 24. αἱματα. εὑρεθησαν (*hanc lectionem delet Jackson*).

XIX. 1. *init.* *—*και. μεγαλην οχλου πολλου. λεγοντων. ἡ δυναμις και ἡ δοξα (*—*και ἡ τιμη). του θῡ (*pro* κῳ̄ τῳ θῳ̄). 2. ὁς εκρινε την πολιν (*—*ὁτι) *Mill., at* οἱ *pro* ὁτι *posterius Wetst.* (*silet Jackson.*). διεφθειρε. *—*της. 3. ειρηκασιν. 4. *—*και *secund. Jackson.* τω θρονω του ουρανου. 5. απο του ουρανου *Jackson.*, απο του θρονου απο του ουρανου *Mill.*, *at* ουρανου (*pro* θρονου) *Wetst.* τω θεω. 6. λεγοντες. θεος ἡμων. 8. περιβαλληται. λαμπρον και καθαρον. των ἁγιων εστι. 9. του θῡ εισι. 10. —του (*ante* ιῡ) *bis.* 12. —ὡς. εν τη κεφαλη. ονοματα γεγραμμενα και ονομα γεγραμμενον. 13. κεκληται. αυτου το ονομα. 14. —τα *prius et posterius.* αυτοις. —και *ultim.* 15. διστομος οξεια. παταξη. —και *ultim.* 16. —το (*ante* ονομα). 17. ιδον *Jackson.* —ἑνα. εκραξεν εν. πετομενοις. συναχθητε (—και). το μεγα του θῡ. 18. αυτους. +τε (*post* ελευθερων). —και (*ante* μικρων). +τε (*post* μικρων). 19. τον πολεμον. 20. μετ᾽ αυτου *Mill.* ὁ μετ᾽ αυτου *Jackson. Wetst. semel, at* μετ᾽ αυτου ὁ *Wetst. semel.* —του πυρος. —τῳ (*ante* θειω). 21. εξελθουση.

Cap. XX. 2. ὁ διαβολος. σατανας ὁ πλανων την οικουμενην ὁλην. 3. —αυτον *secund.* πλανα. —ετι *Mill. Jackson.*, *at* ετι τα εθνη *et iterum* τα εθνη *Wetst.* —και *ultim.* λυθηναι αυτον. 4. το θηριον. ουδε (*pro* ουτε). —αὐτων (*post* μετωπον). +του (*ante* χριστου) *Jackson.: nam deest* του *in textu Stephanico.* 5. *Desunt omnia usque ad* αὐτη. 6. —και ἁγιος. επι τουτω. ὁ δευτερος θανατος *Jackson. Griesb.* δευ. θαν. *Wetst.* τα χιλια (τὰ *deest in Millii textu*). 7. μετα (*pro* ὁταν τελεσθῃ) *Mill. Wetst.* (*silet Jackson.*). 8. —τα *posterius.* —ταις. τον πολεμον. αριθμος αυτων. 9. —και ανεβησαν. εκ του ουρανου απο του θῡ. 10. και το θηριον. 11. μεγαν λευκον. —και τον καθημενον επ᾽. αυτον (*pro* αυτου). 12. —τους νεκρους. τους μεγαλους και τους μικρους. —ἑστωτας. θρονου (*pro* θῡ). ηνοιχθησαν. αλλο βιβλιον. —εν. 13. τους νεκρους τους εν αυτη. τους ἑαυτου νεκρους *Mill.*, *at* τους νεκρους τους εν αυτοις *Jackson. Wetst.* εκριθησεν *Jackson. fin.* αυτου. 14. εβληθη. "*Post* θανατος *addit* ἡ λιμνη του πυρος" *Mill.*, *at* ὁ θανατος ὁ δευτερος *Jackson.*, ὁ θανατος ὁ δευτερος εστιν *Wetst.* 15. τω βιβλιω. *Post fin. capitis* xx. *desiderantur omnia.*

ΤΩ. ΘΕΩ. ΔΟΞΑ.

ADDENDUM.

In the course of my Biblical studies I met with not a few other MSS. of portions of the Greek Testament which are not only uncollated, but have not yet appeared in any general Catalogue. I have incidentally alluded to several in the foregoing pages (*vid.* pp. v. lxxiv. note), I will now mention a few others, which nothing but hard necessity has hindered me from subjecting to a closer examination.

At Middle Hill, in that wonderful collection of more than twenty thousand MSS. in various languages, besides the copy described above, p. lxxvi., I inspected:

(1) A noble MS. of the Gospels (13975) in large folio, with a very full commentary in minute letters surrounding the text. It may be of the 12th century, and once belonged to Lord Strangford.

(2) A copy of the Acts and all the Epistles (7681), dated A.D. 1107. This MS. (as well as that in the British Museum, Additional 16943) once formed part of the collection made by the Hon. F. North for the University of Corfu.

(3) An Evangelistarium of the 12th or 13th century was described to me by Sir T. Phillipps, but could not be found at the time.

At Parham, besides the four MSS. I collated, and the two specially named above (p. xlvii.), are about ten more copies of different dates, of which seven contain the Gospels, four the Acts and Epistles. A complete collation of all the N. T. MSS. in this Library would be no unworthy task for any one who desired to do good service to Biblical literature.

I am indebted to the kindness of Archdeacon Hale for my acquaintance with three Lectionaries which have long been deposited in Sion College Library, but even there seem to have been quite forgotten. The Archdeacon is engaged in compiling a critical Catalogue of Biblical Manuscripts now in this country, a work of which I should have been glad indeed to have been able to avail myself.

In addition to those mentioned above, I know of but five MSS. of the Apocalypse in these islands (making only twenty in all), which though they have been previously used for Mill's or Wetstein's editions, doubtless need renewed examination; they are the following:

(1) Bodleian: Huntingdon 131, vellum of the 12th century, very poorly collated by Mill, whom I followed in capp. x. and XXII.

(2) Bodleian: Barocc. 3, collated by Caspar Wetstein after Mill. The margin of this beautiful little book, of the eleventh century, is crowded with a very full and unique Commentary, published by J. A. Cramer, in his Catena on the Apocalypse, Oxon. 1840. It ends xx. 1, ἔχον. I collated cap. x.

(3) and (4) Christ Church, Oxford, Wake 1 and 2, both collated by C. Wetstein.

(5) Cambridge Public Library, Dd. 9, 69, contains besides the Gospels of the 13th century, a more recent copy of the Apocalypse which has not been used since Mill's time.

I cannot help indulging the hope that health and leisure may yet be granted me to pursue my researches among these and similar treasures of our English libraries. But while the harvest is plenteous, the labourers have hitherto been few indeed; and I should much rejoice if some of those younger scholars who have so generously appreciated my efforts would devote a portion of their own time to investigations which have thus far borne some fruit, and seem to promise yet more, in a department of sacred learning which yields to none in its interest or importance.

CAMBRIDGE: PRINTED BY C. J. CLAY, M.A. AT THE UNIVERSITY PRESS.

By the same Editor.

A full and exact Collation of about twenty Greek **Manuscripts of the Holy Gospels, (hitherto unexamined), deposited in the British Museum, the Archiepiscopal Library at Lambeth, &c. with a Critical Introduction. Pp. 252, 6*s*.**